T0181117

Lecture Notes in Computer Science 14104

Founding Editors

Gerhard Goos
Juris Hartmanis

The series Lecture Notes in Computer Science (LNCS), including its subseries Lecture Notes in Artificial Intelligence (LNAI) and Lecture Notes in Bioinformatics (LNBI), has established itself as a medium for the publication of new developments in computer science and information technology research, teaching, and education.

LNCS enjoys close cooperation with the computer science R & D community, the series counts many renowned academics among its volume editors and paper authors, and collaborates with prestigious societies. Its mission is to serve this international community by providing an invaluable service, mainly focused on the publication of conference and workshop proceedings and postproceedings. LNCS commenced publication in 1973.

Osvaldo Gervasi · Beniamino Murgante ·
Ana Maria A. C. Rocha · Chiara Garau ·
Francesco Scorza · Yeliz Karaca ·
Carmelo M. Torre
Editors

Computational Science and Its Applications – ICCSA 2023 Workshops

Athens, Greece, July 3–6, 2023
Proceedings, Part I

Springer

Editors
Osvaldo Gervasi 🆔
University of Perugia
Perugia, Italy

Beniamino Murgante 🆔
University of Basilicata
Potenza, Italy

Ana Maria A. C. Rocha 🆔
University of Minho
Braga, Portugal

Chiara Garau 🆔
University of Cagliari
Cagliari, Italy

Francesco Scorza 🆔
University of Basilicata
Potenza, Italy

Yeliz Karaca 🆔
University of Massachusetts Medical School
Worcester, MA, USA

Carmelo M. Torre 🆔
Polytechnic University of Bari
Bari, Italy

ISSN 0302-9743   ISSN 1611-3349 (electronic)
Lecture Notes in Computer Science
ISBN 978-3-031-37104-2   ISBN 978-3-031-37105-9 (eBook)
https://doi.org/10.1007/978-3-031-37105-9

This Springer imprint is published by the registered company Springer Nature Switzerland AG
The registered company address is: Gewerbestrasse 11, 6330 Cham, Switzerland

Preface

These 9 volumes (LNCS volumes 14104–14112) consist of the peer-reviewed papers from the 2023 International Conference on Computational Science and Its Applications (ICCSA 2023) which took place during July 3–6, 2023. The peer-reviewed papers of the main conference tracks were published in a separate set consisting of two volumes (LNCS 13956–13957).

The conference was finally held in person after the difficult period of the Covid-19 pandemic in the wonderful city of Athens, in the cosy facilities of the National Technical University. Our experience during the pandemic period allowed us to enable virtual participation also this year for those who were unable to attend the event, due to logistical, political and economic problems, by adopting a technological infrastructure based on open source software (jitsi + riot), and a commercial cloud infrastructure.

ICCSA 2023 was another successful event in the International Conference on Computational Science and Its Applications (ICCSA) series, previously held as a hybrid event (with one third of registered authors attending in person) in Malaga, Spain (2022), Cagliari, Italy (hybrid with few participants in person in 2021 and completely online in 2020), whilst earlier editions took place in Saint Petersburg, Russia (2019), Melbourne, Australia (2018), Trieste, Italy (2017), Beijing, China (2016), Banff, Canada (2015), Guimaraes, Portugal (2014), Ho Chi Minh City, Vietnam (2013), Salvador, Brazil (2012), Santander, Spain (2011), Fukuoka, Japan (2010), Suwon, South Korea (2009), Perugia, Italy (2008), Kuala Lumpur, Malaysia (2007), Glasgow, UK (2006), Singapore (2005), Assisi, Italy (2004), Montreal, Canada (2003), and (as ICCS) Amsterdam, The Netherlands (2002) and San Francisco, USA (2001).

Computational Science is the main pillar of most of the present research, industrial and commercial applications, and plays a unique role in exploiting ICT innovative technologies, and the ICCSA series have been providing a venue to researchers and industry practitioners to discuss new ideas, to share complex problems and their solutions, and to shape new trends in Computational Science. As the conference mirrors society from a scientific point of view, this year's undoubtedly dominant theme was the machine learning and artificial intelligence and their applications in the most diverse economic and industrial fields.

The ICCSA 2023 conference is structured in 6 general tracks covering the fields of computational science and its applications: Computational Methods, Algorithms and Scientific Applications – High Performance Computing and Networks – Geometric Modeling, Graphics and Visualization – Advanced and Emerging Applications – Information Systems and Technologies – Urban and Regional Planning. In addition, the conference consisted of 61 workshops, focusing on very topical issues of importance to science, technology and society: from new mathematical approaches for solving complex computational systems, to information and knowledge in the Internet of Things, new statistical and optimization methods, several Artificial Intelligence approaches, sustainability issues, smart cities and related technologies.

In the workshop proceedings we accepted 350 full papers, 29 short papers and 2 PHD Showcase papers. In the main conference proceedings we accepted 67 full papers, 13 short papers and 6 PHD Showcase papers from 283 submissions to the General Tracks of the conference (acceptance rate 30%). We would like to express our appreciation to the workshops chairs and co-chairs for their hard work and dedication.

The success of the ICCSA conference series in general, and of ICCSA 2023 in particular, vitally depends on the support of many people: authors, presenters, participants, keynote speakers, workshop chairs, session chairs, organizing committee members, student volunteers, Program Committee members, Advisory Committee members, International Liaison chairs, reviewers and others in various roles. We take this opportunity to wholehartedly thank them all.

We also wish to thank our publisher, Springer, for their acceptance to publish the proceedings, for sponsoring part of the best papers awards and for their kind assistance and cooperation during the editing process.

We cordially invite you to visit the ICCSA website https://iccsa.org where you can find all the relevant information about this interesting and exciting event.

July 2023

Osvaldo Gervasi
Beniamino Murgante
Chiara Garau

Welcome Message from Organizers

After the 2021 ICCSA in Cagliari, Italy and the 2022 ICCSA in Malaga, Spain, ICCSA continued its successful scientific endeavours in 2023, hosted again in the Mediterranean neighbourhood. This time, ICCSA 2023 moved a bit more to the east of the Mediterranean Region and was held in the metropolitan city of Athens, the capital of Greece and a vibrant urban environment endowed with a prominent cultural heritage that dates back to the ancient years. As a matter of fact, Athens is one of the oldest cities in the world, and the cradle of democracy. The city has a history of over 3,000 years and, according to the myth, it took its name from Athena, the Goddess of Wisdom and daughter of Zeus.

ICCSA 2023 took place in a secure environment, relieved from the immense stress of the COVID-19 pandemic. This gave us the chance to have a safe and vivid, in-person participation which, combined with the very active engagement of the ICCSA 2023 scientific community, set the ground for highly motivating discussions and interactions as to the latest developments of computer science and its applications in the real world for improving quality of life.

The National Technical University of Athens (NTUA), one of the most prestigious Greek academic institutions, had the honour of hosting ICCSA 2023. The Local Organizing Committee really feels the burden and responsibility of such a demanding task; and puts in all the necessary energy in order to meet participants' expectations and establish a friendly, creative and inspiring, scientific and social/cultural environment that allows for new ideas and perspectives to flourish.

Since all ICCSA participants, either informatics-oriented or application-driven, realize the tremendous steps and evolution of computer science during the last few decades and the huge potential these offer to cope with the enormous challenges of humanity in a globalized, 'wired' and highly competitive world, the expectations from ICCSA 2023 were set high in order for a successful matching between computer science progress and communities' aspirations to be attained, i.e., a progress that serves real, place- and people-based needs and can pave the way towards a visionary, smart, sustainable, resilient and inclusive future for both the current and the next generation.

On behalf of the Local Organizing Committee, I would like to sincerely thank all of you who have contributed to ICCSA 2023 and I cordially welcome you to my 'home', NTUA.

On behalf of the Local Organizing Committee.

Anastasia Stratigea

Organization

ICCSA 2023 was organized by the National Technical University of Athens (Greece), the University of the Aegean (Greece), the University of Perugia (Italy), the University of Basilicata (Italy), Monash University (Australia), Kyushu Sangyo University (Japan), the University of Minho (Portugal). The conference was supported by two NTUA Schools, namely the School of Rural, Surveying and Geoinformatics Engineering and the School of Electrical and Computer Engineering.

Honorary General Chairs

Norio Shiratori	Chuo University, Japan
Kenneth C. J. Tan	Sardina Systems, UK

General Chairs

Osvaldo Gervasi	University of Perugia, Italy
Anastasia Stratigea	National Technical University of Athens, Greece
Bernady O. Apduhan	Kyushu Sangyo University, Japan

Program Committee Chairs

Beniamino Murgante	University of Basilicata, Italy
Dimitris Kavroudakis	University of the Aegean, Greece
Ana Maria A. C. Rocha	University of Minho, Portugal
David Taniar	Monash University, Australia

International Advisory Committee

Jemal Abawajy	Deakin University, Australia
Dharma P. Agarwal	University of Cincinnati, USA
Rajkumar Buyya	Melbourne University, Australia
Claudia Bauzer Medeiros	University of Campinas, Brazil
Manfred M. Fisher	Vienna University of Economics and Business, Austria
Marina L. Gavrilova	University of Calgary, Canada

| Sumi Helal | University of Florida, USA and University of Lancaster, UK |
| Yee Leung | Chinese University of Hong Kong, China |

International Liaison Chairs

Ivan Blečić	University of Cagliari, Italy
Giuseppe Borruso	University of Trieste, Italy
Elise De Donker	Western Michigan University, USA
Maria Irene Falcão	University of Minho, Portugal
Inmaculada Garcia Fernandez	University of Malaga, Spain
Eligius Hendrix	University of Malaga, Spain
Robert C. H. Hsu	Chung Hua University, Taiwan
Tai-Hoon Kim	Beijing Jaotong University, China
Vladimir Korkhov	Saint Petersburg University, Russia
Takashi Naka	Kyushu Sangyo University, Japan
Rafael D. C. Santos	National Institute for Space Research, Brazil
Maribel Yasmina Santos	University of Minho, Portugal
Elena Stankova	Saint Petersburg University, Russia

Workshop and Session Organizing Chairs

| Beniamino Murgante | University of Basilicata, Italy |
| Chiara Garau | University of Cagliari, Italy |

Award Chair

| Wenny Rahayu | La Trobe University, Australia |

Publicity Committee Chairs

Elmer Dadios	De La Salle University, Philippines
Nataliia Kulabukhova	Saint Petersburg University, Russia
Daisuke Takahashi	Tsukuba University, Japan
Shangwang Wang	Beijing University of Posts and Telecommunications, China

Local Organizing Committee Chairs

Anastasia Stratigea	National Technical University of Athens, Greece
Dimitris Kavroudakis	University of the Aegean, Greece
Charalambos Ioannidis	National Technical University of Athens, Greece
Nectarios Koziris	National Technical University of Athens, Greece
Efthymios Bakogiannis	National Technical University of Athens, Greece
Yiota Theodora	National Technical University of Athens, Greece
Dimitris Fotakis	National Technical University of Athens, Greece
Apostolos Lagarias	National Technical University of Athens, Greece
Akrivi Leka	National Technical University of Athens, Greece
Dionisia Koutsi	National Technical University of Athens, Greece
Alkistis Dalkavouki	National Technical University of Athens, Greece
Maria Panagiotopoulou	National Technical University of Athens, Greece
Angeliki Papazoglou	National Technical University of Athens, Greece
Natalia Tsigarda	National Technical University of Athens, Greece
Konstantinos Athanasopoulos	National Technical University of Athens, Greece
Ioannis Xatziioannou	National Technical University of Athens, Greece
Vasiliki Krommyda	National Technical University of Athens, Greece
Panayiotis Patsilinakos	National Technical University of Athens, Greece
Sofia Kassiou	National Technical University of Athens, Greece

Technology Chair

Damiano Perri	University of Florence, Italy

Program Committee

Vera Afreixo	University of Aveiro, Portugal
Filipe Alvelos	University of Minho, Portugal
Hartmut Asche	University of Potsdam, Germany
Ginevra Balletto	University of Cagliari, Italy
Michela Bertolotto	University College Dublin, Ireland
Sandro Bimonte	CEMAGREF, TSCF, France
Rod Blais	University of Calgary, Canada
Ivan Blečić	University of Sassari, Italy
Giuseppe Borruso	University of Trieste, Italy
Ana Cristina Braga	University of Minho, Portugal
Massimo Cafaro	University of Salento, Italy
Yves Caniou	Lyon University, France

Ermanno Cardelli	University of Perugia, Italy
José A. Cardoso e Cunha	Universidade Nova de Lisboa, Portugal
Rui Cardoso	University of Beira Interior, Portugal
Leocadio G. Casado	University of Almeria, Spain
Carlo Cattani	University of Salerno, Italy
Mete Celik	Erciyes University, Turkey
Maria Cerreta	University of Naples "Federico II", Italy
Hyunseung Choo	Sungkyunkwan University, Korea
Rachel Chieng-Sing Lee	Sunway University, Malaysia
Min Young Chung	Sungkyunkwan University, Korea
Florbela Maria da Cruz Domingues Correia	Polytechnic Institute of Viana do Castelo, Portugal
Gilberto Corso Pereira	Federal University of Bahia, Brazil
Alessandro Costantini	INFN, Italy
Carla Dal Sasso Freitas	Universidade Federal do Rio Grande do Sul, Brazil
Pradesh Debba	The Council for Scientific and Industrial Research (CSIR), South Africa
Hendrik Decker	Instituto Tecnológico de Informática, Spain
Robertas Damaševičius	Kausan University of Technology, Lithuania
Frank Devai	London South Bank University, UK
Rodolphe Devillers	Memorial University of Newfoundland, Canada
Joana Matos Dias	University of Coimbra, Portugal
Paolino Di Felice	University of L'Aquila, Italy
Prabu Dorairaj	NetApp, India/USA
Noelia Faginas Lago	University of Perugia, Italy
M. Irene Falcao	University of Minho, Portugal
Cherry Liu Fang	U.S. DOE Ames Laboratory, USA
Florbela P. Fernandes	Polytechnic Institute of Bragança, Portugal
Jose-Jesus Fernandez	National Centre for Biotechnology, CSIS, Spain
Paula Odete Fernandes	Polytechnic Institute of Bragança, Portugal
Adelaide de Fátima Baptista Valente Freitas	University of Aveiro, Portugal
Manuel Carlos Figueiredo	University of Minho, Portugal
Maria Celia Furtado Rocha	PRODEB–PósCultura/UFBA, Brazil
Chiara Garau	University of Cagliari, Italy
Paulino Jose Garcia Nieto	University of Oviedo, Spain
Raffaele Garrisi	Polizia di Stato, Italy
Jerome Gensel	LSR-IMAG, France
Maria Giaoutzi	National Technical University, Athens, Greece
Arminda Manuela Andrade Pereira Gonçalves	University of Minho, Portugal

Louiza de Macedo Mourelle	State University of Rio de Janeiro, Brazil
Nadia Nedjah	State University of Rio de Janeiro, Brazil
Laszlo Neumann	University of Girona, Spain
Kok-Leong Ong	Deakin University, Australia
Belen Palop	Universidad de Valladolid, Spain
Marcin Paprzycki	Polish Academy of Sciences, Poland
Eric Pardede	La Trobe University, Australia
Kwangjin Park	Wonkwang University, Korea
Ana Isabel Pereira	Polytechnic Institute of Bragança, Portugal
Massimiliano Petri	University of Pisa, Italy
Telmo Pinto	University of Coimbra, Portugal
Maurizio Pollino	Italian National Agency for New Technologies, Energy and Sustainable Economic Development, Italy
Alenka Poplin	University of Hamburg, Germany
Vidyasagar Potdar	Curtin University of Technology, Australia
David C. Prosperi	Florida Atlantic University, USA
Wenny Rahayu	La Trobe University, Australia
Jerzy Respondek	Silesian University of Technology Poland
Humberto Rocha	INESC-Coimbra, Portugal
Jon Rokne	University of Calgary, Canada
Octavio Roncero	CSIC, Spain
Maytham Safar	Kuwait University, Kuwait
Chiara Saracino	A.O. Ospedale Niguarda Ca' Granda - Milano, Italy
Marco Paulo Seabra dos Reis	University of Coimbra, Portugal
Jie Shen	University of Michigan, USA
Qi Shi	Liverpool John Moores University, UK
Dale Shires	U.S. Army Research Laboratory, USA
Inês Soares	University of Coimbra, Portugal
Elena Stankova	St. Petersburg University, Russia
Takuo Suganuma	Tohoku University, Japan
Eufemia Tarantino	Polytechnic of Bari, Italy
Sergio Tasso	University of Perugia, Italy
Ana Paula Teixeira	University of Trás-os-Montes and Alto Douro, Portugal
M. Filomena Teodoro	Portuguese Naval Academy and University of Lisbon, Portugal
Parimala Thulasiraman	University of Manitoba, Canada
Carmelo Torre	Polytechnic of Bari, Italy
Javier Martinez Torres	Centro Universitario de la Defensa Zaragoza, Spain

Giuseppe A. Trunfio	University of Sassari, Italy
Pablo Vanegas	University of Cuenca, Equador
Marco Vizzari	University of Perugia, Italy
Varun Vohra	Merck Inc., USA
Koichi Wada	University of Tsukuba, Japan
Krzysztof Walkowiak	Wroclaw University of Technology, Poland
Zequn Wang	Intelligent Automation Inc, USA
Robert Weibel	University of Zurich, Switzerland
Frank Westad	Norwegian University of Science and Technology, Norway
Roland Wismüller	Universität Siegen, Germany
Mudasser Wyne	SOET National University, USA
Chung-Huang Yang	National Kaohsiung Normal University, Taiwan
Xin-She Yang	National Physical Laboratory, UK
Salim Zabir	France Telecom Japan Co., Japan
Haifeng Zhao	University of California, Davis, USA
Fabiana Zollo	University of Venice "Cà Foscari", Italy
Albert Y. Zomaya	University of Sydney, Australia

Workshop Organizers

Advanced Data Science Techniques with Applications in Industry and Environmental Sustainability (ATELIERS 2023)

Dario Torregrossa	Goodyear, Luxemburg
Antonino Marvuglia	Luxembourg Institute of Science and Technology, Luxemburg
Valeria Borodin	École des Mines de Saint-Étienne, Luxemburg
Mohamed Laib	Luxembourg Institute of Science and Technology, Luxemburg

Advances in Artificial Intelligence Learning Technologies: Blended Learning, STEM, Computational Thinking and Coding (AAILT 2023)

Alfredo Milani	University of Perugia, Italy
Valentina Franzoni	University of Perugia, Italy
Sergio Tasso	University of Perugia, Italy

Advanced Processes of Mathematics and Computing Models in Complex Computational Systems (ACMC 2023)

Yeliz Karaca	University of Massachusetts Chan Medical School and Massachusetts Institute of Technology, USA
Dumitru Baleanu	Cankaya University, Turkey
Osvaldo Gervasi	University of Perugia, Italy
Yudong Zhang	University of Leicester, UK
Majaz Moonis	University of Massachusetts Medical School, USA

Artificial Intelligence Supported Medical Data Examination (AIM 2023)

David Taniar	Monash University, Australia
Seifedine Kadry	Noroff University College, Norway
Venkatesan Rajinikanth	Saveetha School of Engineering, India

Advanced and Innovative Web Apps (AIWA 2023)

Damiano Perri	University of Perugia, Italy
Osvaldo Gervasi	University of Perugia, Italy

Assessing Urban Sustainability (ASUS 2023)

Elena Todella	Polytechnic of Turin, Italy
Marika Gaballo	Polytechnic of Turin, Italy
Beatrice Mecca	Polytechnic of Turin, Italy

Advances in Web Based Learning (AWBL 2023)

Birol Ciloglugil	Ege University, Turkey
Mustafa Inceoglu	Ege University, Turkey

Blockchain and Distributed Ledgers: Technologies and Applications (BDLTA 2023)

Vladimir Korkhov　　　　　　Saint Petersburg State University, Russia
Elena Stankova　　　　　　　Saint Petersburg State University, Russia
Nataliia Kulabukhova　　　　Saint Petersburg State University, Russia

Bio and Neuro Inspired Computing and Applications (BIONCA 2023)

Nadia Nedjah　　　　　　　　State University of Rio De Janeiro, Brazil
Luiza De Macedo Mourelle　　State University of Rio De Janeiro, Brazil

Choices and Actions for Human Scale Cities: Decision Support Systems (CAHSC–DSS 2023)

Giovanna Acampa　　　　　　University of Florence and University of Enna
　　　　　　　　　　　　　　　Kore, Italy
Fabrizio Finucci　　　　　　　Roma Tre University, Italy
Luca S. Dacci　　　　　　　　Polytechnic of Turin, Italy

Computational and Applied Mathematics (CAM 2023)

Maria Irene Falcao　　　　　　University of Minho, Portugal
Fernando Miranda　　　　　　University of Minho, Portugal

Computational and Applied Statistics (CAS 2023)

Ana Cristina Braga　　　　　　University of Minho, Portugal

Cyber Intelligence and Applications (CIA 2023)

Gianni Dangelo　　　　　　　University of Salerno, Italy
Francesco Palmieri　　　　　　University of Salerno, Italy
Massimo Ficco　　　　　　　　University of Salerno, Italy

Conversations South-North on Climate Change Adaptation Towards Smarter and More Sustainable Cities (CLAPS 2023)

Chiara Garau	University of Cagliari, Italy
Cristina Trois	University of kwaZulu-Natal, South Africa
Claudia Loggia	University of kwaZulu-Natal, South Africa
John Östh	Faculty of Technology, Art and Design, Norway
Mauro Coni	University of Cagliari, Italy
Alessio Satta	MedSea Foundation, Italy

Computational Mathematics, Statistics and Information Management (CMSIM 2023)

Maria Filomena Teodoro	University of Lisbon and Portuguese Naval Academy, Portugal
Marina A. P. Andrade	University Institute of Lisbon, Portugal

Computational Optimization and Applications (COA 2023)

Ana Maria A. C. Rocha	University of Minho, Portugal
Humberto Rocha	University of Coimbra, Portugal

Computational Astrochemistry (CompAstro 2023)

Marzio Rosi	University of Perugia, Italy
Nadia Balucani	University of Perugia, Italy
Cecilia Ceccarelli	University of Grenoble Alpes and Institute for Planetary Sciences and Astrophysics, France
Stefano Falcinelli	University of Perugia, Italy

Computational Methods for Porous Geomaterials (CompPor 2023)

Vadim Lisitsa	Russian Academy of Science, Russia
Evgeniy Romenski	Russian Academy of Science, Russia

Workshop on Computational Science and HPC (CSHPC 2023)

Elise De Doncker	Western Michigan University, USA
Fukuko Yuasa	High Energy Accelerator Research Organization, Japan
Hideo Matsufuru	High Energy Accelerator Research Organization, Japan

Cities, Technologies and Planning (CTP 2023)

Giuseppe Borruso	University of Trieste, Italy
Beniamino Murgante	University of Basilicata, Italy
Malgorzata Hanzl	Lodz University of Technology, Poland
Anastasia Stratigea	National Technical University of Athens, Greece
Ljiljana Zivkovic	Republic Geodetic Authority, Serbia
Ginevra Balletto	University of Cagliari, Italy

Gender Equity/Equality in Transport and Mobility (DELIA 2023)

Tiziana Campisi	University of Enna Kore, Italy
Ines Charradi	Sousse University, Tunisia
Alexandros Nikitas	University of Huddersfield, UK
Kh Md Nahiduzzaman	University of British Columbia, Canada
Andreas Nikiforiadis	Aristotle University of Thessaloniki, Greece
Socrates Basbas	Aristotle University of Thessaloniki, Greece

International Workshop on Defense Technology and Security (DTS 2023)

Yeonseung Ryu	Myongji University, South Korea

Integrated Methods for the Ecosystem-Services Accounting in Urban Decision Process (Ecourbn 2023)

Maria Rosaria Guarini	Sapienza University of Rome, Italy
Francesco Sica	Sapienza University of Rome, Italy
Francesco Tajani	Sapienza University of Rome, Italy

Carmelo Maria Torre	Polytechnic University of Bari, Italy
Pierluigi Morano	Polytechnic University of Bari, Italy
Rossana Ranieri	Sapienza Università di Roma, Italy

Evaluating Inner Areas Potentials (EIAP 2023)

Diana Rolando	Politechnic of Turin, Italy
Manuela Rebaudengo	Politechnic of Turin, Italy
Alice Barreca	Politechnic of Turin, Italy
Giorgia Malavasi	Politechnic of Turin, Italy
Umberto Mecca	Politechnic of Turin, Italy

Sustainable Mobility Last Mile Logistic (ELLIOT 2023)

Tiziana Campisi	University of Enna Kore, Italy
Socrates Basbas	Aristotle University of Thessaloniki, Greece
Grigorios Fountas	Aristotle University of Thessaloniki, Greece
Paraskevas Nikolaou	University of Cyprus, Cyprus
Drazenko Glavic	University of Belgrade, Serbia
Antonio Russo	University of Enna Kore, Italy

Econometrics and Multidimensional Evaluation of Urban Environment (EMEUE 2023)

Maria Cerreta	University of Naples Federico II, Italy
Carmelo Maria Torre	Politechnic of Bari, Italy
Pierluigi Morano	Polytechnic of Bari, Italy
Debora Anelli	Polytechnic of Bari, Italy
Francesco Tajani	Sapienza University of Rome, Italy
Simona Panaro	University of Sussex, UK

Ecosystem Services in Spatial Planning for Resilient Urban and Rural Areas (ESSP 2023)

Sabrina Lai	University of Cagliari, Italy
Francesco Scorza	University of Basilicata, Italy
Corrado Zoppi	University of Cagliari, Italy

Gerardo Carpentieri   University of Naples Federico II, Italy
Floriana Zucaro   University of Naples Federico II, Italy
Ana Clara Mourão Moura   Federal University of Minas Gerais, Brazil

Ethical AI Applications for a Human-Centered Cyber Society (EthicAI 2023)

Valentina Franzoni   University of Perugia, Italy
Alfredo Milani   University of Perugia, Italy
Jordi Vallverdu   University Autonoma Barcelona, Spain
Roberto Capobianco   Sapienza University of Rome, Italy

13th International Workshop on Future Computing System Technologies and Applications (FiSTA 2023)

Bernady Apduhan   Kyushu Sangyo University, Japan
Rafael Santos   National Institute for Space Research, Brazil

Collaborative Planning and Designing for the Future with Geospatial Applications (GeoCollab 2023)

Alenka Poplin   Iowa State University, USA
Rosanna Rivero   University of Georgia, USA
Michele Campagna   University of Cagliari, Italy
Ana Clara Mourão Moura   Federal University of Minas Gerais, Brazil

Geomatics in Agriculture and Forestry: New Advances and Perspectives (GeoForAgr 2023)

Maurizio Pollino   Italian National Agency for New Technologies, Energy and Sustainable Economic Development, Italy
Giuseppe Modica   University of Reggio Calabria, Italy
Marco Vizzari   University of Perugia, Italy
Salvatore Praticò   University of Reggio Calabria, Italy

Geographical Analysis, Urban Modeling, Spatial Statistics (Geog-An-Mod 2023)

Giuseppe Borruso	University of Trieste, Italy
Beniamino Murgante	University of Basilicata, Italy
Harmut Asche	Hasso-Plattner-Institut für Digital Engineering Ggmbh, Germany

Geomatics for Resource Monitoring and Management (GRMM 2023)

Alessandra Capolupo	Polytechnic of Bari, Italy
Eufemia Tarantino	Polytechnic of Bari, Italy
Enrico Borgogno Mondino	University of Turin, Italy

International Workshop on Information and Knowledge in the Internet of Things (IKIT 2023)

Teresa Guarda	Peninsula State University of Santa Elena, Ecuador
Modestos Stavrakis	University of the Aegean, Greece

International Workshop on Collective, Massive and Evolutionary Systems (IWCES 2023)

Alfredo Milani	University of Perugia, Italy
Rajdeep Niyogi	Indian Institute of Technology, India
Valentina Franzoni	University of Perugia, Italy

Multidimensional Evolutionary Evaluations for Transformative Approaches (MEETA 2023)

Maria Cerreta	University of Naples Federico II, Italy
Giuliano Poli	University of Naples Federico II, Italy
Ludovica Larocca	University of Naples Federico II, Italy
Chiara Mazzarella	University of Naples Federico II, Italy

Stefania Regalbuto   University of Naples Federico II, Italy
Maria Somma   University of Naples Federico II, Italy

Building Multi-dimensional Models for Assessing Complex Environmental Systems (MES 2023)

Marta Dell'Ovo   Politechnic of Milan, Italy
Vanessa Assumma   University of Bologna, Italy
Caterina Caprioli   Politechnic of Turin, Italy
Giulia Datola   Politechnic of Turin, Italy
Federico Dellanna   Politechnic of Turin, Italy
Marco Rossitti   Politechnic of Milan, Italy

Metropolitan City Lab (Metro_City_Lab 2023)

Ginevra Balletto   University of Cagliari, Italy
Luigi Mundula   University for Foreigners of Perugia, Italy
Giuseppe Borruso   University of Trieste, Italy
Jacopo Torriti   University of Reading, UK
Isabella Ligia   Metropolitan City of Cagliari, Italy

Mathematical Methods for Image Processing and Understanding (MMIPU 2023)

Ivan Gerace   University of Perugia, Italy
Gianluca Vinti   University of Perugia, Italy
Arianna Travaglini   University of Florence, Italy

Models and Indicators for Assessing and Measuring the Urban Settlement Development in the View of ZERO Net Land Take by 2050 (MOVEto0 2023)

Lucia Saganeiti   University of L'Aquila, Italy
Lorena Fiorini   University of L'Aquila, Italy
Angela Pilogallo   University of L'Aquila, Italy
Alessandro Marucci   University of L'Aquila, Italy
Francesco Zullo   University of L'Aquila, Italy

Modelling Post-Covid Cities (MPCC 2023)

Giuseppe Borruso	University of Trieste, Italy
Beniamino Murgante	University of Basilicata, Italy
Ginevra Balletto	University of Cagliari, Italy
Lucia Saganeiti	University of L'Aquila, Italy
Marco Dettori	University of Sassari, Italy

3rd Workshop on Privacy in the Cloud/Edge/IoT World (PCEIoT 2023)

Michele Mastroianni	University of Salerno, Italy
Lelio Campanile	University of Campania Luigi Vanvitelli, Italy
Mauro Iacono	University of Campania Luigi Vanvitelli, Italy

Port City Interface: Land Use, Logistic and Rear Port Area Planning (PORTUNO 2023)

Tiziana Campisi	University of Enna Kore, Italy
Socrates Basbas	Aristotle University of Thessaloniki, Greece
Efstathios Bouhouras	Aristotle University of Thessaloniki, Greece
Giovanni Tesoriere	University of Enna Kore, Italy
Elena Cocuzza	University of Catania, Italy
Gianfranco Fancello	University of Cagliari, Italy

Scientific Computing Infrastructure (SCI 2023)

Elena Stankova	St. Petersburg State University, Russia
Vladimir Korkhov	St. Petersburg University, Russia

Supply Chains, IoT, and Smart Technologies (SCIS 2023)

Ha Jin Hwang	Sunway University, South Korea
Hangkon Kim	Daegu Catholic University, South Korea
Jan Seruga	Australian Catholic University, Australia

Spatial Cognition in Urban and Regional Planning Under Risk (SCOPUR23)

Domenico Camarda	Polytechnic of Bari, Italy
Giulia Mastrodonato	Polytechnic of Bari, Italy
Stefania Santoro	Polytechnic of Bari, Italy
Maria Rosaria Stufano Melone	Polytechnic of Bari, Italy
Mauro Patano	Polytechnic of Bari, Italy

Socio-Economic and Environmental Models for Land Use Management (SEMLUM 2023)

Debora Anelli	Polytechnic of Bari, Italy
Pierluigi Morano	Polytechnic of Bari, Italy
Benedetto Manganelli	University of Basilicata, Italy
Francesco Tajani	Sapienza University of Rome, Italy
Marco Locurcio	Polytechnic of Bari, Italy
Felicia Di Liddo	Polytechnic of Bari, Italy

Ports of the Future - Smartness and Sustainability (SmartPorts 2023)

Ginevra Balletto	University of Cagliari, Italy
Gianfranco Fancello	University of Cagliari, Italy
Patrizia Serra	University of Cagliari, Italy
Agostino Bruzzone	University of Genoa, Italy
Alberto Camarero	Politechnic of Madrid, Spain
Thierry Vanelslander	University of Antwerp, Belgium

Smart Transport and Logistics - Smart Supply Chains (SmarTransLog 2023)

Giuseppe Borruso	University of Trieste, Italy
Marco Mazzarino	University of Venice, Italy
Marcello Tadini	University of Eastern Piedmont, Italy
Luigi Mundula	University for Foreigners of Perugia, Italy
Mara Ladu	University of Cagliari, Italy
Maria del Mar Munoz Leonisio	University of Cadiz, Spain

Smart Tourism (SmartTourism 2023)

Giuseppe Borruso	University of Trieste, Italy
Silvia Battino	University of Sassari, Italy
Ainhoa Amaro Garcia	University of Alcala and University of Las Palmas, Spain
Francesca Krasna	University of Trieste, Italy
Ginevra Balletto	University of Cagliari, Italy
Maria del Mar Munoz Leonisio	University of Cadiz, Spain

Sustainability Performance Assessment: Models, Approaches, and Applications Toward Interdisciplinary and Integrated Solutions (SPA 2023)

Sabrina Lai	University of Cagliari, Italy
Francesco Scorza	University of Basilicata, Italy
Jolanta Dvarioniene	Kaunas University of Technology, Lithuania
Valentin Grecu	Lucian Blaga University of Sibiu, Romania
Georgia Pozoukidou	Aristotle University of Thessaloniki, Greece

Spatial Energy Planning, City and Urban Heritage (Spatial_Energy_City 2023)

Ginevra Balletto	University of Cagliari, Italy
Mara Ladu	University of Cagliari, Italy
Emilio Ghiani	University of Cagliari, Italy
Roberto De Lotto	University of Pavia, Italy
Roberto Gerundo	University of Salerno, Italy

Specifics of Smart Cities Development in Europe (SPEED 2023)

Chiara Garau	University of Cagliari, Italy
Katarína Vitálišová	Matej Bel University, Slovakia
Paolo Nesi	University of Florence, Italy
Anna Vaňová	Matej Bel University, Slovakia
Kamila Borsekova	Matej Bel University, Slovakia
Paola Zamperlin	University of Pisa, Italy

Smart, Safe and Health Cities (SSHC 2023)

Chiara Garau	University of Cagliari, Italy
Gerardo Carpentieri	University of Naples Federico II, Italy
Floriana Zucaro	University of Naples Federico II, Italy
Aynaz Lotfata	Chicago State University, USA
Alfonso Annunziata	University of Basilicata, Italy
Diego Altafini	University of Pisa, Italy

Smart and Sustainable Island Communities (SSIC_2023)

Chiara Garau	University of Cagliari, Italy
Anastasia Stratigea	National Technical University of Athens, Greece
Yiota Theodora	National Technical University of Athens, Greece
Giulia Desogus	University of Cagliari, Italy

Theoretical and Computational Chemistry and Its Applications (TCCMA 2023)

Noelia Faginas-Lago	University of Perugia, Italy
Andrea Lombardi	University of Perugia, Italy

Transport Infrastructures for Smart Cities (TISC 2023)

Francesca Maltinti	University of Cagliari, Italy
Mauro Coni	University of Cagliari, Italy
Francesco Pinna	University of Cagliari, Italy
Chiara Garau	University of Cagliari, Italy
Nicoletta Rassu	University of Cagliari, Italy
James Rombi	University of Cagliari, Italy

Urban Regeneration: Innovative Tools and Evaluation Model (URITEM 2023)

Fabrizio Battisti	University of Florence, Italy
Giovanna Acampa	University of Florence and University of Enna Kore, Italy
Orazio Campo	La Sapienza University of Rome, Italy

Urban Space Accessibility and Mobilities (USAM 2023)

Chiara Garau	University of Cagliari, Italy
Matteo Ignaccolo	University of Catania, Italy
Michela Tiboni	University of Brescia, Italy
Francesco Pinna	University of Cagliari, Italy
Silvia Rossetti	University of Parma, Italy
Vincenza Torrisi	University of Catania, Italy
Ilaria Delponte	University of Genoa, Italy

Virtual Reality and Augmented Reality and Applications (VRA 2023)

Osvaldo Gervasi	University of Perugia, Italy
Damiano Perri	University of Florence, Italy
Marco Simonetti	University of Florence, Italy
Sergio Tasso	University of Perugia, Italy

Workshop on Advanced and Computational Methods for Earth Science Applications (WACM4ES 2023)

Luca Piroddi	University of Malta, Malta
Sebastiano Damico	University of Malta, Malta
Marilena Cozzolino	Università del Molise, Italy
Adam Gauci	University of Malta, Italy
Giuseppina Vacca	University of Cagliari, Italy
Chiara Garau	University of Cagliari, Italy

Sponsoring Organizations

ICCSA 2023 would not have been possible without the tremendous support of many organizations and institutions, for which all organizers and participants of ICCSA 2023 express their sincere gratitude:

Springer Nature Switzerland AG, Switzerland
(https://www.springer.com)

Computers Open Access Journal
(https://www.mdpi.com/journal/computers)

National Technical University of Athens, Greece
(https://www.ntua.gr/)

University of the Aegean, Greece
(https://www.aegean.edu/)

University of Perugia, Italy
(https://www.unipg.it)

University of Basilicata, Italy
(http://www.unibas.it)

 MONASH University   Monash University, Australia
                            (https://www.monash.edu/)

   Kyushu Sangyo University, Japan
                            (https://www.kyusan-u.ac.jp/)

        University of Minho, Portugal
                            (https://www.uminho.pt/)

Universidade do Minho
Escola de Engenharia

Referees

Francesca Abastante	Turin Polytechnic, Italy
Giovanna Acampa	University of Enna Kore, Italy
Adewole Adewumi	Algonquin College, Canada
Vera Afreixo	University of Aveiro, Portugal
Riad Aggoune	Luxembourg Institute of Science and Technology, Luxembourg
Akshat Agrawal	Amity University Haryana, India
Waseem Ahmad	National Institute of Technology Karnataka, India
Oylum Alatlı	Ege University, Turkey
Abraham Alfa	Federal University of Technology Minna, Nigeria
Diego Altafini	University of Pisa, Italy
Filipe Alvelos	University of Minho, Portugal
Marina Alexandra Pedro Andrade	University Institute of Lisbon, Portugal
Debora Anelli	Polytechnic University of Bari, Italy
Mariarosaria Angrisano	Pegaso University, Italy
Alfonso Annunziata	University of Cagliari, Italy
Magarò Antonio	Sapienza University of Rome, Italy
Bernady Apduhan	Kyushu Sangyo University, Japan
Jonathan Apeh	Covenant University, Nigeria
Daniela Ascenzi	University of Trento, Italy
Vanessa Assumma	University of Bologna, Italy
Maria Fernanda Augusto	Bitrum Research Center, Spain
Marco Baioletti	University of Perugia, Italy

Ginevra Balletto	University of Cagliari, Italy
Carlos Balsa	Polytechnic Institute of Bragança, Portugal
Benedetto Barabino	University of Brescia, Italy
Simona Barbaro	University of Palermo, Italy
Sebastiano Barbieri	Turin Polytechnic, Italy
Kousik Barik	University of Alcala, Spain
Alice Barreca	Turin Polytechnic, Italy
Socrates Basbas	Aristotle University of Thessaloniki, Greece
Rosaria Battarra	National Research Council, Italy
Silvia Battino	University of Sassari, Italy
Fabrizio Battisti	University of Florence, Italy
Yaroslav Bazaikin	Jan Evangelista Purkyne University, Czech Republic
Ranjan Kumar Behera	Indian Institute of Information Technology, India
Simone Belli	Complutense University of Madrid, Spain
Oscar Bellini	Polytechnic University of Milan, Italy
Giulio Biondi	University of Perugia, Italy
Adriano Bisello	Eurac Research, Italy
Semen Bochkov	Ulyanovsk State Technical University, Russia
Alexander Bogdanov	St. Petersburg State University, Russia
Letizia Bollini	Free University of Bozen, Italy
Giuseppe Borruso	University of Trieste, Italy
Marilisa Botte	University of Naples Federico II, Italy
Ana Cristina Braga	University of Minho, Portugal
Frederico Branco	University of Trás-os-Montes and Alto Douro, Portugal
Jorge Buele	Indoamérica Technological University, Ecuador
Datzania Lizeth Burgos	Peninsula State University of Santa Elena, Ecuador
Isabel Cacao	University of Aveiro, Portugal
Francesco Calabrò	Mediterranea University of Reggio Calabria, Italy
Rogerio Calazan	Institute of Sea Studies Almirante Paulo Moreira, Brazil
Lelio Campanile	University of Campania Luigi Vanvitelli, Italy
Tiziana Campisi	University of Enna Kore, Italy
Orazio Campo	University of Rome La Sapienza, Italy
Caterina Caprioli	Turin Polytechnic, Italy
Gerardo Carpentieri	University of Naples Federico II, Italy
Martina Carra	University of Brescia, Italy
Barbara Caselli	University of Parma, Italy
Danny Casprini	Politechnic of Milan, Italy

Omar Fernando Castellanos Balleteros	Peninsula State University of Santa Elena, Ecuador
Arcangelo Castiglione	University of Salerno, Italy
Giulio Cavana	Turin Polytechnic, Italy
Maria Cerreta	University of Naples Federico II, Italy
Sabarathinam Chockalingam	Institute for Energy Technology, Norway
Luis Enrique Chuquimarca Jimenez	Peninsula State University of Santa Elena, Ecuador
Birol Ciloglugil	Ege University, Turkey
Elena Cocuzza	Univesity of Catania, Italy
Emanuele Colica	University of Malta, Malta
Mauro Coni	University of Cagliari, Italy
Simone Corrado	University of Basilicata, Italy
Elisete Correia	University of Trás-os-Montes and Alto Douro, Portugal
Florbela Correia	Polytechnic Institute Viana do Castelo, Portugal
Paulo Cortez	University of Minho, Portugal
Martina Corti	Politechnic of Milan, Italy
Lino Costa	Universidade do Minho, Portugal
Cecília Maria Vasconcelos Costa e Castro	University of Minho, Portugal
Alfredo Cuzzocrea	University of Calabria, Italy
Sebastiano D'amico	University of Malta, Malta
Maria Danese	National Research Council, Italy
Gianni Dangelo	University of Salerno, Italy
Ana Daniel	Aveiro University, Portugal
Giulia Datola	Politechnic of Milan, Italy
Regina De Almeida	University of Trás-os-Montes and Alto Douro, Portugal
Maria Stella De Biase	University of Campania Luigi Vanvitelli, Italy
Elise De Doncker	Western Michigan University, USA
Luiza De Macedo Mourelle	State University of Rio de Janeiro, Brazil
Itamir De Morais Barroca Filho	Federal University of Rio Grande do Norte, Brazil
Pierfrancesco De Paola	University of Naples Federico II, Italy
Francesco De Pascale	University of Turin, Italy
Manuela De Ruggiero	University of Calabria, Italy
Alexander Degtyarev	St. Petersburg State University, Russia
Federico Dellanna	Turin Polytechnic, Italy
Marta Dellovo	Politechnic of Milan, Italy
Bashir Derradji	Sfax University, Tunisia
Giulia Desogus	University of Cagliari, Italy
Frank Devai	London South Bank University, UK

Piero Di Bonito	University of Campania Luigi Vanvitelli, Italy
Chiara Di Dato	University of L'Aquila, Italy
Michele Di Giovanni	University of Campania Luigi Vanvitelli, Italy
Felicia Di Liddo	Polytechnic University of Bari, Italy
Joana Dias	University of Coimbra, Portugal
Luigi Dolores	University of Salerno, Italy
Marco Donatelli	University of Insubria, Italy
Aziz Dursun	Virginia Tech University, USA
Jaroslav Dvořak	Klaipeda University, Lithuania
Wolfgang Erb	University of Padova, Italy
Maurizio Francesco Errigo	University of Enna Kore, Italy
Noelia Faginas-Lago	University of Perugia, Italy
Maria Irene Falcao	University of Minho, Portugal
Stefano Falcinelli	University of Perugia, Italy
Grazia Fattoruso	Italian National Agency for New Technologies, Energy and Sustainable Economic Development, Italy
Sara Favargiotti	University of Trento, Italy
Marcin Feltynowski	University of Lodz, Poland
António Fernandes	Polytechnic Institute of Bragança, Portugal
Florbela P. Fernandes	Polytechnic Institute of Bragança, Portugal
Paula Odete Fernandes	Polytechnic Institute of Bragança, Portugal
Luis Fernandez-Sanz	University of Alcala, Spain
Maria Eugenia Ferrao	University of Beira Interior and University of Lisbon, Portugal
Luís Ferrás	University of Minho, Portugal
Angela Ferreira	Polytechnic Institute of Bragança, Portugal
Maddalena Ferretti	Politechnic of Marche, Italy
Manuel Carlos Figueiredo	University of Minho, Portugal
Fabrizio Finucci	Roma Tre University, Italy
Ugo Fiore	University Pathenope of Naples, Italy
Lorena Fiorini	University of L'Aquila, Italy
Valentina Franzoni	Perugia University, Italy
Adelaide Freitas	University of Aveiro, Portugal
Kirill Gadylshin	Russian Academy of Sciences, Russia
Andrea Gallo	University of Trieste, Italy
Luciano Galone	University of Malta, Malta
Chiara Garau	University of Cagliari, Italy
Ernesto Garcia Para	Universidad del País Vasco, Spain
Rachele Vanessa Gatto	Università della Basilicata, Italy
Marina Gavrilova	University of Calgary, Canada
Georgios Georgiadis	Aristotle University of Thessaloniki, Greece

Ivan Gerace	University of Perugia, Italy
Osvaldo Gervasi	University of Perugia, Italy
Alfonso Giancotti	Sapienza University of Rome, Italy
Andrea Gioia	Politechnic of Bari, Italy
Giacomo Giorgi	University of Perugia, Italy
Salvatore Giuffrida	Università di Catania, Italy
A. Manuela Gonçalves	University of Minho, Portugal
Angela Gorgoglione	University of the Republic, Uruguay
Yusuke Gotoh	Okayama University, Japan
Mariolina Grasso	University of Enna Kore, Italy
Silvana Grillo	University of Cagliari, Italy
Teresa Guarda	Universidad Estatal Peninsula de Santa Elena, Ecuador
Eduardo Guerra	Free University of Bozen-Bolzano, Italy
Carmen Guida	University of Napoli Federico II, Italy
Kemal Güven Gülen	Namık Kemal University, Turkey
Malgorzata Hanzl	Technical University of Lodz, Poland
Peter Hegedus	University of Szeged, Hungary
Syeda Sumbul Hossain	Daffodil International University, Bangladesh
Mustafa Inceoglu	Ege University, Turkey
Federica Isola	University of Cagliari, Italy
Seifedine Kadry	Noroff University College, Norway
Yeliz Karaca	University of Massachusetts Chan Medical School and Massachusetts Institute of Technology, USA
Harun Karsli	Bolu Abant Izzet Baysal University, Turkey
Tayana Khachkova	Russian Academy of Sciences, Russia
Manju Khari	Jawaharlal Nehru University, India
Vladimir Korkhov	Saint Petersburg State University, Russia
Dionisia Koutsi	National Technical University of Athens, Greece
Tomonori Kouya	Shizuoka Institute of Science and Technology, Japan
Nataliia Kulabukhova	Saint Petersburg State University, Russia
Anisha Kumari	National Institute of Technology, India
Ludovica La Rocca	University of Napoli Federico II, Italy
Mara Ladu	University of Cagliari, Italy
Sabrina Lai	University of Cagliari, Italy
Mohamed Laib	Luxembourg Institute of Science and Technology, Luxembourg
Giuseppe Francesco Cesare Lama	University of Napoli Federico II, Italy
Isabella Maria Lami	Turin Polytechnic, Italy
Chien Sing Lee	Sunway University, Malaysia

Marcelo Leon	Ecotec University, Ecuador
Federica Leone	University of Cagliari, Italy
Barbara Lino	University of Palermo, Italy
Vadim Lisitsa	Russian Academy of Sciences, Russia
Carla Lobo	Portucalense University, Portugal
Marco Locurcio	Polytechnic University of Bari, Italy
Claudia Loggia	University of KwaZulu-Natal, South Africa
Andrea Lombardi	University of Perugia, Italy
Isabel Lopes	Polytechnic Institut of Bragança, Portugal
Immacolata Lorè	Mediterranean University of Reggio Calabria, Italy
Vanda Lourenco	Nova University of Lisbon, Portugal
Giorgia Malavasi	Turin Polytechnic, Italy
Francesca Maltinti	University of Cagliari, Italy
Luca Mancini	University of Perugia, Italy
Marcos Mandado	University of Vigo, Spain
Benedetto Manganelli	University of Basilicata, Italy
Krassimir Markov	Institute of Electric Engineering and Informatics, Bulgaria
Enzo Martinelli	University of Salerno, Italy
Fiammetta Marulli	University of Campania Luigi Vanvitelli, Italy
Antonino Marvuglia	Luxembourg Institute of Science and Technology, Luxembourg
Rytis Maskeliunas	Kaunas University of Technology, Lithuania
Michele Mastroianni	University of Salerno, Italy
Hideo Matsufuru	High Energy Accelerator Research Organization, Japan
D'Apuzzo Mauro	University of Cassino and Southern Lazio, Italy
Luis Mazon	Bitrum Research Group, Spain
Chiara Mazzarella	University Federico II, Naples, Italy
Beatrice Mecca	Turin Polytechnic, Italy
Umberto Mecca	Turin Polytechnic, Italy
Paolo Mengoni	Hong Kong Baptist University, China
Gaetano Messina	Mediterranean University of Reggio Calabria, Italy
Alfredo Milani	University of Perugia, Italy
Alessandra Milesi	University of Cagliari, Italy
Richard Millham	Durban University of Technology, South Africa
Fernando Miranda	Universidade do Minho, Portugal
Biswajeeban Mishra	University of Szeged, Hungary
Giuseppe Modica	University of Reggio Calabria, Italy
Pierluigi Morano	Polytechnic University of Bari, Italy

Filipe Mota Pinto	Polytechnic Institute of Leiria, Portugal
Maria Mourao	Polytechnic Institute of Viana do Castelo, Portugal
Eugenio Muccio	University of Naples Federico II, Italy
Beniamino Murgante	University of Basilicata, Italy
Rocco Murro	Sapienza University of Rome, Italy
Giuseppe Musolino	Mediterranean University of Reggio Calabria, Italy
Nadia Nedjah	State University of Rio de Janeiro, Brazil
Juraj Nemec	Masaryk University, Czech Republic
Andreas Nikiforiadis	Aristotle University of Thessaloniki, Greece
Silvio Nocera	IUAV University of Venice, Italy
Roseline Ogundokun	Kaunas University of Technology, Lithuania
Emma Okewu	University of Alcala, Spain
Serena Olcuire	Sapienza University of Rome, Italy
Irene Oliveira	University Trás-os-Montes and Alto Douro, Portugal
Samson Oruma	Ostfold University College, Norway
Antonio Pala	University of Cagliari, Italy
Maria Panagiotopoulou	National Technical University of Athens, Greece
Simona Panaro	University of Sussex Business School, UK
Jay Pancham	Durban University of Technology, South Africa
Eric Pardede	La Trobe University, Australia
Hyun Kyoo Park	Ministry of National Defense, South Korea
Damiano Perri	University of Florence, Italy
Quoc Trung Pham	Ho Chi Minh City University of Technology, Vietnam
Claudio Piferi	University of Florence, Italy
Angela Pilogallo	University of L'Aquila, Italy
Francesco Pinna	University of Cagliari, Italy
Telmo Pinto	University of Coimbra, Portugal
Luca Piroddi	University of Malta, Malta
Francesco Pittau	Politechnic of Milan, Italy
Giuliano Poli	Università Federico II di Napoli, Italy
Maurizio Pollino	Italian National Agency for New Technologies, Energy and Sustainable Economic Development, Italy
Vijay Prakash	University of Malta, Malta
Salvatore Praticò	Mediterranean University of Reggio Calabria, Italy
Carlotta Quagliolo	Turin Polytechnic, Italy
Garrisi Raffaele	Operations Center for Cyber Security, Italy
Mariapia Raimondo	Università della Campania Luigi Vanvitelli, Italy

Bruna Ramos	Universidade Lusíada Norte, Portugal
Nicoletta Rassu	University of Cagliari, Italy
Roberta Ravanelli	University of Roma La Sapienza, Italy
Pier Francesco Recchi	University of Naples Federico II, Italy
Stefania Regalbuto	University of Naples Federico II, Italy
Rommel Regis	Saint Joseph's University, USA
Marco Reis	University of Coimbra, Portugal
Jerzy Respondek	Silesian University of Technology, Poland
Isabel Ribeiro	Polytechnic Institut of Bragança, Portugal
Albert Rimola	Autonomous University of Barcelona, Spain
Corrado Rindone	Mediterranean University of Reggio Calabria, Italy
Maria Rocco	Roma Tre University, Italy
Ana Maria A. C. Rocha	University of Minho, Portugal
Fabio Rocha	Universidade Federal de Sergipe, Brazil
Humberto Rocha	University of Coimbra, Portugal
Maria Clara Rocha	Politechnic Institut of Coimbra, Portual
Carlos Rodrigues	Polytechnic Institut of Bragança, Portugal
Diana Rolando	Turin Polytechnic, Italy
James Rombi	University of Cagliari, Italy
Evgeniy Romenskiy	Russian Academy of Sciences, Russia
Marzio Rosi	University of Perugia, Italy
Silvia Rossetti	University of Parma, Italy
Marco Rossitti	Politechnic of Milan, Italy
Antonio Russo	University of Enna, Italy
Insoo Ryu	MoaSoftware, South Korea
Yeonseung Ryu	Myongji University, South Korea
Lucia Saganeiti	University of L'Aquila, Italy
Valentina Santarsiero	University of Basilicata, Italy
Luigi Santopietro	University of Basilicata, Italy
Rafael Santos	National Institute for Space Research, Brazil
Valentino Santucci	University for Foreigners of Perugia, Italy
Alessandra Saponieri	University of Salento, Italy
Mattia Scalas	Turin Polytechnic, Italy
Francesco Scorza	University of Basilicata, Italy
Ester Scotto Di Perta	University of Napoli Federico II, Italy
Nicoletta Setola	University of Florence, Italy
Ricardo Severino	University of Minho, Portugal
Angela Silva	Polytechnic Institut of Viana do Castelo, Portugal
Carina Silva	Polytechnic of Lisbon, Portugal
Marco Simonetti	University of Florence, Italy
Sergey Solovyev	Russian Academy of Sciences, Russia

Maria Somma	University of Naples Federico II, Italy
Changgeun Son	Ministry of National Defense, South Korea
Alberico Sonnessa	Polytechnic of Bari, Italy
Inês Sousa	University of Minho, Portugal
Lisete Sousa	University of Lisbon, Portugal
Elena Stankova	Saint-Petersburg State University, Russia
Modestos Stavrakis	University of the Aegean, Greece
Flavio Stochino	University of Cagliari, Italy
Anastasia Stratigea	National Technical University of Athens, Greece
Yue Sun	European XFEL GmbH, Germany
Anthony Suppa	Turin Polytechnic, Italy
David Taniar	Monash University, Australia
Rodrigo Tapia McClung	Centre for Research in Geospatial Information Sciences, Mexico
Tarek Teba	University of Portsmouth, UK
Ana Paula Teixeira	University of Trás-os-Montes and Alto Douro, Portugal
Tengku Adil Tengku Izhar	Technological University MARA, Malaysia
Maria Filomena Teodoro	University of Lisbon and Portuguese Naval Academy, Portugal
Yiota Theodora	National Technical University of Athens, Greece
Elena Todella	Turin Polytechnic, Italy
Graça Tomaz	Polytechnic Institut of Guarda, Portugal
Anna Tonazzini	National Research Council, Italy
Dario Torregrossa	Goodyear, Luxembourg
Francesca Torrieri	University of Naples Federico II, Italy
Vincenza Torrisi	University of Catania, Italy
Nikola Tosic	Polytechnic University of Catalonia, Spain
Vincenzo Totaro	Polytechnic University of Bari, Italy
Arianna Travaglini	University of Florence, Italy
António Trigo	Polytechnic of Coimbra, Portugal
Giuseppe A. Trunfio	University of Sassari, Italy
Toshihiro Uchibayashi	Kyushu University, Japan
Piero Ugliengo	University of Torino, Italy
Jordi Vallverdu	University Autonoma Barcelona, Spain
Gianmarco Vanuzzo	University of Perugia, Italy
Dmitry Vasyunin	T-Systems, Russia
Laura Verde	University of Campania Luigi Vanvitelli, Italy
Giulio Vignoli	University of Cagliari, Italy
Gianluca Vinti	University of Perugia, Italy
Katarína Vitálišová	Matej Bel University, Slovak Republic
Daniel Mark Vitiello	University of Cagliari

Plenary Lectures

A Multiscale Planning Concept for Sustainable Metropolitan Development

Pierre Frankhauser

Théma, Université de Franche-Comté, 32, rue Mégevand, 20030 Besançon, France
pierre.frankhauser@univ-fcomte.fr

Keywords: Sustainable metropolitan development · Multiscale approach · Urban modelling

Urban sprawl has often been pointed out as having an important negative impact on environment and climate. Residential zones have grown up in what were initially rural areas, located far from employment areas and often lacking shopping opportunities, public services and public transportation. Hence urban sprawl increased car-traffic flows, generating pollution and increasing energy consumption. New road axes consume considerable space and weaken biodiversity by reducing and cutting natural areas. A return to "compact cities" or "dense cities" has often been contemplated as the most efficient way to limit urban sprawl. However, the real impact of density on car use is less clear-cut (Daneshpour and Shakibamanesh 2011). Let us emphasize that moreover climate change will increase the risk of heat islands on an intra-urban scale. This prompts a more nuanced reflection on how urban fabrics should be structured.

Moreover, urban planning cannot ignore social demand. Lower land prices in rural areas, often put forward by economists, is not the only reason of urban sprawl. The quality of the residential environment comes into play, too, through features like noise, pollution, landscape quality, density etc. Schwanen et al. (2004) observe for the Netherlands that households preferring a quiet residential environment and individual housing with a garden will not accept densification, which might even lead them to move to lower-density rural areas even farther away from jobs and shopping amenities. Many scholars emphasize the importance of green amenities for residential environments and report the importance of easy access to leisure areas (Guo and Bhat 2002). Vegetation in the residential environment has an important impact on health and well-being (Lafortezza et al. 2009).

We present here the Fractalopolis concept which we developed in the frame of several research projects and which aims reconciling environmental and social issues (Bonin et al., 2020; Frankhauser 2021; Frankhauser et al. 2018). This concept introduces a multiscale approach based on multifractal geometry for conceiving spatial development for metropolitan areas. For taking into account social demand we refer to the fundamental work of Max-Neef et al. (1991) based on Maslow's work about basic human needs. He introduces the concept of satisfiers assigned to meet the basic needs of "Subsistence, Protection, Affection, Understanding, Participation, Idleness, Creation, Identity and Freedom". Satisfiers thus become the link between the needs of everyone and society and may depend on the cultural context. We consider their importance, their location and their accessibility and we rank the needs according to their importance for individuals or households. In order to enjoy a good quality of life and to shorten trips and to reduce automobile use, it seems important for satisfiers of daily needs to be easily accessible. Hence, we consider the purchase rate when reflecting on the implementation of shops which is reminiscent of central place theory.

The second important feature is taking care of environment and biodiversity by avoiding fragmentation of green space (Ekren and Arslan 2022) which must benefit, moreover, of a good accessibility, as pointed out. These areas must, too, ply the role of cooling areas ensuring ventilation of urbanized areas (Kuttler et al. 1998).

For integrating these different objectives, we propose a concept for developing spatial configurations of metropolitan areas designed which is based on multifractal geometry. It allows combining different issues across a large range of scales in a coherent way. These issues include:

- providing easy access to a large array of amenities to meet social demand;
- promoting the use of public transportation and soft modes instead of automobile use;
- preserving biodiversity and improving the local climate.

The concept distinguishes development zones localized in the vicinity of a nested and hierarchized system of public transport axes. The highest ranked center offers all types of amenities, whereas lower ranked centers lack the highest ranked amenities. The lowest ranked centers just offer the amenities for daily needs. A coding system allows distinguishing the centers according to their rank.

Each subset of central places is in some sense autonomous, since they are not linked by transportation axes to subcenters of the same order. This allows to preserve a linked system of green corridors penetrating the development zones across scales avoiding the fragmentation of green areas and ensuring a good accessibility to recreational areas.

The spatial model is completed by a population distribution model which globally follows the same hierarchical logic. However, we weakened the strong fractal order what allows to conceive a more or less polycentric spatial system.

We can adapt the theoretical concept easily to real world situation without changing the underlying multiscale logic. A decision support system has been developed allowing to simulate development scenarios and to evaluate them. The evaluation procedure is based on fuzzy evaluation of distance acceptance for accessing to the different types of amenities according to the ranking of needs. We used for evaluation data issued from a great set of French planning documents like Master plans. We show an example how the software package can be used concretely.

References

Bonin, O., et al.: Projet SOFT sobriété énergétique par les formes urbaines et le transport (Research Report No. 1717C0003; p. 214). ADEME (2020)

Daneshpour, A., Shakibamanesh, A.: Compact city; dose it create an obligatory context for urban sustainability? Int. J. Archit. Eng. Urban Plann. 21(2), 110–118 (2011)

Ekren, E., Arslan, M.: Functions of greenways as an ecologically-based planning strategy. In: Çakır, M., Tuğluer, M., Fırat Örs, P.: Architectural Sciences and Ecology, pp. 134–156. Iksad Publications (2022)

Frankhauser, P.: Fractalopolis—a fractal concept for the sustainable development of metropolitan areas. In: Sajous, P., Bertelle, C. (eds.) Complex Systems, Smart Territories and Mobility, pp. 15–50. Springer, Cham (2021). https://doi.org/10.1007/978-3-030-59302-5_2

Frankhauser, P., Tannier, C., Vuidel, G., Houot, H.: An integrated multifractal modelling to urban and regional planning. Comput. Environ. Urban Syst. **67**(1), 132–146 (2018). https://doi.org/10.1016/j.compenvurbsys.2017.09.011

Guo, J., Bhat, C.: Residential location modeling: accommodating sociodemographic, school quality and accessibility effects. University of Texas, Austin (2002)

Kuttler, W., Dütemeyer, D., Barlag, A.-B.: Influence of regional and local winds on urban ventilation in Cologne, Germany. Meteorologische Zeitschrift, 77–87 (1998) https://doi.org/10.1127/metz/7/1998/77

Lafortezza, R., Carrus, G., Sanesi, G., Davies, C.: Benefits and well-being perceived by people visiting green spaces in periods of heat stress. Urban For. Urban Green. **8**(2), 97–108 (2009)

Max-Neef, M. A., Elizalde, A., Hopenhayn, M.: Human scale development: conception, application and further reflections. The Apex Press (1991)

Schwanen, T., Dijst, M., Dieleman, F. M.: Policies for urban form and their impact on travel: The Netherlands experience. Urban Stud. **41**(3), 579–603 (2004)

Graph Drawing and Network Visualization – An Overview – (Keynote Speech)

Giuseppe Liotta

Dipartimento di Ingegneria, Università degli Studi di Perugia, Italy
giuseppe.liotta@unipg.it

Abstract. Graph Drawing and Network visualization supports the exploration, analysis, and communication of relational data arising in a variety of application domains: from bioinformatics to software engineering, from social media to cyber-security, from data bases to powergrid systems. Aim of this keynote speech is to introduce this thriving research area, highlighting some of its basic approaches and pointing to some promising research directions.

1 Introduction

Graph Drawing and Network Visualization is at the intersection of different disciplines and it combines topics that traditionally belong to theoretical computer science with methods and approaches that characterize more applied disciplines. Namely, it can be related to Graph Algorithms, Geometric Graph Theory and Geometric computing, Combinatorial Optimization, Experimental Analysis, User Studies, System Design and Development, and Human Computer Interaction. This combination of theory and practice is well reflected in the flagship conference of the area, the *International Symposium on Graph Drawing and Network Visualization*, that has two tracks, one focusing on combinatorial and algorithmic aspects and the other on the design of network visualization systems and interfaces. The conference is now at its 31st edition; a full list of the symposia and their proceedings, published by Springer in the LNCS series can be found at the URL: http://www.graphdrawing.org/.

Aim of this short paper is to outline the content of my Keynote Speech at ICCSA 2023, which will be referred to as the "Talk" in the rest of the paper. The talk will introduce the field of Graph Drawing and Network Visualization to a broad audience, with the goal to not only present some key methodological and technological aspects, but also point to some unexplored or partially explored research directions. The rest of this short paper briefly outlines the content of the talk and provides some references that can be a starting point for researchers interested in working on Graph Drawing and Network Visualization.

2 Why Visualize Networks?

Back in 1973 the famous statistician Francis Anscombe, gave a convincing example of
why visualization is fundamental component of data analysis. The example is known
as the *Anscombe's quartet* [3] and it consists of four sets of 11 points each that are
almost identical in terms of the basic statistic properties of their x– and y– coordinates.
Namely the mean values and the variance of x and y are exactly the same in the four
sets, while the correlation of x and y and the linear regression are the same up to the
second decimal. In spite of this statistical similarity, the data look very different when
displayed in the Euclidean plane which leads to the conclusion that they correspond to
significantly different phenomena. Figure 1 reports the four sets of Anscombe's quartet.
After fifty years, with the arrival of AI-based technologies and the need of explaining and
interpreting machine-driven suggestions before making strategic decision, the lesson of
Anscombe's quartet has not just kept but even increased its relevance.

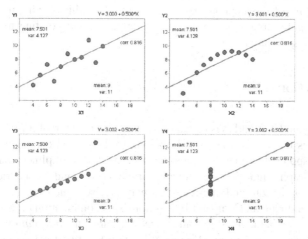

Fig. 1. The four point sets in Anscombe's quartet [3]; the figure also reports statistical values of
the x and y variables.

As a matter of fact, nowadays the need of visualization systems goes beyond the
verification of the accuracy of some statistical analysis on a set of scattered data. Recent
technological advances have generated torrents of data that area relational in nature and
typically modeled as networks: the nodes of the networks store the features of the data
and the edges of the networks describe the semantic relationships between the data features. Such networked data sets (whose algebraic underlying structure is a called graph
in discrete mathematics) arise in a variety of application domains including, for example,
Systems Biology, Social Network Analysis, Software Engineering, Networking, Data
Bases, Homeland Security, and Business Intelligence. In these (and many other) contexts, systems that support the visual analysis of networks and graphs play a central role
in critical decision making processes. These are human-in-the-loop processes where the

continuous interaction between humans (decision makers) and data mining or optimization algorithms (AI/ML components) supports the data exploration, the development of verifiable theories about the data, and the extraction of new knowledge that is used to make strategic choices. A seminal book by Keim et al. [33] schematically represents the human-in-the-loop approach to making sense of networked data sets as in Fig. 2. See also [46–49].

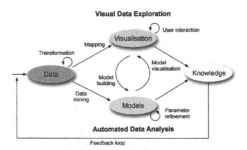

Fig. 2. Sense-making/knowledge generation loop. This conceptual interaction model between human analysts and network visualization system is at the basis of network visual analytics system design [33].

To make a concrete application example of the analysis of a network by interacting with its visualization, consider the problem of contrasting financial crimes such as money laundering or tax evasion. These crimes are based on relevant volumes of financial transactions to conceal the identity, the source, or the destination of illegally gained money. Also, the adopted patterns to pursue the illegal goals continuously change to conceal the crimes. Therefore, contrasting them requires special investigation units which must analyze very large and highly dynamic data sets and discover relationships between different subjects to untangle complex fraudulent plots. The investigative cycle begins with data collection and filtering; it is then followed by modeling the data as a social network (also called *financial activity network* in this context) to which different data mining and data analytic methods are applied, including graph pattern matching, social network analysis, machine learning, and information diffusion. By the network visualization system detectives can interactively explore the data, gain insight and make new hypotheses about possible criminal activities, verify the hypotheses by asking the system to provide more details about specific portions of the network, refine previous outputs, and eventually gain new knowledge. Figure 3 illustrates a small financial activity network where, by means of the interaction between an officer of the Italian Revenue Agency and the MALDIVE system described in [10] a fraudulent pattern has been identified. Precisely, the tax officer has encoded a risky relational scheme among taxpayers into a suspicious graph pattern; in response, the system has made a search in the taxpayer network and it has returned one such pattern. See, e.g., [9, 11, 14, 18, 38] for more papers and references about visual analytic applications to contrasting financial crimes.

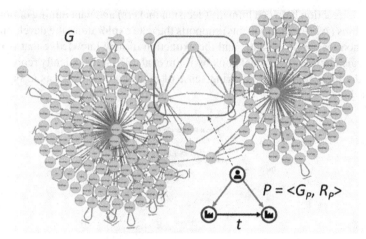

Fig. 3. A financial activity network from [10]. The pattern in the figure represents a Sup-pliesFromAssociated scheme, consisting of an economic transaction and two shareholding relationships.

3 Facets of Graph Drawing and Network Visualization

The Talk overviews some of the fundamental facets that characterize the research in Graph Drawing and Network Visualization. Namely:

– Graph drawing metaphors: Depending on the application context, different metaphors can be used to represent a relational data set modeled as a graph. The talk will briefly recall the matrix representation, the space filling representation, the contact representation, and the node-link representation which is, by far, the most commonly used (see, e.g., [43]).
– Interaction paradigms: Different interaction paradigms have different impacts on the sense-making process of the user about the visualized network. The Talk will go through the full-view, top-down, bottom-up, incremental, and narrative paradigms. Pros and cons will be highlighted for each approach, also by means of examples and applications. The discussion of the top-down interaction paradigm will also consider the hybrid visualization models (see, e.g., [2, 24, 26, 28, 39]) while the discussion about the incremental paradigm will focus on research about graph storyplans (see, e.g., [4, 6, 7]).
– Graph drawing algorithms: Three main algorithmic approaches will be reviewed, namely the force-directed, the layered), and the planarization-based approach; see, e.g., [5]. We shall also make some remarks about FPT algorithms for graph drawing (see, e.g., [8, 19, 20, 25, 27, 40, 53]) and about how the optimization challenges vary when it is assumed that the input has or does not have a fixed combinatorial embedding (see, e.g., [12, 13, 16, 17, 23]).
– Experimental analysis and user-studies: The Talk will mostly compare two models to define and experimentally validate those optimization goals that define a "readable"

network visualization, i.e. a visualization that in a given application context can easily convey the structure of a relational data set so to guarantee efficiency both in its visual exploration and in the elaboration of new knowledge. Special focus will be given to a set emerging optimization goals related to edge crossings that are currently investigated in the graph drawing and network visualization community unedr the name of "graph drawing beyond planarity" (see, e.g., [1, 15, 29, 35]).

The talk shall also point to some promising research directions, including: (i) Extend the body of papers devoted to user-studies that compare the impact of different graph drawing metaphors on the user perception. (ii) Extend the study of interaction paradigms to extended reality environments (see, e.g., [21, 30, 36, 37]); (iii) Engineer the FPT algorithms for graph drawing and experimentally compare their performances with exact or approximate solutions; and (iv) Develop new algorithmic fameworks in the context of graph drawing beyond planarity.

We conclude this short paper with pointers to publication venues and key references that can be browsed by researchers interested in the fascinating field of Graph Drawing and Network Visualization.

4   Pointers to Publication venues and Key References

A limited list of conferences where Graph Drawing and Network Visualization papers are regularly part of the program includes *IEEE VIS, EuroVis, SoCG, ISAAC, ACM-SIAM SODA, WADS,* and *WG.* Among the many journals where several Graph Drawing and Network Visualization papers have appeared during the last three decades we recall *IEEE Transactions on Visualization and Computer Graphs, SIAM Jounal of Computing, Computer Graphics Forum, Journal of Computer and System Sciences, Algorithmica, Journal of Graph Algorithms and Applications, Theoretical Computer Science, Information Sciences, Discrete and Computational Geometry, Computational Geometry: Theory and Applications, ACM Computing Surveys,* and *Computer Science Review.* A limited list of books, surveys, or papers that contain interesting algorithmic challenges on Graph Drawing and Network Visualization include [5, 15, 22, 29, 31–35, 41–45, 50–52].

References

1. Angelini, P., et al.: Simple k-planar graphs are simple (k+1)-quasiplanar. J. Comb. Theory, Ser. B, **142**, 1–35 (2020)
2. Angori, L., Didimo, W., Montecchiani, F., Pagliuca, D., Tappini, A.: Hybrid graph visualizations with chordlink: Algorithms, experiments, and applications. IEEE Trans. Vis. Comput. Graph. **28**(2), 1288–1300 (2022)
3. Anscombe, F.J.: Graphs in statistical analysis. Am. Stat. **27**(1), 17–21 (1973)
4. Di Battista, G., et al.: Small point-sets supporting graph stories. In: Angelini, P., von Hanxleden, R. (eds.) Graph Drawing and Network Visualization. GD 2022, LNCS, vol. 13764, pp. 289–303. Springer, Cham (2022). https://doi.org/10.1007/978-3-031-22203-0_21

5. Battista, G.D., Eades, P., Tamassia, R., Tollis, I.G.: Graph Drawing: Algorithms for the Visualization of Graphs. Prentice-Hall, Hoboken (1999)
6. Binucci, C., et al.: On the complexity of the storyplan problem. In: Angelini, P., von Hanxleden, R. (eds.) Graph Drawing and Network Visualization. GD 2022. LNCS, vol. 13764, pp. 304–318. Springer, Cham (2023). https://doi.org/10.1007/978-3-031-22203-0_22
7. Borrazzo, M., Lozzo, G.D., Battista, G.D., Frati, F., Patrignani, M.: Graph stories in small area. J. Graph Algorithms Appl. 24(3), 269–292 (2020)
8. Chaplick, S., Giacomo, E.D., Frati, F., Ganian, R., Raftopoulou, C.N., Simonov, K.: Parameterized algorithms for upward planarity. In: Goaoc, X., Kerber, M. (eds.) 38th International Symposium on Computational Geometry, SoCG 2022, June 7–10, 2022, Berlin, Germany, LIPIcs, vol. 224, pp. 26:1–26:16. Schloss Dagstuhl - Leibniz-Zentrum für Informatik (2022)
9. Didimo, W., Giamminonni, L., Liotta, G., Montecchiani, F., Pagliuca, D.: A visual analytics system to support tax evasion discovery. Decis. Support Syst. 110, 71–83 (2018)
10. Didimo, W., Grilli, L., Liotta, G., Menconi, L., Montecchiani, F., Pagliuca, D.: Combining network visualization and data mining for tax risk assessment. IEEE Access 8, 16073–16086 (2020)
11. Didimo, W., Grilli, L., Liotta, G., Montecchiani, F., Pagliuca, D.: Visual querying and analysis of temporal fiscal networks. Inf. Sci. 505, 406–421 (2019)
12. W. Didimo, M. Kaufmann, G. Liotta, and G. Ortali. Didimo, W., Kaufmann, M., Liotta, G., Ortali, G.: Rectilinear planarity testing of plane series-parallel graphs in linear time. In: Auber, D., Valtr, P. (eds.) Graph Drawing and Network Visualization. GD 2020. LNCS, vol. 12590, pp. 436–449. Springer, Cham (2020). https://doi.org/10.1007/978-3-030-68766-3_34
13. Didimo, W., Kaufmann, M., Liotta, G., Ortali, G.: Rectilinear planarity of partial 2-trees. In: Angelini, P., von Hanxleden, R. (eds.) Graph Drawing and Network Visualization. GD 2022. LNCS, vol. 13764, pp. 157–172. Springer, Cham (2023). https://doi.org/10.1007/978-3-031-22203-0_12
14. Didimo, W., Liotta, G., Montecchiani, F.: Network visualization for financial crime detection. J. Vis. Lang. Comput. 25(4), 433–451 (2014)
15. Didimo, W., Liotta, G., Montecchiani, F.: A survey on graph drawing beyond planarity. ACM Comput. Surv. 52(1), 4:1–4:37 (2019)
16. Didimo, W., Liotta, G., Ortali, G., Patrignani, M.: Optimal orthogonal drawings of planar 3-graphs in linear time. In: Chawla, S. (ed.) Proceedings of the 2020 ACM-SIAM Symposium on Discrete Algorithms, SODA 2020, Salt Lake City, UT, USA, January 5–8, 2020, pp. 806–825. SIAM (2020)
17. Didimo, W., Liotta, G., Patrignani, M.: HV-planarity: algorithms and complexity. J. Comput. Syst. Sci. 99, 72–90 (2019)
18. Dilla, W.N., Raschke, R.L.: Data visualization for fraud detection: practice implications and a call for future research. Int. J. Acc. Inf. Syst. 16, 1–22 (2015)
19. Dujmovic, V., et al.: A fixed-parameter approach to 2-layer planarization. Algorithmica 45(2), 159–182 (2006)
20. Dujmovic, V., et al.: On the parameterized complexity of layered graph drawing. Algorithmica 52(2), 267–292 (2008)

21. Dwyer, T., et al.: Immersive analytics: an introduction. In: Marriott, K., et al. (eds.) Immersive Analytics, LNCS, vol. 11190, pp. 1–23. Springer, Cham (2018)

22. Filipov, V., Arleo, A., Miksch, S.: Are we there yet? a roadmap of network visualization from surveys to task taxonomies. Computer Graphics Forum (2023, on print)

23. Garg, A., Tamassia, R.: On the computational complexity of upward and rectilinear planarity testing. SIAM J. Comput. **31**(2), 601–625 (2001)

24. Di Giacomo, E., Didimo, W., Montecchiani, F., Tappini, A.: A user study on hybrid graph visualizations. In: Purchase, H.C., Rutter, I. (eds.) Graph Drawing and Network Visualization. GD 2021. LNCS, vol. 12868, pp. 21–38. Springer, Cham (2021). https://doi.org/10.1007/978-3-030-92931-2_2

25. Giacomo, E.D., Giordano, F., Liotta, G.: Upward topological book embeddings of dags. SIAM J. Discret. Math. **25**(2), 479–489 (2011)

26. Giacomo, E.D., Lenhart, W.J., Liotta, G., Randolph, T.W., Tappini, A.: (k, p)-planarity: a relaxation of hybrid planarity. Theor. Comput. Sci. **896**, 19–30 (2021)

27. Giacomo, E.D., Liotta, G., Montecchiani, F.: Orthogonal planarity testing of bounded treewidth graphs. J. Comput. Syst. Sci. **125**, 129–148 (2022)

28. Giacomo, E.D., Liotta, G., Patrignani, M., Rutter, I., Tappini, A.: Nodetrix planarity testing with small clusters. Algorithmica **81**(9), 3464–3493 (2019)

29. Hong, S., Tokuyama, T. (eds.) Beyond Planar Graphs. Springer, Singapore (2020). https://doi.org/10.1007/978-981-15-6533-5

30. Joos, L., Jaeger-Honz, S., Schreiber, F., Keim, D.A., Klein, K.: Visual comparison of networks in VR. IEEE Trans. Vis. Comput. Graph. **28**(11), 3651–3661 (2022)

31. Jünger, M., Mutzel, P. (eds.) Graph Drawing Software. Springer, Berlin (2004). https://doi.org/10.1007/978-3-642-18638-7

32. Kaufmann, M., Wagner, D. (eds.): Drawing Graphs, Methods and Models (the book grow out of a Dagstuhl Seminar, April 1999), LNCS, vol. 2025. Springer, Berlin (2001). https://doi.org/10.1007/3-540-44969-8

33. Keim, D.A., Kohlhammer, J., Ellis, G.P., Mansmann, F.: Mastering the Information Age - Solving Problems with Visual Analytics. Eurographics Association, Saarbrücken (2010)

34. Keim, D.A., Mansmann, F., Stoffel, A., Ziegler, H.: Visual analytics. In: Liu, L., Özsu, M.T. (eds.) Encyclopedia of Database Systems, 2nd edn. Springer, Berlin (2018)

35. Kobourov, S.G., Liotta, G., Montecchiani, F.: An annotated bibliography on 1-planarity. Comput. Sci. Rev. **25**, 49–67 (2017)

36. Kraus, M., et al.: Immersive analytics with abstract 3D visualizations: a survey. Comput. Graph. Forum **41**(1), 201–229 (2022)

37. Kwon, O., Muelder, C., Lee, K., Ma, K.: A study of layout, rendering, and interaction methods for immersive graph visualization. IEEE Trans. Vis. Comput. Graph. **22**(7), 1802–1815 (2016)

38. Leite, R.A., Gschwandtner, T., Miksch, S., Gstrein, E., Kuntner, J.: NEVA: visual analytics to identify fraudulent networks. Comput. Graph. Forum **39**(6), 344–359 (2020)

39. Liotta, G., Rutter, I., Tappini, A.: Simultaneous FPQ-ordering and hybrid planarity testing. Theor. Comput. Sci. **874**, 59–79 (2021)

40. Liotta, G., Rutter, I., Tappini, A.: Parameterized complexity of graph planarity with restricted cyclic orders. J. Comput. Syst. Sci. **135**, 125–144 (2023)

41. Ma, K.: Pushing visualization research frontiers: essential topics not addressed by machine learning. IEEE Comput. Graphics Appl. **43**(1), 97–102 (2023)

42. McGee, F., et al.: Visual Analysis of Multilayer Networks. Synthesis Lectures on Visualization. Morgan & Claypool Publishers, San Rafael (2021)

43. Munzner, T.: Visualization Analysis and Design. A.K. Peters visualization series. A K Peters (2014)

44. Nishizeki, T., Rahman, M.S.: Planar Graph Drawing, vol. 12. World Scientific, Singapore (2004)

45. Nobre, C., Meyer, M.D., Streit, M., Lex, A.: The state of the art in visualizing multivariate networks. Comput. Graph. Forum **38**(3), 807–832 (2019)

46. Sacha, D.: Knowledge generation in visual analytics: Integrating human and machine intelligence for exploration of big data. In: Apel, S., et al. (eds.) Ausgezeichnete Informatikdissertationen 2018, LNI, vol. D-19, pp. 211–220. GI (2018)

47. Sacha, D., et al.: What you see is what you can change: human-centered machine learning by interactive visualization. Neurocomputing **268**, 164–175 (20170

48. Sacha, D., Senaratne, H., Kwon, B.C., Ellis, G.P., Keim, D.A.: The role of uncertainty, awareness, and trust in visual analytics. IEEE Trans. Vis. Comput. Graph. **22**(1), 240–249 (2016)

49. Sacha, D., Stoffel, A., Stoffel, F., Kwon, B.C., Ellis, G.P., Keim, D.A.: Knowledge generation model for visual analytics. IEEE Trans. Vis. Comput. Graph. **20**(12), 1604–1613 (2014)

50. Tamassia, R.: Graph drawing. In: Sack, J., Urrutia, J. (eds.) Handbook of Computational Geometry, pp. 937–971. North Holland/Elsevier, Amsterdam (2000)

51. Tamassia, R. (ed.) Handbook on Graph Drawing and Visualization. Chapman and Hall/CRC, Boca Raton (2013)

52. Tamassia, R., Liotta, G.: Graph drawing. In: Goodman, J.E., O'Rourke, J. (eds.) Handbook of Discrete and Computational Geometry, 2nd edn., pp. 1163–1185. Chapman and Hall/CRC, Boca Raton (2004)

53. Zehavi, M.: Parameterized analysis and crossing minimization problems. Comput. Sci. Rev. **45**, 100490 (2022)

Understanding Non-Covalent Interactions in Biological Processes through QM/MM-EDA Dynamic Simulations

Marcos Mandado

Department of Physical Chemistry, University of Vigo, Lagoas-Marcosende s/n, 36310 Vigo, Spain
mandado@uvigo.es

Molecular dynamic simulations in biological environments such as proteins, DNA or lipids involves a large number of atoms, so classical models based on widely parametrized force fields are employed instead of more accurate quantum methods, whose high computational requirements preclude their application. The parametrization of appropriate force fields for classical molecular dynamics relies on the precise knowledge of the noncovalent inter and intramolecular interactions responsible for very important aspects, such as macromolecular arrangements, cell membrane permeation, ion solvation, etc. This implies, among other things, knowledge of the nature of the interaction, which may be governed by electrostatic, repulsion or dispersion forces. In order to know the balance between different forces, quantum calculations are frequently performed on simplified molecular models and the data obtained from these calculations are used to parametrize the force fields employed in classical simulations. These parameters are, among others, atomic charges, permanent electric dipole moments and atomic polarizabilities. However, it sometimes happens that the molecular models used for the quantum calculations are too simple and the results obtained can differ greatly from those of the extended system. As an alternative to classical and quantum methods, hybrid quantum/classical schemes (QM/MM) can be introduced, where the extended system is neither truncated nor simplified, but only the most important region is treated quantum mechanically.

In this presentation, molecular dynamic simulations and calculations with hybrid schemes are first introduced in a simple way for a broad and multidisciplinary audience. Then, a method developed in our group to investigate intermolecular interactions using hybrid quantum/classical schemes (QM/MM-EDA) is presented and some applications to the study of dynamic processes of ion solvation and membrane permeation are discussed [1–3]. Special attention is paid to the implementation details of the method in the EDA-NCI software [4].

References

1. Cárdenas, G., Pérez-Barcia, A., Mandado, M., Nogueira, J.J.: Phys. Chem. Chem. Phys. **23**, 20533 (2021)
2. Pérez-Barcia, A., Cárdenas, G., Nogueira, J.J., Mandado, M.: J. Chem. Inf. Model. **63**, 882 (2023)

3. Alvarado, R., Cárdenas, G., Nogueira, J.J., Ramos-Berdullas, N., Mandado, M.: Membranes **13**, 28 (2023)
4. Mandado, M., Van Alsenoy, C.: EDA-NCI: A program to perform energy decomposition analysis of non-covalent interactions. https://github.com/marcos-mandado/EDA-NCI

Contents – Part I

Assessing Urban Sustainability (ASUS 2023)

**Advanced Data Science Techniques with Applications in Industry and
Environmental Sustainability (ATELIERS 2023)**

Advances in Web Based Learning (AWBL 2023)

**Blockchain and Distributed Ledgers: Technologies and Applications
(BDLTA 2023)**

Bio and Neuro Inspired Computing and Applications (BIONCA 2023)

**Choices and Actions for Human Scale Cities: Decision Support
Systems (CAHSC DSS 2023)**

Computational and Applied Mathematics (CAM 2023)

Advances in Artificial Intelligence Learning Technologies: Blended Learning, STEM, Computational Thinking and Coding (AAILT 2023)

Building a Network Knowledge Base Based on a Belief Revision Operator

Reynold Osuna-González and Guillermo De Ita-Luna[✉]

Benemérita Universidad Autónoma de Puebla, Puebla, México
deitaluna63@gmail.com

Abstract. We present a proposal for negotiation in a network knowledge base (*NKB*) formed by a set of k intelligent agents, in order to decide the acceptance (or not) of a new information ϕ that is expressed in propositional logic.

Each one of the agents Ai, $i = 1,\ldots,k$ has associated a knowledge base (*KB*) Ki expressed as propositional formulas in conjunctive form. In order to decide the acceptance of ϕ, the belief revision operator *Ind* is applied on each *KB* Ki and ϕ, then $Si = Ind(\phi, Ki)$, and each one of the literals that form Si is weighed in order to estimate the cost that is required by Ai to accept ϕ.

Si expresses the required information by the agent Ai such that $(Ki \cup Si) \models \phi$. The *NKB* uses a constant value γ that is the threshold of acceptance of *NKB*. Thus, a piece of new information ϕ will be accepted by all the agents in NKB if the average of the weights of the requested formulas Si is greater than γ. Otherwise, ϕ is rejected by all the agents in the *NKB*.

Only in the case that ϕ will be accepted collectively, each one of the Ki in the network *NKB* is updated, as $Ki = (Ki \bigwedge Si)$. Otherwise, there are no changes to any *KB* Ki in the *NKB*.

Keywords: Propositional · Inference Belief Revision · Network Knowledge Base

1 Introduction

The automation of deductive reasoning is a basic and challenging logic problem [1]. Deductive propositional reasoning is usually abstracted as follows: Given a propositional formula K (capturing the knowledge about a domain), and a propositional formula ϕ (a query capturing the situation at hand), then the goal of reasoning is to determine whether K implies ϕ, which is presented as $K \vDash \phi$. This is known as the propositional inference problem (or the entailment problem).

Since automatic reasoning is one of the purer forms of human intellectual thought, the automation of such reasoning by means of computers is a basic and challenging scientific problem [1]. Thus, one of the fundamental problems in automatic reasoning is the propositional inference problem. This last problem is a relevant task in many other issues such as: estimating the degree of belief, belief revision, abductive explanation, logical diagnosis, and many other procedures in Artificial Intelligence (AI) applications.

© The Author(s), under exclusive license to Springer Nature Switzerland AG 2023
O. Gervasi et al. (Eds.): ICCSA 2023 Workshops, LNCS 14104, pp. 3–14, 2023.
https://doi.org/10.1007/978-3-031-37105-9_1

Inference operations are present not only in logic but in many areas of mathematics. The concept of logical inference has proven to be more fruitful for the development of a general logic theory than the concept of theorem and of logical validity. Abstract inference operations are known as closure operators in universal algebra and lattice theory [2].

The current techniques that are most used to automatically check $K \models \phi$, when K and ϕ are conjunctive normal forms (CF), are the resolution method [3] and the systems type Gentzen [4]. However, these processes have not only an inherent exponential complexity, but also, they lack a recovery proposal when the inference does not hold. On the contrary, our proposal for checking $K \models \phi$ allows to build a new CF S for repairing the inference, such that $(S \cup K) \models \phi$. In our proposal, $(S \cup K)$ continues as a CF; therefore, our proposal is closed on conjunctive forms. If K represents a knowledge base (KB) associated with an intelligent agent A, then S expresses the required information by the agent A such that $(K \cup S) \models \phi$.

Belief revision problem consists in incorporate new beliefs to a knowledge base already established, changing as little as possible the original beliefs and maintaining consistency of the KB. We propose a method for belief revision, first considering a unique intelligent agent, and afterward, a network of intelligent agents that want to consider if new information is or not accepted in a collective form.

Although different types of logic have been used in decision-making processes by intelligent agents, such as modal logic, fuzzy logic, temporal logic, etc. In our case, we have circumscribed our work within propositional logic because our proposal for group decision-making of agents is based on using a belief revision operator, which we have already developed and analyzed their behavior and consistency in propositional logic [5]. Furthermore, we have extended our original proposal of a belief revision operator to be applied in the revision of consistency of a knowledge base [6].

People are becoming increasingly more connected to each other as social networks continue to grow both in number and variety [7]. Taking them as a collection, a network agents can be seen as one complex network with many different types of relations, different degrees of strength for each relation, and a wide range of information on each agent. In this context, a network agents formed by intelligent agents are reflections of the content of their own individual (or local) knowledge bases; modeling how knowledge flows over the network—or how this can possibly occur—is therefore of great interest from a knowledge representation and reasoning perspective.

In this article, we provide an introduction to the *network knowledge base* (*NKB*) model, and then focus on the problem of how a single agent's knowledge base changes when exposed to a stream of new items coming from the reality. Afterwards, we show how to make a collective decision of acceptance, if new information is considered for the network knowledge base.

2 Preliminaries

Let $X = \{ x_1, \ldots, x_n \}$ be a set of n Boolean variables. A literal, denoted as *lit*, is a variable x or a denied variable $\neg x$. As usual, each $x \in X$, $x^0 = \neg x$ and $x^1 = x$.

A *clause* is a disjunction of different literals. For $k \in N$, a *k-clause* is a clause with exactly k literals, and $(\leq k)$-*clause* is a clause with at most k literals. Sometimes, we consider a clause as a set of literals.

A *phrase* is a conjunction of literals. A *k-phrase* is a phrase with exactly k literals. A variable $x \in X$ appears in a clause C (or phrase) if x or $\neg x$ is an element of C.

A conjunctive normal form (*CF*) is a conjunction of clauses, and *k-CF* is a *CF* containing only *k-clauses*. A disjunctive normal form (*DF*) is a disjunction of sentences, and *k-DF* is a *DF* containing only *k-phrases*. A *CF* F with n variables is a *n-ary* Boolean function $F:\{0,1\}^n \to \{0,1\}$. Rather, any Boolean function F has infinitely many equivalent representations, among these, some in *CF* and *DF*.

We denote with Y any of the basic logic elements that we are using, such as a literal, a clause, a phrase, a *DF* or a *C*. $v(Y)$ denotes the set of variables involved in the object Y. For example, $Y(\neg x_1 \bigvee x_2) = \{x_1, x_2\}$. While $Lit(Y)$ denotes the set of literals involved in object Y. For example, if $X = v(Y)$ then $Lit(Y) = X \cup \neg X = \{x_1, \neg x_1, ..., x_n, \neg x_n\}$. We also use $\neg Y$ as the negation operator on the object Y. We denote the cardinality of a set A by $|A|$.

An *assignment s* for a formula F is a Boolean mapping $s: v(F) \to \{1, 0\}$. An assignment s can also be considered as a non-complementary set of literals: $l \in s$ if and only if s assigns true to l and $\neg l$ false. s is a partial *assignment* for the formula F when s has determined a logical value only to variables of a proper subset of F, namely $s: Y \to \{1, 0\}$ and $Y \subset v(F)$. A *CF* F is satisfied by an assignment s if each clause F is satisfied by s; A model of F is an assignment on $v(F)$ satisfying F. Considering s as a set of literals, notice that s has not any complementary pair of literals, this is, if $l \in s$, then $\neg l \notin s$.

A phrase f is satisfiable by an assignment s, if $f \subseteq s$. Otherwise, s falsifies f. A *DF* F is satisfiable by s if a sentence in F is satisfiable by s. F is contradicted by s if all sentences in F are contradicted by s.

Given a formula F, $S(F)$ is the set of all possible mappings defined on $v(F)$. If $n = |v(F)|$ then $|S(F)| = 2^n$. $s \vDash F$ denotes that the assignment s is a model of F (s satisfies F). $s \nvDash F$ denotes that s is an assignment falsifying F. We denote by $Sat(F)$ to the set of assignment in $S(F)$ which they are models for F. $Fals(F)$ denotes the set of assignments in $S(F)$ that falsifies F. Similarly, $\#Sat(F)$ and $\#Fals(F)$ denotes the number of models and falsifying assignments of F, respectively.

2.1 Construction of Independent Sets of Clauses

As K and ϕ are *CF*'s, the falsifying assignments $Fals(K)$ y $Fals(\phi)$ can be calculated efficiently [8]. Review $K \vDash \phi$ is equivalent to checking whether $Sat(K) \subseteq Sat(\phi)$, or that: $Fals(\phi) \subseteq Fals(K)$. The result of applying the operator of belief revision between a KB K and the new evidence ϕ is denoted as $K' = K \circ \phi$.

When $K \vDash \phi$, then we define $K = K \circ \phi$, because the new evidence is inferred from K, end then K does not need any information to accept ϕ. If $K \nvDash \phi$ then $Fals(\phi) \not\subseteq Fals(K)$, which implies that there is a set of assignments S such that $S \subseteq Fals(\phi)$ and $S \not\subseteq Fals(K)$.

When $K \nvDash \phi$, we propose a method to build $S = (Fals(\phi) - Fals(K)) \neq \emptyset$ which allows to recognize a new *CF Fs*, such that $S = Fals(Fs)$ and $K' = (K \bigwedge Fs)$, and it holds $K' \vDash \phi$. $K' = (K \wedge Fs)$ has less information than K (because K' has more clauses than K). In fact, if $S \neq 0$ then $Fals(K) \subset Fals(K')$, and therefore, $Sat(K') \subset Sat(K)$.

Let K be a CF, i.e., $K = \bigwedge_{i=1}^{m} C_i$, where each C_i, $i = 1, \ldots, m$ is a disjunction of literals. The set of assignments forming $Fals(C_i)$ can be represented through a string A_i from the set $\{0, 1, *\}$. If $C_i = \{x_{i1} \vee \ldots \vee x_{ik}\} \in K$, then the value for each position from i_1 - th to i_k – th of the string A_i, has to falsify the literals of C_i. If $x_{ij} \in C_i$ then the ij – th element of A_i is set to 0. If $\neg x_{ij} \in C_i$ then the ij – th element of A_i is set to 1. The variables in $v(K)$ which do not appear in C_i are represented by the symbol *, meaning that they could take any logical value $\{0, 1\}$. In this way, the string A_i of length $n = |v(K)|$ represents the set of assignments falsifying the clause C_i.

We will denote the formation of the string representing $Fals(C_i)$ as $A_i = string(Fals(C_i))$. It is easy to build $Fals(K)$ since each clause C_i determines a subset of falsifying assignments of K.

In this article, we will express $Fals(C)$ as the falsifying string or as the set of literals in an indistinct way, since both expressions denote the set $Fals(C)$. The following property expresses how to form the falsifying set of assignments of a CF.

Property 1. *Given a CF $K = \bigwedge_{i=1}^{m} Ci$, it holds $Fals(K) = \bigcup_{i=1}^{m} \{\sigma \in S(K) \mid Fals(C_i) \subseteq \sigma\}$.*

Definition 1. *Given two Clauses C_i and C_j, if they have at least one complementary literal, they will be called independent clauses. Otherwise, it is said that both are dependent clauses.*

Two independent clauses C_i and C_j have complementary pair of literals, therefore their falsifying assignments must also have complementary literals, that is, $Fals(C_i) \cap Fals(C_j) = \emptyset$.

Definition 2. *Let $K = \{C_1, C_2, \ldots, C_m\}$ be a CF. K is called independent if for any pair of clauses $C_i, C_j \in K, i \neq j$, the property of independence is met.*

Definition 3. *Given two falsifying strings A and B each of length n, if there is an $i = 0, \ldots, n$, such that $A[i] = x$ and $B[i] = 1 - x, x \in \{0, 1\}$, it is said that they have the independence property. Otherwise, we say that both strings are dependent.*

Notice that falsifying strings for independent clauses have complementary values (0 and 1) in at least one of their fixed values. Let $C_i \in K$ and $x \in v(K) \backslash v(C_i)$ be any variable, we have that

$$C_i \equiv (C_i \vee \neg x) \bigwedge (C_i \vee x) \tag{1}$$

Furthermore, this reduction preserves the number of falsifying assignments of C_i. Since $\#Fals(C_i) = 2^{n-|Ci|} = 2^{n-(|Ci|+1)} + 2^{n-(|Ci|+1)} = \#Fals((C_i \vee \neg x) \bigwedge (C_i \vee x))$, because $(C_i \vee x)$ and $(C_i \vee x)$ are two independent clauses.

Definition 4. *Given a pair of dependent clauses C_1 and C_2, if $Lit(C_1) \subseteq Lit(C_2)$ we say that C_2 is subsumed by C_1.*

If C_1 subsumes C_2 then $Fals(C_2) \subseteq Fals(C_1)$. On the other hand, if C_2 is not subsumed by C_1 and they are dependents, there is a set of indices $I = \{1, ..., p\} \subseteq \{1, ..., n\}$ such that for each $i \in I$, $x_i \in C_1$ but $x_i \notin C_2$. There exists a reduction to transform C_2 to be independent with C_1, we call this transformation the independent reduction between two clauses.

The independent reduction works as follows: let C_1 and C_2 be two dependent clauses. Let $\{x_1, x_2, ..., x_p\} = Lit(C_1) - Lit(C_2)$. By (1) we can write: $C_1 \bigwedge C_2 = C_1 \bigwedge (C_2 \vee \neg x_1) \bigwedge (C_2 \vee x_1)$. Now C_1 and $(C_2 \vee \neg x_1)$ are independent. Applying (1) to $(C2 \vee x_1)$:

$$C_1 \bigwedge C_2 \equiv C_1 \bigwedge (C_2 \vee \neg x_1) \bigwedge (C_2 \vee x_1 \vee \neg x_2) \bigwedge (C_2 \vee x_1 \vee x_2) \qquad (2)$$

The first three clauses are independent. If we repeat the process of making the last clause independent with the previous ones until xp is considered; we have that $C1 \bigwedge C2$ can be written as:

$$C_1 \bigwedge (C_2 \vee \neg x_1) \bigwedge (C_2 \vee x_1 \vee \neg x_2) \bigwedge \ldots \bigwedge (C_2 \vee x_1 \vee x_2 \vee \ldots \vee \neg x_p) \bigwedge (C_2 \vee x_1 \vee x_2 \vee \ldots \vee x_p) \qquad (3)$$

The last clause contains all literals of C_1, so it is subsumed by C_1, and then.

$$C_1 \bigwedge C_2 \equiv C_1 \bigwedge (C_2 \vee \neg x_1) \bigwedge (C_2 \vee x_1 \vee \neg x_2) \bigwedge \ldots \bigwedge (C_2 \vee x_1 \vee x_2 \vee \ldots \vee \neg x_p) \qquad (4)$$

We obtain on the right side of (4) an independent set of $p + 1$ clauses, which we denote as $ind\_red(C_1, C_2)$.

We consider a new information ϕ that is a conjunction of clauses φ_j, $j = 1, ..., m$ in propositional calculus. In order to review if each clause is inferred from a *KB K*, we must consider when $K \vDash \varphi$, for φ in ϕ, and for this, we must review if $C \vDash \varphi$, for any clause C in K. Then, we introduce a belief revision operator in order to review if $C \vDash \varphi$.

We will use the independent reduction between two clauses C_1 and φ (or between their respective falsifying strings) to define:

$$Ind(\varphi, C) = \begin{cases} \varphi & \text{if } \varphi \text{ and } C \text{ are independent} \\ \emptyset & \text{if } Lit(C) - Lit(\varphi) = \emptyset \\ ind\_red(C, \varphi) - C & \text{in other case} \end{cases} \qquad (5)$$

It is easy to redefine the operator *Ind* in terms of the falsifying strings representing $Fals(C)$ and $Fals(\varphi)$, see for example [8] for a construction based on falsifying strings. The operation $Ind(\varphi, C)$ forms a conjunction of clauses whose falsifying assignments are exactly $Fals(\varphi) - Fals(C)$.

3   A Belief Revision Operator

The paradigm best known for belief revision is the AGM paradigm [9]. Subsequently, Mendelzon and Katsuno [10] unified the different belief revision approaches to semantic, and reformulated the AGM postulates, which were called: KM postulates. Subsequently, Darwiche and Pearl [11] proposed the iterated revision, where his proposal establishes a representation based on model assumptions.

The problem of belief revision initially requires knowing whether $K \vDash \phi$, which involves solving a difficult problem (a Co-NP complete problem). One way to practically solve these types of problems is to introduce approximate algorithms for changing beliefs, as well as algorithmic proposals for revising finite belief bases. However, this leads to generating non-optimal solutions.

In this work, instead of computing the set of models of the involved formulas, the revision operator works on the sets of falsifying assignments of the formulas. And our belief revision's method is based on the following property.

Theorem 1. Given φ and C two clauses, it holds: $(C \wedge Ind(\varphi,C)) \vDash \varphi$.

Proof: If φ and C are independent, then $Ind(\varphi,C) = \varphi$. Therefore, $(C \wedge Ind(\varphi,C)) \cong (C \wedge \varphi)$, and in this case we have that $(C \wedge \varphi) \vDash \varphi$ by the propositional property $(p \wedge q) \vDash q$, and by the reflexivity $\varphi \vDash \varphi$. Otherwise, it holds that $(C \wedge \varphi) \cong (C \wedge Ind(\varphi,C))$ since $Ind(\varphi,C)$ is a set of clauses independent with C and by (2), then $(C \wedge Ind(\varphi,C)) \vDash \varphi$.

Theorem 2. Let φ and C be two clauses, then $Fals(Ind(\varphi,C)) = Fals(\varphi) - Fals(C)$.

Proof: If $Ind(\varphi,C) = \emptyset$, then $Fals(\varphi) \subseteq Fals(C)$. Therefore, $Fals(\varphi) - Fals(C) = \emptyset$. Now, let us assume that $Ind(\varphi,C) \neq \emptyset$. Let s be an assignment such that $s \in Ind(\varphi,C)$. We will show that $s \in Fals(\varphi)$ and $s \notin Fals(C)$. If $s \in Fals(Ind(\varphi,C))$, then s falsifies φ because each clause in $Ind(\varphi,C)$ has the form $(\varphi \vee R)$ where R is a disjunction (R could be empty, for example in the case $Ind(\varphi,C) = \emptyset$). If s falsifies $(\varphi \vee R)$, then s has to falsify φ, and thus $s \in Fals(\varphi)$. On the other hand, the clause $(\varphi \vee R) \in Ind(\varphi,C)$ is independent from C because of the construction of the operator Ind; therefore, $(Fals(C) \cap Fals(Ind(\varphi,C))) = \emptyset$. Thus, $s \notin Fals(C)$.

Given two clauses φ_i and C_j, the operator $Ind(\varphi_i, C_j)$ forms a set of strings that represents the set of falsifying assignments: $Fals(\varphi_i) - Fals(C_j)$. This is, $Ind(\varphi_i, C_j)$ determines the assignments that are in $Fals(\varphi_i)$, but which are not contained in $Fals(C_j)$.

Let φ be a clause, and $K = \bigwedge_{i=1}^{m} Ci$ be a CF. If we apply the independence's operator between each C_j and φ, we get as result S_{ij}. The union of each S_{ij}, $S_{\varphi_i} = \bigcup_{i=1}^{m} S_{ij}$ holds that $S_{\varphi_i} \subseteq Fals(\varphi)$ and $S_{\varphi_i} \not\subseteq Fals(K)$.

When the operator $Ind(\varphi_i, C_j)$ is applied on all $C_j \in K$, a set S of strings is obtained. Furthermore, S holds that $S \subseteq Fals(\varphi_i)$ and $S \not\subseteq Fals(K)$.

The sets $Ind(\varphi_i, C_j)$ allows to build a CF Fs_i such that $S_{\varphi_i} = (D_1 \wedge D_2 \wedge ... D_t)$, and $S_{\varphi_i} = Fals(Fs_i)$. When the new clauses Fs_i are added to K, a new KB $K'_i = K \wedge Fs_i$ is obtained. K'_i holds $K'_i \vDash \varphi_i$, meanwhile K'_i remains as a CF.

K is extended with the clauses Fs_i obtained by $Ind(\varphi_i,K)$ forming $K' = (K \wedge Fs_i)$. Thus K' also extends the space of falsifying assignments of K, adding the falsifying assignments in $Fals(\varphi_i)$ that were initially not included in $Fals(K)$. In fact, $Fals(Ind(\varphi_i, K))$ and $Fals(\varphi_i)$ are disjointed, meaning that $Fals(K) \bigcap Fals(Ind(\varphi_i, K)) = \emptyset$. In other words, the set of models of K' is now a subset of the models of K, that is, $Sat(K') \subseteq Sat(K)$.

But, the application of the operator $Ind(\varphi_i, K)$ on each $\varphi_i \in \phi$, $i = 1,...,k$ could not produce a minimum number of clauses. A reduction that we call *Varcom* allows to reduce the number of clauses formed by $Ind(\phi, K)$.

Hence, after obtaining the set of clauses Fs from $Ind(\varphi, K)$, we reduce its cardinality, eliminating subsumed clauses and when two clauses $Ind(\varphi_{i1}, K)$ and $Ind(\varphi_{i2}, K)$ are different only by a complementary literals, then both clauses are the same only changing its complementary literals by the symbol '*'.

In order to generate a minimum set of independent clauses as a result of $Ind(\varphi, K)$, it is crucial to sort the clauses $C_j \in K$ in ascending order according to the length.

$|S_j| = |Lit(C_j) - Lit(\varphi)|$. This is done since the number of literals in C_j, different to the literals in φ, determine the number of independent clauses to be generated. Hence, we have a strategy for reducing the number of independent clauses to be generated by each $Ind(\varphi_i, C_j)$.

This is done in order to obtain minimal set of clauses for $Ind(\varphi, K)$. Notice that all reductions maintain conjunctive forms as outcome.

Our proposal is based on the construction of a CF: $Ind(\varphi, C)$, that is necessary to fulfill $(C \bigwedge Ind(\varphi, C)) \vDash \varphi$.

The definition of the operator $Ind(\varphi, C)$ is constructive. The operator $Ind(\varphi, C)$ allows us to propose a new way to solve the problem of belief revision between conjunctive forms.

4 Multi Agent Systems

An agent is an entity enabled to perceive its environment and capable of acting in it, according to what it senses but an intelligent agent is expected not only to act as a response to predefined stimulus, but adapting to the changes in the environment while, possibly, learning from it [12]. Multi agent systems can be seen as a distributed system composed by a network of autonomous agents with its own objectives to satisfy [13].

A Multi agent system is like a society of individuals interacting with each other, exchanging information and negotiating between them to reach its own goals [14]. This leads to the need for a mechanism that allows coordination between the actions of the agents without external supervision, as agents must reach an agreement on their own [15].

Multi agent technology is applied by intelligent systems to solve the problems of analysis of complex systems and intelligent management activities. Intelligent Multi Agent Systems (MAS) based learning combine collection of information from their environment, recognition data, intelligent classification data and prediction future data, storage data, delivery data to knowledge management systems such as Decision Support System (DSS) and Management Information System (MIS) [16].

Agent based system and intelligent agents are two important issues in research area. Intelligent multi agent systems have great potentials to use in different purposes [16] like MAS learning, MAS in development of ambient intelligence, MAS and simulation and use of MAS for Smart Cities planning and control [13].

The knowledge of each agent in a multi agent system may be different from each other and even the knowledge of one agent may be in conflict with the knowledge of another. With the purpose that a MAS can make a collective decision given a new information φ, and where each agent $A_i \in NK$ has associated an own KB K_i, we propose that each agent apply a belief revision operator of K_i on the new information φ, and according to the degree of acceptation of φ by A_i, then to make a collective decision of all MAS. We present in the following section how to make such collective decision.

5 A Network Knowledge Base

According to [17], a network knowledge base (*NKB*) is a directed graph with a labeling function for vertices and another for edges. The labels express attributes and its values. Each of the vertices is associated with an user of a social network with its own knowledge base and the edges are the relationship between users. This approach aims to predict reactions of users of a social network to the news received thru the network.

In this work, a more general approach will be used, using a MAS for deciding the acceptance of new information. Let $NK = \{A_1, A_2, ..., A_k\}$ be a network knowledge base formed by a set of k intelligent agents. Each agent A_i, $i = 1, ..., k$ has associated a local knowledge base *KB* K_i representing the beliefs currently held by the agent A_i.

Each knowledge base K_i is expressed by conjunctive forms, this is $K_i = C_{i,1} \wedge ... \wedge C_{i,m_i}$ where each $C_{i,j} \in K_i$ is a clause. We will omit the subindex i, when it is not necessary to identify the agent A_i.

Given a KB K_i, each clause $C_{ij} \in K_i$ has associated a weight $W_{ij}, j = 1, ..., m_i$. Each weight $0 < W_{ij} \leq 1$ indicates the degree of trust that the agent A_i has on the veracity of the clause C_{ij}. In this way, a same clause C can have different weights (different degree of trust) assigned by the different agents in the *NKB*.

The weight of the degree of belief of an agent A_i is $weight(A_i) = \sum_{j=1}^{mi} W_{ij}$. In order to normalize the knowledge of an agent in regards to the knowledge of the collective of agents, the relative weight of the agent in the network knowledge base is $rel\_weight(A_i) = weight(A_i) / \sum_{j=1}^{k} weight(A_j)$.

Afterwards, we address the broad issue of understanding how new information is accepted or not in a collective way for the network of agents. For this task, we must determine first, the degree of relevance of any literal $l \in Lit(A_i)$ into the set of beliefs of the agent A_i, denoted as $rel(l, A_i)$.

We determine the importance of the literal l in the degree of belief of A_i in the following way:

$$rel(l, A_i) = \sum_{l \in C_{ij}} (W_{ij}/|C_{ij}|) \tag{6}$$

The function rel: $Lit(A_i) \times NK \to R^+$ measures the degree of relevance of a literal l into the beliefs of the agent A_i. The relative weight of a literal l in a K_i is relevant because it allows us to calculate for each agent, the relative weight of the new information. Thus, we assume that each agent adopts its own degree of belief from any new information.

The relative weight of a literal l is normalized with respect to the sum of the weights of the literals involved in the KB of the agent A_i. For this, we must consider first the total weight of the literals involved in K_i as: $W_l(A_i) = \sum_{l \in Lit(A_i)} rel(l, A_i)$. Therefore, the strategic value of a literal l with respect to all literals involved in a KB K_i of an agent A_i is: $w\_rel(l, A_i) = rel(l, A_i)/W_l(A_i)$. Note that in this case, we have that $\sum_{l \in Lit(A_i)} w\_rel(l, A_i) = 1$.

It is known that there are distinct strategies for collective decision-making (see e.g. [18]) depending on whether speed or accuracy is imperative and, more broadly, shed light on how intelligence is best attained. Our proposal for the collective decision-making is based on the logical value of each literal composing the new information ϕ that is shared in our MAS model.

We address the broad issue of understanding how new information ϕ is shared in the MAS model, and which is the degree of belief of each agent A_i in the MAS on ϕ. For example, we could define the strategic value of a new clause C (or new rule) to be considered by any agent $A_i \in NK$. Given a clause $C = (l_1 \lor \ldots \lor l_r)$ of literals in $Lit(A_i)$, we define the relative weight of the clause C by the agent A_i as $weight(C, A_i) = \sum_{l \in C} w\_rel(l, A_i)$, because we assume that each agent adopts its own degree of belief from any new information. Let us consider that the new information is a CF, it is $\phi = \varphi_1 \bigwedge \ldots \bigwedge \varphi_m$.

Let S_{φ_i} be the additional information that a KB K_i requests in order to infer any $\varphi \in \phi$, this is $S_{\varphi_i} = Ind(\varphi, K_i)$. Thus, for each agent $A_i \in NK$, S_{φ_i} will be the information (given as a conjuctive formula) that is necessary to hold $(K_i \cup S_{\varphi_i}) \models \varphi$. Hence, S_{φ_i} is the information that K_i does not have, but that is necessary to add to the beliefs of A_i in order to make A_i believes in φ.

In this way, we can weigh how much information is missing from an agent's belief set K_i, so that A_i believes in the new information φ. The information required by A_i is S_{φ_i}, which must be weighed in terms related to the importance of the literals that compose it.

We can measure the information contained in S_{φ_i}, denoted as $weight(S_{\varphi_i})$. First, we separate from S_{φ_i} the new literals in S_{φ_i} but that are not in φ. Those set of new literals are necessary to infer φ from K_i. Let us consider that $S_{\varphi_i} = (C_1 \land \ldots \land Cr)$. Let $S_{-\varphi_i} = (C'_1 \land \ldots \land C'r)$ be the set of clauses from S_{φ_i} without the literals of φ, this is, for all C_j in S_{φ_i}, $C'_j = C_j - \varphi$. And then, we can associate a weight to S_{φ_i}, denoted as $weight(S_{\varphi_i})$, which is made according to the weight of the literals in $(S_{\varphi_i} - \varphi)$ and by the following rules:

1. If $S_{\varphi_i} = \emptyset$ then $weight(S_{\varphi_i}) = 0$.
2. If $l = (S_{\varphi_i} - \varphi), l \in Lit(A_i)$, then $weight(S_{\varphi_i}) = w\_rel(l, A_i)$.
3. If $C = (S_{\varphi_i} - \varphi), C$ a clause, then $weight(S_{\varphi_i}) = \sum_{l \in C} w\_rel(l, A_i)$.
4. If $S_{-\varphi_i} = (C'_1 \land \ldots \land C'r)$ is a conjunctive form, then $weight(S_{\varphi_i}) = min\{1, \sum_{C \in S_{-\varphi_i}} weight(C, A_i)\}$.

Then, an agent A_i, $i = 1, \ldots, k$ has a degree of belief on φ given by the formula: $belief(A_i, \varphi) = 1 - (weight(S_{\varphi_i}))/(weight(A_i))$. And the degree of belief of the collective NKB on φ is given by $belief(NK, \varphi) = average_{i=1}^k (belief(A_i, \varphi))$.

Given the new information ϕ to be considered by the network knowledge base, the objective is to determine if the information ϕ is accepted by the collective NKB, and which is its degree of acceptance. For this, the *NKB* determines a constant value γ that is the threshold of acceptation of *NKB*. Thus, a new information ϕ will be accepted by all the agents in *NKB* if $belief(NK, \phi) > \gamma$. Otherwise, ϕ is rejected by all the agents in *NKB*.

In this case, when $average_{i=1}^{k}(belief(A_i,)) < \gamma$, then the new information ϕ is rejected by *NKB* and no change is performed on each $K_i, i = 1, \ldots, k$. Otherwise, all K_i in the NKB is updated as $K_i = (K_i \cup S_{\varphi_i})$, and each clause C_j in S_{φ_i} that is aggregated to K_i will be weighted as $Wij = weight(C_j, A_i)$.

Given the expressive power of the *NKB* model, there are plenty of domains in which this model can be useful since the integration of new information in organizations continues to be a topic of intensive research and immense practical importance [18]. For instance, in the problem of selecting the best users to be included in a marketing campaign based on social media, since users who have the greatest number of connections are not always the best candidates for being chosen as "seeds" of online marketing campaigns [7].

As one limitation of this work, is that the belief revision operator used in this model has been developed to work in propositional logic. In order to express the richness of language in social media, it will be necessary to extend the revision operator to other higher logics, as well as to consider other AI tools that capture negotiations between intelligent agents into different logics.

The proposed NKB model could be used in predicting people's reactions to information that they receive, modeling a society as a directed graph where nodes represent individuals with their respective set of beliefs, represented in the form of weighted clauses, i.e., the degree of confidence the individual has on each clause. This network could then be subjected to different news one by one, studying at each step the percentage of individuals who accept the information and predicting whether the society will collectively accept or reject the news.

This model can also be applied to small groups, such as a work team, where each member has their respective belief system, depending on their studies and experience. Each member can have different levels of confidence in their own beliefs and the confidence they have in the rest of the team members and their abilities, helping in possible collective decision-making.

For example, we have a practical application of the belief review operator in the diagnosis about the possible strain of covid that a patient may have contracted, based on the symptomatology that it shows. An immediate extension of our application is to consider a team of doctors, and based on the opinion of each one, obtain a diagnosis of the group.

Another possible application of this model is as a support tool—in combination with NLP and ML tools, among others—for detecting unfair competition. In this setting, a *NKB* could be useful in detecting information flow patterns that are typical of sock puppet campaigns.

6   Conclusions

Given a *KB* K_i associated with an intelligent agent A_i, and a new information φ, both expressed as conjunctive forms in propositional calculus, we have developed a belief revision operator on propositional logic that allows us to construct the missing information S_{φ_i} that is needed to hold $(K_i \cup S_{\varphi_i}) \models \varphi$.

A logical operator, called $Ind(\varphi, K_i)$, is proposed. $Ind(\varphi, K_i)$ finds a minimal set S_{φ_i} of clauses whose falsifying assignments cover $Fals(\varphi) - Fals(K_i)$, and therefore, $(K_i \bigwedge S_{\varphi_i}) \models \varphi$.

We extend this belief revision process to allow us to consider a collective decision-making by a network knowledge base *NKB*. Therefore, given new information φ, a collective decision of acceptance of φ can be made by the entire *NKB*.

In order to decide the acceptance (or not) of φ, the belief revision operator *Ind* is applied on each *KB* K_i and φ. Afterward, $S_{\varphi_i} = Ind(\varphi, K_i)$, and each one of the literals that form S_{φ_i} is weighed in order to estimate the cost that is required by A_i to accept φ.

Only in the case that φ will be accepted collectively, each one of the K_i in the network *NKB* is updated, as $K_i = (K_i \bigwedge S_{\varphi_i})$. Otherwise, there are no changes to all *KB* K_i in the *NKB*.

Given the expressive power of the *NKB* model, there are plenty of domains in which this model can be useful since the integration of new information in organizations continues to be a topic of intensive research and immense practical importance.

Acknowledgment. The authors wish to thank to the Conacyt (Consejo Nacional de Ciencias y Tecnología) – México.

References

1. Shankar, N.: Metamathematics, machines and gödel's proof. In: Cambridge Tracts in Theoretical Computer Science, No. 38. Cambridge University Press (1997)
2. Jansana, R.: Propositional Consequence Relations and Algebraic Logic. In: Zalta, E.N. (ed.) (2006)
3. Bordeaux, L., Hamadi, Y., Zhang, L.: Propositional satisfiability and constraint programming: a comparative survey. ACM Comput. Surv. **38**, 1–54 (2006)
4. Gallier, J.: SLD-resolution and logic programming (PROLOG). In: Logic for Computer Science, Foundations of Automatic Theorem Proving, pp. 410–447. University of Pennsylvania, Department of Computer and Information Science (2003)
5. De Ita, G., Marcial-Romero, R., Bellor, P., Contreras, M.: Belief revision between conjunctive normal forms. J. Intell. Fuzzy Syst. **34**(5), 3155–3164 (2018)
6. Bello, P., De Ita, G.: An algorithm to belief revision and to verify consistency of a knowledge base. IEEE Latin America Trans. **19**(11), 1867–1874 (2021)
7. Gallo, F., Simari, G., Martinez, M.V., Santos, N.A., Falappa, M.A.: Local belief dynamics in network knowledge Bases. ACM Trans. Comput. Logic **23**(1), 1–36 (2021)

8. De Ita, G., Marcial-Romero, R., Hernández, J., Pozos-Parra, P.: Using binary patterns for counting falsifying assignments of conjunctive forms. Elect. Notes in Theoretical Comput. Sci. **315**, 17–30 (2015)
9. Alchourron, C., Gardenfords, P., Makinson, D.: On the logic of theory change: partial meet contraction and revision functions. J. Symbolic Logic **50**, 510–530 (1985)
10. Katsuno, H., Mendelzon, A.O.: On the difference between updating a knowledge base and revising it. In: KR'91 Cambridge, MA, USA, pp. 387–394 (1991)
11. Darwiche, A., Pearl, J.: On the logic of iterated belief revision. Artif. Intell. **89**, 1–29 (1997)
12. Russell, S., Norvig, P.: Artificial Intelligence: A Modern Approach, 2nd edn. Prentice Hall Press, Upper Saddle River, NJ, USA (2009)
13. Julian, V., Botti, V.: Multi-agent systems. In: Applied Sciences (Switzerland), vol. 9, Issue 7. MDPI AG (2019). https://doi.org/10.3390/app9071402
14. Oprea, M.: Applications of multi-agent systems (2004). https://doi.org/10.1007/1-4020-815 9-6_9
15. Wooldridge, M.: An Introduction to MultiAgent Systems. John Wiley & Sons, Chichester (2002)
16. Asadi, R., Mustapha, N., Sulaiman, N.: A framework for intelligent multi agent system based neural network classification model. Int. J. Comput. Sci. Inf. Secur. **5**(1), 168–174 (2009)
17. Gallo, F.R., Simari, G.I., Martinez, M.V., Falappa, M.A.: Predicting user reactions to Twitter feed content based on personality type and social cues. Future Generation Comput. Syst. **110**, 918–930 (2020). https://doi.org/10.1016/j.future.2019.10.044
18. van Veen, D.-J., Kudesia, R.S., Heinimann, H.R.: An agent-based model of collective decision-making: how information sharing strategies scale with information overload. IEEE Trans. Comput. Soc. Syst. **7**(3), 751–767 (2020). https://doi.org/10.1109/TCSS.2020.2986161

Classification of Text Writing Proficiency of L2 Learners

Giulio Biondi[1], Valentina Franzoni[1,2(✉)], Alfredo Milani[1],
and Valentino Santucci[2,3]

[1] Department of Mathematics and Computer Science, University of Perugia,
Via Vanvitelli 1, Perugia, Italy
{giulio.biondi,valentina.franzoni,alfredo.milani}@unipg.it
[2] Department of Computer Science, Hong Kong Baptist University, Kowloon Tong,
Hong Kong, China
valentino.santucci@unistrapg.it
[3] University for Foreigners of Perugia, Perugia, Piazza Grimana, Italy

Abstract. In this study, we present a novel system for the automatic classification of text complexity in the Italian language, focusing on the phraseological dimension. This quantitative assessment of text complexity is crucial for various applications, including text readability measurement, text simplification, and support for educators during evaluation processes. We use a dataset comprising texts written by Italian L2 learners and classified according to the levels of the Common European Framework of Reference for Languages. The dataset texts serve as a basis for calculating phraseological features, which are then used as input for multiple machine-learning classifiers to compare their performance in predicting proficiency levels. Our experimental results demonstrate that the proposed framework effectively harnesses phraseological complexity features to achieve high classification accuracy in determining proficiency levels.

Keywords: Text Complexity · Natural Language Processing · Text Classification

1 Introduction

In recent years, the analysis and evaluation of text complexity have garnered significant attention in the field of Natural Language Processing (NLP) and education, given its crucial role in various applications, such as readability assessment, text simplification, and assisting teachers in evaluation procedures [9,13,16,19]. The ability to accurately measure the complexity of a text is especially relevant for second language (L2) learners, as it allows for the selection of appropriate learning materials and the tailoring of teaching methods to individual student needs.

The Common European Framework of Reference for Languages (CEFR) [6] provides a widely recognized standard for language proficiency assessment,

O. Gervasi et al. (Eds.): ICCSA 2023 Workshops, LNCS 14104, pp. 15–28, 2023.
https://doi.org/10.1007/978-3-031-37105-9_2

encompassing various skills such as reading, writing, listening, and speaking. However, the automatic classification of text complexity according to CEFR levels remains a challenging task. This challenge is further exacerbated when considering the phraseological dimension, a crucial aspect of language proficiency that has been relatively underexplored in previous research.

In this study, we aim to bridge this gap by proposing a novel system for automatically assessing text complexity in the Italian language, focusing specifically on the phraseological dimension and targeting CEFR proficiency levels. To achieve this goal, we utilize a dataset of texts produced by Italian L2 learners for written examinations, classified according to CEFR levels. We extract several phraseological features from the texts and employ multiple machine-learning classifiers to predict CEFR proficiency levels based on these features.

The rest of the paper is organized as follows: Sect. 2 provides an overview of related work in the field of text complexity assessment and phraseological analysis. Section 3 presents our methodology. Section 4 details the dataset, feature extraction, and machine learning classifiers used. Section 5 discusses the experimental results, demonstrating the effectiveness of the proposed framework in achieving high classification accuracy. Finally, Sect. 5 concludes the paper and outlines potential avenues for future research.

2   Related Work

In [19], an automatic classification system for measuring the complexity level of a given Italian text is introduced from a linguistic point of view. The task of measuring the complexity of a text is cast to a supervised classification problem by exploiting a dataset of textual instructions purposely produced by linguistic experts for second language teaching and assessment purposes. The commonly adopted levels from the Common European Framework of Reference for Languages were used as target classification classes, the exam instructions were elaborated by considering a large set of numeric linguistic features, and an experimental comparison among ten widely used machine learning models was conducted. The results show that the proposed approach is able to obtain good prediction accuracy on a dataset comprising lexical, morphological, syntactical, and morpho-syntactical features computed from a corpus of texts written by Italian L2 learners, while a further analysis was conducted in order to identify the categories of features that influenced the prediction. The maximum accuracy of 74.2% was achieved using a Random Forest classifier.

Previous attempts at classifying texts according to their complexity for the Italian language include [4,7]. The first presents a new resource for automatically assessing text difficulty in the context of Italian as a second or foreign language learning and teaching, called MALT-IT2, which automatically classifies input texts according to the CEFR level they are more likely to belong to. The second proposes a new approach to readability assessment with a specific view of the task of text simplification. The intended audience includes people with low literacy skills or mild cognitive impairment. READ-IT represents the first advanced readability assessment tool for Italian, which combines traditional raw text features with lexical, morpho-syntactic, and syntactic information. In READ-IT, readability assessment is carried out for both documents and sentences where the latter represents an important novelty of the proposed approach creating the prerequisites for aligning the readability assessment step with the text simplification process.

Regarding measures of text complexity, in [16], the author proposes the use of Pointwise Mutual Information (PMI) [2] to determine the phraseological complexity of texts; PMI was also used Logdice association measure [18] estimating the complexity of reading comprehension texts classified with CEFR [14].

3 Method

In this work, the task of determining the complexity of a text is defined as a supervised classification problem; several machine learning classifiers are trained with features computed from texts extracted from the CELI corpus, [13] which includes texts of students' responses to the teachers' essay instructions. The texts in the corpus were produced by Italian L2 learners and are classified according to the learner's level, i.e. the CEFR proficiency levels B1, B2, C1, and C2. The texts are analyzed from the phraseological complexity point of view; more specifically, the work focuses on the text diversity and text sophistication dimensions.

3.1 Text Pre-processing

In Natural Language Processing applications, during the pre-processing phase techniques are employed to produce a structured output from unstructured texts; in particular, after tokenizing the texts, lemmatization and dependency parsing were performed to analyze the texts from the dimensions of interest. The texts in the CELI corpus were pre-processed by means of the UDPIPE software [20], coupled with the *italian-isdt-ud-2.10-220711* treebank. UDPIPE processes texts following the Universal Dependencies framework (UD) [15], which provides consistent grammar annotation rules for texts in several human languages; in particular, for texts in the Italian language, 17 Parts-of-speech tags and 45 dependency relations tags are defined. The following dependency relations were considered to analyze the phraseological complexity of the text:

- **obj**: the direct object of a verb
- **amod**: adjective modifying the meaning of a nominal head
- **advmod**: a (non-clausal) adverb or adverbial phrase modifying the meaning of the head.
- **conj**: a relation between two elements connected by a coordinating conjunction (e.g. *and* and *or*.

The conj dependency was considered to account for cases in which, for example, a verb had multiple direct objects, as in the following example taken from the dataset:

Cambiare stile di vita, luogo, lavoro è sempre comunque un'esperienza positiva che ci rendi più forti.
Changing lifestyle, place, job is, in any case, a positive experience that strengthens us.
As visible in Fig. 1, the word *stile* is tagged by the parser as a direct object (*obj*)

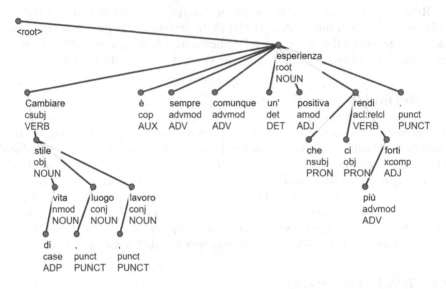

Fig. 1. UDPIPE parsing tree of the example sentence

of the head verb *cambiare*, while *luogo* and *lavoro* as coordinated (*conj*) with the head noun *stile*, although both are syntactically direct objects of *cambiare* too. For this reason, conjuncts with words tagged as *obj*, *amod*, or *advmod* were also considered for the computation of statistics. Words selected according to the criteria mentioned above were selected and used to compute the features in Sects. 3.2 and 3.3.

3.2 Text Sophistication

According to [16], the text sophistication dimension can be calculated [1,17] following two main approaches: the first is based on selecting uncommon word combinations in a text according to a list of sophisticated word collocations or by exclusion from a list of most frequent combinations; however, such resources are usually not available for a language, including Italian. Another strategy requires estimating the association between words by means of an appropriate frequency-based word association measure; collocations scoring high association values usually carry a rather distinctive meaning, and can therefore be associated with the sophistication level of a text. In this work, a frequentist approach is adopted, and the sophistication of collocations is estimated through the

Pointwise Mutual Information (PMI) or LogDice measures. Pointwise Mutual Information is an association measure frequently employed in NLP applications; it measures the association between two terms x and y with their occurrence and co-occurrence values as measured in a sufficiently large reference corpus; it is defined as

$$PMI = \log_2 \frac{p(x,y)}{p(x)p(y)}$$

where the numerator is the co-occurrence probability and the denominator the product of the occurrence probabilities of the two terms. In this work, two tokens x and y, where $xDEPy$ for some dependency DEP, are considered co-occurring each time they appear under the same dependency link in the reference corpus. PMI has been used in literature for several NLP applications, including text emotion recognition [8], topic modelling [22] and text generation [21]. LogDice is a standardized measure to quantify the tendency of two tokens to occur together in a corpus, defined as:

$$14 + \log_2 \frac{2*O_{11}}{R1 + C1}$$

where O_{11} is the observed frequency of the collocation and $R1$ and $C1$ are the frequencies of the two tokens in the reference corpus. In this work the Paisa corpus [11] was used as the reference corpus, to draw the occurrence and co-occurrence values used to compute PMI/Logdice association measures for each pair of words.

3.3 Text Diversity

The phraseological diversity dimension can be substantially measured in analogy with lexical diversity, by defining adequate type-token ratio measures. To measure the lexical diversity of a text, Root Type Token Ratio (RTTR) is frequently used in NLP to measure the degree of lexical variation and is defined as:

$$RTTR = \frac{t}{\sqrt{n}}$$

where t is the count of different types in the text and n is the total number of tokens. In this work the following variations of RTTR were also considered and employed as features:

- Lemma-TTR, where t is the count of different lemmas in the text;
- Obj-TTR, where t is the count of different tokens dependency-tagged as *obj* and n the total count of tokens tagged as *obj*;
- Amod-TTR, where t is the count of different tokens dependency-tagged as *amod* and n the total count of tokens tagged as *amod*;
- Advmod-TTR, where t is the count of different tokens dependency-tagged as *advmod* and n the total count of tokens tagged as *advmod*;

4 Experiments Settings

4.1 Dataset

The dataset is composed of 3041 texts, with an average of 12.3913 sentences and $\approx$ 210 tokens per text. 13 texts contain no occurrences of one or more of the considered dependencies, and thus the calculation of the corresponding measures was impossible. For this reason, such texts were excluded, bringing the total down to 3028.

In Table 1 the class distribution of the dataset is shown; the dataset is unbalanced, with B1 accounting for more than 33% of the total texts, and C2, i.e. the highest proficiency level being the less represented class. In Table 2 the number

Table 1. Dataset statistics

Class	#Texts	#Types	#Tokens
B1	1212	6656	161776
B2	840	8484	159017
C1	585	11377	158289
C2	404	12782	159120
Total	3041	22039	638202

of tokens tagged with each of the dependencies and the total number of tokens in the CELI Corpus are reported; $\approx$ 16% of the tokens were selected for further analysis [3,5].

Table 2. Tokens by dependency

Dependency	Count
Obj	35747
Amod	27714
Advmod	42473
Conj/Obj	1722
Conj/Amod	1214
Conj/Advmod	77
Total	638202

4.2 Features

Five different features combinations were extracted, to assess the contribution of the sophistication and diversity aspects in determining the complexity of a text:

- **Test 1**: diversity features only
- **Test 2**: Sophistication (PMI) features
- **Test 3**: Sophistication (PMI) + diversity features
- **Test 4**: Sophistication (LogDice) features
- **Test 5**: Sophistication (LogDice) + diversity features

4.3 Classification Models

In this work, for each feature subset, 12 different classification models, listed in Table 3, were trained: Support Vector Machines classify records by projecting

Table 3. Classification models

Model	Description
SVM_Linear	Support Vector Machine with Linear kernel
SVM_RBF	Support Vector Machine with Radial Basis Function kernel
SVM_Poly	Support Vector Machine with Polynomial kernel
RF_Gini	Random Forest classifier with Gini criterion
RF_Entropy	Random Forest classifier with Entropy criterion
RF_Log_loss	Random Forest classifier with Log_loss criterion
MLP_1	Multi Layer Perceptron with one hidden layer
MLP_2	Multi Layer Perceptron with two hidden layers
MLP_3	Multi Layer Perceptron with three hidden layers
NB	Naive Bayes classifier fitting Gaussian distributions
QDA	Quadratic Discriminant Analysis classifier
AdaBoost	AdaBoost boosting classifier

them in a higher dimensional space where they are separable by a set of hyperplanes. The choice of the kernel function determines how the original records are represented in the vector space; in this work, three different kernels, i.e. Linear, Radial Basis Function, and Polynomial were tested. Random Forest is an ensemble classification method that fits a large set of decision trees (100 in this work) on a dataset and adopts a majority classification scheme to aggregate the outputs of the decision trees and classify an unknown record. Decision trees are built by learning decision rules which iteratively split data into different subsets. During the tree learning process, the quality of each split is measured by a criterion; the Gini, Entropy, and Log_loss criteria were considered here. The Multi-Layer Perceptron (MLP) classifier is a conventional feed-forward neural network trained with the gradient descent algorithm. The input layer has as many neurons as the number of features fed to the classifier, and the output layer has one neuron per different class (in this work four, corresponding to the CEFR B1 to C2 classes); between the input and the output layer other hidden layers are responsible for learning patterns in the data. Three models, with a different number of hidden layers, were designed in accordance with experiments in [19]; for MLP_1 one hidden layer of 25 neurons was used, while MLP_2 and MLP_3 introduce respectively one and two additional hidden layers of the same size. The AdaBoost Classifier is an ensemble method fitting a series of weak estimators on the same dataset, focusing iteratively on more difficult and specific records; in its default Scikit-Learn settings, the base estimator for Adaboost is a Decision Tree classifier with maximum depth 1. Finally, Gaussian Naive Bayes and QDA are two classification algorithms based on Bayesian theory; the former aims at learning a Bayesian network model to perform predictions, while the latter builds, for each of the target classes, a multivariate probabilistic model and classifies unknown records by maximizing the posterior probability.

4.4 Performance Metrics

The performance of the model is evaluated through the common metrics used for classification tasks, i.e. Accuracy, Precision, Recall, and F1-Score. The confusion matrices obtained by the best classifier for each feature subset are also reported. The scores are calculated by adopting a 10-fold Cross-Validation approach: each text belongs to one test set and is classified using the model trained on the corresponding training set.

5 Experimental Results

In Table 4 the results of the experiments considering diversity features only are reported; QDA proves to be the best performer according to all the metrics. There are no significant differences among classifiers, except for AdaBoost and Gaussian Naive Bayes, showing sensibly lower figures.

Table 4. Test 1 (diversity) results

Classifier	Accuracy	Precision	Recall	F1
SVM, Linear	0.6889	0.6839	0.6709	0.6756
SVM, RBF	0.6869	0.6907	0.6600	0.6691
SVM, Poly	0.6889	0.6858	0.6688	0.6743
RF, Gini	0.6711	0.6664	0.6528	0.6578
RF, Entropy	0.6622	0.6563	0.6424	0.6476
RF, Log_loss	0.6622	0.6563	0.6424	0.6476
MLP_1	0.6849	0.6814	0.6630	0.6688
MLP_2	0.6846	0.6788	0.6630	0.6677
MLP_3	0.6879	0.6851	0.6674	0.6708
AdaBoost	0.6354	0.6065	0.6088	0.5952
Gaussian Naive Bayes	0.6539	0.6408	0.6381	0.6380
QDA	**0.6922**	**0.6886**	**0.6744**	**0.6793**

Table 5. Test 1 normalized confusion matrix, QDA (diversity)

QDA	B1	B2	C1	C2
B1	**0.8421**	0.1397	0.0175	0.0008
B2	0.3792	**0.5024**	0.1100	0.0084
C1	0.0530	0.1795	**0.6427**	0.1248
C2	0.0099	0.0248	0.2550	**0.7104**

Table 6. Test 2 (sophistication-PMI) results

Classifier	Accuracy	Precision	Recall	F1
SVM, Linear	0.7332	0.7303	0.7200	0.7246
SVM, RBF	0.7325	0.7318	0.7169	0.7234
SVM, Poly	**0.7381**	**0.7377**	0.7164	**0.7247**
RF, Gini	0.7249	0.7229	0.7120	0.7165
RF, Entropy	0.7242	0.7212	0.7105	0.7148
RF, Log_loss	0.7242	0.7212	0.7105	0.7148
MLP_1	0.7351	0.7273	0.7196	0.7229
MLP_2	0.7358	0.7346	**0.7212**	0.7272
MLP_3	0.7318	0.7252	0.7157	0.7196
AdaBoost	0.6625	0.6419	0.6442	0.6391
Gaussian Naive Bayes	0.7157	0.7103	0.6964	0.7019
QDA	0.7199	0.7161	0.7015	0.7070

Table 7. Test 2 normalized confusion matrix, SVM Poly (PMI)

SVM_Poly	B1	B2	C1	C2
B1	**0.8969**	0.0956	0.0075	0.0000
B2	0.3325	**0.5634**	0.0981	0.0060
C1	0.0308	0.2325	**0.6479**	0.0889
C2	0.0025	0.0223	0.2178	**0.7574**

In Table 6 the results of the experiments including the text sophistication features are reported; the confusion matrix for the best classifier, i.e. SVM with linear kernel, is reported in Table 7. In Table 8 the results of the experiments including the base, text sophistication, and text diversity features are reported (Table 5). The confusion matrix for the best-performing classifier, i.e. SVM with Linear Kernel, is shown in Table 9. In Fig. 2 the F1 scores of all the classifiers are plotted for Test 5, i.e. LogDice-based sophistication and diversity features; the best-performing group is represented by SVM classifiers, followed by Random Forests, MLP3 and QDA groups with substantially similar performance, while

Gaussian Naive Bayes and, most notably, AdaBoost generally achieve lower figures. Such behaviour is generally consistent across experiments, with notable
exceptions being MLP1 and MLP2 scoring higher than some RF-based classifiers in Test 1 and Test 2. Complete results for Test 5 are reported in Table 12;
the best performance is achieved by SVM with linear kernel, with an Accuracy of 76.85%, 2.7% higher than the best one so far for Italian CEFR reported
in [19]. Furthermore, in linguistics the CEFR B1, B2 and C1, C2 levels are
often grouped in two macro-levels B and C; the confusion matrix for Test 5 in
Table 13 shows that misclassification errors occur mostly between classes of the
same macro-level and distant classes, e.g. B1 and C2, are seldom confused. If
the classification output is aggregated according to the grouped categorization,
the system achieves an overall accuracy of $\approx$ 93%; a similar behaviour can be
observed for all the test cases (Tables 10 and 11).

Table 8. Test 3 (diversity+sophistication-PMI) results

Classifier	Accuracy	Precision	Recall	F1
SVM, Linear	0.7589	0.7597	**0.7508**	**0.7545**
SVM, RBF	0.7517	0.7544	0.7378	0.7444
SVM, Poly	**0.7606**	**0.7639**	0.7468	0.7534
RF, Gini	0.7325	0.7322	0.7213	0.7261
RF, Entropy	0.7312	0.7306	0.7158	0.7220
RF, Log_loss	0.7312	0.7306	0.7158	0.7220
AdaBoost	0.6628	0.6393	0.6416	0.6320
Gaussian Naive Bayes	0.7223	0.7132	0.7128	0.7121
QDA	0.7378	0.7338	0.7212	0.7259
MLP_1	0.7272	0.7174	0.7092	0.7127
MLP_2	0.7348	0.7277	0.7189	0.7230
MLP_3	0.7437	0.7417	0.7330	0.7366

Table 9. Test 3 normalized confusion matrix, SVM Linear (diversity+PMI)

SVM_Linear	B1	B2	C1	C2
B1	**0.8587**	0.1313	0.0100	0.0000
B2	0.2763	**0.6148**	0.1005	0.0084
C1	0.0239	0.1538	**0.7350**	0.0872
C2	0.0025	0.0198	0.1832	**0.7946**

Table 10. Test 4 (sophistication-LogDice) results

Classifier	Accuracy	Precision	Recall	F1
SVM, Linear	0.7368	0.7316	**0.7215**	0.7261
SVM, RBF	0.7361	0.7356	0.7187	0.7262
SVM, Poly	**0.7424**	**0.7410**	0.7185	**0.7278**
RF, Gini	0.7269	0.7185	0.7074	0.7123
RF, Entropy	0.7325	0.7254	0.7144	0.7193
RF, Log_loss	0.7325	0.7254	0.7144	0.7193
MLP$_1$	0.7338	0.7239	0.7158	0.7192
MLP$_2$	0.7341	0.7260	0.7165	0.7207
MLP$_3$	0.7384	0.7317	0.7219	0.7262
AdaBoost	0.6648	0.6328	0.6396	0.6296
Gaussian Naive Bayes	0.7249	0.7160	0.7032	0.7084
QDA	0.7269	0.7205	0.7077	0.7128

Table 11. Test 4 normalized confusion matrix, SVM Poly (LogDice)

SVM_Poly	B1	B2	C1	C2
B1	**0.8978**	0.0948	0.0075	0.0000
B2	0.3086	**0.5933**	0.0909	0.0072
C1	0.0308	0.2564	**0.6256**	0.0872
C2	0.0074	0.0198	0.2153	**0.7574**

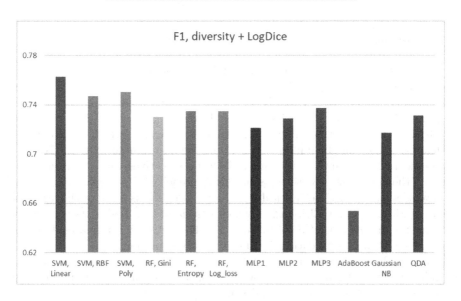

Fig. 2. Classifiers' F1 Score for Test 5, (features: diversity + sophistication-LogDice)

Table 12. Test 5 (diversity + sophistication-LogDice) results

Classifier	Accuracy	Precision	Recall	F1
SVM, Linear	**0.7685**	**0.7684**	**0.7583**	**0.7628**
SVM, RBF	0.7550	0.7562	0.7406	0.7470
SVM, Poly	0.7599	0.7619	0.7428	0.7503
RF, Gini	0.7394	0.7372	0.7243	0.7301
RF, Entropy	0.7447	0.7433	0.7287	0.7349
RF, Log_loss	0.7447	0.7433	0.7287	0.7349
MLP$_1$	0.7375	0.7269	0.7165	0.7211
MLP$_2$	0.7427	0.7377	0.7224	0.7288
MLP$_3$	0.7470	0.7405	0.7352	0.7372
AdaBoost	0.6800	0.6593	0.6583	0.6537
Gaussian Naive Bayes	0.7289	0.7185	0.7173	0.7170
QDA	0.7444	0.7382	0.7277	0.7313

Table 13. Test 5 normalized confusion matrix, SVM Linear (diversity+LogDice)

SVM_Linear	B1	B2	C1	C2
B1	**0.8703**	0.1205	0.0091	0.0000
B2	0.2596	**0.6352**	0.0969	0.0084
C1	0.0205	0.1675	**0.7282**	0.0838
C2	0.0025	0.0223	0.1757	**0.7995**

6   Conclusions

In this work, a framework is proposed for the automated classification of texts produced by Italian language L2 learners according to the Common European Framework of Reference (CEFR) B1 to C2 levels. The proposed approach focuses on phraseological text complexity features. Phraseological complexity is defined by the notions of text sophistication and text diversity, which are modelled with appropriate statistical metrics (i.e. Pointwise Mutual Information, LogDice, Type-token Ratios), applied to lemmas, objects, adjectives, and adverbial modifiers in the text. The effectiveness of this approach and possible metrics and feature sets has been experimentally evaluated on various state-of-the-art classifier algorithms. The CELI corpus, which is a dataset of real texts written by L2 students in official CEFR exams and classified with the candidates' levels of Italian competence certification, has been used in experiments.

Results show a promising capability of the framework to assess the text complexity level with different sets of features; the best outcomes were obtained by combining diversity features and sophistication features based on LogDice measures, with an accuracy of 76.85% and an F1 of 76.28% when using Support

Vector Machines. For CEFR Italian language L2 learners, the proposed strategy improves previous results obtained in the literature [19].

Future work will explore whether it is possible to further improve performance, with the integration of the proposed pure phraseological framework with an approach considering lexical and morphological quantitative indices as that in [19]; another potentially promising innovative direction is to explore the role of text embedding vectorial representations [10,12] in reflecting text complexity.

Acknowledgment. This work is partially supported by the Italian Ministry of Research under PRIN Project "PHRAME" Grant n.20178XXKFY.

References

1. Carpi, A., D'Alessandro, F.: On the hybrid Černý-road coloring problem and Hamiltonian paths. In: Gao, Y., Lu, H., Seki, S., Yu, S. (eds.) DLT 2010. LNCS, vol. 6224, pp. 124–135. Springer, Heidelberg (2010). https://doi.org/10.1007/978-3-642-14455-4_13
2. Church, K.W., Hanks, P.: Word association norms, mutual information, and lexicography. Comput. Linguist. **16**(1), 22–29 (1990)
3. D'Alessandro, F., Carpi, A.: On incomplete and synchronizing finite sets. Theoret. Comput. Sci. **664**, 67–77 (2017). https://doi.org/10.1016/j.tcs.2015.08.042
4. Dell'Orletta, F., Montemagni, S., Venturi, G.: READ-IT: assessing readability of Italian texts with a view to text simplification. In: Proceedings of the Second Workshop on Speech and Language Processing for Assistive Technologies, pp. 73–83. Association for Computational Linguistics, Edinburgh, Scotland, UK (2011)
5. Carpi, A., D'Alessandro, F.: On the commutative equivalence of context-free languages. In: Hoshi, M., Seki, S. (eds.) DLT 2018. LNCS, vol. 11088, pp. 169–181. Springer, Cham (2018). https://doi.org/10.1007/978-3-319-98654-8_14
6. Council of Europe. Council for Cultural Co-operation. Education Committee. Modern Languages Division: Common European Framework of Reference for Languages: Learning, Teaching, Assessment. Cambridge University Press, Cambridge (2001)
7. Forti, L., Grego Bolli, G., Santarelli, F., Santucci, V., Spina, S.: MALT-IT2: a new resource to measure text difficulty in light of CEFR levels for Italian L2 learning. In: Proceedings of the Twelfth Language Resources and Evaluation Conference, pp. 7204–7211. European Language Resources Association, Marseille, France (2020)
8. Franzoni, V., Milani, A., Biondi, G.: SEMO: a semantic model for emotion recognition in web objects. In: Proceedings of the International Conference on Web Intelligence, pp. 953–958. WI 2017, Association for Computing Machinery, New York, NY, USA (2017). https://doi.org/10.1145/3106426.3109417
9. Franzoni, V., Poggioni, V., Zollo, F.: Automated classification of book blurbs according to the emotional tags of the social network zazie. ESSEM@ AI* IA **1096**, 83–94 (2013). CEUR-WS
10. Li, Y., Yang, T.: Word embedding for understanding natural language: a survey. In: Srinivasan, S. (ed.) Guide to Big Data Applications. SBD, vol. 26, pp. 83–104. Springer, Cham (2018). https://doi.org/10.1007/978-3-319-53817-4_4
11. Lyding, V., et al.: The PAISÀ corpus of Italian web texts. In: Proceedings of the 9th Web as Corpus Workshop (WaC-9), pp. 36–43. Association for Computational Linguistics, Gothenburg, Sweden (2014). https://doi.org/10.3115/v1/W14-0406

12. Mikolov, T., Sutskever, I., Chen, K., Corrado, G., Dean, J.: Distributed representations of words and phrases and their compositionality. In: Proceedings of the 26th International Conference on Neural Information Processing Systems, vol. 2, pp. 3111–3119. NIPS 2013, Curran Associates Inc., Red Hook, NY, USA (2013)
13. Milani, A., Franzoni, V., Biondi, G.: Parsing tools for Italian phraseological units. In: Gervasi, O., et al. (eds.) ICCSA 2021. LNCS, vol. 12955, pp. 427–435. Springer, Cham (2021). https://doi.org/10.1007/978-3-030-87007-2_30
14. Natova, I.: Estimating CEFR reading comprehension text complexity. Lang. Learn. J. **49**(6), 699–710 (2021). https://doi.org/10.1080/09571736.2019.1665088
15. Nivre, J., et al.: Universal dependencies v2: an evergrowing multilingual treebank collection. In: Proceedings of the Twelfth Language Resources and Evaluation Conference, pp. 4034–4043. European Language Resources Association, Marseille, France (2020)
16. Paquot, M.: The phraseological dimension in interlanguage complexity research. Second. Lang. Res. **35**(1), 121–145 (2019). https://doi.org/10.1177/0267658317694221
17. Poggioni, V., Bartoccini, U., Carpi, A., Santucci, V.: Memes evolution in a memetic variant of particle swarm optimization. Mathematics **7**(5), 423 (2019). https://doi.org/10.3390/math7050423
18. Rychlý, P.: A lexicographer-friendly association score. In: RASLAN (2008)
19. Santucci, V., Santarelli, F., Forti, L., Spina, S.: Automatic classification of text complexity. Appl. Sci. **10**(20), 7285 (2020). https://doi.org/10.3390/app10207285
20. Straka, M.: UDPipe 2.0 prototype at CoNLL 2018 UD shared task. In: Proceedings of the CoNLL 2018 Shared Task: Multilingual Parsing from Raw Text to Universal Dependencies, pp. 197–207. Association for Computational Linguistics, Brussels, Belgium (2018). https://doi.org/10.18653/v1/K18-2020
21. Takayama, J., Arase, Y.: Relevant and informative response generation using pointwise mutual information. In: Proceedings of the First Workshop on NLP for Conversational AI, pp. 133–138. Association for Computational Linguistics, Florence, Italy (2019). https://doi.org/10.18653/v1/W19-4115
22. Vishal, K., Deepak, G., Santhanavijayan, A.: An approach for retrieval of text documents by hybridizing structural topic modeling and pointwise mutual information. In: Mekhilef, S., Favorskaya, M., Pandey, R.K., Shaw, R.N. (eds.) Innovations in Electrical and Electronic Engineering. LNEE, vol. 756, pp. 969–977. Springer, Singapore (2021). https://doi.org/10.1007/978-981-16-0749-3_74

Advanced Processes of Mathematics and Computing Models in Complex Computational Systems (ACMC 2023)

Decision Support for Effective Urban Regeneration Projects: A Model Based on Community Interests – Project Costs Analysis

Ivan Blečić, Emanuel Muroni, and Valeria Saiu[✉]

University of Cagliari, Via Corte d'Appello 78, Cagliari, Italy
{ivanblecic,emanuel.muroni,vsaiu}@unica.it

Abstract. In the realm of public policy-making, identifying and prioritizing regeneration interventions represent a critical challenge for the development of effective strategies and actions. This requires a comprehensive approach to understanding of the interplay between physical spaces, their users, and social practices and to evaluate the convenience of different projects both in economic and social terms. Among the decision-support methods that policymakers have at their disposal there are the Participatory Cost-Benefit Analysis (PCBA) that can guide in planning and investment programs towards optimal choices. This paper presents a methodology to perform a novel PCBA, based on two criteria: (1) the declared interest of the local community in the use of a specific space and (2) the estimated economic costs of the intervention needed for using a space. An exploratory case study within the city of Cagliari (Italy) is presented to evaluate advantages and limitations in the proposed method. This study was undertaken using qualitative economic analysis and through a participatory process that involved local stakeholders as part of a large collaborative project lead by the University of Cagliari.

The results provide a clearer understanding of the trade-offs/synergies involved in urban regeneration and a possible explanation of long-term poor results, which is likely to occur when investments do not consider both spatial and social dimensions. In particular, the integrated approach based on community interests and project costs can produce a more cost-effective social effects and can have a greater influence on the economic value of the intervention, representing a potential predictor of choice, over alternative scenarios.

Keywords: multi-criteria decision making · collaborative/participatory approaches · cost-benefit analysis · urban regeneration · neighbourhood scale

1 Introduction

Urban regeneration is a complex and multifaceted field of research, public policy and practice that seeks to revitalize urban areas and stimulate social and economic growth, with the ultimate goal of improving the quality of life for residents. Achieving this goal requires an integrated, multi-dimensional, and multi-level approach that considers the interplay between social and spatial dimensions, and the unique characteristics of each locality that influence their effectiveness of a project.

© The Author(s), under exclusive license to Springer Nature Switzerland AG 2023 2023
O. Gervasi et al. (Eds.): ICCSA 2023 Workshops, LNCS 14104, pp. 31–43, 2023.
https://doi.org/10.1007/978-3-031-37105-9_3

The importance of context-specific interventions has been recognized by the European Union as crucial for maximizing impact and sustainability [1]. By adopting a nuanced approach that considers the specific needs and aspirations of local communities, urban regeneration projects can be more responsive and effective in achieving their intended outcomes. In this context, social characteristics such as community engagement, social cohesion, and access to services and amenities are crucial for addressing underlying social issues and promoting inclusive growth. At the same time, the physical environment, including infrastructure, transportation, and public spaces, plays a significant role in shaping the social environment and residents' capabilities [2–6]. By carefully assessing these aspects, decision-makers can make informed choices about which projects are most likely to succeed and generate the greatest impact for communities.

The interlinkages between space characteristics and their perceived value are crucial, as they can determine investment priorities and influence project success. For instance, an urban area with good access to public transportation is likely to be perceived as valuable by residents and potential users or investors. This perception of value can influence investment priorities and decision-making choices. However, if investment priorities are not aligned with the values and needs of the community, the project may fail to achieve its intended outcomes and even create unintended negative consequences.

To avoid this, well-structured methodologies have been studied to make informed choices about which projects are most likely to succeed and generate the greatest impact for communities. Decision support tools based on multi-criteria decision-making (MCDM) techniques have been used extensively in the assessment of urban regeneration to evaluate the most performing interventions [7–11]. Many of these, incorporate social visions, preferences, and feelings of the stakeholders involved to ensure that decisions are more inclusive and reflect the diverse needs and values of the community [12, 13].

Within the scope of these studies, the aim of this article is to present a novel MCDM tool that aims to assist planners and public policy makers in their selection and prioritization of urban interventions. This tool operates based on two critical criteria that aim to ensure optimal outcomes for the community. The first criterion considers the expressed interest of the community – social and cultural associations and groups – in utilizing a particular space, while the second criterion assesses the estimated economic costs linked to the interventions required for utilizing a space.

Through this approach, the tool serves as a crucial resource for decision-makers seeking to strike a balance between community interests (benefits) and project costs (public expenditure) and in their efforts to promote sustainable urban development.

To demonstrate the efficacy and potential uses of our evaluation framework for urban analysis and policy design, we present the outcomes of a case study conducted within the city of Cagliari (Italy). The findings of this study provide a convincing explanation for the suboptimal long-term outcomes that may result from investments that do not incorporate the proposed cost-benefit assessment. The proposed approach has the potential to generate more cost-effective social effects and exert greater influence on the economic value of the intervention, serving as a crucial predictor of choice when compared to alternative scenarios.

The novelty and significance of this paper can be traced to its contribution to the growing body of knowledge in the field of innovative digital tools for the management of public buildings, open spaces, and community empowerment. Furthermore, the application of this framework in the case study provides a tangible demonstration of the utility and effectiveness of the proposed tool for policy design.

The paper is structured as follows: Sect. 2 provides an overview of the main MCDM tools utilized in urban regeneration, emphasizing the distinctiveness of our approach; Sect. 3 outlines the evaluation methodology and describes the protocol used for the community scoping and economic analysis of regeneration costs; Sect. 4 showcases a case study to illustrate the practical application of our approach; Sect. 5 analyzes the results; and finally, Sect. 6 presents concluding remarks, and outlines potential future perspectives.

2 Background and Previous Research

In the field of urban regeneration, the selection and prioritization of interventions poses a pivotal challenge for the formulation of effective policies and strategies. This involves optimizing economic resources while simultaneously improving social impacts, which requires a comprehensive evaluation of the spatial and physical characteristics of sites, as well as their current and potential uses [14]. Attention must be paid to not-for-profit cultural, social, and recreational activities managed by the community [15]. As highlighted by Voinov and Bousquet [13], in fact, the stakeholders' engagement is often only nominal in nature and this is one of the causes of projects' failure [16, 17].

Numerous studies have attempted to determine the optimal model for guiding and assisting stakeholders in making the best decisions, utilizing various criteria and procedures. Tasheva – Petrova [18] explores the feasibility of combining social dimensions and physical features to achieve sustainable management of open public spaces in large housing estates within the Nadezhda district of Sofia. The research utilizes qualitative and quantitative methods, spatial analysis, and participatory activities to examine the attitudes, perceptions, aspirations, and motivations towards public spaces from the perspective of pupils, citizens, and administration staff. By doing so, the study aims to enhance the community's engagement and commitment to public spaces.

A multitude of studies employ Cost-Benefit Analysis (CBA) to compare the social benefits against the costs of a particular investment. In recent years, in fact, several researchers have endeavored to address certain inherent limitations of the conventional CBA approach. For instance, challenges pertaining to the identification and quantification of intangible benefits, such as community-based values, have been highlighted [19, 20]. To tackle these limitations, a more effective approach is to combine economic evaluation with participatory evaluation, incorporating qualitative indicators based on the perceptions of citizens. This match is known as Participatory Cost-Benefit Analysis (PCBA), which leads to more informed and equitable decisions that better serve the interests of society at large. Among the first studies that focus on this topic, Sager [21] underlined the potential advantages of integrating cost-benefit analysis with participatory methods as a means of obtaining a more comprehensive understanding of transportation planning projects.

Drawing upon the insights of Campos et al. [22], PCBA can be described as a hybrid methodology that combines both quantitative and qualitative elements to enable a more comprehensive appraisal of economic projects. This approach involves the use of diverse sources and methods, including interpersonal deliberation, to generate a deeper and broader understanding of the valuation and appraisal processes.

As an exemplar, García de Jalón et al. [20] implemented a PCBA to evaluate the economic benefits and costs associated with public initiatives that seek to facilitate citizen access to urban green spaces.

In order to understand the complex and ever-evolving dynamics of urban development, Haoyu [23] devised a game model, which takes into account the interplay of costs and benefits, as well as the actions and outcomes of various actors involved in the process. This model provides a useful framework for optimizing the integration and coordination of diverse interests in the development of urban spaces and can serve as a valuable resource for decision-making oriented towards ensuring inclusive and sustainable forms of urban planning and governance.

The proposed methodology offers a novel approach by placing emphasis on the impact of public expenditure for urban regeneration projects on potential community benefits. This is achieved through a dual analysis that integrates a comprehensive understanding of potential space utilization with the interception, evaluation, and normalization of community interests in these spaces.

The "projection" of interests from diverse individuals interviewed on different open spaces/buildings provides a means of prioritizing projects, serving as a valuable decision-support tool for local administrations in resource allocation. It is essential to evaluate the social impact of project costs to ensure that regeneration interventions have a positive effect on the community.

This approach also ensures that the community's voice is heard and considered in the decision-making process, promoting a sense of ownership and participation in the project. Ultimately, assessing the social impact of public expenditure for urban regeneration projects is critical in promoting sustainable and inclusive urban development that benefits all members of the community.

3 Methodology

To achieve this twofold goal – maximize the social impacts and minimize costs of interventions – the model combines two different methodologies:

1) *Interest – Social analysis:* qualitative research design accomplished through the community scoping step, a technique for participatory design and analysis employed to better understand local conditions and to describe community needs, perceptions, and interests in using different public spaces. This step includes semi-structured in-depth interviews with different social actors (formal and informal organizations and associations, key individuals) that provide detailed information and data to be implemented in the evaluation model.

2) *Cost – Space analysis:* documentation, observation, surveying and cataloging of all public spaces into four main categories – ecological sites, urban parks, little gardens, sport areas – according to their potential uses and unique characteristics. Furthermore,

the current state of each space, as the level of intervention required for their use –
no interventions, little interventions, great interventions – is defined to estimate the
costs.

The results of these two steps are combined to define a community interests – project
costs analysis that reveals what are: (1) the dominant or priority interventions (high
effective – low expensive); (2) the inferior intervention options (low effective – low
expensive) and (3) the questionable interventions (low effective – low expensive/high
effective – high expensive). The data are synthetized into a two-dimensional chart (see
Fig. 1).

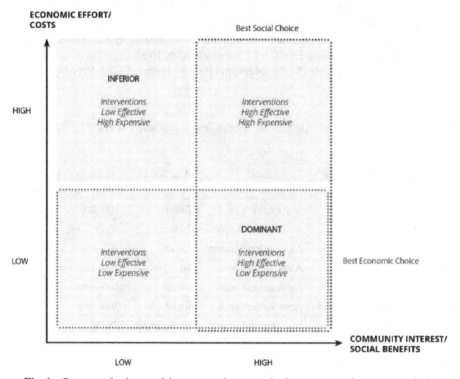

Fig. 1. Conceptual scheme of the proposed community interests – project costs analysis.

4   Case Study: Is Mirrionis – San Michele Neighbourhoods

The proposed methodology was validated by applying it to the case study of two neighbourhoods in the city of Cagliari (Italy). We have mapped and characterized using
traditional on-the-ground techniques and open data sources, 21 public open spaces and

14 groups and associations that operate in these urban areas (see Tables 1 and 2). Then, we have conducted in parallel both social and spatial analysis and evaluation.

Social analysis. We have engaged in a process of dialoguing with a range of stakeholders to gain a deeper understanding of the intricate social dynamics that affect the current use of public spaces. Subsequently, we conducted interviews with representatives from 14 associations to gather their perspectives and interests on the mapped spaces. These insights are crucial in ensuring that any interventions in urban regeneration are sustainable, inclusive, and reflective of the needs and desires of the community.

To further refine our understanding, we asked them to indicate their level of interest in suggested spaces on a three-level ordinal scale, ranging from low to high. To aggregate the resulting scores, we employed the Borda count method [24], which assigned points of 0, 1, and 2 to the low, intermediate, and high levels of interest, respectively.

The overall score for each space was determined by adding up the points assigned to each level of interest. As a result, we have established five categories of community interest: Very low (<5); Low (5–10); Medium (10–15); High (15–20); Very high (>20) (see Table 2).

Table 1. Case study analysis. Associations, groups, and social actors selected for the in-depth analysis.

Code	Name of social actor	Type/Level	Main Sector	Number of associates/ involved residents
A01	Casa del Quartiere	Association/Local	Culture	100–200
A02	Acli Cagliari	Association/National	Culture	4500–5000
A03	Istituto Gramsci	Association/National	Culture	100–150
A04	Teatro del Segno	Association/Local	Arts	100–150
A05	Mutuo Soccorso	Association/Local	Social	100–150
A06	Associazione Anziani	Association/Local	Social	300–350
A07	Amici Naturalmente	Association/Local	Environment	25–50
A08	TDM 2000	Association/Local	Culture	50–100
A09	Sarditinera Onlus	Association/Local	Culture	25–50
A10	Aladin Pensiero	Association/Local	Comunication	25–50
A11	Legambiente Sardegna	Association/National	Environment	500–550
A12	Sant'Eusebio	Church	Religion	-
A13	S.M. Kolbe	Church	Religion	-
A14	SS. Pietro e Paolo	Church	Religion	-

Spatial analysis: To evaluate the potential for future projects, we conducted a comprehensive mapping of public spaces. This involved gathering documentation, conducting observations, and surveying and cataloguing each open public space. We classified these spaces into four main categories, namely ecological sites, urban parks, small gardens, and sports areas, based on their unique characteristics and potential uses.

To refine our assessment, we conducted a comprehensive evaluation of the current state of each public space and estimated the level of intervention required to make them usable. To obtain accurate and reliable evaluative judgments, we consulted with a panel of experts, who considered various factors, such as direct costs of construction or site upgrading, the local construction market, the type of proposed intervention, the conservation state of buildings and the quality of the open spaces.

Furthermore, the experts also considered costs related to possible overheads due to legal and ownership issues, such as private/public ownership and property fragmentation, as well as planning and conservation constraints established during the surveying of each individual space [25]. These additional considerations are crucial for a comprehensive understanding of the costs and feasibility of urban regeneration projects.

Based on these evaluations, we classified the required interventions into five categories of project costs: Very Low (<50 k€), Low (50–200 k€), Medium (200–500 k€), High (500–2.000 k€), and Very High (>2.000 k€) (see Table 2). This classification provides a useful tool for urban planners and decision-makers to determine the appropriate level of investment needed for each public space, based on its unique characteristics and potential uses.

Table 2. Case study analysis. For each public open space: code/name, type of space, estimated cost of intervention and declared interest of social actors (associations and groups)

Code	Name of space	Type/current state	Estimated Cost (k€)	Interest
S01	Piazza Mercato Quirra	Square	400	16
S02	Spazio aperto Quirra/Brianza	Little Garden	500	10
S03	Parco San Michele	Urban Park	200	24
S04	Spazio aperto via Sirai	Little Garden	3.000	0
S05	Spazio aperto via Cinquini	Little Garden	2.000	12
S06	Parco di Monte Claro	Urban Park	100	21
S07	Tuvixeddu-Tuvumannu	Ecological Area	9.000	15
S08	Polisportiva Johannes	Sport Area	650	2
S09	Campi via Argonne	Sport Area	250	5
S10	Campi via Montesanto	Sport Area	650	6
S11	Piazza Is Maglias	Square	100	11
S12	Piazza San Michele	Square	50	21
S13	Piazza Medaglia M	Square	500	13

(continued)

Table 2. (*continued*)

Code	Name of space	Type/current state	Estimated Cost (k€)	Interest
S14	Piazza Paese di Seui	Square	100	0
S15	Piazza Premuda/Abruzzi	Square	250	4
S16	Piazza Paese di Desulo	Square	500	0
S17	Giardino via Barigadu	Little Garden	50	4
S18	Giardino Montevecchio	Little Garden	50	20
S19	Campi via Cornalias	Sport Area	350	12
S20	Piazza Scuola Popolare	Square	250	23

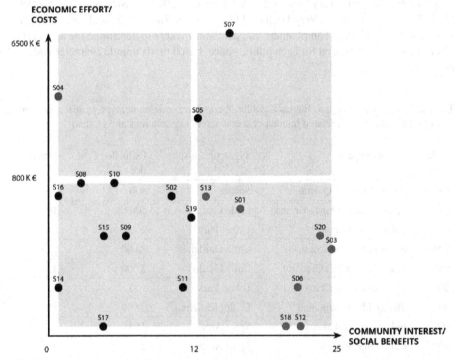

Fig. 2. Case study analysis: the community interests – project costs analysis. The dots indicate: the priority interventions (green); the questionable interventions (black) and the secondary interventions (red).

5 Discussion

The findings revealed that out of the 20 spaces considered: seven were categorized as priority spaces for intervention (35%); one as a secondary space for intervention (5%); and 12 as questionable spaces for interventions (60%) (Fig. 2). An additional evaluation of the level of priority was conducted for the eight spaces belonging to the first two categories (Fig. 3), and the results are presented in the last column of Table 3.

Table 3. Case study analysis: priority and secondary spaces for intervention.

Code	Name of space	Interest	Estimated Cost	Priority
S12	Piazza San Michele	Very High	Very Low	Very High
S18	Giardino Montevecchio	Very High	Very Low	Very High
S06	Parco di Monte Claro	Very High	Low	High
S03	Parco San Michele	Very High	Medium	High
S20	Piazza Scuola Popolare	Very High	Medium	High
S01	Piazza Mercato Quirra	High	Medium	Medium
S13	Piazza Medaglia M	Medium	Medium	Medium
S04	Spazio aperto via Sirai	Very Low	Very High	Very Low

Fig. 3. Image of the priority (green) and secondary (red) spaces for intervention.

Among the seven identified priority spaces for intervention, two large urban parks (S03 and S06) were perceived by the majority of interviewees as neighborhood landmarks and were found to be in good condition, requiring minimal intervention to accommodate a variety of activities that could cater to different user categories.

Another priority area is Piazza San Michele (S12), situated strategically in front of a church and at the intersection of urban connecting roads. Recently redeveloped, the square no longer functions as a temporary open-air market, which had previously made it a vital space during the day. The interviewees expressed their desire to use the square for various purposes and restore its previous functions, including that of the market.

Similarly, the gardens of Montevecchio (S18) is a recently redeveloped space which has great potential but requires additional interventions to fully enhance its social potential. In particular, the presence of criminal activities that are favoured by the urban design and the particular conformation of streets, is underlined by the interviews. To deal with this, they suggest integrating the gardens with the services and other surrounding open spaces.

The square that accommodates the building of the former Popular School (S20) was deemed a highly significant space by the interviewees. It holds a special historical value as the site of the popular school that was established in the 1970s to provide education for workers. Additionally, it is located in the heart of the district, serving as a suitable area for both the residents of neighbouring buildings and those seeking access to other activities, such as the hospital.

Piazza Mercato (S01) currently serves two primary functions. During the day, it hosts a large open market that attracts visitors to the city market located within it. In the afternoon, once the market closes, it transforms into a large, but scarcely used, car park. The interviewees strongly perceived the potential of this space, viewing its redevelopment as an opportunity to revitalize the area where many disadvantaged families reside.

Piazza Medaglia (S13) is a square surrounded by buildings, forming a central block at the intersection of the main urban connecting roads in the San Michele district. The adjacent kindergarten, serving as a meeting point for many families in the area, adds to the square's significance. Despite its poor state of maintenance, the square remains of great interest to the interviewees due to its strategic location and the presence of the kindergarten.

On the contrary, the area of Via Sirai (S04) is not considered a priority by the interviewees. This largely depends on the conformation of the space itself. It is, in fact, a large disused area requires major interventions and investments.

6 Conclusions

In this paper, a method for evaluating priority regeneration interventions is presented. Our approach involves an analysis of the relationship between community interest and project costs, which is designed to support policy makers in their decision-making process.

To ensure a comprehensive evaluation, our methodology incorporates both social and spatial analysis methods. The social analysis component allows for more effective and targeted interventions that are tailored to the specific needs and priorities of the community. Furthermore, our community scoping activity promotes a collaborative and participatory approach to research, fostering a positive and productive relationship that can be leveraged for future projects and initiatives.

In terms of spatial analysis, our methodology takes a systematic approach to mapping and categorizing public spaces, which provides a more accurate understanding of their unique features and potential for future development. By considering the current state of each space and the level of intervention required, we are able to provide detailed and accurate cost estimates that are useful for decision-making and planning.

The case study results show that our procedure has promising feasibility and efficiency. The Participatory Cost-Benefit Analysis used to carry out a comparative analysis of the economic costs of a project and their community benefits, expressed by the declared interests of local populations and groups, allows for a better understanding of of the potential role of urban regeneration in promoting social inclusion objectives. At the same time, the qualitative analysis used to estimate the economic expenditure that could be covered by public administrations for each project allows to increase awareness of the importance of proper decision-making in the early design process.

Moreover, two potential directions for the future of this study can be identified. Firstly, social evaluation may be partially automated through digital participation platforms that enable participants to engage in decision-making processes in a structured manner. Specifically, online forums and surveys could be employed ex ante to assess subjective interests and identify community priorities, and ex post to evaluate the effectiveness of programmes, policies, or projects.

Accordingly, spatial analysis can be significantly enhanced through the utilization of Geographical Information System (GIS) platforms [26–28]. Through GIS, detailed databases can be constructed that combine geographical information with data on the present and potential uses of a space, as well as its overall condition, thereby enabling the estimation of regeneration costs. By employing GIS in this manner, it is feasible to obtain more profound insights into the complexities of urban spaces. This approach also facilitates the development of cost-benefit analyses that are tailored to the unique requirements and proclivities of the community. By so doing, decision-makers can make informed choices regarding which interventions are most likely to be efficacious and offer the highest return on investment.

Second, the synthetic evaluation of places based on two criteria is merely a preliminary step towards a more intricate evaluation process. By introducing further criteria to the model, it is conceivable to develop more refined and precise tools for ranking or rating places, or for evaluating and selecting places for a range of purposes.

References

1. European Commission: A European Green Deal. https://ec.europa.eu/info/strategy/priorities-2019-2024/european-green-deal_en (2019). Accessed 25 Jun 2022
2. Blečić, I., Cecchini, A., Congiu, T., Fancello, G., Trunfio, G.A.: Evaluating walkability: a capability-wise planning and design support system. Int. J. Geogr. Inf. Sci. **29**, 1350–1374 (2015). https://doi.org/10.1080/13658816.2015.1026824
3. Sassen, S.: Urban capabilities: an essay on our challenges and differences. J. Int. Aff. **65**, 85–95 (2012)
4. Sen, A.: The Idea of Justice. Harvard University Press (2011)
5. Nussbaum, M.C.: Creating Capabilities: The Human Development Approach and Its Implementation. Mass. Harvard University Press, Cambridge (2011)
6. Pinna, F., Saiu, V.: Greenways as integrated systems: a proposal for planning and design guidelines based on case studies evaluation. Sustainability **13**, 11232 (2021). https://doi.org/10.3390/su132011232

7. Nesticò, A., Elia, C., Naddeo, V.: Sustainability of urban regeneration projects: novel selection model based on analytic network process and zero-one goal programming. Land Use Policy **99**, 104831 (2020). https://doi.org/10.1016/j.landusepol.2020.104831

8. Bottero, M., Mondini, G., Oppio, A.: Decision support systems for evaluating urban regeneration. Procedia. Soc. Behav. Sci. **223**, 923–928 (2016). https://doi.org/10.1016/j.sbspro.2016.05.319

9. Guarini, M.R., Battisti, F., Chiovitti, A.: A methodology for the selection of multi-criteria decision analysis methods in real estate and land management processes. Sustainability **10**, 507 (2018). https://doi.org/10.3390/su10020507

10. Lee, J.: Spatial ethics as an evaluation tool for the long-term impacts of mega urban projects: an application of spatial ethics multi-criteria assessment to canning town regeneration projects, London. In: Brebbia, C.A., Sendra, J.J. (eds.) Sustainability and the City, pp. 51–66. WIT Press, Southampton, Boston (2018)

11. Roy, B.: Multicriteria Methodology for Decision Aiding. Springer US, Boston, MA (1996)

12. Marta, B., Giulia, D.: Addressing social sustainability in urban regeneration processes. An application of the social multi-criteria evaluation. Sustainability **12**(18), 7579 (2020). https://doi.org/10.3390/su12187579

13. Voinov, A., Bousquet, F.: Modelling with stakeholders. Environ. Model. Softw. **25**, 1268–1281 (2010). https://doi.org/10.1016/j.envsoft.2010.03.007

14. Bottero, M., Mondini, G., Datola, G.: Decision-making tools for urban regeneration processes: from Stakeholders Analysis to Stated Preference Methods. TeMA – J. Land Use, Mobility Env. **10**, 193–212 (2017). https://doi.org/10.6092/1970-9870/5163

15. Jessop, B., Brenner, N., Jones, M.: Theorizing Sociospatial Relations. Environ Plan D **26**, 389–401 (2008). https://doi.org/10.1068/d9107

16. Saiu, V.: The three pitfalls of sustainable city: a conceptual framework for evaluating the theory-practice gap. Sustainability **9**, 2311 (2017). https://doi.org/10.3390/su9122311

17. Saiu, V.: Evaluating outwards regeneration effects (OREs) in neighborhood-based projects: a reversal of perspective and the proposal for a new tool. Sustainability **12**, 10559 (2020). https://doi.org/10.3390/su122410559

18. Tasheva Petrova, M.: Sustainable management of open public space in a large housing estate in sofia: integrating physical characteristics and social dimensions. In: ICUP2020: International Conference on Urban Planning. Faculty of Civil Engineering and Architecture, pp 187–196. University of Nis, Serbia, Niš (2020)

19. Harris, G.T.: Cost benefit analysis: its limitations and use in fully privatised infrastructure projects. Aust. J. Public Adm. **50**, 526–538 (1991). https://doi.org/10.1111/j.1467-8500.1991.tb02324.x

20. García de Jalón, S., et al.: Providing access to urban green spaces: a participatory benefit-cost analysis in Spain. Int. J. Environ. Res. Public Health **17**, 2818 (2020). https://doi.org/10.3390/ijerph17082818

21. Sager, T.: Citizen participation and cost-benefit analysis. Transp. Plan. Technol. **5**, 161–168 (1979). https://doi.org/10.1080/03081067908717160

22. Campos, I., et al.: The diversity of adaptation in a multilevel governance setting. Adapting to Climate Change in Europe: Exploring Sustainable Pathways – from Local Measures to Wider Policies, pp. 49–172 (2018). https://doi.org/10.1016/B978-0-12-849887-3.00003-4

23. Haoyu, C.: "Conflict" or "Cooperation": a study on the spontaneous order of urban public space development from the perspective of stakeholders. IOP Conf. Ser.: Mater. Sci. Eng. **960**, 042043 (2020). https://doi.org/10.1088/1757-899X/960/4/042043

24. Emerson, P.: The original Borda count and partial voting. Soc. Choice Welf. **40**, 353–358 (2013). https://doi.org/10.1007/s00355-011-0603-9

25. Blečić, I., Cecchini, A., Minchilli, M., Tedeschi, L.F., Trunfio, G.A.: A decision support tool on derelict buildings for urban regeneration. ISPRS Ann. Photogramm. Remote Sens. Spatial Inf. Sci. **IV-4/W7**, 19–25 (2018). https://doi.org/10.5194/isprs-annals-IV-4-W7-19-2018

26. Blečić, I., Saiu, V., Trunfio, G.A.: Towards a high-fidelity assessment of urban green spaces walking accessibility. In: Gervasi, O., et al. (eds.) ICCSA 2020. LNCS, vol. 12252, pp. 535–549. Springer, Cham (2020). https://doi.org/10.1007/978-3-030-58811-3_39

27. Blečić, I., Saiu, V.: Assessing urban green spaces availability: a comparison between planning standards and a high-fidelity accessibility evaluation. In: La Rosa, D., Privitera, R. (eds.) INPUT 2021. LNCE, vol. 146, pp. 339–347. Springer, Cham (2021). https://doi.org/10.1007/978-3-030-68824-0_37

28. Blečić, I., Cecchini, A., Saiu, V., Trunfio, G.A.: Evaluating territorial capital of fragile territories: the case of Sardinia. In: Gervasi, O., Murgante, B., Misra, S., Rocha, A.M.A.C., Garau, C. (eds.) Computational Science and Its Applications – ICCSA 2022 Workshops: Malaga, Spain, July 4–7, 2022, Proceedings, Part III, pp. 531–545. Springer International Publishing, Cham (2022). https://doi.org/10.1007/978-3-031-10545-6_36

Sensitivity Analysis of a Cardiac Electrophysiology Model for the Occurrence of Electrical Alternans

Rodrigo B. Pigozzo[ID], Rodrigo Weber dos Santos[ID], and Bernardo M. Rocha[✉][ID]

Graduate Program in Computational Modeling, Universidade Federal de Juiz de Fora, Juiz de Fora, Brazil
rodrigo.pigozzo@estudante.ufjf.br,
{rodrigo.weber,bernardomartinsrocha}@ice.ufjf.br

Abstract. Cardiac arrhythmias are a serious health problem that can lead to sudden cardiac arrest, heart failure, and ultimately death. Electrical alternans is often seen in patients with cardiac arrhythmias, particularly those affecting the ventricles. Alternans is a beat-to-beat variation in the duration or amplitude of cardiac action potentials, which can be reflected in alterations of the electrocardiogram. Identifying and monitoring electrical alternans in patients with cardiac arrhythmias can be important in preventing serious complications and improving outcomes. In the context of computational modeling of the heart, there are several mathematical models representing the generation of the action potential on cardiac cells. Some of these models do exhibit alternans, while others do not manifest this behavior. Therefore, considering the relevance of alternans in the study of deadly arrhythmias, it is of great interest to identify which are the parameters from a given mathematical cell model that contribute the most to the occurrence of alternans. The main objective of this study was to understand the parameters that most impact quantities of interest related to alternans behavior using local and global sensitivity analysis. To this end, we focused in this work on a simplified model of the cardiac action potential and evaluated the significance of its parameters for the action potential duration and the maximum slope of the restitution curve, which are relevant for alternans behavior. Overall, this study provides initial insights into the mathematical models of cardiac electrophysiology and how to evaluate the impact of parameters on alternans.

Keywords: cardiac electrophysiology · action potential alternans · Mitchell-Schaeffer model · Sensitivity Analysis · Sobol Indices

1 Introduction

Cardiac arrhythmias affect the heart's rhythm, causing it to beat too fast, too slow, or irregularly, leading to serious health problems, including sudden car-

Supported by organization x.

diac arrest, heart failure, and death. Electrical alternans is often seen in patients with cardiac arrhythmias, particularly those affecting the ventricles. Alternans is a phenomenon in which there is a beat-to-beat variation in the duration or amplitude of cardiac myocytes action potentials, which are the electrical signals that stimulate the heart muscle to contract. Clinical experiments and measurements indicate that electrical alternans can be a precursor to dangerous arrhythmias, such as ventricular fibrillation or sudden death [21]. The alterations of properties at the cellular level can also be reflected in variations in the amplitude or shape of the electrocardiogram (ECG) waveform. Therefore, identifying and monitoring electrical alternans in patients with cardiac arrhythmias can prevent serious complications and improve outcomes.

Despite the importance of alternans in studying heart diseases, many mathematical models for the electrophysiology of cardiac myocytes cannot reproduce this phenomenon, while others do [4,6]. Although some techniques for promoting alternans in specific cardiac cell models exist [2], there is a lack of studies in the literature evaluating the role and impact of model parameters on the occurrence of alternans. A recent study [10] using a technique known as population modeling identified the ion channel that maximally affected the occurrence of APD alternans and found that relevant quantities of interest were sensitive to changes in the plateau calcium current of the cardiac cell model under consideration.

In this work, we identify the most relevant parameters for quantities of interest related to alternans promotion, such as the action potential duration and the maximal slope of the restitution curve. A simplified mathematical model of the cardiac action potential, such as the modified Mitchell-Schaeffer (MMS), was used in this study to limit the number of parameters under investigation since it consists of a two-variable model with four parameters. Both local and global sensitivity analysis (SA) methods [15], such as the one-at-a-time and Sobol indices, were used in this initial investigation to provide insight into the impact of the model parameters. The choice of the MMS model for this work is also based on the fact that analysis is available, which allows the evaluation of the model dynamics for a given set of parameters and a comparison with the results obtained via the sensitivity analysis. This is important for validating the approach presented in this work, especially considering that most realistic cardiac cell models in the literature have several variables and parameters for which no mathematical analysis is available to describe their dynamics.

The remainder of this document is organized as follows: in the next section, we present the mathematical models for cardiac electrophysiology and the computational methods used to analyze their alternans behavior. In Sect. 3, we present some numerical experiments using the sensitivity analysis tools, and in Sect. 4, our concluding remarks on the results and findings of this work are presented.

2   Mathematical Model and Methods

We begin this section by presenting the mathematical model for the generation of cardiac action potential used to investigate the electrical alternans phenomenon.

Some basic concepts related to alternans, such as the restitution curve, are introduced in the sequence. Mathematical and computational tools for sensitivity analysis of the cardiac cell model are also presented in this section.

2.1 Cardiac Cell Model

There is a vast literature on cell models for generating cardiac action potential based on ordinary differential equations (ODEs). The models range from the seminal model of Hodgkin and Huxley [7] to more recent human ventricular models [18]. For this work, we used the modified Mitchell-Schaeffer Model (MMS) [1], a simple model with two variables capable of reproducing electrical alternans, for which some analytical results are available. The MMS model modifies the original Mitchell-Schaeffer (MS) model to avoid pacemaker behavior when exploring the parameter space, which is crucial for sensitivity analysis and could hinder the exploratory analysis of alternans classification. The unwanted pacemaker behavior manifests as the transmembrane potential cyclically depolarises and repolarises without any applied external stimulus (see [1] for further details).

The MMS model consists of two variables: the transmembrane potential or voltage $v_m(t)$, and the gating variable $h(t)$, which satisfy the following ODEs:

$$\frac{dv_m}{dt} = h\frac{(v_m + a)(v_m + a - \lambda)(1 - v_m)}{\tau_{in}} - \frac{v_m}{\tau_{out}} + J_{stim}, \tag{1}$$

$$\frac{dh}{dt} = \begin{cases} \frac{1-h}{\tau_{open}} & v_m \leq v_{gate} \\ -\frac{h}{\tau_{close}} & v_m > v_{gate} \end{cases}, \tag{2}$$

where J_{stim} is an externally applied stimulus current, v_{gate} is the activation threshold potential and the parameters τ_{in}, τ_{out}, τ_{open}, τ_{close} are time constants controling important features of the action potential. The parameters a and λ are set to 0 and v_{gate}, respectively, in the MMS model [1].

The first term on the right-hand side of Eq. (1) represents the inward current (J_{in}) whose strength is specified by the time constant τ_{in}. The second term is the outward current (J_{out}), which consists of a combination of the currents which decrease the membrane voltage, such as the potassium current. Likewise, in the inward current, the time constant τ_{out} controls the strength of the outward current. The gating variable h is open when $h = 1$ and closed when $h = 0$, as can be seen from Eq. (2). The parameters τ_{close} and τ_{open} are the time constants with which the gate controlled by the h variable closes and opens, respectively.

An action potential of the MMS model is presented in Fig. 1, which was generated using the baseline parameter values presented in Table 1.

2.2 Alternans

In cardiac electrophysiology, alternans is a beat-to-beat alternation in cellular action potential shape and duration [17], despite a constant pacing period (basic cycle length - BCL), that may lead to alternans in the T-wave of the ECG [22].

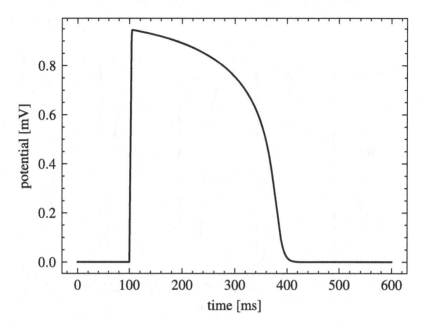

Fig. 1. Action potential generated by the MMS model when a external stimulus is appled at $t = 100$ ms for the baseline parameters: $v_{gate} = 0.13$, $\tau_{in} = 0.3$, $\tau_{out} = 6.0$, $\tau_{open} = 120$, and $\tau_{close} = 150$.

Table 1. Baseline parameter values for the MMS model, and the interval used for the SA of alternans behavior.

Parameter	Baseline value	Interval
τ_{in}	0.3	[0.1, 0.5]
τ_{out}	6.0	[2.0, 10.0]
τ_{open}	120.0	[40.0, 200.0]
τ_{close}	150.0	[50.0, 250.0]

An example of alternans of action potential for the MMS model is presented in Fig. 2 below.

The BCL can be expressed as the sum of the diastolic interval (DI) and APD. Alternans are often associated with dangerous arrhythmias like ventricular fibrillation [5]. Alternans can be observed in single cardiac cell simulations through the action potential restitution protocols, which are commonly used in cardiac electrophysiology to investigate the APD and the rate adaptation properties of cardiac cells. Essentially, APD restitution refers to the natural shortening of APD in response to faster heart rates.

2.3 Restitution Curve

The dynamics of a paced cardiac cell can be described through the restitution curve, which is obtained by plotting APD as a function of the basic cycle length

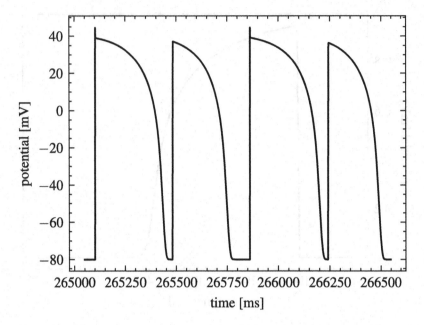

Fig. 2. APDs of the MMS Model and the occurrence of alternans. The model parameters used for generating this pulses are: $\tau_{in} = 0.1$, $\tau_{out} = 9.0$, $\tau_{open} = 100$, and $\tau_{close} = 120$.

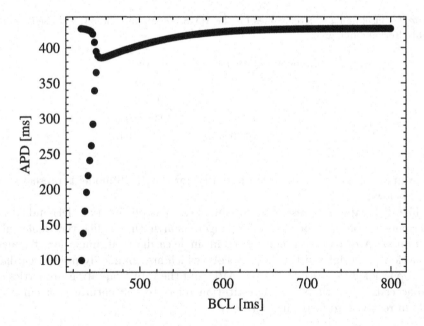

Fig. 3. Restitution curve of the MMS model and the occurrence of alternans at BCL of 320 ms. The model parameters used for generating this curve are: $\tau_{in} = 0.1$, $\tau_{out} = 4.3$, $\tau_{open} = 50.1$, and $\tau_{close} = 177.5$.

(period). Alternans occur when a period-doubling bifurcation appears on the restitution curve. Figure 3 shows an example of the restitution curve for the MMS model for a specific set of parameters $\{\tau_{in}, \tau_{out}, \tau_{open}, \tau_{close}\}$ which results in alternans (as observed near the BCL of 320 ms).

Two different pacing protocols are usually employed to generate the restitution curve: the S1S2 and dynamic protocols [13,19]. The S1S2 pacing protocol involves applying two stimuli (S1 and S2) to a cardiac cell at different intervals to study its response. In the protocol, a basic cycle length (BCL) and a certain number of beats (n_{beats}) are selected for the pacing of the S1 stimuli. Following n_{beats} of the S1 pacing, a second stimulus (S2) is applied at a range of coupling intervals (CI). When using a dynamic pacing protocol, a number of beats of the S1 pacing are given, and then the S1 cycle length is decremented until the minimum CI is reached.

The restitution curve can also be studied using the graphical approach proposed by [12], which is characterized by the dependence of APD on the preceding diastolic interval (DI). Defining the action potential duration of the next cycle as

$$APD_{i+1} = f(DI_i) = f(BCL - APD_i) \tag{3}$$

gives an iterative map (for a fixed period $BCL = APD_i + DI_i$), where f represents the function relating the new APD to its previous DI. As detailed in [12], it is said the restitution curve is stable when

$$|f'(DI_i)| < 1, \tag{4}$$

and when

$$|f'(DI_i)| > 1, \tag{5}$$

it represents a predictor for the occurrence of alternans. In other words, if the maximum slope of the restitution curve is greater than one, alternans may occur. Figure 4 shows an example of the APD and DI relation for the MMS.

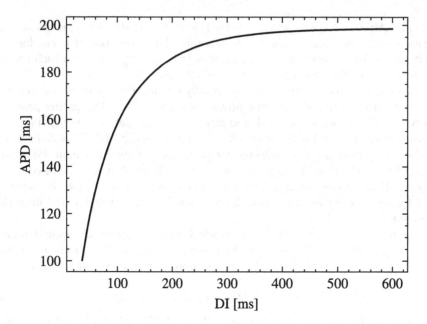

Fig. 4. Another example of restitution Curve for the MMS Model showing APD as a function of DI.

2.4   Restitution Curve for the MMS

Both the original MS [11] and the MMS [1] models, present an asymptotic derivation of the restitution curve, which is a closed expression relating APD and DI. For the MMS model it is given by:

$$\text{APD}_{n+1} = f(DI_i) = \tau_{\text{close}} \, \ln \left(\frac{1 - \left(1 - h_{\text{min}}^{\text{MMS}}\right) e^{-\frac{DI_i}{\tau_{\text{open}}}}}{h_{\text{min}}^{\text{mMS}}} \right), \tag{6}$$

where $h_{\text{min}}^{\text{MMS}}$ is given by

$$h_{\text{min}}^{\text{MMS}} = \left(1 + \frac{\tau_{\text{out}}}{4\tau_{\text{in}}} \left(1 - v_{\text{gate}}\right)^2 \right)^{-1}. \tag{7}$$

Therefore, to determine if, for a given set of parameters, the MMS model predicts the occurrence of alternans, the criterion was to verify if Eq. (6) satisfied the condition $|f'(DI_i)| > 1$.

2.5   Quantities of Interest

To evaluate the occurrence of alternans or not, two quantities of interest (QoI) were defined and evaluated via sensitivity analysis. The action potential duration (APD) and the maximum slope of the restitution curve (MaxSlope) for single cardiac cells were considered QoIs. These quantities were defined and computed as follows:

- APD: Action potential duration measures the time taken from the depolarization to the repolarization during an action potential (see Fig. 1). We considered APD measured at 90% repolarization (APD90) as the metric for APD. It is calculated by determining the time interval between the peak of the action potential and the point at which the membrane potential has repolarized to 90% of its initial value.
- MaxSlope: This quantity was defined as the maximum slope of the restitution curve generated for the single cardiac cell using the dynamic pacing protocol. The maximum slope of the restitution curve (MaxSlope) was calculated using the gradient of the restitution curve (see Fig. 4), which was computed using second-order accurate central differences in the interior points.

2.6 Sensitivity Analysis

The investigation of how changes or fluctuations in model inputs impact the output of a mathematical model, whether it can be distinguished qualitatively or quantitatively, is known as sensitivity analysis (SA) [3]. There exists several techniques for performing SA in the literature, such as the local one-at-a-time (OAT), the elementary effects method (EE), Sobol' indices, and others.

SA can be used for many purposes: identifying important input variables, model calibration and validation, risk assessment, decision-making, and optimization [15]. SA can help better understand the behavior of complex systems, such as in the present case of alternans occurrence in mathematical cell models of the action potential.

In this work, we used the well-known Sobol indices [16] for conducting global sensitivity analysis of the MMS model with respect to quantities of interest relevant to the occurrence of alternans. Local SA through the OAT method was also evaluated to complement the results. Let Y be a scalar quantity of interest for which we want to assess the impact of the input parameters $\mathbf{X} = \{X_1, X_2, \ldots, X_D\}$. The first-order Sobol index expresses the direct influence of a parameter X_i on the variance of the quantity of interest Y and is given by:

$$S_i = \frac{\mathbb{V}\left[\mathbb{E}\left(Y \mid X_i\right)\right]}{\mathbb{V}(Y)} \tag{8}$$

where $\mathbb{E}$ denotes the expected value, $\mathbb{V}$ represents the variance, and $\mathbb{E}\left(Y \mid X_i\right)$ denotes the expected value of the output Y when the parameter X_i is fixed. The first order Sobol sensitivity index represents the expected reduction in the variance of the analyzed quantity when the parameter X_i is fixed.

The total Sobol index represents possible interactions between the input parameters and their effects on the Y quantity. For the input X_i it is denoted by S_{T_i}, and is given by:

$$S_{T_i} = \frac{\mathbb{E}\left[\mathbb{V}\left(Y \mid X_{\sim i}\right)\right]}{\mathbb{V}(Y)} = 1 - \frac{\mathbb{V}\left[\mathbb{E}\left(Y \mid X_{\sim i}\right)\right]}{\mathbb{V}(Y)} \qquad (9)$$

where $X_{\sim i}$ represents all input parameters except the X_i parameter.

3   Numerical Experiments

In this section, we present details on the implementation and design of the numerical experiments, as well as the results of sensitivity analysis in terms of APD and the maximum slope of the restitution curve for the MMS model.

3.1   Implementation

The numerical simulations carried out in this work were performed using the openCARP simulation environment for cardiac electrophysiology [13]. To this end, the MMS model had to be implemented as a cell model in the environment. In particular, the simulations were based on existing openCARP modules for computing the APD of a single cardiac cell. The restitution curve was generated using the expression for the MMS model given by Eq. (6).

The computational experiments of this work were all carried out in a code implemented in the Python programming language with support for scientific computing through the NumPy and SciPy libraries [20].

In this work, the first order and total order Sobol sensitivity indices were calculated for quantities of interest (QoI) from the MMS Model using the Saltelli method [14] available in the SAlib library [9] for the Python programming language.

3.2   Design of Experiments

Table 1 shows the parameter space used for conducting the SA of the MMS model, which was selected such that the baseline values were centered between the lower and upper limits and considering a coefficient of variation of approximately 66%. Considering a total of $D = 4$ parameters under investigation, a total of $N * (2D + 2) = (N * 10)$ samples were used to carry out the sensitivity analysis via *Sobol indices*. The value of N was chosen as $N = 2^{10} = 1024$, resulting in a total of 10240 samples from which APD and the restitution curve had to be computed.

In addition, the one-at-a-time approach was performed by exploring the parameters using the lower limit, baseline value, and upper limit values (from Table 1) for the analysis of each parameter.

3.3   Sensitivities for APD

We begin by presenting the results of the OAT study for the APD of the MMS, which is presented for each parameter on Fig. 5. The results show that reducing τ_{in} increases the APD, while increases in the values of both τ_{out} and τ_{close} increases the APD. Results also indicates that τ_{open} has negligible effects on the APD.

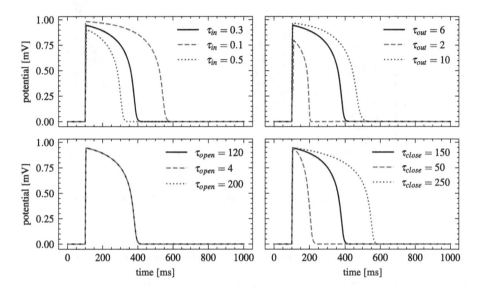

Fig. 5. Local one-at-a-time SA of the parameters of the MMS model for APD.

Figure 6 shows the results of the main and total Sobol indices for the APD considering the for time constant parameters. The results in terms of the main Sobol indices reiterates the OAT analysis made earlier since it indicates that the most influential parameter in the APD is, in fact, τ_{close}, and that τ_{open} parameter that does not impact the APD. From the total Sobol indices, one can observe that a small interaction between the parameters contribute to the variation on APD.

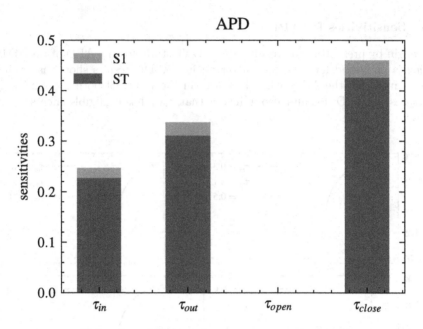

Fig. 6. The main (S1) and total (ST) Sobol indices calculated for the APD of the MMS model.

3.4 Sensitivities for Maximum Slope of the Restitution Curve

Here we present the results of sensitivity analyses for the maximum slope of the restitution curve, which can be used for the prediction of alternans. Figure 7 presents the results of the OAT study for MaxSlope, which indicate that τ_{in}, τ_{out}, and τ_{close} parameters influence this quantity significantly. The only exception is τ_{open} whose influence on the variation of the maximum slope is small.

Sobol sensitivity indices are reported in Fig. 8, which show that except for τ_{open}, the other three parameters have a significant impact on the analyzed QoI, as demonstrated via the main indices. For this quantity, it is interesting to observe that high-order interactions between the parameters are present, as can be observed via the total Sobol indices (when they are greater than the main indices).

3.5 Discussion

It is interesting to confront the results of the SA based on Sobol indices with knowledge from the analysis of the MS model which provide a reparametrization to allow a direct classification of the alternans behavior in terms of two parameters. This analysis is not yet available for the modified MS used in this work, however, it is expected that it should not be much different from the one available for the MS model, which we recall next, since the difference between the models is minimal.

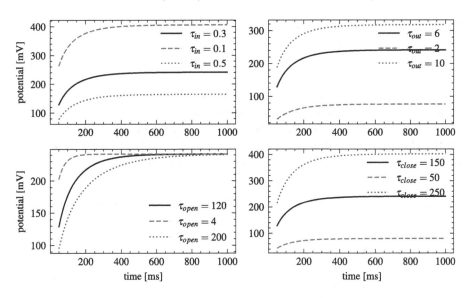

Fig. 7. Local one-at-a-time SA of the parameters of the MMS model for MaxSlope

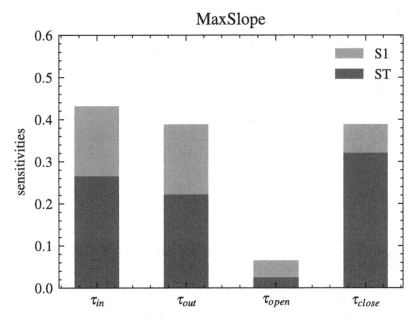

Fig. 8. The main (S1) and total (ST) Sobol indices calculated for the MaxSlope (maximum slope of the restitution curve) of the MMS model.

For the MS model [11] one can define dimensionless quantities that can be used to classify the behavior of the solutions. The following quantities are defined:

$$h_{\min} = 4\left(\frac{\tau_{\mathrm{in}}}{\tau_{\mathrm{out}}}\right), \quad h_{\mathrm{thr}} = \frac{\tau_{\mathrm{in}}}{\tau_{\mathrm{out}}} \frac{1}{v_{\mathrm{stim}}(1 - v_{\mathrm{stim}})} \quad r = \frac{\tau_{\mathrm{open}}}{\tau_{\mathrm{close}}}. \quad (10)$$

The region in the parameter space defined by $r < 1$ and below the curve defined by the following relation

$$h_{\text{thr}} = \left(\frac{1}{1 + r} \right), \tag{11}$$

characterizes solutions with alternans behavior, whereas the remaining regions of the parameter space do not present alternans.

Figure 9 below shows the parameter space defined in terms of r and h_{thr} for the classification of the solutions. The lines in blue is the curve represents Eq. (11), and the region denoted by γ is where alternans occurs.

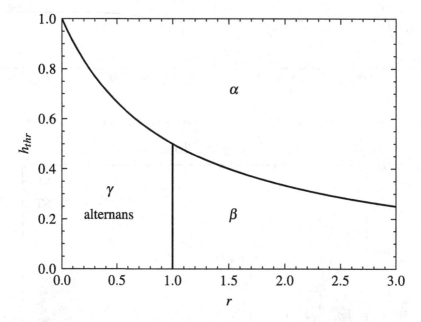

Fig. 9. Classification of the parameter space in the original MS model and the region γ where alternans occurs.

Comparing this information from the MS model and the results of the SA for the MMS in terms of the QoIs relevant for alternans behavior, one can notice that the role of the τ_{open} parameter has been neglected in both the local and global SA (via OAT and Sobol indices). However, analyzing the r parameter from Eq. (10), one can notice that τ_{open} is present, and it is relevant to result in values of r smaller than 1 (which is one of the conditions for the MS model to present alternans). From the graphical or schematic classification of the solution presented in Fig. 9 together with Eq. (10) for r, one can see that a given set of parameters on the right of $r = 1$ line and above the r_{thr} curve for which alternans does not occur, can be classified on the left where alternans occur by simply changing the value of the τ_{open} parameter. Therefore, its influence on the alternans behavior is relevant and was not captured by the local and global SA studies carried out.

4   Conclusions

In this work, we evaluated a mathematical model of cardiac electrophysiology with respect to complex dynamics known as alternans, a beat-to-beat variation in the shape and duration of the action potential. Local and global sensitivity analyses of quantities of interest, such as action potential duration and maximum slope of the restitution curve, which are relevant for the alternans behavior, were carried out for the modified Mitchell-Schaeffer model in terms of its four time constant parameters.

The results indicate that three of the four parameters significantly impact APD and the restitution curve's maximum slope for the parameter space explored in this work. However, previous analyses of the original model indicate that the four parameters are important for generating alternans dynamics. These findings clearly show the limitation of the classic Sobol indices for sensitivity analysis as the only metric for the classification of model behaviors. To summarize, these results highlight the need of other tools like regional sensitivity analysis [8,23,24] for the task of binary classification of model outputs based on the specified behavior definition.

Future works should explore techniques for the identification of the parameters that are more relevant for the alternans behavior. In addition to that, other possibilities for the extension of this work include the usage of surrogate models to accelerate the sensitivity analysis, the usage of other analytical findings of the MMS model to corroborate with computational studies, and also conducting the same type of study for more complex cardiac electrophysiology models with dozens of variables.

References

1. Corrado, C., Niederer, S.A.: A two-variable model robust to pacemaker behaviour for the dynamics of the cardiac action potential. Math. Biosci. **281**, 46–54 (2016)
2. Eastman, J., Sass, J., Gomes, J.M., Dos Santos, R.W., Cherry, E.M.: Using delay differential equations to induce alternans in a model of cardiac electrophysiology. J. Theor. Biol. **404**, 262–272 (2016)
3. Eck, V.G., et al.: A guide to uncertainty quantification and sensitivity analysis for cardiovascular applications. Int. J. Numer. Methods Biomed. Eng. **32**(8), e02755 (2016)
4. Elshrif, M.M., Cherry, E.M.: A quantitative comparison of the behavior of human ventricular cardiac electrophysiology models in tissue. PLoS ONE **9**(1), e84401 (2014)
5. Gizzi, A., Cherry, E.M., Gilmour, R.F., Jr., Luther, S., Filippi, S., Fenton, F.H.: Effects of pacing site and stimulation history on alternans dynamics and the development of complex spatiotemporal patterns in cardiac tissue. Front. Physiol. **4**, 71 (2013)
6. Gomes, J.M., Dos Santos, R.W., Cherry, E.M.: Alternans promotion in cardiac electrophysiology models by delay differential equations. Chaos: Interdisc. J. Nonlinear Sci. **27**(9), 093915 (2017)

7. Hodgkin, A.L., Huxley, A.F.: A quantitative description of membrane current and its application to conduction and excitation in nerve. J. Physiol. **117**(4), 500 (1952)
8. Hornberger, G.M., Spear, R.C.: Approach to the preliminary analysis of environmental systems. J. Environ. Mgmt. **12**(1), 7–18 (1981)
9. Iwanaga, T., Usher, W., Herman, J.: Toward SALib 2.0: advancing the accessibility and interpretability of global sensitivity analyses. Socio-Environ. Syst. Model. **4**(18155), 10 (2022). https://doi.org/10.18174/sesmo.18155, https://sesmo.org/article/view/18155
10. Jeong, D.U., Marcellinus, A., Lim, K.M.: Sensitivity analysis of cardiac alternans and tachyarrhythmia to ion channel conductance using population modeling. Bioengineering **9**(11), 628 (2022)
11. Mitchell, C.C., Schaeffer, D.G.: A two-current model for the dynamics of cardiac membrane. Bull. Math. Biol. **65**(5), 767–793 (2003)
12. Nolasco, J.: A graphic method for the study of alternation in cardiac action potentials. J. Appl. Physiol. **25**(2), 191–196 (1968)
13. Plank, G., et al.: The openCARP simulation environment for cardiac electrophysiology. Comput. Methods Programs Biomed. **208**, 106223 (2021). https://doi.org/10.1016/j.cmpb.2021.106223
14. Saltelli, A., Annoni, P., Azzini, I., Campolongo, F., Ratto, M., Tarantola, S.: Variance based sensitivity analysis of model output. design and estimator for the total sensitivity index. Comput. Phys. Commun. **181**(2), 259–270 (2010)
15. Saltelli, A., et al.: Global Sensitivity Analysis: The Primer. Wiley, Hoboken (2008)
16. Sobol, I.M.: Global sensitivity indices for nonlinear mathematical models and their monte Carlo estimates. Math. Comput. Simul. **55**(1–3), 271–280 (2001)
17. Surawicz, B., Fisch, C.: Cardiac alternans: diverse mechanisms and clinical manifestations. J. Am. Coll. Cardiol. **20**(2), 483–499 (1992)
18. Tomek, J., et al.: Development, calibration, and validation of a novel human ventricular myocyte model in health, disease, and drug block. Elife **8**, e48890 (2019)
19. ten Tusscher, K.H., Noble, D., Noble, P.J., Panfilov, A.V.: A model for human ventricular tissue. Am. J. Physiol. Heart Circulatory Physiol. (2004)
20. Virtanen, P., et al.: SciPy 1.0 contributors: SciPy 1.0: fundamental algorithms for scientific computing in python. Nat. Methods **17**, 261–272 (2020). https://doi.org/10.1038/s41592-019-0686-2
21. Wilson, L.D., Rosenbaum, D.S.: Mechanisms of arrythmogenic cardiac alternans. Europace 9(suppl_6), vi77-vi82 (2007)
22. You, T., Luo, C., Zhang, K., Zhang, H.: Electrophysiological mechanisms underlying t-wave alternans and their role in arrhythmogenesis. Front. Physiol. **12**, 614946 (2021)
23. Young, P.: Data-based mechanistic modelling, generalised sensitivity and dominant mode analysis. Comput. Phys. Commun. **117**(1–2), 113–129 (1999)
24. Young, P., Parkinson, S., Lees, M.: Simplicity out of complexity in environmental modelling: Occam's razor revisited. J. Appl. Stat. **23**(2–3), 165–210 (1996)

Estimating the Effect of TEC Data on Rain with Modelling and Wavelet Transformation Analysis

Selcuk Doven[1]([✉]) [iD], Büşranur Güdar[1] [iD], Khaled Al-Nimer[1] [iD], and Zafer Aslan[2] [iD]

[1] Institute of Graduate Study, Istanbul Aydın University, 34295 Istanbul, Turkey
{selcukdoven,busranurgudar,khaledalnimer}@stu.aydin.edu.tr
[2] Faculty of Engineering, Department of Computer Engineering, Istanbul Aydın University, 34295 Istanbul, Turkey
zaferaslan@aydin.edu.tr

Abstract. Events such as geomagnetic storms and solar winds cause significant changes and deterioration in the upper layers of the earth's atmosphere. These distortions have a significant effect on the waves and signals used by the satellites and radios we use. Based on different satellite observations, studies on geomagnetic storms, ionosphere TEC (Total Electron Content) samples, and GPS observations, we can obtain some measurements. Another important natural event in measuring temperature data and investigating its effects is rain. In this study, it is aimed to determine the effect of TEC change in the ionosphere on the daily precipitation for Izmir, Trabzon and Istanbul provinces of Turkey and to determine whether the success of the algorithms used for different regions will change according to the region, that is, the data. The temporal variation of TEC data for the period January 1–December 31, 2017 has been examined and modelled. In this study 60% of the one-year daily data was used for training, 20% for evaluation, and 20% for testing. In the first part of the study, wavelet transforms and large, medium, and small scale changes in TEC and precipitation data were examined. In the second part of the study, TEC data are modelled with artificial neural networks, support vector machines, and decision tree-based estimation methods. And in the last stage, machine learning algorithms and wavelet were used together to predict TEC data, and the prediction success ratio was tried to be related. There is a sufficient evidence of observed and estimated TEC data with alpha = 0, 05 significant level.

Keywords: Total Electron Concentration · Wavelet · Artificial Neural Network · Support Vector Machine · Decision Tree

1 Introduction

Today, data mining and machine learning are used in almost every field, from health to communication, from education to security. One of these fields is the TEC (Total Electron Content) field. With the estimation studies carried out in this field, we continue our daily

---

These authors Contributed equally to this work.

O. Gervasi et al. (Eds.): ICCSA 2023 Workshops, LNCS 14104, pp. 59–72, 2023.
https://doi.org/10.1007/978-3-031-37105-9_5

lives with minimal interruptions, especially in the field of satellite and communication. Another important area is rain forecasting. It takes place in our lives as an important issue in many areas, from the drinking water we use in our daily lives to its use in agricultural areas.

When the recent academic studies are examined, it is seen that there are not many academic publications on whether there is a linear relationship between TEC and rain fall rate. The relationship between increasing and decreasing in TEC data is another important issue, and was examined. Within the scope of this study, similar studies in two areas were analyzed.

TEC causes an important error component in the global positioning system (GPS) by ionospheric delays. Ionospheric error can be reduced by a dual-frequency receiver using a linear combination. However, accurate ionospheric error modelling is required for single-frequency receivers. El-Diasty developed a short-term forecasting model based on a short data set [2]. In their study, they used five GPS stations with five-day ionospheric datasets along with time and location to develop the Wavelet network (WN)-based ionospheric model. He also made a comparison between the WN-based ionospheric model developed to validate the WN-based ionospheric model and the CODE, JPL, and IGS Global Ionospheric Map (GIM) models.

Sorkhabi used the deep learning method of artificial neural networks so that SF users could estimate the TEC value [10]. By using the ionosphere code observation method, which is a single-layer model, 24 permanent GNSS stations in the northwest of Iran were selected and modelled independently of the geometry called L4 between the satellite and the receiver with a linear combination. This modelling was used to train the error ANN with a hyperbolic tangential sigmoid activation function and two 5-day periods of high and low solar and geomagnetic activity intervals.

Estimating where and when space weather events such as solar flares and X-ray bursts are likely to occur in a given area of interest poses a significant challenge in space weather research. Asaly et al. have focused on X-ray time series predictions. In their study, they used a support vector machine to classify daily Total Electron Content spatial changes prior to solar flare events [1].

With the importance of knowing the extreme TEC values in readiness for danger-ous ionospheric conditions, Nishioka and others have derived a cumulative distribution function of TEC to estimate the extreme TEC values that occur annually, every 10 years, and every 100 years in Japan. To estimate the extreme values of TEC, they examined their daily distribution using 22 years of TEC data from 1997 to 2018. They used two methods. In the first method, the distribution of slab thickness is artificially inflated to estimate excess TEC values. In the second method, excessive slab thicknesses are applied to estimate excessive TEC values [7].

Inyurt et al. aimed to estimate the daily ionospheric total electron content (TEC) using the Gaussian process regression (GPR) model and multiple linear regression (MLR) in their work. First of all, the daily TEC values of two Global Navigation Satellite System (GNSS) stations in Turkey were collected from 2015 to 2017. The performance of the GPR model is compared with the classical MLR model using Taylor diagrams and relative error plots. Six models with various input parameters were realized for both GPR and MLR techniques [4].

Tang et al. studied accurate corrections for ionospheric total electron content (TEC) and early warning information, and a short-term ionospheric prediction model for global navigation satellite system (GNSS) applications under the influence of space weather. They used a new machine learning model, the Prophet model, to predict the global ionospheric TEC [11].

Iyer and Mahajan recommend using the regression method to estimate TEC using an online machine learning model with new training data at regular intervals in their work. They tested the model for both quiet and disturbed days for the IISC, Bangalore, India location near the magnetic equator. The model is adaptive and chooses the appropriate regression method to reduce computation time and make it suitable for short-term predictions in real time [5].

Lei et al. proposed two different new methods for estimating TEC data based on time. (1) Introduced the Bidirectional Gate Repeater Unit BiGRU to enhance capabilities to predict TEC with both past and future time step. (2) To highlight critical time step information, an attention mechanism was used to give weight to each time step. Using Deep Neural Network (DNN), Artificial Neural Network (ANN), Recurrent Neural Network (RNN), Long Short-Term Memory (LSTM), Bidirectional Long Short-Term Memory (BiLSTM) and Gated Repetitive Unit (GRU) as machine learning algorithms estimation of TEC ta has been carried out [12].

Benoit et al. conducted a study on the estimation of TEC data over a 6 year period. Linear Regression, Polynomial Regression, Support Vector Machine algorithms were used as estimation algorithms and Elastic Net regularization method was used to reduce the RMSE value [13].

Momin et al. present statistical distributions of rain velocity measured in Malaysia with integration times of 10 s, 20 s, 30 s, 1 min and 2 min. The ITU-R P.618–13 estimation method was used to estimate the rain attenuation of the ground-to-satellite link using the rain rate measured with integration times of 10 s, 20 s, 30 s, 1 min and 2 min [14].

Ahuna et al., together with their studies containing 4 years of data, conducted a study to predict the rain precipitation situation. They tried to increase the success ratio by using back propagation neural network (BPNN) in examinations made in different regions [15].

Sodunke et al., in their study, studied the effects of rain during the communication of satellite devices. In this study, the estimation of precipitation in a particular region at different times was made. In this study, the Feed Forward Neural Networks (FFNN) algorithm was used as the estimation method [16].

Nandi et al., time series prediction of rain attenuation from rain velocity measurement during rain was made for the temperate place Vigo, Spain using Synthetic Storm Technique (SST) for Ka and Q band signal. Rain velocity and rain attenuation data for the three-year measurement period from 2016 to 2018 were used to test the validity of the SST model at the current location [17].

Eyigüler analysed Magnetic and Electric field variations during Geomagnetically active days over Turkey. This paper covers same result on Geomagnetically induced currents (GIS) at mid-latitudes magnetic field perturbations are in the order of 0.5 nT/s and near vicinity of Bozcaada and Çanakkale in Turkey [19].

This paper shows some result of temporal variation of TEC data in selected areas in Turkey. Advanced machine learning helps to understand and to model temporal variation of daily TEC data.

2 Data and Study Area

2.1 Data Set

This study was carried out to cover the cities of Istanbul, Izmir and Trabzon within the borders of the Republic of Turkey in 2017. The dataset contains 365 rows. The data set consists of 3 columns of daily TEC data, historical data, rain fall rate (mm/m^2) data and rain series transformed with the Wavelet technique.

2.2 Study Area

TEC values based on in this study cover the cities of Istanbul, Izmir and Trabzon in Turkey. TEC data is taken from Germany's open source IMPC DLR (Ionosphere Monitoring and Prediction Center) site. These values are TEC values taken daily for 1 year from 01.01.2017 to 31.12.2017.

The latitude and longitude information is as follows (Table 1 and Fig. 1):

Table 1. Geographic Description of Study Area

No	Study Area	Latitude	Longitude
1	Istanbul	41.0082° N	28.9784° E
2	Izmir	38.4333° N	38.4333° N 27.1528
3	Trabzon	41.0052° N	39.7179° E

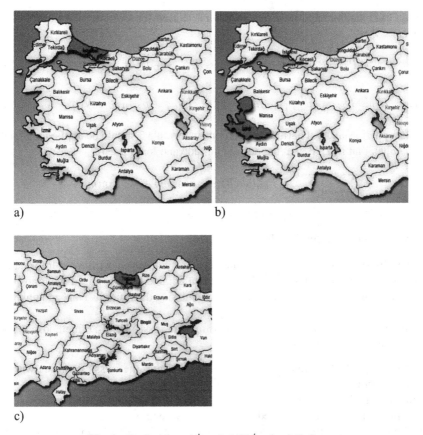

Fig. 1. Study Area, a) İstanbul, b) İzmir, c) Trabzon

3 Models and Algorithms

3.1 TEC – Total Number of Electrons

The number of free electrons per unit area up to 1000 km from the ground is called TEC, that is, the total number of electrons. The main factors affecting the total number of electrons are as follows [8].

1. Geographical Location
2. Seasons
3. Local time difference
4. Magnetic activities
5. Variability in extreme ultraviolet radiation

The smallest value in the total number of electrons occurs at midnight, while the largest value occurs at noon. In addition, the total number of electrons increases from north to south [8].

In local TEC determination studies, the following formulas for differential code differences for satellites and receivers are obtained by taking the differences of signals between each satellite and receiver. Formula 1 is used for satellites and formula 2 for receivers. [8].

$$P_4 = P_{1J}^i - P_{2J}^i = d_{ion,1,J}^i - d_{ion,2,J}^i + DCB^i + DCB_J \tag{1}$$

$$L_4 = L_{1J}^i - L_{2J}^i = \left(d_{ion,1,J}^i - d_{ion,2,J}^i\right) - \lambda\left(b_{1,J}^i - b_{2,J}^i\right) - \lambda(N_{1,J}^i - N_{2,J}^i) \tag{2}$$

The ionospheric spherical harmonic functions in formula 3 should be applied to find the VTEC value, that is, E (β,s) at the desired latitude and longitude [8].

$$\sum_{n=0}^{n_{max}} \sum_{m=0}^{n} \widetilde{P_{nm}}(\sin \beta)(a_{nm} \cos(ms) + b_{nm} \sin(ms)) \tag{3}$$

3.2 Methods of Completing the Missing Data

Istanbul TEC data consists of two columns. The first column shows the day information, the second swarm shows the total electron count obtained as a result of the ionosphere observations. It is of great importance to define missing data such as NaN and unknown in databases.

Fill – missing code is used to fill in missing data in MATLAB. 6 methods are used most frequently in MATLAB.

1. Fill missing (A, 'previous'): It is a method of filling the missing entries with the previous entry.
2. Fill missing (A, movmethod, window): a method of filling in missing entries using a moving window average or median with window length.
3. Fill missing (A, fillfun, gapwindow): Fills in the gaps of missing entries using a special method fill – fun, specified by a function descriptor, and a fixed window surrounding each gap from which padding values are calculated and must have the input arguments, and fillfun, which are vectors containing length sample data, length sample data locations, and missing data locations and the positions in it are a subset of the vector of sample points (Fig. 2).

3.3 Multilayer Perceptron Neural Networks Algorithm (MLP NN)

Artificial neural networks (ANNs) are in a network-like structure formed by neurons that make up the nervous system of humans. ANNs are divided into two as the most known types. In ANN, the model consisting of three input layers and an output layer is called Single-Layer Neural Networks (SLNN), while the model consisting of input, output and hidden layers is called Multi-Layer Perceptron Neural Networks (MLP NN). MLP NN was used in this study. Multilayer Perceptron Neural Networks have a feed-forward structure and are a simple and reliable type of ANN. Output values from MLP NN must be binary. Binary results mean that the output values in the output layer are Yes/No, 0/1, True/False etc. means [3, 9] (Fig. 3).

344	4.5085
345	4.9495
346	5.9215
347	4.7205
348	NaN
349	NaN
350	NaN
351	NaN
352	NaN
353	5.0835

344	4.5085
345	4.9495
346	5.9215
347	4.7205
348	4.7810
349	4.8415
350	4.9020
351	4.9625
352	5.0230
353	5.0835

a)   b)

Fig. 2. Missing Data from the File

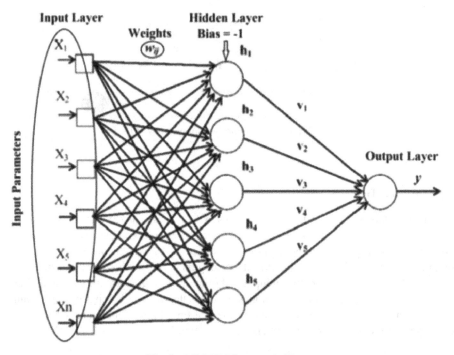

Fig. 3. MLP NN Structure's Flow

3.4 Support Vector Machine (SVM)

One of the main differences between Artificial Neural Networks (ANNs) and SVM is that
SVM trains any system focusing on a single solution (a single optimal solution), while

ANN compares multiple solutions and trains by finding the best optimal solution. This is an advantage for SVM in terms of getting the result more practical and faster, but also a disadvantage as it focuses on a single solution. SVM works similar to MLP NN working logic. If this similarity is explained in more detail, firstly the dataset (whether passively or dynamically obtained from experimental results) is introduced to the algorithm. Then the attributes are evaluated in turn. Although the determination of the features is not for MLP NN, it has been seen that this algorithm is very important for classifying the outputs. Then, training and test datasets are created based on the real dataset. In another similarity, MSE is calculated in order to control and evaluate the system performance, as in the MLP NN algorithm [6] (Fig. 4).

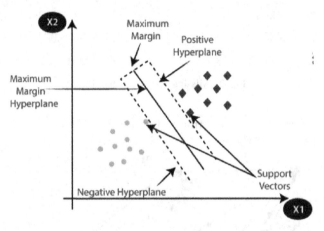

Fig. 4. Example Decision Boundary of SVM [21]

3.5 Decision Tree

KA, detects statistically significant data groups in the data set and shows these significant relationships in the form of tree diagrams. Because this notation is easy and understandable, it is used in many machine learning applications. KA, which consists of input and output data sets, works with a supervised learning method. In this supervised structure, KA detects the connection between input and output. In the KA structure created, there are roots, branches, leaves and the nodes between them. Data belonging to the same class are in leaves on the same branch. In the leaf on a branch, there are result values corresponding to all possible output classes [18] (Fig. 5).

3.6 Wavelet Method

A wave is usually referred to an oscillating function of time or space, such as sinusoid. Wave transformation of signals has proven to be extremely valuable in mathematics, science, and engineering, especially for periodic, time-invariant, or stationary phenomenon. A wavelet is a small wave with finite energy, which has its energy concentrated in time

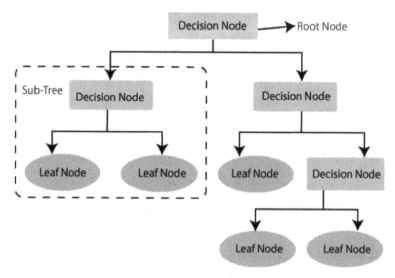

Fig. 5. Genel structure of Decision Tree [21]

or space to give a tool for the analysis of transient, non-stationary, or time-varying phenomenon. The wavelet still has the oscillating wavelike characteristics, but also has the ability to allow simultaneous time, or space, and frequency analysis with a flexible mathematical foundation. Following figures illustrate the difference between wave and wavelet [20] (Fig. 6).

4 Results

In this section, you can observe the results of the application for the cities of Istanbul, Izmir and Trabzon. For each province, an application was made with artificial neural networks, support vector machines, and decision tree-based estimation, which are machine learning algorithms. The r2, mse and rmse values of each application are listed. Then, the rain data was transformed with Wavelet as d1, d2, d3. With this transformed wavelet data, machine learning algorithms work as a hybrid model to increase the success ratio (Table 2).

Table 3 Shows comparison of model results for estimating daily variation of TEC. Result of Support Vector Machine shows better and much reliable results with alpha = 0,10.

Table 4 Shows comparison of model results for estimating daily variation of TEC. Result of AAN (d2 hybrit model) shows better results with alpha = 0,05.

Table 4 Shows comparison of model results for estimating daily variation of TEC. Result of Decision Tree (d3 hybrid model) shows better results with alpha = 0,01.

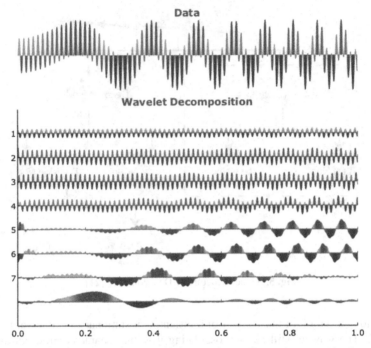

Fig. 6. Example of Visualize Wavelet transform using common x axis plot

Table 2. Comparison of Model Results for Izmir

Machine Learning Algorithm	Artificial Neural Network	Decision Tree	Support Vector Machine
r	−0.0001	−0.01	−0.02
mse	59.6231	0.9871	0.9945
rmse	6.5206	0.9935	0.9972
Machine Learning Algorithm D1	Artificial Neural Network	Decision Tree	Support Vector Machine
r	−0.0001	0.32	0.09
mse	935.2481	67.441	90.816
rmse	22.1084	8.2123	9.5298
Machine Learning Algorithm D2	Artificial Neural Network	Decision Tree	Support Vector Machine
r	−0.0051	0.36	0.00

(*continued*)

Table 2. (*continued*)

Machine Learning Algorithm D2	Artificial Neural Network	Decision Tree	Support Vector Machine
mse	19.3029	63.1	99.027
rmse	3.4068	7.9435	9.9512
Machine Learning Algorithm D3	Artificial Neural Network	Decision Tree	Support Vector Machine
r	−0.0137	0.23	−0.04
mse	19.1358	0.000	104.7
rmse	2.9027	8.8086	10.232

Table 3. Comparison of Model Results for Trabzon

Machine Learning Algorithm	Artificial Neural Network	Decision Tree	Support Vector Machine
r	0.00083	−0.02	−0.14
mse	0.3648	29.461	32.781
rmse	0.4906	5.4278	5.7255
Machine Learning Algorithm D1	Artificial Neural Network	Decision Tree	Support Vector Machine
r	−0.0230	0.57	0.34
mse	0.0926	12.314	18.959
rmse	0.2587	3.5091	4.3542
Machine Learning Algorithm D2	Artificial Neural Network	Decision Tree	Support Vector Machine
r	−0.0004	0.46	0.20
mse	0.1176	15.629	23.052
rmse	0.3095	3.9534	4.8012
Machine Learning Algorithm D3	Artificial Neural Network	Decision Tree	Support Vector Machine
r	−0.0369	0.16	−0.02
mse	4.9844	24.309	29.48
rmse	2.1198	4.9304	5.4295

Table 4. Comparison of Model Results for Istanbul

Machine Learning Algorithm	Artificial Neural Network	Decision Tree	Support Vector Machine
r	0.12	−0.18	−0.01
mse	724.83	974.84	832.58
rmse	26.923	31.222	28.854
Machine Learning Algorithm D1	Artificial Neural Network	Decision Tree	Support Vector Machine
r	0.32	0.19	0.40
mse	0.67781	0.81789	0.59808
rmse	0.823289	0.90437	0.77335
Machine Learning Algorithm D2	Artificial Neural Network	Decision Tree	Support Vector Machine
r	−0.0004	0.46	0.20
mse	0.1176	15.629	23.052
rmse	0.3095	3.9534	4.8012
Machine Learning Algorithm D3	Artificial Neural Network	Decision Tree	Support Vector Machine
r	0.75	0.82	0.82
mse	0.24969	0.18411	0.18209
rmse	0.49968	0.42908	0.42672

5 Conclusions

This study was carried out within the scope of several purposes. First of all, it is determined whether there is a relationship between the TEC-historical data and temporal variation of precipitation. If there is a relationship, estimating it and increasing the accuracy by using the estimation rate as a hybrid of Wavelet and machine learning algorithms. And finally, by examining the data of three different cities of Turkey with the same algorithms, it is observed how the performances of the algorithms change according to the changing data set.

As a result of the study, it has been determined that there is a linear partial relationship between TEC-historical data and rain. Although this situation is at different rates for all 3 cities, it has been observed that there is a strong relationship to a certain extent.

It has been determined that the prediction accuracy rate has increased significantly in some provinces with the use of machine learning algorithms first and then the Wavelet signal analysis method performed in the application part. It has been determined that the ANN algorithm for the city of Trabzon works with the wavelet d1 frequency and the rmse ratio is 0.82, which is the most appropriate algorithm. With the DT algorithm, D2, r = 0.36 value was reached for the city of Izmir. Likewise, D2, r = 0.57 values were reached for the city of Trabzon with the DT algorithm. It has been determined that the support decision tree algorithm works most efficiently for the city of Izmir and it is the most appropriate algorithm with an rmse ratio of 0.99. It has been determined that of the Decision Tree (d3 hybrid model) algorithm works most efficiently for the city of Istanbul, and it is the most appropriate algorithm with an rmse ratio of 0.45.

When we analyzed the outputs of the application work, it was revealed that the algorithms did not perform the same for every dataset, even though they were working with similar datasets for the same problem. With this result, it has been observed that different problems work with different accuracy rates by different algorithms, and that the success ratio of algorithms with different data in the same problem significantly changes.

Significant levels have been changes from 0,01 to 0,10 for three selected study areas with TEC data observations and estimations.

As a result of the study, the results of the three targeted cases were reached. After this study, other studies can be done to increase the reliability of the results. First of all, performance conditions can be observed by working with different machine learning algorithms in these regions. As another study, the dataset of 2017 from this study can be expanded and a wider dataset by using long term results can be examined. Finally, with the expansion of the data set, performance conditions can be compared by working with deep learning algorithms, which is an approach covered by the field of machine learning.

References

1. Asaly, S., Gottlieb, L.A., Reuveni, Y.: Using support vector machine (SVM) and ionospheric total electron content (TEC) data for solar flare predictions. IEEE J. Sel. Top. Appl. Earth Obs. Remote Sens. **14**, 1469–1481 (2020)
2. El-Diasty, M.: Regional ionospheric modeling using wavelet network model. The J. Global Positioning Syst. **15**(1), 2 (2017)
3. Gogou, G., Maglaveras, N., Ambrosiadou, B.V., Goulis, D., Pappas, C.: A neural network approach in diabetes management by insulin administration. J. Med. Syst. **25**, 119–131 (2001)
4. Inyurt, S., Hasanpour Kashani, M., Sekertekin, A.: Ionospheric TEC forecasting using Gaussian process regression (GPR) and multiple linear regression (MLR) in Turkey. Astrophys. Space Sci. **365**, 1–17 (2020)
5. Iyer, S., Mahajan, A.: Predicting the ionospheric total electron content using adaptive regression model. In: 2021 6th International Conference for Convergence in Technology (I2CT), pp. 1–11. IEEE (2021)
6. Karamizadeh, S., Abdullah, S.M., Halimi, M., Shayan, J., Javad Rajabi, M.: Advantage and drawback of support vector machine functionality. In: 2014 international conference on computer, communications, and control technology (I4CT), pp. 63–65. IEEE (2014)
7. Nishioka, M., Saito, S., Tao, C., Shiota, D., Tsugawa, T., Ishii, M.: Statistical analysis of ionospheric total electron content (TEC): long-term estimation of extreme TEC in Japan. Earth, Planets and Space **73**(1), 1–12 (2021)
8. Şentürk, E.: Küresel İyonosfer Haritalarının Türkiye'deki Performansının GNSS Verileriyle İstatistiksel Olarak İncelenmesi. Dokuz Eylül Üniversitesi Mühendislik Fakültesi Fen ve Mühendislik Dergisi **23**(67), 247–255 (2021)
9. Uğuz, S.: Makine öğrenmesi teorik yönleri ve Python uygulamaları ile bir yapay zekâ ekolü. Nobel Yayıncılık. Ankara (2019)

10. Sorkhabi, O.M.: Deep learning of total electron content. SN Appl. Sci. **3**(7), 1–9 (2021). https://doi.org/10.1007/s42452-021-04674-6
11. Tang, J., Li, Y., Yang, D., Ding, M.: An approach for predicting global ionospheric TEC using machine learning. Remote Sens. **14**(7), 1585 (2022)
12. Lei, D., et al.: Ionospheric TEC prediction base on attentional BiGRU. Atmosphere **13**(7), 1039 (2022)
13. Benoit, A.G.M.D.S., Petry, A.: Evaluation of F10.7, sunspot number and photon flux data for ionosphere TEC modeling and prediction using machine learning techniques. Atmosphere **12**(9), 1202 (2021)
14. Momin, M., Alam, M.M., Mahfuz, M.H., Islam, M.R., Habaebi, M.H., Badron, K.: Prediction of rain attenuation on earth-to-satellite link using rain rate measurement with various integration times. In: 2021 8th International Conference on Computer and Communication Engineering (ICCCE), pp. 385–390. IEEE (2021)
15. Ahuna, M.N., Afullo, T.J., Alonge, A.A.: Rain attenuation prediction using artificial neural network for dynamic rain fade mitigation. SAIEE Africa Res. J. **110**(1), 11–18 (2019)
16. Sodunke, M.A., Ojo, J.S., Adedayo, K.D., De, A., Sulaimon, M.O.: Prediction and analysis of seasonal rain attenuation in the South-western region of Nigeria for future microwave applications. Adv. Space Res. (2022)
17. Nandi, D.D., Pérez-Fontán, F., Pastoriza-Santos, V., Machado, F.: Application of synthetic storm technique for rain attenuation prediction at Ka and Q band for a temperate Location, Vigo, Spain. Adv. Space Res. **66**(4), 800–880 (2020)
18. Metlek, S., Kayaalp, K.: Makine Öğrenmesinde, Teoriden Örnek MATLAB Uygulamalarına Kadar Destek Vektör Makineleri. İksad Yayınevi (2020)
19. Palmer, J.M., Theisen, J.M., Duran, R.M., Grayburn, W.S., Calvo, A.M., Keller, N.P.: Secondary metabolism and development is mediated by LlmF control of VeA subcellular localization in Aspergillus nidulans. PLoS Genet. **9**(1), e1003193 (2013)
20. Kalafatoğlu, E., Ceren, E., Kaymaz, Z.: Magnetic and electric field variations during geomagnetically active days over Turkey. Adv. Space Res. **60–9**, 1921–1948 (2017). https://doi.org/10.1016/j.asr.2017.07.019
21. SVM Algorithm: https://www.javatpoint.com/machine-learning-support-vector-machine-algorithm. Erişim Tarihi: 12 Mayıs 2023, Erişim Saati: 13:25

Prediction of Wind Speed by Using Machine Learning

Uğur Şener[1]([⊠]) [ID], Buket İşler Kılıç[2] [ID], Ahmet Tokgözlü[3] [ID], and Zafer Aslan[4] [ID]

[1] Faculty of Administrative Sciences, Department of Business Management, Istanbul Aydın
University, 34295 Istanbul, Turkey
usener@aydin.edu.tr
[2] Department of Computer Engineering, Istanbul Topkapi University, 34087 Istanbul, Turkey
buketisler@topkapi.edu.tr
[3] Faculty of Science and Literature, Süleyman Demirel University, Isparta, Turkey
tokgozlu68@gmail.com
[4] Faculty of Engineering, Department of Computer Engineering, Istanbul Aydın University,
34295 Istanbul, Turkey
zaferaslan@aydin.edu.tr

Abstract. Due to the depletion of fossil fuel resources and environmental concerns caused by traditional fuel systems in recent years, the share of renewable energy sources in current energy production has been increasing. Among these energy sources, wind and solar energy stand out compared to other sources. Wind energy is a clean, sustainable and low-cost energy source. Wind and solar energies vary considerably according to the stochastic environment of meteorological conditions. Solar and wind energy variability and uncontrollability lead to power quality, generation-consumption balance and reliability problems of solar and wind energy systems. For this reason, it is important to know and predict the wind speed and solar radiation characteristics of the regions where the systems are installed. In this study, meteorological data of Antalya Serik Region were analyzed using statistical methods and wavelet transform. Thus, the potentials of wind and solar energies in the study area and large and small-scale events affecting these potentials were determined. In addition, a short-term estimation study was made for wind intensity and solar radiation using the time series of meteorological data. Besides SARMA, SARMAX and NAR models, Wavelet-NARX, SARMAX-NAR and NAR-SARMAX hybrid models are employed. Hybrid models are successfully produced better results than component forecasts.

Keywords: ANN · Wind speed forecasting · Hybrid forecasting · NAR · NARX · SARMA · SARMAX · Wavelet

1 Introduction

Wind energy and other renewables are emerging energy sources since European Green Deal and other similar decrees force nations to decrease their carbon emission levels. Wind energy forecasts have economic value for both short and long term considerations. Wind speed of Serik, Antalya region is forecasted in this paper which is the first one in the region. Results may contribute also Mediterranean wind speed predictions in general.

O. Gervasi et al. (Eds.): ICCSA 2023 Workshops, LNCS 14104, pp. 73–86, 2023.
https://doi.org/10.1007/978-3-031-37105-9_6

Depending on the advancing technology all over the world, the needs of people for electrical energy are also increasing. Since the existing fossil resources used in electrical energy production are limited, they are decreasing day by day and they will be exhausted one day, on the one hand, electrical energy saving studies are carried out, on the other hand, studies on generating electrical energy using renewable resources continue at a great pace. The importance of the studies for the use of renewable resources in the production of electricity is obvious for the future of the countries, since they reduce the dependence on foreign sources. One of the studies carried out in this context is the generation of electrical energy by using the wind potentials, which have shown great development in the world, especially in Europe and Turkey in recent years.

Considering the cost of the wind turbine, it includes the decision of the region where the wind turbine will be installed and the measurement of the wind. Long-term wind measurements are made in the region where the wind turbine is planned to be installed, and as a result, it is decided whether it is suitable for installing a turbine, that is, the selection of the wind turbine becomes important. In our study, determining the place where the wind turbine will be installed and knowing how the wind values will be in the future will be a great gain for the investment to be made by the establishment to be established and the calculation of its return. In this study, it is planned that the changes in the future wind situation, which has not been done until now, that is, the wind modeling, and the determination of the situation, so that the operator will have the opportunity to make comfortable investments. In the study area, which is a tourism region, it is planned to meet the energy need with clean energy.

Both statistical and machine learning forecasting approaches are used to predict wind speed. Seasonal auto-regressive moving average (SARMA), SARMA with explanatory variable (SARMAX), nonlinear auto-regressive neural network (NAR), NAR with explanatory variable (NARX) and Wavelet transform are used as component forecasts and also their hybrid models are employed to reduce forecast error. ARIMA method uses differencing when trend exists in the data which can be detected by correlogram and unit root tests. When the forecast completed first term and differenced series are summed or integrated to reach the final forecast. Forecasting process combines auto regressive components with a finite moving average process. Auto regressive component consists of lagged response variables, while residual series obtained from a regression equation and also lagged series constitute the latter component. Auto regressive neural networks (NAR) is a specialized ANN model for time series forecasting. The input nodes consist of actual response variable and its lagged versions while output node presents the forecast series. In general, one hidden layer with multiple nodes is used between input and output layers. When explanatory variables are included to NAR model, it is called NARX model.

Combination and hybrid forecasting procedures use more than one forecasting technique in order to improve forecast accuracy measures. The forces generating series and underlying process behind the data are generally not visible to the forecaster to combining forecast models is can produce better results than the component forecasts. The idea behind combining is that disadvantages of component forecasts can be eliminated by supporting it with another model. For instance, ARIMA model is a very strong and versatile tool for short term time forecasting but forecast function of it is the linear combination of lagged variables and residuals. However, NAR models have the ability to model nonlinear patterns. ARIMA-NAR and NAR-ARIMA hybrid models combine the advantages of both models and so improve forecast accuracy [1, 2]. Combination procedures started with simple average of component forecasts. Then, weighted averaging with different approaches is employed. Correlation coefficients did not work well, but regression coefficients are strong estimates for weights. When heterocedasticity exists in the component forecast series, it is better to use WLS. Constraining coefficients to be nonnegative and sum to one also improves forecast accuracy. Multi-layer perceptron of ANN model can be used also as a nonlinear combination procedure [3].

Zhang [1] combined ARIMA and ANN models in his hybrid models where instead of ARIMA, SARMAX model is used because of the fact that data contain seasonality but not trend. Zhang forecasted the response variable with the first model. Then, residual series obtained from first model is forecasted with second model. After that, residual forecasts are summed to first models forecast results to reach final forecast. He used both ARIMA and ANN as first and second models.

One approach to support nonlinear autoregressive time series forecasting model is to support it with explanatory variables obtained from Wavelet transform. By doing so, the impact of wavelet transforms and data preprocessing on the performance of estimation using NARX was demonstrated. The comparison of the relationship between model outputs and observations, as well as the reliability and precision of the models, were thoroughly discussed.

2 Study Area and Methodology

Selected region represents Mediterranean region of Turkey. Therefore, this paper is a pilot study for the general impacts of climate change on wind speed and wind energy potential on the Mediterranean region. Selected region is available below. Then, literature review and methodology is presented in this section.

2.1 Study Area

Serik is a district of Antalya, located in the Mediterranean Region of Turkey. The district, situated in the central part of Antalya province, is located between 36–37° latitude and 31–32° longitude. It is an important tourist center of our country, with an increasing population during the summer season due to tourism, but decreasing in the winter season when students leave the district. The district center, which is approximately 38 km east of Antalya city center, is located 7 km inland from the coast and at an altitude of 26 m above sea level.

The district center of Serik is 30 km east of Antalya. The district has a 22 km coastline on the Mediterranean Sea and its center is located 8 km inland at an altitude of 26 m above sea level on a partly undulating plain terrain. The district's area is 1,550 km², of which 45,360 hectares are agricultural land and 65,764 hectares are forest land. Serik constitutes an eastern extension of the Antalya Plain. The district is bordered by Aksu district of Antalya in the west, Manavgat district in the east, Bucak district of Burdur and Sütçüler district of Isparta in the north, and the Mediterranean Sea in the south.

Livestock farming and forestry are carried out in the mountainous areas, while agriculture, especially early vegetable cultivation, is common in the plain areas. The district's commercial life is connected to the Antalya city center. The western Taurus Mountains begin to rise in the north of the district.

The district has a Mediterranean climate. Summers are dry and hot, and winters are mild and rainy (although this can sometimes vary). As a result of this climate, the natural vegetation is maquis. The region's most important rivers are Köprüçay and Aksu Stream (Fig. 1).

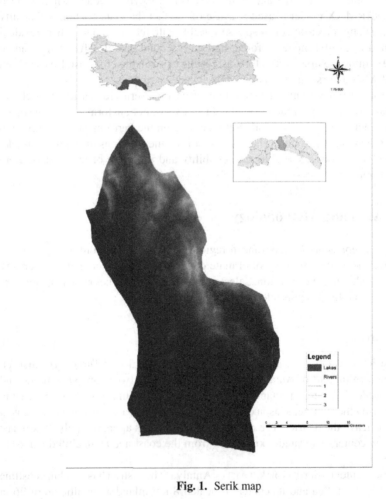

Fig. 1. Serik map

2.2 Nonlinear Autoregressive Neural Network (NAR, NARX)

The term "artificial intelligence," which is used frequently nowadays, is quite difficult to define. This is because artificial intelligence is a notion that gets into numerous academic fields, including computer science, psychology, physics, medicine, and philosophy. The simplest definition of artificial intelligence is the effort to simulate the behaviors that we refer to as human intelligence in machines—reasoning, making sense, generalizing, learning from past mistakes, etc. This method, which was created for a variety of goals, is becoming more and more common, which increases the dependency of individuals on technology. The idea of artificial intelligence, which was introduced by John McCarthy in 1956 at the Dartmouth Conference, has evolved over time with the theory that creating tailored answers to the issues encountered can improve the success of the models. ANN technique was one of the several models developed for this study. As is usually observed in the literature, artificial neural networks have demonstrated effectiveness in a wide range of domains, including prediction, modeling, and classification applications [4–6]. ANN model is constructed with connected nodes of weights which is used also for multivariate forecasting purposes. Multi-layer Perceptron (MLP) is the most often used network structure for forecasting. MLP generally contains three layers in which first layer is used for explanatory variables, second layer is the hidden one and third layer is for predicted variables [7, 8].

ANN has specialized networks for time series forecasting which are nonlinear autoregressive neural network (NAR) and nonlinear autoregressive neural networks with exogenous inputs (NARX). The NARX neural network approach has frequently been discovered in the literature for providing successful results in modeling studies of chaotic data [9, 10]. A kind of feedback ANN model known as NARX networks is renowned for its ability to forecast time series data accurately. It is noted that it delivers more effective learning and converges faster than conventional feedback network architectures [11, 12]. NARX model can be expressed mathematically with the following function [13];

$$y(t) = f(y(t-1), y(t-2), \ldots, y(t-ny), x(t-1), x(t-2), \ldots, x(t-nx)) \quad (2.1)$$

The equation's terms $y(t-1)$, $y(t-2)$, ..., $y(t-ny)$ represent in for net outputs, and $x(t-1)$, $x(t-2)$, ..., $x(t-nx)$ stand for network inputs. The number of inputs is represented by the nx parameter. The ny parameter displays how many previous outputs will be used as feedback. By returning the signal of the prior output value and the prior independent input signal, the $y(t)$ depending on the output parameter is determined.

The literature review showed that merging an additional analysis technique with an ANN model improved prediction accuracy [14, 15]. In Wavelet transform (WT), it is well recognized that choosing the right main wavelet and deciding on the decomposition level effectively capture the properties of the data and improve performance. In order to improve the accuracy of wind forecasting, a hybrid Wavelet-NARX method has been created in this study. We compared performances of component forecasts with hybrid ones including Wavelet-NARX, SARIMAX-NAR and NAR-SARIMAX.

2.3 Wavelet

Alfred Haar introduced the term "wavelet" for the first time in 1909. Many significant researchers have worked on the wavelet transform, one of the preprocessing approaches for signal processing, including Daubechies, Coifman, and Wickherhouser.

Any signal is split into smaller signals by the wavelet transform, which analyzes the changes in chaotic data over time. This is done through multiple stages of processing in the time frequency domain. It establishes which sub components of this time series' major modes of variability are and how these modes evolve over time. In other words, it enables the transformation of the original dataset into a different format that offers a clearer justification. The discrete wavelet transform produces two complimentary signals, the approximation (A) and detail (D) components, from the original signal, which is represented by the symbol S. The generated coefficients can be examined at various frequency and resolution ranges. The A data exhibits the general properties of the original signal in its abridged form during the decomposition process. On the other hand, detail components assist us in identifying time series with high-frequency rapid changes.

Mathematically, the discrete wavelet transform (ADD) is defined as follows [16];

$$cD1 = \sum_{-\infty}^{+\infty} (f[n].g[2n - k])$$ (2.2)

$$cA1 = \sum_{-\infty}^{+\infty} (f[n].h[2n - k])$$ (2.3)

The original signal is represented by f[n], which is given in the equation. The filter level is represented here by n. In the formula, the value of k indicates the level of dissociation. Decomposition can be accomplished by processing both g(k) and h(k) through high-low pass filters, respectively. Discrete wavelet transform detail data was used in the study's analysis to access the wind data's specific characteristics and catch unexpected changes.

2.4 ARIMA

Auto regressive (AR) models use lagged predicted variables as explanatory variables, because they are correlated with predicted variables when the time series data have serial correlation. In this case, serial correlation problem is used for the benefit of the model. ACF/PACF figures reveal whether serial correlation exists which can be observed in almost all of the time series data sets. Auto regressive moving average (ARMA) models combine AR component with a finite moving average process (MA). MA component of the model relies on the interdependency between error series and predicted series so lagged residual series obtained from the regression is included to model similar to AR component. If differencing is employed to the predicted series of ARMA model, it is called auto regressive integrated moving average (ARIMA) model. When there is trend pattern in the series, ARIMA model employs differencing for removing trend before combining AR and MA variables. After forecast series calculated, it is integrated (summed) to reach final forecast.

ARIMA is actually univariate forecasting technique but explanatory variables can be included to the model with transfer function [17].

2.5 Forecast Accuracy

Regression based models fit the forecasting function with respect to minimization of sum of squares error $SSE = \sum_{t=1}^{n}(Y_t - \hat{Y}_t)^2$ so conventional regression models are called ordinary least squares (OLS), where t is the period number, n is the quantity of periods, $\hat{Y}_t$ is the forecast at period t and Y_t is the actual data at period t [18]. When we divide SSE to the quantity of periods in the models we will reach mean square error $MSE = \frac{\sum_{t=1}^{n}(Y_t - \hat{Y}_t)^2}{n}$. Square root of MSE is called $RMSE = \sqrt{\frac{\sum_{t=1}^{n}(Y_t - \hat{Y}_t)^2}{n}}$ which is a popular forecast accuracy measure. SSE and MSE are in square level compared with actual data but after taking square root, RMSE is converted back to the level of actual figures, so this fact makes it comparable with Y_t. All forecast accuracy measures explained here which are based on SSE have the range of $[0,\infty)$ and lower values indicate better forecasts [19, 20].

Many researchers prefer using forecast accuracy measures based on percentages of error term e_t in actual data Y_t. This scaling error term with respect to actual data makes forecast accuracy measure more comparable between the forecasting techniques even for different data sets. Mean percentage error MPE is used to determine whether model underestimates or overestimates the actual figures which is calculated by MPE $= \sum_{t=1}^{n} \frac{Y_t - \hat{Y}_t}{Y_t}$. Negative MPE indicates that forecast figures are greater than actual data so model overestimates the real situation. Conversely, positive MPE means underestimation. Mean absolute percentage error is the most popular forecast accuracy measure and calculated with the formula MAPE $= \sum_{t=1}^{n} \frac{|Y_t - \hat{Y}_t|}{|Y_t|}$ [18]. Percentage error based forecast accuracy measures explained here have the range of $[0,1]$ and forecast accuracy is better when it is close to zero. Symmetric mean absolute percentage error $SMAPE = \sum_{t=1}^{n} \frac{|Y_t - \hat{Y}_t|}{(|Y_t| + |\hat{Y}_t|)/2}$ is percentage of the error term in the absolute averages of actual d predicted data [11]. Absolute operator is not the part of original formula but added to make statistic a positive percentage. Theil's U is another measure we would like to present in this paper which is calculate by Theil's $U = \frac{\sum_{t=1}^{n-1}\left(\frac{Y_{t+1} - \hat{Y}_{t+1}}{Y_t}\right)^2}{\sum_{t=1}^{n-1}\left(\frac{Y_{t+1} - Y_t}{Y_t}\right)^2}$ [21].

3   Results

Missing values in the hourly data set from 2015 to 2022 were estimated using linear interpolation. Out of 69.503 data points, only 200 were missing, indicating that the data set is reliable. The data for 2022 was separated as out-of-sample periods. The data from 2015 to 2021 was used to fit the Wavelet-NARX model, while the data from 2022 to 2021 was used for other models.

The SARMA model is fitted with 52 weeks periodicity, including MA, AR, SAR (seasonal autoregressive) and SMA (seasonal moving average) components. 2020–2021 in sample data set is used for model fitting and stationary R square is for selecting best model. Data does not contain trend, so differencing is not required theoretically. Seasonal ARMA(1,0,2)(2,0,1) model bested other ARIMA procedures in all error measures. Selected model is used to forecast 2022 out of sample periods.

For SARMAX model, seasonal exponential smoothing forecast of wind speed with 24 h periodicity is included to the model as explanatory variable with transfer function in order to represent a daily average wind speed to SARMA model. SARMAX-NAR model is applied to normalized data set. Z-score normalization is used because it produced lower error measures compared with the min-max method. Mean of in sample periods is subtracted from data point and result is divided to the standard deviation of the in sample periods. 2020–2021 in sample data is used for training model. In sample data is divided as 60% for training, 20% for validation and 20% for test. 77 autoregressive components are included to the model and 129 hidden nodes are used between input and output layer. MSE is minimized for training. Optimized net is used to forecast out of sample periods.

NAR-SARMAX and SARMAX-NAR hybrid models are formulated such that forecast started with forecasting wind speed with the former method which is NAR in NAR-SARMAX. Residual series obtained from NAR is forecasted with latter SARMAX model. SARMAX residual forecast results is summed with NAR forecast of wind speed to have final forecast. SARMAX-NAR model is formulated with reverse order.

Wavelet-NARX hybrid were employed to evaluate a dataset of 69.503 hourly wind speed data for the years 2015–2022. Both approaches utilized the hourly data set from 2015 to 2021 as the input for the network, and the out-of-sample period of 2022 was projected using a selected model. The 2022 out-of-sample dataset was used for model fitting, and the stationary R square was employed to select the best model. 60% percent of the data were used for training, while the remaining 40% were used for validation and testing. The number of hidden layer neurons varied based on the performance of the network. All error measures demonstrated that the Wavelet-NARX model outperformed all other alternatives. The section on results presents the accuracy of the predictions made for both past periods and also first future year.

In the study, multiple methods were used to predict wind speed, and NAR was one of them. The success of the network was evaluated by comparing the R test results. The study found that the best R performances were 0.79 for training, 0.79 for validation, and 0.78 for test values. The analysis results were presented in Fig. 2, which showed the graphic and prediction outcomes.

For Wavelet-NARX hybrid methodology started with wavelet analysis and wind speed series are divided into wavelets. The d4 wavelet, which is known to produce effective results in the literature, was used to divide the data into three levels. The study found that large and medium-sized events had an impact on the change in wind speed for the Serik region. As a result, data related to these events were introduced to the network as input along with the NARX data, while actual wind data were used as output.

The hybrid model, which was developed by using wavelet transform analysis, showed more successful results than the model that was developed using only NAR. The hybrid study resulted in R values of 0.92 for training, 0.92 for validation, and 0.91 for test data. The study found that the average wind speed in 2022 was 2.97 m/s. Based on the hybrid model, the wind prediction for 2023 was determined to be 2.98 m/s. The results suggest that there will be a slight increase in the average wind speed in 2023 compared to 2022. Figure 3 presents the graphic and prediction outcomes generated based on the analysis results.

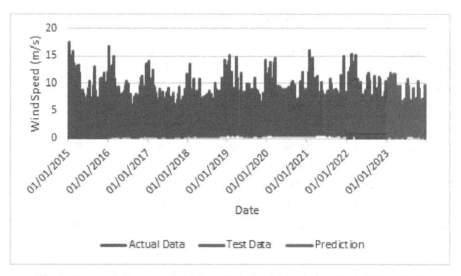

Fig. 2. Temporal wind speed variation of ANN model between 2015–2023 in Serik

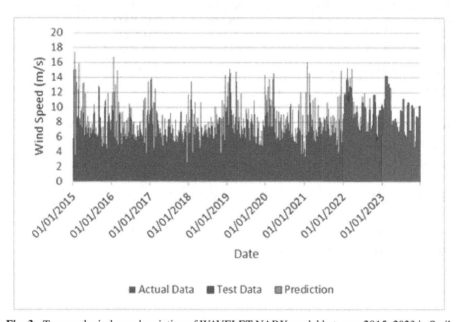

Fig. 3. Temporal wind speed variation of WAVELET-NARX model between 2015–2023 in Serik

According to in sample periods, NAR-SARIMA model produced better error measures compared with other models in general. In percentage error measures of MPE and MAPE, NAR model is slightly better. Among component forecasts NAR model is better than SARIMA and SARIMAX models. SARIMA-NAR hybrid model did not improved results than component forecasts (Tables 1, 2 and 3, Figs. 4 and 5).

Table 1. Forecast accuracy measures for training data (2020–2021)

2020–2021 Training	SARMA	SARMAX	NAR	SARMAX NAR Hybrid	NAR SARMAX Hybrid
MSE	0.97	1.01	0.57	1.07	0.58
RMSE (m/s)	0.98	1.00	0.76	1.03	0.76
MAE	0.63	0.63	0.54	0.62	0.54
MPE (%)	−10.2%	−10.1%	−10.9%	−10.0%	−6.7%
MAPE (%)	24.2%	24.3%	22.4%	24.6%	21.4%
SMAPE (%)	21.5%	21.5%	19.9%	22.0%	19.7%
U1	0.14	0.14	0.11	0.14	0.11
U2	1.07	1.09	0.90	1.21	0.89

Table 2. Forecast accuracy measures for test period of next month

Test with next month (01/2022)	SARMA	SARMAX	NAR	SARMAX-NAR Hybrid	NAR SARMAX Hybrid	Wavelet-NARX Hybrid
MSE	1.87	1.83	2.49	6.60	2.37	1.01
RMSE (m/s)	1.37	1.35	1.58	2.57	1.54	1.00
MAE	1.00	0.97	1.16	1.92	1.12	0.73
MPE (%)	N/A	N/A	N/A	N/A	N/A	N/A
MAPE (%)	N/A	N/A	N/A	N/A	N/A	N/A
SMAPE (%)	33.7%	31.9%	39.0%	62.5%	38.1%	25.2%
U1	0.18	0.18	0.20	0.30	0.20	0.13
U2	0.86	0.12	0.29	1.36	0.39	0.37

2022 data set of 8060 data points contain 84 h as zero so MPE and MAPE cannot be calculated for out of sample periods. For short-term forecasting of first consecutive month; Wavelet-NARX model bested others.

Table 3. Forecast accuracy measures for test period of next year

Test with next year (2022)	SARMA	SARMAX	NAR	SARMAX-NAR Hybrid	NAR SARMAX Hybrid	Wavelet-NARX Hybrid
MSE	1.49	1.47	1.92	4.99	1.76	0.86
RMSE	1.22	1.21	1.39	2.23	1.33	0.93
MAE	0.88	0.85	1.01	1.56	0.96	0.68
MPE	N/A	N/A	N/A	N/A	N/A	N/A
MAPE	N/A	N/A	N/A	N/A	N/A	N/A
SMAPE	33.3%	31.5%	37.7%	55.6%	36.5%	26.9%
U1	0.18	0.17	0.19	0.29	0.19	0.13
U2	0.90	0.52	0.77	0.92	0.72	0.37

For long-term forecasting Wavelet-NARX model bested others in almost all statistics.

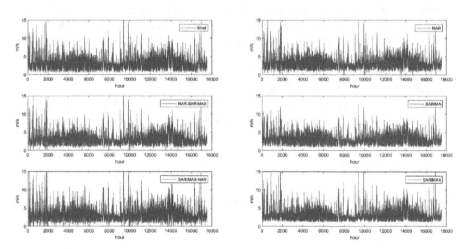

Fig. 4. Training period estimations

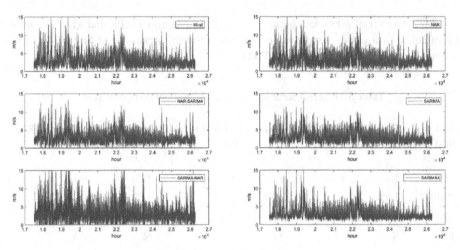

Fig. 5. Test period estimations

4 Discussion

Objective of the paper is presenting wind speed forecast and also testing hybrid forecasting models with hourly wind data in order to see whether they improve forecast accuracy measures or not. SARMA, SARMAX, NAR and Wavelet transform are used as component forecasts in SARMAX-NAR, NAR-SARMAX and NARX-Wavelet hybrid models in which NARX-Wavelet performed best. While the prediction accuracy of the ARIMA and NAR methods are high for time series forecasting, it is well-established that utilizing hybrid models can further improve performance [22, 23]. Results showed that the NARX-Wavelet outperformed the NAR model, while achieving an R value of 0.91 on the test data, compared to 0.78 for the ANN model. This resulted in a 16% increase in prediction accuracy when using the hybrid model.

Considering the vast alternatives of hybrid models to be employed in the future; Wavelet transform can be included to SARMA with transfer function model as explanatory variable or with the methodology presented by Zhang (2003). Combination forecasting approaches can be used to combine given component forecasts. Decomposition models can be applied to formulate seasonality indices.

Acknowledgement. This paper is conducted under the Cube4EnvSec project of NATO Science for Peace Program.

References

1. Kim, S., Choi, C.Y., Shahandashti, M., Ryu, K.R.: Improving accuracy in predicting city-level construction cost indices by combining linear ARIMA and nonlinear ANNs. J. Manage. Eng. **38**(2), 1–47 (2022). https://doi.org/10.1061/(asce)me.1943-5479.0001008
2. Zhang, G.P.: Time series forecasting using a hybrid ARIMA and neural network model. Neurocomputing **50**, 159–175 (2003). www.elsevier.com/locate/neucom

3. Terregrossa, S.J., Sener, U.: Employing a generalized reduced gradient algorithm method to form combinations of steel price forecasts generated separately by ARIMA-TF and ANN models. Cogent Econ. Finance **11**(1), 1–25 (2023). https://doi.org/10.1080/23322039.2023.2169997

4. Kurani, A., Doshi, P., Vakharia, A., Shah, M.: A comprehensive comparative study of artificial neural network (ANN) and support vector machines (SVM) on stock forecasting. Ann. Data Sci. **10**(1), 183–208 (2023)

5. Coelho, L.B., Zhang, D., Van Ingelgem, Yves, Steckelmacher, Denis, Nowé, Ann, Terryn, Herman: Reviewing machine learning of corrosion prediction in a data-oriented perspective. npj Materials Degradation **6**(1), 8 (2022). https://doi.org/10.1038/s41529-022-00218-4

6. Kechagias, J.D., Tsiolikas, A., Petousis, M., Ninikas, K., Vidakis, N., Tzounis, L.: A robust methodology for optimizing the topology and the learning parameters of an ANN for accurate predictions of laser-cut edges surface roughness. Simul. Model. Pract. Theory **114**, 102414 (2022)

7. Zhang, G.P., Qi, M.: Neural network forecasting for seasonal and trend time series. Eur. J. Oper. Res. **160**(2), 501–514 (2005). https://doi.org/10.1016/j.ejor.2003.08.037

8. Zhang, G.P.: Neural Networks in Business Forecasting (2011). https://doi.org/10.4018/978-1-59140-176-6

9. Sunny, J., Schmitz, J., Zhang, L.: Artificial neural network modelling of Rossler's and Chua's chaotic systems. In: 2018 IEEE Canadian Conference on Electrical & Computer Engineering (CCECE), pp. 1–4. IEEE (2018)

10. Koschwitz, D., Frisch, J., Van Treeck, C.: Data-driven heating and cooling load predictions for non-residential buildings based on support vector machine regression and NARX Recurrent Neural Network: a comparative study on district scale. Energy **165**, 134–142 (2018)

11. Shin, Y., Smith, R., Hwang, S.: Development of model predictive control system using an artificial neural network: a case study with a distillation column. J. Clean. Prod. **277**, 124124 (2020)

12. Wunsch, A., Liesch, T., Broda, S.: Groundwater level forecasting with artificial neural networks: a comparison of long short-term memory (LSTM), convolutional neural networks (CNNs), and non-linear autoregressive networks with exogenous input (NARX). Hydrol. Earth Syst. Sci. **25**(3), 1671–1687 (2021)

13. Sum, J.P.F., Kan, W.-K., Young, G.H.: A note on the equivalence of NARX and RNN. Neural Comput. Appl. **8**(1), 33–39 (1999)

14. Reşat, H.G.: Design and development of hybrid forecasting model using artificial neural networks and ARIMA methods for sustainable energy management systems: a case study in tobacco industry. J. Fac. Eng. Archit. Gazi Univ. **35**(3), 1130–1140 (2020)

15. İşler, B., Aslan, Z.: Modeling of vegetation cover and spatio-temporal variations. J. Fac. Eng. Archit. Gazi Univ. **36**(4), 1863–1874 (2021)

16. Küçük, M., Agiralioglu, N.: Wavelet regression technique for streamflow prediction. J. Appl. Stat. **33**(9), 943–960 (2006)

17. Box, G.E.P., Jenkins, G.M.R.G.C., Ljung, G.M.: Time Series Analysis Forecasting and Control, 5th edn. Wiley, New Jersey (2016)

18. Makridakis, S., Wheelwright, S.C.: Forecasting Methods and Applications, 3rd edn. John Wiley & Sons (1997)

19. Adli, K.A., Sener, U.: Forecasting of the US steel prices with LVAR and VEC models. Bus. Econ. Res. J. **12**(3), 509–522 (2021). https://doi.org/10.20409/berj.2021.335

20. Şener, U.: Türkiye'de Binek Otomobili Endüstrisinin Talebine Kantitatif Bir Yaklaşım, Istanbul Aydin University (2015)

21. Bliemel, F.: Theil's forecast accuracy coefficient: a clarification. J. Market. Res. **10**(4), 444 (1973). https://doi.org/10.2307/3149394

22. Kreinovich, V., Nguyen, H.T., Ouncharoen, R.: How to Estimate Forecasting Quality: A System-Motivated How to Estimate Forecasting Quality: A System-Motivated Derivation of Symmetric Mean Absolute Percentage Error Derivation of Symmetric Mean Absolute Percentage Error (SMAPE) and Other Similar Characteristics (SMAPE) and Other Similar Characteristics, pp. 1–11 (2014). https://scholarworks.utep.edu/cs_techrep
23. Jadhav, V., Reddy, B.V., Gaddi, G.M.: Application of ARIMA model for forecasting agricultural prices. J. Agric. Sci. Technol. **19**(5), 981–992 (2017). www.SID.ir

Analytic Solutions of Fractional Differential Equation Associated with the k-Symbol Tremblay Differential Operator

Rabha W. Ibrahim[1,2] , Suzan J. Obaiys[3] , Nur Amalina Binti Jamaludin[4] , and Yeliz Karaca[5,6(✉)]

[1] Mathematics Research Center, Department of Mathematics, Near East University, Near East Boulevard, 99138 Nicosia/Mersin, Turkey
[2] Department of Computer Science and Mathematics, Lebanese American University, Beirut, Lebanon
[3] Department of Computer System and Technology, Faculty of Computer Science and Information Technology, University of Malaya, Kuala Lumpur, Malaysia
suzan@um.edu.my
[4] Centre Foundation Studies, UPNM (National Defense University of Malaysia), 57000 sg besi camp, Kuala Lumpur, Malaysia
amalinajamaludin@upnm.edu.my
[5] University of Massachusetts Chan Medical School (UMASS), 55 Lake Avenue North, Worcester, MA 01655, USA
yeliz.karaca@ieee.org
[6] Massachusetts Institute of Technology (MIT), 77 Massachusetts Avenue, Cambridge, MA 02139, USA

Abstract. A generalization of Tremblay differential operator is obtained in terms of the $k-$symbol fractional calculus in a complex domain. By using this operator, the analytic solutions of fractional differential equation are investigated. Our approach is based on a variety of ideas, spanning subordination and superordination as well as the use of Jack Lemma. For the normalized operator, some geometric characteristics are researched and discovered, including univalency and convexity. In order to find an analytical response to a class of fractional differential equations, the bounded turning characteristic will be investigated. Examples are illustrated in the sequel.

Keywords: Fractional calculus · Fractional differential equation · Fractional differential operator · Analytic function · Univalent function

1 Introduction

The Tremblay differential operator (TDO) is a special structure of fractional differential operator (usually uses the classic fractional differential operator) used

© The Author(s), under exclusive license to Springer Nature Switzerland AG 2023
O. Gervasi et al. (Eds.): ICCSA 2023 Workshops, LNCS 14104, pp. 87–104, 2023.
https://doi.org/10.1007/978-3-031-37105-9_7

in the study of special functions and mathematical physics. The TDO has applications in various fields such as quantum mechanics, signal processing, and image processing. It is also used in the study of special functions such as the Bessel function and the hypergeometric function and the Whittaker functions [1]. Ibrahim and Jahangiri studied TDO with a complex variable. Later, Esa et al. [2] considered a modification of the TDO of a complex variable. Recently, Irmak [3] presented different geometric studies including TDO. In this work, we aim to introduce a generalization of TDO in view of the $k-$symbol calculus.

The concept k-symbol fractional calculus is the overview of the gamma function to take account of the parameter k (see [4]). This simplification yields the recognized $k-$symbol fractional differential and integral operators. This postponement shields the fractional operators of complex variables. The k-symbol fractional calculus is a influential implement for analyzing and modeling complex schemes that display non-integer order dynamics (see [5–7]).

Global analytic solutions refer to mathematical solutions that provide a formula or expression for the function being studied over its entire domain. In other words, a global analytic solution provides a complete description of the behavior of a function, without any gaps or singularities. Examples of functions that have global analytic solutions include polynomials, trigonometric functions, exponential functions, and logarithmic functions. These functions can be expressed using finite combinations of elementary functions (see [8–10]). However, not all functions have global analytic solutions. For example, some transcendental functions such as the gamma function and the Riemann zeta function do not have closed-form expressions that can be evaluated for all inputs. In these cases, numerical methods may be used to approximate the function over its domain (see [11–13]).

The $k-$symbol TDO is formulated in the open unit disk. A global solution for a fractional differential equation involving it is formulated analytically. Our method is found by different concepts including the subordination and superordination together with the application of Jack Lemma. Some geometric properties, such as univalency and convexity, are investigated and found for the normalized operator. The bounded turning characteristic will be looked at in order to discover an analytical solution to a class of fractional differential equations. Instances are provided in the follow-up.

2   The $k-$Symbol Process

The concept of k-symbol calculus [4] is first proposed in order to alter the well-known fractional calculus based on the $k-$gamma function

$$\Gamma_k(t) = \int_0^\infty \exp(\frac{-t^k}{k}) t^{\eta-1} dt, \quad \Re(\eta) > 0, \ k \in \mathbb{R}^+.$$

Definition 1

$$\Gamma_k(\eta) = \lim_{n \to \infty} \frac{n! k^n (nk)^{\frac{\eta}{k}-1}}{(\eta)_{n,k}}, \tag{1}$$

where

$$(\eta)_{n,k} := \eta(\eta + k)(\eta + 2k)...(\eta + (n-1)k) = \frac{\Gamma_k(\eta + nk)}{\Gamma_k(\eta)}.$$

Note that $\Gamma_k(\eta) \to \Gamma(\eta)$ when $k = 1$, and $\Gamma_k(\eta + k) = \eta\Gamma_k(\eta)$, $\Gamma_k(k) = 1$.

By utilizing $\Gamma_k(\eta)$, the $k-$symbol Riemann-Liouville operators are formulated in [11, 12], as follows:

Definition 2. *The following formula can be applied to the $k-$symbol Riemann-Liouville fractional integral*

$$\mathcal{R}^{\mu}_{a,k}u(\eta) = \frac{1}{k\Gamma_k(\mu)} \int_a^{\eta} (\eta - \xi)^{\mu/k-1} u(\xi)d\xi, \quad \mu > 0.$$

Note is that, for $u(\eta) = 1$, then

$$\mathcal{R}^{\mu}_{a,k}u(\eta) = \frac{(\eta - a)^{\frac{\mu}{k}}}{\Gamma_k(\mu + k)}, \quad \mu \in (0, 1].$$

As a specific value of $a = 0$, the integral becomes

$$\mathcal{R}^{\mu}_k u(\eta) = \frac{1}{k\Gamma_k(\mu)} \int_0^{\eta} (\eta - \xi)^{\mu/k-1} u(\xi)d\xi.$$

The $k-$symbol Riemann-Liouville fractional derivative has the structure

$$D^{\mu}_k u(\eta) = \frac{d}{d\eta} \left(\mathcal{R}^{1-\mu}_k u(\eta) \right).$$

The formula for the Caputo derivative with the sign k is

$$^C_k \Delta^{\mu} u(\eta) = \begin{cases} k^w \mathcal{R}^{wk-\mu}_k u^{(w)}(\eta) = \dfrac{k^{w-1}}{\Gamma_k(wk - \mu)} \int_0^{\eta} \dfrac{u^{(w)}(\xi)}{(\eta - \xi)^{\mu/k - w + 1}} d\xi, & \mu \in ((w-1)k, wk] \\ \dfrac{d^w}{d\eta^v} u(\eta), & wk = \mu. \end{cases}$$

$$(2)$$

For example, when $k = 1$, the classical Caputo derivative is obtained.

Keep in mind that the function of the k-Riemann-Liouville singular kernel is expressed, as follows:

$$\Bbbk_{\mu,k}(\eta) = \frac{\eta^{\mu/k-1}}{k\Gamma_k(\mu)}, \quad \mu \in (0,1), \ k > 0.$$

Hence, the integral operator changes in terms of the convolution product

$$\mathcal{R}^{\mu}_k u(\eta) = \Bbbk_{\mu,k}(\eta) * u(\eta).$$

As an instance, when $u(\eta) = 1$ then

$$D^{\mu}_k u(\eta) = \frac{\eta^{\frac{1-\mu}{k}-1}}{\Gamma_k(1 - \mu)}.$$

Generally, if $u(\eta) = \eta^m$ then

$$D_k^\mu u(\eta) = \left(\frac{\Gamma_k(k(m+1))}{\Gamma_k(1-\mu+km)} \right) \eta^{\frac{1-\mu}{k}+m-1}.$$

Clearly, for $k = 1$, the operator has the regular formula [14]

$$D_1^\mu u(\eta) = \left(\frac{\Gamma(m+1)}{\Gamma(1-\mu+m)} \right) \eta^{m-\mu}.$$

2.1   The k−Symbol TDO

By using D_k^μ, the k−symbol TDO is defined as follows:

$$^T D_k^{\mu,\nu} := \frac{\Gamma_k(\nu)}{\Gamma_k(\mu)} \eta^{1-\nu} D_k^{\mu-\nu} \eta^{\mu-1} \tag{3}$$

$$\left(\mu, \nu \in [0,1]; \; \mu > \nu; \; \eta \in \mathbb{C} \right).$$

Next, we discuss the upper bound of $^T D_k^{\mu,\nu}$ acting on the class of univalent analytic functions when $|\eta| < 1$.

Proposition 1. *For a complex variable η with $|\eta| < 1$, let $u(\eta)$ be univalent. If $0 < \rho := \mu - \nu < 1$, then*

$$|^T D_k^{\mu,\nu} u(\eta)| \le \frac{\Gamma_k(\nu)}{\Gamma_k(\mu)\Gamma_k(2-\mu+\nu)} r \left(r F_k(2,1;2-\rho;r) \right)', \tag{4}$$

$$(r = |\eta| < 1, \, 0 < \rho < 1)$$

where F_k indicates the k−symbol hypergeometric function. The inequality is sharp for the Koebe function

$$B(\eta) := \frac{\eta}{(1-\eta)^2}, \; |\eta| < 1.$$

Proof. Since u is univalent function then it has the expansion series

$$u(\eta) = \eta + \sum_{n=2}^\infty u_n \eta^n, \tag{5}$$

with $|u_n| < n$. A computation yields, when $u_1 = 1$

$$|^T D_k^{\mu,\nu} u(\eta)| \le \frac{\Gamma_k(\nu)}{\Gamma_k(\mu)} \sum_{n=1}^\infty \frac{\Gamma_k(n+1)}{\Gamma_k(n+1-\rho)} n r^n = \frac{r\Gamma_k(\nu)}{\Gamma_k(\mu)} \sum_{n=0}^\infty \frac{(n+1)\Gamma_k(n+2)}{\Gamma_k(n+2-\rho)} r^n$$

$$= \frac{r\Gamma_k(\nu)}{\Gamma_k(\mu)\Gamma_k(2-\rho)} \sum_{n=0}^\infty \frac{(2)_{n,k}(1)_{n,k}}{(2-\rho)_{n,k}} \frac{(n+1)r^n}{\Gamma_k(n+1)}$$

$$= \frac{r\Gamma_k(\nu)}{\Gamma_k(\mu)\Gamma_k(2-\mu+\nu)} \left(r F_k(2,1;2-\rho;r) \right)',$$

where $F_k(.)$ presents the k−symbol hypergeometric function. The equality is indicated when $u(\eta)$ is replaced by the Koebe function.

Note that when $r \to 1$, Proposition 1 yields

$$|^T D_k^{\mu,\nu} u(\eta)| \leq \frac{\Gamma_k(\nu)}{\Gamma_k(\mu)\Gamma_k(2-\mu+\nu)}\left(F_k(2,1;2-\rho;1)\right)'.$$

Proposition 2. *The operator* $^T D_k^{\mu,\nu}$ *is normalized by the formula*

$$\mathfrak{T}_k^{\mu,\nu} u(\eta) := \frac{\nu}{\mu}\left(^T D_k^{\mu,\nu} u(\eta)\right) = \eta + \sum_{n=2}^{\infty}\left(\frac{\Gamma_k(\nu+k)\Gamma_k(\mu+n)}{\Gamma_k(\mu+k)\Gamma_k(\nu+n)}\right) u_n \eta^n \quad (6)$$

$$:= \eta + \sum_{n=2}^{\infty} \hbar_n(\nu,\mu,k) u_n \eta^n, \quad \left(0 < \nu \leq \mu \leq 1, k \geq 1\right)$$

where u is given in (5).

Proposition 3. *For a complex variable η with $|\eta| < 1$, let $u(\eta)$ be convex. If $0 < \rho := \mu - \nu < 1$, then*

$$|^T D_k^{\mu,\nu} u(\eta)| \leq \frac{r\Gamma_k(\nu)}{\Gamma_k(\mu)\Gamma_k(2-\mu+\nu)}\left(F_k(2,1;2-(\mu-\nu);r)\right), \quad (7)$$

$$(r = |\eta| < 1, 0 < \rho < 1)$$

where F_k indicates the $k-$symbol hypergeometric function. The inequality is sharp for the Koebe function

$$J(\eta) := \frac{\eta}{(1-\eta)}, \ |\eta| < 1.$$

Proof. Since u is convex function then it has the expansion series

$$u(\eta) = \eta + \sum_{n=2}^{\infty} u_n \eta^n, \quad (8)$$

with $|u_n| < 1$. A computation yields, for $u_1 = 1$

$$|^T D_k^{\mu,\nu} u(\eta)| \leq \frac{\Gamma_k(\nu)}{\Gamma_k(\mu)}\sum_{n=1}^{\infty}\frac{\Gamma_k(n+1)}{\Gamma_k(n+1-\rho)}r^n = \frac{r\Gamma_k(\nu)}{\Gamma_k(\mu)}\sum_{n=0}^{\infty}\frac{\Gamma_k(n+2)}{\Gamma_k(n+2-\rho)}r^n$$

$$= \frac{r\Gamma_k(\nu)}{\Gamma_k(\mu)\Gamma_k(2-\rho)}\sum_{n=0}^{\infty}\frac{(2)_{n,k}(1)_{n,k}}{(2-\rho)_{n,k}}\frac{r^n}{\Gamma_k(n+1)}$$

$$= \frac{r\Gamma_k(\nu)}{\Gamma_k(\mu)\Gamma_k(2-\mu+\nu)}\left(F_k(2,1;2-(\mu-\nu);r)\right).$$

The equality is indicated when $u(\eta)$ is replaced by the Koebe function.

Proposition 4. *Consider the operator* $[\mathfrak{T}_k^{\mu,\nu} u(\eta)]$. *If it satisfies the inequality*

$$\sum_{n=2}^{\infty} n(n - (1 - \sqrt{6}))|\hbar_n(\nu,\mu,k)||u_n| < \sqrt{6}$$

then $[\mathfrak{T}_k^{\mu,\nu} u(\eta)]$ *is univalent in* Σ.

Proof. A computation yields

$$\left| \frac{\eta[\mathfrak{T}_k^{\mu,\nu} u(\eta)]''}{[\mathfrak{T}_k^{\mu,\nu} u(\eta)]'} \right| = \left| \frac{\sum_{n=2}^{\infty} n(n-1)\hbar_n(\nu,\mu,k)u_n\zeta^{n-1}}{1 + \sum_{n=2}^{\infty} n\hbar_n(\nu,\mu,k)u_n\eta^{n-1}} \right| \le \frac{\sum_{n=2}^{\infty} n(n-1)|\hbar_n(\nu,\mu,k)||u_n|}{1 - \sum_{n=2}^{\infty} n|\hbar_n(\nu,\mu,k)||\psi_n|}.$$

To prove that $[\mathfrak{T}_k^{\mu,\nu} u(\eta)]$ is univalent, by the condition inequality of the result yields that

$$\left| \frac{\eta[\mathfrak{T}_k^{\mu,\nu} u(\eta)]''}{[\mathfrak{T}_k^{\mu,\nu} u(\eta)]'} \right| < \sqrt{6}.$$

Then in virtue of the Umezawa lemma [17], we obtain univalency of the operator $[\mathfrak{T}_k^{\mu,\nu} u(\eta)]$.

Due to the severe nature of the Koebe function as a univalency function, we will analyze some key characteristics of a special example of $[\mathfrak{T}_k^{\mu,\nu} u(\eta)]$ when u is the Koebe function.

Proposition 5. *Consider the operator* $[\mathfrak{T}_k^{\mu,\nu} u(\eta)]$. *If it satisfies the inequality*

$$\frac{\eta^2 [\mathfrak{T}_k^{\mu,\nu} u(\eta)]^{(3)}}{[\mathfrak{T}_k^{\mu,\nu} u(\eta)]'} - \left(\frac{\eta[\mathfrak{T}_k^{\mu,\nu} u(\eta)]''}{[\mathfrak{T}_k^{\mu,\nu} u(\eta)]'} \right)^2 + \frac{(2\eta[\mathfrak{T}_k^{\mu,\nu} u(\eta)]'')}{([\mathfrak{T}_k^{\mu,\nu} u(\eta)]')} + 1$$

$$\prec \chi + (1 - \chi) \left(\frac{1+\eta}{1-\eta} \right)^{3/2}, \quad \chi \in [0,1)$$

Then $[\mathfrak{T}_k^{\mu,\nu} u(\eta)]$ *is convex of order* χ.

Proof. Let

$$\Phi(\eta) = 1 + \left(\frac{\eta[\mathfrak{T}_k^{\mu,\nu} u(\eta)]''}{[\mathfrak{T}_k^{\mu,\nu} u(\eta)]'} \right), \quad \Psi(\eta) = \frac{\Phi(\eta) - \chi}{1 - \chi}.$$

Obviously, $\Psi(0) = 1$ and

$$\eta\Psi'(\eta) = \frac{\eta\Phi'(\eta)}{1 - \chi}.$$

Then, in view of Miller and Mocanu lemma [16], we obtain

$$\Psi(\eta) + \eta\Psi'(\eta) \prec \left(\frac{1+\eta}{1-\eta} \right)^{3/2}$$

where $\Psi(\eta) \prec \dfrac{1+\eta}{1-\eta}$. But

$$\Phi(\eta) + \eta\Phi'(\eta) = \frac{\eta^2[\mathfrak{T}_k^{\mu,\nu}u(\eta)]^{(3)}}{[\mathfrak{T}_k^{\mu,\nu}u(\eta)]'} - \left(\frac{\eta[\mathfrak{T}_k^{\mu,\nu}u(\eta)]''}{[\mathfrak{T}_k^{\mu,\nu}u(\eta)]'}\right)^2 + \frac{(2\eta[\mathfrak{T}_k^{\mu,\nu}u(\eta)]'')}{([\mathfrak{T}_k^{\mu,\nu}u(\eta)]')} + 1$$

$$\prec \chi + (1-\chi)\left(\frac{1+\eta}{1-\eta}\right)^{3/2}, \quad \chi \in [0,1)$$

Then $\Phi(\eta) \prec \dfrac{1+(1-2\chi)\eta}{1-\eta}$ or $\Re(\Phi(\eta)) > \chi$; which yields that $[\mathfrak{T}_k^{\mu,\nu}u(\eta)]$ is convex of order χ.

2.2   Fractional Differential Equation (FDE)

In this part, we have study the generalized FDE in terms of the suggested k−symbol TDO, as follows:

$$\mathcal{V}(\eta) = \left(\frac{\eta}{\mathfrak{T}_k^{\mu,\nu}u(\eta)}\right)^2 [\mathfrak{T}_k^{\mu,\nu}u(\eta)]' - 1, \quad \eta \in \Sigma := \{\eta \in \mathbb{C} : |\eta| < 1\}, \quad (9)$$

where $\mathcal{V}(\eta)$ is analytic in Σ with $|\mathcal{V}(\eta)| < 1$.

Example 1. Let $\mathcal{V}(\eta) = \eta/(1-\eta)$. Then the solution of Eq. (9) is given by the formula (see Fig. 1)

$$\begin{aligned}
\mathfrak{T}_k^{\mu,\nu}u(\eta) &= -\frac{\eta}{(c\eta - \eta\log(1-\eta) + \eta\log(\eta) - 1)} \\
&= \eta + \eta^2(c+\log(\eta)) + \eta^3(2c\log(\eta) + c^2 + \log^2(\eta) + 1) \\
&\quad + \eta^4(c(3\log^2(\eta) + 2) + 3c^2\log(\eta) + c^3 + \log^3(\eta) + 2\log(\eta) + 1/2) \\
&\quad + \eta^5(c(4\log^3(\eta) + 6\log(\eta) + 1) + c^2(6\log^2(\eta) + 3) + 4c^3\log(\eta) \\
&\quad + c^4 + \log^4(\eta) + 3\log^2(\eta) + \log(\eta) + 4/3) + O(\eta^6),
\end{aligned}$$

where c is a constant.

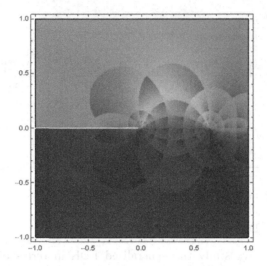

Fig. 1. Plot of the solution in Example 1

Example 2. Let $\mathcal{V}(\eta) = \eta/(1-\eta)^2$. Then the solution of Eq. (9) is given by the formula (see Fig. 2)

$$\mathfrak{T}_k^{\mu,\nu} u(\eta) = \frac{(\eta - \eta^2)}{(c\eta^2 - c\eta - 2\eta - (\eta-1)\eta \log(1-\eta) + (\eta-1)\eta \log(\eta) + 1)}$$

$$= \eta + \eta^2(c + \log(\eta) + 1)$$

$$+ \eta^3(2c(\log(\eta) + 1) + c^2 + \log^2(\eta) + 2\log(\eta) + 3)$$

$$+ \eta^4(c(3\log^2(\eta) + 6\log(\eta) + \eta) + 3c^2(\log(\eta) + 1) + c^3 + \log^3(\eta) + 3\log^2(\eta)$$

$$+ 7\log(\eta) + 13/2)$$

$$+ \eta^5(6c^2(\log^2(\eta) + 2\log(\eta) + 2) + c(4\log^3(\eta) + 12\log^2(\eta) + 24\log(\eta) + 19)$$

$$+ 4c^3(\log(\eta) + 1) + c^4 + \log^4(\eta) + 4\log^3(\eta) + 12log^2(\eta) + 19\log(\eta) + 46/3) + O(\eta^6)$$

where c is a constant.

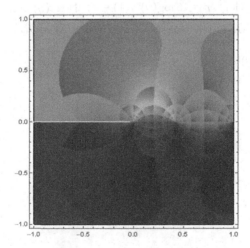

Fig. 2. Plot of the solution in Example 2

A univalent solution of a differential equation is a solution that is unique for a given set of initial or boundary conditions. In other words, there is only one solution that satisfies the differential equation and the given conditions. Univalent solutions are important in many applications of differential equations, particularly in physics and engineering, where unique solutions are necessary to make predictions and design systems. In the next section, we deal with the univalent solution of Eq. (9) in Σ. Our method is to present sufficient conditions to get a bounded turning behavior of k−symbol TDO. For this process, we have use the following information.

3 Information

3.1 Bounded Turning

A bounded turning analytic function is a complex function that has a property of bounded turning. A function is said to have a bounded turning at a point if the argument of the function remains within a bounded range as the function approaches that point [14,15]. More formally, a function $u(\eta)$ is said to have a bounded turning at a point η_0 if there exists a positive constant M such that $|\arg[u(\eta)] - \arg[u(\eta_0)]| < M$ for all z in some neighborhood of η_0. In simpler terms, the function does not oscillate rapidly as it approaches the point η_0. This property is often used in the study of complex analysis, where it is useful in understanding the behavior of functions near singularities and poles.

Examples of bounded turning analytic functions include the exponential function, the trigonometric functions, and any rational function that has simple poles. These functions have a smooth behavior near their singularities, and the argument of the function remains bounded as it approaches these points. In general, a bounded turning analytic function is a well-behaved function that does not exhibit any wild or erratic behavior near its singularities. This property is important in many areas of mathematics, including complex analysis, differential equations, and harmonic analysis.

Definition 3. *An analytic function $u(\eta)$ of the normalized form $u(0) = 0$ and $u'(0) = 1$ is called bounded turning in Σ if and only if $\Re(u'(\eta)) > 0$, $\eta \in \Sigma$.*

3.2 Subordination

Differential subordination [16] is a technique used in complex analysis to compare two analytic functions. Given two analytic functions $u(\eta)$ and $v(\eta)$, we say that $u(\eta)$ is differentially subordinate to $v(\eta)$ if there exists an analytic function $w(\eta)$ satisfying the conditions: $w(\eta)$ maps the unit disk $|\eta| < 1$ onto itself, i.e., $w(\eta)$ is a conformal mapping of the unit disk onto itself. $w(0) = 0, w'(0) > 0$ such that $u(\eta) = v(w(\eta))$ for all η in the unit disk, denoting by $u \prec v$. Intuitively, differential subordination means that $u(\eta)$ is "controlled" by $v(\eta)$ in a certain sense. Specifically, the function $w(\eta)$ provides a change of variable that transforms the unit disk into itself, and maps $u(\eta)$ to $v(\eta)$ in such a way that

$\Re w'(\eta) > 0$ for all $\eta \in \Sigma$. This condition ensures that the conformal mapping preserves the orientation of the unit disk, so that the angle between any two curves is preserved under the mapping.

Differential subordination has many applications in complex analysis, particularly in the study of univalent and starlike functions. By comparing two analytic functions using differential subordination, one can often derive useful information about their geometric properties, such as their radii of convexity or starlikeness.

3.3   Jack Lemma

The Jack Lemma states that if a function $u(\eta)$ is analytic Σ in the complex plane, and if $u(\eta)$ is not identically zero on Σ, then the zeros of $u(\eta)$ are isolated. In other words, if there is a point $\eta_0 \in \Sigma$ such that $u(\eta_0) = 0$, then there exists a small disk centered at η_0 in which $u(\eta)$ is also zero only at η_0. This result is important because it shows that the zeros of an analytic function are always isolated, which is not true for general continuous functions. The proof of the Jack Lemma relies on the fact that analytic functions can be locally represented by power series expansions, and that the zeros of a power series are also isolated. The Jack Lemma has many applications in complex analysis, such as in the study of the zeros of entire functions, the factorization of meromorphic functions, and the proof of the fundamental theorem of algebra.

We need the following result.

Lemma 1. *[16]- p.19*
For $\eta_0 \in \Sigma$ and $\rho_0 = |\eta_0|$, we assume that $u(\eta) = u_n \eta^n + u_{n+1} \eta^{n+1} + \cdots$ is analytic on $\Sigma_{\rho_0} \cup \{\rho_0\}$ such that $u \not\equiv 0$ and $n \geq 1$. If $|u(\eta_0)| = \max\{|u(\eta)| : \eta \in \Sigma_{\rho_0}\}$, then there is an $m \geq n$ with

$$-\Re\left(\frac{\eta_0 u'(\eta_0)}{u(\eta_0)}\right) = m, \text{ and}$$
$$-\Re\left(\frac{\eta_0 u''(\eta_0)}{u'(\eta_0)} + 1\right) \geq m.$$

3.4   Janowski Starlike Functions (JSFs)

JSFs are a family of holomorphic functions in the unit disk that are important in complex analysis. They were introduced by Stefan Janowski in 1929. A function $u(\eta)$ is said to be JSF in the unit disk if it has the form (13), where u_n are complex coefficients satisfying the condition $|u_2|2$. A function is JSF if it is analytic in the unit disk, maps it onto a domain that is starlike with respect to the origin, and satisfies a certain inequality involving the second coefficient of its power series expansion. JSFs are a generalization of the class of starlike functions introduced by Bieberbach. They have many interesting properties, including sharp distortion theorems and connections to geometric function theory. One important subclass of JSFs are the Janowski close-to-convex functions, which are functions that satisfy the condition $|(\eta u'(\eta))/u(\eta)|1/2$ in the unit disk. These functions have a particularly simple geometric interpretation: they map the unit disk onto a domain that is contained in a convex domain with diameter at most 2.

Definition 4. *The class of JSFs is defined as follows.*
$\mathbb{J}[\aleph, \flat]$ *is the class of all functions* $\wp : \Sigma \to \mathbb{C}$ *with* $\wp(0) = 1$ *fulfilling*

$$\wp(\eta) \prec \frac{1 + \aleph\eta}{1 + \flat\eta}, \quad -1 \le \flat < \aleph \le 1.$$

Lemma 2. *[18] Suppose that* $\wp$ *satisfies* $\wp(0) = 1$ *and* $|\wp_n| \le 2$. *If* $(\wp(\eta), \eta\wp'(\eta)) \in \Delta$, *where* Δ *is a complex domain; and* $\Re\top(\wp(\eta), \eta\wp'(\eta)) > 0$, *then* $\Re\wp(\eta) > 0$ *for* $\eta \in \Sigma$.

4   Solvability

Our aim is to present the sufficient conditions to obtain $\Re\left([\mathfrak{T}_k^{\mu,\nu} u(\eta)]'\right) > 0$

Theorem 1. *Assume the following inequality*

$$\mathrm{Re}\left(1 + \frac{\eta[\mathfrak{T}_k^{\mu,\nu} u(\eta)]''}{[\mathfrak{T}_k^{\mu,\nu} u(\eta)]'}\right) < 1 + \frac{\kappa}{2}, \quad \eta \in \Sigma, \kappa > 0. \tag{10}$$

(i) If $2 \ge 1 + \kappa$, *and* $[\mathfrak{T}_k^{\mu,\nu} u(\eta)]/\eta \ne 0$, *then* $\mathrm{Re}\,[\mathfrak{T}_k^{\mu,\nu} u(\eta)]' > 0$, $\eta \in \Sigma$.
(ii) If $2 \ge 1 + \kappa$, *and* $[\mathfrak{T}_k^{\mu,\nu} u(\eta)]/\eta \ne 0$, *then*

$$\frac{\eta[\mathfrak{T}_k^{\mu,\nu} u(\eta)]'}{[\mathfrak{T}_k^{\mu,\nu} u(\eta)]} \prec (1 - \eta)/(1 - k\eta), \quad \eta \in \Sigma, \quad k = 1/(1 + \kappa).$$

(iii) If $2 \ge 1 + \kappa$ *and* $[\mathfrak{T}_k^{\mu,\nu} u(\eta)]/\eta \ne 0$, *then* $[\mathfrak{T}_k^{\mu,\nu} u(\eta)]$ *is univalent.*

Proof. (i) We aim to show that $[\mathfrak{T}_k^{\mu,\nu} u(\eta)]' \ne 0$ for all $\eta \in \Sigma$ and $\eta \ne 0$ (since $[\mathfrak{T}_k^{\mu,\nu} u(0)]' = 1$ in Proposition 2). If there is η_1, $0 < |\eta_1| < 1$ and $[\mathfrak{T}_k^{\mu,\nu} u(\eta)]' = (\eta - \eta_1)^{m_1} \psi(\eta)$, where $m_1 \ge 1$ and ψ is analytic in Σ and $\psi(\eta_1) \ne 0$, then

$$1 + \frac{\eta\,[\mathfrak{T}_k^{\mu,\nu} u(\eta)]''}{[\mathfrak{T}_k^{\mu,\nu} u(\eta)]'} = 1 + \frac{m_1\eta}{\eta - \eta_1} + \frac{\eta[\mathfrak{T}_k^{\mu,\nu} u(\eta)]'}{\psi(\eta)}.$$

Therefore, $1 + \dfrac{\eta\,[\mathfrak{T}_k^{\mu,\nu} u(\eta)]''}{[\mathfrak{T}_k^{\mu,\nu} u(\eta)]'} \to \infty$ when $\eta \to \eta_1$, which contradicts (26).
Let

$$[\mathfrak{T}_k^{\mu,\nu} u(\eta)]' = (1 - w(\eta))^{\frac{\kappa}{n-1}}, \tag{11}$$

where $0 < \kappa/(n-1) \le 1$. Since $[\mathfrak{T}_k^{\mu,\nu} u(\eta)]' \ne 0$ for all $\eta \in \Sigma$, then $w(\eta) = w_{n-1}\eta^{n-1} + \cdots$ is analytic in Σ with $w(0) = 0$. In addition, we have

$$\left(1 + \frac{\eta[\mathfrak{T}_k^{\mu,\nu} u(\eta)]''}{[\mathfrak{T}_k^{\mu,\nu} u(\eta)]'}\right) = 1 - \frac{\kappa\eta w'(\eta)}{(n-1)(1 - w(\eta))}.$$

Consider the equality $\max_{|\eta| \leq |\eta_0|} |w(\eta)| = |w(\eta_0)| = 1$. By Lemma 1, we get

$$\eta_0 w'(\eta_0) = k w(\eta_0); \quad (k \geq n-1; w(\eta_0) = e^{i\theta}; \theta \in \mathbb{R}).$$

Thus,

$$\mathrm{Re}\left(1 + \frac{\eta_0 [\mathfrak{T}_k^{\mu,\nu} u(\eta_0)]''}{[\mathfrak{T}_k^{\mu,\nu} u(\eta_0)]'}\right) = 1 - \frac{\kappa}{n-1} \mathrm{Re}\left(\frac{k\, e^{i\theta}}{1 - e^{i\theta}}\right).$$

Hence, the following fact is obtained

$$\mathrm{Re}\left(1 + \frac{\eta_0 [\mathfrak{T}_k^{\mu,\nu} u(\eta_0)]''}{[\mathfrak{T}_k^{\mu,\nu} u(\eta_0)]'}\right) = 1 + \frac{k\kappa}{2} \geq 1 + \frac{\kappa}{2},$$

which contradicts (26). That is $|w(\eta)| < 1, \eta \in \Sigma$, and by (11), we have

$$|\arg([\mathfrak{T}_k^{\mu,\nu} u(\eta)]')| = \kappa |\arg((1 - w(\eta))| < \frac{\kappa}{(n-1)} \frac{\pi}{2} \leq \frac{\pi}{2},$$

where $2 \geq 1 + \kappa$, which leads to $\mathrm{Re}\,[\mathfrak{T}_k^{\mu,\nu} u(\eta)]' > 0, \eta \in \Sigma$,

(ii) Formulate a function w as follows:

$$\frac{\eta [\mathfrak{T}_k^{\mu,\nu} u(\eta)]'}{[\mathfrak{T}_k^{\mu,\nu} u(\eta)]} = \frac{1 - w(\eta)}{1 - kw(\eta)}, \tag{12}$$

where $k = 1/(1+\kappa)$, then $w(\eta) = c_1\eta + \cdots$ is analytic in Σ. Now, let $\eta_0 \in \Sigma$ with $\max_{|\eta| \leq |\eta_0|} |w(\eta)| = |w(\eta_0)| = 1$. According to Lemma 1, we have

$$\eta_0 w'(\eta_0) = k w(\eta_0); \quad (k \geq 1; w(\eta_0) = e^{i\theta}; \theta \in \mathbb{R}).$$

In view of (12), a logarithmic differentiation implies

$$\mathrm{Re}\left(1 + \frac{\eta_0 [\mathfrak{T}_k^{\mu,\nu} u(\eta_0)]''}{[\mathfrak{T}_k^{\mu,\nu} u(\eta_0)]'}\right) = \mathrm{Re}\left(a \frac{\eta_0 w'(\eta_0)}{1 - k w(\eta_0)} - \frac{\eta_0 [\mathfrak{T}_k^{\mu,\nu} u(\eta_0)]'}{1 - w(\eta_0)} + \frac{1 - w(\eta_0)}{1 - k w(\eta_0)}\right)$$

$$= \mathrm{Re}\left(k \frac{k\, e^{i\theta}}{1 - k\, e^{i\theta}} - \frac{k\, e^{i\theta}}{1 - e^{i\theta}} + \frac{1 - e^{i\theta}}{1 - k\, e^{i\theta}}\right)$$

$$= \left(\frac{1+k}{2}\right) f(t), \quad t = \cos\theta$$

where

$$f(t) = \frac{k(1-k) + 2(1-t)}{1 - 2kt + k^2}, \quad -1 \leq t \leq 1.$$

Since $\kappa > 0$, $0 < k = 1/(1+\kappa) < 1$ and $2 \geq 1 + \kappa$, then $2k - 1 \geq 0$. Hence,

$$f'(t) = 2(1-k) \frac{(k+1)k - 1}{(1 - 2kt + k^2)^2} \geq 2(1-k) \frac{2k - 1}{(1 - 2kt + k^2)^2} \geq 0,$$

which gives that f is a non-decreasing function and

$$f(t) \geq f(-1) = \frac{(n-1)(1-k)+4}{(1+k)^2}.$$

Hence, the previous relation shows that

$$\text{Re}\left(1 + \frac{\eta_0[\mathfrak{T}_k^{\mu,\nu}u(\eta_0)]''}{[\mathfrak{T}_k^{\mu,\nu}u(\eta_0)]'}\right) \geq \frac{(1-k)+4}{2(1+k)} \geq 1 + \frac{\kappa}{2},$$

which contradicts (26). In virtue of $|w(\eta)| < 1, \eta \in \Sigma$ then (12) shows that the argument of the theorem is occurred.

(iii) Assume that

$$\left(\frac{\eta}{[\mathfrak{T}_k^{\mu,\nu}u(\eta)]}\right)^2 [\mathfrak{T}_k^{\mu,\nu}u(\eta)]' - 1 = V(\eta). \tag{13}$$

Then $V(\eta) = d_1\eta + \cdots$ is analytic in Σ. A logarithmic differentiation implies

$$1 + \frac{\eta[\mathfrak{T}_k^{\mu,\nu}u(\eta)]''}{[\mathfrak{T}_k^{\mu,\nu}u(\eta)]'} = \frac{\eta V'(\eta)}{1+V(\eta)} + 2\frac{\eta[\mathfrak{T}_k^{\mu,\nu}u(\eta)]'}{[\mathfrak{T}_k^{\mu,\nu}u(\eta)]} - 1. \tag{14}$$

In view of (14), we obtain

$$\text{Re}\left(\frac{\eta V'(\eta)}{1+V(\eta)} + 2\frac{\eta[\mathfrak{T}_k^{\mu,\nu}u(\eta)]'}{[\mathfrak{T}_k^{\mu,\nu}u(\eta)]} - 1\right) < 1 + \frac{\kappa}{2}. \tag{15}$$

Consequently, we have

$$\frac{\eta[\mathfrak{T}_k^{\mu,\nu}u(\eta)]'}{[\mathfrak{T}_k^{\mu,\nu}u(\eta)]} \prec \frac{1-\eta}{1-k\eta},$$

where $0 < k = 1/(1+\kappa) < 1, \kappa > 0$ which yields $\text{Re}\left(\frac{\eta[\mathfrak{T}_k^{\mu,\nu}u(\eta)]'}{[\mathfrak{T}_k^{\mu,\nu}u(\eta)]}\right) > 0$. Thus, (15) presents

$$\text{Re}\left(\frac{\eta V'(\eta)}{1+V(\eta)} - 1\right) < 1 + \frac{\kappa}{2} - 2\text{Re}\left(\frac{\eta[\mathfrak{T}_k^{\mu,\nu}u(\eta)]'}{[\mathfrak{T}_k^{\mu,\nu}u(\eta)]}\right) < 1 + \frac{\kappa}{2}. \tag{16}$$

For $\eta_0 \in \Sigma$ with $|V(\zeta_0)| = 1$. According to Lemma 1, we get

$$\eta_0 V'(\eta_0) = kV(\eta_0); \quad (k \geq 1; V(\eta_0) = e^{i\theta}; \theta \in \mathbb{R}).$$

Thus,

$$\text{Re}\left(\frac{\eta_0 V'(\eta_0)}{1+V(\eta_0)} - 1\right) = \text{Re}\left(\frac{ke^{i\theta}}{1+e^{i\theta}}\right) - 1 = \frac{k}{2} - 1.$$

Hence, Re $\left(\frac{\eta_0 V'(\eta_0)}{V(\eta_0)} - 1\right) \geq 1 + \frac{\kappa}{2}$, where $k \geq 1$, which contradicts the assumption. That is $|V(\eta)| < 1, \eta \in \Sigma$. In addition, (13) shows that

$$\left|\left(\frac{\eta}{[\mathfrak{I}_k^{\mu,\nu} u(\eta)]}\right)^2 [\mathfrak{I}_k^{\mu,\nu} u(\eta)]' - 1\right| < 1, \quad \eta \in \Sigma$$

which concludes the desired assertion.

Theorem 2. *Let $\kappa \geq 0$ and*

$$\text{Re}\left(1 + \frac{\eta[\mathfrak{I}_k^{\mu,\nu} u(\eta)]''}{[\mathfrak{I}_k^{\mu,\nu} u(\eta)]'}\right) > -\kappa, \quad \eta \in \Sigma. \tag{17}$$

(i) If $k \geq 2\kappa + 3$, then $\text{Re}\left([\mathfrak{I}_k^{\mu,\nu} u(\eta)]'\right) > 0, \eta \in \Sigma$.
(ii) If $k \geq 2\kappa + 2$, and $[\mathfrak{I}_k^{\mu,\nu} u(\eta)]/\eta \neq 0$, then

$$\frac{\eta[\mathfrak{I}_k^{\mu,\nu} u(\eta)]'}{[\mathfrak{I}_k^{\mu,\nu} u(\eta)]} \prec \frac{1}{(1-\eta)}.$$

Proof. (i) Let

$$[\mathfrak{I}_k^{\mu,\nu} u(\eta)]' = \frac{1}{(1 - w(\eta))^{\frac{2(\kappa+1)}{k-1}}}, \quad k > 1 \tag{18}$$

where $0 < 2(1+\kappa)/(k-1) \leq 1$. As in the above result, $[\mathfrak{I}_k^{\mu,\nu} u(\eta)]' \neq 0$ for all $\eta \in \Sigma$, which yields $w(\eta) = b_{k-1}\eta^{k-1} + \cdots$ is analytic in Σ with $w(0) = 0$. Additionally, by (18), a logarithmic differentiation leads to

$$\left(1 + \frac{\eta[\mathfrak{I}_k^{\mu,\nu} u(\eta)]''}{[\mathfrak{I}_k^{\mu,\nu} u(\eta)]'}\right) = 1 + \frac{2(\kappa + 1)(\eta w'(\eta))}{(k-1)(1 - w(\eta))}. \tag{19}$$

Assume that $\eta_0 \in \Sigma$ is such that $\max_{|\eta| \leq |\eta_0|} |w(\eta)| = |w(\eta_0)| = 1$. Then according to Lemma 1, we have $\eta_0 w'(\eta_0) = q w(\eta_0), (q \geq k - 1; w(\eta_0) = e^{i\theta}; \theta \in \mathbb{R})$. Thus,

$$\text{Re}\left(1 + \frac{\eta_0[\mathfrak{I}_k^{\mu,\nu} u(\eta_0)]''}{[\mathfrak{I}_k^{\mu,\nu} u(\eta_0)]'}\right) = 1 + \frac{2(\kappa + 1)}{k - 1} \text{Re}\left(\frac{q e^{i\theta}}{1 - e^{i\theta}}\right)$$

$$= 1 - \frac{q(\kappa + 1)}{k - 1} \leq -\kappa,$$

which contradicts (17). That is $|w(\eta)| < 1, \eta \in \Sigma$. Also, (18) implies that

$$|\arg([\mathfrak{I}_k^{\mu,\nu} u(\eta)]')| = \frac{2(\kappa + 1)}{k - 1}|\arg((1 - w(\eta))| < \frac{2(\kappa + 1)}{k - 1}\frac{\pi}{2} \leq \frac{\pi}{2},$$

where $k \geq 2\kappa + 3$. Hence, $\text{Re}\left([\mathfrak{I}_k^{\mu,\nu} u(\eta)]'\right) > 0, \eta \in \Sigma$.

(ii) Formulate a function w by

$$\frac{\eta[\mathfrak{T}_k^{\mu,\nu}u(\eta)]'}{[\mathfrak{T}_k^{\mu,\nu}u(\eta)]} = \frac{1}{1-w(\eta)}. \tag{20}$$

Then $w(\eta) = c_{k-1}\eta^{k-1} + \ldots$ is analytic in Σ with $\max_{|\eta|\le|\eta_0|}|w(\eta)| = |w(\eta_0)| = 1$. In view of Lemma 1,

$$\eta_0 w'(\eta_0) = qw(\eta_0); \quad (q \ge k-1; w(\eta_0) = e^{i\theta}; \theta \in \mathbb{R}).$$

Thus, (20) gives

$$\mathrm{Re}\left(1 + \frac{\eta_0[\mathfrak{T}_k^{\mu,\nu}u(\eta_0)]''}{[\mathfrak{T}_k^{\mu,\nu}u(\eta_0)]'}\right) = \mathrm{Re}\left(\frac{\eta_0 w'(\eta_0)}{1-w(\eta_0)} + \frac{1}{1-w(\eta_0)}\right)$$

$$= \mathrm{Re}\left(\frac{qe^{i\theta}+1}{1-e^{i\theta}}\right) = \frac{1-q}{2} \le -\kappa,$$

where $q - 1 \ge (k-1) - 1 = k - 2 \ge (2\kappa + 2) - 2 = 2\kappa$. Which contradicts (17). Hence, $|w(\eta)| < 1, \eta \in \Sigma$. This completes the proof.

Next, we proceed to show that the $[\mathfrak{T}_k^{\mu,\nu}u(\eta)]'$ is dominated by the JSF. Let $M_{\wp_m}$ is the set of all holomorphic functions of the form $\wp(\eta) = 1 + \wp_m\eta^m + \wp_{m+1}\eta^{m+1}, \ldots, \quad \eta \in \Sigma$.

Theorem 3. *Consider the following assumptions:*

(i) $-1 \le \flat < \aleph \le 1, -1 \le \jmath < \imath \le 1,$ *and* $\Bbbk\jmath \le 0.$
(ii) $0 < \wp_1' = 2\wp_1/(\aleph - \flat) \le 2.$
(iii)

$$\left((\imath - \jmath)(1-\flat)^2 + 16\Bbbk\jmath(\aleph - \flat)\right)^2 + (\imath - \jmath)^2(1+\flat)^4(2-\wp_1')^2$$

$$\le 16\Bbbk^2(\aleph - \flat)^2 + 2(\imath - \jmath)(1+\flat)^2\left((\imath - \jmath)(1-\flat)^2 - \Bbbk\jmath(\aleph - \flat)\right)4(2-\wp_1'). \tag{21}$$

If

$$1 + \Bbbk\eta[\mathfrak{T}_k^{\mu,\nu}u(\eta)]'' \prec \frac{1+\imath\eta}{1+\jmath\eta}, \tag{22}$$

then

$$[\mathfrak{T}_k^{\mu,\nu}u(\eta)]' \in \mathbb{J}[\aleph,\flat].$$

Proof. Define $\eth : \Sigma \to \mathbb{C}$ by

$$\eth(\eta) = \frac{(\aleph - 1) + (1-\flat)[\mathfrak{T}_k^{\mu,\nu}u(\eta)]'}{(\aleph + 1) - (1+\flat)[\mathfrak{T}_k^{\mu,\nu}u(\eta)]'}, \tag{23}$$

where $[\mathfrak{T}_k^{\mu,\nu}u(\eta)]' \in \mathcal{H}_{\wp_1}$. Clearly, $\eth$ is analytic on Σ and

$$\eth(\eta) = 1 + 2\wp_1'\eta^m + \eth_{m+1}\eta^{n+1} + \cdots \in \mathcal{H}_{\wp_1'},$$

whenever $0 < \wp_1' = 2\wp_1/(\aleph - \flat) \le 2$. By (22) and (23), we have

$$\Re\left\{\frac{(\imath - \jmath)\big((1+\flat)\eth(\eta) + (1-\flat)\big)^2 + 2\Bbbk(1-\jmath)(\aleph-\flat)\eta\eth'(\eta)}{(\imath - \jmath)\big((1+\flat)\eth(\eta) + (1-\flat)\big)^2 - 2\Bbbk(1+\jmath)(\aleph-\flat)\eta\eth'(\eta)}\right\} > 0.$$

Define $\mathsf{T} : \mathbb{C}^2 \to \mathbb{C}$ by

$$\mathsf{T}(r, s) = \frac{(\imath - \jmath)\big((1+\flat)r + (1-\flat)\big)^2 + 2\Bbbk(1-\jmath)(\aleph-\flat)s}{(\imath - \jmath)\big((1+\flat)r + (1-\flat)\big)^2 - 2\alpha(1+\jmath)(\aleph-\flat)s}.$$

Then T is continuous of r and s on $\triangle =: \mathbb{C}^2 - \{(r,s) : M(r,s) = 0\}$, where

$$M(r, s) = (\imath - \jmath)\big((1+\flat)r + (1-\flat)\big)^2 - 2\alpha(1+\jmath)(\aleph-\flat)s.$$

Note that $(1,0) \in \triangle$ and $\Re(\mathsf{T}(1,0)) > 0$. Moreover, for all $(ia, b) \in \triangle$,

$$\Re\{\mathsf{T}(ia, b)\} =$$
$$\Re\left\{\frac{(\imath - \jmath)(1-\flat)^2 + 2(1-\flat^2)(\imath-\jmath)i\rho - (\imath-\jmath)(1+\flat)^2 a^2 + 2\Bbbk(1-\jmath)(\Bbbk-\flat)\flat}{(\imath - \jmath)(1-\flat)^2 + 2(1-\flat^2)(\imath-\jmath)ia - (\imath-\jmath)(1+\flat)^2 a^2 - 2\Bbbk(1+\jmath)(\aleph-\flat)\flat}\right\}.$$

Denoting by

$$x = (\imath-\jmath)(1-\flat)^2, \quad y = 2\alpha(1-\jmath)(\aleph-\flat),$$
$$z = -(\imath-\jmath)(1+\flat)^2, \quad w = 2(\imath-\jmath)(1-\flat^2), \quad v = -2\Bbbk(1+\jmath)(\aleph-\flat).$$

Then $\Re\mathsf{T}(ia, b) = \Re\{(x + \flat y + za^2 + wia)/(x + v\flat + za^2 + wia)\}$. For $\Re\mathsf{T}(ia, b) < 0$, we have to prove

$$x^2 + x(y + v)\flat + yv\flat^2 + \big(2xz + w^2 + z(y + v)\flat\big)a^2 + z^2a^4 < 0.$$

But $\flat \le -1/2$, and $\Bbbk\jmath < 0$, then, we have

$$2xz + w^2 + (y + v)z\flat \geqslant 2xz + w^2 - \frac{1}{2}(y + v)c$$
$$= 2(\imath-\jmath)(1+\flat)^2\big((\imath-\jmath)(1-\flat)^2 - \Bbbk\jmath(\Bbbk-\flat)\big) > 0. \quad (24)$$

In addition, we have $a^2 \le -\big(\frac{2(2+\wp_1')\flat}{(2+\wp_1')+(2-\wp_1')} + 1\big)$, where $\wp_1' = 2\wp/(\Bbbk-\flat)$; thus if (24) holds, then we get

$$x^2 + x(y + v)\flat + yv\flat^2 + \big(2xz + w^2 + (y + v)z\flat\big)a^2 + z^2a^4$$
$$\le \left(yv - \frac{2(2+\wp_1')(y+v)z}{(2+\wp_1')+(2-\wp_1')} + \frac{4(2+\wp_1')^2z^2}{\big((2+\wp_1')+(2-\wp_1')\big)^2}\right)\flat^2$$
$$+ \left((x-z)(y+v) + (2xz+w^2)\right)\left(\frac{-2(2+\wp_1')}{(2+\wp_1')+(2-\wp_1')}\right)$$
$$+ \frac{4(2+\wp_1')z^2}{(2+\wp_1')+(2-\wp_1')}\right)\flat + \big(x^2 - 2xz - w^2 + z^2\big). \quad (25)$$

According to (25) when $\ell(b) =: rb^2 + sb + t$, where

$$r = yv - \frac{2(2 + \wp_1')(y + v)z}{(2 + \wp_1') + (2 - \wp_1')} + \frac{4(2 + \wp_1')^2 z^2}{\left((2 + \wp_1') + (2 - \wp_1')\right)^2},$$

$$s = (x - z)(y + v) + (2xz + w^2)\left(\frac{-2(2 + \wp_1')}{(2 + \wp_1') + (2 - \wp_1')}\right) + \frac{4(2 + \wp_1')z^2}{(2 + \wp_1') + (2 - \wp_1')},$$

$$t = x^2 + z(z - 2x) - w^2.$$

In view of the relation

$$\ell(b) \leq \max_{b \leq -\frac{1}{2}} \ell(b) = \frac{4t - 2s + r}{4}, \tag{26}$$

we have $\max_{\sigma \leq -\frac{1}{2}} \ell(b) \leq 0$ is equivalent to

$$
\begin{aligned}
4t - 2s + r = {}& \left(4x^2 + yv - 2x(y + v)\right)\left((2 + \wp_1') + (2 - \wp_1')\right)^2 \\
& - 2\left(2w^2 + 4xz - (y + v)z\right)\left((2 + \wp_1') + (2 - \wp_1')\right)(2 - \wp_1') \\
& + 4z^2\left(2 - \wp_1'\right)^2 \leq 0.
\end{aligned}
$$

Replacing x, y, z, w and v in above formula, we get

$$
\begin{aligned}
\ell(b) \leq {}& 4\left(\left((\imath - \jmath)(1 - \flat)^2 + \alpha\jmath(\aleph - \flat)\right)^2 - 16\Bbbk^2(\aleph - \flat)^2\right) + 4(\imath - \jmath)^2(1 + \flat)^4(2 - \wp_1') \\
& - 8(\imath - \jmath)(1 + \flat)^2\left((\imath - \jmath)(1 - \flat)^2 - \Bbbk\jmath(\aleph - \flat)\right)4(2 - \wp_1') \leq 0.
\end{aligned}
$$

If inequality (21) occurs, then this yields that $\top(r, s)$ achieves the conditions of Lemma 2, which ends the proof.

5   Conclusion

In a complex domain, an extension of the Tremblay differential operator is derived using the k−symbol fractional calculus. This operator is used to look at the analytical solutions of fractional differential equation. Our strategy is founded on a number of concepts, including Jack Lemma, subordination, and superordination. Some of the geometric properties are investigated and explored for the normalized operator, such as univalency and convexity. The bounded turning property is also studied to provide an analytic solution of a class of fractional differential equations, using the expression $[\mathfrak{T}_k^{\mu,\nu} u(\eta)]'$. Our last result is about the upper bound of the expression in terms of the Janowski starlike functions

$$[\mathfrak{T}_k^{\mu,\nu} u(\eta)]' \prec \frac{1 + \aleph\eta}{1 + \flat\eta}, \quad \eta \in \Sigma.$$

References

1. Tremblay, R.: Some operational formulas involving the operators xD, xΔ and fractional derivatives. SIAM J. Math. Anal. **10**(5), 933–943 (1979)
2. Ibrahim, R.W., Jahangiri, J.M.: Boundary fractional differential equation in a complex domain. Bound. Value Probl. **2014**(1), 1–11 (2014). https://doi.org/10.1186/1687-2770-2014-66
3. Irmak, H.: Characterizations of some fractional-order operators in complex domains and their extensive implications to certain analytic functions. Ann. Univ. Craiova-Math. Comput. Sci. Ser. **48**(2), 349–357 (2021)
4. Diaz, R., Pariguan, E.: On hypergeometric functions and pochhammer k-symbol. Divulgaciones Matemticas **15**, 179–192 (2007)
5. Suthar, D., Baleanu, D., Purohit, S., Ucar, F.: Certain k-fractional calculus operators and image formulas of k-Struve function. AIMS Math. **5**(3) (2020)
6. Singh, Y., Dubey, R.S.: Fractional calculus operator with generalize k-Mittag-Leffler function. J. Interdisc. Math. **23**(2), 545–553 (2020)
7. Ibrahim, R.W.: K-symbol fractional order discrete-time models of Lozi system. J. Differ. Equat. Appl. 1–20 (2022)
8. Hadid, S.B., Ibrahim, R.W.: Geometric study of 2D-wave equations in view of k-symbol airy functions. Axioms **11**(11), 590 (2022)
9. Tassaddiq, A.: A new representation of the k-gamma functions. Mathematics **7**(2), 133 (2019)
10. Yadav, A., Mathur, T., Agarwal, S., Yadav, B.: Fractional boundary value problem in complex domain. J. Math. Anal. Appl. 127178 (2023)
11. Foukrach, D., Meftah, B.: Some new generalized result of Gronwall-Bellman-Bihari type inequality with some singularity. Filomat **34**(10), 3299–3310 (2020)
12. Rahman, G., Nisar, K.S., Ghaffar, A., Qi, F.: Some inequalities of the Gruss type for conformable k-fractional integral operators. Revista de la Real Academia de Ciencias Exactas, Fisicas y Naturales. Serie A. Matematicas **114**(1), 1–9 (2020)
13. Zhao, S., Butt, S.I., Nazeer, W., Nasir, J., Umar, M., Liu, Y.: Some Hermite-Jensen-Mercer type inequalities for k-Caputo-fractional derivatives and related results. Adv. Differ. Equat. **2020**(1), 1–17 (2020)
14. Ibrahim, R.W.: Normalized symmetric differential operators in the open unit disk. In: Daras, N.J., Rassias, T.M. (eds.) Approximation and Computation in Science and Engineering. SOIA, vol. 180, pp. 417–434. Springer, Cham (2022). https://doi.org/10.1007/978-3-030-84122-5_22
15. Hadid, S.B., Ibrahim, R.W., Momani, S.: A new measure of quantum Starlike functions connected with Julia functions. J. Funct. Spaces **2022** (2022)
16. Miller, S.S., Mocanu, P.T.: Differential Subordinations. Marcel Decker Inc., New York. Basel (2000)
17. Umezawa, T.: On the theory of univalent functions. Tohoku Math. J. Second Series **7**(3), 212–228 (1955)
18. Ali, R.M., Nagpal, S., Ravichandran, V.: Second-order differential subordination for analytic functions with fixed initial coefficient. Bull. Malays. Math. Sci. Soc. (2) **34**, 611–629 (2011)

A Computational Content Analysis on Representation in Mental Health News Media with Global Perspectives

Ahu Dereli Dursun$^{(\boxtimes)}$ (iD)

Institute of Social Sciences, Communication Studies, Istanbul Bilgi University, Istanbul, Türkiye
`ahu.dereli.dursun@bilgiedu.net, ahudereli@yahoo.com`

Abstract. Media representations can provide important symbolic resources in the construction of perception and agendas in diverse domains particularly concerning public health and social awareness. In view of this standpoint, dominant media frames are said to be powerful in defining social problems and shaping public discourses. The majority of the relevant literature demonstrates that representations of people with mental disorder are often negative, individuals being depicted in a passive role. A grammatical analysis of language use in press reveals different perspectives regarding the assignment of a more or less prominent role. The use of active and passive verb voice is one constituent of such analysis. Framing process constitutes another mode of analysis of news media content, which is stated to be dynamic in the concept of communication. Accordingly, this study aims to provide insights into the representation of individuals that experience mental health problems. For this purpose, newspaper stories are analyzed by examining the volume and content of a sample of selected news stories on mental illness in Türkiye for a time period of six years. Six national daily newspapers make up the sample of the study which provides a content analysis on the news media dataset. The analysis results demonstrate statistical findings on the depiction of people with mental disorder. Based on the findings and considering the sensitivity of the issue, it can be noted that more emphasis can be placed on humanizing mental illness by indicating that mental disorder is real, common and possible to be treated. In addition, coverage of other success stories with positive frames can be an alternative way to balance the multitude of news stories that link mental illness with violence or other negative elements.

Keywords: Computational content analysis · News frames · Journalistic news media · Categorical level of representation · Degree of agency · Mental health news · Public discourses · Computational journalism · Computational linguistics · Computational and multi-way frequency analysis · Systematic language description · Grammatical analyses

Supported by organization x.

1   Introduction

The news media are known to have an influential role in shaping public attitudes regarding a wide range of issues including health. Mental health and mental disorders are stated to stand worldwide as one of the most stigmatized of all human conditions [1]. This statement is regarded as an alarming one particularly when the challenges experienced by numerous individuals within this particular group of representing themselves are considered [2]. Even though there has been a shift in the recent years towards improved advocacy, more 'voice' being developed and greater social awareness pertaining to people that experience mental health problems as a result of campaigns and initiatives upholding positive mental health messages and challenging some commonly misrepresentations and commonly held myths [2], negative representation of mental illness continues and people with mental illness belong to the groups subject to thoughtless labeling. Negative aspects and assumptions get reinforced continuously as a result of such processes that reveal the insidious and perpetuating nature of stigma [3].

Language is able to construct meanings and maintain the dialogue among participants, allowing them to build up a culture of shared understandings and interpret the world more or less in the same ways. This is because language, in which written words sounds, objects and so forth, operates as a representational system by representing the concepts, feelings and ideas in a culture to other people, and thus, representation through language, which is one of the media, is considered to be central to the processes through which meaning is produced [4]. Frames, as alternative ways of defining issues related to social and political world, are parts of journalistic norms, social movements and political arguments [5]. Despite variations of definitions of news frames on theoretical and empirical dimensions, they are generally viewed as devices for seeing the world in a certain way and making sense of the complicated nature thereof [6]. The frames of meaning, constituting the mainstays of the construction process of social reality, are called cognitive schemas one hand acting as available templates for interpretation of people, facts and events. On the other hand, frames are said to yield a mechanism allowing the storage of realities in our minds so that they can be retrieved when needed. It is this mechanism which contains the reality focusing on a certain frame and excluding the other realities [7]. Considering these elements and mechanisms, frame building and frame setting are included in framing process, which is stated to be dynamic in the concept of communication.

Content analysis, as one of the most significant research techniques in social sciences, acknowledges that society is enacted in texts, talk and other modalities of communication, and hence, without understanding the way language operates in the social world, it will not be possible to understand social phenomena. In that regard, data at stake cannot be treated as physical events, but rather as communications formed and disseminated to be read, seen, interpreted, enacted and reflected on based upon the meanings on the side of the recipients. One aspect that differentiates content analysis from other empirical methods of inquiry is that the communications are interpreted as texts in their social uses. In natural sciences, in contrast, investigative methods are seldom slanted towards contents, meanings, communications, references and intentions [8].

In social science research, computer-based methods of analysis have been in the upward trend with the advent of common computing facilities, which have made varying types of content such newspaper articles, medical records, answers to open-ended questions possible to be a subject to systematic analysis of textual data. Thereby, the input can be analyzed in terms of frequencies and coded into categories to draw on inferences owing to the opportunity of having such contents of communication available in the form of machine readable texts. While computer-assisted analysis can facilitate with volumes electronic data sets by reducing time burden and eliminating the need for multiple human coders to establish inter-coder reliability, it is still important that human coders be employed for purposes of content analysis due to the fact that they are can pull out latent and/or nuanced meanings in a particular text, which is verified by the study that demonstrated the outcome of human coders being able to evaluate a broader array and to make inferences from latent meanings [9]. Likewise, this point of caution related to the harnessing of computational techniques is also stated by Walter and Ophir who point out that the interpretation of findings still requires a qualitative analysis by experts in the related field of interest even if the computer-assisted approach/method can automatically identify frame elements and packages [10]. Krippendorff also discusses related limitations related to computer applications while he acknowledges the fact that the use of computers has revolutionized the manipulation of texts in ways that are attractive to content analysts who can, thereby, circumvent the burden in manual data handling and eliminate instances of unreliable coding owing to the capability of computers as tools for processing large volumes of textual data [8]. By applying logical or algebraic operations to the internal representations of data, entered as inputs, computers produce new representations [8].

Across this strand, as the growth of news media in the context of rapid technological change has brought about certain novelties in methods, so has computational content analysis proved to be a convenient, robust and reliable tool. Accordingly, computational content analysis has enabled the application of computational methods related to the extraction of content features from digital texts as well as images. Other than the technical affordances, computational content analysis as a method, has lent itself to gaining knowledge on both current and historical social issues through analyzing observations of media messages and communication. Some of the computational content analysis techniques which are most frequently employed within the social sciences are natural language processing (NLP) and computer vision owing to their connection to artificial intelligence (AI) and machine learning. A study in light of these developments with a focus of objective understanding of media content provides a review of representative methodologies and algorithms, tools as well as systems that advance the area of human-centered media understanding by means of machine intelligence to enable detailed and nuanced characterization of media content and to help understand its effect extending from individual experiences to behavioral, cultural and societal inclinations to commercial consequences. The study also puts forth the importance of text mining and natural language processing (NLP) to ensure a nuanced understanding of language use as well as spoken interactions in media to be able to track trends and patterns across different contexts [11]. A another study demonstrates the applicability of a new method concerned with inductive identification and measurement of media frames in complex and large corpora by unsupervised machine learning techniques. Apart from reducing bias and costs of earlier methods, the authors prove the benefit of integrating a novel computational tool with established theoretical perspectives to improve the understanding of social phenomena [10].

In tandem with the developments of computing technologies, content analysis, as a technique with initially journalistic roots, has also evolved into a stock of research methods that have the potential to derive inferences from all sorts of communication data whether they be verbal, pictorial and symbolic. Currently, its growth is said to be exponential, mainly as a result of the computers' widespread uses in different types of text processing [8]. The present study aims at providing a different perspective in news media content analysis around the issue of the representation of individuals that experience mental health problems through grammatical analysis of voice of verbs and the frame of personalization to shed light on some nuances by means of a computational application approach.

2 Material and Methods

2.1 Dynamic Media News Dataset

The newspaper items on the themes of mental health and mental illness, with key words that include mental health, mental distress, mental disorder, mental illness, depression, depressive, bipolar disorder and affective disorder, printed between 2014 and 2019 in six daily newspapers in Türkiye (*Hürriyet, Sabah, Milliyet, Sözcü, Cumhuriyet* and *Posta*), which are accessible via electronic means, constitute the dataset handled in this study. The total number of news items amounts to 725 (*Hürriyet* (n = 218), *Sabah* (n = 168), *Milliyet* (n = 158), *Sözcü* (n = 110), *Cumhuriyet* (n = 38) and *Posta* (n = 33)) with Hürriyet having the highest circulation rate (185.655) followed by *Sabah* (179.341), *Sözcü* (153.773) and *Milliyet* (121.754) while *Posta* ranking sixth with a circulation rate of 105.003 [12]. Even though *Cumhuriyet* does not have a high circulation in the country, it is a newspaper whose audience is known to have a high educational level. The focus on the news items in this study is on representation of people with mental disorder and grammatical language analysis of active/passive voice use in their depiction. The dataset belongs to the dissertation thesis entitled "News Media Portrayal of Mental Health and Psychological Problems: An Analysis of Daily Newspapers in Turkey". Table 1 presents the number of news items covered in the aforementioned six newspapers.

Table 1. The number of news items by newspapers.

Name of the newspaper	The total number of news items (N = 725)
Hürriyet	218
Sabah	168
Milliyet	158
Sözcü	110
Cumhuriyet	38
Posta	33

2.2 Methods

Computational and Statistical Dynamic Models with Real-Time Mental Health-Related News

Dynamic processes both deterministic and stochastic can serve as tools to provide answers to different questions. Likewise, dynamic models, as simplified representations of real-world entities, expressed in equations or computer codes aim at mimicking some of the needed features of the system in question while leaving out the inessential ones. The reason why these models are called 'dynamic' is owing to their description of the change system properties show over time. They are useful in the process of model formulation, analysis and deriving conclusions therefrom. formulating models, analyzing them, and drawing conclusions [13]. Such models enable the examination of relationships that cannot be handled based on only experimental methods and projections that would not be possible to make by the extrapolation of data; therefore, their usefulness is evident. In addition to these advantageous points, computational modeling has become another approach set in context that can enable the integration of diverse sources of data to test the probability of working hypotheses and bringing about novel ones, while statistical models are directed towards the proving of null hypothesis. Whereas outputs of statistical models are fed into computational models, outputs from computational models can yield more empirical data collection and further statistical models. In short, this kind of a systems science methodology elicits a set of innovative approaches so that intricate problems in social science, behavioral science and public health research can be addressed [14]. The ultimate goal is to serve a deeper understanding of the problem and its possible solutions.

Figure 1 provides a visual illustration of this complementary approach in the context of mental health news via a Computational frame and news media content analysis.

Accordingly, multi-way frequency analysis is considered to be an appropriate means of analysis in the case when the objective of the research is to determine whether a statistically significant relationship among three or more discrete variables exists. Another point about this kind of frequency analysis is related to its

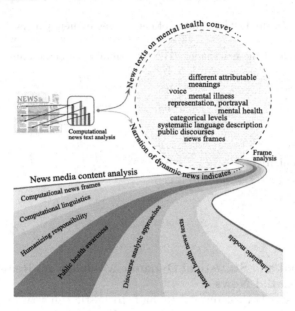

Fig. 1. Computational frame and news media content analysis.

use when all variables are considered variables of interest and none of the variables in the analysis are dependent variables [15]. If the calculated X^2 value is larger than the critical value, given the degrees of freedom and alpha value, statistical significance is stated to exist, and the following equations are employed to calculate the related degrees of freedom:

$(r - 1)(s - 1)(p - 1)$, where

$r=$ number of levels variable X

$s=$ number of levels variable Y

$p=$ number of levels variable Z [15]

The related analyses and depictions were carried out by Matlab [16].

3   Experimental Results and Discussion

Grammatical analysis of language use in media news texts can reveal the perspectives of the newspapers or journalists. Sentence syntax conveys the participants' semantic roles in an event by relational functions such as subject or object or the use of active or passive voice [17]. Consequently, when active voice is used the subject in the sentence has a prominent role, when passive voice is used, the agent is assigned a less prominent role. In addition, the issue of disempowerment also comes to the picture when health experts are conferred grammatical agency through the use of active voice, whereas individuals with mental illness are deprived of this kind of agency by the use of passive voice [18].

The dataset analyzed based on this grammatical device of active and passive forms has revealed that individuals that have mental disorder are represented by active voice in 524 of the news items and by passive voice in 393 of the news items. Table 2 provides the breakdown of this linguistic aspect by newspapers, while Fig. 2 and Fig. 3 show the histogram depictions by newspapers and over the six-year time period, respectively.

Table 2. The breakdown of this linguistic aspect by newspapers.

Name of the newspaper	The number of news stories with active voice used for the representation of the individual through active voice (N = 393)
Hürriyet	137
Sabah	98
Milliyet	73
Sözcü	50
Cumhuriyet	24
Posta	11

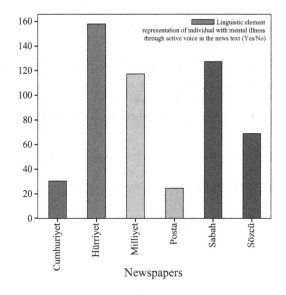

Fig. 2. Histogram depiction of the use of active voice in the representation of individuals in the news items analyzed.

Entman identified five popular ways for framing news stories, which are conflict, human interest/personalization, consequence, morality and responsibility [19]. Based on this point of view, this study provides the human interest/personalization element with the frame of the success story of the people with mental illness in the news items analyzed. Out of the total 725 news items, only 43 (13.79%) of the stories mention a success element, which indicates an insignificant percentage. A very similar percentage of finding was revealed in a study

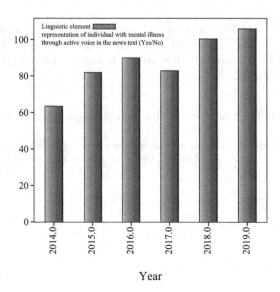

Fig. 3. Histogram depiction of stories with success content.

by [20] which found out that only 14% of the news stories provided a description of treatment or recovery from mental illness.

Table 3 shows the breakdown of the success stories by newspapers and Fig. 1 provides the histogram depiction of the success stories by newspapers analyzed.

Table 3. The breakdown of the success stories by newspapers.

Name of the newspaper	The number of news stories with success content (N = 43)
Hürriyet	17
Sabah	12
Milliyet	9
Sözcü	1
Cumhuriyet	-
Posta	4

Figure 4 provides the histogram depictions of stories with success content in the news items analyzed.

The success stories are mostly on recovery from mental illness, which is a process of change through which the individuals improve their health and well-being, and struggle against the mental disorder, which is a step towards living a self-directed life following the striving of reaching their potential. The subsequent related themes are integration into social life by finding a job, philanthropic acts

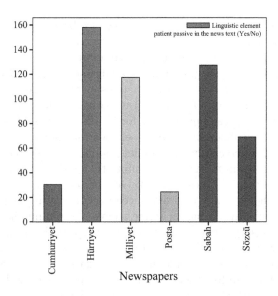

Fig. 4. Histogram depiction of the use of active voice in the representation of individuals in the news items analyzed over the six-year period.

like doing voluntary work, educating others and helping their community (i.e. donation of organs), conforming to socially accepted norms like getting married and engaging in creative activities like producing work of art (handcrafts, acting on stage, making a music album, composing music and writing poems). Compatibly, reporting stories of systemic issues around the topic of mental illness by giving place to the profiles of people with a mental illness who have become a part of their community and leading satisfactory lives with fulfilling relationships corresponds to positive framing with personalization type. Despite making up a relatively smaller proportion of the entire news coverage, an emphasis on the success stories with positive frames through the favorable developments in the lives of those who have mental illness fits within the recommendations of some mental health and media initiatives as well as related councils [21].

4   Conclusion and Future Directions

A subtle change in language may pinpoint a change in perspective as well since language is a critical tool of meaning and interpretation. Grammatical analysis of language use in news media texts reveal the perspectives of the newspapers or journalists. The linguistic aspect of verb voice, namely the use of active or passive constructions, in sentence syntax conveys the participants' semantic roles in an event by relational functions such as subject or object. When individuals with mental health problems are situated in the same news context with the health experts, the issue of disempowerment arises when health experts are conferred grammatical agency through the use of active voice, whereas individuals with mental illness are deprived of this kind of agency by the use of passive voice. Even though the number of news stories analyzed in this study has shown a higher number in active voice construction compared to passive voice, this level of agency and instrument of grammatical analysis can be paid more attention in terms of reporting and journalistic practices in the future. The second point of analysis, namely framing of news stories, rests on the conceptualization of Entman who identified five popular ways for framing news stories. Among these, human interest/personalization has been selected for the analysis of the dataset. Despite indicating a percentage that is not significant, the inclusion of success stories like recovery from the treatment hints that a diagnosis of mental illness is not forever, and mental illness is treatable with recovery being possible. In a parallel fashion, the coverage of other success stories with positive frames like integration into social life, being an active member of community and maintaining positive relationships, as indicated in the dataset analyzed in this study, can be one alternative way to balance the preponderance of news stories that link mental illness with violence or that include sensational and exaggerated dramatic elements. Such shifts in news content and coverage, with a humanizing global perspective, with the changing face of newspaper representations of those with mental illness, can spark a wealth of movement towards fostering a new culture of positive change, acceptance, reducing misconceptions and prevention of social exclusion, which will benefit broader society in the long run.

References

1. Bloch, S., Singh, B.: Understanding Troubled Minds: A Guide to Mental Illness and its Treatment. Melbourne University Press, Melbourne (1997)
2. Morris, G.: Mental Health Issues And The Media: An Introduction For Health Professionals. Routledge, Abingdon-on-Thames (2006)
3. Wahl, O.: Media Madness: Public Images of Mental Illness. Rutgers University Press, New Brunswick (1995)
4. Hall, S.: The Work of Representation. In Representation: Cultural Representations and Signifying Practices, pp. 13–74. Sage (1997)
5. De Vreese, C.H.: News framing: theory and typology. Inf. Des. J.+ Doc. Des. **13**(1), 51–62 (2005)
6. Balabanova, E.: The Media and Human Rights: The Cosmopolitan Promise. Routledge, Abingdon-on-Thames (2014)
7. Goffman, E.: Frame Analysis: An Essay on the Organization of Experience. Harvard University Press, Cambridge (1974)
8. Krippendorff, K.: Content Analysis: An Introduction to its Methodology, pp. 215–276. Sage publications, Thousand Oaks (2018)
9. Conway, M.: The subjective precision of computers: a methodological comparison with human coding in content analysis. Journalism Mass Commun. Q. **83**(1), 186–200 (2006)
10. Walter, D., Ophir, Y.: News frame analysis: an inductive mixed-method computational approach. Commun. Methods Meas. **13**(4), 248–266 (2019)
11. Somandepalli, K., Guha, T., Martinez, V.R., Kumar, N., Adam, H., Narayanan, S.: Computational media intelligence: human-centered machine analysis of media. Proc. IEEE **109**(5), 891–910 (2021)

12. Gazeteler. https://www.gazeteler.tv/tiraj_raporu.php. Accessed 9 Apr 2022
13. Assets. http://assets.press.princeton.edu/chapters/s8124.pdf. Accessed 5 Mar 2023
14. Mabry, P.L., Hammond, R., Ip, E.H.-S., Huang, T.T.-K.: Computational and statistical models: a comparison for policy modeling of childhood obesity. In: Salerno, J., Yang, S.J., Nau, D., Chai, S.-K. (eds.) SBP 2011. LNCS, vol. 6589, pp. 87–88. Springer, Heidelberg (2011). https://doi.org/10.1007/978-3-642-19656-0_14
15. Tabachnick, B.G., Fidell, L.S.: Using Multivariate Statistics, 6th edn. Pearson, Boston (2012)
16. MATLAB, version 9.12.0 (R2022a): The Math-Works Inc., Natick, Massachusetts (2022)
17. Van Dijk, T. A.: News analysis. Case Studies of International and National News in the Press. New Jersey: Lawrence (1988)
18. Rowe, R., Tilbury, F., Rapley, M., O'Ferrall, I.: About a year before the breakdown i was having symptoms': sadness, pathology and the Australian newspaper media. Soc. Health and Mental Illness **25**, 680–696 (2003)
19. Entman, R.M.: Framing US coverage of international news: contrast in narratives of KAL and Iran AirIncidents. J. Commun. **41**(4), 6–27 (1991)
20. McGinty, E.E., Kennedy-Hendricks, A., Choksy, S., Barry, C.L.: Trends in news media coverage of mental illness in the United States: 19952014. Health Aff. **35**(6), 1121–1129 (2016)
21. TEAM Up.: Style guide: Reporting on mental health. Entertainment (2012)

A Simple Implementation of an Entangler Circuit by Using Quantum Linear Optics

Marco Simonetti[1,2]([✉]) [iD], Damiano Perri[1,2] [iD], and Osvaldo Gervasi[2] [iD]

[1] Department of Mathematics and Computer Science, University of Florence,
Florence, Italy
[2] Department of Mathematics and Computer Science, University of Perugia,
Perugia, Italy
m.simonetti@unifi.it

Abstract. The topic of quantum computing is one that is expanding quickly and has the potential to completely change how some difficult problems can be resolved. In recent years, there has been considerable advancement in the research and application of quantum computing technologies. The use of this technology to address challenging or impractical tasks for conventional computers is an area of ongoing research.

By creating an optical entangler, a quantum-helpful circuit for generating pairs of intensely entangled states, which are useful in numerous applications including quantum teleportation, quantum dense coding, and quantum error correction, this work has demonstrated a potential application of these technologies. Although the Optical Dual Rail Mode has shown to be extremely helpful for scaling up optical quantum circuits, there are still many obstacles and issues that need to be resolved before it can be widely applied in quantum computing.

Keywords: Quantum Computing · Optical Quantum Processing Unit · Entangler · Dual Rail Mode

1 Introduction

Photon chips are one of the most promising platforms for quantum computing. They have several advantages over other physical systems, such as ions or superconducting qubits, that make them particularly suitable for specific quantum computing tasks. Photons' inherent ability to travel long distances without significant loss of coherence is an important advantage. That makes them ideal for use in quantum communication, where quantum information is transmitted over large distances through optical fibres or free-space channels. Photons are already a well-established technology for quantum communication, with several commercial applications such as quantum key distribution and secure transmission. Another benefit of photons is their ability to be manipulated using linear optical devices such as beam splitters, phase shifters, and polarizers.

O. Gervasi et al. (Eds.): ICCSA 2023 Workshops, LNCS 14104, pp. 116–129, 2023.
https://doi.org/10.1007/978-3-031-37105-9_9

The main difficulty in using photons for quantum computing is their lack of strong interactions with each other. So, to perform entangling operations between two photons, it is necessary to use a non-linear optical element, which is typically weak and hard to control. However, recent advances in materials science have led to the development of new types of non-linear optical materials, such as diamond nitrogen-vacancy centres that can be used to implement high-fidelity two-qubit gates between photons. Another challenge to performing quantum computation with photons is the problem of detecting single photons with high efficiency: it is necessary to detect individual photons with high efficiency reliably. Several technologies for photon detection exist, including single-photon avalanche photodiodes (SPADs) and transition-edge sensors (TESs), but each has its strengths and weaknesses. However, the use of photons in quantum computing has already led to several impressive demonstrations of quantum algorithms, including reduced and simplified versions of Shor's algorithm for factoring large numbers and Grover's algorithm for database search or some applications in Machine Learning.

A Discrete Variable quantum circuit may be implemented using an optical circuit. There are several alternative encodings, such as *spatial modes encoding* and *polarisation modes encoding*. Each qubit in a quantum circuit has a pair of spatial qumodes when using spatial modes encoding. One photon in one of the spatial modes corresponds to each qubit state in a Fock state[1]: so, the quantum state $|0\rangle$ can be encoded as $|1, 0\rangle$ in spatial mode, where one photon is in the first qumode, and no photons are in the second one; consequently, the quantum state $|1\rangle$ can be encoded as $|0, 1\rangle$. This model is called *Dual Rail Mode*.

In other words, two spatial modes are used to represent each qubit, with one mode corresponding to the logical 0-state (0_L) and the other mode corresponding to the logical 1-state (1_L). The qubit state is then encoded as a superposition of the two spatial modes, with the relative amplitudes of the modes determining the probability of measuring the qubit in the 0 or 1 state [1].

The uses of Quantum Computing, even if the technology is still in its infancy, are remarkable: they have the potential to revolutionize fields such as cryptography, drug discovery, financial modeling, weather forecasting, and optimization problems in logistics and transportation, among others [2–4]. Quantum computers can solve certain complex problems exponentially faster than classical computers, which makes them promising for tasks that require significant computing power [5]. Additionally, quantum computing can enable the development of new technologies such as quantum sensing and quantum communication, which could

---

[1] The Fock space is a mathematical construction used to describe the quantum states of a system of identical particles, such as electrons, photons, or atoms. It is a Hilbert space that is built up from a vacuum state, which represents the absence of any particles, and a set of creation and annihilation operators, which create and destroy particles. The Fock space is a powerful tool for calculating the probabilities of different quantum states of a system of identical particles.

have significant implications for various industries. While quantum computing is still in its early stages, its potential applications and impact are vast and exciting to consider.

2 Related Works

One of the topics that contributed to the development of quantum computing based on optical properties is the *Quantum Optical Linear Circuit* (QOLC), which is a linear optical circuit that is used to manipulate quantum states of light [6–8]. It is composed of passive linear optical elements, such as beam splitters and phase shifters, and single-photon detectors. The beam splitter and the phase shifter can be described mathematically through a unitary Gaussian matrix. The main components of a QOLC are:

- **Input port**: it is a physical port where the quantum state of light is introduced into the circuit. The input port can be a single-mode or multi-mode fibre, depending on the application; it must be designed to minimise losses and maintain the coherence of the quantum state. A *single photon source* is always present upstream of the input port. During its propagation within the quantum circuit, its distribution wave is processed to enable computation. Single photon sources are defined by specifying parameters such as *brightness*, *purity* or *indistinguishability* [9–11]. The model that describes a single photon source is the perfect/imperfect quantum-dot-based single-photon source obtained by a statistical combination of Fock states.
- **Phase shifters**: they are passive linear optical elements that change the phase of a beam of light. Phase shifters are used to adjust the photon's phase to create interference patterns and manipulate the quantum state of light.
- **Beam splitters**: they are passive linear optical elements that split a beam of light into two or more beams. They are used to separate and recombine photons. By adjusting the reflectivity and transmissivity of the beam splitter, interference patterns can be created to manipulate the quantum state of light. In certain encoding forms, such as Single Photon Mode, they are also used to produce entangled states, a critical resource for quantum communication and quantum computing.
- **Detectors**: they detect the photons that exit the circuit. Single-photon detectors are typically used in QOLC, as they can detect individual photons. They must also be designed to maximise detection efficiency and minimise noise.

The results obtained from the circuit are filtered and sampled according to the methods of Boson Sampling [12–15]. Thanks to VR and Cloud technology advancements [16–21], researchers now have access to valuable resources that allow them to study and gain a deeper understanding of quantum phenomena. They can also experiment and test their ideas on remote platforms that use real quantum processors.

3   The Entangler Circuit in Dual Rail Mode

A quantum optical spatial dual rail circuit is a type of quantum circuit that operates on photons using a spatial encoding scheme called dual-rail encoding. This scheme divides a single photon into two separate spatial modes: the *signal* and *idler* modes. These two modes can be considered two separate paths. The dual rail encoding scheme helps to perform quantum computations because it allows for the encoding of quantum information in a robust way against certain types of errors. For example, the dual rail encoding can be used to encode a qubit, where the presence or absence of a photon in the signal mode represents the logical state $|0\rangle_L$, and the presence or absence of a photon in the idler mode means the logical state $|1\rangle_L$.

So, in this specific case, the state $|1,0\rangle$ has been chosen for logic state $|0\rangle_L$ and the state $|0,1\rangle$ for logic state $|1\rangle_L$. In this work, we present the circuit implementation of an Entangler (Fig. 1, Eq. 1), helpful in generating Bell's states [22–24].

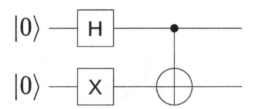

Fig. 1. Entangler Circuit

$$
\begin{aligned}
|\psi_{out}\rangle &= CX \cdot (H \otimes X) \cdot |00\rangle = \\
&= (|0\rangle\langle0| \otimes \mathbb{I} + |1\rangle\langle1| \otimes X) \cdot (H \otimes X) \cdot |00\rangle = \\
&= (|0\rangle\langle0| \otimes \mathbb{I} + |1\rangle\langle1| \otimes X) \cdot (H \otimes X) \cdot (|0\rangle \otimes |0\rangle) = \\
&= (|0\rangle\langle0| \otimes \mathbb{I} + |1\rangle\langle1| \otimes X) \cdot (H|0\rangle \otimes X|0\rangle) = \\
&= (|0\rangle\langle0| \otimes \mathbb{I} + |1\rangle\langle1| \otimes X) \cdot \frac{1}{\sqrt{2}}((|0\rangle + |1\rangle) \otimes |1\rangle) = \\
&= \frac{1}{\sqrt{2}}(|0\rangle \langle0|0\rangle + |0\rangle \langle0|1\rangle) \otimes (\mathbb{I}|1\rangle) + \\
&+ \frac{1}{\sqrt{2}}(|1\rangle \langle1|0\rangle + |1\rangle \langle1|1\rangle) \otimes (X|1\rangle) = \\
&= \frac{1}{\sqrt{2}}(|0\rangle \otimes |1\rangle) + \frac{1}{\sqrt{2}}(|1\rangle \otimes |0\rangle) = \frac{1}{\sqrt{2}}|01\rangle + \frac{1}{\sqrt{2}}|10\rangle
\end{aligned}
\tag{1}
$$

The first stage of the entangler, i.e. $H \otimes X$, can be implemented as in Fig. 2, having got their equivalent representation utilising a beam splitter and four phase shifters to constitute gates H and X; that is possible employing some unit matrix decomposition schemes [25–28]. This section will present the circuit implementation of an Entangler [29–32] using linear quantum optics. The circuit was built and tested with the Perceval software[2] [33], and the results obtained were later compared with the outcome got from a true quantum optical computer in the cloud, Quandela Cloud[3]. Consequently, for displaying the various gates in the circuit, the graphical and mathematical conventions given by the software are followed[4].

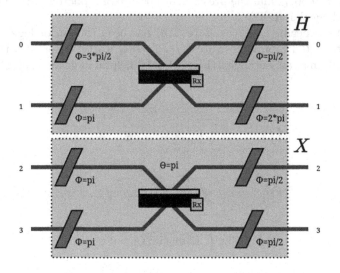

Fig. 2. Optical equivalent gates: H (in pink) and X (in green) (Color figure online)

Relating to the implementation of CNOT, it is essential to empathise that, in dual-rail encoding, deterministic two-qubit gates are impossible, and a chance of failure always exists. This nonsuccess can be detected in two ways: by using additional photons, known as *ancillas*, that are measured independently from the information photons to determine if the gate was successful on the information qubits (these gates are known as *heralded*); or by directly measuring the information qubits and assessing whether the gate was successful based on the result (these gates are known as *postselected*). The CNOT gate operates on two qubits (two couples of modes), a *control* and a *target*, and inverts the value of the target if the control qubit is in the logical state $|1\rangle_L$. Two types of CNOT gates occur most in the literature: the **postselected CNOT** of Ralph [34] and the **heralded CNOT** of the KLM (Knill-Laflamme-Milburn) protocol [35].

---

[2] https://perceval.quandela.net/docs/index.html.

[3] https://cloud.quandela.com/webide/login.

[4] https://perceval.quandela.net/docs/components.html.

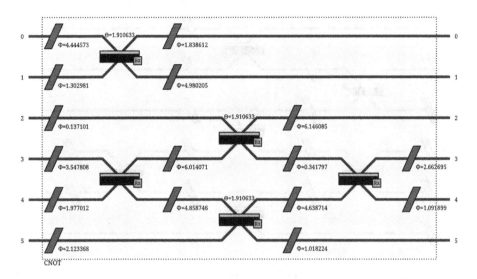

Fig. 3. Proposed Optical CNOT schema

A CNOT gate of the first type, which is less sophisticated but much more straightforward to build than the other one, is sufficient to implement the proposed entangler circuit (Fig. 3 and Fig. 4). On the Entangler in Fig. 4, however, it is possible to operate some significant simplifications, which help to make the physical realisation of the circuit easier and reduce noise due to unnecessary additional components. An optical Entangler like the one in Fig. 5 is therefore proposed. Some useful tools provided by the simulation software allow one to verify the equivalence between the circuits in Fig. 4 and Fig. 5: both have the same unitary matrix (Eq. 2).

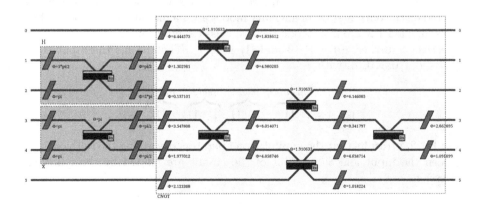

Fig. 4. Entangler built from the two previous blocks

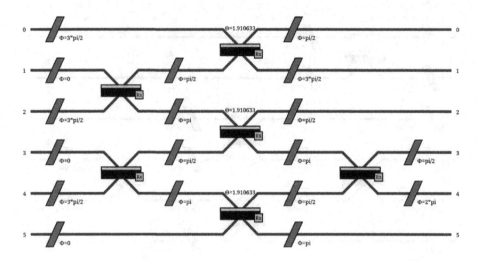

Fig. 5. Simplified proposed Entangler

$$U = \begin{pmatrix} \frac{\sqrt{3}}{3} & -\frac{\sqrt{3}i}{3} & -\frac{\sqrt{3}i}{3} & 0 & 0 & 0 \\ -\frac{\sqrt{6}i}{3} & \frac{\sqrt{6}}{6} & \frac{\sqrt{6}}{6} & 0 & 0 & 0 \\ 0 & \frac{\sqrt{6}}{6} & -\frac{\sqrt{6}}{6} & -\frac{\sqrt{3}i}{3} & -\frac{\sqrt{3}i}{3} & 0 \\ 0 & -\frac{\sqrt{6}i}{6} & \frac{\sqrt{6}i}{6} & 0 & \frac{\sqrt{3}}{3} & \frac{\sqrt{3}}{3} \\ 0 & -\frac{\sqrt{6}i}{6} & \frac{\sqrt{6}i}{6} & \frac{\sqrt{3}}{3} & 0 & -\frac{\sqrt{3}}{3} \\ 0 & 0 & 0 & -\frac{\sqrt{3}}{3} & \frac{\sqrt{3}}{3} & -\frac{\sqrt{3}}{3} \end{pmatrix} \qquad (2)$$

Modes labelled 0 and 5 are the ancillary modes. No photons are provided into them; the output state is guaranteed to be correct only if no photons are detected on the output stage of ancillary modes after a measurement process. The modes labelled 1,2 and 3,4 encode the two classical input qubits $|0\rangle \otimes |0\rangle = |00\rangle$, respectively; further, $|0\rangle$ is $|1,0\rangle$ and $|1\rangle$ is $|0,1\rangle$. That means the input state $|\psi_{in}\rangle$ is $|0,1,0,1,0,0\rangle$, with

$$|\psi_{in}\rangle = | \overbrace{0}^{ancilla}, \overbrace{1, 0}^{qubit_1}, \overbrace{1, 0}^{qubit_0}, \overbrace{0}^{ancilla} \rangle$$

From Eq. 2, it results that the annihilation operators describing the relationships between the input and the output of the circuit are related by the following expressions

$$\begin{pmatrix}\hat{b}_0\\\hat{b}_1\\\hat{b}_2\\\hat{b}_3\\\hat{b}_4\\\hat{b}_5\end{pmatrix}=\begin{pmatrix}\frac{\sqrt{3}}{3}&-\frac{\sqrt{3}i}{3}&-\frac{\sqrt{3}i}{3}&0&0&0\\[4pt]-\frac{\sqrt{6}i}{3}&\frac{\sqrt{6}}{6}&\frac{\sqrt{6}}{6}&0&0&0\\[4pt]0&\frac{\sqrt{6}}{6}&-\frac{\sqrt{6}}{6}&-\frac{\sqrt{3}i}{3}&-\frac{\sqrt{3}i}{3}&0\\[4pt]0&-\frac{\sqrt{6}i}{6}&\frac{\sqrt{6}i}{6}&0&\frac{\sqrt{3}}{3}&\frac{\sqrt{3}}{3}\\[4pt]0&-\frac{\sqrt{6}i}{6}&\frac{\sqrt{6}i}{6}&\frac{\sqrt{3}}{3}&0&-\frac{\sqrt{3}}{3}\\[4pt]0&0&0&-\frac{\sqrt{3}}{3}&\frac{\sqrt{3}}{3}&-\frac{\sqrt{3}}{3}\end{pmatrix}\cdot\begin{pmatrix}\hat{a}_0\\\hat{a}_1\\\hat{a}_2\\\hat{a}_3\\\hat{a}_4\\\hat{a}_5\end{pmatrix}$$

$$(3)$$

$$\begin{pmatrix}\hat{a}_0^\dagger\\\hat{a}_1^\dagger\\\hat{a}_2^\dagger\\\hat{a}_3^\dagger\\\hat{a}_4^\dagger\\\hat{a}_5^\dagger\end{pmatrix}=\begin{pmatrix}\frac{\sqrt{3}}{3}&-\frac{\sqrt{6}i}{3}&0&0&0&0\\[4pt]-\frac{\sqrt{3}i}{3}&\frac{\sqrt{6}}{6}&\frac{\sqrt{6}}{6}&-\frac{\sqrt{6}i}{6}&-\frac{\sqrt{6}i}{6}&0\\[4pt]-\frac{\sqrt{3}i}{3}&\frac{\sqrt{6}}{6}&-\frac{\sqrt{6}}{6}&\frac{\sqrt{6}i}{6}&\frac{\sqrt{6}i}{6}&0\\[4pt]0&0&-\frac{\sqrt{3}i}{3}&0&\frac{\sqrt{3}}{3}&-\frac{\sqrt{3}}{3}\\[4pt]0&0&-\frac{\sqrt{3}i}{3}&\frac{\sqrt{3}}{3}&0&\frac{\sqrt{3}}{3}\\[4pt]0&0&0&\frac{\sqrt{3}}{3}&-\frac{\sqrt{3}}{3}&-\frac{\sqrt{3}}{3}\end{pmatrix}\cdot\begin{pmatrix}\hat{b}_0^\dagger\\\hat{b}_1^\dagger\\\hat{b}_2^\dagger\\\hat{b}_3^\dagger\\\hat{b}_4^\dagger\\\hat{b}_5^\dagger\end{pmatrix}$$

Equations 3 and 4 show the procedure for calculating the output state, starting from the initial state. That will allow comparing the correctness of the results obtained with the simulator and with the real optical quantum computer.

$$\begin{cases}\hat{a}_0^\dagger=\dfrac{\sqrt{3}}{3}\hat{b}_0^\dagger-\dfrac{\sqrt{6}i}{3}\hat{b}_1^\dagger\\[8pt]\hat{a}_1^\dagger=-\dfrac{\sqrt{3}i}{3}\hat{b}_0^\dagger+\dfrac{\sqrt{6}}{6}\hat{b}_1^\dagger+\dfrac{\sqrt{6}}{6}\hat{b}_2^\dagger-\dfrac{\sqrt{6}i}{6}\hat{b}_3^\dagger-\dfrac{\sqrt{6}i}{6}\hat{b}_4^\dagger\\[8pt]\hat{a}_2^\dagger=-\dfrac{\sqrt{3}i}{3}\hat{b}_0^\dagger+\dfrac{\sqrt{6}}{6}\hat{b}_1^\dagger-\dfrac{\sqrt{6}}{6}\hat{b}_2^\dagger+\dfrac{\sqrt{6}i}{6}\hat{b}_3^\dagger+\dfrac{\sqrt{6}i}{6}\hat{b}_4^\dagger\\[8pt]\hat{a}_3^\dagger=-\dfrac{\sqrt{3}i}{3}\hat{b}_2^\dagger+\dfrac{\sqrt{3}}{3}\hat{b}_4^\dagger-\dfrac{\sqrt{3}}{3}\hat{b}_5^\dagger\\[8pt]\hat{a}_4^\dagger=-\dfrac{\sqrt{3}i}{3}\hat{b}_2^\dagger+\dfrac{\sqrt{3}}{3}\hat{b}_3^\dagger+\dfrac{\sqrt{3}}{3}\hat{b}_5^\dagger\\[8pt]\hat{a}_5^\dagger=\dfrac{\sqrt{3}}{3}\hat{b}_3^\dagger-\dfrac{\sqrt{3}}{3}\hat{b}_4^\dagger-\dfrac{\sqrt{3}}{3}\hat{b}_5^\dagger\end{cases}$$

$$(4)$$

$$|0,1,0,1,0,0\rangle = \hat{a}_1^\dagger \hat{a}_3^\dagger |0,0,0,0,0,0\rangle$$

$$\hat{a}_1^\dagger \hat{a}_3^\dagger = \left(-\frac{\sqrt{3}i}{3}\hat{b}_0^\dagger + \frac{\sqrt{6}}{6}\hat{b}_1^\dagger + \frac{\sqrt{6}}{6}\hat{b}_2^\dagger - \frac{\sqrt{6}i}{6}\hat{b}_3^\dagger - \frac{\sqrt{6}i}{6}\hat{b}_4^\dagger\right)\left(-\frac{\sqrt{3}i}{3}\hat{b}_2^\dagger + \frac{\sqrt{3}}{3}\hat{b}_4^\dagger - \frac{\sqrt{3}}{3}\hat{b}_5^\dagger\right)$$

$$= \left(-\frac{1}{3}\hat{b}_0^\dagger \hat{b}_2^\dagger - \frac{i}{3}\hat{b}_0^\dagger \hat{b}_4^\dagger + \frac{i}{3}\hat{b}_0^\dagger \hat{b}_5^\dagger - \frac{\sqrt{2}i}{6}\hat{b}_1^\dagger \hat{b}_2^\dagger + \frac{\sqrt{2}}{6}\hat{b}_1^\dagger \hat{b}_4^\dagger - \frac{\sqrt{2}}{6}\hat{b}_1^\dagger \hat{b}_5^\dagger - \frac{\sqrt{2}i}{6}\hat{b}_2^{\dagger 2} + \right.$$

$$\left. -\frac{\sqrt{2}}{6}\hat{b}_2^\dagger \hat{b}_3^\dagger - \frac{\sqrt{2}}{6}\hat{b}_2^\dagger \hat{b}_5^\dagger - \frac{\sqrt{2}i}{6}\hat{b}_3^\dagger \hat{b}_4^\dagger + \frac{\sqrt{2}i}{6}\hat{b}_3^\dagger \hat{b}_5^\dagger - \frac{\sqrt{2}i}{6}\hat{b}_4^{\dagger 2} + \frac{\sqrt{2}i}{6}\hat{b}_4^\dagger \hat{b}_5^\dagger\right)$$

$$|\psi_{out}\rangle = \hat{a}_1^\dagger \hat{a}_3^\dagger |0,0,0,0,0,0\rangle =$$

$$= -\frac{1}{3}\hat{b}_0^\dagger \hat{b}_2^\dagger |0,0,0,0,0,0\rangle - \frac{i}{3}\hat{b}_0^\dagger \hat{b}_4^\dagger |0,0,0,0,0,0\rangle + \frac{i}{3}\hat{b}_0^\dagger \hat{b}_5^\dagger |0,0,0,0,0,0\rangle +$$

$$-\frac{\sqrt{2}i}{6}\hat{b}_1^\dagger \hat{b}_2^\dagger |0,0,0,0,0,0\rangle + \frac{\sqrt{2}}{6}\hat{b}_1^\dagger \hat{b}_4^\dagger |0,0,0,0,0,0\rangle - \frac{\sqrt{2}}{6}\hat{b}_1^\dagger \hat{b}_5^\dagger |0,0,0,0,0,0\rangle +$$

$$-\frac{\sqrt{2}i}{6}\hat{b}_2^{\dagger 2} |0,0,0,0,0,0\rangle - \frac{\sqrt{2}}{6}\hat{b}_2^\dagger \hat{b}_3^\dagger |0,0,0,0,0,0\rangle - \frac{\sqrt{2}}{6}\hat{b}_2^\dagger \hat{b}_5^\dagger |0,0,0,0,0,0\rangle +$$

$$-\frac{\sqrt{2}i}{6}\hat{b}_3^\dagger \hat{b}_4^\dagger |0,0,0,0,0,0\rangle + \frac{\sqrt{2}i}{6}\hat{b}_3^\dagger \hat{b}_5^\dagger |0,0,0,0,0,0\rangle - \frac{\sqrt{2}i}{6}\hat{b}_4^{\dagger 2} |0,0,0,0,0,0\rangle +$$

$$+\frac{\sqrt{2}i}{6}\hat{b}_4^\dagger \hat{b}_5^\dagger |0,0,0,0,0,0\rangle$$

Now applying the creation operators $\hat{b}_i^\dagger$ to the appropriate mode i-th of the vector $|0,0,0,0,0,0\rangle$, we obtain the output state of the optical quantum system under consideration:

$$|\psi_{out}\rangle = \hat{a}_1^\dagger \hat{a}_3^\dagger |0,0,0,0,0,0\rangle =$$

$$= -\frac{1}{3}|1,0,1,0,0,0\rangle - \frac{i}{3}|1,0,0,0,1,0\rangle + \frac{i}{3}|1,0,0,0,0,1\rangle +$$

$$-\frac{\sqrt{2}i}{6}|0,1,1,0,0,0\rangle + \frac{\sqrt{2}}{6}|0,1,0,0,1,0\rangle - \frac{\sqrt{2}}{6}|0,1,0,0,0,1\rangle +$$

$$-\frac{i}{3}|0,0,2,0,0,0\rangle - \frac{\sqrt{2}}{6}|0,0,1,1,0,0\rangle - \frac{\sqrt{2}}{6}|0,0,1,0,0,1\rangle + \quad (5)$$

$$-\frac{\sqrt{2}i}{6}|0,0,0,1,1,0\rangle + \frac{\sqrt{2}i}{6}|0,0,0,1,0,1\rangle - \frac{i}{3}|0,0,0,0,2,0\rangle +$$

$$+\frac{\sqrt{2}i}{6}|0,0,0,0,1,1\rangle$$

The space dimension describing this transformation is given by the formula $C_n^{m+n-1} = \binom{m+n-1}{n}$, where m is the number of modes in system and n is the number of photons in input; here, the dimension is $\binom{6+3-1}{3} = 21$: the components of the state vector given by Eq. 5 have only 13 non-zero probability amplitudes, while the remaining eight are zero.

Since modes 0 and 5 are heralded (it means 0 photons in them, 0 photons expected out of them), the output state $|\psi_{out}\rangle$ collapses after a measurement process and the relative filtering step to eliminate all the states with mode 0 or mode 5 different from zero; the new output state consequently becomes $|\psi'_{out}\rangle$ (in order to improve readability, the ancillary states have been omitted).

$$|\psi'_{out}\rangle = -\frac{\sqrt{2}i}{4}|1,1,0,0\rangle + \frac{\sqrt{2}}{4}|1,0,0,1\rangle - \frac{i}{2}|0,2,0,0\rangle$$
$$- \frac{\sqrt{2}}{4}|0,1,1,0\rangle - \frac{\sqrt{2}i}{4}|0,0,1,1\rangle - \frac{i}{2}|0,0,0,2\rangle \qquad (6)$$

Subsequently, because the modes encoding the individual qubits can only contain a single photon alternatively, all those states that do not respect this constraint are discarded. The final state remaining after this post-selection operation, hence, results $|\psi''_{out}\rangle$.

$$|\psi''_{out}\rangle = +\frac{\sqrt{2}}{2}|1,0,0,1\rangle - \frac{\sqrt{2}}{2}|0,1,1,0\rangle \qquad (7)$$

The outcome is correct because the final state is a Bell's state, as expected. So, output outcomes for probability distribution for the state in $|\psi''_{out}\rangle$ are $\frac{1}{2}$ for the state $|1,0,0,1\rangle$ and $\frac{1}{2}$ for the state $|0,1,1,0\rangle$. Circuit simulations with Perceval (Table 1, Fig. 6, Fig. 7 and Fig. 8) show perfect agreement with the theoretically obtained results.

Table 1. Probability of each state composing final output state for the Dual Rail Entangler with input $|0,1,0,1,0,0\rangle$; results obtained with Perceval.

state	probability
$|1,0,1,0,0,0\rangle$	0.111111
$|2,0,0,0,0,0\rangle$	0.000000
$|1,0,0,0,1,0\rangle$	0.111111
$|0,2,0,0,0,0\rangle$	0.000000
$|0,1,0,1,0,0\rangle$	0.000000
$|0,0,0,1,0,1\rangle$	0.055556
$|0,0,0,0,2,0\rangle$	0.111111
$|0,1,0,0,0,1\rangle$	0.055556
$|0,0,1,0,1,0\rangle$	0.000000
$|0,0,0,2,0,0\rangle$	0.000000
$|0,0,0,0,0,2\rangle$	0.000000
$|1,1,0,0,0,0\rangle$	0.000000
$|1,0,0,1,0,0\rangle$	0.000000
$|1,0,0,0,0,1\rangle$	0.111111
$|0,1,1,0,0,0\rangle$	0.055556
$|0,1,0,0,1,0\rangle$	0.055556
$|0,0,1,0,0,1\rangle$	0.055556
$|0,0,0,1,1,0\rangle$	0.055556
$|0,0,1,1,0,0\rangle$	0.055556
$|0,0,0,0,1,1\rangle$	0.055556
$|0,0,2,0,0,0\rangle$	0.111111

```
Initial State: |0,1,0,1,0,0>
------------------------------------------------------------------
Ouput State:
|1,0,1,0,0,0> (-0.3333333333333333-1.263373392013101e-09j)
|1,0,0,0,1,0> (8.603854712019301e-10-0.33333333333333337j)
|1,0,0,0,0,1> (-3.7847472817382997e-10+0.3333333333333334j)
|0,1,1,0,0,0> (8.917603877556248e-10-0.23570226039551578j)
|0,1,0,0,1,0> (0.23570226039551584+6.068048979956943e-10j)
|0,1,0,0,0,1> (-0.23570226039551584-2.66042558938492e-10j)
|0,0,2,0,0,0> (7.459158944326773e-11-0.33333333333333315j)
|0,0,1,1,0,0> (-0.23570226039551584+7.985322125758645e-10j)
|0,0,1,0,0,1> (-0.23570226039551578+5.72973640755592e-10j)
|0,0,0,1,1,0> (-9.62582347163732e-10-0.23570226039551578j)
|0,0,0,1,0,1> (1.363797379137784e-09+0.23570226039551584j)
|0,0,0,0,2,0> (-6.458912113628097e-10-0.33333333333333326j)
|0,0,0,0,1,1> (7.974764182350216e-10+0.23570226039551584j)


-1/3*|1,0,1,0,0,0>
-I/3*|1,0,0,0,1,0>
+I/3*|1,0,0,0,0,1>
-sqrt(2)*I/6*|0,1,1,0,0,0>
+sqrt(2)/6*|0,1,0,0,1,0>
-sqrt(2)/6*|0,1,0,0,0,1>
-I/3*|0,0,2,0,0,0>
-sqrt(2)/6*|0,0,1,1,0,0>
-sqrt(2)/6*|0,0,1,0,0,1>
-sqrt(2)*I/6*|0,0,0,1,1,0>
+sqrt(2)*I/6*|0,0,0,1,0,1>
-I/3*|0,0,0,0,2,0>
+sqrt(2)*I/6*|0,0,0,0,1,1>
------------------------------------------------------------------
```

Fig. 6. Output state from simulation on Perceval of Dual-Rail Entangler Circuit

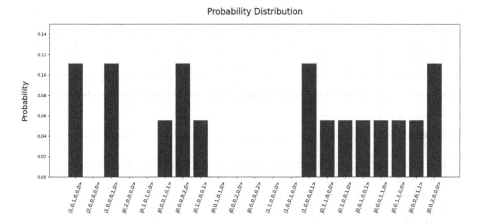

Fig. 7. Probability distribution for state $|\psi_{out}\rangle$ on Perceval of Dual-Rail Entangler Circuit

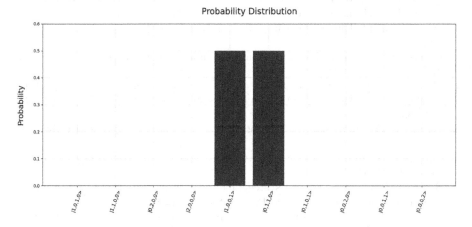

Fig. 8. Probability distribution for state $|\psi''_{out}\rangle$ on Perceval of Dual-Rail Entangler Circuit

4   Conclusions

Quantum computing is a rapidly growing area that has the potential to revolutionise the way some complex problems can be solved. The development and usage of quantum computing technology have made significant progress in recent years. Researchers are continuously exploring new ways to leverage this technology to solve complex or impossible problems for classical computers. Quantum computing's unique properties, such as superposition and entanglement, enable it to perform specific calculations exponentially faster than classical computers.

This paper has illustrated a possible application of these technologies by realizing an optical entangler, a quantum helpful circuit for producing pairs of maximally entangled states intensely used in many applications such as quantum teleportation, quantum dense coding and quantum error correction. The Optical Dual Rail Mode has proved to be very useful for scaling up optical quantum circuits but still has many challenges and problems to be solved to be widely used in quantum computing.

We intend to deepen this line of studies in successive works, especially by implementing quantum algorithms using linear and non-linear optics.

References

1. Isaac, L.: Chuang and Yoshihisa Yamamoto. Simple quantum computer. Phys. Rev. A **52**(5), 3489 (1995)
2. Simonetti, M., Perri, D., Gervasi, O.: An example of use of variational methods in quantum machine learning. In: Gervasi, O., Murgante, B., Misra, S., Rocha, A.M.A.C., Garau, C. (eds.) Computational Science and Its Applications –ICCSA 2022 Workshops. ICCSA 2022. LNCS, vol. 13382, pp. 597–609. Springer, Cham (2022). https://doi.org/10.1007/978-3-031-10592-0_43
3. Abdelgaber, N., Nikolopoulos, C.: Overview on quantum computing and its applications in artificial intelligence. In: 2020 IEEE Third International Conference on Artificial Intelligence and Knowledge Engineering (AIKE), pp. 198–199. IEEE (2020)
4. Bayerstadler, A., et al.: Industry quantum computing applications. EPJ Quantum Technol. **8**(1), 25 (2021)
5. Möller, M., Vuik, C.: On the impact of quantum computing technology on future developments in high-performance scientific computing. Ethics Inf. Technol. **19**, 253–269 (2017)
6. Fox, A.M., Fox, M.: Quantum Optics: An Introduction, vol. 15. Oxford University Press, Oxford (2006)
7. Cerf, N.J., Adami, C., Kwiat, P.G.: Optical simulation of quantum logic. Phys. Rev. A **57**(3), R1477 (1998)
8. Ralph, T.C.: Quantum optical systems for the implementation of quantum information processing. Rep. Progress Phys. **69**(4), 853 (2006)
9. Somaschi, N., et al.: Near-optimal single-photon sources in the solid state. Nat. Photonics **10**(5), 340–345 (2016)
10. Ollivier, H., et al.: Reproducibility of highperformance quantum dot single-photon sources. ACS Photonics **7**(4), 1050–1059 (2020)
11. Loredo, J.C., et al. Scalable performance in solid-state single-photon sources. Optica **3**(4), 433–440 (2016)
12. Tillmann, M., Dakić, B., Heilmann, R., Nolte, S., Szameit, A., Walther, P.: Experimental boson sampling. Nat. Photonics **7**(7), 540–544 (2013)
13. Hamilton, C.S., Kruse, R., Sansoni, L., Barkhofen, S., Silberhorn, C., Jex, I.: Gaussian boson sampling. Phys. Rev. Lett. **119**(17), 170501 (2017)
14. Spring, J.B., et al.: Boson sampling on a photonic chip. Science **339**(6121), 798–801 (2013)
15. Brod, D.J., Galvão, E.F., Crespi, A., Osellame, R., Spagnolo, N., Sciarrino, F.: Photonic implementation of boson sampling: a review. Adv. Photonics **1**(3), 034001 (2019)
16. Perri, D., Simonetti, M., Gervasi, O.: Deploying efficiently modern applications on cloud. Electronics **11**(3) (2022). ISSN: 2079-9292. https://doi.org/10.3390/electronics11030450. https://www.mdpi.com/2079-9292/11/3/450

17. Perri, D., Simonetti, M., Tasso, S., Ragni, F., Gervasi, O.: Implementing a scalable and elastic computing environment based on cloud containers. In: Gervasi, O., et al. (eds.) ICCSA 2021. LNCS, vol. 12949, pp. 676–689. Springer, Cham (2021). https://doi.org/10.1007/978-3-030-86653-2_49 ISBN: 978-3-030-86653-2

18. Perri, D., Simonetti, M., Gervasi, O.: Synthetic data generation to speed-up the object recognition pipeline. Electronics **11**(1) (2022). ISSN: 2079-9292. https://doi.org/10.3390/electronics11010002. https://www.mdpi.com/2079-9292/11/1/2

19. Perri, D., Fortunelli, M., Simonetti, M., Magni, R., Carloni, J., Gervasi, O.: Rapid prototyping of virtual reality cognitive exercises in a tele-rehabilitation context. Electronics **10**(4) (2021). ISSN: 2079-9292. https://doi.org/10.3390/electronics10040457. https://www.mdpi.com/2079-9292/10/4/457

20. Perri, D., Simonetti, M., Lombardi, A., Faginas-Lago, N., Gervasi, O.: Binary classification of proteins by a machine learning approach. In: Gervasi, O., et al. (eds.) ICCSA 2020. LNCS, vol. 12255, pp. 549–558. Springer, Cham (2020). ISBN: 978-3-030-58820-5. https://doi.org/10.1007/978-3-030-58820-5_41

21. Laganà, A., Gervasi, O., Tasso, S., Perri, D., Franciosa, F.: The ECTN virtual education community prosumer model for promoting and assessing chemical knowledge. In: Gervasi, O., et al. (eds.) ICCSA 2018. LNCS, vol. 10964, pp. 533–548. Springer, Cham (2018). ISBN: 978-3-319-95174-4. https://doi.org/10.1007/978-3-319-95174-4_42

22. Mermin, N.D.: Hidden variables and the two theorems of john bell. Rev. Mod. Phys. **65**(3), 803 (1993)

23. Zeilinger, A.: Experiment and the foundations of quantum physics. Rev. Mod. Phys. **71**(2), S288 (1999)

24. Lee, H.-W., Kim, J.: Quantum teleportation and Bell's inequality using single-particle entanglement. Phys. Rev. A **63**(1), 012305 (2000)

25. Clements, W.R., Humphreys, P.C., Metcalf, B.J., Kolthammer, W.S.. Walmsley, I.A.: Optimal design for universal multiport interferometers. Optica **3**(12), 1460–1465 (2016)

26. Reck, M., Zeilinger, A., Bernstein, H.J., Bertani, P.: Experimental realization of any discrete unitary operator. Phys. Rev. Lett. **73**(1), 58 (1994)

27. de Guise, H., Di Matteo, O., Sánchez-Soto, L.L.: Simple factorization of unitary transformations. Phys. Rev. A **97**(2), 022328 (2018)

28. Kumar, S.P., Dhand, I.: Unitary matrix decompositions for optimal and modular linear optics architectures. J. Phys. A Math. Theor. **54**(4), 045301 (2021)

29. Imre, S., Balazs, F.: Quantum Computing and Communications: An Engineering Approach. John Wiley & Sons, Hoboken (2005)

30. Asbóth, J.K., Calsamiglia, J., Ritsch, H.: Computable measure of nonclassicality for light. Phys. Rev. Lett. **94**(17), 173602 (2005)

31. Rezakhani, A.T.: Characterization of two-qubit perfect entanglers. Phys. Rev. A **70**(5), 052313 (2004)

32. Zhang, J., Vala, J., Sastry, S., Whaley, K.B.: Geometric theory of nonlocal two-qubit operations. Phys. Rev. A **67**(4), 042313 (2003)

33. Heurtel, N., et al.: Perceval: a software platform for discrete variable photonic quantum computing. Quantum **7**, 931 (2023). ISSN : 2521–327X. https://doi.org/10.22331/q-2023-02-21-931

34. Ralph, T.C., Langford, N.K., Bell, T.B., White, A.G.: Linear optical controlled-NOT gate in the coincidence basis. Phys. Rev. A **65**(6), 062324 (2002)

35. Knill, E., Laflamme, R., Milburn, G.J.: A scheme for efficient quantum computation with linear optics. Nature **409**(6816), 46–52 (2001)

Hopf Bifurcation of a Delayed SVEIS Worm Propagation Model with Nonlinear Incidence Rate

Zizhen Zhang[1]($\boxtimes$) , Weishi Zhang[1] , and Anwar Zeb[2]

[1] School of Management Science and Engineering, Anhui University of Finance and Economics, Bengbu 233030, China
zzzhaida@163.com
[2] Department of Mathematics, COMSATS University Islamabad, Abbottabad, Pakistan
anwar@cuiatd.edu.pk

Abstract. In the present internet age, worms pose a great threat to network security. It is urgent to explore the spreading law of worms through networks. To this end, an SVEIS(Susceptible-Vaccinated-Exposed-Infectious) worm propagation model with nonlinear incidence rate and time delay is proposed in this study. A series of sufficient conditions for local stability and appearance of Hopf bifurcation are derived through taking the time delay as bifurcation parameter. Moreover, direction and stability of the Hopf bifurcation are established with aids of center manifold method. Finally, a numerical example is demonstrated to certificate theoretical findings.

Keywords: Hopf bifurcation · Delay · SVEIS model · Nonlinear incidence rate · Stability

1 Introduction

The advent of the internet age has given rise to enormous changes in modern society. For example, we can easily access data and information by simply clicking a button, and we can buy what we need without leaving home. However, in the meantime, the rapid development of internet technologies has brought about severe challenges for safeguarding the valuable data or information stored in computers and for the data or information in transit [1]. Worms act like communicable diseases and they are epidemic in nature. Therefore, it is possible to establish mathematical models to represent the behavior of a computer worm, which is a self contained program. In fact, there have been some works about mathematical models for worm propagation in networks. Feng et al. [2] formulated an SIRS(Susceptible-Infectious-Recovered-Susceptible) worm propagation model in wireless sensor network. Nevertheless, one of the significant characteristics of

Supported by Anhui University of Finance and Economics.

worms such as the Code Red worm [3] and the Witty worm [4] is their incubation. In another word, when a worm enters into a susceptible computer, it hides
itself and becomes infectious after a period. From this point of view, the SIRS
model [2] ignores the incubation period during the propagation process of computer worms. Due to this fact, Hosseini et al. [5–7] formulated and investigated
different forms of SEIRS(Susceptible-Exposed-Infectious-Recovered-Susceptible)
worm propagation model. Considering the effect of quarantine, some scholars
have proposed and analyzed some worm propagation models including quarantine [8–10].

Vaccination is proverbially thought of one of the most significant measures to
struggle against the propagation of computer viruses in networks. Some mathematical models on the propagation of worms have been developed [11–14]. Nevertheless, the aforementioned models include vaccination strategy on the basis
of the bilinear incidence rate, which is suitable just for the situation when the
fraction of the infected computers is not large. With the popular use of networks
in our daily life, the number of infected computers in networks maybe large
in real network world. To overcome the defect of the bilinear incidence rate,
Upadhyay and Kumari [15] established the following worm propagation model
incorporating nonlinear incidence rate and vaccination:

$$
\begin{cases}
\frac{dS(t)}{dt} = \Lambda - \mu S(t) - \omega S(t) + \theta V(t) - \frac{\beta S(t)I(t)}{S(t)+I(t)+c} + (1-q)\gamma I(t), \\
\frac{dV(t)}{dt} = \omega S(t) - \theta V(t) - \mu V(t) + \xi E(t) + q\gamma I(t), \\
\frac{dE(t)}{dt} = \frac{\beta S(t)I(t)}{S(t)+I(t)+c} - \mu E(t) - \xi E(t) - \sigma E(t), \\
\frac{dI(t)}{dt} = \sigma E(t) - \mu I(t) - \gamma I(t),
\end{cases}
\tag{1}
$$

where $S(t)$, $V(t)$, $E(t)$ and $I(t)$ denote the numbers of the susceptible nodes,
the vaccinated nodes, the exposed nodes and the infectious nodes, separately.
Λ is the constant recruitment rate of the susceptible nodes; μ is the crashing
rate of all the nodes; β is the contact rate between the susceptible and the
infectious nodes; c is the half saturation constant and q is the proportion of
recovered nodes gaining worm-acquired immunity. ω, θ, ξ, σ and γ are the state
transition probabilities. Upadhyay and Kumari [15] examined stability analysis
of the model system (1).

Actually, dynamics of mathematical models not only implicate stability, but
also include bifurcation and periodic phenomenon [16]. Although the law of
motion of a system is related to the state of motion at the present moment, it
can also be influenced by the state of motion at some moments or some moments
in the past. Time delay phenomenon is a kind of physical phenomenon that
exists widely in the actual engineering control process. Considering the effect
of time delay in the mathematical model would be more relevant to real life.
Particularly, differential equations incorporating time delays experience much
more tanglesome dynamical behaviors compared to ordinary differential equations. Consequently, we shall explore the Hopf bifurcation induced by time delay
because of incubation period of worms into the model system (1) and consider
the delayed worm propagation model described in the following form:

$$
\begin{cases}
\frac{dS(t)}{dt} = \Lambda - \mu S(t) - \omega S(t) + \theta V(t) - \frac{\beta S(t)I(t)}{S(t)+I(t)+c} + (1-q)\gamma I(t), \\
\frac{dV(t)}{dt} = \omega S(t) - \theta V(t) - \mu V(t) + \xi E(t) + q\gamma I(t), \\
\frac{dE(t)}{dt} = \frac{\beta S(t)I(t)}{S(t)+I(t)+c} - \mu E(t) - \xi E(t) - \sigma E(t-\tau), \\
\frac{dI(t)}{dt} = \sigma E(t-\tau) - \mu I(t) - \gamma I(t),
\end{cases}
\tag{2}
$$

in which τ is the time delay because of incubation period of worms.

The skeleton of this study is as follows. Local stability and Hopf bifurcation is analyzed and crucial point of the time delay at which a Hopf bifurcation appear is determined in the next section. Direction and stability of the Hopf bifurcation are determined in Sect. 3. A numerical example is presented to certificate the correctness of the analytical findings in Sect. 4. Section 5 concludes our study.

2   Analysis of Local Stability and Hopf Bifurcation

On the basis of the calculation by Upadhyay and Kumari [15], it can be concluded that if the basic reproduction number $R_0 = \frac{\Lambda\beta\sigma(\mu+\theta)}{\kappa_2(\mu+\gamma)(\Lambda(\mu+\theta)+c\mu\kappa_1)} > 1$ where $\kappa_1 = \mu + \theta + \omega$ and $\kappa_2 = \mu + \xi + \sigma$, then the model system (2) exists an unique endemic equilibrium $W_*(S_*, V_*, E_*, I_*)$, where

$$
S_* = \frac{I_* + c}{\Delta_1}, E_* = \frac{(\mu+\gamma)I_*}{\sigma},
$$

$$
V_* = \frac{(\omega + \Delta_1\Delta_2)I_* + c\omega}{\Delta_1(\mu+\theta)},
$$

$$
I_* = \frac{\sigma\Lambda\Delta_1(\mu+\theta) - c\mu\sigma\kappa_1}{\mu(\Delta_1\Delta_3 + \sigma\kappa_1)},
$$

with

$$
\Delta_1 = R_0 - 1 + \frac{cR_0}{S^0},
$$

$$
\Delta_2 = \frac{\xi(\mu+\gamma)}{\sigma} + q\gamma,
$$

$$
\Delta_3 = (\mu+\gamma)(\mu+\xi+\theta) + \sigma(\mu+q\gamma+\theta),
$$

$$
S^0 = \frac{\Lambda(\mu+\theta)}{\mu\kappa_1}.
\tag{3}
$$

The Jacobian matrix Q_* at $W_*(S_*, V_*, E_*, I_*)$ is presented by

$$
Q_* = \begin{bmatrix}
k_{11} & k_{12} & 0 & k_{14} \\
k_{21} & k_{22} & k_{23} & k_{24} \\
k_{31} & 0 & k_{33} + l_{33}e^{-\lambda\tau} & k_{34} \\
0 & 0 & l_{43}e^{-\lambda\tau} & k_{44}
\end{bmatrix},
\tag{4}
$$

where

$$k_{11} = -\mu - \omega - \frac{\beta I_*(I_* + c)}{(S_* + I_* + c)^2}, k_{12} = \theta,$$

$$k_{14} = (1 - q)\gamma - \frac{\beta S_*(S_* + c)}{(S_* + I_* + c)^2},$$

$$k_{21} = \omega, k_{22} = -\mu - \theta, k_{23} = \xi, k_{24} = q\gamma,$$

$$k_{31} = \frac{\beta I_*(I_* + c)}{(S_* + I_* + c)^2}, k_{33} = -\mu - \xi,$$

$$k_{34} = \frac{\beta S_*(S_* + c)}{(S_* + I_* + c)^2}, l_{33} = -\sigma,$$

$$k_{44} = -\mu - \gamma, l_{43} = \sigma.$$

The characteristic equation of Jacobian matrix W_* can be obtained with

$$\lambda^4 + \Theta_3\lambda^3 + \Theta_2\lambda^2 + \Theta_1\lambda + \Theta_0 + (\Delta_3\lambda^3 + \Delta_2\lambda^2 + \Delta_1\lambda + \Delta_0)e^{-\lambda\tau} = 0, \quad (5)$$

with

$\Theta_0 = k_{33}k_{44}(k_{11}k_{22} - k_{12}k_{21}),$

$\Theta_1 = k_{12}k_{21}(k_{33} + k_{44}) - k_{11}k_{33}(k_{22} + k_{44}) - k_{22}k_{44}(k_{11} + k_{33}),$

$\Theta_2 = k_{11}k_{33} + k_{22}k_{44} - k_{12}k_{21} + (k_{11} + k_{33})(k_{22} + k_{44}),$

$\Theta_3 = -(k_{11} + k_{22} + k_{33} + k_{44}),$

$\Delta_0 = k_{44}l_{33}(k_{11}k_{12} - k_{12}k_{21}) + k_{12}l_{43}(k_{21}k_{34} - k_{24}k_{31}) + k_{22}l_{43}(k_{31}k_{14} - k_{34}k_{11}),$

$\Delta_1 = k_{12}k_{21}l_{33} - k_{14}k_{31}l_{43} + k_{34}l_{43}(k_{11} + k_{22}) - l_{33}(k_{11}k_{22} + k_{11}k_{44} + k_{22}k_{44}),$

$\Delta_2 = l_{33}(k_{11} + k_{22} + k_{44}) - l_{34}l_{43}, \Delta_3 = -l_{33}.$

Lemma 1 [16]. $W_*(S_*, V_*, E_*, I_*)$ is locally asymptotically stable if $\sigma\beta(S_* + c)S_* \le \kappa_2(\mu + \gamma)(S_* + I_* + c)^2$ is satisfied when $\tau = 0$.

For $\tau > 0$, assume that $\lambda = iv(v > 0)$ is a root of Eq. (5). Thus

$$\begin{cases} (\Delta_1 v - \Delta_3 v^3)\sin(\tau v) + (\Delta_0 - \Delta_2 v^2)\cos(\tau v) = \Theta_2 v^2 - v^4 - \Theta_0, \\ (\Delta_1 v - \Delta_3 v^3)\cos(\tau v) - (\Delta_0 - \Delta_2 v^2)\sin(\tau v) = \Theta_3 v^3 - \Theta_1 v, \end{cases} \quad (6)$$

leading to

$$v^8 + \Upsilon_3 v^6 + \Upsilon_2 v^4 + \Upsilon_1 v^2 + \Upsilon_0 = 0, \quad (7)$$

where

$$\Upsilon_0 = \Theta_0^2 - \Delta_0^2,$$

$$\Upsilon_1 = \Theta_1^2 - \Delta_1^2 + 2\Delta_0\Delta_2 - 2\Theta_0\Theta_2,$$

$$\Upsilon_2 = \Theta_2^2 - \Delta_2^2 + 2\Delta_1\Delta_3 + 2\Theta_1\Theta_3 - 2\Theta_0,$$

$$\Upsilon_3 = \Theta_3^2 - \Delta_3^2 - 2\Theta_2.$$

Define $v^2 = \varpi$. Equation (7) equals

$$\varpi^4 + \Upsilon_3\varpi^3 + \Upsilon_2\varpi^2 + \Upsilon_1\varpi + \Upsilon_0 = 0. \quad (8)$$

Discussion regarding the distribution of roots for Eq. (8) is similar to that analyzed by Li and Wei [17]. For the mathematical convenience, we suppose that Eq. (8) exists at least one ϖ_0 ($\varpi_0 > 0$) and moreover, Eq. (7) exists $v_0 = \sqrt{\varpi_0}$ leading to that Eq. (5) has a pair of purely imaginary roots $\pm iv_0$. From Eq. (6), one has

$$\tau_i = \frac{1}{v_0} \arccos\left[\frac{P_1(v_0)}{P_2(v_0)}\right] + \frac{2i\pi}{v_0}, \tag{9}$$

with

$$P_1(v_0) = (\Delta_2 - \Delta_3\Theta_3)v_0^6 + (\Delta_1\Theta_3 + \Delta_3\Theta_1 - \Delta_0 - \Delta_2\Theta_2)v_0^4$$
$$+ (\Delta_0\Theta_2 + \Delta_2\Theta_0 - \Delta_1\Theta_1)v_0^2 - \Delta_0\Theta_0,$$
$$P_2(v_0) = \Delta_3^2 v_0^6 + (\Delta_2^2 - 2\Delta_1\Delta_3)v_0^4 + (\Delta_1^2 - 2\Delta_0\Delta_2)v_0^2 + \Delta_0^2.$$

Let

$$\tau_0 = min\{\tau_i\}, i = 0, 1, 2, \cdots. \tag{10}$$

Based on Eq. (5), one has

$$\left[\frac{d\lambda}{d\tau}\right]^{-1} = -\frac{P_3(\lambda)}{P_4(\lambda)} + \frac{P_5(\lambda)}{P_6(\lambda)} - \frac{\tau}{\lambda}, \tag{11}$$

where

$$P_3(\lambda) = 4\lambda^3 + 3\Theta_3\lambda^2 + 2\Theta_2\lambda + \Theta_1,$$
$$P_4(\lambda) = \lambda^5 + \Theta_3\lambda^4 + \Theta_2\lambda^3 + \Theta_1\lambda^2 + \Theta_0\lambda,$$
$$P_5(\lambda) = 3\Delta_3\lambda^2 + 2\Delta_2\lambda + \Delta_1,$$
$$P_6(\lambda) = \Delta_3\lambda^4 + \Delta_2\lambda^3 + \Delta_1\lambda^2 + \Delta_0\lambda.$$

This gives

$$Re\left[\frac{d\lambda}{d\tau}\right]^{-1}_{\lambda=iv_0} = \frac{Q'(\varpi_0)}{P_2(v_0)}, \tag{12}$$

where $Q(\varpi) = \varpi^4 + \Upsilon_3\varpi^3 + \Upsilon_2\varpi^2 + \Upsilon_1\varpi + \Upsilon_0$ and $\varpi_0 = v_0^2$. Clearly, if $Q'(\varpi_0) \neq 0$, in accordance withs of the Hopf bifurcation theorem proposed by Hassard et al. in [18], we can stated the obtained results in the following theorem.

Theorem 1. *If $R_0 > 1$, then endemic equilibrium $W_*(S_*, V_*, E_*, I_*)$ is locally asymptotically stable whenever $\tau \in [0, \tau_0)$; while a Hopf bifurcation experiences near $W_*(S_*, V_*, E_*, I_*)$ when $\tau = \tau_0$ and a cluster of periodic solutions exhibit around $W_*(S_*, V_*, E_*, I_*)$.*

3   Direction and Stability of the Hopf Bifurcation

In this section, we derive the explicit formula governing direction and stability of the Hopf bifurcation exhibits at $W_*(S_*, V_*, E_*, I_*)$ when $\tau = \tau_0$. Denote $\sigma = \tau + \tau_0$, $\sigma \in \Re$, $t = s\tau$, $S(s\tau) = S(s)$, $V(s\tau) = V(s)$, $E(s\tau) = E(s)$, $I(s\tau) = I(s)$.

Define $X_1(t) = S(t) - S_*$, $X_2(t) = V(t) - V_*$, $X_3(t) = E(t) - E_*$ and $X_4 = I(t) - I_*$, then the model system (2) is equivalent to

$$\dot{X}(t) = L_\sigma(X_t) + F(\sigma, X_t), \tag{13}$$

where $X(t) = (X_1(t), X_2(t), X_3(t), X_4(t))^T \in C = C([-1, 0], \Re^3)$, $X_t(\vartheta) = X(t + \vartheta) = (X_1(t + \vartheta), X_2(t + \vartheta), X_3(t + \vartheta), X_4(t + \vartheta))^T \in C$ and $L_\sigma : C \to \Re^4$, $F : \Re \times C \to \Re^4$ are

$$L_\sigma(\varsigma) = (\sigma + \tau_0)[K\varsigma(0) + L\varsigma(-1)], \tag{14}$$

and

$$F(\sigma, \varsigma) = (\sigma + \tau_0)(F_1, 0, F_3, 0)^T, \tag{15}$$

where

$$K = \begin{pmatrix} k_{11} & k_{12} & 0 & k_{14} \\ k_{21} & k_{22} & k_{23} & k_{24} \\ k_{31} & 0 & k_{33} & k_{34} \\ 0 & 0 & 0 & k_{44} \end{pmatrix}, L = \begin{pmatrix} 0 & 0 & 0 & 0 \\ 0 & 0 & 0 & 0 \\ 0 & 0 & l_{33} & 0 \\ 0 & 0 & l_{43} & 0 \end{pmatrix},$$

and

$$F_1 = k_{15}\varsigma_1^2(0) + k_{16}\varsigma_1(0)\varsigma_3(0) + k_{17}\varsigma_3^2(0) + k_{18}\varsigma_1^2(0)\varsigma_3(0)$$
$$+\varsigma_{19}\varsigma_1(0)\varsigma_2^2(0) + k_{110}\varsigma_1^3(0) + k_{111}\varsigma_2^3(0) + \cdots,$$
$$F_3 = k_{35}\varsigma_1^2(0) + k_{36}\varsigma_1(0)\varsigma_3(0) + k_{37}\varsigma_3^2(0) + k_{38}\varsigma_1^2(0)\varsigma_3(0)$$
$$+\varsigma_{39}\varsigma_1(0)\varsigma_2^2(0) + k_{310}\varsigma_1^3(0) + k_{311}\varsigma_2^3(0) + \cdots,$$

where

$$k_{15} = \frac{\beta I_*(I_* + c)}{(S_* + I_* + c)^3}, k_{16} = -\frac{2\beta S_* I_* + c\beta(S_* + I_* + c)}{(S_* + I_* + c)^3},$$

$$k_{17} = \frac{\beta S_*(S_* + c)}{(S_* + I_* + c)^3}, k_{18} = \frac{6\beta S_* I_* + c\beta(S_* + I_* + c) - \beta I_*(I_* + c)}{(S_* + I_* + c)^4},$$

$$k_{19} = \frac{6\beta S_* I_* + c\beta(S_* + I_* + c) - \beta S_*(S_* + c)}{(S_* + I_* + c)^4},$$

$$k_{110} = -\frac{\beta I_*(I_* + c)}{(S_* + I_* + c)^4}, k_{111} = \frac{\beta S_*(S_* + c)}{(S_* + I_* + c)^4},$$

$$k_{35} = -k_{15}, k_{36} = -k_{16}, k_{37} = -k_{17}, k_{38} = -k_{18},$$

$$k_{39} = -k_{19}, k_{310} = -k_{110}, k_{311} = -k_{111}.$$

Thus, there exists $\eta(\varsigma, \sigma)$ for $\sigma \in [-1, 0]$ satisfying

$$L_\sigma(\phi) = \int_{-1}^0 d\eta(\varsigma, \sigma)\phi(\varsigma). \tag{16}$$

Define

$$\eta(\varsigma, \sigma) = (\tau_0 + \sigma)(K\delta(\varsigma) + L\delta(\varsigma + 1)). \tag{17}$$

For $\phi \in C([-1,0], \Re^4)$,

$$A(\sigma)\phi = \begin{cases} \frac{d\phi(\varsigma)}{d\varsigma}, & -1 \leq \varsigma < 0, \\ \int_{-1}^{0} d\eta(\varsigma,\sigma)\phi(\varsigma), & \varsigma = 0, \end{cases} \tag{18}$$

and

$$R(\sigma)\phi = \begin{cases} 0, & -1 \leq \varsigma < 0, \\ F(\sigma,\phi), & \varsigma = 0, \end{cases} \tag{19}$$

Then system (13) becomes

$$\dot{X}(t) = A(\sigma)X_t + R(\sigma)X_t. \tag{20}$$

For $\varphi \in C^1([0,1], (\Re^4)^*)$,

$$A^*(\varphi) = \begin{cases} -\frac{d\varphi(s)}{ds}, & 0 < s \leq 1, \\ \int_{-1}^{0} d\eta^T(s,0)\varphi(-s), & s = 0 \end{cases} \tag{21}$$

and

$$\langle \varphi(s), \phi(\varsigma) \rangle = \bar{\varphi}(0)\phi(0) - \int_{\varsigma=-1}^{0} \int_{\rho=0}^{\varsigma} \bar{\varphi}(\rho - \varsigma) d\eta(\varsigma)\phi(\rho)d\rho. \tag{22}$$

Suppose that the eigenvector $\Psi(\varsigma) = (1, \Psi_2, \Psi_3, \Psi_4)^T e^{iv_0\tau_0\varsigma}$ of $A(0)$ related to $+iv_0\tau_0$ and the eigenvector $\Psi^*(\varsigma) = M(1, \Psi_2^*, \Psi_3^*, \Psi_4^*) e^{iv_0\tau_0 s}$ of $A^*(0)$ related to $-iv_0\tau_0$. Then it is not difficult to validate that

$$\Psi_2 = \frac{iv_0 - k_{11} - k_{14}\Psi_4}{k_{12}},$$

$$\Psi_3 = \frac{iv_0 - k_{34}}{(iv_0 - k_{34})(iv_0 - k_{33} - l_{33}e^{-i\tau_0 v_0}) - k_{34}l_{43}e^{-i\tau_0 v_0}},$$

$$\Psi_4 = \frac{l_{43}e^{-i\tau_0 v_0}\Psi_3}{iv_0 - k_{44}},$$

$$\Psi_2^* = -\frac{k_{12}}{iv_0 + k_{22}},$$

$$\Psi_3^* = \frac{k_{12}k_{21}}{k_{31}(iv_0 + k_{22})} - (iv_0 + k_{11}),$$

$$\Psi_4^* = -\frac{k_{23}\Psi_2^* + (iv_0 + k_{33} + l_{33}e^{iv_0\tau_0})\Psi_3^*}{l_{43}e^{iv_0\tau_0}}.$$

and

$$\langle \Psi^*, \Psi \rangle = 1, \langle \Psi^*, \bar{\Psi} \rangle = 0,$$

where

$$M = \frac{1}{1 + \Psi_2\bar{\Psi}_2^* + \Psi_3\bar{\Psi}_3^* + \Psi_4\bar{\Psi}_4^* + \Psi_3e^{-iv_0\tau_0}(l_{33}\bar{\Psi}_3^* + l_{43}\bar{\Psi}_4^*)}.$$

The detailed expressions of coefficients w_{20}, w_{11}, w_{02} and w_{21} can be determined on the basis of the calculation process in [18]:

$$w_{20} = 2\bar{M}\tau_0[k_{15} + k_{16}\Psi_3 + k_{17}\Psi_3^2 + \bar{\Psi}_3^*(k_{35} + k_{36}\Psi_3 + k_{37}\Psi_3^2)],$$

$$w_{11} = \bar{M}\tau_0[2k_{15} + k_{16}(\bar{\Psi}_3 + \Psi_3) + 2k_{17}\bar{\Psi}_3\Psi_3 + \bar{\Psi}_3^*(2k_{35} + k_{36}(\bar{\Psi}_3 + \Psi_3) + 2k_{37}\bar{\Psi}_3\Psi_3)],$$

$$w_{02} = 2\bar{M}\tau_0[k_{15} + k_{16}\bar{\Psi}_3 + k_{17}\bar{\Psi}_3^2 + \bar{\Psi}_3^*(k_{35} + k_{36}\bar{\Psi}_3 + k_{37}\bar{\Psi}_3^2)],$$

$$w_{21} = 2\bar{M}\tau_0[k_{15}(2B_{11}^{(1)}(0) + B_{20}^{(1)}(0)) + k_{16}(B_{11}^{(1)}(0)\Psi_3 + \frac{1}{2}B_{20}^{(1)}(0)\bar{\Psi}_3 + B_{11}^{(3)}(0) + \frac{1}{2}B_{20}^{(3)}(0))$$

$$+ k_{17}(2B_{11}^{(3)}(0) + B_{20}^{(3)}(0)) + k_{18}(\bar{\Psi}_3^2 + 2\Psi_3) + k_{19}(\Psi_3^2 + 2\Psi_3\bar{\Psi}_3) + 3k_{110} + 3k_{111}\Psi_3^2\bar{\Psi}_3$$

$$+ \bar{\Psi}_3^*(k_{35}(2B_{11}^{(1)}(0) + B_{20}^{(1)}(0)) + k_{36}(B_{11}^{(1)}(0)\Psi_3 + \frac{1}{2}B_{20}^{(1)}(0)\bar{\Psi}_3 + B_{11}^{(3)}(0) + \frac{1}{2}B_{20}^{(3)}(0))$$

$$+ k_{37}(2B_{11}^{(3)}(0) + B_{20}^{(3)}(0)) + k_{38}(\bar{\Psi}_3^2 + 2\Psi_3) + k_{39}(\Psi_3^2 + 2\Psi_3\bar{\Psi}_3) + 3k_{310} + 3k_{311}\Psi_3^2\bar{\Psi}_3)],$$

with

$$B_{20}(\varsigma) = \frac{iw_{20}}{v_0\tau_0}\Psi(\varsigma) + \frac{i\bar{w}_{02}}{3v_0\tau_0}\bar{\Psi}(\varsigma) + \Omega_1 e^{2iv_0\tau_0\varsigma}, \tag{23}$$

$$B_{11}(\varsigma) = -\frac{iw_{11}}{v_0\tau_0}\Psi(\varsigma) + \frac{i\bar{w}_{11}}{v_0\tau_0}\bar{\Psi}(\varsigma) + \Omega_2, \tag{24}$$

where

$$\begin{pmatrix} 2iv_0 - k_{11} & -k_{12} & 0 & -k_{14} \\ -k_{21} & 2iv_0 - k_{22} & -k_{23} & -k_{24} \\ -k_{31} & 0 & 2iv_0 - k_{33} - l_{33}e^{-2iv_0\tau_0} & -k_{34} \\ 0 & 0 & -l_{43}e^{-2iv_0\tau_0} & -k_{44} \end{pmatrix} \Omega_1 = \begin{pmatrix} \Omega_{11} \\ 0 \\ \Omega_{13} \\ 0 \end{pmatrix}, \tag{25}$$

$$\begin{pmatrix} k_{11} & k_{12} & 0 & k_{14} \\ k_{21} & k_{22} & k_{23} & k_{24} \\ k_{31} & 0 & k_{33} + l_{33} & k_{34} \\ 0 & 0 & l_{43} & k_{44} \end{pmatrix} \Omega_2 = \begin{pmatrix} \Omega_{31} \\ 0 \\ \Omega_{33} \\ 0 \end{pmatrix}, \tag{26}$$

where

$$\Omega_{11} = k_{15} + k_{16}\Psi_3 + k_{17}\Psi_3^2,$$

$$\Omega_{13} = k_{35} + k_{36}\Psi_3 + k_{37}\Psi_3^2,$$

$$\Omega_{31} = 2k_{15} + k_{16}(\bar{\Psi}_3 + \Psi_3) + 2k_{17}\bar{\Psi}_3\Psi_3,$$

$$\Omega_{33} = 2k_{35} + k_{36}(\bar{\Psi}_3 + \Psi_3) + 2k_{37}\bar{\Psi}_3\Psi_3.$$

Thus, we have

$$\begin{aligned} C_1(0) &= \frac{i}{2v_0\tau_0}\left(w_{11}w_{20} - 2|w_{11}|^2 - \frac{|w_{02}|^2}{3}\right) + \frac{w_{21}}{2} \\ \Pi_0 &= -\frac{Re\{C_1(0)\}}{Re\{\lambda'(\tau_0)\}}, \\ \Pi_1 &= 2Re\{C_1(0)\}. \end{aligned} \tag{27}$$

Theorem 2. The Hopf bifurcation at $\tau = \tau_0$ is supercritical (subcritical) if $\Pi_0 > 0$ ($\Pi_0 < 0$); The periodic solutions exhibiting around the endemic equilibrium point $W_*(S_*, V_*, E_*, I_*)$ is stable (unstable) if $\Pi_1 < 0$ ($\Pi_1 > 0$).

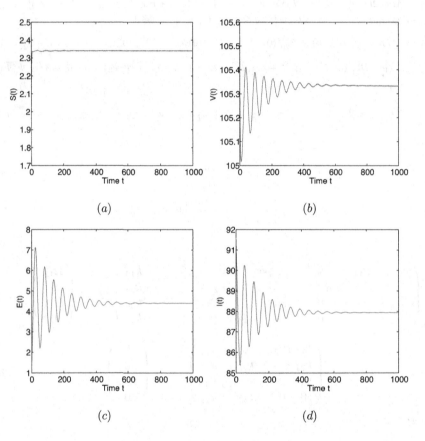

Fig. 1. The time plots for $\tau = 14.4705 < \tau_0 = 15.6626$.

4   Numerical Simulations

In the current section, we utilize the numerical simulations to verify the obtained analytical results in Sect. 2 and Sect. 3. The parameter values are fixed as follows: Choosing $\Lambda = 0.4$, $\mu = 0.002$, $\theta = 0.014$, $\omega = 0.6$, $\beta = 0.24$, $c = 10$, $q = 0.9$, $\gamma = 0.003$, $\xi = 0.01$, $\sigma = 0.1$. Then the model system (2) becomes

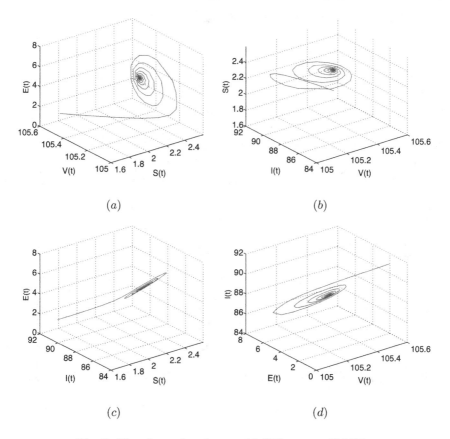

Fig. 2. The phase plots for $\tau = 14.4705 < \tau_0 = 15.6626$.

$$\begin{cases} \frac{dS(t)}{dt} = 0.4 - 0.602\, S(t) + 0.014\, V(t) - \frac{0.24\, S(t)I(t)}{S(t)+I(t)+10} + 0.0003I(t), \\ \frac{dV(t)}{dt} = 0.6\, S(t) - 0.016\, V(t) + 0.01E(t) + 0.0027I(t), \\ \frac{dE(t)}{dt} = \frac{0.24\, S(t)I(t)}{S(t)+I(t)+10} - 0.012E(t) - 0.1E(t-\tau), \\ \frac{dI(t)}{dt} = 0.1E(t-\tau) - 0.005I(t), \end{cases} \qquad (28)$$

from which one has $R_0 = 14.6520 > 1$ and then the unique endemic equilibrium point $W_*(2.3398, 105.3279, 4.3968, 87.9355)$ is obtained. By calculations, we obtain $\sigma\beta(S_* + c)S_* = 0.6929$ and $\kappa_2(\mu + \gamma)(S_* + I_* + c)^2 = 5.6309$. Thus, $\sigma\beta(S_* + c)S_* \leq \kappa_2(\mu + \gamma)(S_* + I_* + c)^2$ is satisfied. Accordingly, we can know that the model system (28) is locally asymptotically stable whenever $\tau = 0$.

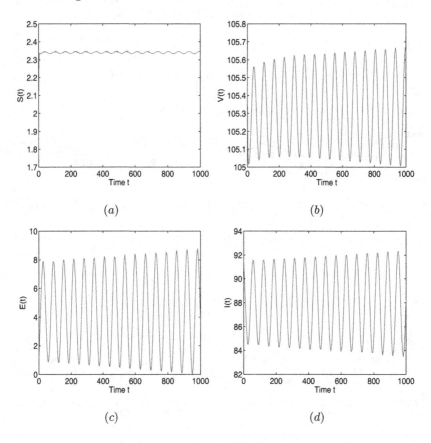

Fig. 3. The time plots for $\tau = 17.2562 > \tau_0 = 15.6626$.

For $\tau > 0$, we obtain $v_0 = 0.7195$, $\tau_0 = 15.6626$ and $\lambda'(\tau_0) = 0.009308 + i2.003327$. That is to say, the sufficient criteria for appearance of Hopf bifurcation at $\tau_0 = 15.6626$ hold. We first fix $\tau = 14.4705 \in (\tau_0 = 15.6626)$, it can be illustrated in Figs. 1–2 that the model system (28) is locally asymptotically stable. By contrary, when we fix $\tau = 17.2562 > \tau_0 = 15.6626$, them model system (28) loses its stability. Numerical simulation figures are shown as in Figs. 3–4. Specially, we have $C_1(0) = -0.000604 - i0.003251$ through some complicated computations, and then we have $\Pi_0 = 0.064890 > 0$ and $\Pi_1 = -0.001208 < 0$. Therefore, in accordance with Theorem 2, we have the conclusion that the Hopf bifurcation experiences at $\tau_0 = 15.6626$ is supercritical and the bifurcating periodic solutions exhibiting around $W_*(2.3398, 105.3279, 4.3968, 87.9355)$ are stable.

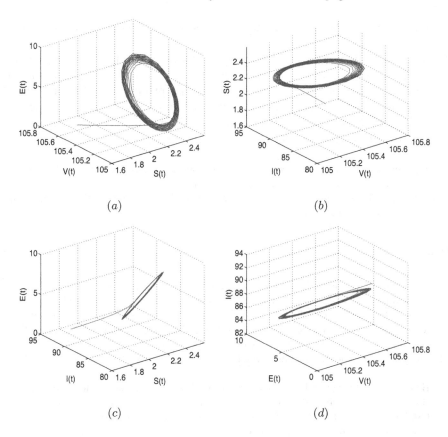

Fig. 4. The phase plots for $\tau = 17.2562 > \tau_0 = 15.6626$.

5   Conclusions

With more and more applications of networks in our daily life, the damage caused by computer viruses is also gradually obvious. Therefore, it is imperative to grope for the law governing the dissemination of computer viruses. Towards this goal, a delayed SVEIS worm propagation model concludes nonlinear incidence rate by drawing the time delay because of the incubation interval of worms into the model formulated by Upadhyay and Kumari [15]. We mainly investigate the impact of the time delay on the proposed model, and the main findings are demonstrated in the form of local stability and Hopf bifurcation.

The basic reproduction number R_0 and existence of the unique endemic equilibrium $W_*(S_*, V_*, E_*, I_*)$ are obtained. A series of sufficient criteria for local stability and exhibition of Hopf bifurcation are derived with aids of eigenvalue method. It is found that the proposed model is locally asymptotically stable when the value of the time delay is fixed below the crucial value τ_0 under some specified conditions. In this situation, the numbers of the susceptible nodes, the vaccinated nodes, the exposed nodes and the infectious nodes tend to the equilibrium $W_*(S_*, V_*, E_*, I_*)$, and the law governing the dissemination of worms can be forecasted. Otherwise, the propagation of worms will be out of control whenever the value of the time delay exceeds the crucial value τ_0. Therefore, by taking measures to control the incubation period time delay of the worm, we can get a stable system that will be beneficial to control the spread of the worm on the network. Furthermore, direction and stability of the Hopf bifurcation are determined by center manifold method. Our study's findings supplement the work by Upadhyay and Kumari [15].

Acknowledgements. Thanks very much for your kind work on this conference. On behalf of my co-authors, we would like to express our great appreciation to editor and reviewers. We sincerely hope to get your suggestions for this paper and may this conference enjoy complete success.

References

1. Mishra, B.K., Pandey, S.K.: Dynamic model of worms with vertical transmission in computer network. Appl. Math. Comput. **217**(21), 8438–8446 (2011)
2. Feng, L.P., Song, L.P., Zhao, Q.S., Wang, H.B.: Modeling and stability analysis of worm propagation in wireless sensor network. Math. Probl. Eng. **2015**, 1–8 (2015)
3. Berghel, H.: The code red worm. Commun. ACM **44**(12), 15–19 (2001)
4. Shannon, C., Moore, D.: The spread of the witty worm. IEEE Secur. Priv. **3**(2), 46–50 (2004)
5. Hosseini, S., Azgomi, M.A., Rahmani, A.T.: Malware propagation modeling considering software diversity and immunization. J. Comput. Sci. **13**, 49–67 (2016)
6. Guillen, J.D.H., Rey, A.M.D., Encinas, L.H.: Study of the stability of a SEIRS model for computer worm propagation. Phys. A **479**, 411–421 (2017)
7. Geetha, R., Madhusudanan, V., Srinivas, M.N.: Influence of clamor on the transmission of worms in remote sensor network. Wirel. Pers. Commun. **118**(1), 461–473 (2021)
8. Xiao, X., Fu, P., Dou, C.S., Li, Q., Hu, G.W., Xia, S.T.: Design and analysis of SEIQR worm propagation model in mobile internet. Commun. Nonlinear Sci. Numer. Simul. **43**, 341–350 (2017)
9. Srivastava, P.K., Ojha, R.P., Sharma, K., Awasthi, S., Sanyal, G.: Effect of quarantine and recovery on infectious nodes in wireless sensor network. Int. J. Sens. Wirel. Commun. Control **8**, 26–36 (2018)
10. Khanh, N.H.: Dynamics of a worm propagation model with quarantine in wireless sensor networks. Appl. Math. Inf. Sci. **10**(5), 1739–1746 (2016)
11. Mishra, B.K., Keshri, N.: Mathematical model on the transmission of worms in wireless sensor network. Appl. Math. Model. **37**(6), 4103–4111 (2013)
12. Singh, A., Awasthi, A.K., Singh, K., Srivastava, P.K.: Modeling and analysis of worm propagation in wireless sensor networks. Wirel. Pers. Commun. **98**(3), 2535–2551 (2018)
13. Nwokoye, C.H., Umeh, I.I.: The SEIQR-V model: on a more accurate analytical characterization of malicious treat defense. Int. J. Inf. Technol. Comput. Sci. **9**(12), 28–37 (2017)
14. Mishra, B.K., Pandey, S.K.: Dynamic model of worm propagation in computer network. Appl. Math. Model. **38**(7), 2173–2179 (2014)

15. Upadhyay, R.K., Kumari, S.: Global stability of worm propagation model with nonlinear incidence rate in computer network. Int. J. Netw. Secur. **20**(3), 515–526 (2018)
16. Zhang, J.F.: Bifurcation analysis of a modified Holling–Tanner predator–prey model with time delay. Appl. Math. Model. **36**(3), 1219–1231 (2012)
17. Li, X.L., Wei, J.J.: On the zeros of a fourth degree exponential polynomial with applications to a neural network model with delays. Chaos, Solitons Fractals **26**(2), 519–526 (2005)
18. Hassard, B.D., Kazarinoff, N.D., Wan, Y.H.: Theory and Applications of Hopf Bifurcation. Cambridge University Press, Cambridge (1981)

Fractional Order Computing and Modeling with Portending Complex Fit Real-World Data

Yeliz Karaca[1,2]($\boxtimes$)(iD), Mati ur Rahman[3](iD), and Dumitru Baleanu[4,5](iD)

[1] University of Massachusetts Chan Medical School (UMASS),
55 Lake Avenue North, Worcester, MA 01655, USA
yeliz.karaca@ieee.org
[2] Massachusetts Institute of Technology (MIT), 77 Massachusetts Avenue,
Cambridge, MA 02139, USA
[3] Department of Computer Science and Mathematics, Lebanese American University,
Beirut, Lebanon
[4] Department of Mathematics, Çankaya University, 1406530 Ankara, Türkiye
[5] Institute of Space Sciences, Magurele, Bucharest, Romania

Abstract. Fractional computing models identify the states of different systems with a focus on formulating fractional order compartment models through the consideration of differential equations based on the underlying stochastic processes. Thus, a systematic approach to address and ensure predictive accuracy allows that the model remains physically reasonable at all times, providing a convenient interpretation and feasible design regarding all the parameters of the model. Towards these manifolding processes, this study aims to introduce new concepts of fractional calculus that manifest crossover effects in dynamical models. Piecewise global fractional derivatives in sense of Caputo and Atangana-Baleanu-Caputo (ABC) have been utilized, and they are applied to formulate the Zika Virus (ZV) disease model. To have a predictive analysis of the behavior of the model, the domain is subsequently split into two subintervals and the piecewise behavior is investigated. Afterwards, the fixed point theory of Schauder and Banach is benefited from to prove the existence and uniqueness of at least one solution in both senses for the considered problem. As for the numerical simulations as per the data, Newton interpolation formula has been modified and extended for the considered nonlinear system. Finally, graphical presentations and illustrative examples based on the data for various compartments of the systems have been presented with respect to the applicable real-world data for different fractional orders. Based on the impact of fractional order reducing the abrupt changes, the results obtained from the study demonstrate and also validate that increasing the fractional order brings about a greater crossover effect, which is obvious from the observed data, which is critical for the effective management and control of abrupt changes like infectious diseases, viruses, among many more unexpected phenomena in chaotic, uncertain and transient circumstances.

© The Author(s), under exclusive license to Springer Nature Switzerland AG 2023
O. Gervasi et al. (Eds.): ICCSA 2023 Workshops, LNCS 14104, pp. 144–159, 2023.
https://doi.org/10.1007/978-3-031-37105-9_11

Keywords: Fractional computing models · crossover behavior · complex fit real-world data · mathematical biology · computational biology · fractional calculus · piecewise global fractional derivatives · Newton interpolation formula · ABC fractional derivatives · equicontinuous mapping · Schauder's fixed point theorem · dynamics of multi-compartment models · fractional order compartment models · stochastic differential equations · differential equations

1   Introduction

The integration of advanced mathematics towards the solution of fractional-order calculus/systems and achieve the feasible designs for various applications of fractional-order systems. Accordingly, fractional-order modeling of dynamic systems with applications is utilized to describe various real-world phenomena and processes. Dynamical systems are often modeled based on algebraic, differential/integral or difference equations, while the majority of real-world processes as well as phenomena have been modeled by using nonlinear differential or integral and difference equations. This particular domain has diverse applications in most fields of engineering, physics, chemistry, control theory, mathematical biology and epidemiology. Several illnesses and viral diseases have significantly affected human populations, ranging from measles, to TB, malaria, HBV, HCV, tumor cancers, the Spanish flu and COVID-19, among many others, resulting in high mortality rates.

As a result of such abrupt developments, various strategies have been designed and implemented to control and reduce the spread of infections within their communities. While many epidemics have been effectively controlled through the discovery of cures and treatments, there are still some diseases that remain incurable and lack proper medications or treatments. Among the aforesaid diseases, Zika disease, is one of the most infectious ones, caused by the bite of infectious Aedes insects. Outbreaks due to Zika virus have been recorded in different counties of Africa (for further details please see [1]). The symptoms of disease are laziness and sudden disease cause other signs like rashes of skins, sudden fever, conjunctness and feeling of pains in all parts of the body. The said signs may remain for two to seven days, and sometimes the signs do not appear in the infecting individual. This virus may also impact all the women whom have pregnancy and may transferred to the new born easily (see further detail in [2,3]). In this way, the new fetal may also faces abnormality, small head, weak muscles and weak system of nerves.

It is remarkable that researchers are increasingly use different tools and analysis for investigating epidemiological disease, and one of the powerful tools is the mathematical formulation. Mathematical models have been increasingly used as robust means for the predictions and accurate analyses pertaining to the transmission dynamics of infectious diseases. Given these, varying degrees of mathematical models have been formulated, used for the description of different diseases. Different studies have provided the formulation of the ZV disease by using nonlinear differential equations. For instance, the Kucharsk et al. [4] formulated the ZV disease which spread during 2013–14 in France. By the applications of controlling theory of optimality, Okosun and Bonyah [5] investigated some procedural means to minimize the transition dynamics of the infection, and another study posited that the usage of cure and spray for mosquitos could reduce its spread (see the details in [6]). For some remarkable applications of fractional differential operators, the following references can be referred to [7–9]. It should be noted that fractional order integral and differential operators are nonlocal in nature and have the ability to provide global dynamics which include the traditional order dynamics as special case (see further details in [10,11]). As a result of the aforementioned observations, researchers have been prompted to investigate various dynamic problems in the context of fractional order derivatives utilizing different operators, as evident in [12–14].

There are differential operators of two classes of operators on the basis of kernels: while one class includes operators such as Riemann-Liouville and Caputo operators with singular kernel type operators, others such as Caputo-Fabrizio and Atangana-Baleanu, many others, are included in non-singular kernel type class. It can be stated that both kinds have a variety of applications in mathematical modeling of various real-world problems, having been used in many studies some of which are in [15–17]. To study the phenomenon of crossover behavior, numerous differential operators have been proposed in the literature, such as fractal derivatives, non-integer order derivatives with singular or nonsingular kernels, fractal-fractional operators, among many others (see [19–21] for more details). Although randomness can be modeled using stochastic equations with some degree of success, the phenomenon of crossover behavior in dynamics remains a challenging problem to explain. In the field of fractional calculus, exponential and Mittag-Leffler mappings have limitations in determining the time of crossovers. To address this issue, new approaches involving various piecewise differentiations and integrations have recently been introduced (see [22] for more details). In this paper, we provide an introduction of classical and global piecewise derivatives and integral, along with some applicable examples and numerical schemes with feasible design. Towards these manifolding processes, this study, with the unique solution of the proposed problem, aims to introduce new concepts of fractional calculus that manifest crossover effects in dynamical models. In addition, as inspired from the above discussion, we initially investigate the mathematical model given in [18] by using the Caputo and Atangana-Baleanu piecewise differential operators. We formulated the proposed model in the

$$
\begin{aligned}
&{}_{0}^{CABC}D_{t}^{\varpi}(\mathcal{X}(t)) = \lambda_{h} - \alpha_{1}\beta_{1}\mathcal{X}\mathcal{U} - \delta_{1}\mathcal{X}, \\
&{}_{0}^{CABC}D_{t}^{\varpi}(\mathcal{Y}(t)) = \alpha_{1}\beta_{1}\mathcal{X}\mathcal{U} - \delta_{1}\mathcal{Y}, \\
&{}_{0}^{CABC}D_{t}^{\varpi}(\mathcal{Z}(t)) = \lambda_{m} - \alpha_{2}\beta_{2}\mathcal{Y}\mathcal{Z} - \delta_{2}\mathcal{Z}, \\
&{}_{0}^{CABC}D_{t}^{\varpi}(\mathcal{U}(t)) = \alpha_{2}\beta_{2}\mathcal{Y}\mathcal{Z} - \delta_{2}\mathcal{U}, \\
&\mathcal{X}(0) = \mathcal{X}_{0}, \ \mathcal{Y}(0) = \mathcal{Y}_{0}, \\
&\mathcal{Z}(0) = \mathcal{Z}_{0}, \ \mathcal{U}(0) = \mathcal{U}_{0},
\end{aligned}
\tag{1}
$$

In a more explicit form, the model (1) can also be written as

$$
{}^{CABC}_{0}D_t^{\varpi}(\mathcal{X}(t)) = \begin{cases} {}^{C}_{0}D_t^{\varpi}(\mathcal{X}(t)) = {}^{C} H_1(\mathcal{X},\mathcal{Y},\mathcal{Z},\mathcal{U},t), & 0 < t \le t_1, \\ {}^{ABC}_{0}D_t^{\varpi}(\mathcal{X}(t)) = {}^{ABC} H_1(\mathcal{X},\mathcal{Y},\mathcal{Z},\mathcal{U},t), & t_1 < t \le T, \end{cases}
$$

$$
{}^{CABC}_{0}D_t^{\varpi}(\mathcal{Y}(t)) = \begin{cases} {}^{C}_{0}D_t^{\varpi}(\mathcal{Y}(t)) = {}^{C} H_2(\mathcal{X},\mathcal{Y},\mathcal{Z},\mathcal{U},t), & 0 < t \le t_1, \\ {}^{ABC}_{0}D_t^{\varpi}(\mathcal{Y}(t)) = {}^{ABC} H_2(\mathcal{X},\mathcal{Y},\mathcal{Z},\mathcal{U},t), & t_1 < t \le T, \end{cases}
$$

$$
{}^{CABC}_{0}D_t^{\varpi}(\mathcal{Z}(t)) = \begin{cases} {}^{C}_{0}D_t^{\varpi}(\mathcal{Z}(t)) = {}^{C} H_3(\mathcal{X},\mathcal{Y},\mathcal{Z},\mathcal{U},t), & 0 < t \le t_1, \\ {}^{ABC}_{0}D_t^{\varpi}(\mathcal{Z}(t)) = {}^{ABC} H_3(\mathcal{X},\mathcal{Y},\mathcal{Z},\mathcal{U},t), & t_1 < t \le T, \end{cases}
$$

$$
{}^{CABC}_{0}D_t^{\varpi}(\mathcal{U}(t)) = \begin{cases} {}^{C}_{0}D_t^{\varpi}(\mathcal{U}(t)) = {}^{C} H_4(\mathcal{X},\mathcal{Y},\mathcal{Z},\mathcal{U},t), & 0 < t \le t_1, \\ {}^{ABC}_{0}D_t^{\varpi}(\mathcal{U}(t)) = {}^{ABC} H_4(\mathcal{X},\mathcal{Y},\mathcal{Z},\mathcal{U},t), & t_1 < t \le T, \end{cases} \tag{2}
$$

where ${}^{C}_{0}D_t^{\varpi}$ and ${}^{ABC}_{0}D_t^{\varpi}$ are Caputo and ABC derivative respectively. We investigate the existence results and uniqueness of at least one approximate solution.

The remainder of this paper is outlined as follows: Sect. 2 provides Preliminary definitions, Sect. 3 presents information on Existence and uniqueness demonstrative results and Sect. 4 on Numerical Scheme. The next section, namely Sect. 5, addresses Experimental Results and Discussion: Numerical performances of the piecewise global fractional derivatives for Zika virus infection and finally Sect. 6 provides Conclusion and Future Directions.

2   Preliminary Definitions

Foundational definitions can be provided in this part of the study [19, 21].

Definition 1. *Let $V(t) \in \mathcal{H}^1(0,T)$ be a function, the ABC derivative can be written as*

$$
{}^{ABC}_{0}D_t^{\varpi}(V(t)) = \frac{ABC(\varpi)}{1-\varpi} \int_0^t \frac{d}{d\wp}V(\wp)E_\varpi\left[\frac{-\varpi}{1-\varpi}\left(t-\wp\right)^\varpi\right]d\wp, \tag{3}
$$

where the normalization function is defined as $ABC(0) = ABC(1) = 1$.

And the integration can be written as

$$
{}^{ABC}_{0}I_t^{\varpi}V(t) = \frac{1-\varpi}{ABC(\varpi)}V(t) + \frac{\varpi}{ABC(\varpi)\Gamma(\varpi)} \int_0^t (t-\wp)^{\varpi-1}V(\wp)d\wp. \tag{4}
$$

Definition 2. *The Caputo derivative for a function $V(t)$ is defined as*

$$
{}^{C}_{0}D_t^{\varpi}V(t) = \frac{1}{\Gamma(1-\varpi)} \int_0^t (t-\wp)^{n-\varpi-1}[V^{'}(\wp)]d\wp.
$$

Definition 3. *Consider a differentiable increasing functions be $V(t)$ and $g(t)$, then the classical piecewise derivative is given as*

$$
{}_{0}^{PG}D_t V(t) = \begin{cases} V(t), & 0 < t \leq t_1, \\ \dfrac{V'(t)}{g'(t)} & t_1 < t \leq T, \end{cases}
$$

while the integration is

$$
{}_{0}^{PG}I_t V(t) = \begin{cases} \displaystyle\int_0^t V(\tau)d\tau, & 0 < t \leq t_1, \\ \displaystyle\int_{t_1}^t V(\tau)g'(\tau)d(\tau) & t_1 < t \leq T, \end{cases}
$$

here ${}_{0}^{PG}D_t V(t)$ and ${}_{0}^{PG}I_t V(t)$ stands for classical derivative and integration in $0 < t \leq t_1$ and for global derivative and integration in $t_1 < t \leq T$.

Definition 4. *Consider a differentiable function be $V(t)$, then the classical and fractional piecewise derivative is defined as*

$$
{}_{0}^{PC}D_t^{\varpi}V(t) = \begin{cases} V'(t), & 0 < t \leq t_1, \\ {}_{0}^{C}D_t^{\varpi}V(t) & t_1 < t \leq T, \end{cases}
$$

and the integration can be written as

$$
{}_{0}^{PC}I_t V(t) = \begin{cases} \displaystyle\int_0^t V(\tau)d\tau, & 0 < t \leq t_1, \\ \dfrac{1}{\Gamma \varpi} \displaystyle\int_{t_1}^t (t-\wp)^{\varpi-1}V(\wp)d(\wp) & t_1 < t \leq T, \end{cases}
$$

here ${}_{0}^{PC}D_t^{\varpi}V(t)$ and ${}_{0}^{PC}I_t V(t)$ present classical derivative and integration in $0 < t \leq t_1$ and fractional derivative and integration in $t_1 < t \leq T$.

Definition 5. *If a differentiable function be $V(t)$, then the Caputo and ABC piecewise derivative is given by*

$$
{}_{0}^{PCABC}D_t^{\varpi}V(t) = \begin{cases} {}_{0}^{C}D_t^{\varpi}V(t), & 0 < t \leq t_1, \\ {}_{0}^{ABC}D_t^{\varpi}V(t) & t_1 < t \leq T, \end{cases}
$$

while the integration can be written as

$$
{}_{0}^{PCABC}I_t V(t) = \begin{cases} \dfrac{1}{\Gamma \varpi} \displaystyle\int_{t_1}^t (t-\wp)^{\varpi-1}V(\wp)d(\wp), & 0 < t \leq t_1, \\ \dfrac{1-\varpi}{ABC\varpi}V(t) + \dfrac{\varpi}{ABC\varpi\Gamma\varpi} \displaystyle\int_{t_1}^t (t-\wp)^{\varpi-1}V(\wp)d(\wp) & t_1 < t \leq T. \end{cases}
$$

here ${}_{0}^{PCABC}D_t^{\varpi}V(t)$ and ${}_{0}^{PCABC}I_t V(t)$ is Caputo derivative and integration in $0 < t \leq t_1$ and ABC derivative and integration in $t_1 < t \leq T$.

Lemma 1. *The piecewise derivable equation solution for the right sides vanishes at $t = 0$*

$$_0^{PCABC}D_t^\varpi \mathcal{V}(t) = H(\mathcal{V}, t), \quad 0 < \varpi \leq 1$$

is given by

$$\mathcal{V}(t) = \begin{cases} \mathcal{V}_0 + \dfrac{1}{\Gamma(\varpi)}\displaystyle\int_0^t H(\wp, \mathcal{V}(\wp))(t - \wp)^{\varpi-1}d\wp, \ 0 < t \leq t_1 \\[3mm] \mathcal{V}(t_1) + \dfrac{1-\varpi}{ABC(\varpi)}H(\mathcal{V}, t) + \dfrac{\varpi}{ABC(\varpi)\Gamma(\varpi)}\displaystyle\int_{t_1}^t (t - \wp)^{\varpi-1}H(\wp, \mathcal{V}(\wp))d(\wp). \end{cases}$$

3 Existence and Uniqueness Demonstrative Results

In order to demonstrate the existence and uniqueness of a solution to the problem at hand, we can express the system can be stated (2) in a manner similar to that shown in Lemma 1. Building on this, we can then proceed to provide a more detailed explanation, as follows, can be provided:

$$_0^{PCABC}D_t^\varpi \mathcal{V}(t) = H(t, \mathcal{V}(t)), \quad 0 < \varpi \leq 1,$$

is

$$\mathcal{V}(t) = \begin{cases} \mathcal{V}_0 + \dfrac{1}{\Gamma(\varpi)}\displaystyle\int_0^t H(\wp, \mathcal{V}(\wp))(t - \wp)^{\varpi-1}d\wp, \ 0 < t \leq t_1, \\[3mm] \mathcal{V}(t_1) + \dfrac{1-\varpi}{ABC(\varpi)}H(\mathcal{V}, t) + \dfrac{\varpi}{ABC(\varpi)\Gamma\varpi}\displaystyle\int_{t_1}^t (t - \wp)^{\varpi-1}H(\wp, \mathcal{V}(\wp))d(\wp), \end{cases} \tag{5}$$

where

$$\mathcal{V}(t) = \begin{cases} X(t) \\ Y(t) \\ Z(t) \\ U(t), \end{cases} \quad \mathcal{V}_0 = \begin{cases} X_0 \\ Y_0 \\ Z_0 \\ U_0, \end{cases} \quad \mathcal{V}_{t_1} = \begin{cases} X_{t_1} \\ Y_{t_1} \\ Z_{t_1} \\ U_{t_1}, \end{cases} \quad H(t, \mathcal{V}(t)) = \begin{cases} H_i = \begin{cases} {}^C H_i(\mathcal{X}, \mathcal{Y}, \mathcal{Z}, \mathcal{U}, t) \\ {}^{ABC} H_i(\mathcal{X}, \mathcal{Y}, \mathcal{Z}, \mathcal{U}, t), \end{cases} \end{cases} \tag{6}$$

where $i = 1, 2, 3, 4$. Take $\infty > T \geq t > 0$ with Banach space as $E_1 = C[0, T]$ endowed with norm

$$\|\mathcal{V}\| = \max_{t \in [0, T]} |\mathcal{V}(t)|.$$

In order to obtain the desired outcome, we examine the growth condition of the non-linear function, which can be expressed as:

(C1) There exists constants $L_\mathcal{V} > 0$; for every $H, \bar{\mathcal{V}} \in E \ni$

$$|H(t, \mathcal{V}) - H(t, \bar{\mathcal{V}})| \leq L_H |\mathcal{V} - \bar{\mathcal{V}}|.$$

(C2) Let one has constants $C_H > 0$ and $M_H > 0, \ni$

$$|H(t, \mathcal{V})| \leq C_H |\mathcal{V}| + M_H$$

holds.

Theorem 1. *Assuming that H is continuous piecewisely on the subintervals $0 < t \leq t_1$ and $t_1 < t \leq T$ of $[0, T]$, and subject to the hypothesis $(C2)$, it can be concluded that the piecewise problem expressed in Eq. (2) has at least one solution on every of these subintervals.*

Proof. We can use the Schauder fixed point theorem to define a closed subset B of E on both subintervals $0 < T \leq t_1$ and $t_1 < T \leq T$.

$$B = \{\mathcal{V} \in E : \|\mathcal{V}\| \leq R_{1,2}, \ R_{1,2} > 0\},$$

Considering the operator $\mathcal{T} : B \to B$ and using Eq. (5) as

$$\mathcal{T}(\mathcal{V}) = \begin{cases} \mathcal{V}_0 + \dfrac{1}{\Gamma(\varpi)} \displaystyle\int_0^{t_1} H(\wp, \mathcal{V}(\wp))(t - \wp)^{\varpi - 1} d\wp, \ 0 < t \leq t_1 \\ \mathcal{V}(t_1) + \dfrac{1 - \varpi}{ABC(\varpi)} H(t, \mathcal{V}(t)) + \dfrac{\varpi}{ABC(\varpi)\Gamma(\varpi)} \displaystyle\int_{t_1}^t (t - \wp)^{\varpi - 1} H(\wp \mathcal{V}(\wp)) d(\wp). \end{cases} \tag{7}$$

On any $\mathcal{V} \in B$, we get

$$|\mathcal{T}(\mathcal{V})(t)| \leq \begin{cases} |\mathcal{V}_0| + \dfrac{1}{\Gamma(\varpi)} \displaystyle\int_0^{t_1} (t - \wp)^{\varpi - 1} |H(\wp, \mathcal{U}(\wp))| d\wp, \\ |\mathcal{V}_{t_1}| + \dfrac{1 - \varpi}{ABC(\varpi)} |H(t, \mathcal{V}(t))| \\ + \dfrac{\varpi}{ABC(\varpi)\Gamma(\varpi)} \displaystyle\int_{t_1}^t (t - \wp)^{\varpi - 1} |H(\wp \mathcal{V}(\wp))| d(\wp), \end{cases}$$

$$\leq \begin{cases} |\mathcal{V}_0| + \dfrac{\mathbf{T}^\varpi}{\Gamma(\varpi + 1)} [C_H |\mathcal{V}| + M_H] = R_1, \ 0 < t \leq t_1, \\ |\mathcal{V}_{t_1}| + \dfrac{1 - \varpi}{ABC(\varpi)} [C_H |\mathcal{V}| + M_H] \\ + \dfrac{\varpi(T - \mathbf{T})^\varpi}{ABC(\varpi)\Gamma\varpi + 1} [C_H |\mathcal{V}| + M_H] d(\wp) = R_2, \end{cases}$$

$$\|\mathcal{T}(\mathcal{U})\| \leq \begin{cases} R_1, \ 0 < t \leq t_1, \\ R_2, \ t_1 < t \leq T. \end{cases}$$

Fixing $R_{1,2} = \max\{R_1, R_2\}$, we see that $\|\mathcal{T}(\mathcal{V})\| \leq R_{1,2}$ which demonstrate that $\mathcal{T}$ is bounded and also $\mathcal{T}(\mathcal{V}) \in B$. Thus, $\mathcal{T}(B) \subset B$. Further, for completely continuity, $t_i < t_j \in [0, t_1]$ is taken in Caputo sense such that

$$|\mathcal{T}(\mathcal{V})(t_j) - \mathcal{T}(\mathcal{V})(t_i)| = \left| \dfrac{1}{\Gamma(\varpi)} \int_0^{t_j} (t_j - \wp)^{\varpi - 1} H(\wp, \mathcal{V}(\wp)) d\wp, \right.$$

$$\left. - \dfrac{1}{\Gamma(\varpi)} \int_0^{t_i} (t_i - \wp)^{\varpi - 1} H(\wp, \mathcal{V}(\wp)) d\wp \right|$$

$$\leq \dfrac{(C_H \mathcal{V} + M_H)}{\Gamma(\varpi + 1)} [t_j^\varpi - t_i^\varpi + 2(t_j - t_i)^\varpi]. \tag{8}$$

From (8), it is observed that as t_i tends to t_j, then

$$|\mathcal{T}(\mathcal{V})(t_j) - \mathcal{T}(\mathcal{V})(t_i)| \to 0, \text{ as } t_i \to t_j.$$

Since $\mathcal{T}$ is bounded on $[0, t_1]$, so is uniformly continuous also over $[0, t_1]$. Hence, it can be concluded that $\mathcal{T}$ over the said interval is equi-continuous as well.

Next we take the other interval $t_i, t_j \in [t_1, T]$ in the ABC sense as

$$|\mathcal{T}(\mathcal{V})(t_j) - \mathcal{T}(\mathcal{V})(t_i)| = \left| \frac{1 - \varpi}{ABC(\varpi)} H(t, \mathcal{V}(t)) + \frac{\varpi}{ABC(\varpi)\Gamma(\varpi)} \int_{t_1}^{t_j} (t_j - \wp)^{\varpi - 1} H(\wp, \mathcal{V}(\wp)) d\wp, \right.$$

$$\left. - \frac{1 - \varpi}{ABC(\varpi)} H(t, \mathcal{V}(t)) + \frac{(\varpi)}{ABC(\varpi)\Gamma(\varpi)} \int_{t_1}^{t_i} (t_i - \wp)^{\varpi - 1} H(\wp, \mathcal{U}(\wp)) d\wp \right| \tag{9}$$

$$\leq \frac{\varpi(C_H \mathcal{V} + M_H)}{ABC(\varpi)\Gamma(\varpi + 1)} [t_j^{\varpi} - t_i^{\varpi} + 2(t_j - t_i)^{\varpi}].$$

Also from (9), we see that

$$|\mathcal{T}(\mathcal{V})(t_j) - \mathcal{T}(\mathcal{V})(t_i)| \to 0, \text{ as } t_i \to t_j.$$

Due to uniform continuity of $\mathcal{T}$ over the said interval, It can be concluded that the mapping $\mathcal{T}$ is equicontinuous over the interval $[t_1, T]$, making it an equicontinuous mapping. By applying the Arzelà-Ascoli theorem, it can be shown that the operator $\mathcal{T}$ is both completely continuous and uniformly continuous, and has bounds. Hence, using Schauder's fixed point theorem, it can be deduced that the piecewise differentiable problem stated in Eq. (2) has at least one solution on each subinterval.

Theorem 2. *In view of hypothesis (C1) together with the condition that*

$$\max \left\{ \frac{\mathbf{T}^{\varpi}}{\Gamma(\varpi + 1)} L_H, L_H \left[\frac{1 - \varpi}{ABC(\varpi)} + \frac{\varpi(T - \mathbf{T})^{\varpi}}{ABC(\varpi)\Gamma(\varpi + 1)} \right] \right\} < 1,$$

the proposed model has unique solution.

Proof. We define the operator $\mathcal{T} : E \to E$, where E is a certain set, and consider $\mathcal{V}$ and $\bar{\mathcal{V}} \in E$ on the interval $[0, t_1]$ in the Caputo sense

$$\|\mathcal{T}(\mathcal{V}) - \mathcal{T}(\bar{\mathcal{V}})\| = \max_{t \in [0, t_1]} \left| \frac{1}{\Gamma(\varpi)} \int_0^t (t - \wp)^{\varpi - 1} H(\wp, \mathcal{V}(\wp)) d\wp \right.$$

$$\left. - \frac{1}{\Gamma(\varpi)} \int_0^t (t - \wp)^{\varpi - 1} H(\wp, \bar{\mathcal{V}}(\wp)) d\wp \right|$$

$$\leq \frac{\mathbf{T}^{\varpi}}{\Gamma(\varpi + 1)} L_H \|\mathcal{V} - \bar{\mathcal{V}}\|.$$

Using Eq. (10), we obtain

$$\|\mathcal{T}(\mathcal{V}) - \mathcal{T}(\bar{\mathcal{V}})\| \leq \frac{\mathbf{T}^{\varpi}}{\Gamma(\varpi + 1)} L_H \|\mathcal{V} - \bar{\mathcal{V}}\|. \tag{10}$$

Assuming that $\mathcal{T}$ is a contraction, according to the Banach contraction theorem, the considered problem has a unique solution in the given sub-interval. For $t \in [t_1, T]$ and in the sense of the ABC derivative, we can proceed to the next step.

$$\|\mathcal{T}(\mathcal{V}) - \mathcal{T}(\bar{\mathcal{V}})\| \leq \frac{1 - \varpi}{ABC(\varpi)} L_H \|\mathcal{V} - \bar{\mathcal{V}}\| + \frac{\varpi(\mathbf{T} - T^{\varpi})}{ABC(\varpi)\Gamma(\varpi + 1)} L_H \|\mathcal{V} - \bar{\mathcal{V}}\|. \quad (11)$$

or

$$\|\mathcal{T}(\mathcal{V}) - \mathcal{T}(\bar{\mathcal{V}})\| \leq L_H \left[\frac{1 - \varpi}{ABC(\varpi)} + \frac{\varpi(T - \mathbf{T})^{\varpi}}{ABC(\varpi)\Gamma(\varpi + 1)} \right] \|\mathcal{V} - \bar{\mathcal{V}}\|. \quad (12)$$

Assuming that $\mathcal{T}$ is a contraction, we can apply the Banach contraction theorem to conclude that the considered problem has a unique solution in the given sub-interval. Furthermore, based on relations (10) and (12), it can be confirmed that the problem proposed in this study has a unique solution.

4   Numerical Scheme

In order to solve the system of piecewise differential equations given in Eq. (2), it is essential to design a numerical scheme, and accordingly, the approach of the study has been develop a scheme that works for the two subintervals, or strains, of the interval $[0, T]$, using the Caputo and ABC formulations. To achieve this, the numerical scheme for the piecewise derivative of integer order is handled, as has been presented in reference [22]. To apply the scheme, we use piecewise integration on the first Eq. (2), has been employed separately for the Caputo and ABC formats, which yields:

$$\mathcal{X}(t)) = \begin{cases} \mathcal{X}_0 + \dfrac{1}{\Gamma(\varpi)} \displaystyle\int_0^{t_1} (t - \wp)^{\varpi - 1}{}^C H_1(\wp, \mathcal{X}) d\wp, & 0 < t \leq t_1, \\[2ex] \mathcal{X}(t_1) + \dfrac{1 - \varpi}{ABC(\varpi)} {}^{ABC} H_1(t, \mathcal{X}) \\[2ex] + \dfrac{\varpi}{ABC(\varpi)\Gamma(\varpi)} \displaystyle\int_{t_1}^{t} (t - \wp)^{\varpi - 1}{}^{ABC} H_1(\wp, \mathcal{X}) d\wp, \end{cases} \quad (13)$$

To obtain the numerical scheme for the system of equations given in (2), we will start with the first equation of the system is addressed, which is denoted by (13). It should be noted that the procedure we will describe can be repeated for the other compartments and partitions of the system as well.

At $t = t_{n+1}$, one has

$$\mathcal{X}(t_{n+1})) = \begin{cases} \mathcal{X}_0 + \dfrac{1}{\Gamma(\varpi)} \displaystyle\int_0^{t_1} (t - \wp)^{\varpi - 1}{}^C H_1(\mathcal{X}, \wp) d\wp, \\[2ex] \mathcal{X}(t_1) + \dfrac{1 - \varpi}{ABC(\varpi)} {}^{ABC} H_1(\mathcal{X}, t_n) \\[2ex] + \dfrac{\varpi}{ABC(\varpi)\Gamma(\varpi)} \displaystyle\int_{t_1}^{t_{n+1}} (t - \wp)^{\varpi - 1}{}^{ABC} H_1(\wp, \mathcal{X}) d\wp. \end{cases} \quad (14)$$

Equation (14) can be presented using the Newton interpolation approximation, which is described in detail in reference [22].

$$
x(t_{n+1}) = \begin{cases} x_0 + \begin{cases} \frac{(\Delta t)^{\varpi-1}}{\Gamma(\varpi+1)} \sum\limits_{k=2}^{i} \left[{}^C H_1(x_{k-2}, t_{k-2}) \right] \Pi + \frac{(\Delta t)^{\varpi-1}}{\Gamma(\varpi+2)} \sum\limits_{k=2}^{i} \left[{}^C H_1(x_{k-1}, t_{k-1}) \right. \\ \left. - {}^C H_1(x_{k-2}, t_{k-2}) \right] \Sigma + \frac{\varpi(\Delta t)^{\varpi-1}}{2\Gamma(\varpi+3)} \sum\limits_{k=2}^{i} \left[{}^C H_1(x_k, t_k) - 2 {}^C H_1(x_{k-1}, t_{k-1}) \right. \\ \left. + {}^C H_1(x_{k-2}, t_{k-2}) \right] \Delta \\[6pt] x(t_1) + \begin{cases} \frac{1-\varpi}{ABC(\varpi)} {}^{ABC} H_1(x_n, t_n) + \frac{\varpi}{ABC(\varpi)} \frac{(\delta t)^{\varpi-1}}{\Gamma(\varpi+1)} \sum\limits_{k=i+3}^{n} \left[{}^{ABC} H_1(x_{k-2}, t_{k-2}) \right] \Pi \\ + \frac{\varpi}{ABC(\varpi)} \frac{(\delta t)^{\varpi-1}}{\Gamma(\varpi+2)} \sum\limits_{k=i+3}^{n} \left[{}^{ABC} H_1(x_{k-1}, t_{k-1}) + ABC H_1(x_{k-2}, t_{k-2}) \right] \Sigma \\ + \frac{\varpi}{ABC(\varpi)} \frac{\varpi(\delta t)^{\varpi-1}}{\Gamma(\varpi+3)} \sum\limits_{k=i+3}^{n} \left[{}^{ABC} H_1(x^k, t_k) - 2 {}^{ABC} H_1(x_{k-1}, t_{k-1}) \right. \\ \left. + {}^{ABC} H_1(x_{k-2}, t_{k-2}) \right] \Delta. \end{cases} \end{cases} \end{cases} \quad (15)
$$

Similarly, we can apply the Newton interpolation approximation can be applied to the remaining three compartments of the system of equations as well.

$$
y(t_{n+1})) = \begin{cases} y_0 + \begin{cases} \frac{(\Delta t)^{\varpi-1}}{\Gamma(\varpi+1)} \sum\limits_{k=2}^{i} \left[{}^C H_2(y_{k-2}, t_{k-2}) \right] \Pi + \frac{(\Delta t)^{\varpi-1}}{\Gamma(\varpi+2)} \sum\limits_{k=2}^{i} \left[{}^C H_2(y_{k-1}, t_{k-1}) \right. \\ \left. - {}^C H_2(y_{k-2}, t_{k-2}) \right] \Sigma + \frac{\varpi(\Delta t)^{\varpi-1}}{2\Gamma(\varpi+3)} \sum\limits_{k=2}^{i} \left[{}^C H_2(y_k, t_k) - 2 {}^C H_2(y_{k-1}, t_{k-1}) \right. \\ \left. + {}^C H_2(y_{k-2}, t_{k-2}) \right] \Delta \\[6pt] y(t_1) + \begin{cases} \frac{1-\varpi}{ABC(\varpi)} {}^{ABC} H_2(y_n, t_n) + \frac{\varpi}{ABC(\varpi)} \frac{(\delta t)^{\varpi-1}}{\Gamma(\varpi+1)} \sum\limits_{k=i+3}^{n} \left[{}^{ABC} H_2(y_{k-2}, t_{k-2}) \right] \Pi \\ + \frac{\varpi}{ABC(\varpi)} \frac{(\delta t)^{\varpi-1}}{\Gamma(\varpi+2)} \sum\limits_{k=i+3}^{n} \left[{}^{ABC} H_2(y_{k-1}, t_{k-1}) + ABC H_2(y_{k-2}, t_{k-2}) \right] \Sigma \\ + \frac{\varpi}{ABC(\varpi)} \frac{\varpi(\delta t)^{\varpi-1}}{\Gamma(\varpi+3)} \sum\limits_{k=i+3}^{n} \left[{}^{ABC} H_2(y^k, t_k) - 2 {}^{ABC} H_2(y_{k-1}, t_{k-1}) \right. \\ \left. + {}^{ABC} H_2(y_{k-2}, t_{k-2}) \right] \Delta. \end{cases} \end{cases} \end{cases} \quad (16)
$$

$$
z(t_{n+1})) = \begin{cases} z_0 + \begin{cases} \frac{(\Delta t)^{\varpi-1}}{\Gamma(\varpi+1)} \sum\limits_{k=2}^{i} \left[{}^C H_3(z_{k-2}, t_{k-2}) \right] \Pi + \frac{(\Delta t)^{\varpi-1}}{\Gamma(\varpi+2)} \sum\limits_{k=2}^{i} \left[{}^C H_3(z_{k-1}, t_{k-1}) \right. \\ \left. - {}^C H_3(z_{k-2}, t_{k-2}) \right] \Sigma + \frac{\varpi(\Delta t)^{\varpi-1}}{2\Gamma(\varpi+3)} \sum\limits_{k=2}^{i} \left[{}^C H_3(z_k, t_k) - 2 {}^C H_3(z_{k-1}, t_{k-1}) \right. \\ \left. + {}^C H_3(z_{k-2}, t_{k-2}) \right] \Delta \\[6pt] z(t_1) + \begin{cases} \frac{1-\varpi}{ABC(\varpi)} {}^{ABC} H_3(z_n, t_n) + \frac{\varpi}{ABC(\varpi)} \frac{(\delta t)^{\varpi-1}}{\Gamma(\varpi+1)} \sum\limits_{k=i+3}^{n} \left[{}^{ABC} H_3(z_{k-2}, t_{k-2}) \right] \Pi \\ + \frac{\varpi}{ABC(\varpi)} \frac{(\delta t)^{\varpi-1}}{\Gamma(\varpi+2)} \sum\limits_{k=i+3}^{n} \left[{}^{ABC} H_3(z_{k-1}, t_{k-1}) + ABC H_3(z_{k-2}, t_{k-2}) \right] \Sigma \\ + \frac{\varpi}{ABC(\varpi)} \frac{\varpi(\delta t)^{\varpi-1}}{\Gamma(\varpi+3)} \sum\limits_{k=i+3}^{n} \left[{}^{ABC} H_3(z^k, t_k) - 2 {}^{ABC} H_3(z_{k-1}, t_{k-1}) \right. \\ \left. + {}^{ABC} H_3(z_{k-2}, t_{k-2}) \right] \Delta. \end{cases} \end{cases} \end{cases} \quad (17)
$$

$$u(t_{n+1})) = \begin{cases} u_0 + \begin{cases} \left[\dfrac{(\Delta t)^{\varpi-1}}{\Gamma(\varpi+1)} \sum\limits_{k=2}^{i} \left[{}^C H_4(u_{k-2}, t_{k-2})\right]\Pi + \dfrac{(\Delta t)^{\varpi-1}}{\Gamma(\varpi+2)} \sum\limits_{k=2}^{i} \left[{}^C H_4(u_{k-1}, t_{k-1})\right.\right. \\ \left. - {}^C H_4(u_{k-2}, t_{k-2})\right]\Sigma + \dfrac{\varpi(\Delta t)^{\varpi-1}}{2\Gamma(\varpi+3)} \sum\limits_{k=2}^{i} \left[{}^C H_4(u_k, t_k) - 2\,{}^C H_4(u_{k-1}, t_{k-1})\right. \\ \left.\left. + {}^C H_4(u_{k-2}, t_{k-2})\right]\Delta \right. \end{cases} \\[2em] u(t_1) + \begin{cases} \left[\dfrac{1-\varpi}{ABC(\varpi)} {}^{ABC} H_4(u_n, t_n) + \dfrac{\varpi}{ABC(\varpi)} \dfrac{(\delta t)^{\varpi-1}}{\Gamma(\varpi+1)} \sum\limits_{k=i+3}^{n} \left[{}^{ABC} H_4(u_{k-2}, t_{k-2})\right]\Pi \right. \\ + \dfrac{\varpi}{ABC(\varpi)} \dfrac{(\delta t)^{\varpi-1}}{\Gamma(\varpi+2)} \sum\limits_{k=i+3}^{n} \left[{}^{ABC} H_4(u_{k-1}, t_{k-1}) + ABC H_4(u_{k-2}, t_{k-2})\right]\Sigma \\ + \dfrac{\varpi}{ABC(\varpi)} \dfrac{\varpi(\delta t)^{\varpi-1}}{\Gamma(\varpi+3)} \sum\limits_{k=i+3}^{n} \left[{}^{ABC} H_4(u^k, t_k) - 2\,{}^{ABC} H_4(u_{k-1}, t_{k-1})\right. \\ \left.\left. + {}^{ABC} H_4(u_{k-2}, t_{k-2})\right]\Delta. \right. \end{cases} \end{cases} \tag{18}$$

Here

$$\Delta = \begin{bmatrix} (1+n-k)^{\varpi}\left(2(n-k)^2 + (3\varpi+10)(n-k) + 2\varpi^2 + 9\varpi + 12\right) \\ -(n-k)\left(2(n-k)^2 + (5\varpi+10)(-k+n) + 6\varpi^2 + 18\varpi + 12\right) \end{bmatrix},$$

$$\Sigma = \begin{bmatrix} (1+n-k)^{\varpi}\left(3 + 2\varpi - k + n\right) \\ -(n-k)\left(n-k+3\varpi+3\right) \end{bmatrix},$$

$$\Delta = \begin{bmatrix} (1+n-k)^{\varpi} - (n-k)^{\varpi} \end{bmatrix}.$$

and

$$\begin{aligned} {}^C H_1(\mathcal{X},\mathcal{Y},\mathcal{Z},\mathcal{U},t) &= {}^{ABC} H_1(\mathcal{X},\mathcal{Y},\mathcal{Z},\mathcal{U},t) = \lambda_h - \alpha_1\beta_1\mathcal{X}\mathcal{U} - \delta_1\mathcal{X}, \\ {}^C H_2(\mathcal{X},\mathcal{Y},\mathcal{Z},\mathcal{U},t) &= {}^{ABC} H_2(\mathcal{X},\mathcal{Y},\mathcal{Z},\mathcal{U},t) = \alpha_1\beta_1\mathcal{X}\mathcal{U} - \delta_1\mathcal{Y}, \\ {}^C H_3(\mathcal{X},\mathcal{Y},\mathcal{Z},\mathcal{U},t) &= {}^{ABC} H_3(\mathcal{X},\mathcal{Y},\mathcal{Z},\mathcal{U},t) = \lambda_m - \alpha_2\beta_2\mathcal{Y}\mathcal{Z} - \delta_2\mathcal{Z}, \\ {}^C H_4(\mathcal{X},\mathcal{Y},\mathcal{Z},\mathcal{U},t) &= {}^{ABC} H_4(\mathcal{X},\mathcal{Y},\mathcal{Z},\mathcal{U},t) = \alpha_2\beta_2\mathcal{Y}\mathcal{Z} - \delta_2\mathcal{U}. \end{aligned}$$

5   Experimental Results and Discussion: Numerical Performances of the Piecewise Global Fractional Derivatives for Zika Virus Infection

This section is concerned with the numerical scheme proposed by this study for simulating the considered model from which the simulation will be carried out over the time interval $[0,T]$, as shall be split into two sub-intervals: $[0,t_1)$ and $(t_1,T]$. To demonstrate the effectiveness of the numerical scheme of the study,

Table 1. Different numerical values for the considered model (1) with Data-I [22].

Symbol	value	Symbol	value	Symbol	value
$\mathcal{X}_0$	100	λ_h	1.2	α_2	0.005
$\mathcal{Y}_0$	60	λ_m	0.3	β_2	0.0003
$\mathcal{Z}_0$	40	α_1	0.0004	δ_1	0.004
$\mathcal{U}_0$	20	β_1	0.02	δ_2	0.0014

Table 2. Initial and parameters numerical values for ZV disease model (1) Data-II [18].

Symbol	value	Symbol	value	Symbol	value
$\mathcal{X}_0$	400	λ_h	1.2	α_2	0.005
$\mathcal{Y}_0$	100	λ_m	0.3	β_2	0.0003
$\mathcal{Z}_0$	600	α_1	0.0004	δ_1	0.004
$\mathcal{U}_0$	140	β_1	0.02	δ_2	0.0014

two different datasets have been used: the first data set is taken from [22], and the second one is from [18]. The data for both datasets are shown in Tables 1 and 2, respectively.

Numerical simulations are at stake for Data-I at various fractional orders, which are presented in Figs. 1a through 1d. In order to simulate the system of equations, we have utilized the idea of piecewise fractional derivatives, which are defined over the interval $[0, T]$. The graphical presentations are arranged and designed in the Matlab through which all the analysis and applications are conducted [23].

Caputo derivatives have specifically been utilized for the simulations on $[0, t_1]$, while we have employed ABC derivative representations have been employed for the simulations over $[t_1, T]$, where $t_1 = 25$ and $T = 50$. The simulations presented are based on different fractional orders. As can be seen from the results, the healthy population increases due to the high recruitment rate, while the infected human population decreases as healthy individuals enter the population. The same trend is observed for healthy and infected mosquitoes at various fractional orders, indicating that the disease is under control.

The graphical representation of the piecewise derivative for the two subintervals, utilizing two distinct concepts of fractional derivatives provides certain findings, and this representation exhibits a bending or cut, illustrated by the arrow, which can aid in understanding the crossover behavior phenomenon. Such a behavior is frequently witnessed when an infection undergoes sudden decay or growth, beyond the explanatory capacity of deterministic methods.

Simulations using Data-II have also been carried out, as presented in Figs. 2a to 2d. We have employed the notion of piecewise fractional derivative on the interval $[0, T]$, where Caputo derivative simulations were performed on $[0, t_1]$,

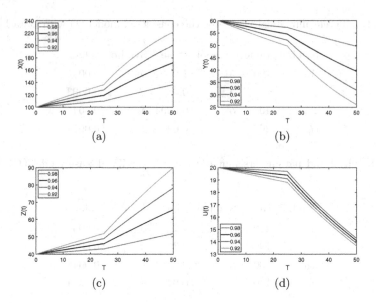

Fig. 1. Dynamics of $\mathcal{X}, \mathcal{Y}, \mathcal{Z}, \mathcal{U}$ classes at various fractional order ϖ for the set of Data-I on sub interval $[0, t_1]$ and $[t_1, T]$ of $[0, T]$, where $t_1 = 25$, $T = 50$.

and ABC derivative representations were illustrated over $[t_1, T]$. Two scenarios, namely $t_1 = 25$ and $T = 50$, and $t_1 = 60$ and $T = 120$ have been taken into consideration in this study. In these simulations, we observe that the healthy population initially declines but eventually stabilizes. In contrast, the infectious human population initially grows but eventually stabilizes. To clarify, it has been found that the identical behavior is exhibited by both healthy and infected mosquitoes, across various fractional orders, which suggests that the infection is not initially under control, but can potentially be managed through appropriate and effective treatment and care strategies and interventions.

As with the previous simulations, we have examined the piecewise derivative graphical representation for the two sub-intervals using two different concepts of fractional orders. As demonstrated by the arrow, the graphical representation displays bends or cuts in the middle of the curves, and consequently, these features aid in elucidating the crossover behavior observed in the simulations.

6   Conclusion and Future Directions

Formulating fractional order compartment models through the consideration of differential equations based on the underlying stochastic processes can point towards a systematic approach to ensure predictive accuracy allowing that the model remains plausible at all times. Such a scheme is capable of providing a convenient interpretation and feasible design with regard to all the parameters and partitions of the model. Towards these multi-stage processes, this study

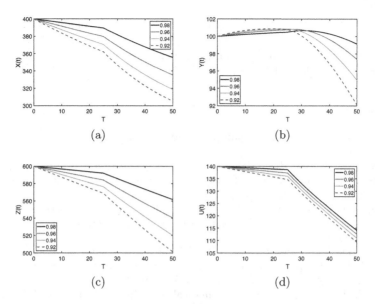

Fig. 2. Dynamics of $\mathcal{X}, \mathcal{Y}, \mathcal{Z}, \mathcal{U}$ classes at various fractional order ϖ for the set of Data-II on sub interval $[0, t_1]$ and $[t_1, T]$ of $[0, T]$.

aims to introduce new concepts of fractional calculus that manifest crossover effects in dynamical models. To this end, piecewise global fractional derivatives in sense of Caputo and Atangana-Baleanu-Caputo (ABC) have been utilized, and they are applied to formulate the Zika Virus (ZV) disease model. In order to have a predictive analysis of the behavior of the model, the strain is divided into two subintervals and the piecewise behavior is investigated. Thereafter, the fixed point theory of Schauder and Banach is employed for proving the existence and uniqueness of at least one solution in both senses for the considered problem. With respect to the numerical simulations based on the data, Newton interpolation formula has been modified and extended for the considered nonlinear system in the study where graphical presentations and illustrative examples are based on the data for various multi-compartments of the systems with respect to the applicable real-world data for different fractional orders. The obtained results verify that increasing the fractional order results in a greater crossover effect, which is clearly observable, and reducing the fractional order reduces the abrupt changes. This effect cannot be demonstrated using ordinary fractional order or stochastic differential equations. Based on the impact of fractional order reducing the abrupt changes, the results obtained from the study demonstrate and also validate that increasing the fractional order yields a greater crossover effect, as evident from the observed data, which is critical for the effective management and control of abrupt changes like infectious diseases, viruses, among many more unexpected dynamic and nonlinear phenomena in chaotic, uncertain and transient circumstances. Taken together, as future directions, the established analysis can be extended to more complex dynamical problems of fractional order involving piecewise differential equations. The developed models with the proposed scheme can be used for other illnesses and diseases as well as pertinent data for the estimation, prediction, management as well as control purposes in the ever-evolving global landscape.

References

1. Zika virus, World Health Organization (2015). http://www.who.int/mediacentre/factsheets/zika/en/
2. Calvet, G., Aguiar, R.S., Melo, A.S.O., et al.: Detection and sequencing of Zika virus from amniotic fluid of fetuses with microcephaly in Brazil: a case study. Lancet Infect. Dis. **16**, 653–660 (2016)
3. Perkins, T.A., Siraj, A.S., Ruktanonchai, C.W., et al.: Model-based projections of Zika virus infections in childbearing women in the Americas. Nat. Microbiol. **1**, 16126 (2016)
4. Kucharski, A.J., Funk, S., Eggo, R.M.M., et al.: Transmission dynamics of Zika virus in island populations: a modelling analysis of the 2013–14 French Polynesia outbreak. PLoS Neglect. Trop. D. **10**, 38588 (2016)
5. Bonyah, E., Okosun, K.O.: Mathematical modeling of Zika virus. Asian Pac. J. Trop. Dis. **6**, 637–679 (2016)
6. Bonyah, E., Khan, M.A., Okosun, K.O., et al.: A theoretical model for Zika virus transmission. PLoS ONE **12**, 1–26 (2017)
7. Machado, J.T., Kiryakova, V., Mainardi, F.: Recent history of fractional calculas. Commun. Nonl. Sci. Num. Simul. **16**(3), 1140–1153 (2011)
8. Hilfer, R.: Threefold Introduction to Fractional Derivatives, Anomalous Transport: Foundations and Applications. Germany (2008)
9. Agarwal, R.P., Lakshmikantham, V., Nieto, J.J.: On the concept of solution for fractional differential equations with uncertainty. Nonlinear Anal.: Theory Methods Appl. **72**(6), 2859–2862 (2010)
10. Grace, S., Agarwal, R., Wong, P., Zafer, A.: On the oscillation of fractional differential equations. Fractional Calculus Appl. Anal. **15**(2), 222–231 (2012)
11. Xu, C., Liao, M., Li, P., Yuan, S.: Impact of leakage delay on bifurcation in fractional-order complex-valued neural networks. Chaos Solitons Fractals **142**, 110535 (2021)
12. Liu, X., Rahmamn, M.U., Ahmad, S., Baleanu, D., Anjam, Y.N.: A new fractional infectious disease model under the non-singular Mittag-Leffler derivative. Waves Random Complex Media 1–27 (2022)
13. Riaz, M.B., Awrejcewicz, J., Rehman, A.U.: Functional effects of permeability on Oldroyd-B fluid under magnetization: a comparison of slipping and non-slipping solutions. Appl. Sci. **11**(23), 11477 (2021)
14. Riaz, M.B., Saeed, S.T.: Comprehensive analysis of integer-order, Caputo-Fabrizio (CF) and Atangana-Baleanu (ABC) fractional time derivative for MHD Oldroyd-B fluid with slip effect and time dependent boundary condition. Discret. Continuous Dyn. Syst.-S **14**(10), 3719 (2021)
15. Rahman, M.U., Arfan, M., Shah, Z., Kumam, P., Shutaywi, M.: Nonlinear fractional mathematical model of tuberculosis (TB) disease with incomplete treatment under Atangana-Baleanu derivative. Alex. Eng. J. **60**(3), 2845–2856 (2021)
16. Rahman, M.U., Alhawael, G., Karaca, Y.: Compartmental analysis of middle eastern respiratory syndrome coronavirus model under fractional operator with next-generation matrix methods. Fractals (2023)

17. Baleanu, D., Ghassabzade, F.A., Nieto, J.J., Jajarmi, A.: On a new and generalized fractional model for a real cholera outbreak. Alex. Eng. J. **61**(11), 9175–9186 (2022)
18. Khan, M.A., Ullah, S., Farhan, M.: The dynamics of Zika virus with Caputo fractional derivative. AIMS Math. **4**(1), 134–146 (2019)
19. Atangana, A., Baleanu, D.: New fractional derivatives with non-local and non-singular kernel. Therm. Sci. **20**(2), 763–769 (2016)
20. Karaca, Y.: Computational complexity-based fractional-order neural network models for the diagnostic treatments and predictive transdifferentiability of heterogeneous cancer cell propensity. Chaos Theory Appl. **5**(1), 34–51 (2023)
21. Atangana, A.: Extension of rate of change concept: from local to nonlocal operators with applications. Results Phys. **19**, 103515 (2020)
22. Atangana, A., Araz, S.I.: New concept in calculus: piecewise differential and integral operators. Chaos Solitons Fractals **145**, 110638 (2021)
23. MATLAB, 2022 version 9.12.0 (R2022a). The Math-Works Inc., Natick, Massachusetts

Awareness of Space and Earth Systems by Musical Actions

E. Özel Ay[1](✉) , O. A. Büyükbayram[2] , Z. Aslan[1] , and G. Özdemir[3]

[1] Faculty of Engineering, Department of Computer Engineering, Istanbul Aydın University, 34295 Istanbul, Turkey
{elifozelay,zaferaslan}@aydin.edu.tr
[2] Faculty of Education, Istanbul Aydın University, 34295 Istanbul, Turkey
aylinbuyukbayram@aydin.edu.tr
[3] Anatolian BIL Professional School of Higher Education, Istanbul Aydın University, 34295 Istanbul, Turkey
guvenozdemir@aydin.edu.tr

Abstract. The aim of the study is to show interest of primary school students' to our solar system, planets, space weather and to raise awarenes on these issues. In this research, awareness of 8-year-old students at Istanbul Halkalı Cumhuriyet Primary School on "space and earth system" was analysed. Training methodologies solar – earth systems, weather conditions, astronomy and related contents have been supported by art, music, literature, language and philosophy. An integrated education and awareness program were implemented by making use of body percussion. In the first stage, a questionnaire consisting of 15 questions was applied to 20 students and the students were sung with a ukulele and a song written on the subject. Afterwards, the song was repeated several times with the accompaniment of the students. Then, the students were asked to perform body percussion movements as they wanted by singing a song. Video and audio recordings were taken from the students. At the second stage, these students were given a presentation about space, earth and planets, and then they were asked to answer the same survey questions and to perform body percussion movements again. In both stages, the survey questions were analysed by using SPSS Package Program and screenshots of music audio signals analysed. Video records were digitalized and data was transferred to the computer. The project Results show that there is no a serience differences between boys and girls reactions. The awareness of space and earth sciences showed slightly an increasing trend at the 1st stage and the the second one.

Keywords: Music-based education · sun-space-earth system · body percussion

O. Gervasi et al. (Eds.): ICCSA 2023 Workshops, LNCS 14104, pp. 160–176, 2023.
https://doi.org/10.1007/978-3-031-37105-9_12

1   Introduction

Adams J. and his friends [1] have established a curriculum for K-12 Education in astronomy. According to this curriculum, students in K-4 class; must acquire a geocentric perspective on objects and motion in the sky. 5–8 classrooms, students should learn about solar system motion from a heliocentric perspective. 9–12 ages students should learn about stellar evolution and the structure of the universe.

Meyer, A. O. et al. [2] presented their Moon phases projects to improve students' understanding of the causes ans process of the Moon phases. They implemented this project with a sample of undergraduate ans non-science major students enrolled at a medium-sized public university located in the southeastern part of the United States.

Rollins et al. [3] articulated a vision for science education that would make science literacy a reality for everyone on Earth. They emphasized that science empowers people to solve problems creatively, think critically, work collaboratively and use technology effectively. Thompson end his friends [4] have shown how scientific imagination and research power can bring together people from all continents, in almost all countries of the World. In presenting this impressive result, they aimed to help us understand the unifying power of the questions to understand our universe and use space for this purpose.

J. M. Davila, N. Gopalswamy and B. J. Thompson [4, 16] said that The International Heliophysical Year (IHY) is a UN-sponsored international scientific cooperation program for understanding the external effects of planetary environments and universal processes in solar-terrestrial-planetary-heliospheric physics. IHY focuses on developments in all aspects of the heliosphere and its interaction with the interstellar medium. The term heliophysics was coined specifically to refer to the activity of studying the entire solar-heliospheric-planetary system. In fact, it is a concept that extends the connections from Earth to the Sun and between planets. It is an extension of the concept of "geophysics".

IHY 2007 is planned to coincide with the fiftieth year of 1957–1958 IGY (International Geophysical Year), one of the most successful international science programs of all time. IGY has resulted in tremendous progress in Sun - Earth connections, planetary science and the heliosphere in general, the tradition of the International Years of Science started almost 125 years ago with the first "International Polar Year". It started as "IPY" in 1882–1883, the second IPY was organized in 1932. But the World-Wide Observation Network was implemented by Carl Freidrich Gouss in 1832 after Alexander Humbolt's suggestion. With the support of the British Crown and the Russian Tsar, Gauss succeeded in establishing a network of 53 stations in places such as Greenwich, Dublin, Toronto, Cape of Good Hope. It later added 4 more in India and Singapore. The reason why the law is important is because, in fact, the structure of objects in the universe is largely determined by gravity and magnetism. Gravity is responsible for structuring planets, planetary systems, stars, galaxies. Magnetic forces at work in the solar system's plasma environment are responsible for the storage and subsequent release of large amounts of energy in solar flares, mass ejections, and magnetic storms. The IHY, organized after the IGY, has 3 main purposes:

1) To improve our understanding of the heliophysical processes that govern the Sun, Earth and Heliosphere.
2) Continuing the tradition of international research and advancing the legacy on the 50th anniversary of the International Year of Geophysics,
3) To show the world the importance of Space and Earth Science.

Scientific Goals are listed below:

1) To develop the basic science of heliophysics through interdisciplinary work,
2) To determine the response of terrestrial and planetary magnetospheres and atmospheres to external factors,
3) To determine the solar heliosphere and to encourage the research on the interstellar medium, that is, towards the new frontier,
4) To encourage international cooperation in the research of heliophysical phenomena, now and in the future,
5) To convey the results of IHY to the scientific community and the public on the IHY website.

Since 1988, the UN, through its Space Applications Programme, has supported the establishment of UN Regional Centers for Space Science and Technology in Africa, Asia and the Pacific, Latin America and the Caribbean, and the West.

It publishes reports submitted by all countries on its website. Reports were presented from many centers such as Austria, Moscow, Greater Arab Emirates, Italy, Romania, China, Pakistan, Germany, Brazil, South Africa, Iran, Mexico, Japan, USA, Canada, Czech Republic, Korea, Croatia, and symposiums were held. It was last reported in 2021 by Russia and the Greater Arab Emirates. In Turkey, a symposium was held in September 2010.

Tulunay underlines that space weather shows by conditions in the Sun and solar wind, Earth's magnetosphere, ionosphere and atmosphere. Space weather is primarily an astronomical phenomenon that encompasses various fields of science, such as interdisciplinary physics, engineering, due to solar activity and cosmic rays.

Tulunay and her friends [6, 14, 17] have a project named I love my Sun. It is an educational Project for primary school children aged 4–11. Firstly, as the European COST 724 project, it was made by Y. Tulunay and her team. Throughout the Project, students were asked to draw pictures about the Sun. Afterwards, a 20 –minute presentation was made by a scientist from the related field and students were asked to draw a picture again. These drawn pictures were compared as before and after. The Czech Republic version of the Project was made in 2014 in 16 classrooms. In Spain, it was made for 60 students.

Weather in space, which has numerous satellites and has become the field of activity of many countries, has also become important. The one-to-one effects of changes in space weather in daily life on Earth are very limited, but satellites are very affected. When we say space, we usually mean over 100 km. So, what effect does it have on us at ground level? As a matter of fact, the effects that we can see in daily life are very limited. Because it depends on many factors. But at higher levels it usually has a huge impact on satellites. It causes some electrification on satellites. It makes the atmosphere expand. Increases drag force. It can cause them to fall out of their orbits or change their orbits. It affects the activities of astronauts on the International Space Station, located 400–500 km away. Although they are protected, they are still exposed to radiation. Many airline flights are around 10 km and it causesan increasein the radiation at these levels. Therefore, the amount of radiation dose should be measured in these flights. It also causes ground-level power outages. "Possible effects are more visible in higher latitudes. A solar storm in 1989 caused a power outage in a Canadian province for 6 h. These effects depend on latitude and the intensity of solar activity. We see it mostly at higher latitudes. We see at latitudes above 50–60 °, the best example of this is the polar auroras. Aurora is actually the release of energy from the sun into the atmosphere. From there, we understand that some particles from the sun filled the atmosphere with mass energy. Therefore, we see its effects more frequently in higher latitudes. As a result of a very strong solar storm and geomagnetic storm in 1989, all these electrical structures, railways or bridges in the Upper latitudes, and their expansion and contraction in the latitudes below these aurora belts are affected by the currents coming from above. Or pipelines carrying oil and natural gas have wear limits, there are loads exceeding those limits. Countries in the latitudes that put more satellites and are affected by it usually map out which regions will be exposed to power cuts in advance and take some precautions accordingly."

Kaymaz Z. et al. [39, 43] say high-energy particles enter the atmosphere, which happens during solar flares. There are more events that increase the radiation dose. It's also something to do with solar radiation. Especially with the development of the computer age, meteorologists for a long time make weather forecasts. Especially the space weather, which we call 'Space Weather', gained a great speed after the 2000 s. Therefore, according to the studies done in the world, the duration of the predictions is a bit long, but we have models and measurements that make the predictions. Measurements are made in different regions with satellites. Meteorology is so developed that there is a meteorology station in every village. We can calculate when the mass from the sun will reach the earth. So predictions are made. Space weather studies in Turkey are carried out for the first time in the Upper Atmosphere and Space Weather Laboratory established at Istanbul Technical University. Modelling studies and measurements are being made.

Space weather is closely related to satellite construction. Scientists believe that solar air can cause satellites to fall out of their orbits. Over the past year, the European Space Agency's Swarm constellation, which measures magnetic fields around Earth, has begun displacing the atmosphere ten times faster than before. European Space Agency (ESA) officials said that the Swarm satellite, which studies the Earth's magnetic field, has sunk into the atmosphere due to solar storms [40]. More solar wind activity, sunspots, solar flares, and coronal mass ejections are being produced at an increasing rate. "There's a lot of complex physics that we still don't fully understand going on in the upper layers of the atmosphere where it interacts with the solar wind [41].

Space Weather forecasting is the prediction of abnormal or intense eruptions on the Sun and their effects on the Earth's Magnetosphere. Space Weather forecast products also contain information about the geomagnetic latitudes affected by this event. National Space Program and Strategic 10 Goals [42]: The National Space Program has been prepared for the coordinated and integrated execution of our country's vision, strategies, goals and projects in the field of space policies in order to evaluate the current potential in our country, considering the developments in the world. The National Space Program is a comprehensive project prepared for the coordinated and integrated execution of our country's vision, strategies, goals and projects in the field of space policies in order to evaluate the current potential in our country, considering the developments in the world.

Objectives of the National Space Program is listed below: Developing technologies and necessary infrastructures that will stand out within the framework of the needs and capabilities in the field of space technologies, reducing the foreign dependency, planning for the use of space technologies as a tool in the development. They carry existing talents and achievements in the field of space further with national technologies, contributing to the scientific knowledge and experience of humanity, increasing space awareness the country's people, especially young people.

In the 100th anniversary of the Republic, a hard landing will be made on the Moon with a national and original hybrid rocket that will be fired in close Earth orbit with international cooperation. In the second stage, the first launch will be made, this time with a national rocket, and a soft landing will be made on the Moon. By sending a traveling vehicle to the lunar surface with national technologies and more experience in launch technologies and space systems operating in deep space and providing space history will increase awareness with space, ıt is aimed to contribute to world science and technology with scientific experiments on the traveling vehicle.

Space and Astrophysics awareness will be created in order to develop effective and competent human resources in the field of space. Graduate and doctorate scholarships will be awarded in clearly defined fields. National and international summer schools, courses and workshops will be organized.

Bangir Alpan and his friends [25] searched that mental arithmetic education on the visual perception development of five-year old children. The study was conducted at Ministry of Agriculture and kindergartens. Demirci [24] studied to identify the effect of visual perception education on the development of visual perception in the children of five-six ages. Yildirim S. et al. [22] studied the effect of Montessori and mandala education provided to pre-schoolers to visual perception behaviours. They used Frostig Visual Perception Test was applied which was developed by Frostig.

Kurtz [26] explain the concept of visual perception is explained as the ability to recognize, distinguish, group and interpret visual stimuli with previous experiences. A. Reinartz and E. Reinartz [29], while describing visual perception, emphasized that visual perception is not just the ability to see. On the other hand İ. B. Orhon [27] stated that the interpretation of a visual stimulus is realized by the brain, not by the eye. Frostig examined the basis of visual perception behaviour by dividing it into five sub-areas. These sub-fields are; eye-motor coordination, shape-ground distinction, shape constancy, perception of location with space, perception of space relations.

[32] One of the similar study is to raise social awareness about space weather, earth, space air and sun through extra-curricular education and body percussion work. It is known that children are familiar from the time they are in the mother's womb. Rhythm studies, education and training programs, which are thought to contribute positively to each of the fields of it can be designed for children of all age groups, primitive since ages, body music has been applied in pre-school institutions in early childhood at the primary

school level, which the Ministry of National Education (MEB) deems appropriate. It can be seen that rhythm study groups have a special place in their weekly programs and different activities can be seen. It can be used actively in education and teaching methods. Saraç [35, 36] underlines that it is appropriate to organize for primary school children. It is observed that he talks about the importance of rhythmic skills in activities and music studies.

When the musical achievements and indicators of 8-year-old children attending MEB Primary School are examined, it is observed that preschool, primary school 1-2-3 achievements, rhythm. Their development related to body movements can be noticed and it can be said that they can accompany with basic body music practices. According to Açılmış and Kayıran [30], it appeals to many senses. With such studies, developmental areas can be supported and positive contributions can be made to the education process in terms of children's learning while having fun (pp.221–222). With the approval of the Ministry of Education. It can be said that one of the most basic of the rhythm activities used in for education and training is the use of body percussion, that is, body music [38]. It can be mentioned that the sounds created by the use of different parts of the body are transformed into a kind of music. Çetin [33] predicted, it can be said that body music exercises can also be used actively in line with the skills and needs of children in rhythm practice (p.74). Body music, which is known to be made by using different forms of sound, such as clapping hands, snapping fingers, hitting the chest and the tops of the legs with the help of the hands, tapping the feet on the ground. Although its effect on children's cognitive, psychomotor, emotional and social development can be mentioned, it can be said that its contribution to children's learning skills is also important. It can be observed that the realization of rapid learning with the help of rhythm studies also allows the use of rhythm studies in education and training. It can be said that the contribution of rhythm studies to children's emotional and social skills is also related to their self-expression skills. Türkmen [37], within the scope of Special Teaching Methods, emphasizes the importance of teaching music with rhythm and the use of rhythm studies in general teaching methods in terms of children's skills (pp. 80–98). The fact that children can express themselves with body music in line with their developmental level also contributes to many learning and teaching practices. It can be said that it has caused its inclusion in the method children's creativity development. It can also be said that the improvisation studies, which are thought to support the children, are more efficient than the choreographies taught to children by imitation, and that these studies are important in terms of gaining self-confidence. Alpagut et al. [31] underlines the need and importance of improvisation in terms of the development of self-confidence in children (p. 75). In the Specific Music Teaching Methods, in which improvisation studies are actively involved. [19] Bentz studied with students in different arts and climate change project.

Mentioning the importance of improvisation and rhythm studies, [35]'s rhythmic. It is also observed that it emphasizes the importance of studies and their use in education (pp. 137–198). In the music study carried out within the scope of the Scientific Research Project (B.A.P.), body music used to observe their attitudes towards awareness, in other words, measurement was expected to contribute as an intermediary. Understanding students' sun awareness in the study.

For the purpose of singing, a study of singing was done without using the sun and related terms and again together. It is provided to be accompanied by the body percussion movements studied. Lyrics for children the study, which was prepared to arouse curiosity, in itself, the awareness of the sun. It was evaluated in two stages, before and after the information. Ozgül and friends [34] researched researched the importance of learning by having fun and improvising on the subject for primary school children. It can be said that it emphasizes and predicts that learning will be easier (p.119). Önal [7] carried out a study in order to determine autistic children's responsiveness and predisposition towards music education. Savan Anna [8], says music effects people physiological and biochemical, so it is important for education. Gürbüz and his friends [9] studied the effects of the lessons taught with educational songs and games in the "Let's Get to Know the Matter" unit of the 4th grade primary school science lesson on the academic success and permanence of the students. Yangın et al. [10] determined the effect of applications supported with children's songs in primary school 4th grade science lesson on students' learning. Ata P. [11] searched the effect of music and drama on learning. Aydın S. et al. [12] investigated the effect of the use of the process evaluation method on the academic success and permanence of the student in the unit of study. Başer A. [13] searched that if music clearly contributes to language, social life, personality, mental and emotional situation. Sen Y. [15] studied recent developments in the importance of music in the preschool period, to enrich the preschool programs by using the effect of music on children, to determine the role of music. They make the art of music popular in these institutions. N. Devi et al. [23] aimed to development, standardize and validate a 'Questionnaire on Music Perception Ability' that can be used as a tool to classify the individuals as with and without musical abilities. Tugrul B. and her friends [28] study of the effect of the frostig developmental visual perception educational program on the visual perception levels of six aged children.

In the first stage of the present paper, students were asked to answer the questionnaire, it was determined whether children had knowledge about sun awareness and related topics. The purpose of the study was not mentioned in order to evaluate them. At this stage it was expected that they would reflect their knowledge with body music, thus sound intensity. To the music of the song children, accompanied by body movements and sounds, express themselves through improvisation expected and recorded.

The children, who were informed about the awareness of the sun, performed the same music for the second time. They were asked to do this and they were expected to think about the information they learned together with the lyrics. They were asked to reflect on the loudness in body music. Then students were asked to answer the questionnaire again. As a result of the studies evaluation of questionnaires were analysed. The next part is related with methodology. The third part of the paper covers results.

2 Material and Method

In this section, the research model, sampling, how the data were collected and data analysis are included. Flow chart of this study is below (see Fig. 1):

Fig. 1. Application of the research on music perception ability

2.1 Study Area

Our survey work; was built in Halkalı Cumhuriyet Primary School in Küçükçekmece district of Istanbul.

In line with the basic objectives of Turkish National Education, the school aims to raise our children as individuals with personality, adhering to the Principles of Atatürk, loving their homeland, nation and flag, in accordance with the National Education Basic Law, in accordance with the 2023 Education Vision Plan of the Ministry of National Education. There are 37 teachers and 918 students in school.

In addition, the school is involved in many different international projects under the headings of e twinning, e-safety, Erasmus, waste material recycling, reading to my brother, white flag, nutrition-friendly. At the school, between 2020–2022, with the cooparation of Poland and Germany, the Erasmus Project has been realized eithin the scope of Erasmus K229 named "Making Math More Motivating". In 2021, an e-twinning project conducted with international teachers from Poland, Albania, Italy, Portugal, Romania and Turkey. In the project, students would find solutions to the problems they encountered while traveling in space with STEM education. They provided STEM education to their students. They conducted interdisciplinary studies using the disciplines of Science, Mathematics, Engineering and Technology. Their students got chance to meet with international students at different schools. Their students did many activities with different schools. The goals of their project are:

1- To enable the students to learn interdisciplinary topics
2- The students get to know different cultures
3- To develop students' knowledge in engineering projects
4- Students learn web 2.0 tools

2.2 Method

The first stage of the survey study was conducted on students in the 8-year-old group. In the continuation of the work, the first questionnaire was applied to all students, then a song related to the subject was sung with the students accompanied by the ukulele and the body percussion was worked on. Afterwards, a 20-min presentation on space, space air, earth, planets was given by expert professors. The following questionnarie was filled by all students again. The video and voice records were taken from students.

3   Results

The sample of the study consisted of 8-year-old children studying at Halkalı Cumhuriyet Primary School in Küçükçekmece district of Istanbul in the 2022–2023 academic year.

Table 1. Demographic information of students

Gender	N	Age
Female	10	8
Male	10	8
Total	20	20

The demographic information of the sample group included in the study is given in Table 1, 2 and 3.

As seen in Table 1, 20 students participated in our study. Half of them are girls and half of them are boys, but all of them are 8 years old.

Table 2. Educational status of the parents

Mother	Father	Other	Literacy
1	1	0	İlliterate
0	0	0	Primary school
1	5	0	High School
18	14	0	University
20	**20**	**0**	**Total**

When the educational status of the parents was analyzed, it was found that 90% of the mothers have university degree, 5% have high school degree, and 5% were illiterate; It was concluded that 70% of the fathers have university degree, 25% have high school degree, and 5% were illiterate, (Table 2).

Table 3. Distribution of answers to some questions

	Yes	No	1 year and lower	2 years	3 years and more	not watching documentaries	nature and science	nature and science + culture and art	Total
Q_4	18	2							20
Q_5			4	9	7				20
Q_6	18	2							20
Q_7	15	5							20
Q_8						5	8	7	20

According to **Q_4**, 10% of the students did not receive early childhood education, (Table 3). According to **Q_5**, 20% of those who receive early childhood education have a period of 1 year or less, 40% 2 years, the remaining 40% have received early childhood education for 3 years or more. According to **Q_6**, 10% of the students do not have a library at home. According to the question **Q_7**, 75% of the students who have a library at home have books on space, nature and planets in their library. According to **Q_8**, 25% of the students do not watch any documentaries, 40% only watch documentaries about nature and science, 35% watch documentaries on nature, science, culture and art (Table 3). In our research, Wilcoxon signed-rank test was used to investigate the effectiveness of education [20–22].

Table 4. Evaluation of Questions (**Q_4, Q_5, Q_6, Q_7, Q_8**) Before Presentation.

	Q_4	Q_5	Q_6
Mean	1.1000	2.1500	1.1000
Median	1.0000	2.0000	1.0000
Mode	1.0000	2.0000	1.0000
Std. Dev	0.3077	0.7451	0.3077
Variance	0.0950	0.555	0,095
Minimum	1.0000	1.0000	1.000
Maximum	2.0000	3.0000	2.000

Table 4 indicate that mean value of Q_4 is 1.1000, Q_5 is 2.1500 and Q_6 is 1.1000. Standart deviation of these questions are 0.3077, 0.7451 and 0.3077. A small differences in the standart deviation shows that the values in the data set are close to each other.In addition the standart deviation values in questions 4 and 6 are equal to each other.

Tables 4 and 5 show some differences and slight increase between standard deviation and variance of questions before and after presentation.

Table 5. Evaluation of Questions (**Q_7** and **Q_8**) Before Presentation & After Presentation

	Q_7	Q_8_1	Q_8_2	Q_8_3	&	Q_7	Q_8_1	Q_8_2	Q_8_3
Mean	1.2500	0.7000	0.6000	1.2000		**1.3000 ↑**	0.6000	**0.7000 ↑**	1.2000
Median	1.0000	1.0000	0.0000	0.0000		1.0000	1.0000	0.0000	0.0000
Mode	1.0000	1.0000	0.0000	0.0000		1.0000	1.0000	0.0000	0.0000
Std. Deviation	0.4442	0.4701	0.9403	1.5078		**0.4701↑**	**0.5026↑**	**0.9787 ↑**	1.5078
Variance	0.1970	0.2210	0.8840	2.2740		**0.2210 ↑**	**0.2530 ↑**	**0.9580↑**	2.2740
Minimum	1.0000	0.0000	0.0000	0.0000		1.0000	0.0000	0.0000	0.0000
Maximum	2.0000	1.0000	2.0000	3.0000		2.0000	1.0000	2.0000	3.0000

Table 5 shows that the value of mean and standart deviation of Q_7 and Q_8_2 are increased before presentation and after presentation. On the other hand the value of mean of Q_8_1 is decreased and the value of standart deviation of Q_8_1 is increased. But the values of Q_8_3 don't show any differences in comparison with the before and after presentation.

4   Conclusion

In this section, the results of the analysis made with SPSS are given by dividing them into sub-headings.

4.1   Gender and Score Relationship Analysis

Relational data on gender score is given at Table 6.

Table 6. Descriptive statistics

	N	Mean	Std. Deviation	Minimum	Maximum
Gender	20(pre+post)	1.5000	0.5063	1.0000	2.000
Score	40(pre+post)	2.4500	0.4748	1.0000	3.00

Table 7. Evaluation of wilcoxon test

		N	Mean Rank	Sum of Ranks	Z	p
Score-gender	Negative Ranks	1	3.50	3.50	−3.702	0.000
Score-gender	Positive Ranks	18	10.36	186.50	−3.702	0.000
Score-gender	Ties	1				
	Total	20				

12th, 14th and 15th questions in the questionnaire, when we assign a score value to the average of the questions and investigate the effect of this average score on gender, since our research group's N value is less than 30, when we apply the Wilcoxon Test, one of the non-parametric tests, since the score and gender averages are different from each other, and the p value is less than 0.005. There is a significant difference between the mean score of the questions and the gender (Table 6).

Table 7 shows results of Evaluation of Wilcoxon Test. P values (0.000) explain that there is a significant difference between mean score of questions, 12, 14 and 15 and gender distribution.

Table 8. Descriptive statistics for gender-presentation relation

	N	Mean	Std. Deviation	Minimum	Maximum
Gender	40	1.5000	0.5063	1.000	2.000
Presentation	40	1.5000	0.5063	1.00	2.00

4.2 Analysis for Students Awareness of Solar and Earth System

Analyses descriptive statistics for questions number 10 and 11 after presentation for boys and girls do not show an important difference. Table 9 shows values are same for pre presentation and post presentation activity for boys and girls.

Table 9 shows values are same for pre presentation and post presentation activity.

Table 9. Presentation differences

		N	Mean Rank	Sum of Ranks	Z	p
Gender-Presentation	Negative Ranks	10	10.50	105.00	.000	1.000
Gender-Presentation	Positive Ranks	10	10.50	105.00	.000	1.000
Gender-Presentation	Ties	20			.000	1.000
	Total	40				

According to the Tables 8 and 9, about the survey, when the relationship between presentation and gender was examined, it was observed that presentation did not make a significant difference on gender, since the mean values were equal to 10.50 and the p = 1 value was greater than 0.005. As a conclusion, there is no difference was observed between female students and male students in terms of the permanence of the presentation. When the 9th, 10th and 13th questions are examined, there is a significant difference between the 9–1 question and the presentation since the mean values are different and the p value is less than 0.005. The training provided was beneficial in terms of sun, solar and earth system awareness.

When the question numbered 9–2, namely space air, in the questionnaire was examined, it was observed that the presentation raised awareness about the subject of solar system, since the average values were different from each other and the p value was less than 0.005.

After the values for the earth item no. 9–3; since the mean values are close to each other and the p value is greater than 0.005, it has been observed that the presentation given to the students does not make a significant difference in the formation of their awareness on solar and earth systems. It is concluded that the students have participated in another pilot space supported by EU. For this reason, awareness level of the students are high.

In the 11th question and since the p value was greater than 0.005, it was observed that the presentation given to the students was not related to the student's previous participation in a science workshop. In the chosen institution, students already have prior knowledge in this field; It would be beneficial to make a similar application in schools in other geographical regions and with different dermographic characteristics. Similar studies would be extended and beneficial to outreach. These activities would be some part of future plans and an infrastructure on this subject in the future, and this will raise awareness in the society. For this reason we build a web site for outreach of the subject. It is www.ssaoutreach.aydin.edu.tr [18].

4.3 Conslusions and Recommendations

This study has a contribution to primary school education programs, considering the combination of music and survey work and the effect of art on the learning speed of individuals. Similar to the study of Tulunay Y. [6] and her team, positive results were obtained. Considering that the group selected for the study have already knowledge some information on this field, a positive result were still observed in comparison with pre and post training programs. Boys and girls have no difference for the first and second stage reactions. In addition to this specific situation, the sample group can be selected wider so that the social contribution will be more meaningful. For the future work, the study would become more comprehensive if this study is applied among student groups with different demographic structures.

Acknowledgements. Authors would like to thank, (BAP) IAU-Scientific Research Program, AKEV (Anatolian Education and Culture Foundation), HALKALI Cumhuriyet Primary School and Assist. Prof. Dr. Uğur ŞENER. They also very much obliged to Prof. Dr. Yurdanur Tulunay and Prof. Dr. Ersin Tulunay for their support.

APPENDIX- Questionnarie

SPACE AIR, EARTH AWARENESS LEVEL DETERMINATION SURVEY

Dear Participant,

Thank you very much for taking the time to complete this survey. The purpose of this survey is to determine the awareness levels of students aged 7-11 about space weather, earth, sun and planets. Your answers and evaluation that will guide us are very important for the next stages of this research.

It is not possible to access the data to be obtained in this study within the scope of the protection of personal information and to use the shared information for other than its purpose.

All questions must be marked. None of the questions asked will be used for scoring you.

SECTION 1

1. How old are you?   ( ) lower than 8   ( ) 9 -10   ( ) 11
2. Gender: ( ) Female ( ) Male
3. Educational Status of Your Elders With Whom You Live At Home (Mother, Father, Other...)

Mother: ( ) illiterate	Father: ( ) illiterate
( ) primary school	( ) primary school
( ) high school	( ) high school
( ) university	( ) university

Other : ( ) illiterate
          ( ) primary school
          ( ) high school
          ( ) university

4. Did you receive early childhood education before starting primary school (like nursery, kindergarten)?
          ( ) Yes   ( ) No
5. If you received early childhood education (nursery, kindergarten), how many years did you take?
          ( ) 1 year or lower than   ( ) 2 years   ( ) 3 years and more
6. Do you have a library in your home?
          ( ) Yes, I have   ( ) No, I have not
7. If your answer to question 6 is yes, do you have books about nature, space, planets in your library?
          ( )   Yes, I have   ( ) No, I have not

SECTION 2

8. What kind of documentaries do you prefer to watch on television and other digital media? (More than one option can be ticked)
   ( ) Nature and Science   ( ) Art or Culturel   ( ) I don't watch documentary

9. Which of the following concepts have you heard before? (More than one option can be ticked, you can mark by putting an X in the boxes.)

Space weather includes the environmental conditions created by the sun and solar winds in the earth's and atmosphere layers. These conditions, electronics etc. on earth demands affect human health. Studies are underway to estimate the effects on biological and technological systems.
          ( ) Sun   ( ) Space Weather   ( ) Earth

10. **Which of the following concepts have you heard before? (More than one option can be ticked, you can mark by putting an X in the boxes.)**

The plasma emitted as a result of solar activities collides with these charged particles and ripples, forming a tail in the opposite direction and takes the form of a drop. The particles trapped in the tail section accelerate towards the poles of the Earth, which is a giant magnet, as a result of fluctuations. Particles reaching the upper layers of the atmosphere transfer their energy to the atoms and molecules there. After this energy transfer in the polar regions where the magnetic field lines of the Earth are concentrated, atoms and molecules that gain extra energy emit this energy in the form of light. The light show, which is as intense as the amount of particles in the solar wind, continues until all the extra energy transferred is transformed into light. Particles flowing from the magnetic tail towards the poles reach both poles at the same time, and aurora lights occur at both poles at the same time. Aurora lights, which contain high amounts of particles, give an impressive spectacle to the audience, but can interfere with radio and GPS signals or cause power outages.

( ) Northern Lights   ( ) Solar System   ( ) Planets

11. **Have you ever attended a science workshop or an event such as a science camp?** ( ) Yes, I joined   ( ) No, I did not joined

12. **The education I received at school; arouses my curiosity about space weather, sun, planet, earth.**

( ) I don't agree   ( ) I am undecided   ( ) I agree

13. **When I hear about space weather and universe in the cartoons and documentaries I watch, I read these subjects from the internet, books, etc. I search**

( ) I don't agree   ( ) I am undecided   ( ) I agree

14. **Space weather is an important concept for the earth.**

( ) I don't agree   ( ) I am undecided   ( ) I agree

15. **There is a relationship between space weather and the earth.**

( ) I don't agree   ( ) I am undecided   ( ) I agree

References

1. Adams, J., Slater, T.: Astronomy in the national science education standards. J. Geosci. Edu. **48**(1), 39–45 (2000)
2. Meyer, A.O., Mon, M.J., Hibbard, S.T.: The lunar phases project: a mental model-based observational project for undergraduate nonscience majors. Astron. Edu. Rev. **10**(1), (2011). http://aer.aas.org/ resource/1/aerscz/v10/i1/p010203s1
3. Rollins, M.M., Dentton, J.J., Janke, D.L.: Attainment of selected earth science concepts by Texas high school seniors. J. Edu. Res. **77**(2), 81–88 (1983)
4. Thompson, B.J., Gopalswamy, N., Davila, J.M., Haubold, H.J. (eds.) Putting the "I" in IHY, XV, pp.371 (2009)
5. Tulunay, Y.: Space weather and Europe – an educational tool with the sun (SWEETS), Final Report, (2008). http://cordis.europa.eu/ documents/documentlibrary/126792761EN6.pdf
6. RESULTS OF THE I LOVE MY SUN PROJECT 2014–2016, Mosna Zbysek, Macusova Eva, Kouba Daniel, Blanch Estefania, Humlova Danka)

7. Önal, O.: Otistik Çocuklarda Müzik Eğitimi, Kırıkkale Üniversitesi, Yüksek Lisans Tezi (2010)
8. Anna, S.: The effect of background music on learning, the society for research in psychology of music and music. Education **27**, 138–146 (1999)
9. Fatih, G., Ezelnur, Ç., Ufuk, T.: Eğitsel Şarkı ve Oyun Tekniklerinin Öğrencilerin Akademik Başarıları ve Kalıcılığı Üzerine Etkileri. Bayburt Eğitim Fakültesi Dergisi **12**(24), 593–612 (2017)
10. Selami, Y., Mustafa, S., Sinan, B., Nesrin, Y.: Fen Bilimleri Dersinde Çocuk Şarkıları İle Desteklenmiş Öğretimin İlkokul 4. Sınıf Öğrencilerinin Başarısına Etkisi, Uluslararası Eğitim Bilimleri Dergisi **8**, 44–57 (2016)
11. Pesen, A., Çiftçi, Y.E.: The effect of traditional teaching method and teaching with drama and music on academic achievement and permanence. In: International Engineering, Science and Education Conference, 01–03 December 2016, Diyarbakir/Turkey (2016)
12. Aydın, S.: Ural Keleş Pınar ve Ürün Nesrin, SÜREÇ DEĞERLENDİRME YÖNTEMİNİN 7. SINIF "GÜNEŞ SİSTEMİ VE ÖTESİ: UZAY BİLMECESİ" ÜNİTESİNDE ÖĞRENCİLERİN AKADEMİK BAŞARILARI VE KALICILIK DÜZEYLERİNE ETKİSİ, Türk Eğitim Araştırmaları Dergisi, 1, 11–17 (2016)
13. Başer, F.A.: MÜZİĞİN OKUL ÖNCESİ DÖNEMDE ÇOCUK GELİŞİMİNE KATKISI, Sakarya Üniversitesi Eğitim Fakültesi Dergisi, 0, 8 (2004)
14. Tulunay Yurdanur, Crosby Bock Norma, Tulunay Ersin, Calders Stijn, Parnowski Aleksei, Sulic Desanka, The COST example for outreach to the general public: I love my Sun, J. Space Weather Space Climate, 3 (2013)
15. Yavuz, Ş.: Okulöncesi Dönemde Çocuğun Gelişiminde Müziğin Önemi. Atatürk Üniversitesi Sosyal Bilimler Enstitüsü Dergisi **7**(1), 337-343 (2010)
16. Davila, J.M., Gopalswamy, N., Thompson, B.J.: Preparing for the International Heliophysical Year (IHY), NASA Goddard Space Flight Center, Greenbelt, MD 20771, USA (2007)
17. Url 1, http://ilovemysun.net/. Last accessed 11 Apr 2023
18. Url 2, www.ssa.outreach.aydin.edu.tr. Last accessed 11 Apr 2023
19. Bentz, J.: Learning about climate change in, with and through art. Clim. Change **162**(3), 1595–1612 (2020)
20. Sosyal Bilimler İçin Veri Analizi El Kitabı, Şener Büyüköztürk, Pegem Yayınevi, 2021
21. Sidney, S.: Non Parametric Statistics for The Behavioral Science. McGraw-Hill Book Company, Inc., New York Toronto London (1956)
22. Yildirim, S., Akman, B., Alabay, E.: A review on the effect of montessori and mandala education provided to pre-schoolers to visual perception behaviors, Buca Egitim Fakultesi Dergisi **32**, 2012
23. Devi, N., Kumar, A., Arpitha, V., Khyathi, G.: Development and standardization of "Questionnaire on Music Perception Ability", **6**(1), (2017)
24. Demirci, A.: The effect of visual perception education on the development of visual perception in the children of five-six ages, Gazi University Phd Thesis (2010)
25. Bangir, A.G., Ozbalci, M.: Does visual aritmetics education support visual perception development of children. Uluslararası Egitim Programlari ve Ögretim Calismalari Dergisi **5**, 10 (2015)
26. Kurtz, L.A.: Visual Perception Problems in Children with AD/ HD, Autism and Other Learning Disabilities, A Guide for Parents and Professionals, Jessica Kingsley Publishers (2006)
27. Orhon, İB.: Gorsel Algı ve Temel Sanat Eğitimi. Gazi Universitesi Mesleki Egitim Dergisi **5**, 135–156 (2003)
28. Tugrul, B., Aral, N., Erkan, S., Etikan, İ: Altı Yasindaki Cocuklarin Gorsel Algilama Duzeylerine Frostig Gelisimsel Gorsel Algi Egitim Programinin Etkisinin Incelenmesi. Kafkas Universitesi Dergisi **8**, 67–84 (2001)

29. Reinartz, A., Reinartz, E.: Wahrnehmun Gstraining (M. Won Frostig, B. A. David Horne and Ann Maria Miler, M.A.), Dortmund: An Weisung self (2001)

30. Açılmış, H., Kayıran, B.K.: Muzik Ogretimi (1.baskı). Pegem Akademi. Ankara (2021)

31. Alpagut, U., et al.: Teoriden Uygulamaya Yeni Yönelimler ve Yeni Yaklaşımlarla Müzik Öğretimi. Alpagut, U. ve Yöndem, S. (ed.) Nobel Yayıncılık. Ankara (2019)

32. Aytaç, B., Tan, M.K., Gök, Z., Can, Ü.K., Orff-Schulwerk Elementer Müzik Ve Hareket Pedagojisinin Temelleri" Kitap İncelemesi. https://doi.org/10.31811/ojomus.708189. ONLINE J. Music Sci. 5(1), 83–96. Kitap İncelemesi (2020)

33. Çetin, G.Ç.: Etkinliklerle Müzik Öğretimi (3. baskı). Kök Yayıncılık. Ankara (2016)

34. Özgül, İ.: Müzik Eğitimi ve Öğretimi. (8. baskı). Pegem Akademi. Ankara (2020)

35. Saraç, A.G.: Müzik Eğitiminde Özel Öğretim İlke, Yöntem ve Teknikleri 1. (1. baskı). Nobel Yayıncılık. Ankara (2016)

36. Saraç, A.G.: Müzik Eğitiminde Özel Öğretim İlke, Yöntem ve Teknikleri 2. (1. baskı). Nobel Yayıncılık. Ankara (2016)

37. Türkmen, E.F.: Müzik Eğitiminde Öğretim Yöntemleri. (8. baskı). Pegem Akademi. Ankara (2021)

38. Aytaç, B., Tan, M.K., Gök, Z., Can, Ü.K.: Orff-Schulwerk Elementer Müzik Ve Hareket Pedagojisinin Temelleri" Kitap İncelemesi. https://doi.org/10.31811/ojomus.708189 .ONLINE, J. Music Sci. 5(1), 83–96. Kitap İncelemesi (2020)

39. Url 3: https://www.trthaber.com/haber/bilim-teknoloji/uzayda-hava-durumu-nasil-663408. html. Last accessed 11 Apr 2023

40. Url 4: https://www.space.com/. Last accessed 11 Apr 2023

41. Url 5: https://hezarfen.mgm.gov.tr/Aylik/gecmis/sweather/sweather.aspx. Last accessed 11 Apr 2023

42. Url 6: https://www.millisavunma.com/milli-uzay-programi-ve-stratejik-10-target/. Last accessed 11Apr 2023

43. Kalafatoğlu, E.C., Kaymaz, Z., Moral, A.C.: Geomagnetically induced current (GIC) observations of geomagnetic storms in Turkey: Preliminary results (2019)

Forecasting Multivariate Time Series with a Dynamic-System-Based Hybrid Model

Daria Ganaeva⬤ and Anna Golovkina$^{(\boxtimes)}$⬤

Saint Petersburg State University, Saint Petersburg, Russia
`a.golovkina@spbu.ru`

Abstract. This paper proposes a time series forecasting approach that integrates nonlinear dynamic systems reconstruction with statistical forecasting methods. The suggested technique is as follows: the time series is decomposed into dynamic and stochastic components, each of which is used to build independent predictive models. In the end, the forecasting results are combined together. The research compares the prediction results and errors values for with the suggested technique, ARIMA, SVR, and a sparse identification method SINDy on synthetic and real-world data sets. Forecasting accuracy utilizing the suggested technique outperforms that of competing methods. Thus, the proposed approach may be utilized to solve practical issues involving the prediction of the behavior of diverse processes for which the mathematical model is unknown but data are accessible at discrete periods.

Keywords: Dynamic system reconstruction · Time series forecasting · Time series decomposition

1 Introduction

Forecasting is a method for making predictions about the direction of future trends based on historical data and current inputs. Forecasting is the most important optimization concept in terms of energy savings, material savings, boosting efficiency, and making appropriate control decisions.

The forecasting problem can be solved from two angles: building univariate or multivariate time series models. Traditional universal forecasting methods predict variables using only information contained in their own past values and possibly the current and past values of an error term. In contrast, multivariate models attempt to explain changes in a variable by reference to movements in the current or past values of other (explanatory) variables.

One of the most popular univariate methods is autoregressive integrated moving average (ARIMA) modeling, which uses past values of the variable and its differences and moving averages to make future predictions [13,17,19]. Other univariate methods include exponential smoothing and trend analysis. Univariate methods are easy to implement and interpret and can provide accurate forecasts

Supported by Saint Petersburg State University, project ID: 94062114.

for simple time series data with a single trend or seasonality. However, they may not perform well for complex data with multiple trends or seasonalities or when external factors are influencing the data.

Multivariate methods, on the other hand, involve modeling multiple time series variables that may be related to each other. One popular multivariate method is vector autoregression (VAR) modeling, which models the relationships between multiple time series variables using lagged values of each variable [2]. Multivariate methods can provide more accurate forecasts for complex data as they can capture the effects of multiple variables and external factors.

Besides the mentioned traditional statistical approaches, in recent years, there has been an increasing interest in machine learning [20] and deep learning-based [5,8,21] methods for time series forecasting, which have shown promising results in both univariate and multivariate settings.

One popular deep learning-based method is the long short-term memory (LSTM) model [11], which is a variant of recurrent neural networks (RNNs) that can capture long-term dependencies in data. LSTMs have been shown to outperform traditional methods such as ARIMA and exponential smoothing for time series forecasting, especially for data with complex patterns and seasonality. Another neural network-based approach is the convolutional neural network (CNN) [12], which can be applied to time series data by treating it as an image and extracting relevant features using convolutional layers.

Among machine learning methods for time series forecasting, the most promising are regression models with different kernels [9] and ensemble methods that combine multiple models to improve the accuracy and robustness of forecasts [7]. One popular ensemble method is the random forest (RF) model [6], which combines multiple decision trees to make predictions. RF has been shown to perform well for time series data with multiple predictors and non-linear relationships. Another ensemble method is the gradient boosting machine (GBM) [16], which combines multiple weak models to create a strong model.

However, these methods also have some limitations. For neural network-based methods, one of their main limitations is their black-box nature, which makes it difficult to interpret the results and understand the underlying relationships between variables. Additionally, these methods may require a large amount of data and computational resources for training and may suffer from overfitting if the data is not carefully preprocessed.

For ensemble methods, the main limitation is that they may be computationally expensive to train and may require careful tuning of hyperparameters to achieve optimal performance. Additionally, these methods may not perform well for data with complex temporal dependencies or non-linear relationships.

Dynamical systems reconstruction approaches are a different class of methods for time series forecasting that involve reconstructing the underlying dynamics of the system from the observed data [1,14,15,23,24]. These methods can potentially overcome some of the limitations of neural network-based and ensemble methods, as they can provide a more interpretable model and do not require extensive hyperparameter tuning. In addition, unlike traditional univariate and multivariate time series forecasting techniques, this method enables the inclusion of nonlinear behavior in the underlying process.

One popular method for dynamical system reconstruction is the Takens embedding theorem [22], which involves embedding the time series data in a higher-dimensional to capture the underlying dynamics of the system. Other approaches include delay-coordinate embedding and state-space reconstruction.

A state-space dynamical system usually models the causal relationships between variables using a system of differential equations [3]. Reconstruction methods identify a model of the system's dynamics based on the measurements to estimate the state of the system, which can then be used to predict its future behavior.

The paper proposes a strategy for increasing the predictability and generalization properties of predictive models by combining traditional statistical univariate forecasting approaches with nonlinear dynamic system reconstruction. The suggested technique has the advantage of being able to deal with unevenly distributed and noisy time series data. This is accomplished by additional data creation with spline approximation as well as the decomposition of time series data into dynamic and stochastic components. A dynamic component is used to reconstruct dynamic systems in the form of a system of differential equations, the structure of which is unknown in advance. The stochastic component is fed to the traditional univariate forecasting method like ARIMA. In the end, the predictions from both models are summarized to get the final result.

The remaining part of the paper is structured as follows: Sect. 2 describes time series preprocessing steps, such as data decomposition and regularization; Sect. 3 introduces the components of a hybrid forecasting model and the principles guiding their design; and Sect. 4 compares the proposed approach to established methods on synthetic and real-world time series data.

2   Time Series Preprocessing

Real-world time series often include components with different frequencies, contain noise, or are impacted by external, unknown stochastic factors. Also, the measurements that comprise a time series may contain inconsistent time stamps. These characteristics can affect the effectiveness of a forecasting model. That is why preprocessing steps with the original time series are required.

Recent studies show that incorporating decomposition algorithms with forecasting algorithms usually yields more accurate predictions. What is more, this step is vital for dynamic system reconstruction in state-space form, which is the basis of the proposed hybrid model.

We selected singular spectrum analysis (SSA) over other decomposition methodologies because it does not rely on specific assumptions about the regularity or stationarity of the data. We apply it to decomposing the original time series into dynamic and stochastic components, which are then used independently for ODE-based model identification and statistical model training.

Because ODE reconstruction algorithms are sensitive to the regularity of the data used for identification, we undertake regularization of the dynamical component with spline approximation among other preprocessing steps to generate additional data.

If time series data is of high dimension, it would be ineffective to identify dynamic systems in high-dimensional space. To avoid this, it is proposed to apply clustering-based dimensionality reduction techniques. The steps listed above are discussed in further detail below.

2.1   Time Series Decomposition

Singular spectrum analysis (SSA) is a data-driven technique for analyzing time series data. It involves decomposing a time series into a set of components, each of which represents a different frequency or timescale of the data. SSA is particularly useful for analyzing non-stationary or noisy time series data, as it can effectively separate the signal from the noise.

The SSA algorithm involves several steps. First, the time series data is embedded in a higher-dimensional space using a sliding window technique. Next, the embedded data is decomposed into a set of eigenvectors and eigenvalues using a singular value decomposition. The eigenvectors represent the different components of the time series, while the eigenvalues provide information about their relative importance.

After the decomposition, the components can be reconstructed by combining the eigenvectors with the original time series data. The resulting components can be analyzed separately to identify patterns or trends in the data, or they can be combined to reconstruct the original time series.

One advantage of SSA is that it does not require any prior assumptions about the underlying dynamics of the time series. It is also relatively easy to implement and can be used with a wide range of time series data, including irregularly sampled data. That is why it was selected as a decomposing tool in the proposed algorithm. The basic algorithm consists of two complementary steps: decomposition and reconstruction [10] which are briefly reproduced below for convenience.

Stage 1. Decomposition

Step 1. Embedding. Consider a time series $T = (x(t_0), \ldots, x(t_{M-1})) = (x_0, \ldots, x_{M-1})$ of length M. Let L be a window length, where $1 < L < M$. The embedding procedure forms $K = M - L + 1$ lagged vectors:

$$X_i = (x(t_{i-1}), \cdots, x(t_{i+L-2}))^{\mathsf{T}}, \quad 1 \leq i \leq K,$$

of length L. Trajectory matrix $\mathbf{X}$ of time series T has lagged vectors as its columns.

Step 2. Singular value decomposition. The result of this step is the singular value decomposition of the trajectory matrix $\mathbf{X}$. It can be written as:

$$\mathbf{X} = \mathbf{X}_1 + \cdots + \mathbf{X}_d.$$

Here $d = \max\{i : \lambda_i > 0\}$, where $\lambda_1, \ldots, \lambda_L$ are the eigenvalues of matrix $\mathbf{S} = \mathbf{X}\mathbf{X}^\top$ taken in the decreasing order; $\mathbf{X_i} = \sqrt{\lambda_i}U_iV_i^\top$, where $U_1, \ldots, U_L$ is the orthonormal system of the eigenvectors of matrix $\mathbf{S}$, and $V_i = \frac{\mathbf{X}^\top U_i}{\sqrt{\lambda_i}}$.

Stage 2: Reconstruction

Step 3. Grouping. The next step is grouping the terms of the singular value decomposition, which correspond to the separable dynamic (including trend and periodicity) and statistical (residual) components of the series.

The grouping operation divides the set of indices $\{1, \cdots, d\}$ into separate subsets $\{I_1, \cdots, I_m\}$. The previous step's decomposition can be written in a grouped form as follows:

$$\mathbf{X} = \mathbf{X}_{I_1} + \cdots + \mathbf{X}_{I_m}.$$

Here $\mathbf{X}_{I_k} = \mathbf{X}_{i_1} + \cdots + \mathbf{X}_{i_{p_k}}, k = \overline{1, m}, I_k = \{i_1, \ldots, i_{p_k}\}$.

Step 4. Diagonal averaging. Each matrix from the grouped decomposition is converted into a new series of length M in this stage. An $L \times K$ matrix $\mathbf{Y}$ with components of y_{ij} is transformed into a series of $(g_0, \ldots, g_{N-1})$, according to the formula:

$$g_k = \begin{cases} \dfrac{1}{k+1}\displaystyle\sum_{m=1}^{k+1} y^*_{m,k-m+2}, & 0 \le k \le L^* - 1, \\[3mm] \dfrac{1}{L^*}\displaystyle\sum_{m=1}^{L^*} y^*_{m,k-m+2}, & L^* - 1 \le k \le K^*, \\[3mm] \dfrac{1}{M-k}\displaystyle\sum_{m=k-K^*+2}^{M-K^*+1} y^*_{m,k-m+2}, & K^* \le k \le M. \end{cases}$$

Here $L^* = \min\{L, K\}, K^* = \max\{L, K\}, M = L + K - 1; y^*_{ij} = y_{ij}$ if $L < K$ and $y^*_{ij} = y_{ji}$ if $L \ge K$.

Diagonal averaging applied to matrices X_{I_k} produces series $\widetilde{T}^{(k)} = (\tilde{x}_0^{(k)}, \ldots, \tilde{x}_{M-1}^{(k)})$. The initial series $(x_0, \ldots, x_{M-1})$ is decomposed into the sum of m series:

$$x_n = \sum_{k=1}^{m} \tilde{x}_n^{(k)}.$$

2.2   Time Series Clustering

Real-world data sets typically contain multidimensional time series with large dimensions, making the reconstruction of dynamic systems in high dimensional space impractical. To address this issue, it is advocated that time series data be clustered based on their similarity, with the premise that one time series has a limited influence on the others. The time series assigned to one cluster are then used to reconstruct intra-cluster dynamic system. The k-Shape [18] technique is used to group data based on correlation.

The k-Shape is a partitional clustering approach that uses an iterative refining procedure similar to the k-means procedure. It employs a shape-based distance measure (SBD) and a centroid computing approach that takes time series shapes into consideration.

The SBD measure is based on cross-correlation with which the similarity of two sequences $\vec{x} = (x_1, \cdots, x_m)$ and $\vec{y} = (y_1, \cdots, y_m)$ can be determined. It can be written as follows:

$$SBD(\vec{x}, \vec{y}) = 1 - \max_{w}\left(\frac{CC_w(\vec{x}, \vec{y})}{\sqrt{R_0(\vec{x}, \vec{x})R_0(\vec{y}, \vec{y})}}\right),$$

zero value of which indicates perfect similarity for time series sequences. Here, $CC_w(\vec{x}, \vec{y}) = (c_1, \cdots, c_w) = R_{w-m}(\vec{x}, \vec{y})$, $w \in \{1, 2, \cdots, 2m-1\}$ is the cross-correlation sequence with length $2m-1$, where $R_{w-m}(\vec{x}, \vec{y})$ is computed, in turn, as:

$$R_k(\vec{x}, \vec{y}) = \begin{cases} \sum_{l=1}^{m-k} x_{l+k} \cdot y_l, & k \geq 0, \\ R_{-k}(\vec{y}, \vec{x}), & k < 0. \end{cases}$$

Centroids are calculated as optimization problems with the goal of minimizing the sum of squared distances to all other time series sequences, as opposed to centroids being calculated as the arithmetic mean of the corresponding coordinates of all sequences of a cluster. The computed sequence, however, is expressed as the maximizer of the squared similarities to all other time series sequences since cross-correlation captures the similarity of time series. A more detailed formulation can be found in [18].

Every time a refinement step is repeated, k-Shape completes two steps: updating the cluster memberships by comparing each time series to all computed centroids and assigning each time series to the cluster with the closest centroid using the SBD measure (assigning step); and updating the cluster centroids to account for the changes in cluster memberships (refinement step). Until there is no change in cluster membership or the allotted number of iterations has been reached, the algorithm repeats these processes.

2.3   Data Regularization Using Splines

In some cases time series data points may be located sparsely or irregularly. To address this problem, it is proposed to perform data regularization, which consists of two successive steps: data approximation; generation of additional data using the approximating function.

Interpolation splines are the main candidate for the role of the approximating function, because, firstly, for the right side of the system of differential equations to be restored in polynomial form, the use of polynomial functions will give better results than, for example, trigonometric ones, and even more so if there is no reason to assume that the process described by the time series is periodic.

Secondly, considering polynomial functions, if the time interval on which the process is described is large, and there is no reason to consider the function describing the process to be smooth enough, then there is no point in using a single polynomial to approximate this function, and there is no point in improving the quality of approximations through the use of polynomials of high degrees - in this case it is better to use a piecewise function, composed of individual polynomials of low degrees, defined on a part of the global time interval.

Finally, since non-linear continuous functions which are complex differentiable in an open set can be represented as power series in the neighbourhood of any given point with any accuracy, and the partial sums of this series are polynomials, it was decided to use approximation by piecewise polynomial functions.

Cubic spline interpolation, the most popular piecewise-polynomial approximation, employs cubic polynomials between each subsequent pair of nodes [4].

3   Hybrid Forecasting Model

3.1   Dynamic Component Forecasting Based on ODE Reconstruction

The proposed method for the reconstruction of a system of ordinary differential equations in polynomial form uses an approach based on the artificial generation of new data.

Let the values of components $X_j(t), j = (1, n)$, of vector $\mathbf{X}(t) \in \mathbb{R}^n$ be known at time points $t_0, \cdots, t_{M+1}$. It is assumed that the time series corresponds to some dynamic process, which can be represented by a system of ordinary differential equations with constant coefficients:

$$\frac{d\mathbf{X}}{dt} = \sum_{k=0}^{N} P^k \mathbf{X}^{[k]}, \tag{1}$$

where $\mathbf{X}(t) \in \mathbb{R}^n$ is a vector describing the state of the system at time point t, $\mathbf{X}^{[k]}$ is k-th Kronecker power of vector $\mathbf{X}$, N is the maximum Kronecker power to which $\mathbf{X}$ is raised, and P^k are coefficient matrices.

To address the problem of sparse or irregular time series, it is proposed first to approximate the components $X_j(t_i), j = \overline{1, n}, i = \overline{1, M}$ of the measurement vector using splines and then generate additional data points using approximating function.

Matrices P^k are unknown and should be found from available measurements $\mathbf{X}(t_0), \cdots, \mathbf{X}(t_{M+1})$ combined with artificially generated data. Similarly to the SINDy method proposed in [3], P^k are found as solution to sparse regression problem:

$$P = \arg\min_{\tilde{P}} \left(\left\| \dot{\mathbf{X}} - A\tilde{P} \right\|_2 \right) \tag{2}$$

where $\dot{\mathbf{X}}$ is obtained by replacing the derivatives in the left side of (1) with finite differences, A is the matrix of measurements and $P = (P^0, \cdots, P^k)$. This problem can be solved using sparse optimization algorithms, for example, LASSO or sequential thresholded least-squares [3] with additional L_1 regularization term in (2). This helps to identify the most valuable features in the system and eliminate others that are less important.

Considering the assumption that one time series does not affect the other immediately, but with some delay, the right side of the system 1 contains polynomial components with $X_j(t - \tau_j)$, where the delay parameters τ_j are selected experimentally.

Forecasting of the dynamic component of time series is carried out using a numerical solution of the reconstructed system (1).

3.2   Stochastic Component Forecasting Model

The statistic components of time series are approximated and predicted using the ARIMA [13] method. It is based on the use of moving average models and autoregressive models. A linear combination of the variable's previous values is used to forecast the variable of interest in an autoregression model. The formula for an autoregressive model of order p is the following

$$y_t = c + \phi_1 y_{t-1} + \phi_2 y_{t-2} + \cdots + \phi_p y_{t-p} + \varepsilon_t,$$

where ε_t is white noise. This model is referred to as an $AR(p)$ model.

A moving average model uses previous prediction errors in a regression-like model rather than prior values of the forecast variable

$$y_t = c + \theta_1 \varepsilon_{t-1} + \theta_2 \varepsilon_{t-2} + \cdots + \theta_q \varepsilon_{t-q} + \varepsilon_t,$$

where ε_t is white noise. This model is referred to as an $MA(q)$ model.

Combining differencing with autoregression and a moving average model, a non-seasonal ARIMA model (AUtoRegressive Integrated Moving Average) is obtained. The full model can be written as

$$y_t' = c + \phi_1 y_{t-1}' + \cdots + \phi_p y_{t-p}' + \theta_1 \varepsilon_{t-1} + \cdots + \theta_q \varepsilon_{t-q} t + \varepsilon_t,$$

where y_t' is the differenced series. This model is referred to as an $ARIMA(p, d, q)$ model, where p is the order of the autoregressive part, d is the degree of differencing and q is the order of the moving average part.

Once the model order (p, d, q) has been identified, the parameters $c, \phi_1, \cdots, \phi_p, \theta_1, \cdots, \theta_q$ need to be estimated. It can be done by using maximum likelihood estimation (MLE) and Akaike's Information Criterion (AIC).

MLE determines the parameter values that maximize the likelihood of obtaining the observed data. MLE is comparable to the least squares estimates that would be obtained by minimizing the error

$$\sum_t \varepsilon_t^2.$$

AIC can be written as

$$AIC = -2\log L + 2(p + q + k + 1),$$

where L is the likelihood of the data, $k = 1$ if $c \neq 0$ and $k = 0$ if $c = 0$.

3.3   Composite Forecast

To predict future values of time series data, it is necessary to sum up at each moment of time the numerical solution of a dynamical system (1) with predictions based on a stochastic model. It should be emphasized, that time discretization of both parts of hybrid models should be consistent.

4   Experiments

This section contains the results of two numerical experiments: a toy example of identifying a dynamic system using synthetic data and the construction of a hybrid forecasting model based on the Abilene real-world data set.

4.1   Synthetic Data

The time series for the system reconstruction was synthetically generated using the numerical solution $(x(t), y(t))$ of the Van der Pol oscillator ODEs:

$$\begin{cases} \dfrac{dx}{dt} = y, \\ \dfrac{dy}{dt} = \mu(1 - x^2)y - x. \end{cases} \tag{3}$$

Specifically, a particular solution of the system (3) obtained on the interval $[0, 10]$ with the initial condition was $(x_0, y_0) = (1, 4)$ and step $h = 0,01$ used as training data. From it, two time series were formed: a regular one with a given thinning step and an irregular one, for which the required number of points was randomly taken.

A particular solution of the system (3) obtained on the interval $[5, 15]$ with the initial condition was $(x_0, y_0) = (1, 1)$ was used as testing data. The results are shown in the Fig. 1, 2. The graphs on the left show data points used as the input dataset, and the graphs on the right show true phase trajectory $y(x)$ of the system, as well as the trajectory of the reconstructed system using the proposed method and SINDy. In the case with regular data points mean absolute errors of the proposed algorithm and SINDy are 0.008 and 0.028 respectively, and in the case with regular data points they are 0.009 and 0.136 respectively.

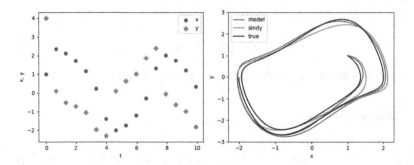

Fig. 1. Reconstruction using 15 regular data points

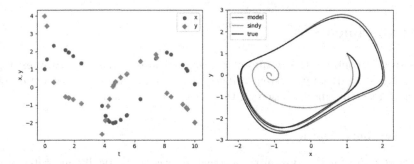

Fig. 2. Reconstruction using 30 irregular data points

4.2   Abilene Real-World Data Set

The proposed hybrid approach is applied to develop a predictive model for the Abilene data set, which describes the transmission of traffic between 12 nodes of the telecommunications network shown in Fig. 3. Each edge means the transmission of traffic between the nodes it connects.

The graphics below depict the intermediate steps described above and applied to the Abilene time series data. Figure 3 shows how the original time series with traffic levels via one edge is divided up into dynamic and stochastic components. Figure 4 demonstrates forecasts with each component of hybrid predictive model as well as the results of a composite forecast.

The proposed technique is contrasted with two well-known time series forecasting methods: ARIMA and SVR. The predicting outcomes from these models under identical conditions are shown in Fig. 5 . The forecasts from the hybrid model are clearly more accurate than those from the ARIMA and SVR models. To support this conclusion, we use a recursive approach to examine the models for multi-step forecasting tasks. The forecasts are created 1, 2, 3, 4, 6, 8, 12, and 24 h ahead. Mean Absolute Error (MAE) values for the proposed hybrid model, ARIMA, and SVR models are shown in Figs. 6–8, respectively. In these figures, values along ax x correspond to the transmission network's edges (traffic between two linked nodes). It is clear that, in addition to having reduced error values, the suggested hybrid model produces prediction results with an error that is robust to the forecasting horizon. Table 1 summarizes the numerical values of MAE and Mean Absolute Percentage Error (MAPE) computed as the average between all the edges in the network for the compared models.

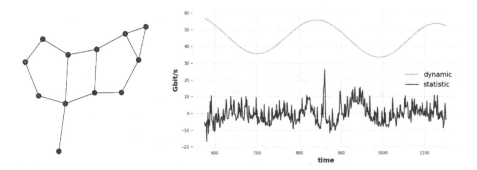

Fig. 3. Abilene network scheme and example of one edge time series decomposition

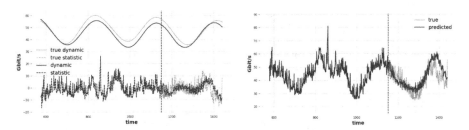

Fig. 4. Forecasting with dynamic and stochastic components forecast (left) and a composite forecast (right)

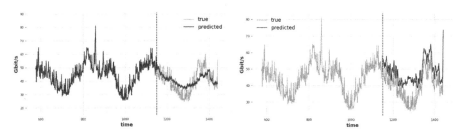

Fig. 5. Forecasting with ARIMA single model (left) and forecasting using SVR single model (right)

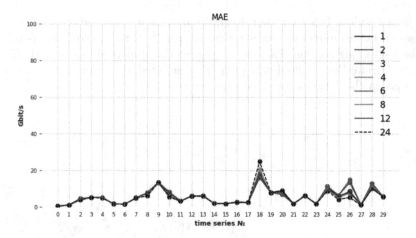

Fig. 6. Proposed hybrid model MAE

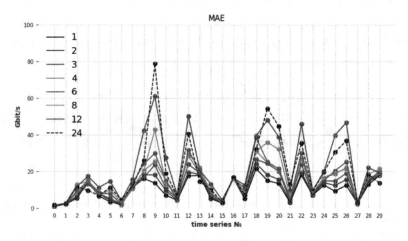

Fig. 7. ARIMA MAE

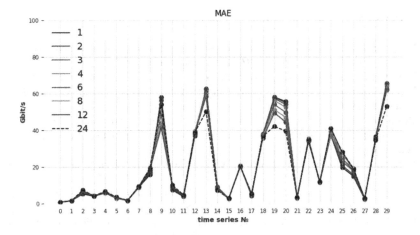

Fig. 8. SVR MAE

Table 1. Mean MAE and MAPE values for hybrid, ARIMA, and SVR models in multi-step forecasting up to 24 h

Step	Our method		ARIMA		SVR	
	MAE Gbit/s	MAPE %	MAE Gbit/s	MAPE %	MAE Gbit/s	MAPE %
1	5.64	7.72	9.93	13.75	19.25	21.41
2	5.45	7.57	11.12	15.37	19.36	21.61
3	5.72	7.76	12.59	16.81	19.61	21.82
4	5.37	7.47	13.89	18.19	19.78	21.99
6	5.66	7.58	15.02	19.25	20.01	22.12
8	5.28	7.39	15.82	20.53	19.21	21.13
12	5.38	7.29	22.55	26.27	20.12	22.26
24	5.36	7.15	19.82	25.87	16.75	18.95

5 Conclusion

The research provides a method for multivariate time series forecasting that combines decomposition, approximation, and statistical modeling approaches, as well as methods for nonlinear dynamic system reconstruction and sparse optimisation. The experimental findings reveal that employing the suggested technique on synthetic and real-world data sets resulted in greater prediction accuracy than SINDy, ARIMA, and SVR. In addition, the suggested hybrid model is verified for extrapolation properties in multi-step forecasting, where it shown error robustness to forecasting horizon in contrast to ARIMA and SVR.

References

1. Bongard, J., Lipson, H.: Automated reverse engineering of nonlinear dynamical systems. Proc. Natl. Acad. Sci. **104**(24), 9943–9948 (2007)
2. Box, G.E.P., Jenkins, G.M., Reinsel, G.C., Ljung, G.M.: Time Series Analysis: Forecasting and Control. Wiley series in probability and statistics, Wiley, Hoboken. fifth edn. (2016)
3. Brunton, S.L., Proctor, J.L., Kutz, J.N.: Discovering governing equations from data by sparse identification of nonlinear dynamical systems. Proc. Natl. Acad. Sci. **113**(15), 3932–3937 (2016)
4. Burden, R.L., Faires, J.D., Burden, A.M.: Numerical Analysis. Cengage Learning. Boston 10 edn. (2016)
5. Chang, Y.Y., Sun, F.Y., Wu, Y.H., Lin, S.D.: A memory-network based solution for multivariate time-series forecasting (2018)
6. Fan, G.F., Zhang, L.Z., Yu, M., Hong, W.C., Dong, S.Q.: Applications of random forest in multivariable response surface for short-term load forecasting. Int. J. Electr. Power Energy Syst. **139**, 108073 (2022)
7. Galicia, A., Talavera-Llames, R., Troncoso, A., Koprinska, I., Martínez-Álvarez, F.: Multi-step forecasting for big data time series based on ensemble learning. Knowl.-Based Syst. **163**, 830–841 (2019)
8. Geng, X., He, X., Xu, L., Yu, J.: Graph correlated attention recurrent neural network for multivariate time series forecasting. Inf. Sci. **606**, 126–142 (2022)
9. Girard, A., Rasmussen, C., Candela, J.Q., Murray-Smith, R.: Gaussian process priors with uncertain inputs application to multiple-step ahead time series forecasting. In: Advances in Neural Information Processing Systems, vol. 15. MIT Press (2002)
10. Golyandina, N., Nekrutkin, V., Zhigljavsky, A.A.: Analysis of Time Series Structure. Chapman and Hall/CRC, London (2001)
11. Hochreiter, S., Schmidhuber, J.: Long short-term memory. Neural Comput. **9**(8), 1735–1780 (1997)
12. Huang, S.C., Le, T.H.: Chapter 8 - convolutional neural network architectures. In: Huang, S.C., Le, T.H. (eds.) Principles and Labs for Deep Learning, pp. 201–217. Academic Press (2021)
13. Hyndman, R.J., Athanasopoulos, G.: Forecasting: Principles And Practice. Otexts, Online Open-Access Textbooks, Melbourne, Australia, third print edition edn (2021)
14. Kramer, D., Bommer, P.L., Tombolini, C., Koppe, G., Durstewitz, D.: Reconstructing Nonlinear Dynamical Systems from Multi-Modal Time Series (2022)
15. Kutz, J.N., Brunton, S.L., Brunton, B.W., Proctor, J.L.: Dynamic Mode Decomposition: Data-Driven Modeling of Complex Systems. Society for Industrial and Applied Mathematics, Philadelphia (2016)
16. Lainder, A.D., Wolfinger, R.D.: Forecasting with gradient boosted trees: augmentation, tuning, and cross-validation strategies: winning solution to the M5 uncertainty competition. Int. J. Forecast. **38**(4), 1426–1433 (2022)
17. Lütkepohl, H.: New Introduction to Multiple Time Series Analysis. Springer, Heidelberg (2005)
18. Paparrizos, J., Gravano, L.: k-shape: efficient and accurate clustering of time series. ACM SIGMOD Rec. **45**(1), 69–76 (2016)
19. Sapankevych, N.I., Sankar, R.: Time series prediction using support vector machines: a survey. IEEE Comput. Intell. Mag. **4**(2), 24–38 (2009). conference Name: IEEE Computational Intelligence Magazine

20. Shah, S.Y., et al.: AutoAI-TS: AutoAI for time series forecasting (2021)
21. Song, W., Fujimura, S.: Capturing combination patterns of long- and short-term dependencies in multivariate time series forecasting. Neurocomputing **464**, 72–82 (2021)
22. Stark, J., Broomhead, D., Davies, M., Huke, J.: Takens embedding theorems for forced and stochastic systems. Nonlinear Anal. Theory Methods Appl. **30**(8), 5303–5314 (1997)
23. Tandeo, P., Ailliot, P., Sévellec, F.: Data-driven reconstruction of partially observed dynamical systems. preprint, Predictability, probabilistic forecasts, data assimilation, inverse problems/Climate, atmosphere, ocean, hydrology, cryosphere, biosphere/Theory (2022)
24. Williams, M.O., Kevrekidis, I.G., Rowley, C.W.: A data-driven approximation of the Koopman operator: extending dynamic mode decomposition. J. Nonlinear Sci. **25**(6), 1307–1346 (2015)

Mobile Platform Based on ROS and LIDAR for Mapping in Civil Construction

Gerson Lima Serejo[1](✉), Viviane Almeida dos Santos[2],
Alexandre Francisco Barral Silva[3], and Carlos Gustavo Resque dos Santos[1]

[1] Federal University of Pará, Graduate Program in Computer Science, Augusto Corrêa Street, 01, Belem, Para 66.075-110, Brazil
gerson.serejo@tucurui.ufpa.br, carlosresque@ufpa.br

[2] Federal University of Pará, Graduate Program in Applied Computing, BR 422 Highway Km 13 Construction Site UHE, Tucurui, Para 68.455-695, Brazil
vsantos@ufpa.br

[3] Barral Robotics and Automation BRA LTDA, Antônio Ramos Alvim Avenue, 1450, apt 202, Floresta, Joinville, Santa Catarina 89.211-460, Brazil

Abstract. The civil construction industry is one of the fastest growing industries in Brazil economically, but it is one of the less grown in terms of application of technologies and innovations. There is a scarce number of studies related to the development and use of mobile platforms applied to construction site environments. With these motivations, this paper presents the development of a mobile platform to be used as a tool to help and improve the inspection process in the construction industry and minimize the costs of acquiring an industrial mobile platform. We explain the materials used in its construction, its electrical schematic and its modeling in Solidworks 3D. The vehicle was shipped with the Robot Operation System (ROS), which used the SLAM algorithm, along with the Rplidar S2 sensor to generate 2D maps. The comparison of the work floor plan with the 2D maps resulted in values very close to the actual measurements. The results ensure that the application of the platform is successful in hostile environments. As a scientific contribution, this innovative study validated the platform navigation planning in horizontal and vertical directions to obtain less shadow in the scene, using the work floor plan as a reference.

Keywords: LIDAR · SLAM · Hector · ROS · Civil construction · Mobile platform

1 Introduction

According to Delgado et al. [1], the construction industry is one of the most important economic sectors in the world. Construction expenses represent a growth from 9% to 15% of most countries' economic performance and, in many cases, represent half of the country's investment in civil construction. The civil construction performance in Brazil in 2022 grew 6%, compared to the industrial segment, which in the same year grew 4.5%, according to the Brazilian Construction Industry Chamber[1]. Despite this,

---

[1] Available at: https://cbic.org.br/construcao-civil-deve-crescer-6-em-2022-diz-cbic/.

O. Gervasi et al. (Eds.): ICCSA 2023 Workshops, LNCS 14104, pp. 192–205, 2023.
https://doi.org/10.1007/978-3-031-37105-9_14

the construction industry has suffered from labor shortages, security risks, and low automation worldwide [2].

Robotics has emerged as a promising technology in the construction industry with the potential to improve productivity and safety. Nonetheless, the adoption of robotics in the construction industry still faces many challenges due to the unique characteristics of each building. According to Xiao et al. [2], the civil construction process presents a lower standardization and control level at the construction site.

Additionally, mobile robotics have been widely used in industry, performing complex tasks in different working conditions and environments [3]. Efficient navigation is one crucial capability of autonomous mobile robots. For navigation, mobile platforms need a map for path planning, known as SLAM (Simultaneous Localization and Mapping) [15, 16].

Due to fewer academic works in this area, this paper presents the development of a mobile platform built to be used in rough terrain, usually found on construction sites in civil construction. This vehicle was shipped with the Robot Operation System (ROS) to integrate the Hector SLAM package, along with the RPlidar S2 sensor for carrying out the environment mapping through 2D maps. These maps were compared with the floor plan of a medium-sized building at the city of Breu Branco, Pará, Brazil. The search shows the details of the objects inside the construction site identified in the 2D maps. This study presents the results through the comparison between two experiments that carried out the construction site scanning in two different directions, and the best result was obtained with the experiment that used the movement in the vertical direction and presented the lower uncertainty measurement when comparing the areas of the floor plan with 2D map.

This article is organized as follows: in the 2nd Section, the related works are presented; in the 3rd Section, the methodology applied in the study is described; in the 4th Section, the results and discussions are presented; and in the 5th Section, the conclusions and future work are described.

2 Related Works

Searches were carried out in scientific databases, such as the IEEE Xplore, Science Direct, MDPI, Scopus, and Google Scholar to find studies related to ROS and SLAM mapping algorithm, using the LIDAR laser sensor in complex unstructured environments.

Ding et al. [4] conducted a review about using SLAM taking into account rough and complex terrain. The agricultural environment was selected where SLAM is applied using three main fundamental types: light detection and range SLAM, Visual SLAM, and Sensor Fusion SLAM. Their work discusses the applications and perspectives of SLAM as a technology in agricultural mapping and navigation.

Yu et al. [5] proposed to improve the Hector SLAM algorithm using sensor fusion. The experiments demonstrated the accuracy of robot positioning and mapping. The final results also show the effectiveness and validity of the proposed algorithm.

Asadi et al. [6] designed a robotic computer vision system to generate a map of the real world and the obstacles present in a walkable space. The map was generated by the

SLAM algorithm with a camera to perform the navigation and capture of the objects in the scene. The system was applied in three outdoor environments, demonstrating real-time applicability to different outdoor scenes.

Shen et al. [7] developed a ROS-based platform using the LIDAR laser sensor for building 2D-SLAM maps in a real environment. In the map building stage, they used three algorithms: Gmapping, Hector-SLAM, and Cartographer, which were compared and evaluated. The results show that Gmapping has the highest mapping accuracy in small and simple areas. The second algorithm, Hector-SLAM, is more suitable for a prolonged environment like a corridor. And the third algorithm, Cartographer, seems to present more advantages in complex environments, such as a maze format.

Zhao et al. [8] developed a mobile platform with an adaptive robot navigation and positioning system that works with four-wheel drive based on ROS. The platform built maps using Gmapping, Karto SLAM, and Hector SLAM algorithms. Karto SLAM stood out as the one that presented high robustness to improve the accuracy of map building. The system can accurately locate, build an environmental map, and achieve accurate navigation, through simulation and practical application in a real environment.

Çelik et al. [3] designed an autonomous mobile robot using a LIDAR laser sensor based on ROS technology. The robot was developed to execute different SLAM algorithms for planning the best path. Thus, the user can define the robot's movement from the initial to the desired final point. In the Gazebo simulation environment, it was observed that the proposed algorithm produced a 1% to 3% shorter path compared to Dijkstra's shortest path algorithm.

Najim et al. [9] designed a mobile robot with multidirectional wheels to move indoors with narrow corridors controlled by ROS. The SLAM algorithm and the LIDAR laser sensor were used to create the environmental map and determine the robot location and position. This research conducted practical experiments of moving the robot inside a corridor to create an environmental map to avoid obstacles. The real-time map estimation results were efficient for robot positioning and navigation.

The presented works are recent research about using LIDAR sensor and SLAM algorithm in map building, navigation and positioning. The experiments mentioned above do not involve or develop robots adapted for construction sites but for controlled environments, such as corridors or laboratories [3, 5, 7–9]. Studies carried out in platforms at irregular terrains, such as agriculture, mostly use commercial platforms, such as the Husky A200 [4, 6]. Therefore, there is a shortage of studies on developing and using mobile platforms aimed at civil construction and minimizing the acquisition costs of a mobile industrial platform.

3 Methodology

This research aims at developing a mobile platform to be used in a rough terrain of construction sites. This section explains the platform's modeling and development, the materials used, the electrical diagram, and the experiments carried out with the platform.

3.1   Mobile Platform Modeling in Solidworks 3D

The platform was initially modeled in Solidworks 2023 as a way to measure the amount of material that would be needed for its construction. Also, its dimensions were analyzed to verify the feasibility of the supported equipment within its internal space. Figure 1 displays the 3D model of the mentioned mobile platform.

Fig. 1. Mobile platform 3D model.

3.2   Mobile Platform Development

The mobile platform was developed for rough terrain, so a closed chassis design was adopted as a way to not expose the electronic equipment loaded on the platform to the hostile environment of the construction site. The vehicle's chassis was made entirely of 20 × 20 mm structural aluminum and it was covered with 2 mm aluminum sheets. The vehicle's structure is composed of four off-road wheels, and each wheel contains an motor coupled to its axle, allowing four-wheel drive. Figure 2 shows the mobile platform and its structural items.

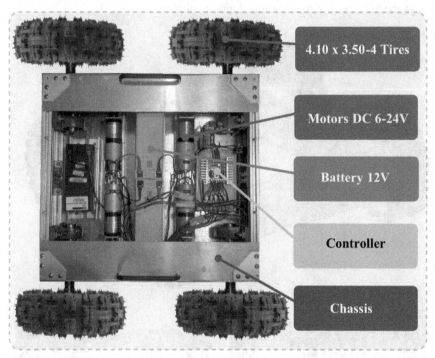

Fig. 2. Mobile platform made up of the following components: tires, motors, battery, controller, and chassis.

Table 1 presents the description and justification of the structural and electrical items used in the mobile platform construction.

A manual control panel was developed at the back of the vehicle, containing buttons and a display with the following functions: green button to turn on/off the platform; orange button to turn on/off the power of the onboard electronic components; display to show batteries charging; the red emergency button used to cut off the batteries supply voltage and the motor controller, causing the platform to stop working, in case there is a risk of accident in data collection. Figure 3 shows the mobile platform control panel.

3.3 Platform Electrical Diagram

The platform electrical scheme was developed to work teleoperated, using the 6-channel FLYSKY radio transmitter that transmits to a receiver of the FS iA6B. This receiver was switched to channels CH5 and CH6, which send a 5V signal to channels S1 and S2 of the Sabertooth controller, which controls the motors. The controller was initially configured

Table 1. List of structural and electrical items in the platform

Item	Description	Justification
Tire	*Scott Ottobock, Off-Road type, measuring 4.10 X 3.50 and Rim 4*	Because it is suitable for rough terrain
Motor	*Chihai, model CHP-42GP-775, voltage ~ 6-24V, planetary gearbox, torque 4.0 N.m, shaft diameter 8mm, weight ~ 730g and speed 120rpm*	Because it offers high torque and planetary gearbox
Battery	*Moura, 12v voltage, 9ah current and No-break type*	Due to its high longevity and current
Controller	*Sabertooth 2x12, voltage ~ 18-24V and current 12A*	Because it enables control of high current and high voltage
Chassis	20 × 20 mm structural aluminum and 2mm aluminum sheets	Because aluminum minimizes the structure weight

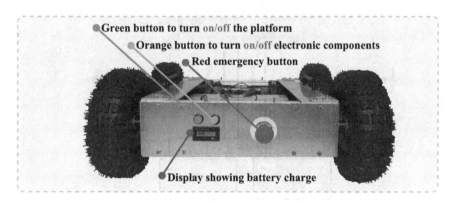

Fig. 3. Manually operated mobile platform panel.

by switching its switch in positions 1 and 5 for OFF and 2, 3, 4, and 6 for ON to enable its control via radio signal. This board controls the motors through channels S1 and S2. Each channel fed two motors on the right side and two on the left. This pair connection allowed four degrees of freedom for the platform, moving forwards, backward, and turning around its axis to the right and left sides. Each motor works with 24V, therefore the vehicle has two 12V batteries, connected in series at ports B+ and B-, providing 24V and a 9ah current, necessary to power the motors. The motors on the left side are connected to the M1A positive and M1B negative ports, and those on the right side are connected to the M2A positive and M2B negative ports. Figure 4 shows the electrical connections for the receiver, controller, motors, and batteries.

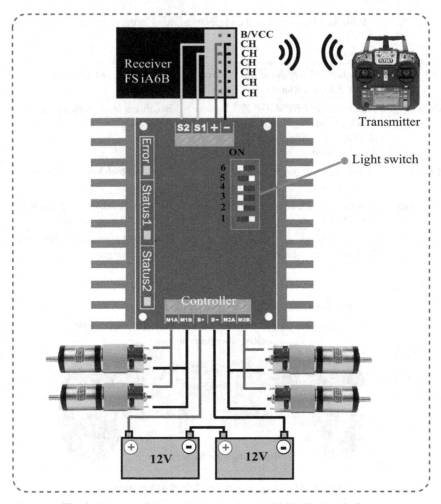

Fig. 4. Scheme of electronic components embedded in the platform.

3.4 Mobile Platform Experiments

A laptop computer with a RPlidar S2 sensor was attached to the mobile platform to scan the surface of the work. The platform was teleoperated through radio control.

This project used the Ubuntu 20.04 operating system to run the ROS middleware, which integrates running programs called nodes for mapping a civil construction environment. The laser scanner node links with the ROS master node to enable message exchange between low-level devices and the ROS. Figure 5 schematically shows the laser scanner node /rplidarNode, sending a /scan message to the ROS master.

For data entry, the RPlidar S2 sensor scans the walls through its laser that measures the properties of the reflected light to obtain the distance between the object and the sensor. The maximum range of the RPlidar S2 sensor is 18m. This sensor writes the

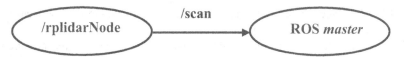

Fig. 5. Message exchange flowchart of between the /rplidarNode node and the ROS master node.

scanned data to the computer's USB port. Data is read from the USB port to be sent to ROS.

The Hector SLAM package was installed on ROS to create the SLAM environmental map, which uses the hector mapping function to generate an environmental map and simultaneously estimate the 2D pose of the platform in the environment. This map will be displayed over lines in a grid format in the RViz interface. The generated map can be saved containing two files, one of which has the extension TFW, which is used by GIS applications that contain the map's location, scale, and rotation; the second file is a TIF-type image stored. Combining these two files makes it possible to locate and navigate in SLAM. Figure 6 shows the overall system block diagram.

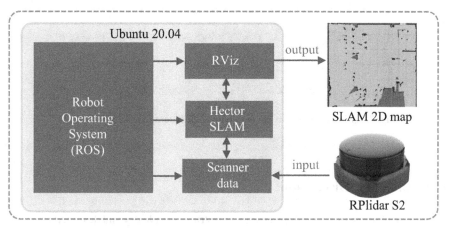

Fig. 6. Flowchart of input and output steps. At the input, data is generated by the RPlidar S2 sensor, and at the output, the SLAM map is displayed on the RViz interface.

3.5   SLAM Map Generation and Comparison with the Work Floor Plan

To create the 2D map, the mobile platform embedded with a laptop containing ROS was used to control the RPlidar S2 sensor. In the environment in which the research was carried out, the experiments took place on the first floor of a medium-sized construction site during business hours, when workers were moving. In the first experiment, the platform was scanned using the movement in the vertical direction of the work floor plan. The second experiment performed the scanning with the movement in the horizontal direction. These scanning types were selected from the experiment performed by Köseoğlu et al. [10]. The objective was to verify the best way to reduce the shadow areas of the 2D map and reach better measurement accuracy.

The grid measurement of the generated 2D map was used to get the area measurement of each experiment for performing comparisons between the floor plan area and the 2D map area. Figure 7 shows the grid generated in the 2D map. Each square generated in the image measures 1×1 m and enables the comparison of the floor plan with the 2D map.

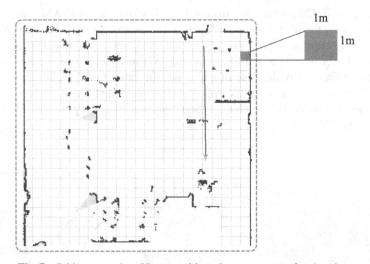

Fig. 7. Grid generated on 2D map with each square measuring 1×1 m.

4 Results and Discussion

The mobile platform was developed for the construction industry and designed for rough off-road terrain. Its electronics were shipped and protected from construction site waste, and its system relies on ROS, according to Zhao et al. [8].

This platform made it possible to inspect the work without the need for high financial expenses with the acquisition of a mobile industrial platform. Compared with existing platforms in the literature, two significant differences were observed. The first difference is that authors who did not develop the platform used mobile industrial platforms adapted for construction sites [11–13]. As for the second difference, the authors who developed the platforms did not adapt the platforms to irregular terrain found in civil construction [3, 7, 14]. Figure 8 shows the comparison of mobile industrial platforms adapted for construction sites with platforms developed in the academic environment and generally used in laboratories.

Before using the mobile platform in a real environment, it was submitted to the evaluation of a robotics specialist, who is the director of a robotics and automation company in Brazil. The platform was analyzed and submitted to tests to validate its

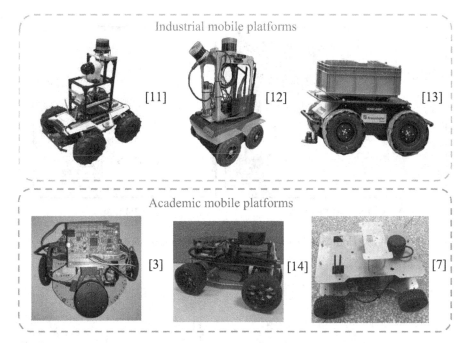

Fig. 8. Comparison between industrial and academic mobile platforms found in the literature.

electronics and mechanics. The expert's assessment was described in a technical report[2]. After the evaluation, it was possible to verify that the platform can be used in construction sites with the supervision of a human being, since, in case of emergency, it is possible to stop the platform quickly.

After completing the development of the mobile platform, the first test was carried out in a real environment to observe its ability to move and overcome common obstacles in construction. To this end, the platform was placed in a room containing two environments separated by a small wall and three support columns. The vehicle was teleoperated to navigate the environment to construct the 2D map. Figure 9 shows the correlation of the structures in the environment compared to the generated 2D map. The red arrow shows the wall separating the environments, and the blue arrows show the columns distributed on the construction site, presenting the level of accuracy of the 2D map generated.

Communication between the operator and the mobile platform has not failed during the experiment, showing that the communication system is safe and can be used in this environment. The platform battery spent 1.7V to conduct the experiments in an operating time of 20 min. Consumption was within the expected range for the two batteries connected in series. The platform traveled around the environment and recorded the evolution of the 2D map from 0 m to 6 m. With this technique, it was possible to observe the best direction of movement in the environment, detecting the shadow areas for each interval. Figure 10 shows the intervals and evolution of the 2D map.

---

[2] The complete technical report is available at the link: bit.ly/3NaKlgC.

(a) Construction site

(b) 2D map

Fig. 9. Correlation between the construction site and the 2D map.

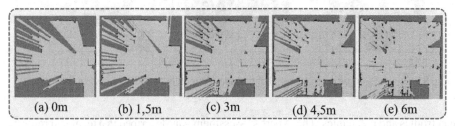

(a) 0m   (b) 1,5m   (c) 3m   (d) 4,5m   (e) 6m

Fig. 10. Evolution of the 2D map according to the distance covered by the platform.

In the image acquisition stage, we noted the importance of moving the platform around the construction site, defining the best direction for the platform to move around the site, and generating a 2D map with few shadow areas. Figure 11 shows the test conductor teleoperating the platform to perform the movements inside the construction site. First, the movement of the platform is in the vertical direction. In this sense, there were few shadow areas, and when comparing the floor plan with the 2D map generated, we obtained an area of ~130.35 ± 0.75 (m²). In the second experiment, the platform movement was in the horizontal direction. In this sense, they presented many shadow areas in the created 2D map, and comparing the floor plan with the 2D map, we obtained the following area ~129.75 ± 1.33 (m²). We obtained the same area with small measurement uncertainty compared to the first experiment. The shadow areas were created by three columns, a small wall that separated two environments, and the rubble scattered on the floor.

Among the contributions of this work, we highlight the detailed process explanation and the knowledge transmitted when carrying out the mobile platform development to meet civil construction demands. In this area, the adoption of technologies is still scarce compared to other areas [17]. We also emphasize that the level of assertiveness of the 2D mapping compared with the floor plan was satisfactory, as well as the reduced uncertainty values verified in the analyzed areas. Another contribution also consists of

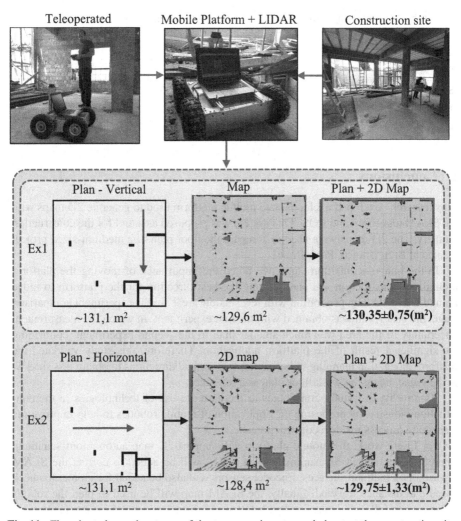

Fig. 11. Flowchart shows the stages of the two experiments carried out at the construction site with the mobile platform.

the richness of details observed in the mapping concerning the real environment, in which columns, walls, and objects found in the scene through mapping can be specified. Finally, in Table 2, we present the price comparison between industrial mobile platforms and the proposed platform, showing that it is possible to reduce costs for developing a mobile platform for construction industry.

This mobile platform can be applied in several construction areas and serve as a tool for workplace inspections, as a mobile agent to communicate between teams, and as support in improving the evolutionary construction process. This work is innovative in the use of mobile robotics in the construction industry, a segment where the inclusion of technological innovations is still very scarce.

Table 2. Price comparison between industrial platforms and the proposed platform.

Platform	Price
Proposed platform	$ 1,565.00
Scout 2.0[3]	$ 12,900.00
Jackal J100[4]	$ 19,092.00
Husky A200[5]	$ 20,328.00

5   Conclusions

This research developed a teleoperated mobile platform used to generate 2D maps with the SLAM algorithm and ROS. This system was proposed as a tool for the construction industry. The 2D maps were used to compare the floor plan of a medium-sized project located at Breu Branco, Pará, Brazil.

In the image acquisition stage, we noted the importance of moving the platform around the construction site and defining the best direction for the platform to move around it and 2D map generation with few shadow areas. In the experiment comparison stage, the best result was obtained with the first experiment, in which the measurement uncertainty of the area was much smaller than in the second experiment, confirming the significant result of the platform application. Therefore, this study validated the platform navigation planning in horizontal and vertical directions to obtain less shadow in the scene, using the work floor plan as a reference.

As novelty, this study contributes to increase the use of technologies in the construction industry, by proposing the application of mobile robotics to help improve the inspection process inside a construction site.

For future work, the mobile platform will support 2D map autonomous scanning. Therefore, an Inertial Measurement Unit (IMU) will be added to correct the SLAM algorithm on inclined surfaces. Encoder sensors will also be added for motors to check speed and distance traveled. Finally, the SLAM map will be used to plan the robot's navigation to follow a determined path and avoid obstacles in a real environment.

References

1. Delgado, J.M.D., et al.: Robotics and automated systems in construction: understanding industry-specific challenges for adoption. J. Build. Eng. **26**, 100868 (2019)
2. Xiao, B., Chen, C., Yin, X.: Recent advancements of robotics in construction. Autom. Constr. **144**, 104591 (2022)
3. Çelik, O.M., Köseoğlu, M.: A modified dijkstra algorithm for ros based autonomous mobile robots. J. Adv. Res. Nat. Appl. Sci. **9**(1), 205–217 (2023)
4. Ding, H., Zhang, B., Zhou, J., Yan, Y., Tian, G., Gu, B.: Recent developments and applications of simultaneous localization and mapping in agriculture. J. Field Robot. **39**(6), 956–983 (2022)

---

[3] Available at: https://global.agilex.ai/products/scout-2-0.

[4] Available at: https://clearpathrobotics.com/jackal-small-unmanned-ground-vehicle/.

[5] Available at: https://clearpathrobotics.com/husky-unmanned-ground-vehicle-robot/.

5. Yu, N., Zhang, B.: An improved hector SLAM algorithm based on information fusion for mobile robot. In: 2018 5th IEEE International conference on cloud computing and intelligence systems (CCIS), pp. 279–284. IEEE (2018)
6. Asadi, K., et al.: Building an integrated mobile robotic system for real-time applications in construction. arXiv preprint arXiv:1803.01745 (2018)
7. Shen, D., Xu, Y., Huang, Y.: Research on 2D-SLAM of indoor mobile robot based on laser radar. In: Proceedings of the 2019 4th International Conference on Automation, Control and Robotics Engineering, pp. 1–7 (2019)
8. Zhao, J., Liu, S., Li, J.: Research and implementation of autonomous navigation for mobile robots based on SLAM algorithm under ROS. Sensors **22**(11), 4172 (2022)
9. Najim, H.A., Kareem, I.S., Abdul-Lateef, W.E.: Omnidirectional mobil robot with navigation using SLAM. Eng. Technol. J. **41**(01), 196–202 (2023)
10. Köseoğlu, M., Çelik, O.M., Pektaş, Ö.: Design of an autonomous mobile robot based on ROS. In: 2017 International Artificial Intelligence and Data Processing Symposium (IDAP), pp. 1–5. IEEE (2017)
11. Ilyas, M., Khaw, H.Y., Selvaraj, N.M., Jin, Y., Zhao, X., Cheah, C.C.: Robot-assisted object detection for construction automation: data and information-driven approach. IEEE/ASME Trans. Mechatron. **26**(6), 2845–2856 (2021)
12. Karimi, S., Braga, R.G., Iordanova, I., St-Onge, D.: Semantic navigation using building information on construction sites: arXiv preprint arXiv:2104.10296 (2021)
13. Follini, C.: Bim-integrated collaborative robotics for application in building construction and maintenance. Robotics **10**(1), 2 (2020)
14. Di, H., Chu, Z.: Design of indoor mobile robot based on ROS and lidar. In: 2022 2nd International Conference on Robotics and Control Engineering, pp. 62–66 (2022)
15. Alhmiedat, T., et al.: A SLAM-based localization and navigation system for social robots: the pepper robot case. Machines **11**(2), 158 (2023)
16. Li, B., Ma, Z., Zhao, Y.: 2D Mapping of mobile robot based on micro-ROS. In: Journal of Physics: Conference Series, Vol. 2402, No. 1, p. 012030. IOP Publishing (2022)
17. Okpala, I., Nnaji, C., Karakhan, A.A.: Utilizing emerging technologies for construction safety risk mitigation. Pract. Period. Struct. Des. Constr. **25**(2), 04020002 (2020)

Artificial Intelligence Supported Medical Data Examination (AIM 2023)

Social Media Text Analysis on Public's Sentiments of Covid-19 Booster Vaccines

Yohan Kristian[1], Adira Valdi Yesenia[1], Safina Safina[1],
Anindya Apriliyanti Pravitasari[1], Eka Novita Sari[2], and Tutut Herawan[3,4(✉)]

[1] Departement of Statistics, Universitas Padjadjaran, Jl. Ir. Soekarno KM. 21, Jatinangor,
Sumedang, West Java 45363, Indonesia
{yohan19001,adira19001,safina19001}@mail.unpad.ac.id,
anindya.apriliyanti@unpad.ac.id
[2] AMCS Research Center, Sleman, Yogyakarta, Indonesia
eka@amcs.co
[3] Sekolah Tinggi Pariwisata Ambarrukmo Yogyakarta, Jl. Ringroad Timur No. 52, Bantul,
Daerah Istimewa Yogyakarta 55198, Indonesia
[4] Institute for Big Data Analytics and Artificial Intelligence, UiTM Shah Alam, Selangor Darul
Ehsan, 40450 Shah Alam, Malaysia
tutut@um.edu.my

Abstract. Two years of the COVID-19 Pandemic, countries across the world
have started the process of vaccination in two-step doses. WHO stated that six
months after the second dose injection, the effectiveness of the EUL (emergency
use listing) vaccines has decreased by about 8%. Therefore, booster vaccines are
recommended to be developed. Indonesia launched booster vaccinations with the
objective of restoring decreased immunity and giving clinical protection. This
study assesses the opinions of Indonesian citizens regarding the booster vaccine
through social networks (Twitter and Youtube), which are mined through the Twitter
API and Python Selenium Web Driver. Several algorithms have been employed
to evaluate the best predictions of public sentiment. Each of them is given four
scenarios to handle the imbalanced data: not handling the imbalance, and handling
it with SMOTE, random oversampling and random undersampling. Support Vector
Machines, Random Forest, Bidirectional Recurrent Neural Network, Gaussian
Naive Bayes, Logistic Regression, Bernoulli Naive Bayes, and CatBoost Classifiers
are executed under the same experimental setup. The best performance is
given by CatBoost with ROS for handling the imbalance data; the accuracy is 88%,
the weighted average f1-score is 88%, while the precision and recall averages are
89% and 88%, respectively.

Keywords: sentiment analysis · COVID-19 · booster vaccine · social media ·
text analysis

1 Introduction

The first case of Covid-19 was reported in late 2019 in Wuhan, China, and since then
WHO has recorded over 500 million positive cases around the world [1]. The first action
many countries took to control the virus' outbreak was to implement social distancing,

O. Gervasi et al. (Eds.): ICCSA 2023 Workshops, LNCS 14104, pp. 209–224, 2023.
https://doi.org/10.1007/978-3-031-37105-9_15

national border closing and quarantine. It quickly becomes clear that these regulations are not enough to contain the virus that has killed more than 156,673 people in Indonesia alone [1]. There needs to be another strategy to protect citizens, particularly health-care workers, seniors and those with underlying health conditions [2]. To meet the imminent need for stronger protection, a new pandemic vaccine development paradigm has been proposed [3]. Although the need for vaccines is widely accepted all over the world, the development of Covid-19 vaccines is not without its challenges: such as deciding over the best approach to creating the vaccines, side effects that may occur, testing strategies, unknown duration of immunity, and last but not least, funds. Finally, a large demand for vaccines will arise due to the pandemic. Thus, clinical and serologic investigations will be needed to confirm which are still at risk once vaccinations are accessible, and studies that could serve as the foundation for developing a globally equitable vaccine-allocation system [3].

In Presidential Decree No. 18 of 2020, which was stipulated on September 3, 2020, President of Republic Indonesia, Joko Widodo, developed the National Team for Accelerating the Development of Coronavirus Disease 2019 (Covid-19). The team has 4 goals: first to accelerate the development of the Covid-19 vaccine in Indonesia, second to realize the national resilience and independence of the nation in the development of the Covid-19 vaccine, third to increase the synergy of research, development, study, and application of science and technology, as well as inventions and innovations, production, distribution, and use and/or utilization of the Covid-19 vaccine between the government and science and technology institutions as well as technological resources in Covid-19 vaccine development, and finally to utilized and increased capacity, as well as national capabilities in the development of the Covid-19 vaccine [4]. After a rigorous process of testing in clinical trials to prove that they meet the standards of safety and effectiveness, scientists were able to manufacture safe and efficacious Covid-19 vaccines in record speed [5]. The first vaccination in Indonesia took place on 31 January, 2021 with the President of Republic Indonesia Joko Widodo, as the first person who was vaccinated with a dose of Sinovac vaccine [6]. To date, 66,3% of the world has received at least one dose of a Covid-19 vaccine [7]. In Indonesia, over 201 million have received the first dose, and over 168 million have received the second dose of Covid-19 vaccines [8]. Nonetheless, COVID-19 immunization efforts must continue to focus on reducing death and serious diseases, as well as protecting the health-care system [9].

Despite the growing number of vaccinated citizens around the world, a few nations face new challenges, such as viral variant emergence and concerns about fading protection following immunization [10]. Mizrahi et al., looked at data from Israel's Ministry of Health and Maccabi Healthcare Services (MHS). They discovered that with time, protection against infection and disease deteriorated (from December 2020 to July 2021). People who were vaccinated in January and February, for example, were 53 percent more likely than those who were vaccinated in March and April, to test positive for COVID-19 [11]. WHO stated that six months after the second dose injection, the effectiveness of the EUL (emergency use listing) vaccines has decreased by about 8% over a period of 6 months in all age groups [9]. Those, and several other research determined the need for a third vaccine dose. Indonesia has started their third vaccine dose program on Wednesday, 12 January, 2022. For the third dose of vaccines, it can be done with the same type of vaccine (homologous) or by giving a different vaccine from the first and second dose (heterologous). The ministry of Health prioritizes health workers on the grounds of an emergency due to the Delta variant [12] invasion. And its current expansion has taken into account vaccine safety, efficacy and quality [13].

The news of the third dose of vaccination of Covid-19 in Indonesia has gotten a variety of responses from the citizens, particularly on social media. Facebook, Twitter and Instagram, for example, offer a lot of untapped potential for providing non-trivial knowledge and might be utilized to analyze changes in the social, public health, and economic arenas [14]. When a rapid decision is necessary, obtaining information directly from the public via social media is very beneficial, as traditional communication methods such as surveys and interviews do not allow this. This research aims to analyze the public's sentiment towards COVID-19 booster vaccination in Indonesia while also reviewing the most appropriate method of social media text analysis for this type of data. From a political perspective, the massive demand for political information can be regarded as an important factor. Thus, sentiment analysis plays an important role in national security and public opinion analysis [15]. The result of this research not only could play a part in the next decision-making process regarding COVID-19 vaccination by giving insight to the government into how Indonesia's citizens responded towards the third dose vaccination of COVID-19, but also highlight the best method of social media text analysis.

This research will fill the gap of the previous research from the total of data collected, method of data cleaning and analysis, and the programming language used in analysis. In the research done by Khoiril Hikmah, the data collected from Twitter with a total of 100 tweets are used to analyze the sentiment using Naive Bayes Algorithm with PHP programming language [16]. The data used in this research is collected by Rapid Miner from Twitter tweets and Youtube comments, containing 647 neutral comments, 374 negative comments, and 282 positive comments. Each of them is given four scenarios to handle the imbalanced data, which are: not handling the imbalance, and handling it with random oversampling (ROS), random undersampling (RUS), and synthetic minority over-sampling technique (SMOTE). The method compared to analyze the sentiments on this research are CatBoost Classifier, Support Vector Machine (SVM), Random Forest, Logistic Regression, GaussianNB, BernoulliNB, and Bidirectional Gated Recurrent Unit (BiGRU) method using python programming language.

Further research in this topic can be done to fill the gap that this research can not reach. Since this research only analyzes the sentiment of Indonesia's citizens on social media, the result of this research only applies to the situation in Indonesia and can not in any way be generalized to other countries or territories. Moreover, the result of this research can be improved by a larger data set collected from other sources, a more thorough cleaning process of the data and the use of a more standard language on the data collection.

The remainder of the paper is organized as follows. In Sect. 2, more comparable studies are provided and discussed in order to lead to the research question. Section 3 details the methodology, including the tools used to gather tweets and comments, as well as to support the method employed in this research. For Sect. 4, the findings are presented and discussed, and in Sect. 5, we conclude this research and highlight future research.

2 Related Works

Using unigram and bigram (*n*-gram) and supervised learning with simple Support Vector Machines (SVM), research of Balahur [17] was written, with the topic of emotional analysis of Twitter datasets. On the paper result, it is concluded that on one hand, the best method to be used for emotional analysis is a combined form of unigram and bigram. Also by using unique tags, such as emotive words and modifiers, are seen to strongly improve the performance rating of emotions. (joy, happiness, sadness, fear, and etc.) In another study by Narasamma and Sreedevi [18], they introduced a hybrid machine learning model named Catboost Recurrent Neural Framework (CRNF) with an error pruning mechanism to analyze the Twitter data based on user opinion. Initially, a twitter-based dataset on the coronavirus COVID-19 vaccine is obtained, which is then pre-processed and trained to the system. Furthermore, the suggested CRNF model divides sentiments into three categories: positive, negative, and neutral. Furthermore, the sentiment analysis procedure is carried out using Python, and the parameters are determined.

Employing the Naive Bayes Algorithm method, Pristiyono, *et al.* [19] analyses sentiment analysis of COVID-19.The data crawling process in the article was done manually by using the access token received from the Twitter API using the rapid miner tools to extract the requested information and data. Hikmah, *et al.* [16] wrote another paper about vaccine booster sentiment analysis. The dataset was retrieved from Twitter about Indonesian netizen perspective towards the booster vaccine. Case folding, tokenizing, filtering, and stemming are all part of the data preprocessing stage. While the sentiment classification is divided into positive sentiment, negative emotion and neutral sentiment by using the Naive Bayes algorithm. Another study about sentiment analysis on COVID-19 vaccine booster was written by Ong, Pauzi and Gan [14]. The data was gathered from Twitter users in Malaysia and identified three important latent Dirichlet allocation (LDA) topics: (1) type of vaccination booster; (2) effects of vaccination booster; (3) vaccination program operation.

This study builds on the related work by employing several known methodologies to determine the optimal model for predicting public sentiment towards the COVID-19 booster vaccine. The models compare each other with the imbalanced data that was previously handled. Table 1 summarizes the previous state of the art, which related to this research.

Table 1. Related work of sentiment analysis

References	Topic	Model	Accuracy (%)
Balahur [17]	Sentiment Analysis in Social Media Texts	SVM	79.96%
Narasamma and Sreedevi [18]	Twitter based Data Analysis in Natural Language Processing using a Novel Catboost Recurrent Neural Framework	CRNF	99.34%
Pristiyono, Ritonga, Ihsan, Anjar and Rambe [21]	Sentiment Analysis of COVID-19 Vaccine in Indonesia Using Naive Bayes Algorithm	Naive Bayes	-
Hikmah, Fauzan, and Harliana [11]	Sentiment Analysis of Vaccine Booster during Covid-19: Indonesian Netizen Perspective Based on Twitter Dataset	Naive Bayes	89.00%
Ong, Pauzi and Gan [13]	Text Mining and Determinants of Sentiments Towards the COVID-19 Vaccine Booster of Twitter Users in Malaysia	LDA	-

3   Material and Proposed Method

Several steps were done to achieve the results. After mining the data required to run the algorithms, the process of cleaning the data and labeling each comment was needed. A case of imbalance data was found after labeling each comment, therefore three methods to handle the imbalance were applied alongside the classification algorithms. The accuracy of each model combination was compared to evaluate which model is the best for the data. The specification and flow of analysis system is visualized in Fig. 1.

3.1   Data Processing

The proposed approach utilized the Twitter and YouTube comment data for analyzing the sentiments. Here, both of the data sources are based on COVID-19 booster vaccine, collected by using the keywords "vaccine" and "booster" in Indonesian language. The data crawling operation is done manually using the Twitter API access token and the Rapid miner tools to extract the desired information and data. YouTube comments from several videos reporting on booster vaccine were also mined using Rapid miner tools. The utilized dataset details about the 1282 numbers of tweets and YouTube comment altogether that involves the aftereffect of booster vaccine, information about the availability of the vaccine, and so on. In this, the collected data are based on the category of "positive" reviews, negative reviews and neutral reviews. Moreover, the collected dataset is given to the developed Catboost model for further processing. The comments that are categorized as negative comments are those containing bad words, ridicule, or

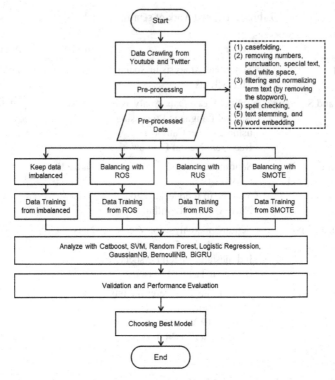

Fig. 1. The specification and flow of analysis system

opposition towards COVID-19 booster vaccine. The category of neutral comments are given if the comments only contain information or question without stating partiality. Finally, the comments that are deemed as positive comments contain praises, statements of agreement, even encouragement to others to participate in the third dose of COVID-19 vaccination. Table 2 below are examples of labeled data for this study.

Table 2. Examples of the categorized comments

Comments	Label/ Category
Saya vaksin 1,2, dan booster di Indonesia. Alhamdulillah taat aturan dan protokol kesehatan. Kita sehat, Indonesia kuat	Positive
Sementara itu, mekanisme Heterolog, yaitu pemberian vaksin booster dengan menggunakan jenis vaksin yang berbeda dengan vaksin primer dosis lengkap yang telah didapat sebelumnya	Neutral
Semua orang yang sudah booster dan taat prokes kena covid. Jadi apa gunanya vaksin dan prokesnya itu?	Negative

Figure 2 shows the number of comments each label has after the labeling process. It shows that the data is unbalanced, with the Positive category making up the minority and the Neutral category the majority.

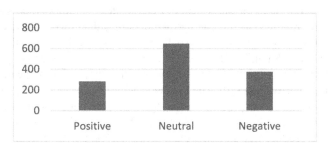

Fig. 2. Histogram of labeled comments

At the preprocessing stage, the data will be uniform in shape and format. This stage consists of (1) casefolding, (2) removing numbers, punctuation, special text, and white space, (3) filtering and normalizing term text (by removing the stopword), (4) spell checking, (5) text stemming, and (6) word embedding. This stage produces terms or basic words that are free from prefixes or suffixes. As part of preprocessing, the data that has been categorized were then labeled word by word. This labeling process is to identify the raw data that will provide context to it, and enable machine learning to use the data and learn from it. Table 3 are the results of the cleaned data that is used in this study.

Table 3. Examples of the cleaned comments

No	Label	Comment	Cleaned comment
1	0	['tinjau', 'kena', 'vaksi', 'boster', 'pfizer',…]	Tinjau kena vaksi boster Pfizer astrazeneca
2	0	['vaksin', 'booster', 'hanya', 'tahan', 'bulan',…]	Vaksin booster hanya tahan bulan telah apa
3	2	['saya', 'tunggu', 'efek', 'samping',…]	Saya tunggu efek samping vaksin booster kok
4	2	['saya', 'tidak', 'demam', 'sama', 'sekali',…]	Saya tidak demam sama sekali sampai suah sore

3.2 Methodology for Handling Imbalance Data

The condition of imbalanced data poses a risk to classification fairness because of uneven data representations in which the minority class is usually also an important one. Therefore, we require methods to improve its recognition rates by balancing the dataset and reducing the risk of analysis or machine learning algorithms skewing toward the majority. Several methods for handling imbalance data are employ in this study, i.e. ROS, RUS, and SMOTE, that compared each other and also with data that remains imbalanced. The method of Random Over Sampling (**ROS**) is used to address data imbalances. Without increasing the variation of the class data, ROS replicates the minority class data sample and adds it to the training data set. The size of the training data set is increased by ROS by repeating the original sample in order to balance the class distribution [20]. On the other side, Random Under Sampling (**RUS**) is yet another method for addressing data imbalance. In RUS, as opposed to ROS, specific samples are removed from the majority class to balance the minority class [20]. The Synthetic Minority Over-sampling Technique or **SMOTE** is another oversampling technique for imbalance data. The interpolation approach used in this technique increases the amount of new minority class instances. Before they are used to produce new minority class instances, the minority class instances that lie together are recognized. Because this technique can construct synthetic examples rather than replicating minority class instances, it avoids the problem of overfitting [21].

3.3 Model Evaluation

3.3.1 Confusion Matrix

There are numerous techniques to assess the effectiveness of learning algorithms and the classifiers they create in supervised machine learning (ML). A confusion matrix, which tracks successfully and erroneously recognized instances for each class, is used to build measures of the quality of categorization [23].

Table 4. A confusion matrix for multiclass classification

		Actual		
		Positive	Negative	Neutral
Predicted	**Positive**	TP	FP_1	FP_2
	Negative	FN_1	TN	$FNeutral_1$
	Neutral	$FNeutral_2$	FN_2	$TNeutral$

Table 4 above is the example of a confusion matrix of three class classification. *TP* (True Positive) stands for the number of comments correctly classified as positive comments, whereas *FP* (False Positive) stands for comments that are classified as positive when they are actually negative/neutral. The amount of positive comments that are classified as negative/neutral when they are actually positive is called *FN* (False Negative) or *FNeutral* (False Neutral). If a comment is predicted as negative or neutral correctly, it is considered as *TN* (True Negative) or *TNeutral* (True Neutral).

3.3.2 Precision

True positives and examples that are incorrectly categorized as positives (false positives) are two factors that affect precision [23]. The precision of a classification model is its ability to identify only the relevant data points [24]. Calculating precision mathematically involves dividing the total number of true positives by the sum of true positives and false positives, as shown in Eq. (1).

$$precision = \frac{TP}{TP + FP} \qquad (1)$$

It expresses the proportion of the data points of our model that is said existed in the relevant class.

3.3.3 Recall

Recall depends on the data that were correctly classified (true positives) and incorrectly classified (false negatives) [23]. This function assesses a model's capacity to locate every relevant examples in a data set [24]. According to the mathematical model, recall is determined by dividing the total number of true positives by the total number of true positives + the total number of false negatives, as shown in Eq. (2).

$$recall = \frac{TP}{TP + FN} \qquad (2)$$

It expresses the ability to find all relevant instances of a class in a data set.

3.3.4 F1-Score

F1-score gauged the model's accuracy. The formula determines it based on accuracy and reminders [25]. F1-Score is a composite metric that rewards algorithms with better sensitivity and challenges those with higher specificity [23].

$$F1 - score = \frac{2 \times precision \times recall}{precision \times recall} \qquad (3)$$

3.3.5 Accuracy

By displaying the likelihood of the class label's true value, accuracy provides an approximation of the algorithm's efficacy; in other words, it evaluates the algorithm's overall performance [23]. Accuracy is calculated as the sum of accurate predictions divided by the total number of data sets. Accuracy ranges from 0.00 to 1.0, with 1.0 being the best and 0.00 being the worst [25].

$$accuracy = \frac{TP + TN + TNeutral}{P + N + Neutral} \qquad (4)$$

4 Results and Discussion

4.1 Result

The data is divided to 80% for training data and 20% for testing. Data imbalances are overcome by three methods namely SMOTE, Random Over Sampling (ROS), Random Under Sampling (RUS). Therefore, the amount of training data and testing data will follow the results of the data imbalance processing. For the analysis, seven different classification methods are used in this study, such as CatBoost Classifier, SVM, Random Forest, Logistic Regression, GaussianNB, BernoulliNB, and Neural Network for Natural language processing (NLP) with BiGRU method. The CatBoost Classifier is tuned by the 1000 iterations parameter, 1% learning rate parameter, 42 random seeds parameter, 8 depth of the tree parameter, with accuracy and auc as loss parameter. The SVM, Random Forest, Logistic Regression, GaussianNB, and BernoulliNB are tuned by the default parameter, with 5 fold cross validation. The Bidirectional Gated Recurrent Unit (BiGRU) is created by some layers, the first layer is the embedding layer which uses a vector with dimensions of 100 words long, to represent each word. The second layer is the Bidirectional Gated Recurrent Unit (BiGRU) layer. The third layer is the Dense layer with dropout and ReLU activation function. The last layer is the Output Layer with 3 neurons and softmax as the activation function.

Table 5 below shows the comparison accuracy of each methodology with the balancing scenarios. Turns out, the best classifier methods are CatBoost Classifier with 88% accuracy and BiGRU with 83% accuracy, after the imbalance data are handled by Random Over Sampling (ROS). However, it also can be shown that the powerful classification method with the highest accuracy is the CatBoost Classifier with 75% or above in both imbalance and balanced data with ROS, RUS, and SMOTE.

Table 5. Comparison Methods Accuracy

	Imbalancd	SMOTE	ROS	RUS
CatBoost	0.75	0.76	0.88*	0.75
SVM	0.58	0.52	0.64	0.49
Random Forest	0.59	0.47	0.76	0.49
Logistic Regression	0.58	0.52	0.57	0.49
GaussianNB	0.49	0.40	0.39	0.39
BernoulliNB	0.52	0.43	0.47	0.46
BiGRU	0.56	0.58	0.83*	0.46

* indicate the high accuracy

Table 6 shows the comparison of F1-Score for each methodology with the balancing scenarios. Same as accuracy, the best classifier methods are CatBoost Classifier with 88% accuracy and BiGRU with 83% accuracy, after the imbalance data are handled by Random Over Sampling (ROS). Moreover, in Table 5 it also can be shown that the powerful classification method with the highest F1-Score is the same as the best method for the accuracy.

Table 7 shows the comparison of precision for each methodology with the balancing scenarios. The comparison of precision produces the same result as the comparison of accuracy and F1-Score. When compared by the precision, CatBoost Classifier and BiGRU, handled by ROS, still get the highest points with 89% and 84% respectively.

Table 6. Comparison Methods F1-Score

	Imbalanced	SMOTE	ROS	RUS
CatBoost	0.73	0.77	0.88*	0.75
SVM	0.49	0.51	0.65	0.50
Random Forest	0.52	0.48	0.75	0.49
Logistic Regression	0.53	0.51	0.57	0.49
GaussianNB	0.45	0.35	0.36	0.38
BernoulliNB	0.52	0.43	0.47	0.46
BiGRU	0.55	0.58	0.83*	0.46

* indicate the high F1-Score

Table 7. Comparison Methods Precision

	Imbalanced	SMOTE	ROS	RUS
CatBoost	0.81	0.79	0.89*	0.77
SVM	0.49	0.52	0.66	0.51
Random Forest	0.59	0.47	0.78	0.53
Logistic Regression	0.54	0.53	0.58	0.50
GaussianNB	0.46	0.39	0.40	0.47
BernoulliNB	0.53	0.44	0.48	0.47
BiGRU	0.55	0.58	0.84*	0.47

* indicate the high precision

Table 8 shows the comparison of Recall for each methodology with the balancing scenarios. Catboost with the recall of 88% is still the highest, followed by BiGRU with the recall of 83%. This shows that from every comparison of evaluation model, Catboost continuously produces the highest score and therefore can be said as the best classification model for this data.

Catboost and BiGRU with balance handling utilizing ROS are the best models for the full analysis employing metrics of evaluation using accuracy, precision, recall, and F1-score. The explanation for the best model, i.e. BiGRU and Catboost Classifier, will briefly show as the example of analysis process.

4.1.1   BiGRU

For the Random Over Sampling handled data, the total parameters number of BiGRU is 369.163 parameters, with 15.963 trainable parameters and 353.200 non-trainable parameters. The output will be dense to 3 neuron layers with softmax activation layers. Model summary for BiGRU is visualized by Fig. 3.

Table 8. Comparison Methods Recall

	Imbalanced	SMOTE	ROS	RUS
CatBoost	0.75	0.76	0.88*	0.75
SVM	0.58	0.52	0.64	0.49
Random Forest	0.58	0.49	0.76	0.51
Logistic Regression	0.58	0.52	0.58	0.49
GaussianNB	0.49	0.4	0.39	0.40
BernoulliNB	0.52	0.43	0.47	0.46
BiGRU	0.56	0.58	0.83*	0.46

* indicate the high recall

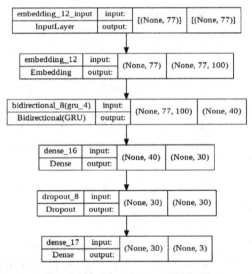

Fig. 3. Model summary of BiGRU

The BiGRU fine-tuned-based best network has a 100 epoch. In this scenario, the highest recognition rate of 89% is reached when the network is trained with Adam Optimizer, batch size of 64, and maximum epoch of 20. However, as in Fig. 4, these data show that there is underfitting in recognizing train and validation loss, so the resulting model is not very accurate.

Figure 5 shows the confusion matrix and the value of evaluation metric. After evaluating the BiGRU model, the accuracy rate of this model is 83% with an average precision level of 84%. The precision for every variable is 88% for neutral comments, 91% for negative comments, and 72% for positive comments. Negative comments is the variable with the highest precision.

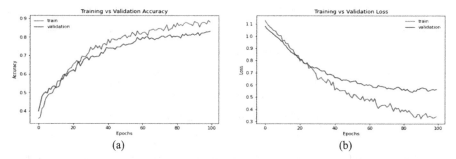

Fig. 4. Training vs validation plot for (a) accuracy and (b) loss

	precision	recall	f1-score	support
0	0.88	0.74	0.80	99
1	0.91	0.85	0.88	117
2	0.72	0.91	0.81	92
accuracy			0.83	308
macro avg	0.84	0.83	0.83	308
weighted avg	0.84	0.83	0.83	308

Fig. 5. Confusion matrix and the value of evaluation metric

4.1.2 Catboost

Another powerful model which has best accuracy is the CatBoost classifier with ROS. This algorithm is fine-tuned-based best network has 1000 iterations and is trained with 8 depths of tree, 1% learning rate, and 42 random seeds. The Figs. 6 and 7 show the Train and validation accuracy plot and matric of evaluation value, respectively.

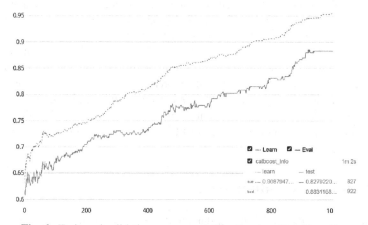

Fig. 6. Train and validation accuracy plot for Random Over Sampling

	precision	recall	f1-score	support
0	0.78	0.90	0.84	99
1	0.91	0.85	0.88	117
2	0.99	0.91	0.95	92
accuracy			0.88	308
macro avg	0.89	0.89	0.89	308
weighted avg	0.89	0.88	0.88	308

Fig. 7. Metric of Evaluation

For the Random Over Sampling handled data, the highest classification rate of 90% is reached and after evaluating the model, the accuracy rate of this model is 88% with an average precision level of 89%. The precision for every variable is 78% for neutral comments, 91% for negative comments, and 99% for positive comments. Positive comments is the variable with the highest precision.

4.2 Discussion

As discussed before in the literature review, there have been some studies about social media sentiment analysis. Hikmah, Fauzan, and Harliana [11] are using Naive Bayes to classify the sentiment from Twitter comments about Indonesian netizen perspective towards the booster vaccine, by consisting 23% of positive sentiment, 15% of neutral sentiment, and 76% of negative sentiment with the result 89% of accuracy rate. With an accuracy rate of 92.96%, Lestari and Saepudin [20] discovered tweets with positive sentiment of up to 86% and tweets with negative sentiment of up to 14% using the Naive Bayes Algorithm on sentiment analysis of the Sinovac vaccine. Ananda [22] discovered 63% of accuracy rate within Bidirectional GRU (BiGRU) methods for analyzing Indonesia's netizen sentiment to COVID-19 vaccine consisting 59% neutral sentiment, 71% negative sentiment, and 41% positive sentiment.

Based on the results of the three studies including our own, it is clear that utilizing the CatBoost Classifier to categorize sentiments is the most appropriate. It achieves 88% accuracy for overall class, 78% accuracy for neutral sentiment, 91% for negative sentiment, and 99% for positive sentiment. The data was treated with a comment using Random Over Sampling. Additionally, the use of the BiGRU method in sentiment classification can be considered, with a classification accuracy result of 83 percent accuracy for each sentiment category, namely 88 percent for neutral sentiment, 91% for negative sentiment, and 72% for positive sentiment, using the same data handling method. However, the issue of data underfitting must be revisited for the implementation of this method.

5   Conclusion and Future Research

According to our research, the Indonesian public has mixed feelings about the COVID-19 vaccine booster. After comparing 7 different methods with 4 scenarios imbalance data handling methods, the best method with the highest accuracy is CatBoost Classifier with Random Over Sampling method. The result of the analysis showed 78% for neutral comments, 91% for negative comments, and 99% for positive comments. After preprocessing the data by categorizing the data, cleaning the data from typo, tokenizing the data, embedding the data, handling the imbalance data, the BiGRU shows there's some problem with the fitting data (underfitting).

Mining data from social media sometimes required permit that could take sometimes to acquire. Due to many vernaculars and dialect in Indonesia, many comments contained or were fully in other dialect which complicate the cleaning process. Further researches with the same type of data are expected to use more data and more cleaning of the data collection in an attempt to fix the fitting problem.

Acknowledgement. The authors thanks to the Department of Statistics and Research Center for Artificial Intelligence and Big Data, Universitas Padjadjaran which supports this research. The work of Tutut Herawan and Eka Novita Sari is supported by AMCS Research Center.

References

1. WHO Coronavirus (COVID-19) Dashboard, https://covid-19.who.int retrieved 16 June 2022
2. Jeyanathan, M., Afkhami, S., Smail, F., Miller, M.S., Lichty, B.D., Xing, Z.: Immunological considerations for COVID-19 vaccine strategies. Nature Reviews Immunology **20**, 615–632 (2020)
3. Lurie, N., Saville, M., Hatchett, R., Halton, J.: Developing Covid-19 vaccines at pandemic speed. N. Engl. J. Med. **382**, 1969–1973 (2020)
4. Jokowi Bentuk timnas Percepatan Pengembangan Vaksin Covid-19, Jokowi Bentuk Timnas Percepatan Pengembangan Vaksin Covid-19 | Republika Online Retrieved 18 June 2022
5. What You Need To Know About COVID-19 Vaccines, What you need to know about COVID-19 vaccines | UNICEF Indonesia Retrieved 18 June 2022
6. Program Vaksinasi COVID-19 Mulai Dilakukan Presiden Orang Pertama Penerima Suntikan Vaksin COVID-19, http://p2p.kemkes.go.id/program-vaksinasi-covid-19-mulai-dilakukan-presiden-orang-pertama-penerima-suntikan-vaksin-covid-19/ Retrieved 18 June 2022
7. Coronavirus (Covid-19) Vaccinations, Coronavirus (COVID-19) Vaccinations - Our World in Data Retrieved 18 June 2022
8. Vaksinasi COVID-19 Nasional, Vaksin Dashboard (kemkes.go.id) Retrieved 18 June 2022
9. Interim Statement on Booster Dose for COVID-19 Vaccination, Interim statement on booster doses for COVID-19 vaccination (who.int) Retrieved 18 June 2022
10. Shekhar, R., Garg, I., Pal, S., Kottewar, S., Sheikh, A.B.: COVID-19 vaccine booster: to boost or not to boost. Infectious disease reports **13**(4), 924–929 (2021)
11. Mizrahi, B., et al.: Correlation of SARS-CoV-2-breakthrough infections to time-from-vaccine. Preliminary Study (2021)
12. Zhan, Y., Yin, H., Yin, J.Y.B.: 1.617. 2 (Delta) Variant of SARS-CoV-2: features, transmission and potential strategies. International journal of biological sciences **18**(5), 1844 (2022)
13. Vaksin Booster Bertujuan Melindungi Dan Menjadi Modal Pemulihan Ekonomi, Vaksin Booster Bertujuan Melindungi Dan Menjadi Modal Pemulihan Ekonomi | Covid19.go.id Retrieved 18 June 2022
14. Ong, S., Pauzi, M.B.M., Gan, K.H.: Text Mining and Determinants of Sentiments Towards the COVID-19 Vaccine Booster of Twitter Users in Malaysia. MDPI, Basel, Switzerland (2022)
15. Yue, L., Chen, W., Li, X., Zuo, W., Yin, M.: A survey of sentiment analysis in social media. Knowl. Inf. Syst. **60**(2), 617–663 (2018). https://doi.org/10.1007/s10115-018-1236-4

16. Hikmah, K., Fauzan, A.C., Harliana. Sentiment Analysis of Vaccine Booster during Covid-19: Indonesian Netizen Perspective Based on Twitter Dataset. Teknologi Komputer dan Sistem Informasi, STMIK Pringsewu (2022)
17. Balahur, A.: Sentiment Analysis in Social Media Texts, pp. 120–128 (2013)
18. Narasamma, V.L., Sreedevi, M.: Twitter based Data Analysis in Natural Language Processing using a Novel Catboost Recurrent Neural Framework. European Commission Joint Research Centre (2021)
19. Pristiyono, R., Ihsan, M., Anjar, M.A.A.A., Rambe, F.H.: Sentiment Analysis of COVID-19 Vaccine in Indonesia Using Naive Bayes Algorithm IOP Conf. Ser.: Mater. Sci. Eng. **1088**, 012045
20. Ananda, D.: Analisis Sentimen Pengguna Media Sosial Terhadap Kebijakan Pemerintah Dalam Program Vaksinasi Covid-19 Di Indonesia Menggunakan Metode Bidirectional Gated Recurrent Unit (BiGRU). Bachelor thesis. Department Of Statistics, Universitas Padjadjaran, Sumedang (2022)
21. Jeatrakul, P., Wong, K.W., Fung, C.C.: "Classification of Imbalanced Data by Combining the Complementary Neural Network and SMOTE Algorithm" School of Information Technology. Murdoch University, Australia (2010)
22. Sabarmathi, G., Chinnaiyan, R.: Sentiment Analysis for Evaluating the Patient Medicine Satisfaction. Int. J. Computat. Intell. Cont. **13**, 113–118 (2021)
23. Sokolova, M., Japkowicz, N., Szpakowicz, S.: Beyond Accuracy, F-Score and ROC: a Family of Discriminant Measures for Performance Evaluation. In: Sattar, A., Kang, Bh. (eds.) AI 2006: Advances in Artificial Intelligence. Lecture Notes in Computer Science(), vol 4304. Springer, Berlin, Heidelberg (2006)
24. When Accuracy Isn't Enough, Use Precision and Recall to Evaluate Your Classification Model, When Accuracy Isn't Enough, Use Precision and Recall to Evaluate Your Classification Model Retrieved 22 June 2022
25. Vujovic, Z.D.: Classification Model Evaluation Metrics. Int. J. Adv. Comput. Sci. Appl. **12**(6), 1–8 (2021)

TECD: A Transformer Encoder Convolutional Decoder for High-Dimensional Biomedical Data

Luca Zedda, Alessandra Perniciano, Andrea Loddo(✉),
and Barbara Pes

Department of Mathematics and Computer Science, University of Cagliari,
via Ospedale 72, 09124 Cagliari, Italy
{luca.zedda,alessandra.pernician,andrea.loddo,pes}@unica.it

Abstract. In recent years, machine learning and deep learning methods have been increasingly explored in a variety of application domains, including healthcare. Despite the rapid advances in this field, several challenges still need to be addressed to properly model complex biomedical datasets, such as genomic datasets or physiological signals from wearable sensors, that exhibit a very high dimensionality, i.e., a high number of variables or features which can be mutually related. As evidenced by the literature, the induction of reliable predictive models becomes intrinsically harder as the data dimensionality increases. To give a contribution to this field, this paper explores a new deep learning approach that leverages the emerging paradigm of *Transformers*, which can capture long-range dependencies among the input features and combines them with a *Convolutional Neural Network*, which is suited for capturing local patterns and dependencies. The resulting architecture has shown very promising results on six biomedical datasets with high dimensionality (several thousands of features), paving the way for further research in this area.

Keywords: Biomedical data · High-dimensional data · Machine learning · Deep learning · Transformers

1 Introduction

Machine learning (ML) and deep learning (DL) have revolutionized the way data is analyzed and interpreted and have, indeed, been applied to a wide range of fields such as computer vision (CV), natural language processing (NLP), and sensor-based human activity recognition (HAR). These approaches are also increasingly being exploited in the context of healthcare data analytics, e.g., for improving the clinical decision-making process and diagnostic purposes, with a fast-growing number of reported applications [8,16].

However, as the dimensionality of data increases, the performance of traditional machine learning algorithms can degrade significantly, making it quite

O. Gervasi et al. (Eds.): ICCSA 2023 Workshops, LNCS 14104, pp. 225–240, 2023.
https://doi.org/10.1007/978-3-031-37105-9_16

challenging to develop robust predictive models that can be reliably deployed in the real world. More specifically, high dimensionality refers to the presence in the data of a considerable number of variables (or *features*), which can even greatly exceed the number of data records available, as is often the case in healthcare applications [2]. This can lead to the issue of *overfitting*, i.e., to the development of models that, while perfectly describing the data used to train the machine learning algorithm, do not generalize well when applied to new, previously unseen data.

In recent years, a large amount of research has focused on devising suitable approaches to deal with high-dimensional biomedical datasets, investigating learning methods that scale well on high-dimensional feature spaces [17,43] as well as adequate dimensionality reduction techniques, such as *feature extraction* and *feature selection* [30]. Furthermore, high dimensionality often comes with other issues embedded in the nature of the data, including class imbalance and noise, which require proper strategies at both pre-processing and learning stages [14,26]. Several approaches have been proposed to deal with such complex datasets, including hybrid learning strategies that combine feature selection with data-balancing or cost-sensitive approaches [27,40]. As well, methods have been devised for enriching data by ontological annotations that can reveal valuable semantic relationships among the features in order to improve the variable selection process and the classification itself [9,13].

To address the challenges associated with high-dimensional biomedical data, some works have also started to explore deep learning methods that have the potential to learn very complex non-linear relationships among the features [33, 35], albeit at a higher computational cost. In the presence of datasets with many more features than instances, hybrid models have also been investigated based on a suitable combination of feature selection and deep neural networks [19].

In this paper, we propose a new deep learning approach for classifying high-dimensional biomedical data based on a *Transformer Encoder Convolutional Decoder* architecture. Our approach, hereinafter referred to as TECD, combines the strengths of *transformers* and *convolutional neural networks* (CNNs) to effectively capture complex relationships that may be hidden in datasets containing a large number (on the order of thousands) of features.

The proposed TECD architecture has been validated in two different biomedical case studies. Specifically, the first study involved five genomic datasets for cancer diagnosis, while the second study focused on a high-dimensional dataset for Covid-19 detection. Our method obtained promising results in both studies, showing satisfactory performance also in the presence of imbalanced data distributions.

The remainder of this paper is organized as follows. In Sect. 2, an overview of the background concepts used in this study and an exploration of related work are provided. Following this, Sect. 3 presents the proposed architecture and its functional components. Section 4 illustrates the materials and methods used in this work, focusing on the presentation of the genomic and Covid-19 detection datasets. Next, Sect. 5 presents the experimental setup, the results obtained with the associated findings, and a comparison with state-of-art machine learning methods. Finally, Sect. 6 gives the concluding remarks and outlines future work.

2 Background Concepts and Related Work

In the last decade, the impact of DL techniques has grown exponentially, revolutionizing several areas of machine intelligence, including CV [6], NLP [24], automatic speech recognition [18], drug discovery and toxicology [41], recommender systems [11], or medical analysis [4], to name a few.

Since the proposal of AlexNet's Convolutional Neural Network (CNN) [20], CNNs have begun to achieve outstanding performance in the ImageNet contest, making them one of the most notable DL approaches in the CV field. However, deep approaches are not limited to CNNs but include other techniques such as Multi-Layer Perceptron (MLP), Recurrent Neural Networks (RNN) and its variants, deep generative or unsupervised learning networks (e.g., GANs) [32].

In addition, one of the most recent approaches is certainly the transformer [37]. It uses the self-attention mechanism, differentially weighing the importance of each part of the input data. Transformer's success in NLP enabled researchers to explore its applicability to other fields, such as CV [10], using it for several tasks. Examples include object detection [5], image classification [29], or image segmentation [42].

In medicine and healthcare, pathologists have a keen interest in computer-aided diagnosis (CAD) systems because they can extract meaningful information from clinical and imaging data, provide personalized patient care by analyzing the patient's medical history, symptoms, and tests, or detect and classify diseases [7,39]. It is in this context that our approach is inspired. In fact, encoder-decoder architectures are widely used for various image segmentation tasks. FCN [23] introduces the encoder-decoder architecture and significantly improves the segmentation performance, while U-Net [31] and its evolution build on the idea of FCN by introducing a U-shaped network with lateral connections between the downsampling path and the upsampling path, which propagate context information for better localization. Although upsampling has been widely used in semantic segmentation to restore the low-resolution feature maps obtained from the downsampling path [21], more recently, attention mechanisms have improved the performance by weighting the channels before outputting them to the next layer.

Our work also exploits the concept of attention, but instead of focusing on the pixels of an image or using traditional feature selection approaches, it aims to refine tabular feature data within an encoding-decoding architecture while reducing computation through a feature selection strategy inherent to the architecture itself. Although a few works have recently tried out deep learning approaches to dealing with high-dimensional data matrices in the biomedical field [33], including methods based on CNNs [19,35], our approach is highly innovative as it jointly exploits the potential of transformers and CNNs. To our knowledge, no previous work has investigated a similar DL approach to model complex high-dimensional biomedical data, such as the genomic datasets and the Covid-19 dataset used in this study.

3   The Proposed Architecture

This section presents the proposed approach and the basic building blocks. Specifically, Sect. 3.1 and Sect. 3.2 describe two key concepts underlying the proposed architecture, i.e., attention mechanisms and transformers, respectively, while the CNN is briefly illustrated in Sect. 3.3. Finally, the structure of the architecture proposal is presented in its entirety in Sect. 3.4.

3.1   Attention Mechanism

As mentioned above in Sect. 2, there has been considerable interest in attention mechanisms in recent years for NLP or CV tasks since the introduction of the transformer architecture and multi-head self-attention (MHSA) [37].

The primary goal of attention mechanisms is to focus on relevant parts of the input while ignoring irrelevant parts, allowing the model to selectively attend to specific parts of the input. More in detail, the MHSA formulation is represented by Eq. (1):

$$MultiHead(Q, K, V) = Concat(head_1, \ldots, head_h)W^O \tag{1}$$

where:

$$head_i = Attention(QW_i^Q, KW_i^K, VW_i^V) \tag{2}$$

$$Attention(Q, K, V) = softmax(\frac{QK^T}{\sqrt{d_k}})V \tag{3}$$

Here, Q, K, and V represent the query, key, and value matrices. W_i^Q, W_i^K, and W_i^V represent the learned projection matrices for the ith head. W^O represents the learned output projection matrix. h is the number of heads. d_k is the dimensionality of the key vectors.

3.2   Transformers

Transformers [37] are a type of neural network architecture that aims to capture long-range dependencies between input sequences, allowing the model to better understand the context and meaning of the input.

Indeed, traditional neural networks, such as RNNs and CNNs, have been widely used for sequence modeling tasks. However, these networks have limitations in handling long sequences due to the vanishing gradient problem and the limited receptive field of CNNs. Transformers address these limitations using a self-attention mechanism to capture dependencies between all positions in the

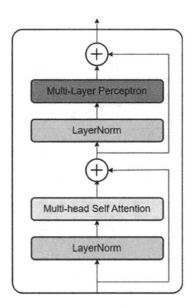

Fig. 1. A schematic illustration of a transformer block. The block takes a sequence of input tokens and produces a sequence of transformed tokens. A rectangle with its name represents each layer of the block. The block has three main components: a multi-head self-attention layer (in pink), a feed-forward layer (in turquoise), and two residue connections with layer normalization (in lilac). (Color figure online)

input sequence. The self-attention mechanism computes a weighted sum of the input based on the similarity between each input token and each other token, allowing the model to attend to relevant parts of the input at each processing step. A schematic representation of the transformer block architecture is depicted in Fig. 1.

While transformers were initially developed for sequential modeling tasks in NLP, they have also been applied to tabular data, where they have achieved state-of-the-art performance in various machine learning tasks. Recently, novel deep learning approaches, such as TabNet [1] and TabFormer [25], have aimed to exploit the transformer architecture for tabular data applications.

3.3 Convolutional Neural Networks (CNNs)

CNNs are a class of artificial neural networks that rely on a mathematical operation called convolution to automatically extract key features from the input data. They also use a proper regularization method to deal with the problem of over-fitting, which may occur in a fully connected network [32].

CNNs were initially designed for 2D shapes and used extensively in image classification and visual recognition tasks. However, they can also be applied to tabular data, where they can effectively capture local dependencies between features.

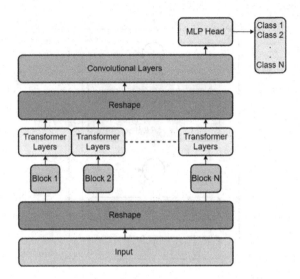

Fig. 2. A schematic illustration of the proposed TECD architecture that relies on an encoder-decoder structure. The encoder, composed of transformer layers, computes attention by reweighting features in relation to each other. At the same time, the convolutional decoder serves as a dimensional reduction tool or to enrich the input data through convolution operations.

In particular, 1D-CNNs are effective for tabular data classification [34]. 1D-CNNs apply a sequence of 1-dimensional convolutional operations to the input data, which can capture local patterns and dependencies between adjacent features. This makes them suitable for tasks where the order of features may be important.

3.4   TECD: Transformer Encoder Convolutional Decoder

Our proposed approach involves preprocessing the input data by padding it to form sequences divisible by a predetermined block size. Each block is passed through a transformer encoder, and the resulting outputs are merged. This merged output is then given to a CNN consisting of n residual blocks. Each residual block reduces the dimensionality of the input using an average pooling layer, and the final output is passed through a linear classification layer to generate predictions for the number of classes.

More specifically, the above process can be formalized as follows. Let X be the input data and B be the predetermined block size. We pad X so that its length is a multiple of B, resulting in a new sequence X'. We then divide X' into m B-sized blocks, denoted as $X_1, X_2, ..., X_m$, where m is the number of blocks. Each block X_i is then passed through a transformer encoder to generate an output tensor H_i. The output tensors $H_1, H_2, ..., H_m$ are then merged using a concatenation operation along the sequence dimension, resulting in a single output tensor H.

The output tensor H is then passed through a convolutional neural network (CNN) consisting of n residual blocks, denoted as $ResBlock_1$, $ResBlock_2, ..., ResBlock_n$. Each residual block reduces the dimensionality of the input using an average pooling layer. The final output is passed through a linear classification layer to generate predictions for the number of classes.

A schematic illustration of the proposed architecture is shown in Fig. 2.

4   Materials and Methods

We validated our innovative approach on two challenging case studies: the first refers to cancer classification from genomic data, while the second refers to Covid-19 detection from blood test data. For each case study, we conducted an extensive experimental investigation comparing the performance of our TECD architecture with that of state-of-the-art machine learning methods widely used in biomedical data analysis. In the following, we provide an overview of the datasets employed in our experiments (Sect. 4.1) and of the machine learning algorithms included in the comparative study (Sect. 4.2).

4.1   Datasets

Genomic Datasets. Gene expression data has proven to be very useful for various clinical applications, such as the diagnosis and prognosis of several types of cancer. However, one of the most serious problems in the analysis of such kind of data is the extremely low instances-to-features ratio, being the number of samples (i.e., biological tissues) very small compared to the number of features (i.e., genes). In this work, we exploit one of the largest publicly available repositories of gene expression data, namely the *Gene Expression Machine Learning Repository* (GEMLeR), that was collected by the International Genomics Consortium [36]. Specifically, we used the five datasets reported in Table 1, characterized by an instances-to-features ratio of 0.14: although low, this ratio is higher than that reported in most studies in the literature [15].

Each dataset refers to a binary classification task that discriminates a specific type of tumor (coded as a positive class) against other types of tumors (negative class). In particular, we chose five datasets that exhibit different levels of class imbalance, as shown in Table 1, to explore the performance of our approach across different data distributions. Precisely, the *Breast* and *Colon* datasets are moderately imbalanced, with 22% and 19% of minority instances, respectively. Instead, the *Uterus* and *Omentum* datasets present more skewed data distributions. In contrast, the *Ovary* dataset has a degree of imbalance that is in the middle of the others.

Covid-19 Detection Dataset. This dataset, which represents a very challenging case study [22], contains information from blood samples collected through a blood scanner. It was published by Hilab[1], a laboratory company based in

---

[1] https://hilab.com.br/.

Table 1. List of datasets from GEMLeR repository used in this work. The table indicates the number of instances and features of every dataset, along with the percentage of minority instances available.

Dataset	No. of Instances	No. of Features	Minority Instances
Breast	1545	10936	22%
Colon	1545	10936	19%
Ovary	1545	10936	13%
Uterus	1545	10936	8%
Omentum	1545	10936	5%

Brazil that operates thousands of blood scanner points throughout the country, primarily in hospitals and pharmacies.

The digitization technology of the devices and the large number of tests performed have generated enough data to create a significant benchmark for machine learning and deep learning tasks. Indeed, the dataset consists of 40,044 instances equally distributed into two classes representing positive or negative samples for Covid-19, as labeled by expert biomedical scientists. Each piece is described by 12,210 numerical features, resulting in a classification problem with very high dimensionality.

4.2   Machine Learning Methods

To validate our TECD architecture and demonstrate its effectiveness in biomedical data classification, we performed a comparative analysis involving the following machine learning algorithms:

- *Bayesian Network* (BayesNet);
- *Naïve Bayes* (NB);
- *Support Vector Machine* (SVM);
- *k-Nearest Neighbor* (k-NN);
- *Ripper* (JRip);
- *One Rule* (OneR);
- *Decision Tree* (J48);
- *Random Forest* (RF).

We observe that the methods considered are representatives of different families of classifiers [22]. Indeed, BayesNet and NB are probabilistic models that represent the conditional dependency relationships among the variables involved in the task. SVM, known to scale well to high-dimensional feature spaces, exploits a statistical learning framework to model linear decision boundaries and more complex boundaries in dependence on the adopted kernel function. The k-NN algorithm is an instance-based learner that assigns the class to unknown instances based on their similarity to the training records. JRip and OneR are rule-based classifiers that induce simple yet effective models in the form of *if-then* prediction rules. Finally, J48 and RF are tree-based classifiers: in particular, J48 builds a single decision tree exploiting the well-known C4.5 method originally proposed by Quinlan [12]. At the same time, RF is an ensemble method combining multiple decision tree predictions.

5   Experimental Study

In this section, we summarize our experimental investigation, first presenting the experimental settings (Sect. 5.1) and then discussing the results obtained (Sect. 5.2).

5.1   Experimental Setup

The experiments were performed on a workstation with an NVIDIA GeForce RTX 3060 GPU and 32 GB of RAM. The configuration of both types of experiments is described below.

Experimental Setup for TECD. To ensure reproducibility, we set the random seed for data partitioning and model initialization. The experiment was repeated 5 times. In each run, the dataset was partitioned using the 80-10-10 rule: 80% for training, 10% for validation, and the remaining 10% for testing. In particular, in each run, the best model was selected based on the performance of the validation set; this model was then evaluated on the test of that particular run. The final performance was obtained by averaging the results of the five runs.

The training phase lasted a maximum of 250 epochs, with the following hyperparameters: learning rate of 1×10^{-5}, Lion optimizer [38], cross-entropy loss, a warmup learning rate of 1×10^{-7}, 25 warmup epochs, and batch size of 128. The Lion optimizer is a novel algorithm for training deep neural networks proposed by Google Brain using genetic algorithms. It is more memory efficient than Adam because it only keeps track of the moment.

Experimental Setup for Machine Learning Algorithms. For the machine learning algorithms, we leveraged the implementations provided by the WEKA library [12]. For a fair comparison, we used the same experimental protocol for the TECD architecture, i.e., 5 training-testing runs (with 10% of the data reserved for testing at each run).

The settings adopted for the classifiers correspond, in most cases, to the default parameters provided by the WEKA library. In particular, we used a linear kernel for the SVM method. At the same time, the RF classifier was implemented with 100 trees and $log_2(N) + 1$ random features (where N is the dimensionality, i.e., the number of features, of the dataset at hand). For the k-NN approach, we considered two versions of the method: with and without instance weighting; in both cases, the number of nearest neighbors (i.e., the k parameter) was set to 5 to reduce the risk of overfitting. In what follows, we will refer to the weighted version of k-NN as k-NNw.

Furthermore, since the performance of machine learning algorithms can degrade in the presence of a large number of features, we also conducted experiments in which the data dimensionality was reduced by applying proper feature selection methods. Specifically, we used a ranking-based selection approach [3] to assign weights to the features based on their correlation with the target class; then, a subset containing the first 110 top-ranked features (1% of the original dimensionality) was employed for model induction. For a broad comparison, we experimented with different feature ranking criteria, as implemented by the WEKA library, namely *Information Gain* (IG), *Symmetrical Uncertainty* (SU), *Gain Ratio* (GR), *Pearson's Correlation* (Corr), and *ReliefF*, which have proven to be effective in the context of biomedical data analysis [3, 28].

5.2   Experimental Results and Discussion

For our evaluation, we considered two metrics: the F-measure and the accuracy. Specifically, the F-measure is the harmonic mean of precision and recall (see Eq. (4)), where precision is the ratio of true positives to the total predicted positives and recall is the ratio of true positives to the total actual positives.

$$F - measure = \frac{2 * precision * recall}{precision + recall}, \tag{4}$$

The F-measure is commonly used in information retrieval and binary classification in the presence of imbalanced datasets. For this reason, we considered the F-measure for evaluating the experiments conducted on the genomic datasets, which present an imbalanced class distribution, as shown in Table 1.

On the other hand, accuracy is defined as the ratio of correct predictions (true positives and true negatives) to the total number of cases, as reported in Eq. (5):

$$Accuracy = \frac{TP + TN}{TP + TN + FP + FN}, \tag{5}$$

where TP is the number of true positives, TN is the number of true negatives, FP is the number of false positives, and FN is the number of false negatives. Since the accuracy considers both classes equally, it is well suited for performance evaluation in the presence of balanced data distributions, as in the Covid-19 detection dataset considered here.

Results on the GEMLeR Datasets. Table 2 summarizes the results of the first comparative analysis conducted on the five GEMLeR datasets included in our study (*Breast, Colon, Ovary, Uterus,* and *Omentum*). Specifically, the performance of our TECD architecture is compared with that of the nine machine learning methods described in Sect. 4.2.

As can be seen, our proposed approach performs robustly across all genomic benchmarks considered. Precisely, in four out of five cases (i.e., in *Breast, Colon, Uterus,* and *Omentum* datasets), it achieved the highest F-measure value, while in the *Ovary* dataset it was outperformed only by SVM and JRip. Thus, overall,

Table 2. Results obtained on the GEMLeR datasets in terms of F-measure.

Dataset	TECD	BayesNet	NB	SVM	KNN	KNNw	OneR	JRip	J48	RF
Breast	**0.93**	0.91	0.90	0.90	0.82	0.81	0.79	0.81	0.85	0.87
Colon	**0.96**	0.85	0.88	0.89	0.87	0.87	0.85	0.88	0.88	0.85
Ovary	0.68	0.60	0.58	0.72	0.50	0.50	0.61	**0.74**	0.67	0.47
Uterus	**0.72**	0.47	0.57	0.60	0.62	0.62	0.18	0.48	0.50	0.24
Omentum	**0.53**	0.44	0.49	0.44	0.39	0.39	0.37	0.41	0.38	0.00

our TECD architecture has proved to be effective in classifying different cancer types based on the patient's genetic profile, despite the low instances-to-features ratio of this kind of data (see Sect. 4.1).

Table 3. Accuracy results obtained on the Covid-19 dataset.

Method	Accuracy
RF [22]	0.74
ANN [22]	0.84
TECD (Our)	**0.86**

Results on the Covid-19 Dataset. In a previous work [22], we already explored the same Covid-19 dataset examined here by conducting an extensive comparative analysis of different machine learning methods, including those considered in this paper, and of different deep learning methods, including 1D-CNN, TabNet, Node as well as an ANN network specially designed for that purpose. Among the machine learning methods, RF was the best-performing one in [22], with an overall accuracy of 0.74. However, the ANN model turned out to be significantly more accurate, with an overall accuracy of 0.84. Such a model, designed after exploring different neural network architectures and settings, is used here as a reference method to evaluate the performance of our new TECD architecture. As seen in Table 3, TECD shows superior performance, confirming it can be a suitable approach for handling complex high-dimensional datasets.

Discussion. Although not exhaustive, the results of our experimental analysis showed that the proposed encoding-decoding architecture has the potential to capture meaningful patterns across different types of biomedical datasets, even in the presence of imbalanced data distributions, with an inherent capability of reducing the input dimensionality. High-dimensional feature spaces represent indeed a primary challenge for most machine learning algorithms, which often require a preliminary preprocessing aimed at reducing the number of input features, especially in the presence of a low instances-to-features ratio, as in the case of the genomic datasets.

On these datasets, as mentioned in Sect. 5.1, we conducted further experiments to evaluate the impact of a preliminary dimensionality reduction on the nine machine learning methods involved in our comparative analysis. Specifically, each classifier was evaluated in conjunction with different feature selection methods, namely IG, Corr, SU, GR, and ReliefF, for a total of 45 selector-classifier combinations. As shown in Table 4, in most cases, the experiments with feature selection showed better performance for the machine learning algorithms. However, the final F-measure may strongly depend on the adopted selection approach, and no single selector-classifier combination performs consistently better than the others.

Table 4. F-measure performance obtained on the GEMLeR datasets using machine learning classifiers in conjunction with different feature selection methods (IG, Corr, SU, GR, ReliefF).

Dataset	IG	Corr	SU	GR	ReliefF	BayesNet	NB	SVM	KNN	KNNw	OneR	JRip	J48	RF
Breast	✓					0.92	0.89	0.91	0.91	0.90	0.79	0.90	0.86	0.92
		✓				0.88	0.80	0.90	0.89	0.88	0.79	0.87	0.85	0.89
			✓			0.90	0.88	0.91	0.90	0.90	0.79	0.89	0.88	0.92
				✓		0.88	0.79	0.89	0.89	0.88	0.79	0.89	0.86	0.91
					✓	0.90	0.85	0.91	0.88	0.88	0.79	0.88	0.86	0.90
Colon	✓					0.87	0.84	0.90	0.89	0.89	0.85	0.91	0.84	0.88
		✓				0.86	0.82	0.89	0.88	0.88	0.85	0.90	0.88	0.88
			✓			0.86	0.84	0.90	0.88	0.88	0.85	0.89	0.86	0.88
				✓		0.86	0.84	0.90	0.89	0.88	0.85	0.90	0.85	0.89
					✓	0.86	0.82	0.89	0.86	0.85	0.85	0.92	0.91	0.91
Ovary	✓					0.71	0.65	0.79	0.68	0.67	0.61	0.77	0.74	0.84
		✓				0.66	0.67	0.77	0.56	0.56	0.61	0.73	0.69	0.81
			✓			0.75	0.66	0.79	0.66	0.65	0.61	0.78	0.75	0.86
				✓		0.76	0.68	0.80	0.54	0.54	0.61	0.80	0.69	0.81
					✓	0.66	0.63	0.82	0.59	0.59	0.61	0.79	0.78	0.79
Uterus	✓					0.55	0.51	0.52	0.42	0.42	0.18	0.47	0.51	0.46
		✓				0.53	0.54	0.51	0.39	0.39	0.18	0.46	0.41	0.50
			✓			0.57	0.52	0.51	0.42	0.42	0.22	0.47	0.54	0.45
				✓		0.56	0.53	0.49	0.43	0.43	0.24	0.55	0.43	0.42
					✓	0.52	0.52	0.45	0.32	0.32	0.21	0.56	0.52	0.48
Omentum	✓					0.50	0.42	0.37	0.43	0.43	0.37	0.53	0.34	0.48
		✓				0.48	0.41	0.31	0.56	0.56	0.37	0.50	0.40	0.42
			✓			0.46	0.40	0.32	0.37	0.37	0.37	0.46	0.38	0.45
				✓		0.47	0.41	0.23	0.29	0.29	0.37	0.41	0.34	0.37
					✓	0.39	0.33	0.39	0.34	0.34	0.37	0.65	0.37	0.53

Overall, comparing the results in Table 4 with those previously shown in Table 2, we can still observe that our TECD architecture turns out to be quite effective overall. Indeed, in three out of five datasets (*Breast, Colon,* and *Uterus*) it outperformed each of the 45 selector-classifier combinations, while in the *Omentum* dataset, it outperformed 40 combinations out of 45; the *Ovary* dataset in the only one, among those examined, in which TECD did not perform significantly better.

Finally, as regards the second case study considered in this paper, related to Covid-19 detection from blood test data, we observe that the instances-to-features ratio is not a critical concern in this case, as a vast number of instances is available along with many features. In a so different setting, as previously observed in Table 3, our TECD architecture also showed promising performance, prompting us to enlarge our experimentation in order to further validate our approach on multiple and heterogeneous scenarios.

6 Conclusions

Computer-aided diagnosis systems are becoming increasingly effective in assisting clinical staff with a wide range of diseases and cancers. Artificial intelligence methods have been successfully applied in this field in recent years. However, several issues still need to be addressed to cope with the inherent complexity of biomedical datasets, which pose multiple challenges, including high dimensionality.

In this work, we presented a new deep learning architecture designed to classify high-dimensional biomedical data. The main innovative contribution of this work is the realization of a novel approach able to combine the strengths of transformers and convolutional neural networks to effectively capture complex relationships that may be hidden in datasets containing a large number of features. In addition, within the encoding-decoding architecture, the concept of attention has been applied, which aims to refine the input data through a feature selection strategy inherent to the architecture itself.

Overall, the experiments performed on six public datasets produced results that are in line with or better than other state-of-the-art methods in the literature, making our proposed TECD architecture an effective contribution to deep learning models in addressing the challenges associated with high-dimensional datasets. In future work, we plan to further validate our approach on different real-world case studies, encompassing various problem settings, e.g., in terms of the number of instances, features, instances-to-features ratio, and class imbalance level.

Acknowledgements. This research was supported by the ASTRID project (Fondazione di Sardegna, L.R. 7 agosto 2007, n°7, CUP: F75F21001220007).

References

1. Arik, S., Pfister, T.: TabNet: attentive interpretable tabular learning. In: Proceedings of the AAAI Conference on Artificial Intelligence, vol. 35, pp. 6679–6687 (2021)
2. Berisha, V., et al.: Digital medicine and the curse of dimensionality. NPJ Digit. Med. **4**(1), 153 (2021)

3. Bolón-Canedo, V., Sánchez-Maroño, N., Alonso-Betanzos, A.: Feature Selection for High-Dimensional Data. Springer, Cham (2015). https://doi.org/10.1007/978-3-319-21858-8

4. Budd, S., Robinson, E.C., Kainz, B.: A survey on active learning and human-in-the-loop deep learning for medical image analysis. Medical Image Anal. **71**, 102062 (2021)

5. Carion, N., Massa, F., Synnaeve, G., Usunier, N., Kirillov, A., Zagoruyko, S.: End-to-end object detection with transformers. In: Vedaldi, A., Bischof, H., Brox, T., Frahm, J.-M. (eds.) ECCV 2020, Part I. LNCS, vol. 12346, pp. 213–229. Springer, Cham (2020). https://doi.org/10.1007/978-3-030-58452-8_13

6. Chai, J., Zeng, H., Li, A., Ngai, E.W.: Deep learning in computer vision: a critical review of emerging techniques and application scenarios. Mach. Learn. Appl. **6**, 100134 (2021)

7. D'Ancona, G., et al.: Deep learning to detect significant coronary artery disease from plain chest radiographs AI4CAD. Int. J. Cardiol. **370**, 435–441 (2022)

8. Davenport, T., Kalakota, R.: The potential for artificial intelligence in healthcare. Future Healthc. J. **6**(2), 94–98 (2019)

9. Dessì, N., Pascariello, E., Pes, B.: Integrating ontological information about genes. In: 2014 IEEE 23rd International WETICE Conference, pp. 417–422. IEEE (2014)

10. Dosovitskiy, A., et al.: An image is worth 16×16 words: transformers for image recognition at scale. In: 9th International Conference on Learning Representations, ICLR 2021, 3–7 May 2021, Austria (2021)

11. Elkahky, A.M., Song, Y., He, X.: A multi-view deep learning approach for cross domain user modeling in recommendation systems. In: WWW 2015 (2015)

12. Frank, E., Hall, M.A., Witten, I.H.: The WEKA Workbench. Online Appendix for 'Data Mining: Practical Machine Learning Tools and Techniques', 4th edn. Morgan Kaufmann (2016)

13. Gillies, C.E., Siadat, M.R., Patel, N.V., Wilson, G.D.: A simulation to analyze feature selection methods utilizing gene ontology for gene expression classification. J. Biomed. Inform. **46**(6), 1044–1059 (2013)

14. Gupta, S., Gupta, A.: Dealing with noise problem in machine learning data-sets: a systematic review. Procedia Comput. Sci. **161**, 466–474 (2019)

15. Hambali, M.A., Oladele, T.O., Adewole, K.S.: Microarray cancer feature selection: review, challenges and research directions. Int. J. Cogn. Comput. Eng. **1**, 78–97 (2020)

16. Javaid, M., Haleem, A., Singh, R.P., Suman, R., Rab, S.: Significance of machine learning in healthcare: features, pillars and applications. Int. J. Intell. Netw. **3**, 58–73 (2022)

17. Kalina, J.: Classification methods for high-dimensional genetic data. Biocybern. Biomed. Eng. **34**(1), 10–18 (2014)

18. Kaur, A.P., Singh, A., Sachdeva, R., Kukreja, V.: Automatic speech recognition systems: a survey of discriminative techniques. Multim. Tools Appl. **82**(9), 13307–13339 (2023)

19. Kilicarslan, S., Adem, K., Celik, M.: Diagnosis and classification of cancer using hybrid model based on ReliefF and convolutional neural network. Med. Hypotheses **137**, 109577 (2020)

20. Krizhevsky, A., Sutskever, I., Hinton, G.E.: ImageNet classification with deep convolutional neural networks. In: Proceedings of the 25th International Conference on Neural Information Processing Systems. NIPS 2012, vol. 1, pp. 1097–1105 (2012)

21. Li, Y., Cai, W., Gao, Y., Li, C., Hu, X.: More than encoder: Introducing transformer decoder to upsample. In: Adjeroh, D.A., et al. (eds.) IEEE International Conference on Bioinformatics and Biomedicine, BIBM 2022, Las Vegas, NV, USA, 6–8 December 2022, pp. 1597–1602. IEEE (2022)

22. Loddo, A., Meloni, G., Pes, B.: Using artificial intelligence for COVID-19 detection in blood exams: a comparative analysis. IEEE Access **10**, 119593–119606 (2022)

23. Long, J., Shelhamer, E., Darrell, T.: Fully convolutional networks for semantic segmentation. In: Proceedings of the IEEE Conference on Computer Vision and Pattern Recognition, pp. 3431–3440 (2015)

24. Madsen, A., Reddy, S., Chandar, S.: Post-hoc interpretability for neural NLP: a survey. ACM Comput. Surv. **55**(8), 155:1–155:42 (2023)

25. Padhi, I., et al.: Tabular transformers for modeling multivariate time series. In: ICASSP 2021–2021 IEEE International Conference on Acoustics, Speech and Signal Processing (ICASSP), pp. 3565–3569. IEEE (2021)

26. Pes, B.: Learning from high-dimensional biomedical datasets: the issue of class imbalance. IEEE Access **8**, 13527–13540 (2020)

27. Pes, B.: Learning from high-dimensional and class-imbalanced datasets using random forests. Information **12**, 286 (2021)

28. Pes, B., Lai, G.: Cost-sensitive learning strategies for high-dimensional and imbalanced data: a comparative study. PeerJ Comput. Sci. **7**, e832 (2021)

29. Radford, A., et al.: Learning transferable visual models from natural language supervision. In: International Conference on Machine Learning, pp. 8748–8763. PMLR (2021)

30. Ray, P., Reddy, S.S., Banerjee, T.: Various dimension reduction techniques for high dimensional data analysis: a review. Artif. Intell. Rev. **54**(5), 3473–3515 (2021). https://doi.org/10.1007/s10462-020-09928-0

31. Ronneberger, O., Fischer, P., Brox, T.: U-net: convolutional networks for biomedical image segmentation. In: Navab, N., Hornegger, J., Wells, W.M., Frangi, A.F. (eds.) MICCAI 2015. LNCS, vol. 9351, pp. 234–241. Springer, Cham (2015). https://doi.org/10.1007/978-3-319-24574-4_28

32. Sarker, I.H.: Deep learning: a comprehensive overview on techniques, taxonomy, applications and research directions. SN Comput. Sci. **2**(6), 420 (2021)

33. Sevakula, R.K., Singh, V., Verma, N.K., Kumar, C., Cui, Y.: Transfer learning for molecular cancer classification using deep neural networks. IEEE/ACM Trans. Comput. Biol. Bioinf. **16**(6), 2089–2100 (2019)

34. Shwartz-Ziv, R., Armon, A.: Tabular data: deep learning is not all you need. Inf. Fusion **81**, 84–90 (2022)

35. Singh, R., Lanchantin, J., Robins, G., Qi, Y.: DeepChrome: deep-learning for predicting gene expression from histone modifications. Bioinformatics **32**(17), i639–i648 (2016)

36. Tiglic, G., Kokol, P.: Stability of ranked gene lists in large microarray analysis studies. J. Biomed. Biotechnol. **2010** (2010)

37. Vaswani, A., et al.: Attention is all you need. In: Guyon, I., et al. (eds.) Advances in Neural Information Processing Systems 30: Annual Conference on Neural Information Processing Systems 2017, 4–9 December 2017, Long Beach, CA, USA, pp. 5998–6008 (2017)

38. Yazdani, M., Jolai, F.: Lion optimization algorithm (LOA): a nature-inspired metaheuristic algorithm. J. Comput. Design Eng. **3**(1), 24–36 (2016)

39. Zedda, L., Loddo, A., Di Ruberto, C.: A deep learning based framework for malaria diagnosis on high variation data set. In: Sclaroff, S., Distante, C., Leo, M., Farinella, G.M., Tombari, F. (eds.) ICIAP 2022. LNCS, vol. 13232, pp. 358–370. Springer, Cham (2022). https://doi.org/10.1007/978-3-031-06430-2_30
40. Zhang, C., Zhou, Y., Guo, J., Wang, G., Wang, X.: Research on classification method of high-dimensional class-imbalanced datasets based on SVM. Int. J. Mach. Learn. Cybern. **10**, 1765–1778 (2019)
41. Zhavoronkov, A., et al.: Deep learning enables rapid identification of potent DDR1 kinase inhibitors. Nat. Biotechnol. **37**(9), 1038–1040 (2019)
42. Zheng, S., et al.: Rethinking semantic segmentation from a sequence-to-sequence perspective with transformers. In: IEEE Conference on Computer Vision and Pattern Recognition, CVPR 2021, virtual, 19–25 June 2021, pp. 6881–6890. Computer Vision Foundation/IEEE (2021)
43. Zou, H.: Classification with high dimensional features. Wiley Interdisc. Rev.: Comput. Stat. **11**(1), e1453 (2019)

Advanced and Innovative Web Apps (AIWA 2023)

A New Exercise Environment for the Experimental Treatment of Visual Snow

Damiano Perri[1,2]([✉]) [ID], Osvaldo Gervasi[2] [ID], and Marco Simonetti[1,2] [ID]

[1] Department of Mathematics and Computer Science, University of Florence, Florence, Italy
damiano.perri@unifi.it
[2] Department of Mathematics and Computer Science, University of Perugia, Perugia, Italy

Abstract. The Visual Snow Syndrome is a neurological condition that causes flickering dots to appear across a person's entire field of vision. Those who suffer from this syndrome report seeing an unending stream of flickering dots throughout their visual field. Although patients often experience concurrent migraines, Visual Snow Syndrome appears to be a distinct phenomenon from prolonged migraine aura. The cause of this syndrome is not yet fully understood, but it has been linked to various eye and brain dysfunctions. The aim of this work is to make improvements to the environment in which exercises affected by this condition are developed. Currently, the Visual Snow Initiative provides an online platform where it is possible to carry out a 30-day exercise cycle during which patients are shown videos with noise that simulates Visual Snow and only affects certain areas of the visual field. This video noise moves and shifts along the screen occupying different areas of the screen. The video stream is sent from the servers to the users and requires a modern and efficient internet connection. A single video file occupies about 2GB of disk space. Modern codecs that deal with compressing video and encoding it into browser-supported formats have great difficulty encoding a stream where the pixel matrix of the video is in constant motion. The purpose of this work is to reconstruct the noise that is displayed within the video files for the exercises by means of JavaScript algorithms in such a way as to reduce the download required from users to a few kilobytes and to generate client-side the video that will then be used for the exercise.

Keywords: Augmented Reality · Eyes disease · Visual Snow Syndrome · Web Programming

1 Introduction

For some years now, researchers have been focusing on the study of a chronic condition called Visual Snow. Visual Snow is a visual pathology that affects a small

O. Gervasi et al. (Eds.): ICCSA 2023 Workshops, LNCS 14104, pp. 243–252, 2023.
https://doi.org/10.1007/978-3-031-37105-9_17

but significant percentage of people worldwide. Characterised by the perception of a constant visual disturbance, similar to television noise that appears when the antenna is not properly tuned. Visual Snow can be extremely disabling for sufferers. The condition is characterised by bright spots, sparkles, mists and lines moving within the visual field. These symptoms can cause severe visual discomfort, interfere with daily activities and impair patients' quality of life. Currently, there is no definitive cure for this condition and available therapies mainly focus on symptom management. An innovative approach being tested today consists of a 21-day cycle where the patient has to watch 30-minute films showing video noise. This is also described on the official page of the Visual Imagery Project (VSP)[1]. It is important to point out that VSI is an experimental treatment and its efficacy rate is still a matter of scientific investigation.

The idea is that these films help patients focus their attention on the external visual stimulus and reduce the perception of internal visual disturbance. However, this therapy has some limitations. First of all, it requires a large video stream, which means that patients must have access to a fast and stable internet connection in order to benefit from the therapy. In addition, video streaming can consume a significant amount of data, which could be a problem for patients with bandwidth limitations. In this article, a new approach for the treatment of Visual Snow will be presented, based on the generation of video noise through a client-side JavaScript code. To overcome these limitations, we propose an improvement to the experimental approach currently used to treat Visual Snow. Our approach is based on generating video noise through a client-side JavaScript code. The code can be downloaded and executed within the user's browser, and does not require real-time video streaming, greatly reducing the amount of data required to utilise the treatment. This method is intended to contribute to the valuable work carried out by the Visual Snow Initiative[2], which consists of feeding users films with video noise moving across the visual screen. The goal is to reduce the amount of data needed to deliver the videos with visual noise to patients, eliminating the need for a large video stream. This will reduce loading times and the amount of data to be downloaded, simplifying access to therapy for anyone who needs it.

In this article, we will detail the development process of our JavaScript code, the experiments conducted to test its effectiveness, and the potential future applications of this technology for the treatment of other similar visual pathologies. With our proposed JavaScript code for client-side video noise generation, we hope to offer a new and improved therapy for Visual Snow patients. Section 2 the most recent literature addressing the Visual Snow problem is discussed. Section 3 the steps and techniques used for the realisation of the JavaScript code and the application are discussed. Section 4 outlines the main objectives obtained after the development of the mobile app and anticipates the future developments.

---

[1] https://visualsnowproject.com/.
[2] https://www.visualsnowinitiative.org/.

2   Related Works

This section reviews the modern scientific literature dealing with Visual Snow pathology.

According to epidemiological and clinical studies, VSS is linked to other perceptual disorders such tinnitus, fibromyalgia, and vertigo. There may be clinical similarities and pathophysiological analogies in migraine [1]. The clinical characterization of visual snow syndrome is currently undergoing development, with proposed modifications to the diagnostic criteria. Two recent studies have investigated the possibility of dysfunctional visual processing and hyperexcitability in the occipital cortex through the use of electrophysiology. Additionally, advanced functional imaging techniques show potential for providing more detailed understanding of the underlying disease mechanisms [2,3].

In some individuals, their keen observation skills allow them to perceive their own white blood cells flowing through the retinal microvasculature, appearing as small cells or dots moving in a squiggly path, particularly when observing the blue sky. This phenomenon is referred to as the blue field entoptic [4,5] or Scheerer's phenomenon and can be elicited using a blue field entoptoscope. Research indicates that this phenomenon is present in up to 80% of individuals with visual snow [6].

Modern technologies can, in our opinion, contribute to helping people with this condition. Augmented Reality (AR) and Virtual Reality (VR) [7,8] are also increasingly being used in the medical field, and science is discovering potentials that were not even imaginable a few years ago [9]. In this article, a mobile programme for Android is proposed that allows one to simulate what people with Visual Snow see [10].

The recent experience we all had with COVID-19 made it clear that new technologies are essential [11–13] and should be used as much as possible to improve people's quality of life. Artificial intelligence [14,15], neural networks [16,17] and Cloud technologies [18–20] enable and will increasingly enable the provision of services to citizens even remotely. Telemedicine [21] and telerehabilitation [22] are and will be increasingly common themes.

The authors of this article [23] carried out an effective survey involving thousands of people and found that individuals with visual snow syndrome had an average age of 29 and no significant difference in sex prevalence. Black and white static was the most frequently reported visual symptom. Other commonly reported visual symptoms included floaters [24,25], afterimages [26], and photophobia [27]. The disorder typically manifests in early life, with approximately 40% of patients experiencing symptoms for as long as they can remember [23]. In this study, concentrated in a sample of 1015 people in the United Kingdom, it was found that approximately 2 percent of people are affected by Visual Snow [28].

3   The Proposed Solution

The JavaScript programming language is extremely versatile and allows the programmer to write code that can then be executed on users' devices regardless of the operating system they use. JavaScript is in fact executed within the browser, and it is therefore the browser that is responsible for interpreting and executing the code. For this reason, it was decided to develop the code that deals with rendering directly client-side and in a high-level language such as JavaScript. It is important to note that, between the various browsers, there may be small but important differences in the interpretation of JavaScript code and in the performance that can be achieved. As of March 2023, the most popular browsers are Chrome with 64.8% market share, followed by Safari with 19.5%, Edge with 4.63%, Firefox with 2.93% and then other smaller browsers such as Samsung Internet and Opera[3]. In developing the code that will be presented in this section, we have therefore focused mainly on compatibility with the Chrome browser and Safari.

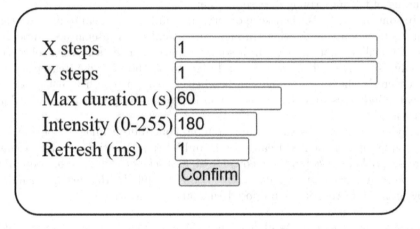

Fig. 1. User interface for the developers

Figure 1 shows the graphic interface used by the developers to calibrate some of the parameters used to generate the video noise that is represented on the screen. The first two parameters are called "X steps" and "Y steps". These identify the density of points to be handled by the algorithm. If for example "X steps" is set equal to 1, then the algorithm will scan the matrix of pixels in steps of 1 pixel at a time in a horizontal direction. If a value of 10 is set, then the algorithm will then process every 10th pixel. The same mechanism is defined for the variable 'Y steps'. This makes it possible to test different exercises with different densities of video noise on the screen, e.g. one might want to create a stream with extremely dense noise on the left eye and a stream with little video noise on the right eye.

The 'Max durations' parameter allows the maximum duration of an exercise to be expressed in seconds. This will allow experts to define exercises with a pre-determined time, for example 60 s or several minutes, and allows us to test how the software behaves when performing sequential exercises with a predetermined duration.

---

[3] https://www.similarweb.com/browsers/.

The "Intensity" parameter is used to calibrate the colour level that the pixels must take on: In the current project, noise is generated by the constantly changing colouration of the pixels. The pixels take on two types of colour: black or coloured. In the case where the pixel under consideration is to be coloured black then its RGB component will be equal to (0,0,0). In the case where the pixel is to be coloured its RGB component will be equal to (X,X,X) with X equal to *Intensity*.

The 'Refresh' parameter indicates the refresh time of the noise shown on the screen. This allows you to define how quickly the screen shown on the display should change. A value of 1ms means that every millisecond the screen containing the noise will be refreshed, generating a new one randomly.

The proposed algorithm for generating video noise uses a canvas that expands across the width and height of the page to occupy 100% of its space. The canvas is an HTML object compatible with all browsers and is predefined at the implementation level[4]. Each point on the canvas will represent one pixel of the monitor. Through a double for loop, the list of pixels is scrolled. For each pixel, the Math.random function is called, which generates a random flaot number between 0 and 1. If the extracted number is greater than 0.5 then the pixel will be coloured with the value of *Intensity* requested by the programmer, otherwise it will be coloured black. Iterating this block of code in accordance with the set refresh rate results in a random, constant generation of video noise.

```
function setColor(i,color){ //0=black; 1=colored
    if(color==0) {
        buffer32[i] = 0; // R
        buffer32[i+1] = 0; // G
        buffer32[i+2] = 0; // B
    }else{
        buffer32[i]=intensity; // R
        buffer32[i+1]=intensity; // G
        buffer32[i+2]=intensity; // B
    }
}
for(let x=0;x<c.width;x+=xSteps){
    for(let y=0;y<c.height;y+=ySteps){
        let i = 4 * (x + y * c.width);
        if(Math.random()<0.5){
            setColor(i,1);
        }
        else{
            setColor(i,0);
        }
    }
}
```

Listing 1.1. Sample of the algorithm

---

[4] https://developer.mozilla.org/en-US/docs/Web/API/Canvas_API.

Figure 2 shows an example of video noise simulated by the proposed algorithm with *Intensity* set to 188. Figure 3 shows an example of video noise simulated by the proposed algorithm with *Intensity* set to 255. An example of video noise simulated by the proposed algorithm with *Intensity* set to 255, *Xsteps* set to 3, and *Ysteps* set to 2 is shown in Fig. 4.

Fig. 2. Noise sample, intensity 188, Xsteps 1, Ysteps 1

Fig. 3. Noise sample, intensity 255, Xsteps 1, Ysteps 1

The comparative Table 1 shows a comparison between the two approaches, the one involving the presentation of noise via video clips and the one generating

Fig. 4. Noise sample, intensity 255, Xsteps 2, Ysteps 3

Table 1. Comparative table between the two approaches

Comparison	Video Streaming	Noise locally generated
Data downloaded	2 GB	1 MB
CPU usage	12%	16%
GPU usage	36%	12%

it client-side. The table shows the difference in terms of data download and the difference in terms of CPU and GPU usage. The data was calculated with a Workstation with an Intel CPU i7-5820K@3.2 GHz, 64 GB of ram and an NVIDIA 2700 GPU. As can be seen, much less data is downloaded if a script is used to generate the noise. In addition, local computation increases CPU utilisation but reduces the use of the GPU, which is generally well utilised when displaying films. In order to make the application even more versatile and to be able to run on machines with little computational power, a future development will be to increase the use of the GPU and reduce that of the CPU, by moving the calculations related to editing and processing the colour of pixels to the GPU.

4   Conclusions and Future Work

This work aimed to realise an improvement to be submitted to the Visual Snow Initiative. The aim is to improve the platform with which videos are delivered of the exercises that people with Visual Snow use to try to improve their health condition. What has been realised is a JavaScript algorithm that can be effectively modelled and adapted for all the exercises currently delivered by the platform and is made available to users on the GitHub platform in such a way that anyone can access this code freely and for free[5]. The use of JavaScript has made it possible to reduce the download required for users to perform the exercise. Each exercise currently on the platform occupies 1.5 to 2 GB of data space. This makes it difficult for people who have a slow Internet connection or are in areas with poor network coverage to access the media files with which to perform the daily exercise. On the other hand, generating the exercise on the client side by downloading a small JavaScript file of just a few KB, which encodes the exercise to be performed, makes it possible to expand the audience of people who can use and perform these exercises even in those areas where network coverage is slow or even partially absent. In addition, the ease with which the code can be manipulated allows new exercises to be generated by the experts involved in devising them, speeding up and hopefully improving the quality of scientific research for the benefit of people and their physical and mental health. In the future we will try to expand this work in two ways: First of all, we plan to expand what we have created for the use of virtual reality visors so that these exercises can be carried out in an immersive environment that thus enables greater effectiveness in treatment, and to do this we will use the environment provided by the Unity software. The second way is to extend the code realised in this article to interface only with web platforms in relation to the needs that will be described by the experts of the Visual Snow Initiatives.

Acronyms

The following acronyms are used in this manuscript:

API Application Programming Interface
AR   Augmented Reality
JS   JavaScript
MB   MegaByte
KB   KiloByte
VR   Virtual Reality
VSI Visual Snow Iniziative
VSS Visual Snow Syndrome

References

1. Klein, A., Schankin, C.J.: Visual snow syndrome, the spectrum of perceptual disorders, and migraine as a common risk factor: a narrative review. Headache: J. Head Face Pain **61**(9), 2021, 1306–1313. https://doi.org/10.1111/head.14213. https://headachejournal.onlinelibrary.wiley.com/doi/pdf/10.1111/head.14213
2. Traber, G.L., Piccirelli, M., Michels, L.: Visual snow syndrome: a review on diagnosis, pathophysiology, and treatment. Curr. Opin. Neurol. **33**(1), 2020, 74–78. ISSN: 1350-7540. https://journals.lww.com/co-neurology/Fulltext/2020/02000/Visual_snow_syndrome__a_review_on_diagnosis,13.aspx

---

[5] https://github.com/DamianoP/VisualSnow_NoiseGenerator.

3. Liu, G.T., Schatz, N.J., Galetta, S.L., Volpe, N.J., Skobieranda, F., Kosmorsky, G.S.: Persistent positive visual phenomena in migraine. Neurology **45**(4), 1995, 664–668. ISSN: 0028–3878. https://doi.org/10.1212/WNL.45.4.664. https://n.neurology.org/content/45/4/664.full.pdf
4. Riva, C.E., Petrig, B.: Blue field entoptic phenomenon and blood velocity in the retinal capillaries. J. Opt. Soc. Am. **70**(10), 1234–1238 (1980). https://opg.optica.org/abstract.cfm?URI=josa-70-10-1234. https://doi.org/10.1364/JOSA.70.001234
5. Sinclair, S.H., Azar-Cavanagh, M., Soper, K.A., Tuma, R.F., Mayrovitz, H.N.: Investigation of the source of the blue field entoptic phenomenon. Invest. Ophthalmol. Vis. Sci. **30**(4), 668–673 (1989). ISSN: 1552–5783. https://arvojournals.org/arvo/content_public/journal/iovs/933148/668.pdf
6. Puledda, F., Schankin, C., Digre, K., Goadsby, P.J.: Visual snow syndrome: what we know so far. Curr. Opin. Neurol. **31**(1) (2018). ISSN: 1350–7540. https://journals.lww.com/co-neurology/Fulltext/2018/02000/Visual_snow_syndrome__what_we_know_so_far.9.aspx
7. Gervasi, O., Perri, D., Simonetti, M., Tasso, S.: Strategies for the digitalization of cultural heritage. In: Gervasi, O., Murgante, B., Misra, S., Rocha, A.M.A.C., Garau, C. (eds.) Computational Science and Its Applications - ICCSA 2022 Workshops. ecture Notes in Computer Science, vol. 13382, pp. 486–502. Springer, Cham (2022). https://doi.org/10.1007/978-3-031-10592-0_35 ISBN: 978-3-031-10592-0
8. Santucci, F., Frenguelli, F., De Angelis, A., Cuccaro, I., Perri, D., Simonetti, M.: An immersive open source environment using Godot. In: Gervasi, O., et al. (eds.) ICCSA 2020. LNCS, vol. 12255, pp. 784–798. Springer, Cham (2020). https://doi.org/10.1007/978-3-030-58820-5_56
9. Perri, D., Simonetti, M., Gervasi, O.: Synthetic data generation to speed-up the object recognition pipeline. Electronics **11**(1) (2022). ISSN: 2079–9292. https://www.mdpi.com/2079-9292/11/1/2. https://doi.org/10.3390/electronics11010002
10. Perri, D., Simonetti, M., Gervasi, O., Amato, N.: A Mobile app to help people affected by visual snow. In: Gervasi, O., Murgante, B., Misra, S., Rocha, A.M.A.C., Garau, C. (eds.) Computational Science and Its Applications - ICCSA 2022 Workshops, ICCSA 2022, pp. 473–485. Springer Cham (2022). https://doi.org/10.1007/978-3-031-10592-0_34
11. Perri, D., Simonetti, M., Gervasi, O., Tasso, S.: Chapter 4 - high-performance computing and computational intelligence applications with a multi-chaos perspective. In: Karaca, Y., Baleanu, D., Zhang, Y. D., Gervasi, O., Moonis, M. (Eds.) Multi-Chaos, Fractal and Multi-Fractional Artificial Intelligence of Different Complex Systems, pp. 55–76. Academic Press (2022). ISBN: 978-0-323-90032- 4. https://doi.org/10.1016/B978-0-323-90032-4.00010-9. https://www.sciencedirect.com/science/article/pii/B9780323900324000109
12. Perri, D., Simonetti, M., Tasso, S., Gervasi, O.: Learning mathematics in an immersive way. In: Castro, L.M., Cabrero, D., Heimgärtner, R. (eds.) Software Usability. IntechOpen, Rijeka (2021). https://doi.org/10.5772/intechopen.96533
13. Simonetti, M., Perri, D., Amato, N., Gervasi, O.: Teaching math with the help of virtual reality. In: Gervasi, O., et al. (eds.) ICCSA 2020. LNCS, vol. 12255, pp. 799–809. Springer, Cham (2020). https://doi.org/10.1007/978-3-030-58820-5_57
14. Perri, D., Simonetti, M., Lombardi, A., Faginas-Lago, N., Gervasi, O.: Binary classification of proteins by a machine learning approach. In: Gervasi, O., et al. (eds.) ICCSA 2020. LNCS, vol. 12255, pp. 549–558. Springer, Cham (2020). https://doi.org/10.1007/978-3-030-58820-5_41

15. Labini, P.S., et al.: On the anatomy of predictive models for accelerating GPU convolution Kernels and beyond. ACM Trans. Archit. Code Optim. **18**(1), 1–24 (2021). ISSN: 1544–3566. https://doi.org/10.1145/3434402
16. Perri, D., Simonetti, M., Lombardi, A., Faginas-Lago, N., Gervasi, O.: A new method for binary classification of proteins with machine learning. In: Gervasi, O., et al. (eds.) ICCSA 2021. LNCS, vol. 12958, pp. 388–397. Springer, Cham (2021). https://doi.org/10.1007/978-3-030-87016-4_29
17. Benedetti, P., Perri, D., Simonetti, M., Gervasi, O., Reali, G., Femminella, M.: Skin cancer classification using inception network and transfer learning. In: Gervasi, O., et al. (eds.) ICCSA 2020. LNCS, vol. 12249, pp. 536–545. Springer, Cham (2020). https://doi.org/10.1007/978-3-030-58799-4_39
18. Laganà, A., Gervasi, O., Tasso, S., Perri, D., Franciosa, F.: The ECTN virtual education community prosumer model for promoting and assessing chemical knowledge. In: Gervasi, O., et al. (eds.) ICCSA 2018. LNCS, vol. 10964, pp. 533–548. Springer, Cham (2018). https://doi.org/10.1007/978-3-319-95174-4_42
19. Perri, D., Simonetti, M., Tasso, S., Ragni, F., Gervasi, O.: Implementing a scalable and elastic computing environment based on cloud containers. In: Gervasi, O., et al. (eds.) ICCSA 2021. LNCS, vol. 12949, pp. 676–689. Springer, Cham (2021). https://doi.org/10.1007/978-3-030-86653-2_49
20. Perri, D., Simonetti, M., Gervasi, O.: Deploying efficiently modern applications on cloud. Electronics **11**(3), 450 (2022). ISSN: 2079–9292. https://www.mdpi.com/2079-9292/11/3/450. https://doi.org/10.3390/electronics11030450
21. Perri, D., Fortunelli, M., Simonetti, M., Magni, R., Carloni, J., Gervasi, O.: Rapid prototyping of virtual reality cognitive exercises in a tele-rehabilitation context. Electronics **10**(4), 457 (2021). ISSN: 2079–9292. https://www.mdpi.com/2079-9292/10/4/457. https://doi.org/10.3390/electronics10040457
22. Perri, D., Simonetti, M., Gervasi, O.: Deploying serious games for cognitive rehabilitation. Computers **11**(7), 103 (2022). ISSN: 2073–431X. https://www.mdpi.com/2073-431X/11/7/103. https://doi.org/10.3390/computers11070103
23. Puledda, F., Schankin, C., Goadsby, P.J.: Visual snow syndrome. Neurology **94**(6), e564–e574 (2020). ISSN: 0028–3878. https://n.neurology.org/content/94/6/e564.full.pdf. https://doi.org/10.1212/WNL.0000000000008909
24. Milston, R., Madigan, M.C., Sebag, J.: Vitreous floaters: etiology, diagnostics, and management. Surv. Ophthalmol. **61**(2), 211–227 (2016). ISSN: 0039–6257. https://doi.org/10.1016/j.survophthal.2015.11.008. https://www.sciencedirect.com/science/article/pii/S003962571530014X
25. Cipolletta, S., Beccarello, A., Galan, A.: A psychological perspective of eye floaters. Qual. Health Res. **22**(11), 1547–1558 (2012). PMID: 22910587. https://doi.org/10.1177/1049732312456604
26. Virsu, V., Laurinen, P.: Long-lasting afterimages caused by neural adaptation. Vis. Res. **17**(7), 853–860 (1977). ISSN: 0042–6989. https://doi.org/10.1016/0042-6989(77)90129-8. https://www.sciencedirect.com/science/article/pii/0042698977901298
27. Katz, B.J., Digre, K.B.: Diagnosis, pathophysiology, and treatment of photophobia. Surv. Ophthalmol. **61**(4), 466–477 (2016). ISSN: 0039–6257. https://doi.org/10.1016/j.survophthal.2016.02.001. https://www.sciencedirect.com/science/article/pii/S0039625715300072
28. Kondziella, D., Olsen, M.H., Dreier, J.P.: Prevalence of visual snow syndrome in the UK. Eur. J. Neurol. **27**(5), 764–772 (2020). https://doi.org/10.1111/ene.14150. https://onlinelibrary.wiley.com/doi/pdf/10.1111/ene.14150. https://onlinelibrary.wiley.com/doi/abs/10.1111/ene.14150

Evolution of Applications: From Natively Installed to Web and Decentralized

Adrian Petcu$^{(\boxtimes)}$ ⓘ, Madalin Frunzete, and Dan Alexandru Stoichescu

Faculty of Electronics, Telecommunications, and Information Technology,
University Politehnica of Bucharest, Bucharest, Romania
adrian.petcu@stud.etti.upb.ro
https://sdetti.upb.ro/

Abstract. Applications evolve from year to year either to fit consumer needs or to increase productivity and simplify work for developers. With the rapid development of web technologies, there has been a significant shift towards web applications as a means to distribute software instead of traditional, installable packages. This paper analyses the evolution of applications along with challenges and strategies to overcome them. More specifically, we discuss the trend of applications being shifted to online versions rather than native-oriented ones, which must be installed on the users' devices. Comparisons for performance and speed of development have been studied, considering current limitations and advantages/disadvantages. Ultimately, we conclude that while transitioning to web applications requires careful planning and execution, the benefits of this shift make it a worthwhile endeavor for many organizations.

Keywords: evolution · application · native · native · pwa · web3

1 Introduction

Throughout the past few decades, software distribution has seen significant evolution. Formerly, software was distributed via installable packages, requiring manual installation on each device, whereas, currently, software applications take the form of websites. The introduction of web technologies has led to a shift toward web applications accessed via a web browser and do not require installation. This change offers various benefits, including more straightforward accessibility, enhanced scalability, and decreased maintenance expenses. In addition, consumers' ability to use web applications from any device with an internet connection has increased their popularity.

As a result, more and more businesses are considering migrating their programs from installable packages to online applications. Nevertheless, this change presents several obstacles, including technological needs, user experience, and cultural and organizational constraints. This study examines these obstacles and proposes solutions for migrating from installable packages to web applications successfully. By identifying these obstacles and options, companies can make

O. Gervasi et al. (Eds.): ICCSA 2023 Workshops, LNCS 14104, pp. 253–270, 2023.
https://doi.org/10.1007/978-3-031-37105-9_18

educated decisions regarding whether or not to migrate their applications and how to do so successfully.

Transitioning applications from native platforms to the web poses several user experience and technical challenges. This transition can be further explored in the area of achieving decentralization using blockchain. In the first section, we explore the evolution of applications, their contents, and the types of applications. Further on, we explore challenges posed by migrating applications, and we conclude with a performance analysis of a popular document editing application available both as an installable package and as a web application, measuring the time required to open documents and RAM consumption.

2   Applications

An application is any material (software or hardware) designed for end-users to use in order to fulfill specific needs or for entertainment. Initially, the term "application" in the software world referred to bundles of code written in various programming languages (C++, Java, etc.) meant to be executed on a device containing an operating system (Windows/Linux).

Operating systems are system software designed to ensure proper functionality of a hardware device (personal computer, laptop, mobile phone) and provide common services for applications. For example, an application designed to interact with hardware peripherals (mouse, keyboard) would communicate with the operating system and not with the device directly.

Applications usually require "installation" on the operating system as a step before being executed and used. As a user, you would have to download the bundle (executable), install it (or unpackage it), and execute the entry point of the application (an executable file ".exe" or ".sh"), then the entry point would manage the dependencies and static assets.

Users would have to verify the source of the application in order to protect themselves from malicious software design to gain control of their operating system and personal data.

2.1   Application Package Contents

Application bundles usually follow the same pattern - an entry point, libraries, and static assets. The entry point of an application, depending on the technology, is an executable file or a simple HTML (Hyper-Text-Markup-Language) file.

The installation step of an application consists of unpacking a file in a user-predefined location along with adding entries in the operating system for the proper functioning of the application (user settings and low-level configurations) in the registry.

When installing Windows OS-based applications, low-level configurations are stored in the Windows Registry, which is a hierarchical database designed to store information, settings, and options for applications and hardware. For example, when a program is installed, a new subkey containing settings such as a program's location, its version, and how to start the program are all added to the Windows Registry.

For Linux-based applications, the installation step is simplified as there is no central "registry" of configurations for the applications. Unpacking the application bundle contents into a predefined user folder will suffice as the configuration files and settings are stored in the same folder as the application.

As presented in Fig. 1 applications usually have a single entry point and may contain multiple layers in which the information is organized. File types may vary between libraries, binary executables, configurations, and internal storage.

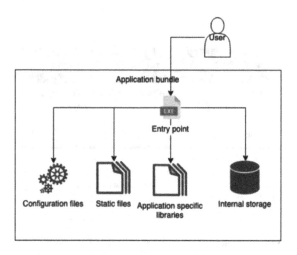

Fig. 1. Application bundle contents

2.2   Types of Applications

As stated in the previous part, applications rely on operating systems to provide core functionality and access to hardware. With the rapid expansion of the internet and its benefits, several types of applications have become available for end-users.

Native, User-Installed Applications. These applications require a physical device where the user manually performs the installation step, whether by downloading an executable and running it or by using a third-party application designed to download and install applications (e.g., Windows Store, Google Play, Apple AppStore) [7].

User-installed applications require regular updates to protect the user from potential security breaches and bring new features and functionalities.

Depending on the nature of the application, internet connectivity is not required. The user can benefit from the feature in an isolated environment with fast response [9] and interaction as there are no other dependencies. Hardware resources and storage would become problematic if the desired application performed multiple tasks demanding more storage and computational memory. For example, from one version to another, the user might encounter a situation requiring upgrading his hardware/operating system to continue using the application.

Web-Based Applications. Web-based applications mimic the behavior and interaction of a typical native application but with limited or no access to physical hardware.

Fig. 2. Website from 1996

Due to browser limitations, web-based applications were initially trivial and provided a not-so-friendly user experience as the user would have to wait between screens [3] as seen in Fig. 2. Compared with native applications, where the end-user would get instant feedback, this was considered a disadvantage. With the evolution of browsers, applications did not require the user to wait for a full-page refresh to continue to the next screen. This provided a bridge between native applications and web-based applications in which the users would benefit from faster feedback.

The main difference between a web-based and a user-installed application is the installation step. The end-user must only access a web page to start using the application, skipping the installation step (procuring the installable package, running it, configuring the product, etc.). Resources and storage would no longer be a problem as the web server would handle the computational and storage load and only static resources and plain text would be sent to the user. The evolution of browsers paved the way for hardware interaction, such that users could access and interact with physical hardware like cameras, file systems, etc.

Web applications can be accessed anywhere and from any device as long as it has a browser installed. The information is saved in real-time [12], and hand-off can be made quickly between devices to continue working on the task at hand from a different device, thus, increasing mobility. Even though web applications provide easy access to the user, they are costly to the entity hosting them. The computational and hardware resources which initially were the responsibility of the end-user now lie in the responsibility of the server hosting the application, which means that the costs of maintaining and hosting the applications would be transferred to the application owner.

Unlike regular personal computers, application servers can scale when the load increases to keep the response time in parameters for an increase in user number and even for surges like multiple users accessing the web app after clicking an advert. Server scaling can be either vertical, which means increasing the resources of a particular server (RAM, CPU, storage), or horizontal, which means creating more virtual instances of the same server to handle the temporary increase in requests as seen in Fig. 3.

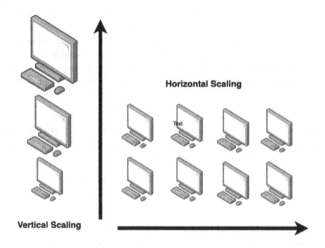

Fig. 3. Horizontal vs vertical scaling

Hybrid Web Applications. These applications combine the benefits of web-based and native applications, providing offline availability and one source code for all platforms, making the development of applications more accessible. Hybrid web applications are written primarily on web-oriented programming languages (HTML, CSS, JS) and are executed within a browser extended to communicate with the native elements of the specific device [5].

For example, communication with the camera or surfing through the phone agenda can be achieved using the cross-native library already developed by third-party vendors, thus enabling interaction with the native hardware from the web application.

The main advantage of hybrid application development has mostly been based on the philosophy of write-once, run everywhere where companies would try to create a cross-platform application using a single code base [13]. Hybrid applications can be distributed through app stores like native applications and are typically developed using frameworks like Apache Cordova, PhoneGap, and Ionic/Capacitor.

Developing hybrid mobile applications becomes more and more accessible as developers oriented on web development can be assigned to mobile development projects in no time as the initial setup is fast and code is written in widely known frameworks like (Angular, React, and Vue).

Table 1. Advantages of hybrid web and native applications

Application	Advantages	Disadvantages
Web Hybrid	– Uses Web technologies – Write once deploy anywhere – Large developer community – Offline support	– Lower performance – Limited access to native features – Dependance on 3rd party frameworks – Limited offline access
Native	– High Performance – Access to native functionality – Improved user experience – Offline capabilities	– Platform-specific development – App distribution – Limited cross-platform capabilities – Higher development costs

As we can observe from Table 1, there are some disadvantages of developing hybrid web applications, generated mainly by the smoothness of the transitions in the UI and the general consistency [6] with the native elements like menus, dropdowns, and selectors but also in performance and native functionality access.

To close the gap between hybrid web and native development, there are some frameworks that allow developers to write code only once and build/bundle the code for multiple devices. The general layout of these applications is written in a meta-syntax which is converted by tools in native code, and, by selecting the desired OS output [17], the framework will generate the application bundle for the specific OS (Windows, Android, iOS).

Progressive Web Applications (PWA). Developing multiple platforms has become a popular alternative for companies without resources or wanting to hire specialized mobile developers for each target platform. Until recently, the web platform lagged behind mobile-centric innovation [1] in its ability to compete with native applications or multiple platforms. Instead, a new set of standards backed by the Google Web Fundamentals group is trying to bridge this gap by introducing features such as offline support, background synchronization, and installation on the web home screen [19] (very similar to how native applications behave).

Progressive Web Applications (PWA) refers to a term created by Russel and Bermanan (2015) in a blog post that covers initial implementation ideas. PWAs are defined by a set of concepts and keywords, including progressive, responsive, independent of connectivity, application-like, fresh, secure, discoverable, reusable, installable, and connectable (Addy Osmani, 2015).

These are PWA's contributions to unifying the mobile experience, where web applications can be installed and distributed without application markets, work without Internet connectivity, receive push notifications [4] and look like native applications.

PWAs would be a better alternative to both native applications and hybrid web applications. For example, both would require installing and searching with an internet search engine that would not find application-specific content meaning that application owners [10] would lose traffic as install conversion would be low, plus the applications with content could not be found via a search engine.

The core of PWA's functionality is assured by the Service Worker API, which allows developers to use a background script that acts as a network and device proxy.

The advantages of using progressive web applications are as follows:

1. Offline functionality
2. Great performance (seamless transitions and page loads)
3. No installation and updates are required (installing is done by saving the link to the homepage, which then acts like an app)
4. Platform-specific features (push notifications)
5. Low data consumption
6. App store independent
7. Discoverable (appear in search engines)
8. Linkable (installing an app is just navigating to a specific link)
9. Responsive (adapt to the browser size)

2.3   Advantages and Disadvantages of User-Installed Applications

User-installed applications generally require the user to own the hardware on which the application is installed. However, in the fast-evolving world of the internet, this is a significant disadvantage. Some applications provide online synchronization of users' configurations and contents. However, to access that information [2], the user must install the same application on multiple devices connected to the internet.

There is also the problem of version compatibility. Often users need to keep the application's version installed on multiple devices [14] in sync to benefit from internet synchronization. This provides discomfort for the end-user as he needs to check and install the latest version of the application regularly.

The information stored on local devices is often lost in case of a hardware malfunction or natural disasters. This results in a very low resilience, and for

Table 2. Advantages and disadvantages of user-installed applications

Advantages	Disadvantages
– Application isolation for highly sensitive documents – No need for internet connection and synchronization	– Low level of resilience – Version compatibility – Regular application updates need to be installed – Access to user documents is limited by hardware – Cannot be accessed unless the application is installed

the user to protect himself against such events, he might be needed to perform regular backups [8] of the data and configuration (if the application provides such functionality).

From the data security point of view, applications installed on personal hardware are more secure as the user can decide whether to connect the device to the internet. The user can interact with the application in isolation on a local machine if the information is highly sensitive.

As presented in the Table 2 there are several advantages and disadvantages to using a user-installed application compared to web applications.

3   User Experience and Technical Challenges

It has been shown that the user experience (UX) of software has a substantial influence on adoption and usage. As enterprises contemplate migrating their programs from installable packages to online applications, it is crucial to consider their impact on user experience (UX). There are multiple technical considerations involved in achieving a migration of software from the choice of technologies to security. This chapter presents an overview of the most significant user experience (UX) difficulties posed by the move to online applications as well as the technical difficulties associated with techniques for overcoming them.

3.1   User Experience

Challenges. The transition from installable packages to online applications presents a number of UX difficulties. Performance poses a significant concern. Web applications may be slower than locally installed applications due to factors such as network latency, server load, and browser compatibility issues. This can lead to resistance from users as locally installed applications might be faster and more responsive to user commands.

Online applications usually require an internet connection to operate, limiting their use in regions with poor access. In addition, web applications may not offer the same functionality or capabilities as locally installed software, resulting in user frustration and resistance. While switching to online applications, users may be required to learn new interfaces or procedures, which can be complex and time-consuming.

Strategy. Numerous techniques can be used to overcome the UX difficulties posed by the migration to online applications. One strategy is performance optimization. This involves approaches for improving the performance of online applications, including server-side rendering, caching, and minification. Providing offline access to web applications is another method [20]. This may be accomplished with service workers and local data caching, as presented previously using PWA.

Feature parity is another essential factor to consider as users might get frustrated if features are missing from an application that is intended to replace a legacy solution. Using native browser APIs and frameworks is one method for guaranteeing that online applications have the same capabilities and functionality as locally installed applications.

Users can adjust to new interfaces or processes with the aid of user training and assistance. Techniques for offering training materials, tutorials, and support resources can simplify the shift to online applications.

Device Hand-Off Between Applications. Working with installed applications might not be very convenient if the user is always on the move and must shift from one device to another in order to continue work.

The term hand-off or handover originally came from the ability of cellular networks to transfer an ongoing call or data session from one channel connected to the core network to another channel for the phone user to have a seamless experience during a call and in transit.

At the time of writing this article, application hand-off allows users with devices with the same core operating system to instantly shift from one device to another for basic actions and applications (writing emails, surfing the web). Operating systems provide this functionality for core applications as it requires elevated access to the operating system kernel. Application developers are provided with access and documentation to implement this feature, but a limited number of applications do so.

3.2 Technical Requirements

Challenges. Transitioning from installable packages to online applications presents several technological difficulties. Data security is a significant challenge. Cross-site scripting (XSS) and SQL injection may make online applications more susceptible to attack than locally installed programs. This might result in data breaches and other security problems, which can be mitigated with careful consideration of the differences between online environments and local environments.

Another area for improvement is data storage. Online applications may require a different approach to data storage than locally installed programs, posing a challenge for enterprises with an established data architecture. In addition, online applications require additional resources than locally installed programs, which can be costly and require the purchase of expensive hardware or cloud infrastructure.

Access to specific machine data is also an important factor to consider, as some factory applications might require interaction with machinery in order to extract data and act according to it.

Limitations of web browsers for more complex actions performed by specialized applications is another factor to consider when migrating applications to a web environment. Connectivity to computer ports to interact with hardware might also present a challenge.

Strategy. Various approaches might be utilized to address the technical difficulties associated with the migration to online applications. Using secure development methods, such as regular code reviews, penetration testing, and encryption is one strategy, similar to the ways of work when developing a native application. Using secure hosting and cloud infrastructure [18] is another method. This usually involves utilizing suppliers with robust security protocols and updating software and systems regularly.

Data splitting and encryption can be employed to handle data storage. Using techniques like server-side rendering and caching, it is possible to optimize performance and improve user experience. Lastly, resource demands can be met via strategies such as load balancing and auto-scaling.

4 Web3 and Decentralization

4.1 Web3

As previously researched, Web3 is based on blockchain technology [16], a decentralized and immutable ledger that enables secure and transparent transactions without the need for intermediaries. Web3 uses blockchain technology to provide decentralized data storage, identity management, and user-to-user transactions.

As opposed to Web2, also known as the "Social Web" which is the current stage of the internet which is rather dominated by social media, mobile devices and cloud computing, web3 has a strong focus on decentralization and open web.

The most popular stack for developing decentralized applications relies on the Ethereum Virtual Machine (EVM) blockchain platform which benefits the support of numerous APIs and libraries that help application developers achieve their goals in a shorter amount of time.

Ethereum is a public blockchain that allows decentralized applications to be deployed and run inside it [15]. Smart contracts are the most significant enablers for transitioning to a decentralized application as they allow developers to write code directly in the blockchain. They execute automatically and autonomously when specific predetermined conditions are met. In the Ethereum context, smart contracts are written in a high-level programming language named Solidity and are compiled into bytecode that can be executed on the EVM.

As seen in Fig. 4 Web3 heavily relies on peer-to-peer interaction and decentralization of data, thus, reducing the risk of having a single source of truth or failure.

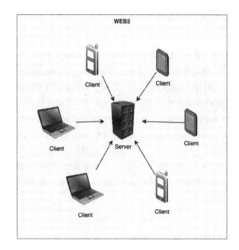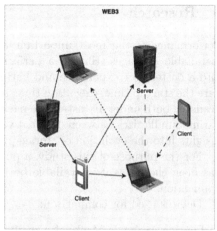

Fig. 4. Web2 vs Web3

4.2   Key Points into Transitioning to a Decentralized Infrastructure

The transition from Web2 to Web3 involves a substantial move toward decentralization and an analysis of the core business of the application in scope must be taken into consideration before proceeding with the transition. Applications designed for private use inside a company may benefit from a decentralized architecture since the nature of blockchain transactions relies on immutability, thus, better tracking of resources can be put in place.

When migrating to a public blockchain and a decentralized architecture, governance, security, interoperability, and privacy must be considered.

From a governance perspective, the nature of Web3 implies that there should not be any controlling authority; instead, decisions should be made by consensus among network participants. Transparency of the governance is important and it should be inclusive and open to all network participants.

Since using a public blockchain involves that data is public, a proper audit of the smart contracts should be put in place to avoid any attacks. Secure communication between the application and the blockchain should be considered.

Applications designed to run in a decentralized environment must consider that Web3 networks are interoperable, meaning they can communicate and share data with other networks. The adoption of open standards and protocols should be considered to ensure that the application operates as designed and can be seamlessly integrated with other networks.

Web3 networks must protect the privacy of network participants while also ensuring transparency and accountability. Scenarios in which the full identity of a user is not known are often and might require changing the business logic of the intended application to allow anonymous participants.

5   Research

Performance is the most important aspect of web applications compared to installable packages. Having a performant application can also be translated into a better user experience and better productivity. This study aims to compare the startup time, execution time, and memory usage of an application being available both under an installable package form as well a web application. Comparing bundle sizes between different versions of the same product might provide insights into the evolution of storage required to run a specific application.

For the purpose of this study, a popular document editing software solution has been chosen as it is available both as an installable package and as a web application.

Devices used for comparison:

- **Device 1:** Apple Macbook Pro, 13 in., CPU: Apple M2, Memory: 32 GB
- **Device 2:** Apple Macbook Pro, 16 in., CPU: Apple M1 Max, Memory: 64 GB

Internet connectivity:

- 230 Mbps, Bucharest, Romania

Browser:

- Google Chrome, Version 111.0.5563.64 (arm64)

Running multiple simulations of opening a file using both laptops and both solutions will provide valuable insights into the performance difference between the online version and the user-installed version of the same application.

Time to first paint and RAM consumption are essential factors to consider [11] as they provide information regarding the user experience. Browser resource caching has not been deactivated, and the installed application has been completely closed after each file opens.

6   Results

The study has been carried out successfully using two different types of files (small and large) - 390kb and 32MB. Comparing the loading times and RAM consumption on both devices offers a good overview of the differences.

User reaction times and network request times have been measured in order to observe whether the online version of the same application loads faster compared to the locally-installed version.

The time spent opening the files has been measured from the start of the process (double-click the executable file for the natively installed application and click the link for the web application) to the time when the document becomes first interactive for some 20 consecutive runs using the two mentioned devices.

Calculation of relative improvement has been achieved using Eq. 1 formula, where N represents the new value and O represents the original value.

$$RI = \frac{N - O}{O} \tag{1}$$

It has been observed that using the installed application, the time spent opening a small file is an average of 3.994 s, while opening the same file on the web version has an average of 2.160 s on **Device 1**. Running the same tests on a larger file, the average load time for the native app was 4.396 s compared to the web version, which had an average of 3.032 s. This represents a 45.93% respectively 31.03% improvement in time spent on the online version compared to the installed application as seen in Fig. 5a. Overall average time decrease has been roughly 38%.

RAM consumption on **Device 1** for the operation of opening the two files using the local application has been observed to have an average of 351MB and 367MB for the small and large files, while for the web version, averages were 227MB and 239MB respectively which represents an average of 36% less RAM consumption as seen in Fig. 6a.

Running the same tests on **Device 2** apart from the overall decrease in time spent compared to **Device 1** (which is expected since the specifications of the devices are different), we have observed that opening the small file on the native application and on the web version took an average of 2.640 s and 1.282 s respectively. For the larger file, the results were 2.836 s and 1.630 s. An average 51.43% respectively 42.5% decrease in time spent has been observed. Overall the time decreased by 47%. Figure 5b shows the evolution of tests on device 2.

RAM consumption on **Device 2** for the operations using the local application has been observed to have an average of 250 MB and 262 MB for the small and large files, while for the web version, averages were 275 MB and 205MB respectively which represents an average of 6.25% less RAM consumption as seen in Fig. 6b.

The expected time for performing both operations, using the web application and the locally installed application, may vary based on network load, internet speed, and device load.

Computing the results, we can assume that using the web version of the same application requires 42% less time until the application becomes interactive and RAM consumption is 20% smaller.

7 Discussion

Migrating applications to a web version might bring many benefits to both private and public companies. As presented in this paper, many of the advantages outweigh the disadvantages as internet connectivity is relatively common and internet speed improves from year to year.

Limitations in terms of hardware interaction can be overcome with the rapid development and evolution of browsers. Security should always be a priority when migrating to an online environment since internet connectivity might expose potential vulnerabilities inside organizations.

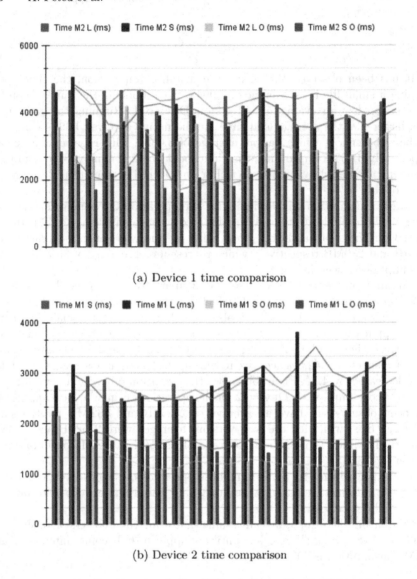

(a) Device 1 time comparison

(b) Device 2 time comparison

Fig. 5. Time spent till interactive. S: Small File, L: Large file, O: Web application, M1: Device 1, M2: Device 2

Removing the need to install an application and quickly accessing it using a link provides faster onboarding to both new customers and employees. Results show that the studied application performs better on the web version, most likely due to caching and better optimization. Nevertheless, this cannot be generalized for all applications, especially those requiring lots of computational and GPU power.

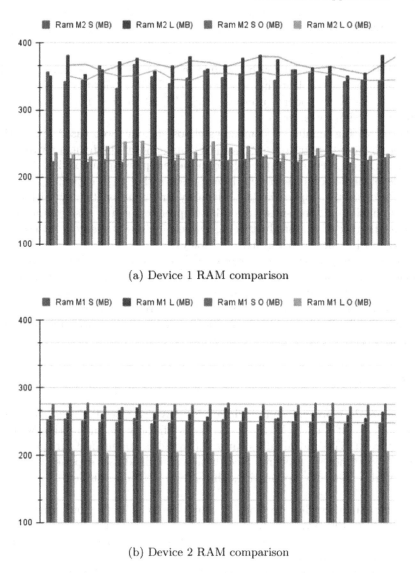

(a) Device 1 RAM comparison

(b) Device 2 RAM comparison

Fig. 6. RAM Consumption. S: Small File, L: Large file, O: Web application, M1: Device 1, M2: Device 2

Migrating applications to an online version might bring more benefits than advantages, but a thorough assessment needs to be made before deciding to migrate applications (e.g., Specialized applications for factories and 3d graphic design).

These challenges are an intriguing expansion for this study, and the authors want to broaden the results of the current work by expanding the research to include a more in-depth review of the migration implications.

7.1 Current Trends

Many companies choose to migrate their products online due to the fact that they can reach more clients with a simple registration and payment step rather than downloading and installing the product. This provides flexibility and ease of user access in a modern, user-friendly GUI in the web browser and offers better conversion rates.

An increasing number of companies choose to offer web-based applications nowadays rather than native ones, as developing and maintaining a native application can be cumbersome, especially from the manpower point of view. However, more developers specialize in web development rather than native.

Updates to the application functionality are done on the fly without the user's manual input, and subscription-based products can be easily implemented without the risk of the product being hacked (access is granted via username and password rather than through a CD-key).

The operating system is no longer considered an issue, as all user interaction is done using the browser. However, some applications may require more system resources to perform complex tasks.

Even though implementing PWA standards is straightforward and brings benefits by default, such applications are not marketed as such due to the lack of popularity.

8 Conclusions

As software development and the internet evolve, so does the need to keep up with the current trends. In the early times of software, interaction with the systems was trivial and mainly achieved through a command terminal. Recent trends rely on modern user interfaces with a simplified user experience as interaction with day-to-day applications shifts from desktop-installed to web applications.

In this paper, we have provided an overview of the previous, current, and future state of the development of applications, both native and web. We have studied the current state of development and preferred approaches. In addition, studied the trends and directions for the software development of applications.

Furthermore, the decentralization of the application and its implication has been studied and key points on performing this step have been taken into account and documented.

Shifting an application from desktop-installed to web poses many challenges, which have been outlined in the presented sections. Directions to overcome those challenges have been considered for every specific scenario.

A study has been carried out to compare the time spent on performing a similar task on both a desktop-installed and a web version of the same piece of software. The results show that the web application loaded faster and consumed fewer resources than the desktop version.

References

1. Biørn-Hansen, A., Majchrzak, T.A., Grønli, T.-M.: Progressive web apps for the unified development of mobile applications. In: Majchrzak, T.A., Traverso, P., Krempels, K.-H., Monfort, V. (eds.) WEBIST 2017. LNBIP, vol. 322, pp. 64–86. Springer, Cham (2018). https://doi.org/10.1007/978-3-319-93527-0_4
2. Despa, M.L.: Comparative study on software development methodologies. Database Syst. J. **5**(3), 37–56 (2014)
3. Dingli, A., Seychell, D.: The New Digital Natives. JB Metzler, Stuttgart (2015)
4. Fortunato, D., Bernardino, J.: Progressive web apps: an alternative to the native mobile apps. In: 2018 13th Iberian Conference on Information Systems and Technologies (CISTI), pp. 1–6. IEEE (2018)
5. Georgiev, M., Jana, S., Shmatikov, V.: Breaking and fixing origin-based access control in hybrid web/mobile application frameworks. In: NDSS symposium, vol. 2014, p. 1. NIH Public Access (2014)
6. Gonsalves, M.: Evaluating the mobile development frameworks Apache Cordova and Flutter and their impact on the development process and application characteristics. California State University, Chico (2019)
7. Ickin, S., Petersen, K., Gonzalez-Huerta, J.: Why do users install and delete apps? A survey study. In: Ojala, A., Holmström Olsson, H., Werder, K. (eds.) ICSOB 2017. LNBIP, vol. 304, pp. 186–191. Springer, Cham (2017). https://doi.org/10.1007/978-3-319-69191-6_13
8. Jazayeri, M.: Some trends in web application development. In: Future of Software Engineering (FOSE 2007), pp. 199–213. IEEE (2007)
9. Jobe, W.: Native apps vs. mobile web apps. Int. J. Interact. Mob. Technol. **7**(4) (2013)
10. Kotane, I., Znotina, D., Hushko, S.: Assessment of trends in the application of digital marketing. Sci. J. Polonia Univ. **33**(2), 28–35 (2019)
11. Kounev, S., Lange, K.D., von Kistowski, J.: Systems Benchmarking: For Scientists and Engineers, vol. 1. Springer, Heidelberg (2020)
12. Lim, S.H.: Experimental comparison of hybrid and native applications for mobile systems. Int. J. Multimed. Ubiquit. Eng. **10**(3), 1–12 (2015)
13. Malavolta, I., Ruberto, S., Soru, T., Terragni, V.: Hybrid mobile apps in the Google play store: an exploratory investigation. In: 2015 2nd ACM International Conference on Mobile Software Engineering and Systems, pp. 56–59. IEEE (2015)
14. Montelius, A.: An exploratory study of micro frontends. Master's thesis, Linköping University, Software and Systems (2021)
15. Panda, S.K., Satapathy, S.C.: An investigation into smart contract deployment on Ethereum platform using Web3.js and solidity using blockchain. In: Bhateja, V., Satapathy, S.C., Travieso-González, C.M., Aradhya, V.N.M. (eds.) Data Engineering and Intelligent Computing. AISC, vol. 1407, pp. 549–561. Springer, Singapore (2021). https://doi.org/10.1007/978-981-16-0171-2_52
16. Petcu, A., Pahontu, B., Frunzete, M., Stoichescu, D.A.: A secure and decentralized authentication mechanism based on Web 3.0 and Ethereum blockchain technology. Appl. Sci. **13**(4), 2231 (2023)
17. Qu, C., Calheiros, R.N., Buyya, R.: Auto-scaling web applications in clouds: a taxonomy and survey. ACM Comput. Surv. (CSUR) **51**(4), 1–33 (2018)
18. Selvarajah, K., Craven, M.P., Massey, A., Crowe, J., Vedhara, K., Raine-Fenning, N.: Native apps versus web apps: which is best for healthcare applications? In: Kurosu, M. (ed.) HCI 2013. LNCS, vol. 8005, pp. 189–196. Springer, Heidelberg (2013). https://doi.org/10.1007/978-3-642-39262-7_22

19. Tandel, S., Jamadar, A.: Impact of progressive web apps on web app development. Int. J. Innov. Res. Sci. Eng. Technol. **7**(9), 9439–9444 (2018)
20. Torchiano, M., Ricca, F., Marchetto, A.: Are web applications more defect-prone than desktop applications? Int. J. Softw. Tools Technol. Transfer **13**, 151–166 (2011)

Hybrid Security Approach
for Behavioural Privacy of Business
Processes in a Cloud Environment

Farah Abdmeziem[1]([envelope]) [iD], Saida Boukhedouma[1],
and Mourad Chabane Oussalah[2]

[1] LSI Laboratory, University of Science and Technology Houari Boumediene,
Algiers, Algeria
{fabdmeziem,sboukhedouma}@usthb.dz
[2] LS2N Laboratory, University of Nantes, Nantes, France
Mourad.oussalah@univ-nantes.fr

Abstract. Business processes are surely at the heart of companies but
they are also the target of numerous security attacks, especially when
using nowadays technologies like Cloud computing. Hence, ensuring business processes' security is one of the main concerns in both industry
and research area. Securing a business process involves securing its three
main aspects namely, the informational, the logical (behavioural), and
the organisational aspect. While most of the works in the literature
focus on the security of the informational aspect, Goettelmann et al.
in [9] propose an obfuscation technique that aims to guarantee explicitly
the security of the logical aspect of a business process i.e. persevering
the privacy of the company's know-how expressed through the business
process. This paper proposes an alternative solution to the obfuscation
technique that is based on the strengths of this latter while addressing
its identified limits. Our approach combines the ideas of the obfuscation
technique and security annotations. The proposed solution is described
via a metamodel that exhibits the main concepts it is based on, and a
global functional architecture describing the principal steps of the solution, mainly a deployment configuration of the business process, meeting
a set of defined constraints (and rules). A comparison between the obfuscation technique and our proposed approach according to security level
and deployment costs is also illustrated, through examples.

Keywords: Business process · Security · Multi-Cloud environment ·
Obfuscation · Security annotation · Know-how privacy · Constraints ·
Process fragment

1 Introduction

A business process (BP) is a set of tasks (activities) that are to be performed
in a logical manner by actors (human or system) using and producing resources
(data and artefacts), so as to fulfil an overall business objective. A business

O. Gervasi et al. (Eds.): ICCSA 2023 Workshops, LNCS 14104, pp. 271–289, 2023.
https://doi.org/10.1007/978-3-031-37105-9_19

process is defined through three main aspects namely the informational aspect which pertains to the data used and generated throughout the life-cycle of the business process; the logical aspect that encapsulates the company's know-how and expertise; and finally the organisational aspect which concerns the allocation of tasks to stakeholders within the company. Given that business processes are essential to a company's operations, they are often targeted by security attacks. This is especially true now that companies are increasingly leveraging new technologies such as cloud computing to build and deploy their business processes, which introduce new security risks. In this vein, in our previous work [8], we studied business processes security and we gave an overview of security mechanisms used in the literature. During our study we found out that most of research works focus on the security of the informational view [1,6,7,18] and to the best of our knowledge, the work of Goettelmann et al. in [9] is the first to focus solely on securing the logical aspect of business processes, by proposing an obfuscation technique. The present work is founded on the strengths of the obfuscation technique while seeking to address its limits. We propose an hybrid security approach by first proposing a multi-level security annotation step that consists in annotating business processes tasks with four labels namely Highly-sensitive, Sensitive, Complementary or non-sensitive according to the sensitivity degree of each task. Then, we describe a global functional architecture that exhibits all steps of the proposed solution. Specifically, we describe an algorithm to build a deployment configuration (meeting a set of defined constraints) of the business process in a set of available Clouds (multi-Cloud environment). Notice that the set of constraints (and rules) used for building a deployment configuration is checked for consistency using a SAT solver, in order to avoid constraints violation. The principal concepts of our solution are also described through a meta-model that globally outlines the links between these concepts. The remain of this paper is structured as follows: Sect. 2 gives an overview of research works proposed to ensure business processes security. In Sect. 3, we detail the obfuscation technique proposed in [9] and we highlight its strengths and limits. To palliate this limits we present, first, in Sect. 4 our meta-model that represents the core concepts of our hybrid security solution. Followed by the details of this latter in Sect. 5. Finally, we illustrate our solution on a motivating example in Sect. 6 before concluding and outlining future work directions in Sect. 7.

2   State of the Art

In this section, we give a glimpse of the approaches tackling business processes security. We categorize the proposed solutions according to the business process aspect tackled by the approach especially, the logical and the informational (data) aspects.

Security of the Informational Aspect: In [2], Altuhhova et al. propose an extension to the Business Process Modelling Language (BPMN) to take into consideration security concerns. The extension is based on Dubois et al. work [5], which propose a domain language that helps to extend different languages with the notion of risk management. Furthermore, Ahmed et al. in [1], propose a method to assign security requirements to business processes, the solution is based on risk-oriented patterns. Jensen et al. propose in [12], through three architectural patterns to achieve security in a cloud environment by using multiple distinct clouds (Multi-cloud environment). One of the patterns consist in *Partition of application system into tiers* and aims to protect from data leakage by separating the logic from data. Turki et al. propose in [20] to enrich BPMN with security notations described as padlocks. Different padlocks are proposed to match security requirements as confidentiality, integrity and, privacy. In the same vein, Rodriguez et al. in [19] also propose graphical annotations in the form of padlocks with specific codes to specify the security requirements, for example, the code CO refers to confidentiality. Another interesting solution is proposed by Watson in [22], it is based on the Bell-LaPadula Multi-level security model [4], where subjects represent the business process services and objects the data in input and output to/from the services. At last, we have the work in [10] where Goettelmann et al. propose an approach to ensure sensitive data exchange of business processes in a Cloud environment. The solution consists in transforming a centralized orchestration into a choreography under security constraints. Moreover, In [11], Han et al. propose an optimal distribution of business processes using a cloud and user-end resources, with the aim to protect sensitive data. In the same line, Pavoa et al. in [18] propose an approach to decompose business processes for cloud deployment, while preserving data safety constraints, monetary costs and performances requirements. Furthermore, the authors of [6], propose an automatic decomposition of a business process for its deployment on premises and on a Cloud resources to preserve sensitive data. At last, in [7] an approach that consists in obfuscating sensitive data before its storage in the Cloud services is proposed. The solution is based on ASCII characters to obfuscate data and reduce its size.

Security of the Logical Aspect: To protect the logical aspect, Jensen et al. in [12], propose through another architectural pattern, to split the logic into fine-grained fragments that could be deployed in distinct clouds. However, the solution does not provide specific details on how the splitting process could be carried out. On similar note, Gottelmann et al. in [9], propose a semi-automatic solution that consists in splitting the business process logic into fragments that should be deployed into distinct clouds. The fragmentation is based on the AND split and X(OR) gateways of BPMN[1]. We have built our work around this solution, and in Sect. 3, we provide further details about it. Nacer et al. in [17], go one step further and tackle the issue of malicious clouds collusion in case of deploying a business process into a multi-cloud environment. Indeed, splitting a business process into different fragments can surely preserve the know-how of companies but can not prevent from an eventual coalition between the involved clouds, to trace back the business logic. For that, Nacer et al. propose to add fake

---

[1] Business Process Modelling Notation.

fragment to the business process into strategic points, this can result in increased complexity of the business process and may require the involvement of multiple clouds, making it more challenging to orchestrate a collusion between them. In the same vein, Nacer et al. propose in [16] a metric for evaluating the privacy level of the business process logic because they claim that even though adding fake fragments can reduce cloud collusion but a risk persists and it is important to be able to measure it. Such a metric is important for cloud clients who want to compare different deployments solutions. However, adding fake fragments could result in increasing the deployment costs of the business process. Hence, in their further work Nacer et al. in [15] consider this issue and propose a solution to find a balance between costs and security risks of the logical aspect of a business process deployed in a multi-cloud environment.

3   The Obfuscation Technique

In this section, we give more details about the obfuscation technique proposed in [9] to preserve the companies know-how. After analysing a number of business processes, the authors found that sensitive tasks of a business process are those tasks where decisions are taken and where synthesis are made. Furthermore, they established a link between decisions tasks and the opening X(OR) BPMN gateways (Fig. 2) and, between synthesis tasks and, the closing AND join BPMN gateways (Fig. 1). Finally, the authors found that generally, a decision task has a complementary fragment that comes after the closing X(OR) gateway (Fig. 2) and, the complementary task of a synthesis task is, the task or fragments that triggers an AND gateway (Fig. 1).

Fig. 1. Synthesis task   **Fig. 2.** Decision task

This analysis helps to automate the detection of sensitive task. For a secure deployment of a business process in a cloud environment, the authors proposed to split the business process into fragments and to deploy them into a multi-cloud environment. The solution is based on three main constraints: the trust-level, the co-locate and the separate constraints as follows: The co-locate and separate constraints state whether two fragments of a business process can be deployed in a same or, separate clouds respectively.

1. Separate the complementary fragments;
2. Separate the different alternatives of a X(OR) split gateway.
3. Deploy the synthesis and the decision fragments in clouds providing high trust level.

The solution is applicable only in the context of well-defined BPMN-based work-flows and is based specifically, on the AND-join and X(or) split gateways whilst, the solution does not take into consideration the sequential pattern which is one of the most commonly used patterns in BPMN diagrams. Indeed, we could easily have the case of a BPMN diagram with only a sequence of sensitive tasks. Plus, while the proposed solution can provide satisfactory results in certain scenarios (e.g., when the fragments before an opening X(OR) gateway and after a closing AND gateway are highly sensitive), we contend that this is not always the case. To illustrate this point, consider the example depicted in Fig. 3, which outlines the process for creating a new customer bank account. After the evaluation of the client's supporting documents, the bank employee decides whether to accept or reject the request. In case of acceptance, an account number is allocated to the client and then, simultaneously, the service in charge of making credit card is notified and, a welcome pack for the client is prepared. At the end of the process, a notification is sent to inform the client if his/her request has been accepted or rejected. Following the proposed constraints in [9] we have come to the process partitioning depicted in Fig. 4 that shows the partitioning of the business process on three clouds. Notice the use of the tasks send/receive that allow the communication between the different fragments, which is a commonly used method in process choreographies, and the fictive task added in the exclusive OR gateway when one of the alternative is deployed on another Cloud. Hence, three clouds are needed for a secure deployment of this business process. Upon analysing the fragments or tasks that are identified as sensitive according to the Synthesis/Decision and Synthesis-dependency/decision-dependency constraints, we observe that the majority of these tasks are not actually sensitive, with the exception of the "allocate account number" task. Indeed, a bank may want to keep secret its strategy of allocating accounts to the client. Moreover, the tasks "Evaluate supporting document" and "Send final notification" are considered as dependent. However, in this case, deploying these two tasks on a same Cloud would not reveal a strategic and important information about the bank know-how. To conclude, the strengths and the drawbacks of the obfuscation technique could be summarized in the following items:

1. Strengths:
   - Automatic detection without human intervene;
   - The notion of complementary tasks is important as non-sensitive tasks once put together could reveal important know-how;
   - The separate and co-locate constraints that indicate how and where to deploy each fragment of the business process.
2. Drawbacks:
   - Relying only on the X(or) split and AND join gateways would not cover all the sensitive tasks of a business process. Hence, in some cases the fragmentation of the business process won't be efficient in term of security;

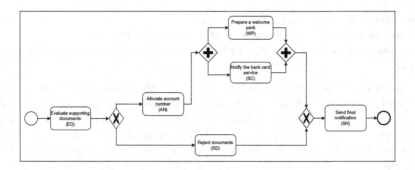

Fig. 3. BPMN process for Bank account creation

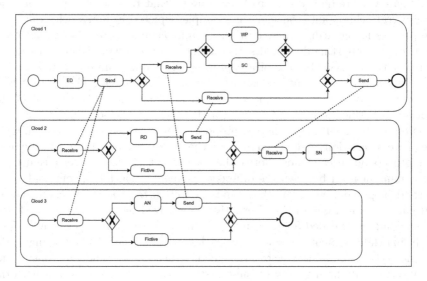

Fig. 4. Fragmentation of the bank account creation BP according to the obfuscation technique

- Conversely, sensitive tasks of a business process would not be necessarily the fragments before an opening X(OR) gateway and after a closing AND gateways;
- Same for the complementary task that could be at any location of the business process and not necessarily before/after X(OR) split and AND join gateways.

Consequently, these drawbacks can result in a fragmentation of business processes, which may not be effective in terms of security, or incurring significant costs due to the use of unnecessary multiple clouds in some cases.

In the next section, we propose an alternative solution to detect the sensitive tasks and, we enrich the proposed co-locate and separate rule and constraints, to ensure a secure deployment of business processes in a cloud environment.

4   Meta-model of Concepts: Hybrid Security Solution

Before digging into the details of our proposed approach, we introduce, first, a meta-model that serves as a conceptual foundation for our proposed security approach, which relies on the obfuscation and the annotation techniques. The meta-model, illustrated in Fig. 5, is designed to safeguard the know-how privacy of companies that are at risk of compromising their sensitive information by migrating to a cloud environment. Our hybrid approach leverages annotations to achieve this goal. Specifically, the know-how of a company is encapsulated in a business process, which can be modeled using BPMN (Business Process Modeling Notation) and is, by definition, composed of a set of tasks, and may contain X(or) /AND gateways to synchronize and link tasks. We distinguish two types of tasks namely business tasks, which encapsulate the business logic, and communication tasks, which permits the communication between different tasks. Business tasks can be annotated with sensitivity levels (i.e., highly-sensitive, sensitive, non-sensitive, or complementary). These annotations trigger security constraints "Separate," and security rules "Co-locate," between tasks. Applying these constraints and rules generates a deployable fragments of the business process. Finally, cost metrics could be used to evaluate the deployment cost of a business process in a multi-cloud environment using our hybrid security technique. This meta-model can be easily extended and instantiated to ensure the business process' behavioural privacy in a Cloud environment.

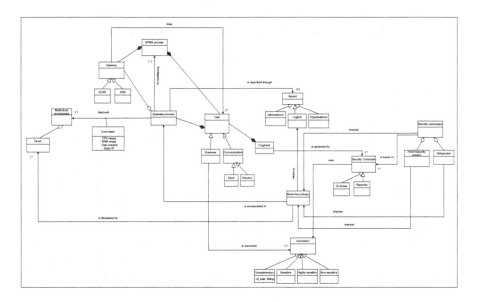

Fig. 5. Meta-model for the hybrid security solution

5   Hybrid Security Solution: Annotation and Obfuscation Based

In this section, we introduce our hybrid solution that combines security annotations and security constraints proposed in [9]. The primary aim of our solution is to secure the companies' confidential know-how encapsulated in business processes. The functional schema of our approach is depicted in Fig. 6 and comprises of four main phases: annotation, generation of constraints and rules, consistency check of the generated constraints and rules, and configuration generation. The output of each step of the process is represented with an ellipse form in Fig. 6. We provide further details on each phase in the following subsection.

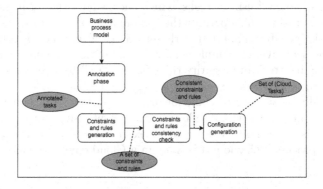

Fig. 6. Functional schema of the hybrid security solution

5.1   Annotation Phase

Annotations are a popular means of securing business processes, and they can be broadly classified into three categories: textual, graphical, and hybrid (a combination of textual and graphical). However, security annotations are often used to ensure business processes' data confidentially, integrity and availability [3,14,21]. In this work, we have managed to use textual security annotation to guarantee the privacy of the companies' know-how. Hence, a business analyst can use three annotations namely H.S: for highly-sensitive tasks, S: for Sensitive tasks, and CS for Complementary tasks to annotate the business process. In order to help the designer further in using these annotations, we give a brief definition of a highly-sensitive, sensitive and complementary tasks as follows: A **highly-sensitive** task is a task that encompasses strategic decisions or operations and at the same time, it uses or produces highly sensitive data.

A **sensitive** task is a task that either encompasses strategic decisions or uses/ produces sensitive data.

Finally, the **complementary tasks**: in line with the authors of [9], we also distinguish the complementary tasks that are tasks that could be non-sensitive in their own but if deployed together in a sequential/alternative/parallel manner they could disclose confidential information about a company's knowledge or expertise. However, in our proposed solution, we do not associate these complementary tasks with specific AND/OR gateways; instead, they could occur at any stage of the workflow.

5.2   Fragmentation Constraints and Rules

After the annotation step, fragments of the business process are generated according to a set of constraints (Separate) and rules (Co-locate). The proposed constraints in [9] were adapted based on our proposed security annotations as follows:

1. Separate (H.S,H.S): deploy a pair of highly-sensitive tasks into different clouds;
2. Deploy H.S tasks into Clouds that satisfies the security level required by the highly sensitive task;
3. Separate (Tx,CS): deploy a task Tx and its complementary task CS into different clouds;
4. Separate(S,S): deploy a pair of sensitive tasks into different clouds;
5. Separate (H.S,S): deploy a pair of highly-sensitive and sensitive tasks into different clouds;
6. Co-locate(N.S,S): sensitive tasks and non-sensitive tasks can be deployed in the same Cloud;
7. Co-locate (N.S,S): highly-sensitive tasks and non-sensitive tasks can be deployed in the same Cloud;
8. Co-locate(N.S,N.S): non-sensitive tasks can be deployed in the same Cloud;

Constraint Consistency. After the constraints generation, it is important to check the consistency of these latter i.e. that a given constraint does not violate another one, for that we relied on a SAT solver to check the consistency of the conjunction of all the constraints. The SAT solver returns "SAT" i.e. there exits at least one configuration where tasks are allocated to Clouds while satisfying all the constraints and rules together, and "UNSAT" otherwise. For that, we encoded each constraint as a Boolean formula as follows:

(sensitive separate constraint) AND (co-locate constraint) AND (highly sensitive task separate constraint) AND (highly sensitive and sensitive tasks separate constraint) AND (separate complementary) AND (deploy highly sensitive in clouds with trust_level $\geq$ trust_level required).

Where as an indication, the sensitive separate constraint could be expressed as: (s1 AND NOT s2 AND c1 AND NOT c2) OR (NOT s1 AND s2 AND NOT c1 AND c2); Such as: s1: Sensitive task1, s2: Sensitive task2, c1: Cloud 1, c2: Cloud 2. Whereas, the Co-locate constraint could be expressed as: (ns1 AND s1 AND c1 AND NOT c2) AND ((ns2 AND c2) OR (ns2 AND NOT c1 AND s2 AND c2)); Such as: ns1: Non-sensitive task1, ns2: Non-sensitive task2.

5.3   Algorithm for the Configuration Generation

The Algorithm 1 is designed to return the final configuration, i.e., the set of tasks deployed in their corresponding clouds while ensuring the "Separate" constraints and "Co-locate" rule. To achieve this, the algorithm iterates over the set of business process tasks, which are sorted in descending order based on their sensitivity level. The highly-sensitive tasks, denoted by the H.S. annotation, are deployed first, followed by sensitive and complementary tasks. This deployment strategy is important to ensure that the clouds with the highest trust level are reserved for the highly-sensitive tasks. For each task in the set, the "TaskDeploymentScheme" procedure detailed in Algorithm 2 is called. This procedure checks the "Separate" constraint and returns a map of (tasks, cloud), i.e., where tasks should be deployed based on its sensitivity level. It is important to note that Algorithm 2 allows a task to be deployed in the first cloud that meets the security constraints stated above. However, there might be multiple clouds that meet these constraints without violating security. In these cases, a balance needs to be found between deployment costs and security constraints. While this is not considered in this work, it constitutes the object of one of our future research.

Table 1. Algorithm parameters notation

Parameters	
S	The set of the N available Clouds
C	The set of constraints on each task Ti
L	The minimum trust value required to deploy a highly sensitive task in a Cloud
B	The set of business process' tasks sorted in descending order
CloudByTask	A map to store the pairs (Task, Cloud) denoting that a given task is affected to a specific Cloud
isHsensitive	A function that checks if a task is annotated with the S annotation
isSensitive	A function that checks if a task is annotated with the H.S or S annotations respectively
Cid	ID of the complementary task of Tx

Algorithm 1. Final configuration

1: Input: N, C, S, L, B   ▷ B is sorted in a descending order according to tasks' sensitivity level.
2: Output: Config
3: **for each** (task Tx in B) **do**
4:     $Config \leftarrow TaskDeploymentScheme(Tx, N, C, S, L)$

Algorithm 2. Procedure: TaskDeploymentScheme

1: Input: Tx, N, C, S, L
2: Output: CloudByTask
3: *bool* ← *true*;
4: *j* ← 1;
5: **if** (isHSensitive(Tx)) **then**
6:     **while** (*j* <= *N*) **do**
7:         **if** (TrustLevel(Sj)>= L) **then**
8:             **if** (isEmpty(Sj)) **then**
9:                 Deploy(Sj,Tx);
10:                 CloudByTask.add(Tx,Sj);
11:                 *break*;
12:             **else**
13:                 **for each** (Ti in Sj) **do**
14:                     **if** (isHSensitive (Ti) or isSensitive (Ti) or equal(Ti.cid,Tx.id)) **then**
15:                         Separate(Ti,Tx);
16:                         *j* ← *j* + 1;
17:                         *bool* ← *false*;
18:                         *break*;
19:                 **if** bool **then**
20:                     Deploy(Sj,Tx);
21:                     CloudByTask.add(Tx,Sj);
22:                     *break*;
23:         **else**
24:             *j* ← *j* + 1;
25: **else**
26:     **if** (isSensitive(Tx)) **then**
27:         **while** (*j* <= *N*) **do**
28:             **if** (isEmpty(Sj)) **then**
29:                 Deploy(Sj,Tx);
30:                 CloudByTask.add(Tx,Sj);
31:                 *break*;
32:             **else**
33:                 **for each** (Ti in Sj) **do**
34:                     **if** (isHSensitive (Ti) or isSensitive(Ti) or equal(Ti.cid,Tx.id)) **then**
35:                         Separate(Ti,Tx);
36:                         *j* ← *j* + 1;
37:                         *bool* ← *false*;
38:                         *break*;
39:                 **if** bool **then**
40:                     Deploy(Sj,Tx);
41:                     CloudByTask.add(Tx,Sj);
42:                     *break*;
43:     **else**
44:         **while** (*j* <= *N*) **do**
45:             **for each** (Ti in Sj) **do**
46:                 **if** (equal(Ti.cid,Tx.id)) **then**
47:                     *j* ← *j* + 1;
48:                     *bool* ← *false*;
49:                     *break*;
50:             **if** bool **then**
51:                 Deploy(Sj,Tx);
52:                 CloudByTask.add(Tx,Sj);
53:                 *break*;
54: return *CloudByTask*

---

6 Use Case Scenario

Figure 7, depicts a BPMN process followed by a bank to grant or not a loan to a client, the process is inspired from [13]. When the client deposits his/her application, the process begins by retrieving the data needed from the application like the age and the salary of the client. Then, the installments are computed. With the retrieved data and the computed installments, the bank proceed the client's application according to its policy and, according to the results of this step the bank decides to reject or accept the client's application. The bank recognizes the potential gains that could be achieved by leveraging cloud computing environments to improve its operational efficiency. However, it is also concerned about the risk of disclosing its proprietary know-how to potential competitors or fraudulent cloud providers. Figure 8, depicts the Bank's business process annotated with our proposed security annotations. Indeed, the bank encapsulated the bulk of its know-how in the task "Process application" that computes sensitive data produced by the task "Compute installments". Hence, the "Process application" is a highly-sensitive task annotated with the annotation **H.S** and, should be deployed in a Cloud with high level of trust. The "compute installment" task is a sensitive task annotated with **S**, because the bank do not want to expose, on what the installments computation is based. Furthermore, the "retrieve data" task does not reveal any information about the bank strategy, but it produces the data in input to the "Compute installment" task, hence, these two tasks are complementary and have to be separated. Finally, the tasks "Notify eligibility" and "Notify rejection" are not sensitive (they do not encapsulate any of the bank know-how and, do not manipulate any sensitive data) but, if these two tasks are deployed with the highly sensitive task "Process application" they could reveal in which case the bank accepts or rejects a loan application. Hence, these two tasks are complementary with the "process application" task and should be separated.

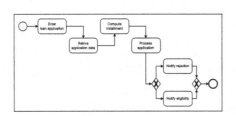

Fig. 7. Bank's loan process

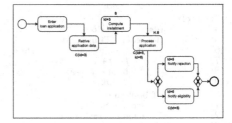

Fig. 8. Annotated loan process

Fragmentation. Following the constraints and rules detailed in Sect. 5.2, we obtain:

- Deploy "Process application" task in a Cloud with a high-level of trust. Let L1 be the level of trust determined by the designer, hence Trust-level(C3) **>=** L1;

- Separate ("Compute installements", "Process application");
- Separate ("Retrieve data", "Compute installments");
- Separate ("Process application", "Notify eligibility");
- Separate ("Process application", "Notify rejection");
- Separate ("Notify rejection", "Notify eligibility");
- Co-locate ("Enter loan application", "Retrieve data").

After that, given these constraints and the co-locate rule, the output of the application of the Algorithm 1 detailed in Sect. 5.3 would be as follows: (**Cloud1**, "Enter loan application", "Retrieve application data", "Notify rejection"), (**Cloud2**, "Compute installments", "Notify eligibility"), (**Cloud3**, "Process application").

The set of tasks for each cloud constitute a fragment of the business process and these latter exchange with the communication tasks Send and Receive (Fig. 9).

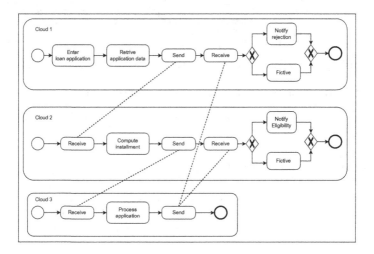

Fig. 9. The loan process fragments according to the hybrid security solution

Some Implementation Details: The implementation of the proposed approach is according to the architecture depicted in Fig. 10. In this architecture, the system is composed of the following components:

- **Security Annotation Tool**: This tool allows to annotate a business process by a designer and generates security rules and constraints.
- **Constraint Solver**: This component takes the generated security rules and constraints as input and checks their consistency. In our case we used the SAT solver MiniSAT[2].

---

[2] http://minisat.se/MiniSat.html.

– **Task Allocator**: This component takes the set of consistent constraints and allocates the tasks of the business process to the appropriate Clouds.
– **Multi-cloud environment**: This component represents the environment where the business process' tasks will be deployed. We simulated a multi-cloud environment using the container Docker[3]. We also relied on Jenkins[4] in order to automatically deploy the tasks in their respective virtual machines. Lastly, the tasks exchange using the Rest API[5].

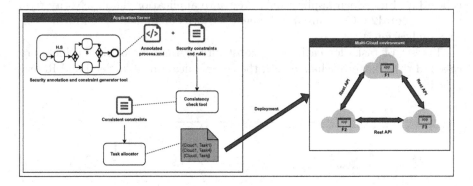

Fig. 10. Deployment architecture of the hybrid security solution

7   Results and Discussion

In this section, we discuss and compare our proposal to the one in [9]. The comparison is proceed according to two criteria *Security* and *Cost*.

7.1   Security

Figure 11, depicts the fragmentation and deployment of the loan business process detailed in Sect. 6, following the solution proposed in [9] (using the obfuscation technique). We can notice that, like with our proposed solution, the deployment requires three distinct Clouds, but in the case of the obfuscation technique the logic of the loan process is half preserved. Indeed, one Cloud has already 80% of the bank know-how through the tasks "Compute installment" and "Process Application" and this is due to the fact that sequential BPMN pattern is not taken into consideration. In this case, one can easily notice that the bank know-how is more secure with the annotation-based solution.

---

[3] https://www.docker.com/.
[4] https://www.jenkins.io/.
[5] https://www.redhat.com/en/topics/api/what-is-a-rest-api.

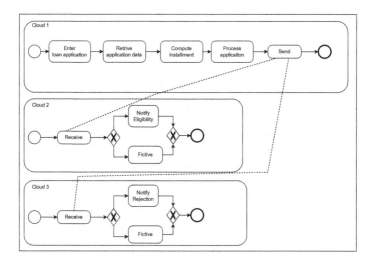

Fig. 11. Loan process fragments according to the obfuscation technique

7.2 Cost Evaluation

Costs (monetary and performance costs) are one of the reasons that makes companies postpone the security requirements of a system to be developed. That is why it is important to find a balance between security and these costs. In this section, we are interested in the monetary costs induced by the proposed solutions. Hence, we propose a cost model to estimate the deployment costs as the sum of the following resources:

- CPU usage: corresponds to the CPU cores needed to execute the process' tasks (CPU/GHz).
- RAM usage: corresponds to the size (in GB) of the needed RAM.
- Data transfer: corresponds to the amount of the exchanged data between the Clouds fragments. (Data transfer/GB)

Both solutions consist in splitting the business process and deploy it in a multi-cloud environment. If we resume the bank account process presented in Sect. 3, securing its know-how with the solutions proposed in [9] requires its deployment into three distinct Clouds. However, as depicted in Figs. 12 and 13, with the hybrid approach the deployment of **the bank account BP**(already described in Fig. 3 in Sect. 6) requires two clouds. Hence, if we consider the proposed Cost model with an example of three Cloud provider's pricing given in Table 2, and supposing that fragment1, fragment2 and fragment3 (generated in case of the obfuscation technique) will be deployed in Cloud1, Cloud2 and Cloud3 respectively, the deployment of the bank account process will cost 423.23$ with the obfuscation technique and 262.45$ with the hybrid approach. Thus, we can notice that the fragmentation according to the obfuscation technique proposed in [9] will generates unnecessary deployment costs whereas as stated in Sect. 3, the solution will not bring a gain regarding the process know-how.

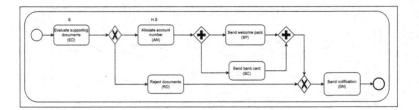

Fig. 12. Annotated Bank Account process

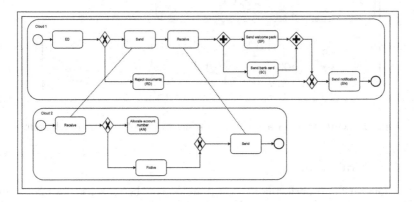

Fig. 13. Bank account process fragments

7.3   The Approach Limitations

Even though this approach ensures the security of the logical aspects of business processes, it has some limitations. In particular, the number of Clouds to be used to deploy the fragments of the business process, relates mainly to the number of highly-sensitive and sensitive tasks which could be quite high depending on the size of the business process in question. Hence, in this work, we are tackling business processes with a moderate number of highly-sensitive and sensitive tasks. However, to deal with larger number of highly-sensitive and sensitive tasks and, in order to reduce the number of the considered clouds, we are currently working on updating the Separate constraints to consider the structure of the business process. Specifically, we argue that the sequential order of the tasks

Table 2. Cloud provider's pricing

Cloud provider	CPU usage ($/GHz/mo)	RAM usage ($/GB/mo)	Data transfer ($/GB)
Cloud1	20.56	4.20	0.02
Cloud2	25.46	4.23	0.04
Cloud3	30.67	5.11	0.08

could play a role in the Separate constraint and the co-locate rule. Hence, we can for example co-locate two sensitive tasks that are not successive. Overall, this work is ongoing and we will provide further details on our findings in future updates.

8 Conclusions and Future Work Directions

This work focuses on enhancing the security of the logical aspect of business processes. Building upon our previous work in [8], where we provided an overview of proposed mechanisms for ensuring business process security, this study specifically examines the obfuscation technique and identifies its limitations in detecting sensitive tasks. We argue that the semi-automatic detection of sensitive tasks proposed in [9] is not always valid. In fact, we demonstrated through business processes examples the fact that sensitive tasks are not always bound to the X(Or) split and the And join gateways. Hence, the human intervene from the start is necessary to specify which task is sensitive and which one is not, according to our definition of sensitive tasks. As an alternative, we proposed an hybrid approach based on textual annotations where we distinguished four types of tasks namely highly-sensitive, sensitive, complementary and non-sensitive, and we adapted the security constraints proposed in the obfuscation technique in order to separate two highly-sensitive tasks, two sensitive tasks, a highly-sensitive task and a sensitive task and a task for its complementary tasks. Even though the obfuscation technique proposed in [9] showed its efficiency, in some cases it can be costly and less effective regarding security. In those cases, the proposed hybrid approach is preferable. In addition of updating the Separate constraints as discussed in Sect. 7.3, we plan to update our algorithm to take into consideration the deployment costs. Indeed, a task Tx could be deployed into different clouds without violating the security deployment constraints. However, regarding monetary costs, one deployment could be preferable to another. Finally, as future work, we intend to explore the impact of business processes changes at runtime on the security constraints and the deployed fragments.

References

1. Ahmed, N., Matulevičius, R.: Securing business processes using security risk-oriented patterns. Comput. Standards Interfaces **36**(4), 723–733 (2014)
2. Altuhhov, O., Matulevičius, R., Ahmed, N.: An extension of business process model and notation for security risk management. Int. J. Inf. Syst. Model. Des. (IJISMD) **4**(4), 93–113 (2013)
3. Argyropoulos, N., Kalloniatis, C., Mouratidis, H., Fish, A.: Incorporating privacy patterns into semi-automatic business process derivation. In: 2016 IEEE Tenth International Conference on Research Challenges in Information Science (RCIS), pp. 1–12. IEEE (2016)
4. Bell, D.E., LaPadula, L.J.: Secure computer systems: mathematical foundations. Technical report, Mitre Corp, Bedford (1973)

5. Dubois, É., Heymans, P., Mayer, N., Matulevičius, R.: A systematic approach to define the domain of information system security risk management. In: Nurcan, S., Salinesi, C., Souveyet, C., Ralyté, J. (eds.) Intentional Perspectives on Information Systems Engineering, pp. 289–306. Springer, Heidelberg (2010). https://doi.org/10.1007/978-3-642-12544-7_16

6. Duipmans, E.F., Ferreira Pires, L., Bonino da Silva Santos, L.O.: A transformation-based approach to business process management in the cloud. J. Grid Comput. **12**(2), 191–219 (2014)

7. Enireddy, V., Somasundaram, K., Prabhu, M.R., Babu, D.V., et al.: Data obfuscation technique in cloud security. In: 2021 2nd International Conference on Smart Electronics and Communication (ICOSEC), pp. 358–362. IEEE (2021)

8. Farah, A., Saida, B., Mourad, O.C.: On the security of business processes: classification of approaches, comparison, and research directions. In: 2021 International Conference on Networking and Advanced Systems (ICNAS), pp. 1–8. IEEE (2021)

9. Goettelmann, E., Ahmed-Nacer, A., Youcef, S., Godart, C.: Paving the way towards semi-automatic design-time business process model obfuscation. In: 2015 IEEE International Conference on Web Services, pp. 559–566. IEEE (2015)

10. Goettelmann, E., Fdhila, W., Godart, C.: Partitioning and cloud deployment of composite web services under security constraints. In: 2013 IEEE International Conference on Cloud Engineering (IC2E), pp. 193–200. IEEE (2013)

11. Han, Y.B., Sun, J.Y., Wang, G.L., Li, H.F.: A cloud-based BPM architecture with user-end distribution of non-compute-intensive activities and sensitive data. J. Comput. Sci. Technol. **25**(6), 1157–1167 (2010)

12. Jensen, M., Schwenk, J., Bohli, J.M., Gruschka, N., Iacono, L.L.: Security prospects through cloud computing by adopting multiple clouds. In: 2011 IEEE 4th International Conference on Cloud Computing, pp. 565–572. IEEE (2011)

13. de Leoni, M., Dumas, M., García-Bañuelos, L.: Discovering branching conditions from business process execution logs. In: Cortellessa, V., Varró, D. (eds.) FASE 2013. LNCS, vol. 7793, pp. 114–129. Springer, Heidelberg (2013). https://doi.org/10.1007/978-3-642-37057-1_9

14. Menzel, M., Warschofsky, R., Meinel, C.: A pattern-driven generation of security policies for service-oriented architectures. In: 2010 IEEE International Conference on Web Services, pp. 243–250. IEEE (2010)

15. Nacer, A.A., Godart, C., Rosinosky, G., Tari, A., Youcef, S.: Business process outsourcing to the cloud: balancing costs with security risks. Comput. Ind. **104**, 59–74 (2019)

16. Nacer, A.A., Godart, C., Youcef, S., Tari, A.: A metric for evaluating the privacy level of a business process logic in a multi-cloud deployment. In: 2017 IEEE 21st International Enterprise Distributed Object Computing Conference (EDOC), pp. 153–158. IEEE (2017)

17. Nacer, A.A., Goettelmann, E., Youcef, S., Tari, A., Godart, C.: Obfuscating a business process by splitting its logic with fake fragments for securing a multi-cloud deployment. In: 2016 IEEE World Congress on Services (SERVICES), pp. 18–25. IEEE (2016)

18. Povoa, L.V., de Souza, W.L., Pires, L.F., do Prado, A.F.: An approach to the decomposition of business processes for execution in the cloud. In: 2014 IEEE/ACS 11th International Conference on Computer Systems and Applications (AICCSA), pp. 470–477. IEEE (2014)

19. Rodríguez, A., Fernández-Medina, E., Trujillo, J., Piattini, M.: Secure business process model specification through a UML 2.0 activity diagram profile. Decis. Support Syst. **51**(3), 446–465 (2011)

20. Turki, S.H., Bellaaj, F., Charfi, A., Bouaziz, R.: Modeling security requirements in service based business processes. In: Bider, I., et al. (eds.) BPMDS/EMMSAD 2012. LNBIP, vol. 113, pp. 76–90. Springer, Heidelberg (2012). https://doi.org/10.1007/978-3-642-31072-0_6

21. Varela-Vaca, A.J., Warschofsky, R., Gasca, R.M., Pozo, S., Meinel, C.: A security pattern-driven approach toward the automation of risk treatment in business processes. In: Herrero, Á., et al. (eds.) International Joint Conference CISIS'12-ICEUTE'12-SOCO'12 Special Sessions. AISC, vol. 189, pp. 13–23. Springer, Heidelberg (2013). https://doi.org/10.1007/978-3-642-33018-6_2

22. Watson, P.: A multi-level security model for partitioning workflows over federated clouds. J. Cloud Comput. **1**(1), 1–15 (2012). https://doi.org/10.1186/2192-113X-1-15

Assessing Urban Sustainability (ASUS 2023)

Pedestrian Isochrones Facilities Overlapping with Openrouteservice. An Easy, Fast and Opensource Indicator in Novara, Italy

Mattia Scalas[1,2(✉)] [iD]

[1] Interuniversity Department of Regional and Urban Studies and Planning (DIST), Politecnico
Di Torino, 10128 Turin, Italy
mattia.scalas@polito.it
[2] Centro Euro-Mediterraneo Sui Cambiamenti Climatici (CMCC), 73100 Lecce, Italy

Abstract. The concept of proximity in planning requires the attention of schol-ars and decision-makers to the issue of accessibility to services within a walking distance, as part of the more general effort to make cities more resilient, sustain-able, and healthy. From an operational side, rethinking cities according to the paradigm of proximity and accessibility to services on foot implies the need for time-based methodologies that can identify the areas that can be reached within a given time interval. These methodologies often use GIS network analy-sis tools, but can require long analysis times and high financial costs for software. This con-tribution proposes an indicator of walking accessibility to facilities that is simple, quick to compute, and built using free and open-source tools such as QGIS and Openrouteservice, in order to allow its broad replicability on different contexts. The indicator was successfully tested in the city of Novara, Italy, using the 5-, 10- and 15-min isochrones, identifying the areas from which all the selected facilities can be reached within this time interval.

Keywords: Openrouteservice · 15-min City · Chrono-urbanism · GIS

1 Introduction

Making cities more inclusive, safe, resilient and sustainable [1] requires an understanding and assessment of a substantial number of variables through a holistic and multidisci-plinary perspective that addresses cities understood as complex systems. Many of the goals and pathways leading to urban resilience and sustainability are related to health and well-being, also with regard to the relationship with land-use and travel behaviour [2]: moreover, accessibility and transportation are key factors to consider in climate change mitigation actions and policies [3].

From this perspective, walkability improvement, pedestrian walk zones, traffic restrictions and nature-based solutions in public spaces impact on congestion, urban microclimate [4], quality of space [5] and consequently on individual health, improv-ing the conditions of the commuting environment and promoting sustainable mobility. Basically, a walkable environment is positively correlated with effectively stimulating

O. Gervasi et al. (Eds.): ICCSA 2023 Workshops, LNCS 14104, pp. 293–307, 2023.
https://doi.org/10.1007/978-3-031-37105-9_20

walking and cycling, influences the built environment quality [6]. One of the factors affecting the successful implementation of the above-mentioned measures relies on the distribution of the facilities and their accessibility on foot, that need to be assessed in order to identify the target areas. In this sense, methodologies based on network analysis are widely used, but may present problems of financial cost and data accessibility.

This research proposes an open-source, replicable, expeditious indicator based on the isochrones overlapping to identify basins of pedestrian accessibility to a set of everyday services. The indicator was tested in the municipality of Novara, Italy.

This contribution is structured in parts: Sect. 2 provides a brief State of the Art framing some proximity models and accessibility assessment methodologies. Section 3 illustrates, and the materials and methods used. Section 4 provides the results obtained, which are discussed in Sect. 5. Section 6 contains the conclusions. Appendix A includes some instructions for the usage of the software adopted.

2 State of the Art

Proximity as an element on which to build urban quality can be traced back to Howard's Garden City, Perry's Neighbourhood Unit, Christaller's Central Place Theory and the studies of Edward T. Hall, Jane Jacobs and French chrono-urbanism [7–9], but it has gained momentum and has been able to go outside the academic with the dissemination of models such as the Supermanzana [10] and Carlos Moreno's 15-min City [11], with additional influence among decision-makers during and after the Covid-19 pandemic [12, 13]. Despite a certain amount of criticism [14, 15], institutions such as the Cities Climate Leadership Group (C40) have officially promoted some of these models [16]. At a practical level, the evaluation of proximity services and accessibility is often performed through the use of GIS, network analysis and isochrones, that can be found in the work of Capasso Da Silva in Tempe [17], Ferrer-Ortiz in Barcelona [18], Pellicelli et al. in Cagliari [19] or through the space syntax methodology as in the work of Yamu & Garau in Vienna [20]. Other approaches employ multiple source data and methodologies, for example using cell phone data [21] or deep learning technologies [22].

Sometimes, especially with regard to models based on network analyses, the network used is made available under a proprietary licence. Other times, the data are both government data or from private providers: both of these conditions can raise challenges in the reproducibility of analyses and the standardisation of calculation procedures.

Starting from this context this contribution proposes a fast, cost-free, and open-source methodology for the calculation of a pedestrian service accessibility indicator, to help identify the areas from which it is possible to walk to all the identified services within a certain timeframe and the areas lacking services within a specific pedestrian accessibility radius, in order to provide a starting point for the identification and spatialisation of appropriate policies for the reduction of vehicular traffic and an increase in the liveability and health of the environment. Furthermore, this indicator could be integrated into broader evaluation frameworks of urban sustainability. The indicator is based on isochrones with respect to a set of Points of Interest (POIs), evaluating the overlap of the service areas originating from the calculation of POIs isochrones. This procedure employs the open source software QGIS and Openrouteservice, and open data from OpenStreetMap via the QuickOSM plugin.

3   Materials and Methods

In this section are presented the steps involved in designing a methodology for calculating a walking accessibility indicator, designed to be quick to calculate, simple and opensource.

This methodology seeks to spatialise and quantify those areas within the city characterised by the possibility of reaching or not reaching a series of facilities within a given walking time.

The methodology was tested on the municipality of Novara in north-western Italy, and consists of three main steps:

1. Points of Interests identification;
2. Isochrones calculation;
3. Isochrones overlapping and scoring.

The GIS software used is QGIS Desktop 3.30.0-s-Hertogenbosch in combination with the QuickOSM plugin using Openstreemap data for downloading, the Openrouteservice software installed as a local server for calculating isochrones, and the QGIS model Count Polygon Overlap.

After a brief description of the case study, the steps will be illustrated in the following sections. Please refer to Appendix A for an explanation of how to install and use Openrouteservice, which it is considered appropriate to describe in detail as it is relatively complex to deploy.

3.1   Description of the Case Study

Novara is a city of 101,727 inhabitants -163,654 with the urban agglomeration - (Euromobility, 2022) in eastern Piedmont, capital of the province of the same name and located barycentrically to Turin and Milan, the capital of Lombardy. The city has the second largest population in the entire Piedmont region, covers an area of 103.05 km2, is an important logistics and rice-growing centre and is home to the University of Eastern Piedmont (UPO).

The municipality is characterised by an urban fabric of Roman origin and subsequent expansions along the main road axes towards Milan, Alessandria, Turin, Valsesia and Lakes Orta and Maggiore, with a development that has resulted in a highly anthropised landscape: the current Regulatory Plan dates from 2003.

As far as mobility is concerned, Novara was endowed with a Urban Sustainable Mobility Plan (PUMS) in 2022, which contains some useful guidelines to orientate the application of the indicator. According to the plan, the city is subject to significant traffic being a logistic centre between Milan and Turin, which is not followed by an adequate level of infrastructure and local public transport service. In particular, the lack of closure of the outer ring road precludes a hierarchy of roads that loads some of the most important city streets with improper traffic, giving rise to congestion phenomena that are further aggravated by the modal habits of residents: 50% of residents prefer the car for movements within a radius of 4–5 kms. PUMS transposes the national PUMS guidelines into twenty specific objectives for the city of Novara and twenty-two actions. Among these actions are

- Az.4) New pedestrian and bicycle accessibility in Novara Nord;
- Az.9) New pedestrian areas;
- Az.10) Low Emission Zones (LEZ);
- Az.11) Novara city of proximity: the '15 blocks.

These actions can be traced back to the pedestrian and proximity dimension at the centre of attention of the methodology presented in this contribution, synthesised by the PUMS in a post-pandemic perspective as the idea of *'transforming Novara into a neighbourhood city thanks to the combined arrangement of Zones 30 (real proximity areas) and pedestrian-cycling corridors where inhabitants can find themselves in a new community'* [23].

PUMS has already adopted the isochrones methodology in the context of A.11 by identifying seven 'blocks' from whose centroid the service area was presumably drawn. The seven blocks are: Historic Centre, Major Hospital, New Hospital Complex, University Area - Perrone Complex, University Area - Sant'Agabio Complex, Railway Station - Novara FS, Railway Station - Novara Nord (Fig. 1).

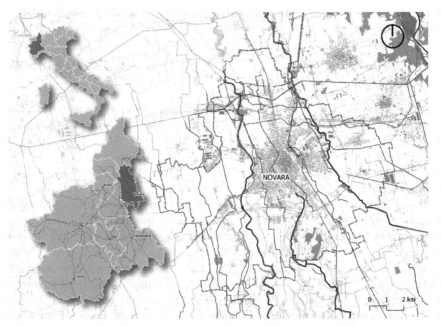

Fig. 1. Novara localization. Author's elaboration from OpenStreetMap and Regione Piemonte data.

3.2 Points of Interests Identification

This research refers to four of the six categories identified by Carlos Moreno in his 15-min City model: Commercial, Health care, Education, Entertainment, and the POIs identified by Staricco [9] further selected by the author in order to return a group of typical facilities of everyday life. The selected POIs, represented in Table 1 and mapped in Fig. 2, were all obtained from OpenStreetMap data downloaded through the QuickOSM plugin. If no point data were available, the centroid was calculated from the polygonal data. The process of choosing the POIs was conditioned by the availability of the data provided by OpenStreetMap and its structure. Since OSM is a volunteered geographic information (VGI) see [24, 25] and [26] for quality and reliability investigations: in particular, the third contribution focuses on POIs reliability.

Table 1. POIs selection for the isochrones analysis

Cluster	POIs name	Description	OSM key/value	Source
Commercial	Supermarket	Self-service large area store	'shop' = 'supermarket'	OSM
	Food and Drink	Includes cafes, bars and pubs	'amenity' = 'bar' AND 'amenity' = 'pub' AND 'amenity' = 'café'	
Health care	Pharmacy	Shop where a pharmacist sells medications	'amenity' = 'pharmacy'	
Education	Kindergarten	Education facility for children too young for regular schools	'amenity' = 'kindergarten'	
	School	Primary, middle and secondary school	'amenity' = 'school'	
Entertainment	Leisure Park	A municipal park	'leisure' = 'park'	
	Sport	Includes most common sport facilities: swimming, tennis, basketball, running, soccer	'sport' = 'swimming' AND 'sport' = 'tennis' AND 'sport' = 'basketball' AND 'sport' = 'running' AND 'sport' = 'soccer'	

3.3 Isochrones Calculation

In this stage, isochrones calculation was performed in three time intervals: 5, 10 and 15 min based on the literature consulted. The City of Novara in its PUMS explicitly refers to the 15-min City model, but literature considers also 5, 10 and 20 min (Staricco, 2022).

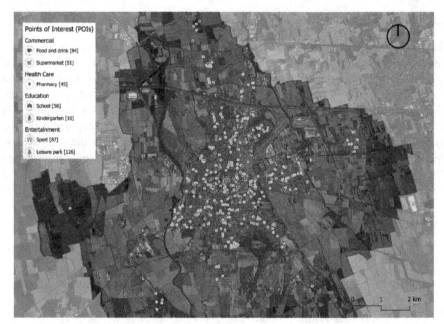

Fig. 2. Municipality of Novara – Points of Interest (POIs). Author's elaboration from Open-StreetMap data. Basemap Google Satellite.

In general, the choice of this parameter is closely related to factors such as the objectives of the analysis and the physical structure of the case study.

The software used for the isochrones is Openrouteservice, with a deployment in a local server running on Docker and through the interface offered by the QGIS ORS tools plugin with the Isochrones geoprocessing from Point Layer. Details can be found in Appendix A. Openrouteservice makes use of the Openstreetmap (OSM) network, and the isochrones are constructed on a pedestrian with an average speed of 5 km/h travelling through a set of segments classified according to the OSM attribute system. The parameters have not been changed from the default provided by Openrouteservice.

In order to speed up the calculation process, the algorithms were executed serially with the Execute as batch process command: from each layer containing POIs, isochrones were derived at 5, 10 and 15 min to allow the three different parameters to be visualised. The batch process for all 22 categories of POIs took 70,324 s to execute, which took place on an Intel Core i7 computer with 2.60 GHz, 16 GB of RAM and 4 GB of RAM dedicated to Docker where the Tomcat server with Openrouteservice was running. In Table 2, some summary statistics of the operations performed.

3.4   Isochrones Overlapping and Scoring

The counting of the number of overlaps was performed on three layers obtained from a dissolve process, also performed in batch, applied to the isochronous layers of the individual POIs. A QGIS model developed by Jenkins and in the public domain under

Table 2. POIs and Isochrones calculation statistics

Tomcat server ORS Docker container allocated RAM	4 GB
Number of POIs layers	22
Number of points	424
Isochrones calculated	1272
Total calculation time	70.324 s

the Creative Commons CC-0 licence was used to count the overlaps. The model, which can be visualised and edited directly from QGIS via the graphical modeler, is a chain of simpler geoprocessings, executed serially until a new layer is obtained with a column in the attribute table showing the number of overlaps.

The counting was performed on the 5-, 10- and 15-min isochrones in order to have three final results to analyse and compare.

As far as scoring is concerned, if the construction of the indicator is taken as a stand-alone activity as in this case, one can simply use the number of counted overlaps, possibly grouped and divided into classes.

If, on the other hand, the counting of overlapping isochrones is part of broader evaluative frameworks, it will be necessary to adapt the scale used to that of the general framework.

4   Results

In this section the results are described, dividing them into the three time-categories over which the analysis was performed: 5, 10, 15 min. Results interpretation and maps were performed within QGIS using the geoprocessing functions of the Plot family via the Python console. The results are analysed according to seven classes defined by the number of overlaps counted: class 7 indicates the maximum number of overlaps (positive) and so on down to the minimum of 1 overlap (negative).

4.1   5-min Overlapping

The analysis identifies four main polarities, which are developed around the five most relevant polygons out of the 11 total class seven. These areas, the most extensive, are distributed along the north-south axis of the built-up area and in the occidental area.

Of the five areas, the largest is the one extending in the quadrants defined by the intersection of Via Pina Ballario and Via Giulio Cesare. Within this area, characterised by the coexistence or the presence within a five-minute walk of all the services selected for the analysis, there are several recently built residential buildings along Via Paolo Fornara, Via Pina Ballario and Via Spreafico. The second largest area is located slightly further north along the axis of via Giuseppe Verdi and revolves around a commercial structure that is barycentric with respect to the identified overlays. Significant is the presence of residential buildings. The third and fourth areas tend to be contiguous and are located east and west of the axis defined by Via Giulio Biglieri and Corso Torino. The area thus defined, west of the historic centre, contains a fair number of residential buildings. The last class seven area considered is defined by the presence of the 11 September 2011 park and is characterised by a mainly low-intensity residential fabric.

It is interesting to note that around the remaining class 7 polygons some clusters are generated that include class 6 polygons, in particular in the area between the railway line and the Sant'Agabio district, to the east of the historic centre. Other class 6 clusters are present along Via Luigi Camoletti, east of the San Paolo district, near Sant'Antonio to the north and near Pernate to the north-east (Fig. 3).

Fig. 3. Isochrones overlaps: 5-min walking. Author's elaboration from OpenStreetMap data. Basemap Google Satellite.

4.2 10-Min Overlapping

Compared to the analysis within five minutes, the one on 10 shows a continuous class 7 polygon that occupies a large part of the built-up area, excluding the peripheral areas that fall in class 6 anyway, except for the south-eastern edges of the built-up area in the prison area, east along the Corso Milano, north along the Via Verbano and in the Vignale area. Outside the main built-up area, it is evident that the inhabited areas south of Torrion Quartara and Olengo to the south-east and the hamlet of Casalgiate to the west remain outside the first two classes. As is to be expected, the north-west area hosting the Novara logistics hub is completely outside the identified polygons (Fig. 4).

Fig. 4. Isochrones overlaps: 10-min walking. Author's elaboration from OpenStreetMap data. Basemap Google Satellite.

4.3 15-Min Overlapping

In the latter case, the class 7 polygon indicating walking accessibility to all selected POIs tends to cover almost the entire built-up area, with the exception of the south-west area along Strada Statale 211 and the two northern expansions along Via Verbano and the Vignale area. On the other hand, the Sant'Agabio area along Corso Trieste falls into class 6. The logistics hub area is also excluded in this case (Fig. 5).

5 Discussion

The results obtained show a different level of capacity in capturing the distinctions between internal areas of the city depending on the time parameter chosen. The 15-min parameter, in particular, tends to be not very explanatory if the objective is to categorise the inhabited area of the city of Novara. Even the 10-min parameter may not be able to capture internal variations in the distribution of services, in a sense overlapping with the information in parameter 15. A comparison of the three visualization can be found in Fig. 6.

More interesting, however, is the analysis that emerged from the use of the 5-min parameter, where a number of polarities emerge that allow one to distinguish areas within the built-up area. These areas, which tend to be those that gather around the highest scoring polygons in class 7, define portions of the territory in a favourable condition from the point of view of accessibility on foot to POIs used for the construction of the

Fig. 5. Isochrones overlaps: 15-min walking. Author's elaboration from OpenStreetMap data. Basemap Google Satellite.

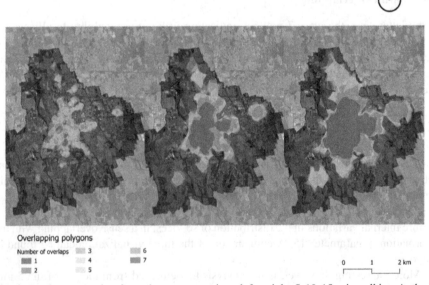

Fig. 6. Isochrones overlapping polygons comparison: left to right, 5, 10, 15-min walking. Author's elaboration from OpenStreetMap data. Basemap Google Satellite.

study. Similarly, the analysis with parameter 5 min highlights lower scoring territories (classes 2, 3, 4) always within the urbanised fabric of the city.

It is considered that the number of overlaps between the isochrones generated by the POIs considered may constitute a meaningful indicator which can serve both as a quick exploratory evaluation aimed at identifying areas to be analysed with other methodologies, and as an indicator that can be integrated into evaluation frameworks. It is believed that some operational pointers can also emerge from a semi-simple GIS analysis with the overlay of other information layers. For example, as shown in Fig. 7, some of the routes identified inside one of the highest-scoring polygons can be improved in terms of walkability, traffic and quality of space.

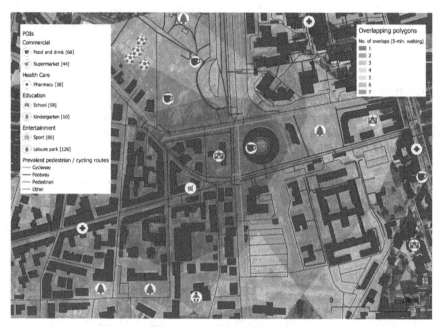

Fig. 7. A 5-minute highest overlap area with reachable POIs and route network classification. Author's elaboration from OpenStreetMap and Regione Piemonte data. Basemap from Google Satellite.

It is believed that the of isochrones overlapping can provide a general overview to identify the "pedestrian potential" of some portions of the city, contributing to locating and implementing interventions towards public space quality.

The presented methodology has a number of advantages: once all the necessary software has been correctly installed, operations are carried out very quickly and with a fair degree of automation. The use of opensource data also allows high level of generalisation and replicability.

However, a number of critical issues emerged. First of all, a certain complexity in the software deployment of Openrouteservice should be noted.

Secondly, it is necessary to highlight the issue of data availability: in this study, it was decided to use the open data made available by OpenStreetMap and downloaded via QuickOSM, but it should be noted that the OSM data may present errors and imprecisions. It is therefore suggested to evaluate government data as an alternative to OSM data. Also in this regard, also a cross-check with demographic and occupational data could extend the level of detail of the analysis to include the dimension of living and workplaces.

A third issue concerns the selection of POIs: In this study, a literature review based on similar studies and empirical experience was adopted. However, the use of participatory methodologies for selection, and the weighting of individual POIs could be of some interest to further detail the analysis.

The fourth and final point to be highlighted concerns the choice of time parameter. This study used the 5-, 10- and 15-min time periods and then compared the results obtained. However, the choice of the time parameter depends on numerous factors and further research could investigate this further.

6 Conclusion

The experimentation conducted in the City of Novara showed that it is possible to use isochrones overlapping through the Openrouteservice software to obtain an indicator of pedestrian accessibility basins to a given service, which in the case study was most significant for the time threshold of 5 min compared to 10 and 15 min. The proposed indicator and its calculation methodology overcomes dependence on commercial services that may limit the use of network analysis techniques with GIS software. Despite some limitations, the tested methodology is considered promising for the technologies adopted, the speed of application, widespread availability of data, high level of automatization, open source nature and good replicability. Future developments may consider the use of this indicator in the context of broader sustainability assessment frameworks or use the presented methodology to identify areas of the city where analyses of spatial quality and liveability can be carried out. Also, similar analysis based on specific target groups can be investigated, considering for example children, elderly, etc. The main future developments of the research concern the use of this methodology to identify suitable areas for microclimate analysis, aimed at building the knowledge base for the implementation of resilience actions and policies. The identified 'super isochrones', because they represent areas potentially suitable for pedestrians, can serve as a focus for the development of quality urban blocks capable of stimulating modal diversion and implementing adaptation and mitigation actions. These areas, for example, can be conceived as the nodes of a pedestrian network designed to ensure high climate comfort through measures - such as nature-based solutions - that can achieve multiple objectives.

Acknowledgements. The author would like to thank Dr. Guglielmo Ricciardi of the Euro-Mediterranean Centre on Climate Change for his valuable comments and the association GFOSS.IT APS, the Italian OSGeo local chapter, for their commitment to opensource software.

Also, the author would like to thank the Openrouteservice staff for their availability and support in solving issues concerning the use and deploy of the software, and Syntaxbyte for the clear explanations concerning the set-up procedure via Docker.

Appendix A. Openrouteservice Deployment on Windows

Openrouteservice (ORS) is maintained by the GIScience Research Group of the Department of Geography at the University of Heidelberg [27], and offers opensource routing services built on OpenStreetMap (ORS), OpenAddresses, GeoNames and Who's On First data. ORS can be used via `maps.openrouteservice.org`, requesting a personal API key or configuring a localhost Tomcat server via Docker, allowing to avoid any use restriction. Docker, Git and WSL are required.

ORS GitHub repository can be cloned from command line with `git clone` https://github.com/GIScience/openrouteservice. To build the container in `openrouteservice` folder these subfolders should be created: `mkdir -pconf elevation_cache graphs logs/ors logs/tomcat`. The container can be generated with `docker compose up`, and is it possible to check the installation at http://localhost:8080/. Default geographical data can be changed cleaning the old data in folders `elevation_cache, data e graphs`, downloading the required `.pbf` (e.g. from http://download.geofabrik.de/) and modifying some settings in `docker-compose.yml` file, decommenting line `# -./your_osm.pbf:/ors-core/data/osm_file.pbf` and replacing with the name of the new `.pbf`. Regarding profiles, default installation only activates car profile. For other profiles, `docker/conf/ors-config.json` should be modified identifying the active profiles array and adding the new one.

References

1. United Nations: Transforming our world: the 2030 agenda for sustainable development A/RES/70/1 (2015). [Online]. Available: https://sdgs.un.org/sites/default/files/publications/21252030%20Agenda%20for%20Sustainable%20Development%20web.pdf
2. Tonne, C., et al.: Defining pathways to healthy sustainable urban development. Environ. Int. **146**, 106236 (2021). https://doi.org/10.1016/j.envint.2020.106236. Jan.
3. Raven, J., et al.: Urban planning and design. In: Rosenzweig, C., Solecki, W., Romero-Lankao, P., Mehrotra, S., Dhakal, S., Ali Ibrahim, S. (eds.) Climate Change and Cities: Second Assessment Report of the Urban Climate Change Research Network, pp. 139–172. Cambridge University Press, New York (2018)
4. Sodoudi, S., Zhang, H., Chi, X., Müller, F., Li, H.: The influence of spatial configuration of green areas on microclimate and thermal comfort. Urban Forestry & Urban Greening **34**, 85–96 (2018). https://doi.org/10.1016/j.ufug.2018.06.002. Aug.
5. Talen, E.: Pedestrian Access as a Measure of Urban Quality. Plan. Pract. Res. **17**(3), 257–278 (2002). https://doi.org/10.1080/026974502200005634. Aug.
6. Kim, E.J., Kim, J., Kim, H.: Does Environmental Walkability Matter? The Role of Walkable Environment in Active Commuting. Int. J. Environ. Res. Pub. Heal. **17**(4), Art. no. 4 (Jan. 2020). https://doi.org/10.3390/ijerph17041261
7. Bartzokas-Tsiompras, A., Bakogiannis, E.: Quantifying and visualizing the 15-Minute walkable city concept across Europe: a multicriteria approach. Journal of Maps **0**(0), 1–9 (Dec. 2022). https://doi.org/10.1080/17445647.2022.2141143
8. Osman, R., Ira, V., Trojan, J.: A tale of two cities: The comparative chrono-urbanism of Brno and Bratislava public transport systems. Moravian Geographical Reports **28**(4), 269–282 (2020). https://doi.org/10.2478/mgr-2020-0020. Dec.

9. Staricco, L.: 15-, 10- or 5-minute city? A focus on accessibility to services in Turin, Italy. Journal of Urban Mobility **2**, 100030 (2022). https://doi.org/10.1016/j.urbmob.2022.100030. Dec.

10. Rueda, S.: Un nuevo urbanismo para abordar los retos de la sociedad actual. Neutra 15, Art. no. 15 (2007). Accessed: 24 Mar. 2023. [Online]. Available: https://www.revistaneutra.org/RN/article/view/536

11. Moreno, A., Allam, Z., Chabaud, D., Gall, C.: Introducing the '15-Minute City': Sustainability, Resilience and Place Identity in Future Post-Pandemic Cities. Smart Cities **4**(1), 93–111 (2021)

12. Allam, Z., Moreno, C., Chabaud, D., Pratlong, F.: Proximity-Based Planning and the '15-Minute City': A Sustainable Model for the City of the Future, pp. 1–20 (2021). https://doi.org/10.1007/978-3-030-38948-2_178-1

13. Pinto, F., Akhavan, M.: Scenarios for a Post-Pandemic City: urban planning strategies and challenges of making 'Milan 15-minutes city.' Transportation Research Procedia **60**, 370–377 (2022). https://doi.org/10.1016/j.trpro.2021.12.048. Jan.

14. Khavarian-Garmsir, A.R., Sharifi, A., Sadeghi, A.: The 15-minute city: Urban planning and design efforts toward creating sustainable neighborhoods. Cities **132**, 104101 (2023). https://doi.org/10.1016/j.cities.2022.104101. Jan.

15. Marchigiani, E., Bonfantini, B.: Urban Transition and the Return of Neighbourhood Planning. Questioning the Proximity Syndrome and the 15-Minute City. Sustainability **14**(9), Art. no. 9 (Jan. 2022). https://doi.org/10.3390/su14095468

16. Cities Climate Leadership Group C40: C40, NREP to collaborate on 15-minute city pilots. C40 Cities. https://www.c40.org/news/c40-nrep-collaborate-15-minute-city/. Accessed 12 May 2023

17. Capasso Da Silva, A., King, D.A., Lemar, S.: Accessibility in Practice: 20-Minute City as a Sustainability Planning Goal. Sustainability **12**(1) (2020). https://doi.org/10.3390/su12010129

18. Ferrer-Ortiz, B., Marquet, O., Mojica, L., Vich, G.: Barcelona under the 15-Minute City Lens: Mapping the Accessibility and Proximity Potential Based on Pedestrian Travel Times. Smart Cities **5**(1), Art. no. 1 (Mar. 2022). https://doi.org/10.3390/smartcities5010010

19. Pellicelli, G., Caselli, B., Garau, C., Torrisi, V., Rossetti, S.: Sustainable Mobility and Accessibility to Essential Services. An Assessment of the San Benedetto Neighbourhood in Cagliari (Italy). Computational Science and Its Applications – ICCSA 2022 Workshops: Malaga, Spain, July 4–7, 2022, Proceedings, Part VI, pp. 423–438. Springer-Verlag, Malaga, Spain (2022). [Online]. Available: https://doi.org/10.1007/978-3-031-10592-0_31

20. Yamu, C., Garau, C.: The 15-Min City: A Configurational Approach for Understanding the Spatial, Economic, and Cognitive Context of Walkability in Vienna. In: Gervasi, O., Murgante, B., Misra, S., Rocha, A.M.A.C., Garau, C. (eds.) Computational Science and Its Applications – ICCSA 2022 Workshops, pp. 387–404. Springer International Publishing, Cham (2022)

21. Zhang, S., Zhen, F., Kong, Y., Lobsang, T., Zou, S.: Towards a 15-minute city: A network-based evaluation framework. Environment and Planning B: Urban Analytics and City Science **50**(2), 500–514 (2023). https://doi.org/10.1177/23998083221118570. Feb.

22. Zhou, H., He, S., Cai, Y., Wang, M., Su, S.: Social inequalities in neighborhood visual walkability: Using street view imagery and deep learning technologies to facilitate healthy city planning. Sustain. Cities Soc. **50**, 101605 (2019). https://doi.org/10.1016/j.scs.2019.101605

23. Comune di Novara: Piano urbano della mobilità sostenibile dell'area urbana di Novara (P.U.M.S.) e piani di settore ad esso formalmente e funzionalmente connessi (2022)

24. Jacobs, K.T., Mitchell, S.W.: OpenStreetMap quality assessment using unsupervised machine learning methods. Trans. GIS **24**(5), 1280–1298 (2020). https://doi.org/10.1111/tgis.12680

25. Teimoory, N., Ali Abbaspour, R., Chehreghan, A.: Reliability extracted from the history file as an intrinsic indicator for assessing the quality of OpenStreetMap. Earth Sci. Inf. **14**(3), 1413–1432 (2021). https://doi.org/10.1007/s12145-021-00675-6

26. Bright, J., De Sabbata, S., Lee, S., Ganesh, B., Humphreys, D.K.: OpenStreetMap data for alcohol research: Reliability assessment and quality indicators. Health Place **50**, 130–136 (2018). https://doi.org/10.1016/j.healthplace.2018.01.009. Mar.

27. Neis, P., Dietze, L., Zipf, A.: A Web Accessibility Analysis Service based on the OpenLS Route Service (2008)

GeoBIM for Urban Sustainability Measuring: A State-of-the-Art in Building Permit Issuance

Valerio Della Scala[1] , Caterina Quaglio[1] , and Elena Todella[2]([✉])

[1] Department of Architecture and Design (DAD), Politecnico di Torino, Viale Mattioli 39, 10122 Turin, Italy
[2] Department of Regional and Urban Studies and Planning (DIST), Politecnico di Torino, Viale Mattioli 39, 10122 Turin, Italy
elena.todella@polito.it

Abstract. The integration of Geographic Information System (GIS) and Building Information Modelling (BIM) has shown promising applications in different sectors related to urban transformation and at various scales, ranging from the district to the building level. This approach, also known as GeoBIM, presents opportunities and challenges for assessing urban indicators, with both technical and social implications. This paper aims to define the state-of-the-art and to explore the possibilities opened by GeoBIM for urban transformation measurement, with a focus on planning and building permits issuance. Accordingly, a literature and project review is conducted, to better understand the challenges and potential of GeoBIM. The results show that there are still technical problems to be addressed (e.g., data acquisition approaches and interoperability). Moreover, further research can be directed at the social implications of GeoBIM in practice, including updating political and cultural frameworks, enhancing competencies, and rethinking conventional practices from digitalization to re-coding processes.

Keywords: Geographic Information System (GIS) · Building Information Modelling (BIM) · GeoBIM · Urban sustainability · Building permits

1 Introduction: GeoBIM and Urban Sustainability

Digital technologies are becoming increasingly relevant to solving urbanization problems and ensuring sustainable development [1]. In particular, smart cities have become an increasingly widespread concept in public and scientific debate as an urban development model aimed at achieving these goals [2–4], capable of meeting resilient and sustainable city transformation goals [3]. Information is therefore essential to treat cities as systems and, consequently, as devices that can be addressed and improved through technologies [5].

To make sustainable smart cities possible in operational terms, City Information Modeling (CIM) is recognized as a tool that can improve city management, consisting of an urban model – both spatial and temporal [3] – that allows modeling, monitoring, analysis and simulation actions [2, 4, 6]. Indeed, a CIM model makes it possible to automatically manage information and conduct advanced simulations on complex problems from both economic, social and spatial parameters, with the possibility of integrating different scales [1]. CIM is understood as a tool that combines and integrates data from different sources, including geographic information systems (GIS) and building information modeling (BIM), into a comprehensive and up-to-date urban database, which should have open data, be accessible and interactive for all stakeholders [5]. Accordingly, CIM has relevant technical potential for understanding urban data, visualizing public policies, measuring and monitoring urban indicators, and even project evaluation and planning [3, 7, 8]. It can thus improve decision-making processes related to urban transformation and city management by providing information to administrations, urban planners, designers, and citizens [5, 7, 9] through a constantly updated spatial database. Moreover, by fostering stakeholders' understanding of public management actions, it can stimulate social participation and reconciliation and negotiation between the needs of different parties [10, 11]. The dissemination of open and quality data is important to strengthen the link between citizens and local government in understanding and discussing the planning actions that shape cities [5], from the district to the building level [12, 13].

Sustainable smart cities can be achieved, and urban sustainability can be assessed through the smart, multidisciplinary and holistic approach of CIM, aimed at [5, 7, 8, 14]:

(i) helping to achieve the global goals related to reducing human activity in the environment;
(ii) accounting for the systemic impacts of resource and waste flows over the entire life cycle of projects;
(iii) visualizing integrated data and models with different levels of detail on the whole set of urban development operations;
(iv) promoting the negotiation and discussion among the instances of different stakeholders.

The integration of BIM and GIS, henceforth referred to as GeoBIM [3, 5, 15, 16], is a topic that has attracted much attention in recent years as an integrated and systemic approach to urban sustainability and measurement [8, 17, 18]. Indeed, GeoBIM has the potential to overcome current information barriers [1], with a mutual fulfillment of BIM and GIS in terms of scale and system accuracy, allowing the entire built environment, from building to urban space, to be represented and controlled in a single solution [3]. Currently, BIM contains detailed building information, but excludes anything that does not relate to the architectural model; in contrast, GIS can conduct large-scale spatial analysis, but does not report building information [1, 8]. The development of GeoBIM stems precisely from the need to integrate these functions and achieve all urban design goals with one system.

The differences between the two systems, however, necessarily imply numerous technical challenges [15, 16], in terms of different modeling methods, representation, scale chosen for data restitution, purposes for which data are produced, and local or supra-local reference of coordinate systems. At the same time, a general professional inadequacy and lack of expertise in both fields also imply societal challenges with respect to city decision-making processes [3, 16], in terms of informed stakeholder involvement, the need for knowledge in the specific fields, and the urgency for changes in legislation and regulations regarding planning at the institutional level [19]. The implementation of GeoBIM is then a socio-technical issue, which needs problematization to move from manual analysis to automation of some procedures.

This paper aims precisely to define the state-of-the-art and explore the possibilities opened by GeoBIM for urban indicators, focusing on building permit issuance. Accordingly, a literature and project review is conducted, to better understand the challenges and potential of GeoBIM, both in terms of technical problems to be addressed, and social implications in practice and operationalization of such technology.

The application of GeoBIM to the realm of issuing building permits, with a more efficient authorization process, is an emerging area of research. Recently, the creation of cadastral databases through GeoBIM integrations has enabled developments in the direction of managing information more interactively and automating some measurements and verifications [1, 16, 20]. In particular, verification of project compliance with building permits, widely approached and managed in Europe through manual verification work against regulations by technical experts from municipalities, is being tested in the possibility of standardizing and automating the process by automatically issuing building permits [16]. Such an approach, through GeoBIM, could ensure not only the requirements, but also to measure several urban indicators, at different scales, to guarantee a sustainable and controlled development of the built environment.

Accordingly, the paper is organized as follows: Sect. 2 proposes the research design and defines the steps and aims of the literature and project review; Sect. 3 presents the background on GeoBIM technology, with a focus on building permits issuance; Sect. 4 presents the results of the literature and projects review, highlighting its technical and social challenges; Sect. 5 introduces conclusions and future work.

2   Research Design

This section illustrates the research design in conducting the literature review.

In the earliest stage of the review process, the Web of Science database has been chosen to support the literature search, with a query related to "GIS", "BIM", "urban", and "sustainability indicators". The selection of the papers has been filtered by considering the following criteria: (i) English language papers; (ii) the study must be related to the integration of GIS and BIM; (iii) the papers must explore a specific project application to be deepened in the review.

Then, given the goal of this paper to review the state-of-the-art of the challenges and potential of BIM and GIS integration both in technical and societal terms, a screening process has been conducted. First, the abstracts of all the references have been read in order to select and identify the most related research to the aims of this study. Second, the full paper texts of the appropriate references have been included in the research database. Finally, the 24 selected papers have been read, in order to collect information about the state-of-the-art and theoretical background of GeoBIM applications, to be included in a textual analysis.

The results of the analysis are reported in Sect. 4, aimed at defining the state-of-the-art and exploring the possibilities opened by GeoBIM for urban indicators, focusing on building permit issuance.

3 GIS and BIM Integration: An Operational Perspective

As briefly explored in the introduction, GeoBIM can facilitate urban development as integrating BIM and GIS can provide spatial analyses that combine an efficient architecture/building-scale flexible management with a broader city-level visualization and information [1, 8, 21]. The two systems are able to compensate for reciprocal shortcomings.

BIM, as a 3D digital model at the building scale, provides geometric and semantic information for the project and enables detailed visualization of components and continuous updating of information, in a single platform for data processing [3, 22]. This, made available to multiple professionals, allows control of large volumes of data on the components of the project itself, with collaborative and circular digital management coordinated through the description of geospatial information. This technology thus allows for improved performance of the built environment, but also improved information quality with impacts on decision-making processes.

However, the hardware costs and resources required to process the BIM data of an entire city are unimaginable [22], making it impossible to exclusively use this technology for urban development, planning, and construction of smart sustainable cities. On the other hand, GIS makes it possible to obtain and manage spatial and geographic information at the city level, with a hierarchical data processing logic that reduces the amount of hardware computation [8, 23] to display and analyze it. In addition, the type of data that GIS effectively handles is derived from multiple sources, including not only morphological elements, but distributive ones, related to distances, location, and especially potential analyses of relationships between different dimensions. Therefore, GIS enables analysis from not only representations of space, but also of events occurring in it.

The integration of a process of digital management of information related to a work (BIM) and the representation with geographic information systems of a territory and what happens on it (GIS) allows the exchange of data between the systems in a single database, without loss of information and indeed with a mutual feeding of them.

The literature analyzes the potentials and criticalities of GeoBIM from different points of view. As highlighted in the introduction, the differences between the two systems necessarily imply numerous technical problems, and at the same time a general professional inadequacy and lack of expertise in both fields also imply societal issues. Given the operational objectives of the literature and project review proposed, to better understand the challenges and potential of GeoBIM and socio-technical implications in the operationalization of such technology, this work specifically addresses a recent line of research that emphasizes the need to bridge the gap between theory and practice [16]. As Ohori et al. clearly state "most of the research conducted so far has covered only the high-level and semantic aspects of GIS-BIM integration" [24]. On the contrary, an "application-oriented perspective" is introduced as a key to investigating the actual problems and opportunities in the use of GeoBIM and the broader implications it might have on research and professional work contexts [25]. The assumption underlying this perspective is that operational issues concerning the potential of BIM-GIS integration can only be addressed with respect to specific scenarios and use cases [26, 27].

Many possible GeoBIM application areas are discussed in the literature. Some of the most common fields of operation in the built environment include, for example, 3D mapping [28], city analysis, infrastructure and building design and monitoring [8, 16, 29], urban development [5], energy performance assessment [30].

GeoBIM is therefore used as a support to urban planning and performance assessment at very different scales, ranging from single buildings to much wider systems as in the case of infrastructure asset management or underground networks [8, 31, 32]. In addition, the literature review suggests the possible use of this tool at different stages of the process, from decision-making to construction, to management throughout the entire life cycle of an asset [31, 33].

Given this overview, this research adopts an application-oriented approach to question how GeoBIM can support the measuring of sustainability in urban transformation processes. To this end, the result analysis presented in the next chapter focuses on a specific use case, namely building permit issuing, with specific attention to automation in code-check compliance. Several reasons motivate our interest in this specific field of application. First, although sustainability goals are now increasingly adopted by public institutions operating at various levels, it is rarely questioned how they can be included in ordinary planning and design processes. This means moving from the level of exceptional pilot projects to their actual possibility to be scaled up to produce results on the large scale. Second, building permits extend the scope of sustainability measurement to private processes and buildings, for which data and assessment tools are often lacking. Finally, the application of GeoBIM to building permit issuing would allow laying the foundations in the design phase for the measurement of performance in the subsequent project life cycle.

4   Digital Building Permit for Urban Sustainability Assessment: Opportunities and Challenges

In recent years there has been increasing interest in automated code-checking systems for issuing building permits. Actually, academic papers show that themes pertaining to the digital building permit (DBP) problem have been surfacing since the early 2000s, although a systematic approach only emerged recently. In the last ten years, the number of research and experiments has grown exponentially. Generally, the building permit process is part of the broader framework of digitalization in the construction sector [26]. Nonetheless, the research for automation remains strongly linked to the condition of locality, and it still suffers technical, methodological and social difficulties. In the following sections, first of all we focus on what kind of diffusion such systems are having, also highlighting some geographical trends in this regard. Then, we explore the most common implementation difficulties highlighted in the literature, identified in three macro-aspects. Finally, we briefly emphasize the implications – and related difficulties – opened up by GeoBIM for urban indicators, starting from the in-depth focus on building permits issuance.

4.1 State of the Art of DBP Projects: A Geographical Overview

Recent papers focused on the global state of DBP have tried to frame the geographical distribution of projects related in some ways to this sphere, providing an articulated state of the art [27, 34, 35]. On a general level, a broad geographic distribution emerges, with a good concentration of projects and initiatives located in Europe (and especially Central and Northern Europe). Among the non-European cases, which enclose Australia, Brazil, Canada, Chile and the United Arab Emirates, among others, there are also some of the pioneering initiatives. In particular the Corenet project developed in Singapore since the 1990s for e-submission and recently transformed into one of those processes trying to adopt BIM technology for partial code compliance checking. Similarly, the Seumter digital submission system adopted by Korea since 2009 is recently undergoing implementations aimed at integrating BIM and Industry Foundation Classes (IFC) models in the partial automation of project compliance assessment [35].

In Europe, the state of the art is fragmented. The most fertile area seems to be the northern part of the continent, with Estonia, Finland, Germany, Norway, the Netherlands, the United Kingdom, and Sweden engaged in one or more projects targeting the development of DBP systems. It should be mentioned, however, that experiments along these lines are also taking place elsewhere, such as in France, Slovenia, Spain, Switzerland and Portugal.

In particular, one of the first attempts to evaluate the possibilities of translating the set of regulations in a computational sense, with a view to a possible automation of inspections related to building permits, was carried out in 2014 in England: in collaboration with Solibri and Butler & Young, the National Building Specification (NBS) developed a pilot to evaluate the tools currently available to perform automatic code compliance checking using a BIM model [36]. Among the most recent applications and attempts in this regard, the Finnish Kira-HUB platform [37] is gaining momentum, becoming one of the most interesting paradigms on the continent and beyond. The digital ecosystem that contains a three-dimensional environment, in addition to being used by both the private user for a compliance pre-verification and the public entity to monitor the compliance check process, is currently being used to incrementally characterize the very model of the three-dimensional space.

In general, there are some issues concerning the various projects and the state of the digital building permit in a global sense. Considering the evaluation parameters of the Building Smart International, many of the projects at the most advanced stage fall into level 2: hybrid, the BIM value is actively used in code checking, but some manual procedures may still be present. This is because level 3, the one in which "laws are readable by machines, open standards that do not depend on the software environment are used, and holistic code checking is performed" is difficult to achieve at the present stage, even for a context historically characterized by greater legislative and regulatory simplification [34]. This mainly depends on the difficulty of translating into a computational sense the entire apparatus of codes and standards, which by their nature are heterogeneous and ontologically different, but we will go further on this later. Among the few advances produced in this regard, many have been made in automating the extraction and transformation of rules directly from regulatory codes and documents. Artificial intelligence (AI) methods use natural language processing algorithms such as text analysis, content monetization, automatic content classification, and text mining. These methods allow computers to automatically derive meaning from text and generate logic rules for checking purposes [38].

Definitely, the greatest common denominator among the cases, both the ones discussed and those which have been only mentioned here, is precisely the intention to produce a platform for the three-dimensional digital submission of projects and partial automation of compliance checking. Almost all of the projects focus on the goal of using BIM models, which highlights how BIM and GIS integration is still a complex road ahead.

4.2 The Implementation of DBP Systems: Three Open and Critical Issues

In parallel to applications and developments, it is essential to analyze the problems and major obstacles to implementing this type of system. To do so, we will once again draw on the literature reviewed so far, enlarging the reference discussion of one of the previously cited papers [27]. Indeed, the work highlights a series of subtopics corresponding to the different stages of progress of studies and experiments. By treating them as consequential problems, the study allows not only to delineate which aspects catalyze to a greater extent the efforts of experts, rather it allows to identify which are the most common issues and aspects to be implemented, with a view to DBP diffusion. Starting from this framework, we specifically highlight three macro-aspects that are most closely related to the orientation of our analysis.

Data Availability and Convertibility
The issue of data availability and convertibility touches several spheres with regard to the automation of DBP. First of all, the aspect of the translation of standards and codes into "computer-interpretable" and "computational objects" must be considered. It is plausible to argue that almost every particular context presents a code structure characterized by objects that can be easily translated in this sense, others less so and others not at all. In this sense, a 2015 study [39] classifies standards (in general terms) into three categories: those which are computer-interpretable (declarative) and those which are not (informative); finally, those which can be considered as unsuitable. Among operational developments, however, some hypothesize the use of NLP-based methods, which essentially involve implementing IFC to incorporate compliance checking-related information [40], while in the Netherlands, experiments are being carried out aimed at the storage of spatial planning information in 3D based on CityGML [27], a conceptual model and exchange format for the representation, storage and exchange of virtual 3D city models, promoted by the Open Geospatial Consortium.

In general, the topic is crucial, but developments are still isolated and strongly context-specific.

Standard and Interoperability CityGML/IFC
Another aspect refers on the one hand to the conversion of normative data into spatial format (in terms of IFC models), and on the other hand to how BIM data in IFC format can be converted into 3D geodata [41], in order to support an uninterrupted digital data

flow and consequently enrich the system incrementally, while continuing to record the transformation of current conditions.

In fact, rather than the issue strictly related to the accessibility and quantity of information available, which is certainly fundamental but concerns local policies and actions for the implementation of databases, the most urgent issue at the methodological level concerns how to make information, or rather geoinformation, reliable but above all interoperable data. This can only pass through standardization and conversion: to date, the most suitable system seems to be CityGML, (especially in relation to general urban rules such as zoning) [42].

The few works focusing on possible solutions to the issue point out that, although there are tools that would already support the conversion and georeferencing of data, a clear definition of the necessary requirements for conversion is still lacking, and this affects the coherence of the results. The GeoBIM benchmark 2019 – funded by ISPRS and EuroSDR [43] – had as its aim precisely the evaluation of implementations of coherent conversions between 3D city models and BIM, also involving external experts [29]. It emerges precisely how the issue of checking the coherence and truthfulness of geometric and semantic information is considered the most critical [29, p. 12], so much so that a further manual check of the conversion still remains necessary.

Other works are attempting to deal with the problem from a strictly technical point of view, and trying to evaluate advances, net of the aforementioned difficulties. Still starting from the general assumption that "municipalities invest a lot of time and person-hours into manual building permit checks" [44, p. 529], and that the implementation of DBP systems could guarantee an improvement "of both the efficiency and transparency of building permit checks" [44, p. 534], a team based at Tu Delft is trying to convert data corresponding to a set of regulatory parameters and constraints, extracted mostly from zoning documents, into JSON formats, in order to immediately explore the possibilities of web interaction of a partially automatic check-compliance system. The reference case study is the aforementioned Rotterdam project and involves investigating the possibility of a system running on an online server. The hypothesis is to load and display IFC files directly on a browser, and then convert them into glTF files to be finally displayed with BIMSurfer2 [44]. But beyond exquisitely technical aspects, this research also highlights the limitations with regard to the truthfulness of the output, leading to the conclusion that the generalization of standards and other parameters to be converted, and the construction of a common basic ground upstream of the process, are unavoidable aspects.

Back on a more general level, this problem also relates to the preliminary analysis and evaluation phases of planners (both private and internal to public facilities). In other words, the issue of converting data into CityGML models, or other related systems, concerns both the evaluation and check-compliance of a project in relation to its enabling and the preliminary analyses to its development.

In this case, several solutions are explored, including: automated methods to extract design information from BIM models in IFC to insert it into a semantic logic-based representation, aligned with a corresponding semantic logic-based representation of normative information [27] (a modality proposed for example by [40]); another more popular and well-known system is the use of Solibri Model Checker (SMC), "to validate the information content of BIM models prior to code checking" [27]; or, again, one avenue evaluated in the aforementioned Korean KBIM case is that of "a design quality control process whereby architects create OpenBIM data using specific guidelines and previously developed BIM libraries" [27]. But even in this case, implementations are still numerically very limited.

GeoBIM Automation

In general, the issues outlined concern the automation of building-related permits, while on a more specific level can be all referred to a field that is indicated as GeoBIM - although, as above mentioned, this definition has only recently begun to spread. The basic problem can be summarized as follows: the need to place the designed building (BIM) in its geographical context (GIS).

Linking this to the theme of translatability and computer-interpretability of standards, it should be considered that the BIM model must be examined against specific requirements defined by codes and regulations. Recently, there has been an increase in studies and research in this direction, many of them concentrated in the Netherlands [41] and the Scandinavian area [45] but also in other geographical areas, as highlighted above through the state-of-the-art analysis of real-world applications.

Eventually, the reason why these aspects are the most relevant for us is that they are closely linked both to the topic of assessing the sustainability of an intervention (and its inclusion among the objectives of the automation of building permit procedures) and, more generally, to the effects such automation would generate on coding in general. The pivotal question in this regard is: how, in view of the possible need to make standards computational, could the norm-making paradigm change?

4.3   GeoBIM and Urban Indicators

The three highlighted macro problematic aspects – data availability, interoperability and automation – are correlated to some difficulties with respect to the operationalization of indicators for urban sustainability [20, 49–53].

Regarding the national context [53], data are often unavailable because they are obsolete or linked to episodic collections, and/or the databases are difficult to consult. Moreover, existing data are often not homogeneous in terms of spatial scale, reference time span and disaggregation levels. Consequently, potential interoperability between databases is not feasible, because partial information does not allow cross-queries, e.g., between statistical and geospatial information. In line with these issues, the possibility of supporting an uninterrupted and incrementally enriched flow of digital data clashes with non-open or non-standard technologies [48, 53], making even real-time and automatic updating complex. In this sense, a political discussion and local action for the implementation of accessible and integrable databases [46–48] and related codes and regulations [20] is more urgent than ever.

With respect to the need to measure the sustainability of projects, in the context of building permits, urban indicators could allow for both quantitative and qualitative assessments that are not only statistical but visualizable and spatialized [20, 48, 54, 55] thus a GeoBIM integration would be a key support for the spatialization of sustainability measurement. Furthermore, since observing one indicator at a time, rather than their relationship to each other, limits the possibility of capturing multiple and interrelated implications of urban transformation processes, GeoBIM could guide the process from measurement and monitoring to the actual evaluation of project performance [56].

The use of GeoBIM models can help to make more informed decisions by making use of several key indicators that can lead to better and more reliable results through a multi-criteria approach [57, 58]. BIM makes it possible to quickly extract data and information from the components of a project and aid in the evaluation [58], mainly due to the potential offered by the IFC file format, while GIS integrates such assessments into the broader urban decision-making by incorporating multiple location and environmental information and criteria – as social, environmental and economic indicators – thus bringing GeoBIM technology to potentially more effective use in multi-criteria decision-making [59, 60].

5 Discussion and Conclusions

The analysis of the literature and ongoing experimental projects developed in the previous sections brought to light both potentials and criticalities in the integration of BIM and GIS systems for building permit issuing.

The results of the analysis show, on the one hand, the potentials offered by Geo-BIM systems in this respect. Some elements, particularly critical in the measurement of sustainability in urban transformation processes, are worth highlighting. First, the integration of BIM and GIS systems could foster greater integration and uniformity of measurements and reference systems at all scales – from the building to the territorial one – through the introduction of common interoperability standards. Second, the implementation of three-dimensional digital urban models could make it possible to localize and spatialize measurements that are usually solely statistical, laying the foundations for a quanti-qualitative evaluation of urban transformation processes. Thirdly, GeoBIM technologies pave the way for extending the scope and time of urban sustainability assessment, providing a constantly updatable platform for the systemic measurement and monitoring of a wide variety of indicators over a period of time covering the entire design process and project life cycle.

On the other hand, the literature review also shows how, for these perspectives to become operational, a number of limitations must still be overcome. More specifically, technical issues concerning the integration of GIS and BIM systems, widely discussed in the literature, are traced back in this paper to three issues particularly critical for addressing GeoBIM implementation for digital building permit: (i) data availability and convertibility; (ii) standard and interoperability; and (iii) automation. Nevertheless, other cultural and social aspects raised by the spread of GeoBIM systems are still understudied, highlighting a gap in the literature in this respect. Among the most relevant social issues are, for example, the lack of technical skills and structures within technical offices and design agencies; the inertia of cultural and professional working contexts; the change of perspective and role required to public and private actors operating in the building sector; the ethical problems related with the acquisition and storage of personal data; etc. In addition, most of the studies developed on this topic do not explicitly address the implications of adopting GeoBIM systems – and in particular automated check-coding systems – on the overall regulatory paradigm. Indeed, the partial automation of building compliance verification processes opens new possibilities for the streamlining and updating of administrative procedures on the one hand and for the implementation of data-based multi-criteria decision-making processes on the other.

In conclusion, the paper envisage the potential of GeoBIM systems for disseminating urban sustainability measurement in ordinary building processes. It also suggests, however, the need to develop further research from at least three understudied perspectives: (i) the actual potential of developing sustainability assessment tools and methods through GeoBIM systems; (ii) the socio-cultural limitations related to GeoBIM operationalization for digital building permit; and (iii) the possibilities it opens up for a more comprehensive process of re-coding and revision of current regulatory frameworks.

References

1. Xia, H., Liu, Z., Efremochkina, M., Liu, X., Lin, C.: Study on city digital twin technologies for sustainable smart city design: A review and bibliometric analysis of geographic information system and building information modeling integration. Sustain. Cities Soc. **84**, 104009 (2022)
2. Camero, A., Alba, E.: Smart City and information technology: A review. Cities **93**, 84–94 (2019)
3. Al Furjani, A., et al.: Enabling the City Information Modeling CIM for Urban Planning with OpenStreetMap OSM. In: The Fourth International Conference for Geospatial Technologies. Libya GeoTec 4, Tripoli, Libya (2020)
4. Nochta, T., Wan, L., Schooling, J.M., Parlikad, A.K.: A socio-technical perspective on urban analytics: The case of city-scale digital twins. J. Urban Technol. **28**(1–2), 263–287 (2021)
5. Souza, L., Bueno, C.: City information modelling as a support decision tool for planning and management of cities: A systematic literature review and bibliometric analysis. Build. Environ. **207**(16), 108403 (2022)
6. Stojanovski, T., Partanen, J., Samuels, I., Sanders, P., Peters, C.: Viewpoint: city information modelling (CIM) and digitizing urban design practices. Built Environment **46**, 637–646 (2020)
7. Dantas, H.S., Sousa, J.M.M.S., Melo, H.C.: The importance of city information modeling (CIM) for cities' sustainability. In: IOP Conf. Ser. Earth Environ. Sci., Institute of Physics Publishing (2019)
8. Wang, M., Deng, Y., Won, J., Cheng, J.C.P.: An integrated underground utility management and decision support based on BIM and GIS. Autom. Constr. **107**, 102931 (2019)
9. Chen, K., Lu, W., Xue, F., Tang, P., Li, L.H.: Automatic building information model reconstruction in high-density urban areas: augmenting multi-source data with architectural knowledge. Autom. Constr. **93**, 22–34 (2018)
10. Thompson, E.M., Greenhalgh, P., Muldoon-Smith, K., Charlton, J., Dolník, M.: Planners in the future city: using city information modelling to support planners as market actors. Urban Planning **1**, 79–94 (2016)
11. Ungureanu, T.: The potential of city information modeling (CIM) in understanding and learning from the impact of urban regulations on residential areas in Romania. In: New Technol. Redesigning Learn, pp. 422–428. SPACES (2019)
12. Abastante, F., Lami, I.M.: An integrated assessment framework for the requalification of districts facing urban and social decline. In: Seminar of the Italian Society of Property Evaluation and Investment Decision, pp. 535–545. Springer, Cham (2016)
13. Abastante, F., Lami, I.M., Mecca, B.: How to revitalise a historic district: A stakeholders-oriented assessment framework of adaptive reuse. In: Values and Functions for Future Cities, pp. 3–20. Springer, Cham (2020)

14. Yigitcanlar, T., Kamruzzaman, M., Foth, M., Sabatini-Marques, J., da Costa, E., Ioppolo, G.: Can cities become smart without being sustainable? A systematic review of the literature. Sustain. Cities Soc. **45**, 348–365 (2019)

15. Ellul, C., Stoter, J., Harrie, L., Shariat, M., Behan, A., Pla, M.: Investigating the state of play of geobim across Europe. In: ISPRS Annals of the Photogrammetry, Remote Sensing and Spatial Information Sciences, pp. 19–26. ISPRS Archives (2018)

16. Noardo, F., et al.: Opportunities and challenges for GeoBIM in Europe: developing a building permits use-case to raise awareness and examine technical interoperability challenges. J. Spat. Sci. **65**(2), 209–233 (2020)

17. Amirebrahimi, S., Rajabifard, A., Mendis, P., Ngo, T.: A data model for integrating GIS and BIM for assessment and 3D visualisation of flood damage to building. CEUR Workshop Proceedings, pp. 78–89 (2015)

18. Liu, X., Wang, X., Wright, G., Cheng, J., Li, X., Liu, R.: A state-of-the-art review on the integration of building information modeling (BIM) and geographic information system (GIS). ISPRS Int. J. Geo Inf. **6**, 53 (2017)

19. Gaballo, M., Mecca, B., Abastante, F.: Adaptive reuse and sustainability protocols in Italy: Relationship with circular economy. Sustainability **13**(14), 8077 (2021)

20. Della Scala, V., Quaglio, C.: Sustainability assessment in the authorisation process of urban transformation: the meta-design of a GeoBIM platform. Valori e Valutazioni 32 (2023)

21. Pauwels, P., Zhang, S., Lee, Y.C.: Semantic web technologies in AEC industry: A literature overview. Autom. Constr. **73**, 145–165 (2017)

22. Rathore, M.M., Paul, A., Hong, W.H., Seo, H., Awan, I., Saeed, S.: Exploiting IoT and big data analytics: Defining smart digital city using real-time urban data. Sustain. Cities Soc. **40**, 600–610 (2018)

23. Zhao, L.J., Chen, L.J., Ranjan, R., Choo, K.K.R., He, J.J.: Geographical information system parallelization for spatial big data processing: A review. The Journal of Networks Software Tools and Applications **19**(1), 139–152 (2016)

24. Ohori, K.A., Diakité, A., Krijnen, T., Ledoux, H., Stoter, J.: Processing BIM and GIS Models in Practice: Experiences and Recommendations from a GeoBIM Project in The Netherlands. ISPRS International Journal of Geo-Information **7**, 311 (2018)

25. Beck, S.F., Abualdenien, J., Hijazi, I.H., Borrmann, A., Kolbe, T.H.: Analyzing contextual linking of heterogeneous information models from the domains BIM and UIM. ISPRS Int. J. Geo Inf. **10**, 807 (2021)

26. Noardo, F., Wu, T., Ohori, K.A., Krijnen, T., Stoter, J.: IFC models for semi-automating common planning checks for building permits. Autom. Constr. **134**, 104097 (2022)

27. Noardo, F., et al.: Unveiling the actual progress of digital building permit: getting awareness through a critical state of the art review. Build. Environ. **213**, 108854 (2022)

28. Sun, J., Mi, S., Olsson, P., Paulsson, J., Harrie, L.: Utilizing BIM and GIS for Representation and Visualization of 3D Cadastre. ISPRS Int. J. Geo Inf. **8**, 503 (2019)

29. Noardo, F., et al.: Tools for BIM-GIS Integration (IFC Georeferencing and Conversions): Results from the GeoBIM Benchmark 2019. ISPRS Int. J. Geo Inf. **9**, 502 (2020)

30. Yamamura, S., Fan, L., Suzuki, Y.: Assessment of urban energy performance through integration of BIM and GIS for smart city planning. In: International High-Performance Built Environment Conference, Procedia Engineering **180**, 1462–1472 (2017)

31. Garramone, M., Moretti, N., Scaioni, M., Ellul, C., Re Cecconi, F., Dejaco, M.C.: BIM and GIS integration for infrastructure asset management: a bibliometric analysis. ISPRS Annals of the Photogrammetry, Remote Sensing and Spatial Information Sciences, pp. 77–84 (2020)

32. Slongo, C., Malacarne, G., Matt, S.T.: The IFC file format as a means of integrating BIM and GIS: the case of the management and maintenance of underground networks. ISPRS Annals of the Photogrammetry, Remote Sensing and Spatial Information Sciences 4, (2022)

33. Moretti, N., Ellul, C., Cecconi, F.R., Papapesios, N., Dejaco, M.C.: GeoBIM for built environ-ment condition assessment supporting asset management decision making. Autom. Constr. **130**, 103859 (2021)
34. Brito, D.M., Costa, D.B., Ferreira, E.A.M.: Code Checking using BIM for Digital Build-ing Permit: a case study in a Brazilian municipality. In: IOP Conference Series: Earth and Environmental Science **1101**, 022049 (2022)
35. Kim, I., Choi, J., Teo, E.A.L., Sun, H.: Development of K-BIM e-Submission prototypical system for the openBIM-based building permit framework. J. Civ. Eng. Manag. **26**(8), 744–756 (2020)
36. National Building Specification website: https://www.thenbs.com/knowledge/nbs-and-open-standards-for-bim, last accessed 06 April 2023
37. Finnish Kira-HUB platform: (https://kirahub.org/en/home/, last accessed 06 April 2023
38. Shahi, K., McCabe, B.Y., Shahi, A.: Framework for automated model-based e-permitting system for municipal jurisdictions. Journal of Management Engineering **35**, 1–10 (2019)
39. Malsane, S., Matthews, J., Lockley, S., Love, P.E.D., Greenwood, D.: Development of an object model for automated compliance checking. Autom. Constr. **49**, 51–58 (2015)
40. Zhou, P., El-Gohary, N.: Text and information analytics for fully automated energy code checking. Sustainable Civil Infrastructures, 196–208 (2019)
41. van Berlo, L.A., Papadonikolaki, E.: Facilitating the BIM coordinator and empowering the suppliers with automated data compliance checking. In: Proceedings of the 11th European Conference on Product and Process Modelling, pp. 145–154. ECPPM (2016)
42. Gröger, G., Kolbe, T. H., Nagel, C., Häfele, K.H.: OGC City Geography Markup Language (CityGML) Encoding Standard, 344 (2012)
43. Ellul, C., Noardo, F., Harrie, L., Stoter, J.: The EUROSDR GeoBIM project - developing case studies for the use of GeoBIM in practice. In: 3rd BIM/GIS Integration Workshop and 15th 3D GeoInfo Conference, The International Archives of the Photogrammetry, Remote Sensing and Spatial Information Sciences (2020)
44. Hobeika, N., van Liempt, J., Noardo, F., Ohori, K.A., Stoter, J.: GeoBIM Information to check Digital Building Permit regulations. The International Archives of the Photogrammetry, Remote Sensing and Spatial Information Sciences (2022)
45. Eriksson, H., et al.: Requirements, development, and evaluation of a national building standard: A Swedish case study. ISPRS Int. J. Geo Inf. **9**(2), 78 (2020)
46. Abastante, F., Lami, I.M., Mecca, B.: How Covid-19 influences the 2030 Agenda: do the practices of achieving the Sustainable Development Goal 11 need rethinking and adjustment? Valori e Valutazioni **26**, 11–23 (2020)
47. Fattinnanzi, E.: The quality of the city: The role of assessment in plan and project drafting methodologies. Valori e Valutazioni **20**, 3–12 (2018)
48. Abastante, F., Gaballo, M.: Assessing the SDG11 on a Neighborhood Scale Through the Integrated Use of GIS Tools. An Italian Case Study. In: Calabrò, F., Della Spina, L., Piñeira Mantiñán, M.J. (eds.) New Metropolitan Perspectives. NMP 2022. Lecture Notes in Networks and Systems 482. Springer, Cham (2022)
49. Zall Kusek, J., Rist, R.C.: A Handbook for Development Practitioners. Ten Steps to a Results-Based Monitoring and Evaluation System. The International Bank for Reconstruction and Development/The World Bank, Washington D.C (2004)
50. Hák, T., Janoušková, S., Moldan, B.: Sustainable Development Goals: A need for relevant indicators. Ecol. Ind. **60**, 565–573 (2016)
51. da Silva, J., Fernandes, V., Limont, M., Bonino Rauen, W.: Sustainable development assess-ment from a capitals perspective: Analytical structure and indicator selection criteria. J. Environm. Manage. **260** (2020)
52. van Vuuren, D.P., et al.: Defining a sustainable development target space for 2030 and 2050. One Earth **5**(2), 142–156 (2022)

53. Lami, I.M, Abastante, F., Gaballo, M., Mecca, B., Todella, E.: Fostering sustainable cities through additional SDG11-related indicators. Valori e Valutazioni, 32 (2023)
54. Fattinnanzi, E., Acampa, G., Forte, F., Rocca, F.: The overall quality assessment in architectural design. Valori e Valutazioni **21**, 3–14 (2018)
55. Forte, F.: Architectural quality and evaluation: a reading in the European framework. Valori e Valutazioni 23 (2019)
56. Mecca, B., Gaballo, M., Todella, E.: Measuring and evaluating urban sustainability. Valori e Valutazioni 32 (2023)
57. Anelli, D., Tajani, F.: Spatial decision support systems for effective ex-ante risk evaluation: An innovative model for improving the real estate redevelopment processes. Land Use Policy **128**, 106595 (2023)

Hypotheses of a Heterodox Evolutionary Assessment Approach for the Sustainable City

Maria Rosa Trovato[2(✉)], Cheren Cappello[1], Ludovica Nasca[2], and Vittoria Ventura[2]

[1] Department of Architecture, Design and Urban Planning, Sassari, Italy
c.cappello@studenti.uniss.it
[2] Department of Civil Engineering and Architecture, Catania, Italy
mariarosa.trovato@unict.it, ludovica.nasca@phd.unict.it

Abstract. This contribution outlines a path of analysis, evaluation, and interpretation of the concept of sustainability in its most challenging context, the city. It proposes a twofold approach that looks behind the concept of value as utility or efficiency in view of the potential arising from the constitutive ambiguity of urban signs: objects, circumstances, phenomena, processes. The first part of this experiment presents an orthodox approach mostly based on the description functions; the second one proposes a heterodox approach based on wider assessment functions according to an evolutionary approach articulated in the capacities of inertia, adaptation and ex-aptation that redefine the value functions defined to represent the main aspects of urban sustainability.

Keywords: Urban sustainability · Evolutionary approach · Data analysis · Urban assessment · Urban ex-aptation

1 Introduction

One of the main reasons of interest in evaluating the complexity of urban eco-systems is the polysemy of the objects identified as 'value-bearers'; value, in its multiple declinations and articulations, is the essential content of their relevance for the organisation of settled communities.

Based on the value contents implied by their socio-economic order, communities establish and evolve extrasystemic (with the environment) and intrasystemic (between subsystems) complementarity relationships.

Complementarities and divergences between subsystems result in asymmetries in the allocation of the social surplus, which cause the set and hierarchies of codes and programmes to evolve.

These programmes interpret the prospect of continuous growth in the volume and value of the capital stock differently [1]; in fact, each of them refers to economic policy directions that differ in the position in which they place the same values in the means-end chain.

Within this unified and monolithic narrative stand the pillars of urban sustainability: society, economy, environment [2].

© The Author(s), under exclusive license to Springer Nature Switzerland AG 2023
O. Gervasi et al. (Eds.): ICCSA 2023 Workshops, LNCS 14104, pp. 322–338, 2023.
https://doi.org/10.1007/978-3-031-37105-9_22

It is common knowledge, however, that once the entropic watershed is crossed, wealth can no longer grow, and it is necessary to address the ecological, urban, and social issue through new narratives and new value/price relations.

The present work, with reference to the case study of the Municipality of Syracuse (Italy), proposes a multidimensional assessment model [3, 4] based on two complementary approaches with the aim of representing most of the value that tangible and intangible occurrences actually and potentially express, overcoming the limitations of an orthodox approach based on a misunderstood concept of progress. In fact, the city presents the greatest opportunities for this further capacity precisely because of the density and rapidity of the communication that spreads and self-sustains in it, fostering the evolution and accumulation of additional urban capital surplus [5].

Consequently, the city is an **eco-socio-system** whose **hyper-complexity** must be reduced by means of the basic cognitive functions, **observation, interpretation,** and **communication**, which typically select value-based representations, in particular the **home-city-landscape system**. The latter is a mental construction that transcends the occurrences of dwelling, living together and contemplating into corresponding axiological essences. The home-city-landscape system is the value essence of its object references: the building organism, the functional and infrastructural apparatus, the spatial-institutional extension. The home-city-landscape system is the essence of the resilient forms in which the **surplus** of the social product is consolidated and accumulated and can referred to the human and urban capital. [6]. **Human surplus** is made of **consciousness, personality and creativity**; **Urban surplus** is made of **shape, normativity and sharing**.

Surplus is the energy of **evolution**: city evolves through the different times and shapes of **Inertia, Adaptation** and **Ex-a**ptation.

These three forms support the reinterpretation of the traditional multiple trade-off relationships between **Efficiency, Effectiveness, Convenience** and **Equity** from the perspective of the city as the highest value **shape** of capital [7] (Fig. 1).

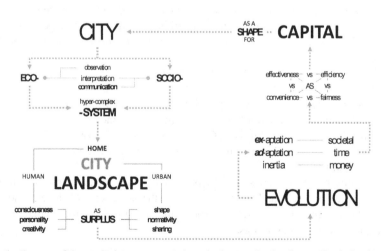

Fig. 1. Pattern of the evolutionary approach to the home-city-landscape Capital valuation.

The above pattern is the conceptual-operational basis of a value-based cognitive process [8], coordinating a twofold approach, orthodox and heterodox, each of which selects and combines differently the information units from the perspectives of which the urban-territorial unit surveyed and represented.

The paper is divided into five parts: the second outlines a synthetic spatial profile of the studied context by identifying the areas most exposed to convergence between development prospects and conservation instances; the third summarises the method with reference to the information sources and the articulation of the contents of the applied multi-criteria analysis model; the fourth provides the results of the GIS mapping of the evaluation syntheses deriving from the aggregation of the information units at the different levels of evaluation and interpretation; the fifth concludes the paper with a discussion of the operational and conceptual results.

2   Materials. The Municipal Context of Syracuse (Italy)

Syracuse, the capital of the homonymous province, the sixth city for population in Sicily and one of the most relevant for the complex heritage value, synthesizing natural, and cultural systems in a landscape unity listed as a World Heritge Site by UNESCO since 2005. The municipality has 117,053 inhabitants, a housing stock of 10,596 units on a total area of approximately 7.5 square kilometers.

The municipal territory is articulated in six areas (Fig. 2):

- Ortigia, the ancient fortified nucleus built from the 8th century B.C. onwards, whose historic-artistic value has driven significant redevelopment and restoration processes that have supported significant functional, economic and social transformations resulting in an unexpected real estate and valorization;
- The Umbertino district which arose at the end of the 19th century after the demolition of most of the original city walls; it was formed according to a modern orthogonal layout principle, along the main axis (Corso Umberto I), a continuation of the main bridge connecting Ortigia to the mainland. The district is characterised by wide streets and large architecturally qualified buildings aggregated in large quadrangular blocks, which include shops and businesses, as well as residential and accommodation facilities.
- the "Borgata di Santa Lucia", built shortly after the previous one, until the early 20th century, was created as a working-class neighbourhood to allow the petty bourgeoisie that crowded Ortigia to have worthy dwellings in a modern context;
- the neighbourhoods in the northern area, built mainly since the 1960s: Grottasanta, Akradina, Tiche, Neapolis, Epipoli, Canalicchio, Targia, Belvedere;
- the area comprising the Canalicchio and Carrozziere quarters in the western part of the municipality;
- in the southern part, the coastal settlement of Fontane Bianche and, behind it, the Borgo di Cassibile, whose history is linked to the last events of the Second World War, and which preserves a rural settlement (the "Borgo di Cassibile") that maintains its original layout and buildings.

The territory of the municipality of Syracuse borders the petrochemical industrial district of Augusta-Priolo to the north, which extends along a 27 km coastal area.

The articulated and heterogeneous waterfront is of great interest as it includes areas of absolute historical, artistic and landscape value, as well as opportunities for entrepreneurial and socio-cultural development that are not without significant criticalities. These are:

- the landscape complex formed by the islet of Ortigia and the bays of Porto Piccolo and Porto Grande represents a meaningful part of Syracuse's complex value, even though it is affected by the typical criticalities of the gentrification processes: a fast modification of the socio-economic structure; drastic filtering-up phenomena; a dramatic reduction of residents; massive real estate investments from outside; distortion of the map of property values.
- the northern area, bordering the aforementioned petrochemical settlement, is a densely built-up context whose building stock could be affected in the medium to long term by development prospects arising from the redevelopment processes in the field of industrial archaeology of some parts of the plant;
- the Maddalena Peninsula is the richest area in terms of natural landscape, but it too, despite the constraining regime affecting the Plemmirio nature reserve area, is experiencing worrying real estate pressures;
- the southern part of the waterfront is of great scenic and recreational interest due to the value of the beaches and, along the municipal boundary, the mouth of the Cassibile river; this has deterred the formation of the settlements of Ognina and Fontane Bianche, which have significantly reduced the naturalistic value of the area.

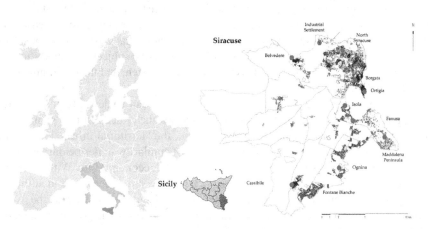

Fig. 2. Territorial frame of the Syracuse Municipality.

3   Methods. Patterns and Contents of a Heterodox Assessment Evolutionary Approach

The proposed method concerns the organisation of the cognitive process of the studied territorial-urban system, coordinating the description and evaluation functions according to a dual approach, orthodox and heterodox.

Description involves observation and denotation, while evaluation involves connotation and interpretation as further elaborations of higher axiological density.

A different degree of "neutrality" of the observer characterises the four functions: observation is predominantly neutral, whereas interpretation expresses the intentionality of the observer. Neutrality characterises an orthodox approach, conversely, intentionality supports heterodox approach and the consequent greater responsibility of the evaluation involving axiological and praxeological coordinations [9]; the former involve values, the latter choices.

An Orthodox Valuative Approach (OVA) merely provides evaluations within the range of significance of what is ordinary, probable, generally acknowledged; it uses semantics (relations of signification) related to current circumstances, efficiency criteria and conventions with a low gradient of agency, i.e. predominantly unintentional. As a result, evaluations are reduced to the "positive" sphere of factual judgement where an occurrence is assumed to be valid for the public and within a limited spatio-temporal range of validity, disregarding further possibilities of worthiness.

In the development of urban eco-socio-systems, such an approach has supported the most unscrupulous and irreversible transformations by sacrificing important components of historical, artistic and naturalistic value that are now regretted.

A Heterodox Evaluative Approach (HVA), on the contrary, looking as much at errors of the past as at threats from the future: 1. Extends the sphere of meaningfulness to what is extra-ordinary, possible, specifically valid; 2. Practices semantics that encompass the entire spectrum of experience that unfolds from memory to expectations, formulating in various cases hypotheses of resemantisation that enhance the potential of what is contingently judged inefficient, ineffective, not cost-effective; 3. Identifies as many reasons for which it is possible to discern reserves of hidden value in what is ordinarily considered rejects; 4. Supports the bottom-up agency of the collective subject, especially in view of further instability of the balance between the social system and the environment and reduction of distributive fairness.

With reference to the concrete characteristics of urban settlements, the proposed description and evaluation model basically replicates the structure of a "signification process" applied to each significance-bearing unit, the "territorial-urban sign", within a "semantic field", the city, bounded by relations of similarity and/or belonging. These links are spatial, administrative, anthropic, social, legal, economic, etc. Within this network, the elementary Signifiers, or significance-bearers, are selected and identified by simplifying reduction, i.e. the set of characteristics by aggregation of which the overall Significance of each sign – i.e. the individual land-urban units – is provided; the latter, consequently, is not taken as a physical referent, but as a synthesis between the structured set of its characteristics and its complex value, i.e. between Signifier and Significance. Two filters are thus interposed between the physical referent and the sign, one cognitive, the other evaluative. In this sense:

– according to an OVA, the sign is bound to the referent insofar as the latter is represented by significance bearers; thus on the basis of a link of dependence of the significance on the signifier preceding it: according to a signification process, it is commonly agreed that "price depends on value";

– according to an HVA, the sign is bound to the referent insofar as the latter retains a memory of its past value and a hope as to its future worth and therefore has a value in itself; such an "iconic value" is independent of the signifier and rather operates on it by restoring semantic dignity to components normally neglected, in relation to which the sign itself gains a different physiognomy; according to a resemantisation process: "the stone which the builders rejected has become the cornerstone!"

The signification and resemantisation processes [10] supporting the two approaches are summarised in Fig. 3.

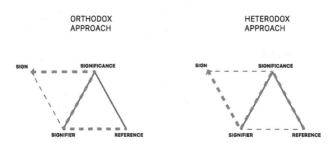

Fig. 3. Semiotic interpretation of the Orthodox and Heterodox approaches.

Transposing this scheme to the case of urban analysis and evaluation, a city can be represented as a semantic chain whose signs assume the function of mutual interpreters. This capacity depends on sharing the same criteria of identification (the topology of land-urban units) and signification (the official information units) and thus on the aptitude to be represented in terms of the same significance bearers.

The latter, in economic-estimative language, can be regarded as the multiple measures of its "capacity to count" as a driver of civil progress. This capacity is differently represented – i.e. evaluated – depending on the type of approach applied, orthodox or heterodox.

The proposed model has the structure of a database that contains as records (references) the elementary land-urban units (urban signs) delimited by the National Statistics Institute (NSI), in this case the Census Sections (CS), and as fields (the elementary signifiers) [11, 12], i.e. the observations accessible in the NSI portal, grouped in the five main topicals, Population, Foreigners, Dwellings, Households, Buildings [13–16];

In general, the cognitive process is developed through a typical Work Breakdown Structure (WBS) [17, 18] which:

– in the construction process it is structured by a progressive top-down disaggregation of the two main socio-economic categories of the city: according to the OVA, Human Capital (HC) and Urban Capital (UC) [19, 20]; according to the HVA Civic Eco-System (CES) and the Social Eco-System (SES);

– in the operational process, the WBS is covered from the bottom up, i.e. by subsequent aggregation of the measures assigned to each CS from the perspective of the attributes selected and identified as the most significant "value bearers".

A specific WBS was created for each of the two above mentioned approaches (Figs. 4 and 5).

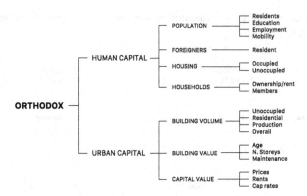

Fig. 4. WBS of the Valuation Orthodox Approach.

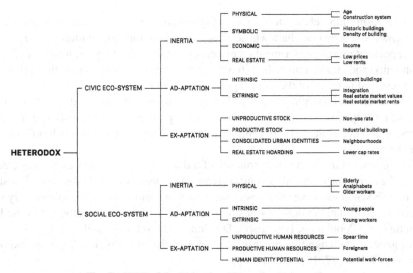

Fig. 5. WBS of the Valuation Heterodox Approach.

The overall process of knowledge of facts and values unfolds according Multi-Attribute Value Theory-based model [21, 22], for the principles of which we refer to the qualified literature on the method and applications most relevant to this experience [23].

The cognitive-valuation process is developed in the following steps:

– for each record (CS) each unit of elementary information is standardised into a score according to a semantic, in this case a four-linear standardisation function anchored to the minimum and maximum values and the three quartiles of each observation in the semantic field;

– this semantic is assigned a "polarity" that identifies the elementary signifier as a value-bearer or disvalue-bearer; each elementary information unit (observation from the official dataset is normalized according a standard 0–2 scale score. Finally, a hierarchical system of weights measures the relative importance of each of the characteristics in relation to all others at the same level of aggregation, in accordance with the organisation of each of the two information frameworks.

At each level of aggregation and for each group of attributes, the CS's final score S is calculates by the weighted average scores of the attributes from the lower (the standardized scores) to the higher level:

$$S = \sum_{i=1}^{n} \lambda_i s_i$$

where λ_i is the weight of the i_{th} attribute and s_i the normalized elementary score, under the following condition:

$$\sum_{i=1}^{n} \lambda_i = 1$$

4 Application e Results

4.1 Orthodox Approach: Human and Urban Capital

The data base provided by the official sources and the subsequent evaluative elaborations – developed at the different levels of abstraction of the primary observation, addressing the two dimensions of human and urban capital [24] – are linked to an interoperable Geographical Information System (GIS). This consultation platform enriches numerical processing with synthetic knowledge supported by thematic comparisons between the different areas and neighbourhoods by cross-referencing in several cases the levels of denotation and connotation.

4.1.1 Human Capital

The aforementioned interpretative process provided an initial assessment of Human Capital represented through 46 elementary information units variously aggregated, relating to the size and articulation of the Resident population, the presence and integration of Foreigners, the Housing Condition and the condition of Households (Fig. 6).

The CS detailed database does not provide income data and therefore the survey on socio-professional status and income is associated with the educational level. Moreover, the observations on the residents are unsuitable to display education level in areas such as Fontane Bianche or Ortigia where second houses prevail. Also the Mobility indices representation doesn't correspond to a situation typically characterized by the presence of commutants students whose mapping should display similar values in the coastal area of Cassibile as in the area between Isola and Fanusa neighbourhoods.

Similarly, mapping of the foreigners integration in affected on the one hand by the concentration of farms in the central part of the rural area nearby Cassibile, on the other hand by different favourable location drivers in various areas of the Borgata and the northern area.

Similarly, the overview of the representation of the two forms of capital should be approached with reference to the number of occupied dwellings and the ratio of rented to owned dwellings. Some examples:

- high-income households are concentrated in the Pizzuta district, which is charac-terised by a high level of settlement quality;
- in Ortigia the prevalence of renting depends on the lack of residents, as properties purchased from outside are put on the rental market or left vacant. This is the effect of the excess of intangible values over functional ones, which identifies real estate as a target for just such a hoarding; Ortigia is an exemplary case of the convergence of inefficiency and property inequity;
- the Borgata, on the other hand, is characterised by significant unexpressed potential, anticipated by rents but not by market prices, nor by the quality of maintenance and urban furnishings.

In general, the composition of households is poorly correlated with location and settlement quality, except in the case of Ortigia from which young and medium-sized households move towards the Borgata, but especially towards the northern area, due to the better building performance offered by buildings meeting contemporary housing standards (Fig. 6).

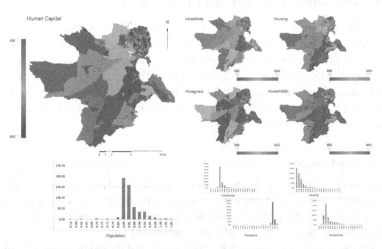

Fig. 6. Maps and probability density graphs of the main axiological components of the Human Capital (our valuation and GIS elaborations of the NSI dataset).

4.1.2 Urban Capital

Urban Capital was also observed and interpreted based on the normalisation and aggregation and combination of data into indices with reference to the general categories of the volume and value of building stock.

The observations concerned the volumes and functions of residential and productive uses and the total building stock in the CS.

The entire descriptive framework addresses, in its original aspirations, the category of urban landscape and thus distinguishes and emphasises the considerable amount of historic buildings and their integration into the overall urban fabric.

Again, the lack of information on actual volumes made it necessary to use an indirect representation, obtained by integrating observations on the rates of buildings of different age classes, number of above-ground elevations and properties. Excluding the suburban areas, the maps showed significant differences between the landscape quality of the historic urban fabric, Ortigia and the Borgata, and that of the more recent ones in the northern part of the city. In spite of the effects of a representation influenced by measurements at different scales, it can be seen that the most heavily built-up sections, i.e. those of the densest urban fabrics, often show average evaluations due to the wide range of maintenance conditions that characterise buildings dating back to the 1960s-80 (Fig. 7).

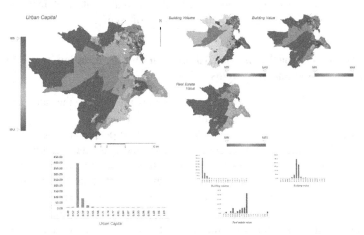

Fig. 7. Maps and probability density graphs of the main axiological components of the Urban Capital (our valuation and GIS elaborations of the NSI dataset).

4.1.3 Synthesis

The complexity and contradictions of this particular spatial context are finally summarised in the results of the overall assessments of the two complementary and converging categories of the home-city-landscape system. Here again, it is an abstraction that reflects the original aspirations of the economic-estimative tradition engaged in defining the most effective (monetary and non-monetary) assessment information contents and attributes for the purposes of economic communication, thus reducing to synthetic indices the complexity of the multiple aptitudes to be worth, prices or preference relations, according to the task and purpose of the assessment.

Among the contradictions that emerge from this experience of "reasoned mapping" – that is, traced back to the numerical evidence of the available territorial information apparatus – the divergence of landscape values and environmental disvalues stands out. The latter, especially in the face of the successes of the 'cultural industry' that are recognised by the "Ortiga" brand, must be constantly brought to the attention of the public.

The effects of the sudden development of this sector can also be seen in this analysis, just in the relationship between human and urban capital, which is significantly – and now also irreversibly – affected by the accumulation of liquidity in the real estate asset, mostly consolidated in the old nucleus of Ortigia and seeking new opportunities in the Borgata di S. Lucia. Further ways and forms of this trend can also be seen in the extra-urban areas, in particular on the Maddalena Peninsula and on the southern coast in the area of Cassibile and Fontane Bianche, whose naturalistic and landscape values complement the architectural and testimonial ones, completing the basket of real estate performances with relevant alternatives for both productive and speculative investment.

These expectations imply certain threats of irreversible impacts generated by transformations inspired by entrepreneurial success and real estate that increase the gap between the reasons of efficiency and the demands of equity.

4.2   Heterodox Approach: Inertia, Adaptation and Ex-aptation at the Levels of the Civic and Social Systems

The prospect of a heterodox approach overcomes the dimension of the category of capital by turning to that of eco-system, particularly civic and social.

The civic eco-system involves the relations between people and the city with reference to the way in which the city responds to the instances that the community expresses in the view of a more rapid and consistent affirmation of the principles of civic progress; the social eco-system looks at the way in which the urban dimension constitutes the catalyst of social fairness through the reduction of communicative barriers between social sub-systems and between the system and the environment: in the former case, aspects of social justice are taken into account, in the latter those of environmental justice.

This perspective is taken here to reinterpret the official information system in light of three evolutionary capacities: Inertia, Adaptation and Ex-aptation. These are three ways in which a social-urban eco-system, as a whole, on the one hand acquiesces to individual and social demands and pressures from mainly economic-productive drivers of development, and on the other hand reveals the tensions arising from the inevitable gaps in social communication between colliding sub-systems that make the social system increasingly vulnerable to environmental fluctuations. These three attitudes of the social-urban system toward its living space have been represented through the indices relating to the above three concepts:

- Inertia is that condition represented in the barriers to the rapid transformation of the human/urban landscape, which hints at margins of value contained in depth apart from that contingently attributed;
- Adaptation is the condition of an urban eco-system that has responded to the triggers of material progress according to the directions of urban land policies by exhausting the entire spectrum of potential implicit in the heritage that has been irreversibly erased;
- Ex-aptation is an evolutionist concept, introduced by two paleontologists, S. J. Gould and E. S. Vrba [25], in disagreement with that of adaptation, because it assumes unemployed resources as a condition of new unexplored possibilities in spite of most likely low use or functional value.

4.2.1 Inertia

The Inertia index summarizes the scoring of the two Civic and Social eco-systems groups of drivers.

The first one concerns the building volume components due to its scarce reversibility and flexibility. A fortiori, architectural heritage constitutes a component of the building asset whose historic-architectural value consolidates the perspective of the preservation of the multiple cultural identities stratified over time [26, 27]. The synthesis of inertia identifies consolidated urban contexts as invariants of the development policies of the city as a whole. Even some peripheral coastal urban units, albeit in continuous and subdued expansion, prospect the consolidation of an image capable of opposing the real estate attack, as in the areas of Ognina, Fontane Bianche and the Maddalena peninsula.

The second one concerns the fragile and non-independent social fabrics due to old age and low educational attainment; nevertheless, these constitute a significant presidium of the local identities [28] facing imminent dissolution.

The maps of Inertia at the levels of the two eco-systems are displayed in Fig. 8.

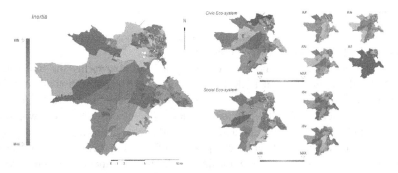

Fig. 8. Maps of the main drivers of Inertia at the levels of civic and social eco-systems (our valuation and GIS elaboration of the NSI dataset).

4.2.2   Adaptation

The synthesis of the adaptation maps suggests that the expansion of the city and the vibrancy of these areas due to the presence of the younger people can prospect, especially in the Borgata, co-evolutionary processes of neighbourhood identities aimed at public spaces and the life quality enhancement.

With reference to the civic eco-system, the areas of the new city that have rapidly developed in response to the prospects of renewal and expansion of the urban building stock have also failed to complete and evolve the secondary urbanization system beyond the minimum legal standards. As a result, the measures of this rapid adaptation referring to the rate of urban expansion over time, the typological and functional mix of the built heritage among different areas does not reflect the profile of a context that has developed organically.

The social eco-system is also affected by these critical issues as to the difficulties of maintaining and developing neighbourhood identities around key social and cultural facilities (Fig. 9).

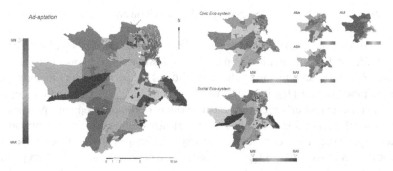

Fig. 9. Maps of the main drivers of Adaptation at the levels of civic and social eco-systems (our valuation and GIS elaboration of the NSI dataset).

4.2.3   Ex-aptation

The sequence of the aspects of Ex-aptation also outlines a complex framework of resources with has yet unexpressed potential.

From the perspective of the civic eco-system, it is noteworthy the underutilized residential building stock which, traditionally regarded as a manifestation of inefficiency, implies a tendency for real hoarding in view of positive expectations of future real estate performances in terms of both yield and capital gains measured by the low cap rates especially in Ortigia, in the Borgata and in the Maddalena Peninsula.

However, these aspects also underlie positive effects in terms of social rebalancing due to the high heterogeneity of the housing stock, the assortment of which provides a wide set of opportunities in the different areas of the city in response to the multiple needs, of personal use, of renting, of seasonal activities that can as much alternate as integrate. A further aspect concerning prospects for social promotion concerns an extensive stock of old, disused industrial buildings in the areas close to the central station that outline significant undefined urban inclusive development prospects [29] (Fig. 10).

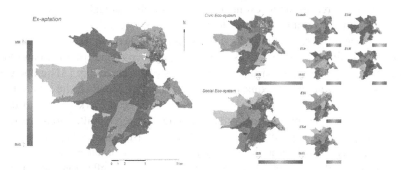

Fig. 10. Maps of the main drivers of Ex-aptation at the levels of civic and social eco-systems (our valuation and GIS elaboration of the NSI dataset).

4.2.4 Synthesis

The three perspectives of the heterodox approach highlight the different ways of considering the same urban context as valuable depending on its variables, with the perspective of not neglecting any potential or residual fraction of the past/future capacity of parts of the territory and city to become important for someone and in certain aspects. The mapping of Inertia as the capacity of the territorial-urban system to resist transformations with a high social and urban impact, does not reveal a clear correspondence between the most resistant areas and the least dynamic social components.

Similarly, and inversely, the Adaptation map indicates the areas that have already exhausted their entire transformative potential, unless a massive rethinking of urban policy lines, hopefully in the wake of the opportunities of ecological transition.

In this prospect emerges the capacity for Ex-Adaptation that in the whole context takes the different forms of real hoarding, on the one hand motivated by the expansion of the real estate sector, on the other identifiable in the expectations about new intended uses of the abandoned ancient industrial asset that can integrate the now saturated lines of expansion of the existing building stock.

5 Conclusions

This study aims to suggest a research path on the sustainability of urban development [30] based on the fertile and multiple notion of value, often taken in the reductive forms of utility in hedonic terms on the one hand and efficiency, functional and economic, on the other.

The proposal of a dialectic between an orthodox and a heterodox approach, supported by a multidimensional assessment model applied in a complex, stratified and in various respects even contradictory urban context, is aimed at highlighting the polysemy of different occurrences (objects, facts, processes, trends) with respect to the possibility of expressing a multiplicity of values. In the prospect of a twofold (orthodox/heterodox) approach, all of them has been recognised relevant even if not predominantly highlighted by location and/or real estate investment choices, as well as not adequately valued at the level of the political-administrative system.

In this perspective, if the orthodox approach based on efficiency and cost-effectiveness defines clear objectives and non-contradictory criteria of urban redevelopment processes, the emergence of the instances of sustainability [31] empower the science of evaluations in applying heterodox approaches showing the contradictions of the traditional development model, which has leveraged market rules to transfer irreducible costs to the environment (mainly natural, but more guiltily to human).

This study, also consistent with the most recent sustainability approaches, which propose measurements of embodied energy and residual performances, proposes – especially considering the concepts of Inertia and Ex-aptation – a reflection and experimentation on how to think and represent by values the fabric of occurrences and relationships that denotate and connotate the home-city-landscape system in a centripetal perspective, from planet to home.

More generally, the heterodox approach is an important stage of "suspension of judgment" in the awareness that values are all the more important the more the facts themselves are recognized as values, and that values are not relative or absolute, but false or authentic, and always present, irreducible and unamendable across the entire spectrum of the shared experience.

Acknowledgements. Conceptualization, M.R.T.; methodology, M.R.T.; software, M.R.T., C.C. and L.N.; validation, and M.R.T., C.C. and L.N.; formal analysis, M.R.T.; investigation, C.C., L.N. and V.V.; resources, C.C., L.N. and V.V.; data curation, C.C. and L.N.; writing—original draft preparation, M.R.T.; writing—review and editing, M.R.T. and V.V.; visualization, M.R.T., C.C. and L.N.; supervision, M.R.T.; project administration, M.R.T.; funding acquisition, M.R.T.

References

1. Glaeser, E.L., Redlick, C.: Social Capital and Urban Growth; Working Paper 14374; National Bureau of Economic Research: Cambridge, MA, USA. http://www.nber.org/papers/w14374 (2008). Last accessed 10 Oct 2021
2. United Nations: The 2030 Agenda for Sustainable Development. http://sdps.un.org/goals (2015). Last accessed 2 Apr 2023
3. Della Spina, L.: Strategic planning and decision making: a case study for the integrated management of cultural heritage assets in southern Italy. In: Bevilacqua, C., Calabrò, F., Della Spina, L. (eds.) NMP 2020. SIST, vol. 178, pp. 1116–1130. Springer, Cham (2021). https://doi.org/10.1007/978-3-030-48279-4_104
4. Tajani, F., Guarini, M., Sica, F., Ranieri, R., Anelli, D.: Multi-criteria analysis and sustainable accounting. Defining indices of sustainability under Choquet's integral. Sustainability **14**(5), 2782 (2022). https://doi.org/10.3390/su14052782
5. Camagni, R., Capello, R.: Regional competitiveness and territorial capital: a conceptual approach and empirical evidence from the european union. Reg. Stud. **47**, 1383–1402 (2013). https://doi.org/10.1080/00343404.2012.681640

6. Coleman, J.S.: Social Capital in the Creation of Human Capital. In: Coleman, J.S. (ed.) Networks in the Knowledge Economy. Oxford University Press (2003). https://doi.org/10.1093/oso/9780195159509.003.0007

7. de Hart, J., Dekker, P.: A tale of two cities: local patterns of social capital. In: Hooghe, M., Stolle, D. (eds.) Generating Social Capital: Civil Society and Institutions in Comparative Perspective, pp. 153–170. Palgrave, New York, NY, USA (2003)

8. Keeney, R.L.: Applying value-focused thinking. Military Oper. Res. 13(2), 7–17 (2008). https://doi.org/10.5711/morj.13.2.7

9. Giuffrida, S., Ventura, V., Nocera, F., Trovato, M.R., Gagliano, F.: Technological, axiological and praxeological coordination in the energy-environmental equalization of the strategic old town renovation programs. In: Mondini, G., Oppio, A., Stanghellini, S., Bottero, M., Abastante, F. (eds.) Values and Functions for Future Cities. GET, pp. 425–446. Springer, Cham (2020). https://doi.org/10.1007/978-3-030-23786-8_24

10. Giuffrida S., Trovato M.R.: A semiotic approach to the landscape accounting and assessment. an application to the urban-coastal areas. In: Salampasis, M., Theodoridis, A., Bournaris, T. (eds.) 8th International Conference on Information and Communication Technologies in Agriculture, Food and Environment, HAICTA 2017, vol. 2030, pp. 696–708. Chania, Crete Island; Greece; 21–24 Sep 2017, CEUR Workshop Proceedings ISSN: 16130073

11. Trovato, M.R., Nasca, L.: An axiology of weak areas: the estimation of an index of abandonment for the definition of a cognitive tool to support the enhancement of inland areas in sicily. Land 11(12), 2268 (2022). https://doi.org/10.3390/land11122268

12. Trovato, M.R., Cappello, C.: Climate adaptation heuristic planning support system (HPSS): green-blue strategies to support the ecological transition of historic centres. Land 11, 773 (2022). https://doi.org/10.3390/land11060773

13. ISTAT. Rapporto Annuale 2020—La Situazione del Paese. 2020. https://www.istat.it/it/archivio/244848. Last accessed 1 Aug 2021

14. ISTAT. Data Set 8mila Census. http://ottomilacensus.istat.it/. Last accessed 1 Aug 2021

15. ISTAT: Territorial bases and census variables. https://www.istat.it/it/archivio/104317. Last accessed 1 Aug 2021

16. ISTAT. Index of Social and Material Vulnerability. http://ottomilacensus.istat.it/fileadmin/download/Indice_di_vulnerabilit%C3%A0_sociale_e_materiale.pdf (2011). Last accessed 1 Aug 2021

17. Berg, C., Colenso, K.: Work breakdown structure practice standard project—WBS vs activities. PM Netw. 14(4), 69–71 (2000)

18. Haugan, G.T.: Effective Work Breakdown Structures. Management Concepts, Inc., Vienna VA USA (2001)

19. Goodwin, N.R.: Five Kinds of Capital: Useful Concepts for Sustainable Development. http://ageconsearch.umn.edu/bitstream/15595/1/wp030007.pdf (2003). Last accessed 10 Oct 2021

20. Trovato, M.R.: Human capital approach in the economic assessment of interventions for the reduction of seismic vulnerability in historic centres. Sustainability 12, 8059 (2020). https://doi.org/10.3390/su12198059

21. Keeney, R.L., Raiffa, H., Rajala, D.W.: Decisions with multiple objectives: preferences and value trade-offs. IEEE Trans. Syst. Man Cybern. 9(7), 403 (1979). https://doi.org/10.1109/TSMC.1979.4310245

22. Trovato, M.R.: A multi-criteria approach to support the retraining plan of the Biancavilla's old town. In: Calabrò, F., Della Spina, L., Bevilacqua, C. (eds.) ISHT 2018. SIST, vol. 101, pp. 434–441. Springer, Cham (2019). https://doi.org/10.1007/978-3-319-92102-0_46

23. Belton, V.: Multi-criteria problem structuring and analysis in a value theory framework. In: Gal, T., Stewart, T.J., Hanne, T. (eds.) Multicriteria Decision Making, pp. 335–366. Springer US, Boston, MA (1999). https://doi.org/10.1007/978-1-4615-5025-9_12

24. Nasca, L., Giuffrida, S., Trovato, M.R.: Value and quality in the dialectics between human and urban capital of the city networks on the land district scale. Land **11**(1), 34 (2022). https://doi.org/10.3390/land11010034

25. Gould, S.J.: Exaptation: a crucial tool for an evolutionary psychology. J. Soc. Issues **47**(3), 43–65 (1991). https://doi.org/10.1111/j.1540-4560.1991.tb01822.x

26. Winchell, K.M., Losos, J.B., Verrelli, B.C.: Urban evolutionary ecology brings exaptation back into focus. Trend Ecol. Evol. (2023). https://doi.org/10.1016/j.tree.2023.03.006

27. Associazione Nazionale Centri Storico Artistici (ANCSA): Centro Ricerche Economiche e Sociali del Mercato dell'Edilizia (Cresme). Centri Storici e Futuro del Paese. Indagine Nazionale sulla Situazione dei Centri Storici. ANCSA, Cresme, Italy (2017)

28. Cappello, C., Giuffrida, S., Trovato, M.R., Ventura, V.: Environmental identities and the sustainable city the green roof prospect for the ecological transition. Sustainability **14**(19), 12005 (2022)

29. Belsky, E.S., DuBroff, N., McCue, D., Harris, C., McCartney, S., Molinsky, J.: Advancing Inclusive and Sustainable Urban Development: Correcting Planning Failures and Connecting Communities to Capital. Joint Center for Housing Studies of Harvard University, Cambridge, MA, USA (2013)

30. Tanguay, G.A., Rajaonson, J., Lefebvre, J.-F., Lanoie, P.: Measuring the sustainability of cities: an analysis of the use of local indicators. Ecol. Indic. **10**, 407–418 (2010). https://doi.org/10.1016/j.ecolind.2009.07.013

31. Steiniger, S., et al.: Localising urban sustainability indicators: the CEDEUS indicator set, and lessons from an expert-driven process. Cities **101**, 102683 (2020). https://doi.org/10.1016/j.cities.2020.102683

Sustainable Aging in Aix-Marseille-Provence Metropolis: Assessment Indicators and Interactive Visualizations for Policy Making

Joan Perez[1(✉)] [iD], Araldi Alessandro[1], Boyer Thomas[1], Bridier Sébastien[2], Decoupiny Fabrice[1], Fusco Giovanni[1], Laperrière Vincent[2], and Trémélo Marie-Laure[2]

[1] Université Côte-Azur, CNRS, ESPACE, Nice, France
joan.perez@univ-cotedazur.fr
[2] Aix-Marseille Université, CNRS, ESPACE, Aix-en-Provence, France

Abstract. As the world's population continues to age and urbanization accelerates, the focus of urban sustainability has evolved towards promoting the needs and well-being of older adults in addition to environmental concerns. Urban environments have a significant impact on the experiences of city dwellers, particularly of older adults, and from this perspective certain neighborhoods present greater challenges than others. To address issues related to aging, cities around the world have launched initiatives to improve urban sustainability for older adults, ranging from redesigning public spaces to providing opportunities for social interaction. However, to design effective interventions, open-access data related to urban environments must be collected and analyzed to identify neighborhoods with the greatest need for improvement. This paper presents a case study of the Aix-Marseille-Provence metropolis in France, showing that a range of assessment indicators focused on walkability and urban form can be calculated using open-access data. Through the presentation of these indicators and exploratory analysis results in a visual and interactive format (HTML-based platform), planners and policymakers can quickly identify patterns and trends, thereby helping them identify neighborhoods with the most significant needs and create more effective policies.

Keywords: Aging · walkability · urban form · data visualization · urban sustainability

1 Introduction

As the world's population ages and more people choose to live in urban areas, the focus of urban sustainability has evolved beyond environment issues to also encompass the needs and well-being of older adults. This evolution has been driven by a growing recognition of the important role that urban environments play in promoting healthy aging and social inclusion, as highlighted by academics and intergovernmental organizations [1, 2]. The locations are significantly impacting the experiences and possibilities of all city dwellers,

O. Gervasi et al. (Eds.): ICCSA 2023 Workshops, LNCS 14104, pp. 339–353, 2023.
https://doi.org/10.1007/978-3-031-37105-9_23

and especially of older adults, and from this perspective certain neighborhoods are presenting greater challenges than others. This is for example the case of car-dependent suburbs made of single-family homes, hard to walk areas because of obstacles or steep slopes, or the presence/absence of close-by shops and services which leads to different degrees of vitality for neighborhoods [3]. The challenge for cities and policy makers is to ensure that older adults are, regardless of their residential location, fully integrated into the urban environment. In recent years, cities around the world have launched initiatives aimed at improving urban sustainability for older adults. These initiatives have included everything from redesigning public spaces to better meet the needs of older adults [4], to providing more opportunities for social interaction and community engagement [5]. To summarize, the aim is to make urban spaces more livable, sustainable, and resilient for generations to come.

Built environments yet require improvements and modifications to varying degrees of urgency, depending of course on the type of issues at hand, but also on the requirements of the inhabitants living in different locations. From this perspective, the collection, analysis, and interpretation of open-access data related to urban environments can help identify the level of immediacy to which different neighborhoods, associated to different ratio of older adults, are exposed to sustainability and walkability issues. Urban planners and policy makers can for example use the output of a different range of assessment indicators to design, implement and modify urban locations within the aim of improving the overall quality of life for aging residents. However, to reach that aim, it is important for assessment indicators to be designed to address specific issues and for their results to be easily comprehensible and accessible at a metropolitan scale. This paper thus focuses on a test metropolitan area, the Aix-Marseille-Provence metropolis in southern France, and shows that a wide range of assessment indicators focusing on the link between locations and aging can be calculated using specific data in open-access. The range of indicators addressed in this paper focuses on the ratio of older adults, walkability issues (steep slopes and accessibility to amenities) as well as on the physical features of urban spaces (morphotypes), as they could be perceived by people. By presenting data in a visual and interactive way, planners and makers can then quickly identify patterns and trends that might not be immediately apparent.

This paper is organized as follows. Section 2 introduces the case study Aix-Marseille-Provence Metropolis and the different datasets gathered for this study. Section 3 presents the assessment indicators that have been calculated. Section 4 presents preliminary results obtained by cross-analyzing the different indicators presented in Sect. 3. Section 5 introduces an interactive platform to visualize and explore the spatial results calculated in the previous sections. Section 6 concludes the paper with a discussion on future applications.

2   Case Study and Data Presentation

2.1   Aix-Marseille-Provence Metropolis

The Aix-Marseille-Provence Metropolis is an intercommunal organization made of 92 communes in southern France (Fig. 1). Its area is about 3,150 km^2 for a population of 1,9 million inhabitants in 2019. Marseille and Aix-en-Provence are the main cities of this intercommunal organization. The urban agglomeration, defined by the French Statistical Institute INSEE as the continuously built-up area with gaps up to 200 m, covers 1,758 km^2, with a population of 1,614,500 in 2019. Spatially, the urban agglomeration includes the city of Aix-en-Provence and the industrial and logistic area around the coastal lagoon of Berre, and covers most of the Bouche-du-Rhône administrative department (5,087 km^2 and 2,034,000 inhabitants in 2019).

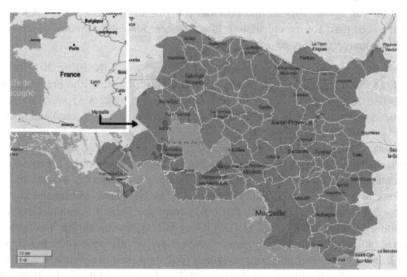

Fig. 1. Administrative boundaries of the 92 communes belonging to Aix-Marseille-Provence Metropolis [6].

The *«Logements, individus, activité, mobilités scolaires et professionnelles, migrations résidentielles»* database of the French National Institute of Statistics and Economic Studies (INSEE) [7] provides variables and information related to the French housing units and the households occupying them. Over the last decade (2008–2018) and across the entire metropolitan area, the population of people aged over 80 has grown by 25%, while the total population has only grown by 3.5%. However, the growth of the elderly population is significantly more pronounced in the least densely populated municipalities on the outskirts of urban areas, while in the center of the Marseille and Aix agglomerations, the trend is towards stagnation or even a decrease in the proportion of people aged over 80.

Across the Aix-Marseille-Provence metropolitan area, households consisting of a single senior, known as "isolated seniors," represent 52.3% (68,782 out of 131,522) of the households possessing at least one senior aged 75 or older. 43% of the households with at least one senior aged over 75 live in single-family houses, 90% of which owner-occupied. Among the remaining 57% living in apartments, only 53% of which are owner-occupied, and half of the remaining 47% are tenants living in social housing and the other half in private rental apartments. In the metropolitan area as a whole, 50% of apartments that elderly people occupy lack elevators, making it difficult for those living on higher floors. This lack of elevator access is equally prevalent among isolated seniors.

2.2 Data collection

With the availability of census data accessible through open data access, it is possible to delve deeper and to conduct a more comprehensive analysis of spatial disparities associated with aging. This section provides a list of all the datasets, in open access, that have been used for the calculation of assessment indicators (Sect. 3) focusing on walkability and readability of urban spaces.

- The « *localised disposable income system (Filosofi®)*» of INSEE in 2017 [8]. The scale of data collection corresponds to a square tessellation of the French territory with tiles measuring of 200 m on each side. This file gathers 35 variables related to the structure and characteristics of both households (size, age, etc.) and housings (sqm of housing units, owner, etc.).
- The «*Permanent database of facilities (BPE®)*» of INSEE in 2019 [9]. This dataset gathers all the amenities in France with their geolocation. Amenities are divided into several categories and sub-categories such as service, commerce, education, health and social services, transportation and mobility, sports-leisure-culture and tourism.
- The «*Topographic dataset (BD TOPO®)*» from the French National Geographic Institute (IGN) in 2019 [10]. BD TOPO® are GIS layers containing, amongst other things, building footprints (polygons on a two-dimensional plane) where buildings are digitized as single-part polygons and roads (polylines on a two-dimensional plane).
- The 30-m resolution digital elevation model (DEM) of the Shuttle Radar Topography Mission of the NASA Earthdata program [11].

As the next sections will show, municipalities and policymakers can gain insights that were previously unavailable by leveraging and cross analyzing the aforementioned data sources.

3   Indicators

It is important for assessment indicators to be designed to address specific issues in order to maximize their impact and ensures their comprehensibility. Within this research, we put the focus on walkability as well as on the physical features of urban spaces as they could be perceived by an aging population. Walkability typically refers to various factors that make an environment conductive to walking. As discussed in Lo [12] different pedestrian performance metrics have been developed within various disciplines such as traffic engineering, transportation planning, urban design, public health or sociology, and all these fields have varying definitions and methods on how to assess walkability. In the context aging and urban planning, walkability mostly refers to creating a resilient and healthy city [13] while the physical features of urban spaces refer to morphotypes around street segments.

3.1 Share of Individuals Aged 65 Years or Older

The concept of the third age is a term that is often used interchangeably with old age. The third age is generally associated with individuals who have retired from full-time work and are no longer raising children, but are not yet considered to be in the final stages of life, also referred to as the fourth age. People belonging to the third and fourth age are commonly referred to as "seniors", "elderly persons" or "older adults" and are often recognized as a distinct demographic group with specific needs and challenges. The age structure of the population is available within the 2017 « *localised disposable income system (Filosofi®)*» database of INSEE [8]. First, the population aged 65 years or older, which roughly corresponds to both the third and the fourth age, has thus been extracted and divided by the total population per tile to obtain the share of older adults per location. On a given tile, if the number of households is less than 11, the data are imputed in order to respect the confidentiality threshold set by the French government. Overall, most of the tiles (79%) contain less than 11 households but they only account for 20% of the population.

3.2 Slope Averages

Older adults have weaker muscles and joints, making it more difficult for them to navigate steep slopes. This can lead to increased fatigue and discomfort, which can further increase the risk of falls. Moreover, walking on a steep slope enhances the intensity of physical activity, resulting in an elevation of heart rate, which in turn increases the risk of cardiovascular complications for older adults [14]. When considering the needs of aging populations, it's important to consider the slope of the terrain, above all in the case of Aix-Marseille-Provence metropolis, which includes a contrasted topography. Even if an area has pedestrian-friendly amenities, steep slopes can create difficulties for older adults who may have limited mobility. For this project, for the second assessment indicator, we thus computed the slope average using the 30-m resolution elevation data from the Shuttle Radar Topography Mission (SRTM) of the NASA Earthdata program [11], at the very same scale than the previous indicator i.e., the tiles measuring 200 m on each side of the Filosofi® database. The indicator has been named "slope average".

3.3 Accessibility to Amenities

The concept of the "15-min walk city" or of hyper-proximity has gained traction in urban planning in the last decade. The idea is that cities should be designed so that residents can access most of their daily needs within a 15-min walk, bike ride, or public transit trip, thus contributing to more vibrant, compact and sustainable communities [15, 16]. Studies have also highlighted an association between a lack of shops and weak walkability scores, within neighborhoods that could be described as food deserts [17]. Given both these rationales, the number of accessible amenities has been calculated in a queen's topological space of contiguity from the scale of the 200-m tiles of the Filosofi® dataset [8] using the *permanent database of facilities* of INSEE [9]. A queen's topological space of contiguity corresponds to a maximum of 600 m of walk from edge to edge, or of 300 m from the center to an edge, and thus look in perfect adequation to the concept of the "15-min walk city". From this perspective, *SSi* (Shops and Services) expresses the sum of amenities accessible within a given tile *i* based on the occurrences within the said tile and within the contiguous tiles. Amenities within the queen's neighborhood of *i* have been weighted according to the slope average. In other words, the steeper the slope, the less the amenities are contributing to the final score of *SSi*. The *permanent database of facilities* of INSEE contains hundreds of categories of shops and services. For this research, we operated a subset on categories of shops and services that could be used by the elders, such as health services, convenience stores, supermarkets, post offices, etc. A specific list of amenities used by older adults does not stand out in the academic literature and thus, the detail of the retained categories we decided to select for the research has been made available in Appendix A. From now on, this subset will be referred to as amenities.

$$SS_i = i + \left(\sum_{j=0}^{n} L_j + \left(\frac{M_j}{2} \right) + \left(\frac{H_j}{4} \right) \right)$$

Given *i* the number of amenities within a tile, *Lj* (low slope) are the values observed in the queen's neighborhood of *i* where the slope average is <5%, *Mj* (medium slope) are the values observed in the queen's neighborhood of *i* where the slope average is between 5% and 8%, and *Hj* (high slope) are the values observed in the queen's neighborhood of *i* where the slope is > 8%.

3.4 Morphotypes Around Street Segments

The urban landscape of Aix-Marseille-Provence Metropolis is made of a patchwork of very diverse forms of the urban fabric. Within this project, a first analysis of the diverse urban fabric of Marseille was carried out [18]. The Multiple Fabric Assessment protocol [19] was used to identify and characterize morphotypes around street segments, i.e. typical forms of the urban fabric, using street-based morphometrics of buildings, streets and plots, and their mutual relations, as they can be perceived by pedestrian moving on the street using the *BD TOPO®* from the French National Geographic Institute (IGN) in 2019 [10] as the primary source of data. A new version of the MFA protocol implements several improvements related to precision, robustness and scalability to analyse larger study areas, and compare them between one another. The new protocol was applied to the whole department of Bouches-du-Rhône, roughly corresponding to the Aix-Marseille-Provence Metropolis, and allowed detecting and characterizing 19 different morphotypes (Fig. 2).

Five morphotypes make up the compact urbanization in around the old city centres: **UF1**. Old compact village centres and densified faubourgs, organic or planned, made of townhouses and small adjoining buildings (2.4% of the street segments of the study area) **UF15**. Compact grid-based heterogeneous urban fabric, with varied adjoining buildings aligned on regularly meshed networks, including some specialised buildings (1% of the street segments). **UF16**. Compact and dense fabric of small-to-mid-sized adjoining buildings and townhouses aligned on meshed and irregular networks, with strong presence of specialised buildings (1%). **UF9**. Densified urban subdivisions of

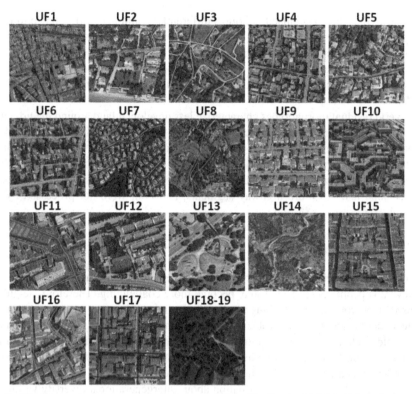

Fig. 2. The 19 morphotypes around street segments identified by the Multiple Fabric Assessment protocol in Aix-Marseille-Provence Metropolis

townhouses and houses moderately aligned and close to dense partially meshed and irregular networks (2.8%). **UF17**. Fabric of townhouses and adjoining buildings aligned on a regular grid (negligible).

Two morphotypes characterize modernist urbanization, together with specialized space: **UF11**. Modernised mid-rise continuous/discontinuous fabric alternating fragments of buildings and houses aligned on irregularly meshed networks (1%). **UF10**. Discontinuous modernist fabrics of elongated apartment blocks and towers with setback on irregularly meshed networks (3.2%). **UF0**. Specialized space is a specific morphotype characterized by the over-representation of specialized buildings (factories, commercial buildings, logistic buildings, hospitals, university campuses) (5.1%).

Seven morphotypes make up the vast low-rise peripheral and suburban urbanization: **UF6**. Fabric of urban subdivisions of aligned houses (1.1%). **UF7**. Suburban residential fabric of homogeneous subdivisions of houses and villas (or houses) with setback on organic or tree-like networks (4.7%). **UF4**. Subdivisions of partially aligned houses and 1-storey villas with setback and partially aligned on meshed/tree-like and irregular network (1.6%). **UF5**. Heterogeneous suburban fabric of houses and villas moderately aligned on tree-like and/or sloped networks (1%). **UF2**. Heterogeneous suburban fringe

of houses, villas and specialised buildings differently positioned with refence to irregularly meshed or tree-like networks (3.7%). **UF12**. Heterogeneous and discontinuous
suburban fabrics alternating fragments with houses/villas and fragments with buildings,
setback on tree-like networks (5.4%). **UF3**. Heterogeneous ex-urban fabric of houses,
villas and specialized low-rise buildings, differently positioned on tree-like networks
(14.4%).

Several residual morphotypes characterize less developed land around the urbanisa-
tion: **UF14**. Suburban/exurban fabric interfacing with undeveloped land (10.4%). **UF13**.
Empty connective fragments (negligible). **UF8**. Rural space with scattered buildings
(17.2%). of the study area. **UF18-UF19** are a single morphotype of undeveloped land
interfaced with suburban and exurban fabric (10.2%). 12% of the study area are undeveloped land and 1.8% are highway segments, and both were not processed by the
protocol.

4   Exploratory Analysis

The outskirts of towns often trade off pedestrian-friendliness in favor of car mobility.
However, as people age, driving may become more challenging. Therefore, neighborhoods that are for example lacking nearby shops and services, or that are constructed
on steep slopes may become problematic in the long run regarding the level of autonomy of older adults. This section thus aims at exploring the vulnerability and autonomy
levels of the elderly population within the Aix-Marseille-Provence Metropolis based on
three indicators calculated within the previous section: the share of individuals aged 65
years or older which provides information about intergenerational diversity within the
neighborhoods, the slope average to evaluate walkability and accessibility to amenities.
The scale of analysis is once again the 200-m tiles gridded data of the Filosofi® census
in 2017 [8].

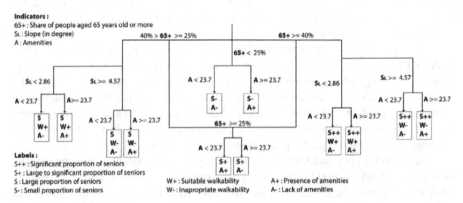

Fig. 3. A tree-like classificatory model to evaluate the degree of vulnerability/autonomy of the
elderly population

An expert-based classification system has been developed to classify each 200-m tile
based on the three aforementioned indicators. First, the share of individuals aged 65 years

or older has been divided into three categories using the following thresholds: less than 25% (S-), between 25 and 40% (S), and more than 40% (S+ for very aged population). This segmentation relies on the analysis of the density distribution of this indicator. Second, the slope average has also been divided into three categories. According to Alves *et al.,* [14] normal heartbeats are generally between 60 and 90 bpm, while a measurement of 120 'bpm is the outcome of great efforts for an elderly person. The authors then deduce the following categories related to the difficulty of a senior's walk according to the slope: <5%—suitable, 5% < x < 8%—acceptable and >8%—inappropriate. We thus used the very same thresholds to evaluate walkability (W+ and W−) within a neighborhood. Lastly, using SS*i* (Sect. 3), we operated a division into two categories: presence and lack of amenities. The threshold between these two categories has been set to 23.7. Despites many studies on accessibilities to shops and services, as well as on the concept of walkability and walkability for the older adults [20, 21], a single and clear threshold of a given number of reachable amenities for an urbanized area to be considered as properly equipped does not stands out from the academic literature. As a result, we decided to pick three peripheral locations where amenities are present: *Septèmes-les-Vallons*, *Gardanne* and *Fuveaux*. The mean of SS*i* of these three locations allowed defining 23.7 as a threshold for the following two categories: properly equipped in amenities (A+) and lack or few amenities (A−). The tree-like classificatory model using these thresholds allowed obtaining 12 different class labels (Fig. 3).

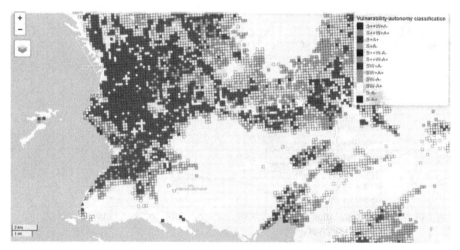

Fig. 4. Sample of the classificatory results in Marseille (source: HTML-based platform, see Sect. 5)

Several sub-categories and spatial clusters emerge (Fig. 4), based on how the proportion of seniors, walkability and accessibility to amenities are combined. As summarized in Table 1, the statistical results of this application allow locating and quantifying the number of seniors concerned by walkability and accessibility to amenities issues. It is for example interesting to note that the worst-case scenario (S++W−A−: significant proportion of older adults, a bad score of walkability and a lack of amenities) only concerns

Table 1. Statistical results by class label

Label	Description	% of Tot Pop	% of 65 yo+	% of urbanized surface
S++W+A−	Significant proportion of seniors, suitable walkability, lack of amenities	0.28	0.66	0.51
S++W+A+	Significant proportion of seniors, suitable walkability, presence of amenities	0.40	0.93	0.28
S+A+	Large to significant proportion of seniors, presence of amenities	4.00	6.36	1.56
S+A−	Large to significant proportion of seniors, lack of amenities	2.19	3.65	5.21
S++W−A−	Significant proportion of seniors, inappropriate walkability, lack of amenities	0.72	1.74	1.66
S++W−A+	Significant proportion of seniors, inappropriate walkability, presence of amenities	0.20	0.45	0.12
SW+A−	Large proportion of seniors, suitable walkability, lack of amenities	2.09	3.34	5.34
SW+A+	Large proportion of seniors, suitable walkability, presence of amenities	3.99	6.22	1.88
SW−A−	Large proportion of seniors, inappropriate walkability, lack of amenities	4.83	7.70	12.48
SW−A+	Large proportion of seniors, inappropriate walkability, presence of amenities	3.38	5.16	1.08
S−A−	Small proportion of seniors, lack of amenities	29.42	23.00	56.89
S−A+	Small proportion of seniors, presence of amenities	48.49	40.78	12.98

1.74% of the total population of 65-year-old or more within the Aix-Marseille-Provence metropolitan area for 1.66% of the total urbanized surface. In contrast, the best-case scenario (S++W+A +: Significant proportion of older adults, suitable walkability, presence of amenities) concerns 0.40% of the total population of 65-year-old or more for 0.28% of the total urbanized surface. Yet, those two examples are not sub-spaces where intergenerational diversity prevails, but rather areas where the older adults are overrepresented. Intergenerational diversity is better within the S− and S sub-categories which represent together 86.2% of the 65-year-old or more living in Aix-Marseille-Provence Metropolis.

5 Open Access to Data, Code, and Interactive Visualizations

All four indicators discussed in Sect. 3 as well as the results of the exploratory analysis that involves classification in Sect. 4 have been compiled into a geopackage file. Furthermore, an HTML-based interactive visualization platform using these indicators has been set up using the package *mapview* on R [22]. The Aix-Marseille-Provence Metropolis uses the same kind of HTML-based interactive visualization within the open-access project MData [6] (e.g. Fig. 1). Launched in 2021, this service allows accessing and visualizing data at the scale of the metropolis, related for example to urban planning, water management, road traffic and their regulation, sport, sanitation, waste management, construction.

Within this research, all indicators have been calculated at the scale of the 200-m tiles, except for the urban fabric typology which is at the scale of the street segments. The geopackage, the version 1.0 of the platform, as well as an R code have been made available (Appendix B). The R code provides information on the session, load the packages and the layers from the geopackage, simplify and prepare the color ramps for each layer, and finally produce the platform. In this version of the platform (v1.0), the urban fabric indicator has been filtered according to the tiles possessing population, and the segments below 10 m of length have been removed. This was done with the intention of reducing the platform's size, which now stands at 93 megabytes. The HTML-based platform can be easily accessed on any computer, making it simple to engage and solicit feedback from the public. The panels on the left side allow activating-deactivating the different layers, as well as zooming in and out any neighborhood part of Aix-Marseille-Provence Metropolis. Figure 5 displays a selection of the assessment indicators calculated within this research accessible in the version 1.0 of the platform.

6 Conclusion and Discussions

The aim of this paper was to show that it was possible to produce detailed new information about aging for the case of a metropolitan area such as Aix-Marseille-Provence Metropolis based only on open-source data. Within this study, we decided to put the focus on two dimensions: walkability and urban form. However, the challenge for us as researchers was not only to produce and analyze new data, but also to effectively

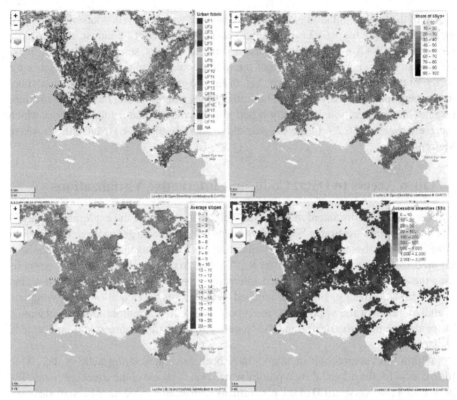

Fig. 5. v1.0 HTML-based platform related to Aging in Aix-Marseille-Provence Metropolis; top left: morphotypes around street segments in 2019, top right: share of 65-year-old or more in 2017; bottom left: average slopes; bottom right: accessible amenities in 2017.

communicate our findings to a broader audience. We recognized that sharing complex research results in a clear and concise manner is essential for policymakers, urban planners, and the public to make informed decisions about the future of their communities. To overcome this challenge, in addition to sharing our data, we integrated our results into an interactive viewing platform to spatially visualize and share our data in a user-friendly manner with interactive maps. Thanks to the MData initiative of Aix-Marseille-Provence Metropolis, data access and visualization has become a tool to help people in making strategic decisions about the future of the metropolis. The data format of the indicators calculated within the research project is compliant with the MData initiative, and we are thus in contact with the metropolis to add our results to the official platform.

From a thematic point of view, a future perspective for this project is to combine the identified morphotypes within the Aix-Marseille-Provence Metropolis with sociodemographic indicators of the resident population. We will thus be able to identify the urban forms which are more often associated with the different age classes within the resident population and/or with trends of aging or rejuvenation. The distribution of services can also be assessed with respect to the morphotypes where they are located. Aging also relates to certain concepts about urban form, such as readability or legibility, which refers to how easily people can understand and navigate the physical layout of a city [23], or intelligibility which is the degree to which the spatial layout of an urban environment can be understood by its inhabitants [24]. An intelligible urban environment is likely to be accessible and efficient, while less intelligible environments can lead to confusion, disorientation, or even social isolation for older adults. As MFA focuses on perceptible elements of urban form, this perspective could well be carried out integrating our outcomes with surveys of intelligibility-readability by seniors within different morphotypes.

Finally, our study does not consider other factors besides slope, accessibility to amenities, and physical features of urban spaces. Yet, many other factors can make an environment conducive to walking, especially for elder people, and we plan to investigate other factors in future research.

Acknowledgment. This research was funded by a grant from Région Sud, Provence-Alpes-Côte d'Azur, France (ForVie).

Appendix A: List of Retained Categories from the 2019 BPE® Dataset

A203, A101, A104, A206, A207, A208, A501, A502, A504, B101, B102, B201, B202, B203, B204, B205, B206, B301, B302, B303, B304, B305, B306, B307, B311, B312, B313, B315, D106, D108, D112, D113, D201, D202, D203, D206, D207, D208, D209, D211, D212, D213, D214, D221, D232, D233, D235, D236, D237, D238, D239, D240, D241, D242, D301, D302, D303, D305, D401, D402, D403, D404, E101, E107, E108, E109, F304, F101, F102, F108, F109, F113, F120, F201, F303, F306.

Full list of categories:

https://www.insee.fr/fr/metadonnees/source/fichier/BPE19_Liste_%C3%A9quip ements_insee-fr.pdf

Appendix B: Files Upload

https://zenodo.org/record/7818160

This upload contains a geopackage file, R code, Readme file and an HTML-based platform with interactive maps created using the geopackage and R code. This upload presents various indicators and a HTML-based platform with interactive maps to help planners and policymakers to quickly identify patterns and trends related to aging within Aix-Marseille metropolis, France.

Files.

- 'AGING_AMP_INDICATORS.gpkg': The geopackage file contains spatial data used in the R code to create the maps.
- 'code_R_platform_v1.0_ForVie.R': The R code used to create the interactive maps.

- 'ForVie_platform_v1.0.html': The platform for visualizing the interactive maps.
- 'Readme.txt'

Instructions
To use this upload, follow these steps:

1. Download the geopackage file, R code, and index.html file.
2. Open the R code in RStudio or another R environment.
3. Install any necessary packages as listed in the first section of the R code.
4. Run the code in R to create the HTML-based platform with interactive maps.

Alternatively, it is possible to directly open the ForVie_platform_v1.0.html file in a web browser to view the maps.

References

1. Verderber, S.: Sprawling Cities and Our Endangered Public Health. Routledge, London, United Kingdom (2012)
2. Buffel, T., Phillipson, C., Scharf, T.: Ageing in urban environments: developing 'age-friendly' cities. Critical Soc. Policy **32**(4), 597–617 (2012)
3. Wood, G.E.R., et al.: The role of urban environments in promoting active and healthy aging: a systematic scoping review of citizen science approaches. J. Urban Health **99**, 427–456 (2022)
4. Hanson, J.: The inclusive city: delivering a more accessible urban environment through inclusive design. In: (Proceedings), RICS Cobra, International Construction Conference: responding to change, York (2004)
5. Phillipson, C.: Developing age-friendly urban communities: critical issues for public policy. Pub. Policy Aging Rep. **25**(1), 4–8 (2015)
6. MData: GEO-visualization platform of Aix-Marseille-Provence Metropolis. https://data.amp metropole.fr/map. Accessed 2023
7. INSEE: «Logements, individus, activité, mobilités scolaires et professionnelles, migrations résidentielles». https://www.insee.fr/fr/statistiques/4508161
8. INSEE : Localised disposable income system («Dispositif Fichier localisé social et fiscal», Filosofi®). https://www.insee.fr/fr/statistiques/6215138?sommaire=6215217
9. INSEE : Permanent database of facilities («Base permanente des équipements», BPE®). https://www.insee.fr/fr/metadonnees/source/operation/s1524/presentation
10. IGN: «Base de données topographique» (topographic dataset, BD TOPO®). https://geoser vices.ign.fr/bdtopo
11. NASA Earthdata program 30-Meter SRTM Tile Downloader https://dwtkns.com/srtm30m/
12. Lo, R.-H.: Walkability: what is it? J. Urbanism: Int. Res. Placemaking Urban Sustain. **2**(2), 145–166 (2009). https://doi.org/10.1080/17549170903092867
13. Abastante, F., Lami, I.M., La Riccia, L., Gaballo, M.: Supporting resilient urban planning through walkability assessment. Sustainability **12**, 8131 (2020)
14. Alves, F., Cruz, S., Ribeiro, A., Bastos Silva, A., Martins, J., Cunha, I.: Walkability index for elderly health: a proposal. Sustainability **12**, 7360 (2020)
15. Moreno, C., Allam, Z., Chabaud, D., Gall, C., Pratlong, F.: Introducing the "15-minute city": sustainability, resilience and place identity in future post-pandemic cities. Smart Cities **4**, 93–111 (2021)
16. Speck, J.: WALKABLE CITY: How Downtown Can Save America, One Step at a Time, 312 p. North Point Press (2012)

17. Calise, T.V., Chow, W., Ryder, A., Wingerter, C.: Food access and its relationship to perceived walkability, safety, and social cohesion. Health Promot. Pract. **20**(6), 858–867 (2019)
18. Fusco, G., Araldi, A., Perez, J.: The city and the metropolis: urban form through multiple fabric assessment in Marseille, France. In: Annual Conference Proceedings of the XXVIII International Seminar on Urban Form, pp. 884–894. University of Strathclyde Publishing, Glasgow (2021)
19. Araldi, A., Fusco, G.: From the street to the metropolitan region: pedestrian perspective in urban fabric analysis. Env. Plann. B: Urban Anal. City Sci. **46**(7), 1243–1263 (2019)
20. Musselwhite, C., Haddad, H.: Mobility, accessibility and quality of later life. Qual. Ageing Older Adults **11**(1), 25–37 (2010)
21. Diyanah, I.A., Hafazah, A.K.: Implications of walkability towards promoting sustainable urban neighbourhood. Procedia. Soc. Behav. Sci. **50**, 204–213 (2012)
22. Appelhans, T., et al.: mapview: Interactive Viewing of Spatial Data in R. Package on CRAN (2022). https://cran.r-project.org/web/packages/mapview/index.html
23. Lynch, K.: The Image of a City, 194 p. The MIT Press (1960)
24. Hillier, B., Hanson, J.: The Social Logic of Space, 296 p. Cambridge University Press (1984)

Urban Sustainability Towards European Missions and Challenges: Where Do We Stand?

Marika Gaballo[ID], Beatrice Mecca[ID], and Elena Todella[✉][ID]

Interuniversity Department of Regional and Urban Studies and Planning (DIST), Politecnico di Torino, Viale Mattioli 39, 20125 Turin, Italy
elena.todella@polito.it

Abstract. The centrality of cities and urban processes in sustainable development and the green transition has been recognized by the 2030 Agenda for Sustainable Development, the New Urban Agenda and the Green Deal. In this context, this paper aims to explore the conceptualizations of cities that have received attention, such as "inclusive city", "knowledge city", "low carbon city", "resilient city", "smart city", and "sustainable city". Since measuring progress through the reaching of sustainable development in contemporary cities is a current and relevant issue, the paper reflects on both theory and practice levels: (i) by developing a conceptualization of current challenges in pursuing urban sustainability; (ii) by discussing available (and/or needed) measurement and assessment tools, such as indicators, to support the construction and evaluation of such sustainable urban policies. In doing so, the research specifically focuses on the European Union's (EU) framework for urban sustainability, outlined in the Horizon Europe Program for Research and Innovation for 2021–2027. Accordingly, the Strategic Plan 2021–2024 and the work programmes 2023–2024 of "Clusters" and "Missions" are analyzed to understand where we stand towards European challenges in urban sustainability. Moreover, the paper explores indicators provided by different European institutions in order to outline a set of indicators useful for monitoring the city conceptualizations encouraged at the European level.

Keywords: Sustainable Cities · European Union · Urban Sustainability · Indicator framework · Horizon Europe

1 Introduction

Over the last decades, several conceptualizations of "cities" emerged in the literature and policy discourse [1], which have gradually developed, modified and, to some extent, hybridized [2, 3]. Accordingly, scholars and practitioners from different fields defined a variety of sustainable approaches to contribute to sustainability and its improvement. Some of these conceptualizations have been deepened in the literature and are considered conceptually distinct enough to define their key aspects in relation to ongoing sustainability challenges [1–7]. The categories that received more attention than others are: "eco-city"; "low carbon city"; "global city"; "creative city"; "knowledge city"; "resilient city"; "inclusive city"; "smart city"; "sustainable city" [2, 3].

O. Gervasi et al. (Eds.): ICCSA 2023 Workshops, LNCS 14104, pp. 354–373, 2023.
https://doi.org/10.1007/978-3-031-37105-9_24

Contemporary debates in both academic and policy contexts focus on the role of sustainability in urban development, to respond to the substantial challenges implied by cities [5, 8]. Planners and policymakers play a crucial role in shaping cities, given the power to choose which urban concepts to adopt [6, 9]. This decision-making process should be informed by an awareness of the different dimensions of urban conceptualizations. Accordingly, clarifying these conceptualizations, in theory, have implications for how they are pursued in policies and in practice, as concrete frameworks for action through strategic plans [6, 10].

The abovementioned reflection on both theory and practice levels is pursued by addressing the following questions: *what are the key aspects, debates, and challenges relating to each conceptualization of "city"? What are the available and worth exploring indicators to evaluate them?*

In answering these questions, the aim of this paper is twofold: i) to outline which city conceptualizations are encouraged in the EU framework and define the related key aspects to assess their development; ii) to define a set of indicators to monitor these aspects starting from existing indicator frameworks.

In a short overview of these conceptualizations, the "sustainable city", as the most frequently occurred, is intricately linked with the majority of the others, as a comprehensive umbrella [1] addressing the different pillars of sustainability. A "sustainable city" aims to meet present needs without compromising future generations [11], balancing human activity and the environment while promoting social equality, economic well-being, and environmental quality [1, 5, 6, 12].

The "eco-city" [1, 5, 7] encompasses ecological and cultural diversity, renewable resources, and sustainable transportation, while the "low-carbon city" [1, 7, 13] prioritizes policies that promote low-carbon urban development. The "global city" requires specialized infrastructure and a critical mass of functions to support a comprehensive modernization plan, while the "creative city" [1, 4, 6] aims to attract young professionals but has been criticized for promoting inequality and gentrification. The "knowledge city" [1, 5, 7] emphasizes the knowledge and innovation economy but does not centrally promote ecological sustainability. An "inclusive city" fosters social cohesion and quality of life for all citizens, and addresses social inequalities, through smart and sustainable urban planning, citizen participation and co-creation, and digital and technological solutions for urban challenges (Sharifi and Salehi, 2022). The "smart city" [4–7] connects residents to urban infrastructure and services through technology and data analytics but focuses more on social and economic aspects. Finally, the "resilient city" [2, 3, 7] refers to a city's ability to withstand and recover from the effects of hazards in a timely and efficient manner, promoting smart growth and building social cohesion.

In exploring these conceptualizations, a focus can be proposed in terms of both the context of reference and the time scale of observation, to circumscribe theoretical observation and to direct practical action in the short term. In doing so, this paper does not pretend to provide an exhaustive overview in terms of theoretical conceptualization since such categories are not universally recognized in the literature, neither in their use in practices worldwide [6].

Specifically, this paper focuses on which of these "cities" conceptualizations are encouraged by the European Union (EU) and are present in the framework of the "Horizon Europe Program for Research and Innovation" for the period 2021–2027, as a guiding program of future research and innovations, in order to observe which city concept is encouraged for future urban developments. In particular, we refer here to the Strategic Plan 2021–24 [14], that defines the key strategic orientations for the first four years and sets the priorities towards sustainable development. The focus of the Strategic Plan is on the "Global challenges and European industrial competitiveness" pillar, and it has been prepared through a co-design process involving Member States, EEA members, the European Parliament, stakeholders and the public. In particular, the current work programmes 2023–2024 on "Clusters" and "Missions" are taken into account, to understand where we stand towards European missions and challenge in urban sustainability. For further details on the structure of the "Horizon Europe Program for Research and Innovation" 2021–2027, see [15].

The following section describes the research design and approach to categorizing "cities" and explores relevant indicators. Sections 3 and 4 present results from analyzing city categorization and identifying indicators. Section 5 discusses the findings and implications for future research and actions.

2   Research Design

To answer the provided questions, the research is structured into two phases, namely: (i) a content analysis of the selected documents, to outline which city conceptualizations encouraged in the EU framework, defining key aspects to assess their development; (ii) a screening of the existing institutional frameworks of indicators, to define a set of indicators to monitor these aspects.

2.1   Phase 1: Content Analysis

The selected documents on Horizon Europe are reviewed and analyzed, in the first phase, via a textual analysis through ChatGPT (Chat Generative Pretrained Transformer, see [16]), as a tool for Natural Language Processing (NLP), in different steps (Fig. 1):

1) a textual analysis of the Strategic Plan 2021–2024 [14] is provided, to define which conceptualizations of "city" are mentioned into the document;
2) starting from the highlighted categories, a textual analysis of the 7 work programmes 2023–2024 on "Clusters" [17–22] and "Missions" [23] is provided, to define which of the abovementioned conceptualizations are mentioned or envisaged in the documents, to define which documents touch the totality of the conceptualizations (as a selection criterion);
3) starting from the previous selection, a textual analysis of the selected "Clusters" and "Missions" is provided, to highlight which are the key aspects related to each city conceptualization that need to be assessed. It has to be specified that, starting from the analysis provided by ChatGPT, all the results have been revised and elaborated by the authors of this paper.

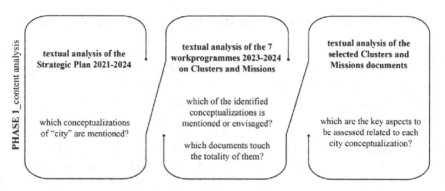

Fig. 1. The steps in Phase 1 of the research.

2.2 Phase 2: Indicators' Screening

The actual institutional framework at the European level includes the following leading Institutes that provide sustainable development indicators on cities [24–29]: i) Eurostat provides statistical data on European cities, while the ii) Joint Research Centre (JRC) of the European Commission, iii) the European Environment Agency (EEA), and iv) the Organization for Economic Co-operation and Development (OECD) provide indicators for monitoring sustainable urban development across Europe.

Considering the key aspects related to each city conceptualization identified in Phase 1, the research starts from the institutional European frameworks outlined above, to detect how they can be assessed. Thus, a screening of the existing institutional frameworks of indicators is provided consisting of the following steps (Fig. 2):

1) analysis of European institutional publications to select those with existing sustainable development indicators for cities;
2) screening of selected publications to identify which indicators assess the key aspects identified in Phase 1.

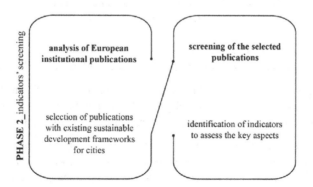

Fig. 2. The steps in Phase 2 of the research.

3   City Conceptualizations and Related Aspects in EU Framework

The aim of this section is to define which conceptualizations of city are mentioned and are meant to be pursued in the Strategic Plan 2021–2024 and work programmes 2023–2024 of "Clusters" and "Missions", at the European level.

In this phase, a textual analysis is conducted through ChatGPT. It's increasingly recognized how ChatGPT, as an advanced AI language model, can contribute to research by supporting researchers in NLP [30–32] and improving data analysis and interpretation [33] without human involvement. This experimental analysis proposes to define conceptualizations of cities, searching for their mentions, and to identify related key aspects in the documents more efficiently. Due to the risk of inconsistent performance or biased output [31], traditional qualitative analysis is used for refinement.

3.1   Step 1: Strategic Plan 2021–2024

A textual analysis of the Strategic Plan 2021–2024 is provided through ChatGPT, to define which conceptualizations of "city" are mentioned into the document and how they are defined. This step aims at setting such definitions as a starting point to frame the subsequent analyses.

Accordingly, ChatGPT has been questioned through the following formula: "Please make a textual analysis of the document at this link https://www.eeas.europa.eu/sites/default/files/horizon_europe_strategic_plan_2021-2024.pdf to find a definition of *city conceptualization*", substituting from time to time the city conceptualizations already mentioned, in both the singular and plural forms ("creative city"; "eco-city"; "global city"; "inclusive city"; "knowledge city"; "low carbon city"; "resilient city"; "smart city"; "sustainable city").

With respect to the "creative", "eco", "global", and "knowledge" city conceptualizations, ChatGPT highlighted that not a mention, neither a specific definition could be found in the document, answering through different formulas, such as:

- *After conducting a thorough textual analysis of the Horizon Europe Strategic Plan (2021 – 2024) document, I could not find a specific definition of "creative city". [...] it does not appear to be a central concept in the Horizon Europe Strategic Plan (2021 – 2024) [...];*
- *After reviewing the Horizon Europe Strategic Plan (2021 – 2024) document, I could not find any specific sections where the term "just city" is explicitly mentioned [...].*

With respect to the "inclusive", "low carbon", "resilient", "smart", and "sustainable" city conceptualizations, ChatGPT highlighted that a specific mention and a definition could be found in the document, answering through different formulas, such as:

- *Upon analyzing the document, the phrase "inclusive city" appears several times, primarily in the context of research and innovation activities related to urban development. [...] Despite the lack of a direct definition, the document does provide some guidance on the characteristics of an inclusive city [...];*

- *The term "low carbon city" is mentioned in several places throughout the document, particularly in the section titled "Building a climate-neutral, green, and circular economy [...].*

Then, ChatGPT has been further questioned through the following formula: "In which sections of the document is mentioned the *city conceptualization*?", only with respect to the five city conceptualizations emerged in the document.

Accordingly, the city conceptualizations for which a mention and a definition are provided, through ChatGPT, are reported in Table 1, with the specific sections in which they are found.

Table 1. City conceptualizations and mentions in the Strategic Plan 2021–2024.

Conceptualization	Definition	References
Inclusive city	An inclusive city fosters social cohesion and quality of life for all citizens, while addressing social inequalities and exclusion. Specific research and innovation areas that can contribute to creating more inclusive cities are smart and sustainable urban planning; citizen participation and co-creation; and digital and technological solutions for urban challenges	Sections: "Global Challenges and European Industrial Competitiveness"; "Culture, Creativity and Inclusive Society"; "Civil Security for Society"; "Digital, Industry and Space"
Low carbon city	A low-carbon city reduces greenhouse gas emissions and negative environmental impacts while enhancing the well-being of its citizens. It is designed and managed to minimize carbon emissions from energy production, buildings, transport, and waste, while maximizing the use of renewable energy and promoting circular economy practices. Collaboration between different sectors and deployment of low-carbon technologies and systems in urban areas are crucial to achieving this goal	Sections: "Executive Summary"; "Building a climate-neutral, green, and circular economy"; "Sustainable and smart mobility"; "Food, bioeconomy, natural resources, agriculture and environment"; "Health"

(continued)

Table 1. (*continued*)

Conceptualization	Definition	References
Resilient city	A resilient city is able to adapt to and recover from shocks and stresses while maintaining its essential functions, structures, and identity. It can thrive in the face of uncertain and changing conditions. Building resilient cities requires addressing key areas including climate adaptation, digital transformation, circular economy, and social cohesion. It is emphasized the importance of resilience in urban areas, as critical for building resilient cities	Sections: "Introduction"; "Europe in a changing world – inclusive, innovative and reflective societies"; "Global challenges and European industrial competences"; "Innovative Europe"; "A climate-neutral, green, fair, and social Europe"; "Digital, industry and space"
Smart city	Smart cities use digital technologies and sustainable solutions to address societal challenges and improve urban services. It is emphasized the importance of data and digital technologies in developing, testing, and deploying innovative solutions, such as improving mobility and other urban services	Sections: "Societal Challenges"; "Digital, Industry and Space"; "Climate, Energy and Mobility"; "Bioeconomy, Natural Resources, Agriculture and Environment"
Sustainable city	A sustainable, liveable, and resilient city can adapt to climate change and resource scarcity. It requires a holistic approach that considers social, economic, and environmental dimensions, involving citizens and stakeholders. Key priorities include innovative and low-carbon urban technologies, sustainable mobility options, circular economy principles, and investing in green spaces and social infrastructure. Overall, sustainable cities promote well-being in a socially, economically, and environmentally sustainable manner	Sections: "Introduction"; "Civil Security for Society"; "Digital and Industry Transformation"; "Climate, Energy, and Mobility"; "Food, Bioeconomy, Natural Resources, Agriculture, and Environment"; "Health"

3.2 Step 2: Clusters and Missions 2023–2024

After highlighting analyzing the Strategic Plan, a textual analysis of the 7 work programmes 2023–2024 "Clusters" and "Missions" is conducted through ChatGPT, to define if the five city conceptualizations emerged are mentioned or envisaged in the documents. The aim of this step is to define which "Clusters" and "Missions" can be related to the totality of the city conceptualizations highlighted, as a selection criterion to circumscribe the research on the work programmes that fully cover the several aspects of urban sustainability, and as a starting point to go in-depth in the subsequent screening.

In this step, the 7 documents analyzed namely are: Cluster 1, "Health" [17]; Cluster 2, "Culture, creativity and inclusive society" [18]; Cluster 3, "Civil security for society" [19]; Cluster 4, "Digital, industry and space" [20]; Cluster 5 "Climate, energy and mobility" [21]; Cluster 6, "Food, bioeconomy, natural resources, agriculture and environment" [22]; Missions [23].

According to each document, ChatGPT has been questioned through the following formula: "Please make a textual analysis of the document at this link *link* to find mentions of *city conceptualization*", substituting from time to time the city conceptualizations already mentioned, in both the singular and plural forms ("inclusive city"; "low carbon city"; "resilient city"; "smart city"; "sustainable city").

The search produced three different sorts of caseloads:

- the city conceptualization is explicitly mentioned in the work programme ($\in$);
- the city conceptualization is not explicitly mentioned in the work programme, however related concepts can be identified and linked to it ($\cong$);
- the city conceptualization is not explicitly mentioned, neither related concepts can be identified.

A synthesis of this analysis is reported in Table 2.

Table 2. City conceptualizations in "Clusters" and "Missions".

Conceptualization	Clusters' work programmes 2023–2024						Missions' work programme 2023 2024
	1	2	3	4	5	6	
Inclusive city		$\cong$		$\cong$	$\in$		$\cong$
Low carbon	$\cong$	$\in$	$\cong$	$\cong$	$\in$	$\cong$	$\in$
Resilient city		$\cong$	$\in$	$\cong$	$\cong$		$\cong$
Smart city		$\cong$		$\cong$	$\cong$		$\in$
Sustainable city	$\cong$	$\cong$		$\cong$	$\cong$		$\in$

As an example of each case:

- the city conceptualization "low carbon city" results as explicitly mentioned in the work programme of "Cluster 2", namely: *After conducting a textual analysis of the document at the provided link, I have found the following mentions of "low carbon city" or "low carbon cities" [...]*;
- the city conceptualization "smart city" results as not explicitly mentioned in the work programme of "Cluster 4", however related concepts can be identified and linked

to it, namely: *After analyzing the document at the provided link, I have found that there are no direct mentions of "smart city" or "smart cities" in the document. [...] However, there are some indirect references to topics related to smart cities [...]*;

- the city conceptualization "resilient city" results as not explicitly mentioned in, neither related concepts can be identified: *After conducting a textual analysis of the document at the provided link, I found no mentions of "resilient city" or "resilient cities". [...] there is no specific mention of "resilient city" or "resilient cities".*

According to this screening, the selected documents for further analysis are "Cluster 2", "Cluster 4", "Cluster 5", and "Missions", as related to the totality of the city conceptualizations highlighted.

3.3 Step 3: Key Aspects

Starting from the previous selection, a textual analysis of the selected "Clusters" and "Missions" is provided through ChatGPT, to highlight which are the key aspects related to each city conceptualization that need to be assessed.

Indeed, if the previous steps provide a general definition and positioning in the work programmes of the different ways in which cities are defined, this step aims at exploring the implications of these definitions for sustainable urban development, in terms of key aspects to be assessed. Accordingly, this step is preliminary to give guidance for decision-making, enable target setting for cities as well as allow assessing whether the development is proceeding, through the definition of existing or worth exploring indicators.

According to each document, and in relation to each city conceptualization, ChatGPT has been questioned through the following formula:

"Please define which are the key aspects to be assessed related to the *city conceptualization* in the document at this link *link of the specific work programme*", substituting from time to time the different city conceptualizations.

The results of this analysis were elaborated by the authors and synthesized in Fig. 3, in which the circles represent the key aspects emerged and the surrounding arches relates to the city conceptualizations to which they are linked.

Based on this analysis, it can be highlighted that: (i) the key aspects related to all the 5 conceptualizations are "citizen participation" and "sustainable urbanization", which are quite broad and likely related to different aspects of urban sustainable development; (ii) some other key aspects emerged as in common among different conceptualizations of the city, at least 3 or 4, and punctually cover the different sustainability pillars (e.g., "energy efficiency", "social inclusion", and "circular economy"); (iii) each city conceptualization has at least one key aspect that is strictly related to that particular one, or at maximum two (e.g., "renewable energy" for "low carbon city", or "risk assessment" for "resilient city" and "smart city"). Accordingly, it can be defined that, even if there are overlaps among city conceptualizations, these differ and should be pursued precisely on the basis of certain aspects that are completely absent in others.

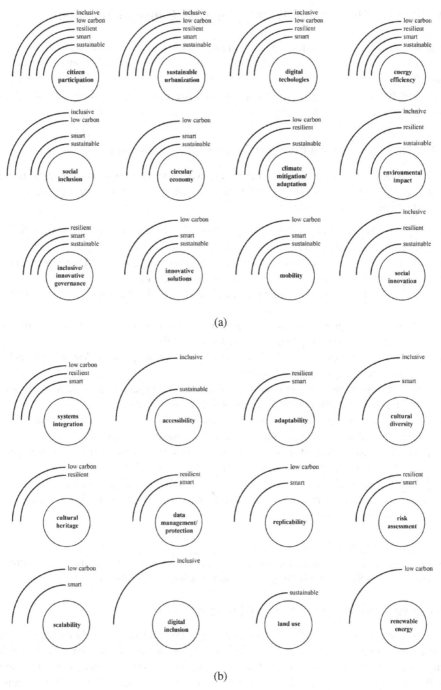

Fig. 3. The key aspects emerged from the analysis of "Cluster 2", "Cluster 4", "Cluster 5" and "Missions", related to each city conceptualization.

4 Set of Indicators for Monitoring City Conceptualizations

The aim of this section is to provide a set of indicators through which assess the development of the emerged city conceptualization – namely "inclusive city", "low carbon city", "resilient city", "smart city", "sustainable city" – by detecting a connection between the identified key aspects (Fig. 3) and the existing European institutional indicators frameworks.

4.1 Step 1: Institutional European Framework of Indicators

Publications from Eurostat, JRC, EEA and OECD have been screened to select those that include sustainable development indicators for cities. This screening led to the identification of 11 publications:

- [34]: this publication provides a comprehensive set of statistics on urban areas in the EU, including indicators related to sustainable development.
- [35]: this report provides an overview of the progress made by the EU and its member states towards achieving sustainable cities and communities.
- [36]: this publication provides an updated version of the Regional Yearbook with a focus on the latest data available.
- [37]: this report proposes a reference framework for sustainable cities that aims to help cities monitor their progress toward sustainability goals.
- [38]: this report presents a set of indicators for measuring progress towards a circular economy from a systemic perspective.
- [39]: this report provides an overview of sustainable urban development in Europe, focusing on key environmental, social, and economic indicators.
- [40]: this report explores how cities can facilitate sustainable transitions, including the use of sustainable development indicators to measure progress.
- [41]: this report provides an overview of the state and outlook of Europe's environment, including urban sustainability indicators.
- [42]: this report presents an overview of the challenges facing regions and cities, including the use of indicators to measure progress and inform policy in areas such as sustainable development.
- [43]: this report assesses progress towards green growth in Southeast Europe, including the use of indicators to measure progress and inform policy in urban areas.
- [44]: this report provides an assessment of progress toward the Sustainable Development Goals (SDGs), including indicators for urban sustainability.

4.2 Step 2: Indicators to Assess the Emerging Key Aspects

An in-deep exploration of selected documents was conducted to identify indicators that can be used for assessing the emerging key aspects of sustainable development for each city conceptualizations identified in Phase 1. Table 3 reports the 114 indicators identified in the existing frameworks that can be traced back to the evaluation of the 24 key aspects.

Based on this analysis, it can be highlighted that: (i) at least one indicator is available for all the emerged key aspects; (ii) some key aspects, the environmental ones, are the most supplied by available indicators, namely "energy efficiency", and "renewable

Table 3. The available indicators for each emerging key aspect.

Key aspects	Indicators	References
Citizen participation	Voter turnout [%]	[35, 36]
	Participation in civil society organizations [n.]; Trust in government, and public satisfaction with public services [%]	[37]
Sustainable urbanization	Share of urban population [%]; Green space per inhabitant [sqm/inhab.]; Number of people living in overcrowded households [n.]	[34, 37, 39–41]
	Urban sprawl [%]; Population density [n.]; Green infrastructure [sqm]; Urban land uptake [sqm]; Green urban areas [smq]; Housing affordability [%]	[37, 39–41]
Digital technologies	Broadband penetration rate [%]; Percentage of internet users [%]	[38, 44]
Energy efficiency	Energy intensity of gross domestic product (GDP) in Purchasing Power Standards (PPS) per kg of oil equivalent (kgoe) [kgoe/GDP]; Share of renewable energy [%]; Share of cogeneration in electricity production [%]	[35, 38]
	Carbon intensity [CO2]; Energy productivity [kWh]; Energy efficiency [kWh/€]; Energy subsidies [€]	[38]
	Primary energy consumption [kWh]; Final energy consumption [kWh]; Energy-related greenhouse gas emissions [CO2]	[38, 44]
Social inclusion	At-risk-of-poverty rate [%]; Material deprivation rate [%]; Gender pay gap [%]	[36, 37, 39–41]
	Poverty and social exclusion rate [%]; Share of low-wage earners [%]	[37, 39–41]
	Unemployment rate [%]	[37, 39–42]

(*continued*)

Table 3. (*continued*)

Key aspects	Indicators	References
Circular economy	Material footprint [tons]; Recycling rate of municipal waste [%]; Share of recycled material in material consumption [%]	[34, 38–41]
	Resource productivity [€/tons]; Waste generation per capita [kg/inhab.]	[38–41]
	Circularity rate [%]	[38–41, 43]
Climate mitigation/adaptation	Greenhouse gas emissions [CO2]; Renewable energy share [%]; Energy consumption from renewable sources [kWh]	[35–41]
	Climate change vulnerability [%]	[37, 39–41, 43]
Environmental impact	Environmental footprint [tons of CO2]; Air and water quality [micrograms/cbm]; Waste and recycling rates [%]	[37, 39–41]
	Carbon footprint [CO2]	[37, 43]
Inclusive/innovative governance	Public expenditure on education [€]; Health and social protection [€]	[34, 38, 44]
Innovative solutions	Research and development expenditure [€]; Patents applications [patent unit]	[35, 36, 44]
Mobility	Modal split of transport [%]; Average commute time [minutes]	[34, 37, 39–41, 44]
	Transport-related emissions [CO2]	[37, 39–41, 44]
Social innovation	Social investment [€]; Social protection expenditure [€]	[35, 37, 39, 41, 44]
	Social impact investment [€]	[37, 39, 41, 44]
Systems integration	Energy and water use efficiency [kWh]; Green public procurement [%]	[34, 37, 40, 41, 44]
	Resource efficiency [€/tons]; Sustainable public procurement [%]	[37, 38, 40, 41, 44]
Accessibility	Share of population with access to broadband internet [%]	[34, 39, 41, 44]

(*continued*)

Table 3. (*continued*)

Key aspects	Indicators	References
	Accessibility to natural areas and green spaces [sqm]; Access to basic services (e.g., healthcare, education, water, sanitation) [n.]	[39, 41, 44]
Adaptability	Share of employed population with high level of education and training [%]	[35, 39, 41]
	Diversity of economic activities and employment opportunities [n.]	[39, 41]
	Resilience to economic shocks and natural disasters [%]	[39, 41–43]
Cultural diversity	Share of foreign-born population and language diversity [n.]	[34]
	Diversity of cultural heritage sites and institutions [n.]; Cultural diversity in natural areas and landscapes [n.]	[39, 41]
	Ethnic and linguistic diversity and integration [%]	[39, 41, 42]
Cultural heritage	Number of cultural heritage sites and institutions [n.]	[36, 39, 41]
	Conservation and restoration of cultural heritage sites [%]; Protection and management of cultural heritage in natural areas [%]	[39, 41]
	Investment in cultural heritage preservation and promotion [€]	[39, 41, 42]
Data management/protection	Compliance with data protection regulations [%]	[35]
	Adoption of open data policies and measures [%]	[43]
Replicability	Standardized data collection methods and metadata availability [%]	[34]

(*continued*)

Table 3. (*continued*)

Key aspects	Indicators	References
	Availability of detailed information on the methodology used, including sources, data collection and processing procedures [%]; Data and methodology transparency, replicability, and availability of quality assurance and control procedures [%]; Transparency of data sources, methodologies, and assumptions, with clear documentation and traceability [%]	[35]
Risk assessment	Assessment of the probability and consequences of environmental risks and their impacts on human health and ecosystems [%]; Assessment of the likelihood and potential impact of risks on economic, social, and environmental outcomes [%]	[38, 41]
Scalability	Deployment of sustainable technologies and infrastructure in different cities and regions [n.]	[34–36]
Digital inclusion	Individuals using the internet for personal purposes [%]; Households with internet access at home [%]	[34, 41]
	Broadband coverage and quality [%]; Access to digital devices [%]; Access to high-speed internet [%]; Access to mobile broadband [%]; Access to online public services [%]; Internet usage rate [%]	[41]
Land use	Land use by type [sqm]; Land cover by type [sqm]; Agricultural land use [sqm]; Forest land use [sqm]; Urban land use [sqm]	[34, 38, 41, 42]

(*continued*)

Table 3. (*continued*)

Key aspects	Indicators	References
	Density [n.]; Green spaces [sqm]; Built environment [sqm]; Land use and land cover [sqm]; Land take [sqm]; Land cover change [%]; Land area per capita [sqm/ per capita]; Agricultural land area per capita [sqm/ per capita]; Forest area per capita [sqm]; Urban land area per capita [sqm/ per capita]	[38, 41, 42]
Renewable energy	Share of renewables in gross final energy consumption [%]; Renewable energy production [kWh]; Renewable energy consumption [kWh]; Share of renewable electricity in gross electricity consumption [%]; Installed capacity [MW]; Energy production [kWh]; Investment [€]; Renewable electricity generation [kWh]; Renewable heating and cooling [kWh]; Share of renewables in total primary energy supply [%]	[35, 41, 42]

energy"; (iii) some key aspects, the socio-cultural ones, are less investigate, namely "cultural diversity", and "cultural heritage". Accordingly, it can be defined that, even if there are available indicators for all the emerged key aspects, further research can be directed to the ones for which the available ones are less.

5 Discussion and Conclusions

This paper underscores the importance of assessing the development of the urban models according to the EU demands and missions, with the ultimate goal of achieving sustainable development. By scrutinizing how various city categories are employed and questioned in the EU Strategic Plan and work programmes, this research explicates the objectives and delineates crucial aspects of each emerging city model: (i) by developing a conceptualization of current challenges in pursuing urban sustainability; (ii) by presenting available (and/or needed) measurement and assessment tools, such as indicators, to support the evaluation of such sustainable urban policies.

Two main contributions can be highlighted in this research.

First, the research defines through the support of ChatGPT the five conceptualizations of cities encouraged in the European framework and identifies 24 key aspects, which are the elements that characterize them and to be pursued.

Second, it highlights 114 available indicators for the assessment of the 24 key aspects. Although at least one indicator is available for each emerging key aspect, some of them are more explored than others. As an example, environmental key aspects (e.g., energy efficiency, renewable energy) emerge as more endowed with measures to monitor them, than socio-cultural ones (e.g., cultural diversity, or cultural heritage). Moreover, the key aspect of the scalability of cities reports only one indicator, since within the analyzed publications this concept relates more than indicators important qualitative issues to keep in mind for its measurement. Therefore, although indicators are available for all of the key aspects that have emerged, this paper allows us to focus first on those aspects that are less in-depth and on which further research may be needed.

Such contributions have implications on both theory and practice levels.

First of all, at a theoretical level, these findings about the city conceptualizations that can be found, and the overlapping among conceptualizations, can be the basis for further research that – at a critical level – can serve to refine and sharpen the conceptualizations themselves.

Second, at a practical level, the complexity given by the high amount of available indicators should be managed, on the one hand, by identifying some indicators more suitable than others, in a choice oriented: (i) by the specific city concept addressed and its specificities; (ii) by distinguishing their use in a measurement process, to frame the state or condition of a system or process, or in an evaluation process, to define the performance of an action, alternative, or element. On the other hand, based on the abovementioned distinction, possible evaluation methodologies to bring these indicators into an assessment process could be provided, to support monitoring activities through a stated correspondence between goals, indicators, and measures of these indicators – e.g., as in the Agenda 2030 framework – or to provide an assessment of urban sustainable development in a holistic and systemic way, to possibly provide input for cost-benefit analyses (CBA), and similar techniques such as social return on investment analysis (SROI); or Multi-Criteria Analysis (MCA); and finally Sustainability Assessment Tools (SATs).

Specific reflection can be made with respect to the experimental use of ChatGPT for functional text analysis to answer the research question. Since ChatGPT can be used to search for precise information, it has proven to be a useful support. In particular, it has been effective for carrying out repetitive tasks, such as searching for a specific mention or reference to keywords as in the case of this research, speeding up the work exponentially and doing so with the identification of very precise data, referring to punctual sections of the analyzed documents. ChatGPT is not the only tool that can do analysis of this kind, but it ensures useful comparisons between data, being an AI, thus also somehow managing to interpret sections of the text where reference to the conceptualizations sought is not explicit. This is precisely why, as done by the authors of this article, it is necessary to verify and triangulate the results and information received.

Regarding the limitations of the research, first of all it cannot be considered directly as an action framework, as much as a starting point for further actions and research. Moreover, it is important to note that the article focuses on the European Union's framework for urban sustainability, and the identified key aspects and indicators may not be applicable or relevant to other regions or countries. Also, going down to national, regional, and local levels may need to be further localized and declined to capture the specificities of each context. Finally, localizing such indicators would imply reflections on operational aspects and challenges, such as data availability and homogeneity in terms of scale, time, levels of aggregation. Nevertheless, this research already offers insights into bridging the gap between theory and practice in confronting urban challenges and realizing sustainable development objectives within the EU framework.

References

1. de Jong, M., Joss, S., Schraven, D., Zhan, C., Weijnen, M.: Sustainable–smart–resilient–low carbon–eco–knowledge cities; making sense of a multitude of concepts promoting sustainable urbanization. J. Clean. Prod. **109**, 25–38 (2015). https://doi.org/10.1016/j.jclepro.2015.03.005
2. Coaffee, J., O'Hare, P., Hawkesworth, M.: Resilient Urban Futures. Routledge (2018). https://doi.org/10.4324/9781315179049
3. Sharifi, A., Khavarian-Garmsir, A.R.: Sustainable Urban Development: Challenges and Opportunities for Developing Countries. Springer (2023)
4. Ahvenniemi, H., Huovila, A., Pinto-Seppä, I., Airaksinen, M.: What are the differences between sustainable and smart cities? Cities **60**, 234–245 (2017). https://doi.org/10.1016/j.cities.2016.10.009
5. Bibri, S.E., Krogstie, J.: Smart sustainable cities of the future: an extensive interdisciplinary literature review. Sustain. Cities Soc. **31**, 183–212 (2017). https://doi.org/10.1016/j.scs.2017.01.005
6. Hatuka, T., Rosen-Zvi, I., Birnhack, M., Toch, E., Zur, H.: The Political premises of contemporary urban concepts: the global city, the sustainable city, the resilient city, the creative city, and the smart city. Plan. Theory Pract. **19**(2), 160–179 (2018). https://doi.org/10.1080/14649357.2018.1455216
7. Sharifi, A., Salehi, M.: Smart and Sustainable Urban Development: From Vision to Practice. Routledge (2022)
8. Lami, I.M., Abastante, F., Gaballo, M., Mecca, B., Todella, E.: Fostering sustainable cities through additional SDG11-related indicators: Promuovere le città sostenibili attraverso indicatori integrativi dello SDG11. Valori e Valutazioni **32**, 45–61 (2023)
9. Mecca, B., Gaballo, M., Todella, E.: Measuring and evaluating urban sustainability: misurare e valutare la sostenibilità urbana. Valori e Valutazioni **32**, 17–29 (2023). https://doi.org/10.48264/VVSIEV-20233203
10. Lami, I.M., Bottero, M., Abastante, F.: Multiple criteria decision analysis to assess urban and territorial transformations: insights from practical applications. In: Rezaei, J. (ed.) Strategic Decision Making for Sustainable Management of Industrial Networks. GINS, vol. 8, pp. 93–117. Springer, Cham (2021). https://doi.org/10.1007/978-3-030-55385-2_6
11. European Commission. Europe 2000: Outlook for the development of the Community's territory: Communication from the Commission to the Council. Brussels (1987)
12. Abastante, F., Lami, I.M.: An integrated assessment framework for the requalification of districts facing urban and social decline. In: Mondini, G., Fattinnanzi, E., Oppio, A., Bottero, M., Stanghellini, S. (eds.) SIEV 2016. GET, pp. 535–545. Springer, Cham (2018). https://doi.org/10.1007/978-3-319-78271-3_42
13. Rotondo, F., Abastante, F., Cotella, G., Lami, I.M.: Questioning low-carbon transition governance: a comparative analysis of European case studies. Sustainability **12**(24), 10460 (2020)
14. European Union: Horizon Europe. Strategic Plan 2021–2024 (2021). Retrieved from https://op.europa.eu/en/web/eu-law-and-publications/publication-detail/-/publication/3c6ffd74-8ac3-11eb-b85c-01aa75ed71a1

15. European Commission page: https://research-and-innovation.ec.europa.eu/funding/funding-opportunities/funding-programmes-and-open-calls/horizon-europe_en. Last accessed 5 Apr 2023

16. Chat GPT OpenAI homepage: https://chat.openai.com/. Last accessed 5 Apr 2023

17. European Commission: Horizon Europe Work Programme 2023–2024: Cluster 1 – Health (2022). Retrieved from https://ec.europa.eu/info/funding-tenders/opportunities/docs/2021-2027/horizon/wp-call/2023-2024/wp-4-health_horizon-2023-2024_en.pdf

18. European Commission: Horizon Europe Work Programme 2023–2024: Cluster 2 - Culture, Creativity and Inclusive Society (2022). Retrieved from https://ec.europa.eu/info/funding-tenders/opportunities/docs/2021-2027/horizon/wp-call/2023-2024/wp-5-culture-creativity-and-inclusive-society_horizon-2023-2024_en.pdf

19. European Commission: Horizon Europe Work Programme 2023–2024: Cluster 3 – Civil Security for Society (2022). Retrieved from https://ec.europa.eu/info/funding-tenders/opportunities/docs/2021-2027/horizon/wp-call/2023-2024/wp-6-civil-security-for-society_horizon-2023-2024_en.pdf

20. European Commission: Horizon Europe Work Programme 2023–2024: Cluster 4 – Digital, Industry and Space (2022). Retrieved from https://ec.europa.eu/info/funding-tenders/opportunities/docs/2021-2027/horizon/wp-call/2023-2024/wp-7-digital-industry-and-space_horizon-2023-2024_en.pdf

21. European Commissio: Horizon Europe Work Programme 2023–2024: Cluster 5 – Climate, Energy and Mobility (2022). Retrieved from https://ec.europa.eu/info/funding-tenders/opportunities/docs/2021-2027/horizon/wp-call/2023-2024/wp-8-climate-energy-and-mobility_horizon-2023-2024_en.pdf

22. European Commission: Horizon Europe Work Programme 2023–2024: Cluster 6 - Food, Bioeconomy, Natural Resources, Agriculture and Environment (2022). Retrieved from https://ec.europa.eu/info/funding-tenders/opportunities/docs/2021-2027/horizon/wp-call/2023-2024/wp-9-food-bioeconomy-natural-resources-agriculture-and-environment_horizon-2023-2024_en.pdf

23. European Commission: Horizon Europe Work Programme 2023–2024: Mission Areas (2022). Retrieved from https://ec.europa.eu/info/funding-tenders/opportunities/docs/2021-2027/horizon/wp-call/2023-2024/wp-12-missions_horizon-2023-2024_en.pdf

24. Vigar, G., Heidrich, O., Deutz, P.: Greening the brownfield–a simplified LCA tool for the assessment of the sustainability of brownfield regeneration options. Environ. Sci. Policy **55**, 300–308 (2016)

25. Antonioli, M., Marzucchi, A., Montresor, S., Pontoglio, S.: Low-carbon innovation and technology transfer in latecomer countries: Insights from solar PV in the clean development mechanism. Energy Policy **102**, 152–166 (2017)

26. Nijkamp, P., Poot, J.: The future of urban sustainability: towards an integrated approach. Int. J. Sust. Dev. World **24**(3), 197–205 (2017). https://doi.org/10.1080/13504509.2016.1212283

27. Martinez-Fernandez, C., Audirac, I.: Urban planning and governance for sustainable urbanization: the case of Mexico. Cities **106**, 102788 (2020)

28. Wachsmuth, D., Chan, E., Blaisdell, R., Steele, W.: Who is being left behind in the urban renaissance? Mapping gentrification and displacement in American cities. J. Am. Plann. Assoc. **86**(4), 495–509 (2020)

29. European Commission: Urban Agenda for the EU (2022). https://futurium.ec.europa.eu/en/urban-agenda

30. Biswas, S.: Natural language processing using deep learning techniques: a review. Int. J. Artif. Intell. Mach. Learn. **5**(2), 27–41 (2023). https://doi.org/10.4018/IJAIML.20230401.oa3

31. Islam, M.R., Islam, M.S.: ChatGPT: a revolutionary tool for natural language processing. In: Proceedings of the International Conference on Natural Language Processing, pp. 1–7. Springer, Cham (2023)

32. Zaremba, A., Demir, E.: A survey of natural language processing applications in cybersecurity. J. Cybersecurity Inform. Manage. **1**(1), 10–23 (2023). https://doi.org/10.4018/JCIM.202301 01.oa2

33. Guo, B., Zhang, X., Wan, G.Z., et al.: How Close is Chat GPT to Human Experts? Comparison Corpus, Evaluation, and Detection. arXiv preprint arXiv:2301.07597 (2023)

34. Eurostat: Urban Europe – Statistics on Cities, Towns and Suburbs, Eurostat Statistical books, Publications Office of the European Union, Luxembourg (2019). https://doi.org/10.2785/ 12028

35. Eurostat: Sustainable Development in the European Union – Monitoring Report on Progress Towards the SDGs in an EU Context, Eurostat Statistical books, Publications Office of the European Union, Luxembourg (2020). https://doi.org/10.2785/880277. https://ec.europa.eu/ eurostat/web/products-statistical-books/-/KS-02-20-001

36. Eurostat: Eurostat Regional Yearbook – Edition 2021, Eurostat Statistical books, Publications Office of the European Union, Luxembourg (2021). https://doi.org/10.2785/099019

37. Angelidou, M., Psaltoglou, A., Komninos, N., Kakderi, C., Tsarchopoulos, P., Panori, A.: Towards a reference framework for sustainable cities (SMART-U-Green). JRC Science for Policy Report, European Commission, Joint Research Centre, Institute for Prospective Technological Studies, Seville, Spain (2018). https://publications.jrc.ec.europa.eu/repository/han dle/JRC111835

38. Tukker, A., et al.: Environmental and resource footprints in a global context: Europe's structural deficit in resource endowments. Global Env. Change **48**, 20–26 (2018). https://publications.jrc.ec.europa.eu/repository/bitstream/JRC112674/jrc112674_cir cular_economy_indicators_report.pdf

39. European Environment Agency: Sustainable urban development in Europe: A snapshot of the EU cities. EEA Report, No 1/2016

40. European Environment Agency: Sustainability transitions: policy and practice. EEA Report No 9/2019 (2019)

41. European Environment Agency: The European environment — state and outlook 2020: knowledge for transition to a sustainable Europe. EEA Report No 10/2020 (2020). https://www. eea.europa.eu/publications/soer-2020. https://doi.org/10.2800/110793

42. Organization for Economic Co-operation and Development: OECD Regional Outlook 2016: Productive Regions for Inclusive Societies (2016). https://www.oecd-ilibrary.org/urban-rural-and-regional-development/oecd-regional-outlook-2016_9789264260245-en

43. Organization for Economic Co-operation and Development: Towards Green Growth in Southeast Europe: A Review of Progress in 12 Countries. OECD Green Growth Studies (2017). https://www.oecd-ilibrary.org/development/towards-green-growth-in-southeast-europe_9789264278741-en

44. Organization for Economic Co-operation and Development: Measuring Distance to the SDGs Targets (2019). https://www.oecd-ilibrary.org/development/measuring-distance-to-the-sdg-targets-2019_a8caf3fa-en

Exploratory Analysis of Building Stock: A Case Study for the City of Esch-sur-Alzette (Luxembourg)

Antonino Marvuglia[1]([⊠]) [iD] and Mohamed Laib[2] [iD]

[1] Environmental Research and Innovation Department (ERIN), Luxembourg Institute of Science and Technology (LIST), L-4362 Esch-sur-Alzette, Luxembourg
antonino.marvuglia@list.lu
[2] IT for Innovative Services Department (ITIS), Luxembourg Institute of Science and Technology (LIST), L-4362 Esch-sur-Alzette, Luxembourg
mohamed.laib@list.lu

Abstract. One of the main steps in developing urban building energy models (UBEM) is the classification of the building stock according to building archetypes. Different approaches have been proposed to accomplish this task, some based on the application of clustering techniques, or a combination of expert knowledge, deterministic classification, and data driven approaches. This paper proposes the utilization of a hybrid approach where exploratory data analysis is combined with feature extraction and feature selection to support clustering. The proposed methodology was applied to the building stock of the city of Esch-sur-Alzette (Grand Duchy of Luxembourg). The used data set includes buildings' geometrical and physical characteristics, preassigned occupancy estimates, and final energy use simulated with a quasi-steady-state model. According to the variables' combination and deterministic building stock fragmentation schemes used, the number of archetypes identified varied between 12 and 89. The paper shows the potential of clustering techniques for the development of archetypes, even though this must be combined with other (deterministic) fragmentation methods because clustering alone does not allow for the differentiation of building use typologies and construction periods, both of which must be considered to characterize buildings properly.

Keywords: Building archetypes · Building energy models · Clustering

1 Introduction and State of the Art

According to the International Energy Agency (IEA), the building sector has an enormous efficiency potential that is still far from being fully leveraged [1]. In order to help policy makers and energy planners to set up priority actions for renovation at city level, comprehensive building energy models at city scale are and will be increasingly needed [2]. The concept of Urban Building Energy Models (UBEM) has now become a standard way to look at the estimation of citywide energy demand expanding from the building

© The Author(s) 2023
O. Gervasi et al. (Eds.): ICCSA 2023 Workshops, LNCS 14104, pp. 374–391, 2023.
https://doi.org/10.1007/978-3-031-37105-9_25

level [3]. A comprehensive description of the approaches used in large-scale building energy models is given in the reference [3], where the four main steps of a UBEM are identified as: 1. 3D City model, 2. Archetype development, 3. Urban climate data, and 4. UBEM simulation engine. From the reference [3] it emerges that one of the key determinants of building energy models is the building stock aggregation step, whereby one constructs a model of the building stock that reflects as best as possible its characteristics. Due to space constraints, this is the step we will mostly focus on in this paper. As it is well described in [4], building stock aggregation and characterization models can be broadly divided into three categories: top-down models, statistical bottom-up models, and engineering-based or physics-based bottom-up models [5, 6]. Top-down models are macro-scale, and they do not look at individual end-uses. They treat the built environment as a single energy user and utilize historical aggregated data for their estimations. Cities are analyzed from the perspective of techno-socioeconomic drivers (e.g., by econometric equations) [7]. Bottom-up approaches consider urban attributes at the micro-scale, studying individual (or sets of) buildings. The estimation of individual end-uses is then extrapolated to a larger scale (city/regional/national). This approach relies on the availability of extensive data to gather information on uses and impacts [8, 9]. The first step to describe the building stock is the identification of the geometrical properties of buildings (geometry, shape, and geospatial positions) using 3D city models. Subsequently, non-geometrical properties of buildings, like material, system, and occupancy, are normally defined by *building archetypes*. The definition of archetypes is a bottom-up engineering modelling procedure used to classify sets of buildings according to some common characteristics so that the detailed data and model results of the building that are identified as representative of each archetype can be extrapolated to the rest of the buildings belonging to the same group [7]. The last step of UBEM is the thermal model itself using a simulation engine. Archetypes' identification is thus a major step in UBEM. However, there is still no standard method for the definition of buildings' representative archetypes [10], and archetypes development remains still one of the biggest challenges in UBEM [3]. As was clearly stated in [2], despite providing a useful initial rough classification of the building stock, the simplistic classification by building use typologies necessitates a complementary fragmentation to identify variations related to equipment and system technical specifications as well as occupant behavior.

Several approaches have been applied to identify buildings' archetypes. Most of them use statistical techniques [11], while some apply a data-driven methodology [2, 12]. In Sokol et al. [13], a Bayesian method is used to factor in occupants-related characteristics in the definition of the archetypes, using probability distributions to represent uncertain parameters for which reliable data are rarely available. Numerous studies apply cluster analysis to the building stock to identify representative building classes and improve the accuracy of energy use prediction models [10, 14]. In Tardioli et al. [15], a clustering methodology in six steps for building classification is proposed to identify representative buildings and groups of buildings characterized by similar features. This approach has the advantage of not assigning a certain weight to specific features (e.g., the energy index or total energy consumption) but instead balancing the importance of all the building characteristics (i.e., geometry, energy, and occupancy). In Borges et al. [2], building archetypes are identified by combining deterministic buildings classification (based on characteristics like the use of typology and construction period) and clustering carried out using the R package NbClust [16] in various orders. The authors conclude that this approach allows obtaining archetypes of a higher granularity than when applying deterministic and cluster methodologies separately. In Nägeli et al. [17], a synthetic approach is used to generate realistic building stock data. In Costanzo et al. [18], instead of operating through direct archetypes identification, an approach based on using different layers of information is used, with the aim of avoiding oversimplifications. Afterward, the energy use prediction model was realized using a simulation-based approach in EnergyPlus.

The present paper proposes a methodology to achieve the buildings archetypes fragmentation that best represents buildings in terms of their expected operation energy use. The used methodology combines a deterministic method (based on the subdivision of the buildings according to their construction period and a pre-defined list of building typologies) with unsupervised clustering. The methodology is applied to a case study dealing with the city of Esch-sur-Alzette, in the South of Luxembourg.

2   Methodology

2.1   Data Description and Preparation

The proposed methodology in this paper is illustrated in Fig. 1. Each step is illustrated in the following.

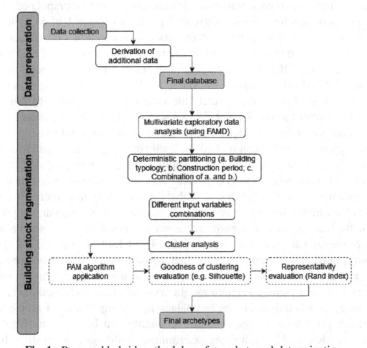

Fig. 1. Proposed hybrid methodology for archetypes' determination.

The data collection step is the same as described in [19] and [20], as here the same building stock data (geometrical characteristics, type of heating, U-values) is used. As described in [19], buildings elements and components were selected and classified according to previous studies [21, 22] and relevant standards [23]. The geospatial dataset consists of georeferenced building footprints (a georeferenced polygon for each building) and related attributes on building characteristics (year of construction, building function, and typology). The derivation of additional data consists in the calculation of geometrical characteristics like average building height (H_{avg}), building gross volume (V_{gross}), useful floor area (A_{useful}), and the area of walls delimiting the building envelope, that were obtained as described in [19], where the procedure to assign materials to each building component in each building by using the respective building type and period of construction information (and making resort to stochastic allocation in case of unknown information, such as the state of renovation) is also detailed.

As detailed in [5] and [20], the final energy use intensity (i.e., the energy used per m^2 of heated floor area) in each building was calculated using a quasi-steady-state energy demand simulation model for which the set of variables listed in Table 1 was available and which was applied to a data set containing 5400 buildings and 6594 cadastral units (see Table 2). Data variables listed in Table 1 represent our final database.

Table 1. List of variables known for each record (building) of the dataset.

Variable #	Variable name	Description
1	building_id	Building ID
2	QUARTIER	District
3	Typology	Building type
4	year_const	Construction year
5	ETPLEINS	Floors over the ground level
6	NBRHABITAN	Number of occupants
7	height_ave	Average building height (m)
8	length_w_out	Perimeter of outer walls (m)
9	surf_w_out	Surface of outer walls (m^2)
10	foot_area	Gross footprint area (m^2)
11	A_n	Heated floor area (m^2)
12	U_w	U-value of walls (W/m^{2}K)
13	U_r	U-value of roof (W/m^{2}K)
14	U_f	U-value of the ground floor (W/m^{2}K)
15	heating_sys	Heating system type
16	window_id	Window typology
17	$q_{E,V}$	Final energy use intensity (kWh/m^{2}a)

Heating system type (heating_sys) can take four values: 1. Conventional boiler of single-family-house (SFH); 2. Condensation boiler of SFH; 3. Conventional boiler of multi-family-house (MFH); 4. Condensation boiler of MFH. Window typology (window_id) can take seven values as described in Table 3, taken from [20].

Table 2. Number of buildings in the database per each building typology.

Building typology	n. of buildings	n. of cadastral units
1. Detached house (DH)	954	1159
2. Row-house (RH)	675	943
3. Mixed usage building (MX)	509	825
4. Multi-family-house (MFH)	3262	3667

Table 3. Window types.

Window type	Glazing type	Frame type	Construction period	U-value (W/m^2K)	g-value (-)
1	Single	Wood	Until 1968	5.00	0.87
2	Double	Aluminium (no thermal break)	1969–1983	4.30	0.75
3	Double	Aluminium (with thermal break)	1984–1994	3.20	0.75
4	Double	PVC	1969–1994	3.00	0.75
5	Double	Wood	Until 1994	2.70	0.75
6	Double	PVC-Aluminium	From 1995	1.90	0.60
7	Double	Wood	From 1995	1.60	0.60

2.2 Multivariate Exploratory Data Analysis

To visually explore the characteristics of the building data set, multivariate data analysis techniques have been applied in this paper. Since the dataset contained numerical and categorical features, Factor Analysis of Mixed Data (FAMD) was applied [24, 25]. The algorithm is a compromise between Principal Component Analysis (PCA) [26] and Multiple Correspondence Analysis (MCA) [27] and is known to handle well numerical and categorical features at the same time. In FAMD, each continuous variable is standardized (i.e., centred and then divided by its standard deviation), and each categorical variable is transformed into a dummy variable and divided by the square root of the proportion of objects taking the associated category [28]. Then, a PCA is applied to the resulting features (standardized for the continuous and transformed for the categorical) [29].

In this paper, FAMD is used to reduce the dimension of data to easily visualise it and gain better insight into the data structure. Moreover, FAMD's new dimensions are also used for clustering and compared to other variables' combinations. Each nominal variable has J_k levels, and the sum of all the J_k equals to J. Each nominal variable is coded using four indicator variables. For example, the four levels of the variable "heating_sys" are coded as 1000; 0100; 0010 and 0001. There are $I = 6594$ observations. We denote $\mathbf{X}$ the I × J indicator matrix (i.e., a matrix whose entries are 0 or 1). The J × J table obtained as $\mathbf{B} = \mathbf{X}^{\mathrm{T}}\mathbf{X}$ is called the *Burt matrix* associated to $\mathbf{X}$.

The proportion of variances explained by the new dimensions is displayed in the scree plot shown in Fig. 2.

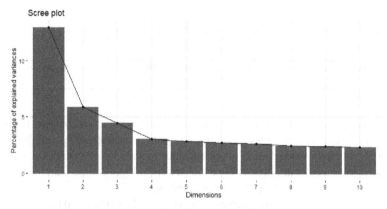

Fig. 2. Scree plot of the eigen values of the Burt matrix.

Only the first three dimensions have around 5% or higher of the explained variance. The remaining axes have an equal contribution of 2% of the variance. In this study, FAMD is applied to get quick insight and visualization of the dataset. However, in our case, the explained variance is too low (e.g., the first 10 dimensions plotted in the figure represent only 41% of the variance), and therefore more than just 10 dimensions were needed to perform the clustering described in the following sections. For the sake of readability, the data were projected into a 2-dimensional space formed by the Burt matrix's first two eigenvectors. Figure 3 shows the representation of the continuous variables on the *circle of correlations* [25], projected on the two first dimensions of FAMD.

The association between each variable is depicted on the graph. Variables that have a positive correlation are grouped. Variables with negative correlation are placed on each side of the origin (opposed quadrants). *Cos2* is a measure of how well the variables are represented on the factor map (square cosine, squared coordinates). A high *cos2* value (around 1) suggests that the variable on the principal component is well represented. In this case, the variable is situated relatively close to the correlation circle's edge. A low *cos2* value (around 0) implies that the principal components do not sufficiently describe the variable. In this case, the variable is very near the circle's centre. If a variable can be accurately described by just two principal components (Dim1 and Dim2), then the sum of the *cos2* on these two principal components is equal to one. The variables will

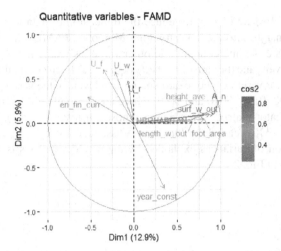

Fig. 3. Representation of the continuous features on the space spanned by the two first principal components.

be placed on the circle of correlations in this case. More than two components may be needed for some of the variables to capture the data completely. The variables in this instance are situated inside the correlation circle. In Fig. 3 the variables are coloured according to their *cos2* variables. As one can see from Fig. 3, some features are highly correlated, such as foot_area, length_w_out, and A_n.

Figure 4 shows the factor map representation of the data on the two first components.

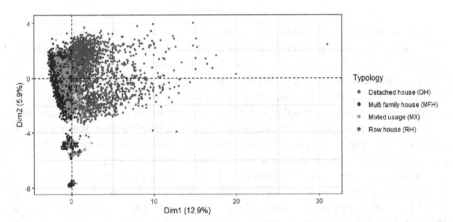

Fig. 4. Factor map representation of individuals on the two first components (coloured by building typology).

In Fig. 4 one can see that in these first two dimensions, the MFH class partially overlaps the MX class, and the DH class partially overlaps the RH class. This result is normal because MFH buildings are usually multi stores buildings, where offices or services can be easily located, and RH ones have several similar characteristics (geometry, shape, materials, etc.) to DH.

2.3 Building Stock Fragmentation

In the building stock fragmentation step, the buildings were divided into smaller subsets using deterministic and data-driven methodologies. The aim is to obtain subsets for which the similarity is also respected in terms of final energy use intensity (energy used per m^2 of the net surface). In other words, each of the obtained buildings' subsets should contain buildings that are not only similar with respect to their physical and functional characteristics (i.e., the features used to perform the fragmentation) but for which also a similar energy use intensity can be expected. In this way, the cluster label attributed to each building can help understand the best scheme to achieve building classifications based on buildings' characteristics that best respond to their actual energy use. This last point will be better explained in Sect. 3.

The building stock fragmentation stage is divided into three steps: (1) Variables' combinations choice; (2) buildings' deterministic classification (based on building typology, on construction period, and the combination of both); (3) PAM-based clustering. Details of each of these procedures and their implementation in the case study are presented in the remainder of the paper.

We decided to use four construction periods: Period 1: Before 1900; Period 2: Between 1900 and 1950; Period 3: Between 1951 and 2000; Period 4: After 2000. These periods reflect three main "construction waves". The first one, at the beginning of the 20th century, was linked to the exploitation of the iron mines and the flourishing of the steel industry, which attracted numerous workers. The second is linked with the reconstruction after World War II. A third wave took place at the end of the 20th century due to the booming of the finance and consulting sector in Luxembourg (and to some extent also the European institutions) that attracted and is still attracting a considerable number of workers.

2.4 Variables' Combinations

The variables' combinations (VC) on which the following steps (deterministic classification and PAM-based clustering) were performed is based on a) expert judgment (schemes from VC1 to VC4 below), b) unsupervised features selection (scheme VC5), and c) features extraction supported by FAMD (VC6).

More specifically, we applied the following variables' combinations schemes:

VC1. All the variables (from #2 to #17) shown in Table 1;

VC2. All the variables from #2 to #16 (the final energy use intensity, $q_{E,V}$, was excluded);

VC3. All the variables, except the U-values (#12, #13 and #14) and the number of occupants (#6);

VC4. All the variables, except the U-values (#12, #13 and #14), the number of occupants (#6) and the final energy use intensity (#17);

VC5. Unsupervised feature selection on the full data set (i.e., including all the variables from #2 to #17 in Table 1) based on the space-filling concept introduced in [30];

VC6. FAMD dimensions that represent 75% of the variance in each fragmentation.

Note that the number of selected variables in VC5, as well as the number of necessary dimensions in VC6, vary for each deterministic partitioning.

The selection of a number of variables lower than the initial dimension of our data manifold is based on the rationale that, when using the entire set of variables, some partitionings contained too few data-points with respect to the number of features. The same problem was encountered in [2]. To curb this problem, we then applied features selection to reduce the number of features used.

The variables' combination choice was repeated for each of the building partitionings obtained with the three following deterministic clustering subdivisions: 1. Division by building typology (called *typ_sep* hereafter); 2. Division by period of construction (called *period_sep* hereafter); 3. Division by both building typology and period of construction (called *typ&period_sep* hereafter).

The applied unsupervised feature selection algorithm eliminates existing data redundancy and keeps only those features that include new information. The algorithm is coded in the R package '*SFtools*' [31].

Table 4 shows the list of selected features for each studied fragmentation using VC5. It is worth mentioning that some of the variables are selected for all fragmentation, such as NBRHABITAN, height_ave, $q_{E,V}$. As Table 4 shows, there are several redundant features, e.g., one can see that the variables length_w_out and surf_w_out are selected alternatively in each fragmentation scenario.

2.5 Cluster Analysis

K-means [32] is one of the most well-known clustering techniques. It is used in many fields and relies on the distance matrix of the data, which is usually calculated using the Euclidian distance metrics. However, since the data set used in this paper is characterized by a mix of categorical and numerical features, other dissimilarity measures, such as the Gower distance [33], have been considered. Furthermore, to minimise the influence of noise and outliers, a medoid-based method was required, namely the Partitioning Around Medoid (PAM) algorithm was applied [34]. The main difference between PAM and K-means is that the latter computes the mean value of the cluster (centroid) to use as a prototype vector to represent the cluster, while the former uses an existing vector (i.e., a data-point) as a representative object. For this reason, the PAM algorithm is less sensitive to the initial choice of medoids than the K-means algorithm. This characteristic of PAM contributes to further limiting the influence of noise and outliers. However, the PAM algorithm is more computationally expensive than K-means, as it requires the calculation of all pairwise distances between points at each iteration.

The R packages '*clust*' [35] and '*factoextra*' [36] have been used to carry out the analyses.

Following the exploratory data analysis result, the data is grouped into classes according to the building typology. Clustering quality has been assessed using the silhouette score [37]. If one takes any object i in the data set and denotes by A the cluster to which it has been assigned, when A contains other objects apart from i, the average distance $a(i)$ of i from all the objects within A can be calculated. If one now considers another cluster

Table 4. List of selected features for each studied fragmentation, which corresponds to VC5.

	DH	RH	MX	MFH	Before 1900	1900 to 1950	1950 to 2000	After 2000	DH & 1900 to 1950	DH & 1950 to 2000	DH & After 2000	RH & 1900 to 1950	RH & 1950 to 2000	MX & 1900 to 1950	MX & 1950 to 2000	MFH & 1900 to 1950	MFH & 1950 to 2000	MFH & After 2000
QUARTIER	✓	✓	✓	✓	✓	✓	✓	✓	✓	✓	✓	✓	✓	✓	✓	✓	✓	✓
Typology																		
Year_const	✓	✓	✓	✓														
ETPLEINS	✓	✓							✓	✓	✓	✓	✓	✓	✓			
NBRHABITAN	✓	✓	✓	✓	✓	✓	✓	✓	✓	✓	✓	✓	✓	✓	✓	✓	✓	✓
height_ave	✓	✓	✓	✓	✓	✓	✓	✓	✓	✓	✓	✓	✓	✓	✓	✓	✓	✓
length_w_out	✓	✓			✓	✓	✓						✓			✓		✓
surf_w_out			✓	✓				✓	✓			✓	✓	✓		✓	✓	
foot_area									✓						✓			✓
A_n			✓						✓			✓	✓			✓		✓
U_w			✓				✓		✓	✓		✓	✓	✓		✓		
U_r	✓	✓	✓	✓	✓	✓	✓	✓	✓	✓	✓	✓	✓	✓	✓	✓	✓	✓
U_f									✓	✓								
heating_sys	✓	✓	✓	✓	✓	✓	✓	✓	✓	✓	✓	✓	✓	✓	✓			✓
window_id	✓	✓	✓	✓	✓	✓	✓	✓	✓	✓	✓	✓	✓	✓	✓	✓	✓	
$q_{E,V}$	✓	✓	✓	✓	✓	✓	✓	✓	✓	✓	✓	✓	✓	✓	✓	✓	✓	✓

$C \neq A$ and computes the mean $d(i, c)$ of the distances from i to all the objects in C, the smallest $(b(i))$ of those distances can be selected. The silhouette width for data-point i in cluster A is defined by:

$$\begin{cases} s(i) = \frac{b(i)-a(i)}{max[a(i),b(i)]} & if \ |C_A| > 1 \\ s(i) = 0 & if \ |C_A| = 1 \end{cases} \tag{1}$$

where $|C_A|$ is the cardinality of A, i.e., the number of elements in A.

The silhouette S_A of cluster A is the average of the silhouette widths of all the objects in A. Given a certain partitioning that separates the data set into K clusters, the overall silhouette score of the partitioning is the mean of the silhouette of the clusters over all

K clusters:

$$S = \frac{1}{K} \sum_{A=1}^{K} S_A \qquad (2)$$

Therefore, the higher the silhouette score, the better the clustering [37]. A good partitioning of the data set yields a silhouette score close to 1.

3   Results and Discussions

The number of clusters identified with the hybrid clustering (i.e., using first the deterministic clustering and then the PAM algorithm) per each VC and each fragmentation scheme varied between 12 and 89, with the lowest number (12) found when using the VC1 or the VC2 scheme coupled with the *typ_sep scheme* deterministic building stock fragmentation, and highest number (89) found when using the VC6 scheme coupled with *typ&period_sep*.

Figure 5 shows a heatmap of the silhouette scores of the different subgroups of buildings obtained by combining building typologies and construction periods (deterministic partitioning cases shown as column headers).

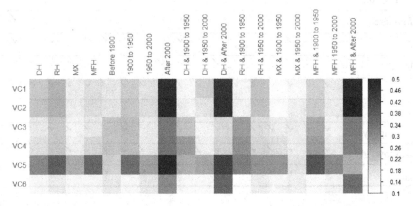

Fig. 5. Silhouette values for the partitionings obtained dividing the buildings by typology (*typ_sep*), by period of construction (*period_sep*), and by a combination of the two (*typ&period_sep*).

From the observation of Fig. 5, one can infer that the typology alone normally does not provide "optimal" clusters from the compactness and separation standpoint (measured by the Silhouette index). This is true in every case, but slightly improves when unsupervised features selection is used (VC5). In all the cases, the separation among clusters is more clear (higher values of the Silhouette index) for the buildings built after 2000. We can partially explain this by the fact that for certain old buildings (or even single dwellings) certain renovation interventions (like internal insulation or windows replacement) could have been realized without having been recorded, therefore this information may be missing from the dataset. This is less likely for newer buildings (built after 2000).

However, as it will be shown later in Fig. 7, in our context, the first objective of clustering is using the descriptors (i.e. the variables from #2 to #16) to obtain sets of buildings that are as similar as possible in their expected energy use intensity, while separation and compactness (reflected by the Silhouette index) becomes the second objective.

Looking at the VC2 row of Fig. 5, one can observe that for this variables' combination scheme, there are three cases (buildings "After 2000", "DH & After 2000", and "MFH & After 2000") with the best partitioning (highest Silhouette values of Fig. 5), that are also reflected in terms of final energy use, i.e., when we repeat the clustering adding the variable $q_{E,V}$, (as the VC1 row of Fig. 5 exhibit nearly the same pattern in terms of Silhouette values). Among these three cases, the box plots of the final energy use of each obtained cluster showed that, in terms of clusters separation, the best case is the one of VC2 for MFH built after 2000 (Fig. 6), as the mean and median values are the best separated from one cluster to the other. Nonetheless, some overlap between the range of variation of the $q_{E,V}$ values of the different clusters is inevitable, as there will always be dwellings with different features but with the same or similar energy use intensity. As mentioned above, one reason for this is that there are buildings belonging to the same construction period but with different renovation states.

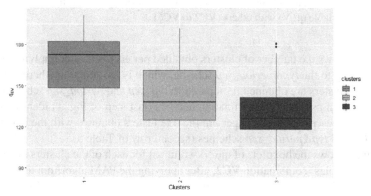

Fig. 6. Box plots of the final energy use intensity ($q_{E,V}$) of each cluster obtained with VC2 for MFH built after 2000.

Finally, the partitionings obtained using all the variables (VC1) have been compared with all the others using Rand's cluster similarity index [38]. This index takes values between 0 and 1, being 0 the scenario in which the two partitionings one is comparing have no similarities (that is, when one only consists of a single cluster and the other is composed of clusters containing single points), and 1 the case in which the partitionings are the same.

The values of the Rand similarity indices obtained are shown as numbers within each cell in Fig. 7. The figure emphasizes the similarity between VC1 and VC2, as the Rand index approaches value 1 in almost all the deterministic partitioning cases. Moreover, the figure shows that when the U-values (variables #12, #13, and #14) and the number of occupants (variable #6) are removed from the data set (namely, the cases of VC3 and VC4) the obtained clusters are not similar (i.e., the values of the Rand index are low) to the ones obtained in the case of VC1 (i.e., when all variables are included). From this perspective, we then argue that the VC2 scheme would be the best option to obtain clusters that can reflect the expected final energy use when this latter is unknown. This conclusion is indeed not very surprising since the final energy use is calculated starting from the variables that express the physical characteristics of the buildings [5, 20].

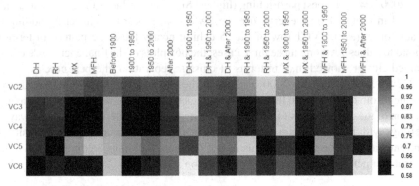

Fig. 7. Rand index values obtained by comparing the clusters resulting from VC1 (i.e., when removing the variable qE,V) with others (VC2 to VC6).

Table 5 shows the number of clusters obtained per each VC after applying the PAM algorithm only to the *typ&period_sep* scheme, which is the situation where the highest numbers of clusters are obtained (compared to *typ_sep* and *period_sep* schemes).

We can then assume that the final archetypes (last step of Fig. 1) identified by the methodology described in this paper are the 43 clusters obtained with the combination of the VC2 and *typ&period_sep* schemes (second row of Table 5).

Figure 8 shows the boxplots of q_{EV} [kwh/m^2 a] for each of the clusters identified by using the variables' combination VC2, after applying the PAM algorithm to the *typ_sep* scheme. The clusters are named using the acronym of the building typology they refer to (e.g. DH for detached houses) and the cluster number within that particular typology (e.g. DH_1 is the first of the clusters that contain detached houses).

The figure shows that the VC2 scheme, even if it does not use q_{EV} as input variable, allowed a reasonably good separation in terms of final energy use intensity (looking at the distancing among the medians and the average values of the clusters, typology by typology). The fact that a similar separation was obtained also with VC1, which, however, includes q_{EV} among the input variables, testifies that the scheme VC2 allowed to obtain a partitioning that represents building clusters (i.e. archetypes) with a reasonably good separation in terms of expected energy use intensity.

Table 5. Number of clusters per each VC scheme after applying the PAM algorithm to the *typ&period_sep* scheme.

	DH & 1900-1950	DH & 1950-2000	DH & After 2000	RH & 1900-1950	RH & 1950-2000	MX & 1900-1950	MX & 1950-2000	MFH & 1900-1950	MFH & 1950-2000	MFH & After 2000	Total n. of clusters
VC1	6	3	3	4	3	8	3	3	3	3	39
VC2	9	3	3	7	3	6	3	3	3	3	43
VC3	9	10	5	4	11	6	11	7	11	3	77
VC4	4	10	11	4	10	6	11	7	9	3	75
VC5	3	3	3	3	3	3	3	3	5	3	32
VC6	11	9	11	11	11	8	4	11	6	7	89

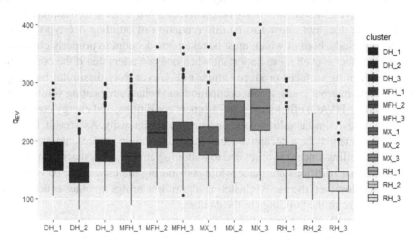

Fig. 8. Clustering applied to each deterministic split (VC2).

4   Conclusion

This research suggests a new hybrid methodology for archetype identification that combines the traditional deterministic approach with cluster analysis. The proposed approach has been applied to the building stock of the city of Esch-sur-Alzette, in the south of Luxembourg. The used building stock comprises 5400 buildings and 6594 cadastral units. The number of archetypes identified varied between 12 and 89 (according to the different schemes detailed in the paper).

The chosen archetypes are the 43 clusters obtained by applying the PAM clustering algorithm to the data set which comprises all the variables in the dataset, excluding the final energy use intensity (variables' combination scheme called VC2 in the paper), but where the buildings had been previously partitioned using the deterministic separation based on building typologies and construction period (called *typ&period_sep* in the paper).

The novelty of the proposed approach, compared to similar analyses proposed in the literature [2, 15], consists mainly in the exploration of different variables' combinations and the application of unsupervised variables selection, in addition to variables' extraction obtained with the FAMD algorithm [24].

Borges et al. [2] suggested that, when building metered energy is used as a unique variable to perform clustering, completing the cluster analysis prior to the building period fragmentation allows to better capture the patterns of energy usage and impacts the cluster analysis' outcome as little as possible. In our case, we do not use directly metered energy data, but energy data derived from a physics-based simplified model. Moreover, the clustering is performed using several variables, and the matching with the energy usage patterns is checked using the Rand index. Therefore, in our case the order of the two steps is still relevant, but to a lower extent.

We confirm the finding already highlighted by Borges et al. [2] that there is strong evidence that the use of clustering techniques has a high potential for the development of archetypes, even though this must be combined with other partitionings, because clustering alone does not allow for the differentiation of building use typologies and construction periods, both of which must be taken into account to properly characterize buildings. This fact is even more important when one considers that if the consumption patterns and heating surfaces produce similar ratios, even very dissimilar buildings in terms of design, internal gains, tenant occupation and behaviour, heating ventilation and air conditioning (HVAC) efficiency, refurbishment conditions, and energy conservation measures may have similar values of the final energy use intensity. As a result, the energy use intensity alone may be a deceptive variable for determining representative buildings for energy modelling since it is unrelated to building geometry. Clustering, on the other hand, ensures that partitions are made while considering the total range of variation in each variable. However, the use of clustering algorithms brings up other concerns, such as the sample size of the buildings in the database.

Future work will involve benefitting from the proposed hybrid approach to use buildings cluster labels (detected archetypes) as one of the input variables to inform UBEMs and validate the results of the new energy simulations using metered energy data. This, however, necessitates collecting new data.

Acknowledgments. This research was developed within the project "Continuous lifecycle assessment of buildings and districts through real-time design and operation data underpinned by semantics" (SemanticLCA), funded by the Luxembourg National Research Fund (FNR) under the Grant INTER/UKRI/19/14106247 and the UK Engineering and Physical Sciences Research Council (EPSRC) under the Grant EP/T019514/1.

References

1. IEA: Buildings - A source of enormous untapped efficiency potential. https://www.iea.org/topics/buildings. Accessed 12 May 2022
2. Borges, P., Travesset-Baro, O., Pages-Ramon, A.: Hybrid approach to representative building archetypes development for urban models – a case study in Andorra. Build. Environ. **215**, 108958 (2022). https://doi.org/10.1016/j.buildenv.2022.108958
3. Johari, F., Peronato, G., Sadeghian, P., Zhao, X., Widén, J.: Urban building energy modeling: state of the art and future prospects. Renew. Sustain. Energy Rev. **128**, 109902 (2020). https://doi.org/10.1016/j.rser.2020.109902
4. Langevin, J., et al.: Developing a common approach for classifying building stock energy models. Renew. Sustain. Energy Rev. **133**, 110276 (2020). https://doi.org/10.1016/j.rser.2020.110276
5. Mastrucci, A., Marvuglia, A., Benetto, E., Leopold, U.: A spatio-temporal life cycle assessment framework for building renovation scenarios at the urban scale. Renew. Sustain. Energy Rev. **126**, 109834 (2020). https://doi.org/10.1016/j.rser.2020.109834
6. Abbasabadi, N., Ashayeri, M.: Urban energy use modeling methods and tools: a review and an outlook. Build. Environ. **161**, 106270 (2019). https://doi.org/10.1016/j.buildenv.2019.106270
7. Swan, L.G., Ugursal, V.I.: Modeling of end-use energy consumption in the residential sector: a review of modeling techniques. Renew. Sustain. Energy Rev. **13**, 1819–1835 (2009). https://doi.org/10.1016/j.rser.2008.09.033
8. Allegrini, J., Orehounig, K., Mavromatidis, G., Ruesch, F., Dorer, V., Evins, R.: A review of modelling approaches and tools for the simulation of district-scale energy systems. Renew. Sustain. Energy Rev. **52**, 1391–1404 (2015). https://doi.org/10.1016/j.rser.2015.07.123
9. Ferrando, M., Causone, F., Hong, T., Chen, Y.: Urban building energy modeling (UBEM) tools: a state-of-the-art review of bottom-up physics-based approaches. Sustain. Cities Soc. **62**, 102408 (2020). https://doi.org/10.1016/j.scs.2020.102408
10. Schaefer, A., Ghisi, E.: Method for obtaining reference buildings. Energy Build. **128**, 660–672 (2016). https://doi.org/10.1016/j.enbuild.2016.07.001
11. Cerezo, C., Sokol, J., AlKhaled, S., Reinhart, C., Al-Mumin, A., Hajiah, A.: Comparison of four building archetype characterization methods in urban building energy modeling (UBEM): a residential case study in Kuwait City. Energy Build. **154**, 321–334 (2017). https://doi.org/10.1016/j.enbuild.2017.08.029
12. Pasichnyi, O., Wallin, J., Kordas, O.: Data-driven building archetypes for urban building energy modelling. Energy **181**, 360–377 (2019). https://doi.org/10.1016/j.energy.2019.04.197
13. Sokol, J., Davila, C.C., Reinhart, C.F.: Validation of a Bayesian-based method for defining residential archetypes in urban building energy models. Energy Build. **134**, 11–24 (2017). https://doi.org/10.1016/j.enbuild.2016.10.050
14. Ghiassi, N., Mahdavi, A.: Reductive bottom-up urban energy computing supported by multivariate cluster analysis. Energy Build. **144**, 372–386 (2017). https://doi.org/10.1016/j.enbuild.2017.03.004
15. Tardioli, G., Kerrigan, R., Oates, M., O'Donnell, J., Finn, D.P.: Identification of representative buildings and building groups in urban datasets using a novel pre-processing, classification, clustering and predictive modelling approach. Build. Environ. **140**, 90–106 (2018). https://doi.org/10.1016/j.buildenv.2018.05.035
16. Charrad, M., Ghazzali, N., Boiteau, V., Niknafs, A.: NbClust: an R package for determining the relevant number of clusters in a data set. J. Stat. Soft. **61**, 1–36 (2014). https://doi.org/10.18637/jss.v061.i06
17. Nägeli, C., Camarasa, C., Jakob, M., Catenazzi, G., Ostermeyer, Y.: Synthetic building stocks as a way to assess the energy demand and greenhouse gas emissions of national building stocks. Energy Build. **173**, 443–460 (2018). https://doi.org/10.1016/j.enbuild.2018.05.055

18. Costanzo, V., Yao, R., Li, X., Liu, M., Li, B.: A multi-layer approach for estimating the energy use intensity on an urban scale. Cities **95**, 102467 (2019). https://doi.org/10.1016/j.cities.2019.102467

19. Mastrucci, A., Marvuglia, A., Popovici, E., Leopold, U., Benetto, E.: Geospatial characterization of building material stocks for the life cycle assessment of end-of-life scenarios at the urban scale. Resour. Conserv. Recycl. 54–66 (2017). https://doi.org/10.1016/j.resconrec.2016.07.003

20. Mastrucci, A., Pérez-López, P., Benetto, E., Leopold, U., Blanc, I.: Global sensitivity analysis as a support for the generation of simplified building stock energy models. Energy Build. **149**, 368–383 (2017). https://doi.org/10.1016/j.enbuild.2017.05.022

21. Nemry, F., et al.: Options to reduce the environmental impacts of residential buildings in the European Union—potential and costs. Energy Build. **42**, 976–984 (2010). https://doi.org/10.1016/j.enbuild.2010.01.009

22. Mastrucci, A., Popovici, E., Marvuglia, A., De Sousa, L., Benetto, E., Leopold, U.: GIS-based life cycle assessment of urban building stocks retrofitting. A bottom-up framework applied to Luxembourg. Presented at the Enviroinfo & ICT4S 2015, Copenhagen, Denmark (2015)

23. Charette, R.P., Marshall, H.E.: UNIFORMAT II elemental classification for building specifications, cost estimating, and cost analysis. NIST US Department of Commerce (1999)

24. Pagès, J.: Analyse factorielle multiple avec R. Presented at the (2013). https://doi.org/10.1051/978-2-7598-1085-7.c004

25. Kassambara, A.: Practical guide to principal component methods in R. STHDA (2017)

26. Hill, M.O., Smith, A.J.E.: Principal component analysis of taxonomic data with multi-state discrete characters. Taxon **25**, 249–255 (1976). https://doi.org/10.2307/1219449

27. Kiers, H.A.L.: Simple structure in component analysis techniques for mixtures of qualitative and quantitative variables. Psychometrika **56**, 197–212 (1991). https://doi.org/10.1007/BF02294458

28. van de Velden, M., Iodice D'Enza, A., Markos, A.: Distance-based clustering of mixed data. WIREs Comput. Stat. **11**, e1456 (2019). https://doi.org/10.1002/wics.1456

29. Vichi, M., Vicari, D., Kiers, H.A.L.: Clustering and dimension reduction for mixed variables. Behaviormetrika **46**(2), 243–269 (2019). https://doi.org/10.1007/s41237-018-0068-6

30. Laib, M., Kanevski, M.: A new algorithm for redundancy minimisation in geo-environmental data. Comput. Geosci. **133**, 104328 (2019). https://doi.org/10.1016/j.cageo.2019.104328

31. Laib, M., Kanevski, M.: SFtools: space filling based tools for data mining (2017)

32. MacQueen, J.: Some methods for classification and analysis of multivariate observations. Presented at the Proceedings of the Fifth Berkeley Symposium on Mathematical Statistics and Probability, Volume 1: Statistics, Berkeley, Calif. (1967)

33. Gower, J.C.: A general coefficient of similarity and some of its properties. Biometrics **27**, 857–871 (1971). https://doi.org/10.2307/2528823

34. Kaufman, L., Rousseeuw, P.J.: Partitioning around medoids (Program PAM). In: Finding Groups in Data, pp. 68–125 (1990). https://doi.org/10.1002/9780470316801.ch2

35. Maechler, M., Rousseeuw, P., Struyf, A., Hubert, M., Hornik, K.: cluster: Cluster Analysis Basics and Extensions. R package version 2.1.4 (2022)

36. Kassambara, A., Mundt, F.: Factoextra: extract and visualize the results of multivariate data analyses. R Package Version 1.0.7 (2020). https://CRAN.R-project.org/package=factoextra

37. Rousseeuw, P.J.: Silhouettes: a graphical aid to the interpretation and validation of cluster analysis. J. Comput. Appl. Math. **20**, 53–65 (1987). https://doi.org/10.1016/0377-0427(87)90125-7

38. Rand, W.M.: Objective criteria for the evaluation of clustering methods. J. Am. Stat. Assoc. **66**, 846–850 (1971). https://doi.org/10.2307/2284239

A Methodological Framework to Assess Individual Sustainable Behavior

Marta Bottero[1] ⓘ, Giulio Cavana[1](✉) ⓘ, and Sara Viazzo[2] ⓘ

[1] Interuniversity Department of Regional and Urban Studies and Planning (DIST), Politecnico di Torino, Viale Mattioli, 39, TO 10125 Turin, Italy
giulio.cavana@polito.it

[2] TEBE-IEEM Research Group, Energy Department, Politecnico di Torino, Corso Duca degli Abruzzi 24, 10129 Torino, Italy

Abstract. Cities are privileged places in which the transition of society towards a sustainable future could be achieved. In this direction, individuals could have a preeminent impact in the attempt to meet such target.

To engage individuals in the more responsible use of resources, more sustainable behavior and environmental identity within citizens has to be promoted. To support the transition of citizens behavioral patterns toward a more sustainable use of resources, several tools have been proposed, especially in the Human-Computer Interaction field. Such tools are rarely used more than once by users, thus usually they fail in promoting a stable engagement of the user, and their efficacy in fostering a change in her environmental behavior is limited. In this paper a methodology to design a gamifyied environment is presented, taking into consideration the possibility to integrate different parameters to promote user's participation and to foster her perseverance in the engagement with the proposed serious game. A specific Sustainability Index is proposed, together with its calculation algorithm, in order to better communicate and compare the environmental performances of individuals, and ultimately to interact among each other through collaboration and competition in the framework of the proposed game itself.

Keywords: Sustainable behavior · Gamification · Environmental Impact

1 Introduction

Cities have a primary impact in the achievement of a more sustainable society [1]. Indeed, nowadays more than half of the world's population lives in urban areas, and their carbon emission related to the energy uses in cities account for more than half of the globally emitted greenhouse gases (GHG) [2]. A large number of initiatives target the city as the place in which to concentrate the actions towards a more sustainable future where to pursue an environmental sustainability and social inclusion [3]. The 2030 Agenda for Sustainable Development, for example, specifically addresses cities with its 11th Sustainable Development Goal (SDG), aiming at making "cities and human settlements inclusive, safe, resilient and sustainable" [3]. Furthermore, cities could also be particularly interested by the new paradigm of the Circular Economy [4] as it has

O. Gervasi et al. (Eds.): ICCSA 2023 Workshops, LNCS 14104, pp. 392–404, 2023.
https://doi.org/10.1007/978-3-031-37105-9_26

been framed by the European Commission in its Circular Economy Action Plan (CEAP) adopted in the wider framework of the European Green Deal [5, 6]. The shift to this new paradigm will influence cities by limiting the loss of biodiversity, and create sustainable growth by generating new jobs [7–9].

The wished transition toward a more sustainable and circular city will inevitably have to consider the complexity of the urban system and the wider plethora of city users, stakeholders and actors, in order to ensure an equitable transition towards a human-centered circular model [10, 11]. In particular, considering the role of individuals in such transition, it has been extensively recognized the impact that they have in several fields related to the consumption of resources. In the building sector, for instance, it has been extensively demonstrated how the way in which the user operate a building has a great impact on its energy consumption [12], limiting the reliability of the assumptions made in the design phase and, thus, resulting in a mismatch between simulated and actual energy consumption [13–15].

Also in the general consumption of resources, the role of individuals is fundamental in achieving higher level of sustainability, as well as a potential shift to a more circular society. Several examples are presented in literature regarding recycling patterns [16, 17], water consumption [18], individual purchase decisions [19, 20].

Some studies have demonstrated that, even when structural barrier are removed, people tend to behave in a more sustainable manner only when they already have a pro-environmental attitude [17, 21], or environmental identity [22]. As such, to promote a better and more efficient use of resources, and thus, a more sustainable behaviour of individuals, the promotion of environmental identity within citizens has been stressed [21], as well as self-efficacy building education [23], and social interaction [24]. In engaging with sustainable behaviour, the amount of information possessed by the individual plays a significant role in this attempt [25], by affecting their perceived behavioural control and self-efficacy conceived, respectively, as the perceived amount of control people have on their actions [26], and their perceived level of control to implement these action regardless the events affecting their lives [27].

In regards to self-efficacy, for example, several are the studies suggesting that increasing the amount of information provided to individuals could reduce their use of energy [28–32], while the comparison to others could promote more sustainable behavioral patterns [17, 33].

Considering all the above, aim of this paper is to propose a methodology to evaluate the sustainability of individuals through self-reported virtuous actions to be implemented on an online application, and to foster their transition towards environmental conscious behaviour. In particular, the proposed methodology will exploit the possibilities of engaging the individual inside context specific virtual communities in gamified environments. These communities could be formed based on common interests or characteristics (employees of the same company, fan-bases of sport events, etc.) and defined in time (in the form of time defined challenges), in order to promote the effect that the push from peers could have in the achievement of higher level of individual sustainable behaviour.

The rest of the contribution is structured as follows: in Sect. 2 different sustainable evaluation protocols are presented with the focus both on the hardware component of the urban infrastructure, and on the available tools to assess and foster individual citizens' sustainable behavioural patterns. In Sect. 3 the methodology to develop the gamified environment is delineated. Finally, in Sect. 4 conclusions and further avenue of the research are presented.

2   Evaluation Methods and Engagement Strategies

2.1   Urban Sustainability Protocols and Methods

The attempt to evaluate sustainability at the urban level is a complex task that comprise several dimensions: from environmental, economic, and social ones, and it is not just a purely technical/scientific evaluation [34]. In the context of urban regeneration projects, the literature presents a variety of methods to assess decision-makers in selecting the most suitable alternative to achieve higher level of sustainability against a wide variety of criteria [35]. Several international and regional protocols originally proposed with the goal of assessing the performance of buildings [36] are now expanding their view in order to provide evaluation tools more balanced toward the assessment of environmental, social and economic dimensions" [37]. Among these, BREEAM Communities, CASBEE-UD, GBI Township, LEED-ND, IGBC Green Township and GRIHA-LD could be named to provide an example of the wide variety of protocol used both internationally and in specific national frameworks. Compared to their "building-focused" counterparts, tailored for the site specific evaluation of aspects of building performance related to its site [38–40] these large scale tools aim to transcend building components or buildings separately [41, 42], in order to take in consideration, at the same time, also the built environment, landscape, infrastructure in their evaluation [43]. The previously mentioned protocols are based on evaluations performed by third party organizations. Other frameworks measure individual assets or portfolio grounding on self-reported data [36]. Tools like the Global ESG Benchmark for Real Assets (GRESB) [44] or European Public Real Estate (EPRA) [45] aim to collect data on environmental, social, and governance performance of buildings in order to provide recommendations on optimization options, and to provide a framework to track their performance over the years.

All these methods assess the urban environment as static assets or in specific moment of time, lacking an integration of the dynamic component represented by the users of spaces. In these sense, a method to engage people in the "on going" sustainability of a city/district/neighborhood is still lacking. Therefore, an assessment tool that could engage the community at different moment (as it could be the case of specific windows of time) could integrate these aspects in the assessment of the sustainability of the urban areas. Nonetheless, these methods allow the comparison between achieved performance (or design option) against benchmark ones, thus guiding towards areas of possible improvements of the former.

2.2   Environmental Footprint as Individual Sustainability Assessment Tool

The evaluation of individuals' behavior in term of sustainability is usually demanded to Ecological footprint calculators. Similar to self-assessment methods [36], these tools are based on self-reported data about user's consumption pattern in order to evaluate her impact on the environment. The results of the calculation are usually presented in kilograms of equivalent CO_2 yearly emitted (thus usually referred to as "carbon footprint calculator"), accompanied by advices and suggestions on how to reduce this figure through behavioral change [25]. Also in this field, a variety of calculators are available in literature [25], both internationally and national specific [46].

The capability of certain calculators of providing continuous information about environmental impact through monitoring and feedbacks aim to influence individual perception of self-efficacy [47], allowing them to be considered behaviour change interventions [25], with proven effects on individual environmental footprint reduction [48–50].

Despite these potentialities, the use of environmental footprint calculator is not so widespread among individuals [51]; furthermore, the majority of these tools are used few times by the same user [46, 52].

This aspect, in particular, has a peculiar hindering effect on the desirable outcomes of the use of environmental footprint calculator [25]. In the household domain, for instance, it is recognized that the efficacy of feedbacks is related on their frequency and continuity [28, 31, 53, 54]. One of the major obstacle in this regard resides in the design itself of the commonly used calculators, structured to provide feedback on a yearly base [55], reducing the likelihood of a repeated use of the tool [25].

Another aspect that has been recognized as culprit for the reduced impact of these calculators is their too narrow focus in solely providing information about carbon footprint, without providing actionable feedbacks [46]. An avenue of improvement in that sense as been proposed in the introduction of gamification aspects in these tools.

2.3 Gamification and Serious Games to Foster Behavioral Change

The promotion of behavioral change toward a more pro-environmental one is a common goal for initiatives in the realm of serious games and gamification in the Human-Computer Interaction (HCI) field [46, 56]. These two concepts refer to the inclusion of game design elements in real-world contexts, to combine entertainment purposes, with other motivations such as learning ones [57–59]. These elements take the form of points, levels, badges to name few, and absorb the player in non-game activities, motivating her to engage in the activity for which the gamified environment has been designed [60]. In this sense then, gamification has been recognized as promising in promoting a shift toward more sustainable behavioral pattern in users and, in general, among members of society [46, 60].

Regarding some of the limitation of the aforementioned environmental footprint calculator, and in particular the issue related to their one-off use by users, gamification specifically address this matter by motivating users (also referred as players in this framework) to repeatedly engage with sustainable actions [60], and, by doing so, promoting habit formation and, consequently, the long-term maintenance of a certain behavior [61].

An interesting aspect related to gamification is the possibility to connect members in a community [46] by sharing experiences and best practices [62] and to foster the engagement of players through competition among them.

Ro et al. [60] highlights how this latter aspect could be related to behavioral change theory, and, especially, on the aspect of group norms. Users playing in groups (teams) are motivated to engage with behavior that would fit with others in seek for a sense of acceptance, further conforming to the group norm [46, 60, 63]. Another positive advantage in the introduction of competitive aspects in the system is also represented by the possibility of pushing slaking members to engage by reminding them of the contribution that they could provide [60].

This role of providing information about other users and, especially, who leads the group in terms of commitment, is fulfilled by leaderboards providing information about individual or group/team achievements [46], thus providing extrinsic rewards [62, 64], and, ultimately, spread the adoption of desirable behaviour through social diffusion [60, 65].

3   Gamified Methodology to Assess Individuals and Collective Sustainability

In light of the considerations above, the present paper aims at presenting an ongoing research about the construction of a platform-based gamified environment (a serious game) with the target of boosting the adoption of sustainable behaviors among users. Such goal will be fostered by the mechanics of the game aiming at promoting the interaction of the user with the platform and with other users.

The game is based on the calculation of a Sustainability Index (SI) proposed as a metric to establish the level of sustainability of the user's behavior. The SI will be calculated as a player's total score, based on three main components that will grant her points: (i) the actual behavior of the player, (ii) the fruition of educational contents provided by the platform, (iii) and the continuity of interaction with the platform itself. The SI will be then normalized in a scale from 0 to 1, representing the percentage of achievement of a fully desirable sustainable behavior, being 0% an unsustainable behavior of the user, and 100% a fully sustainable and desirable behavior.

Considering the first aspect, the actual behavior of the user will be evaluated by means of the self-reported environmental responsible actions that she accomplishes during a day. In particular, on the platform, a set of environmental conscious behaviors (actions) will be proposed; examples of such actions might be, for instance, "increase the set-point of your cooling system", "switch to a plant based diet" and so on. Each day, the player will state which action she has performed, and she will score a number of points according to the number of action she accomplished. The higher the score, the higher the level of commitment of the user with an environmental conscious behaviour. The second aspect (fruition of educational contents) will aim at sensitise the user toward the possible changes in her behaviour in order to reduce her environmental footprint, and also regarding the impact that the actions described above could have in this direction. The mechanics of the game will grant extra points to the player due to her interaction with these educational contents, thus increasing her final SI score. The last way in which the player could score points is by means of a repeated interaction with the platform: the longer the player self-reports actions and make use of the educational contents, the more extra points are granted, and her SI will increase, thus rewarding the continuity of the player's engagement.

The ultimate goal of the integration of these two last additional ways for scoring points in the mechanics of the game (i.e. the fruition of educational content, and the perseverance in interacting with the platform) is to increase the awareness of the user toward the possible impacts that her daily actions and choices could have in terms of environmental sustainability, and to promote a change in her behaviour and the maintenance of the latter in time.

The mechanics presented above will result in the calculation of the individual player's SI. A second step to further boost the engagement of the individual player will be by means of the interaction among users [46, 60]. In this regard, the players could decide to join together forming teams and compete among each other during defined time-windows, so called "challenges". These challenge could be tailored on specific community of users, and promoted during particular events in partnership with different types of promoters, such as sport or cultural events, corporate team-building activities, and so on. During a challenge, a player could voluntary join a team and participate to the construction of the team's SI (SI_{tm}) that will be calculated as an average of each team member's individual SI.

Depending on the type of event for which the challenge is promoted, possible extrinsic rewards could be envisioned such as specific benefits in case of corporate team-building, or intrinsic ones in case of operations such as community building attempts [62]. While the single-mode mechanics (the possibility for the user to calculate her SI) is not time-limited, the competition in teams will be necessarily constrained within specific time-spans in order to act on two temporal levels (continuous and punctual), using the challenge mechanism as singularities to boost users' participation.

The present mechanics share some similarities with several other proposed ones regarding the interaction among different users, but differentiate itself particularly in the way in which the environmental performance of the users are calculated and used to compete against each other, or in teams (See in particular [66]). In particular, the proposed methodology is bases on the calculation of a tailored index (the SI) capable to easily communicate to the users the impacts that individual actions could have on the environment. At the same time, such index will be used in the competition among users and teams to establish the most sustainable one. An aspect of novelty of the proposed methodology reside specifically in the calculation of such index, in analogy with the sustainability assessment protocols presented in Sect. 2.1. Such procedure allows to perform benchmarking evaluations against an optimum common sustainability target independently from other users (differently, for example, from mechanics used in other projects such as [66]), thus providing feedbacks regarding the distance of each user from a desirable goal.

In Fig. 1 a schematization of the architecture of the proposed environment is provided. Starting from self-reporting the accomplishment of virtuous actions {A.1, A.2, A.3...A.n} selected from the set of available options (a) (such as "increase the set-point of your cooling system", "switch to a plant based diet" and so on), and the other forms of engagement with the game such as: access to App-embedded online content (q), repetitive use of the platform during several days (c), each user will score a specific amount of points. Furthermore, the SI individually achieved by each of the users will be averaged

398   M. Bottero et al.

on the number of users to return the overall SI_{tm} that will be used as the metrics to compete with the other teams in the time-defined challenge.

Similar to the building and neighborhood evaluation protocols described above (such as BREEAM, LEEDS, and so on), 5 labels are associated with predefined thresholds. These labels are defined in the form of medals (platinum, gold, silver, bronze, wood), in order to provide the user with an easy to understand metrics to evaluate her own level of sustainability.

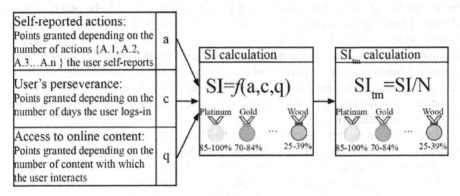

Fig. 1. Architecture of the proposed serious game.

In the next sections, a mathematical description of the game mechanics used to calculate the SI is presented.

3.1 Sustainability Index Calculation

Following the proposed mechanics, each user's individual SI will be calculated daily following Eq. (1):

$$SI = log((a + c + q) * \frac{9}{k} + 1) \tag{1}$$

where a is the total amount of points scored by the user by self-reporting the accomplishment of the virtuous actions, c and q are a number of possible bonus points to account for the interaction of the user with the App, and k is the total amount of points worth of achieving the highest SI. For consistency reasons, the latter parameter must be constrained according to Eq. (2):

$$k \geq (a + c + q) \tag{2}$$

and, furthermore, the value of k should be equal to the maximum points achievable by accomplishing all the actions proposed by the set of predetermined ones in the App:

$$k = a_{max} \tag{3}$$

being a_{max} the sum of all the points granted by self-registering all the actions of the proposed set. In line with the attempt of the proposed mechanics to promote user's participation and to challenge them to achieve higher level of sustainability in their behaviour, the logarithmic function (1) has been proposed against a possible linear one in the normalization of the SI. In Fig. 2 a graphical comparison among the two normalization strategies are displayed.

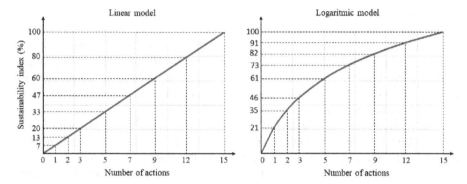

Fig. 2. Comparison between linear and logaritmic model

As it appears clear, the non-linear function (the logarithmic one) grant higher level of SI even to users that score low amounts of points while becoming more and more challenging for users that already achieve higher scores. This could have a double-fold advantage on the linear model: on the one hand, it lessens the punitive results of slacking individuals, while keeping the already virtuous users challenged. The latter aspect might respond to a common issue reported by few Authors highlighting how already pro-environment users report lower interest toward not challenging environmental calculators [46].

3.2 Point Scoring Mechanics

Aa seen before, the user might score points accomplishing certain actions from a set of predefined ones (parameter a), by fruition of contents embedded in the App (parameter q), or logging in the App for more days in a row, thus engaging recurrently with the App and the team (parameter c).

In particular, regarding parameter a, the set of possible virtuous actions {A.1, A.2, A.3…A.n} are individuated. Each action grants a number of points related to its possible environmental impact reduction that a user would achieve by acting according to that behaviour instead of a usual one.

Therefore, the value of parameter a will be calculated as (4):

$$a = \sum V_{A.n,acc} \tag{4}$$

where $V_{A.n,acc}$ is the value $V_{A.n}$ of the actions that user accomplishes and self-register.

Regarding parameter c, it considers the perseverance of the user in interacting with the challenge (the time-defined period of time in which the user joins a team and compete against other teams), granting points depending on the amount of days she log-in the App. The calculation of c is performed according to Eq. (5):

$$c = \left(t * \frac{\sqrt{c_{max}}}{T} \right)^2 \tag{5}$$

where t is the number of days the user logs-in during the challenge, T is total duration of the challenge in days, and c_{max} is the total amount of points grantable by the variable c. The mechanics rewarding the user with more points the longer she interacts with the challenge is quite evident from the shape of the curve that grants points with a quadratic relation to the number of days of log-in (5). The points granted by the parameter c will increase each day of participation of a user to a challenge, motivating her to be perseverant in her engagement.

Finally, parameter q is intended to promote the interaction of the user with educational content regarded sustainability targets that could be achieved by engaging in more pro-environment actions and behaviors: each day the App will provide the user with educational contents the fruition of which will grant her a predefined amount of points to increase her SI level (avoiding the necessity to accomplish each and every one of the possible action defined in the set of actions {A.1, A.2, A.3...A.n}, thus reducing the possible disappointment of the user not capable of doing all the actions every day). One of the main advantages of the presented model is the possibility to specify all the parameter at stake (from the number of actions, to their specific value through the number of possible impacts, to the maximum amount of points granted by parameters c and q). The final step to be performed to calculate the SI at the team level (SI_{tm}) would then be to average the individual SI of the team members and to average them with the number of team members (N_{tm}). The SI_{tm} will then be:

$$SI_{tm} = \frac{SI}{N_{tm}} \tag{6}$$

4 Conclusion and Future Perspectives

In this paper a serious game has been proposed in order to support individual's transition towards a more environmental conscious behaviour. The proposed mechanics make use of a specifically designed index able to easily communicate to the player her degree of sustainability compared to a fully desirable one. Such index could be used to foster user's engagement by means of interaction and competition with other users, and, thus, building on the concept of group norm.

The proposed methodology for the calculation of such index specifically targets the issues that such serious games usually have to face, such as the lack of users' participation or the low number of times that the player interacts with it, by means of the introduction of different parameters in the calculation process.

Regarding the calculation process itself, the aggregated Sustainability Index at the team level could have a counter-productive effect: due to the fact that the former is calculated by averaging the individual member's Sustainability Index, the virtuous behaviour of a single user could be lost in a not so performing one at the team level, thus depressing the individual user's motivation to challenge herself in performing more environmental conscious actions. In this regards, the communication of the performance of each user should not be presented as subordinate to the aggregated communication of the performance of the team as a whole, in order to promote social diffusion and the engagement starting from the individual level.

The present paper is methodological in nature, therefore, both the range of actions to be considered in the point scoring mechanism, and the possible duration of the team challenging mechanism have to be further defined, and the potential to adapt their case by case selection depending on the specific events should be further investigated.

As a future development of the research, the different amount of points granted by the actions should be defined based on the reduction potential that such action could have on the overall footprint of an individual, against different sets of criteria (such as reduction in the use of energy or resources, or the reduction of behaviour induced carbon emissions). Such impact should be adequately evaluated and scientifically sound, in order to further be informative on the potential reduction of one's environmental impacts. Finally, the methodology will be implemented on a web-app, and it will be tested in different context (urban communities, corporate team building events, sport or cultural events) in order to test its capability to foster individuals' engagement, and to evaluate possible context-specific modification to the methodology itself (in terms, for example, of bonus point allocation).

References

1. United Nations: How to make cities more resilient: a handbook for local government leaders. (2017)
2. Schiera, D.S., Minuto, F.D., Bottaccioli, L., Borchiellini, R., Lanzini, A.: Analysis of rooftop photovoltaics diffusion in energy community buildings by a novel gis- and agent-based modeling co-simulation platform. IEEE Access 7, 93404–93432 (2019)
3. United Nations: Transforming our world: the 2030 Agenda for Sustainable Development (2015)
4. Girard, L.F., Nocca, F., Gravagnuolo, A.: Matera: city of nature, city of culture, city of regeneration. Towards a landscape-based and culture-based urban circular economy. Aestimum 74, 5–42 (2019)
5. European Commission: The European Green Deal. Eur. Comm. 53(9), 24. https://eur-lex.eur opa.eu/legal-content/EN/TXT/?uri=CELEX%3A52019DC0640. Accessed 15 May 2023
6. European Commission: Circular Economy Action Plan for a cleaner and more competitive Europe. 28. https://eur-lex.europa.eu/legal-content/EN/TXT/?qid=1583933814386& uri=COM:2020:98:FIN. Accessed 12 May 2023
7. Bonoli, A., Zanni, S., Serrano-Bernardo, F.: Sustainability in building and construction within the framework of circular cities and European new green deal. The contribution of concrete recycling. Sustainability 13(4), 1–16 (2021)
8. Napoli, G., Barbaro, S., Giuffrida, S., Trovato, M.R.: The European green deal: new challenges for the economic feasibility of energy retrofit at district scale. In: Bevilacqua, C., Calabrò,

F., Della Spina, L. (eds.) NMP 2020. SIST, vol. 178, pp. 1248–1258. Springer, Cham (2021). https://doi.org/10.1007/978-3-030-48279-4_116

9. Cerreta, M., Muccio, E., Poli, G., Regalbuto, S., Romano, F.: A multidimensional evaluation for regenerative strategies: towards a circular city-port model implementation. In: Bevilacqua, C., Calabrò, F., Della Spina, L. (eds.) NMP 2020. SIST, vol. 178, pp. 1067–1077. Springer, Cham (2021). https://doi.org/10.1007/978-3-030-48279-4_100

10. Bosone, M., Ciampa, F.: Human-centred indicators (HCI) to regenerate vulnerable cultural heritage and landscape towards a circular city: from the Bronx (NY) to Ercolano (IT). Sustainability 13(10), 5505 (2021)

11. Bosone, M., De Toro, P., Girard, L.F., Gravagnuolo, A., Iodice, S.: Indicators for ex-post evaluation of cultural heritage adaptivreuse impacts in the perspective of the circular economy. Sustainability 13(9), 4759 (2021)

12. Buso, T., Fabi, V., Andersen, R.K., Corgnati, S.P.: Occupant behaviour and robustness of building design. Build. Environ. 94(2), 694–703 (2015)

13. Barthelmes, V.M., Becchio, C., Corgnati, S.P.: Occupant behavior lifestyles in a residential nearly zero energy building: Effect on energy use and thermal comfort. Sci. Technol. Built Environ. 22(7), 960–975 (2016)

14. Fabi, V., Andersen, R.V., Corgnati, S.P., Olesen, B.W.: Occupants' window opening behaviour: a literature review of factors influencing occupant behaviour and models. Build. Environ. 58, 188–198 (2012)

15. Yan, D., et al.: Occupant behavior modeling for building performance simulation: current state and future challenges. Build. Environ. 107, 264–278 (2015)

16. Topf, S., Speekenbrink, M.: Follow my example, for better and for worse: the influence of behavioral traces on recycling decisions. J. Exp. Psychol.: Appl. (2023)

17. Bruchmann, K., Chue, S.M., Dillon, K., Lucas, J.K., Neumann, K., Parque, C.: Social comparison information influences intentions to reduce single-use plastic water bottle consumption. Front. Psychol. 12, 612662 (2021)

18. Schultz, W., Javey, S., Sorokina, A.: Social comparison as a tool to promote residential water conservation. Front. Water 1, 2 (2019)

19. Baul, T.K., Khan, M.A., Sarker, A., Atri, A.C., Jashimuddin, M., Alam, A.: Perceptions and attitudes of tertiary level students towards wood and non-wood furniture and energy fuels in Bangladesh. Trees, Forests and People 10, 100351 (2022)

20. Zapico, J.L., Katzeff, C., Bohné, U., Milestad, R.: Eco-feedback Visualization for Closing the Gap of Organic Food Consumption. In: Proceedings of the 9th Nordic Conference on Human-Computer Interaction, pp. 1–9. ACM, Gothenburg Sweden (2016)

21. Gifford, R.: The dragons of inaction: psychological barriers that limit climate change mitigation and adaptation. Am. Psychol. 66(4), 290–302 (2011)

22. Clayton, S.: Social issues and personal life: considering the environment. J. Soc. Issues 73(3), 667–681 (2017)

23. Estrada, M., Schultz, P.W., Silva-Send, N., Boudrias, M.A.: The role of social influence on pro-environment behaviors in the San Diego region. J. Urban Health 94, 170–179 (2017)

24. Stapleton, S.R.: Environmental identity development through social interactions, action, and recognition. J. Environ. Educ. 46(2), 94–113 (2015)

25. Kok, A.L., Barendregt, W.: Understanding the adoption, use, and effects of ecological footprint calculators among Dutch citizens. J. Clean. Prod. 326, 129341 (2021)

26. Ajzen, I.: The theory of planned behaviour. Organ. Behav. Hum. Decis. Process. 50(2), 179–211 (1991)

27. Bamberg, S.: Applying the stage model of self-regulated behavioral change in a car use reduction intervention. J. Environ. Psychol. 33, 68–75 (2013)

28. Fischer, C.: Feedback on household electricity consumption: a tool for saving energy? Energ. Effi. 1, 79–104 (2008)

29. Grønhøj, A., Thøgersen, J.: Feedback on household electricity consumption: learning and social influence processes. Int. J. Consum. Stud. **35**(2), 138–145 (2011)

30. Darby, S.: Making it obvious: designing feedback into energy consumption. In: Bertoldi, P., Ricci, A., de Almeida, A. (eds.) Energy Efficiency in Household Appliances and Lighting. Springer, Berlin (2001). https://doi.org/10.1007/978-3-642-56531-1_73

31. Abrahamse, W., Steg, L., Vlek, C., Rothengatter, T.: A review of intervention studies aimed at household energy conservation. J. Environ. Psychol. **25**(3), 273–291 (2005)

32. Faruqui, A., Sergici, S., Sharif, A.: The impact of informational feedback on energy consumption—a survey of the experimental evidence. Energy **35**, 1598–1608 (2010)

33. Suls, J., Martin, R., Wheeler, L.: Social comparison: why, with whom, and with what effect? Curr. Dir. Psychol. Sci. **11**(5), 159–163 (2002)

34. Sala, S., Ciuffo, B., Nijkamp, P.: A systemic framework for sustainability assessment. Ecol. Econ. **119**, 314–325 (2015)

35. Suppa, A.R., Cavana, G., Binda, T.: Supporting the EU mission "100 climate-neutral cities by 2030": a review of tools to support decision-making for the built environment at district or city scale. In: Gervasi, O., Murgante, B., Misra, S., Rocha, A.M.A.C., Garau, C. (eds.) Computational Science and Its Applications – ICCSA 2022 Workshops, ICCSA 2022, vol. 13380, pp. 151–168. Springer, Cham. (2022)

36. Bottero, M., Dell'Anna, F.: The role of quality management services (QMSS) in aligning the construction sector to the european taxonomy: the experience of the QUEST project. In: Calabrò, F., Della Spina, L., Piñeira Mantiñán, M.J. (eds.) New Metropolitan Perspectives, NMP 2022, vol. 482, pp. 1732–1741. Springer, Cham (2022)

37. Deng, W., Prasad, P.: Quantifying sustainability for the built environmental at urban scale: a study of three sustainable urban assessment systems. In: Conference on Sustainable Building South East Asia, 4–6th, 2010, Malaysia (2010)

38. Retzlaff, R.C.: Green building assessment systems: a framework and comparison for planners. J. Am. Plann. Assoc. **74**(4), 505–519 (2008)

39. Nguyen, B.K., Altan, H.: Comparative review of five sustainable rating systems. Procedia Eng. **21**, 376–386 (2011)

40. Mattoni, B., Guattari, C., Evangelisti, L., Bisegna, F., Gori, P., Asdrubali, F.: Critical review and methodological approach to evaluate the differences among international green building rating tools. Renew. Sustain. Energy Rev. **82**, 950–960 (2018)

41. Berardi, U.: Beyond sustainability assessment systems: upgrading topics by enlarging the scale of assessment. Int. J. Sustain. Build. Technol. Urban Dev. **2**(4), 276–282 (2011)

42. Haapio, A.: Towards sustainable urban communities. Environ. Impact Assess. Rev. **32**(1), 165–169 (2012)

43. Crit.com: Criterion Planners e a Global Survey of Urban Sustainability Rating Tools. http://crit.com/wp-content/uploads/2014/11/criterion_planners_sustainability_ratings_tool.pdf

44. GRESB: Real Estate Refernce Guide. https://documents.gresb.com/generated_files/real_estate/2021/real_estate/reference_guide/complete.html. Accessed 12 May 2023

45. EPRA: European Public Real Estate Association (EPRA): EPRA Sustainability Best Practices Recommendations Guidelines. (2017)

46. Biørn-Hansen, A., Katzeff, C., Eriksson, E.: Exploring the use of a carbon footprint calculator challenging everyday habits. In: Nordic Human-Computer Interaction Conference (NordiCHI 2022), Article 18, pp. 1–10. Association for Computing Machinery, New York (2022)

47. Kok, G., et al.: A taxonomy of behaviour change methods: an intervention mapping approach. Health Psychol. Rev. **10**(3), 297–312 (2016)

48. Gurusinga, N.: The effectiveness of using carbon footprint calculator to increase students' awareness and motivation to adopt a low-carbon lifestyle. PhD dissertation, University of Melbourne (2016)

49. Gram-Hanssen, K., Christensen, T.H.: Carbon calculators as a tool for a low-carbon everyday life? Sustainability **8**(2), 19–30 (2012)
50. Sutcliffe, M., Hooper, P., Howell, R.: Can eco-footprinting analysis be used successfully to encourage more sustainable behaviour at the household level? Sustain. Dev. **16**(1), 1–16 (2008)
51. Salo, M., Mattinen-Yuryev, M., Nissinen, A.: Opportunities and limitations of carbon footprint calculators to steer sustainable household consumption – Analysis of Nordic calculator features. J. Clean. Prod. **207**, 658–666 (2019)
52. Collins, A., Galli, A., Hipwood, T., Murthy, A.: Living within a one planet reality: the contribution of personal footprint calculators. Environ. Res. Lett. **15**(2), 025008 (2020)
53. Abrahamse, W., Steg, L., Vlek, C., Rothengatter, T.: The effect of tailored information, goal setting, and tailored feedback on household energy use, energy related behaviors, and behavioral antecedents. J. Environ. Psychol. **27**(4), 265–276 (2007)
54. Darby, S.: The effectiveness of feedback on energy consumption. Rev. DEFRA Lit. Meter. Bill. Direct Displays **486**, 26 (2006)
55. Bottrill, C.: Internet-Based Carbon Tools for Behaviour Change. University of Oxford, Environmental Change Institute (2007)
56. Marache-Francisco, C., Brangier, E.: The gamification experience: UXD with a gamification background. In: Blashki, K., Isaias, P. (eds.) Emerging Research and Trends in Interactivity and the Human-Computer Interface, pp. 205–223. IGI Global, Hershey (2014)
57. Deterding, S.: Gamification: designing for motivation. Interactions **19**(4), 14–17 (2012)
58. Ritterfeld, U., Cody, M., Vorderer, P.: Serious Games: Mechanisms and Effects, 1st edn. Routledge, New York (2009)
59. Cravero, S., Strada, F., Lami, I.M., Bottino, A.: Learning sustainability by making games. The experience of a challenge as a novel approach for Education for Sustainable Development. In: 7th International Conference on Higher Education Advances (HEAd 2021), pp. 651–659). Editorial Universitat Politècnica de València (2021)
60. Ro, M., Brauer, M., Kuntz, K., Shukla, R., Bensch, I.: Making cool choices for sustainability: testing the effectiveness of a game-based approach to promoting pro-environmental behaviors. J. Environ. Psychol. **53**, 20–30 (2017)
61. Judah, G., Gardner, B., Aunger, R.: Forming a flossing habit: An exploratory study of the psychological determinants of habit formation. Br. J. Health. Psychol. **18**(2), 338–353 (2013)
62. Cudok, A., Lawrenz, S., Rausch, A., Vietor, T.: Circular economy driven communities – sustainable behavior driven by mobile applications. Procedia CIRP **105**, 362–367 (2022)
63. Hamari, J., Koivisto, J.: "Working out for likes": An empirical study on social influence in exercise gamification. Comput. Hum. Behav. **50**, 333–347 (2015)
64. Duarte, I.C., Afonso, S., Jorge, H., Cayolla, R., Ferreira, C., Castelo-Branco, M.: Tribal love: the neural correlates of passionate engagement in football fans. Soc. Cogn. Affect. Neurosci. **12**(5), 718–728 (2017)
65. McKenzie-Mohr, D.: Fostering Sustainable Behavior: An Introduction to Community-Based Social Marketing, 3rd edn. New Society Publishers, Gabriola (2011)
66. https://www.muv2020.eu/. Accessed 12 May 2023

Advanced Data Science Techniques with Applications in Industry and Environmental Sustainability (ATELIERS 2023)

Application of a Self-supervised Learning Technique for Monitoring Industrial Spaces

V. Magalhães[1]($\boxtimes$), M. Fernanda P. Costa[2], M. J. Oliveira Ferreira[1], T. Pinto[1], and V. Figueiredo[1]

[1] Neadvance - Machine Vision S.A., 4705-002 Sequeira, Braga, Portugal
{vmagalhaes,mferreira,tpinto,vfigueiredo}@neadvance.com
[2] Centre of Mathematics, University of Minho, Campus de Gualtar, 4710-057 Braga, Portugal
mfc@math.uminho.pt
http://www.neadvance.com/, http://www.cmat.uminho.pt/

Abstract. Supervised learning has reached a bottleneck as they require expensive and time-consuming annotations. In addition, in some problems, such as in industrial spaces, it is not always possible to acquire a large number of images. Self-supervised learning helps these issues by extracting information from the data itself, without requiring labels and has achieved good performance, closing the gap between supervised and self-supervised learning. This work presents the application of a self-supervised learning method - SwAV, that classifies anomalies in an industrial space, evaluates its performance and compares the results to the supervised paradigm.

Keywords: Computer Vision · Deep Learning · Self-Supervised Learning · SwAV · Industrial Spaces

1 Introduction

The rise of algorithms capable of detecting and recognizing objects in uncontrolled environments can bring significant benefits to logistics in industrial environments. These technologies provide a more efficient and intelligent management of factory space by automating surveillance and monitoring activities that are mostly performed manually or with CCTV systems that monitor critical areas. These systems are connected to monitors at a control post, where operators manually perceive the monitored areas and detect abnormal situations.

This work was funded by Project "SMARTICS - Platform for Smart Monitoring of Open Industrial Spaces using Computer Vision and Artificial Intelligence", Project n.° LISBOA-01-0247-FEDER-072553, financed by the European Regional Development Fund (ERDF), through the COMPETE 2020 - Competitiveness and Internationalization Operational Program (POCI) and PORTUGAL 2020.

O. Gervasi et al. (Eds.): ICCSA 2023 Workshops, LNCS 14104, pp. 407–420, 2023.
https://doi.org/10.1007/978-3-031-37105-9_27

The use of intelligent logistics solutions reduces the need for human operators to manually monitor specific spaces, reducing the risk of human error and increasing the efficiency of the monitoring process. These algorithms can also process a larger amount of video images and cover a larger area than operators, allowing for more effective monitoring. They increase the efficiency of production by reducing operational and maintenance costs and decreasing waiting times for production and machine downtime.

Deep Learning has brought significant development in automated computer vision systems such as object detection [1], image classification [2], and image segmentation [3], which is useful for monitoring these industrial spaces. However, the success of these systems require a large amount of labeled data, which can be difficult to acquire in industrial settings. Therefore, researchers are working on systems that can adapt to changing conditions without extensive supervision, such as self-supervised learning [4,5,8]. Self-supervised learning methods construct feature representations without manual annotations using pretext tasks, which allows models to solve these tasks by extracting useful information that can later improve downstream tasks. Further self-supervised learning methods use contrastive learning to push positive instances closer together, and negative ones further apart, in the embedding space [9,12]. These methods have shown promising results in closing the performance gap with supervised learning, and some researchers believe that the next AI revolution will be in self-supervised learning rather than supervised learning [12].

In this work, we present the application of a self-supervised learning method - SwAV, for detecting anomalies in two different scenarios in an industrial space. One of the scenarios is to classify whether a shelf is empty or not and the other is to classify if a set of boxes is correctly positioned in a tilted conveyor belt.

The present paper is structured as follows. Section 2 provides some concepts of Self-Supervised Learning. Section 3 presents and explains the SwAV method. Section 4 presents the datasets used to evaluate the performance of the SwAV method. Section 5 presents the experiments made with each dataset and the results obtained. The paper ends with discussion and future work.

2 Self-supervised Learning

Deep Learning has achieved great success in the last decade, especially with supervised learning in computer vision tasks such as image classification [2,13], semantic segmentation [3,14,15], and object detection [1,16,17].

Supervised Learning methods heavily rely on having a large amount of labeled training data, and the quality of deep neural networks is directly impacted by the number of annotated images. However, creating annotated datasets is expensive and time-consuming, and even though there is a lot of data available, labeling it is not always feasible. While there are some datasets, like *Imagenet*, with over a million images [10], it is not always possible to gather labeled data on such a large scale in real-world scenarios. Furthermore, Supervised Learning can sometimes produce errors due to poor generalization and spurious correlations [8,12]. To address these issues, researchers are exploring alternative methods that can make use of the vast amounts of available unlabeled data without requiring extensive labeling.

Self-Supervised Learning (SSL) is gaining attention as a promising alternative to Supervised Learning because it has shown remarkable performance in learning representations without requiring the annotation of large datasets [8,9]. In SSL, unlabelled data is provided to the model, which is then automatically labeled during the training phase by identifying and utilizing the connections between different input features. This compels the network to acquire semantic representations of the data, which can be applied as pre-trained models to downstream tasks to enhance their performance and prevent over-fitting [4,6,7,12].

The cognitive motivation behind SSL is the way infants learn, largely through observation. Within few months of birth, infants have meaningful expectations about the world around them, concepts such as gravity and object permanence. Infants' environment becomes a source of supervision that helps them develop a general understanding of how things work. SSL is an attempt to apply this concept to machines, where the data itself contains inherent features that provide supervision for training the model, rather than labels that tell the network what is right and what is not [12]. Some authors believe that SSL is a promising way to build background knowledge and approximate a kind of common sense in AI systems. Also, when humans do new tasks, information from life experience and prior knowledge is used. SSL mimics this when it transfers the learned features to other tasks [25,26].

During the initial phase of SSL, pretext tasks were introduced to train models to automatically generate labels based on data characteristics, which were used to learn representations. The model acquires features while solving the pretext task, and these features are subsequently transferred to other tasks by transfer learning. Examples of pretext tasks are coloring a grayscale image [27–30], predicting the degree of rotation of an image [31], filling in a missing part of an image [32,33], predicting the relative position of an image [34], solving a jigsaw puzzle [35–37], and more.

Recently, Contrastive Learning has emerged as a highly effective technique that bridges the gap between SSL and supervised learning [38]. It is a discriminative model that uses positive and negative pairs to learn representations by distinguishing between different views of the same image [6]. Essentially, it tries to bring similar views of the same instance closer and different instances farther apart in the representation space [5,9,11,12]. DeepCluster [18], ClusterFit [19], SimSiam [20], PIRL [21], MoCo [22], SimCLR [23], and SwAV [24] are examples of contrastive learning methods.

SwAV is the model used in this work and has achieved state-of-the-art performance on image classification. It is a unique method for learning visual representations by comparing different views of the same image and grouping similar images together. This allows the model to learn a more robust and generalized representation of the visual world. This capability allows companies to use their existing data to train models for a variety of tasks, such as quality control and anomaly detection, without the need for expensive and time-consuming manual labeling. This method is described in more detail in the following section.

3   Swapping Assignments Between Multiple Views (SwAV)

Caron. M., et al. [24] purposed an online clustering-based self-supervised method for learning feature representations named **SwAV**.

The authors purposed a *multi-crop* augmentation strategy that generates multiple views of the same image instead of just one pair without quadratically increasing memory and computational requirements. They use two standard-resolution crops and take V additional low-resolution crops that cover only small portions of the image. Using low resolution images provides only a small increase in computational cost and the model becomes scale invariant. This strategy showed an improvement in performance not only for SwAV but also for other contrastive learning methods [24]. Next, random horizontal flips, color distortions, and Gaussian blur are applied to each resulting crop.

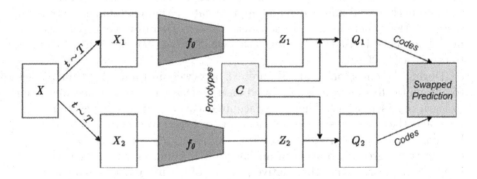

Fig. 1. SwAV Architecture

To generate augmented views of an image x, a random transformation t is selected from a set of image transformations T, and applied to create views x_1 and x_2. For simplicity, only 2 augmented views are listed, but there can be many more. The augmented views are then passed through a convolutional neural network (CNN) f_θ, such as ResNet50, which outputs feature vectors z_1 and z_2 after passing through a projection head (Fig. 1).

The feature vectors z_1 and z_2 are mapped to a set of K trainable prototype vectors $c_1, c_2, ..., c_K$, forming the columns of a matrix C. This mapping is represented by $Q = [q_1, ..., q_B]$ as shown in Fig. 2 (left). The matrix Q is optimized to maximize the similarity between the feature vectors and the prototypes, i.e.,

$$max_Q = Tr(Q^T C^T Z) + \epsilon H(Q), \text{ where } H(Q) = -\sum_{ij} Q_{ij} log Q_{ij} \qquad (1)$$

is the entropy function and ϵ is a parameter that controls the smoothness of the mapping. In practice, the value of ϵ is kept low to prevent a trivial solution, where all samples are mapped to a single representation and are uniformly assigned to all prototypes. To ensure an equal distribution of prototypes, the matrix Q is constrained such that each prototype is selected the same number of times. Once the optimal solution Q^* is found, it takes the form of a normalized exponential matrix:

$$Q^* = Diag(u)exp\left(\frac{C^T Z}{\epsilon}\right) Diag(v) \qquad (2)$$

where $u \in R^K$ and $v \in R^B$ are renormalization vectors. These vectors are computed using the iterative *Sinkhorn-Knopp* algorithm [40].

A "swapped" prediction problem is formulated, consisting of predicting the code q_1 from the feature z_2, and the code q_2 from the feature z_1. The loss function used for this task is as follows:

$$L(z_1, z_2) = \ell(z_1, q_2) + \ell(z_2, q_1) \qquad (3)$$

where $\ell(z_1, q_2)$ is the cross-entropy loss between the code and the probability obtained by taking a *softmax* of the dot products of z_i and all prototypes in C:

$$\ell(z_t, q_s) = -\sum_k q_s^{(k)} log p_t^{(k)}, \text{ where } p_t^{(k)} = \frac{exp((z_t^T c_k)/\tau)}{\sum_{k'} exp((z_t^T c_{k'})/\tau)} \qquad (4)$$

where τ denotes a temperature parameter.

To learn the features, the loss function is minimized with respect to the trainable prototypes C and the parameters θ of the encoder f_θ. The SwAV method compares the features z_1 and z_2 using intermediate codes q_1 and q_2. If these features capture similar information, it should be possible to predict the code from the other feature. SwAV achieves this by swapping assignments between multiple views of the same image (Fig. 2 (right)). This allows the model to compare and learn from different views of the same image, and improve the quality of the learned representations.

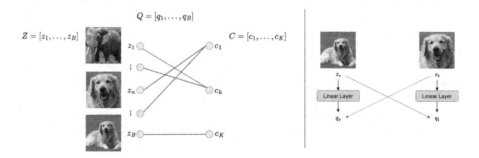

Fig. 2. Left: Assigning B samples to K trainable prototype vectors, **Right**: Swapped prediction problem between two views of the same image

4   Datasets

This work used three datasets for training and evaluating the model, two of which are laboratory scenarios that simulate real anomalies in an industrial setting.

4.1   Dataset 1: Flowers Dataset

One of the datasets used was *Tensorflow's flowers dataset* [39], which comprises of 3670 images of flowers and their respective labels for classification. The dataset consists of five distinct types of flowers, namely Dandelion (represented by 0), Daisy (represented by 1), Tulip (represented by 2), Sunflower (represented by 3), and Rose (represented by 4) (Fig. 3).

0   1   2   3   4

Fig. 3. Examples of images from Tensorflow's flowers dataset with respective labels

4.2   Dataset 2: BookCase Dataset

The *bookcase dataset* created was designed to resemble a real problem in an industrial setting, where the goal is to identify if a shelf is empty or not, so that an alert can be triggered if it is empty, to be consequently refilled by an automated guided vehicle. This is done in real-time where the SwAV algorithm is applied to classify the shelf. In real industrial settings the ranging background, the lighting conditions, obstructions, the different shapes, colors and sizes of the objects all contribute to make the task of teaching the model what to expect difficult.

To prepare the dataset, photographs of a bookcase were taken with different proximity, and the images were cropped and sliced to create individual images of each shelf. The resulting dataset contains 4597 images, out of which 1094 were empty shelves (represented as 0) and 3505 were not empty shelves (represented as 1). Some examples of images from the bookcase dataset are shown in Fig. 4.

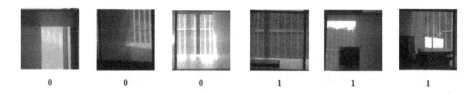

Fig. 4. Examples of images from the created bookcase dataset with respective labels

4.3 Dataset 2: Boxes Dataset

Another industrial problem presented was a tilted conveyor belt where boxes slide. Sometimes the boxes get stuck or mispositioned, ruining the automated process at hand. Again, in real-time SwAV is used to classify this anomaly, so that an alert can be sent and the situation corrected by an operator. The boxes dataset was created to simulate this scenario. Several images were taken with boxes in different positions or even with new, different, and incorrectly present boxes. The goal is to classify if the correct boxes are positioned correctly or if there is an anomaly in the positioning or the presence of other types of boxes.

This dataset contains a total of 116 images, 37 correct images (labelled 1) and 79 incorrect images (labelled 0). Figure 5 shows some image examples from the dataset.

Fig. 5. Examples of images from the created boxes dataset with respective labels

5 Experiments and Results

In this section, we present the experiments made with each dataset and analyze their performance.

5.1 Training

In all the experiments *multi-crop* is applied to every batch of images fed to the network. From each image, two 224×224 high-resolution views and three 96×96 low-resolution views are generated. Random horizontal flips, color distortions, and Gaussian blur are applied to each resulting crop. The images are then fed to the backbone ResNet50 model and through 2 Dense layers with ReLU (projection head). SwAV is trained with mini-batch SGD using batches of 32 different instances. Using the original SwAV article [24] as a reference the temperature parameter τ was set to 0.1 and the Sinkhorn regularization parameter ϵ was set to 0.05 for all runs, as was the number of prototypes that was set to 15. Early stopping was defined to stop training if the loss did not improve in 15 epochs.

We evaluate the features of the ResNet-50 trained with SwAV on these datasets by training a linear classifier on top of the frozen representations. This linear layer is trained during 100 epochs, with categorical cross-entropy loss, Adam optimizer [41], and a learning rate of 0.001. Early stopping was defined to restore the best weights and stop training if the validation loss did not improve in 5 epochs.

5.2 Results Obtained with Dataset 1: Flowers Dataset

SwAV was initially trained on the flowers dataset to see its performance, to then train it on the custom dataset.

For the SwAV training 5 experiments were made. In all these experiments SwAV was trained with 85% of the data, corresponding to 3120 images, and the evaluation of the model was with the remaining 15%, corresponding to 550 images. To evaluate the feature representations a linear classifier is trained on the frozen features with a single dense layer with 5 neurons, with softmax activation function and a l^2 regularizer. This linear layer is trained with the same 85% of data that SwAV is trained with and then evaluated on the 550 unseen images.

The results obtained from all experiments are displayed in Table 1.

Table 1. Results of a linear classifier on SwAVs frozen features with flowers dataset

Experiment	Loss	Accuracy	Precision	Recall	F1-Score
Flowers A	1.298	0.447	0.48	0.46	0.44
Flowers B	0.412	0.856	0.86	0.86	0.86
Flowers C	**0.327**	**0.882**	**0.88**	**0.88**	**0.88**
Flowers D	0.397	0.860	0.86	0.86	0.86
Flowers E	0.348	0.871	0.87	0.87	0.87

Given the experiments done, experiment **Flowers C** was the one that achieved better performance. In more detail, the ResNet50 was initialized with *imagenet* weights. The mini-batch SGD decayed the learning rate to 0.0001, and the number of epochs was set to 300 but stopped at epoch 225 due to early stopping.

The linear classifier achieved 88,2% of accuracy. Table 2 shows the confusion matrix obtained of the best model. The model predicted incorrectly 65 images out of a total of 550 images. Dandelion is the class with the highest recall as it is the class that fewer images were misclassified, only 8.9%. Rose has the highest percentage of misclassified images - 15.9%. Daisy is the class with fewer false positives, having the highest precision.

These experiments could have been optimized to achieve better results but because this dataset was not the focus of the work no more experiments were made.

Table 2. Confusion matrix from experiment Flowers C

True Labels	**Dandelion**	102	3	2	5	0
	Daisy	8	83	1	2	1
	Tulip	0	3	119	3	9
	Sunflower	4	1	5	91	1
	Rose	4	1	10	2	90
		Dandelion	**Daisy**	**Tulip**	**Sunflower**	**Rose**
	Predicted Labels					

5.3   Results Obtained with Dataset 2: BookCase Dataset

As described earlier, the bookcase dataset was created to address a real-world problem in an industrial space context. Since the Flowers C experiment performed best on the flower dataset, SwAV training and the linear classifier were performed on the bookcase dataset with exactly the same settings. The only difference was that the early stopping in the SwAV training was set to 30. The dataset was also split into 85% training and 15% for evaluation, corresponding to 3907 and 690 images, respectively. SwAV was trained during 308 epochs. This experiment was defined as **BookCase F** and the results of the linear classifier on top of the frozen features are shown in Table 3.

Table 3. Results of a linear classifier on SwAVs frozen features with bookcase dataset

Experiment	Loss	Accuracy	Precision	Recall	F1-Score	MCC
BookCase F	0.032	0.988	0.99	0.99	0.99	0.98

The linear classifier achieved 98.8% accuracy, 98% MCC, and 99% on the remaining metrics. The score obtained shows that the binary classifier was able to predict the majority of positive and negative instances.

Table 4 displays the confusion matrix from this experiment. The model only misclassified 6 images from a total of 690: 4 images were misclassified as not empty and 2 as empty.

The bookcase dataset was also trained in a fully supervised manner with hyperparameter optimization to determine the best possible model. The model with the best results achieved 99.6% accuracy. The model was a DenseNet121 with max pooling, 4 dense layers, Adam optimizer, and a learning rate of 0.0001. Table 5 displays the results of a comparison between the self-supervised learning method SwAV and an optimized supervised learning setting. SwAV achieves only −0.8% compared to the supervised learning approach.

Table 4. Confusion matrix from experiment BookCase F

True Lables	Empty (0)	152	4
	Not Empty (1)	2	532
		Empty (0)	Not Empty (1)
		Predicted Labels	

Table 5. Results comparing SwAV and supervised learning with the bookcase dataset

Method	Accuracy
Supervised	0.996
SwAV	0.988

5.4   Results Obtained with Transfer Learning

The other experiment made was with transfer learning. The learned representations from SwAV training on the bookcase dataset were used to solve the classification problem with the boxes dataset. A linear classifier was trained during 500 epochs on the frozen features (learned with the bookcase dataset) with a single dense layer of 2 neurons, with softmax function and a l^2 regularizer. The dataset was split into 70% for training and 30% for evaluation. The dataset was split this way due to the small amount of data. Dividing it as previously 85–15 would only leave 17 images for evaluation, which would not be enough to evaluate the model. Table 6 shows the results achieved. The model correctly predicted all of the 35 images, achieving 100% in all metrics.

Table 6. Confusion matrix of the linear classifier on the boxes dataset with frozen features from the bookcase dataset

True Lables	Incorrect (0)	27	0
	Correct (1)	0	8
		Incorrect (0)	Correct (1)
		Predicted Labels	

This dataset was also trained in a fully supervised manner, with 10 models trained with different hyperparameters to obtain the best possible model. To allow a fair comparison, the dataset was also split into 70–30%. Figure 7 shows the results obtained. The model achieved an accuracy of 81.2% and an MCC of 56.6%, with 8 images being misclassified. These results are due to the dataset containing very few images that the model can learn from.

In this particular case and with these settings, the information from the bookcase dataset was useful to improve the performance compared to the supervised model, outperforming it by 18.8%. Another advantage is reduced training time.

As a result of using information already trained with the bookcase dataset, it is only necessary to train the linear classifier, which is much quicker. If appropriate, the features trained with SwAV can be transferred to various other problems.

Table 7. Confusion matrix of the boxes dataset in a supervised setting

True Lables	**Incorrect (0)**	17	6
	Correct (1)	2	10
		Incorrect (0)	**Correct (1)**
		Predicted Labels	

However, for new images, the model did not classify all of them correctly. Figure 6 was one of these images that the model incorrectly classified as incorrect. As shown the background in these images was quite different from that of the original dataset and contributed to the incorrect classification. This shows that the model did not generalize well. This is also because the dataset is small and very specific.

Fig. 6. New image with different angle and background noise. The model predicted it incorrectly as 0

During the SwAV training on the bookcase dataset, certain features were learned. The linear classifier picked up these features and tried to fit them into the two classes of the boxes dataset. However, the meaningful features of the bookcase problem may cause the model to assign the new images to the wrong classes when looking at the new problem. This happens because the learned features are not appropriate for the new problem. One way to achieve better results would be to acquire more images with different noise and train SwAV with this dataset as well. SwAV would extract specific features from this dataset which would improve performance.

6   Discussion and Future Work

Self-Supervised Learning is progressing and achieving results close to supervised learning. In this work, SwAV was trained with Tensorflow's flowers dataset using different parameters. To evaluate the method a linear classifier, with the frozen representations of the ResNet-50 trained with SwAV, was trained. The SSL method achieved a 88.2% accuracy. SwAV was then trained with the same settings on a custom bookcase dataset that simulated a real-world industrial scenario. It achieved an accuracy of 98.8% and an MCC of 98%, approaching the 99,6% accuracy accomplished by a supervised learning setting.

Regarding transfer learning to downstream tasks, the self-supervised method improved performance compared to the supervised model. However, the model did not generalize well as when given new images the model failed to predict them correctly. The features learned from the bookcase model were not adequate to solve the new problem with the boxes dataset. This is not surprising because SwAV was trained on a very specific dataset with only two classes. It does not extract the same features as if it was trained on, for example, *ImageNet* that has over a million images and 1000 classes.

In general, SwAV extracts useful features that can add information to solve other tasks. However, this depends on the datasets, the task, and the features learned during SwAV training. Also, SSL methods require a lot of computational power which can be a limitation. Depending on the problem and resources, SSL can be a good option.

In terms of future work, the aim is to train SwAV on a big industrial dataset with various images from different projects. There will be a variety of classes and the model will learn better features as it separates the classes in the embedding space and consequently generalize better. We intend to then apply transfer learning of the learned features to other problems and analyze if and how much improvement is made.

References

1. Girshick, R., Donahue, J., Darrell, T., Malik, J.: Rich feature hierarchies for accurate object detection and semantic segmentation. In: Proceedings of the IEEE Computer Society Conference on Computer Vision and Pattern Recognition, pp. 580–587 (2014)
2. Krizhevsky, A., Sutskever, I., Hinton, G.E.: ImageNet classification with deep convolutional neural networks. In: Advances in Neural Information Processing Systems, pp. 1097–1105 (2012)
3. Chen, L.C., Papandreou, G., Kokkinos, I., Murphy, K., Yuille. A.L.: DeepLab: semantic image segmentation with deep convolutional nets, atrous convolution, and fully connected CRFs. In: IEEE Transactions on Pattern Analysis and Machine Intelligence, pp. 834–848 (2018). https://doi.org/10.1109/tpami.2017.269918
4. Kolesnikov, A., Zhai, X., Beyer, L.: Revisiting self-supervised visual representation learning. In: IEEE/CVF Conference on Computer Vision and Pattern Recognition (CVPR), pp. 1920–1929 (2019). https://doi.org/10.1109/CVPR.2019.00202
5. Goyal, P., Mahajan, D., Gupta. A., Misra, I.: Scaling and benchmarking self-supervised visual representation learning. In: Proceedings of the IEEE/CVF International Conference on Computer Vision, pp. 6391–6400 (2019)
6. Albelwi, S.: Survey on self-supervised learning: auxiliary pretext tasks and contrastive learning methods in imaging. Entropy **24**(4), 551. MDPI (2022)

7. Longlong, J., Yingli, T.: Self-supervised visual feature learning with deep neural networks: a survey. IEEE Trans. Pattern Anal. Mach. Intell. **43**(11), 4037–4058 (2020)
8. Xiao, L., et al.: Self-supervised learning: generative or contrastive. IEEE Trans. Knowl. Data Eng. **35**(1), 857–876 (2021)
9. Jaiswal, A., Babu, A.R., Zadeh, M.A., Banerjee, D., Makedon, F.: A survey on contrastive self-supervised learning. Technologies **9**(1), 2. MDPI (2020)
10. Schmarje, L., Santarossa. M., Schröder, S.-M., Koch, R.: A survey on semi-, self- and unsupervised learning for image classification. IEEE Access **9**, 82146–82168. IEEE (2021)
11. Yeh, C.-H., Hong, C.-Y., Hsu, Y.-C., Liy, T.-L., Chen, Y., LeCun, Y.: Decoupled contrastive learning. In: Avidan, S., Brostow, G., Cisse, M., Farinella, G.M., Hassner, T. (eds.) Computer Vision – ECCV 2022. ECCV 2022. LNCS, vol. 13686, pp. 668–684. Springer, Cham (2022). https://doi.org/10.1007/978-3-031-19809-0_38
12. Ohri, K., Kumar, M.: Review on self-supervised image recognition using deep neural networks. Knowl.-Based Syst. **224**, 107090. Elsevier (2021)
13. Simonyan, K., Zisserman, A: Very deep convolutional networks for large-scale image recognition. In: 3rd International Conference on Learning Representations (ICLR), pp. 1–14 (2014)
14. Long, J., Shelhamer, E., Darrell, T.: Fully convolutional networks for semantic segmentation. In: Proceedings of the IEEE Conference on Computer Vision and Pattern Recognition, pp. 3431–3440 (2015)
15. He, K., Gkioxari, G., Dollár, P., Girshick, R.: Mask R-CNN. In: Proceedings of the IEEE International Conference on Computer Vision, pp. 2961–2969 (2017)
16. Girshick, R.: Fast R-CNN. In: Proceedings of the IEEE International Conference on Computer Vision, pp. 1440–1448 (2015)
17. Ren, S., He, K., Girshick, R., Sun, J.: Faster R-CNN: towards real-time object detection with region proposal networks. In: Advances in Neural Information Processing Systems, vol. 28 (2015)
18. Caron, M., Bojanowski, P., Joulin, A., Douze, M.: Deep clustering for unsupervised learning of visual features. In: Proceedings of the European Conference on Computer Vision (ECCV), pp. 132–149 (2018)
19. Yan, X., Misra, I., Gupta, A., Ghadiyaram, D., Mahajan, D.: ClusterFit: improving generalization of visual representations. In: Proceedings of the IEEE/CVF Conference on Computer Vision and Pattern Recognition, pp. 6509–6518 (2020)
20. Chen, X., He, K.: Exploring simple siamese representation learning. In: Proceedings of the IEEE/CVF Conference on Computer Vision and Pattern Recognition, pp. 15750–15758 (2021)
21. Misra, I., Maaten, L.V.D.: Self-supervised learning of pretext-invariant representations. In: Proceedings of the IEEE/CVF Conference on Computer Vision and Pattern Recognition, pp. 6707–6717 (2020)
22. He, K., Fan, H., Wu, Y., Xie, S., Girshick, R.: Momentum contrast for unsupervised visual representation learning. In: Proceedings of the IEEE/CVF Conference on Computer Vision and Pattern Recognition, pp. 9729–9738 (2020)
23. Chen, T., Kornblith, S., Norouzi, M., Hinton, G.: A simple framework for contrastive learning of visual representations. In: International Conference on Machine Learning, pp. 1597–1607. PMLR (2020)
24. Caron, M., Misra, I., Mairal, J., Goyal, P., Bojanowski, P., Joulin, A.: Unsupervised learning of visual features by contrasting cluster assignments. Adv. Neural Inf. Process. Syst. **33**, 9912–9924 (2020)

25. Dickson, B.: Meta's Yann LeCun is betting on self-supervised learning to unlock human-compatible AI, 2020. https://thenextweb.com/news/metas-yann-lecun-is-betting-on-self-supervised-learning-to-unlock-human-compatible-ai. Accessed 16 Jan 2023
26. LeCun, Y., Misra, I.: Self-supervised learning: the dark matter of intelligence (2021). https://ai.facebook.com/blog/self-supervised-learning-the-dark-matter-of-intelligence/. Accessed 16 Jan 2023
27. Zhang, R., Isola, P., Efros, A.A.: Colorful image colorization. In: Leibe, B., Matas, J., Sebe, N., Welling, M. (eds.) ECCV 2016. LNCS, vol. 9907, pp. 649–666. Springer, Cham (2016). https://doi.org/10.1007/978-3-319-46487-9_40
28. Zhang, R., Isola, P., Efros, A.A.: Split-brain autoencoders: unsupervised learning by cross-channel prediction. In: Proceedings of the IEEE Conference on Computer Vision and Pattern Recognition, pp. 1058–1067 (2017)
29. Larsson, G., Maire, M., Shakhnarovich, G.: Learning representations for automatic colorization. In: Leibe, B., Matas, J., Sebe, N., Welling, M. (eds.) ECCV 2016. LNCS, vol. 9908, pp. 577–593. Springer, Cham (2016). https://doi.org/10.1007/978-3-319-46493-0_35
30. Larsson, G., Maire, M., Shakhnarovich, G.: Colorization as a proxy task for visual understanding. In: Proceedings of the IEEE Conference on Computer Vision and Pattern Recognition, pp. 6874–6883 (2017)
31. Komodakis, N., Gidaris, S.: Unsupervised representation learning by predicting image rotations. In: International Conference on Learning Representations (ICLR) (2018)
32. Pathak, D., Krahenbuhl, P., Donahue, J., Darrell, T., Efros, A.A.: Context encoders: feature learning by inpainting. In: Proceedings of the IEEE Conference on Computer Vision and Pattern Recognition, pp. 2536–2544 (2016)
33. Iizuka, S., Simo-Serra, E., Ishikawa, H.: Globally and locally consistent image completion. ACM Trans. Graph. (ToG) **36**(4), 1–14 (2017)
34. Doersch, C., Gupta, A., Efros, A.A.: Unsupervised visual representation learning by context prediction. In: Proceedings of the IEEE International Conference on Computer Vision, pp. 1422–1430 (2015)
35. Noroozi, M., Favaro, P.: Unsupervised learning of visual representations by solving jigsaw puzzles. In: Leibe, B., Matas, J., Sebe, N., Welling, M. (eds.) ECCV 2016. LNCS, vol. 9910, pp. 69–84. Springer, Cham (2016). https://doi.org/10.1007/978-3-319-46466-4_5
36. Kim, D., Cho, D., Yoo, D., Kweon, I.S.: Learning image representations by completing damaged jigsaw puzzles. In: IEEE Winter Conference on Applications of Computer Vision (WACV), pp. 793–802. IEEE (2018)
37. Wei, C., et al.: Iterative reorganization with weak spatial constraints: solving arbitrary jigsaw puzzles for unsupervised representation learning. In: Proceedings of the IEEE/CVF Conference on Computer Vision and Pattern Recognition, pp. 1910–1919 (2019)
38. Ericsson, L., Gouk, H., Hospedales, T.M.: How well do self-supervised models transfer? In: Proceedings of the IEEE/CVF Conference on Computer Vision and Pattern Recognition, pp. 5414–5423 (2021)
39. The TensorFlow Team: Flowers (2019). http://download.tensorflow.org/example_images/flower_photos.tgz
40. Cuturi, M.: Sinkhorn distances: lightspeed computation of optimal transport. In: Advances in Neural Information Processing Systems, vol. 26, pp. 2292–2300 (2013)
41. Kingma, D.P., Ba, J.: Adam: a method for stochastic optimization. arXiv preprint arXiv:1412.6980 (2014)

A Quantum Annealing Solution to the Job Shop Scheduling Problem

Riad Aggoune[1]($\boxtimes$)(iD) and Samuel Deleplanque[2](iD)

[1] ITIS Department, Luxembourg Institute of Science and Technology,
5 Av. des Hauts-Fourneaux, L-4362 Esch-sur-Alzette, Luxembourg
`riad.aggoune@list.lu`
[2] CNRS, Centrale Lille, JUNIA, Univ. Lille, Univ. Valenciennes, UMR 8520 IEMN,
41 boulevard Vauban, 59046 Lille Cedex, France
`samuel.deleplanque@junia.com`

Abstract. We consider in this paper the job shop scheduling problem. We first present a mathematical formulation of the problem, namely a disjunctive model. Then, we show how the model can be reformulated as a Quadratic Unconstrained Binary Optimization (QUBO) problem, that can be solved by an analog quantum computer.

Keywords: quantum computing · optimisation · QUBO · job shop scheduling

1 Introduction

Quantum optimization which is the use of quantum computers and algorithms for solving complex optimization problems, is one of the topics in quantum computing with the highest potential. Two types of approaches are generally used to solve combinatorial optimization problems with quantum computers: exact methods such as the Grover's search algorithm [8], and meta-heuristics such as the Quantum Annealing [9] and the Quantum Approximate Optimization Algorithm (QAOA) [6]. Exact methods and variational methods like QAOA make use of universal gate-based quantum computers, such as the ones developed by the IBM company. Quantum annealing is designed for analog quantum computers developed by D-Wave. Solving a combinatorial optimization problem with heuristics generally requires a transformation of the problem to a format suitable for the quantum computer. While some existing frameworks[1] can cope with Constrained Quadratic Models (CQM), Quadratic Unconstrained Binary Optimization (QUBO) is the best option to map an optimization problem to a quantum computer or simulator. We consider in this paper the job shop scheduling problem. We first review in the following Sect. 2 the quantum-based methods recently proposed in the literature. Then in Sect. 3 we propose a QUBO formulation of the scheduling problem. Finally, in Sect. 4 numerical results obtained with D-Wave quantum annealing machines and conclusions are presented.

---

[1] https://cloud.dwavesys.com/leap.

O. Gervasi et al. (Eds.): ICCSA 2023 Workshops, LNCS 14104, pp. 421–428, 2023.
https://doi.org/10.1007/978-3-031-37105-9_28

2   Problem Definition

The job shop scheduling problem can be stated as follows: A set of n jobs $J = \{J_1, J_2, \ldots, J_n\}$ has to be processed on a set of m machines $M = \{M_1, \ldots, M_m\}$. Each job J_i consists of a linear sequence of n_i operations $(O_{i1}, O_{i2}, \ldots, O_{in_i})$. Each machine can process only one operation at a time and each operation O_{ij} with a processing time of p_{ij} time units needs only one machine. Each job visits the machines according to its own predefined routing. This problem generalizes the flow shop scheduling problem, in which all the jobs are processed following the same routing $(M_1, M_2, \ldots, M_m)$. The objective is to determine the starting date of each operation O_{ij} so that the makespan noted C_{max} is minimized. The problem is NP-hard for $n > 2$ and $m > 2$ [7].

The traditional solution approaches to solve job shop scheduling problems include heuristics and meta-heuristics as well as exact methods, such as branch-and-bound and constraint programming [3].

The linear disjunctive model [11] for the job shop scheduling problem can be expressed as follows. The starting times are represented by the integer variable vector, denoted by x. We use z to denote the binary variable vector, which satisfies the following conditions:

$$z_{ijk} = \begin{cases} 1 \text{ if the job } j \text{ precedes job } k \text{ on machine } i, \\ 0 \text{ otherwise.} \end{cases}$$

We note by $(\sigma_1^j, \ldots, \sigma_h^j, \ldots, \sigma_m^j)$ the processing order of job j through the machines. The minimization of the objective function (1) forces all the jobs to be finished as soon as possible.

$$\sum_{j \in J} x_{\sigma_m^j j} \tag{1}$$

The makespan C_{max} can be minimized by adding the following constraints:

$$C_{max} \geq \sum_{j \in J} x_{\sigma_m^j j} + p_{\sigma_m^j j} \tag{2}$$

Constraints (3) forbid consecutive operations of one job to start before the previous one is finished.

$$x_{\sigma_h^j j} \geq x_{\sigma_{h-1}^j j} + p_{\sigma_{h-1}^j j} \qquad \forall j \in J, h = 2..m \tag{3}$$

Constraints (4) and (5) forbid to have more than one operation at a time on a given machine.

$$x_{ij} \geq x_{ik} + p_{ik} - M z_{ijk} \qquad \forall j, k \in J, j < k, i \in M \tag{4}$$

$$x_{ik} \geq x_{ij} + p_{ij} - M(1 - z_{ijk}) \qquad \forall j, k \in J, j < k, i \in M \tag{5}$$

3   Related Works

The scientific literature on quantum solutions for hard combinatorial optimization problems is becoming significant and diversified. The studies of shop scheduling problems are quite recent and scarce. They can be classified according to the types of quantum computers and algorithms used to solve the problems: analog, universal computers, and simulators. In general, the solution approaches consist in first mapping the decision variables of the considered problems to the qubits of the quantum computer. Then, quantum algorithms are applied to make the qubits value evolve until solutions are found. Solving optimization problems with quantum computers is therefore strongly limited by the number of qubits available, among other hardware constraints.

The first paper in the domain is from Venturelli *et al.* [15]. The authors proposed a QUBO formulation and a quantum annealing solution for the job shop scheduling problem with the makespan objective. The method was implemented on a D-Wave quantum annealer, with 509 working qubits. The authors also introduced window shaving and immediate selections techniques to reduce the number of considered variables. Their model has then been re-used in several studies, as listed below.

In [10] the authors have developed a hybrid quantum annealing heuristic to solve a particular instance of the job shop scheduling problem on the D-Wave 2000Q quantum annealing system that consists of 2041 qubits and a maximum of 6 connections between qubits. The proposed approach includes variable pruning techniques and a processing window heuristic. In [4], job shop instances with unitary operations have been tested on the D-Wave Advantage machine, built upon 5640 qubits and 15 possible connections between qubits. Extensive experiments with the reverse annealing procedure and comparisons with simulated annealing are also described. In [1], a QUBO formulation is proposed for the minimisation of the total completion time in a job shop. The model is solved using the D-Wave hybrid solver and Advantage quantum annealing computer.

A generalization of the job shop scheduling problem with pools of parallel machines available for processing operations was considered in [5]. The authors proposed a QUBO derived from the one of [15] and an iterative procedure to solve relatively large size instances on a specialized hardware[2]. Using the QUBO formulations proposed in [5], the authors in [14], tackle the flexible job shop scheduling problem with the D-Wave solvers. Another QUBO formulation is proposed in [12] for assigning dispatching rules to the machines and scheduling the operations in a flexible job shop system. The problem is solved using the leap hybrid solver. In [13], the authors propose a QUBO formulation for the job shop scheduling with worker assignment considerations. Possible ways to approximate the makespan are discussed and instances solved with the Fujitsu

---

[2] https://www.fujitsu.com/global/services/business-services/digital-annealer.

Digital Annealer are described. In the same environment, the authors in [16] efficiently solve large instances of the job shop scheduling problem with a hybrid approach that combines constraints programming and QUBO models for one-machine problems.

Finally, the only study involving gate-based computers is due to [2]. The authors have proposed four variational quantum heuristics for solving a job shop scheduling problem with early and late delivery as well as production costs, adapted from a steel manufacturing process. They have compared the performance of the heuristics on two-machine flow shop instances using IBM quantum processors with 5 to 23 qubits.

4   QUBO Formulation

The boolean variable x_{ij}^t takes the value 1 if the operation i of the job j starts in period t, with $i = 1..n_i$, $j = 1..n$, $t = 1..T$, and takes the value 0 otherwise. We note $M_{ij}, i = 1..n_i, j = 1..n$, the required machine for the operation i of the job j. The minimization of the Objective function (6) forces the last operations of all jobs to start globally as soon as possible.

$$\sum_j \sum_t t.x_{n_{ij}}^t \tag{6}$$

We force each operation to start exactly once with the following set of constraints (7) to be relaxed in the Objective function.

$$\left(\sum_t x_{ij}^t - 1\right)^2, \qquad i = 1..n_i, j = 1..n \tag{7}$$

Constraints (8) forbid to have more than one operation at a time on a given machine.

$$x_{ij}^t x_{i'j'}^{t'} = 0,$$
$$\forall (i,j,t) \cup (i',j',t') : i,i' = 1..n_i, j, j' = 1..n, (i,j) \neq (i',j'), \tag{8}$$
$$M_{ij} = M_{i'j'}, (t,t') \in T^2, 0 \leq t' - t < p_{ij}$$

Constraints (9) forbid consecutive operations to start before the previous one is finished.

$$x_{ij}^t x_{i+1j}^{t'} = 0, \quad i = 1..(n_i - 1), j = 1..n, (t,t') \in T^2, t + p_{ij} > t' \tag{9}$$

The Quadratic Unconstrained Binary Optimisation (QUBO) model is given with the Objective function (10) to minimize with 4 multipliers, λ_1, λ_2, λ_3 and λ_4, balancing the relaxation of the 4 sets of constraints.

$$\sum_j \sum_t t.x_{n_ij}^t$$

$$+\lambda_1 \sum_j \sum_i (\sum_t x_{ij}^t - 1)^2$$

$$+\lambda_2 \sum_{(i,j,t)\cup(i',j',t')\in T1} x_{ij}^t x_{i'j'}^{t'}$$

$$+\lambda_3 \sum_{(i,j,t,t')\in T2} x_{ij}^t x_{i+1j}^{t'} \qquad (10)$$

with:

$$T1 = (i,j,t) \cup (i',j',t') : i,i' = 1..n_i, j,j' = 1..n, (i,j) \neq (i',j'),$$
$$M_{ij} = M_{i'j'}, (t,t') \in T^2, 0 \leq t' - t < p_{ij}$$
$$T2 = (i,j,t,t') : i = 1..(n_i - 1), j = 1..n, (t,t') \in T^2, t + p_{ij} > t'$$

5 Computational Experiments

As an early result, we present in Fig. 1 the solution we obtained with the D-Wave Hybrid Solution on an instance from the literature [4]. In this instance, 4 jobs with 4 operations have to be scheduled on 4 different machines. The next step will be the direct implementation of the QUBOs for the job shop instances and their solution with the full quantum machines.

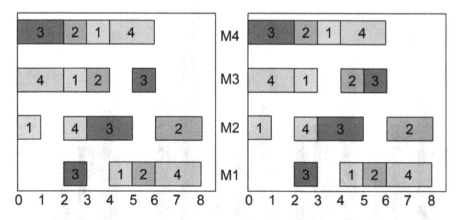

Fig. 1. Representation of the optimal solution from the literature (left, [4]) and the solution obtained with the D-Wave Hybrid Solution (right). The instance has 4 machines (M1, M2, M3, M4), 4 jobs (each represented by a different color), and 4 operations per job.

It should be noted that the solution obtained with our model and the hybrid solver is not an active schedule. Indeed, Job J_2 on machine M_3 could be started earlier.

Five instances with four machines and four operations per job had been solved with T taking values in $\{19, 13, 11, 9, 8, 7, 6, 5\}$. In Table 1, we report the objective function of the best solution obtained with one call of the D-Wave Hybrid Solution, where *n.s.e.* and *s.n.f.* mean *no solution exists* and *solution not found*, respectively. The chart in Fig. 2 shows the evolution of the results according to the number of periods.

Table 1. Results on 5 instances (4 jobs, 4 machines and 4 operations per job) solved by the D-Wave Hybrid Solution.

	T = 19	T = 13	T = 11	T = 9	T = 8	T = 7	T = 6	T = 5
inst1	41	30	25	26	25	24	21	*n.s.e.*
inst2	38	29	26	26	25	21	22	*s.n.f.*
inst3	46	29	27	24	20	20	18	18
inst4	55	38	38	31	29	28	*s.n.f.*	*n.s.e.*
inst5	42	28	25	21	21	20	19	18

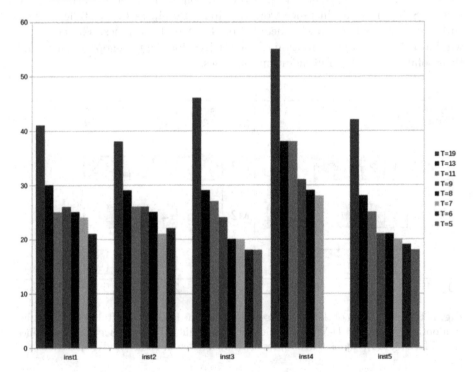

Fig. 2. Objective function evolution according to the number of periods T for 5 instances.

6   Conclusion

In this paper, we first reviewed the recent solutions proposed to solve the job shop scheduling problem on quantum computers, with a focus on QUBO formulations that help integrating constraints that are relevant in practice. We have also proposed a QUBO model that has been solved using D-Wave quantum annealing machines. While the existing hardware are still limited in their ability to handle the number of variables generated, it remains important to progress on the modeling of practical problems. Indeed, the quantum solutions are not yet competitive as compared to classical solutions approaches, but this might change when the number of qubits available is increased. Future works include investigating mechanisms for keeping the number of variables low while integrating efficiently the constraints.

References

1. Aggoune, R., Deleplanque, S.: Solving the job shop scheduling problem: QUBO model and quantum annealing. In: 21st EU/ME meeting - Emerging Optimization Methods: From Metaheuristics to Quantum Approaches, April 2023, Troyes (2023). ⟨hal-04037312⟩
2. Amaro, D., Rosenkranz, M., Fitzpatrick, N., Hirano, K., Fiorentini, M.: A case study of variational quantum algorithms for a job shop scheduling problem. EPJ Quantum Technol. **9**, 100–114 (2022)
3. Da Col, G., Teppan, E.C.: Industrial-size job shop scheduling with constraint programming. Oper. Res. Perspect. **9**, 100249 (2022)
4. Carugno, C., Ferrari Dacrema, M., Cremonesi, P.: Evaluating the job shop scheduling problem on a D-wave quantum annealer. Sci. Rep. **12**, 6539 (2022). https://doi.org/10.1038/s41598-022-10169-0
5. Denkena, B., Schinkel, F., Pirnay, J., Wilmsmeier, S.: Quantum algorithms for process parallel flexible job shop scheduling. CIRP J. Manuf. Sci. Technol. **33**, 12142 (2020)
6. Farhi, E., Goldstone, J., Gutmann, S.: A quantum approximate optimization algorithm (2014). https://doi.org/10.48550/arxiv.1411.4028
7. Garey, Michael R. and Johnson, David S. Computers and Intractability: A Guide to the Theory of NP-Completeness. W. H. Freeman and Co., USA, 1979
8. Grover, L.K.: A fast quantum mechanical algorithm for database search. In: Proceedings of the Twenty-Eighth Annual ACM Symposium on Theory of Computing, pp. 212–219 (1996)
9. Tadashi, K., Nishimori, H.: Quantum annealing in the transverse ising model. Phys. Rev. E **58**(5), 5355 (1998)
10. Kurowski, K., Węglarz, J., Subocz, M., Różycki, R., Waligóra, G.: Hybrid quantum annealing heuristic method for solving job shop scheduling problem. In: Krzhizhanovskaya, V.V., et al. (eds.) ICCS 2020. LNCS, vol. 12142, pp. 502–515. Springer, Cham (2020). https://doi.org/10.1007/978-3-030-50433-5_39
11. Manne, A.S.: On the job-shop scheduling problem. Oper. Res. **8**(2), 223 (1960). https://doi.org/10.1287/opre.8.2.219

12. Rao, P.U., Sodhi, B.: Scheduling with multiple dispatch rules: a quantum computing approach. In: Groen, D., de Mulatier, C., Paszynski, M., Krzhizhanovskaya, V.V., Dongarra, J.J., Sloot, P.M.A. (eds.) ICCS 2022. LNCS, vol. 13353, pp. 233–246. Springer, Cham (2022). https://doi.org/10.1007/978-3-031-08760-8_20
13. Shimada, D., Shibuya, T., Shibasaki, T.: A decomposition method for makespan minimization in job-shop scheduling problem using ising machine. In: 2021 IEEE 8th International Conference on Industrial Engineering and Applications, PP. 307–314 (2021)
14. Schworm, P., Wu, X., Glatt, M., Aurich, J.C.: Solving flexible job shop scheduling problems in manufacturing with Quantum Annealing. Prod. Eng. Res. Dev. **17**, 105–115 (2023). https://doi.org/10.1007/s11740-022-01145-8
15. Venturelli, D., Marchand, D.J., Rojo, G.: Quantum annealing implementation of job-shop scheduling. arXiv preprint:1506.08479, 2015
16. Zhang, J., Lo Bianco, G., Beck, J.C.: Solving job-shop scheduling problems with QUBO-based specialized hardware. In: Proceedings of the International Conference on Automated Planning and Scheduling, vol. 32, no. 1, pp. 404–412 (2022)

Solving 3SAT and MIS Problems with Analog Quantum Machines

Samuel Deleplanque[✉][iD]

CNRS, Centrale Lille, JUNIA, Univ. Lille, Univ. Valenciennes, UMR 8520 IEMN,
41 boulevard Vauban, 59046 Lille Cedex, France
samuel.deleplanque@junia.com

Abstract. This work considers the use of analog quantum machines to solve the boolean satisfiability problem 3SAT by taking Quadratic Unconstrained Binary Optimization models (QUBO) as input. With the aim of using real quantum computers instead of emulators to solve instances of the problem, we choose the D-Wave quantum machines, which have a static topology and limited connectivity. Therefore, the choice of the problem formulation must take these important constraints into account. For this reason, we propose to solve 3SAT instances through polynomial-time reduction to the Maximum Independent Set problem. This is because the resulting graph is less dense and requires lower connectivity than the one that would be produced by directly modeling 3SAT into a QUBO.

Keywords: Quantum Computing · Quantum Annealing · 3SAT · Maximum Independent Set · Combinatorial optimization

1 Introduction

Analog quantum machines are currently the most advanced quantum computers for solving small to medium-sized instances of combinatorial optimization problems. Quantum universal gate-based computers, such a s the IBM numerical machines, are based on NISQ technology (Noisy Intermediate-Scale Quantum) and have an error rate too high to solve anything other than very small instances. Additionally, the number of quantum bits (qubits) in available machines is insufficient in 2023.

There are several types of analog quantum computers, including Pasqal and D-Wave machines. The former is expected to release in 2023 a real (i.e., not an emulator) computer based on Rydberg atoms, but today only the latter offers real quantum machines with a large number of qubits. Both consider transverse-field Ising models, and users can employ Quadratic Unconstrained Binary Optimization models (QUBO) since they are isomorphic to Ising models. The main differences between the two types of analog quantum computers are as follows: while a Pasqal machine can dynamically create a qubits network according to the QUBO, D-Wave machines have a static topology that must be taken into

© The Author(s), under exclusive license to Springer Nature Switzerland AG 2023
O. Gervasi et al. (Eds.): ICCSA 2023 Workshops, LNCS 14104, pp. 429–439, 2023.
https://doi.org/10.1007/978-3-031-37105-9_29

account since the qubits graphs can have a connectivity and topology that do not necessarily correspond to the QUBO graph. From its input (QUBO), the D-Wave machine automatically transforms the model to map it into the qubits graph. This process, called the "embedding process," is another optimization problem and can be very time-consuming. As a result, the number of qubits is larger than the number of vertices from the QUBO, and an embedding solution might not even be found.

In this work, we consider several static topologies from the three latest D-Wave machines: Chimera, Pegasus, and Zephyr, for solving the 3SAT problem. This problem, which we will define in this paper, could directly be modeled by a QUBO by relaxing the clause satisfaction constraints in the objective function. However, it is costly in terms of the number of expressions in the objective function, and this implies a difficult embedding problem. The main contribution of this work is to experiment with the polynomial-time reduction from the 3SAT problem to the Maximum Independent Set problem (MIS) for solving 3SAT instances with a quantum computer. The QUBO of the MIS is relatively simple and seems to be more adaptable to the topologies of the D-Wave machines. In these topologies, the connectivity (i.e., the vertex degrees) is limited.

Even if such a transformation implies that the 3SAT instance is no more difficult than the MIS instance we obtain, the density of the graph might be more convenient to be mapped into the qubits graph compared to the one we would obtain directly from a 3SAT QUBO.

The remainder of this paper is organized as follows. Section 2 introduces the machines used in this work. The 3SAT problem and the MIS optimization problem are described in Sect. 3. The method to transform a 3SAT instance into a MIS instance and the process for obtaining a solution to the 3SAT from a solution to the MIS are presented in Sect. 4. In the final section, Sect. 5, we report on quantum computational experiments.

2   Quantum Annealing and D-Wave Machines

In this work, we focus on the D-Wave quantum machines. These quantum computers are available through the cloud and have up to 5,000 qubits. Although they are not programmable like universal gate-based machines (e.g., IBM quantum machines), their technology directly optimizes Quadratic Unconstrained Binary Optimization models (QUBO). In short, they attempt to reach the ground state of an Ising spin glass system configured in a way that corresponds (indirectly) to the search for the minimum value of a QUBO (Ising models and QUBO are isomorphic; you can refer to [4] and [10] for more information about modeling general optimization problems with QUBO and Ising models, respectively).

The resolution process is adiabatic[1] and is based on quantum annealing [7], which is theoretically proven to be more efficient than the simulated annealing

---

[1] See [1] for more information about adiabatic systems.

meta-heuristic [9] where quantum fluctuations replace temperature changes. The machine intrinsically executes quantum annealing through its hardware. Like universal gate-based quantum machines, quantum annealing machines execute the process several times (the "shots" are here called anneals). The number of anneals is part of the input and is equal to the number of solutions we obtain in the output. An anneal time can also be given as input, and since the machine can be used for approximately one second in total, the number of anneals and the annealing time must respect this bound (some non-linear supplementary times also contribute to the total).

The qubits network is static: the topology cannot be dynamically adapted to the QUBO (or Ising model) given as input. The connectivity of each topology, which can be viewed as the degree of the qubits graph, is crucial. For instance, if a QUBO formulation considers a complete graph, such a specific graph is not directly available in the topology. In such a case, the QUBO must be transformed into another problem, but this time able to be mapped into the machine. This embedding process is automatically done by the machine. The optimization is then performed on a larger graph. The population of qubits used, which is larger than the number of vertices related to the QUBO, sometimes fails to correspond exactly to the initial problem, especially for some qubit pairs called logic qubits that fail to take the same value. This problem is called *Chain Breaks*. The three representations in Fig. 1 show the three latest topologies of D-Wave machines, while Table 1 provides important information such as the number of qubits and the related connectivity.

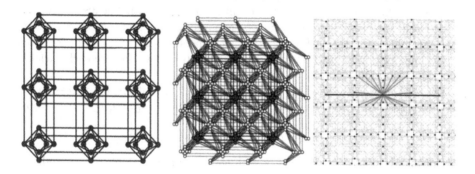

Fig. 1. From left to right: Chimera, Pegasus and Zephir D-Wave machine topologies. More information is given in Table 1.

The embedding process involves solving another optimization problem and can be very time-consuming, to the point of not being able to provide a mapping. To anticipate this significant issue, the user's machine can take it into account while formulating the QUBO. This is an important aspect of this work: we could create a QUBO to solve the 3SAT problem, but its direct formulation as a QUBO tends to have difficulties being embedded in the machine due to the topology of the qubits graph. Taking this into account, we use the polynomial-time reduction

Table 1. D-Wave quantum computing machines

Topology	Chimera	Pegasus	Zephyr
Name Machine	DW_2000Q	Advantage_System	Advantage2_prototype
Machine Version	6	6.1	1.1
Number of working Qubits	2041	5616	563
Connectivity	6	15	20
Annealing Time Range	[1,2000]	[0.5,2000]	[1,2000]

to the MIS to obtain a QUBO more suitable for the topology and, in turn, have a less time-consuming embedding process.

The QUBO model $f^{QUBO}(x)$, which we can provide as input to the machine, is given by the expression (1) with x as a binary vector and Q as the cost matrix.

$$f^{QUBO}(x) = x^T Q x = \sum_i Q_{i,i} x_i + \sum_{i<j} Q_{i,j} x_i x_j. \tag{1}$$

3 A Satisfaction Problem: 3SAT, and a Combinatorial Optimization Problem: MIS

The 3SAT is a Boolean satisfiability problem. The goal is to determine if there exists a solution satisfying a conjunction of clauses, where each clause is a disjunction of 3 literals (i.e., variables or negations of variables). The 3SAT problem is NP-Hard (the proof is given by [8]; you can also refer to [2] for a general survey on satisfiability problems). We denote c_i as a clause with $i = 1, \ldots, |\mathcal{C}|$ from the set of clauses $\mathcal{C}$, and $\mathcal{V}$ as the set of variables such that we denote each variable as $v_j, j = 1, \ldots, |\mathcal{V}|$.

Let's take an example where the 3SAT problem formulated in expression (2) has at least two solutions: ($v_1 = 1$, $v_2 = 1$, $v_3 = 1$) and ($v_1 = 0$, $v_2 = 0$, $v_3 = 0$).

$$(v_1 \vee v_2 \vee \neg v_3) \wedge (\neg v_1 \vee v_2 \vee v_3) \wedge (v_1 \vee \neg v_2 \vee v_3). \tag{2}$$

Not all variables must be part of each clause, but this simple example allows us to introduce the one-in-three 3SAT, where a solution satisfies all the clauses and each clause must be satisfied by exactly one variable. The simple example in expression (2) does not have such a solution.

The MIS problem is a combinatorial optimization problem considering a simple undirected graph $\mathcal{G}$ with a set of vertices $\mathcal{X}$ and a set of edges $\mathcal{E}$. In this problem, we search for the largest subset of vertices $\mathcal{S} \subseteq \mathcal{X}$, also called the maximum independent set, in such a way that no two vertices in $\mathcal{S}$ can be adjacent (i.e., no vertex of $\mathcal{S}$ can be directly connected by an edge of $\mathcal{E}$ to another vertex of the same set). The MIS problem is NP-Hard ([3]; please refer to [5] for an interesting review of this problem).

To model the MIS through a linear program, we denote x as a decision variable vector, where each element $x_k, k \in \mathcal{X}$, takes a $\{0; 1\}$ value such that:

$$x_k = \begin{cases} 1 \text{ if the vertex } k \text{ is in the independent set, i.e., } k \in \mathcal{S}, \\ 0 \text{ otherwise.} \end{cases} \tag{3}$$

Maximizing the cardinality of $\mathcal{S}$ means maximizing the objective function $f_{MIS}(x)$ defined by expression:

$$f_{MIS}(x) = \sum_{k \in \mathcal{X}} x_k. \tag{4}$$

The set of constraints, which, for each edge (k, l) in $\mathcal{E}$, forbids that both vertex k and vertex l are in $\mathcal{S}$, is given by the inequalities:

$$x_k + x_l \leq 1 \qquad \forall (k, l) \in \mathcal{E}. \tag{5}$$

In the scope of using a quantum machine that takes a QUBO as input, we reformulate the set of constraints (5) with the quadratic constraints:

$$x_k x_l = 0 \qquad \forall (k, l) \in \mathcal{E}. \tag{6}$$

We denote λ as the multiplier of the constraints (6) relaxed in the objective function of the QUBO. Considering a correct λ value, searching for a Maximum Independent Set in the undirected graph $\mathcal{G}$ can be done by minimizing the QUBO function $f_{MIS}^{QUBO}(x)$:

$$f_{MIS}^{QUBO}(x) = -\sum_{k \in \mathcal{X}} x_k + \lambda \sum_{(k,l) \in \mathcal{E}} x_k x_l. \tag{7}$$

The minimization of the first expression $-\sum_{k \in \mathcal{X}} x_k$ of $f_{MIS}^{QUBO}(x)$ tends to select the largest number of vertices in the set $\mathcal{S}$ since this is the opposite of the objective function (4). The minimization of the second expression $\lambda \sum_{(k,l) \in \mathcal{E}} x_k x_l$ corresponds to the relaxation of the quadratic constraints (6) weighted by the multiplier λ. We can easily see that, for each constraint not satisfied, which means for two adjacent vertices in $\mathcal{S}$, the objective function will have a penalty of λ.

4   Solving a 3SAT Instance on a Quantum Computer Using Polynomial-Time Reduction to the Maximum Independent Set Problem

Since the QUBO related to a 3SAT instance is difficult to embed into the qubits graph due to its topology, we searched for different methods to solve the boolean satisfiability problem, especially models with a less dense graph. The polynomial-time reduction from SAT to MIS, since $3SAT \leq_p MIS$, allows us to solve 3SAT by resolving MIS.

From an instance of the 3SAT problem, where each binary variable is denoted as $v_j, j = 1..|\mathcal{V}|$, and its negation as $\neg v_j$, we denote a binary variable $y_{i,j}$ with $i = 1..|\mathcal{C}|, j = 1..|\mathcal{V}|$, independently of the negation if applicable. It takes a value from $\{0,1\}$ such that:

$$y_{i,j} = \begin{cases} 1 \text{ if the vertex } (i,j) \text{ is in the independent set } \mathcal{S}, \\ 0 \text{ otherwise.} \end{cases} \tag{8}$$

Each variable $y_{i,j}$ is represented by a vertex in the set $\mathcal{X}$ of a graph $\mathcal{G}$. Each edge e in the set $\mathcal{E}$ exists for one of the following two reasons:

– the two connected variables belong to the same clause $i, i = 1..|\mathcal{C}|$,
– the two connected variables correspond to the same original variable $j, j = 1..|\mathcal{V}|$, and one is the negation of the other.

Even though the total number of variables is always $3 * |\mathcal{C}|$, it is easy to see that the density of the resulting graph is related to the redundancy of each original 3SAT variable and its negation across different clauses. In short, instances with fewer variable occurrences than the graph's connectivity may have a better chance of fitting into the topology of the qubits graph.

The small 3SAT example defined by the expression (2) is transformed into a graph of the MIS problem in Fig. 2. It involves literals that are colored blue or orange, representing variables and their negations, respectively. The binary variables $y_{i,j}$ are associated with clause i and 3SAT variable j. The first clause C_1 is represented by the first K_3 complete subgraph. Each 3-vertex clique enforces a maximum of one y_{ij} to be equal to 1. However, it is notable that a solution to the MIS problem does not necessarily correspond to a one-in-three 3SAT instance since the negation of 3SAT variables is not considered in the MIS variables. Negations are taken into account through edges connecting different clauses. For instance, if a variable v_{SAT} appears in the first clause C_1, while its negation $\neg v_{SAT}$ appears in the second clause C_2, then there is an edge $(y_{C_1, v_{SAT}}, y_{C_2, \neg v_{SAT}})$ in $\mathcal{E}$.

If the resolution of the MIS provides an optimal solution, a solution to the 3SAT problem exists if the cardinality of set $\mathcal{S}$ is equal to the number of clauses. Otherwise, the 3SAT instance cannot be satisfied. In fact, if the MIS resolution does not have exactly one $y_{i,j}$ equal to 1 for each 3-vertex clique i, not all clauses will be satisfied. Assuming such an optimal solution exists, we can deduce the value of the 3SAT variables $v_j, j = 1..|\mathcal{V}|$, from each $y_{i,j} = 1$ as follows:

$$v_j = \begin{cases} 0 \text{ if the variable } v_j \text{ appears as a negation in the clause } i, \\ 1 \text{ otherwise.} \end{cases} \tag{9}$$

Continuing with the example given in expression (2) and the graph obtained in Fig. 2, we can deduce the values of the original variables as follows:

$$\begin{cases} x_1 = y_{1,1} = 1 \\ x_2 = y_{3,2} = 1 \\ x_3 = \neg y_{2,3} = 0. \end{cases} \tag{10}$$

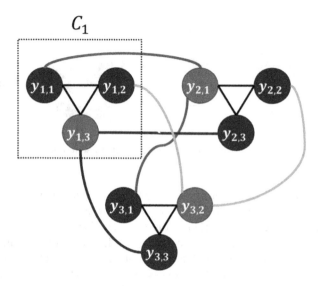

Fig. 2. The MIS graph representation obtained from the boolean satisfiability problem given by the expression (2).

Note that the solution may not be a solution of the one-in-three 3SAT problem, even if the solution of the MIS, with exactly one vertex in $\mathcal{S}$ per 3-vertex clique from the clauses, suggests that exactly one literal will satisfy each clause. For example, all literals satisfy the first clause of the expression (2).

Figure 3 reports the steps of the resolution process from a 3SAT instance to the solution. The main steps of the resolution scheme are as follows. User actions are colored in blue, while machine actions are in green. The 3SAT instance is first reduced to a MIS instance. The latter is formulated through a Quadratic Unconstrained Binary Optimization model (QUBO), which is then given as input to the quantum machine. The machine transforms the QUBO to embed it into the topology of the qubits network. If such an embedding is found, the problem is solved multiple times (i.e., several anneals) by the quantum annealer, which then reconstitutes the MIS solutions. The user can then take all the optimal solutions found. If the number of vertices in the independent set is equal to the number of clauses, all of these solutions, once transformed, satisfy the 3SAT instance.

5   Quantum Computational Experiments

Preliminary results have been obtained on small instances by testing the Chimera and Pegasus topologies. Figure 4 highlights the importance of topology, even if the available connectivity is higher than that required by the graph represented by the QUBO. For instance, the 4 variables and 6 clauses 3SAT instance gives a small graph with 18 variables. We can see from Fig. 4 that the degree of the

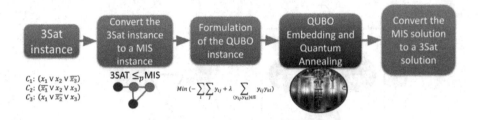

Fig. 3. Main steps of the resolution scheme.

vertices (see A and C) does not exceed 6, which is expected since each vertex is adjacent to the two other vertices in its 3-vertex clique and can also be adjacent to its negation through the 5 other clauses (since all variables have here more than one negation, the degree cannot be 7). Table 1 shows that Chimera has a connectivity of 6 (which seems sufficient for our instance), while Pegasus has a connectivity of 15. The embedding process in the 2000Q machine uses significantly more qubits (61) with its Chimera topology compared to Pegasus of the Advantage machine. After the embedding process, 1000 anneals were executed on the machines, and both gave all the optimal solutions of the MIS and, consequently, all the solutions of the 3SAT instance. The Zephyr topology was also tested with similar success, although not all data about the embedding process were available.

Focusing on the Pegasus topology, we conducted experiments on a challenging instance of the 3SAT problem with 11 clauses and 4 variables. The $3SAT \leq_p MIS$ reduction gives a graph with 33 variables. The graph cannot be considered a sparse graph, but rather a dense graph, since the number of edges is high: all edges for the 11 3-vertex cliques and other edges connecting the same variables and their negations between the different 3-vertex cliques. We used several anneal times balanced by the number of anneals to study the best configuration for such a specific graph. The results are reported in Table 2, which contains the *Chain Breaks Rate* and the number of optimal solutions obtained through the anneals. These results had been obtained on the quantum machine Advantage 6.1 (Pegasus topology).

Table 2. Results on a 4 variables and 11 Clauses 3SAT instance according to the *Annealing Time* et the number of Anneals.

Annealing Time (µs)	|Anneals|	Chain Breaks Rate	|Optimal Solutions|
0.5	7000	High	92
1	7000	Average	6
10	7000	Average	2
100	2500	Average	3
1000	500	Average	1
2000	250	High	0

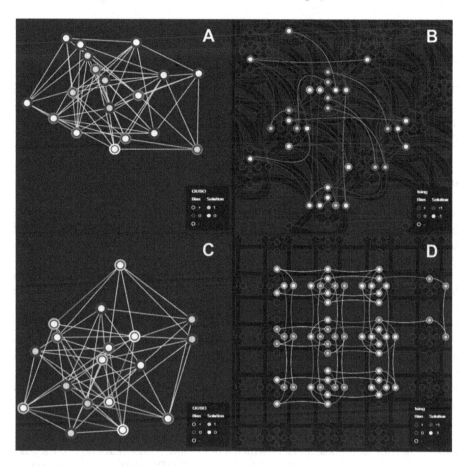

Fig. 4. Results obtained on two different quantum machines: Advantage and D-Wave 2000Q. Graph representations (A) and (C) show the QUBO graphs of the same instance for the two experiments, while qubit graphs (B) and (D) show the result of the embedding process from the QUBO according to the topology of the Advantage machine (Pegasus) and the 2000Q machine (Chimera), respectively. The 3SAT instance has 4 variables and 6 clauses. After transforming the instance to a MIS instance, the problem has 18 variables in the QUBO (3 variables and 6 clauses). We can see the importance of topology: the more recent machine (Advantage) requires 31 qubits (B), while the previous generation (2000Q) needs 61 (D).

Analyzing the results in Table 2, we observed some surprising outcomes. For an annealing time of $\{0.5, 1, 10\}$, the machine allows the execution of 7000 anneals for these three cases, and the number of optimal solutions obtained is higher with a shorter annealing time ($0.5\mu s$) compared to the longest ($10\mu s$) of the three. Since an adiabatic process is related to a system remaining in its state (here: the ground state) by giving slow enough perturbations, we would expect that a longer annealing time would help to stay in the ground state (i.e., give the optimal solution after measurement). However, for these experiments, the *Chain Breaks Rate* reported in Table 2 shows that the machine had more difficulties keeping qubits coupled with the shortest and longest annealing time.

Finally, we conducted experiments to solve small 3SAT literature instances. We tested the 20 variables and 90 clauses of [6]. Although the set of 270 vertices of the MIS graph we obtained from these instances seems small compared to the 5616 qubits available in the Advantage machine, no embedding was found by the machine for any of these instances.

6   Conclusion

In this work, the 3SAT problem is tackled using an analog quantum computer from D-Wave, employing a polynomial-time reduction to the MIS. The aim of this resolution scheme is to generate a QUBO that is easier to map to the qubit graph. This mapping, known as "embedding" is time-consuming due to the static topologies of the qubit graph. When a 3SAT problem instance is reduced to an MIS instance, the embedding seems to have fewer difficulties finding a QUBO mapping, as the degree of the related MIS graph is smaller compared to a direct transformation from a 3SAT instance to a QUBO. The vertex degree is directly linked to the occurrences of the related variables and their negations. Experiments suggest that using such polynomial-time reductions, typically employed in complexity theory, increases the likelihood of solving a 3SAT instance. However, the static topology of D-Wave machines presents challenges not only in terms of degree but also in terms of the topology itself (e.g., a chain of vertices does not necessarily have a corresponding chain in the qubits graph).

Two projects seem to emerge for future work. First, the resolution of combinatorial optimization problems for which a polynomial-time reduction to the MIS exists should be studied, as this problem yields a QUBO that quantum machines can handle relatively easily (e.g., clique, coloring, and cover problems).

Second, other analog computers already exist, and more will be released in the coming years. For example, Pasqal machines also take a QUBO as input but do not have a static topology. It could be interesting to generate benchmarks on both machines based on the resolution scheme presented in this paper.

References

1. Born, M., Fock, V.: Beweis des adiabatensatzes. Zeitschrift für Phys. **51**(3–4), 165–180 (1928)
2. Brailsford, S.C., Potts, C.N., Smith, B.M.: Constraint satisfaction problems: algorithms and applications. Eur. J. Oper. Res. **119**(3), 557–581 (1999)
3. Garey, M.R., Johnson, D.S.: "strong"np-completeness results: motivation, examples, and implications. J. ACM (JACM) **25**(3), 499–508 (1978)
4. Glover, F., Kochenberger, G., Hennig, R., Du, Y.: Quantum bridge analytics i: a tutorial on formulating and using QUBO models. Ann. Oper. Res. **314**(1), 141–183 (2022)

5. Goddard, W., Henning, M.A.: Independent domination in graphs: a survey and recent results. Discrete Math. **313**(7), 839–854 (2013)
6. Hoos, H.H., Stützle, T.: SATLIB: an online resource for research on SAT. Sat **2000**, 283–292 (2000)
7. Kadowaki, T., Nishimori, H.: Quantum annealing in the transverse Ising model. Phys. Rev. E **58**(5), 5355 (1998)
8. Karp, R.M.: Reducibility among combinatorial problems, complexity of computer computations. In: proceedings of Symposium, IBM Thomas, J.W., Research Center, Yorktown Heights, NY, 1972, vol. MR 378476, no. 51, pp. 14644 (1972)
9. Kirkpatrick, S., Gelatt, C.D., Jr., Vecchi, M.P.: Optimization by simulated annealing. Science **220**(4598), 671–680 (1983)
10. Lucas, A.: Ising formulations of many np problems. Front. Phys. **2**, 5 (2014)

Information Retrieval Using Domain Adapted Language Models: Application to Resume Documents for HR Recruitment Assistance

Zakaria Bouhoun[✉], Theo Guerrois, Xianli Li, Mouna Baker,
Nassara Elhadji Ille Gado, Emir Roumili, Francesco Vitillo,
Lies Benmiloud Bechet, and Robert Plana

Assystem EOS, Courbevoie, France
{zbouhoun,tguerrois,xli,mbaker,nelhadji,eroumili,fvitillo,
lbenmiloud,rplana}@assystem.com
https://www.assystem.com

Abstract. To attract and hire the most talented candidate who fit a company's requirements and have the potential to drive its growth, HR professionals spend a significant amount of time sourcing candidates, reviewing their resumes, and assessing their experiences against the needs of open positions. However, with the rise of online recruitment, this process has become increasingly challenging to manage manually. Therefore, job-resume matching has emerged as a crucial technique to automate and streamline the recruitment process. By leveraging machine learning algorithms, job-resume matching allows recruiters to quickly identify the most qualified candidates by comparing their skills and experiences with the requirements of vacant positions. The challenge today is to develop an approach that can effectively encode the semantic meaning of textual information in job descriptions and candidate resumes. In this paper, we propose a novel approach that combines TSDAE and BERT models to create more specialized sentence embeddings for HR data. This approach is powered by clean data extracted using a dedicated CV parsing tool. We also present two methods to automatically create labelled data for training the model. The benchmark of our method against real data shows an improvement of up to 11 points compared to the baseline model without TSDAE, highlighting the effectiveness of our proposed approach.

Keywords: text embedding · job-resume matching · model domain adaptation

1 Introduction

Skills management is a strong strategic stake for all companies. It brings a powerful competitive and economic advantage. In recent years, companies have adopted new recruitment methods to adapt to technological and social changes.

O. Gervasi et al. (Eds.): ICCSA 2023 Workshops, LNCS 14104, pp. 440–457, 2023.
https://doi.org/10.1007/978-3-031-37105-9_30

Online tools, such as professional social networks and online recruitment platforms, have gradually replaced traditional methods, such as newspaper advertising and recruitment agencies.

Today HR (Human Resources) teams often work on time-consuming tasks such as sourcing on social networks or the empirical construction of skills maps, taking time away from more value-added tasks such as the relational and recruitment strategy. The search for CVs (Curriculum Vitae) also concerns sales representatives who must build up files in response to calls for tender. However, this task must often be carried out in a hurry in view of the required response time. In the digital age era, turning to data science solutions is a necessary approach to improve productivity of human resources management.

In this context, Assystem, an industrial consulting company focused on energy (especially nuclear) and digital transition, developed an application called Emoby which is supported by artificial intelligence. Emoby offers a new approach to human resources management and the possibility of cross-referencing internal and external sources of information to define and anticipate customer's technical needs, better allocate resources, forecast tomorrow's jobs, and identify development opportunities. The tool is based on the analysis of data such as CVs, skills maps and job descriptions. Emoby uses the CV matching which is a technology that allows to find the most relevant profile(s) for an expressed need. This feature uses machine learning techniques to identify the most likely matches by comparing the skills and experiences of candidates, which are in resumes, with the requirements of vacant positions which are in job descriptions. It helps automating and speeding up the recruiting process, reducing the time and resources needed to manually go through hundreds of resumes. The goal is to find the candidates who have the most suitable profile for a given position, to facilitate the selection process for employers.

The Emoby matching algorithm was initially developed using the TF-IDF (Term Frequency-Inverse Document Frequency) method followed by LSI (Latent Semantic Indexing) [8]. TF-IDF is a widely used technique in information retrieval that determines the most important words or phrases in a corpus of documents and ranks documents based on their relevance to a given query. While TF-IDF has many advantages, it suffers from some significant drawbacks, such as sparsity, which makes the matrix computation expensive. Furthermore, it does not incorporate semantic information, which is critical for high-quality matching.

To address the sparsity issue, we employed LSI, which is a dimensionality reduction technique that can group together terms with similar meanings and provide a more compact representation of the data. Additionally, LSI can help to incorporate semantic information into TF-IDF and improve the quality of the matching process. However, the TF-IDF followed by LSI approach still suffers from important problems such as language dependence, vocabulary limitation, and the cost of adding new documents. As an international company, Assystem receives CVs from various countries, for example those written in French, English, and Russian, etc. In this case, TF-IDF creates different representations for each language, even if the words have the same meaning. Additionally, since

Assystem works in various sectors, such as nuclear, defense, building, rail, and others, a large TF-IDF matrix with a high number of columns is required to capture the vocabulary from various industries and languages. This large TF-IDF matrix becomes prohibitively expensive and unsuitable for adding new CVs frequently.

To overcome the limitations of the previous matching algorithm, advanced embedding techniques such as CNN (Convolutional Neural Network) [22], BERT (Bidirectional Encoder Representations from Transformers) [1], and Sentence BERT (SBERT) [11] models have been proposed. These techniques allow for accurate capturing of the semantic and contextual meaning of CVs. Additionally, GNN (graph neural network) approaches [19,21] can be combined with embedding techniques to represent the hiring history and interactions between candidates and recruiters.

However, the implementation of these advanced techniques requires certain considerations:

- A sufficient amount of high-quality labeled data is needed to train the models. Obtaining labeled data can be a challenging and time-consuming process, especially in the case of multilingual and multi-sector recruitment.
- Accurate extraction of text from resumes regardless of the structure, the language, or the format of the resume is crucial for effective matching. This may require preprocessing techniques such as OCR (optical character recognition) and NLP (natural language processing) to ensure that the data is in a suitable format for the models.
- Using more specialized models for the HR domain may be necessary to achieve optimal results. These models would need to be adapted on HR specific data to better capture the nuances of the industry and improve the accuracy of the matching process.

To address the challenges faced by current resume matching algorithms, we propose a novel approach that leverages the SBERT model [15] for generating embeddings. Our approach aims to optimize the use of SBERT by applying a technique called TSDAE (Transformer-based Sequential Denoising Auto-Encoder) [17] to enable the model to adapt to various sectors of candidates and accurately capture the semantic meaning of resumes. In addition, we recognize the importance of high-quality data preparation in achieving better results. Thus, we utilize a specialized resume parser that can accurately extract text from resumes, ensuring that our model is trained on clean and reliable data. To further improve our approach, we also introduce a method for automatically generating additional training data for the model. By doing so, we increase the amount of labeled data available for training, which can be particularly valuable in scenarios where obtaining labeled data is a challenging and time-consuming process. Our proposed approach shows promising results in overcoming the limitations of traditional resume matching algorithms and improving the accuracy of candidate selection in recruitment processes. The architecture of our proposed approach is illustrated in Fig. 1 below.

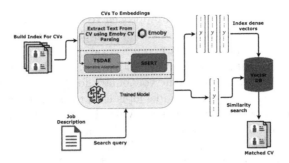

Fig. 1. The overall architecture of our proposed approach

2   Related Works

The task of matching resumes and job descriptions has been the subject of extensive research in recent years. With the increasing number of job postings and job seekers, it has become crucial to find the most suitable candidate for each job offer quickly and efficiently. Various approaches have been proposed to address this challenge, with the common goal of utilizing effective encoding methods to represent the information contained in resumes and job descriptions in a structured and meaningful way, enabling efficient and accurate comparison.

In this section, we will underline the related literature in this research area and discuss the different techniques and algorithms that have been proposed to assist HR in the hiring process. A well-known approach to represent textual data is TF-IDF. [16] suggest clustering resumes into different categories corresponding to different domains of expertise, and then uses a TF-IDF method to represent the text extracted in each resume. The TF-IDF of a resume is then used for two different tasks: binary classification of the resume (accepted, rejected) using models such as Random Forest [2], and ranking using the cosine similarity score. In [13], the same approach based on TF-IDF is used in combination with other features extracted from the resume and JD (job description) including words count, skills, years of experience, spelling errors, and document layout feature. Based on these features, two models are built, one to perform a binary classification (accepted/rejected) and the second for CV ranking using a weighted score function across all features. The approach proposed by [18] is also based on TF-IDF for text representation but applied separately to each section part, including experience, core skills, skill keywords and activity keywords, which means that a CV will not be represented by a single TF-IDF matrix, but by several TF-IDF matrices. To calculate the final ranking, a matching score between each section and the job description is first calculated and then the average of these scores is considered as the final score. To help users find more precise results, the approach in [18] go further and used a Knowledge Graph constructed from relevant information extracted from CV and JD using a NER (Named-entity recognition) based on a fine-tuned BERT model [3] on HR data using the MLM (Masked Language Model) task. In the same objective of building an efficient representation of the CV and JD, [22] proposes an approach to create text embedding using CNN models. The system consists of two stages: Candidate Retrieval that uses a fused embedding strategy to learn representations from CV texts, job skill information graphs and geolocation for candidates and JDs. For this purpose, a CNN model fed by a domain-specific vocabulary for human resources provided by the word2vec (word to vector) model [5] is used to train the embeddings. The second stage, named Reranking, uses a FAISS (Facebook AI Similarity Search) [10] index for clustering and compressing the embeddings, which also allows searching for the closest candidates in real time.

A new approach is proposed in [21] based on GNN. The algorithm consists of constructing a dual-perspective interaction graph that incorporates two different nodes for each candidate (or job): one captures a candidate's preferences for selecting a job and the other captures an employer's preferences for selecting a candidate. Thus, this dual perspective graph approach allows for the modelling of two-way selection intentions. In [19], the authors propose a new method that uses co-attention neural networks in conjunction with GNNs to create semantic representations of candidate profiles and recruitment history. To achieve full semantic representations of both resumes and job postings, they utilize mashRNN (Multi-depth Attention-based Hierarchical Recurrent Neural Network) [9], which extracts data from various structural levels of the documents. The co-attention neural networks are then used to assess the semantic similarity between resumes and job postings. Additionally, GNNs are utilized to generate representations of previous hiring experiences and integrate them into the matching calculation between candidates and job vacancies. Another approach that combined neural networks and GNN is proposed by [1]. The authors used a text matching model based on a pre-trained BERT to obtain a textual representation of resumes and JDs. They also built a relation-based matching model that uses a GNN to learn node representations based on a JD-CV historical matching. The proposed approach also uses a co-teaching mechanism to reduce noise in the training data and improve the model's capability to learn from limited or sparse interaction data.

In [11], the authors presented a new approach of resume matching based on SBERT (Sentence BERT) model. The SBERT has been established as a state-of-the-art model for producing high-quality embeddings that perform extremely well on various natural language processing tasks, including semantic textual similarity and re-ranking tasks [14]. The authors in [11] fine-tuned a multilingual BERT model using the Siamese networks on labelled data extracted from their HR solution. The authors also performed a comparative analysis of the embeddings generated by the TF-IDF, BERT and the fine-tuned SBERT model, using identical data from the HR solution, and the results demonstrated a better performance of the fine-tuned SBERT approach.

3   Contributions

This section highlights the main contributions made during the research work conducted. These contributions include text extraction using a resume parser, the creation of datasets, and the adaptation and training of the model domain. These efforts were essential to the success of the project and are detailed below.

3.1   Text Extraction Using a Resume Parser

To produce meaningful insights and accurate predictions in data science projects, it is essential to prepare and produce a high-quality dataset. A good dataset should be representative of the target population, complete, accurate, and unbiased. Preparing such a dataset is often a complex and challenging process, requiring data scientists to employ various techniques to preprocess and standardize the data.

In our case, the resumes are stored in various file formats, including PDF, DOCX, and image files. This diversity in file types can complicate the process of extracting and analyzing the data, as each format requires a different approach for data extraction. Additionally, each candidate's CV is unique in terms of the domain they have worked in, the language they use, and the overall structure of their document. Therefore, before any analysis can be performed on the CVs, a pre-processing step is required to standardize the data and ensure that it is ready for analysis. This process may include steps such as layout analysis, text recognition and extraction, and entity recognition.

The first stage of the proposed solution is based on the DiT (Document Image Transformer) model [12] which is the first model trained on a large amount of unlabeled text documents. This approach is crucial in the field of document AI due to the time-consuming task of annotating documents and the limited availability of annotated data compared to the wide variety of documents such as CVs, invoices, and articles. The DiT model is considered as document model (similar to language models in the NLP domain) ready to be used as a backbone to feed other models that can perform various tasks, such as document classification or layout analysis. In this project, we used the DiT model as a backbone to extract informative features from CVs, which were then utilized to fine-tune Mask R-CNN (Mask Region-Based Convolutional Neural Networks) [6] as a detection framework on annotated CV data to perform segmentation tasks.

After detecting the sections in the CV, the task of assigning labels to each section is performed through a classification process. Given the visually rich nature of CVs with different layouts and text fonts, a multi-model approach is adopted to leverage both linguistic and spatial features. The commonly used LayoutLM (Layout Language Model) [20] model, inspired by BERT architecture, is ideal for this purpose. LayoutLM incorporates spatial information and visual embeddings to enhance text classification and information extraction tasks. Furthermore, LayoutLM is trained on a significant amount of unlabeled raw documents using a self-supervised approach that enables the model to learn language and layout representations without requiring annotated data. In the second stage for the Emoby CV Parsing, we fine-tune the LayoutLM model on the task of section classification, taking advantage of the text features and spatial features to improve classification accuracy.

We evaluated the performance of the first stage of our system on a test set comprising CVs with varying structures from easy to complex, and it showed a score of 86% of MAP (Mean Average Precision). For the second stage related to section classification, we achieved an F1-Score of 90% for the most important sections, such as Experience, Professional summary, and Personal Information. Additionally, we achieved F1-scores of 85% for Education and 80% for Skills. These promising results encourage us to further develop our approach by incorporating more data, refining the system architecture, and expanding the scope of the project to improve system performance.

3.2   Dataset Creation

According to the official Huggingface explanation [4], to train a sentence transformer model, it is essential to understand how to introduce data into the model and prepare the dataset according to our needs. Furthermore, each configuration has a loss function related to the construction of the dataset. Indeed, there are four general forms to describe different database structures. These also differ according to the purpose and use of artificial intelligence.

Thus, we find:

1. Pairs of sentences with a similarity score for each, from 0 for a contradiction to 2 for an implication.
2. A dataset of similar sentences pairs without similarity score.
3. A dataset of sentences having a discrete score indicating the class to which the sentence belongs.
4. A dataset constructed as triplets (anchor sentence, similar sentence, dissimilar sentence) with no classification nor score.

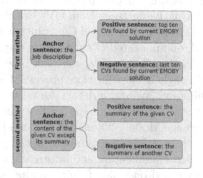

Fig. 2. Dataset structure of our two methods

The present study presents a visual representation of the final dataset structures for each method implemented, as illustrated in Fig. 2. The initial approach involves utilizing the structure proposed by Huggingface, where the job description serves as the anchor sentence, the top ten CVs identified by the current Emoby solution serve as positive sentences, and the last ten CVs identified serve as negative sentences. The second approach entails generating analogous pairs of sentences comprising the contents of a provided CV, except for the summary section and the actual summary. The summary of an alternative CV serves as the negative sentence in this method. Figure 2 demonstrates in a clearer way the final dataset structure of each implemented method in this paper.

During training, positive and negative samples are commonly utilized to enhance the model's ability to comprehend the similarity between different sentences. Positive samples are sentences that are similar to each other, whereas negative samples are dissimilar sentences. Hard negative samples are samples that are challenging for the model to classify correctly, resulting in a significant loss during the training process. Consequently, they are particularly beneficial for accelerating convergence and improving the model's ability to learn the decision boundary. In information retrieval tasks, positive samples are predefined, whereas negative samples can be extracted more easily.

One approach to improve the performance of an existing solution (Emoby) is to use TF-IDF+LSI to retrieve relevant resumes, where the top ten retrieved resumes are considered positive samples, and the last ten resumes in the rank are regarded as hard negative samples. Such dataset structure matches the last case above: we form a dataset of triplets (anchor sentence, similar sentence, dissimilar sentence) with no classification nor score.

In scenarios where similar sentence pairs exist, the summary of a particular resume is utilized as a positive sentence, while negative samples are randomly chosen from the summaries of other resumes. These data structures correspond to various cases of triplets or pairs without classification or similarity score.

The creation of a dataset faces several challenges to overcome or at least to consider. One of the primary challenges is understanding and identifying the relevant information from resumes, which can vary in organization and structure depending on who is writing them. In fact, capturing the correct information, therefore, becomes complicated. To address this challenge, we are using the CV parsing solution describe in Sect. 3.1 that meets our needs.

Another challenge is in the lexical field used. This is specific to the nuclear energy sector. That means some terms may be redundant, so it is necessary to understand the CVs correctly, in order to be sure that the contexts are well affiliated with the right situations. Another challenge is the variation in language structures and grammatical rules across languages. For example, some languages have more complex grammar structures than others, or use different scripts or writing systems.

Moreover, it is important to ensure that there is no gender or language favoritism. This challenge is very important as this could lead to unfair representation of candidates. As French words are involved, adjectives and other words should not influence models. Parity is created to avoid any favoritism.

To represent candidates fairly, the model needs to learn with data from both genders.

One of the key challenges in matching resumes and job descriptions is dealing with multilingual data. Models must be able to handle this variety of languages. To better take this into account, multilingual models are used and amounts of high-quality data in each language are collected. The Assystem job search website includes resumes in French, English, Arabic, etc. The fact that we only use data from our sites is related to the next challenge.

The GDPR (General Data Protection Regulation) is a set of regulations that aim to protect the personal data of individuals in the EU (European Union). As they contain personal data, the consent from the individual is needed. To ensure the security of data, they are collected and analyzed with internally made solutions.

Dataset Based on the Emoby Solution. The first method involves 800 sets of [queries, positives, negatives], in which job descriptions (queries) are paired with information from resumes (positives, negatives). In fact, CVs that are identified as "positive" i.e., they correspond to desired characteristics involved in the field of work, are used as sentences and contexts that match job descriptions. The ones chosen as "negative" i.e., they do not apply to the job, are used to fine-tuned and exclude fields that are not linked to job descriptions. The following format is used:

'query': description of the job, 'positive': List[resume], 'negative': List[resume]

In [4], it is advisable to use TripletLoss for this type of architecture. This is a popular loss function used in tasks that involve learning a similarity metric between triplets of inputs. This loss function encourages the model to learn embeddings that group together similar examples and separate dissimilar examples. The TripletLoss function tries to minimize the distance between the anchor and positive examples while maximizing the distance between the anchor and negative examples.

To train different implemented models, a dataset needs to be built. CVs and vacancies must be collected automatically and quickly.

To achieve this, Emoby, a deployed instance with more than 50 000 active users, is used. This functional version of Emoby is based on the TF-IDF+LSI algorithm which, in addition to matching, will calculate a percentage of correspondence between the CVs found and the job descriptions entered by an HR user. This score will be used to be sure that CV match more than the threshold fixed. The intensive use of the algorithm that sits within the software, i.e., the processes of experts in the field of HR, provides us with solid elements on which to base our increase in data of interest for our training.

Our Human Resources provide job description to be sure that the query suits our nuclear field of work. A pipeline is created to collect resume. It will automatically select a JD, remove special character in the text, do the research in the Emoby database, collect the required CVs, and put them in the right field.

To see if the data collected are relevant. Once all CVs and their matching scores have been retrieved, Fig. 3 emerge from these data. graphics have been made. They represent the distribution of the positive and negative matching scores. To improve the visibility of graphics, each color represents a score of matching. The percentage of scores obtained after data collection is marked for each color. For example, the green color in the Fig. 3 indicate that 14.5% of CV match a JD with a score of 84.

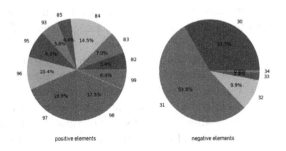

Fig. 3. Distribution of the matching score for all positive and negative items

A confidence interval appears and allows to view the distribution of the data obtained with Emoby. Positive scores are all above 81% of matching i.e., the similarity scores generated for the pairwise JD/resume is high, so similar words are found in both documents. Negative ones do not exceed 34% of matching i.e., the lexicon of the documents is quite disparate

Dataset Based on the CV and Its Summary. Different from the first method based on the correspondence between a job description and a CV, for the second method, we would like to build a dataset taking advantage of the very nature of the CV. We noticed that most resumes contain a summary resuming the experience and education of the given candidate, which reforms a candidate's most valuable qualities differently and accurately. This very nature of a CV summary makes it a positive sentence to the given resume. Thus, during training, our model will consider one's CV and the summary as two sentences having the same meaning. The output model could focus better on the resemblance between a job description and a CV. Since we can't know the similarity score between the CV and its summary, the second configuration, a dataset of similar sentences pairs, is the most suitable option.

It is recommended to use MultipleNegativesRankingLoss [7], one of the most recommended loss functions for datasets consisting of positive pairs. In the case of the second method, the content of a given CV except its summary and the summary form a pair. This loss function takes sentence pairs as input, while summaries related to other summaries are considered as negative samples. It is also possible to determine one or multiple hard negative samples per pair to improve the model's performance.

In contrast to the first method, the second method is independent of the current Emoby solution and involves the acquisition of CVs from the Assystem job search website to supplement the training dataset. However, this approach presents certain challenges as the dataset includes a mixture of cover letters, references, job descriptions, and resumes. Due to the presence of extraneous data, it is imperative to conduct pre-processing of the CV to eliminate irrelevant information before the training process.

To retrieve and classify different sections present in a resume, we use CV parsing, the tool presented in Sect. 3.1. Based on its output, we have identified different types of content, such as education, experience, skills, and personal information etc.

First, we should identify the main characteristics of a resume and how they differ from other types of documents, such as a cover letter and certification. After observing the CV parsing results, we found several missing parts in non-resume documents, especially "education" or "experience", which are the two most valuable content in resumes. The absence of these two allows us not only to remove most cover letters and certifications, but also to filter out resumes that lack these essential elements of education. Also, if the summary is less than 30 words, then it does not contain enough information for training, and we will not consider this CV.

Also, this solution does not preserve a specific tree structure compared to the previous one. Thanks to CV parsing, we managed to identify different content in the CV. We also ranked them based on their importance in recruiting. The reason behind this action is that BERT-based Transformers [3] have tokens limitation, which means a BERT-based model can only take a max length limit of 512 tokens, in case having a long CV and important information gets cut out, we put the important ones like education and experience in the beginning.

Each category is assigned with a weight and priority. So here is the order of priority: firstly, the personal information of the candidates containing their address ranks top to match the most suitable candidates in mobility. Then their project and experience. Their skills, language, and education/certifications rank third. Additionally, this filtering for empty or missing categories can clean up databases of certificates, cover letters, or job descriptions.

In the end, the constructed dataset contains around 9000 CVs, which is useful and usable information for the training of TSDAE and SBERT model.

3.3 Model Domain Adaptation

In this paper, our primary method for matching job descriptions and CVs is using TSDAE as a pre-trained algorithm to improve SBERT models, which has shown superior performance for domain adaptation compared to classical pre-training tasks such as Mask Language Model.

During the pretraining, TSDAE damages the input data by randomly deleting around 60% of tokens as the input noise. The encoder generates fixed-sized vectors, and the decoder tries to reconstruct the original sentences. During the process, the TSDAE model captured well the semantics of input data.

One notable advantage of TSDAE is its ability to function without the need for enormous amounts of labelled data, which are often scarce and costly. Being an unsupervised method, it can discover hidden patterns or groups within the data that may not be immediately apparent. Additionally, these algorithms can adapt to new data or different application domains without requiring a complete retraining of the model, which is particularly important for our constantly evolving CV database.

Furthermore, the introduction of noise with this method can aid in better understanding the CVs. By training the model to reconstruct a corpus, it can account for typographical errors, leading to a better comprehension of the context and situations contained within the data.

As per the TSDAE paper, fine-tuned models are deemed inadequate for TSDAE implementation due to their pre-adaptation to specific sentence embedding tasks. Instead, the recommendation is to use a pre-trained language model, notably the BERT-base-uncased model, which has been proven to achieve superior results. To cater to the linguistic diversity of our CV dataset, which includes English, French, and Arabic, we employed the BERT-base-multilingual-uncased model in the first method. Given the significantly larger size of the dataset in the second method, the use of a BERT-base-uncased model, which is too large to achieve optimal performance, was not viable. Instead, we opted for the second-best pre-trained model, namely the Distil-BERT-base-multilingual-cased model, to effectuate the second method.

As previously mentioned, the SBERT model was fine-tuned using Triplet-Loss in the first method, while MultipleNegativesRankingLoss was used in the second method. However, it is worthwhile to investigate whether TripletLoss can yield superior results in the second method and whether MultipleNegativesRankingLoss can be more effective in the first method. To evaluate the performance of the two pre-trained models under different training loss functions, we fine-tuned them with both MultipleNegativesRankingLoss and TripletLoss based on TSDAE. In addition, to demonstrate the effectiveness of TSDAE, we also fine-tuned two models without utilizing TSDAE.

After completing the stage of fine-tuning, it is imperative to properly evaluate our model through the application of appropriate metrics and methods. A plethora of evaluators for various natural language processing tasks are provided by the sentence transformers package.

When employing TripletLoss in the fine-tuning process, which optimizes the distance between embeddings in the vectorial space, it is advisable to utilize the TripletEvaluator. This evaluator calculates the distance between the embedding of the anchor sentence and those of both the positive and negative sentences. The resulting accuracy is determined by computing the percentage of instances where the distance between the anchor and positive sentence is smaller than the distance between the anchor and negative sentence.

We utilize the RerankingEvaluator for the MultipleNegativesRankingLoss, which optimizes using similarity functions like cosine similarity. This evaluator reorders the mixed list of positive and negative sentences based on the cosine similarity score. The metrics used for evaluation are MAP and MRR@10 (Mean Reciprocal Rank).

MAP considers the number of correct predictions and assigns varying degrees of importance to these predictions. To achieve a higher score, a greater number of correct predictions are required, with greater emphasis placed on the accuracy of the most important predictions. For instance, if we assume that the right prediction is denoted by 1 and a wrong prediction is denoted by 0, then the sequence [1, 1, 1, 0, 0] would receive a superior score of MAP to [1, 0, 1, 0, 1], despite both having an identical number of good predictions.

MRR@10, on the other hand, estimates the likelihood of the first correct prediction being ranked within the number specified after the "@" symbol, in this case, the top ten positions. In this study, only MRR@10 was utilized to evaluate the performance of the models. Therefore, in the subsequent sections of this paper, the term MRR will specifically denote MRR@10.

Results for the First Method. To display results, both loss functions are modified to include wandb (Weights and Biases[1]). This is a platform for developers to track experiments and visualize results. Thanks to it, hyperparameters are easily tracked at each epoch, and the accuracy of the model can be recorded. This enables the model to be adapted by adjusting the parameters in response to the captured accuracy data.

Firstly, a dataset to train the TSDAE model needs to be built in line with the first method. Two datasets are constructed, an unlabeled one to train the model and the other, built by Human Resources, is a "golden" dataset to test the model.

Table 1. Metrics of model MRR and MAP on validation data (200 elements).

Model Name	TSDAE	loss function	MAP	MRR
BERT-base-multilingual	No	MultipleNegativesRankingLoss	0.85	0.91
BERT-base-multilingual	No	TripletLoss	0.89	0.92
BERT-base-multilingual	**Yes**	**MultipleNegativesRankingLoss**	**0.93**	**0.98**
BERT-base-multilingual	Yes	TripletLoss	0.90	0.97

To monitor and measure the performance of models in a reranking task, the benchmark [23] used two metrics, MAP and MRR, which are usually employed to evaluate performance of the models on their evaluation dataset and the golden dataset.

As a reminder, all four models are trained with the same dataset. Overall, incorporating a TSDAE step resulted in an increase in accuracy, despite the limited size of the database, which consisted of only 800 unlabeled samples.

---

[1] https://wandb.ai/site.

However, this small dataset may have a double-edged effect on the outcomes. On the one hand, the addition of a TSDAE layer significantly improved the quality of the embeddings, but on the other hand, the insufficient number of samples could lead to overfitting of the model due to a certain lack of diversity. The database should represent most of the possible cases, so the database created by HR and the validation dataset will show if the model has truly understood the data and if it is applicable on real data.

Table 1 presents the results of the metric on the validation set, which indicate that the MAP (mean average precision) value is greater for the model incorporating TSDAE in comparison to the one without the addition of the layer. Specifically, the MAP value improved from 0.89 for the model without TSDAE to 0.93 for the model with TSDAE. This finding indicates that the model incorporating TSDAE can identify a higher number of relevant CVs for each job description in comparison to the model without TSDAE. Additionally, the MRR value is also higher for the model with TSDAE on the validation set, increasing from 0.92 to 0.98. In the context of reranking tasks, MRR is the average of the reciprocal of the rank of the first relevant result across all queries. Therefore, the improved MRR value for the model with TSDAE indicates that relevant CVs are also graded better since they appear higher up in the list of results.

Using the same evaluation metric, the Human Resources provided dataset was utilized to evaluate the performance of the models. This dataset consisted of manually selected candidates that matched or did not correspond to the job descriptions, representing real cases. However, the dataset only contained around 40 items, which limits our ability to identify trends or make definitive assertions regarding the model's performance. While the quality of the dataset's construction may provide insight into the models' real-world performance, the small sample size does not necessarily enable us to draw conclusions or detect trends that the models may capture.

Table 2. Metrics MAP and MRR on 'golden' dataset.

Model Name	TSDAE	loss function	MAP	MRR
BERT-base-multilingual	No	MultipleNegativesRankingLoss	0.83	0.81
BERT-base-multilingual	No	TripletLoss	0.86	0.88
BERT-base-multilingual	**Yes**	**MultipleNegativesRankingLoss**	**0.89**	**0.91**
BERT-base-multilingual	Yes	TripletLoss	0.85	0.91

As we can see in Table 2, the TSDAE pre-trained model with MultipleNegativesRankingLoss has a better outcome on data that the model had never seen before, i.e., the "golden" dataset. MAP and MRR increased by 0.03 and 0.03 respectively compared to the model without the introduction of a TSDAE model.

In both distinct datasets, the incorporation of TSDAE in the model architecture resulted in a significant improvement in performance. This improvement can be attributed to the model's ability to more accurately capture important features and relationships between words or sentences. This enhanced capability of the model is particularly valuable since the database used in the study was created by HR professionals and represents real cases of individuals who have undergone a recruitment process.

Result for the Second Method. The second method of the study implements two different training loss functions to compare their respective performances. Specifically, the study evaluates the efficacy of MultipleNegativesRankingLoss and TripletLoss in training a model. To evaluate the effectiveness of each loss function in training the model, the study uses two different evaluators. The RerankingEvaluator is utilized to evaluate the ranking quality of the documents retrieved when MultipleNegativesRankingLoss is employed. On the other hand, TripletEvaluator is employed to evaluate the quality of the learned embeddings when TripletLoss is employed.

Meanwhile, we would like to know how effective the TSDAE model is, a comparison of two training results with and without the TSDAE model is shown in Table 3 and 4. We trained two models with the same dataset containing 9000 CVs. We observed that the values of both metrics of the training with TSDAE are higher than the one without TSDAE.

Table 3. Comparison of two MultipleNegativesRankingLoss training results evaluated on validation dataset with and without TSDAE, using RerankingEvaluator.

Model Name	TSDAE	loss function	MAP	MRR
DistilBERT-base-multilingual	No	MultipleNegativesRankingLoss	0.74	0.74
DistilBERT-base-multilingual	**Yes**	**MultipleNegativesRankingLoss**	**0.79**	**0.78**

Table 4. Comparison of two TripletLoss training results evaluated on validation dataset with and without TSDAE, using TripletEvaluator.

Model Name	TSDAE	loss function	Mean accuracy
DistilBERT-base-multilingual	No	TripletLoss	0.91
DistilBERT-base-multilingual	**Yes**	**TripletLoss**	**0.92**

It is evident that utilizing TSDAE as a pre-training method yields improved performance of the model upon completion of the training process. The results presented in both tables pertain to the evaluation of the model's performance on the validation dataset at the conclusion of the training phase. However, it is crucial to ascertain the model's efficacy on the previously mentioned 'golden' dataset. The outcomes of such evaluations are as follows (Table 5):

Table 5. Metrics MAP and MRR on 'golden' dataset.

Model Name	TSDAE	loss function	MAP	MRR
DistilBERT-base-multilingual	No	MultipleNegativesRankingLoss	0.75	0.83
DistilBERT-base-multilingual	No	TripletLoss	0.81	0.90
DistilBERT-base-multilingual	**Yes**	**MultipleNegativesRankingLoss**	**0.86**	**0.95**
DistilBERT-base-multilingual	Yes	TripletLoss	0.84	0.90

The present study investigates the impact of pre-training method, TSDAE, on the performance of fine-tuned models using TripletLoss and MultipleNegativesRank-ingLoss functions. Results indicate that incorporating TSDAE as pre-training method leads to a significant improvement in model performance, as evidenced by a 3-point increase in the case of TripletLoss and an 11-point increase in the case of Multi-pleNegativesRankingLoss. This finding underscores the efficacy of TSDAE in the current context. Notably, models trained with MultipleNegativesRankingLoss outperformed those trained with TripletLoss by 2 and 6 points, contingent on the utilization of TSDAE. In sum, the study concludes that TSDAE as pre-training method and MultipleNegatives-RankingLoss as training loss function led to superior model performance.

4 Conclusion

In conclusion, the introduction of TSDAE in the architecture has proven to be an asset for improving the accuracy of predictions on two distinct datasets. By allowing the model to better capture important features and relationships between words or sentences, TSDAE has demonstrated its ability to enhance the performance of natural language processing models. However, the degree of improvement observed in this study was found to be limited in comparison to the outcomes reported in the TSDAE publication. There are two main reasons for this discrepancy. Firstly, the implementation of the second method was hampered by limitations in GPU capacity, precluding the use of a BERT-based model with a large batch size that could have yielded superior results. Instead, a smaller and quicker alternative, the DistilBERT-based-multilingual-cased model, was employed. To address this issue, a more advanced GPU with higher computational capacity would be required.

Secondly, it is essential to consider the number of input elements during both the TSDAE training and fine-tuning phases. For example, for the first method, increasing the number of input elements can lead to a better accuracy, but it also brings new challenges. Moreover, all of this must be in line with the challenges found. This is particularly significant in the context of recruitment processes, where the ability to accurately predict outcomes can have a significant impact on the selection of candidates. The fact that one of the datasets used in this study was created by HR professionals and represents real cases further highlights the practical value of these findings. By incorporating TSDAE into their models, organizations can improve their recruitment processes and make better-informed decisions when selecting candidates for open positions.

References

1. Bian, S., et al.: Learning to match jobs with resumes from sparse interaction data using multi-view co-teaching network. In: Proceedings of the 29th ACM International Conference on Information & Knowledge Management, pp. 65–74 (2020)
2. Breiman, L.: Random forests. Mach. Learn. **45**, 5–32 (2001)
3. Devlin, J., Chang, M.W., Lee, K., Toutanova, K.: BERT: pre-training of deep bidirectional transformers for language understanding. arXiv preprint arXiv:1810.04805 (2018)
4. Espejel, O.: Train and fine-tune sentence transformers models (1999). https://huggingface.co/blog/how-to-train-sentence-transformers
5. Goldberg, Y., Levy, O.: Word2vec explained: deriving Mikolov et al.'s negative-sampling word-embedding method. arXiv preprint arXiv:1402.3722 (2014)
6. He, K., Gkioxari, G., Dollár, P., Girshick, R.: Mask R-CNN. In: Proceedings of the IEEE International Conference on Computer Vision, pp. 2961–2969 (2017)
7. Henderson, M., et al.: Efficient natural language response suggestion for smart reply. arXiv preprint arXiv:1705.00652 (2017)
8. Hofmann, T.: Probabilistic latent semantic indexing. In: Proceedings of the 22nd Annual International ACM SIGIR Conference on Research and Development in Information Retrieval, pp. 50–57 (1999). https://doi.org/10.1145/312624.312649
9. Jiang, J.Y., Zhang, M., Li, C., Bendersky, M., Golbandi, N., Najork, M.: Semantic text matching for long-form documents. In: The World Wide Web Conference, pp. 795–806 (2019). https://doi.org/10.1145/3308558.3313707
10. Johnson, J., Douze, M., Jégou, H.: Billion-scale similarity search with GPUs. IEEE Trans. Big Data **7**(3), 535–547 (2019). https://doi.org/10.1109/TBDATA.2019.2921572
11. Lavi, D., Medentsiy, V., Graus, D.: conSultantBERT: fine-tuned Siamese sentence-BERT for matching jobs and job seekers. arXiv preprint arXiv:2109.06501 (2021)
12. Li, J., Xu, Y., Lv, T., Cui, L., Zhang, C., Wei, F.: DiT: self-supervised pre-training for document image transformer. In: Proceedings of the 30th ACM International Conference on Multimedia, pp. 3530–3539 (2022). https://doi.org/10.1145/3503161.3547911
13. Menacer, M.A., Hamda, F.B., Mighri, G., Hamidene, S.B., Cariou, M.: An interpretable person-job fitting approach based on classification and ranking. In: Proceedings of The Fourth International Conference on Natural Language and Speech Processing (ICNLSP 2021), pp. 130–138 (2021). https://aclanthology.org/2021.icnlsp-1.15
14. Muennighoff, N., Tazi, N., Magne, L., Reimers, N.: MTEB: massive text embedding benchmark. arXiv preprint arXiv:2210.07316 (2022)
15. Reimers, N., Gurevych, I.: Sentence-BERT: sentence embeddings using Siamese BERT-networks. In: Proceedings of the 2019 Conference on Empirical Methods in Natural Language Processing. Association for Computational Linguistics (2019). https://arxiv.org/abs/1908.10084
16. Roy, P.K., Chowdhary, S.S., Bhatia, R.: A machine learning approach for automation of resume recommendation system. Procedia Comput. Sci. **167**, 2318–2327 (2020). https://doi.org/10.1016/j.procs.2020.03.284

17. Wang, K., Reimers, N., Gurevych, I.: TSDAE: using transformer-based sequential denoising auto-encoderfor unsupervised sentence embedding learning. arXiv preprint arXiv:2104.06979 (2021)
18. Wang, Y., Allouache, Y., Joubert, C.: Analysing CV corpus for finding suitable candidates using knowledge graph and BERT. In: DBKDA 2021, The Thirteenth International Conference on Advances in Databases, Knowledge, and Data Applications (2021)
19. Wang, Z., Wei, W., Xu, C., Xu, J., Mao, X.L.: Person-job fit estimation from candidate profile and related recruitment history with co-attention neural networks. Neurocomputing **501**, 14–24 (2022). https://doi.org/10.1016/j.neucom.2022.06.012
20. Xu, Y., Li, M., Cui, L., Huang, S., Wei, F., Zhou, M.: LayoutLM: pre-training of text and layout for document image understanding. In: Proceedings of the 26th ACM SIGKDD International Conference on Knowledge Discovery & Data Mining, pp. 1192–1200 (2020). https://doi.org/10.1145/3394486.3403172
21. Yang, C., Hou, Y., Song, Y., Zhang, T., Wen, J.R., Zhao, W.X.: Modeling two-way selection preference for person-job fit. In: Proceedings of the 16th ACM Conference on Recommender Systems, pp. 102–112 (2022). https://doi.org/10.1145/3523227.3546752
22. Zhao, J., et al.: Embedding-based recommender system for job to candidate matching on scale. arXiv preprint arXiv:2107.00221 (2021)
23. Zoupanos, S., Kolovos, S., Kanavos, A., Papadimitriou, O., Maragoudakis, M.: Efficient comparison of sentence embeddings. In: Proceedings of the 12th Hellenic Conference on Artificial Intelligence, pp. 1–6 (2022). https://doi.org/10.1145/3549737.3549752

Advances in Web Based Learning
(AWBL 2023)

Gamification in Inclusive Education for Children with Disabilities: Global Trends and Approaches - A Bibliometric Review

Janio Jadán-Guerrero[1] (ID), Fátima Avilés-Castillo[2] (ID), Jorge Buele[3(✉)] (ID), and Guillermo Palacios-Navarro[4] (ID)

[1] Research Center of Mechatronics and Interactive Systems-MIST, Universidad Indoamérica, Quito 170103, Ecuador
janiojadan@uti.edu.ec
[2] Centro de Investigaciones de Ciencias Humanas y de la Educación-CICHE, Universidad Indoamérica, Ambato 180103, Ecuador
faviles@indoamerica.edu.ec
[3] SISAu Research Group, Facultad de Ingeniería, Industria y Producción, Universidad Indoamérica, Ambato 180103, Ecuador
jorgebuele@indoamerica.edu.ec
[4] Department of Electronic Engineering and Communications, University of Zaragoza, 44003 Teruel, Spain
guillermo.palacios@unizar.es

Abstract. Given the growing attention to the intersection between technology and education, gamification has emerged as a strategy with great benefits. This bibliometric review addresses gamification's current and future relevance in the educational field, focusing on its use as a pedagogical strategy to improve the learning and engagement of children with disabilities. Sixty-six studies published between 2001 and 2023 were analyzed, evaluating the most influential articles, main keywords, prominent authors, collaborating institutions, and funding sources. The literature suggests that gamification offers inclusive and personalized learning opportunities covering various disabilities. Methodologies and approaches to implement gamification were identified, including game elements, user-centered design techniques, and emerging technologies such as virtual reality, artificial intelligence, and educational robotics. However, challenges and areas for improvement were also found, such as the need for more long-term empirical evidence and the importance of considering individual differences and specific needs when designing gamification strategies. The review highlights the importance of strengthening collaborative networks between researchers and education professionals to disseminate best practices and promote more effective gamification approaches adapted to the needs of children with disabilities. Collaboration between educators, game developers, researchers, and parents are crucial to ensure that gamification efforts are inclusive and meet the diverse needs of students.

Keywords: Gamification · Inclusive Education · Disabilities · Children

O. Gervasi et al. (Eds.): ICCSA 2023 Workshops, LNCS 14104, pp. 461–477, 2023.
https://doi.org/10.1007/978-3-031-37105-9_31

1 Introduction

Inclusive education is a pedagogical approach that seeks to meet the needs of all students, including those with disabilities and special needs [1, 2]. This approach considers diversity an opportunity to enrich learning and promote equity and equal opportunities in the education system [3, 4]. Attention to diversity involves developing strategies and resources that allow children with disabilities to achieve their educational goals and fully develop in their school and social environment [5].

The scientific literature has reported numerous studies on gamification in education, both in general contexts and those specific to children with disabilities. Studies have addressed various disabilities that affect children, including autism spectrum disorder (ASD) [6], attention deficit hyperactivity disorder (ADHD) [7], learning disabilities, intellectual disabilities, speech and language disorders, and sensory disabilities [8]. In the case of autism spectrum disorder, serious games and video games have been explored to improve social skills, communication, and emotional regulation. Studies have shown promising results, especially in increasing social interaction and effective communication between infants and adults [9]. For attention deficit hyperactivity disorder, gamification has been used to help children improve attention, concentration, and self-control. Educational games that include reward elements and immediate feedback effectively keep these students engaged and motivated in their tasks [10].

Children with learning disabilities, such as dyslexia or dyscalculia, have experienced improvements in their reading, writing, and math skills thanks to gamification-based pedagogical approaches, which offer a playful and personalized approach to teaching [11]. In the context of intellectual disabilities, serious games, and game-based learning environments have been used to teach cognitive and social-emotional skills. Results have shown improvements in cognitive development, adaptability, and problem-solving skills in these students [12]. Gamification has also been applied in speech and language therapies, using specific games and applications to improve articulation, fluency, and language understanding in children with speech and language disorders. Finally, for children with sensory disabilities, such as visual or hearing impairments, gamification has been adapted through assistive technologies, such as devices [13].

In this context, it is essential to explore pedagogical strategies facilitating the active participation and meaningful learning of children with disabilities. Gamification understood as the application of game elements and mechanics in non-game environments, has emerged as an effective tool to improve student motivation, commitment, and learning [14]. This pedagogical approach is beneficial in general education, but its potential in the education of children with disabilities still needs to be fully investigated [15, 16].

This article aims to review the state of the art in applying gamification in the education of children with disabilities and provide an overview of the research carried out in this field through a bibliometric analysis. In addition, it will seek to identify gaps in the existing literature, highlight future research opportunities, and provide recommendations for the effective implementation of gamification in inclusive education. Hopefully, this work will contribute to developing innovative and effective pedagogical practices that promote the learning and well-being of children with disabilities in their educational contexts.

This article consists of four sections, including the introduction in Sect. 1. The methodology is in Sect. 2, and the results are in Sect. 3. The conclusions are presented in Sect. 4.

2 Methodology

2.1 Data Extraction

Before starting to search for relevant articles, a careful selection of the search engine that best suited the needs of the study was carried out. It was decided to use Scopus as a source of information for articles published in the area of interest. The decision was based on several reasons, such as that Scopus is one of the most important and internationally recognized scientific citation indexes and has a rigorous selection process that guarantees the inclusion of high-quality and influential research. This database extensively covers prestigious journals, conference proceedings, and books in many countries. It provides useful analytical tools to comprehensively process the information, making it easy to find and select relevant documents.

2.2 Search

In inclusive education, it is essential to explore different teaching methods that can benefit children with disabilities. One of the emerging areas in this field is gamification, which refers to using game design elements in non-game contexts, such as education. This approach effectively increases student motivation and engagement and can be particularly beneficial for children with disabilities. To better understand how gamification has been applied in inclusive education, we have designed a search equation to identify scientific papers addressing this topic. This equation is divided into three main groups of terms: i) gamification and educational games, ii) children with disabilities and inclusive education, and iii) pedagogical approaches and strategies. These terms represent different approaches and applications of games in educational contexts, the most common disabilities and special needs in children, and concepts related to inclusive education and the practices and strategies used in teaching and learning.

TITLE-ABS-KEY((gamification OR "game-based learning" OR "serious games" OR "digital games" OR "video games" OR "educational games") AND ("children with disabilities" OR "special needs" OR "special education" OR "inclusive education" OR "autism spectrum disorder" OR ASD OR ADHD OR "attention deficit hyperactivity disorder" OR "learning disabilities" OR "intellectual disabilities" OR "speech and language disorders" OR "hearing impairments" OR "visual impairments" OR "physical disabilities" OR "motor disabilities") AND (pedagogical OR pedagogy OR "teaching strategies" OR "learning strategies" OR "instructional methods" OR "educational approaches")).

2.3 Research Questions

Considering the above, the main purpose of this study is to analyze the generation of scientific knowledge related to gamification as a pedagogical strategy to enhance learning and participation in children with disabilities by reviewing documents accessible in Scopus databases. To achieve this objective, several research questions have been formulated:

RQ1: How have the scientific production and citations of gamification for children with disabilities evolved over the years?

This question aims to discover the evolution of scientific production and citations related to using gamification in education for children with disabilities over time. The information obtained will allow the number of publications per year and citation trends to be determined, which will be valuable in anticipating future patterns in this area of research.

RQ2: Which are the countries with the largest number of publications on gamification for children with disabilities?

This question focuses on determining the countries that have generated the largest number of publications to identify the leaders in producing scientific knowledge in this area. In this way, it will be possible to obtain a global perspective of the geographical distribution of the research and determine its importance in different parts of the world.

RQ3: What are the most influential articles in gamification for children with disabilities?

This question seeks to identify which documents have received the highest number of citations on using gamification in education for children with disabilities. By knowing the most influential articles, valuable information can be obtained about the research methods and studies that have been successful, which will make it easier for researchers and professionals to produce high-quality work.

RQ4: What main keywords can be identified in this topic?

This question seeks to identify the most relevant key terms in the topic. This information will be helpful for researchers when searching scientific databases, allowing them to select the most appropriate terms to find relevant documents for their research.

RQ5: Which are the journals/books/proceedings with the highest number of publications and citations?

This question aims to identify the sources that researchers mostly used. This will allow them to make informed decisions about where to publish their research results.

RQ6: Who are the authors with the most publications on this topic?

This question seeks to identify authors who have published many papers. This information will allow researchers to identify the leading experts in the field and make informed decisions about whom they can collaborate with or learn from.

RQ7: Which are the institutions that carried out the most research on gamification for children with disabilities?

This question aims to discover the institutions that have carried out the greatest number of investigations on using gamification in education for children with disabilities. This way, it will be possible to know the leading institutions in researching and producing scientific knowledge in this area.

RQ8: What are the main funding agencies for gamification documents for children with disabilities?

This question offers valuable information for researchers seeking funding for their projects. It will allow them to determine which agencies have funded previous studies in this area and direct their funding search toward these institutions.

2.4 Sample Selection

To carry out this research, scientific articles that are indexed in Scopus and that contain the terms shown in Sect. 2.2 will be used. These articles will be considered the unit of analysis. For the sample selection, inclusion criteria will be applied, including the peer review of the articles, the year of publication, and the appearance of the search terms in the title, abstract, or keywords. Exclusion criteria will also apply for documents not subject to peer review, such as theses or technical reports, review papers, editorials, notes, errata, and retracted, as well as for publications in languages other than English. After applying these criteria, a sample of 66 documents was obtained for analysis. Significantly, the search was last updated on April 4, 2023, which are accessible at the following link https://github.com/faviles7/gamification.

3   Results

RQ1: How have the scientific production and citations of gamification for children with disabilities evolved over the years?

Figure 1 shows the evolution of scientific production over the last 23 years since 2001. According to the data, the number of publications has increased significantly, from three in 2009 to nine in 2020. A decrease is observed after that year, with only one publication in 2023. However, more articles on the subject may continue to be published so that the final figure could be higher.

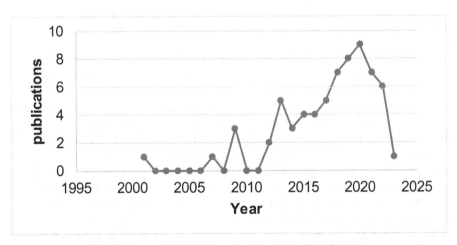

Fig. 1. Annual distribution of articles indexed by Scopus.

Citations are an important measure of the influence and impact of a scientific article in the field of research. In the case of Fig. 2, the citations have varied over the years, with a peak in 2017 (97 citations) and a constant decrease. This pattern could be due to several reasons, such as the topic's popularity at a given time, the quality of the articles published each year, or the impact of the authors and institutions in the research field. It is important to note that citations may continue to increase, as recent articles may take some time to be recognized and cited by other researchers. Therefore, although a decrease has been observed since 2020, there is still potential for the citations of these articles to continue to increase.

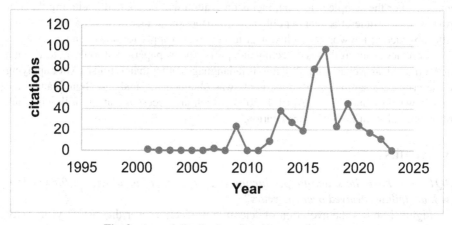

Fig. 2. Annual distribution of citations on this topic.

RQ2: Which are the countries with the largest number of publications on gamification for children with disabilities?

Figure 3 shows the countries with the largest number of publications on this topic: the United Kingdom, Spain, and Greece, with 10, 9, and 8 publications, respectively. Brazil and the United States follow closely with six publications each, and other countries such as Canada, Ecuador, France, India, and Portugal also contribute three publications each.

This geographical distribution of the publications suggests that gamification in the education of children with disabilities has been of interest in different regions, with a notable concentration in Europe. The UK and Spain have shown strong interest in this area of research, which could be related to their respective education systems and the attention they pay to the inclusion of students with disabilities in the educational process.

The bibliometric review also highlights the diversity of approaches. This wide geographical scope indicates that gamification is a pedagogical strategy with the potential to be applied in different cultural and educational contexts. This enriches its knowledge base and facilitates the exchange of experiences and good practices between researchers and education professionals worldwide.

RQ3: What are the most influential articles in gamification for children with disabilities?

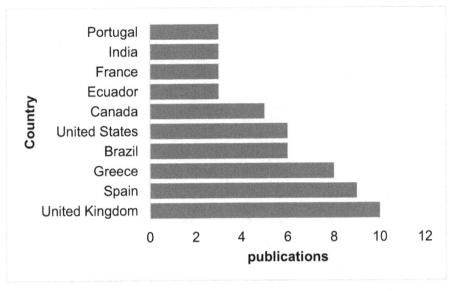

Fig. 3. Summary of the ten countries with the highest number of publications.

Table 1 presents a selection of outstanding research carried out in different countries and years and received a variable number of citations, indicating its impact on the scientific community. Notably, the two most cited studies come from the UK and focus on digital game-based learning for children with dyslexia. The study by Vasalou et al. [17] ranks first in average annual citations, with 8.32, while the study by Gooch et al. [18] ranks second, with 4.97. These works address the importance of the social constructivist approach and the motivation of students with dyslexia in the context of game-based learning.

Studies next on the list address a wide range of topics and populations, from Serious Game Design for Children with Hearing Impairments in Chile, de Cano et al. [19],

Table 1. Summary of the most influential articles.

No.	Authors	Title	Main Findings	Source	Country	Year	Citations	Average
1	Vasalou, A. et al. [17]	Digital games-based learning for children with dyslexia: A social constructivist perspective on engagement and learning during group gameplay	'Words Matter' improves social engagement, provides additional learning opportunities, and boosts self-esteem in children with dyslexia	Computers and Education	United Kingdom	2017	52	8.32 (#1)

(continued)

Table 1. (*continued*)

No.	Authors	Title	Main Findings	Source	Country	Year	Citations	Average
2	Gooch, D. et al. [18]	Using gamification to motivate students with dyslexia	Gamification, through ClassDojo, improves the motivation of students with dyslexia, thanks to the pedagogical personalization of teachers	Conference on Human Factors in Computing Systems - Proceedings	United Kingdom	2016	36	4.97 (#2)
3	Cano, S. et al. [19]	Toward a methodology for serious games design for children with auditory impairments	The MECONESIS methodology for designing serious games is effective for hearing impaired children, enhancing the learning, and gaming experience	IEEE Latin America Transactions	Chile	2016	26	3.59 (#4)
4	Serret, S. et al. [20]	Teaching literacy skills to French minimally verbal school-aged children with autism spectrum disorders with the serious game SEMA-TIC: An exploratory study	The SEMA-TIC serious game significantly improves literacy skills in French children with minimally verbal ASD	Frontiers in Psychology	France	2017	21	3.36 (#5)
5	Díaz-Lauzurica, B., Moreno-Salinas, D. [21]	Computational thinking and robotics: A teaching experience in compulsory secondary education with students with high degree of apathy and demotivation	Increase in student motivation, meaningful learning, better behavior, development of programming and robotics skills	Sustainability	Spain	2019	19	4.47 (#3)

(*continued*)

Table 1. (*continued*)

No.	Authors	Title	Main Findings	Source	Country	Year	Citations	Average
6	Bertacchini, F. et al. [22]	An emotional learning environment for subjects with autism spectrum disorder	Face3D, a 3D modeling system, improves the understanding of emotions and social behaviors in individuals with autism	International Conference on Interactive Collaborative Learning	Italy	2013	19	1.85 (#6)
7	Saridaki, M. et al. [23]	Digital games-based learning for students with intellectual disabilities	Digital games can be an effective educational tool for students with intellectual disabilities under certain conditions and limitations	Games-Based Learning Advancements for Multi-Sensory Human Computer Interfaces: Techniques and Effective Practices	Greece	2009	19	1.33 (#10)
8	Balan, O. et al. [24]	Navigational 3D audio-based game-training towards rich auditory spatial representation of the environment	Training with a 3D audio game improves mental spatial representation and orientation skills	Applications in Software Engineering - Proceedings of the 9th International Conference on Software Process Improvement	Romania	2014	16	1.73 (#7)
9	Leask, M., Pachler, N. [25]	Learning to Teach Using ICT in the Secondary School: A Companion to School Experience: A companion to school experience	ICT possibilities to improve teaching and learning in various subjects	Proceedings - 9th International Conference on Measuring Technology and Mechatronics Automation	United Kingdom	2013	15	1.46 (#9)
10	King, A. et al. [26]	The routledge companion to music, technology, and education	Theoretical and empirical perspectives on technology in music education and its impact on learning	Journal of Intelligent and Fuzzy Systems	United Kingdom	2017	10	1.60 (#8)

to teaching literacy skills in children with autism spectrum disorder using the SEMA-TIC game, Serret et al. [20]. The analysis of this information is crucial to understand the current trends in gamification research applied to the education of children with disabilities.

RQ4: What main keywords can be identified in this topic?

In this section, an analysis was carried out to identify the most relevant topics using the VOSviewer tool to analyze the frequency of keywords in the retrieved documents. To do this, a minimum threshold of 5 occurrences was established to preselect the relevant keywords, resulting in a total of 22 keywords. Table 2 presents a summary of the selected keywords and their frequency and link strength.

Table 2. Summary of the selected keywords.

Keywords	Occurrences	TLS	Keywords	Occurrences	TLS
Serious games	18	61	Diseases	6	28
Education	13	67	Game design	6	3.4
Autism	11	59	Game-based learning	6	18
Gamification	10	56	Learning disabilities	6	19
Learning systems	10	46	Computer aided instruction	5	20
Special education	10	56	Educational computing	5	24
Teaching	10	51	Educational technology	5	24
Computer games	8	48	Human computer interaction	5	27
E-learning	8	34	Including education	5	14
Students	7	38	Intellectual disability	5	20

Examining the data carefully, in Fig. 4 it was possible to identify several important keywords that are relevant to the field of gamification as a pedagogical approach aimed at improving the learning and active participation of children with disabilities. Two sets of main keywords are highlighted: i) those linked to specific disabilities and conditions, such as "adhd", "asd" (autism spectrum disorder), "attention deficit hyperactivity disorder" and "learning disabilities", which demonstrate a trend towards more recent publications, with an average number of years of publication ranging from 2012 to 2017; ii) those related to pedagogical and educational approaches, such as "game-based learning", "educational games", "e-learning", "education", "educational technology", "engagement" and "inclusive education", reflecting a wide range of publications over time, with average publication years ranging from 2011 to 2020.

In addition, terms such as "gamification", "serious games" and "special education" have a greater number of occurrences and links, which suggests that these topics could be of particular interest in the scientific literature related to the application of gamification in the education of children with disabilities.

In addition, there is a diversity of keywords associated with the use of specific technologies, such as "augmented reality", "computer aided instruction", "computer games", "digital games" and "video games".

RQ5: Which are the journals/conferences with the highest number of publications and citations?

Choosing the right publication to share your findings is essential in research, as this decision can affect how often the article will be cited after publication. Therefore, it is essential to identify the most appropriate places of publication to disseminate the research. Table 3 is presented below with the journals and proceedings with the most publications and citations in this field of study.

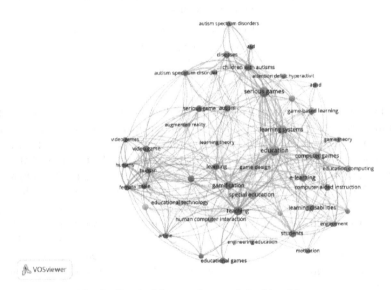

Fig. 4. Cloud of frequent keywords in this subject.

These journals and proceedings allow researchers and practitioners to access up-to-date information, share experiences, and discuss scientific and technological advances in the field. Elsevier's Computers and Education stands out for its high number of citations, suggesting that studies published in this journal could have a greater influence on the academic community and educational practice.

RQ6: Who are the authors with the most publications on this topic?

Based on the information obtained, 193 authors were identified, of which 16 have at least two publications to their credit and the rest only one. This information makes it possible to know those researchers working on this subject, with whom the exchange of experiences, approaches and good practices could be promoted, which will further enrich the understanding and application of similar proposals. This growth in research will also favor the establishment of collaboration networks between experts, strengthening the scientific community around this topic.

Table 3. Summary of the journals, books and proceedings where most articles were published.

Publisher	Journal/Conference	Publications	Citations
Dechema eV	Proceedings of the European Conference On Games Based Learning	3	9
Brazilian Association of Researchers in Special Education	Brazilian Magazine of Special Education	3	4
Associate Iberica de Sistemas e Tecnologias de Informacao	Risti Iberian Magazine of Information Systems and Technologies	3	3
Association for Computing Machinery	ACM International Conference Proceeding Series	2	1
Elsevier	Computers And Education	2	61
Springer	Education And Information Technologies	2	6

Figure 5 shows the authors who are grouped into different clusters (from 1 to 9), which may indicate that they have addressed various themes or approaches within the field of study. Furthermore, the information from VOSViewer shows that the average publication dates vary from 2006 to 2021. This suggests that although the field of research may be at an early stage, there has been sustained interest in the topic throughout the years. Authors such as "Deliyannis, I.", "Fokides, E.", and "Kaimara, P." have more recent publications, with an average publication year of 2021, indicating that they are still active in this field and might be contributing to the most current research in this area. On the other hand, authors such as "Gifford, KE.", "Ouscos, D.", and "Saridaki, M." have an average year of publication older (2006, 2008 and 2008, respectively), which could suggest that their contributions were more relevant in the early years of the field of study.

RQ7: Which are the institutions that carried out the most research on gamification for children with disabilities?

Table 4 allows us to identify the institutions that have conducted the most research on gamification as a pedagogical strategy to improve the learning and engagement of children with disabilities. Two European institutions lead this field with three published articles each: the UCL Institute of Education in the United Kingdom, with 103 citations, and the National and Kapodistrian University of Athens in Greece, with 21 citations.

In addition, several institutions have published two articles each in this field of research. Among them, the University of South Alabama in the United States and the Autonomous University of Aguascalientes in Mexico stand out, as well as other European institutions such as Nottingham Trent University and The Open University in the United Kingdom, the Ionian University and the University of the Aegean in Greece, and the Universitat Autonomous of Barcelona in Spain. Finally, the Universidade do Vale do Itajai in Brazil contributed two articles.

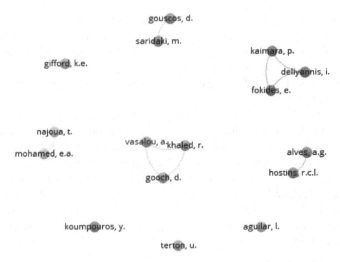

Fig. 5. Co-authors who work in collaborative networks regarding the subject matter.

Table 4. Institutions that have a greater number of publications and citations.

No.	Affiliation	Country	Mainland	Articles	Citations
1	UCL Institute of Education	United Kingdom	Europe	3	103
2	National and Kapodistrian University of Athens	Greece	Europe	3	21
3	University of South Alabama	United States	America	2	1
4	Autonomous University of Aguascalientes	Mexico	America	2	29
5	Nottingham Trent University	United Kingdom	Europe	2	11
6	The Open University	United Kingdom	Europe	2	88
7	Ionian University	Greece	Europe	2	3
8	University of Vale do Itajai	Brazil	America	2	1
9	University of the Aegean	Greece	Europe	2	3
10	University Autonomous of Barcelona	Spain	Europe	2	8

The presence of institutions from different geographical regions, such as Europe and America, indicates a global interest in gamification applied to the education of children with disabilities. The diversity of institutions involved in research also suggests that the field can benefit from a wide range of approaches, perspectives, and methodologies. This information is valuable in the context of the bibliometric review since it helps to understand the geographical distribution and the impact of research in this field and identify the leading institutions in the production of knowledge in the area. In addition, the analysis of these institutions can provide a basis for future collaborations and research projects in gamification and inclusive education.

RQ8: What are the main funding agencies for gamification documents for children with disabilities?

The main funding agencies that have supported these investigations are the Fundação para a Ciência e Tecnologia with two studies. Other important organizations that have financed a single study include the Ministry of Education of the Junta de Castilla y León in Spain, the Conselho Nacional de Desenvolvimento Científico e Tecnológico in Brazil, the Coordenação de Aperfeiçoamento de Pessoal de Nível Superior also in Brazil and the Deanship of science King Saud Research University in Saudi Arabia, among others. While not all the funding agencies involved are listed, these entities represent some of the main sources of support. It is worth noting that 73% of these studies have not been funded or have not been reported.

4 Conclusions

The results showed a growth in scientific production related to gamification and the education of children with disabilities over the years, although with a decrease in recent years. However, the citations of the articles could continue to increase in the future, which indicates that the field continues to be relevant and of interest to the scientific community. In geographical terms, a notable concentration of publications in Europe was identified, with countries such as the United Kingdom and Spain leading the scientific production in the area. This could be related to their education systems and their attention to including students with disabilities. Furthermore, the wide geographical scope of the publications suggests that gamification is a pedagogical strategy applicable in different cultural and educational contexts.

The diversity of approaches and themes addressed in the most influential articles highlights the richness and complexity of the field. In addition, two main sets of keywords were identified: one related to specific disabilities and conditions, and one related to pedagogical and educational approaches. This suggests that the scientific literature addresses the specific needs of children with disabilities and the most effective educational methodologies and strategies for their learning. Several relevant journals and conferences in the field were identified, with Elsevier's Computers and Education being the one that stands out for its high number of citations. This suggests that the studies published in this journal could have a greater influence on the academic community and educational practice. The authors and institutions identified in this bibliometric study show a diversity of geography and approaches. This could facilitate the exchange of experiences and good practices between researchers and education professionals, enriching the knowledge base in the field and fostering future collaborations and research projects. They could receive support from identified funding agencies, both locally and internationally, to gain greater recognition within this area of knowledge.

Within the analyzed literature, several methodologies, and approaches for implementing gamification in the education of children with disabilities were identified. These include the use of game elements such as points, badges, leaderboards, and narratives to motivate students; the application of user-centered design techniques to ensure the accessibility and usability of gamification tools; and the integration of emerging technologies such as virtual and augmented reality, artificial intelligence, and educational robotics to offer immersive and adaptive learning experiences. However, challenges and areas for improvement were also found in the literature. One of the challenges identified is the need for more empirical evidence on the effectiveness of gamification in the education of children with disabilities, especially in the long term. In addition, the importance of considering individual differences and the specific needs of children with disabilities when designing and implementing gamification strategies was recognized, to ensure that these are inclusive and adapted to their learning context.

Regarding future directions, it is necessary to continue investigating the potential of gamification and its relationship with disabilities, considering the specific needs of each group and educational context. It is required: (i) to explore the long-term impact of gamification in the education of children with disabilities, including academic results and socio-emotional skills. (ii) Investigate the best practices and the most effective approaches for gamification in different cultural and educational contexts. (iii) Promote international collaboration between researchers and professionals to share experiences and good practices in applying gamification in the education of children with disabilities. (iv) Identify and address the barriers and challenges for implementing gamification in the education of children with disabilities, including the lack of resources and resistance to change in educational systems.

Acknowledgment. To the Universidad Indoamérica for its support for this research in collaboration with the University of Zaragoza.

References

1. Mitchell, D., Sutherland, D.: What Really Works in Special and Inclusive Education: Using Evidence-Based Teaching Strategies (2020).https://doi.org/10.4324/9780429401923
2. Lindner, K.T., Schwab, S.: Differentiation and individualisation in inclusive education: a systematic review and narrative synthesis. Int. J. Incl. Educ. (2020).https://doi.org/10.1080/13603116.2020.1813450
3. Florian, L.: On the necessary co-existence of special and inclusive education. Int. J. Incl. Educ. **23**, 691–704 (2019). https://doi.org/10.1080/13603116.2019.1622801
4. Ainscow, M.: Promoting inclusion and equity in education: lessons from international experiences. Nord. J. Stud. Educ. Policy **6**, 7–16 (2020). https://doi.org/10.1080/20020317.2020.1729587
5. Sandoval, M., Muñoz, Y., Márquez, C.: Supporting schools in their journey to inclusive education: review of guides and tools. Support Learn. **36**, 20–42 (2021). https://doi.org/10.1111/1467-9604.12337
6. Mubin, S.A., Wee Ann Poh, M.: A review on gamification design framework: how they incorporated for autism children. In: 4th Int. Conf. Work. Recent Adv. Innov. Eng. Thriving Technol. (ICRAIE 2019) (2019). https://doi.org/10.1109/ICRAIE47735.2019.9037765
7. Zhang, M., Vallabhajosyula, R., Fung, D.: Emotional bias modification for individuals with attention deficit hyperactivity disorder: protocol for a co-design study. JMIR Res. Protoc. **9**, e24078 (2020). https://doi.org/10.2196/24078

8. Graham, S., Hebert, M., Fishman, E., Ray, A.B., Rouse, A.G.: Do children classified with specific language impairment have a learning disability in writing? A meta-analysis. J. Learn. Disabil. **53**, 292–310 (2020). https://doi.org/10.1177/0022219420917338

9. Tori, A.A., Tori, R., Nunes, F.D.L.D.S.: Serious game design in health education: a systematic review. IEEE Trans. Learn. Technol. **15**, 827–846 (2022). https://doi.org/10.1109/TLT.2022. 3200583

10. Saleem, A.N., Noori, N.M., Ozdamli, F.: Gamification applications in e-learning: a literature review. Technol. Knowl. Learn. **27**, 139–159 (2021). https://doi.org/10.1007/s10758-020-094 87-x

11. Buele, J., et al.: Interactive system to improve the skills of children with dyslexia: a preliminary study. In: Rocha, Á., Pereira, R.P. (eds.) Developments and Advances in Defense and Security. SIST, vol. 152, pp. 439–449. Springer, Singapore (2020). https://doi.org/10.1007/978-981-13-9155-2_35

12. Vacca, R.A., et al.: Serious games in the new era of digital-health interventions: a narrative review of their therapeutic applications to manage neurobehavior in neurodevelopmental disorders. Neurosci. Biobehav. Rev. **149**, 105156 (2023). https://doi.org/10.1016/j.neubiorev. 2023.105156

13. Furini, M., Mirri, S., Montangero, M.: Gamification and accessibility. In: 2019 16th IEEE Annu. Consum. Commun. Netw. Conf. (CCNC 2019), vol. 36, pp. 104–123 (2019). https:// doi.org/10.1109/CCNC.2019.8651750

14. Fiuza-Fernández, A., Lomba-Portela, L., Soto-Carballo, J., Pino-Juste, M.R.: Study of the knowledge about gamification of degree in primary education students. PLoS ONE **17**, e0263107 (2022). https://doi.org/10.1371/journal.pone.0263107

15. Agran, M., et al.: Why aren't students with severe disabilities being placed in general education classrooms: examining the relations among classroom placement, learner outcomes, and other factors. Res. Pract. Pers. Sev. Disabil. **45**, 4–13 (2020). https://doi.org/10.1177/154079691 9878134

16. Finnerty, M.S., Jackson, L.B., Ostergren, R.: Adaptations in general education classrooms for students with severe disabilities: access, progress assessment, and sustained use. Res. Pract. Pers. Sev. Disabil. **44**, 87–102 (2019). https://doi.org/10.1177/1540796919846424

17. Gooch, D., Vasalou, A., Benton, L., Khaled, R.: Using gamification to motivate students with dyslexia. In: 34th Annual CHI Conference on Human Factors in Computing Systems, (CHI EA 2016), pp. 969–980. Association for Computing Machinery, Open University, Milton Keynes, UK (2016). https://doi.org/10.1145/2858036.2858231

18. Vasalou, A., Khaled, R., Holmes, W., Gooch, D.: Digital games-based learning for children with dyslexia: a social constructivist perspective on engagement and learning during group game-play. Comput. Educ. **114**, 175–192 (2017). https://doi.org/10.1016/j.compedu.2017. 06.009

19. Cano, S., Munoz Arteaga, J., Collazos, C.A., Gonzalez, C.S., Zapata, S.: Toward a methodology for serious games design for children with auditory impairments. IEEE Lat. Am. Trans. **14**, 2511–2521 (2016). https://doi.org/10.1109/TLA.2016.7530453

20. Serret, S., et al.: Teaching literacy skills to French minimally verbal school-aged children with autism spectrum disorders with the serious game SEMA-TIC: an exploratory study. Front. Psychol. **8**, 1523 (2017). https://doi.org/10.3389/fpsyg.2017.01523

21. Díaz-Lauzurica, B., Moreno-Salinas, D.: Computational thinking and robotics: a teaching experience in compulsory secondary education with students with high degree of apathy and demotivation. Sustainability **11**(18), 5109 (2019). https://doi.org/10.3390/su11185109

22. Bertacchini, F., et al.: An emotional learning environment for subjects with Autism Spectrum Disorder. In: 2013 16th International Conference on Interactive Collaborative Learning (ICL 2013), pp. 653–659. IEEE Computer Society, Environmental and Territorial Engineering

and Chemical Engineering Department, University of Calabria, Unical Arcavacata di Rende, Cosenza, Italy (2013). https://doi.org/10.1109/ICL.2013.6644675

23. Saridaki, M., Gouscos, D., Meimaris, M.G.: Digital games-based learning for students with intellectual disability. In: Games-Based Learning Advancements for Multi-Sensory Human Computer Interfaces: Techniques and Effective Practices, pp. 304–325. IGI Global, National and Kapodistrian University of Athens, Greece (2009). https://doi.org/10.4018/978-1-60566-360-9.ch018

24. Balan, O., Moldoveanu, A., Moldoveanu, F., Dascalu, M.-I.: Navigational 3D audio-based game-training towards rich auditory spatial representation of the environment. In: 2014 18th International Conference on System Theory, Control and Computing (ICSTCC 2014), pp. 682–687. IEEE, Bucharest, Romania (2014). https://doi.org/10.1109/ICSTCC.2014.698 2496

25. Leask, M., Pachler, N.: Learing to teach using ICT in the secondary school: a companion to school experience: a companion to school experience. Taylor and Francis, Educational Knowledge Management, University of Bedfordshire, UK (2013)

26. King, A., Himonides, E., Ruthmann, S.A.: The routledge companion to music, technology, and education. Taylor and Francis, University of Hull, UK (2017). https://doi.org/10.4324/9781315686431

Assessment and Visualization of Course-Level and Curriculum-Level Competency Profiles

Viktor Uglev[(✉)] and Ekaterina Shangina

Siberian Federal University, Zheleznogorsk, Russia
`vauglev@sfu-kras.ru`

Abstract. Assessment of the competency development level (CDL) is one of the key tasks in the implementation of e-learning, especially in the dynamics. There is a difficulty in combining competency profiles with respect to the different knowledge blocks (courses and their groups), which allows justifying pedagogical influence. The paper considers the Intelligent Tutoring System (ITS) mechanisms responsible for integration of competency profiles at curriculum level. For this purpose, the mechanism of expert systems (based on Shortliffe criterion) is used. The results of the experiment on supporting the learning process of the master's degree students of the specialty "Informatics and Computer Science" have shown that the CDL assessment method allows recording the individual and group dynamics of competency development. Star diagrams, Cognitive Maps of Knowledge Diagnosis and UGVA method are chosen as the basis for visualization of course-level and curriculum-level competency profiles. It is shown that all of them not only can be built into the ITS automated decision-making chain, but also into the process of synthesizing the text explaining these decisions.

Keywords: e-learning · Intelligent Tutoring Systems · competency development level · competency profile · cognitive visualization · decision-making support

1 Introduction

E-learning in higher education institutions is implemented using modern automation tools (LMS, MOOC, ITS, etc.). The most developed among them are Intelligent Tutoring Systems (ITS) that are based on the potential of artificial intelligence systems. The effectiveness of the learning process is largely determined by how the learning situation is diagnosed and how flexibly the ITS mechanisms are adapted to each learner [17,18]. For this reason, one of the key tasks is to make a diagnosis of the learner's knowledge and skills, based on the results of which the pedagogical influence takes place (the ITS scheduler makes decisions [15]). But since the learning is often based on a set of courses (the curriculum of the whole stage of education), then decisions should be based on the results of a comprehensive (curriculum-level) diagnosis. In the framework of this paper we will consider the issue of determining the competency development level on the course-level and curriculum-levels, as well as their visualization and application in the decision-making mechanism of the ITS scheduler.

The set of the subject disciplines from the curriculum can be represented in the form of a tree, demonstrating the sequence of transitions between the academic semesters (vertical movement) with gradual development of specified competencies. Figure 1 shows the structure of a master's degree program, where each discipline (e-course) contains the subject material to achieve its own goals, but taking into account the system-wide needs of the specialty (profession). Horizontal movement (in the space of semester courses at a particular point in time) is carried out by a learner when interacting with the theoretical and practical material of disciplines, as well as during practical work and testing. Thus, three components are distinguished: structural (subject knowledge level), target (requirements in the form of standards for knowledge and skills in the course metadata and learner's preferences), and functional (direct manifestation of learner's activity in the form of a digital educational footprint) components.

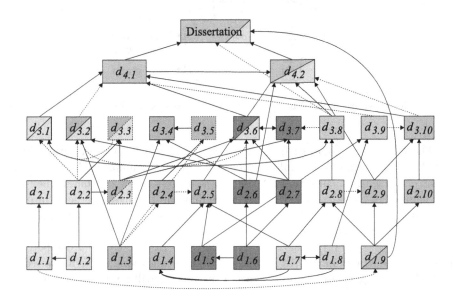

Fig. 1. A specialty discipline tree within the master's degree program curriculum

A fragment of the hierarchy of the learning material organization in each discipline is shown in Fig. 2: each course (d_l) consists of a sequence of topics (t_j), which, in turn, are defined by a sequence of the learning units (u_i). Each learning unit corresponds to a set of tasks or tests (z_m), having an answer option $(a_n,$ the only one in the open form) and links with the corresponding competencies $(c_k \in C)$. Here the values l, i, j, m, n and k are the indices of the corresponding entities from the e-course database. The many-to-many relation between a_n and c_k is responsible for the link between the structural and target components. The diagrams shown in Fig. 2 and subsequent figures will be discussed in more detail in Sect. 4 when describing the pedagogical experiment.

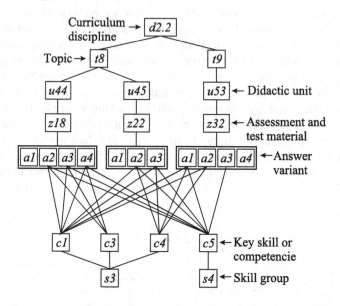

Fig. 2. An example of links between course entities with competencies

The learner's answers to tasks and tests extracted from the digital educational footprint should not only be assessed, but also summarized on the level of the entire learning situation relative to the current point in time in the form of a competency profile. It follows from the diagram that competencies in most cases are developed not only in parallel based on the whole set of disciplines of each semester (horizontal level), but also in the process of transition from course to course (vertical level). Therefore, the question "How to create a competency profile at a curriculum level?" is one of the main questions to be answered so that ITS could develop comprehensive decisions. We will try to answer it.

2   Overview of Existing Solutions

Assessment of the level of competency development during e-learning has limitations, because the ITS capability to record latent indicators [7] about learners is quite scarce [2,25]. From a methodological point of view, competency assessment methods can be divided into psychological (e.g., [16]), course-specific (e.g., [6,10,12]), industry-specific (e.g., [8]), inter-course (comprehensive, such as the Programme for the International Assessment of Adult Competencies (PIAAC)

[14] or VET-PISA [24]). Almost all of them are implemented in the form of specialized activities to change the level of competency development and are of little use while studying the complex of interrelated subject disciplines. This leads to the following disadvantages:

- the learner is aware that he/she is being assessed for certain competencies and can purposefully adjust some of the answers to the desired indicators of the competency profile;
- a different set of questions/tasks is formulated for each competency, making testing of a set of competencies a lengthy and tedious process;
- the result (the competency profile) is presented as a final result, not integrated into the logic of further functioning of the learning environment;
- visualization of the competency profile in the vast majority of cases is limited to a diagram or dashboard, without involving cognitive visualization tools.

All of this reduces the effectiveness of applying the competency profiles as part of ITS. To solve this issue, it is proposed to arrange the assessment and test activities aimed at measuring (assessing) the *competency development level* (CDL) as per [23], but to do it at the curriculum-level. We will describe a CDL assessment model applied to a set of the disciplines taught at the same time and visualize a competency profile (Sect. 3). In Sect. 4 we will describe the results of an experimental application of the curriculum-level assessment of CDL in the ITS-based learning process. We will analyze the results in Sect. 5 and provide recommendations for integrating the CDL curriculum-level method into ITS mechanisms. We conclude with the prospects for the development of the method and our plans for its further application in e-learning.

3 Method

3.1 The Basic Idea of CDL Assessment

Here is a brief description of the CDL assessment method at the course-level. Suppose we have a discipline d_l, the learning units u_i, which are composed of the tasks z_m, each of which has one (for the open form) or more answer options a_n. Then the data on the link q_{nk} between answer options a_n and competencies c_k will be specified as weight coefficients within an interval from 0 to 1 (where 0 means that the competency is not manifested, 1 means that the competency is manifested and 0.5 is the uncertainty threshold).

While processing the log of learner's answers $X_n(t)$, where t is the point in time when testing is carried out, it is possible to calculate not only the assessment of subject knowledge, but also the level of the competency c_k development. For this purpose, each answer associated with the competency and recorded in the log is considered as evidence in favor (MB, where $q_{nk} > 0.5$) or not in favor (MD, $q_{nk} < 0.5$) of the hypothesis about competency development (probability measure) according to formulas (1):

$$MB[c_k, x] = \frac{P(c_k \mid x) - P(c_k)}{1 - P(c_k)} \qquad MD = \frac{P(c_k) - P(c_k \mid x)}{P(c_k)}, \qquad (1)$$

where $x \in X_n(t)$ reflects the quantitative measure of one of the answers to a task or a test in relation to the competency c_k.

Having evaluated the hypotheses about the measure of trust and distrust in the manifestation of the hypothesis about the development of the competency c_k for the discipline with index l we can proceed to the final assessment (the confidence factor Cf as per [5]) according to the formula (2):

$$Cf(c_k, q_k \wedge q_{\overline{k}}) = MB(c_k, q_k) - MD(c_k, q_{\overline{k}}), \qquad (2)$$

where q_k and $q_{\overline{k}}$ are evidence in favor and not in favor of the hypothesis about the competency development level (determined relative to the value q_{nk}).

As a result of calculations using the formulas (1) and (2) we will get a vector of quantitative assessments of the level of competence development AR_k^l for a single discipline with index l. But since the number of answers from $X_n(t)$ is different for the competencies, the results need to be normalized and used in the same scale s as per (3):

$$R_k^l = \frac{AR_k^l * s}{max_k(X_t)}, \qquad (3)$$

where the resulting scale will reduce the CDL values to the interval $[-s; s]$. We will call the vector R_k^l the *course-level competency profile*. For more details on the calculation of CDL values, their normalization, and the calculation of the reference competency profile, see [23].

If it is necessary to allocate qualitative gradation levels in the competency assessment structure, an ordinal scale of the following values is applied: not developed ($R_k^l \rightarrow -1$), rather undeveloped, not determined (evidence is contradictory, i.e. the value R_k^l is equal or close to 0), rather developed and developed ($R_k^l \rightarrow 1$). In contrast to the Likert scale [11], the transition from a quantitative to a qualitative scale can be performed through a fuzzification operation from the fuzzy logic method [26]. An example of the system of characteristic functions formed as the result of a survey of expert opinions among the teaching staff of our department is shown in Fig. 3a (the image is formed in the expert analysis module FLM_modul.py [4], which is a part of the intelligent scheduler subsystem FLM_Builder v.4.b for ITS).

When solving the task of the detailed visualization, the data from competency profiles consisting of only five values, can not be efficiently used. Therefore, we will use the heat map presented in Fig. 3b (see Sect. 5 for examples).

3.2 Curriculum-Level Approach to CDL Assessment

The formation of the course-level competency profile will not reflect the true CDL picture at the point in time t relative to the curriculum, because the development of competencies in different disciplines of the current semester takes place in parallel (see the diagram shown in Fig. 1). We will propose an expansion of the original CDL assessment method for multiple disciplines. We will call this approach *the curriculum-level approach*.

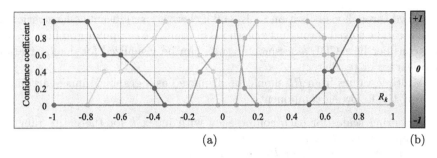

Fig. 3. Translation of the quantitative assessment of the CDL values of individual competencies to a qualitative representation (level, a) and its coding on the heat map scale (b)

The curriculum-level competency profile is formed according to the following steps:

1. All answers to tasks from X_t, which are relevant to the competency with index k in the current academic semester (for all disciplines simultaneously) are selected for the learner according to the presence of links q_{nk} in the metadata of e-courses;
2. Formulas (1) are used to test the hypothesis that competency c_k is developed;
3. The confidence factor Cf is calculated and placed at the position corresponding to the value k in the vector AR_k according to (2);
4. The integral reference competency profile is formed and normalized to s, thus giving R_k;
5. The curriculum-level competency profile is saved in the ITS operation log and visualized, if necessary.

In order to increase the effectiveness of monitoring the learning process in relation to a group of students, one can additionally summarize the indicators of the course-level and curriculum-level competency profiles. This would require calculating the minimum, maximum, and average CDL values for each c_k in a group of students. This results in the *group competency profile* at the point in time t. Although it is of little use for individualizing the tutoring impact of the ITS scheduler, it is useful for finding problematic elements of the learning material.

In general, the CDL method allows organizing the process of competency development level assessment in such a way that the properties of latency, comprehensive coverage, parallel measurement, metric results and visualizability can be implemented.

3.3 Visualization of Competency Profiles

The simultaneous perception of multiple indicators within a single object always has limitations due to the peculiarity of the human mentality [13]. This issue can be solved through visualization tools, and if there is a significant concentration of data it can be solved through the methods of cognitive computer graphics [9]. We will consider how CDL assessment results can be visualized for demonstration to a learner or teacher.

Multiple values from R_k should be displayed as a graphical image accompanied by the following components:

- measuring scales for each competency with index k for the entire range of acceptable values, i.e. from $-s$ to s;
- quantitative values R_k^l or R_k on each of the scales;
- level of uncertainty relative to the development of each competency (zero value);
- (brief or abbreviated) signatures on each scale to quickly find the required indicators.

Examples of this organization of a visual representation of the course-level competency profiles for three different disciplines for one of the learners are shown in Fig. 4. Such star diagrams are built automatically [21]. Their specifics and application will be described in Sect. 4.

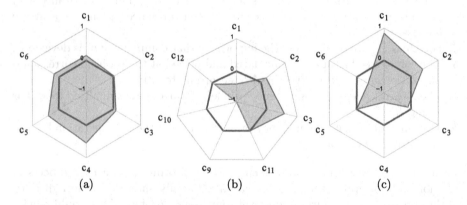

Fig. 4. Examples of visualizations of CDL assessments for three courses in the form of course-level competency profiles of one student

Visualization of the curriculum-level profile will be based on the same principles as for the course-level profile, but the star diagram will include all the competencies of subject disciplines associated with those monitored through ITS. An example of such a profile is shown in Fig. 5a. Figure 5b summarizes such profiles for a study group: the minimum, average, and maximum value thresholds are highlighted.

4   Experiment

We will show the application of the CDL assessment method on a course-level and curriculum-level scale on the example of students of the specialty "Infor-

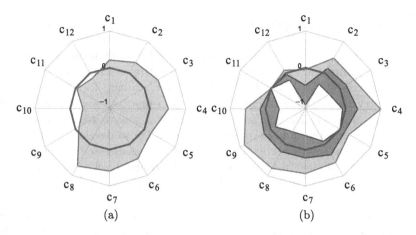

Fig. 5. An example of visual representation of the curriculum-level competency profile of one student (a) and the entire study group (b)

matics and Computer Science" in the Siberian Federal University. We will take the enrollment of 2022 in the academic program "Information Technologies and Mission Control Centers" as an experimental group (group of 8 students).

The specificity of the educational process is that the specialty is based on a unified state standard, which specifies the requirements to the training of students and the list of competencies to be developed in academic disciplines, practices and during writing a graduate qualification work (master's thesis). All 31 disciplines of the curriculum (including the practices) can be conditionally divided into four blocks, represented with different colours on the specialty discipline tree shown in Fig. 1:

- general disciplines (e.g., $d_{3.1}$ "Project management", $d_{1.1}$ "Foreign language", etc. that are highlighted in purple);
- general science disciplines (e.g., $d_{1.7}$ "Data analysis and decision-making", $d_{2.8}$ "System theory", etc. that are highlighted in pink);
- general major disciplines (e.g., $d_{2.5}$ "Artificial intelligence", $d_{3.3}$ "Internet of things", $d_{3.5}$ "Information security", etc. that are highlighted in green);
- special major disciplines (e.g., $d_{1.6}$ "Object-oriented programming", $d_{3.6}$ "Software development technology", etc. that are highlighted in blue);
- industry-specific disciplines (e.g., $d_{1.2}$ and $d_{2.2}$ "Basic spacecraft engineering" that are highlighted in grey);
- scientific and methodological disciplines (e.g., $d_{1.9}$ "Methodology of scientific activity", $d_{2.10}$ "Research seminar", etc. that are highlighted in orange).

Each of the disciplines in the above groups was correlated with competencies from the curriculum through a many-to-many relation. These relations were expressed through the links q_{nk} and allowed selecting data from the digital educational footprint that relate to the individual subjects (with details on the learning units and topics) and to the set of studied disciplines. An example of several links for the discipline $d_{2.2}$ "Basic spacecraft engineering" is shown in Fig. 2. The CDL for 10 disciplines (which was 32.2% of all) and for 12 competencies (which was 2/3 of all) was assessed for the above-mentioned specialty using the experimental ITS AESU[1] during the entire educational cycle.

The experiment was conducted as follows: first, students took a questionnaire and an entry test in each discipline; then the same test was repeated in the middle and at the end of the semester. The goal was to track the dynamics of competency mastery and to apply this knowledge to develop individual and group pedagogical influences by ITS. Each test log was assessed from the subject knowledge point of view (discipline score) and a course-level competency profile was formed (it was not presented to the student) according to the methodology described above.

Each test or set of practical tasks contained from 15 to 70 questions/tasks depending on the content of the discipline and the learning goals (from 4 to 7 competences were tested simultaneously). On average, there were 29 evidences per one log, which could be used to test one or more competencies. For the considered group of students the data covered a academic semester and a half.

5   Results and Analysis

5.1   Competency Profiles

The result of using the CDL assessment method is a set of competency profiles at the time of testing. This allowed forming course-level profiles for each discipline for each student from the experimental study group: Fig. 4 shows the profiles of the student with ID 01041 for the disciplines $d_{1.7}$ "Data analysis and decision-making" (a), $d_{2.2}$ "Basic spacecraft engineering" (b), and $d_{2.5}$ "Artificial intelligence" (c). His curriculum-level competency profile is shown in Fig. 5a. These data demonstrate that when assessing the development of the competency c_4 "Able to develop components of software systems for information processing and computer-aided design" the problems with the discipline $d_{2.5}$ are local, and as for the competency c_{10} "Able to manage a project at all stages of its life cycle" these problems are systematic and require development of a comprehensive pedagogical influence.

Figure 6 shows the course-level competency profiles for the discipline $d_{2.2}$ for another three students with ID 01044 (a), ID 01048 (b) and ID 01049 (c). By comparing these profiles with the profile shown in Fig. 5a and with each other, one can see how the uniform visual representation provides a basis for a quick comparison. For example, it can be seen that all students have difficulties with the development of the competency c_{12} "Able to develop components of hardware and software systems", related to the learning units u_{45} and u_{53} that are tested through the tasks z_{22} and z_{32} (a fragment of links between these entities is shown in Fig. 2).

---

[1] https://aesfu.ru/.

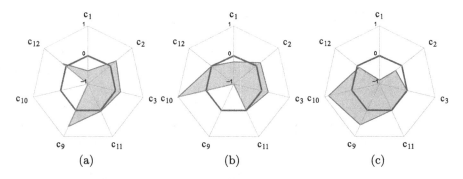

Fig. 6. Examples of visualization of the course-level competency profiles of three students for the discipline "Basic spacecraft engineering"

The dynamics of CDL values in the form of competency profiles is shown in Fig. 7: profiles (a), (b) and (c) correspond to the student with ID 01041 at the beginning (September 12th, 2022), middle (November 8th, 2022) and end (February 14th, 2023) of the first semester/beginning of the second semester for the discipline $d_{1.9}$ "Methodology of scientific activity". Curriculum-level profiles (d), (e) and (f) show the dynamics of this student's competency development for the same dates (in addition, Fig. 5a shows the profile (f) for the middle of the second semester dated April 18th, 2023). Particularly, one can say that the competencies c_9, c_{10}, c_{11} and c_{12} were not formed before the beginning of the second semester (the value R_k is assumed to be -1).

In the current learning situation in mid-April it can be recommended to the student with ID 01041 to give high priority to the material of the discipline $d_{2.2}$ related to the development of competencies c_{12}; c_3 for $d_{1.2}$ and $d_{2.8}$. When analyzing the group's curriculum-level competency profile, the reasons for students' difficulties in developing the competency c_{11} should be clarified and, possibly, the quality of the learning material developing this competency as well as the test materials should be checked.

The group curriculum-level competency profile for a group of students is shown in Fig. 5b (formed based on the mid-semester test data). If we average the data on all competencies for a group of students for one and a half semester, we will get the values presented in Table 1. Their further averaging to a range of values (arithmetic mean for minimum, average, and maximum values) is shown on the chart in Fig. 8, where test stages are plotted on the x-axis, and the factor of confidence in development of the competency from -1 to 1 range is plotted on the left y-axis. The direction of the value change demonstrates not only positive dynamics, but also strong positive correlation (Pearson's correlation coefficient $r = 0.738$) with the dynamics of values of the averaged group assessment of subject knowledge (the right y-axis in percentage of correct answers on the proposed set of tasks and tests). Data on the score are presented in the form of two curves reflecting the indicators of group average performance in the disciplines of the first semester (blue line) and in the disciplines of the second semester (until the

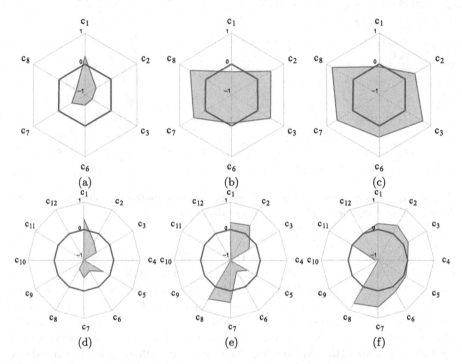

Fig. 7. Examples of the dynamics of course-level competency profiles for the discipline "Methodology of scientific activity" (a–b–c) and curriculum-level competency profiles (d–e–f) for one student

Table 1. Summary of the application of the CDL assessment method to a group of students over a semester and a half

Date	Indicator	c_1	c_2	c_3	c_4	c_5	c_6	c_7	c_8	c_9	c_{10}	c_{11}	c_{12}
September	minimum	−1	−0.4	−0.59	−1	−0.34	−0.61	−0.44	−0.74	−	−	−	−
September	average	−0.14	−0.22	−0.22	−0.28	−0.07	−0.08	−0.8	−0.19	−	−	−	−
September	maximum	1	0.2	0.23	1	0.06	0.37	0.4	0.2	−	−	−	−
November	minimum	−1	−0.4	−0.38	−1	−0.34	−0.44	−0.35	−0.34	−	−	−	−
November	average	−0.23	−0.06	−0.16	−0.28	−0.7	−0.3	−0.23	−0.24	−	−	−	−
November	maximum	0.76	0.4	0.23	1	0.06	0.37	0.56	0.65	−	−	−	−
February	minimum	−1	−0.4	−0.38	−0.42	0	−0.1	−0.35	−0.34	−1	−0.88	0	0
February	average	−0.47	0.06	0.12	0.03	0.11	0.18	0.25	0.29	−0.1	−0.11	0	0
February	maximum	0.29	0.34	0.31	1	0.27	0.37	0.63	0.74	0.4	0.25	0	0
April	minimum	−1	−0.4	−0.38	−0.07	0	−0.1	−0.35	−0.34	−0.1	−0.35	0	−0.2
April	average	−0.56	0.11	0.21	0.25	0.08	0.34	0.25	0.29	0.27	0.15	0	−0.04
April	maximum	−0.04	0.44	0.41	1	0.2	0.59	0.63	0.74	0.86	0.62	0	0.08

end of April 2023, purple line). A visual representation of the last three rows of the table is shown in Fig. 5b based on the test data as of April 18th, 2023.

Similarly to the described experiment, we used the CDL method in the educational process of a number of master's degree programs for the period from 2014

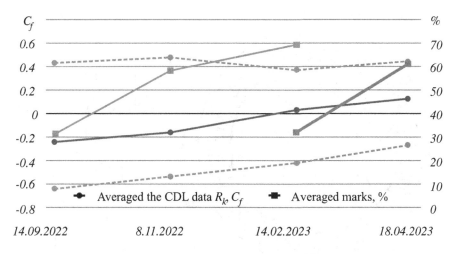

Fig. 8. Summary of data on the dynamics of changes in the CDL values of the group of students (left scale) and subject knowledge (right scale)

to 2023 (about 1500 competency profiles were built based on the test logs). Over the past three years, the data has been integrated into the ITS decision-making chain, which requires a more detailed explanation.

5.2   Integration of CDL Data into ITS Operation Logic

The proposed curriculum-level approach was applied to tracking of CDL dynamics by the ITS and explanation of its decisions, accompanied by the visual representation of competency profiles in the form of star diagrams or in the form of cognitive images in CMKD and UGVA notations. The result of overlaying CDL on cognitive images is shown in Fig. 9. The competency c_3 was chosen as a parameter for visualization, data on which were extracted from the curriculum-level competency profile and the cognitive images of the student's learning situation were projected in structural (left) and functional (right) notation. The heat map shown in Fig. 3b is used as the color scale.

The Cognitive Map of Knowledge Diagnosis (CMKD, [22]) reflects the course-level for the first three semesters (excluding the research seminar $d_{3.1}$ and $d_{3.2}$, research practice $d_{2.9}$): dark gray color indicates disciplines not included in the experiment; light grey color indicates disciplines not yet included in the learning process (the third semester). The disciplines are grouped by semesters (see Fig. 1). There are semantic (inter-course) links between the disciplines, represented by arcs. The block d_0 on the CMKD designates the score of the admission tests when CDL is measured with respect to the competency c_3. It can be seen that the competency under consideration is difficult to be developed in the frame of the course $d_{2.8}$, and these difficulties are originated from the parental discipline $d_{1.7}$ (the link is highlighted in red on Fig. 9a). Similarly, a map is built for the level of semester topics and learning units of the individual course. The

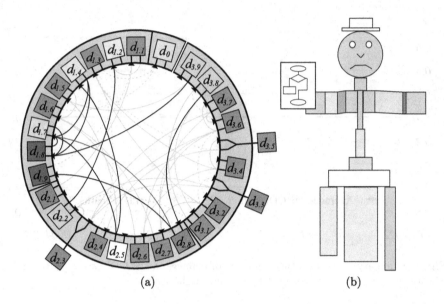

Fig. 9. Results of overlaying data from the curriculum-level competency profile on the CMKD (a) and UGVA (b) graphic notations

digital footprint data, including scores from the competency profile, are overlaid on the CMKD at all scales.

Anthropomorphic images in Unified Graphic Visualization of Activity notation (UGVA, [21]) reflect the functional aspect of the learning process in relation to the key skills of the educational program. Each block of the figure indicates the amount of the learning material responsible for the development of groups of professional skills. The color in Fig. 9b shows the result of overlaying the data from the digital educational footprint on the image: the scores for competency c_3 are interpreted according to the scale from Fig. 3b. In particular, it can be seen that there are difficulties in mastering the learning material of the special major skills s_3 (the upper limb in the right part of the image). Similarly, it is possible to decompose the curriculum-level assessment of any of the checked competencies and display it on the image in UGVA notation.

While incorporating the above cognitive images into the ITS decision-making chain, we used the capability of scaling and changing aspects to draw the cognitive images. This allowed us to form the mixed parametric profiles for each learner, reflecting the problematic issues in the learning process. All assessments of the learners' competencies for the parametric profile and for various visualization options were made on the basis of the CDL assessment method (a special service as part of the experimental ITS AESU). For more details about the cross-cutting approach to the analysis of the learning situation see [20].

At the conclusion of the consideration of examples of application of the CDL assessment method, it should be noted that our work on the processing of competency profiles is still at the stage of developing effective decisions by ITS. But it can already be stated that the curriculum-level CDL assessment allows building more flexible mechanisms for managing the learning process in the implementation of e-learning.

6   Discussion

The CDL method assessment is used in the organization of the educational process not only to support e-learning, but also to arrange admission tests, and to accredit educational programs. Integration of the CDL assessment method into the decision-making chain of the experimental ITS allows synthesizing recommendations for the learner and approaching algorithmic solutions for their automatic explanation (implementing XAI [1] approach).

The obtained results demonstrate not only consistency with the results of the assessment of the competency development dynamics during semester certification (examination), but also reduction of time for performing the tasks and tests. Demonstration of results in graphic form and on the maps while organizing learners' interaction with the ITS was well received by the learners, that is consistent with the findings of Bodily and Verbert [3]: "if students know why they receive a particular recommendation, it could increase their trust in the system along with the likelihood of them following feedback provided by the system".

The recommendations for using the method are as follows:

- formulate tasks/questions in such a way that for each of them it is possible to test hypotheses for 2–3 competencies at once;
- show the learner only those results that relate to the subject assessment at the end of the tasks;
- use the social desirability bias to record guessing attempts (for the test form), particularly to account for attempts to falsify preferences;
- use such wording in the list of tasks/questions that allows revealing subjective preference (recording of motivational component);
- collect learner's responses so that date-specific data can be extracted from the digital educational footprint and changes can be tracked;
- use the metric property of CDL assessment results when automatically processing competency profiles (without visualization) to support ITS decision-making;
- think through the logic of the automated synthesis of the explanation of the reasoning for assigning the relevant values to the competency profile and the methods of calculating the assessments.

7   Conclusion

The practical application of the Competency Development Level (CDL) method allows monitoring the learning process with respect to the competencies. The indirect nature of data collection for competency profiles (especially curriculum-level profiles) makes it a promising tool in e-learning. The CDL method can be positively integrated with cognitive visualization tools.

An important area of our work on improving the method is to expand the types of automatically analyzed answers. We are currently working on integrating the free-text answer processing module [19]. Also, we are adding the remaining disciplines of the academic program "Information Technologies and Mission Control Centers" and a number of related disciplines into the experiment.

References

1. Arrieta, A.B., et al.: Explainable Artificial Intelligence (XAI): concepts, taxonomies, opportunities and challenges toward responsible AI. Inf. Fusion **58**, 82–115 (2020)
2. Baker, R.S.: Stupid tutoring systems, intelligent humans. Int. J. Artif. Intell. Educ. **26**, 600–614 (2016)
3. Bodily, R., Verbert, K.: Trends and issues in student-facing learning analytics reporting systems research. In: Proceedings of the Seventh International Learning Analytics and Knowledge Conference (LAK 2017), pp. 309–318. Association for Computing Machinery, New York, NY, USA (2017). https://doi.org/10.1145/3027385.3027403
4. Bolsunovsky, N.: Implementation of the expert system constructor as a network service. In: Proceedings of the XIV All-Russian Conference Robotics and Artificial Intelligence, pp. 138–143. Litrra-Print, Krasnoyarsk, Russia (2022). https://aesfu.ru/local/conference/_docs/2022/RAI-22_print.pdf
5. Buchanan, B., Shortliffe, E.: Rule-Based Expert System: The MYCIN Experiments of the Stanford Heuristic Programming Project. Addison-Wesley, New York (1984)
6. Gavrilova, T.A., Kokoulina, L.: Using ontology engineering to design an artificial intelligence course. In: Uskov, V.L., Howlett, R.J., Jain, L.C. (eds.) Smart Education and e-Learning 2019. SIST, vol. 144, pp. 201–207. Springer, Singapore (2019). https://doi.org/10.1007/978-981-13-8260-4_19
7. Henry, N.W.: Latent structure analysis. Encyclopedia Stat. Sci. **6** (2004)
8. Huang, Y., Brusilovsky, P., Guerra, J., Koedinger, K., Schunn, C.: Supporting skill integration in an intelligent tutoring system for code tracing. J. Comput. Assist. Learn. **39**(2), 477–500 (2023). https://doi.org/10.1111/jcal.12757
9. Ilves, K., Leinonen, J., Hellas, A.: Supporting self-regulated learning with visualizations in online learning environments. In: Proceedings of the 49th ACM Technical Symposium on Computer Science Education (SIGCSE 2018), pp. 257–262. Association for Computing Machinery, New York, NY, USA (2018)
10. Jensen, M.L., Mondrup, F., Lippert, F., Ringsted, C.: Using e-learning for maintenance of ALS competence. Resuscitation **80**(8), 903–908 (2009). https://doi.org/10.1016/j.resuscitation.2009.06.005
11. Likert, R.: A technique for the measurement of attitudes. Arch. Psychol. **140**, 44–53 (1932)
12. Litovkin, D., Anikin, A., Kulyukin, K., Sychev, O.: Intelligent tutor for designing function interface in a programming language. In: Crossley, S., Popescu, E. (eds.) Intelligent Tutoring Systems, pp. 293–302. Springer, Cham (2022). https://doi.org/10.1007/978-3-031-09680-8_27
13. Miller, G.: The magical number seven, plus or minus two: some limits on our capacity for processing information. Psychol. Rev. **63**(2), 81–97 (1956)
14. Pawlowski, E., Soroui, J.: Analysing PIAAC data with the international data explorer (IDE). In: Large-Scale Cognitive Assessment: Analyzing PIAAC Data, pp. 93–115 (2020). https://doi.org/10.1007/978-3-030-47515-4_5

15. Phobun, P., Vicheanpanya, J.: Adaptive intelligent tutoring systems for e-learning systems. Procedia. Soc. Behav. Sci. **2**(2), 4064–4069 (2010). https://doi.org/10.1016/j.sbspro.2010.03.641

16. Rust, J., Golombok, S.: Modern Psychometrics: The Science of Psychological Assessment. Routledge, NY (2014)

17. Rybina, G.: Intelligent tutoring systems: analysis of basic architectures and features of the application of the ontological approach (on the example of the experience of developing and practical use of tutoring integrated expert systems). Instrum. Syst. Monit. Control Diagn. 2, 23–43 (2023). https://doi.org/10.25791/pribor.2.2023.1388. (in Russian)

18. Shute, V., Towle, B.: Adaptive e-learning. In: Educational Psychologist, pp. 105–114. Routledge (2018)

19. Uglev, V., Dobronets, B.: Methodic of automatic measurement and estimation of the level of competences development. Inf. Educ. **281**(2), 61–65 (2017). https://info.infojournal.ru/jour/article/view/149/150. (in Russian)

20. Uglev, V., Gavrilova, T.: Cross-cutting visual support of decision making for forming personalized learning spaces. In: Krouska, A., Troussas, C., Caro, J. (eds.) Novel & Intelligent Digital Systems: Proceedings of the 2nd International Conference (NiDS 2022). LNNS, vol. 556, pp. 3–12. Springer, Cham (2023). https://doi.org/10.1007/978-3-031-17601-2_1

21. Uglev, V., Sychev, O.: Concentrating competency profile data into cognitive map of knowledge diagnosis. In: Basu, A., Stapleton, G., Linker, S., Legg, C., Manalo, E., Viana, P. (eds.) Diagrams 2021. LNCS (LNAI), vol. 12909, pp. 443–446. Springer, Cham (2021). https://doi.org/10.1007/978-3-030-86062-2_46

22. Uglev, V., Sychev, O.: Evaluation, comparison and monitoring of multiparameter systems by Unified Graphic Visualization of Activity method on the example of learning process. Algorithms **15**(21), 468 (2022). https://doi.org/10.3390/a15120468

23. Uglev, V.A., Ustinov, V.A.: The new competencies development level expertise method within intelligent automated educational systems. In: Bajo Perez, J., et al. (eds.) Trends in Practical Applications of Heterogeneous Multi-Agent Systems. The PAAMS Collection. AISC, vol. 293, pp. 157–164. Springer, Cham (2014). https://doi.org/10.1007/978-3-319-07476-4_19

24. Weber, S., Achtenhagen, F.: Competence domains and vocational-professional education in Germany. In: Competence-Based Vocational and Professional Education: Bridging the Worlds of Work and Education, pp. 337–359 (2017)

25. Woloszynski, T., Kurzynski, M.: On a new measure of classifier competence in the feature space. Comput. Recognit. Syst. **3**, 285–292 (2009)

26. Zadeh, L.A., Aliev, R.A.: Fuzzy Logic Theory and Applications: Part I and Part II. World Scientific Publishing, Singapore (2018)

A Survey of Semantic Web Based Recommender Systems for E-Learning

Cevat Aktas[1] and Birol Ciloglugil[2(✉)]

[1] Institute of Natural Sciences, Department of Computer Engineering,
Ege University, 35100 Bornova, Izmir, Turkey
cevataktas61@gmail.com
[2] Department of Computer Engineering, Ege University,
35100 Bornova, Izmir, Turkey
birol.ciloglugil@ege.edu.tr

Abstract. Recommender systems have been widely used in various domains such as e-commerce, e-learning and the entertainment sector especially for movie and music recommendation. E-learning has gained more attention recently, as the Covid-19 pandemic forced a mandatory shift from face-to-face education to online education. In this regard, taking into consideration the individual differences of learners such as learning styles, prior knowledge level, and motivation level play a vital role in acceptance and usage levels of e-learning systems by the learners and academic success levels of students using these e-learning systems. Semantic web technologies enable modeling these individual differences with ontologies and provide a valuable foundation for knowledge based recommender systems. Various learning resource or learning object ontologies that model learning materials and learner model ontologies that model learner profiles have been developed and used successfully in different educational recommender systems. These ontologies and interaction data of learners with e-learning systems provide valuable data for recommender systems to operate on. Collaborative filtering and content based filtering approaches have been used to analyze these data and implement educational recommender systems. Therefore, in this paper, we provide a review of semantic web based recommender systems conducted at the e-learning domain. We surveyed different aspects of educational recommender systems such as the data sources used for recommendations and the approaches utilized for implementation. Finally, we present the implications, limitations and future work directions in the field of educational recommender systems.

Keywords: E-Learning · Recommender Systems · Semantic Web · Ontology

1 Introduction

Recommender systems have been successfully adopted to various domains that are widely used in daily life, especially in the e-commerce field and for recommendation of movies and music. The usage of recommender systems in the e-learning

O. Gervasi et al. (Eds.): ICCSA 2023 Workshops, LNCS 14104, pp. 494–506, 2023.
https://doi.org/10.1007/978-3-031-37105-9_33

domain is relatively new compared to its usage in the aforementioned domains. There have been numerous educational recommender systems developed in the last decade; however, with the shift from face-to-face education to online education because of the Covid-19 pandemic, the popularity of recommender systems in e-learning has increased [1].

Modeling of the individual differences between learners such as learning styles, prior knowledge level, and motivation level has a significant importance in adoption and usage level of e-learning systems by the learners [2,3]. These individual differences are essential for the personalization support of the e-learning systems [4,5]. Thus, personalization of the recommendations provided to learners effect the academic success levels of students [6–8].

Semantic web technologies enable modeling individual differences of learners with ontologies [9,10] and provide a valuable foundation for knowledge based recommender systems [11,12]. Various learning resource or learning object ontologies that model learning materials and learner model ontologies that model learner profiles have been developed and used successfully in different educational recommender systems [13–17]. These ontologies and interaction data of learners with e-learning systems provide valuable data for recommender systems to operate on [18–20].

Collaborative filtering, content based filtering and knowledge based recommendation are the main approaches for implementing recommender systems [21–23] and have been used to analyze the learner generated data and implement educational recommender systems [22,24]. Other artificial intelligence techniques such as data mining, fuzzy logic and sequential pattern mining are also widely used for implementing recommender systems [25–27].

Therefore, semantic web techniques, recommender system approaches and artificial intelligence methods provide opportunities to facilitate learning progress and enhance learning experiences of learners [13–15]. With this motivation, in this paper, we present a review of other survey studies with similar aims and focus on providing a detailed view of the semantic web based recommender systems conducted at the e-learning domain. We examined different aspects of educational recommender systems such as the data sources used for recommendations and the models and approaches utilized for implementation.

The rest of the paper is organized as follows; Sect. 2 provides a comparison of other surveys conducted to analyze recommender systems and artificial intelligence approaches in general that are applied in the e-learning domain. Section 3 presents a detailed analysis and discussion of recent educational recommender systems that incorporate an ontological component. Section 4 includes a discussion of the implications observed and possible future work directions in the field of educational recommender systems, and lists the limitations of this study. Finally, Sect. 5 concludes the paper.

2   A Review of Surveys Conducted on Personalized E-Learning Systems

There are a lot surveys conducted at the literature that focus on personalized e-learning systems and particularly on the usage of different artificial intelligence techniques in the educational domain. Table 1 presents a brief summary of these survey studies by listing the main aim of each survey paper.

Table 1 contains surveys conducted at a wide range of areas; however, the main aspects considered as inclusion criteria for the examined surveys can be listed as given below:

- "Semantic web, ontology and linked data technologies which are quite related to each other"
- "Recommender system methods"
- "Personalized e-learning systems and usage of artificial intelligence techniques on the educational domain"

Thus, the selected surveys cover a selection of these three criteria; with some surveys meeting at least one of them, while some of them involves both of the criteria listed above. Table 2 presents an analysis of focussed research areas of the recent survey papers examined in Table 1. The studies listed at Table 2 can be categorized in groups as given below:

- "Papers focussing on personalization or usage of artificial intelligence techniques on e-learning systems" [4, 6, 24–27]
- "Surveys that emphasize the application of recommender systems in the e-learning field" [18–22]
- "Papers discussing the semantic web, ontology and linked data technologies in e-learning systems"[16, 17]
- "Review of different recommender system techniques applied in various domains including education"[23]
- "Surveys that cover both semantic web, ontology and linked data related technologies, recommender system methods which are applied in an educational environment"[13–15]

Only three survey studies, namely [13–15] listed in Table 2 are involved with both of the three research areas focussed in this paper. Table 3 provides a more detailed analysis of each survey paper by listing publication year, the publication year interval of studies covered in the survey, and the number of examined studies in each survey.

The number of studies covered by [14] can seem relatively high, that is because this survey also contains studies that do not involve ontologies and focus on other recommender system approaches. When the findings of [14] are anaylzed in detail, it can be seen that only 6 publications were covered when ontology methodologies were investigated, only 10 publications applied ontologies as part of conventional recommender systems, and only 15 publications involved hybrid recommendation approaches, of which only 8 studies involved ontologies as part

Table 1. Surveys Conducted on Personalized E-Learning Systems.

Reference	Year	Main Aim of the Survey
[4]	2015	Focusses on the usage and integration of different learning style models on adaptive e-learning systems.
[6]	2015	Provides content analysis of articles that present adaptive e-learning environments implemented by using learning styles.
[13]	2022	Presents a systematic literature review on ontology usage for implementing recommender systems in the e-learning domain.
[14]	2019	Reviews ontological recommender systems implemented in the e-learning field; however, also provides a review of other machine learning techniques applied for e-learning.
[15]	2018	Knowledge based recommender systems developed by using ontologies are analyzed to present a survey.
[16]	2015	Focusses on ontology usage in e-learning environments; however, the focus of the surveys was not only on recommender systems.
[17]	2018	Provides a systematic mapping study of how ontologies are applied to enhance higher education; thus, the application domain is narrowed down from the e-learning domain in general to higher education context only.
[18]	2015	Presents a more general survey on the usage of recommenders systems on the e-learning domain.
[19]	2022	Reports the state of the art on application of recommender systems on MOOCs (Massive Open Online Courses).
[20]	2022	Provides a more specialized review of the recommender system implementations only for learning path recommendations.
[21]	2020	Dicsusses machine learning based recommender systems implemented in the e-learning domain systematiccally.
[23]	2021	Examines the applications of content-based and context-based recommendation systems; however, not focusses on a particular domain.
[22]	2020	Reviews educational recommender systems by focussing on how to support the learners' agency.
[24]	2015	Surveys the educational content design and learner adaptation aspects of e-learning systems and not focusses on the recommender system related components.
[25]	2022	Presents a more general review of artificial intelligence based personalized e-learning environments and not focusses on recommender systems.
[26]	2020	Discusses the applications and open issues related to artificial intelligence usage in educational systems.
[27]	2020	Provides a survey of the challanges and open research issues of the research field "artificial intelligence in education"

Table 2. Analysis of Focussed Research Areas of Recent Surveys.

Survey Paper	Focussed Research Areas		
	Semantic Web	Recommender System	AI/Personalization in E-Learning
[4]	No	No	Yes
[6]	No	No	Yes
[13]	Yes	Yes	Yes
[14]	Yes	Yes	Yes
[15]	Yes	Yes	Yes
[16]	Yes	No	Yes
[17]	Yes	No	Yes
[18]	No	Yes	Yes
[19]	No	Yes	Yes
[20]	No	Yes	Yes
[21]	No	Yes	Yes
[23]	No	Yes	No
[22]	No	Yes	Yes
[24]	No	No	Yes
[25]	No	No	Yes
[26]	No	No	Yes
[27]	No	No	Yes

Table 3. Details of Surveys Conducted on Usage of Ontologies in Educational Recommender Systems.

Reference	Publication Year	Publication Year Interval of Studies Covered in the Survey	The Number of Examined Studies
[13]	2022	2010–2020	28 journal articles
[14]	2019	2010–2018	108 publications in total (91 journal articles, 10 conference papers, 5 books)
[15]	2018	2005–2014	36 publications

of hybridization strategy (with 3 formal and 5 domain ontologies). Therefore, it can be concluded that when ontologies are considered as the main focus, the number of investigated studies at each survey listed in Table 3 are quite close to each others.

As the most recent survey listed in Table 3, [13] includes only one article from the year 2020, which points out that there is a need for a new survey which will cover more recent research on this topic. With this motivation, this survey focusses on more recent related work on ontology usage in educational recommender systems.

3 Semantic Web Based Recommender Systems Implemented for E-Learning

Some of the pioneering research studies in the field of ontology based educational recommender systems covered by previous systematic literature reviews [13–15] can be listed and briefly discussed as given below:

- [28] : Presents a semantic web based solution to provide personalized feedback to students based on their learning goals for self assessment in lifelong learning environments. It is stated that semantic web technologies are useful to provide more effective learning experiences to students and to make online learning environments more student-oriented.
- [29] : Proposes a smart learning system for the law domain by using knowledge discovery and cognitive computing approaches. The findings of an experimental study conducted with the proposed system show that students achieve higher success when they work with personalized learning materials.
- [30] : Provides a student modeling approach by using ontologies and diagnosis rules. The proposed method is a diagnostic rule-based system that is based on detecting students' mistakes during the learning process to help personalize learning materials.
- [31] : Presents a student modeling approach based on non-monotonic diagnostic methods for training in intelligent virtual environments. The performances of students are continuously monitored to identify students' incorrect answers, and then, the student models are utilized to identify the causes of these errors.
- [32] : Proposes an ontology based personalized feedback generator called "OntoPeFeGe" that takes into account students' learning styles and prior knowledge levels. In this study, student profiles and learning materials are modeled based on an educational domain ontology. The experiments conducted to evaluate the effectiveness of OntoPeFeGe conclude that it improves students' learning performance and helps develop learning strategies.
- [33] : Designs and develops a BDI agents based solution for intelligent tutoring systems. The BDI agents monitor students' performance and offer customized learning plans by taking into account students' learning goals and prior knowledge levels. Experiments conducted to analyze the impact of the proposed system show that students' learning performance was improved significantly and the use of customized learning materials increased students' motivation levels.
- [34] : Provides a problem based learning approach for the IP addressing topic of computer networks course. It is stated that the proposed approach can increase students' motivation and problem-solving skills by offering a more active learning experience.
- [35] : Presents an educational recommender system based on semantic analysis of social networks. With customized recommendations according to students' interests and skills that utilize the semantic analysis of data in learning environments, the learning process of students can become more efficient.

– [36] : Proposes an ontology for representing learners' characteristic features by utilizing different learning style models. It is discussed that learning styles models can be used more effectively by including other characteristics of learners, such as motivation levels, and learning goals.

– [37] : Presents the "ACCESIBILITIC" ontology that supports accessibility of ICT users. The design and development of the ontology that offers solutions to accessibility problems by taking into account the activities and needs of disabled users is explained in detail.

– [38] : Proposes a solution called "OntoSakai" to support learning management systems with semantics and user profiling. The ontology which includes various features of users such as learning styles, preferences, skills, interests and other characteristics is utilized to customize the learning management system and improve learning experiences of students.

– [39] : Provides a personalized social network for academic purposes by using a fuzzy recommender system. The proposed approach collects data through a feedback mechanism that allows users to rate recommended materials, and then, adjusts the recommendations by adapting to the users' preferences and interests to provide more efficient social learning experiences.

– [40] : Presents an adaptive e-learning environment that is based on utilization of semantic web, agents and cloud computing technologies. The ontology-based approach provides a foundation that defines relationships of e-learning materials, and software agents use data mining and data analysis techniques to identify students' strengths and weaknesses. By combining ontologies and software agents, the learning materials are more accurately categorized and presented to students in a more appropriate way.

– [41] : Utilizes semantic web technologies to propose automatic feedback generation for online assessment. In this study, responses of students are automatically evaluated by using semantic web technologies. It is pointed out that these technologies can help provide students with more detailed and personalized feedback and improve their learning processes.

– [42] : Proposes an advisor system that takes into account cultural differences in instructional design processes to provide students more effective learning experiences. This system is used to evaluate the impact of cultural differences on the learning process and to provide students with appropriate learning materials and methods.

– [43] : Presents a hybrid educational recommender system that utilizes ontologies and sequential pattern mining to make recommendations by taking into account students' learning preferences and previous learning experiences. The relationships between learning materials are also analyzed to provide more personalized recommendations.

– [44] : Proposes an agent based context-aware adaptive e-learning system which takes into account the learning needs and characteristics of the students and personalizes the learning materials. It also monitors the learning progress of students and provides feedback to students during their learning processes.

– [45] : Provides the "On-smmile" student model which is based on ontology networks to integrate multiple e-learning systems. This study presents an interesting approach for creation of student models and personalization of learning materials by using ontology networks.

In this paper, more recent research studies that were not covered by [13–15] are also analyzed. Table 4 presents a summary of more recent journal articles by focussing on the main aim of each research paper.

Table 4. Analysis of more recent research articles conducted as ontology based educational recommender systems.

Reference	Year	Main Aim of the Survey
[46]	2021	Addresses the cold-start problem of content recommender systems for the e-learning domain by offering an ontology-based solution.
[47]	2021	Provides a semantic web based hybrid content recommender system for e-learning that alleviates the cold-start problem.
[48]	2023	Presents a personalized e-learning system that supports adaptive access to digital libraries by using ontologies and collaborative filtering.
[49]	2022	Proposes an e-learning recommender system which uses a dynamic ontology.
[50]	2021	Provides a recommender system based on usage of ontologies and machine learning approaches for recommendation of lifelong learning courses.
[51]	2023	Presents a hybrid recommender system that is based on linked data technologies, and description and dialetheic logic.
[52]	2023	Proposes a solution for prediction of students' behaviors based on usage of personalized ontologies and neural networks

4 Discussion of Ontology Usage in Educational Recommender Systems

Implications identified after analyzing previous systematic literature reviews and more recent research articles can be grouped as given below:

- Semantic web technologies and ontologies can be useful for problems such as cold-start, sparsity of ratings, and overspecialization in recommender systems [13,15,46,47].
- Ontologies are generally used for representation of domain knowledge and learner modeling in educational recommender systems [16]. However, there are other areas for using ontologies such as curriculum modeling, data integration among different domains [17].
- The most commonly recommended items to students in educational recommender systems are learning objects [13,14]. Besides that, learning paths [20], feedback [28,32,41], learning devices [37] and pedagogical scenarios [42] can also be recommended to learners.

- Most of the educational recommender systems were evaluated in higher education settings, with only one study reported at pre-school setting [13]. In addition, most of the studies conducted at higher education level are involved with programming and computer/software engineering courses. This is an expected finding, because most of the recommender systems are developed by computer/software engineers and tested in courses of these departments.
- Most of the studies are evaluated as part of a single course [13]. A more diverse evaluation setting is needed to assess the effectiveness of the proposed educational recommender systems.
- Standards for ontology development and engineering are generally not followed or reported in research studies [13, 14].
- Semantic web technologies are frequently used together with software agents [33, 40, 44, 53, 54]. Therefore, more research can be conducted in this area to take advantage of recent technological advancements in this research area.
- There are limited number of studies based on linked data technologies like [51]. More research can me conducted to utilize and combine various technologies.
- Research studies focus more on the technological advancements; however, educational/pedagogical aspects are as important as the technological aspects to provide better learning experiences and to improve the quality of the recommender systems [13].

Future work directions for further research studies can be listed as given below:

- Possible combinations of different recommendation approaches to provide hybrid recommender systems need to be supported with more research [14]. In this regard, traditional recommender system techniques like content-based filtering, collaborative filtering, and knowledge based (ontology based) recommendation can be supported with deep learning and machine learning approaches such as neural networks, support vector machines, and random forest to propose more enhanced hybrid recommendations [13, 55].
- More research should be conducted on methodologies for ontology evaluation. Since most of the studies do not report whether or how they evaluate the ontologies they have developed, there exist a gap in this direction [13].
- The proposed e-learning systems are generally evaluated with runtime performance analysis, simulation studies (with nonreal students), and sometimes quantitative and qualitative observations (in face to face or online classroom settings) [13, 15]. Thus, evaluation aspects of recommenders systems needs more attention in future studies.
- There are recent research studies that focus on providing explainable recommendations to students in personalized e-learning systems [56]
- Utiling new technological advances such as AR/VR technologies and the Metaverse can also facilitate providing more enhanced learning experiences [57].

There are also limitations of this paper. First of all, a systematic approach is not followed, which may effect the findings presented. However, the snowball approach is followed in this paper by checking the citations of other survey articles. Thus, it can be claimed that the overall quality of the papers examined in this paper is relatively high.

5   Conclusion

In this paper, a detailed analysis of previous surveys conducted at the e-learning field by focussing artificial intelligence and personalization, recommender systems, and semantic web/ontology/linked data technologies have been given. Also, a comparison with three other surveys that focus on semantic web based recommender systems in e-learning domain like this review has been provided. A summary of major studies covered by previous surveys is presented and more recent research studies conducted as semantic web based recommender systems in the e-learning field are discussed.

Ontology usage as part of recommender systems provide a huge potential for implementation of future personalized e-learning systems. However, in order to reach the full potential of educational recommender systems, both educational and technological aspects as well as the cultural differences should be considered. In this regard, a diverse set of stakeholders including computer/software engineers, learning content designers, institutional representatives should come together and work in tandem to produce more efficient educational recommender systems, preferably with international collaborations.

References

1. Almaiah, M.A., Al-Khasawneh, A., Althunibat, A.: Exploring the critical challenges and factors influencing the E-learning system usage during COVID-19 pandemic. Educ. Inf. Technol. **25**(6), 5261–5280 (2020). https://doi.org/10.1007/s10639-020-10219-y
2. Essalmi, F., Ayed, L.J.B., Jemni, M., Graf, S.: A fully personalization strategy of e-learning scenarios. Comput. Hum. Behav. **26**(4), 581–591 (2010)
3. Ciloglugil, B., Inceoglu, M.M.: User modeling for adaptive E-learning systems. In: Murgante, B., et al. (eds.) ICCSA 2012. LNCS, vol. 7335, pp. 550–561. Springer, Heidelberg (2012). https://doi.org/10.1007/978-3-642-31137-6_42
4. Truong, H.M.: Integrating learning styles and adaptive e-learning system: current developments, problems and opportunities. Comput. Hum. Behav. **55**, 1185–1193 (2015)
5. Ciloglugil, B.: Adaptivity based on Felder-Silverman learning styles model in e-learning systems. In: 4th International Symposium on Innovative Technologies in Engineering and Science, ISITES 2016, pp. 1523–1532 (2016)
6. Ozyurt, O., Ozyurt, H.: Learning style based individualized adaptive e-learning environments: content analysis of the articles published from 2005 to 2014. Comput. Hum. Behav. **52**, 349–358 (2015)
7. Ciloglugil, B., Inceoglu, M.M.: Exploring the state of the art in adaptive distributed learning environments. In: Taniar, D., Gervasi, O., Murgante, B., Pardede, E., Apduhan, B.O. (eds.) ICCSA 2010. LNCS, vol. 6017, pp. 556–569. Springer, Heidelberg (2010). https://doi.org/10.1007/978-3-642-12165-4_44

8. Ciloglugil, B., Inceoglu, M.M.: A learner ontology based on learning style models for adaptive e-learning. In: Gervasi, O., et al. (eds.) ICCSA 2018. LNCS, vol. 10961, pp. 199–212. Springer, Cham (2018). https://doi.org/10.1007/978-3-319-95165-2_14

9. Berners-Lee, T., Hendler, J., Lassila, O.: The Semantic Web. Sci. Am. **284**(5), 34–43 (2001)

10. Ciloglugil, B., Inceoglu, M.M.: Ontology usage in E-learning systems focusing on metadata modeling of learning objects. In: International Conference on New Trends in Education, ICNTE 2016, pp. 80–96 (2016)

11. Kurilovas, E., Kubilinskiene, S., Dagiene, V.: Web 3.0-Based personalisation of learning objects in virtual learning environments. Comput. Hum. Behav. **30**, 654–662 (2014)

12. Ciloglugil, B., Inceoglu, M.M.: Developing adaptive and personalized distributed learning systems with semantic web supported multi agent technology. In: 10th IEEE International Conference on Advanced Learning Technologies, ICALT 2010, Sousse, Tunesia, 5–7 July 2010, pp. 699–700. IEEE Computer Society (2010)

13. Rahayu, N.W., Ferdiana, R., Kusumawardani, S.S.: A systematic review of ontology use in E-Learning recommender system. Comput. Educ.: Artif. Intell., 100047 (2022)

14. George, G., Lal, A.M.: Review of ontology-based recommender systems in e-learning. Comput. Educ. **142**, 103642 (2019)

15. Tarus, J.K., Niu, Z., Mustafa, G.: Knowledge-based recommendation: a review of ontology-based recommender systems for e-learning. Artif. Intell. Rev. **50**, 21–48 (2018)

16. Al-Yahya, M., George, R., Alfaries, A.: Ontologies in E-learning: review of the literature. Int. J. Softw. Eng. Appl. **9**(2), 67–84 (2015)

17. Tapia-Leon, M., Rivera, A.C., Chicaiza, J., Luján-Mora, S.: Application of ontologies in higher education: a systematic mapping study. In: 2018 IEEE Global Engineering Education Conference (EDUCON), pp. 1344–1353. IEEE (2018)

18. Klašnja-Milićević, A., Ivanović, M., Nanopoulos, A.: Recommender systems in e-learning environments: a survey of the state-of-the-art and possible extensions. Artif. Intell. Rev. **44**(4), 571–604 (2015). https://doi.org/10.1007/s10462-015-9440-z

19. Khalid, A., Lundqvist, K., Yates, A.: A literature review of implemented recommendation techniques used in massive open online Courses. Expert Syst. Appl. **187**, 115926 (2022)

20. Rahayu, N.W., Ferdiana, R., Kusumawardani, S.S.: A systematic review of learning path recommender systems. Educ. Inf. Technol., 1–24 (2022)

21. Khanal, S.S., Prasad, P.W.C., Alsadoon, A., Maag, A.: A systematic review: machine learning based recommendation systems for e-learning. Educ. Inf. Technol. **25**, 2635–2664 (2020)

22. Deschênes, M.: Recommender systems to support learners' agency in a learning context: a systematic review. Int. J. Educ. Technol. High. Educ. **17**(1), 50 (2020)

23. Javed, U., Shaukat, K., Hameed, I.A., Iqbal, F., Alam, T.M., Luo, S.: A review of content-based and context-based recommendation systems. Int. J. Emerg. Technol. Learn. (iJET) **16**(3), 274–306 (2021)

24. Premlatha, K.R., Geetha, T.V.: Learning content design and learner adaptation for adaptive e-learning environment: a survey. Artif. Intell. Rev. **44**(4), 443–465 (2015). https://doi.org/10.1007/s10462-015-9432-z

25. Murtaza, M., Ahmed, Y., Shamsi, J. A., Sherwani, F., Usman, M.: AI-based personalized e-learning systems: Issues, challenges, and solutions. IEEE Access (2022)

26. Chen, X., Xie, H., Zou, D., Hwang, G.J.: Application and theory gaps during the rise of artificial intelligence in education. Comput. Educ.: Artif. Intell. **1**, 100002 (2020)

27. Hwang, G.J., Xie, H., Wah, B.W., Gašević, D.: Vision, challenges, roles and research issues of artificial intelligence in education. Comput. Educ.: Artif. Intell. **1**, 100001 (2020)

28. Belcadhi, L.C.: Personalized feedback for self assessment in lifelong learning environments based on semantic web. Comput. Hum. Behav. **55**, 562–570 (2016)

29. Capuano, N., Toti, D.: Experimentation of a smart learning system for law based on knowledge discovery and cognitive computing. Comput. Hum. Behav. **92**, 459–467 (2019)

30. Clemente, J., Ramírez, J., De Antonio, A.: A proposal for student modeling based on ontologies and diagnosis rules. Expert Syst. Appl. **38**(7), 8066–8078 (2011)

31. Clemente, J., Ramírez, J., De Antonio, A.: Applying a student modeling with nonmonotonic diagnosis to intelligent virtual environment for training/instruction. Expert Syst. Appl. **41**(2), 508–520 (2014)

32. Demaidi, M.N., Gaber, M.M., Filer, N.: OntoPeFeGe: ontology-based personalized feedback generator. IEEE Access **6**, 31644–31664 (2018)

33. Fonte, F.A.M., Burguillo, J.C., Nistal, M.L.: An intelligent tutoring module controlled by BDI agents for an e-learning platform. Expert Syst. Appl. **39**(8), 7546–7554 (2012)

34. Jevremovic, A., Shimic, G., Veinovic, M., Ristic, N.: IP addressing: problem-based learning approach on computer networks. IEEE Trans. Learn. Technol. **10**(3), 367–378 (2016)

35. Khaled, A., Ouchani, S., Chohra, C.: Recommendations-based on semantic analysis of social networks in learning environments. Comput. Hum. Behav. **101**, 435–449 (2019)

36. Labib, A.E., Canós, J.H., Penadés, M.C.: On the way to learning style models integration: a learner's characteristics ontology. Comput. Hum. Behav. **73**, 433–445 (2017)

37. Mariño, B.D.R., RodríGuez-FóRtiz, M.J., Torres, M.V.H., Haddad, H.M.: Accessibility and activity-centered design for ICT users: ACCESIBILITIC ontology. IEEE Access **6**, 60655–60665 (2018)

38. Muñoz, A., Lasheras, J., Capel, A., Cantabella, M., Caballero, A.: OntoSakai: on the optimization of a learning management system using semantics and user profiling. Expert Syst. Appl. **42**(15–16), 5995–6007 (2015)

39. Porcel, C., Ching-López, A., Lefranc, G., Loia, V., Herrera-Viedma, E.: Sharing notes: an academic social network based on a personalized fuzzy linguistic recommender system. Eng. Appl. Artif. Intell. **75**, 1–10 (2018)

40. Rani, M., Nayak, R., Vyas, O.P.: An ontology-based adaptive personalized e-learning system, assisted by software agents on cloud storage. Knowl.-Based Syst. **90**, 33–48 (2015)

41. del Mar Sánchez-Vera, M., Fernández-Breis, J.T., Castellanos-Nieves, D., Frutos-Morales, F., Prendes-Espinosa, M.P.: Semantic Web technologies for generating feedback in online assessment environments. Knowl.-Based Syst. **33**, 152–165 (2012)

42. Savard, I., Bourdeau, J., Paquette, G.: Considering cultural variables in the instructional design process: a knowledge-based advisor system. Comput. Educ. **145**, 103722 (2020)

43. Tarus, J.K., Niu, Z., Yousif, A.: A hybrid knowledge-based recommender system for e-learning based on ontology and sequential pattern mining. Future Gener. Comput. Syst. **72**, 37–48 (2017)
44. Yaghmaie, M., Bahreininejad, A.: A context-aware adaptive learning system using agents. Expert Syst. Appl. **38**(4), 3280–3286 (2011)
45. Yago, H., Clemente, J., Rodriguez, D., Fernandez-de-Cordoba, P.: On-smmile: ontology network-based student model for multiple learning environments. Data Knowl. Eng. **115**, 48–67 (2018)
46. Joy, J., Raj, N.S., VG, R.: Ontology-based E-learning content recommender system for addressing the pure cold-start problem. ACM J. Data Inf. Qual. **13**(3), 1–27 (2021)
47. Jeevamol, J., Renumol, V.G.: An ontology-based hybrid e-learning content recommender system for alleviating the cold-start problem. Educ. Inf. Technol. **26**(4), 4993–5022 (2021). https://doi.org/10.1007/s10639-021-10508-0
48. Senthil Kumaran, V., Latha, R.: Towards personal learning environment by enhancing adaptive access to digital library using ontology-supported collaborative filtering. Library Hi Tech (2023)
49. Amane, M., Aissaoui, K., Berrada, M.: ERSDO: E-learning recommender system based on dynamic ontology. Educ. Inf. Technol. **27**(6), 7549–7561 (2022)
50. Urdaneta-Ponte, M.C., Méndez-Zorrilla, A., Oleagordia-Ruiz, I.: Lifelong learning courses recommendation system to improve professional skills using ontology and machine learning. Appl. Sci. **11**(9), 3839 (2021)
51. Santos, R.D., Aguilar, J.: A hybrid recommender system based on description/dialetheic logic and linked data. Expert. Syst. **40**(2), e13143 (2023)
52. Mary Harin Fernandez, F., Venkata Ramana, T., Shabana, M., Kannagi, V., Nalini, M.: Personalized ontology and deep training tree -based optimal gated recurrent unit -recurrent neural network for prediction of students' behavior. Concurr. Computa.: Pract. Exp. **35**(1), e7420 (2023)
53. Harley, J.M., Taub, M., Azevedo, R., Bouchet, F.: Let's set up some subgoals: understanding human-pedagogical agent collaborations and their implications for learning and prompt and feedback compliance. IEEE Trans. Learn. Technol. **11**(1), 54–66 (2017)
54. Schouten, D.G., Venneker, F., Bosse, T., Neerincx, M.A., Cremers, A.H.: A digital coach that provides affective and social learning support to low-literate learners. IEEE Trans. Learn. Technol. **11**(1), 67–80 (2017)
55. Zheng, X.L., Chen, C.C., Hung, J.L., He, W., Hong, F.X., Lin, Z.: A hybrid trust-based recommender system for online communities of practice. IEEE Trans. Learn. Technol. **8**(4), 345–356 (2015)
56. Barria-Pineda, J., Akhuseyinoglu, K., Želem-Ćelap, S., Brusilovsky, P., Milicevic, A.K., Ivanovic, M.: Explainable recommendations in a personalized programming practice system. In: Roll, I., McNamara, D., Sosnovsky, S., Luckin, R., Dimitrova, V. (eds.) AIED 2021. LNCS (LNAI), vol. 12748, pp. 64–76. Springer, Cham (2021). https://doi.org/10.1007/978-3-030-78292-4_6
57. Inceoglu, M.M., Ciloglugil, B.: Industry 4.0 briefcase: an innovative engineering outreach project for professions of the future. In: Gervasi, O., et al. (eds.) ICCSA 2020. LNCS, vol. 12250, pp. 979–988. Springer, Cham (2020). https://doi.org/10.1007/978-3-030-58802-1_70

COVID-19 Response and Its Aftermath: Experience in Introducing Online Learning Technologies to Diverse Teaching Staff

Elena Berisheva⬭, Oleg Sychev$^{(\boxtimes)}$⬭, Marat Berishev⬭, and Tatyana Chudasova⬭

Volgograd State Technical University, Lenin Ave, 28, Volgograd 400005, Russia
e_berisheva@vstu.ru, o_sychev@vstu.ru

Abstract. The paper is devoted to the experience of developing an online educational system at Volgograd State Technical University. We describe the process of the abrupt transition to online learning during the COVID-19 pandemic and the following process of merging online and on-site learning. The paper discusses how the university's online educational environment was formed and how its staff adapted. We describe the technical, didactic, and organizational measures which resulted in the growing popularity of the online learning environment and other e-learning tools. The online learning environment was created by connecting the existing information system 1C.University with the online learning management system Moodle. The 1C.University software stores the organizational information about the students, their enrollments, teachers, courses, curricula, etc. The custom module that connects 1C.University and Moodle LMS allows keeping student enrollment in the electronic courses up to date and creating additional services for students and teaching staff. The developed education and information electronic environment of the university hosts more than 16 000 online courses. Many courses contain educational videos and interactive learning elements.

Keywords: online learning · technology acceptance · electronic information and educational environment · Moodle

1 Introduction

Online learning—a method of supporting on-site classes and a kind of correspondence learning—has a long history. The University of Phoenix began offering online degrees as early as 1989. But, despite many achievements, including developing Massive Open Online Courses and Intelligent Tutoring systems, most of the pedagogical staff in traditional educational institutions still needed to be convinced about online learning. COVID-19 pandemics and relevant quarantine measures gave a powerful impetus to the implementation of online learning

The reported study was funded by VSTU, project number 60/438-22.

all around the world [16, 20]. Many educational institutions suddenly faced the necessity to move their classes online, which forced the quick adoption of the new form of learning with all its difficulties and problems [14]. However, the same events helped widen the usage of e-learning methods and environments when the initial problems were overcome.

Today, e-learning services and platforms are used for teaching students on all levels of education, professional training and retraining, and adult education. They went beyond a mere medium between a teacher and a learner and became a separate scientific and professional field. The leading world universities actively study and implement e-learning technologies and share open online resources and courses. Developing, implementing, and supporting electronic educational software became a new trend in the IT industry.

E-learning can be considered a complex system with the following basic parts (subsystems):

1. Software and tools for organization and support of educational process;
2. Software and systems for control of learning process, grading, and assessments;
3. Software and systems for organizing interactions of departments of an educational institution for supporting the learning process, including technical support;
4. Software and systems supporting learning analytic and decision-making about the learning process, allowing to get an overall picture of the learning process and increasing its efficiency.

The E-learning process generates a lot of data in the form of the digital learning footprint of each participant of the learning process that can be analyzed. It allows controlling online and on-site classes of each teacher, students' attendance of classes, and the amount of time spent studying the electronic learning materials, gathering and grading assignments, automatic test grading, operative demonstration of the current course grade, and so on, which students, teachers, and university management staff value.

Back in 2020, when educational institutions abruptly had to move their classes online because of the quarantine, many smaller institutions did not have experience in online learning and ready solutions and tools for that [5]. Learning-process participants on all levels of education used the software and solutions they knew. They were used to - or, at least, had easy access to, often without an effort to unify and structurize this new, for them, way of learning. Different teachers in the same institutions often used different tools: for example, some teachers used Skype, others used Zoom, yet others used software messengers or file servers [2]. The institutions encountered the problems like the lack of professional skills in e-learning (and general information and media technologies) among the teaching staff, inadequate communication equipment with low bandwidth that cannot support the stream of e-learning for all the students and teachers at once, and the lack of server space and computing power to keep it all running [4].

These problems were solved with time. New servers were bought; internet bandwidth was enhanced to the level where it could support the workload of fully online classes. Teachers and tutors underwent professional training and developed their electronic materials. When the quarantine ended, many educational of them decided to use this experience and the e-learning tools they learned to support their learning process in class and during homework. Management and the staff of departments that worked on the transition to e-learning encountered new problems, which were deeper [8,11] and required more effort to search, e.g., the following problems:

1. Systematic integration of the learning management systems and educational tools with existing information systems storing administrative data about students and staff.
2. Maintaining the institution's electronic library, integrating it with the learning management system, and enhancing the university's library with seamless access to external digital libraries.
3. Creating a secure platform for qualitative and quantitative grading of online students, including developing electronic question and learning-problem banks and implementing proctoring systems.
4. Creating remote-access laboratories (virtual or giving access to actual physical equipment), which can replace attendance of on-site laboratories [17, 19];
5. Learning-process analysis aimed at identifying hidden opportunities, finding and predicting students' needs, and predicting demand for online courses to maximize the efficiency of the supported online courses and increase competitiveness in the educational service market.

Online learning is a prospective field of development for traditional learning institutions. In the modern world, when people have to keep learning their whole lives to be efficient workers, this way of learning opens new opportunities for educational institutions and people who consider buying their products.

2 Related Works

Responding to the COVID-19 pandemic, different universities adopted online learning platforms and general-purpose online communication tools their staff was most acquainted with: the required speed of the response did not leave enough time to prepare staff for new challenges. Later, these solutions were improved or replaced by institution-wide solutions: some educational institutions developed their own tools, while most of them used standardized learning tools. Many reported their progress in implementing COVID-19 response and adopting e-learning platforms in research papers and articles.

Financial University (Moscow) used the Microsoft Teams platform to hold most of its online lectures, practice lessons, and other online activities. The platform allowed teachers and students to use presentations and demonstrate different software on their screens while videoconferencing. During the quarantine in 2020, they also used Microsoft Skype for Business to hold staff meetings and Zoom for some of their video conferences. The students received assignments in the University's LMS and Microsoft OneNote. Studying information systems in accounting and banking implies practicing using real banking and accounting software. Financial University used Microsoft RemoteApp solutions to allow each student access to remote laboratories with installed commercial-grade software [10], which can be considered establishing an online laboratory with remote access.

In universities of the Kurdistan region of Iraq, the survey of students and teachers about using online learning after COVID-19 showed the following. About 35.6% of survey participants used learning management systems (e.g., Moodle, Google Classroom, Edmodo, or Adobe Captivate Prime) for online learning after the COVID-19 outbreak; 21.6% of participants used mobile messengers (e.g., Viber, WhatsApp, Telegram, Messenger, WeChat) for online learning; while 9.2% of respondents used online classroom applications (e.g., Newrow Smart, Blackboard Collaborate). 33,6% of the survey participants used web-conference and webinar platforms (e.g., Zoom Meetings, Google Meet) [12].

A survey of students (78.5% of participants) and teachers (21.5% of participants) of 65 higher-education institutions in Ukraine (the most active participating institutions were the National University of Aviation and its Summer Academy, Kyiv National Trade and Economic University, Volyn National University named after Lesya Ukrainka, National Technical University named after Igor Sikorsky, and Odesa Agrarian University) had shown active usage of online learning platforms Zoom (88.3% of participants) and Classroom (85.3% of participants). Innovative using of these online platforms improved the students' learning gains. The respondents also used software and tools like YouTube (49.5%), LMS Moodle (47.3%), Microsoft Teams (35.7%), Skype (32.9%), Microsoft one note (12%), Coursera (7.7%), Kahoot (7,6%), etc. [25].

A study conducted in Indonesia with 26 teachers from higher-education institutions in Sumatra, Java, Borneo, and Sulawesi showed similar results. Teachers and students often used learning management systems during the COVID-19 pandemic; Google Class and Edmodo were the most commonly used systems. They also used videoconferencing services Zoom and Skype. One of the unusual findings was that learning management systems hosted by institutions were less attractive for teachers than videoconferencing services [13]. That was likely caused by the lack of skills to develop online learning materials and the significant effort necessary to create necessary online data for using learning management systems.

Universities in Pakistan have also actively transferred their pedagogical and educational activities to the virtual environment. Most universities developed effective online learning systems and switched to online learning. Projects, group work, lessons, and study guides were posted in online learning systems. Teachers have used various tools for virtual classes. Zoom, Google Meet, Microsoft Teams, Webex, and other software applications were used for study and work [18].

3   Online Learning Technologies in VSTU

The timeline of implementing online learning technologies in VSTU is presented in Table 1.

Table 1. Timeline of implementing online learning in VSTU.

Time	Activities
2017	Creation of the university's electronic information and education environment (EIEE)
Summer 2018	Beginning of yearly surveys of students, teachers, and employers regarding the quality of the educational process
March 2020	Emergency mass generation of online courses in EIEE and filling them with content
March–December 2020	Teacher raining in using EIEE and videoconferencing systems
July 2020	The Department of Automation of Educational Activities was created
September 2020	Transition to the EIEE 2.0 platform connected to the 1C.University information system. Appointment of employees responsible for EIEE at departments and faculties
September 2020	Beginning of automatic checks of the EIEE for empty courses and inactive users (twice per year)
December 2020	Approval of the e-course template for basic educational programs
January 2021	Training of teachers with advanced training courses begins
November 2021	Annual competition "The best online course belonging to basic educational programs at the university's EIEE"

3.1   Online Learning in VSTU Before 2020

According to the Federal State Educational Standards, Volgograd State Technical University (VSTU) implemented Electronic Information-Educational Environment (EIEE) years before the spring of 2020. The environment provided access to curricula, course (module) and internship programs, electronic textbooks, and learning material referenced in the course (internship) programs; it allowed students creating their electronic portfolio, including saving their course projects and grades. When undergraduate and graduate curricula include courses using e-learning technologies, the environment must also provide features like building an electronic educational footprint of the learning process, storing the results of exams and the graduate projects and theses, holding online classes and exams which are codified in the curricula for learning programs taught using e-learning tools, and communication between the participants of the learning process using the Internet, including synchronous and asynchronous communication.

EIEE function is supported by educational institution's equipment and staff's (both teaching staff and supporting staff) skills in information-communication technologies (ICT); its use is regulated by the federal law [1].

To conform with these legal regulations, VSTU implemented EIEE and provided teachers access to it. However, it did not gain popularity: teachers were very conservative towards using it in their learning process except in

Table 2. Age categories of Volgograd State Technical University teachers.

Age group	Teachers in 2020	Teachers in 2022
Under 35 years	13%	15%
35–55 years	49%	47%
Over 55 years	38%	38%

some departments of the Faculty of Electronics and Computing. In December 2019, the average number of unique EIEE users was only 73 people per day. The main cause was the low level of development of digital competencies among university teachers and the significant amount of work required to move part of their courses online. Video conferencing tools were used rarely. By 2020, VSTU's teaching staff contained over 800 teachers, only 13% of them young (see Table 2).

According to surveys, 16% of the university's teachers did not even know what Learning Management Systems and Massive Open Online Courses (MOOCs) are. About 65% of teachers have never been trained in MOOCs. 31% of the respondents stated that they are firmly against creating online courses in EIEE.

3.2 Emergencies Measures at Spring 2020

With the advance of the COVID-19 pandemic in the spring of 2020, educational organizations all around the world suddenly had to switch the bulk of their learning process to a remote (primarily online) form. Only a small percentage of universities were fully ready for that transition. VSTU had to solve several problems urgently:

1. creation of online courses in EIEE for all the courses (modules, internships)currently taught in the university;
2. training teachers in e-learning technologies (ELT);
3. teaching students e-learning technologies;
4. control of the learning process in the new form;
5. finding and supporting hardware and software for teachers and students.

A creative team was assembled from employees of the educational-methodological department, teachers of the department "Software for automated systems" and students majoring in Software Engineering to solve the first task. In a week, this team collected the necessary reference data. It developed a set of SQL scripts that prepared information for the Moodle authentication and enrollment plugins External Database and automatically created almost 5 000 online courses with about 1 000 teachers and 14 000 students enrolled in them.

Then it was necessary to teach teachers and professors to develop and publish content in online courses and use video conferencing services to hold online classes. To solve this problem, several of the most experienced teachers filmed tutorial videos that were widely distributed in EIEE. A group of volunteers was assembled from the students of the Faculty of Electronics and Computing; they helped teachers to install software and trained older teachers in using information-communication technologies.

Most of the students already had a higher level of development of digital competencies than teachers. For them, tutorial videos were filmed about using EIEE and video conferencing services. At that time, no single solution for video conferencing was accepted at the university. Most of the teachers used Zoom or Discord.

3.3 Systematization of EIEE in 2020–2021

In July 2020, the Department of Automation of Educational Activities (AEAD) was created at VSTU. It became responsible for the functioning and development of the university's EIEE. Its responsibilities included developing software to connect the university's information system 1C.University with the LMS Moodle, which was used to support the learning process, organize training of the teaching staff, and prepare administrative measures to promote online learning technologies and evaluate their development at the university.

Developed Software. Given the tight deadlines – the first version of the software was developed in just a week – it could not be used to maintain education in the subsequent academic years. So, in time for the next academic year, that began on September 1st 2020, a new application was developed that could provide persistent control over course generation and student and teacher enrollments. The main goal of that application was to connect the university's administrative software 1C.University, which stored information about students, their academic majors and minors, curricula, courses, and teachers who taught them to the Moodle LMS. As it required changing the identification of courses, it was decided to launch a new platform, EIEE 2.0, allowing teachers to import their courses' content from the old platform. The new application consisted of two parts:

1. a *set of SQL plugins* captured university-specific code parts, generating tables of online courses, student groups, and group enrollments;
2. the *Moodle enrollment plugin PoasDatabase*, and extended version of the basic External Database plugin that mostly contained generalized code, not tied to the peculiarities of the learning process at a particular institution.

One of the essential design decisions was determining the exact conditions for creating separate online courses. Students in Russia choose their academic major when enrolling in a higher-education institution, and the relevant curriculum determines which courses they must pass each semester. So common courses with the same names can differ significantly depending on the student's academic major: e.g., a Physics course taught for students majoring in different branches of mechanical engineering is different from a Physics course for future chemists, IT specialists, and managers. Also, courses with many enrolled students can be divided among several lecturers; in this case, not all the lecturers teach the same. Some long courses take several semesters to complete, with different topics for each semester. So we decided to create separate online courses if at least one of the following parameters was different:

- level of education (e.g., undergraduate, graduate);
- semester number;
- academic major;
- kind of learning (e.g., on-site, correspondence, evening, shortened);
- course name;
- lecturer.

If a lecturer wants to use the same online course to teach students from different academic majors or kinds of learning, or two lecturers want to share their materials in a common course, they can use Moodle Course Meta-link functionality to link students enrolled in one online course to the other course.

One of the problems the development team encountered was that VSTU had not employed the scheduling capabilities of the 1C.University system, so the system's database did not contain information about lecturers responsible for different courses in a direct form. It was a serious problem because a big, university-wide course could be taught by several lecturers who adapted their courses to the academic majors of the students they taught. The only place where this information could be found was the module to print grade sheets which lecturers have to fill twice a semester so that faculty staff could track students' progress during the semester. So it was decided to generate online courses based on the grade sheets, which allowed faculty members control over the time of online course creation (i.e., they can be created in advance if the lecturer asks for it).

As students select their academic major at enrollment and their curricula specify exactly which courses they should take each semester (except elective courses), students at VSTU mostly learn in stable groups. So the developed software makes heavy usage of Moodle cohorts (global groups): students are enrolled in courses as groups, not individually. That required enhancing the standard External Database plugin to add automatic cohort enrollment from the external database. We also created bigger cohorts (e.g., combining all students of a certain level of education belonging to a particular academic major or faculty), which allowed heads of learning departments and deans of faculties mass mailing to groups of students.

Another problem that our software-development team solved was dealing with enrolled students who failed their final exams. At VSTU, students are given a grace period to complete the courses they were not able to complete in time; these students had to be enrolled in their previous courses individually, not as a part of the group. So we developed separate software that monitored exam scores, created lists of students in the grace periods, and kept them enrolled in the courses.

The main Moodle installation of the university's EIEE[1] is connected to a smaller Moodle installation[2], supported by "Software for automated systems" department. That second installation hosts innovative learning plugins developed by "Software for automated systems" department:

– assignment module PoasAssignment allows students to select and solve individual variants of assignments distributed using different strategies, which helps avoid cheating;
– Preg question type, which lets teachers specify open answers as regular expressions and can hint next correct character and next correct token in the training mode [21];
– CorrectWriting question type which analyses the sequence of tokens in the answer and reports misplaced, missing, and extraneous tokens [22];
– Supervised block, which opens access to summative and exam quizzes only when the teacher holds classes.

They are used in online courses teaching programming and English as a foreign language.

The developed Moodle plugin PoasDatabase is released under General Public License and can be accessed via its repository site[3]. We plan to submit it to Moodle plugin database once it is made fully compliant with Moodle coding guidelines.

Training of Teaching Staff. At first, teachers and professors of VSTU had significant difficulties filling the online courses generated for them with educational content. To solve that problem, the team governing the transition to online learning developed professional training courses "Organization of teacher's educational activities with the help of tools of university's electronic information and educational environment". Many teachers wanted to study these courses at once, and the registration for courses was immediately filled out for the following year. The course covered the main methods of work in the EIEE, which were necessary for developing online courses and using them in the learning process; they were explained in detail so that the teachers could start using the acquired knowledge immediately. The template online course was created to help teachers satisfy the basic requirements to the online courses they developed; teachers could import elements of the template course into their courses.

The template course includes the following required course elements:

1. News forum (news is published only by teaching staff);
2. General forum (all course participants can participate in discussions);
3. Online consultation with students (the teacher sets the date and time for each group when synchronous online communication takes place);

---

[1] https://eos2.vstu.ru.

[2] https://edu.vstu.ru.

[3] https://bitbucket.org/oasychev/moodle-plugins-poasdatabase/src/master/.

4. General information for course participants (the course program (module, internship), templates for the documents produced by students (title pages, laboratory work protocols, etc.), a list or links to recommended literature and other documents used in the learning process;
5. The course educational content (can be filled before the start of the semester or during it);
6. Mid-semester exams (including the necessary materials to prepare for them);
7. Survey of the course quality (anonymous survey for course participants to evaluate the course effect and quality);
8. The results of students' learning in the course (student grades on a 100-point scale).

Of course, an online course for this training program was also created: it served both as an example and training grounds where teachers could see how their students will experience different elements of online learning. The teachers who participated in the training program especially appreciated video lectures about online learning which they could watch anytime. It was important because many of them could only attend some of the synchronous classes because of their teaching schedule. Access to the online course remained open to the participants after completion of training; according to the Moodle usage statistics, the materials in that course were accessed actively when teachers needed to review the materials after a long break in their usage (e.g., before starting creating online course materials for the next semester). 97% of teachers who participated in training returned to review the material later.

In general, the teachers who completed the training course began to use the EIEE features a lot more actively; after mastering the digital skills, they became creative while developing their online courses. Later, the team developed an advanced training course "Improving the professional competencies of a teacher by using ICT in the context of the implementation of the Federal Education Standards of Higher Education", during which participants learned to record video lectures, edit them by video editor, working with virtual whiteboards and, post the prepared videos to their courses in the EIEE. That made the learning process much more engaging and accessible and increased the learning material's clarity. Even when the university returned to holding in-person classes, video lectures remained in high demand because they allowed students who could not participate in the in-person lecture fully master the topic. They also make online courses more accessible in case of another sudden transition to purely online learning.

Three advanced teacher-training programs in digital competencies were developed between the fall of 2020 and the end of 2022. Four hundred sixty-three people underwent the training and received certificates of professional development. The first program was devoted to working with the university's EIEE and MS Teams video conferencing service. The second program was created to train advanced EIEE users to work with video (MOVAVI[4]) and various interactive

---

[4] https://www.movavi.ru/.

elements in EIEE and virtual boards (IDROO[5], JAMBOARD [3]). The third program was devoted to the automated generation of didactic and methodological documentation.

Administrative Measures. Every department and faculty of the university was required to appoint a designated person responsible for interactions with the environment to organize communications between teachers and the staff implementing EIEE and avoid getting the EIEE staff overwhelmed by trivial questions and requests. These teachers underwent advanced training and could answer most of their peers' questions and perform simple requests (like adding tutors to the courses); they received additional capabilities in the EIEE sections devoted to their departments (faculties) by assigning a special role in Moodle role system. Heads of departments and faculty deans were also assigned a special role at their department (faculties) level to control their subordinates.

The people responsible for the implementation of the EIEE in their departments have the following responsibilities:

1. Adding additional teachers (tutors) in online courses.
2. Assistance in organizing the training of the department staff in using EIEE.
3. Distribution to the department staff passwords and logins to EIEE, institutional e-mails, Office 365 (MS Teams) accounts, etc.
4. Quickly and effectively learn to work with the software used in the university to automate learning.
5. Advising teachers in creating and usage of online learning courses.
6. Collecting questions and requests regarding EIEE from the department staff and communication with the AEAD specialists concerning the requests they cannot perform themselves.

The people responsible for the implementation of the EIEE in their faculties have the following responsibilities:

1. Assistance in detecting and fixing data errors in the learning-process data stored in 1C.University, including interacting with other structural divisions.
2. Coordination of the activities of the staff responsible for the EIEE in the faculty's departments.
3. Distribution to the faculty, students, and staff passwords and logins to EIEE, institutional e-mails, Office 365 (MS Teams) accounts, etc.
4. Assistance in organizing training in online learning and learning analytics for faculty members.
5. Collecting questions and requests regarding EIEE from the faculty students and communication with the AEAD specialists concerning the requests they cannot perform themselves.
6. Quickly and effectively learn to work with the software used in the university to automate learning.

---

[5] https://app.idroo.com/.

Heads of structural divisions have access to all the courses of their structural division. They have read-only access to course content, including assignments, chats, forums, and event logs. That allowed them to control the learning process in their divisions without directly interfering in the learning process. In December 2020, the university's rector officially approved the procedure for the development of online courses at the university's EIEE. The course template was introduced, and lecturers were required to fill all their courses with learning content. AEAD staff periodically performs an automatic check of the EIEE, detecting empty courses and users who have not logged into the system for a month or more. Every year, the university surveys of students, teachers, and employers to assess the quality of the educational process. The results of checking courses and surveys of education quality are distributed to the heads of structural divisions, who can take informed actions based on it. Currently, the AEAD staff is working on a system for assessing the quality of course content at the university's EIEE.

Volgograd State Technical University has been holding a staff contest "The best online course in basic educational programs at the university's EIEE" in order to motivate teachers to create quality, interesting, modern online courses; to identify, support and distribute successful practical experience of university staff in using online learning; to popularize the improvement of course content; to increase competence and professional skills of the staff in creating and implementing educational courses in EIEE, and also to encourage the innovation among the employees involved in the processes of modernization of the university's activities in the development of online courses. The courses are evaluated by the following criteria.

1. Compliance of the online course structure with the "Procedure for creating online courses in the EIEE of the VSTU", approved by order of the rector. The course must contain a scanned copy of the approved course program, forums, didactic content, materials for mid-semester exams, quality assessment survey, and final grades for the previous year. The relevance and availability of the indicated bibliographic sources.
2. Quality and completeness of online-course content. Compliance with didactic content to the approved course program.
3. Completeness and quality of the bank of test questions. Correctness of questions and variety of the question types used. The number of tests to test students' knowledge.
4. Variety of used course elements and variety of their settings.
5. Availability of teacher-created video materials, their quality, and total duration of videos in the course.
6. Organization of teamwork among students (usage of the "Workshop" Moodle activity module; dividing students into teams to perform learning tasks, etc.).
7. Usage of interactive learning elements (Moodle "Lesson" activity module, virtual whiteboards, etc.);
8. Clarity and accessibility of the material (the course materials are presented in understandable terms for the target audience, saturated with illustrative

material (tables, figures, etc.), well structured, main ideas and conclusions are highlighted).

A professional jury is formed to judge the contest. It evaluates each submitted online course according to the criteria described above. The winners receive a monetary reward. University teachers can access the winning courses to learn and adopt best practices. The contest dynamics show a significant increase in the quality and variety of course content. Having mastered the EIEE tools, the course authors introduce creative components; they switch from links to publicly available materials to creating their own engaging videos; the usage of interactive elements also increased. All that contributes to achieving the primary goal of the online educational process—increasing students' interest and engagement in learning their chosen profession, which ultimately makes it possible for the university to prepare professionals who like their job.

4   Evaluation of the Results

4.1   Method

Since 2018, the university has been conducting internal assessments of the quality of education every year by surveying students, teachers, and employers. The questionnaire for teachers includes at least 27 questions. Some of them are dedicated to e-learning technologies. We analyzed answers to these questions (see Table 3) to evaluate the effects of implementing the EIEE and providing training in e-learning. 316 teachers participated in the survey in 2018, 261—in 2020, 257—in 2021, 436—in 2022.

The number of unique users in EIEE was calculated using a special query to the LMS Moodle database. For the calculation, the average value of the number of unique users for each day of the month was taken.

4.2   Results

Currently, EIEE attained high popularity in the university. According to the results of the internal evaluation of education quality, 83% of teachers rate the functioning of EIEE as "good" and "excellent". Less than 1% of them indicated that they do not know the concepts of e-learning and massive open online courses. The average number of MOOCs a VSTU teacher passed successfully is 2. Less than 1% of teachers expressed the desire to use only in-person learning. Most teachers are willing to incorporate online courses in their teaching practice to some extent. Despite the already large number of trained teachers, 78% of them consider it necessary to improve their competence in online learning technologies. 45% of the teachers want to master new tools for educational activities (development of Internet sites, virtual quests, etc.).

Per university regulations, the teaching staff must fill online courses in the university's EIEE with content. A separate document regulating the structure of the course has been developed. For two years now, a university-wide contest of online courses belonging to basic educational programs has been held at

Table 3. Survey of teachers.

Question	Scale of measurement
Do you know what a Learning Management System (LMS) and Massive Open Online Course (MOOC) are?	yes/no
Are you willing to create electronic courses, including video lectures, text lecture notes, virtual laboratories, assignments for homework, tests and final exams?	4-point Likert scale
Please rate the quality of the EIEE functioning	4-point Likert scale
How many MOOCs did you completed (receiving certificate, credential, or diploma)?	number of courses
Are you willing to use the features of EIEE in your educational activities in the future?	8-point Likert scale
Do you need to improve your skills in the field of online learning technologies?	5-point Likert scale

VSTU. New digital services for EIEE are being developed and implemented to facilitate the learning process. In 2022, two massive open online courses were developed at VSTU. All this contributes to the popularity of the EIEE. In 2022, the average number of unique users per day was 2 330 (see Fig. 1). It can be seen that the number of users was very low before the COVID-19 lockdowns; it increased to the maximum during the distance-only learning period, then lowered when the learning became blended (lectures were held online, seminars and laboratory works on-site) and the university returned to fully on-site lessons. Still, it remained sufficiently higher than in pre-COVID-19 time because many teachers and students liked to use the online learning environment. The peaks of user activity occur during exam periods at the end of each semester (December, January, May, June); the highest user activity was registered during the winter exams of 2020–2021 academic year. These exams were held online according to local regulations. The lowest activity was in September, when students began to learn after long summer vacations. In the last year, the difference between the highest and lowest activity decreased because teachers began to use online learning courses in their everyday learning activities.

5   Discussion

Universities that effectively developed the digital transformation strategy of the educational process before the COVID-19 pandemic were relatively calm in switching to e-learning in 2020. However, most educational institutions faced a similar set of problems. These include:

1. Lack of necessary personal technical means for students and teachers;
2. No internet or its low bandwidth;
3. Lack of necessary digital competencies, usually among teachers;

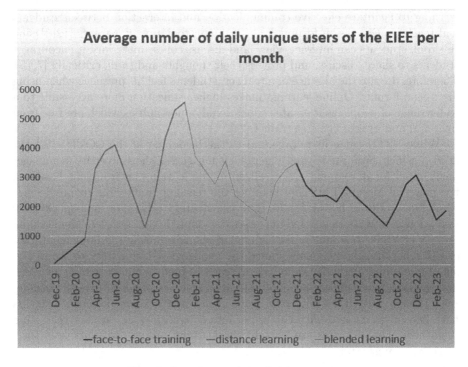

Fig. 1. Average number of unique users.

4. Lack of necessary software from universities and the ability to provide it for personal use for students and teachers;
5. Fear of new learning technologies.

At that moment several companies provided opportunities to use their software products free of charge, which helped a lot. Many platforms have made access to their online courses free. That made immersion in e-learning technologies more accessible and comfortable. The experience gained by universities over the past three years cannot go unnoticed. Students and teachers have found many positive aspects of using e-learning technologies. Personal communication cannot be completely replaced. However, some students are able to master educational programs completely in a remote format at a convenient time and an appropriate pace. The growing account of full e-learning programs in universities confirms this fact. Even with classical in-person teaching, teachers actively began to use new methods and tools (mastered during the COVID-19 pandemic), which made the educational process more interesting for students. The lack of necessary equipment or stable internet in remote areas where students live is sometimes an unsolvable problem. However, with combined learning models, online learning can be successfully developed and improved while addressing inequalities [9]. The lack of live communication can be compensated by video conferencing and chatting. According to [23], the video conferencing feature can be used in online learning to facilitate effective communication and interaction between students and teachers. Discussion forums are a common tool among learners [12]. Using this tool, students can interact, view, and discuss course materials; it encourages students to share, discuss, and process their thoughts and think critically [7,15]. Therefore, despite the absence of a teacher, students feel his presence when using discussion forums. Online learning makes higher education more accessible to a wider range of people as it creates educational opportunities which are free from temporal and geographic constraints [24].

While VSTU came little prepared to the beginning of the COVID-10 lockdowns, which prompted some emergency measures, the university's management opted for developing a centralized online learning environment based on the powerful Moodle LMS and training the teaching staff. This required more effort but produced better results than the strategy relying on non-specialized, well-known software that some universtities adopted (e.g., see [6]). The learning process of VSTU has undergone significant changes during the implementation of EIEE because the pandemic forced the pedagogical community to study and adopt e-learning methods. Many young teachers prefer online teaching as a regular method, while middle-aged and old-aged teachers prefer in-person learning. Even though most of the university teachers are over 55 years old, many teachers have become fascinated with the use of interactive tools and are actively using them now. That engages students in the learning process and increases their motivation in general.

6   Conclusion

The COVID-19 pandemic forced many educational institutions and their teaching staff to consider using online learning tools. Volgograd State Technical University created the Department of Automation of Educational Activities (AEAD) in June 2020. The department's responsibilities include the development and maintenance of the university's electronic information and educational environment (EIEE), training teachers in online learning technologies, and implementing new digital services into the learning process. All the educational departments and faculties elected members responsible for implementing online learning, who work in collaboration with the AEAD staff. The online learning process is based on the Moodle LMS, which was integrated with the university's administrative information system based on 1C.University software to maintaining relevant information about currently taught courses and students enrolled in them.

Much has been done to motivate teachers to use EIEE more actively in the educational process. Local regulations were developed with uniform requirements for the structure of courses and for the obligation to fill them with educational content. Reminder courses are regularly held to form and develop digital competencies among teachers. A competition of online courses with financial rewards for winners and prize-winners is being held. New digital services are being developed; new elements are added to the EIEE to facilitate the teacher's work. Despite the relatively high assessment of the quality of the EIEE by teachers, the quality of the course content still needs to be higher. The fact that the availability of a high-quality online course today is not part of a teacher's job contract and is not considered during competitive selection for a position, unlike articles and textbooks authored by the teacher, for example, also has a negative effect. Nevertheless, the high-quality content of the EIEE affects the motivation for learning and the student body's retention. Therefore, creating an automatic system for checking the quality of content is one of the priorities of the AEAD for further development of educational software.

Acknowledgements. We want to express our thanks to Yaroslav Kamennov and Mikhail Denisov for participating in the implementation of software deployed in the university's electronic information and education environment.

References

1. Order of the ministry of education and science of the russian federation of september 19, 2017 #920 "On approval of the federal state educational standard of higher education - bachelor's degree in the field of study 03.09.04 software engineering" (2017). https://fgosvo.ru/fgosvo/index/24/9
2. Adedoyin, O., Soykan, E.: COVID-19 pandemic and online learning: the challenges and opportunities. Interact. Learn. Environ. **31**, 1–13 (2020). https://doi.org/10.1080/10494820.2020.1813180
3. Ahshan, R.: A framework of implementing strategies for active student engagement in remote/online teaching and learning during the COVID-19 pandemic. Educ. Sci. **11**(9), 483 (2021). https://doi.org/10.3390/educsci11090483
4. Aleshkovskiy, I., Gasparishvili, A., Krukhmaleva, O., Narbut, N., Savina, N.: Russian university students about distance learning: assessments and opportunities. High. Educ. Russia **29**, 86–100 (2020). https://doi.org/10.31992/0869-3617-2020-29-10-86-100
5. Ashraf, M.A., Tsegay, S.M., Meijia, Y.: Blended learning for diverse classrooms: qualitative experimental study with in-service teachers. SAGE Open **11**(3), 21582440211030624 (2021). https://doi.org/10.1177/21582440211030623
6. Benková, M., Bednárová, D., Bogdanovská, G., Pavlíčková, M.: Redesign of the statistics course to improve graduates' skills. Mathematics **10**(15) (2022). https://doi.org/10.3390/math10152569, https://www.mdpi.com/2227-7390/10/15/2569
7. Cendra, A.N., Sulindra, E.: Navigating teaching during pandemic: the use of discussion forum in business English writing class. ELTR J. **6**(1) (2022). https://doi.org/10.37147/eltr.v6i1.127
8. Correia, A.P., Liu, C., Xu, F.: Evaluating videoconferencing systems for the quality of the educational experience evaluating videoconferencing systems for the quality of the educational experience. Dist. Educ. **41**, 429–452 (2020). https://doi.org/10.1080/01587919.2020.1821607
9. Coughlan, T., Goshtasbpour, F., Mwoma, T., Makoe, M., Aubrey-Smith, F., Tanglang, N.: Decision making in shifts to online teaching: analysing reflective narratives from staff working in African higher educational institutions. Trends High. Educ. **2**(1), 123–139 (2023). https://doi.org/10.3390/higheredu2010008
10. Eskindarov, M., Soloviev, V., Anosov, A., Ivanov, M.: University web-environment readiness for online learning during COVID-19 pandemic: case of financial university. In: Gervasi, O., et al. (eds.) ICCSA 2021, Part III. LNCS, vol. 12951, pp. 708–717. Springer, Cham (2021). https://doi.org/10.1007/978-3-030-86970-0_49

11. Hacker, J., vom Brocke, J., Handali, J., Otto, M., Schneider, J.: Virtually in this together - how web-conferencing systems enabled a new virtual togetherness during the COVID-19 crisis. Eur. J. Inf. Syst. **29**(5), 563–584 (2020). https://doi.org/10.1080/0960085X.2020.1814680

12. Hasan, D.O., et al.: Perspectives on the impact of e-learning pre- and post-COVID-19 pandemic-the case of the Kurdistan region of Iraq. Sustainability **15**(5), 4400 (2023). https://doi.org/10.3390/su15054400

13. Irfan, M., Kusumaningrum, B., Yulia, Y., Widodo, S.: Challenges during the pandemic: use of e-learning in mathematics learning in higher education. Infinity J. **9**(2), 147–158 (2020). https://doi.org/10.22460/infinity.v9i2.p147-158

14. Karakaya, F., Üçüncü, G., Çimen, O., Yılmaz, M.: Teachers' views towards the effects of COVID-19 pandemic in the education process in Turkey merve adıgüzel. Participatory Educ. Res. **8**, 17–30 (2021). https://doi.org/10.17275/per.21.27.8.2

15. Kilinc, H., Altinpulluk, H.: Discussion forums as a learning material in higher education institutions. Int. J. High. Educ. Pedag. **2**(1), 1–9 (2021). https://doi.org/10.33422/ijhep.v2i1.25

16. Krishnakumari, S., Subathra, C., Kulandaivel, A.: A descriptive study on the behavior of students in online classes during COVID-19 pandemic. In: AIP Conference Proceedings, vol. 2405, p. 030028 (2022). https://doi.org/10.1063/5.0073115

17. Letowski, B., Lavayssière, C., Larroque, B., Schröder, M., Luthon, F.: A fully open source remote laboratory for practical learning. Electronics **9**(11), 1832 (2020). https://doi.org/10.3390/electronics9111832

18. Rafique, G.M., Mahmood, K., Warraich, N.F., Rehman, S.U.: Readiness for online learning during COVID-19 pandemic: a survey of Pakistani LIS students. J. Acad. Librariansh. **47**(3), 102346 (2021). https://doi.org/10.1016/j.acalib.2021.102346

19. Sanchez-Herrera, R., Mejías, A., Márquez, M., Andújar, J.: The remote access to laboratories: a fully open integrated system. IFAC-PapersOnLine **52**(9), 121–126 (2019). https://doi.org/10.1016/j.ifacol.2019.08.135. 12th IFAC Symposium on Advances in Control Education ACE 2019

20. Singh, J., Singh, L., Matthees, B.: Establishing social, cognitive, and teaching presence in online learning-a panacea in COVID-19 pandemic, post vaccine and post pandemic times. J. Educ. Technol. Syst. **51**(1), 28–45 (2022). https://doi.org/10.1177/00472395221095169

21. Sychev, O.: Write a line: Tests with answer templates and string completion hints for self-learning in a CS1 course. In: Proceedings of the ACM/IEEE 44th International Conference on Software Engineering: Software Engineering Education and Training, ICSE-SEET 2022, pp. 265–276. Association for Computing Machinery, New York (2022). https://doi.org/10.1145/3510456.3514159

22. Sychev, O.: Questions for teaching phrase building with automatic feedback. Softw. Impacts **15**, 100461 (2023). https://doi.org/10.1016/j.simpa.2022.100461

23. Tao, D., Li, W., Qin, M., Cheng, M.: Understanding students' acceptance and usage behaviors of online learning in mandatory contexts: a three-wave longitudinal study during the COVID-19 pandemic. Sustainability **14**(13), 7830 (2022). https://doi.org/10.3390/su14137830

24. Varty, A.K.: Options for online undergraduate courses in biology at American colleges and universities. CBE-Life Sciences Education **15**(4), ar58 (2016). https://doi.org/10.1187/cbe.16-01-0075. pMID: 27856546

25. Zaytseva, I., Grynyuk, S.: University distance learning due to the COVID-19 pandemic in Ukraine. Sci. Heritage **53**, 49–52 (2020). https://doi.org/10.34190/ejel.20.3.2198

Blockchain and Distributed Ledgers: Technologies and Applications (BDLTA 2023)

Are Digital Signatures in Blockchain Functionally Equivalent to Handwritten Signatures?

Victor Dostov[1,2] , Svetlana Krivoruchko[1] , Pavel Shust[3(✉)] , and Victor Titov[2]

[1] Department of Financial Markets and Banks, Financial University Under the Government of the Russian Federation, 49 Leningradsky Prospekt, Moscow 125993, Russia
[2] Modern Financial Technology Laboratory of St Petersburg University, Saint Petersburg State University, 199034 St. Petersburg, Russia
[3] Russian Electronic Money and Remittance Association, Novoslobodskaya ul., 20, of. 25/A5φ, Moscow 127030, Russia
paul.shoust@gmail.com

Abstract. Digital signatures have different uses in a digital world, providing both identification of users and ensuring legal enforceability of digitally signed documents, making them legally binding for the signatories. Purpose of this paper is to review legal aspects of electronic signature application in modern technologies such as on-line banking, DLT and digital lending. As the latter are already well-researched, we use the case of online lending as an illustrative example, yet all conclusions and findings are equally valid for digitally signed transactions and blocks in DLT, for transactions in on-line banking and for many other cases. We look at the challenges presented by the remote conclusion of loan contracts and whether they can be addressed by the usage of electronic signatures. The focus of the research is whether there are technological of procedural solutions that can be used to ensure functional equivalence of electronic and handwritten signatures. The findings may provide grounds for further research of DLT application in electronic signature sphere.

Keywords: Consumer Loan Agreement · Electronic Signature Regulation · Handwritten Signature · Simple Electronic Signature · Distributed Ledgers

1 Introduction

Growing body of the academic literature suggests that distributed ledger technologies might be used to improve the efficiency and security of electronic signatures [1]. Moreover, distributed ledgers rely on electronic signatures to ensure identification, transparency, inalterability [2].

As there are no trust services providers in the blockchain, the trust is based on the e-signature keys and distributed inalterable ledgers. From practical standpoint, this means that private e-signature keys shall be reliably used in multitude of transactions, such as payments, transfer of value, authentication of legal documents, etc. In this regard, as

O. Gervasi et al. (Eds.): ICCSA 2023 Workshops, LNCS 14104, pp. 527–537, 2023.
https://doi.org/10.1007/978-3-031-37105-9_35

blockchain is based on electronic signatures, for legal interpretation of records in DLT there should be an assurance that e-signatures in general are functionally equivalent to handwritten signatures which are still a standard business practice worldwide. This functional equivalence is specifically important for distributed ledgers in particular, as there is no fallback option for handwritten signature.

There is somewhat patchy coverage of signatures (both electronic and handwritten) in academic literature. Legal concept of handwritten signatures is well discussed in in-depth analysis by Stephen Mason [3, pp. 1–94] covering both legal and historical aspects of the phenomenon. Lon L. Fuller [4] contributed significantly to understanding of a handwritten signature in an often-cited work on the functions of legal formalities. Applied aspects in mobile-based e-signatures [5], using electronic watermarks [6] are good examples of such technology-focused research. Another body of research is dedicated to electronic contracts which are intrinsically related to signatures, as well as act of 'signing' and mostly cover consumer protection issues: for example, material clauses disclosure [7], usage of standard electronic contracts and contracts on consuming digital content. But despite seemingly wide coverage of electronic signatures in academic literature, there are still gaps in understanding of relationship between electronic and handwritten signature as well as relation between electronic signature and electronic contract. This paper aims at starting to fill this gap by proposing methodological approach to analyzing practical implications of e-signature usage. From the methodological perspective, Veerpalu's [8] research provides the valuable perspective on functional equivalence regulation for the innovative processes and services.

Methodology of the paper is based on the comparative analysis of the existing handwritten and electronic signature regulation and synthesis of the outcome-focused approaches to achieving similar results in similar circumstances.

In this paper we describe the case of electronic contracts between borrower and lender in online lending services and identify the procedures that may strengthen reliability of online interaction between these two parties. The areas for further research are discussed as well.

2 Signature and Its Functions

In order to explore the potential role of DLT in the application of electronic signatures, it is necessary to first examine the various academic perspectives on the functions of signatures in general. Although electronic signatures are becoming increasingly prevalent, most of the existing academic literature still focuses on handwritten signatures, which remain more widely used. It is also notable that legal considerations are a primary focus of this analysis, rather than technological elements of signatures. However, we contend that an overview of this discussion remains relevant, as the functional equivalence of handwritten and electronic signatures (whether DLT-based or not) must be established within the existing legal framework in order for electronic signatures to gain widespread acceptance among individuals and businesses. It is interesting to note that there is no universally accepted definition of a signature in academic literature. For instance, the United States Commercial Code defines a signature as "any symbol executed or adopted by a party with present intention to authenticate a writing" [9, p. 1185]. A more high-level definition is proposed by the Oxford Dictionary: 'a sign or a mark impressed upon anything'. From the general perspective the signatures are considered a 'legal formality' [4, pp. 800–801].

The definitions of signatures provided by existing academic literature are notably technology and instrument-neutral, which may seem counter-intuitive for subsequent discussions about electronic signatures. However, this approach is justified from a legal standpoint, as it ensures that business practices and courts recognize the varying circumstances and environments in which parties interact. Put simply, a signature may be a sophisticated instrument or a simple mark, made on a piece of paper or a napkin, for a multitude of reasons. This is a critical consideration for understanding the factors that contribute to the success of electronic signatures. While much of the discourse surrounding electronic signatures focuses on the instruments themselves (such as token or cloud-based signatures, or SIM-card-based solutions), or on the storage of qualified electronic signatures, it is important to recognize that the true universality of electronic signatures (including those issued on DLT) will depend on their ability to be used in a wide range of circumstances. Additionally, there is a significant body of literature exploring the various functions that signatures serve.

The approach to handwritten signatures is technology-neutral, making it irrelevant to categorize them based on the instrument or material used. Formally speaking, it is possible to make categorizations based on the type of instrument used to put a handwritten signature (e.g. pen or pencil) or the material on which the handwritten signature is placed (e.g. paper, wood or something else). But the function of the handwritten signature remains the same regardless of these theoretical categories. However, electronic signatures are very technology-specific, which makes them inherently different from handwritten signatures. It is important to consider that by introducing new technologies to the signatures realm, we are not only improving the efficiency of the process but also changing centuries-long business traditions.

There are three types of electronic signatures with varying assurance levels: simple electronic signature (SES), advanced electronic signature (AES), and qualified electronic signature (QES). Simple electronic signatures provide the lowest level of assurance since they do not verify the identity of the signatory and are only associated with electronic data. "I agree" buttons and tickboxes on websites are examples of simple electronic signatures. Even the signature in an email might be recognized as a simple electronic signature. The downside of simple electronic signatures is that their enforceability usually requires a court decision.

Advanced electronic signatures [10] are generally more reliable, as they allow to identify any subsequent changes to the signed documents. Advanced electronic signatures are also uniquely linked to the signatory, specific procedures are used to ensure that the signature cannot be used by anyone, except the signature holder.

Qualified electronic signature is essential and advanced electronic signature that is issued by the reliable third party (qualified trust service provider) which allows to undoubtedly identify the signatory (see Table 1).

Anecdotal evidence and experience shows that there is an inverse relationship between the level of assurance provided by electronic signatures and their adoption rates. This means that people are more willing to use simpler electronic signatures even though they provide less legal protection. This is an important consideration for developers, as technology can provide the highest level of assurance and inalterability, but a higher entry level can negatively affect adoption. Users tend to prioritize convenience over risks unless one of them is critical. Therefore, developers need to balance the level of assurance with the ease of use to ensure wider adoption of electronic signatures.

Table 1. Functional comparison of SES, AES, and QES.[1]

	Simple electronic signature	Advanced electronic signature	Qualified Electronic Signature
Identification function	-	+	+ (highest assurance level as QES is issued by the third party universally trusted by all actors)
Expression of intent	+	+	+
Inalterability function	-	+	+
Evidential function	+	+	+

As previously discussed, signatures must serve specific functions to be of value to economic actors. In the following section, we will examine the evidentiary, cautionary, and inalterability functions of signatures, as well as their ability to record the expression of intent. Additionally, we will explore the risks associated with using signatures and methods for mitigating those risks.

In terms of its evidentiary function, a signature serves to confirm the existence of a legally-binding document, leaving a physical or electronic artifact as evidence. The viability of this artifact is crucial in order to prove the existence of the contract. From the perspective of DLT, viability is based on the distributed nature of information storage and the built-in inability of any single actor to unilaterally delete information. The architecture of DLT must account for the need to maintain evidence over a long period of time, particularly in cases where permissionless DLT relies on the unofficial agreement of its participants. A viable electronic signature based on DLT must ensure that actors cannot simply decide to stop supporting it, which would effectively result in a loss of access to information. However, permissioned DLT systems may be subject to other risks, such as the potential for the central operator to manipulate data in the absence of proper technological safeguards. In such cases, it may be necessary to establish legal obligations to ensure the independence and stability of the system, similar to the specific requirements imposed on qualified trust service providers by relevant regulations.

The cautionary function of a signature requires that it be a significant act for the signatory, signifying their entry into the contract. This is particularly important for contracts that involve new responsibilities and liabilities, such as in the case of lending, which will be discussed in detail below. The importance of the cautionary function

---

[1] Adapted from [11].

may vary significantly depending on cultural circumstances and tradition [12]. From the perspective of electronic signatures, the cautionary function may not be as critical, but the process of using an electronic signature should still entail certain formalities or procedures, rather than being fully automated. While this may seem counter-intuitive from a technical perspective, it is an important consideration in the context of business interactions.

The record-keeping function of a signature is self-explanatory and is similar to the evidentiary function. Handwritten signatures are typically placed on durable material such as paper, but electronic signatures require specific rules and procedures to ensure that they are recorded in an unalterable manner and can be accessed over time. It is also important to ensure reverse compatibility, allowing actors to verify electronic signatures even after the technology has become outdated and is no longer actively supported.

The purpose of signatures is to ensure that the document cannot be altered. However, traditional methods of signing multi-page documents, such as signing every page, are not very reliable. Qualified electronic signatures are a much better option as they allow any changes to be identified. Additionally, DLT can provide an extra layer of reliability as the document or its hash can be stored on a distributed ledger.

There is ongoing debate among practitioners on whether DLT can accommodate legitimate changes to contracts. While some believe that contracts should be fixed, real business practices often require changes to be made to certain clauses. It is possible to simply sign a new version of the document and store it on the distributed ledger as a new version of the existing document. However, it is important to consider whether DLT can handle the growing volume of data.

Another function of the signature is the expression of intent. However, this function does not depend on technological solutions and is largely self-explanatory. Rather, the expression of intent is ensured through the rules and procedures governing the use of electronic signatures.

The functions of a signature discussed above are by no means exhaustive, and different research perspectives may emphasize different types of functions. Nevertheless, the outlined functions have allowed us to identify potential risks associated with the use of signatures, whether handwritten or electronic. This analysis highlights potential gaps in the long-standing tradition of handwritten signatures and provides insight into how DLT considerations can be integrated into electronic signature practices.

The identification of signatories through the use of signatures is limited in its effectiveness. This is because handwritten signatures are not bound to any particular form or technology, unlike identity documents that are commonly used for verification purposes. Consequently, this exposes signatures to the risk of forgery, which can result in identity fraud, significant financial losses, and legal disputes. Furthermore, the occurrence of forgery undermines trust in the economy and the technology used to facilitate electronic signatures.

The implementation of Distributed Ledger Technology (DLT), such as blockchain, in electronic signatures does not wholly address the risk of identity fraud. Permissionless DLT networks, like Bitcoin, lack complete personalization and do not guarantee reliable identification of users. Although software can assist in identifying the identities behind Bitcoin wallets, the possibility of error remains. Moreover, the reliability of identification hinges on the involvement of specific actors in the transaction, which renders DLT-based electronic signatures unreliable for day-to-day use, particularly in lending.

To mitigate the risk of identity fraud, specific identification procedures must be established. Fortunately, such procedures are well-established in the financial sector and other industries. The level of identity verification required should be proportionate to the level of assurance required for a given scenario. Overly strict identification requirements can negatively impact the usability of electronic signatures and give rise to data protection concerns. Therefore, it is essential to consider the specific requirements for various situations when developing DLT-based electronic signature solutions. For example, the level of identification required to purchase groceries differs from that needed to apply for a loan at a bank.

Despite the type of signature used, there is a risk of coercion that individuals may face when signing documents. They could be pressured or tricked into signing a document without fully understanding its contents. This could result from direct fraud or unclear wording in a legal contract [13, p. 731], whether intentional or unintentional. In addition, individuals may be coerced into entering into business relationships under peer pressure, for instance. The risk of coercion is relevant regardless of the type of signature used, including electronic signatures. However, the risks of coercion may be even higher with DLT technology due to the inalterability of records and information included in the ledger. This means that a falsely signed document will be kept on the distributed ledger indefinitely, which raises legal questions in case of disputes. To address this issue, procedures must be introduced to allow for the dispute of signatures if they are proven to have been applied under coercion or not in good faith. Failure to do so would limit the universal usage of DLT-based electronic signatures. Interestingly, the inalterability of DLT may be useful for investigative purposes, as it prevents actors from covering their tracks and hiding illicit activities ex-post. It is important to note that the risk of coercion is distinct from limited knowledge or literacy, as the fact that a document was signed in good faith does not guarantee that the signatory actually read and understood its contents [14]. This applies to both electronic and handwritten signatures.

3 Signatures in the Financial Market: Case of Lending

The case of lending in the financial market provides an excellent opportunity to showcase the multitude of functions that electronic signatures can perform. This is because trust is a major concern in the lending sector, where lenders are often skeptical of borrowers and want to ensure that they receive their money back in a timely manner. At the same time, borrowers are concerned that lenders may abuse their position and charge exorbitant fees and commissions. These issues are further compounded by the fact that lending in the financial market is associated with high legal risks. Potential conflicts between lenders and borrowers may need to be resolved in court, and it is crucial to have an appropriate document trail to protect the interests of both parties.

In addition, lending is a financial service that is subject to specific regulations, such as anti-money laundering regulations. This adds to the complexity of the lending process and underscores the importance of having a secure and reliable system for managing loan agreements and associated documentation. As such, the lending sector provides a perfect illustrative example of a situation where lack of trust is exacerbated by legal risks and specific legal requirements.

By examining the functions of electronic and handwritten signatures in this context, we can also identify areas where distributed ledger technology can be used to improve efficiency, enhance security, and increase reliability.

Table 2. Expected outcomes of the signature function and their business purposes (case of lending).

Outcome	Business purpose
Identification of parties	Money laundering/terrorist financing risks mitigation Enforceable legal redress
Record of expression of intent	Efficient enforceability and protection against fraud, contesting the contracts
Inalterability	Protection against unilateral changes of contract
Contract as evidence	Possibility to enforce the contract through the legal system

Throughout the lending process, the parties use signatures and contracts to ensure the following outcomes (see Table 2):

- *Identification of the parties.*

The lending sector presents a unique case of reverse information asymmetry, where the lenders have limited access to information that is critical to making informed decisions. While it is true that customers may have limited access to information to compare offerings from different financial services providers, in the case of lending, lenders also face significant informational challenges.

Financial institutions must first verify the identity of potential borrowers to ensure that they are not involved in money laundering, terrorist financing, or belong to higher-risk groups, such as politically exposed persons. This is a requirement of specialized regulation, and failure to comply with these regulations can result in severe penalties.

Moreover, lending is data-driven, meaning that lenders need to collect and analyze information about potential borrowers to determine their creditworthiness. This involves evaluating factors such as credit history, income, and other financial indicators to assess the borrower's ability to repay the loan.

Customer due diligence is based on the level of assurance, as mentioned by Shust and Dostov [15]. This process requires the verification of identity, which cannot be accomplished solely through signatures. Handwritten signatures can act as a factor in verifying identity, but only after costly expertise. In contrast, qualified electronic signatures (QES) are efficient in this regard, as they are provided after identity verification, unlike handwritten signatures that can be used without any prerequisites.

It is crucial to ensure that QES certificates are not anonymous if the qualified certificates are issued and stored on the blockchain. However, it is important to note that there are multiple ways to verify identity apart from signatures, such as video identification or biometric identification [16].

Of course, electronic signatures cannot be used to assess creditworthiness of the potential borrower [17] and multitude of other methods are used instead [18]. Below we are looking at particular circumstances where electronic signatures perform these functions. This analysis will be based on the case of loan provision. However, the same consideration will apply in other cases and business scenarios as well.

– *Recording the expression of intent*

In the lending process, financial institutions must ensure that borrowers not only qualify for a loan but also willingly accept all associated terms and conditions. This is crucial not only for regulatory purposes, where financial institutions are mandated to explicitly state the terms and conditions of the contract, but also to prevent potential identity fraud claims. It is essential that the borrower's intent is expressed explicitly and that the evidence of their agreement is admissible in court.

When viewed as a process rather than an instrument, signatures (whether electronic or handwritten) are an efficient tool to express intent. However, they cannot ensure that the customer (potential borrower) has fully read and understood the contract, as the contract can be difficult to comprehend due to legal jargon [19]. Nevertheless, signatures can be used to fix that the borrower has actively agreed to the terms and conditions of the agreement.

To offset this risk, many financial regulators have established requirements towards the form and contents of contracts [20]. These requirements also help to avoid "Russian doll" contracts, which can create cascading complexity as certain clauses reference other contracts that link to additional references.

Electronic signatures are effective in fixing the expression of intent because they imply certain procedures that the customer must follow to ensure that their intent is properly recorded and collected. Even if certificates are stored on a distributed ledger, practitioners need to ensure that the process of using this signature appropriately captures the intent of the customer.

– *Inalterability*

Loan agreements in the lending sector typically contain critical information such as the lending rate, loan amount, and repayment schedule. It is crucial to ensure that these documents are not altered subsequently, as any changes can lead to disputes between the financial institution and the borrower. This is important for both parties, as each can dispute the terms of the agreement in court.

When using paper documents, ensuring inalterability is mostly a logistical issue. It's important to make sure the document is not destroyed or subsequently altered. The same issue is relevant for electronic documents, and in this regard, electronic signatures (namely, qualified electronic signatures) are much more efficient than handwritten signatures. The same is true for distributed ledger technology, which is praised for its inalterability, among other things.

In addition to preventing direct and explicit fraud, inalterability may also help with improper business practices. For example, research shows that unilateral changes to contracts might be against general e-commerce legal requirements [21].

However, ensuring inalterability in current business scenarios can be rather complicated. Financial institutions may be forced to support large document storage facilities, develop specific practices for handling and managing these archives, and keep documents on record for 3–5 years depending on jurisdiction. For public electronic contracts, this requires publishing all versions on the financial institution's website, which is impractical and raises questions about what will happen in case of the closure of the financial service provider.

With distributed ledger technologies and qualified electronic signatures, the same result can be achieved with lower costs. However, to ensure the universal or at least wider implementation of this technology, financial institutions need to ensure that the technology is interoperable and does not create data silos. This is an important issue to consider in the communities' further efforts to expand the usage of DLT in electronic signatures.

– *Evidence*

It is essential to ensure that the documents signed between the lender and the borrower are admissible evidence in court and cannot be tampered with.

The reliability of electronic signatures as evidence in case of disputes depends on their ability to fulfill all necessary functions. The inalterability of distributed ledgers may contribute to ensuring the reliability of electronic signatures stored on them. However, legal recognition of such documents and signatures is also crucial. The legal framework should recognize documents and electronic signatures stored on distributed ledgers to ensure their admissibility in courts. This applies not only to single documents but also to the general audit trail of all documents and transactions in the retail and corporate banking sectors [22, p. 25]. The audit trails should allow the reconstruction of the flow of transactions [23] and underlying contractual documents, which can greatly aid in supervisory and law enforcement activities. As such, the combination of the technological and legal aspects is necessary to ensure the reliability of electronic signatures as evidence in case of disputes.

4 Conclusions and Further Research

Purpose of this paper is to highlight rather counterintuitive nature of signatures as legal formalities. Highest assurance levels do not warrant the universal adoption of electronic signatures, even though they can bring additional benefits to the economic actors.

This consideration shall be taken into account when discussing DLT infrastructure and usage of distributed ledgers in context of electronic signatures. DLT can bring meaningful positive impact on the reliability of electronic signatures and storage of digitally signed documents (i.e. to ensure their inalterability). On the other hand, it is critical to adapt these technological solutions to the business practices and a common sense. The inalterability function is a good illustration of this. Keeping documents in the state as they were initially signed is extremely important to protect against fraud. But this complicates situation in cases of coercion and fraud–victims may have difficulties with rectifying errors.

This makes it extremely important to complement ongoing efforts to improve the efficiency of distributed ledgers with analysis of the business practices, legal considerations, and review of the user experiences. Overlooking these aspects may make technological efforts futile, as they will not be widely adopted.

Electronic and handwritten signatures alone cannot fulfill all of the functions required by business practice. Additional procedures and processes, such as identity verification, must be employed to complement the usage of electronic signatures effectively.

However, despite this limitation, there are areas in which distributed ledger technology (DLT) can improve the usage of electronic signatures in various sectors, including finance. For example, leveraging the inalterability of documentation stored and signed on distributed ledgers can provide greater transparency and confidence in the validity of signatures. Additionally, the use of DLT can enhance the security of electronic signatures by providing an immutable record of transactions that can be audited if necessary.

One area of concern when implementing DLT-based electronic signature systems is the verification of user identity. Legal requirements for identity verification must be taken into consideration to ensure that any new technological proposition is compliant with regulations and ultimately contributes to the attainment of its goals. Ensuring compliance in this area can also help in achieving wider business adoption of DLT and its integration into various business processes.

Thus, while electronic and handwritten signatures may have limitations, the integration of DLT can enhance their functionality and reliability, improving the overall efficiency and effectiveness of business processes.

References

1. Krylov, G., Gaybatova, A., Davydenko, V., Grigoryan, A.: Integration of distributed ledger technology into software electronic signature exchange service. Procedia Comput. Sci. **169**, 479–488 (2020)
2. Sunyaev, A. Distributed ledger technology. In: Internet Computing, pp. 265–299. Springer, Cham (2020). https://doi.org/10.1007/978-3-030-34957-8_9
3. Mason, S.: The Signature. Electronic Signatures in Law. University of London Press (2016)
4. Fuller, L.L.: Consideration and form. Columbia Law Rev. **41**(5), 799-824 (1941).https://doi.org/10.2307/j.ctv5137w8.7
5. Ruiz-Martínez, A., Sánchez-Martínez, D., Martínez-Montesinos, M., Gómez-Skarmeta, A.F.: A survey of electronic signature solutions in mobile devices. J. Theor. Appl. Electron. Commer. Res. **2**(3), 94–109 (2007)
6. Zhu, L., Zhu, L.: Electronic signature based on digital signature and digital watermarking. In: 5th International Congress on Image and Signal Processing, pp. 1644–1647. IEEE, Chongqing (2012). https://doi.org/10.1109/CISP.2012.6469828
7. Kaviar, H.: Consumer protection in electronic contracts. Int. Arab J. e-Technol. **2**(2), 96–104 (2011)
8. Veerpalu, A.: functional equivalence: an exploration through shortcomings to solutions. Baltic J. Law Polit. **12**(2), 134–162 (2019). https://doi.org/10.2478/bjlp-2019-0015
9. Hays, M. J.: The E-sign act of 2000: the Triumph of function over form in American contract law. Notre Dame L. Rev **76** (4,) 1183–1214 (2001)
10. Regulation (EU) No 910/2014 of the European Parliament and of the council of 23 July 2014 on electronic identification and trust services for electronic transactions in the internal market and repealing Directive 1999/93/EC. Official Journal of the European Union. https://eur-lex.europa.eu/legal-content/EN/TXT/HTML/?uri=CELEX:32014R0910&from=EN#d1e2403-73-1. Accessed 21 Apr 2023

11. Titov, V., Shust, P., Dostov, et al.: Digital transformation of signatures: suggesting functional symmetry approach for loan agreements. Computation **10**, 106, 2022, https://doi.org/10.3390/computation10070106

12. Cary, P.: A brief history of the concept of free will: issues that are and are not germane to legal reasoning. Behav. Sci. Law **25**(2), 165–181 (2007). https://doi.org/10.1002/bsl.748

13. Becher, S.I.: Asymmetric information in consumer contracts: the challenge that is yet to be met. Am. Bus. Law J. **45**(4), 723–774 (2008). https://ssrn.com/abstract=1016010. Accessed 20 Mar 2023

14. Stiglitz, J.E.: The contributions of the economics of information to twentieth century economics. Q. J. Econ. **115**(4), 1141–1478 (2000). https://doi.org/10.1162/003355300555015

15. Shust, P., Dostov, V.: Implementing innovative customer due diligence: proposal for universal model. J. Money Laundering Control **23**(4), 871–884 (2020). https://doi.org/10.1108/JMLC-01-2020-0007

16. FATF: Anti-money laundering and terrorist financing measures and financial inclusion - With a supplement on customer due diligence. FATF, Paris, pp. 1–117 (2013–2017). www.fatf-gafi.org/publications/financialinclusion/documents/financial-inclusion-cdd-2017.html. Accessed 21 Mar 2023

17. Hwang, B-H., Tellez, C.: The Proliferation of Digital Credit Deployments. CGAP Brief, World Bank, Washington, DC, pp. 1–4 (2016)

18. Berg, T., Burg, V., Gombović, A., Puri, M.: On the rise of FinTechs: credit scoring using digital footprints. Rev. Finan. Stud. **33**(7), 2845–2897 (2020). https://doi.org/10.1093/rfs/hhz099

19. Gindin, S.E.: Nobody reads your privacy policy or online contract? Lessons learned and questions Raised by the FTC's action against sears. Northwest. J. Technol. Intellect. Prop. **8**(1), 1–39 (2009)

20. Kunz, C., Del Duca, M., Thayer, H., Debrow, J.: Click-through agreements: strategies for avoiding disputes on validity of assent. Bus. Lawyer **57**(1), 401–429 (2001). https://doi.org/10.2307/40688063

21. Loos, M., Luzak, J.: Wanted: a bigger stick. on unfair terms in consumer contracts with online service providers. J. Consum. Policy **39**(1), 63–90 (2015). https://doi.org/10.1007/s10603-015-9303-7

22. English, J., Abdou, H., Adewunmi, P.: An investigation of risk management practices in electronic banking: the case of the UK banks. Banks Bank Syst. **9**(3), 1816–7403 (2014)

23. Westerlund, M., Neovius, M., Pulkkis, G.: Providing tamper-resistant audit trails with distributed ledger based solutions for forensics of IoT systems using cloud resources. Int. J. Adv. Secur. **11**(3,4), 288–300 (2018)

A Decentralized Mechanism to Decouple Vendor-Specific Access Management from IoT Devices Using Blockchain Technology, Smart Contract, and Wallets

Jacobs Jacob Chakola[1]([⊠]) [iD], Garima Sinha[2] [iD], and Deepak K. Sinha[2] [iD]

[1] Cyber Security, CSE, Jain (Deemed-to-be) University, Bangalore, India
Jacobschakola@gmail.com
[2] CSE, Jain (Deemed-to-be) University, Bangalore, India

Abstract. This paper provides a mechanism for distributed access management and authorization transfer for communicating between devices belonging to different wallets and the same wallet. This paper also discusses segregating the IoT network into different groups or levels for fine-grain control. This approach allows Access control and intersystem network communication between authenticated devices and authenticated devices residing in the same system, using the devices layer, smart contract, and wallets. The Device layer is used to transmit data from one device to another, regardless of the wallet they belong to. The smart contract acts as the distributed command and control for access management. The wallet stands as the owner of the IoT in the system. The wallets are generally owned by individuals or end consumers of the IoT product. The approach can be split into three phases: initialization, device authentication, and device-to-device communication.

Keywords: smart contract · blockchain technology · IoT · access management · access control · decentralized mechanism

Abbreviation

A_{PK}	*Public key of device A*
A_{IK}	*Private key of device A*
W_{PK}	*Public key of the wallet that owns the IoT device*
W_{IK}	*Private key of the wallet that owns the IoT device*
SC_{AD}	*Address of the smart contract deployed by IoT device owner*
RG_C	*Registration certificate*
IZ_C	*Initialization certificate*
$Auth_C$	*Authentication Certificate*
Mac_A	*Mac address of IoT devices A*
Mac_B	*Mac address of IoT devices B*
IP_A	*IP address of IoT devices A*
IP_B	*IP address of IoT devices B*

© The Author(s), under exclusive license to Springer Nature Switzerland AG 2023 2023
O. Gervasi et al. (Eds.): ICCSA 2023 Workshops, LNCS 14104, pp. 538–554, 2023.
https://doi.org/10.1007/978-3-031-37105-9_36

PL_A	Privilege-level of IoT devices A
$AuthPacket_A$	Auth Packet of device A
$AuthPacket_B$	Auth Packet of device B
AT_C	Access transfer certificate
AG_C	Access transfer certificate
PLT	level of privilege the transferred user has on the IoT device
Wt	The Wallet that is being granted access to the IoT devices.
WtSC	The smart contract address owned by Wt.
Wt_{PK}	Public key of the Wallet the access is being granted
Wt_{IK}	Private key of the Wallet the access is being granted
WtAddress	the address of the wallet that receives the NFT
NFT	Non-Fungible Token Standard
NFT ID	NFT token ID

1 Introduction

The IoT paradigm represents interconnected networks and heterogeneous devices. The central element of IoT is to expedite sharing of the constrained devices' resources and information with other entities. With the advent of 5G technology, IoT has gained a rapid endorsement in many domains. Where devices with constrained resources are interconnected either through private or public networks, ranging from embedded devices containing sensors such as smart home appliances to vehicle-to-vehicle in supply chain scenarios. The devices or "things" in IoT can be accessed remotely to perform the specified functionality. The solutions for access management are more analogous to the server-client architecture usually owned and managed by the vendors of the IoT devices, designed to manage IoT in the same ecosystem in a centralized fashion.

However, the solutions for IoT access management confront additional challenges as the "things" or devices are conventionally constrained when it comes to memory and processing. Inevitably, the access management solutions must acclimate constrained architecture.

Different vendors enforce their ecosystem and access control that can be used only with their products. That Leads to limited or no interoperability pertaining to access management. This reliance implies the assumption that the vendor's services are always available. This paper intends to decouple the IoT devices and vendor-specific access management using smart-contract deployed on the blockchain, which stands as the command and control for access management. The distributed nature of blockchain technology addresses the constant availability of authentication and access management services regardless of the device vendor.

1.1 Paper Structure

The paper is systematized as follows: Sect. 2 provides a short primer on the workings of blockchain technology, such as hash Pointer, the different consensus algorithms, Smart Contracts, NFTs, and as well as the Limitations of blockchain. Section 3 discusses and examines some related works. Section 4 explains the distributed access management and transfer of authorization mechanism by splitting the approach into four use cases. Section 6 discusses the value proposition of the mechanism. Section 7 discusses the Security Analysis. Finally, Sect. 8 concludes the paper.

2 Background

2.1 Blockchain

Ever since Satoshi Nakamoto made blockchain technologies public debut in 2008 with the whitepaper Bitcoin [1], blockchain has skyrocketed in popularity, expanding beyond the cryptocurrency paradigm into decentralized applications. For most people, blockchain, and bitcoin are synonymous even to this day; blockchain is a distributed, decentralized, immutable ledger that records assets and transactions in a peer-to-peer network with a timestamped block of data chained together as a link list of hash pointers [2].

Blocks in the blockchain act as data storage for the blockchain, each block in the blockchain stores all the transaction information as a database. The critical property that fundamentally distinguishes it from conventional databases is its public verifiability. Public verifiability is achievable by virtue of integrity and transparency. Blockchain facilitates transparency by permitting anyone to verify the state of data and how it was updated; as for integrity, it means data received is not corrupt.

It accomplishes data integrity and authenticity by delivering robust cryptographic proof using elliptic curve cryptographic (ECC) and SHA-256 hashing.

A block in the blockchain contains the hash of the previous block in the header. The genesis block is the first block in the chain and is usually hardcoded (Fig. 1).

Fig. 1. Simplified overview of a blockchain

The blockchain is a trustless architecture where no third parties or centralized authority could corrupt the data in the blockchain, and since it is distributed, there is no single point of compromise.

The different nodes communicate using the gossip protocol. Which inherently creates propagation delays in the network. Potentially create blocks simultaneously.

Consequently, creating two separate branches of the blockchain (Fig. 2) leads to some miners mining on top of the forked branch, fundamentally going against the nature of the blockchain. However, these forked branches will be discarded as the branch with the most combined difficulty will be selected, not the branch with more blocks. The discarded or invalid chains are usually called orphan blocks.

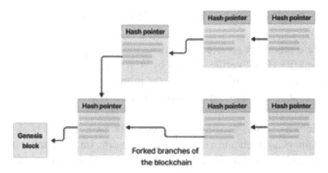

Fig. 2. Forked branch of the blockchain

2.2 Smart Contracts

Blockchain like Ethereum has an Ethereum virtual machine, which makes it a Turing Complete blockchain. This allows Ethereum blockchain the capability to understand and implement any future agreement in the form of smart contracts. Smart contracts are transaction protocols or rather a self-operating computer program or self-executing code when a predetermined condition is satisfied and resides on the blockchain. Which eradicates any involvement of a trusted intermediary [3]. This paper ERC-721: (Non-Fungible Token Standard) for NFT minting [4].

2.3 Hash Pointers

Hash pointer serves two purposes. It uniquely identifies the previous block of data. It also confirms that the data has not been tampered with; due to the properties of the hashing functions. It acts as a tamper-evident log by comparing the previous block's hash to the hash in the next block's header, proving that the block has not been tampered with (Fig. 1).

2.4 NFT

NFTs are non-fungible tokens on the blockchain that are distinguishable with a unique identification code. The NFTs have meta data that is part of the token. These NFTs, unlike cryptocurrencies, are not identical and cannot be exchanged at equivalency [5].

2.5 Consensus

Consensus is the mechanism that achieves the necessary agreement on the blockchain network's state. In the case of bitcoin, the mechanism is proof of work (PoW) [6], also called mining, where the miner computes a hash with leading zeros to meet the difficulty target; once the block is validated, it gets written onto the blockchain and becomes immutable.

There are numerous algorithms for consensus.

Proof-of-Stake (PoS) verifies blocks by staking coins as collateral to become "validators".

Validators are randomly selected to validate the block [7].

Proof of capacity (PoC) verifies blocks by storing possible solutions on the miner's hard drive. The more substantial the drive, the more possible solutions stored. In turn, the greater the chance of matching the required hash. This approach is more analogous to winning a lottery [8].

Proof-of-Activity (PoA) verifies blocks using the two consensus algorithms, PoW and PoS. The miners authenticate a transaction depending on the number of coins staked, using the PoW consensus. The PoA algorithm is designed to reduce the overall power consumption [9].

Proof of burn (POB) operates on the principle of "burning" or sending coins to a verifiably inaccessible wallet address, which burns the coins as the coins sent to this wallet cannot be spent. Doing so grants the privilege to write to block proportionally to the burnt coins [10].

Proof of History (PoH) [11] and Proof of Elapsed Time (PoET) [12] are similar, encoding time passage to determine consensus. PoET is conventionally used in permissioned blockchains, requiring prospective participants to identify them before joining.

Each node in the blockchain sleeps for an assigned random wait time.

A node with the shortest assigned wait time wakes and writes a block to the blockchain.

PoW and PoS consensus algorithm is designed to prevent a situation where a group of miner's controls more than 50% of the blockchain's mining hash rate, including halting new transactions and changing historical blocks granting them the ability to double-spend.

2.6 Limitations of Blockchain

Although blockchain solves some problems in IoT, it is far from a perfect solution. Blockchain still has some limitations. The capabilities and effectiveness of blockchain can be conquered with further investigation.

The Low transaction throughput and high latency resulted in inadequate performance due to the poor scalability of the consensus mechanisms.

The high-power consumption of the blockchain as it scales on constrained devices is due to the complex mining algorithms. However, power-efficient blockchain algorithms could alleviate such difficulty.

Since all transactions on a public/permissionless blockchain are public and participating devices are identified by their public key, they are susceptible to pattern analyses and establishing a connection between addresses, inevitably inferring information and identity of the parties involved [13].

3 Related Work

In [14] proposed a scheme to authenticate, which requires the storage of Symmetric key cryptography on a cloud server. The manufacturers of wearable and smartphones save the devices' details and sensory data on the cloud. The problem with this approach is that all the devices' details, like the symmetric key and the sensory data, are susceptible to a single point of failure attack.

In [15], the proposed approach uses RSS signal variation and RSS-trace concept to prevent physical security attacks like impersonation and device capturing for proximity-based authentication between smartphones and IoT devices. The limitation of this mechanism is that it requires proximity to the IoT and that the authentication data resides on a central local server. As a consequence, it creates a single point of failure.

In [16], the proposed authentication mechanism uses PUFs (physical unclonable Functions) without storing secret keys on centralized servers, which would make it impossible to impersonate but requires the PUF-based authentication data to reside on the server nodes. However, it would make the approach susceptible to single-point failures.

In [17], the proposed two-factor authentication mechanism uses physical properties to identify the IoT devices to prevent impersonation attacks and side-channel attacks. The main drawback to the approach is storing authentication data on a centralized server.

In [18], proposed authentication and a secure communication mechanism between industrial IoT devices. The approach utilizes hash functions and XOR operations for transmitting sensory data and authentication. The limitation of this mechanism is that it mandates the storage of authentication data on a local server, creating a single point of failure.

The mechanism proposed in [19] has three main components, the IoT devices, group leader, and subscriber server. That allows authentication of groups of devices before entering into the system. The registration and authentication data is on the subscriber server. The limitation is that the authentication data of various groups reside on the subscriber server, creating a single point of failure.

[20] proposes a decentralized authentication mechanism using blockchain technology to circumvent several security issues in IoT. However, the primary constraint is that communication is limited to devices within the same system, making it impractical in the IoT paradigm as it is vital for many distributed applications of IoT that require communication between devices of different systems.

4 Proposed Mechanisms

The primary purpose of this work is to provide distributed access control and management for IoT devices irrespective of the vendor allowing for interoperability. This paper provides a mechanism to authenticate IoT devices with IoT devices belonging to the same or different systems. This approach discusses a secure way to transfer access to another user who might not be part of the IoT system as well as segregation of the IoT network.

4.1 Segregation of the IoT Network

The segregation of the IoT network into different levels allows greater control over which devices can communicate with other devices. Only devices that are allowed can intercommunicate between levels. So, if a device or network level gets compromised, it prevents the entire system from being compromised. This segregation should prevent vertical escalation. The network-level segregation acts as the privilege level the IoT device has on the network (Fig. 3).

IoT NETWORK

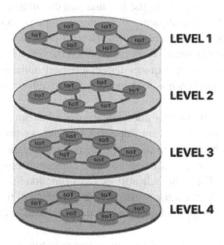

Fig. 3. Segmentation of the IoT network

The network level and its privileges are determined by the Wallet owner. The network level refers to the which segment of the network the IoT reside in, as this determines which other IoT it can intercommunicate. Together with the privilege the IoT has creates the privilege-level (PL_A). An example of what the IoT could have privilege is reading and writing data to a shared database or which IoT devices could communicate with an IoT even on the same network-level. As some IoT device could be programed only communicate with certain other IoT devices. So, there can further segregation within the same network-level. PLT refers to the level of privilege the transferred user has on the IoT device or if the IoT could communicate with other IoT devices own by this wallet/user. P_{code} is 16 characters passcode this was is used to prevent replay and impersonation attacks, each P_{code} is tied to a PLT and privilege-level (PL_A). Not only does this prevent vertical escalation, it allows the IoT to be deployed in environment that require complex segregation of the IoT network for security reasons.

4.2 System Architecture

The mechanism has four components: the device layer, A relay node, Smart Contract, and wallets. The device layer is principally to communicate between the authenticated devices to establish secure communication. The relay node subscribed to the events emitted by the smart contract and relays it to the IoT, there can be more than one reply nodes deployed to provide redundancy as it only purpose is to send the authentication certificate ($Auth_C$) which is emitted by the smart Contract to the IoT devices, this allows for less complexity on the IoT devices as they do not have to directly subscribe to the smart contract, The relay node resides inside the IoT network and is not deployed on the cloud. The Smart Contract is the entity that provides the authentication certificate ($Auth_C$); the authentication between the devices uses this issued authentication certificate ($Auth_C$). The smart Contract acts as distributed access management for the registered IoT devices. The wallet acts as the {owner of the IoT device, and the user interacts with the IoT using the wallet. The approach has three main phases: registration, device authentication, and device-to-device.

Registration phase: The essential principle of this phase is to establish ownership between the IoT (device) and the user (wallet). The user obtains the IoT device's public key (A_{PK}) and mac address and sends a registration certificate (RG_C) containing the public key of the user's wallet (W_{PK}) this public key is not the same as the ethereum public key which is used for making transactions and the smart-contract address (SC_{AD}) as well as a 16 characters passcode (P_{code}) which is tied to a network-level. This registration certificate is signed using the public key of the IoT device. The registration phase mandates the IoT to receive a signed certificate with its public key to establish ownership. The IoT only accepts registration certificate that is signed by its public key as it stores the certificate to use in further validation. The IoT accepts registration certificate only once and would require reset for the devices to accept again. Note that last 40 bytes of the keccak-256 hash public key is the Ethereum address

$$RG_C = A_{PK}\{W_{PK} + SC_{AD} + P_{code}\}. \tag{1}$$

Device authentication phase: This phase is paramount to the mechanism, as the IoT device receives the authentication certificate ($Auth_C$). The IoT device uses this certificate to authenticate itself with other IoT devices. The wallet sends the initialization certificate (IZ_C) to the smart contract. The initialization certificate (IZ_C) contains the mac address (Mac_A), the public key (A_{PK}), and the IP address (IP_A) of the IoT devices, privilege-level (PL_A). Privilege-level contains the network-level and privilege of the device. The initialization certificate (IZ_C) is encapsulated using the wallet's private key (W_{IK}). The initialization certificate also contains a copy of the IP address (IP_A) of the IoT devices that is not encapsulated using the using the wallet's private key (W_{IK}). The smart contract can be programmed to accept transactions only from the wallet that deployed it on the blockchain or from a few assigned wallets, but this paper will focus on the first option. The smart contract crafts the authentication certificate ($Auth_C$) and trigger an event which contains the authentication certificate ($Auth_C$) as well as the IP address of the device (IP_A). The relay node relays the $Auth_C$ to the corresponding IP address in the emitted event. Once the IoT device receives this, the authentication certificate ($Auth_C$) is validated using the registration certificate.

$$IZ_C = W_{IK}\{Mac_A + A_{PK} + IP_A + PL_A\} + IP_A. \tag{2}$$

$$Auth_C = W_{IK}\{Mac_A + A_{PK} + IP_A + PL_A\}. \tag{3}$$

IoT validating the Authentication Certificate.

using Registration Certificate.

$\Rightarrow$ *The IoT device A applies W_{PK} from.*

Registration Certificate on the.

Authentication Certificate.

$$\Rightarrow W_{PK}\{W_{IK}\{Mac_A + A_{PK} + IP_A + PL_A\}\}. \tag{4}$$

$\Rightarrow$ *The IoT devices A check if the Mac Address,*

A_{PK} *and IP Address are the same as its own.*

Device-to-device phase This phase pertains to authenticating the IoT devices with other IoT devices. The device creates an auth packet containing the authentication certificate and the device's IP and mac address. The device's IP and mac address in the pack are signed using the device's private key. The device that receives the broadcast can validate the authenticity by applying the public key of the wallet on the authentication certificate.

The device's public key is provided in the registration certificate, once it obtains the public key of the broadcasting IoT from the authentication certificate. The receiving IoT can validate that the device's IP and mac address provided in both the authentication certificate and the one signed using the device's private key are the same. If all the checks are valid, the IoT device sends back its auth packet signed using the public key of the broadcasting IoT devices. Now since both the IoT devices have each other public keys, they have the facilities to initiate secure communication with each other. The IoT that receives the broadcasting sents a random generated string of characters along with the authentication certificate, which the broadcasting IoT will hash with the passcode (P_{code}) and send back.

Which the receiving IoT verifies by hashing the passcode (P_{code}) with the random string of characters that was send, if they match, this ensure the IoT is not imitated by an adversary on the network,

$$AuthPacket_A = Auth_C \text{ of } Device \, A + A_{IK}\{IP_A + Mac_A\}. \tag{5}$$

The receiving Device B applies the W_{PK} to the.

authentication Certificate of Device.

$$\Rightarrow W_{PK}\{W_{IK}\{Mac_A + A_{PK} + IP_A + PL_A\}\}. \tag{6}$$

The Device B now applies the A_{PK} it just obtained.

for the Authentication Certificate.

$$\Rightarrow A_{PK}\{A_{IK}\{IP_A + Mac_A\}\}. \tag{7}$$

$\Rightarrow$ *The Device B validates if the Mac and.*

IP address are the same as the one.

in the Authentication Certificate.

$$\Rightarrow let \ \delta = random \ generated \ string. \tag{8}$$

$$AuthPacket_B = Auth_C \ of \ Device \ B + B_{IK}\{IP_B + Mac_B + \delta\}. \tag{9}$$

$\Rightarrow$ *The Device A hashes δ with P_{code}.*

$$A_{IK}\{B_{PK}\{hashed \ value \ of \ \delta \ and \ P_{code}\}\}. \tag{10}$$

The Device B validates the hash received from Device A.

By hashing δ with P_{code} and checking is it match.

Case 1: device-to-device communication between devices in the same system owned by the same wallet.

1. The wallet obtained the public key and Mac address of the IoT device, which is to be registered under said wallet and deployed onto the network.
2. The wallet sends a Registration Certificate Eq. (1) to the IoT.
3. Then the wallet sends an Initialization Certificate Eq. (2) to the Smart Contract.
4. The Smart Contract triggers an event and the relay node relays the Authentication Certificate Eq. (3) to the IoT device.
5. The IoT device upon receiving the Authentication Certificate creates Auth packet Eq. (5) and broadcasts it on the network
6. Upon receiving the broadcast, IoT devices validate the Auth Pack and send back their Auth Packet Eq. (8) along with a random generated string of characters to be hashed with passcode (P_{code}). Once this hash is verified, secure connections between the IoT devices are made (Fig. 4).

In a scenario where the IoT system mandates higher security and finer control or the possibility of the authenticated IoT devices being physically accessed by an untrusted

Case: 1

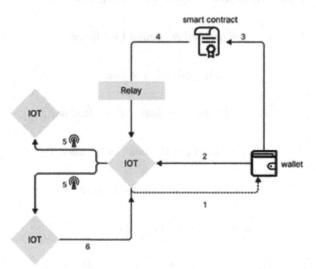

Fig. 4. Device-to-device communication between devices in the same system owned by the same wallet.

Party and the certificate can be stolen. The following steps would mitigate these issues. To increase security in certain networks the IoT device that receives the Broadcasted Eq. (5) can sent the Eq. (8) signed with W_{PK} to the wallet and once the wallet receives the packet, The wallet would apply W_{IK} to extract the Auth packet of device B and then sign it with W_{IP} and send it to the IoT device A.

Case 2: Wallet-to-device communication between wallet and device owned by the same wallet.

Once the device receives the Authentication Certificate and secure communication is established. The Wallet can send packets that are signed with the wallet's private key and then encapsulated with the public key of the IoT device.

1. The packet that was sent from the wallet.

$$\rightarrow A_{PK}\{W_{IK}\{DATA\}\}. \tag{11}$$

2. The IoT device A validates the packet sent from the wallet by applying the device's private key and the public key of the wallet from the registration certificate.

$$\rightarrow A_{IK}\{A_{PK}\{W_{IK}\{DATA\}\}\}. \tag{12}$$

$$\Rightarrow W_{PK}\{W_{IK}\{DATA\}\}. \tag{13}$$

The IoT device has the same facility to send data back in the same manner. This allows the device and wallet to set up a secure connection.

Case 3: device access and communication between wallet and device not owned by the same wallet using non-fungible tokens (NFT).

To allow the IoT device to be accessed by another wallet(user) the steps 1 to 4 from case: 1 must be completed first before the following steps

1. The wallet sends an Access transfer certificate (AT_C) to the smart contract that is encapsulated using the private key of the owner's Wallet except for the wallet address the NFT is sent to which is the same as the wallet the access is being granted (*Wt address*). The Access transfer Certificate also contains public key of the IoT device A (A_{PK}), Mac address of the device A (Mac_A), IP address of the device A (IP_A), public key of the Wallet the access is being granted (Wt_{PK}) this public key is not the same as the ethereum public key which is used for making transactions, the passcode (P_{code}) of the IoT encapsulated using the public key of the Wallet the access is being granted (Wt_{PK}),the passcode (P_{code}) of the IoT encapsulated using the public key of the IoT device A (A_{PK}), level of privilege the user has on the IoT device (PLT). The PLT determines whether the IoT device can be connected to the IoT devices owned by the newly granted wallet(user).

$$\Rightarrow let\ Td = time\ duration\ Wt\ has\ access. \tag{14}$$

$$\Rightarrow let\ \alpha = A_{PK} + Mac_A + IP_A + Wt_{PK} + PLT + Td. \tag{15}$$

$$\Rightarrow let\ \beta = Wt_{PK}\{P_{code} + A_{PK} + Mac_A + IP_A + PLT + Td\}. \tag{16}$$

$$AT_C = W_{IK}\{\alpha + A_{PK}\{P_{code}\}\} + \beta + (Wt\ address) + IP_A. \tag{17}$$

2. The smart contract crafts the Access grant Certificate (AG_C) from Access transfer certificate. Then the smart contract triggers an event that contains an Access grant Certificate (AG_C) and the relay node relays it to the IoT device. The Access grant Certificate (AG_C) contains the data from the Access transfer Certificate and the wallet address the NFT (Wt address) is sent to as well as the NFT token ID (NFT ID). Once the IoT receives the Access grant Certificate it stores it for further use

From the AT_C.

$$\gamma = W_{IK}\{\alpha + A_{PK}\{P_{code}\}\} + (Wt\ address). \tag{18}$$

$$\rightarrow AG_C = \gamma + NFT\ ID + IP_A. \tag{19}$$

3. The smart Contract mints a NFT token and sends it to the Wt. The metadata in the NFT contains the time duration the Wt has access to the IoT devices.

From the AT_C the β is extracted.

$$Wt_{PK}\{P_{code} + A_{PK} + Mac_A + IP_A + PLT + time\ duration\}. \tag{20}$$

4. The Wt crafts Access packet and sends it to the IoT devices. The Access packet contains.

$$Wt_{IK}\{A_{PK}\{NFT\,ID + DATA\}\}. \tag{21}$$

$$DATA = random\ generated\ string\ of\ characters. \tag{22}$$

The IoT validates the Access packet by check applying Wt_{PK} provided in the Access grant certificate and checking the NFT metadata using NFT token ID to validate that access time duration has not expired. Since the NFT token ID can be used to track the NFT and who owns it. Then the random generated string of characters in the Access packet is hashed with P_{code} and is sent back to the wallet. The wallet verifies by hashing the generated string of characters with the P_{code} received in the NFT metadata. By doing so wallet can be ensured that the IoT is not imitated by an adversary and secure connection can be established (Fig. 5).

Case: 3

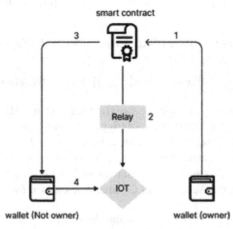

Fig. 5. Device access and communication between wallet and device not owned by the same wallet using non-fungible tokens (NFT).

Case 4: device-to-device communication between different systems belonging to different wallets.

To allow the IoT device to communicate between devices owned by another wallet(user) the steps from case: 3 must be completed first before the following steps. Once the Wt is authenticated to access and the PLT given to the wallet allows the IoT device to connect to the devices owned Wt.

The Wt creates a certificate WtRegistration Certificate which contains the Address of the smart contract (WtSC) owned by Wt as well as a 16 characters passcode (P_{code}) which is tied to a network-level of Wt's network and sends it to the IoT similar to the Registration phase.

And then Wt sends a initialization certificate contains the mac address (Mac_A), the public key (A_{PK}), and the IP address (IP_A) of the IoT devices and the IP address of the device it should communicate with on the Wt system, privilege-level it has on the system owned by Wt (PL_A) as well as the (P_{code}).

The WtSC smart contract triggers an event and the relay node owned by the Wt relays the WtAuthentication certificate to the IoT devices.

The device validates the WtAuthentication certificate then creates and broadcasts its WtAuth packet to the specified IP address of the devices. WtAuth Packet is similar to Eq. (5) but contains the WtAuthentication certificate instead of the Authentication certificate as well as the random generated string of characters which the receiving IoT will hash with the P_{code} from the WtAuthentication certificate. The devices that receive the WtAuth packet sent back its Auth Packet Eq. (8) along with created hashed.

5 Algorithm

ALGORITHM 1 - Smart Contract
---

1. **Inputs:** The certificate.
2. **Output:** An event is emitted, if required mint NFT and send to appropriate wallet.
3. **if** the certificate is sent from the designated wallet.
4. **then**
5. **if** the certificate is an initialization certificate.
6. **then**
   Return Authentication certificate and IP address of IoT as well as emit event.
7. **else if** Access transfer certificate.
8. **then**
   Return Access grant Certificate and IP address of IoT as well as mint NFT sent to appropriate wallet and emit event.
9. **else** Invalid transaction

6 Value Proposition

The value proposition this mechanism provides is an always available distributed access management and transfer of authorization system. That is interoperable regardless of the vendor of the IoT and the system in which the IoT resides. The paper provides solutions for two scenarios. IoT devices that is not connected directly to the internet; case 1 and case 2 are examples of this scenario. The IoT devices that have access to the blockchain and the internet. The example for this is case 3 and case 4. IoT devices for household are prime examples that one may not want the IoT to have access to the internet. Either for privacy or security reasons as the IoT itself may be vulnerable. The other situation is that the IoT devices requires dynamic interaction with other IoT devices such as medical devices lend to a patient for monitoring or smart door locks that would need to interact with other wallets.

7 Security Analysis

7.1 The Adversary Mode

The adversary can intercept communication over the network and have the ability to replay, listen in on, delete, or alter any message, as well as create a new message. There are a few assumptions take into consideration, Authenticity of users and devices initially during the Registration phase and that the public key of the device (A_{PK}) is obtained securely initially for the Registration phase as well as the IP address of the devices is static in the network.

7.2 Secret Disclosure Attack

Registration phase: Once the public key of the IoT (A_{PK}) is obtained. The wallet sends the IoT the registration certificate (RG_C) as mentioned in Eq. (1) it encapsulated using the public key of the IoT device this prevent disclosure Attack and the contents of the RG_C remains secure. as the P_{code} is the information that should remain secure.

Device authentication phase: The wallet sends the initialization certificate (IZ_C) to the smart contract any information present in IZ_C other then IP_A is encapsulated with the wallets private key mentioned is Eq. (2). Once the smart contract verifies that transaction is from the wallet that deployed the smart contract. An authentication certificate ($Auth_C$) is created from the IZ_C. The $Auth_C$ uses the IZ_C which is encapsulated with the Private key (W_{IK}) of the wallet mentioned in Eq. (3). This prevents any disclosure Attack. As mentioned before the public (W_{PK}) and private key (W_{IK}) used for the is not the same as the Ethereum public and private key which is used for making transactions.

Device-to-device phase: once the IoT receives the $Auth_C$ it creates a the $AuthPacket_A$ mentioned in Eq. (5) this includes the $Auth_C$ as well a IP_A and Mac_A where the IP_A and Mac_A are encapsulated using the A_{IK} and the $Auth_C$ as mentioned above is encapsulated with the Private key (W_{IK}). Once both the IoT obtains each other's public key by sending each others their $AuthPackets$ a secure communication can be established preventing any disclosure Attack.

7.3 Replay Attack

Registration phase: Replay attacks do not pose a problem as the registration certificate (RG_C) as mentioned in Eq. (1) is accept only once and require the RG_C to be encapsulated with the public key of the IoT (A_{PK}). The device would require a reset for the IoT to accept a new registration certificate.

Device authentication phase: The smart contract only accept transaction from the wallet that deployed it on to the blockchain. Authentication certificate ($Auth_C$) being replayed would not pose a threat to the mechanism as there would be no advantage gained by the adversary. If the adversary sends the $Auth_C$ the IoT device A would check the $Auth_C$ it already has and if they match, The IoT would just discard the new $Auth_C$ send by the adversary. Since the $Auth_C$ is crafted specify for a particular IoT devices it will do no good sending it to other IoT devices on the network, as when the IoT devices does the verification using the MAC address, IP address and the public key as mentioned in Eq. (3) with its own to check whether they match. If they do not the $Auth_C$ is discarded.

Device-to-device phase: The $AuthPacket_A$ as mentioned in Eq. (5) would not pose a threat to replay attacks as it is crafted using the IP_A and Mac_A of the IoT devices A which is then encapsulated using the private key of the IoT device A (A_{IK}). There is no part in the $AuthPacket_A$ that can be tampered. Once the device B receives $AuthPacket_A$ the device sends back its $AuthPacket_B$ mentioned in Eq. (8). The $AuthPacket_B$ includes a random generated string of characters which is hashed with the P_{code} stored in the RG_C and sent back to device B mentioned in Eq. (10). This acts are defense against impersonation attacks.

7.4 Availability

The segregation of the IoT network into different levels allows greater control and prevents the entire network from being compromised. Even if one level of the network was to be compromised the other level could function as normal. Since the Access management is not depended on the vendors availability but rather the blockchain. The mechanism is always available.

8 Conclusion and Future Work

IoT Devices are expected to communicate between devices from different systems in a secure and distributed environment and by different users. In this paper, a distributed and always available authentication and access management mechanism is proposed that permits IoT devices to authenticate between devices and users, regardless of the device vendor. This approach prevents vendor lockdown of IoT devices in a system. Furthermore, the cost of deploying this mechanism is relatively less as the cost is only at the initial stage and at the transfer of access. The device to device and user to devices authentication is accomplished off-chain. The future work would focus on developing a proof of concept to evaluate and test this approach.

References

1. Nakamoto, S.: Bitcoin: a peer-to-peer electronic cash system. Decentralized Bus. Rev. 21260 (2008)
2. Novo, O.: Blockchain meets IoT: an architecture for scalable access management in IoT. IEEE Internet Things J. 5(2), 1184–1195 (2018). https://doi.org/10.1109/JIOT.2018.2812239
3. Szabo, N.: Formalizing and securing relationships on public networks. FM 2(9) (1997). https://doi.org/10.5210/fm.v2i9.548
4. "EIP-721: Non-Fungible Token Standard". https://eips.ethereum.org/EIPS/eip-721. Accessed 14 Apr 2022

5. Wang, Q., Li, R., Wang, Q., Chen, S.: Non-Fungible Token (NFT): Overview, Evaluation, Opportunities and Challenges. arXiv (2021). https://doi.org/10.48550/arxiv.2105.07447

6. Jakobsson, M., Juels, A.: Proofs of work and bread pudding protocols (extended abstract). In: Preneel, B. (ed.) Secure Information Networks. ITIFIP, vol. 23, pp. 258–272. Springer, Boston (1999). https://doi.org/10.1007/978-0-387-35568-9_18

7. Wood, G.: Ethereum: a secure decentralised generalised transaction ledger. Ethereum Project Yellow Pap. **151**(2014), 1–32 (2014)

8. He, K., Chen, J., Du, R., Wu, Q., Xue, G., Zhang, X.: DeyPoS: deduplicatable dynamic proof of storage for multi-user environments. IEEE Trans. Comput. **65**(12), 3631–3645 (2016). https://doi.org/10.1109/TC.2016.2560812

9. Bentov, I., Lee, C., Mizrahi, A., Rosenfeld, M.: Proof of activity. SIGMETRICS Perform. Eval. Rev. **42**(3), 34–37 (2014). https://doi.org/10.1145/2695533.2695545

10. Azbeg, K., Ouchetto, O., Jai Andaloussi, S., Fetjah, L.: An overview of blockchain consensus algorithms: comparison, challenges and future directions. In: Saeed, F., Al-Hadhrami, T., Mohammed, F., Mohammed, E. (eds.) Advances on Smart and Soft Computing. AISC, vol. 1188, pp. 357–369. Springer, Singapore (2021). https://doi.org/10.1007/978-981-15-6048-4_31

11. Shahaab, A., Lidgey, B., Hewage, C., Khan, I.: Applicability and appropriateness of distributed ledgers consensus protocols in public and private sectors: a systematic review. IEEE Access **7**, 43622–43636 (2019). https://doi.org/10.1109/ACCESS.2019.2904181

12. Bashar, G., Hill, G., Singha, S., Marella, P., Dagher, G.G., Xiao, J.: Contextualizing consensus protocols in blockchain: a short survey. In: 2019 First IEEE International Conference on Trust, Privacy and Security in Intelligent Systems and Applications (TPS-ISA), pp. 190–195 (2019). https://doi.org/10.1109/TPS-ISA48467.2019.00031

13. Li, X., Jiang, P., Chen, T., Luo, X., Wen, Q.: A survey on the security of blockchain systems. Future Gener. Comput. Syst. (2017). https://doi.org/10.1016/j.future.2017.08.020

14. Wu, F., Li, X., Xu, L., Kumari, S., Karuppiah, M., Shen, J.: A lightweight and privacy-preserving mutual authentication scheme for wearable devices assisted by cloud server. Comput. Electr. Eng. (2017). https://doi.org/10.1016/j.compeleceng.2017.04.012

15. Zhang, J., Wang, Z., Yang, Z., Zhang, Q.: Proximity based IoT device authentication. In: IEEE Conference on Computer Communications, IEEE INFOCOM 2017, pp. 1–9 (2017). https://doi.org/10.1109/INFOCOM.2017.8057145

16. Aman, M.N., Chua, K.C., Sikdar, B.: Mutual authentication in IoT systems using physical unclonable functions. IEEE Internet Things J. **4**(5), 1327–1340 (2017). https://doi.org/10.1109/JIOT.2017.2703088

17. Gope, P., Sikdar, B.: Lightweight and privacy-preserving two-factor authentication scheme for IoT devices. IEEE Internet Things J. **6**(1), 580–589 (2019). https://doi.org/10.1109/JIOT.2018.2846299

18. Esfahani, A., et al.: A lightweight authentication mechanism for M2M communications in industrial IoT environment. IEEE Internet Things J. **6**(1), 288–296 (2019). https://doi.org/10.1109/JIOT.2017.2737630

19. Roychoudhury, P., Roychoudhury, B., Saikia, D.K.: Provably secure group authentication and key agreement for machine type communication using Chebyshev's polynomial. Comput. Commun. **127**, 146–157 (2018). https://doi.org/10.1016/j.comcom.2018.06.005

20. Hammi, M.T., Hammi, B., Bellot, P., Serhrouchni, A.: Bubbles of trust: a decentralized blockchain-based authentication system for IoT. Comput. Secur. **78**, 126–142 (2018). https://doi.org/10.1016/j.cose.2018.06.004

Modification of the Algorithm for Dynamic Data Transformation Based on Blockchain Technology for Data Management Systems

Nikita Olimpiev[1]([✉]) [iD], Alexander Vodyaho[2] [iD], and Nataly Zhukova[3] [iD]

[1] ITMO University, Kronverksky Pr. 49, bldg. A, 197101 St. Petersburg, Russia
olimpiev@itmo.ru
[2] Saint Petersburg Electrotechnical University, Professora Popova St. 5, 197022 St. Petersburg, Russia
[3] Laboratory of Big Data Technologies in Socio-Cyberphysical Systems, Saint-Petersburg Federal Research Centre of the Russian Academy of Sciences, 14-th Linia, VI, No. 39, 199178 St. Petersburg, Russia

Abstract. The rapid growth of data and increasing complexity in various domains necessitate advanced data management solutions that address data quality, security, and interoperability challenges. This paper presents a modified algorithm for dynamic data transformation based on blockchain technology for Master Data Management Systems (MDM), incorporating Ethereum, IPFS and semantic data. Based on the proposed algorithm, an architectural approach is also described that allows developing semantic data management systems. The algorithm assumes data validation, enrichment, and deduplication processes, while also ensuring consistency and trust among multiple participants through the decentralized nature of the blockchain. The semantic data management aspect of the system is achieved using Apache Jena and local ontology, which facilitate semantic interoperability and efficient data processing. The proposed approach addresses the challenge of applying blockchain technology to semantic MDM systems and demonstrates an approach to using the system in Semantic Web, as well as in areas such as finance, healthcare, public administration, and logistics. We evaluated the algorithm using a customer information dataset from an e-commerce platform. The results confirmed the potential of blockchain technology in data management and showed improvements in data accuracy, consistency, completeness, but with some loss in storage efficiency due to the use of blockchain. This paper contributes to developing and evaluating a novel algorithm and architecture, combining blockchain technology, MDM principles, and semantic data management for improving data quality, security, and performance in decentralized systems. However, further research and assessment may be required for the full implementation and evaluation of the system.

Keywords: Blockchain Technology · Master Data Management · Ethereum · Semantic Data Management · Data Transformation · Decentralized Systems · Data Quality · Data Security

O. Gervasi et al. (Eds.): ICCSA 2023 Workshops, LNCS 14104, pp. 555–571, 2023.
https://doi.org/10.1007/978-3-031-37105-9_37

1 Introduction

1.1 Background and Motivation

According to Statista, a market and consumer data company, the global data volume reached 79 zettabytes in 2021, with forecasts of a surge to 181 zettabytes by 2025 [1]. This escalating trend prompts researchers to develop and adapt data management systems to satisfy growing demands, while large businesses invest in and deploy systems to optimize their operations. As data volumes expand, concerns related to data security, integrity, and system performance become increasingly crucial, particularly for organizations with multiple branches and teams handling local data.

The Data Management Association International (DAMA) characterizes data management as the capacity to plan, control, and deliver information assets [2]. Master Data Management (MDM) systems, designed to ensure data integrity and provide a unified, up-to-date representation of entities and their relationships in a consolidated form, are highly sought after by corporations dealing with distributed data. According to Gartner, the top 5 MDM market leaders in 2023 are PiLog MDRM, Intelligent Master Data Management Platform, Semarchy xDM, Stibo Systems MDM, and TIBCO EBX [3]. While highly rated, these MDM systems face challenges that could impact their functionality and efficiency. Current MDM systems often rely on a centrally stored tabular data structure, resulting in limitations that only partially fulfill growing organizations' needs for system performance, security, and data integrity.

Blockchain technology offers a potential solution to these issues by facilitating the development of distributed data management systems with robust security, data integrity, and reliability. As highlighted in the study [4], blockchain technology provides a paradigm shift in business process optimization, data exchange, and compatibility across related industries, as well as a novel approach to data management. The technology can be employed to ensure security of data and access when constructing data management systems. In another study on implementing blockchain in data management systems [5], the authors outline possible scenarios and advantages of utilizing this technology, indicating growing interest in the subject. To tackle the challenges of vulnerability, centralization, and scalability in data management, the researchers propose a blockchain-based data collaboration management structure featuring user authentication, data validation, load distribution across nodes, and the introduction of a digital currency called datacoin. However, the practical applicability of the work remains uncertain due to the lack of focus on specific mechanisms used by blockchain platforms, the management systems in operation, and the data employed in the study. Moreover, the authors of another study [6] delineate three levels of data management: blockchain architecture, blockchain data structure, and blockchain data storage mechanism. They conclude that standard blockchains are typically employed for digital currency, hybrid blockchains suit multi-organizational scenarios, and DAG-based blockchains are most appropriate for the Internet of Things. Despite these conclusions, the authors also underscore the shortcomings of hybrid blockchains and the nascent stage of DAG use. To manage excessive data loads, they recommend distributed data storage and encoding methods, as well as the creation of an additional database for queries.

Another significant toolset within data management and transformation is Semantic Web technologies, including RDF, OWL, SPARQL, and Linked Data. These technologies facilitate semantic data processing and offer a standardized methodology for data description and utilization, thereby promoting more efficient processing and application. However, managing semantic data presents complex challenges related to ensuring data integrity and up-to-date representation, which can be addressed using MDM systems. Administering ontology core data enables the realization of semantic technology benefits and allows the implementation of the MDM systems embedded within the Semantic Web concept.

As semantic data is often distributed and its collection involves working with heterogeneous sources, thus issues concerning data integrity and reliability arise. Simultaneously, blockchain technology enables the accumulation of heterogeneous data, ensuring data security and system scalability. For instance, the authors of the study [7] employ blockchain, Ethereum smart contracts, and the InterPlanetary File System (IPFS) network for decentralized data storage to manage ontology data. This stack circumvents the limitations and vulnerabilities of centralized data storage by distributing public ontology among users. While the study demonstrates the efficacy of combining blockchain technology with the Semantic Web for ontology data management, the authors acknowledge the time needed to modify a smart contract in the Ethereum network as a potential limiting factor. Additionally, the implemented ontology consistency checks are performed locally, making it possible for an attacker to bypass them. However, the proposed solution primarily serves as an ontology database manager, rather than a comprehensive data management system. Consequently, the development of an integrated MDM system for managing semantic data based on blockchain remains a pertinent task that warrants further research and development.

The paper is structured into three sections, each addressing a different aspect of the research. Section 1 is dedicated to the introduction, outlining the research issues, author motivation, and the study's goal. In Sect. 2, the basic and proposed modified algorithms for dynamic data transformation are discussed, and the architectural approach for the semantic data management system, based on the proposed algorithm, is presented. Subsequently, an evaluation of the proposed algorithm is provided. Section 3 focuses on the results and their corresponding discussion, elaborating on the research outcomes and the potential of blockchain technology in the realm of data management.

1.2 Research Goal

The analyses of literature sources reveals that prominent MDM systems and blockchain technology implementation methods for data management face certain limitations. There is a scarcity of research in open literature regarding the utilization of data management systems that facilitate interaction with semantic data using blockchain technology. Furthermore, previous studies have not comprehensively addressed the implementation of such a system for managing master data, highlighting the insufficient exploration of this topic, and hindering the assessment of the feasibility of employing Master Data Management systems in the context of the Semantic Web. Illustratively, the paper [8] provides a brief overview of employing blockchain technology for managing master data. The authors highlight the importance for organizations to establish governance rules, processes, and methodologies to efficiently handle master data, thereby facilitating data consolidation across various blockchain networks in which they participate. However, it should be noted that the authors' work is limited to a short paper and does not delve into the implementation details of such a system. The study conducted by the authors [9] assessed the suitability of blockchain technology for storing and exchanging master data in supply chains. Although the application developed for this purpose did not specifically target semantic data, the findings of the study support previous theoretical claims in the literature. Empirical data from the study indicate that permissioned blockchain networks demonstrate enhanced scalability and cost-effectiveness compared to closed networks, including integration with Master Data Management systems. However, it should be noted that the study's results are limited in their applicability due to the lack of focus on semantic technologies and master data usage.

Also, in the context of the algorithms used to manage this data, it should be noted that existing research and industry practices in the field of data management use different approaches. As it turned out from the analysis, the existing academic research in this area is primarily focused on the use of blockchain technology to provide secure, decentralized, and transparent data management solutions [4, 5]. Some of these studies delve deeper into the combination of blockchain and semantic data to further enhance the capabilities of data management systems, offering more efficient and sophisticated ways to process, store, and retrieve information [7].

At the same time, the commercial business sector has witnessed the emergence and growth of Master Data Management (MDM) systems, which typically do not incorporate blockchain technology. These MDM systems are designed to handle vast amounts of structured and unstructured data, ensuring data quality, consistency, and accuracy across different domains and organizations. Instead of leveraging the unique advantages of blockchain and semantic data, MDM systems usually rely on traditional data management techniques, such as relational databases, and tabular data representations, which can limit their ability to adapt to the rapidly evolving data landscape. The main drawback of the listed underlying algorithms is the lack of integration of both blockchain technology and semantic data principles.

Utilizing blockchain and semantic technologies could potentially enhance data management systems, as the individual effectiveness of each technology is supported by the outcomes of reviewed works. However, integrating these technologies into a unified MDM system necessitates further analysis and justification of their implementation approach, drawing upon existing experience.

The goal of this research is to modify the dynamic data transformation algorithm that forms the foundation of a semantic data management system's architecture, and to devise an architectural approach for constructing a data management system utilizing the modified algorithm. This system will employ blockchain technology and conform to master data management (MDM) principles. By incorporating ontologies into MDM systems, the algorithm facilitates data definition, classification, and guarantees accuracy and consistency in the stored information. Additionally, ontologies can facilitate data search and navigation within the system. Blockchain provides data security and system scalability, while master data usage principles maintain the integrity and relevance of semantic data in the system. While the use cases for blockchain for MDM and semantic technologies in organizations are clear, the use of the technology in organizations has yet worked out, which is a key reason for the lack of such systems.

2 Proposed Algorithm and Architectural Approach

2.1 Basic Algorithm of MDM Systems

The basic algorithm that uses only MDM with tabular data representation [10] can be described as follows:

1. Data extraction: Data is retrieved from various sources, such as databases, files, or APIs, in different formats (e.g., XML, JSON, CSV). The extraction process considers the specific data representation (tabular or semantic) and the storage method (centralized or decentralized).
2. Data validation: Before transformation, the algorithm validates the input data to ensure its accuracy and consistency. This step enforces predefined rules and conditions depending on the chosen data representation and storage method. However, it does not utilize the potential of semantic data technologies or the security benefits of blockchain technology.
3. Data transformation: The core of the basic algorithm is the data transformation process. This step converts the validated data into a common intermediate format, applying operations such as data cleansing, filtering, aggregation, and normalization. The transformation process is tailored to the specific data representation but may not take full advantage of the benefits that semantic data formats offer.
4. Data loading: The transformed and validated data is loaded into a target system, such as a data warehouse, database, or another application in the appropriate format and structure.
5. Access control and data retrieval: The basic algorithm employs access control mechanisms depending on the chosen data storage method (centralized or decentralized). Users can retrieve the transformed data, but the level of security and granularity of access control may be limited.

Thus, by systems using the basic algorithm of work, we mean MDM systems with a tabular form of data presentation, which serve to manage the master data of an organization. The purpose of such systems is to ensure that there are no repetitive, incomplete, conflicting data in various areas of the organization. Such systems can interact with external information systems, receive data from them and send back converted data. The basis for the implementation of such systems, as a rule, is an application server with a backend created by the vendor, a relational database and search indexes to speed up work. To sum up, basic MDM systems work centrally, and security is ensured only by the qualifications of the software developers who created the system.

2.2 Development of a Modified Algorithm

The basic sequence of actions can be transformed considering the principles of Master Data Management and the use of blockchain technology for a semantic management system. The modified algorithm assumes combining the principles of Master Data Management (MDM) and the Ethereum 2.0 blockchain technology. Ethereum blockchain was chosen as a platform for the system being developed as it provides a powerful foundation for building decentralized applications, including data management systems, and the transition to Ethereum 2.0 with PoS further enhances its capabilities. Ethereum's transition to Ethereum 2.0, incorporating PoS and sharding, aims to address scalability challenges. Sharding allows the network to process transactions and computations in parallel, increasing the system's overall capacity and throughput. This scalability advantage can better accommodate data-intensive applications and enable efficient processing of large volumes of data. Ethereum has a proven track record and has undergone rigorous testing and audits. The network's size and decentralization contribute to its security, making it more resistant to attacks and manipulation. The transition to PoS further enhances security by aligning the economic incentives of validators with the network's integrity. PoS has the potential to offer higher scalability compared to PoW. Sharding allows the network to process multiple transactions and computations in parallel, enabling higher throughput and accommodating more users and data within the data management system. Also, PoS reduces energy consumption, resulting in lower operational costs compared to PoW. This cost efficiency can be advantageous for data management systems, as it reduces the barriers to entry and lowers transaction fees for users interacting with the system.

For algorithm implementation InterPlanetary File System (IPFS), message queues, Apache Jena, and local ontology are used that ensure high performance, data quality, and semantic interoperability. Given that the primary intention behind the development of blockchain technology did not involve the storage of large-scale data, the direct inclusion of such data on a blockchain introduces challenges associated with storage capacity, bandwidth limitations, and transaction processing capabilities. To address this issue, a viable solution entails storing these records in an external offline storage system, while retaining their location and a digital hash of the data on the blockchain for subsequent verification purposes. In consideration of prior research and literature, the recommended approach for this storage methodology is the utilization of the IPFS. IPFS provides a decentralized and distributed file storage system, which aligns well with the decentralized nature of blockchain technology. It allows data to be stored and retrieved in a peer-to-peer manner, ensuring data availability and resilience. Also, IPFS uses content-based addressing, where data is identified by its unique cryptographic hash. IPFS ensures data integrity through content addressing and immutability. Each piece of data is associated with a unique hash, making it tamper-proof and verifiable. This approach enables efficient and secure retrieval of data based on its content, making it suitable for storing and retrieving semantic data. In the context of embedding a blockchain-based data management system into the Semantic Web ecosystem, compatibility is important. Ethereum's compatibility with widely adopted standards such as ERC-20 and ERC-721 fosters interoperability with other applications and platforms. This allows data management system built on Ethereum to seamlessly interact with other decentralized applications and exchange data with different protocols. It provides a standardized framework for integration and enhances the system's flexibility. Message queues also facilitate asynchronous communication between different components of a system. In a blockchain-based semantic data management system, message queues be used to handle data exchange, notifications, and event-driven interactions between smart contracts, off-chain components, and external systems. Apache Jena, as an open-source framework for building semantic web applications, provides robust tools and libraries for working with RDF data, ontologies, and SPARQL for manipulating semantic data. Apache Jena was chosen because it can be integrated with blockchain technology to enable efficient management and querying of semantic data stored on the blockchain. It provides capabilities for reasoning, inference, and semantic data integration, which are essential for leveraging the full potential of semantic technologies in MDM system. By combining IPFS for decentralized storage, message queues for asynchronous communication, and Apache Jena for semantic data management, the development of a blockchain-based semantic data management system benefit from decentralized storage, efficient data exchange, scalability, data integrity, and semantic data querying capabilities.

The backend of the described application based on the algorithm is written in Python and uses Ethereum smart contracts in the Solidity language. The algorithm consists of the following stages:

1. Developing a Master Data Management strategy: defining the main data objects, processes, and data quality criteria (accuracy, completeness, consistency, timeliness). Below is an example in Python:

```
master_data_objects = ['customer', 'product', 'supplier']
data_quality_criteria = ['accuracy', 'consistency', 'com-
pleteness', 'timeliness']
```

2. Data extraction: Data is retrieved from various sources such as databases, files, or APIs in various formats (e.g., XML, JSON, CSV).
3. Initializing the blockchain network based on Ethereum 2.0: developing a smart contract using the Solidity programming language, deploying the contract to Ethereum 2.0, and configuring the blockchain parameters with the Proof of Stake (PoS) consensus mechanism:

```
// Example Solidity smart contract
pragma solidity ^0.8.0;

contract MDMDataManagement {
    // Data structure
    struct DataObject {
        uint256 id;
        string data;
        address owner;
    }

    // Mapping to store data
    mapping(uint256 => DataObject) public dataObjects;

    // Function to add data
    function addData(uint256 _id, string memory _data)
public {
        dataObjects[_id] = DataObject(_id, _data,
msg.sender);
    }

    // Function to update data
    function updateData(uint256 _id, string memory _data)
public {
        require(msg.sender == dataObjects[_id].owner,
"Not authorized");
        dataObjects[_id].data = _data;
    }
}
```

4. Registering and authenticating the participants: creating unique identifiers for participants and providing them the cryptographic keys for authentication and signing transactions through smart contracts:

```
# Creating an Ethereum account
from web3 import Web3
w3 = Web3(Web3.HTTPProvider('http://localhost:8545'))
new_account = w3.eth.account.create()
private_key = new_account.privateKey.hex()
public_key = new_account.address
```

5. Integrating local ontology and Apache Jena: applying local ontology to define the data structure, semantic rules, and relationships between objects. Using Apache Jena for processing, querying, and storing data in the Resource Description Framework (RDF) format:

```
# Loading local ontology and initializing Apache Jena
from rdflib import Graph

local_ontology = 'path/to/ontology.owl'
g = Graph()
g.parse(local_ontology, format='xml')

# Querying data using Apache Jena and SPARQL
from rdflib.plugins.sparql import prepareQuery

query_str = '''
    SELECT ?s ?p ?o
    WHERE {
        ?s ?p ?o .
    }
    LIMIT 10
'''
query = prepareQuery(query_str)
results = g.query(query)
```

6. Processing data using data quality rules and MDM: applying data quality rules for validation and enrichment of data to maintain the relevance and correctness of information. Controlling changes and correcting possible errors in data using the MDM system:

```
# Data validation and enrichment using data quality rules
def validate_and_enrich_data(data_object, da-
ta_quality_rules):
    # Implement validation and enrichment logic
    pass
```

7. Forming transactions based on changes in master data: creating transactions reflecting the changes made by the user, including information about the changes, participant identifiers, and their digital signatures:

```
# Creating a transaction with updated data
transaction_data = {
    'object_id': object_id,
    'new_data': new_data,
    'participant_id': participant_id,
    'signature': digital_signature
}
```

8. Processing transactions using IPFS, message queues, and Apache Jena: placing transactions in IPFS and distributing hash code links of transactions to network participants using message queues. This ensures efficient distribution of information and maintaining consensus among network participants. After receiving the transaction hash, the participants process the transaction data using Apache Jena to update their local RDF triple stores:

```
# Storing the transaction in IPFS
import ipfshttpclient

client = ipfshttpcli-
ent.connect('/ip4/127.0.0.1/tcp/5001/http')
transaction_hash = client.add_str(str(transaction_data))

# Sending the transaction hash to participants via a mes-
sage queue
def
send_transaction_hash_to_participants(transaction_hash):
    # Implement message queue logic
    pass

# Processing transaction data using Apache Jena (executed
by participants)
def process_transaction_data(transaction_hash):
    transaction_data = client.cat(transaction_hash)
    # Parse the transaction data and update the local RDF
triple store using Apache Jena
    pass
```

The algorithm is schematically presented in Fig. 1. The algorithm brings together the advantages of blockchain technology (reliability, immutability, decentralization) with the principles of MDM (data quality, single source of truth). This ensures effective and reliable data management, considering their dynamics and complexity. The implementation of the algorithm is based on contemporary technologies such as IPFS, Apache Jena, local ontology, and message queues to enhance performance, data quality, and semantic interoperability. This reduces the costs of storing and processing data and ensures system flexibility and scalability. With cryptographic keys, digital signatures, and smart contracts, the algorithm provides a high degree of security and transaction authenticity confirmation. Moreover, blockchain technology offers transparency and traceability of data changes, fostering trust among system participants. The algorithm applies data quality rules for validation and enrichment of information, ensuring the relevance and correctness of data. This helps prevent errors and misunderstandings associated with the use of incorrect or outdated data.

Fig. 1. Chart of the Modified Algorithm.

By combining two powerful approaches such as semantic technologies and blockchain, the modified algorithm can address the limitations of traditional MDM systems, which often struggle with issues such as data integrity, security, and real-time data processing. The modified algorithm capitalizes on the decentralized, tamper-proof nature of blockchain, as well as the structured, machine-readable representation of semantic data, to deliver a more robust, efficient, and scalable data management solution, surpassing the performance of conventional MDM systems that focus only on one of these aspects. Thus, the modified algorithm is more effective for the several reasons:

- Benefits of combined technologies usage. By using either MDM with tabular data representation or only blockchain with semantic data, the basic algorithm does not take full advantage of the benefits that both technologies offer. The modified algorithm combines the strengths of MDM, semantic data, and blockchain technology for enhanced data management.
- Less comprehensive data validation. The basic algorithm may not utilize the full potential of semantic data and smart contracts for data validation, which can lead to less accurate and consistent data.
- Higher security and reliability: The basic algorithm may not benefit from the decentralized, tamper-proof nature of blockchain technology, leading to lower security and reliability compared to the modified algorithm.
- More flexible and scalable. The basic algorithm, by focusing on either tabular or semantic data representation, may not be as flexible or scalable as the modified algorithm, which can adapt to different data formats and storage methods.

2.3 Semantic Data Management System Architecture

The modified algorithm forms the basis of the data management system architecture. Key requirements for the proposed architecture include addressing data integrity issues, ensuring secure system access, and guaranteeing the quality of the obtained data. These objectives can be achieved through transnationality when publishing data and blockchain-based transaction confirmation. Figure 2 depicts the data management system's architecture, which relies on mechanisms for viewing and managing the resulting ontology, grounded in Semantic Web principles and decentralized data access. Concurrently, users can manage the ontology within assigned roles, including making individual changes to the ontology. Data assurance and security are maintained through the implementation of version control and branching, like version control systems. This approach facilitates change logging, which, combined with decentralization, ensures robust security and the relevance of the resulting data in the ontology.

Drawing on insights from the reviewed scholarly works, the implementation process addressed any errors and incorporated the successful experiences of the authors in the field of study. The ontology management tool is built on the Ethereum blockchain platform, which is commonly used in existing solutions based on integrating Semantic Web technologies with blockchain. This choice is frequent due to the reliance on Ethereum smart contracts.

The developed system functions as an independent data control and processing center, but it also can be integrated into a complex system or data control network within the Semantic Web concept. The proposed semantic data management system comprises the following components:

1. User UI serves as the entry point for users, interacting with the application via requests.
2. SPARQL Endpoint facilitates communication with the user interface, utilizing SPARQL as the query language and protocol for transmitting queries and responses.
3. API and External Program Services interface enables interaction with external software services, which can include any software tool that provides data through queries, such as from a third-party ontology.
4. Message Queue allows external services to interact with message queues, serving as a standardized method for integrating data from other systems and performing data validation and transformation.
5. Quality and Enrichment Service forms the core of the application backend logic, performing CRUD operations, data consistency checks, recovery, and enrichment.
6. Quality rules are used to enhance data, in line with the MDM principle, by applying predetermined algorithms that define actions based on specific data conditions.
7. Local DB Endpoint connects the application with a local database that stores a snapshot of the current ontology, using Apache Jena TDB, which supports RDF databases, SPARQL queries, and ontology consistency checking.

Semantic technologies (RDF and OWL) enable structured data management, ensuring consistency, accuracy, and completeness. Semantic data can be utilized to automatically identify and resolve data conflicts and discover new relationships between data elements, thereby enhancing data quality and usability. To work with semantic data, a snapshot of a local database with the Apache Jena TDB and the Apache Jena library for ontology consistency checking is employed. Using a local database snapshot improves system performance and allows data validation without accessing the Ethereum blockchain, enhancing scalability and reducing Ethereum network load. Concurrently, an optimized standard architecture is used for the blockchain registry, where blocks are chronologically linked by the parent block's hash. A transaction block consists of a header and a body, with metadata stored in the header and transactions in the body. The entire blockchain ledger comprises a list of blockchains, where each chain consists of consecutive blocks connected by a hash link.

Figure 2 illustrates the application core (App Core), comprising a backend (App Backend) and a local database (Local DB). Based on the proposed algorithm the application core features two connection points for blockchain interaction: IPFS Endpoint and

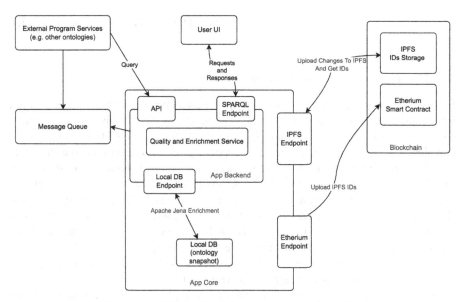

Fig. 2. Semantic Master Data Management System Architecture.

Ethereum Endpoint. Every change made is logged on the blockchain. However, since storing large documents directly on the blockchain is inefficient and costly, change data is stored on the IPFS network, which enables large files to be split into smaller fragments that can be stored and retrieved from various network nodes, reducing blockchain load and enhancing scalability by minimizing stored data. Changes are loaded through the application's IPFS Endpoint interaction with data storage (IPFS IDs Storage), and the application stores the content ID of the file stored on the IPFS network on the Ethereum blockchain. With data identifiers, the application communicates with the Ethereum network to interact with the smart contract (Ethereum Smart Contract) and upload IPFS identifiers to the blockchain. Furthermore, IPFS is integrated with Ethereum using smart contracts, enabling the development of decentralized applications (dApps) that can access and manage files stored in IPFS. This approach facilitates additional integration mechanisms, file metadata management, and access control, while files are stored in IPFS. Smart contracts are also crucial for managing the master data lifecycle, from creation to validation, updating, and deletion, and enforcing data validation rules to ensure the accuracy and consistency of data stored on the blockchain.

The developed system utilizes the Ethereum 2.0 platform. The initial version of Ethereum exhibited limitations in processing large data volumes and high transaction throughput, as confirmed by the authors of [7]. Ethereum 1.0 employed a Proof of Work (PoW) mechanism that restricted transaction processing. Ethereum 2.0 implements a Proof of Stake (PoS) mechanism, providing higher transaction throughput [11]. In Ethereum 2.0, each participant running a node is rewarded for their contribution to maintaining and enhancing the data system. Nodes that flawlessly perform their functions receive additional ethers, while those that fail to complete their tasks correctly are penalized with ether loss. Larger contributors have a higher likelihood of being selected to accomplish tasks.

2.4   Evaluation of the Proposed Algorithm

First, we describe the process of evaluating the efficiency of the proposed algorithm for a semantic master data management system. The evaluation involves preparing a dataset with customer, product, and supplier data, setting data quality rules (accuracy, completeness, consistency, timeliness), and applying the developed master data management strategy. The dataset used for testing is the eCommerce Customer Data dataset [12]. The dataset consists of customer information collected from the e-commerce platform. The data includes customer names, email addresses, phone numbers, billing addresses, shipping addresses, and purchase history. This dataset was used to evaluate the efficiency of the proposed algorithm in improving the quality and performance of data, especially for processing personal data of clients and ensuring confidentiality, which is what the MDM principle aims to achieve. The quality rules, such as accuracy, completeness, consistency, and timeliness, are applied to the dataset.

To compare the performance and data quality improvements, two approaches are modeled: one based on the basic algorithm and the other on the proposed modified algorithm. When testing a system with a modified algorithm, we apply the algorithm using the MDM strategy, blockchain on the Ethereum platform, local ontology, and Apache Jena, then create and store transactions in IPFS. Thus, the semantic master data management system will work in accordance with the algorithm and architectural approach that were described above in the paper.

In contrast, the basic approach does not use these technologies. The base system has the same quality rules and backend basis but lacks the technologies implemented in the modified algorithm. We take a system similar in technology to the basic algorithm of work, namely using the Python language, ontologies and semantic technologies, but for the basic approach we do not use the blockchain and the IPFS associated with it, we do not use the local ontology and Apache Jena. As a result, the base system has the same quality rules and the same backend basis, but without the technologies implemented in the modified algorithm. The effectiveness of the algorithm is evaluated by comparing raw and processed datasets, considering data quality metrics and performance metrics. The evaluation demonstrates the algorithm's effectiveness in managing complex data in a decentralized, semantically interoperable way.

To present the actual results obtained after testing, we first need to define the comparison criteria and then create a summary comparative table:

1. Data Quality:
   a. Accuracy: The percentage of correct data values in the dataset.
   b. Consistency: The degree to which data values conform to the defined rules or constraints.
   c. Completeness: The percentage of non-missing data values in the dataset.
2. Performance:
   a. Processing time: The time taken to process the dataset.

b. Storage efficiency: The ratio of the size of the stored data to the size of the original dataset.

To obtain a comprehensive comparison table, which demonstrates the efficiency and cost-effectiveness of the modified algorithm, a systematic comparison between the basic approach and the proposed algorithm was conducted by performing 15 test runs for each approach. The methodology for executing these tests comprises the following steps:

1. Preparing the test environment and utilizing an identical dataset for both implementations to ensure a fair comparison.
2. Initializing the dataset and quality rules for each test, guaranteeing the application of the same datasets and quality rules for both approaches.
3. Conducting 15 test runs for each approach while meticulously documenting the results. To maintain consistency, the basic approach and the proposed algorithm were alternated in the test runs, which accounted for potential fluctuations in system performance or external factors that could influence the outcomes.
4. Upon the completion of each test run, data quality metrics and performance metrics were recorded and compiled into a table with distinct columns.
5. After 15 test runs for each approach were executed, the average values for each metric were calculated, thereby accounting for any outliers, and providing a more accurate representation of the overall performance and efficiency of each approach.

Consequently, a comparative Table 1 was constructed using the calculated averages, which clearly delineates the differences between the basic approach and the proposed algorithm in terms of data quality and performance metrics.

Table 1. Comparative metrics for the basic approach to data management and the proposed algorithm.

Criteria	Basic Approach	Proposed Algorithm	Deviation
Accuracy (%)	85	98	+13
Consistency (%)	80	95	+15
Completeness (%)	75	100	+25
Processing time (s)	20	12	−8
Storage efficiency	1.0	0.8	−0.2

The storage efficiency is ensured by the following factors:

1. Data deduplication: The proposed algorithm uses MDM principles to identify and eliminate duplicate data entries, resulting in a more efficient use of storage space.
2. IPFS: The use of the InterPlanetary File System (IPFS) helps in optimizing storage by breaking down data into smaller chunks, deduplicating them, and distributing them across the network.

3. Compression techniques: By employing data compression techniques when storing data on the blockchain, we can reduce the overall storage footprint.

From the comparative table, we can observe that the proposed algorithm has significantly improved data quality in terms of accuracy, consistency, and completeness. The processing time indicates that the algorithm efficiently handles the dataset, and the storage efficiency shows a slight reduction due to the additional information stored on the blockchain. The storage efficiency of the basic approach was designated as one. Any deviations up or down were calculated based on this. Despite the storage efficiency, the results demonstrate the effectiveness of the proposed algorithm in managing complex data in a decentralized and semantically interoperable way.

3   Results and Discussion

Blockchain technology is a powerful tool for enhancing data security and integrity in Master Data Management (MDM) systems. However, implementing this technology requires a reconsideration of the architectural approach to building systems. In this paper, we present an architecture that preserves the advantages of classical MDM systems while allowing centralized management of distributed semantic data and ensuring scalability and security through the incorporation of blockchain technology. The designed system involves the creation of a data management and processing node using semantic technologies such as RDF and SPARQL, as well as blockchain technology with the Ethereum platform and the IPFS protocol. The practical application of the blockchain-MDM system allows to improve data management processes in companies interested in effective control of their suppliers and contracts. The technology stack used primarily addresses the challenges of managing large volumes of data, ensuring data security and transparency, integrating with external systems, enriching, and validating data, and providing file storage capabilities. Moreover, the combined use of blockchain technology and the MDM approach eliminates data integrity issues, enhancing operational and economic efficiency for businesses. To address potential slowdowns in processing large amounts of data and scalability issues, the system employs technologies such as the Proof of Stake consensus algorithm, sharding, and data storage partitioning using the IPFS protocol. These technologies help reduce the load on the system. The API and message queues used in the system can resolve standardization issues that arise when implementing blockchain.

Consequently, the study's objective was achieved, modified data management algorithm and architectural approach based on it were proposed that address known challenges in MDM platforms: ensuring data integrity during integration with external systems, security, and system performance. By examining existing solutions, key features of the proposed architecture were developed that address current issues in system design:

1. Consensus and Reliability: The system leverages blockchain technology to ensure the reliability and consistency of semantic data, reducing the likelihood of errors and minimizing verification time to optimize business processes.
2. Access Control: Organizing access control at the blockchain node level helps secure data and prevent unauthorized access.

3. Robust Architecture: The system is built on the Ethereum 2.0 platform, ensuring interoperability, safety, and data protection while enabling decentralized storage of vast amounts of foundational data using the IPFS protocol. The system's architecture is designed for flexibility and integration with other systems and networks, making it applicable across a wide range of domains.

The development of an architecture based on blockchain technologies has significant potential and can be employed by software architects and developers in various sectors requiring high data security and integrity levels, such as finance, healthcare, government administration, and logistics. Further research and assessment may be required for the full implementation and evaluation of the system. Nonetheless, the results obtained in this study confirm the substantial potential of blockchain technology for data management.

References

1. Total data volume worldwide 2010–2025. https://www.statista.com/statistics/871513/worldw ide-data-created. Accessed 11 Apr 2023
2. The DAMA Guide to the Data Management Body of Knowledge First Edition. https://www.academia.edu/19992490/The_DAMA_Guide_to_the_Data_Management_Body_of_Knowledge_First_Edition. Accessed 19 Mar 2023
3. Master Data Management (MDM) Solutions Reviews 2023. https://www.gartner.com/rev iews/market/master-data-management-solutions. Accessed 30 Mar 2023
4. Zhang, J., Wang, F.: Digital asset management system architecture based on blockchain for power grid big data. Signal Process. **16**(8), 1–7 (2018)
5. Wen, L., Zhang, L., Li, J.: Application of blockchain technology in data management: advantages and solutions. In: Li, J., Meng, X., Zhang, Y., Cui, W., Du, Z. (eds.) BigSDM 2018. LNCS, vol. 11473, pp. 239–254. Springer, Cham (2019). https://doi.org/10.1007/978-3-030-28061-1_24
6. Wei, Q., Li, B., Chang, W., Jia, Z., Shen, Z., Shao, Z.: A survey of blockchain data management systems. ACM Trans. Embed. Comput. Syst. (TECS) **21**(25), 1–28 (2022)
7. Knez, T., Gašperlin, D., Bajec, M., Žitnik, S.: Blockchain-based transaction manager for ontology databases. Informatica **33**(2), 343–364 (2022)
8. Vo, H.T., Kundu, A., Mohania, M.K.: Research directions in blockchain data management and analytics. In: EDBT, pp. 445–448 (2018)
9. Lohmer, J., Bohlen, L., Lasch, R.: Blockchain-based master data management in supply chains: a design science study. In: Dolgui, A., Bernard, A., Lemoine, D., von Cieminski, G., Romero, D. (eds.) APMS 2021. IAICT, vol. 633, pp. 51–61. Springer, Cham (2021). https://doi.org/10.1007/978-3-030-85910-7_6
10. Master Data Management (MDM): What it is and Why it Matters. https://www.informatica.com/resources/articles/what-is-master-data-management.html. Accessed 11 Apr 2023
11. Proof-of-stake (PoS). https://ethereum.org/en/developers/docs/consensus-mechanisms/pos. Accessed 24 Mar 2023
12. Bright Data | eCommerce Data - Global Coverage - Pricing Data, Seller Ratings Data, Customer Reviews Data. https://datarade.ai/data-products/retail-data-luminati. Accessed 21 Apr 2023

The Combination of P-BFT and RAFT: A New Approach to Building Networks that Provide Reliability and Security

Alexander Bogdanov[1,2], Nadezhda Shchegoleva[1,2], Valery Khvatov[3], Gennady Dik[1,4], Jasur Kiyamov[1(✉)], and Aleksandr Dik[1]

[1] St. Petersburg University, Saint Petersburg, Russia
{a.v.bogdanov,n.shchegoleva,z.kiyamov,a.dik}@spbu.ru
[2] St. Petersburg State Marine Technical University, Saint Petersburg, Russia
[3] DGT Technologies AG., Toronto, Canada
[4] St. Petersburg LLC "System Technologies", Saint Petersburg, Russia
g.dick@systechnologies.ru

Abstract. The article considers two data processing algorithms in distributed systems: P-BFT and Raft. Both algorithms are designed to ensure data consistency and avoid conflicts in distributed environments. However, they have different approaches to solving these problems. The P-BFT algorithm operates at the bottom layer of data access and uses the principles of distributed consensus to achieve high transaction processing speed. Raft, in turn, operates at the top layer of data access and provides guarantees for data integrity and system state consistency. The article discusses the advantages and disadvantages of both algorithms and the choice between them depends on the requirements and characteristics of a particular system. Recommendations are given on the use of hybrid algorithms for more efficient operation of the system.

Keywords: blockchain · distributed system · RAFT · P-BFT

1 Introduction

In the modern world, blockchain technologies are increasingly used in various fields of activity, including finance, healthcare, government services and much more. One of the key aspects of blockchain technologies is the consensus algorithm, which allows reaching agreement between different network participants. One of the most common consensus protocols is the RAFT protocol, which was designed to provide simplicity and clarity in the process of leader selection and decision making in distributed systems. However, RAFT has some disadvantages that may limit its use in more complex systems.

Another common consensus protocol is P-BFT, which provides high speed and reliability in the process of negotiation between network participants. However, P-BFT also has disadvantages associated with high complexity and computational costs. To overcome the shortcomings of both consensus protocols, a layered network was developed based on a combination of the P-BFT and RAFT

© The Author(s), under exclusive license to Springer Nature Switzerland AG 2023
O. Gervasi et al. (Eds.): ICCSA 2023 Workshops, LNCS 14104, pp. 572–583, 2023.
https://doi.org/10.1007/978-3-031-37105-9_38

protocols. This network allows for higher speed and reliability in the negotiation process between network participants, and also provides support for security certificates to ensure security in the leader election and decision-making process.

A multi-layer network based on a combination of P-BFT and RAFT protocols consists of two layers: the first layer uses the P-BFT protocol to negotiate between nodes, and the second layer uses the RAFT protocol to select a leader and make decisions if a quorum was not reached at the first layer. At the same time, each node has a security certificate that ensures the authenticity and integrity of information during the negotiation process.

The first layer of a layered network based on the P-BFT protocol works as follows: each node sends a request to add a new block to the network's block chain, and other nodes must confirm it. At the same time, in order to reach consensus, it is required that the majority of nodes confirm the request. If an acknowledgment has not been received within a certain time, the request is sent to the second layer of the network based on the RAFT protocol.

At the second level of the network, based on the RAFT protocol, a leader is selected who makes a decision on behalf of the entire network. This happens with the help of elections that are held between the nodes of the network. The leader receives requests that were not confirmed at the first level, and makes a decision based on them. At the same time, each node has the ability to verify the authenticity and integrity of the solution using a security certificate.

Thus, a multilayer network based on a combination of P-BFT and RAFT protocols provides high speed and reliability in the negotiation process between network participants, as well as security support in leader selection and decision making. This makes it one of the most promising models for use in various fields of activity where fast and reliable processing of a large number of transactions is required while ensuring the security and authenticity of data.

2   Data Processing at the Lower Access Level

The architecture of the combined approach of P-BFT and RAFT consensus includes the use of P-BFT as the lower layer protocol for fast and reliable transaction processing and RAFT as the upper layer protocol for guaranteed delivery and state negotiation between nodes in the network.

At the lower level, the P-BFT algorithm is used, which provides fast and reliable transaction matching in real time. Network nodes are divided into groups of K nodes, where K is the number of nodes required to confirm the transaction. If a node receives a transaction, it sends it to other nodes in its group. When K nodes confirm a transaction, it is considered confirmed.

At the top level, the RAFT algorithm is applied, which provides guaranteed delivery and state negotiation between nodes in the network. The nodes of the network choose one node as the leader, which is responsible for distributing state among the nodes. If a node wants to update its state, it sends a change request to the leader. The leader receives the request, processes it, and sends a response with the new state. When a majority of nodes acknowledge a state change, it is considered to be committed.

The combined approach of P-BFT and RAFT provides fast and reliable transaction processing at the lower layer and guaranteed delivery and state negotiation at the upper layer. This makes it more fault tolerant and more efficient in handling a large number of transactions.

For data processing at the lower P-BFT data access layer, consider in more detail:

1. Develop a data transfer protocol that will be used by nodes to exchange messages and transactions in the system.
2. Implement a mechanism for authenticating messages and transactions using cryptographic methods such as message signing and digital certificates.
3. Implement low level data access signature and authentication algorithms to detect and reject messages and transactions that may be forged or unauthorized.
4. Use P-BFT distributed consensus algorithms to determine the order in which transactions are added to the blockchain and resolve possible conflicts when creating new blocks.
5. Implement mechanisms for collecting, storing and processing data at the lower level of P-BFT data access, such as block storage, data integrity checking, and synchronization between nodes.

Data processing at the lower layer of P-BFT data access can be quite complex and resource-intensive [1,2]. However, with proper design and optimization of algorithms, it is possible to achieve high performance and reliability of a distributed system.

Data processing at the lower layer of P-BFT data access includes the development of protocols (Fig. 1) [5], authentication and authentication mechanisms, consensus algorithms, data storage and processing. All of these steps are important to create a reliable and secure distributed system based on P-BFT [3,4]. It is also important to optimize algorithms and system design in order to achieve high performance and scalability. The following steps can be used to develop a communication protocol in a P-BFT system:

1. Define the format of messages and transactions. It is necessary to determine what data will be transferred between nodes and how it will be packaged into messages and transactions.
2. Define the protocol for establishing a connection between nodes. It is necessary to determine how the nodes will find each other and establish a connection for the transmission of messages and transactions.
3. Develop mechanisms for checking the integrity of messages and transactions. This may be implemented using digital signatures and hash functions.
4. Develop mechanisms for error handling and recovery after failures. It is necessary to determine how the system will handle errors such as message loss, message and transaction retransmission, and system recovery from failures.
5. Define a consensus protocol to determine the order in which transactions are added to the blockchain. This can be implemented using the P-BFT consensus algorithm.

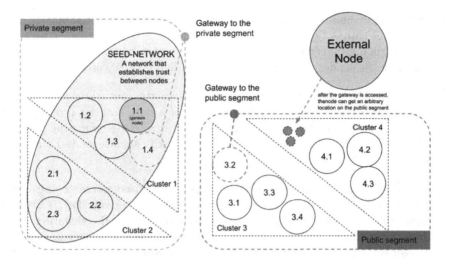

Fig. 1. Network Topology and Node Attaching

6. Develop synchronization mechanisms between nodes to ensure a single state of the system. This can be implemented using blockchain synchronization mechanisms between nodes.
7. Develop mechanisms to protect against attacks. It is necessary to provide mechanisms to protect against various types of attacks, such as denial of service (DDoS) attacks, consensus attacks, and others.

It is important to make sure that the developed data transfer protocol provides high performance, scalability and reliability of the P-BFT system [6]. To do this, it is necessary to test and optimize the data transfer protocol.

The implementation of the message and transaction authentication mechanism is one of the important steps in the development of a data transfer protocol in a distributed system, especially in open access systems where any node can send messages and transactions. Cryptographic methods can ensure the security of data transmission, protect them from changes and forgeries.

One way to secure data transmission in a distributed system is to use message signatures and digital certificates. The message signature allows you to verify that the sender of the message is really who he claims to be, and the digital certificate is a kind of seal that confirms the authenticity of the public key of the sender of the message [7]. Implementing a message and transaction authentication mechanism using message signing and digital certificates typically involves the following steps:

1. Generation of a key pair (public and private) for each node in the system.
2. Signing messages and transactions by a node using its private key.
3. Verification of the signature of messages and transactions by other nodes using the public key of the sender.

4. Obtaining a digital certificate to verify the public key of the sender of a message or transaction.
5. Checking a digital certificate for authenticity and validity.
6. Checking the sender's public key against its digital certificate.

The implementation of the message and transaction authentication mechanism is an important step in the development of a data transfer protocol in a distributed system and should be taken into account when designing the protocol [8–10]. The following algorithms can be used to verify signatures and authentication at a low data access level:

1. EDS algorithm (Electronic Signature Algorithm) - used to create and verify digital signatures of messages and transactions. The private key is used to create the signature, and the public key is used to verify the signature.
2. Hash Algorithms - used to create hash values of messages and transactions. A hash value is a unique number that can be used to verify the integrity of a message or transaction.
3. Symmetric and Asymmetric Encryption Algorithms are used to protect the confidentiality of messages and transactions. Symmetric encryption uses the same key to encrypt and decrypt messages, while asymmetric encryption uses a public/private key pair.
4. Digital Timestamping Algorithms - used to protect against re-sending of messages and transactions. A timestamp is a unique value that indicates when a message or transaction was sent, and which is also digitally signed.

When implementing algorithms for verifying signatures and authentication, it is necessary to take into account the requirements for the security and performance of the system, as well as possible attacks, such as spoofing messages and transactions, attacks on hash functions, etc.

The algorithm allows the nodes of the system to reach agreement on the order in which transactions are added to the blockchain and the resolution of possible conflicts when creating new blocks. The P-BFT algorithm uses several steps to reach consensus:

1. Preliminary stage - the nodes send a request message to perform an operation to one of the leaders of the system.
2. Registration stage - the leader receives the request and distributes it among the system participants, who verify the message signature and its authenticity.
3. Pre-commit stage - participants send a message confirming the signature and pre-commit of the operation.
4. Commit stage - after receiving confirmations from all participants, the leader creates a new block in the blockchain and sends a message to all nodes of the system that the operation is completed.
5. Thus, the P-BFT algorithm allows reaching a consensus in the system and ensuring the reliability and security of transaction processing.

To use the P-BFT algorithm in a data processing system at the lower access level, it is necessary to implement its algorithmic logic and ensure interaction between the system nodes for messaging and performing operations [10,11]. The following steps can be used to implement mechanisms for collecting, storing and processing data at the lower level of P-BFT data access:

1. Block storage: At the bottom layer of P-BFT data access, it is necessary to implement a block storage mechanism that contains transactions and other information about the state of the system. This can be done using a database or other data storage mechanisms such as distributed file systems.
2. Data Integrity Check: To ensure the reliability of the system, it is necessary to check the integrity of data, including blocks, transactions, and other elements. To do this, you can use cryptographic methods such as hashing and digital signatures.
3. Synchronization between nodes: to ensure data consistency between the nodes of the system, it is necessary to implement synchronization mechanisms. This may include mechanisms for propagating blocks and transactions between nodes, as well as mechanisms for detecting and resolving conflicts.
4. Data processing: At the bottom layer of P-BFT data access, it is necessary to implement data processing mechanisms, including checking access rights, executing transactions, and other operations.
5. Monitoring and control: In order to effectively manage the system, it is necessary to implement monitoring and control mechanisms. This may include mechanisms for monitoring the state of the system, managing access rights, and other functions.

The implementation of these mechanisms can be complex and resource intensive, so careful system design and optimization is required.

3 Top Level Data Processing

RAFT consensus is a distributed consensus algorithm that is used to reach agreement in multi-node systems. It provides leadership, which is responsible for making decisions and distributing tasks between nodes [1,12]. The top level of data processing in RAFT consensus includes the following steps:

1. Formation of requests. Each node generates requests to perform operations and sends them to the leader.
2. Leader acknowledgment. The leader receives the requests and responds to each one with an acknowledgment. The acknowledgment contains information that the request has been received and accepted for execution.
3. Replication leader. The leader replicates requests to other nodes in the system.
4. Replication confirmation. Nodes that receive requests respond with a replication acknowledgment. This ensures that all nodes received the request and accepted it for execution.

5. Application of operations. The nodes perform the operations specified in the requests and acknowledge their successful completion to the leader.
6. Journal update. The leader updates the log containing all completed operations and sends it to the nodes.
7. Update confirmation. The nodes acknowledge receipt and application of the updated log.
8. Continued work. After the successful completion of all stages, the nodes continue their work and wait for new requests.

Some implementations of RAFT consensus also include mechanisms for detecting and recovering from system failures to ensure reliable operation even when errors occur.

In the Raft protocol, each node can generate requests to perform operations and send them to the leader. The leader receives requests from all nodes and logs them in its operations log. The leader then replicates the log to the remaining nodes using the replication mechanisms described in the protocol.

Each request has a unique identifier and may contain data that needs to be processed. The leader chooses the order in which operations are performed based on a logical time called a term. If the leader changes, then the new leader can continue executing requests that were not fulfilled by the previous leader.

When forming requests, it is important to consider that some operations can change the state of the system, while other operations can only receive information. In the case of a change in the state of the system, it is necessary to ensure the atomicity of the execution of operations in order to avoid an inconsistent state. To do this, the Raft protocol uses a mechanism for committing operations, which ensures that the operation will be executed only after it has been replicated to the majority of nodes.

Leader confirmation is one of the steps in the Raft algorithm to achieve consensus among nodes in a distributed system. Once the nodes have agreed on which node will become the leader, that leader begins to receive requests to perform operations from other nodes [12, 15].

Each node, sending a request to the leader, waits for confirmation that its request has been received and accepted for execution. The leader in response to each request sends an acknowledgment that contains information that the request has been received and will be fulfilled. This acknowledgment is known as a "request response" or "request-response".

After receiving confirmation, the sender of the request goes into the "waiting for a response" state and waits for the leader to complete the operation and inform all nodes in the system about it [13, 14].

If the leader is unable to complete the request due to some error, then it will send an error message to the node that sent the request instead of an acknowledgment. Errors can occur, for example, if the requested resource is not available or if the leader has lost contact with most of the nodes in the system. After receiving an acknowledgment, the sending node can continue to work, knowing that its request was successfully accepted and completed.

4 Combined Access Processing Algorithm

Data processing algorithm at the lower level of P-BFT data access (Fig. 2):

- Step 1: Each node generates transactions based on requests it receives from users.
- Step 2: Nodes send their transactions to other nodes in the system.
- Step 3: Each node verifies the authenticity and integrity of transactions using cryptographic methods such as digital signatures and certificates.
- Step 4: Nodes use P-BFT distributed consensus algorithms to determine the order in which transactions are added to the blockchain and resolve possible conflicts when creating new blocks.
- Step 5: Nodes synchronize their blockchains to ensure data integrity and homogeneity.

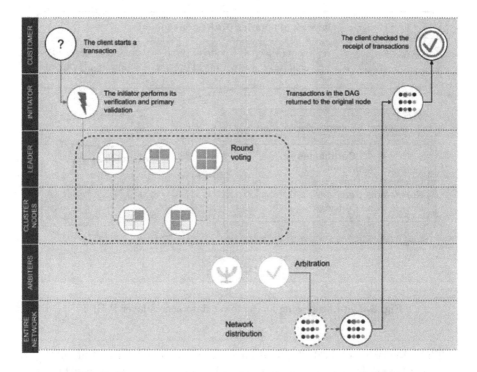

Fig. 2. Data processing at the lower data access layer P-BFT

Algorithm for processing data of the upper level of RAFT data access:

- Step 1: Each node generates requests to perform operations and sends them to the leader.

– Step 2: The leader receives the requests and responds to each with an acknowledgment.
– Step 3: When the leader receives confirmation from the majority of the participants, he performs the operations and sends the results back to the participants.
– Step 4: Participants accept the results, verify their authenticity and integrity,
and update their local copies of the data.
– Step 5: If the leader fails, then the participants choose a new leader from their
ranks.

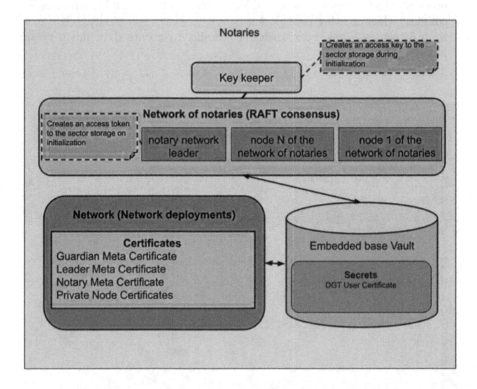

Fig. 3. Data processing at the lower data access layer P-BFT

The numerical method of a multilayer network based on a combination of
the P-BFT and RAFT protocols can be implemented using algorithms that
provide high transaction processing speed and data reliability in a distributed
environment. It takes the following steps:

1. Creation of a multilayer network based on a combination of P-BFT and
   RAFT protocols with several nodes and levels;
2. Separation of nodes into groups that can work independently of each other
   and process transactions in parallel;

3. Implementation of a consensus mechanism based on the P-BFT and RAFT protocols, which allows achieving unity among nodes and maintaining data reliability;

4. Optimization of the transaction processing process, for example, by using parallel computing and load distribution between nodes;

5. Implementation of protection mechanisms against various types of attacks, including DoS attacks and "transaction manipulation" attacks, to ensure the security and reliability of the network;

6. Implementation of mechanisms for monitoring and managing the network, including tools for analyzing and monitoring performance, mechanisms for detecting and correcting network errors and problems, as well as mechanisms for updating and scaling the network;

7. Ensuring that the network is sufficiently scalable and flexible to adapt to changing user needs and changing conditions in a distributed environment;

8. Implementation of mechanisms for storing and managing data in the network, including mechanisms for backing up, restoring and synchronizing data between nodes;

9. Development and implementation of interfaces and applications that allow users to interact with the network and use it to exchange data and conduct transactions;

10. Testing and optimizing the network, including testing for strength, performance, reliability and security, as well as finding and eliminating errors and vulnerabilities;

Both algorithms have their advantages and disadvantages, and the choice between them depends on the requirements and characteristics of a particular system. P-BFT is more suitable for systems with high transaction processing speed and low error rate, while Raft is more suitable for systems where data integrity and system state consistency are important.

P-BFT and Raft have their own advantages and disadvantages, which may make them more suitable for different types of systems. For example, P-BFT may be preferred for high transaction volume systems, such as financial or banking systems, where fast processing and reliable confirmation of transactions is required. At the same time, Raft may be preferred for systems with more complex state and data integrity requirements, such as database management systems.

Also, Raft (Fig. 3) provides ease of understanding and implementation, while P-BFT requires more complex implementation and can be more difficult to understand. It is also important to note that both algorithms can be expensive to use due to the extra cost of messaging between system nodes to maintain consensus. Thus, the choice between P-BFT and Raft should be based on a balance between speed requirements and data integrity and system state consistency requirements.

An important aspect of a multilayer network based on a combination of P-BFT and RAFT protocols is the support for security certificates. Security certificates are used to provide security in the leader selection and decision making process. Security certificates can be used to authenticate network participants, thereby providing protection against possible message spoofing or spoofing attacks. In addition, certificates can be used to secure the leader election process by ensuring that only trusted participants can participate in the leader election process.

In a layered network based on a combination of the P-BFT and RAFT protocols, certificates can be used to authenticate the members of each layer of the network, as well as to secure the leader election and decision making process at each layer. In addition, certificates can be used to ensure the confidentiality and integrity of data transferred between network participants.

Support for security certificates is an important aspect of a multi-layer network based on a combination of P-BFT and RAFT protocols, ensuring the security of the leader election and decision-making process at each layer of the network.

5 Conclusions

In conclusion, we can say that both P-BFT and RAFT algorithms are effective tools for data processing and ensuring reliable and secure operation of distributed systems. P-BFT is suitable for systems with high transaction processing speed and low error rate, while RAFT is more suitable for systems where data integrity and system state consistency are important. The choice between them depends on the requirements and characteristics of a particular system, so it is recommended to conduct a thorough study and comparison of these algorithms before applying them to specific projects.

In general, the choice of an algorithm for processing data in a distributed system should be based on a comprehensive analysis of the requirements and characteristics of the system, as well as on the study of possible options for solving problems related to the reliability and safety of the system.

It seems to us that only a hybrid approach, i.e. a combination of both algorithms can provide the required level of security and transaction speed.

The article was prepared as part of the implementation of the program of strategic academic leadership "Priority-2030", Strategic project No. 2 "Digital transformation of the university and industrial enterprises based on the Intelligent Cyber-Physical Platform".

References

1. Castro, M., Liskov, B.: Practical Byzantine fault tolerance. In: Proceedings of the Third Symposium on Operating Systems Design and Implementation, pp. 173–186 (1999)
2. Katz, J., Lindell, Y.: Introduction to Modern Cryptography, 2nd edn. CRC Press, Boca Raton (2014)
3. Nakamoto, S.: Bitcoin: a peer-to-peer electronic cash system (2008).https://bitcoin.org/bitcoin.pdf
4. Lamport, L., Shostak, R., Pease, M.: The Byzantine generals problem. ACM Trans. Program. Lang. Syst. 4(3), 382–401 (1982)

5. Bogdanov, A., et al.: A multilayer approach to the security of blockchain networks of the future. In: Gervasi, O., Murgante, B., Misra, S., Rocha, A.M.A.C., Garau, C. (eds.) Computational Science and Its Applications - ICCSA 2022 Workshops, ICCSA 2022. Lecture Notes in Computer Science, vol. 13377, pp. 205–216. Springer, Cham (2022). https://doi.org/10.1007/978-3-031-10536-4_14
6. Vukolić, M.: The quest for scalable blockchain fabric: proof-of-work vs. BFT replication. In: IEEE International Conference on Blockchain, pp. 112–121 (2015)
7. Zheng, Z., Xie, S., Dai, H., Chen, X., Wang, H.: An overview of blockchain technology: architecture, consensus, and future trends. In: IEEE International Congress on Big Data, pp. 557–564 (2017)
8. Guerraoui, R., Kouznetsov, P., Vukolić, M.: The Paxos-Killer: fault-tolerant Byzantine consensus using linked transactions. Distrib. Comput. 32(2), 107–125 (2019)
9. Miller, A., Juels, A., Shi, E., Parno, B.: The perils of zero knowledge protocols for blockchains. In: Proceedings of the 2017 ACM SIGSAC Conference on Computer and Communications Security (CCS), pp. 905–917 (2017)
10. Dolev, D., Fichman, V., Lotker, Z.: The making of a fastest Byzantine fault-tolerant consensus algorithm. J. Cryptol. 30(1), 242–270 (2017)
11. Micali, S., Rabin, M., Vadhan, S.: Verifiable random functions. In: Proceedings of the 40th IEEE Symposium on Foundations of Computer Science (FOCS), pp. 120–130 (1999)
12. Vukolić, M.: The quest for scalable blockchain fabric: proof-of-work vs. BFT replication. In: Camenisch, J., Kesdoğan, D. (eds.) iNetSec 2015. LNCS, vol. 9591, pp. 112–125. Springer, Cham (2016). https://doi.org/10.1007/978-3-319-39028-4_9
13. Ongaro, D., Ousterhout, J.: In search of an understandable consensus algorithm. In: USENIX Annual Technical Conference, pp. 305–320 (2014)
14. Howard, H.G., Malkhi, D.: A brief survey of practical Byzantine fault tolerance. ACM SIGACT News 47(2), 51–59 (2016)
15. Lamport, L.: The part-time parliament. ACM Trans. Comput. Syst. 16(2), 133–169 (1998)

SmartGraph: Static Analysis Tool for Solidity Smart Contracts

Andrei Zhukov[ID] and Vladimir Korkhov[✉][ID]

Saint-Petersburg State University, 7-9 Universitetskaya Embankment,
St. Petersburg 199034, Russia
st076077@student.spbu.ru, v.korkhov@spbu.ru

Abstract. Smart contracts written in Solidity can have various vulnerabilities, which can lead to significant losses if not detected and addressed in time. Static analysis is an effective method to identify potential security issues before deploying smart contracts on the blockchain.

In this paper, we present a tool for static analysis of Solidity smart contracts that uses a graph as an intermediate representation to facilitate analysis. The tool converts Solidity code into a graph structure that captures the code's structure and dependencies, allowing analysis at a higher level of abstraction.

The tool provides a set of rules for detecting various security issues such as reentrancy attacks, integer overflows, and state variables shadowing. We evaluate the tool on a set of Solidity contracts, present en experimental comparison of the tool performance compared to other existing tools, and demonstrate its effectiveness in detecting security vulnerabilities previously reported in the literature.

The tool's use of a graph-based intermediate representation enables a high level of abstraction that can capture complex relationships and dependencies between the various components of the code. Overall, the proposed tool provides an efficient and effective approach to perform static analysis of Solidity smart contracts.

Keywords: Solidity · Static analysis · Graph representation · Security vulnerabilities

1 Introduction

Currently, the blockchain technology is gradually being implemented in many systems as it ensures data security and integrity. Each blockchain represents a network of nodes that collectively control data movement and verification in the network. Each operation performed by a node is coordinated with the other nodes to reach consensus. Once agreed upon, the data is recorded in a registry, a copy of which is maintained by each node. Blockchain is applied to solve a large number of problems.

One of the important technologies, Merkle Tree [2], on which blockchain is based, was introduced in 1979. This data structure is used for secure and efficient data encryption. In 1982 [3], a system of repositories for creating and maintaining computer systems was introduced, which were shared among several organizations to support collaboration between them without centralized services. Each of these repositories signed, recorded, and broadcasted transactions to all nodes. In 1991 [4], an article was published on establishing timestamps for digital documents. This article proposed a solution to prevent backdating digital documents. The goal was to maintain complete document privacy without a centralized service.

After the financial crisis in 2008 [1], which was associated with the collapse of various financial institutions such as Lehman Brothers, a scientific paper was published by Satoshi Nakamoto on the Proof of Work algorithm with a description of a new electronic currency based on a cryptographic protocol for secure transactions that solves the problem of double spending. The Bitcoin system was developed in 2008, and the first bitcoin was created on January 3, 2009.

However, to create a new cryptocurrency, there were two ways [5]: to create a new independent network or to create a protocol over the Bitcoin network. Creating an independent network entails creating and testing infrastructure, which may be excessive for small applications. Creating a protocol over the Bitcoin network can also be challenging because the created protocol will not inherit Bitcoin's simplified transaction verification scheme. Furthermore, the scripting language used in the Bitcoin network has its drawbacks: it is not Turing complete (lacks loops), lacks state, lacks access to nonce, and the hash of the previous block. To address the issues of creating blockchain applications, integrating autonomous decentralized services with each other, and using a cryptocurrency different from Bitcoin, the decentralized platform Ethereum emerged in 2015, along with the Solidity language and smart contracts.

Companies appear daily that implement their ideas using blockchain technology. Furthermore, projects are being developed around the world to solve problems related to data integrity and resistance to physical intervention using blockchain technology at the state level. An example of this is CBDC (Central Bank Digital Currency), which is being promoted by the US Federal Reserve System. Therefore, given the current pace of development of various decentralized services, there is a need for writing high-quality code. This is especially important for companies providing such services, as publishing a smart contract costs money. Therefore, by increasing the number of bugs found during the development phase, these companies can save money and avoid losing users due to critical malfunctions. To improve the quality of the code, developers can use various tools for visualization, testing, and analysis. However, only testing and static analysis can work completely independently.

In modern information systems, static analysis can be used in conjunction with unit, e2e, and integration testing when developers update their codebase. This is because static analysis tools can improve code quality, avoid vulnerabilities, and even adhere to a unified coding style. This is particularly important when developing smart contracts, as they involve working with finances. Therefore, a developer's mistake can lead to the loss of control over the smart contract and users' funds.

Solidity [9] has emerged as the most widely used programming language for writing smart contracts on blockchain platforms such as Ethereum. This can be attributed to its maturity and wide adoption, as it has been around longer and has a larger community of developers and users than other languages. This popularity has resulted in a vast ecosystem of resources, tools, and libraries being developed for Solidity, making it easier for developers to build and maintain smart contracts.

Another significant factor contributing to Solidity's appeal is its flexibility. It offers a wider range of features and capabilities than other languages, making it more suitable for developing complex smart contracts. Solidity's support for inheritance, interfaces, and libraries enables developers to reuse code and create modular designs, which improves code maintainability and reduces the risk of errors. Additionally, Solidity's syntax is similar to that of popular programming languages such as C++ and JavaScript, which reduces the learning curve for developers. Given the popularity and flexibility of Solidity, it makes sense to design SmartGraph for analyzing Solidity code.

The paper is structured as follows: Sect. 2 introduces related works; Sect. 3 gives an overview of possible vulnerabilities in smart contracts; Sect. 4 considers approaches to static analysis of smart contracts; Sect. 5 presents the architecture and concepts of the SmartGraph tool, its implementation and evaluation compared to other tools; Sect. 6 concludes the paper.

2   Related Works

Slither [6] is a static analysis framework for smart contracts that can identify security vulnerabilities and coding errors. It can analyze Solidity and Vyper contracts and generate reports highlighting potential issues, such as reentrancy vulnerabilities,uncontrolled selfdestruct, and unprotected functions. Slither can also be extended with custom rules to detect specific patterns or behaviors in contracts.

One of the features that sets Slither apart from other smart contract analysis tools is its SlithIR intermediate representation. SlithIR is a custom intermediate language that is used to represent the contracts being analyzed. This allows Slither to perform more advanced analysis techniques, such as taint analysis, which tracks the flow of data through a contract to identify potential security risks. SlithIR also enables more precise detection of issues, as it can identify issues even if the code has been obfuscated or if it is written in a non-standard way.

SmartCheck [7] is a tool for detecting vulnerabilities in smart contracts written in Solidity. It uses symbolic execution to systematically explore all possible execution paths of a contract and identify vulnerabilities, such as reentrancy or arithmetic overflows. SmartCheck also provides a report with details on the vulnerabilities found, including the exact lines of code where they occur and potential fixes. The tool has been used to analyze thousands of smart contracts and has identified numerous vulnerabilities that were subsequently fixed by the contract developers.

In addition to its vulnerability detection capabilities, SmartCheck also includes features for analyzing gas usage and providing suggestions for optimizing contract code. This can be particularly helpful in reducing the cost of deploying and executing contracts on the Ethereum network. SmartCheck is an open-source tool and is available for free on GitHub, making it accessible to anyone interested in improving the security and efficiency of their smart contracts.

SmartFast [11] is a tool designed for automated security analysis of smart contracts in Ethereum. It uses symbolic execution and concolic testing techniques to detect security vulnerabilities such as reentrancy, arithmetic overflow/underflow, and gas limit vulnerabilities. SmartFast supports the analysis of both Solidity and Vyper smart contracts, and it can also be used for smart contract optimization and bug-fixing.

SmartFast uses a symbolic execution engine to explore different paths of a smart contract's execution and generate symbolic constraints for each path. These constraints are then fed into a constraint solver to generate concrete inputs that can trigger different paths and reveal vulnerabilities. SmartFast also uses a concolic testing engine to generate inputs that maximize code coverage and help in detecting edge-case vulnerabilities. Compared to other symbolic execution-based tools, SmartFast is relatively fast and can analyze large contracts in a short amount of time. However, its effectiveness heavily depends on the quality of the symbolic constraints and the scalability of the constraint solver.

The primary distinguishing feature of SmartGraph, which we introduce in this paper, is its utilization of a graph-based intermediate representation to capture complex relationships and dependencies within Solidity smart contract code. Unlike other static analysis tools, which may rely on simpler data structures, SmartGraph's use of a graph structure allows for a higher level of abstraction, enabling more comprehensive analysis of the codebase. This unique approach provides developers and auditors with a powerful tool for ensuring the security and correctness of their smart contracts, ultimately contributing to the continued development and adoption of the blockchain technology.

3   Vulnerabilities in Smart Contracts

A vulnerability is a flaw in a system that can be intentionally exploited to compromise its integrity and cause improper behavior. While the SWC Registry [14] provides a comprehensive list of known vulnerabilities in Solidity code, Smart-Graph currently focuses on a specific subset of these vulnerabilities as it is still in its early stages of development. This focused approach allows SmartGraph to effectively test its ideas and ensure its tool is working as intended before expanding its capabilities to detect a broader range of security issues.

Default Function Visibility. Functions without defined visibility are public by default. The problem may arise if a malicious actor is able to alter the state of the smart contract through this function. It is recommended to choose the visibility of the function that suits its role in the smart contract to reduce the attack vector.

Variable Overflow. Numeric data types in Solidity versions before 0.8.0 could overflow. This means that a variable of type uint8, for example, will become 0 when one is added to 255. Such behavior can seriously affect the system's operation. For example, if we store a user's balance in the smart contract state, the balance may become zero again due to an addition operation when it exceeds a certain limit. Therefore, it is necessary to use the latest available versions of Solidity or use the special SafeMath library to prevent such issues.

Outdated Solidity Version. It is recommended to use the latest available version of Solidity to write smart contracts, as newer versions fix bugs that can lead to incorrect program behavior.

Unfixed Solidity Version. It is recommended to use a fixed Solidity version, such as pragma solidity 0.8.0, to prevent accidental deployment of a smart contract with an outdated Solidity version and incorrect system behavior.

Use of the Call Method Without Exception Handling. The call function allows interaction with other smart contracts, but errors that may result from its execution need to be handled. If appropriate error handling is not added when calling the call method, subsequent program logic may behave incorrectly.

Unsafe Use of the Selfdestruct Instruction. The selfdestruct function allows termination of a smart contract's operation and transfer of all stored ether to an address specified in the function's argument. The problem arises when an attacker manages to make a call to a function that contains selfdestruct, for example, if the function is public and available for anyone to call within the smart contract.

Reentrancy. One of the most popular and serious vulnerabilities for a smart contract is reentrancy, which involves calling other smart contracts with subsequent interception of the program's execution flow by these contracts. To avoid reentrancy, it is necessary to ensure that all changes to state variables are made before calling other smart contracts, or you can use a function modifier provided by the ReentrancyGuard library from OpenZeppelin.

Default Visibility of State Variables. In Solidity, the visibility of state variables, such as "public", "private", "internal" and "external", determines who can access and modify them. By default, state variables have internal visibility, which means they can be accessed by all functions within the contract, but not by other contracts or external accounts. It is crucial to set the visibility of state variables explicitly to avoid potential security issues and unexpected behavior in the smart contract. If a state variable is left with its default visibility, it may be accessed and modified by any function within the contract, even if it was not intended. This can lead to undesired changes to the state of the contract, making it vulnerable to attacks. Therefore, it is recommended to set the visibility of state variables explicitly, according to the needs of the smart contract and its functions, to ensure that only authorized parties can access and modify them.

Shadowing State Variables. It is not recommended to name variables used in functions or modifiers the same as state variables. In this case, the variable will shadow the state variable, which can lead to misunderstandings.

4   Static Analysis of Smart Contracts

Since the Ethereum network uses the Ethereum Virtual Machine (EVM) as a key component, smart contracts written in high-level languages must be compiled into EVM bytecode to run [9]. Static analysis tools for smart contracts are divided into two types [8]:

- Analysis of EVM bytecode
- Analysis of Solidity code

4.1   Approaches to Analyzing EVM Bytecode

- Using Symbolic analysis, a Control flow graph (CFG) is constructed, on which predefined rules that determine vulnerabilities are examined. Problem: the cumbersome process of constructing CFG [12] and unreadable bytecode make it difficult to form simple rules for vulnerabilities, making this approach to vulnerability detection ineffective.
- To construct an intermediate representation (IR) by extracting the semantics of bytecode and mapping instructions that may be vulnerable to predefined security patterns. Problem: Since bytecode cannot fully represent the semantics of the Solidity language, the analysis is susceptible to false positives and false negatives (FP and FN).

Therefore, analyzing Solidity code is more effective than analyzing EVM bytecode.

4.2   Approach with Solidity Code

The Solidity code analysis approach involves converting Solidity into an intermediate representation (IR) and then using pattern matching to identify vulnerabilities. This approach is adopted by various tools, including Slither and SmartCheck. However, these tools have their limitations. For instance, Slither lacks support for some basic semantics such as var variables, and SmartCheck makes it challenging to create new vulnerability detection rules.

Building IR. Static single assignment [13] (SSA) is a program representation technique used in compiler design and optimization. In SSA form, every variable is assigned exactly once, and each assignment creates a new variable. This allows for easier analysis of the program's control flow and data dependencies, which in turn enables more effective optimizations. SSA has become a popular representation for intermediate code in modern compilers and is widely used in both academia and industry (Fig. 1).

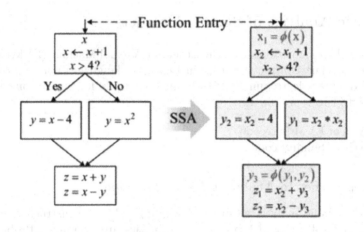

Fig. 1. Example of SSA operation.

In SSA, when a static variable x is assigned, it is represented as x1 and x2, which means that SSA requires each variable to be assigned only once. As a result of this requirement, it is easier to determine the relationships between variables, thus making data dependency analysis more efficient. When different paths are encountered in IR, such as in the case of a conditional block, SSA represents this ambiguity through the phi function, which is calculated based on the current path. If y3 is equal to y1, then z1 will be computed as x2+y1, otherwise as x2+y2.

Definition of Pattern. Often pattern matching is done through brute force search or taint analysis. For example, XPath is a method for detecting information in XML. It traverses the XML document's tags and attributes to find the information. The XML and XPath-based approach is used in SmartFast.

Taint analysis is an analysis of input data obtained from a user. Every variable that is defined by the user is considered as tainted. Every variable based on a tainted variable also gets a similar status. Programs that perform static analysis obtain a complete list of such variables and if they participate in potentially dangerous calls, such as accessing or writing to a database or working with the operating system, the programs will output an appropriate warning.

Abstract Syntax Tree. An abstract syntax tree (AST) [10] represents the structure of a program in an abstract form. The AST is created by the parser during the syntactic analysis of a program. In typical programming languages like Solidity, expressions, statements, and declarations make up the program structure.

Expressions include variable access, literals, unary and binary operators, and function calls. Programming languages offer various statements such as variable declaration, assignment, conditional statements (e.g., if), loops, control flow statements, and code blocks, which define the scope of variables.

Declarations introduce a new named entity, such as a function or a type, to the program. ASTs are useful in detecting vulnerabilities since they can capture the control flow and data flow of a program, allowing static analysis tools to identify patterns that could indicate potential security issues.

Control Flow Graph. CFG is a graph representation of all possible program execution paths. In this graph, each node represents an instruction, and each edge represents a transition from one instruction to another. Typically, the representation includes an entry node where program execution starts and an exit node where the program ends. Let's consider the property of reachability of this graph. This property is very useful for optimization. If there is a subgraph in the graph that cannot be reached from the main program execution flow, then this code is unreachable and can be removed. If the exit node is unreachable, then there may be an infinite loop in the program. Thus, we have discussed concepts that are essential for modern static code analysis, as well as approaches used by tools such as Slither.

In conclusion, our tool utilizes various techniques, such as abstract syntax tree (AST), and control flow graph (CFG), to enable comprehensive analysis of the code. The AST and CFG in our tool enable detailed analysis of the code structure and control flow, thus allowing the detection of complex vulnerabilities. The AST analysis is capable of identifying potential issues with the code's syntax, while the CFG analysis can reveal potential control flow issues. The combination of techniques used in our tool provides a comprehensive approach to identifying security vulnerabilities in smart-contracts.

5   SmartGraph: A Smart Contract Static Analysis Tool

In this section we present the design and evaluation of the SmartGraph [15], the tool based on using graphs as an intermediate representation for detecting vulnerabilities with help of static analysis of smart contracts.

5.1   Architecture

Like any static analysis tool, the smart contract code is inputted into the tool. The code is then transformed using a Solidity parser, which returns the syntax tree of the smart contract. The syntax tree describes the smart contract as a set of contract definitions along with state variables, events, modifiers, and functions defined within them. Functions, in turn, are represented as a set of expressions.

Let's consider the services that the analyzer consists of. The main service is the ParserService, which is responsible for parsing the syntax tree and constructing the Control Flow graph for functions. It can also handle variable types, various Solidity constructs such as while loops, binary operations, unary operations, accessing object properties, and so on.

The GraphService allows building an intermediate representation and using it for analysis. It supports searching for nodes of different types in the graph, adding nodes to the graph, searching for nodes by name, searching for nodes by edges, for example, to construct the Control Flow graph of a function, and searching for nodes in the graph that use state variables.

The IssueService is responsible for finding vulnerabilities in the smart contract based on the intermediate representation constructed. It represents a list of vulnerabilities from the smart contract vulnerability registry, each of which is analyzed.

The ReportService is responsible for generating a report on vulnerabilities, provides an API for adding vulnerabilities to the report, and calculates the number of vulnerabilities (Fig. 2).

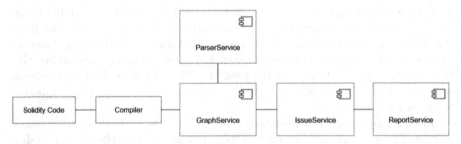

Fig. 2. Architecture.

5.2   Intermediate Representation

The model of this tool includes an intermediate representation in the form of a graph. This means that information about the smart contract is contained in the nodes and edges of a graph. For example, we can record information about a binary operation in a node. In this case, the node will contain the identifier of the line where this binary operation is located in the smart contract, the operator that is applied to the left operand, the left and right operands, which are variables or expressions. Recording information in an edge is used only in one place in the tool: when using a state variable of the smart contract in some expression. In this case, the edge will store information about that expression. Let's examine the intermediate representation in more detail.

Nodes in Intermediate Representation. To build an intermediate representation, the tool traverses the syntax tree. Currently, the traversal goes through the definitions of smart contracts, modifier definitions, Solidity version, event definitions of the smart contract, state variable definitions, using for instructions, and function definitions. From the smart contract definition, the name of the smart contract and all contracts that this contract inherits from are extracted. Accordingly, a node is created in the graph for each definition, which we can manipulate through GraphService.

The definition of a state variable yields nodes in the graph that contain information about the variable's visibility, immutability, type, and name.

From the using for statements, information is extracted indicating the presence of connected libraries such as ReentrancyGuard or SafeMath, as well as the type of variable for which the library is applied.

Finally, a node is added for each function in the smart contract, as well as for each parameter used in that function. The node defining a function contains the following information: name, function parameters, visibility, modifiers, and the function body, which is a Control Flow graph.

Functions. Most potential vulnerabilities are found in function bodies, so their analysis needs to be approached thoroughly. However, it's also important to correctly handle the function definition to obtain important modifiers, visibility, and parameters. The function body consists of instructions, and it can be expressed through a Control Flow graph. Therefore, to construct such a graph, we need to go through each instruction and determine what it represents. For example, if the instruction is a for loop, we need to parse the variable that can be initialized in it, the condition under which it continues to run, the expression that is executed at the end of each iteration, and the body of the for loop itself. If it's an if statement, we need to parse the condition, the body for the true condition, the body for the false condition, but the latter can often be another condition for the if statement, so the process should be recursive.

It is important to note that the body of a function consists of statements that are defined through expressions. For example: address caller = msg.sender;

Here, the statement is the variable declaration, and the expression is accessing the sender property of the msg object. Parsing Solidity involves defining two main operations: parseStatement, which handles parsing statements, and parseExpression, which handles expressions, and applying these two operations recursively, we can obtain information about arbitrarily complex statements. However, different statements can vary greatly, so for ease of working with them, the concept of order was introduced in the node. That is, each node is associated with a string of the form "parameter => use of variable." For example, consider the require(msg.value) instruction. The order property for this statement would look like msg => msg.value => require(msg.value). Thus, we can easily understand which variables are used in the statement and in what order it is executed.

5.3 IR Example

The following code provided is a simple example of a smart contract written in Solidity. The contract is called SimpleDAO and has a single function called donate that allows users to donate Ether to other addresses.

```
pragma solidity 0.4.24;

contract SimpleDAO {
    mapping(address => uint) public credit;

    function donate(address to) public payable {
        credit[to] += msg.value;
    }
}
```

In Fig. 3, you can see the various components of the SimpleDAO contract represented as nodes in the IR. For example, the contract meta information is represented as a version node and contract name node, the mapping of addresses to credits is represented as a state variable node, and the donate function is represented as a function node.

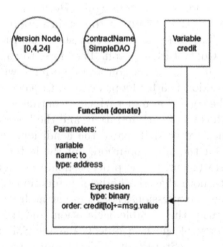

Fig. 3. SimpleDAO contract's intermediate representation.

This contract is written in Solidity, a programming language for building decentralized applications on the Ethereum blockchain. The contract is called ShadowingInFunctions and contains three functions: test1, test2, and test3. Function test3 demonstrates the concept of state variable shadowing (Fig. 4).

```
pragma solidity 0.4.24;

contract ShadowingInFunctions {
    uint n = 2;
    uint x = 3;

    function test1() constant returns (uint n) {
        return n; // Will return 0
    }

    function test2() constant returns (uint n) {
        n = 1;
        return n; // Will return 1
    }

    function test3() constant returns (uint x) {
        uint n = 4;
        return n + x; // Will return 4
    }
}
```

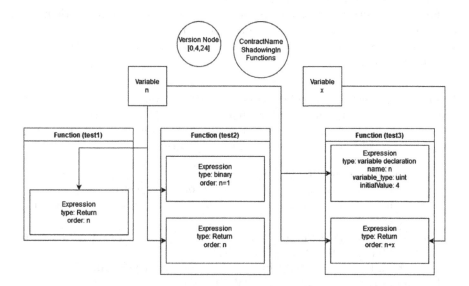

Fig. 4. ShadowingInFunctions contract's intermediate representation.

5.4   Intermediate Representation Analysis

To detect a vulnerability, you need to use the GraphService API to retrieve information about the nodes of the intermediate representation. For example, to analyze the version, you need to refer to the node of the "version" type. In turn, to detect reentrancy, you need to refer to several types of nodes: "using-for", "modifier", and "function", as information about these nodes will allow you to determine whether the state change is a vulnerability or not. Let's consider a few examples of smart contract vulnerability research:

Default Function Visibility. One of the simplest vulnerabilities to detect in this model is as follows:

1. Get all nodes whose type is function.
2. Check the visibility property of the node. If it is equal to default, then the vulnerability is detected and information about this vulnerability needs to be recorded.

Using the Call Method Without Exception Handling. Let's consider a vulnerability that is directly related to the code of the smart contract functions. In this case, it is necessary to analyze the Control Flow graph of the function for the presence of a call function and calls to the assert or require functions. These functions are used to handle exceptions.

1. Get all nodes of type function.
2. From the Control Flow graph of the function body, get all instructions.
3. For each instruction, analyze the order property.
4. If it contains a call and does not contain assert or require, then the vulnerability is detected.

Reentrancy. Let's now consider a vulnerability that relies on the edges between state variables and the instructions that use them. Thanks to these edges, we don't have to look at all the instructions, which simplifies the detection of this vulnerability and reduces the number of false positives.

1. Get all nodes whose type is function.
2. Get inheritance information through nodes of type inherit.
3. Get all instructions that use state variables, in this case, we only need the line numbers.
4. For each function, determine the presence of the nonReentrant modifier from the OpenZeppelin ReentrancyGuard library.
5. Also, check that the contract inherits from ReentrancyGuard.
6. Find all instructions that use the call function.
7. If the function does not have the nonReentrant modifier and there is an instruction that changes the state and comes after the call function call, then the vulnerability is detected.

5.5   Comparative Analysis with Other Analysis Tools

In this comparative analysis, 36 different smart contracts were used, some of which contained vulnerabilities. The smart contracts were taken from the registry of smart contract vulnerabilities [14] (Table 1).

Table 1. Comparative analysis.

Instruments	SmartGraph	Slither	SolHint	Solium
Flagged contracts	31	36	36	36
Detections per contract	3.08	6.19	5.02	4.25
False positives	7	4	0	0
True positives	8	9	4	3
False negatives	14	13	18	19
True negatives	7	10	14	14

Here it is important to understand that the tool described in this work detects only a part of vulnerabilities defined in the registry of smart contract vulnerabilities.

6   Conclusion and Future Work

In this paper, general approaches and concepts used in code analysis, as well as options for static analysis of smart contracts, were considered. SmartGraph, a new instrument for analyzing smart contracts written in Solidity based on an intermediate representation in the form of a graph was presented.

From all of the above, we can conclude that this approach allows us to describe the rules for detecting vulnerabilities quite simply and effectively. Building additional links between nodes in the intermediate representation simplifies the process of analyzing a smart contract to detect vulnerabilities.

However, from the comparative analysis, it can be seen that the next step is to refine the Solidity model since the instrument works incorrectly in 5% of cases. It is also necessary to add the ability to detect all vulnerabilities from the register of smart contract vulnerabilities and to look for places where additional links, built using edges in the graph, will allow for more efficient analysis.

References

1. Guegan, D.: The Digital World: I - Bitcoin: from history to real life. University of Ca' Foscari (2018)
2. Merkle, R.C.: Secrecy, authentication, and public key systems. Stanford University (1979)

3. Chaum, D.: Blind signatures for untraceable payments. In: Chaum, D., Rivest, R.L., Sherman, A.T. (eds.) Advances in Cryptology, pp. 199–203. Springer, Boston, MA (1983). https://doi.org/10.1007/978-1-4757-0602-4_18

4. Haber, S., Stornetta, W.S.: How to time-stamp a digital document. J. Cryptol. **3**(2), 99–111 (1991). https://doi.org/10.1007/BF00196791

5. Buterin, V.: Ethereum: a next-generation smart contract and decentralized application platform (2014)

6. Feist, J., Grieco, G., Groce, A.: Slither: a static analysis framework for smart contracts. arXiv preprint arXiv:1908.09878 (2019)

7. Tikhomirov, S., Voskresenskaya, E., Ivanitskiy, I., Takhaviev, R., Marchenko, E., Alexandrov, Y.: SmartCheck: static analysis of Ethereum smart contracts. In: WETSEB'18: IEEE/ACM 1st International Workshop on Emerging Trends in Software Engineering for Blockchain (WETSEB 2018), 27 May 2018, Gothenburg, Sweden, p. 8. ACM, New York, NY, USA (2018)

8. Striewe, M., Goedicke, M.: A review of static analysis approaches for programming exercises. University of Duisburg-Essen (2014)

9. SolidityLang: Solidity Language Description. https://docs.soliditylang.org/en/v0.8.17/index.html. Accessed 24 Dec 2022

10. ps-group: Abstract Syntax Trees. https://ps-group.github.io/compilers/ast. Accessed 07 Apr 2023

11. Li, Z., Li, S.: SmartFast: an accurate and robust formal analysis tool for Ethereum smart contracts. Inf. Eng. Univ. (2022)

12. Allen, F.E.: Control flow analysis. IBM Corporation (1970)

13. Cytron, R., Ferrante, J., Rosen, B.K., Wegman, M.N.: Efficiently computing static single assignment form and the control dependance graph. IBM Research Division (1991)

14. SWC Registry: Smart Contract Weakness Classification and Test Cases. https://swcregistry.io. Accessed 16 Apr 2023

15. SmartGraph repository. https://github.com/NixoN2/smart-graph. Accessed 22 Apr 2023

Bio and Neuro Inspired Computing and Applications (BIONCA 2023)

Routing in 3D NoCs Using Genetic Algorithm and Particle Swarm Optimization

Maamar Bougherara[1,2], Nadia Nedjah[3], Djamel Bennouar[1],
and Luiza de Macedo Mourelle[4(✉)]

[1] LIMPAF Laboratory, Bouira University, Bouira, Algeria
[2] Département d'Informatique, Ecole Normale Supérieure Kouba, Algiers, Algeria
[3] Department of Electronics Engineering and Telecommunications,
State University of Rio de Janeiro, Rio de Janeiro, Brazil
[4] Department of Systems Engineering and Computation,
State University of Rio de Janeiro, Rio de Janeiro, Brazil
LDMM@ENG.UERJ.BR

Abstract. Networks-on-chip are a new concept in System-on-chip interconnections, facilitating and optimizing complex components integration. However, as it is a new technology, it still requires some research, especially concerning the acceleration and simplification of design phases. Networks-on-chip can be arranged in different topologies, such as hypercube, mesh and torus. Since several data packets can be transmitted simultaneously through the network, an efficient routing strategy must be used in order to avoid congestion delays. In this paper, we propose and evaluate the performance of two routing methods, based on genetic algorithm and particle swarm optimization, for Networks-on-chip with 3D mesh topology. The routing is driven by the minimization of total latency in packets transmission between tasks. The simulation results show that the routing based on genetic algorithm and particle swarm optimization outperforms other routing algorithms in terms of latency.

Keywords: 3D Networks-on-chip · Routing · Genetic algorithm · Particle swarm optimization · Congestion

1 Introduction

Networks-on-Chip (NoCs) provide an infrastructure for on-chip communication, in order to target bottlenecks when running parallel applications. It is based on the well known area of computer network, but driven by the limited resources that a chip design imposes. The basic elements of a NoC are resources (R) and switches (S), connected by links. A resource can be a processor, memory or any kind of functional component [1]. A switch is a component that provides the communication between resources, through links, where packets of information flow.

The topology of the NoC defines the way links are interconnected, which can have the shape of a mesh, torus or hypercube [2]. Figure 1 shows the architecture of a 3D NoC, based on the mesh topology, where, for example, RNI stands for Resource Network Interface, D for Digital Signal Processor, M for Memory, C for Cache, P for Processor, FP for Floating-Point unit and Re for a Reconfigurable component.

© The Author(s), under exclusive license to Springer Nature Switzerland AG 2023
O. Gervasi et al. (Eds.): ICCSA 2023 Workshops, LNCS 14104, pp. 601–613, 2023.
https://doi.org/10.1007/978-3-031-37105-9_40

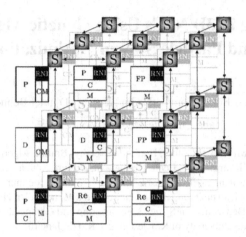

Fig. 1. 3D mesh-based NoC with 27 resources

A NoC is optimised to run a specific application, which is divided into tasks implemented by Intellectual Property (IP) blocks. The design process can be divided into intermediate steps, such as IP assignment of tasks [3] and IP mapping [4,22]. IP assignment consists of associating each task (or set of tasks) to an appropriate IP block, selected among those that are readily available in a repository. The mapping of an application consists of associating the set of assigned IPs to each node in the communication infrastructure of the NoC. Routing defines which paths will be used to establish the communication between IPs. Each of these steps is optimized by computer-aided tools, which use the application specification and generates a full system implementation. These tools optimize the characteristics of the hardware and software in order to obtain a solution that meets the design specifications, as seen in Fig. 2 for a NoC design.

In a NoC architecture, communication delays can occur in congestion situations, when multiple packets require communication through the same switch at the same time [16]. In order to avoid this congestion problem, and thus speed up the overall run-time system, our work explores routing optimization. This paper describes the routing optimization step in the design of NoCs, using static routing based on Genetic Algorithm (GA) and Particle Swarm Optimization (PSO) for NoCs with 3D mesh topology.

The rest of the paper is organized as follows. Previous works on routing algorithms are introduced in Sect. 2. The overview of our routing approach is presented in Sect. 3. In Sect. 4, we discuss the results of the simulation experiments. The conclusion of this work and future work are presented in Sect. 5.

2   Related Work

Many routing algorithms have been proposed for NoCs, but most of them focus only on 2D NoC topologies. Among all the studies conducted for 3D NoCs, few of them

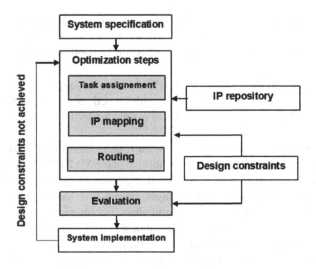

Fig. 2. Typical embedded system design flow for NoCs

targeted routing algorithms and they can be classified into two categories. The first one includes some of the well known routing schemes in 2D NoCs, that were extended to 3D, such as Dimension Ordered Routing (DOR) [5], Valiant [6], O1TURN [7] and Odd-Even [8]. The second one includes some specially related to 3D, such as DyXYZ [9], 3D-FAR [10], MAR [11], Global A (G-CARA) [12], FT-DyXYZ [13].

In 2D mesh topology, the most popular DOR routing algorithm is XY. In this algorithm, each node is characterized by a pair (x,y), representing its position in the network (row and column). By applying the XY algorithm, the packet is, first, routed along the x axis until reaching the destination X and, then, routes along the y axis, until reaching the destination Y. It is a deterministic and minimal algorithm known for its simplicity of implementation. However, it becomes ineffective as soon as the network is overloaded. In this situation, it is not able to avoid congested regions of the network. Therefore, the packets must wait for the channels to become free in order to be transmitted.

The XYZ routing algorithm is the corresponding XY routing algorithm in a 3D mesh topology. Each node is characterized by a triple (x, y, z). The packet is first routed along the X axis, then the Y axis, and finally the Z axis to reach the destination. Although the XYZ algorithm obtains the shortest path, it is not able to avoid congested regions of the network.

The routing algorithm offered by Valiant achieves optimal throughput by balancing the load globally across the entire network. Routing consists of two phases: first, packets are routed from the source to a random intermediate node, followed by routing to the destination. Both phases used DOR algorithm.

O1Turn routing achieves both minimum length and near optimal throughput by simply choosing between 2D turn paths: XY or YX. O1Turn can be extended in 3D topology. In this case, you can choose between several possibilities such as: XYZ, XZY, ZXY, ZYX.

The OE routing protocol, also known as "Odd-Even", uses partially adaptive routing without virtual channels. It relies on specific rules based on column parity to determine allowed and unallowed turns, which helps to avoid circular loops and unwanted blocking states.

Unlike 2D NoCs, a few congestion-aware routing algorithms were proposed for 3D NoCs. DyXYZ [9] applies adaptive routing to solve 3D NoC congestion problems, using congestion information from neighbouring nodes to make handover decision at the current node. 3D-FAR is a regional congestion sensitive routing algorithm proposed in [10]. It presents a clustering structure to collect and propagate congestion information. MAR [11] is an adaptive routing algorithm that routes packets based on Hamiltonian paths without using virtual channels. In [12], a Global A (G-CARA) congestion sensitive routing algorithm is proposed for traffic management in 3D NoC. The algorithm efficiently transmits data packets to regions with low traffic to avoid network congestion. FT-DyXYZ [13] is an adaptive fault tolerant routing algorithm, with the ability to tolerate permanent faulty links in 3D mesh NOCs that uses proximity congestion information in order to balance traffic.

Computational intelligence meta-heuristics have been used as intelligent approaches for efficient routing algorithms. This is the case of AntNet [14], a dynamic routing scheme for telecommunication networks. In [15], the authors applied Ant Colony Optimization (ACO) technique to address the routing problem in 3D NoCs based on three topologies: mesh, torus and hypercube. The results were better than those obtained by deterministic and minimal routing algorithms, such as DOR.

3   Routing Algorithm Approach

To deal with the routing problem, we applied two optimization strategies based on computational intelligence: genetic algorithm and particle swarm optimization. The implementation of the routing algorithm requires the definition of essential parameters. One of them is the definition of the solution.

Each solution contains a possible path for a source-destination pair. The latter is selected at random from an array of several paths of the same source-destination, where this array contains several paths of each pair (source-destination). Figure 3 shows an example of several paths of such pairs and how to define a solution.

Therefore, a solution contains a set of possible paths for all the source-destination pairs needed to transmit data, based on the application mapped onto the NoC. Figure 4 shows a solution. In order to measure the quality of the solutions, we evaluate the fitness function. This function will make it possible to distinguish the best solutions. Therefore, the best solution is the least congested, compared to others.

The fitness function is the congestion. It can be considered as a cost, that we have defined to estimate the rate of use of the network links. Initially, the congestion cost of

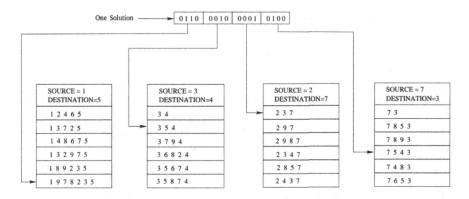

Fig. 3. Example of several paths of pairs (source-destination)

CHROMOSOME	0110 0010 0001 0100
Route 1	1 9 7 8 2 3 5
Route 2	3 5 4
Route 3	2 3 7
Route 4	7 5 4 3

Fig. 4. Exemple of one solution

all links is equal to 0. Each time a link appears in a path, its cost is incremented by 1. The congestion cost of a path of length L is given by the Eq. 1:

$$Congestion\_path_i = \sum_{j=1}^{L} C_j, \tag{1}$$

where C_j is the congestion cost associated with the j-th link of path i in the routing table [17]. The total congestion cost of a solution is the sum of all congestions of all paths used in the solution and calculated according to the Eq. 2:

$$Congestion(S) = \sum_{i=1}^{N} Congestion\_path_i. \tag{2}$$

3.1 Genetic Algorithm

Genetic algorithm (GA) is a special type of stochastic research algorithm that applies evolution as a problem-solving technique [18]. GA works on the research space called population [19]. Each element of the population is called a chromosome, where each one is a solution in itself.

At the beginning, a random population is generated, which represents possible solutions. Each solution is represented by an array, in which the size is the number of source and destination node pairs present in the system. For each pair, a path is selected from multiple distinct paths existing between source and destination.

Once the initial population is generated, a new one is generated based on the following genetic operations [20]:

1) Selection: consists in choosing the individuals who will participate in the reproduction of the future population. The selection function may be random or according to a probabilistic method, such as roulette and tournament. An individual is chosen so that it participates in the reproduction stage to form the new population. In this work, we use random selection.

2) Crossover: recombines two 'parents' to produce two new 'children' in the next generation. We used one-point crossing, where two parent paths are split into two parts, respectively, and recombined. The parts are exchanged to produce the new children. The bit crossing positions are randomly selected along the length of the chromosome, as shown in Fig. 5.

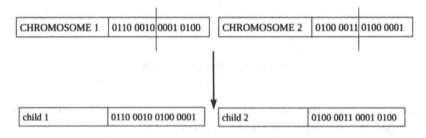

Fig. 5. Crossover operation

3) Mutation: randomly flips a bit position in the chromosome. It consists of choosing a gene at random and replace it with another value, chosen randomly, as shown in the Fig. 6. In the mutation, a mutation rate must be applied which refers to the probability or frequency with which a gene in the chromosome of a solution undergoes a random change or mutation during the evolutionary process.

Algorithm 1 shows the main steps of the genetic algorithm. The stop criterion is the maximum number of iterations, which relates to the number of generations. We applied 500 iterations, a population of 100 chromosomes and a mutation rate of 0.9.

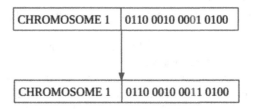

Fig. 6. Mutation operation

Algorithm 1. The main steps of Genetic Algorithm

Initialize the individuals of the population
Evaluate and initialize best solution
iteration := 0
while iteration < max_iteration **do**
    (a) Selection()
    (b) Crossover()
    (c) Mutation()
    iteration := iteration + 1
end while

3.2 Particle Swarm Optimization Algorithm

Particle Swarm Optimization (PSO) [21] is one of the examples of swarm intelligence strategies inspired by a flock of birds in search for food. In PSO, each particle position represents a potential solution of the problem. Each particle is characterized by its position and its performance, i.e., in the case of a function optimization, each particle is characterized by the variable value and the corresponding function value.

Particles are distributed randomly in the search space and move according to a local information. Each particle informs its performance to the neighbouring ones, can remember the position where registered its best perfomance so far and can inform the position of the neightbouring particle with the best performance. The new position x_i of particle i is given by Eq. 3:

$$x_i(t + 1) = x_i(t) + v_i(t + 1). \tag{3}$$

The velocity v_i of each particle i is given by Eq. 4:

$$v_i(t+1) = w.v_i(t)+c_1.r_1(t+1)(Pbest(t)-x_i(t))+c_2r_2(t+1)(Gbest(t)-x_i(t)), \tag{4}$$

where:

    (i) w is the inertia coefficient, used to prevent the particle from drastic changes in direction;

(ii) c_1 is the cognitive coefficient, related to the performance of particle i with respect to its previous one;

(iii) c_2 is the social coefficient, related to the performance of parcicle i with respect to the performance of the swarm;

(iv) $r_1(t)$ and $r_2(t)$ are random values in the interval [0,1], used to characterize the stochastic nature of the cognitive and social contributions;

(v) $Pbest(t)$ is the best position founded by particle i so far;

(vi) $Gbest(t)$ is the best position founded by the swarm.

The cognitive coefficient c_1 and the social coefficient c_2 yield a better performance when they are balanced [23].

In our work, the position of a particle is an array, whose size is the number of pairs (source, destination) implemented in the NoC. For each pair (source, destination), there will be several different paths between the source and the destination. The particle is chosen from each pair among the ones that exist.

Algorithm 2 shows the main steps of the PSO. The stop criterion is the maximum number of iterations. We applied 500 iterations, a swarm of 200 particles, the cognitive coefficient and the social coefficient are 1.35, each, and the inertia coefficient is 0.8.

Algorithm 2. The main steps of PSO

Initialize the particles of the swarm
Evaluate all the particles of the swarm and save Gbest
Initialize the velocity for each particle
iteration := 0
while iteration < max_iteration **do**
   for each particle **do**
      Select a Pbest
      Update the position using Eqs. 3 and 4
      Evaluate the particle fitness
      Update Pbest
   end for
   Update Gbest
   iteration := iteration + 1
end while
Return result from Gbest

---

4 Simulations and Performance Results

We used the Access-Noxim simulator [24], which is an upgraded version of the Noxim simulator. Noxim is a NoC simulator tool [25] written in C++ programming language, based on the SystemC library. The implemented routing strategy can be modified easily by writing and testing code using C++.

In this work, we focus on latency as a measure of performance. Latency is the time between the packet injection in the local port and the consumption of the queue flit in the local port of the destination node. The network was simulated with both 2D and 3D NoCs. We used a 5×5 mesh, for the 2D NoC, and a $3 \times 3 \times 3$ mesh, for the 3D NoC. The total simulation time was 20000 cycles. All the tests were carried out varying the routing algorithms, the traffic models and the packet injection rate (PIR).

Source-destination pairs are generated according to three different distribution traffic models: Complement, Transpose 1 and Transpose 2 [26]. These models are called deterministic patterns. In the three patterns, each node sends messages to a single destination and the destination nodes are selected based on the position of the source nodes, as seen in Table 1. We compared the results obtained with DOR (XYZ) and Odd-Even algorithms. Table 2 shows the full system simulation configuration.

Table 1. Destination nodes of deterministic patterns

Network	Pattern	source node	Destination node
2D Mesh	Complement	(x, y)	(size - x - 1, size - y - 1)
	Transpose 1	(x, y)	(size - y - 1, size - x - 1)
	Transpose 2	(x, y)	(y, x)
3D Mesh	Complement	(x,y,z)	(size - x - 1, size - y - 1, size - z - 1)
	Transpose 1	(x, y, z)	(size - y - 1, size - z - 1, size - x - 1)
	Transpose 2	(x, y, z)	(y, z, x)

Table 2. Parameter settings

Parameter	Setting
Network	2D Mesh vs 3D Mesh
Network dimensions	5×5 vs $3 \times 3 \times 3$
Packet size	8
Virtual channels	4
Warm-up time	1000
Simulation time	20,000 cycles
Routing algorithms	PSO, GA, XYZ and ODD-Even

Figure 7 reports the average latency as a function of PIR for the 2D NoC, using Complement in Fig. 7(a), Transpose 1 in Fig. 7(b) and Transpose 2 in Fig. 7(c). When PIR is very low, all algorithms perform in the same way and have approximately the same average latency values. When PIR is high, GA and PSO outperform the other routing strategies and provide the best results compared to XYZ and Odd-Even.

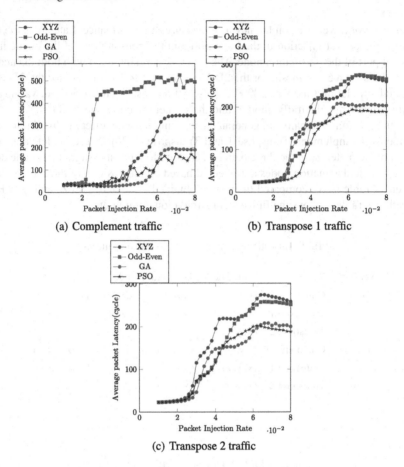

(a) Complement traffic   (b) Transpose 1 traffic

(c) Transpose 2 traffic

Fig. 7. Average latency as a function of PIR in 2D NoC

In Complement traffic, the maximum load, before the network starts saturating using Odd-Even routing, is 0.025 packets/node/cycle. This value increases to 0.045 with XYZ. GA outperforms the other algorithms and PSO starts to give low latency, compared to GA, when PIR it reaches 0.06.

In Transpose 1, the network starts saturating at 0.0135 and 0.015 for Odd-Even and XYZ, respectively. PSO achieves better performance, while GA starts to provide low latency when PIR reaches 0.047, compared to PSO.

Finally, for Transpose 2, XYZ starts saturating at 0.02. When GA and PSO reach 0.01 PIR, the latency becomes better than Odd-Even. PSO begins to provide low latency when it reaches 0.065.

Figure 8 reports the average latency as a function of PIR in the 3D NoC. Figure 8(a) relates to Complement traffic, Fig. 8(b) to Transpose 1 traffic and Fig. 8(c) to Transpose 2 traffic.

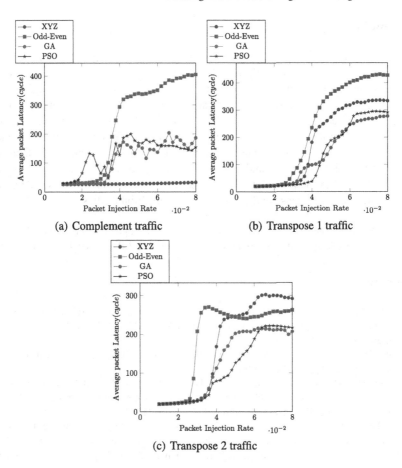

Fig. 8. Average latency as a function of PIR in 3D NoC

In Complement traffic, XYZ outperforms the other routing algorithms in terms of average latency because, in the complementary model, the paths taken by the XYZ routing are static and do not cross in most parts, which does not cause congestion. PSO and GA outperform Odd-Even, when PIR starts saturating at 0.03, while begins to give better performance when it reaches 0.06.

In Transpose1 traffic, 3D Odd-Even performs poorly with regard to XYZ, PSO and GA, and reaches a saturation point at 0.026. The network saturates at 0.046 for XYZ. PSO and GA provide better results, while GA outperforms PSO when PIR is 0.06.

Finally, in Transpose 2 traffic, the network saturation points are 0.046 and 0.042 for Odd-Even and XYZ, respectively. GA and PSO achieve better performance than Odd-Even and XYZ when PIR is 0.04, while PSO outperforms GA when PIR reaches 0.03.

5   Conclusion

This work proposes a routing algorithm based on genetic algorithm and particle swarm optimization, for Network-on-chip in a 3D mesh topology, in order to minimize congestion. A large number of tests were performed, through simulation, using deterministic generated traffic. In most cases, both algorithms performed better than other routing algorithms, such as XYZ and Odd-Even. Despite the promising results that were obtained in deterministic traffic, we have some work to do in order to improvement the approach. In future work, we will use other computational intelligence meta-heuristics, such as differential evolution, and graphs of real application tasks. Besides this, we intend to experiment them on NoCs with larger dimensions than the ones used here, in order to address more intense and complex communication traffics.

Acknowledgments. The authors acknowledge the financial support of Fundação Carlos Chagas Filho de Amparo à Pesquisa do Estado do Rio de Janeiro - FAPERJ - (Proc. E-26/210.044/2021)

References

1. Hu, J., Marculescu, R.: Energy-aware mapping for tile-based NoC architectures under performance constraints. In: Proceedings of the 2003 Asia and South Pacific Design Automation Conference, pp. 233–239. ACM (2003)
2. Davis, W.R., et al.: Demystifying 3D ICs: the pros and cons of going vertical. IEEE Des. Test Comput. **22**(6), 498–510 (2005)
3. Bougherara, M., Nedjah, N., Mourelle, L.D.M., Rahmoun, R., Sadok, A., Bennouar, D.: IP assignment for efficient NoC-based system design using multi-objective particle swarm optimisation. Int. J. Bio-Inspired Comput. **12**(4), 203–213 (2018)
4. Bougherara, M., Nedjah, N., Bennouar, D., Kemcha, R., de Macedo Mourelle, L.: Application mapping onto 3D NoCs using differential evolution. In: Gervasi, O., et al. (eds.) ICCSA 2020. LNCS, vol. 12251, pp. 89–102. Springer, Cham (2020). https://doi.org/10.1007/978-3-030-58808-3_8
5. Sullivan, H., Bashkow, T.R.: A large scale, homogeneous, fully distributed parallel machine, i. In: ACM SIGARCH Computer Architecture News, vol. 5, no. 7, pp. 105–117. ACM (1977)
6. Valiant, L.G., Brebner, G.J.: Universal schemes for parallel communication. In: Proceedings of the Thirteenth Annual ACM Symposium on Theory of Computing, pp. 263–277. ACM (1981)
7. Seo, D., Ali, A., Lim, W.T., Rafique, N.: Near-optimal worst-case throughput routing for two-dimensional mesh networks. In: ACM SIGARCH Computer Architecture News, vol. 33, no. 2, pp. 432–443. IEEE Computer Society (2005)
8. Chiu, G.M.: The odd-even turn model for adaptive routing. IEEE Trans. Parallel Distrib. Syst. **11**(7), 729–738 (2000)
9. Ebrahimi, M., Chang, X., Daneshtalab, M., et al.: DyXYZ: fully adaptive routing algorithm for 3D NoCs. In: 2013 21st Euromicro International Conference on Parallel, Distributed, and Network-Based Processing, pp. 499–503. IEEE (2013)
10. Ebrahimi, M.: Fully adaptive routing algorithms and regionbased approaches for two-dimensional and three-dimensional networkson-chip. IET Comput. Digit. Tech. **7**(6), 264–273 (2013)
11. Ebrahimi, M., Daneshtalab, M., Liljeberg, P., Plosila, J., Flich, J., Tenhunen, H.: Path-based partitioning methods for 3D networks-on-chip with minimal adaptive routing. IEEE Trans. Comput. **63**(3), 718–733 (2014)

12. Nosrati, N., Shahhoseini, H.S.: G-CARA: a global congestion-aware routing algorithm for traffic management in 3d networks-on-chip. In: 2017 Iranian Conference on Electrical Engineering (ICEE), pp. 2188–2193. IEEE (2017)

13. Jouybari, H.N., Mohammadi, K.: A low overhead, fault tolerant and congestion aware routing algorithm for 3D mesh-based Network-on-Chips. Microprocess. Microsyst. **38**(8), 991–999 (2014)

14. Junior, L.S., Nedjah, N., de Macedo Mourelle, L. : ACO approach in static routing for network-on-chips with 3D mesh topology. In : 2013 IEEE 4th Latin American Symposium on Circuits and Systems (LASCAS), pp. 1-4. IEEE (2013)

15. Silva Junior, L., Nedjah, N., De Macedo Mourelle, L.: Efficient routing in network-on-chip for 3D topologies. Int. J. Electron. **102**(10), 1695–1712 (2015)

16. Alfaraj, N., Zhang, J., Xu, Y., Chao, H.J.: Hope: hotspot congestion control for clos network on chip. In: 2011 Fifth IEEE/ACM International Symposium on Networks on Chip (NoCS), pp. 17–24 (2011)

17. Nychis, G.P., Fallin, C., Moscibroda, T., Mutlu, O., Seshan, S.: On-chip networks from a networking perspective: congestion and scalability in many-core interconnects. In: Proceedings of the ACM SIGCOMM 2012 Conference on Applications, Technologies, Architectures, and Protocols for Computer Communication, SIGCOMM 2012, ACM, New York, NY, USA, pp. 407–418 (2012)

18. Holland, J.H.: Adaptation in Natural and Artificial Systems: An Introductory Analysis with Applications to Biology, Control and Artificial Intelligence. MIT Press, Cambridge, MA, USA (1992)

19. Goldberg, D., Holland, J.: Genetic algorithms and machine learning (1988)

20. Mohammed, M.A., Ahmad, M.S., Mostafa, S.A.: Using genetic algorithm in implementing capacitated vehicle routing problem. In: 2012 International Conference on Computer & Information Science (ICCIS), pp. 257-262. IEEE (2012)

21. Zhang, L.B., Zhou, C.G., Liu, X.H., Ma, Z.Q., Ma, M., Liang, Y.C.: Solving multi objective optimization problems using particle swarm optimization. In: Congress on Evolutionary Computation (CEC 2003), vol. 3, pp. 2400–2405 (2003)

22. Bougherara, M., Nedjah, N., Bennouar, D., Kemcha, R., de Macedo Mourelle, L.: Efficient application mapping onto three-dimensional network-on-chips using multi-objective particle swarm optimization. In: Misra, S., et al. (eds.) ICCSA 2019. LNCS, vol. 11620, pp. 654–670. Springer, Cham (2019). https://doi.org/10.1007/978-3-030-24296-1_53

23. Nedjah, N., Mourelle, L.D.M.: Evolutionary multi-objective optimisation: a survey. Int. J. Bio-Inspired Comput. **7**(1), 1–25 (2015)

24. Catania, V., et al.: Noxim: an open extensible and cycle-accurate network on chip simulator. In: IEEE 26th International Conference on Application-specific Systems Architectures and Processors (ASAP), pp. 162–163 (2015)

25. Access Noxim. http://access.ee.ntu.edu.tw/noxim/index.html

26. Duato, J., Yalamanchili, S., Ni, L.: Interconnection Networks. Morgan Kaufmann, Burlington (2002)

More Precise SLAM Using Controlled Filter Augmented with Active Perception

Luigi Maciel Ribeiro[1]([⊠]) [iD], Nadia Nedjah[2] [iD],
and Paulo Victor R. de Carvalho[1] [iD]

[1] Federal University of Rio de Janeiro, Rio de Janeiro, Brazil
luigimaciel@dcc.ufrj.br, paulov@ien.gov.br
[2] State University of Rio de Janeiro, Rio de Janeiro, Brazil
nadia@eng.uerj.br

Abstract. This work presents a new method, called Controlled Filter with Active Perception (CFAP), to approach the problem of Simultaneous Localization and Mapping (SLAM). SLAM aims to map an unknown environment while estimating the trajectory of a mobile agent moving within that environment. CFAP combines the two fundamental pillars of SLAM, which are scan alignment and loop closure, into a single process. The method is inspired by human perception of locating oneself and for this, it uses a mental map to guide itself. CFAP uses a Gaussian distribution to estimate possible poses and performs the alignment process in cycles, where each cycle is influenced by the results of the previous one. The Active Perception mechanism is used in each cycle to determine the quality of each of the possible poses, allowing for more accurate simultaneous localization and mapping. Benchmarking tests were performed on 5 public datasets that demonstrate the effectiveness and efficiency of the proposed method.

Keywords: Active perception · Simultaneous localization and mapping · Optimized search

1 Introduction

Simultaneous Localization and Mapping (SLAM) is a highly complex computational problem that aims to map an unknown environment while simultaneously estimating the trajectory of a mobile agent that is moving within that environment. The fundamental pillars of SLAM are scan alignment and loop closure, which have been extensively studied in numerous works [3,5,12].

The process of scan alignment is common in our daily lives. From a young age, we are trained and encouraged to perform such processes, such as putting a key in a lock, connecting a cell phone charger, or screwing the lid onto a bottle, among others. Human alignment processes demonstrate a systematic methodology, where the process is performed in cycles, with action, observation, and adjustment stages. This concept inspired the creation of a new scan alignment

O. Gervasi et al. (Eds.): ICCSA 2023 Workshops, LNCS 14104, pp. 614–631, 2023.
https://doi.org/10.1007/978-3-031-37105-9_41

method, called Controlled Filter (CF), which uses a Gaussian distribution to estimate possible poses and performs the scan alignment process in stages, with the current stage being fed back with the results from the immediately preceding stage. The main inspirations of CF are Particle Filters [13] and feedback control systems [16].

The other pillar of SLAM is loop closure, which consists of the process of recognizing locations already visited and mapped by the mobile agent. In order to optimize the entire SLAM process, a scan alignment with active perception was developed, which combines the two pillars of SLAM into a single process. To demonstrate the effectiveness of the method, benchmarking tests were performed with five different public datasets.

This paper is divided into five sections: Related Works, Controlled Filter, Active Perception, Performance Results, and Conclusion. Section 2 presents works that propose optimizing the SLAM process. Section 3 demonstrates all the steps of scan alignment using the Controlled Filter. Then, Sect. 4 explains how perception is implemented to improve the SLAM process. Section 5 highlights the entire benchmarking test methodology and concludes with the test results. The paper is concluded with Sect. 6, where the obtained results are analyzed and future work is proposed.

2   Related Works

In [18], an approach to active SLAM in dynamic environments using micro aerial vehicles (MAVs) is presented. In this work, perception is used by a sensitive path planner called the Next-Best-View planner (NBVP) to avoid static and dynamic obstacles in unknown environments. Together with an active loop closure planner (ALCP), it is possible to reduce the uncertainty of SLAM and improve location accuracy. The method is demonstrated in simulated environments and presents results that confirm the effectiveness of this methodology.

In [4], the authors present a visual SLAM (VSLAM) approach with the main objective of tracking and preventing possible failures during the navigation and mapping process. Through continuous identification and association of map points during movement, this proposal can structure a planning that takes into account sensorial restrictions, resulting in reliable navigation. Perception is used in this method to predict the number of map points associated with a given pose, allowing for planning an ideal distance path so that the number of associated points is always above the limit. The results of experiments conducted in two environments demonstrate the performance of this approach.

In [8], an integrated navigation algorithm with visual SLAM is presented with the goal of optimizing the mapping and localization process. This algorithm, called perception-driven navigation (PDN), automatically balances the processes of exploration and revisiting of the environment. To make decisions, the PDN uses a reward structure that takes into account the identification of good areas for loop closure, the uncertainty in the vehicle location, and the quality of area coverage. The method is demonstrated in an autonomous application for inspecting underwater ship hulls, using a hybrid simulation that combines synthetic and real images. The presented results confirm the applicability of the proposed method.

In [17], a method for addressing SLAM in off-road environments is proposed, which presents unique challenges that indoor SLAM does not have. These challenges include issues with direct sunlight, obstruction by foliage, uneven terrain, and chaotic and dynamic environments. To overcome these challenges, the article proposes a panoramic vision-based SLAM method that relies on the collaboration of multiple cameras and a stereo perception system to optimize localization accuracy in off-road environments. The application of this method enabled unmanned ground vehicles (UGVs) to navigate safely and reliably in dynamic and complex off-road environments. Stereo perception is used to improve vehicle motion estimation accuracy and 3D environment reconstruction, allowing for metric scale recovery. The proposed approach offers an effective and reliable solution to the problem of SLAM in off-road environments, with potential for application in a wide range of applications, from autonomous navigation of ground vehicles to mapping natural environments.

In [14], the authors present a new approach to actionable spatial perception using 3D Dynamic Scene Graphs. These graphs allow for characterizing entities in the scene and their relationships, including actionable information for planning and decision-making. The main contribution of the study is the Automatic and Integrated Spatial Perception (SPIN), which constructs a DSG from visual-inertial data. The study also describes algorithms to obtain hierarchical representations of indoor environments and their connections, as well as demonstrating the proposed spatial perception engine in a photo-realistic Unity-based simulator. This method can have a significant impact on various robotics applications, such as planning and decision-making, human-robot interaction, long-term autonomy, and scene prediction. The application of object and human detection techniques, pose estimation, and robust node inference in crowded scenes make this method even more promising for advancing robotics.

In [12], an innovative and promising approach is presented to solve the problem of simultaneous localization and mapping (SLAM) in autonomous robotics. Using derivative-free bio-inspired techniques, the research focuses on scan matching, which is a crucial step for the success of SLAM. Three swarm intelligence optimization methods were investigated: particle swarm optimization, artificial bee colony, and firefly algorithm. The proposed strategy is divided into two main stages, with the aim of reducing scan alignment errors, and uses a posture graph-based approach to maintain estimation consistency. This work was one of the main sources of inspiration for the development of the Controlled Filter with Active Perception method, which will be presented in this article. The main difference between the works is the use of active perception in the new method, which can lead to significant improvements in the accuracy and efficiency of SLAM in autonomous robotics.

3   Controlled Filter

The alignment process compares two scans, one that will be aligned and another that serves as a reference. The goal is to find a pose (x, y, ϕ) that minimizes the mean squared error between the two scans, where x is the robot's horizontal position, y is the robot's vertical position, and ϕ is the robot's angular orientation. The Controlled Filter (CF) updates one parameter at a time, making the process more efficient. For example, if the algorithm has to analyze 50 particles to find the best pose, approximately 125,000 objective function evaluations would be required. However, if the analysis is done separately for each degree of freedom (x, y, ϕ), only 150 objective function evaluations are needed per cycle. The results presented later show that the CF converges in few cycles, and using the adopted strategy, it would take more than 800 cycles to execute the objective function 125,000 times. This illustrates the higher efficiency of the CF compared to other approaches.

The CF consists of five stages: initialization, ϕ adjustment, x adjustment, y adjustment, and stopping criterion. Algorithm 1 presents the complete functioning of the filter. The CF algorithm has some input parameters, such as the bestPose, which is the pose believed to have good alignment; the currentScan, which is the measurements captured by the robot in the current pose; and the referenceScan, which is the measurements captured by the robot in the previous pose.

Algorithm 1. Controlled Filter

Require: bestPose, currentScan, referenceScan
  controlPose $\leftarrow$ bestPose
  standardDeviation $\leftarrow$ 0.1
  sampleSize $\leftarrow$ 100
  maxIterations $\leftarrow$ 100
  maxStagnation $\leftarrow$ 3
  stagnation $\leftarrow$ 0
  for $k \leftarrow 1$ **to** $maxIterations$ **do**
    sΦ, sX, sY $\leftarrow$ **Initialization**(bestPose, standardDeviation, sampleSize)
    bestPose $\leftarrow$ **AdjustΦ**(sΦ, bestPose, currentScan, referenceScan)
    bestPose $\leftarrow$ **AdjustX**(sX, bestPose, currentScan, referenceScan)
    bestPose $\leftarrow$ **AdjustY**(sY, bestPose, currentScan, referenceScan)
    finish, stagnation, controlPose $\leftarrow$ **stopCriterion**(controlPose, bestPose, stagnation, maxStagnation)
    if $finish = Yes$ **then**
      k $\leftarrow$ maxIterations   ▷ Finish
    end if
  end for
  return bestPose

3.1   Initialization

In this stage, the definition of the pose, believed to have a good alignment (bestPose), is performed, which can be the reference pose or a pose calculated from odometry in the first alignment cycle. After this definition, a Gaussian distribution is performed around the bestPose, considering the three degrees of freedom of the pose (x, y, ϕ). The Algorithm 2 illustrates the initialization step, which has three input parameters: the bestPose, which is the initial pose; the standardDeviation, which controls the spread of the Gaussian distribution of samples; and the sampleSize, which is the number of poses generated by the Gaussian distribution and used by the CF.

Algorithm 2. Initialization

Require: bestPose, standardDeviation, sampleSize
   sΦ ← **gaussianDistribution**(bestPose[ϕ], standardDeviation, sampleSize)   ▷
   Equation 1
   sX ← **gaussianDistribution**(bestPose[x], standardDeviation, sampleSize)
   sY ← **gaussianDistribution**(bestPose[y], standardDeviation, sampleSize)
   return sΦ, sX, sY

Figure 1 shows the initial data structure, where the blue points represent the reference scan and the red points represent the current scan. In Fig. 2, we present the initial pose distribution, where the red arrow represents the bestPose, and the black arrows represent the poses generated from a Gaussian distribution, where σ and μ are real values greater than zero, with σ being the mean of the distribution (bestPose) and μ being the standard deviation, according to the Eq. 1:

$$\frac{1}{\sqrt{2\pi\sigma^2}} e^{-\frac{(x-\mu)^2}{2\sigma^2}}. \tag{1}$$

3.2   Coordinate Adjustment

To find the best ϕ, it is necessary to keep the other parameters fixed (bestPose[x] and bestPose[y]). Then, for each ϕ, a new scan and evaluation with the objective function are performed. The objective function used is the mean squared error between the reference scan and the new scan, defined by Eq. 2:

$$\frac{1}{n} \sum_{i=1}^{n} (\hat{y}_i - y_i)^2. \tag{2}$$

After obtaining the best result, the bestPose[ϕ] is updated and we move on to the next step. To update the value of X, it is necessary to keep the other parameters fixed (bestPose[y] and bestPose[ϕ]). Then, for each value of X, the

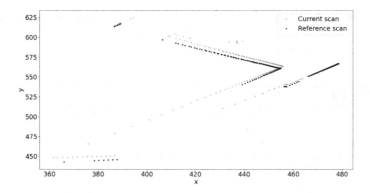

Fig. 1. Data Structure in the Initialization Step.

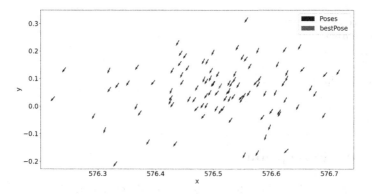

Fig. 2. Initial distribution of poses.

scan is recalculated and an evaluation with the objective function is performed. After obtaining the best result, the bestPose[x] is updated and we move on to the next step. To update the value of Y, it is necessary to keep the other parameters fixed (bestPose[x] and bestPose[ϕ]). Then, for each value of Y, the scan is recalculated and an evaluation with the objective function is performed. After obtaining the best result, the bestPose[y] is updated and we move on to the next step.

3.3 Stop Criterion

This step controls the moment of termination of the CF alignment process by checking whether there was any update in the best pose. If there was an update, the process returns to the first initialization step. If there was no update, the stagnation counter is incremented. Then, it is verified whether the maximum number of stagnation has been reached. If it has not been reached yet, the process returns to the initialization step, otherwise, the process is finished. Algorithm 3 describes the functioning of the stopping criterion and has four input parameters: controlPose, bestPose, stagnation, and maxStagnationNumber. It returns the finalize parameter (Yes or No) and updates the stagnation counter and the controlPose parameter.

Algorithm 3. stopCriterion

Require: controlPose, bestPose, stagnation, maxStagnationNumber
  if $controlPose = bestPose$ **then**
    stagnation ← stagnation + 1
    if $stagnation > maxStagnationNumber$ **then**
      finish ← Yes
    else
      finish ← No
    end if
  else
    controlPose ← bestPose
    stagnation ← 0
    finish ← No
  end if
  return finish, stagnation, controlPose

---

4 Active Perception

Localization, as well as the different alignment processes, are common processes in our daily lives, as mentioned in the introduction of this work. We localize ourselves all the time, whether we are going to work, going from the bedroom to the bathroom, or walking around a mall. To locate ourselves, we use two things: our perception of the space around us - usually from our vision, but it can also be from other senses such as touch, hearing, or even smell - and a mental map that we build, if it is a new location, or a map that is already in our memory [15].

The active perception developed in this work is inspired by our perception when we locate ourselves. The robot, when navigating in an unknown environment, uses the map it has already built to locate itself. With this, the alignment processes of scan matching and loop closure are combined. By aligning the current pose scan to the existing map, the process solves the problem of error accumulation common in traditional alignment processes [2,10] and simultaneously identifies previously visited locations. SLAM can adopt different strategies, such as not adding new readings in already mapped areas, avoiding the inclusion of noise in the map.

SLAM follows the same methodology presented in Sect. 3, but instead of using the *MeanSquaredError* objective function, it uses the new *ActivePerception* function. This function applies a scale of punishments to determine the alignment quality, presented in Fig. 3, which ranges from 100% to 6.25%. The *ActivePerception* function evaluates each point in the scan, and for each empty point within its neighborhood, increments a punishment according to the scale of punishments. Generally, a scan point that is far away from any occupied position receives a maximum punishment, while an occupied point does not receive any punishment.

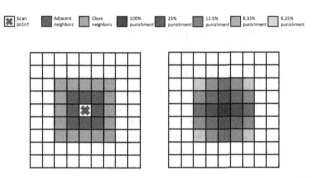

Fig. 3. Representation of the neighborhood of a scan point (on the left) and its respective penalty scale (on the right).

The function *ActivePerception* is presented in Algorithm 4. This function will be used as the objective function for the scan alignment processes performed by the Controlled Filter. As input parameters, the function receives the *adjustedPose*, which represents the pose to be evaluated, the current scan, and the map. It is worth noting that in the first SLAM cycle there is no previous map, therefore, alignment is not required. In this scenario, the map is built based on the first scan performed by the robot. From this point on, the alignment is performed normally, using the map built during previous scans.

The first process performed by the function is the conversion of the scan into coordinates. The scan is a representation of obstacle distances relative to the robot, and this representation needs to be converted to a coordinate representation, compatible with the map, in order to perform an analysis. The *adjustedPose* is defined as $P = (x_p, y_p, \phi_p)$, the coordinate as $c_i = [x_i, y_i]$, where x and y represent a position on the map, and the scan as $V = [v_1, v_2...v_i]$, where v_i is defined as $v_i = (d_i, \theta_i)$, with d representing the distance and θ the measurement angle. The function *scanToCoordinates* is defined by Eq. 3:

$$
c_i = \begin{bmatrix} x_i \\ y_i \end{bmatrix} = \begin{bmatrix} x_p + d_i \cos(\phi_p + \theta_i) \\ y_p + d_i \sin(\phi_p + \theta_i) \end{bmatrix}. \tag{3}
$$

After converting the scan into coordinates, a point-by-point check is performed. For this, the *checkPoint* function is used, analyzing a specific point on

Algorithm 4. ActivePerception

Require: adjustedPose, currentScan, map

  coordinates ← **scanToCoordinates**(adjustedPose, currentScan)

  error ← 0

  penalty ← 4

  numberOfPenalties ← 0

  for *point* **in** *coordinates* **do**

    occupiedPoint ← **checkPoint**(point, map)   ▷ Equation 3

    if *occupiedPoint* = *Yes* **then**

      continue   ▷ Move to next point

    else

      error ← error + penalty

      numberOfPenalties ← numberOfPenalties + 1

      for *neighborX* ← −2 to 2 **do**

        for *neighborY* ← −2 to 2 **do**

          neighbor ← $(point[x] + neighborX, point[y] + neighborY)$

          occupiedNeighbor ← **checkPoint**(neighbor, map)

          if *occupiedNeighbor* = *Yes* **then**

            neighborDistance ← $|neighborX| + |neighborY|$

            error ← error + $\frac{penalty}{4} \frac{1}{neighborDistance}$

          end if

        end for

      end for

    end if

  end for

  return error/numberOfPenalties

---

the map and returning *Yes* if the point is occupied or *No* if the point is empty. The first check occurs at the point being analyzed. If the coordinate of the point is occupied, the process moves on to the next point without incrementing any penalty. Otherwise, a 100% penalty is incremented, and the analysis of all neighbors is initiated. For each unoccupied neighbor coordinate, a penalty is incremented according to the penalty scale presented in Fig. 3.

An example of the *ActivePerception* function's operation in the scan alignment process is presented in Fig. 4. Initially, a poor alignment is presented, as shown in the first figure. This alignment has several penalty points, as can be seen in the second figure. A better alignment is presented the third figure, with consequently fewer penalty points, as shown in the last figure. The goal of the alignment process is to minimize penalty points, which only occurs with an efficient alignment of the current scan to the map.

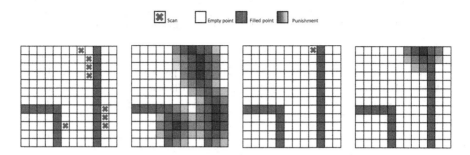

Fig. 4. Scan alignment using *ActivePerception*.

5   Performance Results

In this section, we present the implementation details of the proposed method in this work, Controlled Filter with Active Perception (CFAP). Initially, we conducted an evaluation of the filter, comparing it with a well-established search optimization method. Then, we evaluated the performance of CFAP, aiming to show the results obtained in benchmarking tests and prove its effectiveness. For this, we compared the results with other works that used the same benchmarking tests. The implementation was performed in Python, using the Pandas library for data analysis and conversion, and the PyGame library to create simulation environments. The simulations were executed on a computer equipped with an Intel Core i7-10750H processor and 8 GB of RAM memory.

5.1   Filter Performance Evaluation

The CF is a new method of search optimization, and to justify its use, we performed a comparison with another already established optimization method that has been demonstrating good results, the Particle Swarm Optimization (PSO) [1,7,11]. We compared the results of the CF with the results of the PSO, directing the analysis towards the quality of the alignment. For this, we adjusted the parameters of the CF and PSO so that the convergence time was similar. The dataset used for evaluation was the MIT CSAIL (http://www.ipb.uni-bonn.de/datasets/). Table 1 present the configuration parameters for CF and PSO, respectively. Figure 5 shows the mean squared error of 100 consecutive alignments of CF and PSO, with statistical data in Table 2. Figure 6 shows the map generated by CF and PSO, respectively, on the left and right.

Based on the presented results, the use of the new optimization search method is justified. In relation to this data sample, the CF proved to be more efficient, converging with a lower mean squared error in all alignments. In addition, the CF showed significantly lower variance and standard deviation, which represents greater stability and consistency in the results obtained.

As discussed earlier, the Controlled Filter performs scan alignment in specific degrees of freedom adjustment steps, following a predetermined order, such as

Table 1. CF (left) and PSO (right) configuration parameters.

Parameter	Value	Parameter	Value
Number of samples	100	Number of particles	100
Standard Deviation	0.1	Inertia coefficient	0.8
Maximum Stagnation	3	Cognitive/Social coefficient	1.1
Maximum Cycles	100	Maximum stagnation	10
		Maximum number of iterations	1000

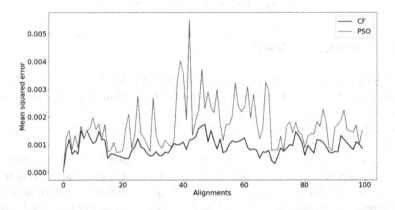

Fig. 5. Mean squared error of 100 consecutive alignments of CF and PSO.

Table 2. Statistical data of the mean squared error of 100 consecutive alignments of CF and PSO

	Mean	Variance	Standard Deviation	Maximum	Minimum
CF	0.002973	9.312295e−07	0.000965	0.005493	1.023563e−04
PSO	0.005394	7.130803e−06	0.002670	0.017439	1.845952e−04

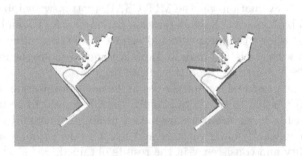

Fig. 6. Map generated by the CF (on the left) and by the PSO (on the right).

adjustment in ϕ, followed by adjustment in x and lastly in y. To verify if the adjustment order impacts the final results, it is necessary to evaluate all possible order variations. For this, an experiment was performed where only the adjustment order was varied, keeping all other simulation parameters constant, such as the scan sample, the objective function ($MeanSquaredError$), and the Controlled Filter settings. 100 consecutive scans of the MIT CSAIL dataset (http:// www.ipb.uni-bonn.de/datasets/) were used for evaluation. Table 1 presents the configuration parameters of the CF, while Fig. 7 presents the results of the different possible adjustment orders in Boxplot format, defining $adjustmentOrder = [(\phi, x, y), (y, \phi, x), (x, y, \phi), (\phi, y, x), (x, \phi, y), (y, x, \phi)]$. Table 3 presents the simulation results.

Analyzing the results, it can be concluded that the variation of the adjustment order does not significantly impact the final result of the Controlled Filter. All adjustment orders present similar medians and dispensation, as well as positive symmetry.

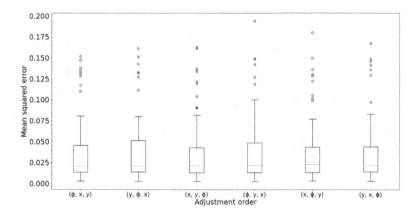

Fig. 7. Boxplots of the mean squared error of 100 consecutive alignments with different adjustment orders.

Table 3. Statistical data of Boxplots from the order of adjustment test

	1^{st}quartile	2^{nd}quartile	3^{rd}quartile	4^{th}quartile	Minimum	Outliers
(x, y, ϕ)	0.0131995	0.021235	0.0431561	0.0817251	0.0026630	9
(x, ϕ, y)	0.0133409	0.022699	0.0436485	0.0769690	0.0034185	9
(y, x, ϕ)	0.0142888	0.021827	0.0438659	0.0830524	0.0034186	7
(y, ϕ, x)	0.0140076	0.020916	0.0514501	0.0799184	0.0028686	7
(ϕ, x, y)	0.0137411	0.020817	0.0458010	0.0804070	0.0029603	8
(ϕ, y, x)	0.0133994	0.021564	0.0488546	0.1001395	0.0028788	6

5.2   CFAP Performance Evaluation

The evaluation methodology adopted was the one proposed by Kümerle in [9]. This methodology is widely applied in other works that propose solutions for SLAM, and therefore, using it makes it possible to compare the performance of the proposed method with other works in a standardized way, facilitating its evaluation. It is important to emphasize that Kümerle's methodology not only evaluates the final result of the maps but also the process of creating them, defining a model to compare the variation between consecutive poses. To evaluate accuracy, two parameters are defined: absolute translational error and absolute rotational error. The absolute translational error is defined by Eq. 4:

$$\lambda_{tranlacional} = \frac{1}{N} \sum_{i,j}^{N} |T(\delta_{i,j} - \delta_{i,i}^*)|, \tag{4}$$

where N is the total number of considered poses; $\delta_{i,j}$ is the variation between poses, defined by Eq. 5:

$$\delta_{i,j} = \begin{bmatrix} \Delta_x \\ \Delta_y \\ \Delta_\phi \end{bmatrix} = \begin{bmatrix} (x_i - x_j) \cos \phi_j + (y_i - y_j) \sin \phi_j \\ -(x_i - x_j) \sin \phi_j + (y_i - y_j) \cos \phi_j \\ \phi_i - \phi_j \end{bmatrix}, \tag{5}$$

where $\delta_{i,j}^*$ is the variation between poses of the reference set; and $T(.)$ separates the translational component (x, y) of the relative pose and calculates the resultant using the Pythagorean theorem. The absolute rotational error, where $R(.)$ separates the rotational component (ϕ) of the relative pose, is defined by Eq. 6:

$$\lambda_{rotacional} = \frac{1}{N} \sum_{i,j}^{N} |R(\delta_{i,j} - \delta_{i,i}^*)|. \tag{6}$$

With the aim of enabling comparison of the results obtained by CFAP with other works and establishing a standardized evaluation method, we chose to use public datasets available at http://www.ipb.uni-bonn.de/datasets/. In Fig. 8, it is possible to visualize the grid maps and robot trajectories corresponding to the datasets INTEL, MIT CSAIL, ACES3, FREIBURG BLDG 79 and MIT KILLIAN COURT, arranged from top to bottom, respectively.

The CFAP demonstrated success in all benchmarking tests performed, proving its ability to deal with various data structures, such as different numbers of Lidar readings, variations in measurement accuracy, and distinct topologies. This diversity is presented in the datasets used in the tests, providing notoriety to the test. The method showed a significant improvement in the generated map when compared to maps generated only with odometry. However, difficulties were identified in datasets with very long corridors and distant loop closures, due to the Active Perception methodology itself. In the case of long corridors, perception is greatly influenced by the robot's current position, which can lead to stagnation, causing the problem of corridor shortening. Regarding distant loop

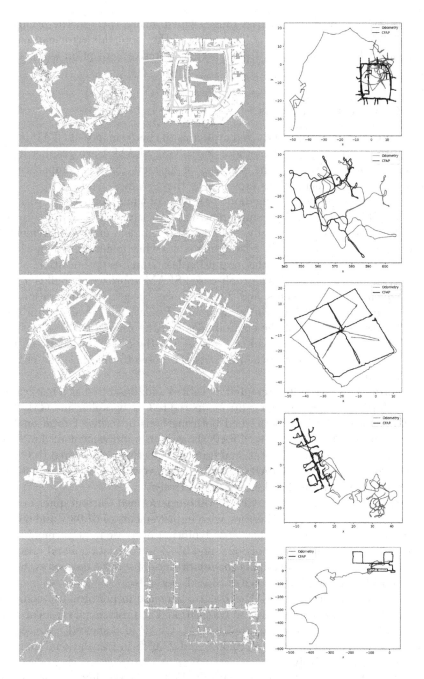

Fig. 8. Grid map and robot trajectory (pink line) obtained using only odometry (left), and using CFAP (center) and comparison of trajectories (right), simulations related to the datasets: INTEL, MIT CSAIL, ACES3, FREIBURG BLDG 79 and MIT KILLIAN COURT, from the first row to the last row, respectively. (Color figure online)

closures, perception has a limited range, which means that, in the occurrence of small alignment errors at the beginning of the loop, this error can cause a significantly large disturbance. In this scenario, Active Perception will not have the reach to correct the error.

5.3   Comparative Analysis

The comparative analysis conducted evaluates the performance of CFAP in comparison to two other popular methods for solving SLAM: Cartographer [6] and Graph Mapping (GM) [9]. The selection of datasets for this comparison was based on the recommendations provided by these studies.

Cartographer proposes a methodology for real-time loop closure with high precision. It achieves this by using branching structures and sub-maps to limit scan correspondences. Essentially, the algorithm builds a map by incrementally matching new sensor data with existing map data while maintaining loop closure. The algorithm also optimizes the map using least-squares optimization.

GM, on the other hand, is a graph-based SLAM approach. It builds a graph from sequential measurements, and then optimizes the graph configuration using a mean squared error minimization approach. Essentially, the algorithm uses a graphical representation of the environment and the robot's path, where nodes in the graph represent poses and edges represent the constraints between those poses. The optimization step then adjusts the poses to minimize the errors in the constraints.

According to the results presented in Table 4 and illustrated as a bar graph in Fig. 9, CFAP shows promising results compared to Cartographer and GM. In the INTEL dataset, CFAP outperformed both methods in terms of rotational and translational errors. Specifically, CFAP showed an improvement of 5.67% and 58.27% in translational and rotational errors, respectively, compared to Cartographer. Compared to GM, CFAP showed an improvement of 30.32% and 85.46% in translational and rotational errors, respectively.

In the MIT CSAIL dataset, CFAP still outperformed Cartographer in terms of translational and rotational errors, with improvements of 67.08% and 65.58%, respectively. However, CFAP showed a significant decrease in performance compared to GM, with an increase of 262% and 254% in translational and rotational errors, respectively. This highlights the importance of specific dataset evaluation when considering the performance of SLAM methods.

In the ACES3 dataset, CFAP showed a decrease in performance compared to Cartographer, with an increase in translational and rotational errors of 43.0% and 33.13%, respectively. Compared to GM, CFAP also showed a decrease in performance, with an increase of 30.66% and 25.65% in translational and rotational errors, respectively.

In the FREIBURG BLDG 79 dataset, FCPA showed improvements compared to Cartographer and GM in terms of rotational and translational errors. Specifically, FCPA showed an improvement of 10.61% and 13.01% in translational and rotational errors, respectively, compared to Cartographer. Compared to GM, FCPA showed an improvement of 27.85% and 22.0% in translational and rotational errors, respectively.

Finally, in the MIT KILLIAN COURT dataset, FCPA showed a 49.93% deterioration in absolute translational error compared to Cartographer. However, there was an 8.8% improvement in absolute rotational error compared to Cartographer. Additionally, FCPA showed a 36.62% deterioration in absolute translational error and a 35.8% improvement in absolute rotational error compared to GM. These results suggest that FCPA is a promising method for SLAM and can provide greater accuracy on certain datasets when compared to commonly used methods.

Table 4. Quantitative comparison of error with [6,9]

	CFAP	Cartographer	GM
INTEL			
$\lambda_{tranlacional}$	0.0216 ± 0.0302	0.0229 ± 0.0239	0.031 ± 0.026
$\lambda_{rotacional}$	0.189 ± 1.854	0.453 ± 1.335	1.3 ± 4.7
MIT CSAIL			
$\lambda_{tranlacional}$	0.0105 ± 0.0114	0.0319 ± 0.0363	0.004 ± 0.009
$\lambda_{rotacional}$	0.127 ± 0.255	0.369 ± 0.365	0.05 ± 0.08
ACES3			
$\lambda_{tranlacional}$	0.0658 ± 0.0708	0.0375 ± 0.0426	0.044 ± 0.044
$\lambda_{rotacional}$	0.538 ± 0.365	0.373 ± 0.469	0.4 ± 0.4
FREIBURG B79			
$\lambda_{tranlacional}$	0.0404 ± 0.0258	0.0452 ± 0.0354	0.056 ± 0.042
$\lambda_{rotacional}$	0.468 ± 0.571	0.538 ± 0.718	0.6 ± 0.6
MIT K. COURT			
$\lambda_{tranlacional}$	0.0789 ± 0.0651	0.0395 ± 0.0488	0.050 ± 0.056
$\lambda_{rotacional}$	0.321 ± 0.278	0.352 ± 0.353	0.5 ± 0.5

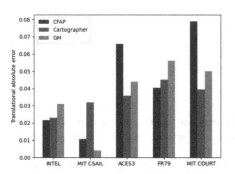 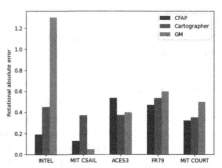

Fig. 9. Comparison graphs of absolute translational error (on the left) and absolute rotational error (on the right).

6   Conclusion

This work presented a new approach to the problem of Simultaneous Localization and Mapping (SLAM) based on scan alignment and loop closure, which are the fundamental pillars of SLAM. The systematic alignment methodology carried out by humans inspired the creation of a new scan alignment method, called Controlled Filter (CF). This method uses a Gaussian distribution to estimate possible poses and performs the scan alignment process in stages. Additionally, an active perception scan alignment was developed that combines the two pillars of SLAM into a single process.

To evaluate the proposed method, the methodology proposed by Kümerle was used, which evaluates both the final results of the maps and the process of creating them. Public data sets were used to allow for comparison of CFAP results with other works and a standardized evaluation method. The CFAP was successful in all benchmarking tests performed, but encountered difficulties in data sets with very long corridors and distant loop closures, due to the active perception methodology itself.

A comparative analysis was carried out with other SLAM methods, such as Cartographer and Graph Mapping, and CFAP obtained better results on average than the others. However, we acknowledge that there is room for improvement in CFAP, especially regarding the difficulties faced in long corridors and distant loop closures. In this sense, future work could explore the development of an auxiliary system to CFAP that detects this type of topology using perception itself, allowing for the adoption of approaches to improve the performance and accuracy of the method.

In summary, this work presented promising results and opened the way for future studies in the field of SLAM, contributing to the development of new methods and techniques that can be applied in various areas, such as robotics, mapping, and autonomous navigation.

Acknowledgments. This work is supported by the Coordenação de Aperfeiçoamento de Pessoal de Nível Superior (CAPES - Brazil, https://www.gov.br/capes), Conselho Nacional de Desenvolvimento Científico e Tecnológico (CNPq - Brazil, https://www.gov.br/cnpq) and by Fundação Carlos Chagas Filho de Amparo à Pesquisa do Estado do Rio de Janeiro (FAPERJ - Brazil, https://www.faperj.br) with grant numbers 201.013/2022, 200.850/2021 and 211.000/2021. We are most grateful for their continuous financial support.

References

1. Amrani, R., et al.: Investigation of structural and electrical properties of ITO thin films and correlation to optical parameters extracted using novel method based on PSO algorithm. Bull. Mater. Sci. **46**(1), 8 (2023)
2. Chen, L.H., Peng, C.C.: A robust 2D-SLAM technology with environmental variation adaptability. IEEE Sens. J. **19**(23), 11475–11491 (2019)
3. Davison, A.J., Murray, D.W.: Simultaneous localization and map-building using active vision. IEEE Trans. Pattern Anal. Mach. Intell. **24**(7), 865–880 (2002)

4. Deng, X., Zhang, Z., Sintov, A., Huang, J., Bretl, T.: Feature-constrained active visual slam for mobile robot navigation. In: 2018 IEEE International Conference on Robotics and Automation (ICRA), pp. 7233–7238. IEEE (2018)
5. Durrant-Whyte, H., Bailey, T.: Simultaneous localization and mapping: part I. IEEE Robot. Autom. Mag. **13**(2), 99–110 (2006)
6. Hess, W., Kohler, D., Rapp, H., Andor, D.: Real-time loop closure in 2D LiDAR SLAM. In: 2016 IEEE International Conference on Robotics and Automation (ICRA), pp. 1271–1278. IEEE (2016)
7. Kennedy, J., Eberhart, R.: Particle swarm optimization. In: Proceedings of ICNN 1995-International Conference on Neural Networks, vol. 4, pp. 1942–1948. IEEE (1995)
8. Kim, A., Eustice, R.M.: Perception-driven navigation: active visual slam for robotic area coverage. In: 2013 IEEE International Conference on Robotics and Automation, pp. 3196–3203. IEEE (2013)
9. Kümmerle, R., et al.: On measuring the accuracy of slam algorithms. Auton. Robot. **27**, 387–407 (2009)
10. Mo, J., Islam, M.J., Sattar, J.: Fast direct stereo visual SLAM. IEEE Robot. Autom. Lett. **7**(2), 778–785 (2021)
11. Moazen, H., Molaei, S., Farzinvash, L., Sabaei, M.: PSO-ELPM: PSO with elite learning, enhanced parameter updating, and exponential mutation operator. Inf. Sci. **628**, 70–91 (2023)
12. Nedjah, N., de Oliveira, P.J.A., et al.: Simultaneous localization and mapping using swarm intelligence based methods. Expert Syst. Appl. **159**, 113547 (2020)
13. Ristic, B., Arulampalam, S., Gordon, N.: Beyond the Kalman Filter: Particle Filters for Tracking Applications. Artech House (2003)
14. Rosinol, A., Gupta, A., Abate, M., Shi, J., Carlone, L.: 3D dynamic scene graphs: actionable spatial perception with places, objects, and humans. arXiv preprint arXiv:2002.06289 (2020)
15. Thornton, I.M., Pinto, J., Shiffrar, M.: The visual perception of human locomotion. Cogn. Neuropsychol. **15**(6–8), 535–552 (1998)
16. Van de Vegte, J.: Feedback Control Systems. Prentice-Hall, Inc. (1994)
17. Yang, Y., Tang, D., Wang, D., Song, W., Wang, J., Fu, M.: Multi-camera visual slam for off-road navigation. Robot. Auton. Syst. **128**, 103505 (2020)
18. Zhao, Y., Xiong, Z., Zhou, S., Wang, J., Zhang, L., Campoy, P.: Perception-aware planning for active SLAM in dynamic environments. Remote Sens. **14**(11), 2584 (2022)

Choices and Actions for Human Scale Cities: Decision Support Systems (CAHSC DSS 2023)

The National Innovative Program for Housing Quality (PINQuA). Strategies and Indicators for Design Quality

Adolfo F. L. Baratta[ID], Massimo Mariani[ID], and Daniele Mazzoni[✉][ID]

Department of Architecture, Roma Tre University, Rome, Italy
{adolfo.baratta,massimo.mariani}@uniroma3.it,
dan.mazzoni1@stud.uniroma3.it

Abstract. In recent years, the debate on new models of living and experiencing urban spaces has been fuelled by events that have highlighted the fragilities and limitations of the contemporary city, which now appears as a changed reality and which, as a result, must be rethought to find new balances. To respond to the "housing issue" in 2020, an ambitious investment program for the implementation of social housing and urban regeneration interventions throughout the Italian territory was promoted by the Ministry of Infrastructure and Transport (MIT), initiated by the Budget Law 2020, creating a special multi-year fund to support the economic scale of the investments. In the program, called the National Innovative Program for Housing Quality (PINQuA), 159 proposals have been accepted for funding, counting more than 900 redevelopment and new construction interventions, involving 15 thousand housing units for a total funding of 2.8 billion euros. The projects were evaluated by a High Commission through scoring in compliance with seven criteria with the help of a matrix composed of several indicators capable of measuring different project impacts. This paper aims to describe the program content, evaluation process and results achieved by PINQuA.

Keywords: Smart City · PINQuA · PNRR · Strategies · Indicators

1 Introduction

In recent years, there has been a gradual increase in the number of households living in absolute poverty in Italy: the incidence has risen from 2.5% in 2005 to 7.5% in 2021, affecting about 5.6 million individuals (ISTAT, 2022). Poverty is a condition closely linked to the economic condition in which families live, consequently it is also connected with the quality of housing condition. On average, the monthly rent of a family in absolute poverty amounts to about 330 €, accounting for 35.9% of total expenses, being significantly higher than the one of families not in state of poverty (1) (ISTAT, 2022). The housing issue is also conditioned by other dimensions that define discomfort (2) and which concern, in addition to the level of decay, the presence of humidity and poor lighting in buildings, elements that combine to affect the healthiness of housing. A further issue related to housing is the widespread condition of overcrowding. In fact,

O. Gervasi et al. (Eds.): ICCSA 2023 Workshops, LNCS 14104, pp. 635–646, 2023.
https://doi.org/10.1007/978-3-031-37105-9_42

in Italy, 28% of the population lives in densely inhabited houses, a figure that is far behind the European average (17%). It is then necessary to point out the decline in public spending on housing hardship support in Italy, which is higher than the average in other European countries. To respond to the growing difficulties developed by housing hardship, the Budget Law 2020 launched the National Innovative Program for Housing Quality (PINQuA), promoted by the Ministry of Infrastructure and Transport (MIT), with the creation of a special multi-year fund to support investment in the sector (MIMS, 2022). The PINQuA, established under Paragraph 437 of Article 1 of Law No. 160 of Dec. 27, 2019, and regulated under I.D. No. 395 of Sept. 16, 2020, is focused on overcoming the monofunctional features typical of 20th century metropolises, and aims to create a new vision of a more fluid, connected and inclusive city. The Program aims to pursue the urban model of the already known smart cities through processes of urban regeneration and reduction of housing and social distress, favoring degraded portions of the territory and revitalizing the suburbs. Urban regeneration refers to all transformation action that affect the structure and use of the city, implying not only spatial and physical changes but also economic, social cultural and creative changes (Galdini, 2008). In Italy, urban regeneration represents in many ways the latest step in a legislative and programmatic path (Mariani, 2022), necessitating a radical transformation in the daily use of spaces (Bernardoni, 2021); in this regard, the Program defines a form of living that aims to move away from the systematic pattern of housing understood as a place to dwell, favoring a model of integrated social living aimed at fostering new networks and transversal ties, redesigning not only housing, but also the spaces available to housing and, therefore, to the city. In line with this approach, PINQuA aims not only to reduce housing and settlement discomfort in the strict sense, but also to positively affect the quality of life of the population through solutions that show themselves durable over time, encouraging the use of innovative models and tools of management, social inclusion, cultural enrichment and quality of artifacts, and support for urban welfare (MIMS, 2022).

2   Contents and Structure of the PINQuA Call for Proposals

PINQuA follows a multilevel governance approach and involves public administrations, which are called upon to plan and submit proposals with the aim of providing concrete responses to the needs of their communities and territories. The proposing entities are Regions, Metropolitan Cities, Provincial Capitals, and Municipalities with more than 60,000 inhabitants. The projects submitted followed the five lines of action provided by the Program referring to: redevelopment and reorganization of the heritage intended for social housing, with an eye to the re-functionalization of areas, spaces and public and private properties including through the regeneration of the urban and socioeconomic fabric and temporary use (MIMS, 2022). One of the main lines of action of the Program concerns the regeneration of areas, spaces and properties that have already been built, to align with the principle of zero land consumption, minimizing the artificialization of urban areas (Ministry of Environment and Energy Security, 2022) also a cornerstone of the Plan for Ecological Transition (3). Regeneration of the socioeconomic fabric, cultural enrichment, improvement of social cohesion, and quality of artifacts, places, and citizens' lives must be durable solutions that all interventions aim to follow, with a view to innovation and sustainability (United Nations, 2015).

The submission of proposals identified two types of interventions i.e., ordinary projects and pilot projects with high strategic impact. The difference lies in the different scale and relevance of the field of intervention: interventions envisaged as pilot projects, in fact, must assume a high strategic impact on the national territory, while ordinary projects must identify a more local scope of intervention, with reference to peripheral areas or areas that present situations of housing and socioeconomic distress and lack adequate urban-local equipment (MIMS, 2022). The size gap between the areas of intervention has a direct reflection on the amounts of funding; ordinary projects could be funded for a maximum of 15 million euros, whereas pilot projects could be up to 100 million euros. Another important difference between the types of proposals concerned the definition of the project to be submitted: while for ordinary projects a level comparable to a Technical and Economic Feasibility Project (PFTE) was sufficient (4), for high performance pilot projects the degree of definition required was the final project.

In addition to the required graphical drawings and administrative and financial documents, a special template containing project responses to physical and impact indicators was required at the proposal submission stage. In fact, in addition to the identification of the project's main data, the values of the indicators were identified so as to bring a summary judgment of the project's overall performance. In total, the number of indicators is 30, divided into 6 groups, defined as in Table 1 below:

Table 1. Physical and impact indicators found in the "PINQuA Sheets".

Indicators	Description
Environmental impact indicators	Energy sustainability, energy efficiency, environmental remediation, material resource consumption and regional resource use
Social impact indicator	Public areas, public buildings, security for garrison, security for inclusiveness, and senior citizen services
Cultural impact indicators	Restoration and enhancement of captive properties, basic educational services, higher educational services, basic entertainment services or facilities, and cultural services or facilities
Urban-territorial impact indicators	Open areas, permeable surfaces, pedestrian and bicycle paths and public mobility
Economic-financial impact indicators	Private funding, employment gains from the project, parametric cost of outdoor areas, parametric cost of the built environment. chrono-economic indicator i.e., ratio of time to cost
Technological impact indicators	Innovative tools and methods, innovative actions and processes, innovative management models, and reversibility of the intervention or technical elements

The introduction of PINQuA within the PNRR's planned investments led to a significant increase in the funds dedicated to the Program. The latter initially foresaw resources of 853.81 million euros, guaranteeing the funding of at least one proposal for each Region to which the proposing party belongs (MIMS, 2022), allocating at least 34% of the resources to interventions from areas in the South (5). Thanks to the inclusion in Mission 5, Component 2 of the PNRR (6), an additional 2.8 billion allocated to the Program was made available, increasing the number of nationally funded works and bringing the resources for the South Italy to 40%.

3   The Set as a Tool for Selection and Evaluation of Proposals

The evaluation process of the proposals submitted in the first phase of the Program was carried out by the High Commission (7). Indicators are used in a wide variety of evaluation applications (Martini, 2002) and, in this case, were useful in the construction of the ranking of proposals. Each set of impact indicators corresponds to an evaluation criterion with which, in turn, a maximum score is associated, as stipulated in the Call for Proposals. An exception to this are the economic-financial impact indicators, which are divided between two different criteria (Table 2). Within each criterion, the indicators take on different specific weights, and the sum of the score obtained in each criterion determines the proposal's final score, for a maximum of 100 points.

The score associated with each criterion is the result of the sum of the scores obtained in the individual indicators by linear interpolation: the value obtained for each indicator was normalized against the maximum observed value and then weighted against the predetermined weights. For dichotomous indicators (Yes/No), on the other hand, the relevant weight was assigned in case of presence and a null score in case of absence of the specific characteristic, operating no normalization (MIMS, 2022).

In this way, a theoretical matrix composed of the 30 indicators is generated for the total number of proposals capable of assessing the multiple performance aspects of the interventions (Baratta et al., 2021), from which the final ranking of the proposals emerged. This method made it possible to carry out an evaluation by assigning scores to the proposals consistent with the seven criteria previously identified in Article 8, paragraph 1 of Ministerial Decree 395/2020.

Table 2. Impact of criteria on the evaluation of proposals.

Score (max)	Criterion	Indicators
15 points	Criterion A	Environmental impact indicators
25 points	Criterion B	Social impact indicators
10 points	Criterion C	Cultural impact indicators
15 points	Criterion D	Urban-territorial impact indicators
15 points	Criterion E	Economic-financial impact indicators
10 punti	Criterion F	
10 points	Criterion G	Technological impact indicators

The assessment made for each group of indicators considers the quality of the proposal and consistency with the purposes envisioned by the PINQuA.

Going into the details of each criterion, the following is specified. For the judgment on criterion A (Table 3), the ability to develop responses to the needs and requirements expressed, the presence of innovative and green economy aspects, the compliance with the Minimum Environmental Criteria (CAM) and the ability to aggregate subjects in an associated form in the key of legality of self-consolidated realities (MIMS, 2022) were evaluated with a maximum weight of 3 units per indicator.

Table 3. P Weight given to environmental impact indicators.

Indicator	Unit of measurement	Attributed weight (max)
Energy Sustainability	0–5	3
Energy efficiency	0–5	3
Environmental remediation	m^2	3
Reduction of material resource consumption	m^3/m^3	3
Regional resource use	m^3/m^3	3

Criterion B consists of the social impact indicators (Table 4), designed to measure the extent of works involving public housing properties, favouring interventions that fit into the most critical contexts of greatest housing tension (Baratta et al. 2017). In terms of social mixitè and diversification of housing supply, the social impact indicators are based on an additional benchmark, namely, on the level of integration both with the context and with interventions related to social housing properties, with reference to the implementation of specific regional policies. As in Criterion A, the weight given to these indicators (Table 4) is a maximum of 3 points.

Table 4. Weight given to social impact indicators.

Indicator	Unit of measurement	Attributed weight (max)
Public areas	m^2/m^2	3
Public buildings	m^2/m^2	3
Security by garrison	m^2/m^2	3
Senior citizen services	m^2/m^2	3
Security by inclusiveness	n. assoc./m^2	3

Criterion C was evaluated on the responsiveness of the cultural impact indicators (MIMS, 2022) designed to measure the work by its capacity to enhance cultural, environmental and landscape assets. This is by rehabilitation and reuse of such assets in the area are cardinal principles of the Program. Criterion C, composed of 5 indicators to which a maximum weight of 2 points is given, totals a maximum score of 10 points (Table 5).

Table 5. Weight given to cultural impact indicators.

Indicator	Unit of measurement	Attributed weight (max)
Asset recovery and enhancement	Yes/No	2
Basic educational services	m^2/m^2	2
Higher services	m^2/m^2	2
Basic entertainment services or facilities	m^2/m^2	2
Cultural services or facilities	m^2/m^2	2

The evaluation of criterion D was carried out through the urban-territorial impact indicators (Table 6), through which it was possible, in addition, to measure the project's focus with respect to the zero balance of land consumption. These indicators turn out to be related to the type of intervention, favoring interventions of rehabilitation and redevelopment of already urbanized areas, or existing buildings, taking into account the significance of the interventions themselves in terms of seismic safety and energy upgrading, including through their demolition and reconstruction (MIMS, 2022). Criterion D, moreover, considers the quantity and quality of open spaces in the proposals, evaluating the attention that is given in the external works and in the use of sustainable road systems.

Table 6. Weight given to urban-territorial impact indicators.

Indicator	Unit of measurement	Attributed weight (max)
Vacant area	m^2/m^2	3
Green area	m^2/m^2	3
Pedestrian way	m^2/m^2	3
Bicycle pathway	m^2/m^2	3
Public mobility	m^2/m^2	2

Criteria E and F (Table 7) were evaluated on the responsiveness of economic-financial indicators. Specifically, the first among them responds to the group of indicators that measure the extent of construction costs (both built and outdoor areas) and the activation of additional economic resources of a private or public nature. The remaining economic-financial indicators, integrating the basis for a development of cost-benefit analysis (Acampa et al. 2022), constitute criterion F, by which the involvement of private operators, including from the third sector, is assessed, with involvement and direct participation of stakeholders also in associative form, especially if they operate in the area of intervention (MIMS, 2022).

Table 7. Weight given to economic and financial impact indicators.

Criterion E		
Indicator	Unit of measurement	Attributed weight (max)
Private financing	€/€	5
Employment indicator	n./m^2	4
Parametric cost of outdoor areas	€/m^2	3
Parametric cost of built	€/m^2	3
Criterion F		
Indicator	Unit of measurement	Attributed weight (max)
Chrono-economic indicator	€/months	7
Number of private and third sector operators involved in the proposal	n.	3

Finally, dichotomous indicators of technological impact were measured for the evaluation of criterion G (Table 8) by examining whether BIM methodology, as well as innovative measures and models of management, social support and inclusion, urban welfare, and proposal activation (MIMS, 2022) were used in proposal writing.

Table 8. Weight given to technology impact indicators.

Indicator	Unit of measurement	Attributed weight (max)
Innovative tools and methods	Yes/No	2
Inclusive actions and processes	Yes/No	2
Innovative products and solutions	Yes/No	3
Innovative management models	Yes/No	3
Reversibility of the intervention or technical elements	Yes/No	1

Following the High Commission's evaluation of the proposals, 93.5% of the requests were considered eligible for funding, an incidence that equates to 271 proposals for a total amount of €4.2 billion: with the resources available under Ministerial Decree No. 383 of 07.10.2021, 159 proposals were actually funded for a total of €2,820,007,520 (Baratta, 2022).

4 A Summary of the Economic Data of the PINQuA Proposals

In addition to the execution of the works, technical expenses for design, verification, validation, construction management and testing are eligible for funding. In this regard, the proposing parties were obliged to submit an economic and financial framework of the works with an attached technical administrative timetable. The composition of the economic framework had to include, in addition to the costs of works and supplies, technical expenses, expenditure related to any purchases of land and expropriations, and other expenses that could not be financed (such as urbanization and management charges). In addition, in sizing the economic resources needed to carry out the intervention, additional financing from other public sources or from the developer's own resources or other private sources could be considered. Additional economic data, mainly related to construction costs, can be transposed through the analysis of the economic-financial impact indicator. This indicator, in fact, makes explicit the parametric costs of construction of building interventions and construction of outdoor areas, which can be identified through the ratio of the total cost to the areas related to them. The following Table 9 summarizes the data of the economic-financial indicator, highlighting the parametric construction data, as well as information on the number of new activities included (services, commercial and other activities) and the estimated time for the realization of the intervention.

Table 9. Detail of economic and financial impact indicator data.

Indicator Description	Description project	Quantity
Private funding indicator	Description funding	Amount €
Overall financing indicator		Amount €
Employment indicator	Description of activities included	Amount no. New activities
Employment indicator (area)		Amount m^2
Indicator of total cost of interventions planned for outdoor areas		Amount €
Indicator surface area of outdoor areas		Amount m^2
Indicator of the parametric cost of outdoor areas		Amount €/m^2
Indicator of the total cost of planned investment in the built environment		Amount €
Indicator surface area of built-up area		Amount m^2
Indicator of the parametric cost of the built		Amount €/m^2
Chrono-economic indicator	Description of estimated time for implementation (months)	Amount €/month
Indicator of private and third sector operators involved in the proposal	Description of operators	Amount no. Operators

Analyzing the distribution of funding across the Italian territory (Fig. 1), the following can be seen:

a. the South was allocated about 1.1 billion euros, or 40.1% of total funding (MIMS, 2022).
b. about 1 billion euros (37.9%) has been allocated to the North.
c. 618 million euros (22%) are earmarked for the Center.

This allocation of funds corresponds to a distribution of interventions (159 proposals), as follows:

a. South and North receive 60 proposals each (equivalent to 37.7% of the works each).
b. the remaining 39 proposals are in the regions of Central Italy, totaling 24.5% of the interventions (MIMS, 2022).

Given the nature of the Program and, consequently, the subjects it was aimed at, the main beneficiaries were municipalities, to which 72% of the investments were allocated, i.e., 114 interventions, of which 98 are ordinary and 6 are pilot projects; the remaining share is attributed to Regions and Metropolitan Cities, totaling 18% and 11%, respectively (MIMS, 2022).

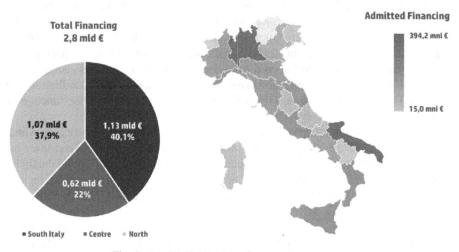

Fig. 1. Spatial distribution of economic resources.

5   Conclusions: A Summary View of the Winning Projects

Some recent regulatory provisions, in particular the so-called Simplification Decree 2021, converted into Law No. 108 of July 29, 2021, provide that, in relation to procedures pertaining to public investments financed, in whole or in part, with the resources provided by the PNRR and the programs co-financed by the European Union Structural Funds, by way of exception to the provisions of paragraphs 1, 1-bis and 1-ter of the Contracts Code, the awarding of design and execution of the related works is also allowed on the basis of the PFTE. The inclusion of the PINQuA within the Missions of the NRP entailed, in addition to the increase in economic resources, a partial revision of the procedure, namely:

- elimination of the second stage of document integration, consistent with the contents of Article 48, paragraph 7, of Decree-Law No. 77 of May 31, 2021, converted into Law No. 108 of July 29, 2021.
- remodulation of the proposal and timetable of the works, consistent with the requirement to conclude the works by January 31, 2026 (Baratta, 2022).

Recalling that one of the objectives of the Program was to favor all those interventions that include actions of recovery, redevelopment, or densification of already urbanized areas, consequently limiting the expansion and use of new land, thus achieving a "zero balance" result (MIMS, 2022), the Program presents only a 2% area of new construction. In fact, the total area of intervention exceeds 14 million square meters, 52% of which is in the southern regions, where only 434,478 square meters are of new construction. Regarding redevelopment interventions, it should be noted that the South is more involved by reaching an important percentage of the existing area to be redeveloped compared to how much is planned nationally (51%) (MIMS, 2022).

With a view to a Low-Density Construction and Urban Regeneration Program, a particular effort on the part of project submitters has been to focus attention on the design of outdoor areas. In fact, nationwide, the area of vegetated open area exceeds 8 million square meters, accounting for 63% of the total open area of interventions. In this, too, the area of the Southland directs the highest percentage of area, 56%, compared to 68% of the total uncovered area. Public spaces cover an area of nearly 10 million square meters (MIMS, 2022) of which, 84% is for outdoor public areas with the function of socialization.

A total of 1.3 million square meters are allocated to the residential area, on which more than 16 thousand housing units are involved, both for redevelopment and new construction, having an average size of 81 square meters per housing unit. Taking the figure back to the national level, 39.8% of these housing units are planned in northern regions (about 6,600 units), 33.2% (5,500 units) in southern regions and 27% (4,500 units) in central Italian regions. MIMS has estimated, based on data provided by Federcasa-Nomisma (8), that the average monthly savings per dwelling in terms of rent, compared to free market prices, amounts to about 479 euros per household (estimate made based on the average size of housing equal to 81 square meters). Still in residential terms, another feature included in the Program's rewarding criteria is the energy efficiency of existing buildings. When considering all interventions eligible for funding, an average energy class advance of about 4 classes was estimated, corresponding to an improvement in annual energy performance of 38% (MIMS, 2022). In this regard, in addition to energy efficiency interventions, many of the projects also include the installation of energy systems from renewable sources in order to ensure an adequate level of energy autonomy of buildings and to help increase the use of renewable sources in cities. Specifically, 60% of interventions include the installation of systems involving at least two renewable sources: 153 interventions involve solar, 59 hydro, 44 geothermal, 24 wind, and 23 biomasses (MIMS, 2022).

Finally, in the Program's view of intervening at the social level in cities, a share of 756,000 square meters is allocated for educational activities involving both childhood and secondary or university education, while about 788,000 square meters is allocated for cultural activities, such as museums, exhibition spaces, libraries, etc. (MIMS, 2022) and to entertainment activities such as theaters, cinemas, or concert spaces. Figure 2 below shows a summary overview of these areas dedicated to cultural and social enrichment nationwide.

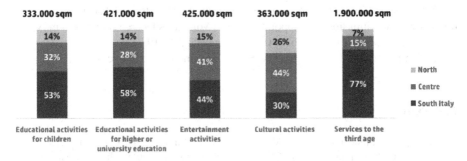

Fig. 2. Surfaces designated for educational and cultural activities.

The ambitious Program aims to intervene throughout the entire national territory, assuming considerable significance, which could have a great impact in transforming the face of the suburbs of many Italian cities (Mariani, 2022) and, by March 2026, Italy has made a commitment to intervene on more than 10,000 housing units and 800,000 square meters of covered and uncovered public spaces (Baratta, 2022).

As the application of PINQuA continued, it was possible to identify certain limitations of the system, both intrinsic and extrinsic in nature. One of the main intrinsic limitations relates to the use of measurement scales articulated in a few steps, which led to an increase in accuracy at the evaluation stage, reaching the fourth significant figure. As the project level advances, a significant difference can be produced between the outcome of the ranking and the performance guaranteed at the preliminary stage, demonstrating an extrinsic limitation that lies in the contingency of the proposed set.

6 Note

(1) The average incidence of rent as a percentage of total spending, which stands at 22.3 percent.

(2) Discomfort studies are a branch of building diagnostics that involves identifying the causes responsible for perceived comfort deficiencies within dwellings (INAIL, 2018).

(3) Plan for Ecological Transition (PTE), approved under Article 57-bis, paragraph 3 et seq. of Legislative Decree No. 152 of April 3, 2006.

(4) In Italy, design levels are regulated by Article 23 of Legislative Decree No. 163 of April 12, 2006, on "Code of public contracts for works, services and supplies"; latest updates: Law No. 122 of 2016, Ministerial Decree No. 248 of 2016. The

aforementioned article defines three levels of design, which in turn define the process of implementation of an intervention, identifiable as the Technical and Economic Feasibility Project, the Definitive Project, and the Executive Project.

(5) In South Italy, based on ISTAT classification, refers to the regions of Abruzzo, Basilicata, Calabria, Campania, Molise, Apulia, Sardinia and Sicily; North refers to the regions of Liguria, Lombardy, Piedmont, Valle d'Aosta, Emilia-Romagna, Friuli-Venezia Giulia, Trentino-Alto Adige and Veneto; Centro refers to the regions of Lazio, Marche, Tuscany and Umbria.

(6) M5C2: social infrastructure, families, communities and the third sector.

(7) The high commission was appointed by the Minister's Decree referred to in Article 1, Paragraph 439 of Law No. 160 of December 27, 2019.

(8) Italian Federation for Housing and Social Housing (www.federcasa.it/).

References

1. Acampa, G., Finucci, F., Grasso, M., Magarò, A.: Preliminary approach for the cost-benefit analysis in the building envelope: study and comparison of actions. In: New Metropolitan Perspectives: Post COVID Dynamics: Green and Digital Transition, between Metropolitan and Return to Villages Perspectives, pp. 786–794 (2022)
2. Baratta, A.F.L.: Una nuova visione dell'abitare e degli spazi dell'abitare nel PNRR. TECHNE-J. Technol. Architect. Environ. **24**, 15–20 (2022)
3. Baratta, A.F.L., Finucci, F., Magarò, A.: Generative design process: multi-criteria evaluation and multidisciplinary approach. TECHNE-J. Technol. Architect. Environ., 304–314 (2021)
4. Baratta, A., Calcagnini, L., Finucci, F., Magaro, A., Molina, H., Ramirez, H.S.Q.: Strategy for better performance in spontaneous building. TECHNE-J. Technol. Architect. Environ., 158–167 (2017)
5. Bernardoni, A., Cossignani, M., Papi, D., Picciotti, A.: Il ruolo delle imprese sociali e delle organizzazioni del terzo settore nei processi di rigenerazione urbana. Indagine empirica sulle esperienze italiane e indicazioni di policy. L'impresa Sociale, un pilastro per le politiche **3**, 7–17 (2021)
6. Galdini, R.: Reinventare la città: strategie di rigenerazione urbana in Italia e Germania. Franco Angeli, Milano (2008)
7. ISTAT: Report povertà in Italia. https://www.istat.it/it/files/2022/06/Report_Povert%C3%A0_2021_14-06.pdf. Accessed 16 Mar 2023
8. Mariani M.: Intervista a Elena Germana Mussinelli. La rigenerazione urbana: una bussola per la qualità della vita. CIL **188**, 42–45 (2022)
9. Martini, A., Sisti, M.: Indicatori o analisi di performance? Implicazione dell'esperienza statunitense di performance measurement. www.uniurb.it/nucleovalutazione/NdV/ReR/Performance_Measurement.pdf. Accessed 15 Mar 2023
10. MIMS: Rapporto del Programma Innovativo Nazionale per la Qualità dell'Abitare. Progetti e prime evidenze. www.mit.gov.it/nfsmitgov/files/media/notizia/2022-06/Report%20PINQuA.pdf. Accessed 18 Mar 2023
11. Ministry of Environment and Energy Security: Piano per la transizione Ecologica. https://asvis.it/public/asvis2/files/Eventi_ASviS/PTE_definitivo.pdf. Accessed 20 Mar 2023
12. Unite Nations: Sustainable development goals. https://www.un.org/sustainabledevelopment/sustainable-development-goals/. Accessed 20 Mar 2023

University Student Housing as a Synergistic Tool Between University and City

Laura Calcagnini⬥, Antonio Magarò⬥, and Luca Trulli(✉)⬥

Department of Architecture, Roma Tre University, Rome, Italy
{laura.calcagnini,antonio.magaro,luca.trulli}@uniroma3.it

Abstract. University student housing has always been a phenomenon that affects the socio-economic community in which it settles. It lends greater importance to the university institution in the role of urban stakeholder, than it would have if deprived of housing and accommodation facilities. Starting with a historical-typological excursus, the paper describes the impacts that university student housing has had through the scientific research that have moved innovation in processes and regulatory procedures, since the dawn of the first *universitas*. In addition, the contribution describes, within the effects in Italy of the application of Law No. 338 of December 14, 2000, and the potential for funding in the sector by the PNRR, two application cases that involved authors with a design experience aimed at the recovery of buildings with historical value in Puglia. The buildings are converted in university student housing and for local University and for the city of Foggia. In this way it allows to summarize the existing value of university student housing and the tools that today allow the architects to intervene on it.

Keywords: University student housing · 5th Public Competition · NRRP · Urban Regeneration

1 University Student Housing During History: From the Right to Study to Urban Regeneration

During the 1230s, Western Europe became the hub of trade with the East, and Italy was the first port for Arab scholars.

This involves a kind of "secularization" of knowledge from which a new kind of cultural pilgrimage arose: that of teachers and students. Without distinction of class or origin, groups of intellectuals emerged within the host city; they were gathered for the purpose of assisting each other.

These groups, which became associations, gave rise to the first *Universitas*, which re-sold autonomy against absolute powers both temporal and religious (Chiarantoni, 2008).

One of the major differences between monastic schools and *Universitas* was that the former were inevitably rooted in the place they were established, because of the inescapable relationship with the monastery and its community. *Universitas*, by contrast, had no classrooms, libraries, or equipment because of the rate of mobility of teachers and students. However, the relationship with the city in which the *Universitas* transited was real: the city took care of the pilgrims' housing needs, taking advantage of their labour. For this reason and to protect their autonomy, the *Universitas* left no traces of their passage, other than the student housing (in Italian: *collegi*) (Coppola Pignatelli, 1969).

At each place, it was necessary to find suitable spaces for cultural settlement: if finding classrooms created few problems because large community halls or church halls were always available, for student housing it was necessary to rely on the private market. It is not uncommon that some municipalities had to intervene to lower rents with the aim of making the *Universitas* stay as long as possible (Chiarantoni, 2008).

Since the presence of *Universitas* was an opportunity for local economies, people began to think of special structures for student housing: (Brizzi and Pini, 1988). Almost simultaneously, for no apparent reason (Kiene, 1997), during the 14th century, buildings, called *collegium*, began to spring up in Italy, France, England, and Spain, with the specific function of providing temporary housing for students. Until then, architecture had not had the opportunity to confront itself with a typological theme such as the *collegium*.

Bologna is among the oldest university seats in Europe having been recognized as *Universitas* by Federico Barbarossa in 1158 and becoming autonomous from municipal power in 1278. The first building intended for university student house is in Bologna and dates to the 13th century: the *Collegio di Spagna*, created to house Spanish pilgrim students. It was desired by Cardinal Arbozon, who entrusted the design to *Matteo Gattapone* from Gubbio (Kiene, 1997).

The connotation as a building for the right to study is clear from the outset since residents could be housed there free of charge if they were of non-wealthy status, as well as of Spanish origin and Christian religion. Its construction lasted only two years, from 1365 to 1367, and it is a typological reference for many of the buildings that would follow it (Belforte, 1996).

The University of Padua was founded in 1222, and the municipality of Padua worked from 1260 to construct buildings for temporary student housing and to lower rents. In four centuries from 1373 to 1771 more than twenty *collegi* will flourish in Padua (Dal Negro, 2003).

Another example of archetypical student housing is in Siena: in the 13th century the municipality established an *Universitas* that already from its foundation had no relationship with either the papacy or the empire. Teachers are paid from the taxes of all citizens, which in fact makes teaching completely free for anyone (the first case in Italy of a public university). In 1408, the municipality is authorized by Papal bull, to build the "house of wisdom" to provide hospitality for poor students. However, the building, once completed in 1416, takes on the character of a residence for wealthy students, attracted by the families of the Sienese bourgeoisie for the purpose of engaging in business dealings (Belforte, 1996).

The Renaissance saw a quest to transform university buildings and those for university student housing, in institutional landmarks, such as public and religious buildings.

One of the main proponents of this change, even from an architectural point of view, was *Cardinal* Branda Castiglioni, who in 1492 founded the first college in Pavia and in 1439 the School of Castiglione d'Olona.

Emerging is the desire to specialize the parts of the building organism, making the educational didactic value of the college prevail. In addition, the sharp distinction between residence spaces, study spaces and collective spaces for socializing practices makes it clear that the desire to frame such buildings as extensions of universities was prioritized, with the aim of placing a higher value on them and making them attractive to students from all over the world.

After the Council of Trento, university institutions underwent a process of strong centralization, aimed at warding off the dangers of spreading heretical theories, associated, increasingly, with the pilgrim student (Chiarantoni, 2008).

Educational *collegi* by the new religious orders such as the Jesuits began to spread in university towns.

The *collegio* acquires, in addition to the function of housing, the function of educational outreach, as happens emblematically in Pavia, with the *Collegio Borromeo*, built between 1561 and 1588: Pellegrino de Pellegrini, known as Tibaldi, was entrusted with the project: he did not pursue the fortress model that had characterized the previous period, but the appearance of Renaissance palaces, openly declaring the residential function.

The relationship with the city is reinforced in the typological evolution as the ground floor is designated to collective spaces.

The 18th century saw the spread of Enlightenment ideas that envisioned a secular revolution in education. The religious monopoly of culture that had been strengthened by the spread of Jesuit educational colleges dissolved, and teaching became a social service administered to citizens by the secular state.

In Turin, Vittorio Amedeo II freed the colleges from religious authority in a move to reform the whole of public education, and, indeed, the King decreed the suppression of all colleges not directly linked to universities.

As it happens in Turin, the goal was to create a widespread network of university seats and supporting facilities such as student housing, under the name of "*Collegi delle Provincie*" (Chiarantoni, 2008).

The first among the *Collegi delleProvincie* was designed by Bernardo Antonio Vittore, who renovated a building in Turin's *Piazza Carlina*.

The building retains the settings of the type defined already by the *Collegio di Spagna*, however, the idea of the single room is abandoned, which comes to accommodate up to four students. Such "crowding" transforms the room into the place for only sleeping, while all other functions are delegated to the common spaces.

Another substantial change concerned the overlooking of the rooms, which, until then, were isolated through distribution from opening to the outside and which now, for the first time, face the city.

In 1810, Napoleon established the *Scuola Normale* in Pisa, following the French model of having the residential structure integrated into the didactive one.

A few years later, King Carlo Felice interrupted the policy of autonomy that had begun with the *Collegi delle Provincie*, returning the management of the student housing to the Jesuits: these resumed the canons of the building type they had devised, while nevertheless retaining the idea of the multiple room, in order to cope with a greater number of students enrolled in higher studies and to be able to have a more lucrative management.

During the Fascism years, some measures, such as the establishment of closed numbers for enrolment in faculties, made the university accessible to a bourgeois elite. However, the principle of the right to study was preserved by the *"Opere Universitarie"* public bodies with the task of organizing forms of material and moral assistance for the underprivileged. Thus, the "Student Houses" were born (Turri, 1935).

After the *Città Universitaria* in Rome, the project for which was coordinated by Marcello Piacentini, who called together the masters of the time, institutional buildings and university student housing became a field of national experimentation for rationalism.

The results of a series of contests held in those years for the design and construction of Student Houses allow us to infer the major typological characters and strengths in the relationship with the city: the mezzanine and basement floors were intended to host the collective spaces, the second floor was for hospitality for non-residents, the cafeteria and administration, and, sporadically there were collective services such as study rooms. On the second floor were private collective facilities such as laundries, kitchens, storage, and technical rooms, as well as sports and recreational facilities. All subsequent floors were for rooms: the model was that of the hotel, and the rooms were predominantly single with specially designed furniture to ensure the *existenz minimum.*

University residences are shifting their function from simple dormitories to more open facilities for urban territories and people and are beginning to be considered important opportunities for the revitalization of urban contexts (Bellini et al. 2020).

Also from this perspective the end of the century is marked by several regulatory interventions managing student housing and allocating the necessary funds for its implementation. The introduction of novelties in the technical field and in relation to dimensional and qualitative standards had to wait until the beginning of the new millennium.

2 The Regulatory Framework and the National Recovery and Resilience Plan

In 2000, Law No. 338 of November 14, bearing "Provisions on accommodation and residences for university students," codified the most qualificative aspects of this type of building, which until then, for other regulations, had been assimilated to hotel or other types (Bologna and Torricelli, 2021). This law constituted a turning point: thanks to implementing decrees over the last two decades it constituted the first national programme aimed at university accommodation and housing, with the purpose of fostering the right to study (Piferi, 2021).

The objectives that the legislation set out to achieve over time intersect in the different scales of intervention by implementing multidisciplinary actions.

The first is of a technical-operational nature: the law aims to increase the number of housing places available to applicants and to define minimum qualitative-quantitative standards for university student housing and accessory spaces.

The second is the socio-cultural ones: it closely relates urban regeneration as a consequence of the regeneration of underutilized buildings, from the integration of offsite students into the urban fabric, to the introduction of innovative forms of teaching.

In the previous four calls, which followed one another over more than two decades, the resources allocated were significant, but, more important was the cultural policy impact, which saw the promotion of financial co-participation by third parties and the increase of those eligible for co-financing, going so far as to include, from the third call onward, local public housing bodies (Baratta and Carlini, 2012).

In relation to urban regeneration, the first three calls enabled the construction and retrofitting of more than 29,000 housing places. The fourth call has provided for the construction and retrofitting of an additional 10,000 housing places: 60% of the interventions in the first three calls are related to the regeneration of existing heritage, while in the fourth call, interventions on the built environment have risen to 80% of the approved co-financing requests (Piferi, 2021).

The first four calls saw the submission of 487 applications for co-financing; the spatial distribution follows the distribution of universities across the territory: 247 applications were in the north, 144 in the centre and 96 in the south. Of these, 395 applications were accepted, for a total co-financing of more than 1,300 million euros.

From the perspective of urban regeneration, successive calls for proposals have always included the possibility of contributing the value of the property to cover the amount charged to the applicant.

This possibility has led to the rehabilitation of buildings, often of great value, nevertheless in disuse, for which it would have been diffi-cult to find the funds even for maintenance work alone. Such buildings, often located within the historic city or at any rate in the consolidated city, once recovered have made it possible to relocate new university receptivity within highly urbanized contexts, in effect fostering a two-way correspondence between residential facilities and local-level urban services.

Demonstrating the value that this possibility of rehabilitating the existing has offered, it should be noted that more than 76% of the interventions that have been carried out and are in progress have as their object the reuse of the existing heritage (Piferi, 2022b).

The National Recovery and Resilience Plan (NRP) fits in by funding a se-rie of additional interventions (Mission 4 - Education and Research, Component M4C1 - Strengthening the supply of education services from kindergartens to universities, Reform 1.7: Reform of student housing legislation and investment in student housing).

Specifically, the decrees aimed at increasing housing places are:

- Ministerial Decree No. 1046 of Aug. 26, 2022, (as amended), which allocates an amount of €300 million to co-finance the purchase and lease of long-term real estate, any necessary upgrades, and the purchase of furniture and equipment;
- Ministerial Decree No. 1252 of Dec. 02, 2022, which uses resources of approximately 150 mi-lion euros as savings derived from the previous decree;
- Ministerial Decree No. 1437 of Dec. 27, 2022, which allocates an amount of 660 mi-lion euros as reimbursement of management expenses for the first three-year period.

All of these programs have provided for or envisage the participation of public and private entities and partnerships. Specifically, Ministerial Decree 1046 co-financed

3,838 housing places of which 904 were in the regions of the South (23.55% of the total) for a total of 200,027,235.96 € (corresponding to state co-financing of 65.15% of this amount).

To these are added the housing places provided by the interventions admitted to co-financing with reserve (797 p.a. equal to 44,395,000.00 € co-financed for 54.97%).

The subsequent Ministerial Decree 1252 co-financed 4,661 units (1,229 of the "purchase" type and 3,432 of the "rental" type) for a total amount of about €135.5 million. Implementing decrees are expected to be published for M.D. 1437 in the coming months.

The regulatory provisions highlight how university student housing is a major topic that attracts a great deal of funding and whose value in terms of impacts and effects in the city is characterized by the different settlement patterns and the possibility of intervention and regeneration of the existing heritage, consistent with the most recent energy and ecological transition objectives.

3 Settlement Patterns in and for the City

The Italian university model is structured, for the most part, in a diffuse manner throughout the territory, with a particular predilection for historical centres. In addition, the Italian heritage is characterized by the presence of buildings, often of great value, that are abandoned or underutilized and in need of rehabilitation.

For these reasons (Del Nord, 2014), the main purpose of Law No. 338 of Nov. 14, 2000, is to encourage the recovery and renovation of existing heritage, introducing a use in which the idea of urban regeneration is inherent, given the lifeblood and economic benefits that university students bring with them.

To the great topicality of this issue, it adds the possibility offered by the legislation to intervene for energy efficiency, which, combined with the possibility of conferring the value of the property to cover the costs borne by the proposing party, zeroes out the expenses for the latter (Baratta and Piferi, 2015).

With the new implementing decrees, the principle of recovering the architectural heritage was further reinforced: Art. 15 of Legislative Decree 152/2021 adds paragraph 4-bis to Art. 1 of the Law, specifying that according to the European Green Deal and the NRRP, "high environmental standards were to be pursued in the implementation and management of interventions."

In addition, Legislative Decree 1257/2021 implementing the Fifth Public Competitive Call, specifies in Art. 4(1) that new green-field construction is not eligible unless it is included in existing campuses or in areas adjoining university settlements.

In addition, the significant advantages in terms of flexibility in dimensional standards, directed at buildings listed for historical architectural merit, consents them to be the preferred target of rehabilitation interventions.

Thus, up to the Fourth Call, more than 76% of the interventions implemented and in progress involve existing buildings (Piferi, 2022a).

The redevelopment of buildings pertaining to the existing heritage is facilitated by the multiplicity of settlement models that the regulations provide, all of which are suitable for student residency and university mobility in general (including that of professors and researchers).

The main types envisaged are hotel-like type, mini lodgement type, integrated cores types and mixed types, solutions that include the *mixité* of the previous types.

If the distribution of housing places determines the settlement type, the other residential services determine the degree of integration with urban spaces (Fig. 1).

Fig. 1. The functional aggregations provided by the regulations: A) hotel-like type, B) mini lodgement type, C) integrated core type.

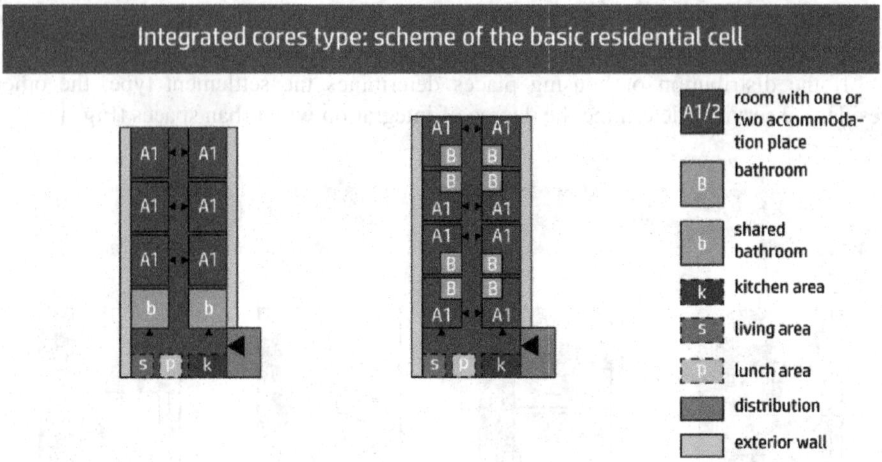

Fig. 1. (*continued*)

The regulations provide for the following functional areas:

- Cultural and educational services, i.e., those functions intended for study, research, reading, meetings, etc., which are carried out by the students individually or in groups, even outside their residential area.
- Cultural and educational services, i.e., the functions intended for study, research, reading, meetings, etc., which are carried out by students individually or in groups, even outside their residential area.
- Support, management, and administrative services, where access and distribution are included, where student meeting and exchange activities take place in addition to spatial connection between and within functional areas, including parking lots and technical rooms or techno-logical services in general.

Such services can be made available to the city, extroverting interior spaces to provide support for citizens as well, fostering the integration of offsite students and transforming the building into an urban landmark. In this sense, residence as understood by the Italian legislation, goes beyond the domestic and private dimension to approach a new model of neighbourhood and city, based on co-neighbourhood i.e., weaving a complex of relationships apt to stimulate the creation of a sharing system that generates transformations.

In the more than 20 years in which the law on university residences in Italy has been operating, the standards on functional areas mentioned above have been considered as minimums and methods have been developed for their verification (Catalano et al. 2022), ensuring that redevelopment interventions can be transformed into opportunities to support the city with new and innovative services: there are been built residences with large libraries, fitness centres with fields and swimming pools, recording rooms, cinemas, restaurants on scenic terraces, and shopping centres.

All these services expand the offer for students (resident and non-resident) and help integrate the student residence into the city.

According to Pike (2002), students who inhabit university residence halls develop a greater predisposition to diversity, since it is in shared spaces that social interaction takes place, the effects of which converge in creating a sense of community and increasing a sense of belonging: these qualities are inversely proportional to the study dropout rate (Berger, 1977) and directly correlated with improved learning activities (Wisley and Jorgensen, 2000).

From what has been written, it can be seen how important it is not only to promote the sharing of spaces and services for students staying in a residence hall, but to encourage wider-ranging actions, initiating redevelopment and re-infrastructure processes extended to the complex of university campuses (Catalano et al. 2022) or urban suburbs where residences are usually located, to ensure effective integration of university residences with city services and functions (Schiaffonati, 2010).

4 The Rehabilitation of Underutilized Heritage Buildings: The Case Study of Foggia

On the occasion of the Fifth Call for Proposals of Law No. 338 of December 14, 2000, the research group of which the authors of this paper are members, participates with different roles in scientific support for the design of a series of interventions, presented by different eligible subjects.

The following details the experience of Foggia, namely the recreation and reuse of a derelict building called the "former Conventino" with the historical function of a women's orphanage. The building is a disused property located near the center of Foggia, whose site area occupies the entire block circumscribed by Via Orientale to the north, Via Carpentieri to the east, Via Barra to the south and Via Diomede to the east.

The original structure of the building, which has a rectangular floor plan of 86 × 30 m and disposed on two levels, had 52 rooms, as well as a gymnasium, two large terraces, a garden, a small church, a parlor, and two schools: an elementary school and a music school.

The building was for a long time used by Caritas as a shelter for the needy, and, later, partially renovated to house a kindergarten of more than 1,700 m^2 between covered and uncovered area by the Azienda Servizi alla Persona "Istituto dell'Addolorata" of Foggia. As of 2018, it has been in a state of abandon.

The building is in good condition today and partly renovated for the still-to-be-completed kindergarten-related work. Less well cared for appear the courtyards, which are difficult to access, in some places infested with wild vegetation and covered with pigeon guano and mouse droppings.

The project proposes a University Student Residence for 64 lodging places, distributed as follows: on the ground floor: 16 lodging places on about 1,200 m^2; on the second floor: 39 lodging places on 900 m^2; on the second floor: 9 lodging places on 250 m^2.

The larger area on the ground floor accommodates a range of support functions for the residence, from play and recreational functions to educational functions, in addition to the actual support services, such as technological services or spaces for carrying out daily household acts. In addition, on the ground floor there are services intended primarily for students, which have an urban-level value since they are also potentially accessible from the outside and serve the city.

The project is characterized by an optimal management of the ground-floor paths, also for the purpose of better usability from the outside of the services, that is, integration with the city. A glazed volume is created that fulfills the function of connecting the wings of the building, recalling the loggia spaces or convent arcades, perimeter to the courtyard (Figs. 2, 3, 4).

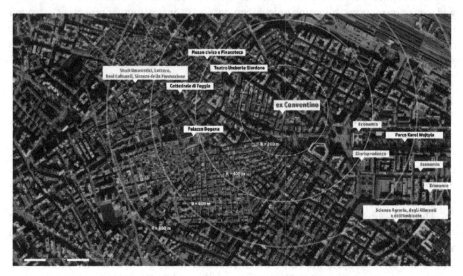

Fig. 2. "Former Conventino." Spatial framing.

Most of the residential spaces are located on the second floor, while on the ground floor it is possible to take advantage of the modular convent layout to create rooms and common spaces of varying sizes that can accommodate different activities.

In particular, the following common spaces that also serve the city are settled in the residence: three study rooms (about 250 m^2); a bar; a newspaper library; and a gymnasium also accessible directly from the outside of about 200 m^2.

The top level is characterized by the presence of a large practicable roof from which there is a privileged view of the city. There is also a series of small attic units, mostly habitable, in which, given the character of independence it is imagined to install mini-housing for different users: visiting professors, visiting researchers, PhD students, etc.

The project, judged eligible for ministerial co-financing, thus becomes an instrument of urban regeneration for several reasons:

– the rehabilitation of a gap in the urban fabric resulting from an abandoned property of historical value, returning a reconnected and redeveloped urban fabric;
– the provision of services that can be enjoyed by the city;
– the inducement of student life on economic activities in the area.

Fig. 3. "Former Conventino." Main elevations on driveways.

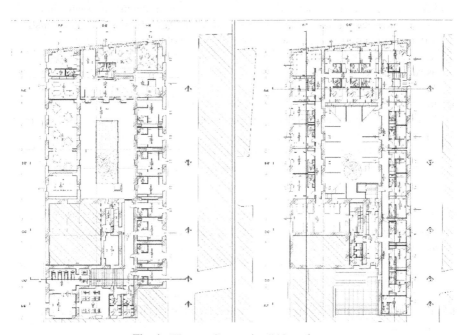

Fig. 4. "Former Conventino." New plants.

5 Conclusions

The brief historical excursus and the case study of Foggia make visible what cultural and political tools, present in regulatory arrangements, make it possible to determine choices in university student housing interventions with positive impacts on the city.

The history of *collegi*, in fact, has evolved by expanding the concept of living from the model of the ecclesiastical cell and of the fortified settlement toward a model in which the functions of living not strictly related to mere rest occupy shared spaces and in which the building for university student housing opens toward the city.

Regulatory arrangements provide the tools for urban regeneration, since as highlighted in the case study they allow for:

- To intervene on the repurposing of built heritage that is often in a state of disuse or obsolete and technologically obsolete, and return a property to the city, often in high-value urban settings.
- To include functions, such as leisure and sports activities to serve not uniquely the university residence hall but the city.
- To intervene with the enrichment of local level services integrated into the building thus allowing for an open project toward the city.

In the more than twenty years of virtuous regulatory leverage, established by Law No. 338 of December 14, 2000, what has certainly come to the fore is that university student housing must be understood as an organism within the urban organism, that is, as a system neither separate nor autonomous from the neighbourhood. They constitute one of the main factors in the growth and development of the social and economic issues of university towns, most likely to a greater extent than the location of industrial or infrastructural facilities of the same size.

Private stakeholders, even those not directly involved in the management or realization of university student housing, have an economic return from them because of the increased consumption paid for by the concentration of off-site students. Moreover, as expected from the design of the interventions in Foggia, the university residence is proposed as a pole of urban regeneration at the small and large scale, since its realization will necessitate the infrastructural innervation of the centre, including through a review of local public transport.

The rental market certainly receives a great advantage from the presence of university student residences: in a wild market situation, rents are those expressed by real estate market operators, however, a market calmed by the presence of such an important entity normalizes all aspects related to normal real estate transactions, depressing speculation and moving in the direction of transparency (Miccoli, Finucci, Murro, 2019).

University student housing provide the city with a range of local-level resources such as recreational spaces, meeting points and educational facilities, while drawing sap from the urban surroundings in terms of commercial, recreational, sports, cultural, etc. activities.

References

Baratta, A. e Carlini, S.: Alloggi e residenze per studenti universitari, l'esperienza del programma 338/2000. Techne J. Technol. Architect. Environ. **4**, 262–270 (2012)

Baratta A. e Piferi C. (2015). Le residenze universitarie come strumento di rigenerazione urbana. L'esperienza del Programma 338/00, in 3° edizione di abitare il futuro. Giornate internazionali di studio, Napoli, 1–2 ottobre, Clean edizioni, pp. 485–493

Belforte, S. (1996). Collegi universitari. Esempi e progetti a confronto, Milano: CELID

Bellini, O.E., Gambaro, M., Mocchi, M.: Living and learning: a new identity for student housing in city suburbs. In: Della Torre, S., Cattaneo, S., Lenzi, C., Zanelli, A. (eds.) Regeneration of the Built Environment from a Circular Economy Perspective. RD, pp. 99–109. Springer, Cham (2020). https://doi.org/10.1007/978-3-030-33256-3_11

Berger, J.B.: Students' sense of community in residence halls, social integration, and first-year persistence. J. Coll. Stud. Dev. **5**, 441–452 (1997)

Brizzi, G.P. e Pini, A.I.: Studenti e Università degli Studenti dal XII al XIX secolo, Bologna: Istituto per la storia dell'Università (1988)

Catalano, G., et al.: Procedures and standards for the sizing of university buildings. Architectural Eng. Des. Manage. **9**, 1–17 (2022)

Chiarantoni, C.: La residenza temporanea per studenti. Atlante italiano, Firenze: Alinea (2008)

Coppola Pignatelli, P.: L'università in espansione, Milano: ETAS Kompass (1969)

Dal Negro, P.: I collegi per studenti dell'Università di Padova. Una storia plurisecolare, Padova: Signum (2003)

Del Nord R.: L'innovazione di processo come strumento per promuovere la qualità delle opere, in Del Nord R. (a cura di), Il processo attuativo del piano nazionale di interventi per la realizzazione di residenze universitarie, Edifir, Firenze, pp. 19–2 (2014)

Kiene, M.: "L'Architettura nel collegio di Spagna e dell'Archiginnasio", in Annali di storia delle Università Italiane, vol. 1, p. 97 (1997)

Miccoli, S., Finucci, F., Murro, R.: Integrating stated preference methods for property valuations in housing markets: an experimental case study in Italy. Int. J. Hous. Markets Anal. **12**(3), 474–486 (2019)

Piferi, C.: La qualità dell'abitare a servizio del diritto allo studio. Edizioni Opera Universitaria, Trento (2021)

Piferi, C.: Processi innovativi per l'abitare sociale. I programmi pluriennali di finanziamento della L 338. Techne J. Technol. Architect. Environ. **24**, 207–217 (2022)

Piferi, C.: "Evoluzione dei luoghi dell'apprendimento: la residenzialità come ambito e strumento di formazione per gli studenti", Contesti Città Territori Progetti, n, pp. 158–171 (2022b)

Pike, G.R.: The differential effects of on-and off-campus living arrangements on students' openness to diversity. NASPA J. **39**(4), 283–299 (2002)

Schiaffonati, F. (2010). "Temi e prospettive di ricerca per l'housing sociale", in Bosio, E. e Sirtori, W., Abitare. Il progetto della residenza sociale fra tradizione e innovazione, Maggioli editore, Rimini, pp. 231–239

Turri, F.: Le case dello studente durante il fascismo. Edilizia popolare **264**(265), 131–136 (1935)

Wisley, N., Jorgensen, M.: Retaining students through social interaction: special assignment residence halls. J. Coll. Admiss. **167**, 16–27 (2000)

Mobility in the City and the University Campus Role: From an Outcome of Urban Anomalies to a Vector of a Sustainable Transition

Jose Kos[1,2]([⊠]) [iD], Lucas Oliveira[1] [iD], Camila Mangrich[1] [iD], Luis Pavan[1] [iD], Renato Almeida[1] [iD], and Areli Santos[1] [iD]

[1] Universidade Federal de Santa Catarina, Florianopolis, SC 88040-900, Brazil
`jose.kos@ufsc.br`
[2] Universidade Federal do Rio de Janeiro, Rio de Janeiro, RJ 21941-901, Brazil

Abstract. The campuses of the most recognized Brazilian universities were an outcome of the country's modernization, which had the automotive industry as one of its most significant symbols. If the automotive industry has attracted massive public funding without much opposition, universities should provide more rigorous and systemic criticism. However, this is not the case. These universities have reproduced the cities' idiosyncrasies, offering free parking and communicating through their campuses the cars' predilection over pedestrians, public transportation, and the natural environment. This article aims to explore digital data from the Federal University of Santa Catarina main campus offering evidence to support deconstructing this message to their students, staff, and society towards a more sustainable and systemic approach, through a significant campus planning shift. To understand current circulation dynamics, we have investigated several university databases, such as the staff and students' home addresses and the Wi-Fi authentication records to the Eduroam network distributed in the campus territory. 538 access points registered nearly 30,000 daily users, who generated around 2 million records every day, containing the authentication time and the access point geographic coordinate. The studies' results illustrate mobility patterns of the academic community inside and outside the campus to support strategies to challenge the current campus planning. We conclude with a proposal for a more resilient campus based on environmental regeneration, particularly along the campus streams to connect the pedestrian entrances, stimulating inclusivity through a diversity of encounters, and promoting active mobility and public transport initiatives associated with parking shrinkage.

Keywords: Active Mobility · Social Inequalities · Campus Planning · Eduroam Authentication · Regenerative Design

1 Introduction

Through the implementation of a multidisciplinary approach, this study aims to examine inflection points in the role of Brazilian public universities regarding mobility and the planning of resilient and regenerative cities. Specifically, we aim to emphasize the

© The Author(s), under exclusive license to Springer Nature Switzerland AG 2023
O. Gervasi et al. (Eds.): ICCSA 2023 Workshops, LNCS 14104, pp. 660–674, 2023.
https://doi.org/10.1007/978-3-031-37105-9_44

data potential, such as the Eduroam Wi-Fi authentication database, to inform campus planning, as well as to explore the campus public open spaces and the surrounding communities through human mobility dynamics. We will shed light on socio-political and mobility infrastructure decision-making in the past that had a lasting impact on Brazilian urban life and has continued to do so to this day on many scales and social spheres. Impacting the car-pedestrian relationship is critical to our study, particularly when we verify the lack of a systemic approach to evaluate these vehicles' complexity that has contributed to severe urban problems, progressively exacerbating Brazilian cities' inequalities.

Private motorized vehicles embody Brazilian inequalities in the cities. During the last decades, the country has led inequality rankings in South America and even in the world. In the late 1980s, this inequality level slightly decreased, with a more significant reduction after the 2000s [1]. However, the cutback in state social benefits, exacerbated by the COVID-19 pandemic, might have changed this scenario in the last few years [2]. Addressing the private vehicles issue in city planning is a major challenge in most developing countries and Brazil has some particularities that make it even harder. Modernization in the country has been closely associated with the automobile industry since its implementation in the mid-XX century. American car companies inaugurated this industry, incorporated by Brazilian discourse as a national product, and advertised to middle-class owners with a message that impacted even those who could not afford them [3]. "This national auto industry played into ideas about the link between consumerism and citizenship, as owning a car became a key component of Brazilian identity" [3 p.9]. Therefore, private vehicles are not only a social status symbol, but carry an image of a progressive country, society, and citizens.

The negotiation to implement the automobile industry in the country was initiated by President Getulio Vargas's (1951–54) administration, but it really launched during Juscelino Kubitschek's government (1956–1961). Kubitschek is known for the slogan "fifty years progress in five" and followed the Fordism approach, conveying the message of turning the poor into consumers and citizens as factory workers [3]. He was able to design, construct and inaugurate, in his five-year administration, the new capital in the heart of the country. Brasília "was the most accomplished symbol of this project of progress, development, and modernization [...] and was designed to mirror to the rest of Brazil, the modern nation that it would become" [4 p.395–396]. Strictly following the CIAM precepts, the city's national-developmentalist project of modernization had the motorized private vehicles as a radical structuring component, making it nearly impossible for the pedestrian experience. Although advertised as a socially egalitarian plan, it displayed the opposite result augmented by cars and garages for every apartment [3, 4]. Most of those who had conditions to own it live in the planned city and most of those who do not have, live in the informal outskirts.

The automotive industry played a significant role in a country urbanized mostly near the coast. The placement of Brasília in the middle of the country represented the power of this industry that provided technological means to deal with the great geographic challenges. Therefore, investment in road infrastructure to connect a large country such as Brazil, which did not have a proper rail infrastructure, was a Kubitschek focus. "Brasília brought about a new sense of mobility, change, and development that would unleash the nation's true potential as a great regional and perhaps even world power" [3 p.137]. Although this industry has been, since then, entirely controlled by international companies, it has been largely funded by the state, with privileged incentives not shared by other industrial sectors [5, 6]. The automotive industry's economic power is gigantic, it represents in the last decades around 15% of the country's GDP [7], and it is intrinsically embedded in the government decision-making from the city to the national levels. Regardless of its ideology, every government since Kubitschek has supported this industry with a significant burden to society.

One needs to consider, among other issues, the onus for the large Brazilian cities of vehicle increments in the last decades. The Brazilian vehicle fleet grew 84.22% from 2006 to 2015, starting with 7.8 inhabitants per vehicle in 2006 to reduce to 4.8 in 2015 [8]. Such a complex issue requires a systemic approach and multiple strategies [9]. Private vehicles have significantly impacted the economy of Brazilian cities, similarly to other Latin American counterparts. Among other expenditures in this region, traffic congestion may cost up to 10 percent of the GDP, and another 5 percent is diverted to road accidents [10]. Public investment in road infrastructure and transportation should focus on these expenses associated with social well-being. However, even when advertised as public transport-oriented initiatives, these enterprises frequently penalize the lower-income population while providing gains to higher-income groups [11]. Furthermore, between 2000 and 2012, bus transport fares costs had much higher growth than items associated with private transport [12]. Another study [13] confirmed these results, demonstrating that between 2006 and 2017 bus fares had a much more significant increase than gasoline prices.

The 2022 presidential campaign promoted an extreme break in Brazilian society [14]. One of the few issues that both candidates and former presidents, Lula (2003–2010) and Bolsonaro (2019–2022), agree on is the support for the automotive industry. Lula's political trajectory and the Workers Party were nurtured in this very industry's labor union. His first two turns as president displayed protection for the automotive industry directly associating it with the nation's economy and the belief that cars should be available to lower-income citizens [3]. Bolsonaro, on the other side, oriented his discourse during his government towards a free-market economy [15] – maintaining the public incentives to the automotive industries, and a few other privileged enterprises of the government supporters –, to the right-wing "growing mistrust and the need to feel safe from others" – embodied in the spread of large Sport Utility Vehicles (SUVs) – [16 p.57], as well as the dissemination of motorized demonstrations as his campaign symbol.

Confronting this national consensus is a major challenge and our argument is that the university has a major responsibility to assume such leadership. Furthermore, it is not enough to disseminate this idea in some research groups, classes, publications, or institutional missions [17]. If the university continuously communicates an opposite message through its own actions – and the campus is one of the most relevant instruments –, this is the one that is disseminated [18]. Therefore, to promote a major shift in the academic community, one that will be multiplied by its students and staff, it is foremost for Brazilian universities to divert from car prioritization to privileging pedestrians, green open spaces, and personal encounters.

Promoting encounters is embedded in the very notion of the university campus existence and should direct every planning action. For Kellerman [19], moving in space is guided by three major needs, curiosity in searching for information and knowledge, desire for proximity, and interaction with other human beings. For the author, these needs are best accomplished while walking or using public transport, while the car serves only the primary function of locomotion. The study by Solnit [20] follows this argument, stating that "the frankness of the encounter and the fluidity of the contact" provided by walking cannot be reproduced even by driving very slowly.

Thus, our study's challenge is to demonstrate, through digital data available at the Universidade Federal de Santa Catarina (UFSC), the feasibility, gains, and obviousness of necessary changes in its main campus. Furthermore, these changes oriented towards walking and environmental regeneration are intrinsic to the university mission [21]. We have summarized above the Brazilian construction of the car's mythos inherited in an indisputable worldview shared by most university decision-makers. Therefore, we aim to geographically display the association of different university databases to support a narrative that could deconstruct such a strong discourse. The studies described below are part of a broader research project on the university campus regenerative development. This research departs from a systemic understanding of the region's ecosystem and its urbanization, particularly related to the campus' rivers. It searches for synergies between campus planning and environmental dynamics. Along these lines, understanding human dynamics is key to pursuing shared positive impacts. Therefore, staff and students' home addresses and the Eduroam Wi-Fi authentication records became the main data sources of these studies, and they exhibit the relevance and feasibility of campus investments' prioritizations concerning walkability and environmental regeneration. The results of the mobility studies within and outside the campus quantify the academic community with a potential to reach the campus by walking or with public transport and when they arrive on campus, the studies illustrate the more used pathways, those that connect to the main campus entrances and those with the capacity to promote interdisciplinary encounters. Furthermore, they display the potential of using the university's streams as circulation axes for pedestrians, for environmental regeneration, and ultimately, for the university's resilience to the climate extreme events that frequently impact the university campus [22].

2   Case Study Context

The Brazilian public universities and other state-financed enterprises guided a series of infrastructure investments linked to land valorization and urban sprawl. A federal decree established the UFSC in 1960 – the year of Brasília's inauguration – as part of the national modernization plan. The new capital proudly represented the national urbanization ideal. Therefore, since the first master plans for the UFSC campus, in the city of Florianópolis, from the late 1950s and early 1960's functionalist zoning and segregation from pedestrians and cars determined the university territory. One emblematic passage from the second master plan emphasized the buildings and its dedicated great parking lots as a symbol of the university nobility [23]. Later, in the 1070s, the most recognized Brazilian landscape architect, Roberto Burle Marx, developed a plan for the university's main square removing the roads that fragmented its space. Burle Marx, notorious for his landscape designs in Brasília, planned an exclusive pedestrian connection to the main buildings of the campus at the square edges. Another symbolic move of Burle Marx's plan implementation is that the square pavement and gardens followed his instructions, but the roads for motorized vehicles have mutilated the square until today [24].

The military regime (1964–1985) followed the coup d'état by the Brazilian Armed Forces in April 1964, through convergences with the United States. Their agreements with territorial implications on Brazilian public campuses are crucial points of the spatial strategies implemented nationwide. UFSC embodied these strategies that promoted strict spatial disciplinary fragmentation on the campus. The fragmentation of different worldviews on campus and its separation from the rest of the city was particularly suitable for the military regime and became an obstacle to a systemic approach to mobility, environmental regeneration, biodiversity, and equity.

The current campus infrastructure and the prioritization of cars as a commuter alternative are entangled factors. Precarious active mobility infrastructure, irregular – or inexistent – deteriorated sidewalks, unsafe bicycle lanes, and, especially, free parking, are among the most conspicuous campus features emphasizing private vehicles over-active and public transportation modes. The faulty physical connectivity between the campus and the city leads to results such as those seen in the survey carried out by the university [25]. More than 70% of faculty and 52% of staff use their own car to reach the university, but 30% of the students prefer walking as their means of commute, according to the results of an online questionnaire. These dynamics have a critical impact on campus, mainly in land occupation and in the suppression of public spaces for encounters and green areas. Today, 34.134 m^2 of the streams' margins on campus, which are environmentally protected under federal law, serve as free parking spaces as well as internal vehicle pathways [26].

The UFSC main campus is the most prominent bus travel attraction hub in the Florianópolis metropolitan region for students [27] and acts as a point of confluence between human and natural flows. Based on the lower areas of the Itacorubi Basin, the campus collects water from the surrounding hills. The implementation of the UFSC campus has a profound impact on the urban landscape, as it influences the expansion of new infrastructure in the Itacorubi Basin region (Fig. 1). However, this expansion has caused frequent floods on campus, traffic congestion, pollution, and the depletion of natural resources.

3 Methodology

We have developed for this paper studies structured from three main specific databases: the vector-based physical information of the campus (buildings, infrastructure, road system, and natural features), the home address registered at the university Identity Management System (idUFSC), and mobility inside the campus, captured by the Eduroam Wi-Fi authentication database. The integration of the university databases in an interdisciplinary process involved the Superintendency of Electronic Governance and Information (SETIC) and other administrative sectors, and researchers from the Computational Security Laboratory (LABSEC) and the Urban Ecology Laboratory (LEUr). Data complexity

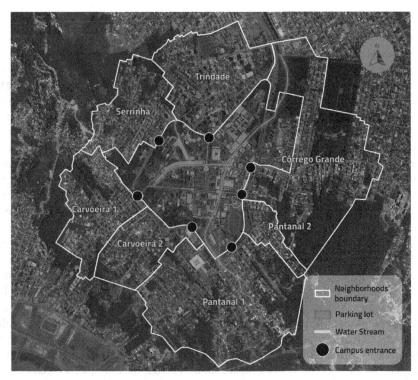

Fig. 1. The urban and natural context of UFSC main campus.

resulting from the large quantity of Eduroam authentication records required specific procedures to manage and dynamically visualize the volume of stored data, according to the Brazilian data protection regulations, which have demanded strict protocols to provide data safety to other interested parties.

We identified a strong potential of the idUFSC platform, which stores records of each university member, such as personal data and academic information. Despite the relevancy of idUFSC's home address records, the database was outdated and obsolete. A partnership established in 2019 with the University President's Office focused on the mobility dynamics and resulted in 39,108 members (74% of total registrations) updating their addresses and authorizing the use of personal data for academic surveys through the SETIC's supervision.

The Eduroam Wi-Fi authentication database represented a central role in these studies, providing relevant data on human dynamics that would be difficult to acquire with other methods. Eduroam service has provided worldwide, since 2002, Wi-Fi access to the larger international research and education community. Each device authentication process generates log files associating user identification and the connection's location and time. Location is given by the access point geographic coordinates, which has an approximately 50-m radius of coverage. Around 500 access points generate millions of daily records.

The queries' definition for the Wi-Fi studies is directly associated with the anonymization process and data manipulation and treatment to guarantee the quality of the results. These queries concentrate on the studies inside the campus, while their association with dynamics outside the campus is mainly regulated by the user's home address. Data group characterization initiates the queries which proceeded to define the patterns evaluated by the search algorithms. After choosing the data groups, the records are selected, extracted, and made available by SETIC to LABSEC, which was responsible for anonymizing the results. One of the techniques for this process is β-k-anonymity, devised by Gomes [28] for the trajectories anonymization and personal data protection, establishing a k value equal to or greater than 5 to define the valid sets. Therefore, more than 4 records are necessary to validate the results. Since the larger the data groups, the better the results' quality due to the anonymization process, electing group categories constituted a major challenge, ensuring a balance between sample quality and avoiding user identification.

Therefore, if we use large disciplinary fields, such as Human Science, Technology, Health, and Social and Economics, we miss less data than if we use every university department to group students circulating in each walkway per hour, for instance. To reduce data losses, it could be better to group results in even larger groups, like undergraduate students, graduate students, staff, and faculty. The same applies to spatial dimensions chosen for the group, such as the access points grouping. The smaller the group of connected users, the greater the risk of data loss due to not meeting the minimum β-k criteria. Thus, we agreed to group data in predefined spatial clusters for each case. To explore the Wi-Fi authentication records, for example, we gathered the 538 access points into sectors named from A to J that, in smaller polygons, define blocks numbered from 1 to 4.

4 Studies on Academic Community Mobility

The work involving digital data and external mobility seeks to understand the university's territory based on its positive or negative impacts in the urban context of the city. The selection of home addresses initiated the studies outside the campus of the active modes of transportation. The challenge was to use logical methods to manipulate postal codes, anonymizing personal data in the records. We have assigned on the QGIS platform each postal code to streets and identified the streets within a polygon calculated by walking time on the routes connecting them to the Campus. Using this strategy, vectorized polygons with origin (residential streets) are grouped by five-minute walking intervals to the destination (campus). The individual home address records, related to the 5-min walking polygons, ensured enough records in the groups to reduce losses in the anonymization process. We have classified the academic community for this study into four categories (undergraduate students, graduate students, staff, and faculty) and the total sample constituted 35,470 individual records (67% of the total). It is noteworthy that 17% of the academic community reaches the university campus within a 10-min walk added by 3% within the 15-min polygon, a total of 7,192 academic members (Fig. 2).

Seeking to understand the dynamics of those who live over the 30-min walking polygon, the study evaluated the potential users of public transport. Crossing the idUFSC database with the Eduroam authentication records provided each individual first and last connection times. These records, grouped in home address neighborhoods, generated two CSV files imported by the graphic tools, one with the entrance time given by the first authentication to the Wi-Fi network and another with the last authentication record, representing the departure time (Fig. 3). An initial sample of 10,284 users from the Eduroam authentication records authorized the use of their registered home addresses for the research. The anonymization process reduced the sample to 7,297 records grouped by home address associated with Wi-Fi authentication records registered every 30 min, starting at 6 a.m.

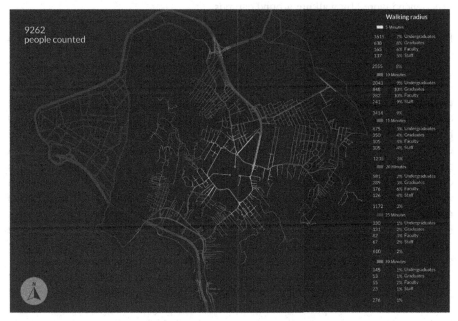

Fig. 2. Home address records classified by category (undergraduate student, graduate student, faculty, and staff) according to walking distance to the campus.

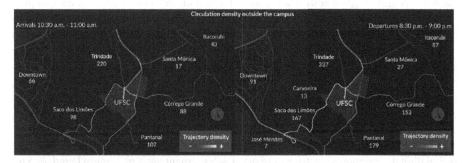

Fig. 3. Arrivals and departures according to a time interval and home neighborhood.

We were able to verify the time that students and staff arrive and depart from various locations in the city, supporting policies to move from private to public transport and reducing the need for parking spaces along the stream banks. The results obtained by crossing address records with the monitoring of authentication data to the Wi-Fi network, bring relevant evidence about the daily variation in the dynamics of entry and exit of members of the academic community. The precariousness and scarcity of infrastructure for active mobility and the little institutional incentive for public transport in line with free parking leads to the preference for individual motorized means in daily commutes. This information may be relevant to encourage municipal public transport, reducing the demand for parking on campus and freeing up free areas for an academic and social experience favored by walking around campus.

A new query developed for SETIC grouped the home address records of those who live within the 10-min polygon, distributed in smaller polygons associated with seven main accesses that connect the campus to the immediate surrounding neighborhoods (Fig. 4). Analyzes of digital data also contribute to meeting other demands of the community, such as the elaboration of inclusion policies at the university for the surrounding residents, increasing the university's extension actions, and leisure areas, and opening the university's social infrastructure to the external community. The number of 1,010 home address records in the Carvoeira neighborhood corroborates the finding that the open areas on the watercourse margins, currently occupied by parking spaces, form a relevant circulation axis for those living within a 10-min walking polygon from the campus. On the right, at the entrance to the other creek, the Pantanal neighborhood is another popular place (1,268 members). Both axes are close to the access to the Trindade neighborhood (1,456 members). The data exploration identified different problems that, based on integrated solutions between the university and municipal administrations, can inhibit the traffic of individual motor vehicles, reduce the demand for parking, enhance the use of active and collective transport, and environmental regeneration.

The choice of the 10-min polygon as a limit for this study was due to the current traffic conditions for active transport, whether on municipal roads or in the internal infrastructure of the campus. Furthermore, the 10-min polygon relates to the university border, or to one of its entrances and was obtained with the isochrone map tool v.net.iso in QGIS, which provides a new polygon with the areas reachable from a starting point within a specific timeframe [29]. For the study, we chose a walking speed of 5 km/h. Individuals may need an additional walk to reach their destinations within the campus.

Thus, to evaluate walking dynamics within the campus we have explored the Wi-Fi authentication records to quantify the trajectories, defined by the origin and destination points as two consecutive access points authentications. The time interval between the consecutive authentications determines the distinction between patterns of *movements* and *stops*. If the interval is longer than 10 min, the algorithm interprets it as a 'stop', otherwise, it indicates that the individual who carries the device is in motion. The trajectories between the origin and destination coordinates were calculated using v.net.path, the shortest path algorithm in QGIS [30]. This process generates a new shapefile representing the trajectories. We computed the sum of all trajectories in each segment of the path within the campus pedestrian network. Each segment has a maximum length of 5 m, totaling 9100 path segments throughout the campus. We highlight that the number of trajectories in each path segment represents the academic pedestrian dynamics throughout 24 h, and the dynamics may vary for each hour, for example, during the opening hours of the university restaurant or at night, when the concentration of people is much higher in CSE (Center of Social and Economic Studies) and CCJ (Center for Law Studies) that have a large course offers in this period. Mapping pedestrian trajectories density as a heat map (Figs. 1 and 4) associated with the campus entries and the number of individuals living up to 10-min walking distance from them displays the paths' potential for internal and external connectivity.

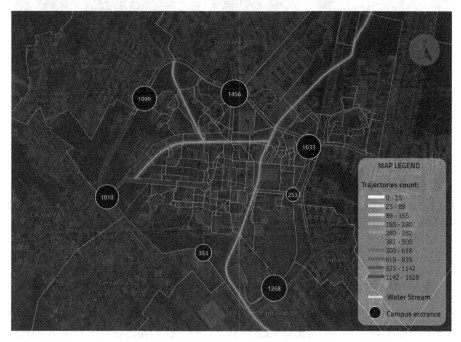

Fig. 4. Internal maps connecting the entrances.

The following study explores the routes, categorized by disciplinary fields, to identify the potential for interdisciplinary encounters among undergraduate students through circulation patterns (Fig. 5). Authentication records in the Eduroam Wi-Fi network from the largest university disciplinary centers – Technology (CTC), Communication (CCE), Health Sciences (CCS), and Philosophy, and Human Sciences (CFH) – structured this study's queries. SETIC provided the results associating the authentication Eduroam data to the idUFSC information, grouping them by the disciplinary fields. LABSEC's anonymization algorithm provided a CSV file with the number of records, with columns for the disciplinary field, the time and location of the authentication access point, with its geographic coordinates. The CSV file imported into QGIS displayed data as trajectories represented as layers of lines along the walkways that connect the origin and destination associated with the two subsequent authentication records. The path selection represented the shortest route between the two consecutive authentication records. Line segments with lighter colors display more overlapping trajectories, suggesting greater chances of encounters between people from different backgrounds. The results allow one to identify the campus areas most visited by undergraduates from different disciplinary fields and the departure points with the highest occurrence of Eduroam authentications. According to the study outcomes, one of the busiest routes is shared by a parking area for more than 500 vehicles along the Carvoeira River' banks with a strong potential to become a new open public space.

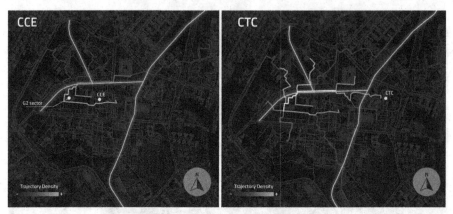

Fig. 5. Trajectories filtered by two centers CCE (left) and CTC (right) between 9:45 a.m. and 10:45 a.m.

5   A Walkable Campus to Impact CITy's Urban Strategies

Universities not only produce knowledge but are also powerful tools for addressing local and global problems, compelling society to act. UFSC's socio-environmental impact extends beyond its physical boundaries, and the university plays a crucial role in identifying and addressing urban challenges that affect daily life in the region where it is situated. Within this context, university territory must be inclusive and engage in a dialogue with the surrounding environment, considering a range of conditioning factors such as climate crises and social inequalities. This approach will enable a more comprehensive identification of problems and the development of project proposals that are better aligned with the specific context of the location. Academic and policy debate has focused on these issues from various perspectives in recent years under multiple nomenclatures: walkable cities, 15-min cities, and isobenefits, for instance [31, 32]. These works underscore how providing a fabric that connects communities, facilities, and services on foot, as well as identifying factors that influence walkability has become a crucial task in promoting life quality, environmental benefits, and social justice.

Information and communication technologies are at the core of critical urban transformations. On one hand, they act as tools to overcome physical and temporal boundaries, on the other, they face critical perspectives over their technocratic pervasiveness and concern with data protection. This scenery persistently posits scientists – and increasingly other practitioners as architects and urban planners – to confront ICTs with newly complexified approaches, especially when dealing with concepts such as territory, the current global context, and its prospects. Data availability, data processing, and even the recent advance in artificial intelligence allowed measuring and visualizing urban dynamics and environmental data with increasing and unprecedented detail.

University campuses reflect the ideas, values, and conceptions of society from their spatial conception to their management and development policies. However, the university also nurtures studies that promote criticism of these ideas, values, and conceptions, particularly nowadays, when studies have demonstrated the vulnerability of life on the planet and the difficulty to implement the necessary changes. It is the university's duty to manifest, through its own actions, that these changes are not only necessary but possible and provide a healthier life to the community. Therefore, as a conclusion of the studies' results, we propose a design for the campus, structured by a campus park network along the campus rivers that provides the regeneration of this ecosystem with pedestrian paths to afford the experience of these noteworthy natural features (Fig. 6).

The results from the studies above demonstrate the feasibility of actions to reduce parking space, particularly along the rivers, that could be associated with charging for parking on campus. The legitimization of these locations can be done on multiple scales, from buildings to territorial planning that demonstrates the interest in caring for this ecosystem that houses it. Thus, the reduction of car parking spaces has been unfolded in proposals such as a linear park that unifies the campus with surrounding neighborhoods, and in which the increase in the section of the university's streams associates spaces for pedestrians, bike paths, and adaptation for the expansion of water in extreme climates. The park challenges a process of denying the quality of these watercourses and privileging private vehicles. Systematically, places like parks and green areas make possible the interconnection of various paradigmatic moments of what is expected for an urban life that respects and integrates with nature in its ways.

The preservation of the edges of the two main streams would allow the creation of walks and bike paths to support longer distances, in green passages that would generate a pleasant experience for traveling to other university areas. New bridges can increase interactions between centers that house the broad disciplinary fields, and these new green areas can stimulate interdisciplinary meetings and exchanges. To ensure the effectiveness of connectivity with the surrounding area, walking axes must be aligned with qualified accesses that increase pedestrian entry to the campus. The guidelines conceived from digital data are based on the principle that it is up to the university to view its streams as a distinction, that is, as an ecological and socio-spatial quality capable of mobilizing the community in environmental preservation and enjoyment, in the valorization of active mobility and in the reaffirmation of the campus as a public space. Ultimately, the proposal aims to communicate to society that these changes that significantly contribute to overall life quality are possible.

1. Laboratory School
2. Court
3. Senior Citizen Study Center & Theater
4. University Library
5. University Hospital
6. Convention Center
7. Univeristy Restaurant
8. Sports Complex

Fig. 6. Proposal for a university park network.

References

1. Alvaredo, F., Gasparini, L.: Recent trends in inequality and poverty in developing countries. Handb. Income Distrib. **2**, 697–805. Elsevier (2015). https://doi.org/10.1016/B978-0-444-59428-0.00010-2
2. Castro, M.C., Gurzenda, S., Turra, C.M., Kim, S., Andrasfay, T., Goldman, N.: Reduction in life expectancy in Brazil after COVID-19. Nat. Med. **27**, 1629–1635 (2021). https://doi.org/10.1038/s41591-021-01437-z
3. Wolfe, J.: Autos and Progress: The Brazilian Search for Modernity. Oxford University Press, Oxford (2010)
4. Caldeira, T., Holston, J.: State and urban space in Brazil: from modernist planning to democratic interventions. In: Managing Urban Futures: Sustainability and Urban Growth in Developing Countries. Routledge, London (2016)
5. Zilbovicius, M., Marx, R., Salerno, M.S.: A comprehensive study of the transformation of the Brazilian automotive industry. IJATM **2**, 10 (2002). https://doi.org/10.1504/IJATM.2002.000054

6. Schapiro, M.G.: O estado pastor e os incentivos tributários no setor automotivo. Rev. Econ. Polit. **37**, 437–455 (2017). https://doi.org/10.1590/0101-31572017v37n02a10
7. Duarte, R.G., Rodrigues, S.B.: Co-evolution of industry strategies and government policies: the case of the Brazilian automotive industry. BAR, Braz. Adm. Rev. **14** (2017). https://doi.org/10.1590/1807-7692bar2017160100
8. ANFAVEA: Anuário da indústria automobilística brasileira 2023, São Paulo (2023). https://anfavea.com.br/site/anuarios/. Accessed 02 Mar 2023
9. Fitzpatrick, S.M.: Complexity blind spots. The Bridge, vol. 50, pp. 13–15 (2020)
10. Mahendra, A., et al.: Towards a more equal city: seven transformations for more equitable and sustainable cities. WRIPUB (2021). https://doi.org/10.46830/wrirpt.19.00124
11. Pereira, R.H.M., Banister, D., Schwanen, T., Wessel, N.: Distributional effects of transport policies on inequalities in access to opportunities in Rio de Janeiro. J. Transp. Land Use **12**, 741–764 (2019)
12. IPEA: Tarifação e financiamento do transporte público urbano. Instituto de Pesquisa Econômica Aplicada, Brasília (2013). https://repositorio.ipea.gov.br/bitstream/11058/1365/1/Nota_Tecnica_Tarifação_e_financiamento_do_transporte_público_urbano.pdf. Accessed 15 Feb 2023
13. IPEA: Avaliação de políticas de redução tarifária dos sistemas de transporte público coletivo no Brasil: evidências empíricas. TD, pp. 1–44 (2022). https://doi.org/10.38116/td2770
14. Ferreira, T., Green, J.N.: Introduction: Brazil under Bolsonaro. Lat. Am. Perspect. **50**, 3–19 (2023). https://doi.org/10.1177/0094582X231157700
15. Rocha, C., Solano, E., Medeiros, J.: The Bolsonaro Paradox: The Public Sphere and Right-Wing Counterpublicity in Contemporary Brazil. Springer, Cham, Switzerland (2021)
16. Wilkinson, R.G., Pickett, K.: The Spirit Level: Why Equality is Better for Everyone. Penguin Books, London (2010)
17. Kenney, D.R., Dumont, R., Kenney, G.: Mission and Place: Strengthening Learning and Community through Campus Design. Praeger Publishers, Westport, Conn (2005)
18. Orr, D.W.: Earth in Mind: On Education, Environment, and the Human Prospect. Island Press, Washington (2004)
19. Wilde, M., Aharon, K.: Daily Spatial Mobilities: Physical and Virtual (2012). RuR. 71, (2013). https://doi.org/10.1007/s13147-013-0221-3
20. Solnit, R.: Wanderlust: A History of Walking. Penguin Books, New York (2001)
21. UFSC, U.F. de S.C.: Plano de desenvolvimento Institucional 2020 a 2024. UFSC, Florianópolis (2020)
22. Kos, J.R., Gebara, M.F., Pompeo, C.A., Pavan, L.H.: Proyecto regenerativo del campus: aprendiendo a través de las dinámicas de la naturaleza y la universidad. Arquitecturas del Sur **35**, 30–41 (2017). https://doi.org/10.22320/07196466.2017.35.052.04
23. UFSC: Plano piloto do conjunto universitário. Editora Universitária, Florianópolis (1965)
24. Kos, J.R., Pavan, L.H., Mangrich, C.P.: The civic potential of the campus: federal university of Santa Catarina and democracy in the city. AS **38**, 80–97 (2020). https://doi.org/10.22320/07196466.2020.38.058.05
25. UFSC: Diagnóstico institucional UFSC. UFSC, Florianópolis (2020)
26. Argenta, V., Orsi, P., Guesser, L.H.: Diagnóstico da ocupação por obras civis em áreas e preservação permanente - Campus Reitor João David Ferreira Lima. Universidade Federal de Santa Catarina (2022). https://repositorio.ufsc.br/handle/123456789/240169. Accessed 01 Mar 2023
27. Logit, C.: PLAMUS: Relatório Final - Consolidação das Propostas e Plano de Implementação, Florianópolis (2015). https://observatoriodamobilidadeurbana.ufsc.br/wp-content/uploads/2019/03/PLAMUS_Produto-19-Relatorio-Final_Volume-Principal.pdf. Accessed 23 Mar 2023

28. Gomes, F.O.: Privacy preserving on semantic trajectories: application on Wi-Fi connections of a university campus (2019). https://repositorio.ufsc.br/handle/123456789/214734. Accessed 22 Mar 2023

29. O'Sullivan, D., Morrison, A., Shearer, J.: Using desktop GIS for the investigation of accessibility by public transport: an isochrone approach. Int. J. Geogr. Inf. Sci. **14**, 85–104 (2000). https://doi.org/10.1080/136588100240976

30. Neteler, M., Beaudette, D.E., Cavallini, P., Lami, L., Cepicky, J.: GRASS GIS. In: Hall, G.B., Leahy, M.G. (eds.) Open-Source Approaches in Spatial Data Handling, pp. 171–199. Springer Berlin, Berlin (2008). https://doi.org/10.1007/978-3-540-74831-1_9

31. D'Acci, L.: Simulating future societies in Isobenefit cities: social isobenefit scenarios. Futures **54**, 3–18 (2013). https://doi.org/10.1016/j.futures.2013.09.004

32. D'Acci, L.: A new type of cities for liveable futures. Isobenefit Urbanism morphogenesis. J. Environ. Manage. **246**, 128–140 (2019). https://doi.org/10.1016/j.jenvman.2019.05.129

Computational and Applied Mathematics (CAM 2023)

Remarks on the Vietoris Sequence and Corresponding Convolution Formulas

Isabel Cação[2] , M. Irene Falcão[1]([⊠]) , Helmuth R. Malonek[2] ,
Fernando Miranda[1] , and Graça Tomaz[2,3]

[1] Centro de Matemática, Universidade do Minho, Braga, Portugal
{mif,fmiranda}@math.uminho.pt
[2] CIDMA, Universidade de Aveiro, Aveiro, Portugal
{isabel.cacao,hrmalon}@ua.pt
[3] Polytechnic of Guarda, Guarda, Portugal
gtomaz@ipg.pt

Abstract. In this paper we consider the so-called Vietoris sequence, a sequence of rational numbers of the form $c_k = \frac{1}{2^k}\binom{k}{\lfloor \frac{k}{2} \rfloor}$, $k = 0, 1, \ldots$. This sequence plays an important role in many applications and has received a lot of attention over the years. In this work we present the main properties of the Vietoris sequence, having in mind its role in the context of hypercomplex function theory. Properties and patterns of the convolution triangles associated with $(c_k)_k$ are also presented.

Keywords: Sequences · Central binomial coefficients · Convolution triangles · Clifford algebra

1 The Vietoris Sequence

For our purpose here, we define the Vietoris sequence $(c_k)_k$ in terms of the "complete central binomial coefficient" as

$$c_k := \frac{1}{2^k}\binom{k}{\lfloor \frac{k}{2} \rfloor}, \quad k = 0, 1, \ldots, \tag{1}$$

where $\lfloor \cdot \rfloor$ is the floor function. The first terms of this sequence are

$$1, \frac{1}{2}, \frac{1}{2}, \frac{3}{8}, \frac{3}{8}, \frac{5}{16}, \frac{5}{16}, \frac{35}{128}, \frac{35}{128}, \ldots.$$

Some years ago, authors of this paper noticed that the sequence (1) appeared in the construction of sequences of multivariate generalized Appell polynomials [11,22]. Since then, several studies on this sequence have been carried out (see e.g. [6,8–10] and the references therein) and the importance of this sequence in hypercomplex context is unquestionable nowadays. For this reason, we thought it would be interesting to collect the properties that have been obtained over the years, presenting them in a unifying way.

O. Gervasi et al. (Eds.): ICCSA 2023 Workshops, LNCS 14104, pp. 677–692, 2023.
https://doi.org/10.1007/978-3-031-37105-9_45

It is worth mentioning that a similar sequence appears in the work [25] of Vietoris in the context of positive trigonometric sums. In fact, in his pioneer work, Vietoris considered the sequence $(a_k)_k$ defined as

$$a_{2k} = a_{2k+1} = \frac{1}{4^k} \binom{2k}{k}, \quad k = 0, 1, \ldots. \tag{2}$$

It follows at once that (1) is a subsequence of (2), since $c_k = a_{k+1}$; $k = 0, 1, \ldots$. Despite this small difference, we have coined (1) as the Vietoris number sequence.

This paper is organized as follows: in Sect. 2 we present equivalent definitions of the Vietoris sequence, while in Sect. 3 we list other important properties of $(c_k)_k$. Finally, the paper ends with some new results on the convolution triangles associated with $(c_k)_k$ and $(c_{2k})_k$.

2 Alternative Definitions

One can find in the literature several ways of writing the Vietoris sequence. Some of these representations were obtained independently and using context-dependent arguments in the framework of hypercomplex analysis. In other cases, the alternative definitions come from very well-known identities. In this section we list several ways of defining the Vietoris sequence, being in most of the cases, trivial to prove the equivalence of the definitions. For each case, we also include in the Appendix A, the Wolfram Mathematica code for defining the sequence.

2.1 Representation in Terms of the Generators of $\mathbb{H}$

Let $\{e_1, e_2\}$ be an orthonormal basis of the Euclidean vector space $\mathbb{R}^2$, with a product according to the multiplication rules

$$e_1 e_2 = -e_2 e_1 \quad \text{and} \quad e_1^2 = e_2^2 = -1.$$

This non-commutative product generates the well-known algebra of real quaternions $\mathbb{H}$ (with the identification $\mathbf{i} := e_1$, $\mathbf{j} := e_2$ and $\mathbf{k} := e_1 e_2$). The Vietoris sequence has the following representation in terms of e_1 and e_2:

$$c_k = \left[\sum_{s=0}^{k} (-1)^s \binom{k}{s} \left(e_1^{k-s} \times e_2^s \right)^2 \right]^{-1} \tag{3}$$

where the so-called symmetric powers with respect to $\times$ are defined recursively as (see e.g. [20]):

$$e_1^m \times e_2^n := \underbrace{e_1 \times \cdots \times e_1}_{m} \times \underbrace{e_2 \times \cdots \times e_2}_{n}$$

$$= \frac{1}{m+n} [m e_1 (e_1^{m-1} \times e_2^n) + n e_2 (e_1^m \times e_2^{n-1})], \quad m, n \in \mathbb{N},$$

and for $m = 0$ or $n = 0$, the powers are understood in the ordinary way.

For an algebraic proof of the equivalence of the representations (1) and (3), we refer to [15] (see also [14]). For more details on the properties of the symmetric powers, we mention [20].

2.2   Double Factorial Representation

The Vietoris sequence can also be written in terms of the double factorial [12,23]. In fact, using the well-known relations

$$(2k)!! = 2^k k! \quad \text{and} \quad (2k+1)!! = \frac{(2k+1)!}{2^k k!},$$

the relation (1) can be written as

$$c_k = \frac{(2\lfloor \frac{k-1}{2} \rfloor + 1)!!}{(2\lfloor \frac{k-1}{2} \rfloor + 2)!!}. \tag{4}$$

2.3   Recursive Definition

It follows immediately from (4) that c_k can be defined recursively as

$$c_k = \begin{cases} \frac{k}{k+1} c_{k-1}, & \text{if } k \text{ odd} \\ c_{k-1}, & \text{if } k > 1 \text{ even} \\ 1 & \text{if } k = 0 \end{cases}.$$

2.4   Pochhammer Symbol Representation

In the works [5,11], the elements of the sequence $(c_k)_k$ were obtained through

$$c_k = \frac{\left(\frac{1}{2}\right)_{\lfloor \frac{k+1}{2} \rfloor}}{(1)_{\lfloor \frac{k+1}{2} \rfloor}},$$

where $(x)_n$ denotes the Pochhammer symbol,

$$(x)_n := x(x+1)\ldots(x+n-1), \ \ n = 1, 2, \ldots; (x)_0 := 1.$$

This is an immediate consequence of the fact that

$$\left(\tfrac{1}{2}\right)_k = \frac{(2k-1)!!}{2^k} \quad \text{and} \quad (1)_k = k!.$$

2.5   Alternating Sum of a Non-Symmetric Triangle

In the work [12], several arithmetic properties of the triangle

$$T_s^k := \frac{1}{k+1} \frac{\left(\frac{3}{2}\right)_{k-s} \left(\frac{1}{2}\right)_s}{(k-s)! s!}, \quad k = 0, 1, \ldots, s = 0, 1, \ldots, k. \tag{5}$$

were derived. One of these properties allows to express the elements c_k of the Vietoris sequence in terms of the alternating row sum of T_s^k:

$$c_k = \sum_{s=0}^{k} (-1)^s T_s^k.$$

2.6   Gamma Function Representation

Recalling the well known identities

$$\Gamma(\tfrac{1}{2}) = \sqrt{\pi}, \quad \Gamma(n+1) = n!, \quad \text{and} \quad \Gamma(n+\tfrac{1}{2}) = \frac{(2n)!\sqrt{\pi}}{2^{2n}n!},$$

we can write

$$c_k = \frac{\Gamma(\tfrac{1}{2} + \lfloor \tfrac{k+1}{2} \rfloor)}{\Gamma(\tfrac{1}{2})\Gamma(1 + \lfloor \tfrac{k+1}{2} \rfloor)} = \frac{\Gamma(\tfrac{1}{2} + \lfloor \tfrac{k+1}{2} \rfloor)}{\sqrt{\pi} \lfloor \tfrac{k+1}{2} \rfloor!}. \tag{6}$$

2.7   Integral Representation

The Wallis integrals are the terms of the sequence $(\mathcal{I}_k)_k$ defined by

$$\mathcal{I}_k = \int_0^{\frac{\pi}{2}} \cos^k x \, dx,$$

which can be evaluated by using the well-known identity

$$\mathcal{I}_k = \frac{\Gamma(\tfrac{k+1}{2})\Gamma(\tfrac{1}{2})}{2\Gamma(\tfrac{k}{2} + 1)}.$$

Having in mind the Gamma-representation (6) of c_k and the properties of the Gamma function, we obtain easily

$$c_k = \frac{2}{\pi} \mathcal{I}_{2\lfloor \frac{k+1}{2} \rfloor}.$$

2.8   Representation in Terms of Catalan Numbers

The popular Catalan numbers,

$$\mathcal{C}_k = \frac{1}{k+1}\binom{2k}{k}; \quad k = 0, 1, \dots,$$

appear in a number of binomial identities. For our purpose here we highlight the following one [1],

$$\mathcal{C}_k = \sum_{s=0}^{k} (-1)^s \binom{k}{s} 2^{k-s} \binom{s}{\lfloor \frac{s}{2} \rfloor} = (-2)^k \sum_{s=0}^{k} (-1)^{k-s} \binom{k}{s} c_s,$$

from where it is trivial to obtain the relation

$$c_k = \sum_{s=0}^{k} \binom{k}{s} (-2)^{-s} \mathcal{C}_s,$$

since $\left(\frac{\mathcal{C}_k}{(-2)^k}\right)_k$ is the binomial transform of $(c_k)_k$.

2.9   Representation in Terms of Values of Legendre Polynomials

In the hypercomplex context, the following special holomorphic polynomial of degree k involving the Vietoris coefficients (or their generalizations) have been constructed and its properties have been studied in a series of papers by authors of this work ([4–6, 11, 14, 22]),

$$\mathbf{P}_k(x_0 + x_1 e_1 + x_2 e_2) = \sum_{s=0}^{k} c_s \binom{k}{s} x_0^{k-s}(x_1 e_1 + x_2 e_2)^s, \tag{7}$$

where e_1 and e_2 are the generators of $\mathbb{H}$. We adopt the following notation in what follows: if $x = x_0 + x_1 e_1 + x_2 e_2 \in \mathbb{H}$, then $|x|^2 = x_0^2 + x_1^2 + x_2^2$, $\mathrm{Re}(x)$ is the real part x_0 of x, $\underline{x}$ designates the vector part of x, i.e., $\underline{x} = x_1 e_1 + x_2 e_2$ and $\omega := \omega(\underline{x}) = \frac{\underline{x}}{|\underline{x}|}$. Since $\omega^2 = -1$, the right-hand side of (7) can be written as

$$\sum_{s=0}^{\lfloor \frac{k}{2} \rfloor} (-1)^s \binom{k}{2s} c_{2s} x_0^{k-2s} |\underline{x}|^{2s} + \omega \sum_{s=0}^{\lfloor \frac{k-1}{2} \rfloor} (-1)^s \binom{k}{2s+1} c_{2s+1} x_0^{k-2s-1} |\underline{x}|^{2s+1}. \tag{8}$$

This means that the polynomials (7) can easily be rewritten in terms of the real variable $t = \frac{x_0}{|x|}$ as

$$\mathbf{P}_k(t, |x|) = |x|^k \left(f_k(t) + \omega(\underline{x}) g_k(t) \right), \tag{9}$$

where $t \in [-1, 1]$ and $f_k(t)$ and $g_k(t)$ are the real functions

$$f_k(t) = \sum_{s=0}^{\lfloor \frac{k}{2} \rfloor} \binom{k}{2s} c_{2s} t^{k-2s} (t^2 - 1)^s$$

and

$$g_k(t) = \sqrt{1 - t^2} \sum_{s=1}^{\lfloor \frac{k+1}{2} \rfloor} \binom{k}{2s-1} c_{2s-1} t^{k-2s+1} (t^2 - 1)^{s-1}.$$

For more details on the representation (9), we refer to [4]. If we recall the Legendre polynomials of degree k written in the form (see e.g. [24])

$$\mathcal{P}_k(t) = t^k \sum_{s=0}^{\lfloor \frac{k}{2} \rfloor} \binom{k}{2s} \binom{2s}{s} \left(\frac{t^2 - 1}{4t^2} \right)^s, \tag{10}$$

it is easy to establish a relation between (10) and the real polynomial $f_k(t)$ in (9), concluding in this way that

$$\mathrm{Re}(\mathbf{P}_k(t, |x|)) = |x|^k \mathcal{P}_k(t).$$

For the special case of $x_0 = 0$ and $|x| = 1$, this last relation provides the following form of representing c_k:

$$c_k = (-1)^{\left\lfloor \frac{k+1}{2} \right\rfloor} \mathcal{P}_{2\left\lfloor \frac{k+1}{2} \right\rfloor}(0). \tag{11}$$

We point out that relation (11) can also be obtained directly by using the following well-known property of the Legendre polynomials:

$$\mathcal{P}_n(0) = \begin{cases} \frac{(-1)^m}{4^m} \binom{2m}{m}, & \text{for } n = 2m \\ 0, & \text{for } n = 2m + 1 \end{cases}.$$

2.10   Representation in Terms of Values of the Derivatives of the Bessel Functions

Consider the Bessel functions of the first kind

$$J_0(z) = \sum_{k=0}^{\infty} (-1)^k \frac{z^{2k}}{2^{2k}(k!)^2} \quad \text{and} \quad J_1(z) = \sum_{k=0}^{\infty} (-1)^k \frac{z^{2k+1}}{2^{2k+1}k!(k+1)!}.$$

Differentiating m-times both Bessel functions we get

$$J_0^{(m)}(z) = \sum_{k=m}^{\infty} (-1)^k \frac{(2k)(2k-1)\cdots(2k-(m-1))z^{2k-m}}{2^{2k}(k!)^2}$$

and

$$J_1^{(m)}(z) = \sum_{k=m}^{\infty} (-1)^k \frac{(2k+1)(2k)\cdots(2k+1-(m-1))z^{2k+1-m}}{2^{2k+1}k!(k+1)!}.$$

Therefore

$$J_0^{(m)}(0) = \begin{cases} (-1)^{\frac{m}{2}} c_m, & \text{if } m \text{ even} \\ 0, & \text{if } m \text{ odd} \end{cases} \quad \text{and} \quad J_1^{(m)}(0) = \begin{cases} 0, & \text{if } m \text{ even} \\ (-1)^{\frac{m-1}{2}} c_m, & \text{if } m \text{ odd} \end{cases}.$$

These two last equalities, allows to write

$$c_k = (-1)^{\left\lfloor \frac{k}{2} \right\rfloor} J_{\frac{1-(-1)^k}{2}}^{(k)}(0),$$

which, in turn, leads together with (8) to the following representation of the hypercomplex polynomial (7)

$$\mathbf{P}_k(x_0 + \omega|\underline{x}|) = \sum_{s=0}^{k} \binom{k}{s} x_0^{k-s} |\underline{x}|^s \left(J_0^{(s)}(0) + \omega(\underline{x}) J_1^{(s)}(0) \right).$$

For more details on this subject we mention the works [11, 23].

3   Other Properties of $(c_k)_k$

Without being exhaustive, we list now several properties of the Vietoris sequence that have been proved in the last years.

1. **Alternating series** [8] $\displaystyle\sum_{k=0}^{+\infty}(-1)^k c_k = 1.$

2. **Combinatorial Identity** [21] $\displaystyle\sum_{s=0}^{k}(-1)^{k-s}\binom{-\frac{3}{2}}{k-s}\binom{-\frac{1}{2}}{s} = (k+1)c_k.$

3. **Trigonometric Identities** [6]   For $0 < \alpha < \pi,$

$$\sum_{k=0}^{\infty} c_k \cos^k \alpha = \frac{2}{1 - \cos\alpha + \sin\alpha} \quad \text{and} \quad \sum_{k=0}^{\infty} c_k \sin^k \alpha = \frac{2}{1 - \sin\alpha + \cos\alpha}.$$

4. **Recurrence Relations** [7,8]

$$(k+2)c_{k+1} = c_k + kc_{k-1}, k \geq 1, \quad c_0 = 1, c_1 = \tfrac{1}{2}$$

and

$$\Delta c_k = -\frac{1}{2}\sum_{s=0}^{k} c_{k-s}\Delta c_{s-1},$$

where $\Delta c_k := c_{k+1} - c_k$ denotes the forward difference with $\Delta c_{-1} := 1.$

5. **Generating Functions**

In [6], an elementary procedure, based on the expansion of the binomial function $(1-t^2)^l$ was used to derive the following generating function of the sequence $(c_k)_k$:

$$F(t) = \frac{\sqrt{1+t} - \sqrt{1-t}}{t\sqrt{1-t}}. \tag{12}$$

Similarly, it can be proved that the even order-terms sequence $(c_{2k})_k$ is generated by the function

$$f(t) = \frac{1}{\sqrt{1-t}}.$$

More recently [7], an exponential generating function of the sequence $(c_k)_k$ was obtained by using methods of the calculus of holonomic differential equations, namely

$$F(t) = I_0(t) + I_1(t),$$

where I_0 and I_1 are the modified Bessel functions of the first kind. This function is closely related to the hypercomplex exponential function that has been studied in the past,

$$\mathrm{Exp}(x_0 + \boldsymbol{\omega}|\underline{x}|) = e^{x_0}\left(J_0(|\underline{x}|) + \boldsymbol{\omega}(\underline{x})J_1(|\underline{x}|)\right).$$

Finally, we mention that the even order-terms sequence $(c_{2k})_k$ has as exponential generating function

$$f(t) = e^{\frac{t}{2}} I_0\left(\tfrac{t}{2}\right).$$

6. **Relation to the central binomial coefficients sequence**

The well-known properties of the central binomial coefficients (CBC) and their relation to the even-order terms of the Vietoris sequence c_{2k}, allows to write down immediately a number of useful relations. In the literature there are a lot of combinatorial identities involving the CBC (see e.g. [19] and the unpublished manuscripts of Gould [16,17]).

In https://w3.math.uminho.pt/VietorisSequence a Mathematica notebook containing the proofs of several well-known properties written in terms of the sequence $(c_{2k})_k$ was made available.

4   Vietoris Convolution Triangles

We recall that the kth convolution of the sequence $(a_n)_n$ is the sequence $(a_n^{(k)})_n$, defined recursively as

$$a_n^{(k)} = \sum_{s=0}^{n} a_s a_{n-s}^{(k-1)},$$

$$a_n^{(0)} = a_n,$$

(see e.g. [3,18]). As it is well known, the convolution of sequences corresponds to the multiplication of their generating functions, i.e., if $F(t)$ is the generating function of the sequence $(a_n)_n$, then the generating function $F_k(t)$ of the kth convolution of the sequence $(a_n)_n$ is $(F(t))^{k+1}$.

For example, in the case of the Vietoris sequence and taking into account (12) we obtain

$$F_0(t) = \frac{\sqrt{t+1} - \sqrt{1-t}}{t\sqrt{1-t}}$$

$$= 1 + \frac{t}{2} + \frac{t^2}{2} + \frac{3t^3}{8} + \frac{3t^4}{8} + \frac{5t^5}{16} + \frac{5t^6}{16} + \frac{35t^7}{128} + \frac{35t^8}{128} + \cdots$$

$$F_1(t) = \frac{2\left(\sqrt{1-t^2} - 1\right)}{(t-1)t^2}$$

$$= 1 + t + \frac{5t^2}{4} + \frac{5t^3}{4} + \frac{11t^4}{8} + \frac{11t^5}{8} + \frac{93t^6}{64} + \frac{93t^7}{64} + \frac{193t^8}{128} + \cdots$$

$$F_2(t) = \frac{\left(\sqrt{t+1} - \sqrt{1-t}\right)^3}{(1-t)^{3/2}t^3}$$

$$= 1 + \frac{3t}{2} + \frac{9t^2}{4} + \frac{11t^3}{4} + \frac{27t^4}{8} + \frac{123t^5}{32} + \frac{281t^6}{64} + \frac{309t^7}{64} + \frac{681t^8}{128} + \cdots$$

The convolution triangle, written in rectangular form, of the sequence $(a_n)_n$ is an array whose k^{th} column is the sequence $(a_n^{(k-1)})_n$, $k = 1, 2, \ldots$ (see e.g. [3,18]).

Tables 1–2 show the convolution triangles $\mathcal{T}_V$ and $\mathcal{T}_{EV}$ corresponding to the Vietoris sequence $(c_n)_n$ and the even order-term sequence $(c_{2n})_n$. Tables 3–4 present the triangles $\mathcal{T}_{CC}$ and $\mathcal{T}_C$ associated to the related sequences

$$u_n = \binom{n}{\lfloor \frac{n}{2} \rfloor} \quad \text{and} \quad v_n = \binom{2n}{n} = u_{2n} \tag{13}$$

of the complete central binomial coefficients and of the central binomial coefficients.

For the sake of better visibility, we also write on the right side of each table, the corresponding left justified triangle. The Mathematica code to produce the tables is presented in the Appendix B.

Table 1. The Vietoris convolution triangle $\mathcal{T}_V$

1	1	1	1	1	1	1	...		1					
$\frac{1}{2}$	1	$\frac{3}{2}$	2	$\frac{5}{2}$	3	$\frac{7}{2}$	...		$\frac{1}{2}$	1				
$\frac{1}{2}$	$\frac{5}{4}$	$\frac{9}{4}$	$\frac{7}{2}$	5	$\frac{27}{4}$	$\frac{35}{4}$	...		$\frac{1}{2}$	1	1			
$\frac{3}{8}$	$\frac{5}{4}$	$\frac{11}{4}$	5	$\frac{65}{8}$	$\frac{49}{4}$	$\frac{35}{2}$	...		$\frac{3}{8}$	$\frac{5}{4}$	$\frac{3}{2}$	1		
$\frac{3}{8}$	$\frac{11}{8}$	$\frac{27}{8}$	$\frac{109}{16}$	$\frac{195}{16}$	$\frac{321}{16}$	$\frac{497}{16}$	...		$\frac{3}{8}$	$\frac{5}{4}$	$\frac{9}{4}$	2	1	
$\frac{5}{16}$	$\frac{11}{8}$	$\frac{123}{32}$	$\frac{69}{8}$	$\frac{541}{32}$	$\frac{483}{16}$	$\frac{805}{16}$	...		$\frac{5}{16}$	$\frac{11}{8}$	$\frac{11}{4}$	$\frac{7}{2}$	$\frac{5}{2}$	1
$\frac{5}{16}$	$\frac{93}{64}$	$\frac{281}{64}$	$\frac{341}{32}$	$\frac{45}{2}$	$\frac{689}{16}$	$\frac{1225}{16}$	...		$\frac{5}{16}$	$\frac{11}{8}$	$\frac{27}{8}$	5	5	3	1
$\vdots$	$\vdots$	$\vdots$	$\vdots$	$\vdots$	$\vdots$	$\vdots$			$\vdots$	$\vdots$	$\vdots$	$\vdots$	$\vdots$	$\vdots$

Denote by $\mathcal{M}_V = (m_{ij})$, $\mathcal{M}_{EV} = (n_{ij})$, $\mathcal{M}_C = (\tilde{n}_{ij})$ and $\mathcal{M}_{CC} = (\tilde{m}_{ij})$ the $r \times r$ matrices formed by using as elements the first r rows of the triangles $\mathcal{T}_V$, $\mathcal{T}_{EV}$, $\mathcal{T}_C$ and $\mathcal{T}_{CC}$ in rectangular form, respectively. It is easy to see that

$$\tilde{m}_{ij} = 2^{i-1} m_{ij} \quad \text{and} \quad \tilde{n}_{ij} = 4^{i-1} n_{ij}; \quad i = 1, 2, \ldots, r, \tag{14}$$

since $c_n^{(k)} = \frac{1}{2^n} u_n^{(k)}$ and $c_{2n}^{(k)} = \frac{1}{4^n} v_n^{(k)}$, $k = 0, 1, \ldots$. In other words,

$$\mathcal{M}_{CC} = \begin{pmatrix} 1 & & & & \\ & 2 & & & \\ & & 2^2 & & \\ & & & \ddots & \\ & & & & 2^{r-1} \end{pmatrix} \mathcal{M}_V \quad \text{and} \quad \mathcal{M}_C = \begin{pmatrix} 1 & & & & \\ & 4 & & & \\ & & 4^2 & & \\ & & & \ddots & \\ & & & & 4^{r-1} \end{pmatrix} \mathcal{M}_{EV}.$$

Table 2. The even order-terms Vietoris convolution triangle $\mathcal{T}_{EV}$

1	1	1	1	1	1	1	$\cdots$		1					
$\frac{1}{2}$	1	$\frac{3}{2}$	2	$\frac{5}{2}$	3	$\frac{7}{2}$	$\cdots$		$\frac{1}{2}$	1				
$\frac{3}{8}$	1	$\frac{15}{8}$	3	$\frac{35}{8}$	6	$\frac{63}{8}$	$\cdots$		$\frac{3}{8}$	1	1			
$\frac{5}{16}$	1	$\frac{35}{16}$	4	$\frac{105}{8}$	10	$\frac{231}{16}$	$\cdots$		$\frac{5}{16}$	1	$\frac{3}{2}$	1		
$\frac{35}{128}$	1	$\frac{315}{128}$	5	$\frac{1155}{128}$	15	$\frac{3003}{128}$	$\cdots$		$\frac{35}{128}$	1	$\frac{15}{8}$	2	1	
$\frac{63}{256}$	1	$\frac{693}{256}$	6	$\frac{3003}{256}$	21	$\frac{9009}{256}$	$\cdots$		$\frac{63}{256}$	1	$\frac{35}{16}$	3	$\frac{5}{2}$	1
$\vdots$	$\vdots$	$\vdots$	$\vdots$	$\vdots$	$\vdots$				$\vdots$	$\vdots$	$\vdots$	$\vdots$	$\vdots$	$\ddots$

Therefore

$$\det \mathcal{M}_{CC} = \prod_{i=1}^{r} 2^{i-1} \det \mathcal{M}_V = 2^{\frac{r(r-1)}{2}} \det \mathcal{M}_V$$

and

$$\det \mathcal{M}_C = 4^{\frac{r(r-1)}{2}} \det \mathcal{M}_{EV}.$$

The determinant of the matrices $\mathcal{M}_C$ and $\mathcal{M}_{CC}$ can be easily computed (see e.g. [2]),

$$\det \mathcal{M}_C = 2^{\frac{r(r-1)}{2}} \quad \text{and} \quad \det \mathcal{M}_{CC} = 1,$$

and this leads to the interesting equality

$$\det \mathcal{M}_V = \det \mathcal{M}_{EV} = 2^{-\frac{r(r-1)}{2}}.$$

For example, for $r = 4$ we obtain

$$\begin{vmatrix} 1 & 1 & 1 & 1 \\ \frac{1}{2} & 1 & \frac{3}{2} & 2 \\ \frac{3}{8} & 1 & \frac{15}{8} & 3 \\ \frac{5}{16} & 1 & \frac{35}{16} & 4 \end{vmatrix} = \begin{vmatrix} 1 & 1 & 1 & 1 \\ \frac{1}{2} & 1 & \frac{3}{2} & 2 \\ \frac{1}{2} & \frac{5}{4} & \frac{9}{4} & \frac{7}{2} \\ \frac{3}{8} & \frac{5}{4} & \frac{11}{4} & 5 \end{vmatrix} = \frac{1}{64}.$$

It is worthwhile to recall that the sequences $(u_n)_n$ and $(v_n)_n$ in (13) have as generating functions,

$$G(t) = \frac{-1 + 2t + \sqrt{1 - 4t^2}}{2t - 4t^2} \quad \text{and} \quad g(t) = \frac{1}{\sqrt{1 - 4t}},$$

respectively, being, as expected, related to the generating functions F and f of $(c_n)_n$ and $(c_{2n})_n$, respectively, through

$$G(t) = F(2t) \quad \text{and} \quad g(t) = f(4t).$$

Table 3. The complete central binomial coefficients convolution triangle $\mathcal{T}_{CC}$

1	1	1	1	1	1	...		1					
1	2	3	4	5	6	...		1	1				
2	5	9	14	20	27	...		2	2	1			
3	10	22	40	65	98	...		3	5	3	1		
6	22	54	109	195	321	...		6	10	9	4	1	
10	44	123	276	541	966	...		10	22	22	14	5	1
$\vdots$	$\vdots$	$\vdots$	$\vdots$	$\vdots$	$\vdots$			$\vdots$	$\vdots$	$\vdots$	$\vdots$	$\vdots$	$\vdots$	$\ddots$

This last relation could also have been used to obtain (14).

Table 4. The central binomial coefficients convolution triangle $\mathcal{T}_C$

1	1	1	1	1	1	...		1					
2	4	6	8	10	12	...		2	1				
6	16	30	48	70	96	...		6	4	1			
20	64	140	256	420	649	...		20	16	6	1		
70	256	630	1280	2310	3840	...		70	64	30	8	1	
252	1024	2772	6144	12012	21504	...		252	256	140	48	10	1
$\vdots$	$\vdots$	$\vdots$	$\vdots$	$\vdots$	$\vdots$			$\vdots$	$\vdots$	$\vdots$	$\vdots$	$\vdots$	$\vdots$	$\ddots$

The Table 2 also reveals another pattern related to the kth convolution of sequence $(\tilde{c}_n)_n = (c_{2n})_n$, when $k = 2m - 1$ is odd, as we next point out.

Observe that the columns $2m$ of $\mathcal{T}_{EV}$ contain the Taylor series coefficients of the functions $(1 - t)^{-m}$ (cf. (12)), which as it is well known is, for each fixed m, the generating function of the sequence $(b_n)_n$, where

$$b_n = \binom{n + m - 1}{m - 1}, \quad n = 0, 1, \ldots.$$

In other words, the triangle formed by the even columns of the triangle $\mathcal{T}_{EV}$, is the rectangular Pascal triangle.

For the particular case of $k = 1$ (i.e., $m = 1$) we find the convolution formula

$$\tilde{c}_n^{(1)} = \sum_{s=0}^{n} \tilde{c}_s \tilde{c}_{n-s} = \binom{n}{0} = 1,$$

which is just a rewrite of the well-known identity for convolution of central binomial coefficients:

$$\sum_{s=0}^{n} \binom{2s}{s}\binom{2(n-s)}{n-s} = 4^n.$$

Acknowledgments. Research at CMAT was partially financed by Portuguese funds through FCT - Fundação para a Ciência e a Tecnologia, within the Projects UIDB/00013/2020 and UIDP/00013/2020. Research at CIDMA has been financed by FCT, within the Projects UIDB/04106/2020 and UIDP/04106/2020.

A   Alternative Definitions

Vietoris sequence

```
c[k_Integer?NonNegative] := 1/2^k Binomial[k, Floor[k/2]]
```

Definition in terms of the generators of $\mathbb{H}$

The implementation of (3) requires the use of the free Mathematica package QuaternionAnalysis [13].

```
e1=Quaternion[0,1,0,0];e2=Quaternion[0,0,1,0];
c1[k_]:=(-1)^k
    Sum[Binomial[k,s]QPower[SymmetricPower[e1,k-s,e2,s],2],{s,0,k}]^-1;
```

The function `Quaternion` defines a quaternion object, while `QPower` implements the usual quaternions powers. Both functions are included in the Mathematica package `QuaternionAnalysis`, where the arithmetic operations are also defined. The code of the function `SymmetricPower` is presented below. For more details on the use of the package we refer to the user guide included in the package documentation.

```
SymmetricPower[q1_, k_, q2_, s_] := SymmetricPower[q1, k, q2, s] =
                1/(k + s) (k q1 ** SymmetricPower[q1, k - 1, q2, s] +
                s q2 ** SymmetricPower[q1, k, q2, s - 1])
SymmetricPower[q1_, 0, q2_, s_] := QPower[q2, s];
SymmetricPower[q1_, k_, q2_, 0] := QPower[q1, k];
```

Double Factorial representation

```
c2[k_Integer?NonNegative] := (2 Floor[(k-1)/2]+1)!!/(2Floor[(k-1)/2]+2)!!
```

Recursive definition

```
c3[k_?((OddQ[#] && Positive[#]) &)] := c3[k] = k/(k + 1) c3[k - 1]
c3[k_?((EvenQ[#] && Positive[#]) &)] := c3[k] = c3[k - 1]
c3[0] = 1;
```

Pochhammer symbol representation

```
c4[k_Integer?NonNegative] :=
                Pochhammer[1/2, Floor[(k + 1)/2]]/Floor[(k + 1)/2]!;
```

Alternating sum of a non-symmetric triangle

```
c5[k_Integer?NonNegative] := Sum[(-1)^s (Pochhammer[3/2, k - s]
                Pochhammer[1/2, s])/((k - s)! s!), {s, 0, k}]/(k + 1);
```

We point out that the function Ck[k,n] included in QuaternionAnalysis defines, for the choice $n = 2$, the Vietoris sequence, using the form (5).

Gamma function representation

```
c6[k_Integer?NonNegative] :=  Gamma[1/2 + Floor[(k + 1)/2]]/
                (Gamma[1/2] Gamma[1 + Floor[(k +  1)/2]]);
```

Integral representation

```
c7[k_Integer?NonNegative] :=
                2/Pi Integrate[Cos[x]^(2 Floor[(k + 1)/2]), {x, 0, Pi/2}]
```

Catalan Numbers

```
c8[k_Integer?NonNegative] := Sum[(-2)^-s Binomial[k, s] CatalanNumber[s],
                                                            {s, 0, k}]
```

Legendre Polynomials

```
c9[k_Integer?NonNegative] := (-1)^Floor[(k+1)/2]
                                LegendreP[2 Floor[(k+1)/2], 0]
```

Bessel functions

```
c10[k_Integer?NonNegative] := Limit[(-1)^Floor[k/2]
                D[BesselJ[1/2 (1 - (-1)^k), x], {x, k}], x -> 0]
```

Bessel functions of the first kind with integer order are entire functions; here we have use the limit to avoid the indetermine form provided by a direct evaluation of the derivatives in Mathematica.

B   Convolution Triangles

To produce the convolution triangle of a sequence in its rectangular form, one can use the function TriangleRect, in one of the following forms:

1. TriangleRect[{a0,a1,...,an},k]
   gives the $(n + 1) \times (k + 1)$ matrix corresponding to the first k convolutions of the sequence whose first $n + 1$ terms are a0,...,an;

2. TriangleRect[exp,n,k]

gives the $(n+1) \times (k+1)$ matrix corresponding to the first k convolutions of the sequence whose general term is given by the expression expr.

```
SeqConv[list1_List, list2_List] :=
    Module[{dim1 = Length[list1], dim2 = Length[list2]},
    If[dim1 == dim2,
        Table[Sum[list1[[k]] list2[[n - k + 1]], {k, 1, n}], {n, 1, dim1}],
        Message[SeqConv::dim]]];
    SeqConv::dim = "Lists in the argument must have the same lenght.";

SeqConv[list_List, k_Integer] := NestList[SeqConv[list, #] &, list, k]
SeqConv[a_, b_, n_] :=
    SeqConv[Table[a[k], {k, 0, n}], Table[b[k], {k, 0, n}]]
SeqConv[a_, n_Integer, k_Integer] :=
    Module[{list = Table[a[j], {j, 0, n}]}, SeqConv[list, k]]

TriangleRect[list_List, k_Integer] := Transpose[SeqConv[list, k]];
TriangleRect[a_, n_Integer, k_Integer] := Transpose[SeqConv[a, n, k]];
```

For example, the code

```
c[k_] := 1/2^k Binomial[k, Floor[k/2]]
TriangleRect[c, 6, 6] // TableForm
```

produces the matrix in the left hand side of Table 1. This result can also be obtained by using

```
TriangleRect[{1, 1/2, 1/2, 3/8, 3/8, 5/16, 5/16}, 6] // TableForm
```

The left justified form of the convolution triangle can be obtained by the use of the function TriangleLeft whose syntax is analogous to that of the function TriangleRect.

```
Matrix2Triangle[matrix_?MatrixQ] :=
    Module[{dim = Dimensions[matrix], m, n}, {m, n} = dim;
    If[n >= m, (Cases[#1, Except[Null]] & ) /@
        Transpose[MapThread[PadLeft[Drop[#1, -#2], m, Null] & ,
        {Take[Transpose[matrix], m], Range[m] - 1}]],
        (Cases[#1, Except[Null]] & ) /@
        Transpose[MapThread[PadLeft[Drop[#1, -#2],
        m, Null] & , {Transpose[matrix], Range[n] - 1}]]]]
```

```
TriangleLeft[list_List, k_Integer] :=
    Module[{n = Length[list]},
    If[n < k + 1, Message[TriangleLeft::order, n - 1]];
        Matrix2Triangle[Transpose[SeqConv[list, k]]]];
        TriangleLeft[a_, k_Integer] := Matrix2Triangle[SeqConv[a, k, k]];
        TriangleLeft::order = "Showing only the triangle of order '1'.";
```

To obtain the table in the right hand side of Table 1 we just have to use:

```
TriangleLeft[c, 6] // TableForm
```

or

```
TriangleLeft[{1, 1/2, 1/2, 3/8, 3/8, 5/16, 5/16}, 6] // TableForm
```

References

1. Aigner, M.: A Course in Enumeration. Springer, Heidelberg (2007). https://doi.org/10.1007/978-3-540-39035-0
2. Bicknell, M., Hoggatt, V.E.: Unit determinants in generalized Pascal triangles. Fibonacci Q. $11(2)$, 131–144 (1973)
3. Bicknell, M.: A primer for the Fibonacci numbers: part XIII. Fibonacci Q. $11(5)$, 511–516 (1973)
4. Cação, I., Falcão, M., Malonek, H.: Matrix representations of a special polynomial sequence in arbitrary dimension. Comput. Methods Funct. Theory $27(1)$, 371–391 (2012)
5. Cação, I., Falcão, M., Malonek, H.: Three-term recurrence relations for systems of Clifford algebra-valued orthogonal polynomials. Adv. Appl. Clifford Algebras 12, 71–85 (2017)
6. Cação, I., Falcão, M.I., Malonek, H.: Hypercomplex polynomials, Vietoris' rational numbers and a related integer numbers sequence. Complex Anal. Oper. Theory $11(5)$, 1059–1076 (2017)
7. Cação, I., Falcão, M.I., Malonek, H.R., Tomaz, G.: A Sturm-Liouville equation on the crossroads of continuous and discrete hypercomplex analysis. Math. Methods Appl. Sci. (2021). https://doi.org/10.1002/mma.7684
8. Cação, I., Irene Falcão, M., Malonek, H.R.: On generalized Vietoris' number sequences. Discret. Appl. Math. 269, 77–85 (2019)
9. Catarino, P., Almeida, R.: A note on Vietoris' number sequence. Mediterr. J. Math. $19(1)$, 41 (2022)
10. Catarino, P., De Almeida, R.: On a quaternionic sequence with Vietoris' numbers. Filomat $35(4)$, 1065–1086 (2021)
11. Falcão, M.I., Malonek, H.R.: Generalized exponentials through Appell sets in $\mathbb{R}^{n+1}$ and Bessel functions. In: AIP Conference Proceedings, vol. 936, pp. 738–741 (2007)
12. Falcão, M.I., Malonek, H.R.: On paravector valued homogeneous monogenic polynomials with binomial expansion. Adv. Appl. Clifford Algebras 22, 789–801 (2012)
13. Falcão, M.I., Miranda, F.: Quaternions: a Mathematica package for quaternionic analysis. In: Murgante, B., Gervasi, O., Iglesias, A., Taniar, D., Apduhan, B.O. (eds.) ICCSA 2011. LNCS, vol. 6784, pp. 200–214. Springer, Heidelberg (2011). https://doi.org/10.1007/978-3-642-21931-3_17
14. Falcão, M., Cruz, J., Malonek, H.: Remarks on the generation of monogenic functions. In: 17th Inter. Conf. on the Appl. of Computer Science and Mathematics on Architecture and Civil Engineering, Weimar (2006)
15. Falcão, M.I., Malonek, H.R.: A pascal-like triangle with quaternionic entries. In: Gervasi, O., et al. (eds.) ICCSA 2021. LNCS, vol. 12952, pp. 439–448. Springer, Cham (2021). https://doi.org/10.1007/978-3-030-86973-1_31
16. Gould, H.W.: Combinatorial identities: Table I: Intermediate techniques for summing finite series, from the seven unpublished manuscripts of H. W. Gould (2010), edited and compiled by Jocelyn Quaintance
17. Gould, H.W.: Combinatorial identities: Table III: Binomial identities derived from trigonometric and exponential series, from the seven unpublished manuscripts of H. W. Gould (2010), edited and compiled by Jocelyn Quaintance
18. Hoggatt, V.E., Jr., Bicknell, M.: Convolution triangles. Fibonacci Q. $10(6)$, 599–608 (1972)
19. Koshy, T.: Catalan Numbers with Applications. Oxford University Press, Oxford (2009)

20. Malonek, H.: Power series representation for monogenic functions in $\mathbb{R}^{n+1}$ based on a permutational product. Complex Var. Theory Appl. **15**, 181–191 (1990)
21. Malonek, H.R., Falcão, M.I.: Linking Clifford analysis and combinatorics through bijective methods. In: 9th International Conference on Clifford Algebras and Their Applications in Mathematical Physics, Weimar, Germany, 15–20 July (2011)
22. Malonek, H., Falcão, M.I.: Special monogenic polynomials–properties and applications. In: Simos, T.E., Psihoyios, G., Tsitouras, C. (eds.) AIP Conference Proceedings, vol. 936, pp. 764–767 (2007)
23. Malonek, H., Falcão, M.I.: On special functions in the context of Clifford analysis. In: Simos, T.E., Psihoyios, G., Tsitouras, C. (eds.) AIP Conference Proceedings, vol. 1281, pp. 1492–1495 (2010)
24. Rainville, E.: Special Functions. Macmillan, New York (1965)
25. Vietoris, L.: Über das Vorzeichen gewisser trigonometrischer Summen. Sitzungsber. Österr. Akad. Wiss **167**, 125–135 (1958)

Verification of the Domains Tracking Algorithm for Solving the System of Allen-Cahn and Cahn-Hilliard Equations

Dmitry Prokhorov[1]([✉]) [ID], Yaroslav Bazaikin[2] [ID], and Vadim Lisitsa[3] [ID]

[1] Institute of Petroleum Geology and Geophysics SB RAS, Koptug ave. 3, Novosibirsk 630090, Russia
prokhorovdi@ipgg.sbras.ru
[2] Faculty of Science, Jan Evangelista Purkyně University in Ústí nad Labem, Pasteurova 3632/15, Ústí nad Labem 400 96, Czech Republic
yaroslav.bazaykin@ujep.cz
[3] Sobolev Institute of Mathematics SB RAS, 4 Koptug ave., Novosibirsk 630090, Russia
lisitsavv@ipgg.sbras.ru

Abstract. The sintering process is widely used in modern industry because it allows for obtaining materials with predefined properties. Chemical or physical techniques can measure these properties. Besides the cost of such methods, it is worth noting that some techniques destroy samples, which causes difficulties in measuring the parameters' evolution. Computer simulation of the sintering process allows for overcoming these difficulties. The sintering models based on the system of Cahn-Hilliard and Allen-Cahn equations require optimization if the number of grains is large. However, optimizations affect the solution; thus, a detailed quality assessment is required. The article presents such a study for our optimization: the Allen-Cahn equations are solved in small subdomains of the whole computational domain, which change over time. We provide comparative tests between solutions obtained by our algorithm and solutions obtained by solving the system in the whole domain. Besides common approaches, we use powerful tools of topology: Hausdorff distance and Betti numbers. The choice of the algorithm parameters is justified by obtained accuracy and efficiency.

Keywords: Sintering · Phase-field · Cahn-Hilliard equation · Allen-Cahn equation

1 Introduction

Sintering is a common way to obtain a material with predefined filtration, strength, and sorptive properties. For example, tungsten and silicon carbides are widely used for extra durable tools, and abrasives [27,33]. Another example

O. Gervasi et al. (Eds.): ICCSA 2023 Workshops, LNCS 14104, pp. 693–707, 2023.
https://doi.org/10.1007/978-3-031-37105-9_46

is the sintering of sorbents for the chemical adsorption of CO_2 [4,5,10]. The process of sintering a granular material with the formation of a porous structure depends on many factors, such as temperature, duration of exposure, external loads, etc., which significantly impact the properties of the resulting material on a macroscale. Thus, computer simulation of sintering is an actual problem of modern material science [6].

We can consider sintering simulation as a moving-boundary problem or Stefan problem. One of the common ways to solve such problems is the level-set method [17,18,24] combined with the immersed boundary method [21,22,25,31,34]. However, the level-set method is more applicable to the simulation of the chemical interaction between fluid and rock [15,28] or to the modeling of the multiphase fluid flows [14,36] than for the sintering simulation [26,30].

Instead of a level-set approach, the phase-field method is often used to model sintering [13,37] and related problems, such bulk phase as solidification [12] and grain growth [23]. The key feature of this method is continuous fields describing the shapes and orientations of different grains. Field variables correspond to physical quantities such as composition and order parameters. They take definite values in grains and smoothly change at the interface.

In the case of a single-component system, the model is described by one conservative Cahn-Hilliard [7] equation and by I Allen-Cahn [2] equations (Sect. 2), where I is the number of grains. Each of the Allen-Cahn equations describes the evolution of the order parameter corresponding to one of the grains [35]. Using finite difference methods for solving this system requires storing values of order parameters for each grain. Thus, increasing the number of grains with a regular grid size causes the growth of computation efforts, but order parameters take zero value on most of the grid.

One method to overcome this difficulty is described in [16]. The principle of this method is that each grid node stores values only of I_c order parameters, where I_c is a predefined constant. Authors of [16] conducted a detailed study about the influence of their algorithm on the grain growth process and determined the optimal parameter.

Similar to [16], we performed a qualitative assessment of our approach (Sect. 3), in which each of the Allen-Cahn equations is solved in a small subdomain corresponding to the current grain. However, we are interested in changes in geometry and topology of sample structure under the influence of high temperature because they are related to chemisorption and strength properties. Therefore, we use topological approaches to the comparison, such as Hausdorff distance [3] and Betti numbers [8] (Sect. 4). The testing results, including the performance, are presented in Sect. 5.

2   Problem Statement

Let us consider a rectangular domain $\Omega = [X_1^{min}, X_1^{max}] \times [X_2^{min}, X_2^{max}] \times [X_3^{min}, X_3^{max}]$. Some part of Ω is occupied by grains; the rest of Ω is called pores. Order parameters $\eta_i(\mathbf{x}, t), 1 \le i \le I$ describe the crystallographic orientation of grains. They vary from 0 to 1. Parameter $\rho(\mathbf{x}, t)$ describes the mass density and varies in the same interval. For example, in Fig. 1, we can see a one-dimensional domain, where $\eta_i = 1$ in the grain i, $\eta_i = 0$ in the pore, and η_i smoothly varies between these values at the interface.

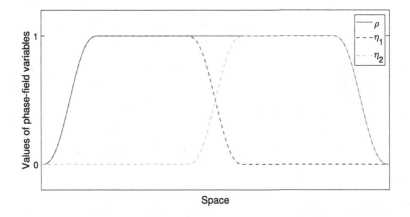

Fig. 1. Phase-field variables

According to [7], the total free energy of a heterogeneous system can be written as

$$F = \int f(\rho, \eta_1, ..., \eta_I) + \frac{1}{2}\beta_\rho |\nabla \rho|^2 + \frac{1}{2}\beta_\eta \sum_i |\nabla \eta_i|^2 d\Omega, \tag{1}$$

where f is a free local chemical energy density, β_ρ and β_η are gradient energy coefficients. The second term describes the impact of surface energy, and the third describes grain boundary energy's impact.

The evolution of ρ is given by the Cahn-Hilliard equation [7]. Mass density changes under the action of flow J, which is proportional to the gradient of the chemical potential μ (Fick's law [9]).

$$\frac{\partial \rho}{\partial t} = \nabla \cdot J \tag{2}$$

$$J = D\nabla \mu \tag{3}$$

$$\mu = \frac{\delta F}{\delta \rho} = \frac{\partial f}{\partial \rho} - \beta_\rho \Delta \rho \tag{4}$$

The Allen-Cahn equation describes the evolution of order parameters η_i [2].

$$\frac{\partial \eta_i}{\partial t} = -L\frac{\delta F}{\delta \eta_i} = -L(\frac{\partial f}{\partial \eta_i} - \beta_\eta \Delta \eta_i) \ \forall i, \tag{5}$$

where L is a constant related to grain boundary mobility.

Free local chemical energy density has the following form:

$$f(\rho, \eta_1, ..., \eta_I) = A\rho^2(1 - \rho)^2 + B\left(\rho^2 + 6(1 - \rho)\sum_i \eta_i^2\right.$$

$$\left. - 4(2 - \rho)\sum_i \eta_i^3 + 3\left(\sum_i \eta_i^2\right)^2\right), \tag{6}$$

where A and B are surface and grain boundary energy constants. Function f has $I + 1$ minima at points $\rho = 0$, $\eta_i = 0 \; \forall i$ and $\rho = 1$, $\eta_i = 1$, $\eta_j = 0 \; \forall j \neq i$, $1 \leq i \leq I$ [35].

Substituting (6) into (2)–(5), we obtain:

$$\frac{\partial \eta_i}{\partial t} = -L(12B\eta_i(1 - \rho - (2 - \rho)\eta_i + \sum_j \eta_j^2) - \beta_\eta \Delta\eta_i) \; \forall i, \tag{7}$$

$$\frac{\partial \rho}{\partial t} = \nabla \cdot D\nabla\left(2A\rho(1 - \rho)(1 - 2\rho) + B(2\rho - 6\sum_i \eta_i^2 + 4\sum_i \eta_i^3) - \beta_\rho \Delta\rho\right). \tag{8}$$

During the sintering, mass transport occurs by several diffuse paths.

1. Volume diffusion is the mass transport from within the grain.
2. Vapor diffusion is the mass transport through the pores.
3. Surface diffusion is the mass transport along the grain surface from the high-curvature areas to low-curvature ones.
4. Grain boundary diffusion is the mass transport along the boundary between grains.

The following form of diffusion coefficient allows taking into account all of these diffusion paths in phase-field terms:

$$D = D_{vol}\phi(\rho) + D_{vap}(1 - \phi(\rho)) + D_{surf}\rho^2(1 - \rho)^2 + D_{gb}\sum_{i<j} \eta_i\eta_j, \tag{9}$$

$$\phi(\rho) = \rho^3(10 - 15\rho + 6\rho^2).$$

$D_{vol}, D_{vap}, D_{surg}, D_{gb}$ are the constants related to material volume, vapor, surface, and grain boundary diffusivity, respectively.

To perform simulation, Eqs. (2) and (5) were discretized with respect to time by explicit forward Euler scheme with step τ. Spatial derivatives were discretized using central finite differences with grid step h for all directions.

3 Algorithm

If I is large, then for each order parameter η_i we define domain $\Omega_i = [X_{i1}^{min}, X_{i1}^{max}] \times [X_{i2}^{min}, X_{i2}^{max}] \times [X_{i3}^{min}, X_{i3}^{max}]$, which fulfills the condition $supp(\eta_i) \subseteq \Omega_i \subseteq \Omega$.

During simulation, grains change their shape and location. Thus, Ω_i should be changed too. Let us denote the minimal distance from grain i to planes bounding Ω_i as a $mindist_i$. Similarly, maximal distance is a $maxdist_i$.

The algorithm for tracking Ω_i consists of the following steps:

1. Initialization: domains Ω_i are chosen so that $mindist_i = maxdist_i = F_{start}, \forall i$.
2. Check: every T_r time steps, conditions $mindist_i > F_{min}, \forall i$ are checked.
3. Increasing: sizes of domains, for which condition $mindist_i > F_{min}$ failed, are increased so that $mindist_i = F_{start}$.
4. Total change: every T_{fr} time steps, all Ω_i change so that $mindist_i = maxdist_i = F_{start}, \forall i$.

Thus, four parameters $F_{min}, T_r, F_{start}, T_{fr}$ define the behavior of the algorithm. However, only two of them, F_{min} and T_r depend on model parameters. If we consider $\eta_i = 0.5$ as a grain surface, then F_{min} should not exceed half of the phase-field interface width. Otherwise, part of the interface will be outside of the domain. Restriction for the T_r depends on normal surface velocity. However, evaluating normal velocity for complex grains configuration is a difficult task. For one spherical grain with radius R, it is:

$$T_r < \frac{F_{min} R^2}{L \beta_\eta}, \tag{10}$$

because normal velocity has the following form [1]:

$$v_\eta = -L \beta_\eta \kappa_b, \tag{11}$$

where κ_b is the grain surface curvature.

4 Comparison Methods

Experiments are conducted in two variants. In the first of them, the evolution of order parameters η_i is computed in the whole domain Ω without tracking the subdomains. Let us denote this variant with subscript S. In the second variant with subscript T tracking algorithm is used.

One of the standard experiments for the sintering model is two spherical grains sintering [13,35]. During sintering, the neck growth between particles occurs. Sintering physics states that neck diameter to particles' diameter ratio has the following time dependence [35]:

$$\frac{X}{D} = K t^n, \tag{12}$$

where n depends on the dominant diffusion mechanism. Thus, we can compare the dynamic of neck growth between solutions.

$$E_X(t) = \frac{|X_S(t) - X_T(t)|}{X_S(t)}. \tag{13}$$

Further, the solutions can be compared in l_∞-norm:

$$E_\rho(t) = \max_{x \in G} |\rho_S(x, t) - \rho_T(x, t)|,$$

where G is the set of grid nodes. Here we use absolute error instead of relative because of the following reasons: ρ varies in the range $[0, 1]$, and the small interface shift cause enormous relative errors, making this measure unrepresentative.

Since we are primarily interested in changes in the sample's surface area, it is reasonable to compare this parameter of solutions.

$$E_A(t) = \frac{|A_S(t) - A_T(t)|}{|A_S(t)|}. \tag{14}$$

The surface area is computed with the Crofton formula [19] in the following way. Points a and b, are randomly chosen on the sphere which circumscribes the sample. Iterating along the line defined by a and b with the step $h/3$ (where h is the grid step), we count the number of intersections with the interface $\rho = 0.5$. The ρ value is trilinear interpolated at the points on the line. Assuming the sphere radius is R and M such experiments is performed with the number of intersections $\{N_1, ..., N_M\}$, than the surface area of the sample is approximately:

$$S \approx \frac{\sum_{i=1}^{M} N_i}{2M} \cdot 4\pi R^2. \tag{15}$$

Finally, the topology tools, such as Hausdorff distance and Betti numbers, allow us to estimate sample differences.

The Hausdorff distance between sets A and B is defined as:

$$d_H(A, B) = \max(\sup_{x \in A} \inf_{y \in B} |x - y|, \sup_{y \in B} \inf_{x \in A} |x - y|). \tag{16}$$

The diameter of set A is defined as:

$$diam(I) = \sup_{x,y \in A} |x - y|. \tag{17}$$

Since the solutions are defined in grid nodes, we can compute Hausdorff distance between sets of points $I_S(t) = \{x \in G | \rho_S(x, t) \geq 0.5\}$ and $I_T(t) = \{x \in G | \rho_T(x, t) \geq 0.5\}$ [32]. However, this approach's minimal possible distance (except zero) is equal to h, which is rather rough. Therefore we upscale grid G into grid G_u with step $0.2\,h$ using trilinear interpolation and then calculate the relation of the interface shift to the diameter of the sample.

$$I_S(t) = \{x \in G_u | \rho_S(x, t) \geq 0.5\},$$
$$I_T(t) = \{x \in G_u | \rho_T(x, t) \geq 0.5\},$$
$$E_H(t) = \frac{d_H(I_S(t), I_T(t))}{diam(I_S(t))}. \tag{18}$$

We can present the solution as a binary digital image, where nodes with value $\rho \geq 0.5$ correspond to the foreground and nodes with value $\rho < 0.5$ correspond to the background. The set of voxels with topology forms topological space. We define 26-connectivity on the foreground [28]. One of the informative characteristics of topology space is the sequence of Betti numbers $\{\beta_0, \beta_1, \beta_2...\}$; β_k is the rank of k–homology group [8]. In 3–dimensional space, all Betti numbers beginning with the third are zero. The first three present the following characteristics of topological space:

1. β_0 - the number of connected components,
2. β_1 - the number of through-holes,
3. β_2 - the number of closed voids.

Thus, we can exactly define if samples are different.

5   Numerical Experiments

To perform the simulation, we use two sets of parameters (Table 1). Both are aluminum oxide properties from [13] non-dimensionalized according to [1].

Table 1. Simulation parameters

Parameter	Two particles simulation	Packing simulation
A	4.933	7.733
B	0.667	0.267
β_ρ	17.5	25
β_η	12.5	5
L	0.203	0.129
D_{vol}	5.559×10^{-5}	3.103×10^{-5}
D_{vap}	2.779×10^{-5}	1.552×10^{-5}
D_{surf}	5.559×10^{-2}	3.103×10^{-2}
D_{gb}	5.559×10^{-2}	3.103×10^{-2}
$h_1 = h_2 = h_3 = h$	1	1
τ	0.05	0.05

All experiments were conducted at the Polytechnic Tornado supercomputer of Saint-Petersburg Polytechnic University equipped with CPU Intel Xeon E5 2697 v3 and GPU NVIDIA K40.

5.1   Simulation of Two Particles

The grid size of the two particles simulation (Fig. 2) is $120 \times 120 \times 200$ nodes. The radius of particles is equal to 40 spatial steps, which correspond to 1.25 μm. The simulations are performed during $5 \cdot 10^6$ time steps, corresponding to 4.5 h.

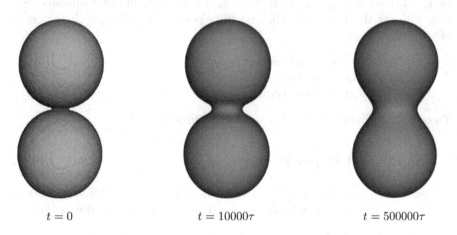

$t = 0$ \qquad $t = 10000\tau$ \qquad $t = 500000\tau$

Fig. 2. Neck growth between two particles

We measure neck diameter 60 times at the steps $\{0, 1, 2, .., 9, 10, 20, .., 100, 200, ..., 5 \times 10^6\}$. Then, using the least square method, parameters of power dependence 19 are defined.

$$\frac{X}{D} = Kt^n + C. \tag{19}$$

Because grid resolution does not allow to define touch of the spheres exactly, the term C is added. The obtained value $n = 0.172$ corresponds to the estimation for grain boundary diffusion [11]. In Fig. 3, neck growth is shown for the solution obtained with the tracking of subdomains.

The value of $E_X(t)$ is less than 10^{-5}, E_ρ is less than 10^{-3}.

Two equal particles are in the equilibrium state. Therefore, the grain boundary does not move, and sizes change slightly. Thus, the only significant parameter of the algorithm is the F_{start}. However, obtained errors allow us to conclude that value $F_{start} = 10h_1$ provides good accuracy.

5.2   Packing Simulation

In this section, we present the results of the sintering simulation of ten packings consisting of 50 equal particles. Packings are prepared using the Lubachevsky-Stillinger algorithm [20]. The snapshots of the samples are saved 56 times at the steps $\{0, 1, 2, .., 9, 10, 20, .., 100, 200, ..., 1 \times 10^6\}$. The grid size is 110^3 nodes.

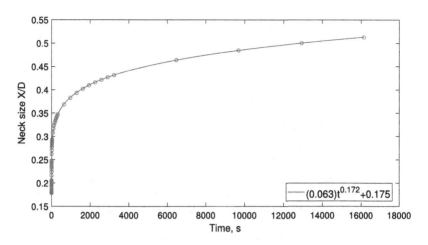

Fig. 3. Time dependence of neck diameter

The particles' radius equals 20 h, corresponding to 250 nm. The simulations are performed during 10^6 time steps, corresponding to 17.5 min.

We perform a simulation with and without tracking subdomains for each of the ten packings. In all experiments, the algorithm has the following parameters:

$$F_{min} = 5\,\text{h}, \qquad T_r = 100\tau,$$
$$F_{start} = 10\,\text{h}, \quad T_{fr} = 1000\tau. \tag{20}$$

For most of the simulations, E_∞ is less than 0.01. The maximal value of $E_\infty = 0.037$ reaches for sample six at the middle of the simulation (Fig. 4 left). This peak also appears in the E_H graph (Fig. 4 right). Nevertheless, E_H has a maximum at the beginning of the simulation for the second sample, where E_∞ has a less significant peak. Even with the peaks, the maximal shift of the interface is less than 0.5% of the sample's diameter. Moreover, E_H values mainly lie on the line corresponding to the minimal possible distance 0.2 h specified by the computation method. The line has an incline because of the shrinkage of the sample during sintering, so the diameters decrease.

The obtained values of the E_A are less than 10^{-3}, which is in the range of Monte-Carlo method error. Thus the time dependence of E_A is not representative.

Then, in order to study the behavior of the algorithm, we perform six additional experiments with the 6th sample (Fig. 5), varying the algorithm parameters (Table 2). In Table 2 "Reference" row corresponds to the experiment without subdomains tracking.

Figures 6 and 7 (right) show that experiments 1, 2, and 5 have much larger error values than others. E_∞ reaches the value 0.25. E_A is less than 1%, but here accuracy of the Crofton formula allows us to differentiate changes in surface area. E_H is up to two percent, approximately 2 h interface shift. It means that in experiments 1 and 2 boundary of subdomains is too close to the interface,

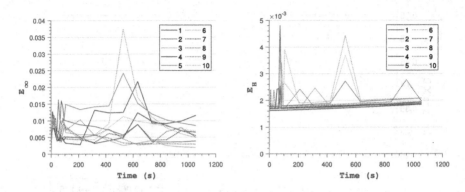

Fig. 4. Time-dependence of E_∞ (left) and E_H (right) for different experiments

Table 2. Algorithm parameters

Number	F_{min}	F_{start}	T_r	T_{fr}	Time (min)
1	3 h	6 h	100τ	1000τ	126
2	3 h	6 h	1000τ	10000τ	120
3	5 h	10 h	100τ	1000τ	133
4	5 h	10 h	1000τ	10000τ	124
5	5 h	10 h	10000τ	100000τ	146
6	10 h	20 h	1000τ	10000τ	220
7	10 h	20 h	10000τ	100000τ	160
Reference					2073

which significantly changes solutions. In experiment 5, domain resizing occurs very rarely, so the interface approaches too close to the boundary.

The sample consists of one connected component and has no void. Also, the sample does not split during the simulation, and voids do not appear. Therefore $b_0 = 1$ and $b_2 = 0$ constantly. The number of holes b_1 decreases during the simulation. At the beginning and end, the number is equal for all experiments. However, in all experiments except 6 and 7, b_1 slightly differs (Fig. 7 right). Graphs for experiments 3 and 4 (graph 4 overlaps the 3-d one in Fig. 7 right) do not feet to the reference in the one point. Graphs 1, 2, and 5 (graph 2 overlaps the 1-st one in Fig. 7 right) differ from the reference in several points. However, the difference in b_1 is equal to one. In spite of differences in b_1, we assume that the evolution of sample structure goes similarly; the cause of discrepancies in graphs are the small changes in the dynamic of pore collapse due to the different parameters of the tracking algorithm.

Thus, we can conclude that parameters 1, 2, and 5 are inappropriate for the current simulation. The four remaining sets of parameters are divided into two groups. Inside each of them, measured errors very close. So, we can choose the best parameters for performance reasons. Between parameters 3 and 4, the

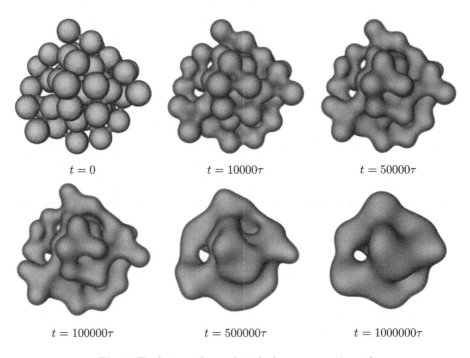

$t = 0$ $t = 10000\tau$ $t = 50000\tau$

$t = 100000\tau$ $t = 500000\tau$ $t = 1000000\tau$

Fig. 5. Evolution of sample 6 (reference experiment)

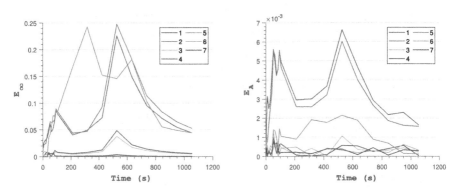

Fig. 6. Time-dependence of E_∞ (left) and E_A (right) for different algorithm parameters

winner is the fourth. Both experiments take a similar amount of memory (Fig. 8), but the fourth runs faster and has fewer errors than the third. There is no obvious winner between parameters 6 and 7. The seventh run faster but use more memory than the sixth. It seems reasonable to use parameters 6 at the beginning of the computation and then switch to parameters 7. The final conclusion, if the experiment is far from the memory limits, then parameters 6/7 are preferred. However, it is not true for the samples with a large number of grains and for the experiments on GPU without domain decomposition between several devices.

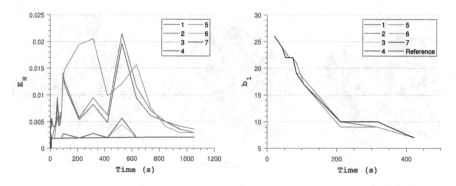

Fig. 7. Time-dependence of E_H (left) and b_1 (right) for different algorithm parameters

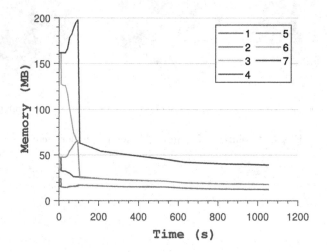

Fig. 8. Time-dependence of memory usage for storing order parameters for different algorithm parameters

6   Conclusion

The article presents a study of the qualitative properties of the algorithm for numerical simulation of sintering based on the system of Cahn-Hilliard and Allen-Cahn equations. The algorithm significantly decreases computational time by narrowing down the Allen-Cahn equations' evolution domains. However, the optimization alters obtained solutions. Besides common approaches, Hausdorff distance and Betti numbers are used to evaluate changes. Numerical experiments show that the solution has good quality if appropriate parameters are chosen. Parameters 3 (Table 2) seems to be the optimal decision. The analysis is performed for the single set of model parameters for packing consisting of 50 spherical grains with a radius of 10 h. However, the results can be generalized without new tests. First of all, the number of grains does not matter; the same parameters can be used for any size of packing (but the amount of device memory should be considered). Secondly, the model parameters are divided into two groups related to surface energy and diffusion mobilities, respectively. Mobilities define the velocity of the interface, so we need to change parameters T_r and T_{fr} proportionally. Energy defines the contact angles, which do not relate much to the algorithm parameters. Also, by the energy parameters, the width of the phase-field interface is defined. For experiments with a large number of grains, small values (like 5 h or 3 h) are used. It is the phase-field method parameter, and it does not depend on material properties, so we do not need to choose parameters for a wide range of interface widths. Thirdly, according to Herring scaling law [29], larger grains sinter slower than the smaller ones, so the same parameter can be used for any grains larger than 10 h by accuracy reasons (by performance reasons, it can be changed). Finally, if the shape of the grain differs from the spherical, then the grain surface has higher curvature and moves faster than the surface of the spherical grain. Therefore, domains should be resized faster, but a rigorous study for this case has not been conducted.

Acknowledgements. Dmitry Prokhorov implemented the pahse-field method and developed algorithms for computing the characteristics of the grains packing digital representation under the support of the basic research program of the Russian Academy of Sciences contract no. FWZZ-2022-0022. Yaroslav Bazaikin analyzed the results under the institutional support of the Faculty of Science, Jan Evangelista Purkyně University in Ústí nad Labem, Czech Republic. Vadim Lisitsa performed a numerical experiments using "Polytechnic RSC Tornado" (SPBSTU, Russia) with the support of the Russian Science Foundation Grant No. 21-71-20003.

References

1. Ahmed, K., Pakarinen, J., Allen, T., El-Azab, A.: Phase field simulation of grain growth in porous uranium dioxide. J. Nuclear Mater. **446**, 90–99 (2014). https://doi.org/10.1016/j.jnucmat.2013.11.036
2. Allen, S., Cahn, J.: Ground state structures in ordered binary alloys with second neighbor interactions. Acta Metallurgica **20**(3), 423–433 (1972)
3. Aspert, N., Santa-Cruz, D., Ebrahimi, T.: Mesh: measuring errors between surfaces using the hausdorff distance. In: Proceedings. IEEE International Conference on Multimedia and Expo, vol. 1, pp. 705–708 (2002). https://doi.org/10.1109/ICME.2002.1035879
4. Bazaikin, Y., Derevschikov, V., Malkovich, E., Lysikov, A., Okunev, A.: Evolution of sorptive and textural properties of cao-based sorbents during repetitive sorption/regeneration cycles: part ii. modeling of sorbent sintering during initial cycles. Chem. Eng. Sci. **199**, 156–163 (2019). https://doi.org/10.1016/j.ces.2018.12.065, https://www.sciencedirect.com/science/article/pii/S0009250919300971
5. Bazaikin, Y., Malkovich, E., Prokhorov, D., Derevschikov, V.: Detailed modeling of sorptive and textural properties of CaO-based sorbents with various porous structures. Sep. Purif. Technol. **255**, 117746 (2021)
6. Bordia, R.K., Kang, S.J.L., Olevsky, E.A.: Current understanding and future research directions at the onset of the next century of sintering science and technology. J. Am. Ceram. Soc. **100**(6), 2314–2352 (2017). https://doi.org/10.1111/jace.14919

7. Cahn, J.W., Hilliard, J.E.: Free energy of a nonuniform system. i. interfacial free energy. J. Chem. Phys. **28**(2), 258–267 (1958). https://doi.org/10.1063/1.1744102
8. Edelsbrunner, H., Harer, J.: Computational topology: an introduction, January 2010. https://doi.org/10.1007/978-3-540-33259-6_7
9. Fick, A.: Ueber diffusion. Annalen der Physik **170**(1), 59–86 (1855)
10. Florin, N., Fennell, P.: Synthetic CaO-based sorbent for co2 capture, vol. 4, pp. 830–838 (2011). https://doi.org/10.1016/j.egypro.2011.01.126, https://www.sciencedirect.com/science/article/pii/S1876610211001287, 10th International Conference on Greenhouse Gas Control Technologies
11. German, R.M.: Sintering Theory and Practice. John Wiley & Sons Inc., New York (1996)
12. Hötzer, J., et al..: Large scale phase-field simulations of directional ternary eutectic solidification. Acta Materialia **93**, 194–204 (2015)
13. Hötzer, J., Seiz, M., Kellner, M., Rheinheimer, W., Nestler, B.: Phase-field simulation of solid state sintering. Acta Materialia **164** (2018). https://doi.org/10.1016/j.actamat.2018.10.021
14. Jettestuen, E., Friis, H.A., Helland, J.O.: A locally conservative multiphase level set method for capillary-controlled displacements in porous media. J. Comput. Phys. **428**, 109965 (2021)
15. K.A. Gadylshina, T.S. Khachkova, V.L.: Numerical modeling of chemical interaction between a fluid and rocks. Numer. Methods Program. (Vychislitel'nye Metody i Programmirovanie) **20**(62), 457–470 (2020). https://doi.org/10.26089/NumMet.v20r440, https://en.num-meth.ru/index.php/journal/article/view/1035
16. Kim, S.G., Kim, D.I., Kim, W.T., Park, Y.B.: Computer simulations of two-dimensional and three-dimensional ideal grain growth. Phys. Rev. E **74**, 061605 (2006)
17. Li, X., Huang, H., Meakin, P.: Level set simulation of coupled advection-diffusion and pore structure evolution due to mineral precipitation in porous media. Water Resour. Res. **44**(12), W12407 (2008)
18. Li, X., Huang, H., Meakin, P.: A three-dimensional level set simulation of coupled reactive transport and precipitation/dissolution. Int. J. Heat Mass Transf. **53**(13), 2908–2923 (2010)
19. Liu, Y.S., Yi, J., Zhang, H., Zheng, G.Q., Paul, J.C.: Surface area estimation of digitized 3d objects using quasi-monte carlo methods. Pattern Recognit. **43**, 3900–3909 (2010). https://doi.org/10.1016/j.patcog.2010.06.002
20. Lubachevsky, B.D., Stillinger, F.H.: Geometric properties of random disk packings. J. Stat. Phys. **60**, 561–583 (1990)
21. Marella, S., Krishnan, S., Liu, H., Udaykumar, H.S.: Sharp interface cartesian grid method i: an easily implemented technique for 3d moving boundary computations. J. Comput. Phys. **210**(1), 1–31 (2005)
22. Mittal, R., Iaccarino, G.: Immersed boundary methods. Annu. Rev. Fluid Mech. **37**(1), 239–261 (2005)
23. Moelans, N., Wendler, F., Nestler, B.: Comparative study of two phase-field models for grain growth. Comput. Mater. Sci. **46**, 479–490 (2009). https://doi.org/10.1016/j.commatsci.2009.03.037
24. Osher, S., Fedkiw, R.P.: Level set methods: an overview and some recent results. J. Comput. Phys. **169**(2), 463–502 (2001)
25. Peskin, C.S.: Flow patterns around heart valves: a numerical method. J. Comput. Phys. **10**, 252–271 (1972)

26. Pino, D., Julien, B., Valdivieso, F., Drapier, S.: Solid-state sintering simulation: surface, volume and grain-boundary diffusions. In: ECCOMAS 2012 - European Congress on Computational Methods in Applied Sciences and Engineering, e-Book Full Papers, September 2012

27. Poetschke, J., Richter, V., Gestrich, T., Michaelis, A.: Grain growth during sintering of tungsten carbide ceramics. Int. J. Refract. Metals Hard Mater. **43**, 309–316 (2014)

28. Prokhorov, D., Lisitsa, V., Khachkova, T., Bazaikin, Y., Yang, Y.: Topology-based characterization of chemically-induced pore space changes using reduction of 3d digital images. J. Comput. Sci. **58**, 101550 (2022)

29. Rahaman, M.N.: Sintering of Ceramics, 1 ed. CRC Press, Boca Raton (2007)

30. Smereka, P.: Semi-implicit level set methods for curvature and surface diffusion motion. J. Sci. Comput. **19**, 439–456 (2003)

31. Sotiropoulos, F., Yang, X.: Immersed boundary methods for simulating fluid-structure interaction. Prog. Aerosp. Sci. **65**, 1–21 (2014)

32. Taha, A.A., Hanbury, A.: An efficient algorithm for calculating the exact hausdorff distance. IEEE Trans. Pattern Anal. Mach. Intell. **37**(11) (2015). https://doi.org/10.1109/TPAMI.2015.2408351

33. Tanaka, H.: Sintering of silicon carbide and theory of sintering. J. Ceramic Soc. Jpn. **110**(1286), 877–883 (2002). https://doi.org/10.2109/jcersj.110.877

34. Tseng, Y.H., Ferziger, J.H.: A ghost-cell immersed boundary method for flow in complex geometry. J. Comput. Phys. **192**(2), 593–623 (2003)

35. Wang, Y.U.: Computer modeling and simulation of solid-state sintering: a phase field approach. Acta Materialia **54**(4), 953–961 (2006)

36. Zhang, J., Yue, P.: A level-set method for moving contact lines with contact angle hysteresis. J. Comput. Phys. **418**, 109636 (2020)

37. Zhang, R.J., Chen, Z.W., Fang, W., Qu, X.: Thermodynamic consistent phase field model for sintering process with multiphase powders. Trans. Nonferrous Metals Soc. China **24**, 783–789 (2014). https://doi.org/10.1016/S1003-6326(14)63126-5

A Two-Step Quaternionic Root-Finding Method

Maria Irene Falcão[1] , Fernando Miranda[1]([✉]) , Ricardo Severino[1] ,
and Maria Joana Soares[2]

[1] CMAT and Departamento de Matemática, Universidade do Minho, Braga, Portugal
{mif,fmiranda,ricardo}@math.uminho.pt
[2] NIPE, Universidade do Minho, Braga, Portugal
jsoares@math.uminho.pt

Abstract. In this paper we present a new method for determining simultaneously all the simple roots of a quaternionic polynomial. The proposed algorithm is a two-step iterative Weierstrass-like method and has cubic order of convergence. We also illustrate a variation of the method which combines the new scheme with a recently proposed deflation procedure for the case of polynomials with spherical roots.

Keywords: Quaternions · Zeros · Weierstrass method

1 Introduction

In this paper we focus on the problem of approximating the zeros of polynomials of the form

$$P(x) = a_n x^n + a_{n-1} x^{n-1} + \cdots + a_1 x + a_0, \ a_n \neq 0, \tag{1}$$

where the coefficients a_k are quaternions.

Newton-like methods, based on quaternion arithmetic, have been considered in the past [6,7,14] to obtain approximations to the zeros of special functions. One important issue in the framework of Newton or any similar derivative-based method is related to the notions of regularity of a quaternionic function and its derivatives, which in turn restrict the application of this class of methods to a certain class of quaternionic functions (see [6] for details).

One of the most frequently used methods for simultaneous approximation of all simple polynomial zeros is the Weierstrass method [22], also known in the literature as the Durand-Kerner method [3] or Dochev method [2]. This is a free-derivative method relying on the factorization of the polynomial which makes its extension to the quaternion setting possible. Such generalization was derived in [5], where it was also proved that, as in the classical case, the method has quadratic order of convergence for the simple roots of a polynomial.

More recently [9], an approach combining a deflation procedure with the Weierstrass method allowed to obtain approximations also to the non-isolated zeros of P. In this work, we suggest an improvement of the quaternionic Weierstrass method, by using a two-step strategy and prove that this new procedure has cubic order of convergence. We also illustrate, by examples, that this new method can be combined with the aforementioned deflation process to obtain the isolated and non-isolated zeros of P.

The paper is organized as follows: in Sect. 2 we recall some results concerning the ring of quaternionic polynomials, fundamental throughout the paper. Section 3 contains the main result of the paper: a two-step Weierstrass method which we prove to have, under certain assumptions, cubic order of convergence. In Sect. 4 we illustrate the performance of the method by considering some examples and computing the corresponding computational order of convergence. We also apply, in Examples 3 and 4, the technique described in [9], to obtain successfully both the isolated and non-isolated zeros of the polynomial under consideration. The paper ends with some remarks and conclusions.

2   Basic Definitions and Results

We start by first recalling some aspects of the algebra of quaternions $\mathbb{H}$ needed for this work; for more details on this algebra, we refer to $[13, 15, 23]$. Here we will adopt the following notation: a quaternion x is an element of the noncommutative division algebra $\mathbb{H}$ of the form $x = x_0 + x_1\mathbf{i} + x_2\mathbf{j} + x_3\mathbf{k}$, $x_i \in \mathbb{R}$, where the imaginary units $\mathbf{i}, \mathbf{j}, \mathbf{k}$ satisfy the multiplication rules

$$\mathbf{i}^2 = \mathbf{j}^2 = \mathbf{k}^2 = -1, \quad \mathbf{ij} = -\mathbf{ji} = \mathbf{k}.$$

In analogy with the complex case, we define the real part of x, $\operatorname{Re}(x) := x_0$, the conjugate of x, $\bar{x} := x_0 - \mathbf{i}x_1 - \mathbf{j}x_2 - \mathbf{k}x_3$ and the norm of x, $|x| := \sqrt{x\bar{x}} = \sqrt{\bar{x}x}$. Any quaternion $x \neq 0$ is invertible and its inverse is given by $x^{-1} = \frac{\bar{x}}{|x|^2}$.

On $\mathbb{H}$, the relation $q \sim q'$ if $\operatorname{Re} q = \operatorname{Re} q'$ and $|q| = |q'|$, is an equivalence relation and, as usual, $[q] := \{q' \in \mathbb{H} : q \sim q'\}$ denotes the equivalence class of q.

In this work we consider polynomials P of the form (1), i.e., polynomials whose coefficients a_k are quaternions located only on the left-hand side of the powers; similar results could be derived by considering the coefficients on the right.

The set of polynomials of the form (1), with the addition and multiplication defined as in the commutative case, is a ring, usually denoted by $\mathbb{H}[x]$ and called the ring of (left) one-sided polynomials.

We introduce now some definitions and results concerning $\mathbb{H}[x]$, which will play an important role in the sequel (see $[11, 15]$ for other details). We mainly follow the notions and notations of $[5, 9]$.

A quaternion q is a zero or a root of P, if $P(q) = 0$, being the evaluation of P at q defined as $P(q) := a_n q^n + a_{n-1} q^{n-1} + \cdots + a_1 q + a_0$. We use the notation $\mathbf{Z}_P$ to represent the set of all the zeros of P. A zero q is called an isolated zero of P, if $[q]$ contains no other zeros of P, otherwise the zero is called a spherical zero of P; in this last case all the elements of $[q]$ are zeros of P (we point out that $[q]$,

$q \in \mathbb{H} \setminus \mathbb{R}$, can be identified with the three-dimensional sphere in the hyperplane $\{(x_0, x, y, z) \in \mathbb{R}^4 : x_0 = q_0\}$, with center $(q_0, 0, 0, 0)$ and radius $\sqrt{q_1^2 + q_2^2 + q_3^2}$).

The conjugate of P, denoted by $\overline{P}$, is obtained by conjugating the coefficients of P; the characteristic polynomial of a quaternion q is the real polynomial

$$\Psi_q(x) := (x - q)(x - \overline{q}) = x^2 - 2\operatorname{Re}(q)\, x + |q|^2. \tag{2}$$

Concerning the zero-structure and the factorization of polynomials in $\mathbb{H}[x]$ we recall the following results (see e.g. [1,11,15,18] for the proofs) essential for next section.

Result 1. *Consider the factorization of a polynomial* $P \in \mathbb{H}[x]$ *in the form* $P(x) = L(x)R(x)$ *with* $L, R \in \mathbb{H}[x]$.

1. *If* $q \in \mathbb{H}$ *is a zero of the right factor* R, *then* q *is a zero of the product* P.
2. *When* q *is a zero of* P *which is not a zero of* R, *we have*

$$P(q) = L(\tilde{q})R(q), \tag{3}$$

   where $\tilde{q} := R(q)qR(q)^{-1}$ *is a zero of* L;
3. *If* $L \in \mathbb{R}[x]$, *then*

$$P(q) = R(q)L(q). \tag{4}$$

Result 2. *Let* P *be a monic polynomial of degree* n $(n \geq 1)$ *in* $\mathbb{H}[x]$. *Then,*

1. P *admits a factorization into linear factors*

$$P(x) = (x - x_n)(x - x_{n-1}) \cdots (x - x_1), \tag{5}$$

   being the quaternions $x_1, \ldots, x_n$ *called factor terms of* P;
2. $\mathbf{Z}_P \subseteq \bigcup_{i=1}^{n} [x_i]$ *and each of the equivalence classes* $[x_i]; i = 1, \ldots, n$, *contains (at least) a zero of* P;
3. *If* $P(x) = (x - y_n)(x - y_{n-1}) \cdots (x - y_1)$ *is another factorization of* P *into linear factors, then there exists a permutation* π *of* $(1, 2, \ldots, n)$ *and* $h_i \in \mathbb{H}$ *such that* $y_{\pi(i)} = h_i x_i h_i^{-1}; i = 1, \ldots, n$.

Result 3. *Let* P *be a monic polynomial of degree* n *in* $\mathbb{H}[x]$ *with* n *isolated roots and let* (5) *be one of its factorizations.*

1. *The equivalence classes of the factor terms* $x_1, \ldots, x_n$ *in* (5) *are distinct;*
2. *Consider the polynomials*

$$R_i := \prod_{j=1}^{i-1} (x - \overline{x}_j).$$

The relation between the roots $\zeta_1, \ldots, \zeta_n$ *and the factor terms* $x_1, \ldots, x_n$ *of* P *is the following:*

$$\zeta_i = R_i(x_i)\, x_i \left(R_i(x_i) \right)^{-1} \quad and \quad x_i = \overline{R}_i(\zeta_i)\, \zeta_i \left(\overline{R}_i(\zeta_i) \right)^{-1}, \tag{6}$$

for $i = 1, \ldots, n$.

3 A Two-Step Weierstrass Method

From now on, we assume, for simplicity, that the polynomial P in (1) is monic, i.e., $a_n = 1$.

In the classical case, i.e., when the coefficients of P are complex, the popular Weierstrass method can be written as

$$\tilde{z}_i = z_i - W_i(z_i); \ i = 1, \ldots, n,$$

where the so-called *Weierstrass correction* W_i is the rational function

$$W_i(x) = \frac{P(x)}{\displaystyle\prod_{j=1 j \neq i}^{n} (x - z_j)}.$$

For simplicity, we use $\tilde{z}_i$ and z_i to denote, respectively, the $k+1$ and the k iterates of the method. If all the zeros of P are simple,[1] and we start with sufficiently close approximations to the roots, this method has quadratic order of convergence [2].

In [5] the authors of this paper extended the Weierstrass method in its sequential version to quaternionic context, by considering the scheme

$$\tilde{z}_i = z_i - \mathcal{P}_i(z_i) \left(\mathcal{Q}_i(z_i)\right)^{-1}; \ i = 1, \ldots, n,$$

where $\mathcal{P}_i(x) = \mathcal{L}_i(x) P(x) \mathcal{R}_i(x)$, with

$$\mathcal{L}_i(x) = \prod_{j=i+1}^{n} \left(x - \overline{z_j}\right), \quad \mathcal{R}_i(x) = \prod_{j=1}^{i-1} \left(x - \overline{z_j}\right) \tag{7}$$

and (cf. (2))

$$\mathcal{Q}_i(x) = \prod_{j=1}^{i-1} \Psi_{\tilde{z}_j}(x) \prod_{j=i+1}^{n} \Psi_{z_j}(x).$$

They also showed that, under certain conditions, the method converges quadratically to the factor terms x_i of P.

One can find in the literature several simultaneous methods based on the Weierstrass corrections with higher order of convergence (see e.g. [20]), which usually depend on the derivatives of the polynomial. If we are looking for a higher order free derivative method, the use of multi-step methods can be a solution. The well-known two-step Newton method [21],

$$\begin{cases} y_i = z_i - \dfrac{P(z_i)}{P'(z_i)} \\[2mm] \tilde{z}_i = y_i - \dfrac{P(y_i)}{P'(y_i)} \end{cases}$$

---

[1] The zeros are all simple if they are all distinct and isolated.

which has a fourth order convergence (see also [16]), can be easily adapted to quaternionic context by replacing first $\frac{P(x)}{P'(x)}$ by $W_i(x)$. In the complex case there are more competitive methods available (see e.g. [19]), but on the contrary, to the best of our knowledge, the quaternionic method that we are going to introduce, based on this strategy, is the one with the highest order of convergence.

Next theorem contains the main result of the paper.

Theorem 1. *Let P be a monic polynomial of degree n in $\mathbb{H}[x]$ with n isolated distinct roots and, for $i = 1, \ldots, n$; $k = 0, 1, 2, \ldots$, let*

$$
\begin{cases}
y_i^{(k)} = z_i^{(k)} - \mathcal{P}_i^{(k)}(z_i^{(k)}) \left(\mathcal{Q}_i^{(k)}(z_i^{(k)}) \right)^{-1} \\[2ex]
z_i^{(k+1)} = y_i^{(k)} - \mathcal{P}_i^{(k)}(y_i^{(k)}) \left(\mathcal{Q}_i^{(k)}(y_i^{(k)}) \right)^{-1}
\end{cases}
\tag{8}
$$

where $\mathcal{P}_i^{(k)}(x) = \left(\mathcal{L}_i^{(k)}(x) P(x) \mathcal{R}_i^{(k)}(x) \right)$ with

$$
\mathcal{L}_i^{(k)}(x) := \prod_{j=i+1}^{n} \left(x - \overline{z_j^{(k)}} \right),
\tag{9}
$$

$$
\mathcal{R}_i^{(k)}(x) := \prod_{j=1}^{i-1} \left(x - \overline{z_j^{(k+1)}} \right)
\tag{10}
$$

and

$$
\mathcal{Q}_i^{(k)}(x) := \prod_{j=1}^{i-1} \Psi_{z_j^{(k+1)}}(x) \prod_{j=i+1}^{n} \Psi_{z_j^{(k)}}(x).
\tag{11}
$$

If the initial approximations $z_i^{(0)}$ are sufficiently close to the factor terms x_i in a factorization of P in the form (5), then the sequences $\{z_i^{(k)}\}$ converge to x_i with cubic order of convergence.

Proof. The proof is an adaptation of the proof in [5], now for the case where each iteration involves two steps. In order to make the document complete, we have included all details.

For simplicity of notation, we write the scheme (8) in the form

$$
\begin{cases}
y_i = z_i - \mathcal{P}_i(z_i) \left(\mathcal{Q}_i(z_i) \right)^{-1} \\[2ex]
\tilde{z}_i = y_i - \mathcal{P}_i(y_i) \left(\mathcal{Q}_i(y_i) \right)^{-1}
\end{cases}
$$

omitting all the superscripts corresponding to the iteration number.

Assume that z_i are approximations to x_i with errors ε_i, i.e.,

$$
\varepsilon_i := x_i - z_i, \quad i = 1, \ldots, n,
\tag{12}
$$

and denote by ε the maximum error, i.e., $\varepsilon := \max_i |\varepsilon_i|$. We assume that ε is *small enough*, i.e., that z_i are *sufficiently good* approximations to x_i. Since, in each iteration, the first step corresponds to the classical quaternionic Weierstrass method, we known that

$$\varepsilon_i' := x_i - y_i, \ i = 1, \ldots, n,$$

are such that

$$\varepsilon' := \max_i |\varepsilon_i| = \mathcal{O}(\varepsilon^2). \tag{13}$$

We now prove, by complete induction on i, that the second step iterates $\tilde{z}_i$ are approximations to x_i with errors $\tilde{\varepsilon}_i$ such that

$$\tilde{\varepsilon}_i = \mathcal{O}(\varepsilon^3).$$

Base Case: We need to prove that $\tilde{\varepsilon}_1 = \mathcal{O}(\varepsilon^3)$.

Observe that the polynomial P can be written, by the use of (12), as

$$P(x) = \prod_{j=1}^{n}(x - x_{n-j+1}) = \prod_{j=1}^{n-1}(x - z_{n-j+1} - \varepsilon_{n-j+1})(x - y_1 - \varepsilon_1')$$

$$= \left(\prod_{j=1}^{n-1}(x - z_{n-j+1}) + \mathscr{E}_1(x)\right)(x - y_1 - \varepsilon_1'),$$

where $\mathscr{E}_1(x)$ designates a remainder polynomial consisting of a sum of $n - 1$ terms of the form

$$-(x - z_n)(x - z_{n-1})\ldots(x - z_{j-1})\varepsilon_j(x - z_{j+1})\ldots(x - z_2), \ j = 2, \ldots, n,$$

with terms consisting of products involving at least two ε_j's. We may assume that we are working in a bounded domain $\mathcal{D}$ of $\mathbb{H}$ (a sufficiently large disk containing all z_i) and therefore, we have

$$\mathscr{E}_1(\alpha) = \mathcal{O}(\varepsilon), \ \forall \alpha \in \mathcal{D}. \tag{14}$$

Taking into account the definition (7) of the polynomial $\mathcal{L}_1$, P can be written as

$$P(x) = \left(\overline{\mathcal{L}}_1(x) + \mathscr{E}_1(x)\right)(x - y_1 - \varepsilon_1') = \overline{\mathcal{L}}_1(x)(x - y_1 - \varepsilon_1') + \mathscr{E}_1(x)(x - y_1 - \varepsilon_1').$$

If we multiply P on the left by $\mathcal{L}_1$ and evaluate the resulting polynomial at the point $x = y_1$, we obtain, recalling the results (3) and (4) in Result 1 and the definition (11) of $\mathcal{Q}_1$,

$$(\mathcal{L}_1 P)(y_1) = -\varepsilon_1' \mathcal{Q}_1(y_1) - \left(\mathcal{L}_1 \mathscr{E}_1\right)(\hat{z}_1) \varepsilon_1',$$

where $\hat{z}_1 = \varepsilon'_1 z_1 (\varepsilon'_1)^{-1}$. Using now (14) we can write

$$(\mathcal{L}_1 P)(y_1) = -\varepsilon'_1 \mathcal{Q}_1(y_1) + \mathcal{O}(\varepsilon \varepsilon'_1).$$

Since we are assuming that the equivalence classes $[x_j]$ are distinct then, for sufficiently small ε, $|\mathcal{Q}_1(y_1)|$ is bounded away from zero and so, by multiplying both sides of the above equality on the right by $(\mathcal{Q}_1(y_1))^{-1}$, we obtain

$$(\mathcal{L}_1 P)(y_1) (\mathcal{Q}_1(y_1))^{-1} = -\varepsilon'_1 + \mathcal{O}(\varepsilon \varepsilon'_1),$$

which means by (8), that

$$x_1 = y_1 - (\mathcal{L}_1 P)(z_1) (\mathcal{Q}_1(y_1))^{-1} + \mathcal{O}(\varepsilon \varepsilon'_1).$$

Finally, we may conclude from (13) that the next approximation to x_1

$$\tilde{z}_1 = y_1 - (\mathcal{L}_1 P)(y_1) (\mathcal{Q}_1(y_1))^{-1}$$

is such that

$$\tilde{\varepsilon}_1 = x_1 - \tilde{z}_1 = \mathcal{O}(\varepsilon \varepsilon'_1) = \mathcal{O}(\varepsilon^3).$$

Induction Step: We now prove that $\tilde{z}_i$ approximates x_i with an error $\mathcal{O}(\varepsilon^3)$, assuming that, for $j = 1, \ldots, i-1$, $\tilde{z}_j$ are $\mathcal{O}(\varepsilon^3)$ approximations to x_j.

Define the polynomials

$$L_i(x) = \prod_{j=i+1}^{n} (x - \bar{x}_j) \quad \text{and} \quad R_i(x) = \prod_{j=1}^{i-1} (x - \bar{x}_j)$$

which can be written as

$$L_i(x) = \prod_{j=i+1}^{n} (x - \tilde{z}_j - \bar{\varepsilon}_j) = \prod_{j=i+1}^{n} (x - \tilde{z}_j) + \mathscr{E}_i(x) = \mathcal{L}_i(x) + \mathscr{E}_i(x)$$

and

$$R_i(x) = \prod_{j=1}^{i-1} (x - \tilde{z}_j - \tilde{\varepsilon}_j) = \prod_{j=1}^{i-1} (x - \tilde{z}_j) + \tilde{\mathscr{E}}_i(x) = \mathcal{R}_i(x) + \tilde{\mathscr{E}}_i(x),$$

where $\mathscr{E}_i$ and $\tilde{\mathscr{E}}_i$ are remainder polynomials defined similarly to $\mathscr{E}_1$, with the appropriate modifications. Since $\mathscr{E}_i$ is a sum of terms, all of which involve at least the product by a $\bar{\varepsilon}_j$ ($j \in \{i+1, \ldots, n\}$), we conclude that $\mathscr{E}_i(\alpha) = \mathcal{O}(\varepsilon)$. On the other hand $\tilde{\mathscr{E}}_i$ is a sum of terms involving at least the product by an $\tilde{\varepsilon}_j$ ($j \in \{1, \ldots, i-1\}$), which means that we can write, using the induction hypothesis,

$$\tilde{\mathscr{E}}_i(\alpha) = \mathcal{O}(\varepsilon^3), \ \forall \alpha \in \mathcal{D}.$$

Therefore the polynomial P can be written as

$$P(x) = \bar{L}_i(x)(x - x_i)\bar{R}_i(x) = \left(\bar{\mathcal{L}}_i(x) + \bar{\mathscr{E}}_i(x)\right)(x - y_i - \varepsilon_i')\left(\bar{\mathcal{R}}_i(x) + \bar{\tilde{\mathscr{E}}}_i(x)\right).$$

Multiplying both sides of the last equality on the left by $\mathcal{L}_i$ and on the right by $\mathcal{R}_i$ and evaluating at $x = y_i$, we obtain

$$(\mathcal{L}_i P \mathcal{R}_i)(y_i) = \left(\mathcal{L}_i \bar{\mathcal{L}}_i \bar{\mathcal{R}}_i \mathcal{R}_i (x - y_i - \varepsilon_i')\right)(y_i) + \left(\mathcal{L}_i \bar{\mathcal{R}}_i \mathcal{R}_i \bar{\mathscr{E}}_i (x - y_i - \varepsilon_i')\right)(y_i)$$
$$+ \left(\mathcal{L}_i \bar{\mathcal{L}}_i (x - y_i - \varepsilon_i')\bar{\tilde{\mathscr{E}}}_i \mathcal{R}_i\right)(y_i) + \left(\mathcal{L}_i \mathscr{E}_i (x - y_i - \varepsilon_i')\bar{\tilde{\mathscr{E}}}_i \mathcal{R}_i\right)(y_i),$$

where we made use of the result that, since $\mathcal{R}_i\bar{\mathcal{R}}_i$ is a real polynomial, it commutes with any other polynomial. Observing that $\mathcal{L}_i\bar{\mathcal{L}}_i\bar{\mathcal{R}}_i\mathcal{R}_i$ is the real polynomial $\mathcal{Q}_i$, using again the results (3) and (4) in Result 1 and having in mind the form of the remainder polynomials $\mathscr{E}_i$ and $\tilde{\mathscr{E}}_i$, we can write

$$(\mathcal{L}_i P \mathcal{R}_i)(y_i) = -\varepsilon_i \mathcal{Q}_i(y_i) - \left(\mathcal{L}_i\bar{\mathcal{R}}_i\mathcal{R}_i\mathscr{E}_i\right)(\hat{y}_i)\varepsilon_i' + \mathcal{O}(\varepsilon^3)$$
$$= -\varepsilon_i' \mathcal{Q}_i(y_i) + \mathcal{O}(\varepsilon\varepsilon_i') + \mathcal{O}(\varepsilon^3), \tag{15}$$

where $\hat{y}_i = \varepsilon_i' y_i (\varepsilon_i')^{-1}$. Since $|\mathcal{Q}_i(y_i)|$ is bounded away from zero, multiplying (15) on the right by $(\mathcal{Q}_i(z_i))^{-1}$ leads to

$$(\mathcal{L}_i P \mathcal{R}_i)(y_i)(\mathcal{Q}_i(y_i))^{-1} = -\varepsilon_i + \mathcal{O}(\varepsilon\varepsilon_i') + \mathcal{O}(\varepsilon^3)$$

or, equivalently, recalling the definition of the errors ε_i',

$$(\mathcal{L}_i P \mathcal{R}_i)(y_i)(\mathcal{Q}_i(y_i))^{-1} = y_i - x_i + \mathcal{O}(\varepsilon^3).$$

This proves that
$$\tilde{z}_i = y_i - (\mathcal{L}_i P \mathcal{R}_i)(y_i)(\mathcal{Q}_i(y_i))^{-1}$$
is an $\mathcal{O}(\varepsilon^3)$ approximation to x_i. □

Remark 1. The use of the Weierstrass method in its sequential version is essential to reach the cubic order of convergence, as a careful analysis of the proof reveals; for more details see [5, Remark 3]. This is the reason why the final order of convergence of this quaternionic two-step method is three instead of four, as in the complex case.

Remark 2. We point out that, for each $\tilde{z}_i$, the scheme performs four polynomial evaluation per iteration, which corresponds to the number of evaluations required by two iterations of the one-step Weierstrass method. However the number of operations involved in each iteration is substantially less, since the demanding process of constructing the polynomials $\mathcal{P}_i$ and $\mathcal{Q}_i$ is done just one time per iteration. Details on evaluation schemes of polynomials with quaternion floating point coefficients from the complexity and stability point of view can be obtained in [4].

As in the case of the classical quaternionic Weierstrass method, the iterative scheme (8) can produce, not only the factor terms, but also the roots of the polynomial. Using the relations (6) between the roots and factor terms of a polynomial and the arguments of the proof of the classical case [5, Theorem 6], the following result can be easily obtained.

Theorem 2. *Let P be a monic polynomial of degree n in $\mathbb{H}[x]$ with n isolated distinct roots and let $\{z_i^{(k)}\}$ be the sequences defined by the two-step Weierstrass iterative scheme (8)–(11) under the assumptions of Theorem 1. Finally, let $\{\zeta_i^{(k)}\}$ be the sequences defined by*

$$\zeta_i^{(k+1)} := \mathcal{R}_i^{(k)}(z_i^{(k+1)}) \, z_i^{(k+1)} \left(\mathcal{R}_i^{(k)}(z_i^{(k+1)}) \right)^{-1}; \quad k = 0, 1, 2, \ldots, \qquad (16)$$

where $\mathcal{R}_i^{(k)}$ are the polynomials given by (10). Then, $\{\zeta_1^{(k)}\}, \ldots, \{\zeta_n^{(k)}\}$ converge to the roots of P with cubic order of convergence.

Remark 3. Observe that the polynomials $\mathcal{R}_i$ in (16) used to obtain the roots are the same polynomials presented in (8) to obtain the factor terms.

4   Numerical Examples

We illustrate the performance of the two-step quaternionic Weierstrass method (8)–(11) by considering several examples.

For the first two experiments we have used the Mathematica add-on application `QuaternionAnalysis` [17] specially designed for symbolic manipulation of quaternion valued functions together with the collection of functions `QPolynomial` [8, 10] for solving polynomial problems in $\mathbb{H}[x]$.

To evaluate the quality of the approximations produced by the numerical scheme, all the examples were constructed so that the exact solution ζ is known. In this way, the error $\varepsilon^{(k)}$ in each iteration k is computed as

$$\varepsilon^{(k)} = \max_i \{ |\zeta_i - z_i^{(k)}| \},$$

where $z_i^{(k)}$ is given by (8). To obtain estimates for ρ, the local order of convergence of the method, we used the following computational estimate (see e.g. [12] for details)

$$\rho \approx \rho^{(k)} := \frac{\log \varepsilon^{(k)}}{\log \varepsilon^{(k-1)}}.$$

We point out that, in some cases, we had to take advantages of the fact that the Mathematica system allows to carry out the numerical computations using arbitrary precision arithmetic.

Example 1. Consider the polynomial

$$P(x) = x^3 + (3 + 3\mathbf{i} + 3\mathbf{j} + 5\mathbf{k})x^2 + (-3 + \mathbf{i} - 3\mathbf{j} + 17\mathbf{k})x + 2 - 16\mathbf{i} - 6\mathbf{j} + 8\mathbf{k}.$$

This polynomial was constructed, with the help of (6), so that its factor terms and roots are, respectively,

$$x_1 = -2 - \mathbf{j} - \mathbf{k}, \quad x_2 = -1 - 2\mathbf{i} - 3\mathbf{j} - 4\mathbf{k} \quad \text{and} \quad x_3 = -\mathbf{i} + \mathbf{j}$$

and

$$\zeta_1 = -2 - \mathbf{j} - \mathbf{k}, \quad \zeta_2 = -1 - \frac{27}{23}\mathbf{i} - \frac{76}{23}\mathbf{j} - \frac{94}{23}\mathbf{k} \quad \text{and} \quad \zeta_3 = \frac{8}{27}\mathbf{i} + \frac{35}{27}\mathbf{j} + \frac{13}{27}\mathbf{k}.$$

Starting with the initial approximation $z^{(0)} = (1, 2, 1+\mathbf{i}+\mathbf{j})$, we reached the precision 10^{-16} after 12 iterations of the quaternionic Weierstrass method (QWM) and just 7 iterations of the two-step quaternionic Weierstrass method (2QWM). Table 1 contains the results concerning the computational order of convergence for both methods. These results agree, as expected, with the conclusions of Theorem 1 (P fulfills its assumptions).

Table 1. Results for Example 1

QWM			2QWM		
k	$\varepsilon^{(k)}$	$\rho^{(k)}$	k	$\varepsilon^{(k)}$	$\rho^{(k)}$
8	7.6×10^{-2}	–	4	1.9×10^{-1}	–
9	1.9×10^{-3}	2.44	5	1.3×10^{-3}	4.08
10	7.1×10^{-7}	2.26	6	6.1×10^{-10}	3.17
11	3.9×10^{-14}	2.18	7	6.0×10^{-29}	3.06
12	7.7×10^{-29}	2.09	8	1.5×10^{-85}	3.01

Example 2. We consider now the polynomial borrowed from [5]:

$$P(x) = (x + 2\mathbf{i})(x + 1 + \mathbf{k})(x - 2)(x - 1)(x - 2 + \mathbf{j})(x - 1 + \mathbf{i}),$$

whose roots are

$$\zeta_1 = 1 - \mathbf{i}, \quad \zeta_2 = 1, \quad \zeta_3 = -1 - \frac{29}{39}\mathbf{i} + \frac{14}{39}\mathbf{j} - \frac{22}{39}\mathbf{k},$$
$$\zeta_4 = 2, \quad \zeta_5 = -\frac{224}{113}\mathbf{i} - \frac{30}{113}\mathbf{k}, \quad \zeta_6 = 2 - \frac{2}{3}\mathbf{i} - \frac{1}{3}\mathbf{j} + \frac{2}{3}\mathbf{k}.$$

We used as initial approximation $z^{(0)} = (\frac{1}{2}, \frac{3}{2}-\mathbf{j}, \frac{3}{2}+\mathbf{i}-\mathbf{j}+\mathbf{k}, \frac{3}{2}+\mathbf{i}-\mathbf{j}, -\frac{1}{2}, -1-2\mathbf{i})$ and reached the precision 10^{-16} after 22 iterations of the quaternionic Weierstrass method and 15 iterations of the two-step quaternionic Weierstrass method. The details about this example are presented in Table 2.

Table 2. Results for Example 2

QWM			2QWM		
k	$\varepsilon^{(k)}$	$\rho^{(k)}$	k	$\varepsilon^{(k)}$	$\rho^{(k)}$
18	9.1×10^{-3}	–	11	2.5×10^{-1}	–
19	1.9×10^{-4}	1.82	12	1.6×10^{-2}	3.06
20	5.4×10^{-8}	1.95	13	6.1×10^{-6}	2.90
21	5.5×10^{-16}	1.96	14	1.3×10^{-16}	3.05
22	1.3×10^{-29}	2.03	15	2.2×10^{-48}	3.00

Example 3. Our next example concerns a polynomial P with a spherical zero, i.e., P does not fulfill the assumptions of Theorem 1.

Recently, we have proposed a deflation algorithm [9] to be used together with the quaternionic Weierstrass method which allows to obtain quadratic order of convergence for isolated and spherical roots without requiring higher order precision. The same technique can be used now for the two-step method. The first part of the method concerns the determination of the spherical roots, while the second one consists of applying the Weierstrass method to a deflate polynomial.

In this example we revisit the first example of [9], where the polynomial

$$P(x) = x^4 + (-1+\mathbf{i})x^3 + (2-\mathbf{i}+\mathbf{j}+\mathbf{k})x^2 + (-1+\mathbf{i})x + 1 - \mathbf{i}+\mathbf{j}+\mathbf{k},$$

was considered. This polynomial has the isolated zeros $-\mathbf{i}+\mathbf{k}$ and $1-\mathbf{j}$ and the sphere of zeros, $[\mathbf{i}]$.

The numerical computations have been performed, as in the aforementioned work, in the Matlab system with double floating point arithmetic.

Starting with the initial guess $z^{(0)} = (1, -2, 0.5\mathbf{i}, 1+\mathbf{i})$, we obtained the results presented in Table 3, without using the deflate strategy. The results of Table 3 can be easily explained if we take into account that in the proof of Theorem 1 we assume that $|Q_i(y_i)|$ is bounded away from zero, which is not the case when we have two factor terms "almost" in the same equivalence class. If arbitrary precision arithmetic is not available, the faster the method, the more quickly this effect is expected to be observed.

Table 3. QWM and 2QMW for Example 3

Roots	Type	Error (QWM)	Error (2QWM)
$1-\mathbf{j}$	Isolated	2.5×10^{-16}	2.4×10^{-12}
$-\mathbf{i}+\mathbf{k}$	Isolated	2.0×10^{-15}	3.6×10^{-13}
$[i]$	Spherical	7.7×10^{-9}	4.5×10^{-8}

Applying now the Weierstrass algorithm to a 2nd degree deflate polynomial with the initial approximation $z^{(0)} = (1, 1+\mathbf{i})$, we obtain, after 11 iterations of QWM and 6 iterations of the 2QWM, the results presented in Table 4.

Table 4. Modified QWM and 2QWM for Example 3

Roots	Method	Type	Error	k
$1 - \mathbf{j}$	Weierstrass	Isolated	7.4×10^{-17}	11
$-\mathbf{i} + \mathbf{k}$	Weierstrass	Isolated	2.3×10^{-18}	11
$1 - \mathbf{j}$	2 step Weierstrass	Isolated	1.6×10^{-16}	6
$-\mathbf{i} + \mathbf{k}$	2 step Weierstrass	Isolated	2.0×10^{-16}	6
$[\mathbf{i}]$	Deflation	Spherical	0	–

Example 4. Consider now the 9th degree polynomial

$$Q(x) = P(x)(x^2 + 4)(x^3 + 9x),$$

where P is the polynomial of Example 3. Apart from the same two isolated roots $-\mathbf{i} + \mathbf{k}$, $1 - \mathbf{j}$ and the spherical zero $[\mathbf{i}]$, this polynomial has also 1 as isolated zero and $[2\mathbf{i}]$ and $[3\mathbf{i}]$ as spherical zeros.

The one- and two-step Weierstrass algorithm applied to the 3rd degree polynomial, obtained by the deflation procedure, with the initial approximation $z^{(0)} = (-1, 2, 1 + \mathbf{i})$, produce, after 12 iterations of QWM and 9 iterations of the 2QWM, the results presented in Table 5.

Table 5. Modified QWM and 2QWM for Example 4

Roots	Method	Type	Error	k
$1.000 - 1.000\mathbf{j}$	Weierstrass	Isolated	3.3×10^{-15}	12
$-1.000\mathbf{i} + 1.000\mathbf{k}$	Weierstrass	Isolated	1.7×10^{-15}	12
1.000	Weierstrass	Isolated	2.7×10^{-15}	12
$1.000 - 1.000\mathbf{j}$	2 step Weierstrass	Isolated	3.4×10^{-15}	9
$-1.000\mathbf{i} + 1.000\mathbf{k}$	2 step Weierstrass	Isolated	1.7×10^{-15}	9
1.000	2 step Weierstrass	Isolated	3.0×10^{-15}	9
$[\mathbf{i}]$	Deflation	Spherical	1.1×10^{-15}	–
$[2\mathbf{i}]$	Deflation	Spherical	1.4×10^{-15}	–
$[3\mathbf{i}]$	Deflation	Spherical	1.9×10^{-15}	–

5   Conclusions

We have derived a two-step method based on the Weierstrass method for computing the roots of a quaternionic polynomial and have proved its cubic order of convergence, under the assumptions that all the roots are isolated and distinct (and the initial guesses are sufficiently "good"). A modified version of the two-step method was also considered allowing to overcome the issues associated to spherical roots.

We hope it is possible to modify the scheme in order to improve its efficiency, in particular, in what concerns the number of evaluation required in each iteration. We intend to focus on this aspect in the near future.

Acknowledgment. Research at CMAT was partially financed by Portuguese funds through FCT - Fundação para a Ciência e a Tecnologia, within the Projects UIDB/00013/2020 and UIDP/00013/2020. Research at NIPE has been financed by FCT, within the Project UIDB/03182/2020.

References

1. Beck, B.: Sur les équations polynomiales dans les quaternions. Enseign. Math. **25**, 193–201 (1979)
2. Dočev, K.: A variant of Newton's method for the simultaneous approximation of all roots of an algebraic equation. Fiz. Mat. Spis. Bŭlgar. Akad. Nauk. **5**(38), 136–139 (1962)
3. Durand, É.: Solutions Numériques des Equations Algébriques. Tome I: Equations du type F(x); Racines d'un Polynôme. Masson et Cie (1960)
4. Falcão, M.I., Miranda, F., Severino, R., Soares, M.J.: Evaluation schemes in the ring of quaternionic polynomials. BIT Numer. Math. **58**(1), 51–72 (2018)
5. Falcão, M.I., Miranda, F., Severino, R., Soares, M.J.: Weierstrass method for quaternionic polynomial root-finding. Math. Methods Appl. Sci. **41**(1), 423–437 (2018)
6. Falcão, M.I.: Newton method in the context of quaternion analysis. Appl. Math. Comput. **236**, 458–470 (2014)
7. Falcão, M.I., Miranda, F.: Quaternions: a Mathematica package for quaternionic analysis. In: Murgante, B., Gervasi, O., Iglesias, A., Taniar, D., Apduhan, B.O. (eds.) ICCSA 2011. LNCS, vol. 6784, pp. 200–214. Springer, Heidelberg (2011). https://doi.org/10.1007/978-3-642-21931-3_17
8. Falcão, M.I., Miranda, F., Severino, R., Soares, M.J.: Mathematica tools for quaternionic polynomials. In: Gervasi, O., et al. (eds.) ICCSA 2017. LNCS, vol. 10405, pp. 394–408. Springer, Cham (2017). https://doi.org/10.1007/978-3-319-62395-5_27
9. Falcão, M.I., Miranda, F., Severino, R., Soares, M.J.: A modified quaternionic Weierstrass method. In: Gervasi, O., Murgante, B., Misra, S., Rocha, A.M.A.C., Garau, C. (eds.) Computational Science and Its Applications – ICCSA 2022 Workshops (ICCSA 2022). LNCS, vol. 13377, pp. 407–419. Springer, Cham (2022). https://doi.org/10.1007/978-3-031-10536-4_27
10. Falcão, M.I., Miranda, F., Severino, R., Soares, M.J.: Computational aspects of quaternionic polynomials - part II: root-finding methods. Math. J. (2018)
11. Gordon, B., Motzkin, T.: On the zeros of polynomials over division rings I. Trans. Am. Math. Soc. **116**, 218–226 (1965)
12. Grau-Sánchez, M., Noguera, M., Grau, À., Herrero, J.R.: On new computational local orders of convergence. Appl. Math. Lett. **25**(12), 2023–2030 (2012)
13. Gürlebeck, K., Sprößig, W.: Quaternionic and Cliford Calculus for Physicists and Engineers. Wiley, NY (1997)

14. Janovská, D., Opfer, G.: Computing quaternionic roots in Newton's method. Electron. Trans. Numer. Anal. **26**, 82–102 (2007)
15. Lam, T.Y.: A First Course in Noncommutative Rings. Graduate Texts in Mathematics, Springer, New York (1991). https://doi.org/10.1007/978-1-4419-8616-0
16. Magreñán Ruiz, A.A., Argyros, I.K.: Two-step newton methods. J. Complex. **30**(4), 533–553 (2014)
17. Miranda, F., Falcão, M.I.: Quaternion analysis package user's guide (2014). http://w3.math.uminho.pt/QuaternionAnalysis
18. Niven, I.: Equations in quaternions. Am. Math. Mon. **48**, 654–661 (1941)
19. Petković, I., Herceg, D.: Computer methodologies for comparison of computational efficiency of simultaneous methods for finding polynomial zeros. J. Comput. Appl. Math. **368**, 112513 (2020)
20. Sakurai, T., Petković, M.: On some simultaneous methods based on Weierstrass' correction. J. Comput. Appl. Math. **72**(2), 275–291 (1996)
21. Traub, J.F.: Iterative Methods for the Solution of Equations. Prentice-Hall, Inc., Englewood Cliffs, NJ (1964)
22. Weierstrass, K.: Neuer Beweis des Satzes, dass jede ganze rationale Function einer Veränderlichen dargestellt werden kann als ein Product aus linearen Functionen derselben Veränderlichen. In: Sitzungsberichte der Königlich Preussischen Akademie der Wissenschaften zu Berlin, vol. II, pp. 1085–1101. Berlin (1891)
23. Zhang, F.: Quaternions and matrices of quaternions. Linear Algebra Appl. **251**, 21–57 (1997)

The Stability of Complex Dynamics for Two Families of Coquaternionic Quadratic Polynomials

Maria Irene Falcão[1] , Fernando Miranda[1] , Ricardo Severino[1(✉)] ,
and Maria Joana Soares[2]

[1] CMAT and Departamento de Matemática, Universidade do Minho, Braga, Portugal
{mif,fmiranda,ricardo}@math.uminho.pt
[2] NIPE, Universidade do Minho, Braga, Portugal
jsoares@math.uminho.pt

Abstract. In this work, we begin by demonstrating that attractors, both periodic and aperiodic, of the one-parameter family of complex quadratic maps $x^2 + c$, where c is a complex number, maintain their stability when we transition from the complex plane $\mathbb{C}$ to the coquaternions $\mathbb{H}_{coq}$ as the map's phase space. Next, we investigate the same question for a different family of quadratic maps, $x^2 + bx$, and find that this is not the case. In fact, the situation for this family of maps turns out to be quite complicated. Our results show that there are complex attractors that undergo changes in their stability, while others maintain it. However, the most intriguing result is that certain regions of the parameter space, known as bulbs, which correspond to the existence of attracting cycles of some fixed period n, exhibit a mixture of stability behavior when we consider coquaternionic quadratics.

Keywords: Iteration of quadratic maps · Coquaternions · Attractors · Coquaternionic polynomials

1 Introduction

The iteration of complex quadratic polynomials has a singular feature: it can be demonstrated that a map $a_2 x^2 + a_1 x + a_0$ is dynamically equivalent to a much simpler quadratic $x^2 + c$. This result offers an apparent advantage: all complex quadratic dynamics can be comprehended by analyzing the dynamics of the family of quadratics $x^2 + c$.

However, there is another side to the story. Despite the wonderful results obtained for the dynamics of the one-parameter family of complex maps $x^2 + c$, see, for example, [5], there is an inevitable sense of lack of diversity. After all, it all boils down to one family of quadratics.

In 2012, we began studying the iteration of quadratic coquaternionic maps with the aim of exploring how their dynamics differ from those of quadratic complex maps. First, in [2], the authors demonstrated that the family of quadratic

O. Gervasi et al. (Eds.): ICCSA 2023 Workshops, LNCS 14104, pp. 722–734, 2023.
https://doi.org/10.1007/978-3-031-37105-9_48

coquaternionic maps $x^2 + c$ possesses non-isolated sets of coquaternionic fixed points and non-isolated sets of periodic coquaternionic points of period two, something that was only possible, see [1], for a much complicated map.

Subsequently, in [3], the authors established that attractor coexistence is possible for the same family of coquaternionic maps, which is known to be untrue for complex quadratics.

Finally, in [4], the authors computed the coquaternionic fixed points for a distinct family of coquaternionic quadratics, $x^2 + bx$, and determined that this family of coquaternionic quadratics is not dynamically conjugate to $x^2 + c$.

In summary, although dealing with coquaternionic functions presents inherent challenges, we can confidently state that the study of coquaternionic quadratic maps has already revealed a remarkable diversity in admissible dynamics, making it one of the most captivating and intriguing topics in the theory of dynamical systems.

2 Basic Results

To ensure completeness, we provide a brief overview of the main concepts and results related to the algebra of coquaternions, which are also referred to as split-quaternions in the literature. This overview is necessary for the remaining sections of the paper.

Let $\{1, i, j, k\}$ be an orthonormal basis of the Euclidean vector space $\mathbb{R}^4$ with a product given according to the following rules:

$$\begin{cases} i^2 = -1, & j^2 = k^2 = 1, \\ ij = -ji = k. \end{cases} \tag{1}$$

A simple computation allows us to prove that this product generates an associative but non-commutative algebra over $\mathbb{R}$, denoted by $\mathbb{H}_{\mathrm{coq}}$, whose elements will be called real coquaternions. It is important to observe that, contrary to what happens in the case of Hamiltonian quaternions, $\mathbb{H}_{\mathrm{coq}}$ is not a division algebra. In fact, $\mathbb{H}_{\mathrm{coq}}$ contains zero divisors and nilpotent elements: for example, we have $(1 + j)(1 - j) = 0$ and $(i + j)^2 = 0$. In the following, we will identify the space $\mathbb{R}^4$ with $\mathbb{H}_{\mathrm{coq}}$ by associating the element $(q_0, q_1, q_2, q_3) \in \mathbb{R}^4$ with the coquaternion $q_0 + q_1 i + q_2 j + q_3 k$.

Given $q = q_0 + q_1 i + q_2 j + q_3 k \in \mathbb{H}_{\mathrm{coq}}$, its conjugate $\bar{q}$ is defined as

$$\bar{q} = q_0 - q_1 i - q_2 j - q_3 k;$$

the number q_0 is called the real part of q and is denoted by $\operatorname{re} q$ and the vector part of q, denoted by $\operatorname{vec} q$, is $\operatorname{vec} q = q_1 i + q_2 j + q_3 k$. In analogy with the complex case, we will identify the set of coquaternions whose vector part is zero with the set $\mathbb{R}$ of real numbers.

It is easy to see that the algebra of coquaternions is isomorphic to the algebra of real 2×2 matrices, with the map $\Phi : \mathbb{H}_{\mathrm{coq}} \to \mathcal{M}_2(\mathbb{R})$ defined by

$$\Phi(q_0 + q_1 i + q_2 j + q_3 k) = \begin{pmatrix} q_0 + q_3 & q_1 + q_2 \\ q_1 - q_2 & q_0 - q_3 \end{pmatrix}$$

establishing the isomorphism. We call the determinant of q, and denote by $\det q$, the quantity given by the determinant of the matrix representative of q, i.e.

$$\det q = q_0^2 + q_1^2 - q_2^2 - q_3^2.$$

It is a straightforward exercise to demonstrate that the determinant of a coquaternion q can be expressed as $\det q = q\,\bar{q}$.

Finally, it can be shown that a coquaternion q is invertible if and only if its determinant is different from zero. In that case, the expression for the inverse is given by

$$q^{-1} = \frac{\bar{q}}{\det q}.$$

Next, we recall some basic definitions of discrete dynamical systems. Let us consider a coquaternionic map $f : \mathbb{H}_{coq} \to \mathbb{H}_{coq}$. For $k \in \mathbb{N}$, we shall denote by f^k the k-th iterate of f, inductively defined by

$$\begin{cases} f^0 = \mathrm{id}_{\mathbb{H}_{coq}} \\ f^k = f \circ f^{k-1}. \end{cases}$$

For a given initial point $q_0 \in \mathbb{H}_{coq}$, the orbit of q_0 under the map f is the sequence

$$\mathcal{O}(q_0) := \left(f^k(q_0) \right)_{k \in \mathbb{N}_0}.$$

A point $q \in \mathbb{H}_{coq}$ is said to be a periodic point of f, with period $n \in \mathbb{N}$, if we have $f^n(q) = q$, with $f^k(q) \neq q$ for $0 < k < n$; in this case, we say that the set

$$\mathscr{C} = \{q, f(q), \ldots, f^{n-1}(q)\}$$

is a n-cycle for f, usually written as

$$\mathscr{C} : q_0 \xrightarrow{f} q_1 \xrightarrow{f} \cdots \xrightarrow{f} q_{n-1}$$

with $q_i = f^i(q)$. Periodic points of period one are called fixed points.

Finally, there is one last definition relevant for the rest of the paper: we say that two coquaternionic maps $f : \mathbb{H}_{coq} \to \mathbb{H}_{coq}$ and $g : \mathbb{H}_{coq} \to \mathbb{H}_{coq}$ are conjugate if there exists an invertible map $\phi : \mathbb{H}_{coq} \to \mathbb{H}_{coq}$ such that

$$f \circ \phi = \phi \circ g.$$

In this case, we say that the corresponding dynamical systems $(\mathbb{H}_{coq}, f)$ and $(\mathbb{H}_{coq}, g)$ are dynamically equivalent, since they share the same dynamical characteristics.

3   Coquaternionic Quadratic Maps $q^2 + c$

We now consider the one-parameter family of coquaternionic quadratic maps

$$f_c : \mathbb{H}_{coq} \rightarrow \mathbb{H}_{coq}$$
$$q \mapsto q^2 + c$$

with the choice of the parameter c limited to the complex plane $\mathbb{C}$. We will use f_c to denote the restriction of the map f_c to the complex plane i.e. $f_c := f_c|_{\mathbb{C}}$. Since our goal is to study what happens to the stability of the attractors of f_c when changing the phase space from $\mathbb{C}$ to $\mathbb{H}_{coq}$, it makes sense to use only complex parameters.

For this family of quadratics f_c, we know that

$$q_1 = \frac{1}{2}(1 - \sqrt{1 - 4c}) \qquad q_2 = \frac{1}{2}(1 + \sqrt{1 - 4c})$$

are the complex fixed points and

$$p_1 = \frac{1}{2}(-1 - \sqrt{-3 - 4c}) \qquad p_2 = \frac{1}{2}(-1 + \sqrt{-3 - 4c})$$

are the complex periodic points of period two. Moreover, from [2], we have that the fixed point q_1 and the 2-cycle $\{p_1, p_2\}$ are attractors for the complex map f_c for parameter values inside the cardioid $|1 - \sqrt{1 - 4c}| = 1$, and inside the circle $|c + 1| = 1/4$, respectively.

Since there is no appropriate concept of derivative for coquaternionic maps, the most suitable method to analyze the stability of a given periodic point of period n is to treat f_c^n as a function from $\mathbb{R}^4$ to $\mathbb{R}^4$ and evaluate the magnitude of the eigenvalues of its corresponding Jacobian matrix. As it is widely recognized, if all eigenvalues of this matrix have a modulus less than one, then the periodic point is considered to be attractive.

From the multiplication rules (1), it follows that

$$f_c(q) = (c_0 + q_0^2 - q_1^2 + q_2^2 + q_3^2, \, c_1 + 2q_0q_1, \, 2q_0q_2, \, 2q_0q_3)$$

for $q = q_0 + q_1 i + q_2 j + q_3 k$ and $c = c_0 + c_1 i$. Hence, the Jacobian matrix of the map f_c, computed at a given point $q = q_0 + q_1 i + q_2 j + q_3 k$, is given by

$$\mathbf{J}_c(q) = \begin{pmatrix} 2q_0 & -2q_1 & 2q_2 & 2q_3 \\ 2q_1 & 2q_0 & 0 & 0 \\ 2q_2 & 0 & 2q_0 & 0 \\ 2q_3 & 0 & 0 & 2q_0 \end{pmatrix},$$

and its four eigenvalues are

$$\lambda_1(q) = \lambda_2(q) = 2q_0$$

$$\lambda_{3,4}(q) = 2q_0 \pm 2\sqrt{-q_1^2 + q_2^2 + q_3^2}.$$

Now, we are ready to present our first result.

Theorem 1. *The complex fixed point* $q_1 = \frac{1}{2}(1 - \sqrt{1 - 4c})$ *is an attractor for* f_c, *for parameter values inside the cardioid* $|1 - \sqrt{1 - 4c}| = 1$.

Proof. First, let us remember that the square root of a complex number $a + b\,\mathrm{i}$ can be written as

$$\sqrt{a + b\,\mathrm{i}} = \frac{1}{2}\sqrt{\sqrt{a^2 + b^2} + a} \pm \frac{1}{2}\sqrt{\sqrt{a^2 + b^2} - a}\,\mathrm{i} \tag{2}$$

Thus, the real part of the complex fixed point q_1 is given by

$$\mathrm{re}\,q_1 = \frac{1}{2} - \frac{1}{4}\sqrt{\sqrt{(1 - 4c_0)^2 + 16c_1^2} + 1 - 4c_0}$$

while its vector part, in this case equal to its imaginary part, is given by

$$\mathrm{vec}\,q_1 = \pm\frac{1}{4}\sqrt{\sqrt{(1 - 4c_0)^2 + 16c_1^2} - 1 + 4c_0}$$

Then, the first two eigenvalues of the Jacobian matrix evaluated at the fixed point q_1 are given by

$$\lambda_1(q_1) = \lambda_2(q_1) = 1 - \frac{1}{2}\sqrt{\sqrt{(1 - 4c_0)^2 + 16c_1^2} + 1 - 4c_0}$$

After a lengthy computation, we can conclude that for parameter values lying inside the parabola $c_0 = -3/4 + 1/4c_1^2$, except for the points on the horizontal half-line from $(1/4, 0)$ to the right, as shown in Fig. 1, the modulus of the first two eigenvalues of the Jacobian matrix evaluated at q_1 is less than one (for the points on the aforementioned half-line, the eigenvalues have modulus equal to one).

On the other hand, the remaining two eigenvalues of the Jacobian matrix evaluated at the fixed point q_1 are given by

$$\lambda_{3,4}(q_1) = 1 - \frac{\sqrt{2}}{2}\sqrt{\sqrt{(1 - 4c_0)^2 + 16c_1^2} + 1 - 4c_0} \pm$$

$$\pm \frac{\sqrt{2}}{2}\sqrt{\sqrt{(1 - 4c_0)^2 + 16c_1^2} - 1 + 4c_0}\,\mathrm{i}$$

for which we can say that their modulus are less than one for parameter values inside the cardioid $|1 - \sqrt{1 - 4c}| = 1$, see Fig. 1. Therefore, we conclude that all four eigenvalues have modulus less than one for parameter values inside the cardioid $|1 - \sqrt{1 - 4c}| = 1$.   □

Based on these results, we can conclude that the complex fixed point q_1 is an attractor for f_c precisely for the same parameter values that it does for the complex map f_c, indicating that its stability remains constant regardless of whether we consider the coquaternion phase space $\mathbb{H}_{\mathrm{coq}}$.

A similar result can be stated for the complex 2-cycle $\{p_1, p_2\}$ of the coquaternionic maps f_c.

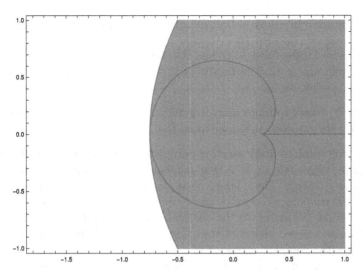

Fig. 1. The regions for which the modulus of the eigenvalues of the Jacobian matrix evaluated at the fixed point q_1 are less than one: the points inside the parabola $c_0 = -3/4 + 1/4c_1^2$, except the horizontal half-line from the point $(1/4, 0)$ to the right, for the first two, and the points inside the cardioid $|1 - \sqrt{1 - 4c}| = 1$, for the others.

Theorem 2. *The complex 2-cycle $\{p_1, p_2\}$, with $p_1 = \frac{1}{2}(-1 - \sqrt{-3 - 4c})$ and $p_2 = \frac{1}{2}(-1 + \sqrt{-3 - 4c})$, is an attractor for f_c, for parameter values inside the circle $|c + 1| = 1/4$.*

Proof. In order to evaluate for which parameter values the complex 2-cycle $\{p_1, p_2\}$ is an attractor of f_c, we are going to compute the products $\lambda_i(p_1)\,\lambda_i(p_2)$, for $i = 1, \dots, 4$. From (2), we have

$$\lambda_1(p_1)\,\lambda_1(p_2) = \lambda_2(p_1)\,\lambda_2(p_2) = 1 + \frac{1}{2}\left(3 + 4c_0 - \sqrt{(3 + 4c_0)^2 + 16c_1^2}\right)$$

$$\lambda_{3,4}(p_1)\,\lambda_{3,4}(p_2) = 1 - \sqrt{(3 + 4c_0)^2 + 16c_1^2}$$

$$\pm \sqrt{2}\sqrt{3 + 4c_0 + \sqrt{(3 + 4c_0)^2 + 16c_1^2}}\, i.$$

These expressions allow us to say that all four products $\lambda_i(p_1)\,\lambda_i(p_2)$ have modulus less than one for parameter values inside the circle $|c + 1| = 1/4$, i.e. we conclude that the complex 2-cycle $\{p_1, p_2\}$ is an attractor for f_c, for c inside the circle $|c + 1| = 1/4$.

$\square$

From this last theorem, we are able to say that the complex 2-cycle $\{p_1, p_2\}$ is an attractor of f_c for exactly the same parameter values for which it is an attractor for f_c, i.e. $\{p_1, p_2\}$ does not change its stability when the phase space goes from the complex plane $\mathbb{C}$ to the coquaternions $\mathbb{H}_{\text{coq}}$.

Since the analytic study of the stability of cycles with period longer than two is not feasible, we decided to investigate computationally whether the results obtained above for the fixed point and the 2-cycle would hold for other attractors of the complex maps f_c. The results of this investigation are now presented in the form of a conjecture.

Conjecture 1. Every complex attractor, either periodic or aperiodic, for f_c is still an attractor for the coquaternionic map f_c.

This assertion resulted from selecting parameter values from 2,000,000 randomly chosen inside the circle $|c| < 2$ that corresponded to maps f_c with a periodic or aperiodic attractor. Then, for each parameter value, we computed the iterate $f_c^n(q)$, for 100 randomly chosen points q within a small coquaternionic neighborhood of a point belonging to the complex attractor of f_c, for a large value of n. In all instances, we observed that $f_c^n(q)$ approached the complex plane and converged to the complex attractor of f_c.   □

The first part of the process described above is easily recognizable as the identification of which of the randomly chosen parameter values belong to the Mandelbrot set $\mathcal{M}(f_c)$. If we generalize the definition of Mandelbrot set for the coquaternionic maps f_c as the complex parameter values for which the map possesses an attractor, either complex or coquaternionic, we have that the conjecture above is equivalent to saying that the Mandelbrot set $\mathcal{M}(f_c)$ is contained in the Mandelbrot set, $\mathcal{M}(f_c)$, for the coquaternionic family f_c.

Let us conclude this section with a comment regarding the Mandelbrot sets associated with these families of maps: in [2], the authors showed that

$$\mathcal{P}_8 = \left\{ -\frac{1}{2} + \frac{c_1}{2}i + q_2j + q_3k : q_2^2 + q_3^2 = \frac{c_1^2 - 4c_0 - 3}{4} \right\},$$

corresponding to the choice of a complex parameter $c = c_0 + c_1 i$, with $c_1^2 > 4c_0 + 3$, is a set of attractive coquaternionic points of period 2, for parameter values inside the ellipse $16(c_0 + 1)^2 + 2c_1^2 = 1$. This means that, for parameter values inside the circle $|c + 1| = 1/4$, the map f_c has a complex 2-cycle attractor but also a coquaternionic attracting 2-cycle. Moreover, one can easily observe that there are parameter values inside the ellipse given above for which f_c has coquaternionic attracting 2-cycles but f_c has no attractor. Therefore, we conclude that the Mandelbrot set for the coquaternionic family f_c contains the Mandelbrot set for the corresponding complex family f_c, but does not coincide with it.

4   Coquaternionic Quadratic Maps $q^2 + bq$

The results presented in the previous section, which allowed us to claim that any attractor of $x^2 + c$, periodic or aperiodic, does not alter its stability by changing the phase space from complex numbers $\mathbb{C}$ to the coquaternions $\mathbb{H}_{coq}$, may actually seem trivial, but let us see what happens when we pose the exact same question for a different family of coquaternionic quadratics maps.

Consider the one-parameter family of coquaternionic quadratic maps

$$\mathsf{f}_b : \mathbb{H}_{\mathrm{coq}} \to \mathbb{H}_{\mathrm{coq}}$$
$$\mathsf{q} \mapsto \mathsf{q}^2 + b\,\mathsf{q}$$

with $b \in \mathbb{C}$, such that $\mathrm{re}\,b \geq 1$. Again, it will be useful to introduce the complex map obtained by restricting f_b to the complex plane $f_b := \mathsf{f}_b|_{\mathbb{C}}$. A straightforward computation, see [4], allows us to say that f_b has two complex fixed points,

$$\mathsf{q}_1 = 0 \qquad \mathsf{q}_2 = 1 - b$$

and two complex periodic points of period two

$$\mathsf{p}_1 = \tfrac{1}{2}(-1 - b + \sqrt{-3 - 2b + b^2})$$

$$\mathsf{p}_2 = \tfrac{1}{2}(-1 - b - \sqrt{-3 - 2b + b^2}).$$

Since this family f_b of complex quadratic maps is conjugated to the simpler complex family $z^2 + c$, its Mandelbrot set is, to the best of our knowledge, not often depicted in the literature. Therefore, we found appropriate to show it here.

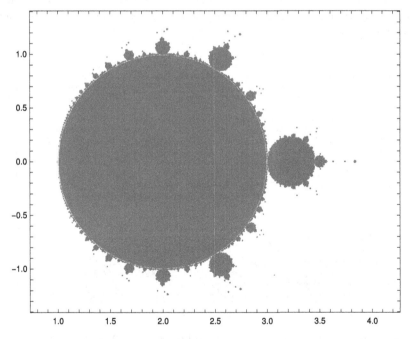

Fig. 2. The Mandelbrot set $\mathcal{M}(f_b)$, for the complex quadratic maps $f_b(z) = z^2 + b\,z$, with $b \in \mathbb{C}$, such that $\mathrm{re}\,b \geq 1$.

In the graphical representation of the Mandelbrot set $\mathcal{M}(f_b)$ given in Fig. 2, we can easily identify both discs $|b - 2| \leq 1$ and $|b - (2 + \sqrt{3/2})| \leq \sqrt{3/2} - 1$

corresponding to parameters values for which the complex fixed point q_2 and the complex 2-cycle $\{p_1, p_2\}$ are attractors, respectively.

In [4], the authors proved the following result.

Theorem 3. *The complex fixed point* $q_2 = 1 - b$ *is an attractor for* f_b*, for parameter values inside the circle* $|b - 2| = 1$.

In the same paper, the authors claimed to have computational evidence for the following statement.

Conjecture 2. The complex 2-cycle $\{p_1, p_2\}$, with $p_1 = \frac{1}{2}(-1 - b + \sqrt{-3 - 2b + b^2})$ and $p_2 = \frac{1}{2}(-1 - b - \sqrt{-3 - 2b + b^2})$, is an attractor for f_b, for parameter values inside the circle $|b - (2 + \sqrt{3/2})| = \sqrt{3/2} - 1$.

Both these results mean that, in agreement with what was stated before for the simpler family of quadratic maps, there is no change in the stability of the complex fixed point and the 2-cycle attractors, when we consider the family of coquaternionic quadratic maps f_b. The point now is whether this is also true for other complex attractors of f_b, e.g. the complex 3-cycle which is an attractor for parameter values in the bulb tangent to the circle $|b - 2| = 1$.

In Fig. 3, we show a zoom of the Mandelbrot set $\mathcal{M}(f_b)$ where we highlighted three bulbs, $\mathcal{B}_4$, $\mathcal{B}_3$, and $\mathcal{B}_5$, tangent to the main circle $|c - 2| = 1$, corresponding to parameter values for which f_b has a 4-cycle, a 3-cycle, and a 5-cycle attractor, respectively.

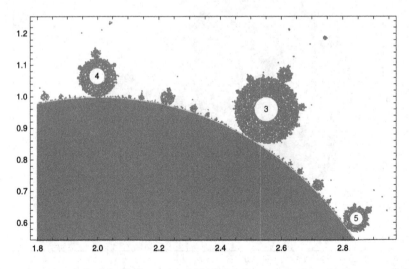

Fig. 3. A zoom of the Mandelbrot set $\mathcal{M}(f_b)$ for the complex quadratic maps $f_b(z) = z^2 + bz$, with $b \in \mathbb{C}$, where the bulbs tangent to the main circle corresponding to the existence of a 4-cycle, a 3-cycle, and a 5-cycle complex attractors are marked.

For the first two bulbs, $\mathcal{B}_4$ and $\mathcal{B}_3$, we have computational evidence to claim the following statements.

Conjecture 3. For every parameter value $b \in \mathcal{B}_4$, the complex 4-cycle, which was an attractor for f_b, is not an attractor for f_b.

Conjecture 4. For every parameter value $b \in \mathcal{B}_3$, the complex 3-cycle, which was an attractor for f_b, is not an attractor for f_b.

Both these claims are the result of selecting which parameter values, from 1,000,000 randomly chosen inside circles containing each bulb, corresponded to the existence of attracting cycles of f_b. Then, for all these values, we computed the iterate $\mathsf{f}_b^n(\mathsf{q})$, for a randomly chosen point q in a small coquaternionic neighborhood of a point of the attractor, again for a large choice of n, and confirmed that it did not converged to the complex plane. □

These results are quite different from everything we had before: for parameter values inside $\mathcal{B}_4$ and $\mathcal{B}_3$, the complex cycle is no longer an attractor for the coquaternionic map f_b, i.e. the cycles change their stability with the phase space going from $\mathbb{C}$ to $\mathbb{H}_{\mathrm{coq}}$. Next, we asked the same question for parameter values inside the bulb $\mathcal{B}_5$ and the answer we obtained was quite unexpected.

Conjecture 5. For parameter values $b \in \mathcal{B}_5$, the complex attracting 5-cycles for f_b exhibit a mixture of stability behavior when we consider the coquaternionic quadratics f_b.

For parameter values belonging to $\mathcal{B}_5$, our computational results are summarized in Fig. 4: in blue we have values such that the attracting complex 5-cycle for f_b is still an attractor for the coquaternionic map f_b, while in orange we have values such that the complex 5-cycle attractor for f_b is not an attractor for f_b. □

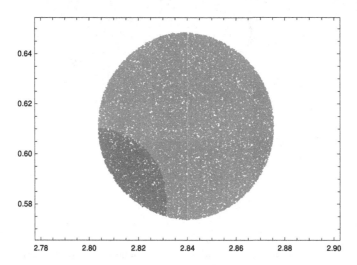

Fig. 4. The bulb from the Mandelbrot set $\mathcal{M}(f_b)$ tangent to the main circle corresponding to the existence of attracting complex 5-cycles: in blue we represent parameter values such that the 5-cycle is an attractor for the coquaternionic map f_b, while in orange we represent parameter values such that the 5-cycle is not an attractor for f_b.

After obtaining these results, the subsequent inquiry was to determine the specific points on the Mandelbrot set $\mathcal{M}(f_b)$ that correspond to the existence of complex attractors, periodic or aperiodic, of the coquaternionic quadratic map f_b. It is worth noting that this task is highly demanding in terms of computation, and therefore, the results presented should be interpreted with caution, as they represent a work in progress.

Our computational results are summarized in Fig. 5, where the values $b \in \mathbb{C}$ such that the coquaternionic map f_b has a complex attractor are represented in blue, while in red are represented parameter values such that f_b has no complex attractor.

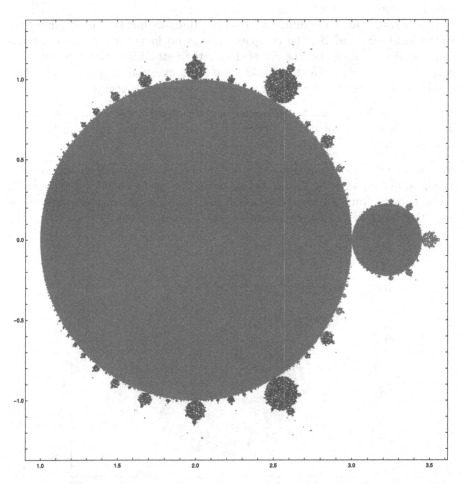

Fig. 5. The parameter space $b \in \mathbb{C}$, with $\mathrm{re}\, b > 1$, where blue points represent values such that the coquaternionic map f_b has a complex attractor, and red points represent values such that f_b has no complex attractor.

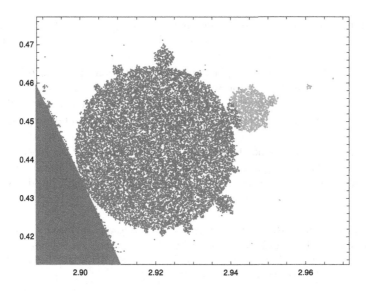

Fig. 6. A detail of the parameter space $b \in \mathbb{C}$, where it is shown a secondary bulb $\mathcal{B}_{13}$, corresponding to values such that f_b has an attracting 13-cycle, for which the coquaternionic map f_b exhibit a mixture of stability behavior: blue points represent values such that f_b has a complex attractor, and orange points represent values such that f_b has no complex attractor.

Upon examining Fig. 5, one might be inclined to assume that only the bulbs tangent the main circle, corresponding to parameter values $b = b_0 + b_1 \mathrm{i}$ with b_1's modulus exceeding a certain threshold, correspond to coquaternionic maps lacking a complex attractor. However, upon closer inspection of the zoomed-in Fig. 4, we can conclude that this is not the case.

To conclude this section, we will take a closer look at the parameter space region where there is a secondary bulb $\mathcal{B}_{13}$, tangent to the $\mathcal{B}_6$ bulb, corresponding to coquaternionic maps that exhibit a mixture of stability behavior. Our computational results for this region are summarized in Fig. 6.

Through this example, we aim to emphasize that the criteria for determining which coquaternionic maps f_b have complex attractors are not expected to be simple.

5   Conclusions

In this work, we begin by showing that attractors, both periodic and aperiodic, of the one-parameter family of complex quadratic maps $x^2 + c$, where c is a complex number, maintain their stability when we change the map's phase space from the complex plane $\mathbb{C}$ to the coquaternions $\mathbb{H}_{\mathrm{coq}}$. Next, we investigate the same question for the one-parameter family of quadratic maps, $x^2 + bx$, and find that this is not the case. In fact, the situation for this family of maps turns out to be quite complicated, since we show that there are complex attractors that undergo changes in their stability, while others maintain it. However, the most intriguing result is that certain regions of the parameter space, known as bulbs, which correspond to the existence of attracting cycles of some fixed period n, exhibit a mixture of stability behavior when we .consider coquaternionic quadratics. Finally, we present the result of our investigation regarding the stability of all complex attracting cycles of f_b when we consider the coquaternionic quadratic maps f_b.

To finish, we would like to emphasize that this study represents the initial step towards investigating the Mandelbrot set for coquaternionic families of quadratics, including $x^2 + c$ and $x^2 + bx$. Future work will build upon these findings.

Acknowledgements. Research at CMAT was partially financed by Portuguese funds through FCT - Fundação para a Ciência e a Tecnologia, within the Projects UIDB/00013/2020 and UIDP/00013/2020. Research at NIPE has been financed by FCT, within the Project UIDB/03182/2020.

References

1. Aulbach, B.: Continuous and Discrete Dynamics near Manifolds of Equilibria. LNM, vol. 1058. Springer, Heidelberg (1984). https://doi.org/10.1007/BFb0071569
2. Falcão, M.I., Miranda, F., Severino, R., Soares, M.J.: Iteration of quadratic maps on coquaternions. Int. J. Bifurcat. Chaos **27**(12), 1730039 (2017)
3. Falcão, M.I., Miranda, F., Severino, R., Soares, M.J.: Basins of attraction for a quadratic coquaternionic map. Chaos, Solitons & Fractals **104**, 716–724 (2017)
4. Falcão, M.I., Miranda, F., Severino, R., Soares, M.J.: Dynamics of the coquaternionic maps $x^2 + bx$. Rend. Circ. Mat. Palermo II. Ser **72**, 959975 (2022). https://doi.org/10.1007/s12215-021-00715-6
5. Peitgen, H.-O., Jürgens, H., Saupe, D.: Chaos and Fractals: New Frontiers of Science. Springer, New York (1992)

Author Index